THE OXFORD HANDBOOK OF

# MODERN
# SCOTTISH
# HISTORY

THE OXFORD HANDBOOK OF

# MODERN

# SCOTTISH

# HISTORY

*Edited by*

T. M. DEVINE

*and*

JENNY WORMALD

OXFORD
UNIVERSITY PRESS

# OXFORD

UNIVERSITY PRESS

Great Clarendon Street, Oxford OX2 6DP

Oxford University Press is a department of the University of Oxford.
It furthers the University's objective of excellence in research, scholarship,
and education by publishing worldwide in

Oxford New York

Auckland Cape Town Dar es Salaam Hong Kong Karachi
Kuala Lumpur Madrid Melbourne Mexico City Nairobi
New Delhi Shanghai Taipei Toronto

With offices in

Argentina Austria Brazil Chile Czech Republic France Greece
Guatemala Hungary Italy Japan Poland Portugal Singapore
South Korea Switzerland Thailand Turkey Ukraine Vietnam

Oxford is a registered trade mark of Oxford University Press
in the UK and in certain other countries

Published in the United States
by Oxford University Press Inc., New York

© Oxford University Press 2012

The moral rights of the authors have been asserted
Database right Oxford University Press (maker)

First published 2012

British Library Cataloguing in Publication Data
Data available

Library of Congress Cataloging in Publication Data
Data available

Typeset by SPI Publisher Services, Pondicherry, India
Printed in Great Britain
on acid-free paper by
MPG Books Group, Bodmin and King's Lynn

ISBN 978-0-19-956369-2

1 3 5 7 9 10 8 6 4 2

# TABLE OF CONTENTS

## PART III  UNION AND ENLIGHTENMENT,
## *c*.1680–1760

# PART IV  THE NATION TRANSFORMED, 1760–1914

# PART V  THE GREAT WAR TO THE NEW MILLENNIUM, 1914–2010

# Contributors

**Michael Anderson**, FRSE, FBA, Honorary Professorial Fellow, School of History, Classics and Archaeology, University of Edinburgh

**Dr Karin Bowie**, Lecturer, School of Humanities, University of Glasgow

**Dr Ben Braber**, Honorary Research Fellow, School of Humanities, University of Glasgow

**Dr Esther Breitenbach**, Research Fellow, School of History, Classics and Archaeology, University of Edinburgh

**Alexander Broadie**, FRSE, Honorary Professorial Research Fellow, School of Humanities, University of Glasgow

**Stewart J. Brown**, FRSE, Professor of Ecclesiastical History and Head of the School of Divinity, University of Edinburgh

**Ewen A. Cameron**, Professor of History, University of Edinburgh

**Dr James Coleman**, University of Glasgow

**Cairns Craig**, FRSE, FBA, Glucksman Professor of Irish and Scottish Studies, University of Aberdeen

**T. M. Devine**, HonMRIA, FRSE, FBA, Personal Senior Research Professor in History and Director of the Scottish Centre for Diaspora Studies, University of Edinburgh

**Robert Dodgshon**, FBA, Emeritus Professor, Institute of Geography and Earth Science, Aberystwyth University

**Elizabeth Ewan**, University Research Chair, History and Scottish Studies, University of Guelph, Canada

**Richard J. Finlay**, Professor of Scottish History, University of Strathclyde

**Dr Patrick Fitzgerald**, Lecturer and Development Officer, Centre for Migration Studies, Ulster American Folk Park, Northern Ireland

**Dr Douglas Hamilton**, Lecturer, Department of History, University of Hull

**Dr Clare Jackson**, Lecturer and Director of Studies in History, Trinity Hall, University of Cambridge

**Colin Kidd**, FRSE, FBA, Professor of Intellectual History and Political Thought, Queen's University Belfast

**Anne-Marie Kilday**, Professor of Criminal History and Associate Dean (Research and Knowledge Transfer), Oxford Brookes University

**Angela McCarthy**, Professor of Scottish and Irish History, University of Otago, New Zealand

**David McCrone**, FRSE, FBA, Professor of Sociology, School of Social and Political Science, University of Edinburgh

**E. W. McFarland**, Professor of History, School of Law and Social Sciences, Glasgow Caledonian University

**Iain McLean**, FBA, Professor of Politics and Official Fellow of Nuffield College, Oxford University

**Dr Catriona M. M. Macdonald**, Reader in Late Modern Scottish History, University of Glasgow

**Dr Esther Mijers**, Lecturer, Department of History, University of Reading

**Graeme Morton**, Scottish Studies Foundation Chair, Department of History, University of Guelph, Canada

**Steve Murdoch**, Professor of History, University of St Andrews

**Dr Stana Nenadic**, Senior Lecturer, School of History, Classics and Archaeology, University of Edinburgh

**G. C. Peden**, FRSE, Emeritus Professor of History, University of Stirling

**Dr Gordon Pentland**, Senior Lecturer in History, School of History, Classics and Archaeology, University of Edinburgh

**Dr Alasdair Raffe**, Lecturer in History, Northumbria University

**Richard Rodger**, Professor of Economic and Social History, School of History, Classics and Archaeology, University of Edinburgh

**T. C. Smout**, FRSE, FBA, Professor Emeritus, School of History, University of St Andrews

**Dr Laura A. M. Stewart**, Lecturer in Early Modern British History, Birkbeck, University of London

**Daniel Szechi**, FRSE, Professor of Early Modern History, School of Arts, Histories and Cultures, University of Manchester

**Dr Andrea Thomas**, Independent Scholar

**Graham Walker**, Professor of Political History, School of Politics, International Studies, and Philosophy, Queen's University Belfast

**Dr Jenny Wormald**, Honorary Fellow, School of History, Classics and Archaeology, University of Edinburgh

# INTRODUCTION

## The Study of Modern Scottish History

### T. M. DEVINE AND JENNY WORMALD

**1**

THE commissioning of *The Handbook of Modern Scottish History* as one of the first in the History series to be published by Oxford University Press confirms the current academic health of the subject. In the past few decades, there has been an outpouring of cutting-edge research; undergraduate classes in Scottish History attract large numbers of students; and public interest in the nation's past has never been higher, as confirmed by the impact of television and radio programmes, as well as features that regularly appear in the print media. In the words of the Historiographer Royal in Scotland, published in 2007: 'Scottish history is pretty vigorous; a structure that was rickety and thinly painted a generation ago is reinforced and much more thickly painted now. It is, as a subject, more deeply understood.'[1] Nevertheless, as indicated below, some weaknesses endure.

T. C. Smout's positive assessment would have been impossible in the later nineteenth century and for several decades thereafter. In 1980 Marinell Ash published her important book, *The Strange Death of Scottish History*. She argued that by late Victorian times 'a general interest in Scottish history had ceased to be the mark of broadly educated Scotsmen and had come instead to be seen as the mark of a narrow parochialism most Scots wished to abandon'. Instead, that period, she suggested, saw Scots embrace 'the emotional trappings of the Scottish past—its symbols are bonnie Scotland of the bens and glens and misty sheiling, the Jacobites, Mary, Queen of Scots, tartan mania and the raising of historical statuary'.[2] Twenty years before Ash's critique, George Elder Davie, in his even more

---

[1] T. C. Smout, 'Scottish History in the Universities since the 1950s', *History Scotland*, vol. 7 (September/October 2007), 49.

[2] Marinell Ash, *The Strange Death of Scottish History* (Edinburgh, 1980), 10.

influential polemic, *The Democratic Intellect: Scotland and her Universities in the Nineteenth Century* (1961), condemned the Scots for 'a failure of intellectual nerve', and made the point that at the very time when nations throughout Europe were becoming increasingly 'history minded', the Scottish people were losing a sense of their past as the universities were 'emphatically resolved . . . no longer to be prisoners of their own history'.

Equally, Bruce Lenman, in his 1973 survey of the teaching of Scottish History in the nation's universities, could conclude that the subject 'was ignored by the Scottish educa-tion system by 1850', while conceding that there had been some bright spots amid the scholarly darkness in the publications of Thomas McCrie, the biographer of John Knox (1811) and Andrew Melville (1819), Patrick Fraser Tytler, whose nine-volume *History of Scotland* (1828–43) covered the period from Alexander III to the Union of the Crowns, and Cosmo Innes, the distinguished scholar of Scottish medieval institutions.[3] These works, however, were devoted to the history of the nation before the Union of 1707. There seemed precious little interest in the more modern period.

Indeed, and more generally, with the exception of Alexander Fraser Tytler, Professor of Universal History and Roman Antiquities in Edinburgh University from 1780 until 1802, and Cosmo Innes, himself Professor of Constitutional Law and History, there had hardly been any teaching of Scottish History in Scottish universities from the time the first History chairs were established in the later seventeenth and early eighteenth cen-turies. Innes assumed his professorship in 1846 after it had been in abeyance for several years. In the hope of reviving interest in Scottish history he first charged no class fees and the numbers who attended grew considerably. As soon as fees were imposed, how-ever, the audience fell to a small handful.[4]

This virtual irrelevance of Scottish History in the universities in the Victorian era poses a fascinating puzzle. After all, in the Age of Enlightenment the Scots had a European-wide reputation as pioneering historical thinkers and writers: 'Hume and Robertson stood alongside Gibbon in a triumvirate which had transformed British and, indeed, European historiography.'[5] Adam Smith was also arguably the world's first-ever economic historian. The Scots *literati* made signal contributions to the methodology of historical study through their elaboration of the stadial theory of development describ-ing how human society moved from the stage of hunter-gatherers to that of farmers and cultivators, and thence to the age of commerce. This was a powerful critique of the dom-inance of narrative history with its continuum of events, uninterrupted by any structural discontinuities. In this way the Scots later influenced some future intellectual develop-ments from historical sociology to Marxist theory.[6]

[3]  Bruce P. Lenman, 'The Teaching of Scottish History in the Scottish Universities', *Scottish Historical Review*, vol. lii (October 1973), 171–3.

[4]  Ash, *Strange Death*, 148.

[5]  Colin Kidd, 'The *Strange Death of Scottish History* Revisited: Constructions of the Past in Scotland, c.1790–1914', *Scottish Historical Review*, vol. lxxvi (April 1997), 100.

[6]  Karen O'Brien, 'Between Enlightenment and Stadial History', *Journal of Eighteenth-Century Studies*, vol. 16 (March 1993), 53–64.

The Enlightenment historians were followed by Sir Walter Scott, the world's first best-selling historical novelist, who, through his Waverley series and *Tales of a Grandfather*, had invested the Scottish past with magical appeal, not only in Britain but throughout Europe and North America. Scott correctly surmised in the introduction to *Waverley* (1814): 'There is no European nation, which in the course of half a century or little more, has undergone so complete a change as the Kingdom of Scotland.' This economic and social transformation, together with the political tensions that it generated, massively expanded the readership for his poetry and novels because they satisfied the nostalgic emotional needs of the propertied classes in a world experiencing unprecedented change from tradition to modernity. So, in the words of one commentator: 'Sir Walter Scott probably did more for Scottish history in this period than all the Scottish universities put together.'[7] Scott was also a potent force in the establishment of the great historical clubs, the Bannatyne, Maitland, Abbotsford, and Spalding, which were active in all the cities of the country apart from Dundee and did an enormous amount of work publishing original Scottish historical sources. But all this creative and editorial activity took place outside the formal structures of Scottish school and university education. Also, the publishing clubs had a short-lived existence. Most were in decline by the mid-nineteenth century and all soon ceased their activities in the decades that followed. Others only arose with the formation of the Scottish History Society in 1886.[8]

Neither the great figures of the Enlightenment nor the mesmerizing historical narratives of Scott, the Wizard of the North, saved Scottish history from academic irrelevance. Pre-1707 Scottish history received a critical pounding from eighteenth-century Enlightenment writers as a subject not worthy of serious study. It was depicted simply as a tale of feudal faction, political turbulence, religious fanaticism, and economic backwardness, in stark contrast to the constitutional, 'civilized', and material progress of England in the medieval and early modern centuries.[9] The only 'usable past', therefore, was English constitutional history, and the English parliamentary experience became the template against which all other British political developments should be measured. Whig Anglo-British history inevitably became the favoured choice. The Enlightenment writers saw themselves as scholarly citizens of the world and such figures as William Robertson and Adam Ferguson came to regard Scottish history as parochial if picturesque. David Hume began a *History of Great Britain* (1754), which was concerned with the seventeenth century. As it moved back to the sixteenth century it became a *History of England*. Likewise, John Millar, a major influence on the development of modern sociology, established his reputation with *An Historical View of the English Government* (1787).

Ironically, the flowering of Scottish culture in which these writers played a prominent part ought to have given the lie to the idea of a backward and uninteresting Scottish

---

[7] Lenman, 'Teaching of Scottish History', 171. The most recent study is Stuart Kelly, *Scott-land: The Man Who Invented a Nation* (Edinburgh, 2010).

[8] Michael Lynch, ed., *The Oxford Companion to Scottish History* (Oxford, 2001), 315–16.

[9] Colin Kidd, *Subverting Scotland's Past* (Cambridge, 1995).

nation. In the nineteenth century, however, the very influential English scholar, H. T. Buckle (1821–1862), forcefully attacked this possibility by describing these earlier Scottish intellectual activities as mere brief and ephemeral aberrations that had faded away before 1800. The Scottish norm in Buckle's view remained a long Scottish history of feudal backwardness and ecclesiastical tyranny.[10] It was a perspective shared by most Scottish authorities at the time. Even Sir Walter Scott's fictional recoveries of the Scottish past could not withstand the intellectually devastating firepower that marginalized the national history as a fit subject for educational purposes. Indeed, his very success and the appeal of his dramatic and colourful tales helped to steer interest in the Scottish past into the intellectual dead end of 'historical kailyards' and romantic appendages.[11]

At root, perhaps, was the problem of the overwhelming dominance of uncritical unionism in Scottish politics before 1870. George Chalmers in his monumental *Caledonia* of 1807–24 was typical of that time in seeing 1707 as a liberation for the Scots, a *sine qua non* of their material and moral progress out of superstition and poverty.[12] In several European countries mid-nineteenth-century nationalism spawned an historiographical revolution. This was not the case in Scotland. As Colin Kidd has suggested: 'Between the mid-eighteenth century and the emergence of the Scottish question in the 1970s there was no credible, sustained or widely supported Scottish critique of the Anglo-Scottish Union, and as such no call for an articulate ideology of Anglo-Scottish unionism.'[13]

For much of the Victorian era in particular, Scotland seemed to enjoy the economic benefits of union and empire without either political interference from outside or the erosion of national identity. Much of the day-to-day administration of Scotland through the burghs, public boards, and courts of the Church remained in Scottish hands. Semi-independence was also guaranteed by the incomplete union that allowed the Scots to retain national powers over private law, the established Church, and education. Through imperial opportunities they not only exploited an abundance of middle-class and professional careers but experienced an enormous boost to national confidence as Scots came to be described in the public prints as natural empire builders. There were some sensitivities aroused, however, especially when the notion of Scotland as a full and equal partner in union seemed threatened (as with the foundation of the National Association for the Vindication of Scottish Rights of 1853) or the Irish were thought to be obtaining unfair advantages at Scottish expense. For the most part, however, a nationalist challenge to the status quo failed to develop because there was no intrinsic political or economic rationale for it to emerge in Scotland.[14]

---

[10] M. Fry, 'The Whig Interpretation of Scottish History', in I. Donnachie and C. Whatley, eds., *The Manufacture of Scottish History* (Edinburgh, 1992).

[11] Richard J. Finlay, 'Controlling the Past: Scottish Historiography and Scottish Identity in the 19th and 20th Centuries', *Scottish Affairs*, 9 (autumn 1994), 124.

[12] George Chalmers, *Caledonia*, 3 vols. (London, 1807–24), vol. I, 866.

[13] Colin Kidd, *Union and Unionisms: Political Thought in Scotland, 1500–2000* (Cambridge, 2008), 24.

[14] There is considerable literature on these issues. For an overview and summation see T. M. Devine, *The Scottish Nation, 1700–2007* (London, 2006), 285–95.

## 2

It might be thought, however, that history was more on the side of Scottish History from the 1880s. Before that decade unionism has rightly been considered 'banal', in the sense employed by Michael Billig, in relation to nationalism, i.e. a political category so omnipresent and unquestioned that no explicit articulation of its importance was required.[15] This changed in the 1880s. As 'Englishness' was redefined to incorporate a more populist concept of 'England', so these terms started to become increasingly used rather than 'Britain' and 'British', to the considerable displeasure of some of the Scottish political elite.[16]

Other factors brought Scottish issues onto the British political agenda. The fear in Scotland that resurgent nationalism was securing preferential treatment for Ireland was one issue. Then there were administrative reforms that were carried out, ostensibly at least, to help the Union function more effectively. These measures included the revival of the office of Secretary of Scotland, the establishment of the Scottish Office in London and a Scottish Standing Committee, within the Westminster Parliament, to consider all Scottish legislation.

The political context behind these initiatives was a movement for Scottish Home Rule within the Union. A Home Rule Association was founded, between 1886 and 1914, and seven Home Rule motions were presented to Parliament. This new impetus for constitutional change came within an ace of success in May 1914 when a Home Rule bill passed its second reading in the House of Commons. The outbreak of the First World War killed off the opportunity for the legislation to reach the statute book. Nonetheless, this political dynamic implied a more serious interest in specifically Scottish matters, which might plausibly be expected to have an impact on a revival in the history and culture of the nation.

Running parallel with these political changes was a widespread concern in influential circles that the Scottish universities, undeniably world-famous in the eighteenth century, were now declining into mediocrity. In the mid-nineteenth century the Indian civil-service examinations became open to public competition. The tradition of Scottish service in India had been long and very rewarding for the landed, professional, and mercantile classes of the country, a crucial mainstay of gentry and middle-class careers.[17] Scottish failure in these new examinations therefore 'amounted almost to a trauma in these sections of the Scottish community which had long traditions in India or who aspired to enter this lucrative career'.[18] More generally, complaints now abounded that

---

[15] Michael Billig, *Banal Nationalism* (London, 1995), and for the Scottish analogy, Kidd, *Union and Unionisms*, 23–31.

[16] R. Colls and P. Dodds, *Englishness: Politics and Culture, 1880–1920* (London, 1986).

[17] See Andrew Mackillop's chapter on Scots in the eastern empire in 'Locality, Nation and Empire: Scots in Asia, c.1695–c.1813', in John M. Mackenzie and T. M. Devine, eds., *Scotland and the British Empire* (Oxford, 2011).

[18] Ash, *Strange Death*, 150.

the products of Scottish universities, had to go to England for advanced training because of their generalist education, that Scottish universities grossly neglected research studies, and that the teaching curricula had hardly changed in three hundred years. Some of the most wounding criticisms came from James Donaldson, rector of Edinburgh High School and editor of the *Educational News*, the journal founded by the Educational Institute of Scotland. Donaldson lamented in 1882: 'The Scottish universities are schools with curricula fixed nearly on the old Reformation programme', and argued that 'an educational revolution' had taken place in the nineteenth century and with it had come much greater 'competition for distinction in science, scholarship, theology and all the higher intellectual pursuits'. In this context, however, the 'Scotsman has to fight with bow and arrow against men armed with rifles and cannon. He is the handloom weaver of the intellectual world.'[19]

Because of the depth of concern a whole series of reform proposals came thick and fast in the later nineteenth century. An Act of Parliament in 1889 established an executive commission under the Court of Session judge, Lord Kinnear, which passed no fewer than 169 ordinances. These included a compulsory entrance examination, changes in arts, law, and medical degrees, including Honours courses. An entrance examination was in place by 1892 and meant that the common age at entry moved upwards from fourteen or fifteen to seventeen, which was facilitated by the introduction of the new leaving certificate for secondary schools. As late as the 1870s, only a small number of Arts students actually took degrees but, by 1914, there had been a transformation with most university students in Scotland now aiming to graduate. New chairs were founded and professorships in English History and Political Economy at Aberdeen, Edinburgh, and Glasgow promoted. Was this to be a new dawn for Scottish History, with the establishment of professorships in the discipline of History backed by state support for the first time in Scotland?[20]

The omens indeed seemed good. Sir William Fraser, clerk to Cosmo Innes and an eminent Edinburgh lawyer, left funds to create a Chair in Scottish History, later founded in 1901, in the University of Edinburgh. Some years afterwards, in 1913, a second professorship was established at the University of Glasgow, from funds realized by the 1911 exhibition of Scottish history, art, and industry at Kelvingrove Park.[21]

It was not an entirely false dawn, even if the skies remained somewhat cloudy for some time to come. Certainly, the admiration of Scottish intellectuals, particularly members of the legal profession, for the constitutional history of England, endured. History in the Scottish universities developed much later than in Oxford and Cambridge, and it was therefore perhaps predictable that the focus of these institutions on Whig constitutionalism would become the pedagogic model for the new chairs of History at Edinburgh and Glasgow, especially in the form of medieval institutional history of the type so

---

[19]  *Contemporary Review*, vol. xli (1882), 150.
[20]  R. D. Anderson, *Education and Opportunity in Victorian Scotland* (Edinburgh, 1983), 269ff.
[21]  Gordon Donaldson, *Sir William Fraser* (Edinburgh, 1985); Lenman, 'Teaching of Scottish History', 177–8.

fashionable in contemporary English scholarship.[22] The first Professor of History at Glasgow in 1894 was Richard Lodge, Fellow of Brasenose College, Oxford, while the new Edinburgh chair went to a Cambridge man, George Prothero:

> Thus, the first two chairs of history in Scotland were filled by Oxbridge candidates... Academic history was [for them] primarily the corporate worship of the origins and development of the contemporary parliamentary establishment at Westminster which both the Scottish and English middle classes regarded as the supreme embodiment of their national class and communal interests.[23]

The persistent anglicization of the curriculum was also fortified by the developing belief that the study of history was not simply to be regarded as a cultural experience but rather as practical study which trained students to be future national statesmen and imperial administrators. These essential skills could only be taught and learned by 'proper history', as articulated by William Stubbs's teaching of the constitutional history of England. Stubbs was the Regius Chair of History at Oxford from 1866 and the most influential academic historian of the age.[24]

It would be most unfair, however, to label the successors of Lodge and Prothero simply as agents of English cultural imperialism in Scotland. Some historians from south of the border did make important contributions to Scottish history. The outstanding example was C. S. Terry, promoted to a professorship at Aberdeen University in 1903, who had an academic background in Cambridge and Durham. He did much in his writings to rehabilitate the pre-1707 Scottish Parliament after the long tradition of negative criticism emanating from the school of Whig historiography.[25] Similarly, but at a later date, Richard Pares, who became a professor at Edinburgh in 1945, introduced the remarkable regulation that all students for Honours in history had to attend a survey course in Scottish History, a requirement later abandoned by his successors when he returned to Oxford in 1954.[26]

Yet, well into the twentieth century, the intellectual orthodoxies remained unfavourable both to the expansion of research and teaching in Scottish history. Since history had come to be regarded as an important and relevant training for future statesmen, civil servants, and imperial administrators, English constitutional history was preferred since it outlined the history of the state in which students were citizens of the United Kingdom rather than Scotland: 'What sort of school for statesmen was the history of a stateless nation? Though rich in heroic characters and dramatic episodes, Scotland's past appeared to lack a whiggish plot.'[27]

In some respects, the first two Scottish History professors, Peter Hume Brown and Robert Rait, at Edinburgh and Glasgow respectively, swam against this tide. Both

[22]  Robert Anderson, 'University History Teaching and the Humboldtian Model in Scotland, 1858–1914', *History of Universities*, vol. 25/1 (2010), 149–50.

[23]  Lenman, 'Teaching of Scottish History', 174.

[24]  Ash, *Strange Death*, 149–50.

[25]  C. S. Terry, *Scottish Parliaments 1603–1707* (Glasgow, 1905).

[26]  J. G., D. H., and L. B. Namier, 'Richard Pares', *English Historical Review*, vol. 73 (October 1958), 577–82.

[27]  Anderson, 'University History Teaching', 167; Kidd, 'Strange Death', 99.

published extensively. Hume Brown produced among other books a three-volume general history of Scotland. He was elected a Fellow of the British Academy, a sign that high-quality academic work was now being done in Scottish history.[28] Rait was an expert on the Scottish Parliament but also wrote for the general public, with *The Making of Scotland* in 1911 and a popular *History of Scotland* in 1914.

But this was not yet an entirely new era. Academic researchers in Scottish history before 1945 were still few and far between, not least because of the premium that the Scottish university system in general at the time placed on teaching rather than original scholarship. Hume Brown's syntheses (1899–1911) remained the standard university textbooks as late as the early 1960s, a half-century after they first appeared.[29] The creation of separate chairs in the subject did in part reflect its relative neglect in general history teaching, but the development was ambiguous because it threatened to isolate Scottish history from mainstream advances in the discipline as a whole.[30] Moreover, most of the new scholarship that was published still tended to concentrate on pre-Union Scotland. To all intents and purposes it seemed that only the 'independent' nation was a worthy and proper focus for academic research. Modern Scottish history remained a Cinderella subject and a tradition that took a long time to die. The first modernist was finally appointed to the Edinburgh chair as late as 2005. Glasgow did only slightly better. Of the six holders of the established Scottish History chair there to date, George Pryde in the 1950s was the only appointment to break the long line of medievalists and early modernists. When J. D. Hargreaves delivered his inaugural lecture as the new Burnett-Fletcher professor at Aberdeen in 1964, he was able to claim that the history of Scotland since 1707 was less studied than that of Yorkshire.[31] Remarkably, William Ferguson's *Scotland: 1689 to the Present*, which appeared in 1968, became the first ever book-length study of the last three hundred years of Scottish political and social history written by an academic historian.

# 3

Scottish research historians in the universities of the early 1950s numbered around fifteen and the expertise of most of them lay in the centuries before 1700. The subject was taught at the undergraduate level in the four ancient Scottish universities of Aberdeen, Edinburgh, Glasgow, and St Andrews, but attracted few students and had a low profile. There was a tiny number of PhD scholars: as late as 1966 only three research degrees in Scottish history were completed in the UK as a whole. Professional Scottish historians felt marginalized and defensive, never being really certain whether their

---

[28] 'The Late Professor Hume Brown', *The Scotsman*, 2 December 1918.
[29] Anderson, 'University History Teaching', 160.
[30] Lenman, 'Teaching of Scottish History', 176.
[31] J. D. Hargreaves, 'Historical Study in Scotland', *Aberdeen University Review*, vol. xi (1964), 237–50.

colleagues in the mainstream of the history discipline regarded them as intellectually respectable. The two Professors of Scottish History in the later 1950s, George Pryde at Glasgow (died 1961) and William Croft Dickinson at Edinburgh (died 1963), were austere scholars of high quality but their publications were unlikely to have much resonance in the world outside the universities. Scottish history had a reputation for being solid but dull, incapable of competing with the exciting momentum being achieved in so many aspects of European, American, and British history at the time.[32]

Nonetheless, important seeds were being sown. Croft Dickinson re-established *The Scottish Historical Review*, the main journal in the subject, which had ended publication earlier in the century. There was institutional expansion in social and economic history, soon to have a powerful impact on modern Scottish history in general. Queen's College, Dundee (still part of St Andrews) appointed a professor in this emerging field in 1955, with other chairs established in Glasgow in 1957 and Edinburgh in 1958. Books of genuine quality began to appear on the modern period, with new and exciting perspectives reflecting the advances in the subject outside Scotland. The works of Henry Hamilton on the Industrial Revolution and Malcolm Gray on the Highlands, both of Aberdeen University, were especially distinguished. But perhaps the most stimulating, and a portent for the future, was Laurance J. Saunders's *Scottish Democracy 1815–1840: The Social and Intellectual Background* (1950). Saunders was not a member of a history department but held a chair of constitutional law at Edinburgh. Nevertheless, he produced a text of innovative and perceptive research, written in clear and appealing prose, on one of the seminal periods of economic, social, and intellectual change in modern Scottish history. D. W. Brogan of Cambridge, reviewing it for the *Scottish Historical Review*, commented fulsomely that the book 'represents both original and penetrating research and a very high degree of synthetic power; and was such a model of clarity and organisation that the critical reviewer is baffled in the performance of his duty'.[33] Saunders had eloquently demonstrated the range of fascinating questions that had never been raised, far less answered, about the recent Scottish past. Here, indeed, it was implied, was a subject full of intellectual challenge and exciting cultural relevance.

Finally, in the 1960s and 1970s, historians of modern Scotland achieved more in two decades than their predecessors had done in two centuries. The four-volume *Edinburgh History of Scotland*, written by Archie Duncan, Ranald Nicholson, Gordon Donaldson, and William Ferguson, gave twentieth-century Scots a professional account of their past from the earliest days to the 1960s. Hume Brown was now finally superseded. R. H. Campbell's *Scotland since 1707* (1965) steered the nation's scholarship towards economic history, the key intellectual dynamic of the 1960s and 1970s. A few years later, T. C. Smout's *A History of the Scottish People 1560–1830* (1969) extended the breadth of the subject into such social issues as demography, social class, culture, and the life experience of ordinary people. Written in luminous prose, it became a best-seller, even attracting

---

[32] Smout, 'Scottish History in the Universities', 45; Lenman, 'Teaching of Scottish History', 178–9; Finlay, 'Controlling the Past', 135.

[33] *Scottish Historical Review*, vol. 31 (April 1952), 82–4.

generous praise in the *TLS* from that notorious Scotophobe, Hugh Trevor Roper, Regius Professor of Modern History at Oxford. Smout's book opened the eyes and expanded the ambitions of an entire generation of undergraduate and graduate students. It became a catalytic force in the study of modern Scottish History.

It was indeed an exciting period, not least for the current editors of this *Handbook* who lived through it. Looking back, it is possible to detect that significant forces were at work. First, the Whig interpretation of history, which had cast such a pall over the study of serious Scottish history for generations, crumbled and eventually became extinct under the assaults of English scholars such as Herbert Butterfield and Lewis Namier. No longer was Scottish historiography imprisoned within a narrative of defective and inadequate development.[34] Second, the Robbins Report in 1964 advised a programme of unprecedented general expansion in British higher education. The results were truly historic. The ancient universities in Scotland grew exponentially in staff numbers, and the new universities of Strathclyde, Dundee, Heriot-Watt, and Stirling soon gained royal charters. All hired more historians than ever before (even the more technically orientated Heriot-Watt for a time). A substantial number of these scholars had expertise in economic or social history. Third, to fill the new posts, apart from a few Scots, historians mainly trained at English universities and at the cutting edge of the discipline were recruited in significant numbers to Scottish academic positions. The bulk of these again were economic and social historians. For them transfers of intellectual interest were reasonably straightforward: studying trade in Hull could easily lead to an examination of the commerce of Glasgow, while poverty issues in Leeds and Liverpool might lead on to consideration of social welfare in Dundee and Edinburgh. Moreover, the study of economic and social history was not fixated with Westminster and its doings. As a result, Scottish history was not only liberated from the old constitutional rut but became embedded within the mainstream of generic European scholarship, where issues very relevant to Scotland—peasant life, rural transformation, emigration, urbanization, industrialization, and much else—were commonplace.

The greatest impact of this scholarly invasion was experienced at Edinburgh, Glasgow, and Strathclyde. The list of the major figures involved was an illustrious one: Michael Anderson, FRSE, FBA; John Butt, FRSE; Neil Buxton; Sydney Checkland, FBA; Baron F. Duckham; Michael Flinn; Gordon Jackson; Clive Lee; Edgar Lythe; Rosalind Mitchison, FRSE; R. J. Morris; Peter Payne, FRSE; Christopher Smout, FRSE, FBA; James Treble; J. T. Ward, to name but a few. Many of the current crop of modern Scottish historians in post benefited from the stimulating teaching and innovative research of this notable generation. In areas of economy and society, at least, Scottish scholarship began rapidly to catch up with the subject elsewhere.

At the same time, the context of Scottish politics was changing. The rise of the SNP from the 1960s, the devolution agenda, and the pollsters' conclusions that in terms of identity 'Scottishness' seemed to be gaining on 'Britishness', provided for a new, public interest in Scottish history. At the start, much of this was satisfied by popular writers such as John Prebble and Nigel Tranter. But academic historians soon made their presence felt in the print, radio, and television media.[35] These political changes above all lent the modern era a relevance and credibility outside the academic domain that it had previously lacked. Many Scots developed a new hunger for understanding the connection between the Scottish past and the Scottish present. Ironically, this appetite for knowledge among adults was partially stimulated by the basic failings in their own school education where, for the most part, Scottish History until more recent times had remained marginal and taught in what one informed observer termed a 'deadly fashion'.[36]

The result of this transformation was a veritable historiographical bonanza. Key works were published in the history of commerce, banking, industry, business, transport, industrial archaeology, and much more. Then the pendulum started to swing to social history in the 1980s and 1990s, with leading-edge research in demography, urbanization, poverty, social class, and much else. Specialist groups were founded in economic history, labour history, history of education, Scottish Catholic history (established long before the revival in the late 1940s), and industrial archaeology. Modern Scottish history came to be situated in a comparative context with a series of Irish–Scottish conferences and their accompanying publications from 1977 and other related innovative work. Large-scale collaborative research projects also developed, often generously funded by external agencies, notably at Aberdeen in Irish–Scottish studies, Stirling and St Andrews in environmental history, St Andrews in the history of the Scottish Parliament, and Edinburgh in diaspora studies. The subject seemed to have developed towards a new intellectual maturity. But what of its current weaknesses?[37]

In an article published in 2007, T. C. Smout was unambiguous, and in response to that question, voiced concern that the gains in research may mean little to scholars outside Scotland; that still too many Scottish historians fail to attempt to relate their work to issues in the international historiographical agenda, so continuing the old accusations of introspection and parochialism; economic history, formerly the catalyst, now virtually disappeared into oblivion; and, he added, that in environmental history, gender studies, modern political history, and cultural history the interest in Scotland, though increasing, remained underdeveloped.[38]

In addition, however, an even more important challenge is the failure thus far to trigger intensive debate, the clash of ideas, in key areas of study, without which the subject cannot renew itself. The Union of 1707 on its tercentenary in 2007 did cause some vigorous discussion and, from time to time, the Highland clearances do still stoke debate in the public prints, though usually along worn ruts and pretty predictable and routine lines of argument.

Part of the difficulty is that there lingers a lack of confidence among some historians of Scotland, a need to search for the way to establish their identity and the importance of

[35]  Smout, 'Scottish History in the Universities', 49.
[36]  Lenman, 'Teaching of Scottish History', 179.
[37]  For example, R. A. Houston and I. D. Whyte, eds., *Scottish Society, 1500–1800* (Cambridge, 1989).
[38]  Smout, 'Scottish History in the Universities', 49–50.

their subject. This was evident very recently in a fascinating and wide-ranging conference on 'Whither Scottish History' in October 2010 sponsored by the *Scottish Historical Review*. This surely relates to the theme already discussed, the lack of serious scholarship until the second half of the twentieth century. Another convention, a much more pernicious one, also endures: the passion for romance, invented or quasi-real. This is above all encapsulated in the early modern period in the obsession with that lamentable figure, Mary, Queen of Scots, but the equally lamentable Bonnie Prince Charlie runs her a close second. The number of books on Mary is vast. Most are dire. But it is surely the responsibility of professional scholars to try to direct attention away from Mary to the much more fascinating kingdom she ruled (very briefly). Visitors to Linlithgow, for example, should be told of the really important and influential monarch in Linlithgow's story, James V, instead of receiving undue emphasis on the fact that Mary, who hardly ever chose to go to Linlithgow, happened to be born there. Any history can shade into myth, romance, fiction. But it is difficult to think of any other society where the two-year antics of a failed ruler—the only failure in a royal house whose kingship was devastatingly impressive for two centuries—have been allowed such a dominant place in early modern historical discussion.

If Mary, Queen of Scots exemplifies one way in which Scottish historians have spent proportionately too much time on a minor issue, at the expense of infinitely more important and interesting ones, another is the uncertainty about whether Scottish history is indeed a subject in its own right, or whether it will only be of interest if set in a wider context, British or international. Ranald Nicholson, mentioned earlier in this introduction, did indeed write a solid and impressive history of the later Middle Ages. But he was informed by his desire to show that Scotland shone as a notable example of concepts then fashionable among historians of other countries. Thus Scotland's 'New Monarchy Triumphant' was—had to be—in the top rank and, as Nicholson argued in a lecture given at Glasgow University, certainly superior to that of England. It was unfortunate that already J. H. Elliott was mounting a convincing critique of the whole idea.[39] What Nicholson was doing—and he was by no means alone in this, and not the last to do it—was writing Scottish history that fitted Scotland into the historiographical fashions of other societies. The problem here was that such an approach came up against the problem that Scotland might not be so readily fitted in; in other words, Scotland had to be considered not as an example of something else, but in its own right. As has already been said, the study of pre-1707 Scottish History used to be seriously neglected, as the history of a backward and violent society. What that really meant was that it did not have the precociously developed governmental and bureaucratic system of England, and therefore another fashionable concept, the overmighty nobility, was predictably portrayed even more overmighty and destructive than any other. Only when the premise was questioned—could a kingdom be civilized only if ruled like England?—did it emerge that Scotland was not a pale reflection of England, but a kingdom with very

---

[39] Ranald Nicholson, *Scotland: The Later Middle Ages* (Edinburgh, 1974). J. H. Elliott, *Imperial Spain, 1469–1716* (London, 1963), ch. 3.

different political and social mores, which actually challenged prevailing ideas, and its history could be used, therefore, to ask a series of different questions.

An offshoot of this problem, and another way in which Scottish historians can be seen to grope for identity, is in that great new fashion, 'British History'. What this could mean, south of the border, could all too often be English history given the name of British. In Simon Schama's much-praised television series, *The History of Britain*, Scotland before 1603 was discussed three times: Skara Brae, Wallace and Bruce, and Knox and Mary. It was ever thus, and not only in works published by English historians on, for example, 'Tudor Britain'.[40] It was exactly what courses in the Scottish universities, euphemistically entitled 'British History', had done. Small wonder, therefore, that Scottish historians had tried to fight back by insisting on the importance of Scotland. But in the second half of the twentieth century, when the new 'British' historiographical problem came into play, that was overtaken by the insistent demand that we all, Scots, English, Irish, Welsh, were British historians now. The late and great Welsh historian Rees Davies determinedly sought to create a British framework for the four societies of the high medieval period. It is questionable whether that really worked.[41] But it did look as if such a framework could really come into its own in the early modern period, when Scotland joined the composite monarchy of England, Wales, and Ireland. Surely it would have much to offer Scottish historians, so long at the mercy in this period of Anglocentric interpretations of the union of the crowns of 1603 and its consequences? And in the flood of publications on early modern British history, Scottish historians found themselves welcome guests and cheerfully became engaged, even though gloomy mutterings about Anglocentricity remained.[42]

# 4

Contributors to this volume were asked to respond to the guidelines in the Oxford University Press *Handbook* series. The *Handbooks* are designed as works of scholarly reference, addressing the need to 'stand back' in order to distinguish the wood from the trees and reflect critically on the state of learning. They are also intended to help shape

---

[40] Thus *The Oxford Illustrated History of Tudor and Stuart Britain*, ed. John Morrill (Oxford, 1996); this is a remarkable example of Anglocentric history under the name of Britain, simply because the editor is a historian who has a notable claim to be genuinely 'British'. It is an indication of the extent of the problem.

[41] For example, Rees Davies, *The Matter of Britain and the Matter of England* (Oxford, 1996), and *The First English Empire* (Oxford, 2000).

[42] The list of 'British' books is a very long one. In the interests of space, only two will be cited here. R. G. Asch, ed., *Three Nations—a Common History? England, Scotland, Ireland and British History c.1600–1920* (Bochum, 1993), and Glenn Burgess, ed., *The New British History: Founding a Modern State, 1603–1715* (London, 1999). Footnotes and, in the second work, a section on Further Reading, provide plenty more examples.

the field by giving primacy to approaches and issues that seem most likely to lift the debate out of excessively worn historical ruts. The chapters, therefore, seek to give succinct accounts of their subjects and be accessible to readers without specialist knowledge but at the same time, unlike a general synthesis, a conventional reference book or a dictionary, they will try to press the limits of current knowledge and address questions that remain unanswered and the agenda for future research. One of the objectives here is to make those controversies that do exist in interpreting the Scottish past more explicit and more amenable to debate, challenge, and disputation, which are the very lifeblood of any vigorous academic discipline.[43]

Within these broad parameters we had to make a number of choices as editors. The most important is that we believe 'the history of modern Scotland' should be analysed from the Renaissance and Reformation periods rather than the previous conventional starting points such as the Union of 1707 or the later seventeenth century. As several of the chapters in the book will demonstrate, there are long-run social, religious, and intellectual forces that shaped the modern Scottish nation which cannot be fully understood without reaching back in time to the sixteenth century.

We have also sought to encourage the existing trend towards the internationalization of Scottish history by commissioning chapters on emigration, immigration, and empire. 'Greater Scotland' arguably needs much attention in light of the long history from the medieval period of the huge numbers of emigrants associated with the Scottish diaspora. In addition, all authors have been advised, whenever appropriate, to make reference to the Scottish historical experience within a comparative framework of reference. We have also been keen to tap into the expertise of other disciplines such as geography, political science, literature, and sociology. All of them have made signal contributions to an understanding of modern Scottish history in recent years. They can often add an important theoretical dimension, still sometimes absent from the strongly empiricist traditions of the subject.

The selection of topics and contributors was especially challenging. There are certain key themes which, of course, had to be included, such as Reformation, the Union of 1707, Industrialization, Enlightenment, the First World War, and the like. But we were also keen to encourage emerging fields. So there are chapters on environment, myth, family, empire, criminality and violence, gender, contemporary society, and economy. We hope that these essays will encourage even more much-needed research into these important areas.

It is one sign of the new energy of the discipline that there are now many more distinguished scholars at work than we could possibly have invited to take part in this project. In the end we used three criteria to decide on the selection of contributors: first, eminent historians in their respective fields; second, younger scholars who by their existing publications are beginning to make fresh and original contributions; third, historians

---

[43] For reviews of the recent historiography see 'Special Issue: "Whither Scottish History":  Proceedings of the Strathclyde Conference', *Scottish Historical Review*, vol. lxxiii (April 1994), and 'Special Issue: "Writing Scotland's History": Proceedings of the Edinburgh Conference', *Scottish Historical Review*, vol. lxxvi (April 1997).

outside Scotland who might be able to see the Scottish experience in a more fresh and interesting light. In fact, sixteen of the authors in the book are based in institutions in England, Ireland, Wales, Canada, and New Zealand. This is itself an indication of the increasing international interest in Scottish history.

# ACKNOWLEDGEMENTS

Completion of a project on the scale of this *Handbook* would not have been possible without the help of many people. We are grateful in the first instance to our contributors for their exemplary patience and support during the two-year gestation of the volume, and for their courteous and speedy responses to our editorial suggestions and queries. We also thank the large number of anonymous external reviewers whom we recruited to help comment on first drafts of chapters. Their contributions were invaluable and did much to enhance the overall quality of the final volume. Our editors at Oxford University Press could not have been more supportive. We thank in particular Christopher Wheeler, who first commissioned the *Handbook*, for his professional advice. Stephanie Ireland, Emma Barber, and Matthew Cotton of OUP were unfailingly helpful and efficient. Richard Mason was a meticulous copy-editor. Last, but by no means whatsoever least, we are very pleased to record our immense gratitude to Margaret Begbie, the anchor of the entire project, who maintained regular contact with contributors, reminded them of various deadlines, and replied with characteristic efficiency and tact to their various questions and concerns.

T.M.D. and J.W.

*June 2011*

## FURTHER READING

Anderson, Robert, 'University History Teaching and the Humboldtian Model in Scotland, 1858–1914', *History of Universities*, vol. 25/1 (2010).

Ash, Marinell, *The Strange Death of Scottish History* (Edinburgh, 1980).

Hargreaves, J. D., 'Historical Study in Scotland', *Aberdeen University Review*, vol. xi (1964).

Lenman, Bruce P., 'The Teaching of Scottish History in the Scottish Universities', *Scottish Historical Review*, vol. lii (October 1973).

Lynch, Michael, ed., *The Oxford Companion to Scottish History* (Oxford 2011).

Smout, T. C., 'Scottish History in the Universities since the 1950s', *History Scotland*, vol. 7 (September/October 2007).

'Special Issue: "Whither Scottish History": Proceedings of the Strathclyde Conference', *Scottish Historical Review*, vol. lxxiii (April 1994).

'Special Issue: "Writing Scotland's History": Proceedings of the Edinburgh Conference', *Scottish Historical Review*, vol. lxxvi (April 1997).

PART I

SOME
FUNDAMENTALS OF
MODERN SCOTTISH
HISTORY

# CHAPTER 1

······································································

# LAND AND SEA: THE ENVIRONMENT

······································································

## T. C. SMOUT

War against the wild forces of nature is, from the point of view of humanity, a constructive and in every way a useful operation, worthy of the attention of all statesmen who have the real welfare of the country at heart.

> H. M. Cadell, *The Story of the Forth* (Glasgow, 1913), p. 225.

SIXTEENTH- and seventeenth-century topographers, like Bishop Leslie and Gordon of Straloch, spoke of the Scottish environment as though it were a given, a gift from a good but often incomprehensible God. Eighteenth-century lairds and philosophers spoke of improvement, nineteenth-century industrialists of the march of progress, Edwardian engineers (like Cadell) of warfare against nature, while modern politicians and environmentalists talk of sustainable development. All are speaking of ways to live comfortably, or more comfortably, in the world around us.

As E. A. Wrigley has emphasized, all life depends on capturing a proportion of the streaming energy of the sun, which even in cloudy northern Britain is equivalent to 22,000 million tons of coal a year.[1] The food of all life on earth rests ultimately on photosynthesis, the process by which vegetable growth is able to capture solar energy, albeit only between one and four parts per thousand. When we eat grain, or meat, or fish we transfer some of this to ourselves, and for an active life a working human population

---

[1] E. A. Wrigley, 'Meeting Human Energy Needs: Constraints, Opportunities and Effects', in P. Slack, ed., *Environments and Historical Change* (Oxford, 1998), 76–95; E. A. Wrigley, 'Energy Constraints and Pre-Industrial Economies', in S. Cavaciocchi, ed., *Economia e Energia secc. XIII–XVIII* (Florence, 2003); E. A. Wrigley, 'The Transition to an Advanced Organic Economy: Half a Millennium of English Agriculture', *Economic History Review*, 59 (2006), 435–80.

needs an intake of 3,500 calories per adult per day, though 1,500 calories will suffice to keep a person alive. When we use thermal energy to keep warm, we use fuel: if it is wood, we use the energy of decades of photosynthesis stored in the trees we fell; if it is peat, we use the stored energy of centuries, even of millennia; if it is coal, gas, or oil, that of possibly tens of millions of years. With good silviculture, trees are a renewable crop. Peat, coal, gas, and oil are not renewable on any human timescale, though until the 1970s they were assumed to be inexhaustible resources—perhaps not locally but certainly globally.

When motive power was needed for ploughing to move goods or to turn machinery, there was once only the choice of simple forms of kinetic energy: muscle power deriving from photosynthesis, either human or animal (a horse is on average ten times stronger than a man), or sources of renewable mechanical energy such as watermills, windmills, and sails. Both the wind and the rain also derive their energy from the sun, the first through differential warming of the earth, the second from solar evaporation in the hydrological cycle. The thermal energy of fuel could not be translated into the kinetic energy of motion until after the invention and development of the rotary steam engine by James Watt and others. With the Industrial Revolution, inorganic fuels swept the board as the prime means by which humanity endeavoured to live more comfortably.

In the last resort the success of economies, of states themselves, has always rested on their access to the sun's energy, current or stored, and on their efficiency in using it. The biggest shift of all is this shift from an organic to an inorganic economy: in the first, humanity used within a year mainly the photosynthesis of that year; in the second, the world now uses annually the accumulated photosynthesis of half a million years, and as we near the peak in oil drilling we realize that a fossil-fuel economy is not sustainable. To speak of the conquest of nature is an oxymoron, since the sun is always inescapably in control of us.

## 1500–1750

In the centuries before 1750, the ability of the Scots and everyone else to capture and use the energy of the sun was not basically different from what it had been in the Iron Age, though changes and improvements had been made at the edges. It depended mostly on photosynthesis through land-extensive methods of husbandry assisted by animals and metal-tipped tools, inefficient by modern standards but good enough to provide a dispersed population with enough calories to survive in most years, and since the Middle Ages also able to support modest urban populations of craftsmen and merchants. To a small degree it also depended on forms of hunter-gathering probably little changed since prehistory, of which fishing with nets and lines on rivers, shores, and from inshore boats, was the most useful. Thermal energy came from peat bogs and turf, seldom from firewood: in the sixteenth and seventeenth centuries it also increasingly came in the Central Belt from coal deposits, which facilitated the growth of Edinburgh, already called Auld Reekie, from a few thousand individuals in 1500 to over forty thousand by

1750. Kinetic energy derived from the muscles of people and horses (still occasionally oxen before 1600), and to a smaller but vital degree from watermills (primarily to process grain) and sailing ships (to trade coastally and overseas). It infrequently came, in blustery Scotland, from windmills.

Compared to other parts of the British Isles, Scotland suffered from two interlinked disadvantages in garnering photosynthetic energy. The first was altitude and slope. Though there were extensive tracts of fertile low arable lands, particularly in the east, only 40 per cent of Scotland is below 500 feet/152 metres (but 79 per cent of England and 78 per cent of Ireland): 31 per cent is above 1,000 feet/305 metres (but 6 per cent of England and 4 per cent of Ireland).[2] This meant that much of the photosynthetic energy had to be gained indirectly from grazing animals rather than directly from crops, at a very low calorie yield per acre. The second disadvantage was climate. Scotland certainly benefited very much from the amelioration of temperature from the warm waters of the Gulf Stream compared to lands at similar latitudes (like Labrador in Canada). But it nevertheless endured more wind and rain, more cold and shorter growing seasons than most other parts of the British Isles.

The configuration of the ground combined with underlying clay soils and schists in the glaciated valleys to turn much low ground into acid bog and marsh, or cover it with standing water. This was so even in Lothian, Fife, and Strathmore, areas of great potential fertility, as well as in the north and west. ' 'Tis almost incredible how much of the mountains they plough', said the visitor Thomas Morer in 1689, because the valleys were so often 'almost useless, on account of frequent bogs and waters in such places.'[3] Yet ground subject to flooding was also cultivated if it was not actually waterlogged, sometimes with catastrophic results: thus at Glen Shira in Argyll around 1700, farmers found themselves washed out of their homes and land, 'catching salmon where they had previously cultivated oats'.[4]

The second disadvantage was climatic. Throughout early modern Europe, the rural economy of marginal and upland areas was severely affected by the prolonged episode of global cooling known as the Little Ice Age.[5] This is best understood as a period between the thirteenth and the mid-nineteenth centuries when the weather became cooler, wetter, and windier than at any time in the last ten thousand years, but it was not itself of uniform and unvarying severity. The fourteenth and earlier fifteenth centuries had very notable years and decades of catastrophic weather characterized by famine and flood, but the period 1500–50 was about as mild as the first half of the twentieth century. Then the nadir of the Little Ice Age is reached between the late sixteenth and the end of the seventeenth centuries with particularly bad episodes in the 1560s, the 1590s, and the

---

[2] B. M. S. Campbell, 'Benchmarking Medieval Economic Development: England, Wales, Scotland and Ireland, c.1290', *Economic History Review*, 61 (2008), 921.

[3] P. Hume Brown, *Early Travellers in Scotland* (Edinburgh, 1891), 267.

[4] R. A. Dodgshon, 'Coping with Risk: Subsistence Crises in the Scottish Highlands 1600–1800', *Rural History*, 15 (2004), 1–25.

[5] J. Grove, *The Little Ice Age* (London, 1988). This account is to be preferred to the more superficial one by B. Fagan, *The Little Ice Age* (New York, 2000).

1620s. Worst of all was the so-called Maunder Minimum between 1645 and 1715 (temperatures were lowest between 1670 and 1700 in Scotland, with spells of hot dry weather in the 1650s and 1660s). The first half of the eighteenth century saw a relative improvement, but with very bad conditions returning in 1739–41, and on several occasions in the second half of the eighteenth century and the early nineteenth century.

Scotland, a high, wet country on the north-western periphery of Europe, bore the full brunt of this climatic variability, not least because the surface of the North Atlantic between the Faeroes and Iceland became some 5°C colder than it is today. There has been as yet relatively little detailed examination of the Scottish weather itself in the Little Ice Age, but H. H. Lamb, doyen of English climate historians, and more recently, Alastair Dawson, have drawn together most of what is known about Scotland.[6] Though there were warm spells in mid-century, there is much evidence of seventeenth-century cold, with permanent snow fields forming in the Cairngorms, permanent ice on high lochans in Strathglass, and in the 1690s a handful of lost Eskimo hunters who found themselves driven in their kayaks, by encroaching Arctic ice, to Orkney and Aberdeen. Lamb suggests that the temperature over the year would have averaged, in the late seventeenth century, 1.5°–2° colder than in the mid-twentieth century, compared to 0.9° colder in England. Cod, which cannot withstand near-freezing temperatures, left the waters around Shetland. There was also much evidence of storms; as the North Atlantic oscillation was turned on, the cold seas created a steep thermal gradient that bred cyclonic winds greater than most storms of modern times. This led to serious episodes of sandblow in the Hebrides (e.g. Tiree and North Uist), at Culbin in Morayshire, and at Rattray and Forvie in Aberdeenshire—at Culbin a mansion house and nine farms covering perhaps 23 square miles were lost. Contrary to popular belief, this would not all have vanished in a single storm but rather have been the consequence of storms over a long period—the formation of the sandbar that closed off Rattray from the sea and formed the Loch of Strathbeg, for example, was first noted in 1413 but became impassable only in 1720. Nor should the effects of storms on shipping be underestimated—the great December hurricane of 1703 sank so many boats that it contributed significantly to the Scottish economic crisis of 1704, 'one of the least years of trade that has been in this age', when the Bank of Scotland ceased payment.[7]

The most serious impact of the Little Ice Age, however, was on the length of the growing season and thus on the photosynthetic abilities of plants. Lamb suggested that the growing season in northern Europe shortened by three weeks or more in the late Middle Ages, and that in the seventeenth century in England by about five weeks in comparison

    [6] A. Dawson, *So Fair and Foul a Day: A History of Scotland's Weather and Climate* (Edinburgh, 2009); H. H. Lamb, *Climate, History and the Modern World* (London, 1982); H. H. Lamb, 'Climate and Landscape in the British Isles', in S. R. J. Woodell, ed., *The English Landscape: Past, Present and Future* (Oxford, 1985), 148–67. See also R. A. Dodgshon, 'The Little Ice Age in the Scottish Highlands and Islands: Documenting its Human Impact', *Scottish Geographical Journal*, 121 (2005), 321–37, and sources cited therein.

    [7] J. A. Steers, *The Sea Coast* (London, 1953), 138–42, 146–8; T. C. Smout, *Scottish Trade on the Eve of Union* (Edinburgh, 1963), 254–5.

to the warmer decades of the twentieth century. In the coldest years like 1695 and 1740, when the summer temperatures were about 2°C lower than the twentieth-century norm, and springs and autumns cold as well, 'the growing season was probably shortened by two months or even more'.[8]

Richard Tipping, investigating the area of the Bowmont Valley on the Scottish side of the Cheviot hills, found an increasing tendency to serious flooding in the late seventeenth and early eighteenth century, an increase in wetness on the bog surface, associated with the growth of sphagnum moss especially in 1550–1600 and 1675–1700, and a lowering of snow-bed plant communities to about 1,200 feet (366 metres), 'well within the daily agricultural "round"'.[9] More local studies of this calibre are badly needed.

All this resulted in a series of Scottish crop failures, dearths, and famines, mainly before the start of the eighteenth century. Scholarly examination of sixteenth-century famines has been quite cursory,[10] but those of the seventeenth century, and especially of the 1690s, have been subject to much more detailed examination. Recent work has emphasized the severity, length, and national depth of 'King William's Ill Years', and suggested that the demographic and economic consequences have been underestimated. Locally in Aberdeenshire and very possibly elsewhere in the Highlands and southern uplands the losses could have amounted to a fifth or more of the population.[11] Similarly, the years 1673–6 and 1681–3, which were associated with heavy snow and disastrous loss of sheep and cattle especially in the south-west, also occasioned a surge in burials and emigration on a scale hitherto unappreciated.

The economic devastation in the Highlands in the seventeenth century has been well delineated by R. A. Dodgshon—here holdings were laid waste and payments of rents of necessity remitted or delayed for years, even decades, following bad years, in an area where parish registers do not survive to measure the loss of human life. I. Whyte shows similarly that in the Borders the problem was not just the bad crop years of the 1690s but a period of 'long-term difficulty extending over at least 15 years during which conditions were consistently unfavourable to cattle-rearing'. Extended wet seasons were even worse at a high altitude than at a low one, and they hit livestock in these areas much more than cereals at low altitudes.[12]

[8]  Lamb, Climate, History, 223ff.

[9]  R. Tipping, 'Palaeoecology and Political History: Evaluating Driving Forces in Historic Landscape Change in Southern Scotland', in I. D. Whyte and A. J. L. Winchester, eds., Society, Landscape and Environment in Upland Britain (Society for Landscape Studies, sup. ser. 2, 2004), 11–20.

[10]  Apart from a comment in Dodgshon, 'Little Ice Age', 238–9, little has appeared since S. G. E. Lythe, The Economy of Scotland in its European Setting, 1550–1625 (Edinburgh, 1960).

[11]  The standard work of M. W. Flinn, ed., Scottish Population History from the Seventeenth Century to the 1930s (Cambridge, 1977), has been expanded in particular by R. E. Tyson, 'Famine in Aberdeenshire, 1695–1699: Anatomy of a Crisis', in D. Stevenson, ed., From Lairds to Louns: Country and Burgh Life in Aberdeen 1600–1800 (Aberdeen, 1986); K. Cullen, C. Whatley, and M. Young, 'King William's Ill Years: New Evidence on the Impact of Scarcity and Harvest Failure During the Crisis of the 1690s in Tayside', Scottish Historical Review, 85 (2006), 250–76.

[12]  Dodgshon, 'Little Ice Age'; I. Whyte, 'Human Response to Short- and Long-Term Climatic Fluctuations: The Example of Early Scotland', in C. D. Smith and M. Parry, eds., Consequences of Climatic Change (Nottingham, 1981), 17–28, quote on 23.

How far holdings were actually abandoned in marginal areas in the Little Ice Age is a disputed question. M. L. Parry's thesis, based on a study of the Lammermuirs, was that the altitudinal range of cultivation retracted appreciably. It is challenged by Tipping, who found no such evidence on the Cheviot edge, while Dodgshon found mixed results in the Highlands and Whyte points out that reduction of cereal acreage and amalgamation of farms is more likely to be the consequence of a run of bad years than actual desertion.[13]

Long-term abandonment of arable land may have depended on more than the weather; the relative movement of prices for animals and oats in the Edinburgh market, for example, may have tempted landlords and farmers to shift towards the former in the Lammermuirs, but might have had little effect in the Cheviots or on Rannoch Moor. On the highland west coast, however, it may have been the sheer force of the storms even more than the cold that forced the abandonment of arable land.

From all this, it might be supposed that the Scots lived on the edge of subsistence in a country only marginally able to support its people. Such was indeed the case over large parts of the Highlands in the seventeenth and eighteenth centuries. Harvest shortfalls occurred (according to some commentators) every fourth or seventh year, though it helped that landowners might then remit or delay grain rents. Even in relatively good seasons there was often a 'hungry gap' in late summer, between the consumption of the last of the stored grain and the onset of a new harvest. At such times the population turned to 'famine foods'—fish if they could get it, shellfish and edible seaweeds gathered from the shore, the blood of cattle tapped from a vein, or the leaves and roots of land plants like nettles and silverweed. The fields of growing oats or bere (a hardy form of barley) abounded in colourful flowers that outsiders considered weeds. Dodgshon has suggested that these were deliberately tolerated by the farmers, because many of them also provided nutrition in the difficult months. The highlanders had a considered strategy for coping with the chronic risk of hunger that beset such marginal areas in these difficult climatic times.[14]

But Scotland, though small, has a highly varied topography, with tracts of relatively fertile land as well as open hill and bog. Outside the Highlands things were less desperate. The country was usually a net exporter of food (fish, meat, and grain), notably so after about 1600. Furthermore, travellers from the outside, however unsympathetic they might be otherwise to the Scots—as so many English were—did not describe the common people of the Lowlands as starving or under-nourished. And when institutions, whether universities or orphanages, left dietary records that can be analyzed, their inmates always turn out to be more than adequately provided with calories.[15] Scottish population increased after the plague-ridden lows of the late Middle Ages, at least to the

---

[13] M. L. Parry, *Climatic Change, Agriculture and Settlement* (Folkestone, 1978); M. L. Parry, 'Climatic Change and the Agricultural Frontier: A Research Strategy', in T. M. L. Wigley, M. J. Ingram, and G. Farmer, eds., *Climate and History* (Cambridge, 1981), 319–36; Tipping, 'Palaeoecology'; Dodgshon, 'Little Ice Age'; Whyte, 'Human Response'.

[14] Dodgshon, 'Coping with Risk'.

[15] Hume Brown, *Early Travellers*; A. J. Gibson and T. C. Smout, *Prices, Food and Wages in Scotland* (Cambridge, 1995).

early seventeenth century, and urban population increased faster still until by 1700 about one Scot in ten lived in a town. None of this would have been possible unless the lowland countryside generally provided more than enough food for the people.

The problem for Scotland as a whole was not chronic Malthusian pressure of population on resources, but inelastic supply when conditions for photosynthesis suddenly deteriorated, as in the 1590s and 1690s. There were no reserves, and the land could not suddenly produce more food. Though in the lowland countryside people might then also turn to famine foods and in the towns they might try to import grain from the Baltic or elsewhere in the British Isles, such shifts could not prevent national malnutrition or famine in these bad years. Yet such years were comparatively unusual except at the close of the sixteenth and seventeenth centuries.

So the Scottish population maintained itself (and increased) through a land-extensive system of husbandry that utilized and ecologically modified every possible inch of land below the highest mountain tops. Timothy Pont in the 1590s could still write on his draft maps of the Highlands, 'extreem wilderness' and 'many wolfs' in north-west Sutherland, and 'all fyr and other wood with great wilderness' at Rynettin in the Abernethy Forest.[16] But the history of animals suggests a steady erosion of truly wild land where large mammals could survive. Elks probably disappeared in the Iron Age, the auroch probably in the Bronze Age, the bear probably in post-Roman times, the wild boar by the thirteenth century. It has been argued that the lynx hung on into the Middle Ages, and beavers lingered into the sixteenth century near Loch Ness. Wolves were still common in the Highlands in the late Middle Ages, and were hunted by Mary, Queen of Scots in the Forest of Atholl in 1563. Robert Gordon of Straloch later in the 1630s said of Aberdeenshire and Banff that 'dangerous animals, hostile to the herds, are lacking, for wolves are now believed to have almost died out, or if there are still any, they are far away from gentler areas and human cultivation'.[17] By 1684 Robert Sibbald, Geographer Royal, believed them extinct in Scotland, and though there are stories of individuals killed by wolves in Perthshire in 1680, and in Sutherland between 1695 and 1700, there are no later plausible records.[18] The largest land bird in Scotland, the capercaillie, the 'cock of the woods' of the pine forests, survived until around 1780 after being in decline for at least a century (it was later successfully reintroduced).[19] Perhaps in this case climate change played a part, but all these species apart from the auroch survived in Scandinavia and in the wilder mountains of Europe, but not in Scotland.

---

[16] J. C. Stone, *The Pont Manuscript Maps of Scotland: Sixteenth-Century Origins of a Blaeu Atlas* (Tring, 1989), 30, 51; D. Yalden, *The History of British Mammals* (London, 1999); *The Blaeu Atlas of Scotland* (Edinburgh, 2006), 93.

[17] Yalden, *The History of British Mammals*; *The Blaeu Atlas of Scotland*, 93.

[18] The story of a wolf slain near Findhorn in 1743 after killing two children 'sounds like a fairy story' (wolves do not kill children) and was first related by the Sobieski Stuarts a century later; Yalden, *The History of British Mammals*, 168.

[19] See G. Stevenson's unpublished PhD thesis, Stirling University, 2007.

# 1750–1950

The most critical developments in the environmental history of Scotland after 1750 related to energy supply. Two forces were at work: a change in the availability of food energy, which enabled more people to be supported from the same area of land, and a revolution in the application of thermal energy, which enabled the concentration of people in cities.

The increasing supply of food energy begins after about 1760; in the central Lowlands, conventional grain yields of oats and barley had by 1800, improved by 200–300 per cent,[20] and in the Highlands the introduction of the potato might enable up to three or four times as many people to live off the same acreage of land as compared to putting it under grain.[21] This had the effect of allowing more people to work at trades and industries divorced from food production, but still, before 1800, using muscle power at hand looms or spinning wheels, or water power at the new cotton- and linen-spinning factories in the countryside.

After 1800, however, it became possible to use Watt's improvements to the steam engine to power rotary motion, so thermal energy was turned into kinetic energy for manufacture and transport. The transition from an organic to an inorganic economy began to gather pace, with enormous consequences. The timing and scale can be judged from the output of Scottish coal mines (Table 1.1), which before the twentieth century were the sole source of inorganic energy available on an industrial scale. The increase, tenfold in the eighteenth century, twentyfold in the nineteenth, was extraordinary.

These developments impacted directly on the growth and redistribution of population, with profound consequences for the natural world, and for the way in which humanity experienced its environment. The reasons for the growth and the details of the distribution are the subject of Chapter 2 below, but population grew fourfold over the period 1750–1950, and the proportion of the Scottish population living in settlements of over five thousand grew from about a fifth to two-thirds of the whole. Partly because of the dual nature of the developments in energy supply (both organic, and inorganic) there was not just a simple shift from country to town. Up until the middle of the nineteenth century both urban and rural populations grew, but thereafter there is only growth in town, and decline in country.

Rural communities lost population for many reasons, but historiographical concentration on the Highland clearances, and more recently on the 'Lowland clearances', has tended to emphasize *force majeur* over voluntary exodus.[22] All over Europe (Scotland

---

[20] T. M. Devine, *The Transformation of Rural Scotland: Social Change and the Agrarian Economy 1660–1815* (Edinburgh, 1994), 57.

[21] M. W. Flinn, ed., *Scottish Population History from the 17th Century to the 1930s* (Edinburgh, 1977), 427; F. H. A. Aalen, K. Whelan, and M. Stout, *Atlas of the Irish Rural Landscape* (Cork, 1997), 85–8, provides a good summary of the environmental and economic pros and cons of the potato.

[22] Eric Richards, *A History of the Highland Clearances*, 2 vols. (London, 1982–5), is the best account; Devine, *The Transformation of Rural Scotland*, esp. chs. 7 and 8.

Table 1.1 Annual output of coal from Scottish fields (million tons)

| 1690 | 0.225 | 1830–4 | 3.22 |
| 1750 | 0.7 | 1860–4 | 12.0 |
| 1775 | 1.0 | 1880–4 | 20.4 |
| 1800 | 2.0 | 1900–4 | 31.1 |
| 1815 | 2.5 | 1910–13 | 41.3 |

*Source*: C. A. Whatley, 'New Light on Nef's Numbers: Coal Mining and the First Phase of Scottish Industrialisation c.1700–1830', in A. J. G. Cummings and T. M. Devine, *Industry, Business and Society in Scotland since 1700* (Edinburgh, 1994), 2–23; M. W. Flinn, *The History of the British Coal Industry, vol. 2, 1700–1830* (1984); R. Church, *The History of the British Coal Industry, vol. 3, 1830–1914* (1986).

was no exception) very remote localities lost their attraction: once, many had seemed in environmental terms the ideal place for life, with a good supply of peat fuel, seaweed, and shell sand for fertilizer, seabirds, fish and rabbits for food, and perhaps free grazing outdoors all year for ponies to supplement human muscle power.[23] There were thousands of such townships in the Highlands, the Hebrides, and the Northern Isles, and though many were forcibly cleared, and some were weakened by voluntary emigration before the laird completed the job, others were deserted entirely voluntarily.

One of these was St Kilda, sixty miles out in the Atlantic but evacuated in 1930 after two thousand years of continuous occupation. In the seventeenth century, it had had a reputation for natural abundance, producing seabird oil, feathers, and flesh, wool, even grain, and supporting perhaps 180 people. By 1930 the population had shrunk to 37 and requested evacuation as an act of charity: what had once seemed a place of natural plenty now seemed to offer nothing but penury and hardship, but it was a society that had changed, not the environment. The seabird colonies benefited from the withdrawal of man. However, the St Kilda house mouse, genetically close to its Norwegian congeners and probably a Viking settler, but one which had in little over a thousand years become a distinctive subspecies (*Mus domesticus muralis*), was still so dependent on people that it became almost immediately extinct.[24]

One main consequence of the growing dominance of inorganic energy was that people flooded in large numbers to the towns and cities, a topic that will be explored in relation to their inhabitants and built environment in Chapter 24. Of the biggest cities, Glasgow with its port and surrounding towns containing nearly two million people by 1901, and Edinburgh with over four hundred thousand, both clearly also had a substantial impact on the environment, though these have not been widely studied.[25] We have

[23] T. C. Smout, *Exploring Environmental History: Selected Essays* (Edinburgh, 2009), ch. 7.

[24] A. Fleming, *St Kilda and the Wider World* (Oxford, 2005); Yalden, *The History of British Mammals*, 221.

[25] But see J. H. Dickson et al., *The Changing Flora of Glasgow: Urban and Rural Plants through the Centuries* (Edinburgh, 2000).

no equivalent yet of William Cronon's work on Chicago to explain the environmental history of a city and its hinterland.[26]

The impact of urban detritus on the surrounding countryside is clearly one major theme in this, and the example of Edinburgh gives an indication of how it developed. Certainly from the late seventeenth century, and perhaps from much earlier, disposal of the town's dung to the farmers nearby was seen as a profitable business, but by the early nineteenth century the latter were forming cartels to oblige the city to moderate its prices. The manure kept agriculture in a ring of Midlothian parishes so well supplied with nitrogen and other nutrients that they no longer needed cattle to supply it, and by this recycling, farms were kept under intensive cropping of wheat and vegetables. Something similar happened on the edge of late eighteenth-century Aberdeen, and nineteenth-century Dundee fertilized the raspberries of the Carse of Gowrie with its sewage. Even quite tiny burghs like Nairn and Pittenweem sold their 'fulzie' to spread on the fields. When the Union canal was built, stretching to Falkirk, Edinburgh waste could reach well into West Lothian.

By the 1840s, however, the growth of population, threefold in Edinburgh since 1750, meant that the problem began to spiral out of control, and the sanitary crisis of the early Victorian city, with its solution, flush toilets that carried the waste away diluted by water into drains, sewers, and ultimately into burns and rivers, brought this tradition of nutrient recycling to a halt. Sewage became waste, not resource. At first, councils were optimistic about continued sales, but as guano and other bagged, dry fertilizers became available to farmers, this was seen to be a false hope. Edinburgh poured her filth into the Water of Leith (it caused disgusting pollution in the harbour), into the River Almond and the Foul Burn, where it irrigated the meadows of a large sewage farm at Craigintinny, which was declared 'a decided financial success'. It was eventually closed in 1922 in response to local complaints about the smell and questions about the wholesomeness of food produced. Thereafter until 1978 all Edinburgh's sewage was poured largely untreated into the sea, through nine outfalls.[27]

The immediate effects of this water pollution, here and in similar cases throughout Scotland where tanneries, bleach and dye works, gas works, paper works, paraffin works, coal washings and similar industrial effluents took effect, was locally catastrophic to the fish life of rivers and streams, notably to salmon and trout. The oyster beds of the Firth of Forth, once perhaps the largest in Britain, had been wiped out through over-fishing, but recovery was made more difficult through pollution. A striking example not of industrial but of agricultural pollution was the effect of reclaiming the peat bogs west of Stirling by throwing the peat into the Forth river, where it floated down to smother sandy beaches and affect the sea bottom as far east as Queensferry.[28]

---

[26] W. Cronon, *Nature's Metropolis: Chicago and the Great West* (New York, 1991).

[27] For an introduction, see N. Goddard, '"A mine of wealth": The Victorians and the Agricultural Value of Sewage', *Journal of Historical Geography*, 22 (1996), 274–90.

[28] D. S. McLusky, 'Ecology of the Forth Estuary', *Forth Naturalist and Historian*, 3 (1978), 10–23.

Burning fossil fuels caused substantial air pollution, the consequences of which embraced both the human and the natural world. The windy weather of central Scotland might be supposed to have diffused the coal smoke from the streets of Auld Reekie and Glasgow, but the blackened buildings of both cities are proof otherwise. The consequences on the health of the population were dire: in Edwardian Glasgow 'experienced newspaper editors left extra space for obituaries during smog sieges', and a fog there in 1909 was calculated to have caused 1,063 extra deaths. As late as 1950, Glaswegians ordinarily inhaled about two pounds of soot each year. The solution came ultimately in the Clean Air Act of 1956, made easier by the substitution of oil and gas for coal without any great economic sacrifice.[29] Smoke pollution also had serious effects on nature, some species of butterflies becoming extinct in the Central Belt and only starting to return late in the twentieth century; the ancient oak wood in Dalkeith Park to the east of the city is still impoverished in its lichen flora because it lay in the path of the smoke plume from Victorian Edinburgh.

In the uplands, the ecological consequences of modernity have also been impoverishing, but by what mechanism is disputed. Fraser Darling famously described the Highlands as a 'wet desert', a zone of former Caledonian forest stripped of its nutrients by the axe and fire of iron-masters and graziers, and by the 'extractive tooth' of animals that consumed but did not recycle nutrients as the animals were driven off and used elsewhere.[30]

Deforestation is now seen to have been a very long drawn-out process, starting as early as the Neolithic and partly climatic in origin. It was substantially complete before 1500, and by 1750 less than a tenth of Scotland was woodland, much of that being open wood pasture and montane scrub.[31] The most obvious parts of a 'wet desert', the mires and flows of the north and west, have been interpreted by James Fenton as the normal ecological climax under the wetter climate of the last four thousand years.[32] Some of the most forested of the remaining areas, the oak woods of Argyll, actually seem to have benefited from the care that the iron-masters took of their fuel supply, and in a similar way those who exploited the belt of oak woods from Dumbartonshire to Perthshire for tanbark, and those who exploited the Scots pine forests of Strathspey and Deeside, contributed to their long-run conservation by taking good care of a profitable resource.[33]

[29] J. R. McNeill, *Something New Under the Sun: An Environmental History of the Twentieth-Century World* (New York, 2000), 63, 66, 70–1.

[30] F. F. Darling, *Pelican in the Wilderness* (London, 1956), 353. See also his *Natural History in the Highlands and Islands* (London, 1947); *West Highland Survey* (Oxford, 1955), 167–76, and 'Ecology of Land Use in the Highlands and Islands', in D. S. Thomson and I. Grimble, *The Future of the Highlands* (London, 1968).

[31] T. C. Smout, A. R. MacDonald, and F. Watson, *A History of the Native Woodlands of Scotland, 1500–1920* (Edinburgh, 2005); R. Tipping, 'The Form and Fate of Scottish Woodlands', *Proceedings of the Society of Antiquaries of Scotland*, 124 (1994), 1–54.

[32] J. H. C. Fenton, 'A Postulated Natural Origin for the Open Landscape of Upland Scotland', *Plant Ecology and Diversity*, 1 (1) (2008), 115–27. For ripostes from G. Peterken and K. D. Bennett, see *Plant Ecology and Diversity*, 2 (1) (2009), 89–94.

[33] Smout et al., *Native Woodlands*, ch. 9; J. M. Lindsay, 'Charcoal Iron Smelting and its Fuel Supply: The example of Lorn Furnace, Argyllshire, 1753–1876', *Journal of Historical Geography*, 1 (1975), 283–98.

The importance of grazing and burning in the open moors, however, can hardly be doubted. If stock is taken off and no fire is used, the drier heaths rapidly revert to birch, willow, and (in some cases) to Scots pine. Using fire to burn the moors, though, was not new, but had been an ancient tool used by farmers to favour grazing for their traditional mix of animals—small sheep, goats, horses, and in particular black cattle. After 1750, but especially after 1800, it was increasingly used to favour either the new flocks of large Cheviot and blackface sheep or in Victorian times to encourage grouse and deer on sporting moors.

The question therefore resolves into asking what were the ecological impacts on the open hill of the new land-management regimes of sheepmaster and sportsman? Fraser Darling's notion that the sale of sheep actually removed significant quantities of critical nutrients from the land has been hard to verify, and the readiness with which birch and willow return once grazing stops also suggests otherwise. The picture is complicated in that aerial deposition of nitrogen and phosphorous in acid rain from factory smoke began to occur from mid-Victorian times, and had the reverse effect to driving off nitrogen and phosphorus in meat and wool: indeed, acid rain seems likely to have been implicated in the decline of heather moorland and the spread of *Nardus strictus* grassland, especially in the west. It also altered the chemical composition and the microscopic fauna of even the highest and most remote lochans in the Cairngorms, as well as other lochs the length and breadth of Scotland.[34]

A more important agent for ecological change on the moors was probably the way the new sheep grazed. Sheep graze close and tread lightly, their small hard dung sits on the surface and oxidizes in the wind, whereas the old black cattle had grazed high, punctured the ground with their hooves, and their runny dung had got into the sward. The new flocks of sheep could also be summered on the hill in far greater numbers than in the past, when stock had been limited by the acute shortage of winter fodder. Now they could be kept on low ground and fed on turnips or (later) artificial feeding stuffs, so that a much bigger breeding stock could occupy the hill in summer and graze all its resources to the utmost.[35]

People at the time noted an environmental transformation over a generation. The montane scrub, full of berries and insects, was eaten off or burned away to improve the grazing: the old summer shielings (mountain pastures), once patches of flowers and sweet herbs high on the hill, became part of the close uniform mat of heather or of *Nardus* and *Molinia* grassland: lower down people noticed a more general decline. Osgoode Mackenzie called Gairloch in his grandfather's time:

> The most perfect wild Highland glen…the braes and wooded hillocks were a perfect jungle of primroses and bluebells and honeysuckle and all sorts of orchids which then quite whitened the ground.[36]

[34] T. C. Smout, *Nature Contested: An Environmental History of Scotland and Northern England, 1600–2000* (Edinburgh, 2000), ch. 5.
[35] Ibid.
[36] O. L. Mackenzie, *A Hundred Years in the Highlands* (Edinburgh, 1988), p. 24.

He made his great artificial garden at Inverewe in Wester Ross to compensate for the great natural garden he had lost. Modern palynological investigation has confirmed contemporary testimony and oral history, and shown a clear decline in floral biodiversity following the arrival of the sheep flocks and the departure of peasant farming.[37]

Scottish landowners, of course, had always hunted game, but sporting estates as a primary land use only began in the early nineteenth century. With the invention of the cartridge and the shotgun they became popular from early Victorian times, and greatly multiplied after 1870 when sheep farming ran into a depression. Most deer forests and grouse moors had therefore already undergone ecological alteration as sheep runs beforehand, and they also used fire as vegetation control. By 1912, 3.6 million acres (and at least 40 per cent of Ross and Cromarty and of Inverness-shire) were deer forest, and what had been a comparatively scarce animal in the well-populated landscape of the eighteenth century became abundant: by 1940 there were reckoned to be 250,000 red deer in the Highlands (but 347,000 by 1990). From early in the nineteenth century they were abundant enough to hinder natural regeneration of pine in Deeside and elsewhere—Fraser Darling reckoned that sixty thousand was the highest population of red deer the land could bear without damage.[38]

Where an estate was used primarily for grouse or salmon, the main ecological impact was in the destruction of raptors. In the case of grouse, this might be rewarded by a short-term surge in the numbers available to shoot, invariably checked by outbreaks of disease and by a longer-term deterioration of habitat where the moors were also grazed by sheep.

The elimination of predators, however, was long-lasting: most of the damage came before 1840, and after around 1870 gamekeepers were mainly engaged in mopping-up operations, as Richard Lovegrove has demonstrated. The records of the fur market held every year in February at Dumfries indicate the scale in the south-west: in 1831, 600 polecat and 226 otter skins were exposed for sale, but none of either by 1869. In the Highlands, the main records are estate vermin returns; there must always be a question where bounties were paid, but owners were not fools and usually demanded the evidence of heads or wings. So we should not dismiss it out of hand when we hear of 143 pine martens and 295 eagles killed at Langwell and Sandside in Sutherland, 1819–26, and similar statistics. Some species of predators became extinct in Scotland as a result (polecat, red kite, osprey, sea eagle) and others were greatly reduced (wild cat, pine marten, otter, hen harrier, golden eagle). It was well into the second half of the twentieth century before there was even limited recovery from this Victorian slaughter.[39]

---

[37] N. Hanley, D. Tinch, K. Angelopoulis, A. Davies, E. B. Barbier, and F. Watson, 'What Drives Long-Run Biodiversity Change', *Journal of Environmental Economics and Management*, 57 (1) (2009), 5–20.

[38] A. Watson, 'Eighteenth-Century Deer Numbers and Pine Regeneration near Braemar, Scotland', *Biological Conservation*, 25 (1983), 289–305; F. F. Darling, *West Highland Survey* (Oxford, 1955), 178; J. S. Smith, 'Changing Deer Numbers in the Scottish Highlands since 1780', in T. C. Smout, ed., *Scotland since Prehistory: Natural Change and Human Impact* (Aberdeen, 1993), 79–88.

[39] R. Lovegrove, *Silent Fields: The Long Decline of a Nation's Wildlife* (Oxford, 2007), ch. 4.

The Victorians became extremely attached to the beauty and wildness of highland scenery, and thanks to the railway and the improved road network, came to enjoy it not only as sportsmen but also as ramblers, mountaineers, and landscape connoisseurs.[40] But the movement for environmental defence came late and was not as strong as in England. The first bird-protection legislation of 1869 was directed to the defence of sea-bird colonies and inspired by a campaign in Yorkshire: it was opposed by fishery interests in Scotland. The National Trust was formed to defend the Lake District in 1895. Not until 1931 was there an equivalent body in Scotland. Knowledge of Scottish biodiversity did not lag—naturalists like William McGillivray and John Harvie-Brown were as industrious and sophisticated as any—and one of the leading proto-ecologists was Patrick Geddes, but somehow knowledge and enthusiasm failed to translate into effective defence of the environment.

Indeed, in one area, the scientists failed to blow the whistle soon enough because they did not believe any harm was being done. The Victorians greatly intensified the exploitation of the sea. Of course, since Mesolithic times fishermen had harvested the marine environment in innumerable ingenious ways, ranging from fish traps and shore-based nets and lines to inshore boats all around the coasts and islands. In the eighteenth century more ambitious herring busses copied the Dutch in making lengthier voyages into the North Sea and Atlantic, but mostly the fisheries were neither well capitalized nor ambitious. Though their prosperity ebbed and flowed, it was not due to any depredation on the stock but rather to the natural vagaries of the fish themselves, and to variations in ocean currents and temperatures that drew them nearer to or further away from human grasp.

The first expansion of the herring industry had nothing to do with steam power, but involved a new design of large, decked, wooden sailing boats capable of venturing further out, and usually equally novel cotton nets, thereby vastly increasing the catch: herring landings went up about eightfold between 1810 and 1880. Steam trawlers were introduced from the 1880s and revolutionized the pursuit of white fish. Steam-driven and steel-hulled drifters followed twenty years later, and dominated the herring fishing on the eve of the First World War. By then the herring catch, at over 2 million barrels, was twentyfold what it had been a century earlier.[41]

Though much more research needs to be done in this area, it seems likely that already by the 1880s more herring were being caught than could be replaced by the breeding stock, as some suspected at the time. But Professor W. E. McIntosh of the new Gatty Marine Laboratory at St Andrews, and the leading Scottish fish scientist of his age, declared there was no need to worry, and he received support from no less a figure than Thomas Huxley, who declared the seas inexhaustible.[42] Despite dissent from some, the dominant voice of science was reassuring, and this combined with the boundless enter-

---

[40]  Smout, *Exploring Environmental History*, ch. 2.

[41]  J. R. Coull, *The Sea Fisheries of Scotland: A Historical Geography* (Edinburgh, 1996): statistics on p. 105.

[42]  D. W. Sims and A. J. Southward, 'Dwindling Fish Numbers Already of Concern in 1883', *Nature*, 439 (9) (2006), 660.

prise of fishermen to prepare the way for emptying the seas of palatable fish. The productivity of the North Sea today is, in these terms, about one-tenth of what it was in 1883.[43]

# 1950–2010

Scotland at the opening of the twenty-first century was apparently set on the road to environmental disaster. It could hardly be otherwise. It was a small but whole-hearted and generally successful part of a global economy growing out of control at an unprecedented rate. *Something New Under the Sun* was the apt title of John McNeill's book on twentieth-century global environmental history, where he lays out the basic figures: between the 1890s and the 1990s world population grew fourfold, urban population thirteenfold, industrial output fortyfold, energy use sixteenfold, carbon dioxide emissions seventeenfold, cattle population fourfold, pig population ninefold, and marine fish catch thirty-fivefold.[44] Scotland did not experience increases in any of these indicators of anything like such magnitudes, mainly because she started from the higher base of early industrialization: but as part of the developed world we have enjoyed rising levels of consumption, which are the primary forces impelling these indices up and up. Scottish GDP rose by an average of 1.9 per cent per year between 1978 and 2008. New registrations of motor vehicles rose from 100,000 a year in 1963 to 250,000 in 2007, when there were 51 vehicles for every 100 people (the figure for Great Britain was 57). Despite gains in the efficiency of energy use, UK consumption of primary energy rose by about 1 per cent per year between 1980 and 2000: it would have been much the same in Scotland.[45]

The Scottish global footprint (the measure of our resource use in relation to the total of the earth's resources) showed in 2009 that if everyone else lived as we do, we would need more than two earths to survive. Our efforts to reduce the impact, however, are not inconsiderable: by 2007 about a fifth of electricity in Scotland was generated by renewables, half from hydro; this was twice the proportion at the start of the century. But our efforts within Scotland are more than outweighed by the consequences of our growing consumption of goods. Thus greenhouse gas emissions for which we are responsible fell by 13 per cent between 1995 and 2004 if we take into account only those generated within Scotland, but if we take into account those emissions generated by Scots buying manufactured imports like cars and TV sets, they actually rose by 11 per cent over the same period.[46]

[43]  Charles Clover, *The End of the Line* (London, 2004), 54.

[44]  McNeill, *Something New Under the Sun*.

[45]  'Key Scottish Environment Statistics 2009', www.scotland.gov.uk/Publications/2009/08/26112651/0; P. Warde, *Energy Consumption in England and Wales 1560–2000* (CNR, Italy, 2007).

[46]  'Production of a Time Series of Scotland's Ecological and Greenhouse Gas Footprints', www.scotland.gov.uk/Publications/2009/10/28101012/0.

There is a lack of easily available environmental statistics specific to Scotland going back any distance of time, and it would be a good academic project to compile them. Climate statistics are the exception, with a good series going back to 1857. Scotland, like the rest of the globe, has become warmer over that period, markedly so in the last half-century: it has also become wetter. Rising consumption of inorganic energy across the world appears to be the root cause, but as Alasdair Dawson reminds us, there are other players in climate change (notably sunspot activity). The outcome of rising temperatures acting on the oceans could either lead to Scotland becoming as cold as Labrador or to an accentuation of present warming trends: we simply do not know.[47]

There is, however, an environmental history of Scotland since 1950 to be written apart from this catastrophe movie, and it concerns changes in agriculture, forestry, and fisheries, advances in pollution control, and the rise of an environmental movement. Not everything in our modern period is gloom and doom.

It is, however, all remarkably little studied. Scottish farming in the twentieth century lacks even an economic history, apart from a useful chapter-length study by Ewen Cameron, which stresses that livestock farming accounted for 76–77 per cent of output (by value) in the 1950s and 1960s, falling to about 64 per cent since 1990, and that about two-thirds of the agricultural area in Scotland is composed of rough grazing—'arable farming, though valuable, is a minority pursuit in Scotland'.[48] This sets parameters for rural environmental history, and explains why the consequences of mechanization, chemicalization, and arable-directed subsidy, which in the post-war period wrought such havoc with farmland biodiversity in England generally, had only a more muted impact on Scotland beyond the main grain-growing areas of Angus, Fife, and Lothian, and even there less severely than in East Anglia and other arable counties in England.

Nonetheless, Scottish farming was severely affected by all the crises and trends that moulded British agriculture as a whole in the late twentieth century. One event that has been studied in appropriate detail is the introduction and spread of myxomatosis in Scotland in 1954–5, which was unreservedly welcomed in Scotland (unlike in England) in the hope that a major pest to agriculture, the rabbit, could be eliminated.[49] Similar detailed treatment awaits historians of the epizootic diseases, of bovine spongiform encephalopathy (BSE, or mad cow disease) in 2000, and foot-and-mouth disease in 1967 and 2001, which affected not pests but the most valuable products of Scottish agriculture. Also worth consideration is the environmental history of agricultural pollution in Scotland, from the devastation caused by organochlorine insecticides (DDT and its allies) in the 1950s and 1960s (particularly to peregrine falcons and other raptors at the head of the food chain), to the pollution caused by excessive use of nitrogen fertilizer, notably to the Ythan river in Aberdeenshire and to parts of Fife.

---

[47] Graphs are conveniently reproduced in 'Key Scottish Environment Statistics in 2005', www.scotland.gov.uk/Publications/2005/08/15135632/56389; Dawson, *So Foul and Fair*, 204, 210–11.

[48] E. A. Cameron, 'The Modernisation of Scottish Agriculture', in T. M. Devine, C. H. Lee, and G. C. Peden, eds., *The Transformation of Scotland: The Economy since 1700* (Edinburgh, 2005), 184–207.

[49] P. Bartrip, 'The Arrival, Spread and Impact of Myxomatosis in Scotland during the 1950s', *Scottish Historical Review*, 88 (2009), 134–53.

The effects of overgrazing by sheep have already been referred to, but the manner in which it was exacerbated by subsidy before and after Britain joined the European Community in 1973 remains under-researched; yet this is reflected in dramatic declines of the characteristic birds of rough grassland, lapwings and curlews. The environmental history of the sporting estate is also largely a blank sheet: two related topics that are frequently in the news are the illegal persecution of raptors and the decline of grouse numbers, both of which have a history spanning much of the twentieth century. Often the latter appears to have been connected, as on the Buccleuch estates in the south of Scotland, with habitat deterioration associated with overgrazing when owners tried to make the most of two sources of income that were perhaps incompatible. Peter Hudson's work on the red grouse has a significant historical dimension utilizing runs of game books back to the nineteenth century, which indicates a way to proceed.[50]

The biggest land-use change in Scotland since 1950 has been afforestation by Sitka spruce and other American conifers: only 6 per cent of the land surface was under wood in 1960, but 17 per cent is afforested today, mostly by conifers. This was a programme initially driven by the forestry commission, but in the later 1970s and early 1980s it was largely executed by private forestry companies, the government agency granting permissions, distributing grants, and setting targets. Some Secretaries of State for Scotland (Willie Ross for one) thought these too low, such were the high and entirely unfulfilled expectations of the economic benefit of forestry to remote areas. The political, administrative, and technological background has been told both in relation to the UK and specifically to Scotland, and the social implications are being explored at the moment in a series of oral history pamphlets.[51] A longer, in-depth, oral history that does justice to the environmental impact of the process is Ruth Tittensor's study of Whitelee Forest in Ayrshire, which stresses the total ecological transformation involved in converting peat bog and open moor into a dense conifer forest. She also demonstrates the disenchantment of the local population when they found that afforestation was not the key to jobs and prosperity, and the loss of access when open country was replaced by an impenetrable and tall barrier of Sitka.[52]

The end of the planting bonanza came in 1986 with the withdrawal of Mrs Thatcher's government from supportive tax breaks for forestry, which had been designed to encourage investment irrespective of where the trees went. The occasion was a dispute over the proposed drainage for planting of the Flow Country in Caithness and Sutherland, which would have obliterated for small returns in timber production one of the last large wilderness areas in Scotland. That this conflict took place at all, and that it had a political outcome favourable to the wilderness, would have been unthinkable earlier. It

[50] P. Hudson, *Grouse in Space and Time* (Fordingbridge, 1992).

[51] D. Foot, 'The Twentieth Century: Forestry Takes Off', in T. C. Smout, ed., *People and Woods in Scotland: A History* (Edinburgh, 2003); J. Tsouvalis, *A Critical Geography of Britain's State Forests* (Oxford, 2000). The pamphlets are the Touchwood History series undertaken by Forestry Commission Scotland with the University of the Highlands and Islands and the University of Aberdeen.

[52] R. Tittensor, *From Peat Bog to Conifer Forest: An Oral History of Whitelee, its Community and Landscape* (Chichester, 2009).

demonstrates the political power of an alliance between ecological science and popular interest in nature conservation, which had Victorian roots but had grown in strength particularly since the 1970s.[53] In a British context such conflicts have been well studied by John Sheail,[54] and in a highland context discussed by several historians and anthropologists.[55] Conflicts between 'use and delight', rural developers or land managers on the one hand, and conservationists and their supporters on the other, were commonplace from 1950 onwards. Early in the twenty-first century they have lessened but not gone away. They do not always have consequences favourable to conservation, as the victory of the American developer Donald Trump demonstrated in 2008 when he gained permission from the Scottish government to destroy the largest mobile dune system left in Scotland in order to build a golf resort. Such battles have been wide-ranging, focusing in the earlier decades particularly on hydroelectric schemes, then on the conservation of habitat, more recently on the placing of wind farms and the reintroduction of lost species like sea eagles and beavers.[56]

These conflicts are often conceptualized as town versus country, or expert versus local knowledge, but the reality is complex. Rural communities have indeed often been hostile to attempts to restrict their development opportunities, but have sometimes rounded on the developers (as with the Lewis windfarm and Harris superquarry in the Western Isles) or have at least failed to support them (as with the Flow Country). And urban populations have been indifferent to some problems, like the siting of waste tips and incinerators beyond their boundaries, or the course of motorways. As Kevin Dunion has shown, local communities have then been left to fight their own corner in a search for environmental justice, with no support from the big conservation charities like the National Trust for Scotland, the Scottish Wildlife Trust, or the RSPB, who fight for nature conservation, and only the relatively impoverished Friends of the Earth as backers. In such cases direct action was often the only realistic course for the objectors (as defenders of their families and communities), and the history of the protests at Greengairs in North Lanarkshire and at Kirknewton in West Lothian, both in the 1990s, read like episodes in radical labour history.[57] Far more work can be done on the structure and social meaning of conflicts over the environment since the end of the Second World War. It is worth noting that the history of biodiversity decline and nature conservation in Scotland has received far more attention than the history of emissions and pollution control, with the history of amenity preservation falling somewhere in between.

---

[53] Smout, *Exploring Environmental History*, 107–8.

[54] J. Sheail, *Nature in Trust: The History of Nature Conservation in Britain* (Glasgow, 1976); J. Sheail, *An Environmental History of Twentieth-Century Britain* (London, 2002).

[55] Smout, *Exploring Environmental History*; Smout, *Nature Contested*; R. A. Lambert, *Contested Mountains: Nature, Development and Environment in the Cairngorm Region of Scotland, 1880–1980* (Cambridge, 2001); K. V. L. Syse, *From Land Use to Landscape: A Cultural History of Conflict and Consensus in Argyll, 1945–2005* (Acta Humaniora 402, University of Oslo, 2009).

[56] C. Warren, *Managing Scotland's Environment*, 2nd edn. (Edinburgh, 2009); C. Warren and R. V. Birnie, 'Re-Powering Scotland: Windfarms and the "Energy or Environment? Debate"', *Scottish Geographical Journal*, 125 (2009), 97–126.

[57] K. Dunion, *Troublemakers: The Struggle for Environmental Justice in Scotland* (Edinburgh, 2003).

What happens on land is always better studied than what happens invisibly below the surface of the sea. Marine fisheries provide the example of the most profligate of all resource exploitations, not only in Scotland but throughout the globe. The Scottish fisheries entered the second half of the twentieth century with replenished stocks (thanks to the interruption of fishing during the war) but with an industry at low ebb following the interwar collapse of the once-enormous herring sales to the Baltic and Russia. The fleet was rebuilt with the help of government subsidy and a remarkable level of technological application. The period of 1945–75 was critical for the introduction of scientific methods of fishing, both mechanical and electronic. Two modern purse seiners (fishing vessels) with a crew of thirty could in 1986 catch more fish than could a thousand boats with five thousand men in the 1840s, even if they only fished for a quarter of the time of their predecessors.[58] Much of the harvest of the purse seiners was used for fertilizer or animal foodstuffs, whereas earlier the catch had been entirely for human consumption except in times of glut.

The 1970s began with closure of the herring fisheries for several years due to depletion of stock: forty years later it was the cod stocks that were in deep trouble. After entry to the Common Market in 1973, the industry was directed through the European Common Fisheries Policy (CFP). Live-weight landings of demersal fish (cod, haddock, flatfish) dropped from around 300,000 tons in 1982 to about 80,000 tons in 2008, and of pelagic fish (mainly mackerel once the herring had declined), from 260,000 tons in 1988 to 140,000 tons in 2008. The number of regularly employed fishermen halved between 1992 and 2002 as stocks fell, and larger boats were used to catch what was left as cheaply as possible.[59] The CFP presided over a marine disaster where each nation's politicians were swayed more by the mutual suspicion of their fishermen than by the warnings of scientists. Scotland reckoned it got a raw deal in the allocation of catch quotas compared to other fishing nations like Spain, but in the widespread evasion of quotas and landings of 'black fish' the Scots were excelled by none. There is an urgent need for an environmental history of modern European sea-fishing, and no less for an environmental history of the salmon farm, which, since the 1970s, has come to supplement and replace wild-caught fish.

Paradoxically, as the open sea was emptied of commercial fish, and the sea-lochs were filled with floating cages of salmon and their heavily polluting waste, other animals that feed on fish flourished in the second half of the twentieth century as never before. Certainly the end of persecution at their breeding stations was a very important factor: fishermen, who had objected to the first protection of the gannet in the 1870s, a hundred years later objected far more vociferously to the protection of the grey seal, which they saw as a serious competitor.[60] Seals and most of the seabirds, however, feed mainly

---

[58] I. Sutherland, *From Herring to Seine Net Fishing on the East Coast of Scotland* (Golspie, 1986).

[59] J. R. Coull, A. Fenton, and K. Veitch, *Boats, Fishing and the Sea, a Compendium of Scottish Ethnology*, vol. 4, esp. the chapters by Coull (Edinburgh, 2009); Coull, *The Sea Fisheries of Scotland*; www.scotland.gov.uk/Publications/2009/09/11100225/0.

[60] R. A. Lambert, 'The Grey Seal in Britain: A Twentieth-Century History of a Nature Conservation Success', *Environment and History*, 8 (2002), 449–74.

on sand-eels: the destruction of most of the cod, herring, and mackerel that also fed on the sand-eels may have led to an increase in food for seals and birds.

To the scholar approaching from the outside, environmental history can appear daunting in the range of knowledge that is expected of its practitioners. To take the last example, surely the skills of a fishery expert and an ornithologist are more appropriate than those of an historian in solving the paradox of declining fish numbers contrasted with increasing seal and bird numbers? The scientists are certainly indispensable here, yet it is the historian who can give the right time perspective and who is best equipped to research how human attitudes towards birds and seals have changed. Very frequently, and probably in this case, a partnership between scientists and historians will produce the best environmental history. Institutional obstructions to such partnerships exist, but they are there to be overcome. There are other cases, though, where an historian could be comfortable working entirely alone with no more than the usual background knowledge of the technicalities of his subject: thus an urgently needed history of the Scottish Environmental Protection Agency and its predecessors back to the inspectorate of the alkali industry in the nineteenth century would not need a pollution scientist as partner. The field of environmental history is so wide, and its questions so far-ranging and intriguing, that there is ample room both for the associational spirit and for the lone practitioner.

## FURTHER READING

Coull, J. R., *The Sea Fisheries of Scotland: A Historical Geography* (Edinburgh, 1996).

Dawson, A., *So Foul and Fair a Day: A History of Scotland's Weather and Climate* (Edinburgh, 2009).

Dickson, J. H., et al., *The Changing Flora of Glasgow: Urban and Rural Plants through the Centuries* (Edinburgh, 2000).

Dodgshon, R. A., 'The Little Ice Age in the Scottish Highlands and Islands: Documenting its Human Impact', *Scottish Geographical Journal*, 121 (2005), 321–37.

Dunion, K., *Troublemakers: The Struggle for Environmental Justice in Scotland* (Edinburgh, 2003).

Lambert, R., *Contested Mountains: Nature, Development and Environment in the Cairngorm Region of Scotland, 1880–1980* (Cambridge, 2001).

Sheail, J., *Nature in Trust: The History of Nature Conservation in Britain* (Glasgow, 1976).

Smout, T. C., *Nature Contested: An Environmental History of Scotland and Northern England, 1600–2000* (Edinburgh, 2000).

—— *Exploring Environmental History: Selected Essays* (Edinburgh, 2009).

—— ed., *People and Woods in Scotland: A History* (Edinburgh, 2003).

—— MacDonald, A. R., and Watson, F., *A History of the Native Woodlands of Scotland 1500–1920* (Edinburgh, 2005).

Syse, K. V. L., *From Land Use to Landscape: A Cultural History of Conflict and Consensus in Argyll, 1945–1980* (Oslo, 2009).

Tittensor, R., *From Peat Bog to Conifer Forest: An Oral History of Whitelee, its Community and Landscape* (Chichester, 2009).

Yalden, D., *The History of British Mammals* (London, 1999).

CHAPTER 2

·····································································································

# THE DEMOGRAPHIC FACTOR

·····································································································

## MICHAEL ANDERSON

As Christopher Smout shows in Chapter 1, for its size, Scotland has a very diverse natural environment. Historically, there have also been major regional differences in land-holding practices, industrial development, and popular and religious culture. All these produced a highly differentiated spatial demography; and this means that we always need to go below the national level if we are fully to understand Scottish population change and its implications for the people of Scotland.

## THE PRE-CENSUS PERIOD

··········································································································································

In practice, however, we have extremely little hard evidence about regional or even national populations before 1801. Robust information on births, marriages, and deaths is only available from 1855. Migration remains a problem even in 2010.

Scotland's first official census, in 1801, showed a national population of somewhat over 1.6 million, with figures for every civil parish. In spite of some problems with data collection, the results for most places are probably accurate for the civilian population to within a few per cent.

By contrast, though widely used by modern historians, Alexander Webster's estimates for 1755 require considerable caution, especially at the local level.[1] Webster did challenge some figures from parish ministers, but many were only estimates. Frequently, ministers only provided rough guesses, especially in the towns, whereas others gave numbers they considered eligible for 'examination' on the Catechism, plus the age at which they treated children as 'examinable'. Webster implies that he estimated children under the examinable age using a standard formula, derived from Halley's Breslau life-table. But Scotland

[1] A late copy of Webster's *Account* is reproduced in James Kyd, *Scottish Population Statistics* (Edinburgh, 1975).

was not Breslau, and variations in mortality and migration meant that age structures between parishes varied widely, so Webster's method could only produce very approximate results at the local level even if he applied it systematically. But in fact he did not, instead frequently adjusting many of the ministers' figures, presumably to make the results look more plausible by removing obvious roundings to zero. One result is that well over a quarter of his parish totals have final two digits in the range '89' to '99', two and a half times the randomly expected number. But the surviving returns from ministers suggest no such pattern in what was sent in.[2]

Use of Webster's parish figures thus requires a strong degree of scepticism, especially in towns and the Highlands, though, at larger levels of aggregation, some errors will cancel out. The most likely conclusion is that Scotland's 1755 population fell somewhere between 1.15 and 1.35 million, possibly towards the higher figure—but, even at 1.2 million, Scotland's growth to 1801 would have been significantly slower than England's.

Most population estimates for earlier dates are largely guesswork.[3] Robert Tyson suggests a total of 1,234,575 for 1691.[4] But this derives from incomplete counts of hearths from tax returns, adjusted by regionally varied estimates of the number of hearths per household, plus data on mean household size by county from a century later. Given these levels of uncertainty, we should not even try to guess more than very rough national population figures before 1801, but focus on what we can infer, from contemporary commentary or data on related matters, about the likely impact of changing opportunities and pressures on people's experienced demographic lives.

On this basis, what might we suggest? Older work mostly assumed that variation in mortality was the key source of demographic change, in a high-pressure world of elevated birth and death rates. So, for example, it was suggested that inoculation against smallpox provided significant stimulus to population growth in the later eighteenth century. Unfortunately, the timing and extent of inoculation makes this unlikely except in the Highlands and the south-west (where there is also supporting contemporary comment).

Above all, however, great stress was laid on fluctuations in death rates, based on contemporary comment and, for the later seventeenth and eighteenth centuries, on counts from parish registers.[5] These suggested that recovery from devastating disease and famine crises of the early fourteenth century was delayed by recurrent outbreaks of bubonic plague before 1500, implying a national population in 1500 of 500,000 to 700,000. Plague and crop failure recurred frequently throughout the sixteenth century, but the number

[2]  Michael Anderson, 'Guesses, Estimates and Adjustments: Webster's 1755 "census" of Scotland Revisited Again', *Journal of Scottish Historical Studies*, 31, i (2011), 26–45.

[3]  Michael Flinn et al., *Scottish Population History from the 17th Century to the 1930s* (Cambridge, 1977), 242.

[4]  Robert Tyson, 'Contrasting Regimes: Population Growth in Ireland and Scotland during the Eighteenth Century', in S. J. Connolly et al., *Conflict, Identity and Economic Development: Ireland and Scotland, 1600–1939* (Preston, 1995), 64–6.

[5]  Flinn et al., *Scottish Population History* is probably the clearest exponent of the mortality-driven position; for a more subtle view, see R. A. Houston, 'The Demographic Regime', in T. M. Devine and Rosalind Mitchison, *People and Society in Scotland, 1760–1830* (Edinburgh, 1988), 17.

of very high food-price years, plus increasing action against vagabonds, hint that the population rose significantly by 1600, perhaps even to one million, but that it probably grew little if at all thereafter.

Nor, in Scotland, did mass mortality linked to harvest failure end after 1600, as it largely did in England, except for the north-west in the 1620s. Seventeen Scottish dearth years in the seventeenth century included major mortality crises in 1623–4, 1650–1, 1673–6, 1681–3, and, above all, in the 1690s, when probably at least a tenth of Scotland's population died—but perhaps as much as a quarter in inland areas of the north-east and much of the western and northern Highlands. Later still, deaths from hunger-related disease were reported in the 1740s and the 1790s, especially in the Northern Isles and the northernmost mainland.[6] Elsewhere, improved market integration, better transport, and proactive steps by local landlords or Poor Law authorities reduced hunger migration and its consequential deaths from famine-related disease (though we still need further research on these developments, from the 1690s onwards).[7]

Locally, before 1700, short-term crises could be severe, a key factor in the constant insecurity of everyday life at this period. In really bad crises, a third of a parish's population could die within a few months. However, most demographers now believe that the medium- and long-term impact of crises on population trends anywhere in north-western Europe was less significant. The only exceptions were crises of exceptional severity (as in the fifteenth century, or in Aberdeenshire in the 1690s, where some parishes took several decades to recover[8]), or if crises followed each other closely clustered in time (as happened in Scotland in the civil-war years).

The main reason for rapid recovery was that most areas in north-western Europe had many young adults quite literally 'waiting' for an opportunity to marry, through land, or another regular source of income, becoming available. When the opportunity arose, because most new households were headed by younger couples, fertility was also boosted. In Scotland, delayed marriage seems to have been normal in lowland farming areas before 1800, with an average age at first marriage for women in their later twenties, and perhaps one in ten not marrying in their fertile years. Scottish Lowlands thus had capacity for rapid recovery after a mortality surge; the same was true in the north-west and the islands, though marriage ages were often rather lower here.[9] Lowland populations

---

[6] For more on this, see ch. 1 above.

[7] Looking ahead, this same set of market, transport, and welfare measures, together with the greater concentration of population near the coasts and lower population densities, saved north-west Scotland from Irish-level mortality when the potato crop failed in the 1840s.

[8] Robert Tyson, 'The Population History of Aberdeenshire, 1695–1755: A New Approach', *Northern Scotland*, 6 (1985), 113–31. Karen Cullen et al., 'King William's Ill Years: New Evidence on the Impact of Scarcity and Harvest Failure during the Crisis of the 1690s in Tayside', *Scottish Historical Review*, 85 (2006), 250–76.

[9] R. A. Houston, 'Age at Marriage of Scottish women, c.1660–1770', *Local Population Studies*, 43 (1989), 63–6; Michael Anderson, 'Population Growth and Population Regulation in Nineteenth-Century Rural Scotland', in Tommy Bengstsson and Osamu Saito, *Population and Economy* (Oxford, 2000), 122–4.

in particular were also highly mobile, so mortality-induced gaps in one community were readily filled by in-migrants from elsewhere.[10]

Most of the time, these processes restricted population growth. For example, Tyson[11] shows that, between 1755 and 1841, many landlords in the north-east and central Highlands not only limited additional household formation by prohibiting subdivision of holdings, but consolidated holdings when the opportunity came up, shifting from mixed farming to stock rearing. In one parish with reasonably robust data (Rothiemay in Banffshire), mean marriage ages rose by over two years for women and four years for men from 1750 to 1800 and 1801 to 1851. In the Western Isles, a similar policy restricted population growth on Coll to less than 10 per cent between 1755 and 1831.

But elsewhere on the west coast and in the islands, restrictions were widely relaxed, especially in the later eighteenth century, as landlords encouraged or even forced holding subdivision to encourage new marriages and in-migration on the coast. The extreme was Tiree, where these policies were reflected, as early as 1779, in a mean female marriage age around 22 and over a quarter of women marrying before they were 20. In 1799, as the kelp boom took off, larger farms were also subdivided and in some areas in-migration was actively encouraged. Population roughly trebled between 1755 and 1831, and subdivision only ceased in the 1840s. Similar processes were widespread around the Argyll coast and the islands at least through to 1815.[12]

However, the consequences were severe when the market for kelp collapsed after 1815, and fishing became increasingly unreliable. In many parishes, populations had only been marginally viable at much lower levels even before the kelp-related boom. Only the potato had made the new numbers sustainable under any contemporary agrarian regime—and, when the potato crop failed dramatically in the 1840s, massive population decline in parishes like Tiree was inevitable, whatever landlords might have sought to do.[13] But, beyond this, ever since the mid-eighteenth century in particular, some landlords in a growing number of areas of Scotland had been actively reducing even populations with more robust means of subsistence in favour of larger- scale arable or livestock farming. The 'Highland clearances' of the first decades of the nineteenth century were merely one part of a longer and much more widespread trend.[14]

Tyson also notes a very contrasting picture, illustrated by a quote in the *New Statistical Account* from the minister of the fishing parish of Rathven in Banffshire; this also has parallels right across western Europe in this period. 'At eighteen years of age they become men, and, whenever they acquire the share of a boat, they marry, as it is a maxim among

---

[10] Ian Whyte, 'Population Movement in Early Modern Scotland', in R. A. Houston and I. D. Whyte, *Scottish Society 1500–1800* (Cambridge, 1989), 37–58.

[11] Robert Tyson, 'Landlord Policies and Population Change in North-East Scotland and the Western Isles 1755–1841', *Northern Scotland*, 19 (1999), 63–74.

[12] Eric Richards, *A History of the Highland Clearances: Agrarian Transformation and the Evictions 1746–1886* (London, 1982), 128–34.

[13] Ibid.; Flinn et al., *Scottish Population History*, 34, 421–30.

[14] For more detail, see ch. 6 below.

them "that no man can be a fisher, and want a wife." [15] The result, it was claimed, was almost universal male marriage, and women typically marrying between 18 and 22. Elsewhere in western Europe, expansion of employment in low capital-base craft and manufacturing activity and in mining created similar opportunities for couples to establish their own homes at earlier ages than in the past, thus stimulating local population growth. New opportunities also encouraged in-migration from rural areas where marriage chances were more limited. The differential regional population trends of the years 1755 to 1851, to be discussed further below, are entirely consistent with this kind of behaviour also occurring in Scotland.

It seems therefore that, as in England and many other countries, opportunities for marriage were a major control over Scottish demographic change in this period. However, in the decades around 1800 there is no sign in Scotland of the significant fall and subsequent rise in mean marriage age that was widespread in England. Given the similar economic and social changes in the two countries by this time, this is surprising, and further research is needed if we are to understand it. However, two areas that were important in the nineteenth century may also have been at work earlier.

First, in early nineteenth-century lowland Scotland, a much higher proportion of agricultural labour than in England was accommodated by farmers, and contracted for at least six months at a time—and there were fewer sites for squatters to settle; the result was greater control over how many single or married people could reside in each parish. Second, the Poor Law in England, especially from the later eighteenth century until 1834, supported casual labourers and their families in their own homes when work was not available, and even subsidized families on the basis of numbers of children. In Scotland, by the mid-nineteenth century, no significant Poor Law support was provided to indigent workers and their families; this was arguably an important risk factor restraining Scottish nuptiality at this time. More work is needed to see whether this also applied in really bad times in Scotland in the eighteenth century, but Poor Law support in many parishes was anyway much less effective at that time. [16]

Finally, what about migration? [17] Even in the medieval period, Scots were renowned in Europe as mobile people. From the sixteenth to the mid-nineteenth centuries at least, much internal migration was of younger men and women moving through a series of short hirings between rural communities as farm workers, or spending time in trading or manufacturing activities, especially in the towns. These needed migrants to grow—and in this period, especially in the larger ones, to counteract their high death rates (though up to the mid-eighteenth century the overall demographic impact of urban centres was limited in Scotland compared with many other parts of Europe, with less than 2 per cent of the population living in towns of more than 10,000 people in 1500 and

---

[15] *New Statistical Account*, vol. 13, 257.

[16] Anderson, 'Population Growth', 120–1; T. M. Devine, 'Urbanisation', in Devine and Mitchison, *People and Society*, 45–7.

[17] The paragraphs that follow rely heavily on Ian Whyte, *Migration and Society in Britain, 1550–1830* (Basingstoke, 2000). On emigration, see also ch. 16 below.

only about 9 per cent in 1750—thereafter was a different story).[18] Until the early eighteenth century, there were also many famine migrants and vagrants in bad times, large numbers of whom died (mostly from disease) as a result. Later, as industrialization and agricultural improvement accelerated, with an accompanying rise or decline of local opportunities in farming, fishing, or manufacturing, growing numbers of families moved in response, which was reflected, for example, in the widespread falls in population in many north-east parishes in the later eighteenth century.

Externally, especially through the sixteenth and seventeenth centuries, many Scots traders went to parts of Continental Europe (more than went to England). Scots also formed major components of continental mercenary armies (over 50,000 on one estimate in the 1620s and 1630s alone)—and many of these never returned. And there were major outflows to Ulster at various points in the seventeenth century (and notably in the 1690s). Overall, probably about 200,000 Scots left the country in the seventeenth century, enough, at an average of two per hundred population per year, to provide an important supplementary safety valve against excessive population pressure.[19]

Overall in the eighteenth century, net emigration was lower as a proportion of national population, not least because, by its end, there was growing net inflow from Ireland, especially into the south-west and the west Central Belt.[20] Emigration probably reduced population growth between 1750 and 1800 by less than 5 per cent, but regionally there was real impact in parts of the north-west, with perhaps 20,000 emigrants to North America between 1765 and 1815 coming from the Highlands, where the average population was well under 200,000.[21] Even more than earlier, in this period many men also moved or were moved out of Scotland as soldiers (up to a fifth of adult males in some areas of the north-west by 1805), as pressed sailors, and, especially in the Northern Isles, in fishing and whaling—and, in all these categories, many died abroad.

# CONTRASTING PATTERNS OF POPULATION CHANGE, 1801–2001

After 1800, information on key aspects of Scotland's population becomes more robust. National populations from the decennial censuses, and changes compared with other parts of Britain and Ireland, are shown in Table 2.1. Census data for 2011 are not available at the time of writing and, given the many uncertainties about the pattern and causes of Scottish demographic change after 2001, discussion of the years 2001–10 is here confined to a short final section of this chapter.

---

[18] Jan de Vries, *European Urbanisation 1500–1800* (London, 1984), 39, 45, 46; see also ch. 24.
[19] For more detail on numbers and destinations of emigrants in this period see chs. 7 and 16.
[20] More detail on this period is covered in chs. 26 and 27.
[21] Marjorie Harper, 'Emigration from the Highlands and Islands since 1750', in Michael Lynch, *The Oxford Companion to Scottish History* (Oxford, 2001), 230.

Table 2.1  Scotland's population, and decadal rates of change for the components of Great Britain and Ireland, 1801–2001

| Census | Scottish population (thousands) | Per cent change over previous 'census'* | | | |
|---|---|---|---|---|---|
| | | Scotland | England | Wales | Ireland |
| 1801 | 1608 | | | | |
| 1811 | 1806 | 12.3 | 14.2 | 14.7 | |
| 1821 | 2092 | 15.8 | 18.1 | 18.0 | |
| 1831 | 2364 | 13.0 | 16.0 | 14.0 | 14.2 |
| 1841 | 2620 | 10.8 | 14.4 | 15.5 | 5.3 |
| 1851 | 2889 | 10.2 | 12.8 | 11.3 | −19.9 |
| 1861 | 3062 | 6.0 | 13.3 | 11.4 | −12.9 |
| 1871 | 3360 | 9.7 | 13.5 | 9.3 | −6.7 |
| 1881 | 3736 | 11.2 | 12.1 | 10.9 | −4.4 |
| 1891 | 4026 | 7.8 | 13.0 | 12.7 | −9.1 |
| 1901 | 4472 | 11.1 | 12.1 | 13.6 | −5.2 |
| 1911 | 4761 | 6.5 | 10.3 | 20.4 | −1.5 |
| 1921 | 4882 | 2.5 | 4.7 | 9.7 | |
| 1931 | 4843 | −0.8 | 6.0 | −2.4 | |
| 1939 | 5007 | 3.4 | 4.7 | −5.4 | |
| 1951 | 5096 | 1.8 | 5.3 | 6.0 | |
| 1961 | 5179 | 1.6 | 5.6 | 1.7 | 0.3 |
| 1971 | 5229 | 1.0 | 5.9 | 3.3 | 3.9 |
| 1981 | 5180 | −0.9 | 1.7 | 3.0 | 10.5 |
| 1991 | 5083 | −1.9 | 2.3 | 2.1 | 2.8 |
| 2001 | 5064 | −0.4 | 2.7 | 1.0 | 7.5 |

* There was no 1941 census, but we have population counts for 29 September 1939. Faster Scottish growth between 1931 and 1939 is largely due to the low emigration of these years.

Compared with England, the Scottish population grew more slowly in every decade between 1801 and 2001. Scottish growth was a little over threefold, England's was nearly sixfold, and Welsh nearly fivefold; only in the 1870s and 1890s did Scottish growth approach England's. From 1921 to 2001, Scotland's population fell in four decades; England's lowest growth was a 1.7 per cent rise in the 1970s. Wales matched Scottish rates in the later nineteenth century, grew rapidly in the 1900s, fell in the interwar period, but rose much faster after 1951. Ireland's population boomed from the mid-eighteenth century until 1841, but the failure of potato crops initiated nearly a century of decline, followed by modest growth, though in the 1970s and 1990s Ireland grew much faster than any country of Great Britain. Even compared with English regions with a large concentration of staple industries, Scotland's growth was in general slower, except marginally for the English North and North-east in the first decades after 1945.

In a wider European context, Scotland's sluggish performance is even more striking. Up to 1911, Scotland's growth, though markedly slower than England's, was much faster than France, and not very different from Belgium, Switzerland, or Sweden, but significantly slower than Denmark, Norway, the Netherlands, or Germany. But, after 1921, Scotland's relative demographic depression dramatically stands out. No significant Western European country, regardless of size, saw decades of actual population decline in the inter-war period. Scottish population rose by only 2 per cent between 1921 and 1951, while that of Belgium, Sweden, Denmark, and Norway increased by between 17 and 41 per cent. The last half of the century was relatively even worse. Scotland's population in 2001 was about 32,000 less than in 1951; everywhere else in north-western Europe, populations grew, in some cases rapidly. The fastest growth was in the Netherlands (over 50 per cent), but Sweden, Norway, and Denmark all exceeded 20 per cent.

Just why Scotland's population was so relatively sluggish for so long cries out for further research, but part of the answer is that there were multiple Scotlands. Published census material at parish level is available from 1801. There are awkward boundary changes in the 1890s, and problems as urban areas extended their boundaries and from local-authority reorganizations in 1975 and 1996. Nevertheless, we can reconstruct six reasonably consistent regional groups; the results are shown in Figure 2.1.

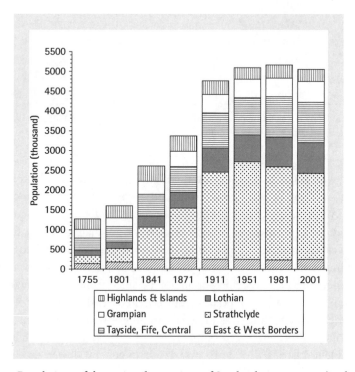

FIGURE 2.1 Populations of the regional groupings of Scotland, 1755 to 2001 (in thousands).

First, note the huge changes in the *relative* shares of the different regions of Scotland. For 1755, Webster's figures suggest that the Highlands and Islands had over a fifth of Scotland's population, at a time when Strathclyde (less Argyll, which is here treated as Highland) held only 15 per cent, and the Lothians 10 per cent. Thereafter, for two centuries, the developing industrial and commercial activities of the west of Scotland meant that Strathclyde's share rose almost continuously, peaking in 1961 at nearly 49 per cent, before falling back below 43 per cent by 2001 (the fall in Glasgow was even larger). In 2001, by contrast, the Highlands and Islands held just 6 per cent of the population (and the East and West Borders together a mere 5 per cent—compared with nearly 12 per cent in Webster's figures).

But if we look at absolute numbers, a rather different picture emerges. The 2001 Highlands and Islands population was around 315,000, up from 298,000 in 1951 and above the 306,000 of 1801 (even if Inverness is excluded, the 1801 figure is still around 297,000 and that for 2001 about 271,000). The Borders, with a population almost identical to that of 1841, had over 100,000 more people in 2001 than in Webster's estimates for 1755. Strathclyde's population in 2001 was eleven times that of 1755 and more than six times that of 1801, but was 15 per cent down on its 1961 peak. No other major manufacturing region in Europe experienced anything approaching this scale of loss, and Strathclyde is a principal cause of Scotland's comparative demographic weakness in the twentieth century.

But even these figures conceal subtler changes in Scotland's population. In 2001 most Scots were spatially highly concentrated, with 63 per cent living in parishes with a population density above five hundred persons per square kilometre (km$^2$); these parishes occupied just 3.3 per cent of the land area, mostly in the Central Belt or around Aberdeen, Perth, or Inverness.[22] At the other extreme, 46 per cent of the land area consisted of parishes with fewer than five people per km$^2$, holding just 1.7 per cent of the population. And in these sparsely populated parishes, excepting some coastal crofting areas, most residents were concentrated into villages or other grouped settlements, thus further boosting the image of the remaining 'deserted lands'.

But, as Map 2.1 suggests, most of these parishes had always been sparsely settled, the only major exceptions being some island parishes and parts of Argyll and Caithness— but even these areas were only settled at a fraction of the density of most of rural Ireland in the years before the famine (for example, even Tiree, which was among the most crowded, had a density in 1841 that was only a third of the average for the County of Cork). Except for a few fishing centres, there was hardly a mainland parish on the north-west coast of Scotland between Fort William and Thurso, and also deep into western

[22] Post-1800 parish data used in this chapter come from the decennial censuses. Data up to 1951 were originally collated by Donald Morse and used, for example, in Michael Anderson and Donald Morse, 'High Fertility, High Emigration, Low Nuptiality: Adjustment Processes in Scotland's Demographic Experience, 1861–1914, Part 1', *Population Studies*, 47 (1993), 5–25. These data have now been thoroughly rechecked and data to 2001 have been added. I am very grateful to Corinne Roughley for her work on the maps.

| | |
|---|---|
| | 0–5 |
| | 5–10 |
| | 10–20 |
| | 20–40 |
| | 40–80 |
| | > 80 |

MAP 2.1 Population density (persons per km²), Scottish parishes, 1801.

Perth and Aberdeenshire, where population density in 1801 exceeded ten per km²; mostly, the average density was much less. Durness in Sutherland where just 1,208 people were settled on 570 km², had an average density of 2.1 people (less than half of a household) per km². These low densities arose because, even *within* highland parishes, most areas were largely empty excepting only parts of the most fertile glens. At the other extreme, the principal clusters of population by 1801 were already located in the Central Belt, up the east coast, around the Moray Firth, and along the coast of Dumfries and Galloway. Two centuries of spatial change, therefore, principally made sparsely populated parishes sparser, and densely populated areas denser—and the same process was also at work within most parishes, as noted above.

But the process of population decline in the now sparsely settled areas was not homogeneous. Map 2.2 shows the widely varying dates, even between neighbouring rural areas, when parish populations peaked.

Some explanations for differences are well studied: the contrast between Argyll and much of Perthshire, where landowners were consolidating holdings (initially mainly for cattle) in the later eighteenth century, compared with eastern Aberdeenshire, where new settlement was actively encouraged for small cattle-breeding farms even in the 1870s; or the mixture of active clearance and flight from deprivation in the Uists, Skye, and Sutherland before 1851, compared with Harris and Lewis, where prosperity from fishing partly backed by landlord investment delayed most decline until the later nineteenth century; or the contrasting fates of smaller and larger east-coast fishing ports, as processing concentrated in those with the largest fleets and best communications.[23] But under-researched puzzles remain: for example, why did almost every parish in Wigtown peak in 1851 (it was more than just an Irish effect); why was decline later in north Berwickshire than in eastern East Lothian (was it because of the water-powered industry in the Whiteadder valley?); and what population effects did turnpikes or railways have?

Map 2.2 also shows that many of the industrial, mining, or commercial parishes that had expanded so rapidly between the later eighteenth century and the First World War, then subsequently peaked long before 1971.[24] This included a swathe of mining districts across south Ayrshire, and, as their mining, shipbuilding, iron and steel and engineering industries went into decline, especially after 1921, most of the parishes north-west and south-east of Glasgow, including the city itself. Less dramatic falls can also be observed after 1951 in the city cores (though not the suburbs) of Edinburgh, Aberdeen, and Dundee.

---

[23] See also ch. 6 below.

[24] Devine, 'Urbanisation', 27–52; R. J. Morris, 'Urbanisation and Scotland', in W. Hamish Fraser and R. J. Morris, eds., *People and Society in Scotland 1830–1914* (Edinburgh, 1990), 73–102.

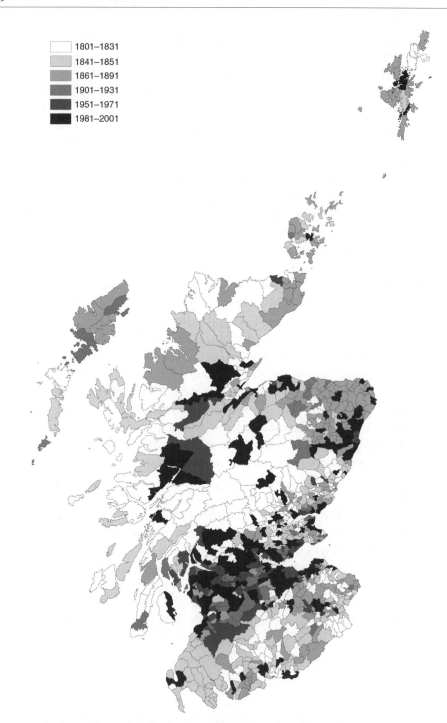

MAP 2.2 Peak population decades for Scottish Civil Parishes, 1801–2000.

# Fertility, Mortality, and Migration: The Processes of Population Change, 1801–2001

How do we understand all this? Before we can link civil registration to the censuses after 1861, it is difficult to be precise about the causes of Scotland's sluggish demographic change. Very high urban mortality from the late 1820s, as rates of town and city growth unparalleled in Europe overwhelmed housing and sanitary infrastructure,[25] was a factor, but more detailed local studies outside the cities are needed to establish its national importance. In spite of the major Irish inflow, net emigration was high in the 1830s and 1840s, as manufacturing experienced the first major trade-cycle depressions, and also in the 1850s (when it spread right across the country). But why Scotland fared much worse than England is still not clear.

After 1861, we can explore for each decade the precise net interplay between numbers of births, numbers of deaths, and net migration. The results are shown in Figure 2.2.

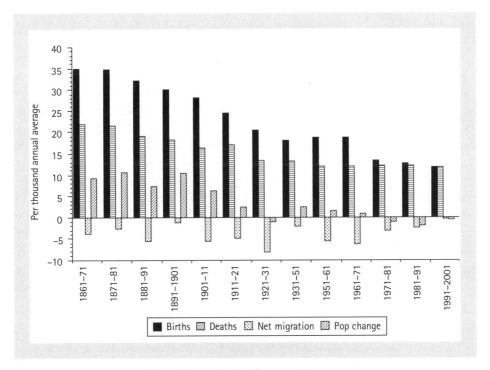

**FIGURE 2.2** Components of Scottish population change, 1861–2001.

[25]  See ch. 24 below.

These data have been explored extensively elsewhere.[26] For present purposes note: the steady decline in natural increase of population from the 1870s to the 1930s, as the birth rate fell faster than the death rate; the stabilizing death rate from the 1950s, as improved survival was offset by an ageing population; and the boom and then collapse of the birth rate, which eventually pushed Scotland into negative natural increase in the last decade of the twentieth century.

In many ways, these trends roughly parallel those of England and Wales, and, indeed, many other parts of Western Europe. Marital fertility began to decline significantly in many parts of most countries from the 1860s at the latest, for reasons that we still do not fully understand. Scotland's pattern is fairly typical: a shift to small families, with their huge implications for living standards and the lives of women, was widely occurring by 1911 among professional middle-class and textile workers (including a growing number of very small families of zero and one), while many large families persisted until the 1950s in mining, heavy industry, and crofting areas—though early fertility decline in farming areas such as East Lothian (where many women worked in the fields) appears in comparative terms unusual.[27]

But two features are internationally special about Scotland's demography over the 150 years to 2001: first, the rate of net emigration (including movement to other parts of the UK); and, second, the substantial variability of birth, marriage, death, and migration rates in different parts of the country.

In the 1880s and the first decade of the twentieth century, net out-migration exceeded 5 per cent of the population and remained high right up to the First World War; between 1904 and 1913, more than 600,000 people left the country (annually more than 1 per cent of population in six of these years and more men than were killed in the First World War). Overall, between 1830 and 1914 about two million people left Scotland for overseas destinations and probably roughly similar numbers went to the rest of the UK, making Scottish emigration per head second in Europe after Ireland. In the 1920s net out-migration exceeded 8 per cent of the population and was the principal factor producing real population decline; some 400,000 people (net) left Scotland in these years, mostly, after the introduction of severe restrictions on migration to the United States in 1923, to the rest of the UK. Net outflow was high again in the 1950s (around 5.5 per cent) and the 1960s (around 6.3 per cent), in total some 600,000 people, about half going overseas. Continued net out-migration at these levels would have produced massive population decline after 1970, but, as natural increase fell, net out-migration declined, to just 2.9 per cent in the 1970s, 2.4 per cent in the 1980s, and 0.3 per cent in the 1990s.[28]

---

[26]  Flinn et al., *Scottish Population History*, Part 5; Anderson and Morse, 'High Fertility'; Michael Anderson, 'One Scotland or Several? The Historical Evolution of Scotland's Population over the Past Century', in Robert Wright, *Scotland's Demographic Challenge* (Glasgow, 2004).

[27]  Michael Anderson and Donald Morse, 'High Fertility, High Emigration, Low Nuptiality: Adjustment Processes in Scotland's Demographic Experience, 1861–1914, Part 2', *Population Studies*, 47 (1993), 319–43; Michael Anderson, 'Highly Restricted Fertility: Very Small Families in the British Fertility Decline', *Population Studies*, 52 (1998), 177–99.

[28]  For more detail on emigration and the destinations of the emigrants, see chs. 7 and 27 below.

The situation in England was dramatically different. In spite of high overseas emigration in terms of numbers, England had relatively low rates of net loss even in the first thirty years of the twentieth century (the highest was 1.7 per cent in 1911–21), and migration was mostly modestly positive thereafter (between 0.8 and a little over 0.9 per cent per decade between 1921 and 1951, and again between 1981 and 2001).

But Scotland also attracted large numbers of in-migrants, actually having a higher proportion of non-natives than England back to at least 1851. The big difference in Scotland's situation was that most Scottish immigrants after the Second World War came from elsewhere in the UK, while a growing majority of those south of the border came from overseas. Thus, in 2001, 9.1 per cent of the population of Scotland was born in the rest of the UK (up from just 5.4 per cent in 1951),[29] whereas in England and Wales this number was just 2 per cent. However, most of this 2 per cent consisted of Scots, the equivalent of 16.2 per cent of Scotland's population in 2001 (up from 11.4 per cent in 1951 and 7.1 per cent in 1901). In 2001 England and Wales had 8.9 per cent of their people born outside the UK; for Scotland it was just 3.8 per cent (though this was significantly above the 2.5 per cent of 1951).

The other remarkable feature of Scotland's net out-migration has been its spatial pervasiveness. When this can first be measured, in the 1860s, over 90 per cent of Scottish parishes, holding over 60 per cent of the 1861 population, had net out-migration. This included all but nine parishes in the Highlands and Islands and Perthshire, all but six in the north-east, and most of the farming parishes in the south-east and south-west, where rates of loss were often far higher than from the Highlands and Islands.[30] But, even this early, it also included many urban and industrial parishes, among them nine with populations of more than 20,000, the largest of which was Paisley. More remarkably in a UK or European context, after 1870 at least one of Glasgow, Edinburgh, Dundee, and Aberdeen (by the 1900s all the four) experienced net outflow in every decade.

The other defining feature of Scottish demographic history right up to the 1970s was a remarkably repressed nuptiality, especially for women.[31] Not only was there a greater reluctance to marry in Scotland than in similar kinds of areas in England, but, in the Highlands and Islands, Scottish nuptiality was among the lowest in the whole of north-western Europe. Possible explanations for this, but with even clearer applicability for the century after 1850, have been discussed above, to which we may add markedly lower real wages than in England, as a discouragement to all but those most confident about their futures from entering into marriage.

Nevertheless, while nuptiality was repressed in the century before the Second World War compared with south of the border, marital fertility was somewhat higher, though also regionally variable. Figure 2.3 illustrates this for different groups of Scottish

---

[29] For English migration to Scotland see Murray Watson, *Being English in Scotland* (Edinburgh, 2003).
[30] Anderson, 'Population Growth', 111–31.
[31] Michael Anderson, 'Why was Scottish Nuptiality so Depressed for so long?', in Isabelle Devos and Liam Kennedy, *Marriage and Rural Economy: Western Europe since 1400* (Turnhout, 1999).

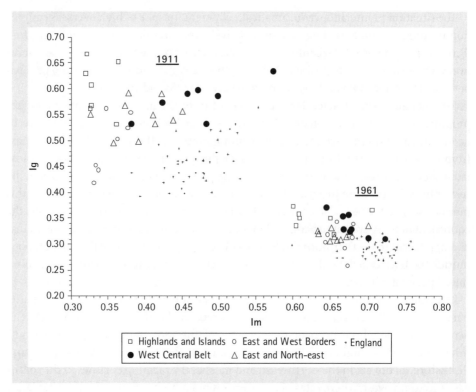

FIGURE 2.3  Age-standardized nuptiality and marital fertility, Scottish and English counties, 1911 and 1961.

counties for 1911 and 1961, and compares them with English counties as a whole. In the absence of detailed information on ages at childbirth, this graph uses the Princeton measure of marital fertility $(I_g)$ and relates it to the Princeton measure of nuptiality $(I_m)$. $I_g$ is an age-standardized proportion of 'potential' (and roughly 'maximal') fertility that a group of women actually produced over a ten-year period around the census date. $I_m$ is most easily interpreted by noting that $1-I_m$ gives the proportion of a woman's potential fertility that is not available for conception within marriage, because of delayed marriage or non-marriage.[32]

The pattern for 1911 shows the highly characteristic features of Scottish nuptiality and fertility before the First World War. Firstly, compared with England, Scottish nuptiality tended to be lower, but, for reasons that we do not yet understand, marital fertility significantly higher; as a result, overall levels of fertility were similar. Second, Scottish fertility and nuptiality were spatially more differentiated than in English: notably, the Highlands and Islands had extremely low nuptiality but high fertility

[32] For further discussion see Anderson and Morse, 'High Fertility', Parts 1 and 2.

within marriage, the industrialized and mining counties of the west Central Belt tended to be high on both (with West Lothian as the UK peak on both), and Roxburgh, Selkirk, and Peebles, with their strong concentration of female employment in textiles, were low on both.[33]

The 1961 pattern was different, even though, overall, age-standardized fertility in Scotland and England had only fallen by 10 and 9 per cent respectively (it had been markedly lower in the 1930s). But, if we break this down into its components, nuptiality was much higher in both countries and marital fertility much lower—yet, for reasons we still do not fully understand, Scotland still tended to rather lower nuptiality and higher marital fertility than England. Within Scotland, a similar regional patterning to that of 1911 was still visible, but with a markedly reduced range of variation.

One caution, however, has recently emerged: in the north-west, high marital fertility may partly reflect a custom whereby women living elsewhere returned to their mothers' homes to bear their first child.[34] The same behaviour also partly explains high non-marital fertility in some parishes, notably in the south-west and parts of Banffshire and Aberdeenshire, where over a fifth of babies were born to non-married mothers in the later nineteenth century.[35] This raises an important issue for further research: it could well be, for example, that highland-born migrant women were as likely as those born elsewhere to marry somewhere, but this is concealed by our only having evidence on the limited numbers who remained at home. The same may also apply to women born in Wigtownshire, for example.

In the later twentieth century, significant changes occurred in both nuptiality and fertility, both within and outside marriage. First, the mean age at first marriage for men, which was about 27 in the late 1850s and peaked at 28.2 in the 1930s, fell after the Second World War to a low of 24.2 in the early 1970s, then rose to 30.7 by 2001. A parallel pattern for women produced a peak of 25.4 for 1911–20, a post-war low of 21.8 in the mid-1970s, and a rise almost to 30 by 2001.

Second, for both men and women, the proportions who married rose markedly in the post-1945 period and fell dramatically in the late twentieth century. In 1971, 58 per cent of women aged 20–24 were married and 91 per cent of those aged 30–34. This compares with 22 per cent and 67 per cent in 1911, and 8 per cent and 61 per cent for 2001.

However, much of the post-1970s marriage decline was substituted by a rise in cohabitation. Cohabitation was very uncommon even among the childless as late as the mid-1970s but, in 2001, despite reduced levels of marriage, a quarter of women aged 20–24 and three-quarters of the 30–34 age group had either at some time been married or were cohabiting, figures well above the proportion who had ever been married in Scotland for

---

[33]  Data and further discussion are in ibid.

[34]  Personal communication from Eilidh Garrett.

[35]  Andrew Blaikie, *Illegitimacy, Sex and Society: Northeast Scotland, 1750–1900* (Oxford 1993), ch. 5, who also summarizes the work of Paddock. For the eighteenth century, see Rosalind Mitchison and Leah Leneman, *Sexuality and Social Control: Scotland 1660–1780* (Oxford, 1989).

any year before 1939 (when cohabitation was extremely uncommon). In the long historical picture of partnership, it is the post-1945 period and not the late twentieth century
that is the anomaly.

The overall trend in fertility was markedly downward in the later twentieth century.
However, this significantly reflected not a flight from childbearing altogether but the
near disappearance of very large families, plus a general shift to later childbearing, which
itself resulted in more very small families. As late as 1981–5 women's median age at childbearing was 25; by 2001–5 it was 29.3. In the same period, births to non-married mothers
rose from 15 per cent to 45 per cent of all births (Dundee's figures were 25 per cent and 60
per cent respectively). Most of this rise was directly linked to the growth in cohabitation.
The first detailed data, for 2001–5, show almost two-thirds of all births to non-married
mothers as registered by couples living at the same address and just 14 per cent by a
mother alone. More generally, however, the whole question of changes and regional dif-
ferentiation in fertility is still poorly understood even for twenty-first-century Scotland,
and there remains great scope for more oral history as well as statistically focused
research for earlier periods.

Detailed examination of mortality changes in the nineteenth and twentieth centuries
is beyond the scope of this chapter; indeed, most of the mass of mortality statistics produced by the General Register Office has not yet been addressed by historians. But a few
key points are clear. In the early twenty-first century, Scotland had the lowest life expectancy at birth in Western Europe. Within the United Kingdom's 432 local authorities
(LAs) in 2005–7, only three Scottish authorities were in the best 200 for women's life
expectation either at birth ($e_0$) or at age 65 ($e_{65}$), and six Scottish LAs in Greater Glasgow
were among the worst ten UK LAs for female $e_0$.[36] In 1999–2001, Glasgow City was four
years below the UK average figure of 80.2, and 2.3 below the Scottish average.

Over the long term, however, there are some brighter signs. Over the previous 150 years,
$e_0$ rose dramatically from 40.3 years for men and 43.9 for women in 1861–70 to 44.7 and
47.4 in 1891–1900; by 1950–2 the figures had climbed to 64.4 and 68.7, and in 1996–8 to
72.4 and 77.9 (note the widening absolute gender gap in the twentieth century).

But this was not the only widening gap. When comparable data first became available,
for the 1870s, $e_0$ for England and Wales was less than six months longer than in Scotland
and about ten months longer for women. The situation in Scotland was better than
France and Germany, but well behind Denmark, Sweden, and Norway. By 1930–2 the gap
compared with England and Wales was 2.7 years for men and over 3.4 years for women
(for women compared with Sweden it was over six years); these gaps only narrowed
slowly over the rest of the century.

However, in one area there was marked relative improvement, at least until after
the Second World War. As Chapter 24 shows, in great part due to their dramatically

---

[36]  Recent data on life expectancy and survival are taken from the General Register Office for
Scotland website at www.gro-scotland.gov.uk/statistics/publications-and-data/life-expectancy/index.
html. For earlier material see the Decennial Supplement to the 48th Detailed Annual Report of the
Registrar General…for Scotland, *Parliamentary Papers*, 1906, xxi.

rapid growth, Scottish nineteenth-century cities had appalling death rates (for example, $e_0$ in Glasgow even in the 1890s was almost ten years below the Scottish average). In the 1860s most rural areas had far lower death rates than small towns, and they in turn than those of the large towns and cities. Over the century up to 1950, marked improvements in sanitation and living conditions brought crude death rates down much faster in larger towns and cities than in the smaller towns and the countryside, though this was helped by the general ageing of rural populations. However, in the last quarter of the twentieth century, most of Greater Glasgow (and also the Western Isles) experienced slower improvement in mortality from key diseases than most of the rest of the country; as male death rates from heart disease fell dramatically for Scotland as a whole, the relative position of people living in many LAs in the west of Scotland worsened; the same was true of female lung-cancer deaths, which rose faster in these areas than in Scotland as a whole.

Figure 2.4 reflects the principal changes in overall mortality in Scotland from the 1860s to 2000–2. It shows the numbers of females born in any year who would have survived to any particular age had the mortality conditions of that year not changed during their lifetimes (for example, at 1860s mortality levels, roughly half of all girl babies would have survived to the age of 50, compared with around three-quarters at 1930–2 levels and over 95 per cent if 2000–2 rates continued). It also captures the relative impact of deaths at different ages on survival chances at any particular point in time. Glasgow in the 1890s is also shown for comparison. The figures for males were always rather worse but broadly moved in parallel.

Over the second half of the nineteenth century, infant death rates actually increased, with more than one in eight babies not reaching their first birthday by the 1890s; this, above all, kept expectation of life at birth so low. Thereafter there was steady improvement as family size fell and sanitation and baby-care improved, but even in the late 1930s infant mortality was still above 70 per 1,000 live births (about 100 in Glasgow, 90 in Dundee). The key change came after the Second World War, and by the end of the century infant mortality was down to about one in 200 births.

By contrast, big improvements from improved sanitation and living standards impacted much earlier on deaths, especially from infectious diseases, of children and young adults. In the 1860s a fifth of baby girls died between their first and fifth birthdays, by the 1890s this was down to one in eight, and by the 1930s to one in eighteen; aided by antibiotics, by 2000–2 it was one in 200. And of women reaching 15 but dying before 45, the parallel figures were a quarter, a fifth, one in nine, and, once mortality associated with childbirth and tuberculosis had been brought under control after the 1930s, one in fifty.

Improvements were much slower at older ages, where most deaths were always from chronic conditions—indeed, increasing tobacco consumption with a consequential marked rise in respiratory cancers was a key factor ensuring that expectation of life for men aged 60 only improved by one year between the 1860s and 1950–2, when it was 14.3 years. It reached 15.3 in 1980–2, and then, as tobacco smoking, cholesterol, and high blood pressure all became more controlled, it rose much faster to 18.5 by 2000–2.

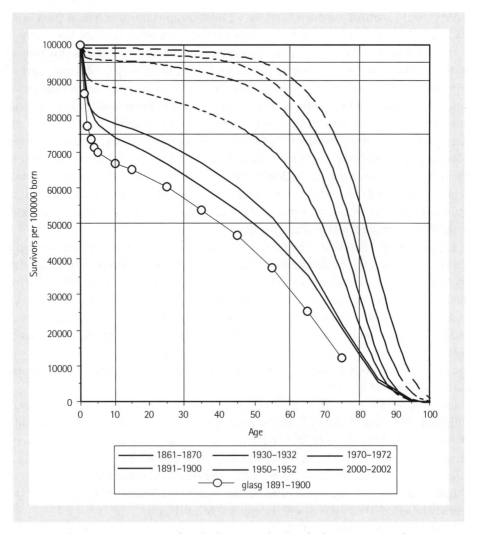

FIGURE 2.4 Survivors per 100,000 females born, Scotland and Glasgow, various dates.

What were the impacts of the combination of fertility, mortality, and migration changes on the age structure of the Scottish population? In 1851, 36 per cent of Scots were aged under 15 and just 4.8 per cent were 65 or over. At censuses from 1911 more detail is available: see Figure 2.5.

The graph for 1911 reflects a society where population had been growing rapidly, with more people born in each decade than in its predecessor, but where relatively high mortality at all ages pulled down the numbers surviving to older age groups. As a result, the proportion of the population aged 65 and over in 1911 was only 5.4 per cent, while the proportion under 15 was 32 per cent.

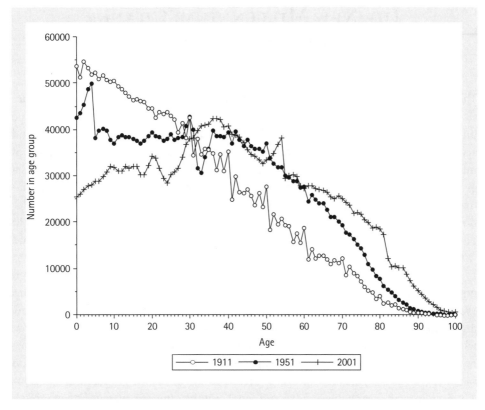

**FIGURE 2.5** Age structures of the Scottish female population, 1911, 1951, and 2001.

By 1951, the pattern had changed. Low fertility in both World Wars was followed by post-war baby booms, but, above all, the graph reflects low interwar fertility and the fertility decline and high emigration before 1914. Fewer than 25 per cent of Scots were under 15. Survival at older ages was still restrained, leaving 9.9 per cent of the population aged 65 and over.

The 2001 pattern changed again. The birth-rate boom of the 1960s and the subsequent erratic decline are well shown: just 18 per cent were aged under 15. But rapidly extending survival chances of the older population meant that 16 per cent were aged 65 and over.

Note finally, however, that even if everyone aged under 20 and over 64 is defined as dependent, this still produces a dependent percentage of 40.1 per cent for 2001, below the figure for 1951 and more than ten percentage points below 1851 (when many people even aged 65 were far less capable of work than at the start of the twenty-first century).

# THE NEW MILLENNIUM: CHANGE
# OR CONTINUITY?

The years 2001–10 saw growing media and political concern over the present and future state of Scotland's population. One contributor was undoubtedly the more accessible information emerging from the General Register Office when the more discursive and accessible *Annual Reviews* replaced the old *Annual Reports*, and a growing range of information was regularly publicized on the GRO(S) website.[37] A second factor was a growing interest by devolved government in population matters, starting with the initiative on migration policy in 2004 and accelerating with the SNP administration's population objectives in 2007. Third, there was, at long last, a resurgence of academic interest in population issues, enthusiastically supported personally by the Registrar General and with funding by the Economic and Social Research Council.

These developments paralleled two marked changes in demographic trends—though only time will tell whether either will survive the post-2008 recession and the 2010 Westminster government's pledge to reduce UK immigration. The change that drew most comment was a marked reversal of the downward trend in national population, which had fallen from a 1971 peak of 5.24 million to a low point of 5.05 million in 2002, on trend to below five million by 2009. Instead it recovered, to an estimated 5.19 million in 2009. This was not the first reversal in three decades of decline (population had actually risen in every year between 1989 and 1995); but this time the average rate of growth for 2003–9 was consistently higher than in any comparable period since the early 1930s.

Positive net migration, a second 'new' feature, was also not new (compare four years in the early 1990s and 1931–2), but it, too, at an annual average of more than 20,000, was the highest figure ever recorded for a period of this length. What was also new was that this positive net migration came mostly, not from falling outflow as in the past, but from increased inflow, especially from the new EU accession states. These immigrants also started to have children and this contributed to another reversed trend, a modest rise in fertility.

But, alongside these new developments, which are still too new for us to judge whether they are more than temporary blips, many of the old patterns and trends continued. While Glasgow City's population showed a small increase for the first time in decades (largely a function of new immigrants), the shifting balance of population from the west Central Belt towards the east continued, with fastest rates of decline for 1999–2009 in Inverclyde and the Western Isles, fastest growth rates in West and East Lothian, and highest absolute growth in the City of Edinburgh. Over the same period, age-standardized death rates for Scotland also fell, with continuing reduced mortality from

---

[37] This section is heavily dependent on information from the most recent editions of *Scotland's Population: The Registrar General's Annual Review of Demographic Trends* (Edinburgh: General Register Office for Scotland), published annually; see also ch. 36 below.

heart and circulatory conditions and respiratory cancers for men; but lung-cancer rates for women rose further, and alcohol-related deaths for both sexes in 2009 were two and a half times their 1989 level. Equally depressingly, between 1996–8 and 2006–8, the gap between the local authorities with lowest and highest expectation of life at birth remained constant for men and actually increased for women. Also, between 1999 and 2009: the mean age at marriage continued to rise (by over two years for both men and women); the number of marriages (after a modest temporary recovery) continued to fall but with no evidence that rates of cohabitation were declining; the proportion of births to non-married women rose by more than a fifth, but the proportion registered solely in the mother's name fell further, implying that much of the increase was to mothers living in a relationship of some kind. But, overall, we still understand so little about the deeper causes of any of the current trends, that guesses as to future trends or the wider implications for Scottish society seem hopelessly premature.

## FURTHER READING

Anderson, Michael, 'Population and Family Life', in Tony Dickson and James Treble, *People and Society in Scotland 1914–1990* (Edinburgh, 1992), 12–47.

—— and Morse, Donald, 'The People', in Hamish Fraser and R. J. Morris (eds.), *People and Society in Scotland 1830–1914* (Edinburgh, 1990), 8–45.

Flinn, Michael et al., *Scottish Population History from the 17th Century to the 1930s* (Cambridge, 1977).

Houston, R. A., 'The Demographic Regime', in T. M. Devine and Rosalind Mitchison, *People and Society in Scotland, 1760–1830* (Edinburgh, 1988), 9–26.

Rothenbacher, Franz, *The European Population*, 2 vols.: *1850–1945* and *Since 1945* (Basingstoke, 2002 and 2005).

*Scotland's Population 2004: The Registrar General's Annual Review of Demographic Trends, 150th Edition* (Edinburgh, 2005).

*Time Series Datasets* (Edinburgh: General Register Office for Scotland), http://www.gro-scotland.gov.uk/statistics/time-series-datasets.html, updated annually.

Tyson, Robert, 'Demographic Change', in T. M. Devine and J. R. Young, *Eighteenth-Century Scotland: New Perspectives* (East Linton, 1999), 195–209.

Whyte, Ian, *Migration and Society in Britain, 1550–1830* (Basingstoke, 2000).

CHAPTER 3

......................................................................................................

# MYTHICAL SCOTLAND

......................................................................................................

## COLIN KIDD AND JAMES COLEMAN

It is generally recognized among Scottish historians that Scotland's national myths are abstractions from reality that tend to force historical, regional, and cultural diversity into a straitjacket; to disregard nuance and hard fact; to embrace gross stereotyping and caricature; and to involve some measure of invention and fabrication.[1] However, rarely is it acknowledged that, historically, Scotland's myths have been subject to the fickleness and changing whims of ideological fashion, and turn out to have had much less staying power than the nation whose supposed enduring essence they are meant to represent. Indeed, not only would an early modern Scot of the sixteenth, seventeenth, or eighteenth centuries have some trouble recognizing the 'mythical Scotland' of the early twenty-first-century imagination, but a nineteenth-century Scot, brought up on the lore of rival denominations, each with its own version of the Presbyterian interpretation of Scottish history,[2] would also be at something of a loss in the Scotland of today, whose imaginings are rarely ecclesiastical. It transpires that the mental underpinnings of communal belonging—the psychological and cultural processes which make the *people* who inhabit the geographical territory of Scotland into a *nation*—are far from robust, notwithstanding Scotland's long and proud history of nationhood. Today's myths of Scotland are not the myths of earlier centuries.

Thus, counter-intuitively perhaps, the history of 'mythical Scotland' is not a singular depiction of a national mindset, but is best negotiated by way of a series of overlapping

---

[1] See e.g. M. and B. Grigor, *Scotch Myths* (Edinburgh, 1981); M. Chapman, *The Gaelic Vision in Scottish Culture* (London, 1978); C. Craig, 'Myths against History: Tartanry and Kailyard in Nineteenth-Century Scottish Literature', in C. McArthur, ed., *Scotch Reels: Scotland in Cinema and Television* (London, 1982); I. Donnachie and C. Whatley, eds., *The Manufacture of Scottish History* (Edinburgh, 1992); D. Broun, R. Finlay, and M. Lynch, eds., *Image and Identity: The Making and Re-making of Scotland through the Ages* (Edinburgh, 1998); E. J. Cowan and R. Finlay, eds., *Scottish History: The Power of the Past* (Edinburgh, 2002).

[2] J. Coleman, 'The Double-Life of the Scottish Past: Discourses of Commemoration in Nineteenth-Century Scotland' (PhD thesis, Glasgow University, 2005); N. Forsyth, 'Presbyterian Historians and the Scottish Invention of British Liberty', *Records of the Scottish Church History Society*, 34 (2004), 91–110.

phases of mythmaking. In spite of the important caveat that these phases were far from watertight, it is nevertheless possible to discern at least four distinct 'moments' of national mythmaking between the sixteenth century and the present. These comprise the refashioning in the sixteenth century by the humanist Hector Boece and the human-ist-reformer George Buchanan of the origin legend of the Scottish nation inherited from the late medieval era; the replacement of this spurious account of Celtic antiquity in the 1760s by an equally fabulous account derived from what was believed to be epic poetry composed by a blind bard by the name of Ossian in the third century AD; the emergence of another romantic myth of Scots highlandism in the late eighteenth and early nine-teenth century, which was not dependent on the historicity of Ossian and therefore proved more resilient, precisely because it bore none of that particular myth's vulnera-bilities; and, finally, in the nineteenth century, the myth of a democratic, Whig–Liberal Presbyterian tradition.[3] This last phase persisted well into the first half of the twentieth century, but was rendered redundant, if not offensive, with the onset of secularization, the rise of a Roman Catholic middle class, and the retreat from a kind of Scots–British political patriotism. The latter was embodied not only by the Unionist Party, which in 1965, significantly, changed its name to the Scottish Conservative and Unionist Party, but also by the Presbyterian socialist ethic of the early Labour movement.[4] Thus, it is the highland myth of romance, formulated in the late eighteenth and early nineteenth cen-turies, which has proved most enduring. Nevertheless, at no stage in the elaboration and transformation of the national myth did a new expression of mythic Scottishness oblit-erate or occlude a mythic version of the medieval War of Independence, which has remained throughout a significant element in the national consciousness.

## EARLY MODERN MYTHS OF ORIGIN

Early modern Scotland inherited a powerful myth of Scottish antiquity from the strug-gles of the Scottish Wars of Independence, which, as historians now recognize, were as much ideological as military. The Plantagenet dream of an English empire of Britain was underwritten by the account of ancient British origins found in the mid-twelfth-century chronicle of Geoffrey of Monmouth.[5] According to Geoffrey's chronicle, Britain had

---

[3] For an alternative typology, see H. Trevor-Roper, *The Invention of Scotland* (New Haven, 2008), which extends his classic of scotophobic muckraking, 'The Invention of Tradition: The Highland Tradition of Scotland', in E. Hobsbawm and T. Ranger, eds., *The Invention of Tradition* (Cambridge, 1983).

[4] E.g James Barr, United Free Church minister, Labour MP, and author of *The Scottish Covenanters* (Glasgow, 1947).

[5] For the influence of Geoffrey's chronicle, see J. Crick, *The Historia Regum Brittaniae of Geoffrey of Monmouth, vol. III: A Summary Catalogue of the Manuscripts* (Cambridge, 1989), and *vol IV: Dissemination and Reception in the Later Middle Ages* (Cambridge, 1991).

been a kingdom of Trojan origin later divided at the death of Britain's first emperor-king, Brut, when Brut's eldest son Locrinus inherited the dominant kingdom of England, and Brut's younger sons Albanacht and Camber were bequeathed Scotland and Wales respectively. Later, so Geoffrey recounted, King Arthur had reunited the realms of Britain under his imperial sway. In response to the imperial vision of Britishness found in Geoffrey's chronicle, late medieval Scots clerics—most prominent among them Baldred Bisset; the anonymous rhetorician who composed the Declaration of Arbroath (possibly Alexander Kinnimonth); and John of Fordun—constructed a counter-mythology that stressed the autonomous origins of the Scottish kingdom. This alternative origin myth emphasized that the Scots were not descended from Troy, but from a Graeco-Egyptian pedigree, in particular the elopement of Scota, the daughter of Pharaoh, with Gathelos, a Greek prince, whose descendants came to Scotland— eventually—by a maritime route via the Mediterranean, Iberia, and Ireland. The kingdom of Scotland had its beginnings, according to Fordun's influential *Chronica gentis Scotorum* (*c.*1363), in 330 BC, when Fergus MacFerquhard made himself king of a Gathelan community settled in the west Highlands of Scotland. Fordun's chronicle formed the basis of Walter Bower's more extended *Scotichronicon* (1441–5), which firmly established the legends of Gathelus–Scota and Fergus MacFerquhard as the accepted origin myth of the Scottish kingdom and principal counter-argument to the English claim of suzerainty over Scotland. The medieval epics, John Barbour's *Bruce*, composed in the late fourteenth century, and the fifteenth-century *Wallace*, ascribed to Blind Harry the minstrel, consolidated the importance of the kingdom's independence at the core of the nation's self-image.

During the early modern period this amalgam of legend and patriotic history was reconfigured in certain ways, but otherwise remained the core of the national myth. In particular, Boece endowed the history of the Scottish kingdom with a humanist veneer. The history of Scotland's kings—whether the real monarchs of medieval times or the fictitious leaders of a shadowy and fabulous antiquity—was told as a 'mirror of princes', that is, an ethical guide to kingship: good kings wisely consulted the community of the realm, ruled happily, and usually died of old age, but the lives of bad kings, or tyrants, tended to end in unfortunate circumstances. Buchanan took this neo-Roman emphasis a stage further, coining an influential myth of an ancient Scottish constitution of 330 BC. According to Buchanan, Fergus had been elected king by the *phylarchi*, or clan chiefs, of the Gathelan Scots. Not only was kingship largely elective within the royal family, but kings were accountable to the community, and it was legitimate to resist tyrants who overstepped the bounds of limited monarchy. Buchanan set out his theory of Scottish kingship in his tract *De Iure regni apud Scotos* (1579) and supplemented it with a range of historical illustration in his history of Scotland, *Historia rerum Scoticarum* (1582). Buchanan's political myths constituted the central matter of Scottish history until the early eighteenth century.[6]

---

[6] For the influence of Buchanan, see J. Durkan, *Bibliography of George Buchanan* (Glasgow, 1994). See also I. D. McFarlane, *Buchanan* (London, 1981).

It would be wrong to conclude that early modern Scots were any more addicted to myths than other nations. Medieval legends of antique origins—as often as not updated in humanistic garb, purloined from a rediscovered Tacitus—contributed enormously to the formation of national consciousness in early modern Europe.[7] In the case of the United Provinces, for instance, the ancient tribe of Batavians provided a foundation charter for Dutch republicanism. Celebrated in Tacitus, the resistance of the Batavians under the leadership of Claudius Civilis to the tyrannical might of Rome prefigured and legitimated the Dutch revolt against Spain. In its most celebrated formulation, the *Liber de antiquitate reipublicae Batavicae* (1610), the Dutch jurist Grotius outlined the decentralized government, estates sovereignty, and elective generalship of the ancient Batavian constitution.[8] Moreover, ancient constitutional myths of the sort fashioned by Buchanan played a central role in political culture across early modern Europe. Romanists and Germanists, for example, debated the provenance of the French monarchy. The Romanists, whose case was formulated in the sixteenth century by Charles Dumoulin and continued in the eighteenth century by Jean-Baptiste Dubos, traced the French monarchy back to Roman imperial authority. On the other hand, the Germanists, whose arguments were devised by François Hotman and rehearsed in the early eighteenth century by Henri de Boulainvilliers, contended that the origins of the French state originated in the Germanic tribal institutions of the Franks.[9] The substance of mythical Scotland was similar in form to the political myths found in other parts of early modern Europe.

Alongside the political myth of the ancient Gaelic past there emerged a parallel ecclesiastical legend. An intriguing reference in Fordun's chronicle to the effect that there had been no bishop among the Scots until Palladius in the early fifth century, Boece's account of the conversion of the Scots around the year 200 in the reign of the fictitious Donald I, and his transposition of the Culdees, an eighth-century Irish monastic reform movement, back into third-century Dalriada—all provided the raw materials for a Presbyterian interpretation of ancient Scottish history, which flourished in the seventeenth century. Its key features were the claim that Scotland had been converted to Christianity by missionaries from the Johannine churches of Asia Minor, not by Petrine

---

[7] F. L. Borchardt, *German Antiquity in Renaissance Myth* (Baltimore, 1971), 25.

[8] Hugo Grotius, *A Treatise of the Antiquity of the Commonwealth of the Batavers* (1610: trans. Thomas Woods, London, 1649); I. Schoffer, 'The Batavian Myth during the Sixteenth and Seventeenth Centuries', in J. Bromley and E. Kossman, eds., *Britain and the Netherlands V* (The Hague, 1975); K. Tilmans, 'Aeneas, Bato and Civilis, the Forefathers of the Dutch: The Origins of the Batavian Tradition in Dutch Humanistic Historiography', in J. Brink and W. Gentrup, eds., *Renaissance Culture in Context* (Aldershot, 1993).

[9] Franklin Ford, *Robe and Sword* (Cambridge, MA, 1953); Quentin Skinner, *The Foundations of Modern Political Thought*, 2 vols. (Cambridge, 1978), vol. ii, 259–318; N. O. Keohane, *Philosophy and the State in France: The Renaissance to the Enlightenment* (Princeton, NJ, 1980), 346–50; R. Briggs, 'From the German Forests to Civil Society: The Frankish Myth of the Ancient Constitution in France', in P. Burke, B. Harrison, and P. Slack, eds., *Civil Histories: Essays Presented to Sir Keith Thomas* (Oxford, 2000).

missionaries from Rome, and that the early Scottish Church had been governed in a proto-Presbyterian fashion by colleges of monks, or Culdees.[10]

Unsurprisingly, the ancient Scottish past was the scene of considerable ideological disputation during the late sixteenth and seventeenth centuries. Royalists upheld the story that Fergus had been the first king of Scotland, but rejected the spin that George Buchanan had imparted to the myth. Rather, a tradition of royalist writers, from Adam Blackwood by way of James VI and I to Sir George Mackenzie of Rosehaugh, argued firmly that Fergus had not been an elected monarch and the kings who had succeeded him had followed by a law of hereditary succession. Blackwood reversed one of Buchanan's central arguments for an elective monarchy, arguing that the ancient clan chiefs constituted a model of unconstrained patriarchal authority, whose hereditary powers had been transferred intact to Fergus I.[11] In the same manner, Mackenzie traced the roots of the Stuarts' indefeasible hereditary monarchy back to the establishment of the Dalriadic kingdom by Fergus MacFerquhard in 330 BC.[12]

Notwithstanding the Union of 1707 with England, the mythical origins of the Scottish kingdom remained a feature of the Scottish ideological landscape into the early eighteenth century. Patrick Abercromby's *Martial Atchievements of the Scots Nation* (1711–15) not only celebrated Scotland's warrior tradition, but also advanced an absolutist interpretation of the supposed events of 330 BC. In addition, the republication of eminent voices from the past reinforced the myth. Sir George Mackenzie's *Works* were published in two lavish volumes in 1716–22, and George Buchanan's complete Latin works were published, surprisingly perhaps, under the auspices of the Jacobite humanist Thomas Ruddiman in 1715.[13] Nor did the Union do anything to silence the popular cults of Wallace and Bruce.[14]

Nevertheless, the Jacobite priest Father Thomas Innes, from the Scots College in Paris, exploded the myth of the ancient kings in 1729 in his *Critical Account of the Ancient Inhabitants of North Britain*. Guided by the new science of diplomatic, or charter, scholarship, pioneered by the French Maurist Jean Mabillon, Innes's scrupulous scholarship unpicked the various layers of material that had accreted as the accepted legend of Scotland's origins. Trawling various archives in Britain and France, Innes compared genealogies in Scottish regnal lists surviving from the Middle Ages. Errors in

---

[10] John of Fordun, *Chronica gentis Scotorum* (Edinburgh, 1871), 64, 93–4; Hector Boece, *Scotorum historiae a prima gentis origine* (1527: Paris, 1574), 86, 99, 128; George Buchanan, *Rerum Scoticarum historia*, in Buchanan, *Opera omnia*, 2 vols. (Edinburgh, 1715), lib. iv, R. 27 R. 35; lib. v, R. 42; lib. vi, R. 69; David Calderwood, *The History of the Kirk of Scotland*, ed. T. Thomson, Wodrow Society, 8 vols. (Edinburgh, 1842–9), vol. i, 34–43; David Buchanan, 'Preface', in John Knox, *The History of the Reformation of the Church of Scotland* (1644: Edinburgh, 1731), lvii–lxxxiv.

[11] Adam Blackwood, *Apologia*, in Blackwood, *Opera Omnia* (Paris, 1644).

[12] George Mackenzie, *Ius Regium* (1684), *A defence of the antiquity of the royal line of Scotland* (1685), *The antiquity of the royal line of Scotland, further cleared and defended* (1686), all in George Mackenzie, *Works*, 2 vols. (Edinburgh, 1716–22).

[13] D. Duncan, *Thomas Ruddiman* (Edinburgh, 1965).

[14] See I. Ross and S. Scobie, 'Patriotic Publishing as a Response to Union', in T. I. Rae, ed., *The Union of 1707* (Glasgow, 1974), 118.

transcription made by lowland monks, which had progressively altered medieval Gaelic names—such as Forco, which became Forgo and eventually Fergus—allowed Innes to date the supposedly ancient sources from which Boece had claimed to compile his history. Moreover, Innes noticed a consensus among the materials he had seen from the eleventh to thirteenth centuries that Fergus MacErch, not Fergus MacFerquhard, had been the first king of Scots in Alba. Therefore, Innes concluded, the first forty kings of Scotland between Fergus MacFerquhard and Fergus MacErch had been spurious, an ingenious and ideologically useful interpolation that he traced to the patriotic needs of the Scottish War of Independence.[15] In the wake of Innes's comprehensive demolition job, mid eighteenth-century Scotland became for a brief period an under-mythologized nation, its sense of self now resting in large measure on the new science of society pioneered in the Scottish Enlightenment. However, ideological detachment, historical scepticism, and a sociological outlook seem to have proved an underwhelming substitute for a collective myth of national origins. At any rate, by the 1760s another myth—that of Ossian—had filled the vacuum.

## THE OSSIAN PHENOMENON

Ossian is the collective name for the two ancient Celtic epics, *Fingal* (1761, dated 1762) and *Temora* (1763), which their opportunistically creative editor and translator, James Macpherson (1736–1796), attributed to Ossian, a blind bard belonging to the ancient Caledonian people of Scotland in the third century AD. Educated at Aberdeen under the influence of the Homeric scholar Thomas Blackwell, Macpherson aimed to reconstitute—as he seems initially to have believed—an ancient Scottish epic that would rival those of Greece and Rome. Was Macpherson an outright forger? That would be a harsh judgement on Macpherson's first airing of the supposed relics of an ancient epic in *Fragments of Ancient Poetry collected in the Highlands of Scotland* (1760). Yet, while the second full-scale epic, *Temora*, was largely Macpherson's own concoction, which allowed him to cash in on the Ossian phenomenon, *Fingal* was indebted to genuine poetic remains composed in the fifteenth and sixteenth centuries as well as to Macpherson's own creativity and editorial laxity; for part of the appeal of the epics lay in the sentimental ethos, so popular in the mid to late eighteenth century, that the 'translator' imported into his incantatory prose-poems. Macpherson's celebrated and notorious 'discovery' not only provided his fellow Scots with an idealized—and, quite literally, *sentimentalized*—picture of a third-century golden age; it was quickly translated into various languages, and came to function as a potent and inspiring fantasy of ancient virtue for other

---

[15]  T. I. Rae, 'Historical Scepticism in Scotland before David Hume', in R. F. Brissenden, ed., *Studies in the Eighteenth Century II* (Canberra, 1973); C. Kidd, *Subverting Scotland's Past* (Cambridge, 1993), 97–107.

national groups. Although Macpherson's own origins were Jacobite, he himself betrayed few signs of this in his writings, and his active political commitments were to Britain and its empire. Moreover, Macpherson had been encouraged in his project, not least his travels to the Highlands in search of source material, by the Moderate Whig–Presbyterian literati of Edinburgh, men such as John Home, Hugh Blair, and Adam Ferguson, who perceived no threat to the Union or the Hanoverian monarchy in Macpherson's quest to recover a supposedly lost Celtic epic.

Yet, by a curious irony, Ossian communicated a myth of Scottish nationhood to the wider world, which sat uneasily with the loyal unionist culture from which Ossian emerged. The poems of Ossian played a central foundational role in the making of modern European nationalism. Indeed, it is arguable that these poems constitute one of the canonical Ur-texts of the romantic nationalisms which spread across the Continent in the century after the sensational discovery of Ossian in the early 1760s.[16] Historians of Continental Europe are agreed upon the importance of Ossian—and a mythical Scotland—to the emergence of an enlightened patriotism and thereafter romantic nationalism. The eminent Italian historian Franco Venturi has argued that the 'extraordinary diffusion' of Ossian across Europe contributed to 'the emerging patriotism of the age of Enlightenment'. In particular, he points to the significance of Ossian's Italian translator and commentator Melchior Cesarotti, whose version appeared in 1763.[17] In *La Création des identités nationales* (1999) Anne-Marie Thiesse assigned a central role first to Ossian, and then to Sir Walter Scott (whose Waverley novels provided inspiration for the *roman national*), in the emergence of European nationalisms. In quick succession they had established a Europe-wide vogue for Scotland that offered a nationalist template for intelligentsias across the Continent. Ossian's critical place in the history of European ideas during the 1760s was to function as a bridge between the ideologies of Jean-Jacques Rousseau and Johann Gottfried von Herder. In particular, Thiesse emphasizes the success of Ossian in insinuating a new set of values that would usurp the cultural authority of the conventional framework of standards—historical, geographical, and social as well as aesthetic—hitherto prevailing in *ancien régime* Europe: no longer was Graeco-Roman antiquity the sole source of cultural legitimacy in Europe.[18] Similarly, Jean Plumyène has explored the phenomenon of 'les nations manuscrites', nationalisms that took their rise from Ossian-like sources, usually heroic narratives of ancient and medieval times discovered in dusty manuscripts or fragments of

---

[16]  See amidst a vast bibliography, P. van Tieghem, *Ossian en France*, 2 vols. (Paris, 1917); Van Tieghem, *Ossian et l'ossianisme dans la littérature européenne au xviiie siècle* (Groningen, 1920); R. Tombo, *Ossian in Germany* (New York, 1901); H. Okun, 'Ossian in Painting', *Journal of the Warburg and Courtauld Institutes*, 30 (1967), 327–56; R. Fiske, *Scotland in Music: A European Enthusiasm* (Cambridge, 1983), ch. 2; G. R. Barratt, 'The Melancholy and the Wild: A Note on Macpherson's Russian Success', *Studies in Eighteenth-Century Culture*, 3 (1973), 125–35; H. Gaskill, ed., *The Reception of Ossian in Europe* (New York, 2004).

[17]  F. Venturi, *The End of the Old Regime in Europe, 1768–1776: The First Crisis*, trans. R. Burr Litchfield (Princeton, NJ, 1989), xvi.

[18]  A-M. Thiesse, *La Création des identités nationales* (Paris, 1999), 23–8, 131–7.

poems and folksongs by patriotic antiquaries enthused with the spirit of 'l'ossianisme'. According to Plumyène, Macpherson's supposed discovery of the fragments of an ancient Gaelic epic provided an international model for nationalist fantasies, a 'mould' that shaped nationalist imaginings. This applied not only to the content and form of these epics, but also to the mysterious circumstances in which they were discovered.[19]

It seemed that every nation, or aspiring nation, was on a quest to find its own domestic Ossian. The Russians, for example, not only translated, imitated, and adapted Ossian;[20] fortuitously, they also happened upon a long-lost medieval epic of their own. During the 1790s Count Musin-Pushkin claimed to have made a discovery in the course of a visit to a monastery of a manuscript containing a Russian epic from about the twelfth century. This epic depicted a medieval campaign in the tenth century between the Russians under Prince Igor at war with a nomadic Turkish people. It is, like Ossian, a tale of defeat. The tale was published in 1800 as 'The Song of the Troop of Igor', though the original manuscript somewhat inconveniently, or perhaps conveniently, perished in the Moscow fire of 1812. 'The Song of Igor' remained a lively component of Russian national consciousness.[21] Moreover, Ossian made an early impact upon Finnish folkloric circles, and would eventually encourage the successful search for a great Finnish epic. Elias Lonnrot, a medical student, made expeditions into the frontier province of Karelia, where he gathered a great body of folk poetry under the title of the *Kalevala*. Published in 1835, the *Kalevala* advertised itself as the old Karelian songs of the ancient times of the Finnish people.[22] By the 1790s Ossian had also become a major cultural force in Polish literary and historical circles. In 1795, the year of the third and last Partition of Poland, Prince Adam Jerzy Czartoryski produced an epic patriotic poem, *Bard polski*, which with its tale of an old bard wandering through a Poland defeated and ravished by the Russians, a poet sunk in grief and haunted by the spirit world, reveals an obvious debt to Macpherson. Scotland's Ossian inspired among Polish scholars a desire to root out in their own peripheries similar sorts of ancient literary and folkloric evidence. Indeed, Nina Taylor remarks upon the 'stamina and vivifying power of the bard that never was', making a persuasive case that the bardic cultural nationalism of nineteenth-century Poland was ultimately built upon the 'frail foundations of a literary fraud' in eighteenth-century Scotland.[23] Such a verdict is even more applicable to the case of Czech nationalism. In September 1817 the Czech scholar Vaclav Hanka was staying with a cleric friend at Kralov Dvor, where he found in a cellar certain fragments of verse in the language of medieval Bohemia, all wrapped around medieval Hussite arrows that had cut them into tatters. A year later the Czech museum in Prague established under the auspices of the Austrians

---

[19] J. Plumyène, *Les Nations romantiques* (Paris, 1979), esp. 123–37.

[20] J. Cassiday, 'Northern Poetry for a Northern People: Text and Context in Ozerov's *Fingal*', *Slavonic and East European Review*, 78 (2000), 240–66.

[21] Thiesse, *La Création*, 44–5; Plumyène, *Les Nations romantiques*, 126.

[22] F. P. Magoun, ed., *The Old Kalevala* (Cambridge, MA, 1969); W. A. Wilson, *Folkore and Nationalism in Modern Finland* (Bloomington, IN, 1976).

[23] N. Taylor, 'Ossian in Poland', in P. Henry, J. MacDonald, and H. Moss, eds., *Scotland and the Slavs* (Nottingham, 1993), 1–14.

received a similar manuscript of apparent medieval Bohemian provenance, which also came into the hands of Hanka. These discoveries—and most especially the poem dealing with 'The Judgement of the Princess Liboucha'—revealed an historic pre-German Czech golden age of constitutionalism, fine manners, and moral purity. By means of this quasi-Ossianic plagiarism-cum-forgery the Czech nation rediscovered itself and declared itself to the world.[24]

Ossian's impact within the British world was, however, more limited. Samuel Johnson found in the Ossian affair 'another proof of Scotch conspiracy in national falsehood',[25] and the Irish complained that Macpherson had stolen Ireland's antiquity and presented it as if it were Scottish.[26] Nevertheless, it was not only English and Irish antiquaries who challenged the authenticity of Ossian. After initially supporting Macpherson, David Hume allowed his ingrained scepticism to reassert itself, and he confessed that he could not believe in the authenticity of Ossian, even if 'fifty bare-arsed Highlanders'[27] should testify on its behalf. The balanced *Report* of the Highland Society in 1805 noted Macpherson's habit of utilizing genuine and historic Gaelic sources (though not, of course, from the third century) and of filling gaps in his material with his own fictions.[28] By the early nineteenth century, Ossian was no longer a shibboleth of Scottish patriotism.

# THE ROMANTIC DISCOVERY OF THE HIGHLANDS

Other elements within the late eighteenth-century re-evaluation of the Highlands were not so vulnerable to the probings of sceptics. In 1782 the anti-Jacobite disclothing measures taken against the highlanders were repealed. The transformation of the highland plaid into the kilt endowed Scotsmen with their own distinctive form of dress-wear. Indeed, the growing cult of sentimental Jacobitism—a safely lost cause—allowed even the late Hanoverian monarchs themselves to patronize Jacobites and their emblems. In particular, George IV's visit to Edinburgh in 1822, a royal pageant of tartanry orchestrated by Walter Scott, ensured that tartan now enjoyed the imprimatur of the establishment.[29] The taste for sublimity in late eighteenth-century aesthetics led to a positive reappraisal of the highland landscape, which had formerly been seen as too rugged and wild to be properly picturesque. The vogue for tartan, the romanticization of the Jacobite cause in poetry and song, and the identification of highland mountains, lochs, and glens as the essential features of Scottish landscape meant

---

[24]  Plumyène, *Les Nations romantiques*, 123–4.

[25]  James Boswell, *Life of Johnson* (Oxford, 1980), 7 February 1775, 578.

[26]  C. O'Halloran, 'Irish Re-Creations of the Gaelic Past: The Challenge of Macpherson's Ossian', *Past and Present*, 124 (1989).

[27]  C. Ryskamp and F. Pottle, eds., *Boswell: The Ominous Years 1774–1776* (London, 1963), 73.

[28]  *Report of the Committee of the Highland Society appointed to enquire into the nature and authenticity of the poems of Ossian* (Edinburgh and London, 1805).

[29]  J. Prebble, *The King's Jaunt* (London, 1988).

that the Highlands became the *pays* not only of highlanders and their descendants in the worldwide highland diaspora, but of all Scots, lowlanders just as much as Gaels. Yet again, it seems, one of the most fascinating puzzles surrounding Scottish self-mythologizing is the absence in a lowland-dominated nation of a clearly articulated myth of lowland identity. The antiquary John Pinkerton tried to supply one in the late eighteenth century, when he traced the ancestry of the Scots-speaking lowlanders back—erroneously—to the aboriginal Picts of the north-eastern Lowlands (who were, in fact, a p-Celtic people). Pinkerton's attempt to fly a Pictish kite enjoyed some success in the first half of the nineteenth century among Scots racialists who perceived, like the Celtophobic Pinkerton, that the lowlanders were of a different ethnic and racial stock from the Celts of the Highlands.[30] However, Pinkerton's Pictish fantasies were ridiculed by Scott in his novel *The Antiquary*, alongside the supposed lineage of Fergus MacFerquhard—derided by Scott as 'the tribe of MacFungus'—and the myth of Ossian, from which Scott was keen to distance himself, notwithstanding his role in promoting Scotland's adopted highland identity.[31] The cult of the Highlands has become one of the most hackneyed features of Scottish popular mythologizing, and, in turn, of cultural history.

From the nineteenth century, mythical Scotland can be appreciated through a wider range of sources, extending beyond the works of an elite circle of chroniclers, historians, and philosophers. The rapid growth of the newspaper press allows us to hear the propagation of myth in the lecture hall, at the public banquet, and at the grand unveilings of monuments and statuary commemorating the Scottish past. Influential studies of historical myth in nineteenth-century Scotland have passed over such sources as unworthy of attention, and have also portrayed the period as an era obsessed with kailyard couthiness and Jacobite swashbuckling.[32] Such analyses give a false impression of the depth to which the 'tartaning' of the Scottish past had rooted itself in Scottish culture. Certainly, tour operators promoted Scotland as a land defined by history: to travel to Scotland was to step back in time and interact with the past as a palpable presence.[33] This commodification of Walter-Scottish history, aligned with Victoria and Albert's enthusiastic endorsement of romantic highlandism, propagated a sanitized manifestation of national myth. For it was Victoria's peculiar synthesis of the Presbyterian and the Jacobite, much more than George IV's spectacular, but brief, excursion to Edinburgh in 1822, that consolidated the modern legend—strikingly at odds with industrial realities—of a tartan Scotland.[34] However, this image of Scotland, so convincingly projected onto the world stage by guide books, kailyard literature, and popular song, did not reflect the dominant myth of Scottish history.

[30] C. Kidd, 'Teutonist Ethnology and Scottish Nationalist Inhibition, 1780–1880', *Scottish Historical Review* (1995).

[31] Kidd, *Subverting Scotland's Past*, 256–8.

[32] M. Ash, *The Strange Death of Scottish History* (Edinburgh, 1980), 10–11, refers to the raising of commemorative statuary as a 'meaningless and highly selective' practice. See also T. Nairn, *The Break-Up of Britain* (London, 1981), 135–43.

[33] K. H. Grenier, *Tourism and Identity in Scotland, 1770–1914* (Aldershot, 2005), 135–65. See also, J. R. Gold and M. M. Gold, *Imagining Scotland: Tradition, Representation and Promotion in Scottish Tourism Since 1750* (Aldershot, 1995).

[34] R. Finlay, 'Queen Victoria and the Cult of Scottish Monarchy', in Cowan and Finlay, eds., *Power of the Past*, 212–14.

# THE PRESBYTERIAN INTERPRETATION
## OF SCOTTISH HISTORY

A Presbyterian narrative of liberty dominated Scottish popular historiography during the nineteenth century. It told how Scots had contributed to the winning of Britain's glorious heritage of civil and religious freedom. This Presbyterian interpretation of British history reached back not only to the revolutions of the seventeenth century and to the Reformation that—ultimately—underpinned them, but further back into the medieval past, to the Scottish Wars of Independence, which constituted the political platform for Scotland's distinctive democratic Reformation and for a Union of equals in 1707. The cult of William Wallace was at the heart of what has come to be known as 'unionist-nationalism'.[35]

Speaking on the six-hundredth anniversary of the Battle of Stirling Bridge (1297), the liberal-imperialist peer and former prime minister Lord Rosebery described Wallace's victory over the English as nothing less than the creation of the Scottish nation. All Britons, he proclaimed, should rejoice 'in the memory of this hero; for he at Stirling made Scotland great, and if Scotland were not great the Empire of all the Britons would not stand where it does.'[36] A letter to the *Ayrshire Advertiser* from December 1854, written under the pseudonym 'Pro-Patria', stated that it was thanks to Wallace and Bruce that the Scots had been able:

> at last to form a permanent union with their more powerful neighbour on the principles of most complete equality.... How much better it is for England, than it would have been if the Scottish nation had been overpowered, conquered, and oppressed.[37]

Since the Middle Ages, it was argued, Scotland had been a beacon of liberty, and nineteenth-century Scots felt an obligation to perpetuate these commitments to the ideal of freedom and, in particular, to the cause of oppressed liberty (though without in any way calling into question the benefits of the Union of 1707). At the laying of the foundation stone of the National Wallace Monument in 1861, the popular author and public speaker James Dodds claimed that had it not been for Wallace's victory, the Scots 'would have been engaged in the same awful and terrible contest in which

---

[35]   G. Morton, *Unionist-Nationalism: Governing Urban Scotland 1830–1860* (East Linton, 1999), 179–80, 188–93; J. Coleman, 'Unionist-Nationalism in Stone? The National Wallace Monument and the Hazards of Commemoration in Victorian Scotland', in E. J. Cowan, ed., *The Wallace Book* (Edinburgh, 2007).

[36]   'Wallace Celebration: Anniversary of Battle of Stirling Bridge', *Glasgow Herald*, 14 September 1897.

[37]   'Monument to Sir William Wallace', Letter from 'Pro-Patria', *Ayrshire Advertiser*, 14 December 1854. The letter concludes with an expression of surprise that the nation has not yet subscribed for a national monument to be erected to Wallace in Edinburgh.

Poland, Italy and Hungary are engaged at this time'.[38] Dodds had befriended Lajos Kossuth during the Hungarian nationalist's exile in London. Attending a meeting in Stirling in 1856 in support of the National Wallace Monument movement, Kossuth himself proclaimed:

> May that liberty dwell with you to the consummation of time, is my prayer, and may the monument you are about to raise to the noblest of your national heroes ... be a monitor of lasting inspiration to Scotland ... Two things at least I can claim to have in common with your William Wallace—that of having struggled for national independence [cheers]—and that of being unfortunate.[39]

In order to prove the bona fides of the Monument movement, and to raise much-needed funds, letters of encouragement were solicited and received from, amongst others, Kossuth and the Italian patriots Garibaldi and Mazzini, which were then framed in fragments of 'the Wallace Oak'.[40]

The elevation of Wallace, it should be noted, conformed to trends found elsewhere in Europe. In 1875 a monument to the Cheruscan chieftain Hermann or Arminius, was completed, which celebrated his defeat of a Roman legion in AD 9. In France a colossal statue was raised to the memory of the Gaulish leader Vercingetorix near the site of the Battle of Gergovia (52 BC).[41] Propagandists found ancient and medieval heroes of this sort rich in mythical potential, for so little was known about them that their lives and achievements could be moulded to fit current concerns. Thus a figure such as Wallace—an icon not burdened by a wealth of biographical detail—has proved capable of serving ideological needs that varied from generation to generation. For the Victorians, Wallace was enlisted as an historic exemplar of self-reliance, hard work, and meritocracy.[42]

Inevitably, Wallace's pre-Reformation Catholicism was conveniently overlooked, but no such problems attached to John Knox's central role in the Scottish Reformation. The Reverend Alexander Duff, a Free Church minister, speaking at the tercentenary of Knox's death in 1872, claimed that by thwarting 'the oft-renewed Popish conspiracies and confederations in the South', Knox had saved the throne of Elizabeth. In so doing, the 'Great Reformer' had guaranteed the success of the Reformation in both England and Scotland, and, by extension, the cause of civil, constitutional, and religious liberty throughout the British Isles.[43] The alternative to Protestantism had been not only

---

[38] 'Laying the Foundation-Stone of The Wallace Monument at the Abbey Craig, Stirling', *Glasgow Herald*, 25 June 1861.

[39] 'Arrival of Kossuth, and the Meeting in St John Church', Mitchell Library, William Burns Papers, B115063.

[40] J. Fyfe, ed., *Autobiography of John McAdam, 1806–1883* (Edinburgh, 1980), 174.

[41] G. L. Mosse, *The Nationalisation of the Masses* (New York, 1975), 47–72.

[42] R. J. Finlay, 'Heroes, Myths and Anniversaries in Modern Scotland', *Scottish Affairs*, 18 (1997), 115–16; G. Morton, 'The Most Efficacious Patriot: The Heritage of William Wallace in Nineteenth-Century Scotland', *Scottish Historical Review*, 77 (1998).

[43] *North British Daily Mail*, 25 November 1872; also J. A. Froude, *History of England from the Fall of Wolsey to the Death of Elizabeth*, 12 vols. (London, 1856–70), vol. x, 457.

Catholicism in the religious sphere, but its political manifestation in tyranny and absolute monarchy.

Ireland was held up as a terrifying example of a nation that lacked the necessary heroic
counterpart to Scotland's great men. By saving Scotland from oppression, Wallace,
Knox, and, later, the Covenanters of the seventeenth century had steered Scotland onto
a path of historical development happily different from Ireland's. At the laying of the
foundation stone of a monument to Knox intended for Edinburgh's High Street, the Free
Church minister William Cunningham depicted Ireland as suffering from the absence
of any 'Reformer or Reformation of her own at all; and the consequence is, that the great
majority of her population are still sunk in Popish ignorance and darkness.'[44] Nineteenth-
century Protestant critics not only denounced Popery as ungodly, but also identified it
as a solvent of nationality. At the United Presbyterian Synod's commemoration of the
Scottish Reformation in 1860, Dr Neil McMichael claimed that whereas Presbyterianism
'sanctified' nationality, Popery attempted to destroy nationalities in order that 'upon the
ruins of national freedom she might set her throne.'[45]

Nineteenth-century Scots aligned their own contemporary causes, such as Chartism,[46]
with earlier phases of Scotland's liberal history. Radicals identified both with Wallace
and with the Covenanters. In 1814 ten thousand 'democratic people' marched from the
Lanarkshire town of Strathaven to the field of Drumclog and then on to the site of what
they believed to be one of 'Wallace's first victories.'[47] During the national commemoration
of the tercentenary of the Reformation in 1860, Patrick Dove, who had been assistant to
Hugh Miller on the Free Church *Witness* newspaper, argued that Wallace and Bruce had
established Scotland's political freedom, paving the way for the Reformation and the
blessings of religious liberty.[48]

The glue that held the disparate elements of this narrative together was a loosely
defined commitment to 'civil and religious liberty'. At the 'national meeting' held to
inaugurate the National Wallace Monument movement, in Stirling in June 1856, Provost
Melville of Edinburgh claimed that it was thanks to Wallace's 'courageous enterprise in
war and prudent administration in peace, [that] the first germ of that civil and religious
liberty which we now enjoy' had been established. Almost half a century later, at the
inauguration in June 1903 of a monument to the Covenanters who fell at the Battle of
Bothwell Bridge, the principal speaker, Lord Overtoun, reminded a crowd of over
twenty-six thousand spectators that those who 'possess in this favoured land the

[44] *Report of Speeches delivered at a Meeting Held in the Music Hall, Edinburgh, on Monday, 18th May
1846, being the day on which the foundation-stone of John Knox's Monument was laid* (Edinburgh, 1846),
25.
[45] 'Proceedings of the United Presbyterian Synod: Tricentenary of the Reformation', *United
Presbyterian Magazine*, June 1860, 261.
[46] D. C. Smith, *Passive Obedience and Prophetic Protest: Social Criticism in the Scottish Church,
1830–1945* (New York, 1987), 164–5.
[47] T. C. Smout, *A Century of the Scottish People 1830–1950* (London, 1986), 236–7.
[48] 'Tricentenary of the Reformation: Celebration in Glasgow', *Glasgow Herald*, 19 December 1860.
Another speaker at the same event went so far as 'to state his belief that Wallace was at heart a Culdee,
not a Papist'.

priceless boon of civil and religious liberty' must remember that the history of Scotland was 'really the story of the Scottish Church, and of the heroic souls who, against fearful odds, stood and died for Christ's Crown and Covenant'.[49]

Notwithstanding the undoubted attractions of the Jacobite cause for Scottish romanticism,[50] within the popular Presbyterian interpretation of British history the Stuarts were viewed less as symbols of a lost Scottish nationhood, but more commonly as villains who thwarted the will of the people. Not that nineteenth-century Scots Presbyterians objected to monarchy per se. In 1887 a monument was unveiled in the Ayrshire village of Muirkirk, dedicated to the memory of several Covenanters who had fallen in that parish. The inauguration ceremony made an unambiguous connection between the civil and religious freedoms bequeathed to Scotland by the Covenanters and the beneficent reign of Queen Victoria; indeed, the inauguration was intended to mark Muirkirk's celebration of Victoria's Golden Jubilee year.[51] The Reverend John Wallace, the parish minister, emphasized the contrast between the 1680s and the 1880s:

> we cannot but feel the great and the happy change that has taken place in the relation between sovereign and people since those trying times when the House of Stuart sat upon the Throne...[Victoria] has not only a constitutional, but a moral right to reign.[52]

The Stuarts' inherited right to govern was as nothing when weighed against the moral right they had forfeited by their odious persecution of the Covenanters.

The public commemoration of the Forty-Five was marked by equivocation. Commentators stressed the folly of the cause that had prompted the rising, and emphasized that it was not the political goals of Jacobitism which made the events of 1745–6 so worthy of remembrance. Instead, nineteenth-century Scots celebrated the heroism and fidelity of the highlanders, whose descendants in the Highland regiments of the British state had risked their lives on behalf of Britain and its empire.[53] A parchment sealed inside the foundation stone of the cairn erected at Culloden stated that the intention was not to remember the Prince or the recovery of the Stuart monarchy but was instead 'dedicated to the memory of brave Highlanders who fell at Culloden...fighting for a cause which they conscientiously believed to be a right one'.[54] Whereas in the twenty-first century the Culloden battlefield of 1746 signifies a national tragedy, a century and a half ago the site had fallen into serious neglect, with several attempts to raise a

---

[49] *Scotsman*, 25 June 1856; 'Battle of Bothwell Bridge, Unveiling of National Memorial', *Glasgow Herald*, 21 June 1903.

[50] M. G. H. Pittock, *The Invention of Scotland: The Stuart Myth and Scottish Identity, 1638 to the Present* (London, 1991), 99–104, 112–20; Pittock, 'The Jacobite Cult', in Cowan and Finlay, eds., *Power of the Past*, 191–8.

[51] 'Muirkirk Martyrs' Monument', *Ayrshire Advertiser and West Country and Galloway Journal*, 23 June 1887.

[52] Ibid.

[53] Finlay, 'Heroes, Myths and Anniversaries', 118–22.

[54] *Aberdeen Journal*, 26 September 1849.

commemorative monument ending in failure through lack of interest.[55] At Glenfinnan, another key site in both Jacobite memory and the Scottish heritage trail, a marble panel placed in the monument erected there in 1815 by MacDonald of Glenaladale describes the Forty-Five as Charles Edward Stuart's 'daring and romantic attempt to recover a throne lost by the imprudence of his ancestors'. The panel states that the monument was raised 'to commemorate the generous zeal and inviolable fidelity' of Glenaladale's forebears who 'fought and bled in that arduous and unfortunate enterprise'.[56] Jacobite traditions were too closely associated with feudal authoritarianism, Catholic tyranny, and a marginal episcopalianism to find a secure and straightforward position within the Presbyterian interpretation of Scottish history. Another canonical icon of today's mythical Scotland, Mary, Queen of Scots, proved similarly problematic for nineteenth-century Scots. Mary's Catholicism rendered it impossible to bind her tragic tale to the national Presbyterian myth. Instead, Mary occupied the same cultural space as Bonnie Prince Charlie: a subject for songs and poetry, for the novelist, the dramatist, and the painter, but not for those who sought to co-opt the power of the past for present purposes.[57]

Nevertheless, by the close of the nineteenth century, the complexion of Scottish nationality was changing. Instead of a loyalist unionist-nationalism, a new hybrid emerged which, under the guise of Home Rule, brought out the nationalist implications of the romantic tradition. This is perhaps most clearly exemplified in the antics of the nationalist-cum-Jacobite Theodore Napier, who not only made several pilgrimages to Culloden on the anniversary of the battle but did the same to Fotheringay, scene of the execution of Mary, Queen of Scots.[58]

Yet the fate of the once-dominant Presbyterian mythology of the nineteenth century was sealed only in the inter-war era, when the intellectuals of the Scottish Renaissance, most prominently Christopher Murray Grieve (Hugh MacDiarmid), began to debunk the sentimental kailyardry of previous generations. For Grieve, authenticity was to be found in the Scots language. This was the only reliable touchstone of national identity, and even here truth was not to be equated with a sentimentalized cult of Robert Burns, but with the vigorous full-blooded poetry of the medieval makars. Moreover, the Scottish Reformation was identified as the ultimate source of the prim Victorianism that had stifled indigenous cultural energies. The poet and literary critic Edwin Muir wrote in 'Scotland 1941' that the Scots had once been 'a tribe, a family, a people', until 'Knox and Melville clapped their preaching palms', rendering 'Burns and Scott, sham bards of a

---

[55] E. Masson and J. Harden, 'Drumossie Moor: Memorialization, Development and Restoration in an Evolving Historic Landscape', in T. Pollard, ed., *Culloden: The History and Archaeology of the Last Clan Battle* (Barnsley, 2009); C. McArthur, 'Culloden: A Pre-Emptive Strike', *Scottish Affairs*, 9 (1994); J. R. Gold and M. M. Gold, 'The Graves of the Gallant Highlanders: Memory, Interpretation and Narratives of Culloden', *History and Memory*, 19 (2007), 23.

[56] Quoted in N. Cameron, 'A Romantic Folly to Romantic Folly: The Glenfinnan Monument Reassessed', *Proceedings of the Society of Antiquaries of Scotland*, 129 (1999), 893.

[57] J. E. Lewis, *Mary Queen of Scots* (London, 1998), 177–221.

[58] M. G. H. Pittock, *The Invention of Scotland*, 127–33.

sham nation/And spiritual defeat wrapped warm in riches.'[59] However, the Covenanting movement—shorn of its full religious significance—did become a source of inspiration for the Labour movement. Nevertheless, the dominant trend was to mythologize Knox and the Reformers as authoritarian dominies who—far from begetting a liberal tradition—were enemies of popular freedom. The Presbyterian interpretation of history had been turned on its head.

Moreover, with industrial dislocation and the retreat from empire, twentieth-century Scotland lost the self-confidence of the unionist-nationalism and popular imperialism that had flourished in the Victorian era. Secularization and the rise of nationalism contributed to the emergence of a mythology of victimhood, grievance, and glorious failure, running from Flodden (1513), via Culloden (1746) and the Highland clearances, to industrial decline. Post-imperial Scotland had become an underdog nation, its people stabbed in the back by a self-serving aristocracy in 1707, and ever since its needs and values had been subordinated to those of a dominant and unforgiving England. Counterbalancing this myth was an apolitical myth of tartanry that had, as both nationalist and socialist intellectuals maintained, anaesthetized the nation during recent centuries of apathetic unionism to the real condition of Scotland.[60] Such arguments were, of course, no less mythological than the myths they criticized. Over time, these views have fashioned a new myth of Scotland's past that emphasizes nationalism and elides Scottish unionism. In 1993 it came as a jolt when the then Conservative Secretary of State for Scotland, Ian Lang, claimed that he would like to have been a fly on the wall at the Battle of Bannockburn (1314); for, had it not been for Bannockburn, Lang stated, Scotland would not have joined in Union with England under such equal terms.[61] Had Lang expressed such an opinion a century or so earlier, he would have been articulating a widely held view. However, as we have seen, political and cultural demands change, and the myths of Scottish history change with them.

## FURTHER READING

Ash, M., *The Strange Death of Scottish History* (Edinburgh, 1980).
Broun, D., Finlay, R., and Lynch, M., eds., *Image and Identity: The Making and Re-making of Scotland through the Ages* (Edinburgh, 1998).
Cowan, E. J., and Finlay, R., eds., *Scottish History: The Power of the Past* (Edinburgh, 2002).
Gaskill, H., ed., *The Reception of Ossian in Europe* (New York, 2004).
Kidd, C., *Subverting Scotland's Past* (Cambridge, 1993).
Thiesse, A-M., *La Création des identités nationales* (Paris, 1999).
Trevor-Roper, H., *The Invention of Scotland* (New Haven, 2008).

[59]  Edwin Muir, 'Scotland 1941', in Muir, *Collected Poems* (London, 1963), 97.
[60]  C. Beveridge and R. Turnbull, *The Eclipse of Scottish Culture* (Edinburgh, 1989); Ash, *Strange Death*; Nairn, *Break-Up of Britain*.
[61]  D. McCrone, 'Tomorrow's Ancestors: Nationalism, Identity and History', in Cowan and Finlay, eds., *Power of the Past*, 254–5; D. McCrone, A. Morris, and R. Kiely, *Scotland—The Brand: The Making of Scottish Heritage* (Edinburgh, 1995).

CHAPTER 4

·······························································································

# RELIGION AND SOCIETY
# TO *c*.1900

·······························································································

STEWART J. BROWN

THE Revolution of 1688, which brought the Dutch Calvinist Stadtholder William of Orange and his consort, Mary, to the English throne, was mainly a political event, led by Whig magnates provoked by royal encroachments on their liberties and property. But it also had important religious dimensions, and this was especially true of Scotland. From late December 1688, as news of the collapsing authority of James VII and II reached Scotland, bands of militant Presbyterians assaulted ministers of the established Church across much of Lowland Scotland, punishing them for their support of the Stuart monarchy by 'rabbling' them from their churches and manses; eventually some two hundred clergy were forcibly ejected. In March 1689 a Convention Parliament met in Edinburgh; it offered the Scottish Crown to William and Mary and ordered all ministers of the Church to pray publicly for the new monarchs. The Convention then turned to the religious settlement and the long-standing struggle between episcopacy and presbytery. In July 1689 it proclaimed that the new monarchs, with the advice of the Scottish Parliament, would establish in Scotland that form of Church government 'which is most agreeable to the inclinations of the people'.

As Lionel Glassey has demonstrated, William was largely uninformed about the Scottish religious situation and evidently promised his support to both Scottish Episcopalians and Presbyterians. While the Dutch Church in which he had been raised was Presbyterian in organization, he was a pragmatist in religious matters; his main concern was to secure a religious settlement that would bring peace and stability to the northern kingdom. There would have been good reason to establish episcopacy and thus move towards uniformity between the established Churches of Scotland and England. But the Scottish Episcopalian cause was soon undermined, first by the refusal of the Scottish bishops to recognize William's claim to the throne, and then by the open support of many Episcopalians for the ill-fated rising in support of James led by Viscount

Dundee in the spring and summer of 1689.[1] In the summer of 1690, after a year's delay, the Convention established Presbyterianism as the form of government for the established Church, and the Calvinist Westminster Confession as the standard of faith. Significantly, the Convention made no reference to God's will in this decision, nor did it renew the Covenants—neither the National Covenant of 1638 nor the Solemn League and Covenant of 1643—by which many believed the Scottish nation had bound itself before God to preserve and maintain the true Church.

As Alec Cheyne observed, 'Generations of historians have made claims and counter-claims about the true balance of religious allegiances at the time of the Revolution' and whether it was presbytery or episcopacy that was truly 'most agreeable to the inclinations of the people'.[2] There is probably no way of resolving this question. What can be said is that the establishment of Presbyterianism in 1690 proved the defining episode in a prolonged struggle over the nature of the Protestant Church and society in Scotland—a struggle that had brought revolutionary upheavals and civil warfare, and contributed to lasting perceptions of Scottish religion as intolerant, severe, persecuting, and divisive. King William's hope was that this struggle would now be brought to a close. 'Moderation', he famously instructed the General Assembly in his King's Letter of 1690, 'is what religion enjoins, neighbouring churches expect from you, and we recommend to you.'[3] To help promote this spirit, William endowed in 1694 a new Chair of Ecclesiastical History at the University of Edinburgh, to give Scottish Presbyterians a sense of perspective about their past. In this chapter, the current holder of that chair will seek to add to this sense of perspective, providing an overview of religion in modern Scotland up to 1900, with emphasis on the movement from a unitary Calvinist state, an aspiring 'godly commonwealth', to a multi-denominational, increasingly pluralist society.

# THE REFORMATION IN SCOTLAND

The Reformation is discussed by Jenny Wormald in Chapter 9, so a few general observations will suffice here. The Reformation came to Scotland in 1560, some forty-three years after Martin Luther had nailed his ninety-five theses to the church door in Wittenberg, and nearly thirty years after the beginning of the English Reformation. The Scottish Reformation reflected the advanced thinking of the second generation of Reformers, especially the Geneva-based, French Protestant theologian and legal scholar John Calvin. It was a relatively non-violent affair, in comparison with Reformations elsewhere

---

[1] L. K. J. Glassey, 'William II and the Settlement of Religion in Scotland, 1688–1690', *Records of the Scottish Church History Society* [hereafter *RSCHS*], 23 (1989), 317–29.

[2] A. C. Cheyne, *Studies in Scottish Church History* (Edinburgh, 1999), 61.

[3] A. L. Drummond and J. Bulloch, *The Scottish Church 1688–1843: The Age of the Moderates* (Edinburgh, 1973), 10.

in Europe. The pre-Reformation Scottish Church, for all its versatility, learning, architectural achievements, and links with Scotland's past, had also grown weak, increasingly ineffective, and unable to reform itself. The Crown, while it opposed the Reformation movement, had to rely on French military force to maintain its authority, and the French presence had become unwelcome among the population. The victory of the Protestant Reformers in Scotland was achieved with English military support against a crumbling resistance in both Church and State. With backing from the Scottish Parliament, the Reformers moved swiftly in the early 1560s to establish in Scotland a godly commonwealth, modelled largely on Calvin's Geneva, with an emphasis on preaching, an innovative educational programme, public order based on biblical commands, and a poor-relief system rooted in parish communities. In 1560 Parliament ratified a new Confession of Faith, or 'Scots Confession'.[4] The Confession was Calvinist in tone and content, emphasizing the 'inscrutable providence' of God, who had determined all things by his 'eternal and immutable decrees'; the total depravity of humankind, all of whom deserved eternal damnation; and God's mercy in electing a portion of sinful humanity to salvation through grace alone. The new Church was loosely governed by a General Assembly of ministers and lay leaders, and by several 'superintendents', parish ministers who were also given the task of visiting parishes, supervising ministers, and planting churches in the surrounding region.

As the valuable work of Jane Dawson has demonstrated, the early phases of the Reformation brought new cultural expressions, including congregational singing, sophisticated musical settings of the Psalms, poetic, vernacular liturgies, the rich cadences of the Geneva Bible, devotional art, and an insistence on a learned ministry. Existing church buildings were adapted for the new forms of worship, with lengthened naves to accommodate seated congregations, high pulpits, and movable Communion tables replacing the old altars.[5] Regular public worship every Sunday brought new patterns to social life, including the enforcement of a Sabbath day of rest for labouring people. The Reformers introduced a system of parish-based social discipline, by which offenders were tried before parish kirk-sessions (consisting of the minister and several laymen, or 'elders', selected for their piety and morals) for such infractions as extramarital sexual relations, drunkenness, brawling, and libel, and if found guilty were required to make public confession and assigned a public penance. The sentence of excommunication was rarely used; rather, the aim was to rehabilitate offenders and reconcile them to the community. The Reformers' educational programme, including a primary school for boys and girls in every parish and a ladder of opportunity for the 'lad o' pairts' (not lassies) to attend a burgh school and university regardless of social background, represented a potent ideal—even if it was never fully achieved. Despite a serious shortage of

---

    [4] *The Scots Confession 1560*, ed. G. D. Henderson (Edinburgh, 1960); W. I. P. Hazlett, 'The Scots Confession 1560: Context, Complexion and Critique', *Archiv für Reformationsgeschichte*, 78 (1987), 287–320.
    [5] J. E. A. Dawson, *Scotland Reformed 1488–1587* (Edinburgh, 2007), 216–39.

ministers in the new Kirk, the Reformation spread rapidly through the country, where its doctrine, worship, and social policies proved broadly popular.

There was, to be sure, also a darker side to the godly commonwealth. In 1563 Parliament passed the Witchcraft Act, which gave the State the power to try and execute witches. In a superb study, Christina Larner discussed how kirk-sessions often took the initiative in seeking out witches, who could include local wise women skilled in the use of herbal remedies; some fifteen hundred women were executed before the odious act was finally repealed in 1735.[6] As Julian Goodare has shown, the witch-hunt in Scotland was directed overwhelmingly against women and involved an intrusive effort by the godly commonwealth to control women and their sexuality.[7] The Reformed authorities also persecuted Roman Catholics, who retreated to more remote parts of the country, especially the north-east, where a remnant survived through the protection of sympathetic noble families and intermittent visits from missionary Jesuits from the 1580s and Franciscans from 1619.[8]

## THE REFORMATION DIVIDED

Early Reformation hopes were shadowed by dissention over the relations of Church and State, and over the nature of Church government. The Reformers had intended to finance their ambitious programme for the godly commonwealth with the resources of the pre-Reformation Church. However, much pre-Reformation Church property, including monastic lands, friaries, and bishops' properties, was seized by the Crown and landed classes, and the new owners had no intention of relinquishing their gains. The Reformation had been achieved against the opposition of Queen Mary. After her forced abdication in 1567, her successor, the hoped-for 'godly king', James VI, remained ever distrustful of the Reformed Church as a rival authority. For many, the best way to achieve the needed cooperation between the Crown, landed elite, and the Church would be for the Scottish Reformed Church to move in a similar direction as the Church of England, and establish government by bishops with the Crown as supreme head of the Church.

Under the leadership of Andrew Melville, however, the Scottish Church moved in a very different direction. From the 1570s, influenced by developments in the continental Reformed Churches, the Church adopted a new system of internal government through a hierarchy of ecclesiastical courts. Fundamental to the system was the classis, or presbytery—made up of the ministers and elders of several neighbouring parishes.

---

[6] C. Larner, *Enemies of God: The Witch-hunt in Scotland* (London, 1981).

[7] J. Goodare, 'Women and the Witch-hunt in Scotland', *Social History*, 23 (1998), 288–308.

[8] M. H. B. Sanderson, 'Catholic Recusancy in Scotland in the Sixteenth Century', *Innes Review*, 21 (1970), 87–107; P. F. Anson, *Underground Catholicism in Scotland 1622–1878* (Montrose, 1970); M. Dilworth, 'The Counter-Reformation in Scotland: A Select Critical Bibliography', *RSCHS*, 22 (1984), 85–100.

Within this 'Presbyterian' system, all ministers were to be equal and none was to exercise individual authority over another. The Presbyterian Church, moreover, was to be independent of the State in its 'spiritual', or specifically religious functions, including the ordination of ministers, administration of the sacraments, and setting of its liturgies. In his seminal study of the Scottish Reformation, Gordon Donaldson portrayed this Presbyterian movement as a radical departure from the early Reformation, which he argued had been moving towards government by bishops as the practice of most of Christendom. He described the superintendents as embryotic bishops and argued that Church and State had been moving towards closer cooperation before the Presbyterian take-over.[9] Others, however, including Alec Cheyne and James Kirk, have viewed Presbyterianism as a logical development of the early Reformation, with its elevation of the laity in Church government and its emphasis on the spiritual independence of the Church.[10] They argued that the superintendents were never intended to be more than an interim measure. They further observed that the Reformers continually looked to Geneva, and not Canterbury, for their ecclesiastical models.

The tensions between presbytery and episcopacy—between the continental Reformed and Anglican models of Reformation—divided the Scottish Reformed Church from the 1580s. King James opposed the Presbyterian movement and sought, through persuasion and force, to bring the Scottish Church into greater conformity with the Church of England. Presbyterians, however, resisted the Crown's efforts to introduce bishops and liturgical changes, perceiving them as moves to undermine Scotland's Reformation. They began depicting Scotland's Reformation in terms of the Old Testament 'covenant' between God and the Hebrew people; in 1596 the General Assembly called for a national 'covenant' to uphold the Presbyterian system.[11] James's moves against Presbyterianism intensified following the Union of the Crowns in 1603. The Crown successfully introduced bishops into the Scottish Church by 1610, and in 1618 it pressured the General Assembly of the Church into accepting liturgical changes (the Five Articles of Perth) that moved Scottish worship closer to that of England. As David Mullan has shown, many Scots believed these ceremonial changes were aimed at introducing an Arminian theology, emphasizing human freedom and an imperative of good works, against the predominant Scottish Calvinist doctrine of salvation by grace alone.[12] During the 1620s Presbyterian ministers and laity, deeply opposed to the changes, began forming 'coventicles', or small groups that met clandestinely for prayer, preaching, and Bible

---

[9]  G. Donaldson, *The Scottish Reformation* (Cambridge, 1960).

[10]  A. C. Cheyne, 'The Scottish Reformation', *Scottish Journal of Theology*, 16 (1963), 78–88; J. Kirk, *Patterns of Reform: Continuity and Change in the Reformation Kirk* (Edinburgh, 1989), 334–67.

[11]  S. A. Burrell, 'The Covenant as a Revolutionary Symbol: Scotland, 1596–1637', *Church History*, 27 (1958), 338–50.

[12]  D. G. Mullan, 'Theology in the Church of Scotland 1618–c.1640: A Calvinist Consensus?', *The Sixteenth-Century Journal*, 26 (1995), 595–617; see also D. G. Mullan, *Scottish Puritanism, 1590–1638* (Oxford, 2000).

reading. The divisions in the Church, to be sure, should not be exaggerated. Most Scottish Protestants were willing to compromise in the interest of Church unity and order, and in the parishes, ministers and kirk-sessions continued the work of preaching, administering the sacraments, pastoral care, supervising discipline and poor relief.[13]

# THE COVENANTS AND THE WESTMINSTER CONFESSION

The tensions, however, were real and they climaxed in 1637, with a popular revolt against efforts by the Crown to introduce further liturgical reforms. The revolt included the drafting of a National Covenant, which called for the restoration of Presbyterianism and which from 1638 was sent to parishes around the country for signature. With the Covenanters' military success against the forces of the Crown in the 'Bishops' Wars' of 1639–40 came a restoration of Presbyterianism. While the Covenanting movement is covered elsewhere in the volume, it is important here to highlight the rigorous Calvinism of the Covenanting period, and especially the Westminster Confession that was adopted in the 1640s and still remains the official standard of faith in the Church of Scotland.

In 1643 Scottish Presbyterians entered into the Solemn League and Covenant with the English parliamentary party against the Crown, providing Scottish military assistance in return for an English promise to adopt Calvinist Presbyterianism within the Church of England. As part of this agreement, an Assembly of English Puritan divines (with several Scottish observers) met at Westminster and between 1643 and 1647 prepared a Confession of Faith and Directory of Worship for what was to be a British Presbyterian Church. The Westminster Confession of Faith provided a systematic, logical, and comprehensive expression of Calvinist doctrine, including the governance of all things by God's eternal decrees, the total depravity of humanity, salvation by grace alone, God's predestination of a portion of humanity for salvation, and God's predestination of the rest for eternal damnation. The Westminster Directory provided for simple, austere worship, centred upon the sermon, Bible readings, and singing of the Psalms. It required that baptism and marriage take place in the presence of the congregation, while it disallowed funeral services or prayers at the graveside, as these might promote the erroneous belief that prayers could have any effect on the eternal prospects of the deceased, whose fate had been predestined from before all time.[14] While never adopted by the English Parliament, the Westminster Confession and Directory were adopted by the General Assembly of the Scottish Church in 1647 and by the Scottish Parliament in 1649. More work is needed on parish life during the Covenanting era; however, it appears that the rigorous Westminster patterns of

---

[13] For a valuable review of the religious debates, see D. Stevenson, 'Scottish Church History, 1600–1660: A Select Critical Bibliography', *RSCHS*, 21 (1982), 209–20.

[14] H. Sefton, 'Occasions in the Reformed Church', in C. MacLean and K. Veitch, eds., *Scottish Life and Society: Religion* (Edinburgh, 2006), 469–78.

thought, worship, and government soon became embedded. This Westminster Calvinism, for all its harshness, could instil an inner strength based on certainty of God's providential ordering of all things, and on a fear of God and none other. As Gordon Marshall has argued (drawing on the work of Max Weber), the Calvinist self-discipline, asceticism, and sense of worldly vocation (or work ethic) shaped national character and contributed to the emergence of a spirit of capitalism in Scotland, evident in commerce and manufactures by the final decades of the seventeenth century.[15]

Following the restoration of the Stuart monarchy in 1660 under Charles II, the Crown reimposed episcopacy within the Scottish Church, proscribed the Westminster Confession, and declared royal supremacy over the Church. The Episcopal settlement was imposed from England, with little sensitivity to Scottish feelings. Some 270 ministers, nearly a quarter of the total, refused to conform to episcopacy and were in consequence deprived of their church livings. Some Presbyterians, mainly in the south-west, again formed conventicles for clandestine worship, holding services on hillsides or in secluded glens. The Crown viewed these conventicles as nests of political rebellion and 'seminaries of treason' and compelled conformity through fines and imprisonment. Presbyterians responded with armed revolts in 1666 and 1679; these were speedily crushed but they left martyrs and popular resistance continued. During the 'killing time' of the 1680s, Covenanters were summarily executed. While the numbers killed were not great—probably fewer than two hundred—some deplorable incidents, including the shooting of John Brown of Priesthill before his wife and children in 1685, or the alleged judicial drowning of two women in the same year at Wigtown (the facts are disputed), became part of a Presbyterian folklore, as did the tales of Covenanting field-preaching on the hillsides, with guards watching for the approach of troopers. The older Presbyterian historiography, which received its classic expression in Robert Wodrow's *History of the Sufferings of the Church of Scotland* (1721–2), has been long discredited. The Crown and ecclesiastical authorities were, after all, responding to armed resistance, and by the declarations of indulgence (in 1669, 1672, 1679, and 1687) the authorities did offer a degree of toleration to Presbyterian beliefs and forms of worship. None the less, the perceptions of an unpopular and persecuting episcopacy, maintained by a despotic State, were compelling in parts of the Lowlands, and these perceptions go far to explain the sweeping away of the Episcopal system and the re-establishment of Presbyterianism in 1689–90.

## The Eighteenth Century

The early eighteenth century was for many Presbyterians the golden age for the Scottish Church, when they believed that the Reformation aspirations for godly commonwealth, based on the preaching of the Word, administration of the sacraments, and enforcement

---

[15] G. Marshall, *Presbyteries and Profits: Calvinism and the Development of Capitalism in Scotland, 1560–1707* (Oxford, 1980).

of ecclesiastical discipline, were at long last being achieved. The Presbyterian settlement of 1690 was confirmed at the Union of 1707, when guarantees were given that the predominantly Anglican Union Parliament would not in future interfere with Scotland's Presbyterian establishment. The relative ease by which Scottish Presbyterians gained these guarantees indicates the pragmatism of the leading politicians, who were more concerned with political stability than with religious uniformity throughout the Union State.[16] The politicians believed that the majority of Scots wanted Presbyterian Church government and the Westminster Confession, and by 1707 they were probably correct. There would, to be sure, be major Jacobite risings, with religious motivations and significant support (mainly from Highlanders and Episcopalians) in 1715 and 1745–6. As Murray Pittock has shown, Jacobites embraced a doctrine of sacred kingship, and believed that the Stuart 'king over the water' represented God's anointed; for them, God's favour had been withdrawn from a corrupt and sinful people, and would not be returned until the Stuarts were restored to the throne.[17] However, for much of the Scottish population, Presbyterianism was shaping beliefs and forging a social order that was increasingly 'agreeable to their inclinations'.

The Presbyterian system, including the hierarchy of Church courts, was by the 1720s in operation throughout Scotland, with the ministers supported by teinds (a notional 10 per cent of agricultural produce) and rentals on seating. The heritors, or principal landowners in each parish, were responsible for the upkeep of church and manse. Each of the country's approximately one thousand parishes had its incumbent minister and its kirk-session. The kirk-sessions had responsibility for the maintenance of social order, education, and poor relief. The next level of ecclesiastical government was the presbytery, made up of the ministers and elders of several neighbouring parishes. There were sixty-nine presbyteries, which normally met monthly to review the work of kirk-sessions and discuss regional and national issues. Above the presbytery was the synod, which consisted of the minister and one elder from each parish within a province representing several presbyteries. There were sixteen synods, and they met twice a year to review presbytery decisions and discuss larger provincial and national issues. At the apex of the system was the General Assembly, made up of commissioners selected by the presbyteries, royal burghs, and universities. The General Assembly met once a year in Edinburgh, and served as both the supreme ecclesiastical court and the highest legislative assembly, considering overtures for new Church laws from the lower courts. This system of representative Church courts, including lay members, provided valuable opportunities for the debate of national issues following the removal of the Scottish Parliament in 1707.

The parish church formed the centre of local communities; it was the place where they assembled and exchanged news, where the ancestors rested in the churchyard, and

---

[16] J. Stephen, 'The Kirk and the Union, 1706–07', *RSCHS*, 31 (2001), 68–96; D. J. Patrick, 'The Kirk, Parliament and the Union', in S. J. Brown and C. A. Whatley, eds., *The Union of 1707: New Dimensions* (Edinburgh, 2008), 94–115.

[17] M. G. H. Pittock, *The Invention of Scotland: The Stuart Myth and the Scottish Identity, 1638 to the Present* (London, 1991), 7–72.

where the rites of passage—baptism, first communion, marriage, and burial—were marked. Sunday services, conducted according to the Westminster Directory, normally lasted about two hours, and included a long sermon and/or lecture on a Scriptural passage, extempore prayer, Bible readings, and the singing of the Psalms without musical accompaniment (organs were expressly banned). The Sabbath was strictly enforced as a day of worship, prayer, and family devotions—while the other holy days of the Christian year (including Christmas and Easter) were not observed. Infants were baptized and marriages celebrated before the congregation, and the dead were buried without religious services or prayers. Parish ministers were expected to visit the homes of all their parishioners regularly, to provide pastoral supervision and religious instruction, and to encourage families to conduct daily household devotions—normally a reading from the family Bible and a prayer.

Parish churches normally celebrated the Lord's Supper once or twice a year, in 'occasions' that continued for four or five days, and brought together the ministers and people from neighbouring parishes. The occasions included a day of fasting and preparation, when communicants were urged to confess their secret sins and be reconciled with their neighbours, a day of examination, in which would-be communicants were examined in doctrine, manners, and morals, and the day of Communion, when communicants were served at table, normally in groups of twelve, while different ministers preached in succession to waiting crowds. All this was followed by a day of thanksgiving. As Leigh Schmidt has shown, these 'holy fairs' were communal festivals, providing opportunities for socializing and exchange of news; people might attend several occasions each year, in their own and in neighbouring parishes. The occasions could also be times of profound psychological tension and all-night prayer. In the address known as the 'fencing of the table', ministers warned would-be communicants, in often terrifying language, that to take the Lord's Supper in an unworthy state was to eat and drink their own damnation, while not to take the sacrament if worthy was to demean the divine grace purchased by Christ's sacrifice and to insult God. It is little wonder that the Communions could foment great inner turmoil. Schmidt has demonstrated how the rituals of the Scottish 'holy fairs' contributed to the emergence of the 'camp meeting' revivals, initially among Scots and Scots-Irish Presbyterian settlers along the western frontier of the United States.[18] In the Scottish Highlands, lay leaders, known simply as the 'Men', emerged from the Communion occasions; they were venerated for their religious knowledge, assisted in examining would-be communicants, dressed in a distinctive manner, and exercised an authority rivalling that of the clergy.[19]

[18] L. E. Schmidt, *Holy Fairs: Scottish Communions and American Revivals in the Early Modern Period* (Princeton, 1989); see also, M. Westerkamp, *Triumph of the Laity: Scots-Irish Piety and the Great Awakening, 1625–1760* (Oxford, 1988), and N. Landsman, *Scotland and its First American Colony, 1683–1760* (Princeton, 1985).

[19] D. M. M. Paton, 'The Myth and the Reality of the "Men": Leadership and Spirituality in the Northern Highlands, 1800–1850', *RSCHS*, 31 (2001), 97–144.

The kirk-sessions maintained communal order. Elders were to search out infractions—including Sabbath-breaking (which could include any form of work or enjoyment), drunkenness, extramarital sex, brawling, or libel—and bring the offenders for trial before the kirk-session. According to the Form of Process adopted in 1707, kirk-sessions had the power to compel evidence under oath. If found guilty, offenders were admonished and required to pay a fine and perform a public penance, which often involved standing in sackcloth before the congregation for a number of Sundays; to refuse the fine and penance could lead to excommunication and alienation from the community.[20] By the testificat system, people could not move from parish to parish to seek work without a letter from a minister testifying to their moral character, which meant there was additional pressure to conform to kirk-session demands. While the grim picture of stultifying parish discipline presented in Grey Graham's classic account, *The Social Life of Scotland in the Eighteenth Century*, is exaggerated, it contains some truth. In close-knit communities with long memories, the shame of public penance could be worse than death. Some women murdered their infants, and were hanged for this, rather than endure 'standing the session'.[21] Work on session records by Leah Leneman and Rosalind Mitchison has demonstrated that the system was largely directed to limiting extramarital pregnancies by controlling women's sexuality.[22] Parish discipline could be severely oppressive, banning theatrical performances, discouraging 'frivolous' popular songs, fiddling and dance, and, in the view of some, throwing a shade over the creative arts in Scotland that would remain into the late nineteenth century, and beyond.

Kirk-sessions managed Scottish poor relief, with funds raised through church-door collections and the rental of the parish mortcloth used to cover coffins when carried for burial. In times of economic crisis, kirk-sessions and heritors were empowered to impose an assessment, or tax on property, to supplement the poor fund.[23] The Scottish poor law restricted relief to those genuinely unable to work, and kirk-sessions determined who qualified and the amounts given. Kirk-sessions and heritors also exercised joint authority over education. Most parishes had a parish school, which represented the twin Reformation aims of universal literacy and a ladder of opportunity for boys of talent. Schoolmasters, appointed by the heritors, had to subscribe to the Westminster Confession; many were able to teach Latin and even Greek. The parish school was periodically examined by the minister and kirk-session, to ensure both quality of instruction and Calvinist orthodoxy. Boys from poorer

---

[20]  I. M. Clark, *History of Church Discipline in Scotland* (Aberdeen, 1929), 138–62; G. D. Henderson, *The Scottish Ruling Elder* (London, 1935), 100–45.

[21]  H. Grey Graham, *The Social Life of Scotland in the Eighteenth Century*, 3rd edn. (London, 1901), 314–34.

[22]  L. Leneman and R. Mitchison, 'Acquiescence and Defiance of Church Discipline in Early-Modern Scotland', *RSCHS*, 25 (1993), 19–39; L. Leneman, 'Seduction in Eighteenth and Early Nineteenth-Century Scotland', *Scottish Historical Review*, 78 (1999), 39–59.

[23]  R. Mitchison, 'The Making of the Old Scottish Poor Law', *Past and Present*, 63 (1974), 58–93; R. A. Cage, 'The Scottish Poor Law, 1745–1845' (PhD Thesis, University of Glasgow, 1974), 25–80.

backgrounds frequently proceeded to a bursary at one of Scotland's five universities. Indeed, it has been a long-standing assumption in Scottish history that the parish school system, a legacy of the Reformation, assured nearly universal literacy, opened careers to talent, and lay behind the extraordinary achievements of the Scottish Enlightenment and Scottish industrialization. This interpretation no longer commands the confidence it once did. R. A. Houston's quantitative research has raised doubts about whether eighteenth-century Scottish literacy was any higher than other Western European countries, while Robert Anderson has questioned the impact of parish schools on social mobility.[24] None the less, for all their failings, the parish schools did represent the ideal of universal literacy, and in much of Scotland they promoted the self-discipline and respect for learning that would, as Richard Saville has argued, provide needed intellectual capital for Scotland's economic development.[25] The whole parish system formed what Tom Devine has described as the 'parish state', in which the established Church exercised authority over vital social functions, including education, poor relief, and the maintenance of order, and helped ensure an unprecedented level of social peace and order.[26]

The unity of the Presbyterian commonwealth, however, began to unravel as the eighteenth century progressed. In part, this resulted from the growth of religious toleration. The reprehensible execution of the Edinburgh University student Thomas Aikenhead for blasphemy in 1697 was the last execution of its kind in Scotland, while the last woman was burned for witchcraft in Scotland in 1727. Increasingly, Scottish government and society (if not the Church courts) were influenced by the notion, advanced by such thinkers as the English philosopher John Locke, that toleration was a virtue, rather than a crime against religious truth and a necessary evil at best. The new attitudes came to include toleration for those who would not conform to the established Church. The process began with the Episcopalians, who had been forced out of the established Church after the Revolution (the process became a gradual one after the initial 'rabblings' of 1688–9), but for whom there was considerable sympathy, especially in England. In 1712, therefore, soon after the Union of 1707, the British Parliament passed a Toleration Act for Scotland, granting legal rights of worship for Scottish Episcopalians who would pray for the monarch and use the English Book of Common Prayer. While it was limited in scope, the Toleration Act meant that the British State would no longer enforce full conformity on the established Church of Scotland.[27]

[24] R. A. Houston, *Scottish Literacy and the Scottish Identity* (Cambridge, 1985); R. D. Anderson, *Education and the Scottish People 1750–1918* (Oxford, 1995), 18–23.

[25] R. Saville, 'Intellectual Capital in Pre-1707 Scotland', in Brown and Whatley, eds., *The Union of 1707*, 45–60.

[26] T. Devine, *The Scottish Nation 1700–2000* (London, 1999), 84–102; C. G. Brown, 'The Myth of the Parish State', in J. Kirk, ed., *The Scottish Churches and the Union Parliament 1707–1999* (Edinburgh, 2001), 57–70.

[27] R. Buick Knox, 'Establishment and Toleration during the Reigns of William, Mary and Anne', *Records of the Scottish Church History Society*, 23 (1989), 330–60.

In 1712 the British Parliament passed another act that would have momentous effects for the established Church and swell the numbers of non-conformists. This was the Patronage Act, which restored lay patronage in the appointment of parish ministers. Patronage had first emerged in the medieval Church; it allowed the original founder of a parish church, and the founder's descendants, to present a clergyman to minister in that church. Patronage had a tempestuous history in the Reformed Church, with the Crown and landed classes, who held nearly all patronage rights, supporting patronage, and committed Presbyterians, with their emphasis on the spiritual independence of the Church, strongly opposing it. Parliament had abolished patronage in 1690, replacing it with a system of election by kirk-sessions and heritors, and its reimposition in 1712 was felt as a blow against Presbyterianism. Lay patrons tended to present 'moderate' ministers, who were less strict about discipline and Calvinist doctrine. For zealous Presbyterians, such ministers were 'worldly' and lukewarm, and their intrusion into parishes would undermine Scotland's Reformation heritage. The result was popular rage and frequent mob violence to halt the induction of a patron's candidates, and confusion in the Church courts about how to respond to the contentious law.

In 1733 a small group of ministers, including the brothers Ebenezer and Ralph Erskine, seceded from the Church of Scotland, together with most of their congregations, in protest against both patronage and what they perceived as a moderate, worldly ethos among Church leaders. They formed an 'Associate Presbytery' made up of the godly; they alone were the true heirs of the Reformation and the Covenants. They famously informed the English evangelical George Whitefield, that he should preach only to their members, as the 'Lord's people', when he visited Scotland in 1741. More and more disaffected ministers and congregations, angered over patronage, joined what became known as the Secession Church. The Seceders split in 1747 over whether their members should take oaths of loyalty to the un-Covenanted British State; both sects claimed to be the one true Church in Scotland, and both continued to grow. Each of these two sects split again in the 1790s over the question of whether or not the union of Church and State, as taught in the Westminster Confession, was God's will. In 1761, meanwhile, there had emerged still another Presbyterian denomination, the Relief Church, which offered a home to Scots who opposed patronage but who were more inclusive in their attitudes to other Christians than the Secession Churches. By 1801 there were over three hundred Secession or Relief congregations, with perhaps 150,000 adherents, representing almost 10 per cent of Scotland's population.[28] They added to the small numbers of Episcopalians and Roman Catholics who were outside the established Church, and also to some little Scottish sects of Baptists, Congregationalists, Quakers, Reformed Presbyterians, and Glassites. What is significant about all this is that Scotland was becoming a multi-denominational society. Considerable numbers were making individual decisions to step out of the parish community, with all

[28]  R. B. Sher and A. Murdoch, 'Patronage and Party in the Church of Scotland, 1750–1800', in N. McDougall, ed., *Church, Politics and Society: Scotland 1408–1929* (Edinburgh, 1983), 201; A. Ranken, *The Importance of Religious Establishments* (Glasgow, 1799), 115–26.

its historic associations and social functions, and to worship in dissenting churches that were essentially voluntary associations.

This growth of denominationalism coincided with a movement of liberal theological thought within the established Church of Scotland. During the 1760s a group of moderate, learned, urban-based clergymen, including William Robertson, Hugh Blair, and Alexander Carlyle—with support from prominent members of the landed and professional classes—came to control the General Assembly and exercise leadership over the Church of Scotland. They embraced the designation of 'Moderate'. They advised the Crown and landed classes on Church patronage, were active in the learned societies and intellectual pursuits of the Enlightenment, promoted toleration, and called for more openness to the theatre, literature, and the other arts. Their sermons appealed to polite sensibility and virtue for its own sake, rather than preaching on divine judgement and the afterlife. The Moderate leadership helped create a liberal social environment in the urban centres in which the Enlightenment could flourish. The Moderate ministers were the subject of a superb book by Richard Sher in 1985 and by a series of studies by Sher, Ian D. L. Clark, Nicolas Phillipson, Alexander Stewart, John Dwyer, Jeffrey Smitten, and others, many of these studies originating in the conferences of the Eighteenth-Century Scottish Studies Society.[29] David Allan has demonstrated the important connections between Renaissance humanism, the Scottish Reformation, and the Enlightenment.[30] John McIntosh has explored how the ethos of the Enlightenment gradually influenced the opponents of the Moderates—who were known variously as the 'Orthodox', 'Evangelical', or 'Popular' party.[31] During the 'Leslie controversy', which involved a hard-fought contest for an Edinburgh professorship in 1805, it was the 'Popular' party that championed freedom of enquiry among professors.[32] The growth of toleration and liberal theological views ensured that the established Church was relatively quiet when Parliament removed most remaining civil disabilities on Scottish Episcopalians in 1792 and most civil disabilities on Roman Catholics in 1793.

Along with the Enlightenment and Moderatism, the second half of the eighteenth century also witnessed an 'evangelical revival' in Scotland. This was part of a larger movement across the North Atlantic world of vital, emotive, personal religion, with an emphasis on the conversion experience and Christ's atonement on the Cross for the sins of all humankind. Evangelical converts gave less attention to the 'parish state', or the doctrines of the Westminster Confession, and more to a simple religion of the heart, an inner assurance of salvation through faith, and the expression of faith through good works. The evangelical movement was connected with the democratic influences associated with the American and French Revolutions, which emphasized the innate moral

---

[29] R. B. Sher, *Church and University in the Scottish Enlightenment: The Moderate Literati of Edinburgh* (Princeton, 1985).

[30] D. Allan, *Virtue, Learning and the Scottish Enlightenment* (Edinburgh, 1993).

[31] J. McIntosh, *Church and Theology in Enlightenment Scotland: The Popular Party, 1740–1800* (East Linton, 1998).

[32] I. D. L. Clark, 'The Leslie Controversy, 1805', *RSCHS*, 14 (1962), 179–97.

sense of the common people rather than deference to the established order in Church and State. The years between 1790 and 1830 brought a burgeoning of dissent until, as Callum Brown has shown, it represented perhaps a third of Scotland's population.[33] While Emma Vincent Macleod and Colin Kidd have both explored the Scottish Churches and the French Revolution, more work is needed on the growth and impact of evangelical and voluntary religion during these years.[34]

# THE EARLY NINETEENTH CENTURY

With industrialization and rapid urbanization from the late eighteenth century, the established Church of Scotland confronted new challenges, including urban overcrowding, mass deprivation, rising crime, prostitution, and unrest among the industrial working classes. There were not enough parish churches for the burgeoning populations of Glasgow and other urban centres, and by 1815 some parishes had populations of ten thousand or more. Under the pressure of such numbers, the urban parish system, including regular church attendance, pastoral visiting, kirk-session discipline, parish poor relief, and parish education, broke down—despite the efforts of some energetic ministers, such as Thomas Chalmers in Glasgow between 1815 and 1823, to sweep back the tide with innovative new methods of urban ministry aimed at reviving the 'parish state' through the mobilization of lay volunteers.[35] By the 1830s, the institutions of the 'parish state' were not coping with the new urban conditions. Moreover, many people were publicly questioning the reasons for maintaining the established Church. Following the expansion of the franchise in 1832, middle-class dissenters launched a political campaign to disestablish the Church of Scotland and end the connection of Church and State.

In 1834 the established Church, under Chalmers's leadership, responded to both the urban challenge and the disestablishment campaign with a series of reforms. These included tackling the vexed patronage issue by giving congregations the power to 'veto' candidates presented by patrons to the parish ministry (the aim was to increase the popular voice in the selection of ministers). Supporters of the veto became known as 'non-intrusionists', because they opposed the 'intrusion' of unpopular patrons' candidates into the parish ministry. There was also a national 'church extension' campaign to build more churches for Scotland's growing population, and new initiatives in extending education and overseas missions. Financial donations to the Church increased fourteenfold between 1834 and 1839, and it appeared that the Reformation ideal of the godly

[33] S. J. Brown, *The National Churches of England, Ireland and Scotland 1801–46* (Oxford, 2001), 41–4; C. G. Brown, *Religion and Society in Scotland since 1707* (Edinburgh, 1997), 20.

[34] E. Vincent, 'The Responses of Scottish Churchmen to the French Revolution', *Scottish Historical Review*, 73 (1994), 191–215; C. Kidd. 'The Kirk, the French Revolution, and the Burden of Scottish Whiggery', in N. Aston, ed., *Religious Change in Europe 1650–1914* (Oxford, 1997), 213–34.

[35] S. J. Brown, *Thomas Chalmers and the Godly Commonwealth in Scotland* (Oxford, 1982), 91–151.

commonwealth might be achieved in an industrializing Scotland. Then in 1838 these hopes were dealt a fatal blow when the Scottish civil courts ruled that the Church's veto act was an illegal infringement upon the property rights of patrons. When the Church insisted on enforcing the veto act despite this civil ruling, the result was a constitutional confrontation between Church and State. The civil courts threatened presbyteries with fines and imprisonment if they enforced the veto act, while the Church courts threatened presbyteries with ecclesiastical discipline if they refused to enforce the veto. The Church became divided between non-intrusionists, who were predominantly evangelical in their piety, and a constitutional party, who were largely heirs of eighteenth-century Moderatism and insisted the Church must relinquish the veto. Non-intrusionists viewed the constitutional conflict as another episode in the long-standing struggle between the Presbyterian Church and State, going back to the 1570s; they perceived themselves to be the heirs of the Reformers and Covenanters, struggling once again for the spiritual independence and authority of Scotland's national Church.

The conflict climaxed with the great Disruption of 1843, when the non-intrusionists— about a third of the ministers and perhaps half the lay membership left—the established Church of Scotland and formed the new Free Church. This Church had particular strength in lowland towns and cities, where as Allan MacLaren has shown, a rising entrepreneurial middle class, opposed to the dominance of the older landed and mercantile elite, found in Free Church evangelicalism an expression of a dynamic new Scotland. Another area of strength was the Highlands, where Free Church membership was associated with both Calvinism and opposition to the landlord class.[36] The Disruption was one of the most important events in Scottish history, and it is the subject of a large literature, much of it highly polemic, but including a number of balanced recent studies.[37] What needs more exploration, however, is the aftermath of the Disruption. Within five years the Free Church had built, through private donations, some 730 new churches, 400 manses, 500 schools, and it was erecting a grand New College on the Mound in Edinburgh. At the same time, as Tom Devine has shown, the Free Church provided more famine relief than any other Scottish denomination during the failure of the potato crops in the later 1840s, and its relief effort spared the western Highlands and Islands massive deaths from famine.[38] How did it manage to raise the funds for all this during arguably the worst economic downturn of the nineteenth century?

The Disruption broke up the Presbyterian establishment, and the Church of Scotland would never recover its national influence and authority. The established Church, which represented only about 32 per cent of churchgoers in 1851, now lacked the resources to fulfil its social roles on a national scale. Two years after the Disruption, Parliament

---

[36] A. A. MacLaren, *Religion and Social Class: The Disruption Years in Aberdeen* (London, 1974); D. M. M. Paton, *The Clergy and the Clearances* (Edinburgh, 2006).

[37] D. J. Withrington, 'The Disruption: A Century and a Half of Historical Interpretation', *RSCHS*, 25 (1993), 118–53.

[38] T. Devine, *The Great Highland Famine: Hunger, Emigration and the Scottish Highlands in the Nineteenth Century* (Edinburgh, 1988).

enacted a new poor law for Scotland, which greatly diminished the role of the established Church in poor relief. The Church's authority over education was severely weakened after 1843 and would be largely removed by Parliament in 1872. Kirk-session discipline steadily declined during the nineteenth century, as offenders chose simply to leave the Church of Scotland rather than submit to the humiliation of public admonishment and penance. After 1901, kirk-session discipline was effectively replaced by private counselling by ministers.[39] During the nineteenth century, moreover, the distinctive Scottish Communion occasions of four or more days' duration ceased in most of Scotland, a victim in part of the demands of industry and commercial agriculture for more regular hours of work. The strict public observance of the Sabbath, however, would continue until late in the twentieth century, as one of the last expressions of the godly commonwealth.

## PLURALISM AND MISSION CULTURE

The years following the Disruption coincided with another set of events that had momentous effects on Scottish religion. This was the great Famine of 1845–50 in Ireland, which brought tens of thousands of Roman Catholic migrants to Scotland, where they joined (though often with ethnic tensions) the small Scottish Catholic population that had survived since the Reformation. Significant Irish migration had begun early in the century, driven by demand for cheap labour in Scotland's industrializing economy. But migration soared during and after the Famine. Migrants arrived impoverished and often ravaged by disease and traumatized; they encountered ethnic and sectarian hatred, and found they had to look to their own communities for support. Many embraced what Emmet Larkin has described as a post-Famine 'devotional revolution', with an emphasis on preserving identity through regular mass-attendance, confessions, Catholic schools, church-building (with sumptuous, 'Italianate' interiors), and frequent missions.[40] Catholics had received nearly full civil rights within the British State with the Catholic Emancipation Act of 1829, and the Catholic migrants proved politically adept, aligning themselves with the Liberal Party from the 1860s, and later, in the 1920s, with the Labour Party. By 1850, there were an estimated 150,000 Catholics in Scotland, by 1878, 332,000, and by 1901, 433,000—which by the latter date represented some 10 per cent of the Scottish population.[41] The territorial Catholic hierarchy in Scotland was restored in 1878. Many Scottish Protestants viewed the growing Catholic population as an intolerable challenge to the Reformation heritage, but found they were powerless to do much about

---

[39] S. J. Brown, 'No More "Standing the Session": Gender and the End of Corporate Discipline in the Church of Scotland, c.1890–1930', *Studies in Church History*, 34 (1998), 447–60.

[40] E. Larkin, 'The Devotional Revolution in Ireland, 1850–1875', *American Historical Review*, 77 (1972), 625–52.

[41] J. McCaffrey, 'Roman Catholics in Scotland in the Nineteenth and Twentieth Centuries', *RSCHS*, 21 (1983), 276.

it. Zealous Protestants, such as James Begg of the Free Church, cried 'no Popery', formed a Reformation Society, issued tracts and periodicals, and inflamed the occasional anti-Catholic riot. The Catholic population, however, remained, and gradually became less Irish and migrant, and more Scottish and settled.

More work is needed on post-1850 Scottish religion, which we now know—largely through the seminal scholarship of Callum Brown—remained robust and socially important up to the 1950s, despite the gradual eroding of the parish state. There were by 1850 three main Presbyterian denominations—the established Church of Scotland, the Free Church, and the United Presbyterians (a denomination formed in 1847 by a union of most of the Secession Churches and the Relief Church). According to the State's Census of Religious Worship in 1851, about 85 per cent of those attending church in Scotland were Presbyterian.[42] However, although they shared the same theology, Church organization, and liturgy, the Presbyterian denominations were bitter rivals. Between the early 1870s and the early 1900s, the Free Church and United Presbyterians revived the political campaign to disestablish the Church of Scotland and have the State appropriate much of its property. The aim was to end all connection between Church and State, and it gained the support of the Liberal Party. But the campaign was conducted with a sectarian rancour that alienated much of the public; as a result disestablishment never became a national cause in Scotland (unlike disestablishment in Ireland and Wales) and the campaign was ultimately unsuccessful.[43] Another reason for the failure of disestablishment was a remarkable revival of the established Church from the 1850s, a phenomenon that needs further research.

The religious landscape became more complex. From 1850, the Scottish Episcopal Church grew in numbers and confidence, benefiting from a steady influx of English and Irish Anglicans. There were also growing numbers of Congregationalists, Baptists, Methodists, and Quakers, along with new evangelical denominations, such as the Catholic Apostolic Church (with its belief in the imminent Second Coming of Christ in glory), the Brethren (with their efforts to return to the practices of the primitive Church before the emergence of an ordained clergy), and, after 1878, the Salvation Army (with its brass bands, uniforms, simple gospel message for the poor, and, from 1890, soup kitchens and hostels). There were non-denominational city missions, holding services in rented rooms, and independent mission halls, such as Carrubber's Close Mission in Edinburgh, which appealed to working people with informal services, short racy addresses, and rousing gospel songs. After 1881, and the wave of pogroms in Russia, there was a sizeable influx of Jews from Russia and Eastern Europe. There were some ten thousand Jews in Glasgow by 1900, about fifteen hundred Jews in Edinburgh, and smaller Jewish communities in other towns.[44]

Later nineteenth-century Scotland had a vigorous evangelical culture—what Callum Brown has described as a 'salvation economy'. Churches reflected the entrepreneurial

[42] Brown, *Religion and Society in Scotland since 1707*, 45.
[43] J. G. Kellas, 'The Liberal Party and the Scottish Church Disestablishment Crisis', *English Historical Review*, 79 (1964), 31–46.
[44] Devine, *Scottish Nation*, 518–22; K. E. Collins, ed., *Aspects of Scottish Jewry* (Glasgow, 1987).

ethos of nineteenth-century Britain by aggressively seeking members, while individuals gave increased emphasis to personal narratives of spiritual growth and redemption.[45] The evangelical culture found expression in a vigorous temperance movement, which sought to combat the destructive impact of hard drink on families. The movement involved all denominations, and reached its peak of activity and influence between 1870 and 1914.[46] There were national revival movements in 1859–62 and 1873–4, which affected most of the Protestant denominations, claimed thousands of converts, and became associated with large, orchestrated meetings, a simple message of personal salvation through acceptance of Christ, sentimental gospel songs, and charismatic preachers, including such visiting American revivalists as James Caughey, Charles G. Finney, and Dwight L. Moody. During the nineteenth century, hundreds of new churches were built, many in the popular neo-Gothic style. From the 1880s, more and more churches also added church halls, to provide accommodation for a growing number of church-based activities through the week, including Sunday schools, mothers' meetings, women's guilds, temperance societies, choirs, sewing circles, literary societies, savings banks, young people's guilds, reading rooms, games rooms, boys' brigades, charitable societies, nursery schools, and boxing clubs. For many young people, especially young women, church-based activities provided their main social outlet.[47] Intense denominational competition, meanwhile, led to an over-building of churches; congregations often believed that a grand church, with a towering steeple, would attract members from neighbouring churches. However, as Robin Gill has argued, many of these ambitious Victorian edifices were never more than half-filled, and they burdened future generations with crippling costs of debt repayment and maintenance.[48]

Churches made their worship more attractive, so as to compete effectively for members in the free marketplace of religion. In the Presbyterian churches stained glass was placed in windows, services grew shorter, sermons were reduced to an average of thirty minutes, and lively hymns were introduced. Beginning in the 1870s, the long-standing ban on instrumental music was set aside and churches began installing organs and developing trained choirs. By 1904, the large majority of Church of Scotland congregations had both an organ and a choir.[49] According to Alec Cheyne's indispensable study, there was a loosening of adherence to the harsher doctrines of the Westminster Confession of Faith, including the total depravity of humanity, predestination, and eternal punishment, while more emphasis was placed on the incarnate Christ, his moral example and human flourishing in this world.[50]

[45] C. G. Brown, *The Death of Christian Britain* (London, 2001), 35–57.

[46] N. D. Denny, 'Temperance and the Scottish Churches, 1870–1914', *RSCHS*, 23 (1988), 217–35.

[47] C. G. Brown and J. D. Stephenson, '"Sprouting Wings?" Women and Religion in Scotland, c.1890–1950', in E. Breitenbach and E. Gordon, eds., *Out of Bounds: Women in Scotland in the Nineteenth and Twentieth Centuries* (Edinburgh, 1992).

[48] R. Gill, *The Myth of the Empty Church* (London, 1993).

[49] A. K. Robertson, 'The Revival of Church Worship in the Church of Scotland' (PhD thesis, University of Edinburgh, 1956), 212–14.

[50] A. C. Cheyne, *The Transforming of the Kirk: Victorian Scotland's Religious Revolution* (Edinburgh, 1983), 60–87.

The Scottish Churches produced a number of exceptionally able theologians and biblical scholars, including A. B. Davidson, Robert Flint, William Robertson Smith, John Tulloch, and the brothers John and Edward Caird; these figures worked to adapt the Reformed Faith, often amid conflicts with traditionalists, to the new scientific understandings of the universe, new historical understandings of the ancient Near East, and new anthropological understandings of world cultures. The openness of such dominant figures as Robert Rainy, Principal of the Free Church's New College, to Darwinism helped ensure there was no major conflict between religion and science in Scotland. As Donald Smith has shown, Church leaders also developed a powerful Bible-based social criticism of Scotland's industrial capitalism, emphasizing the dehumanizing effects of unrestricted competition and the need for state intervention in the economy to achieve greater equality.[51] This fervent 'social gospel' would help position the Church of Scotland to welcome the emergence of the social welfare state in the coming century.

Scotland's major contributions to overseas missions are discussed by Esther Breitenbach in Chapter 28. Suffice it to say here that a Scottish missionary public emerged in the early part of the century; men, women, and children of various denominations devoured missionary publications, supported anti-slavery efforts, joined mission societies, subscribed money, attended lectures, signed petitions in support of missionary causes, participated in circles of prayer, and thrilled to the stories of missionary adventures, and martyrdoms, in exotic lands.[52] Scotland's international reputation in mission work was recognized when it was chosen to host the Edinburgh World Mission Conference of 1910, arguably the most influential conference for planning coordinated Protestant missionary effort and also a formative event in the modern ecumenical movement.

With the waning of the Presbyterian state, there also emerged new expressions of interest in Scottish folk beliefs, many with origins in a pre-Christian past, which had survived witch-hunts, pulpit denunciations, and kirk-session scrutiny. These included beliefs in earth spirits or fairies, second sight (or the ability to see into a spiritual realm), *doppelgängers* and ghosts, the evil eye (the envious glance that could wither and kill), and healing wells. The scholarly collection of folk beliefs began in the late 1870s, and it is interesting that some of the most avid collectors were Highland Presbyterian ministers, including John Gregorson Campbell of the Free Church and James McDougall of the Church of Scotland. The late nineteenth century also witnessed a new interest in 'Celtic spirituality', a conception inspired in part by writers of the Irish literary renaissance who claimed that Celtic peoples lived more closely to spiritual and otherworldly dimensions. Within this 'Celtic twilight', some also discerned, and sought to revive, a distinctive 'Celtic Christianity', with an intuitive grasp

[51] D. C. Smith, *Passive Obedience and Prophetic Protest: Social Criticism in the Scottish Church 1830–1945* (New York, 1987), 245–325.

[52] E. Breitenbach, *Empire and Scottish Society: The Impact of Foreign Missions at Home, c.1790 to c.1914* (Edinburgh, 2009).

of a luminous divinity that infused the natural world.[53] For some, Celtic spirituality was linked with alternative religious beliefs, including spiritualism, or communication with the spirits of the dead through mediums. Modern spiritualism reached Scotland in the 1850s, and found considerable popular interest; in Daniel Dunglas Home, Scotland produced one of the nineteenth century's most celebrated mediums. Some professed 'secularists', moreover, openly rejected any belief in God, but their numbers remained small before the new century.

At the beginning of the twentieth century, religion remained a vital force in Scottish public life. The majority of Scots were Presbyterian: according to the Registrar General's return, nearly 72 per cent of couples were married in a Presbyterian church between 1901 and 1910. Of these, over 45 per cent were married in the established Church of Scotland, which had experienced a significant revival in its numbers and influence after 1850.[54] The legacy of Presbyterian Calvinism, its work ethic, respect for learning, belief in equality before God, moral certainty, lack of deference to human authority, and a certain dourness—all remained recognizable Scottish traits. By 1900, moreover, Presbyterians were putting their rivalries behind them; indeed, a movement had begun that would culminate in the reunion of the three main Presbyterian denominations by 1929. And yet, in crucial ways, the historic social authority of Scottish Presbyterianism, as expressed in the godly commonwealth and parish state, had been irretrievably eroded. The role of the Presbyterian Church in poor relief, education, and maintaining public order had ceased in much of Scotland, and, despite the dreams of some Presbyterian leaders, the Reformation ideal of the godly commonwealth was fading among the population.

The Scottish people were religious, and overwhelmingly Christian, but their Christianity was now more diverse in nature, with choice from a plethora of denominations competing in a free marketplace of religion. Religion was also becoming less communal and more private, less parish-based and more conscience-based. With the waning of kirk-session discipline, it was also less oppressive to women. The nineteenth century, as Callum Brown has argued, saw women making up the majority of congregations and reshaping religion around notions of spiritual growth and nurture (although they would be denied the right to hold office in most Churches until late in the twentieth century).[55] The larger issues of gender and religion in Scotland need further exploration. Another highly significant development of the nineteenth century was the emergence of a large and increasingly confident Roman Catholic Church, whose presence was regarded by probably most Protestants as both alien and a fundamental challenge to Scotland's Reformation heritage, but which was destined by the end of the next century to rival Presbyterianism in numbers and influence.

[53] I. Bradley, *Celtic Christianity: Making Myths and Chasing Dreams* (Edinburgh, 1999), 119–56.
[54] T. C. Smout, *A Century of the Scottish People 1830–1950* (London, 1986), 191.
[55] Brown, *Death of Christian Britain*, 58–87.

## Further Reading

Brown, C. G., *Religion and Society in Scotland since 1707* (Edinburgh, 1997).

Brown, S. J., *Thomas Chalmers and the Godly Commonwealth in Scotland* (Oxford, 1982).

Burleigh, J. H. S., *A Church History of Scotland* (Oxford, 1960).

Cheyne, A. C., *Studies in Scottish Church History* (Edinburgh, 1999).

—— *The Transforming of the Kirk: Victorian Scotland's Religious Revolution* (Edinburgh, 1983).

Donaldson, G., *The Faith of the Scots* (London, 1990).

Drummond, A. L., and Bulloch, J., *The Scottish Church 1688–1843: The Age of the Moderates* (Edinburgh, 1973).

—— *The Church in Victorian Scotland 1843–1874* (Edinburgh, 1975).

—— *The Church in Late Victorian Scotland 1874–1900* (Edinburgh, 1978).

Kirk, J., *Patterns of Reform: Continuity and Change in the Reformation Kirk* (Edinburgh, 1989).

Marshall, G., *Presbyteries and Profits: Calvinism and the Development of Capitalism in Scotland, 1560–1707* (Oxford, 1980).

Orr MacDonald, L. A., *A Unique and Glorious Mission: Women and Presbyterianism in Scotland 1830–1930* (Edinburgh, 2000).

Schmidt, L. E., *Holy Fairs: Scottish Communions and American Revivals in the Early Modern Period* (Princeton, 1989).

Sher, R. B., *Church and University in the Scottish Enlightenment: The Moderate Literati of Edinburgh* (Princeton, 1985).

# CHAPTER 5

......................................................................................................

# THE LITERARY TRADITION

......................................................................................................

## CAIRNS CRAIG

## BEGINNINGS AND ENDINGS

......................................................................................................................................................................

ON 5 June 1819 an event was held in the Freemason's Tavern in London, chaired by the Duke of Sussex, to commemorate Robert Burns and raise funds for the establishment of a 'National Monument to his Memory'. The opening speaker, Sir James Mackintosh, declared that 'this was the first instance in the history of the world, of an assembly of Gentlemen called together, and over which a Prince of the Blood presided, for the purpose of erecting a Monument, in the Capital of his Country, to a Peasant of that country'.[1] The monument proposed was no modest statue but a Greek temple on Calton Hill, designed to acknowledge Burns's equality with classical authors and to establish what would become 'the Acropolis of the Northern Athens'. The proposal aimed to put Burns at the spiritual centre of the nation and create an enduring shrine that would be enhanced by works of commemoration by each generation of Scottish artists. Only twenty-three years after his death in 1796, Scotland and Burns were intimately identified one with the other: Burns's works, according to the duke, 'were calculated to keep alive a spirit of independence, not individual but national, because they brought home to the bosoms of his countrymen in every climate of the globe, recollections of their national language, national dress, and national manners', while the very possibility of a peasant-poet being acclaimed the equal of classical authors was testimony, according to Mackintosh, to 'the benefits resulting from a system of national instruction' that, if imitated elsewhere, would 'incalculably augment the common riches of the intellectual world—would open unnumbered mines of mental treasure, which would otherwise lie unwrought and

---

[1] *Festival in Commemoration of Robert Burns; and to promote a subscription to erect a National Monument to his Memory at Edinburgh: held at the Freemason's Tavern in London, on Saturday, 5 June 1819* (London, 1819), 8.

unvalued'.[2] Burns's works were not the product of individual genius but of the national genius, and, as another speaker predicted, when 'we honour the Memory of our immortal Poet' at the same time '[we] preserve the ardent patriotism and daring spirit, which has distinguished our Countrymen in every land'.[3]

The monument proposed was not built—it metamorphosed into the National Monument to victory in the Napoleonic Wars, which was left unfinished in 1829—but wherever migrant Scots went across the globe, statues to Burns were erected (today, there are estimated to be around 200 full-size memorials and all 3,400 libraries in North America funded by Andrew Carnegie have a bust of Burns) and Burns's birthday is treated as a day of national celebration. This unique identification of poet and nation was made possible by Burns's use, in his most famous poems, of Scots, a language with a literary history that goes back at least to the fourteenth century—and is, therefore, as old as English as a literary vehicle—and which had been the ordinary language of educated Scots until after the Union with England in 1707, when English steadily displaced it as the medium of written culture and public life. As a language, Scots therefore had a double existence. On the one hand, it was the language of the nation's early literary traditions, traditions that became increasingly well known in the eighteenth century through the publication of works by the so-called 'makars' of the fifteenth century—William Dunbar, Robert Henryson, Gavin Douglas, Sir David Lindsay—which had been preserved in the Bannatyne and Maitland manuscripts. These traditions went back to the Wars of Independence with England and some of the most popular poems were ones which, like *The Bruce* by John Barbour and *Wallace* by Blind Harry, celebrated the heroic deeds of the leaders who, in the fourteenth century, had maintained Scotland's independent nationality. It was a version of *Wallace* produced in 1722 by William Hamilton of Gilbertfield that Burns said had 'poured a Scottish prejudice in my veins which will boil along there till the flood-gates of life shut in eternal rest'.[4] On the other hand, the gradual anglicization of Scottish speech among the educated classes meant that Scots was increasingly the language of the lower classes, but one that maintained an oral culture rich in folksong and ballad. Burns, both the son of a peasant and an ardent reader of earlier Scottish poetry, united these two cultural traditions and in doing so made Scots vernacular a key and continuing element in the nation's literary and national identity, even while the nation's eighteenth-century literati were training themselves to avoid 'Scotticisms' and to produce polished English.

The role of Scots gave Scottish literature its defining difference from the English literature that the Scots so assiduously studied in their courses in Rhetoric and Belles Lettres, courses which, as they were imitated in North America, in the empire, and in England itself, were to be the foundation of the modern discipline of English Literature. The vigour of dialect speech and the prominence accorded to lower-class and to peasant characters were to form distinctive features of Scottish writing, ranging from Allan Ramsay's pastoral play *The Gentle Shepherd* in the 1720s through Burns's celebration of the peasantry in 'The Cotter's Saturday

---

[2] *Festival in Commemoration of Robert Burns*, 8.
[3] Ibid., 14.
[4] J. de Lancey Ferguson and G. Ross Roy, eds., *The Letters of Robert Burns*, 2 vols. (Oxford, 1985), vol. 1, 136.

Night' and of beggars and outcasts in 'Love and Liberty', to the prominent place accorded to lower-class Scots speakers in Walter Scott's early novels. Scott's use both of vernacular and of highly specified regional identities made a significant contribution to the development of the novel as a genre—George Eliot and Thomas Hardy would follow in his footsteps—and set a pattern for Scottish novel-writing that was to stretch from John Galt's studies in the local culture of the west of Scotland—such as *Annals of the Parish* (1821) and *The Entail* (1822)—to what many have regarded as Robert Louis Stevenson's masterpiece, the unfinished *Weir of Hermiston* (1896). It was an influence that continued into the twentieth century in the works of distinctively regional novelists such as Nan Shepherd (*The Quarry Wood*, 1928; *The Weatherhouse*, 1930) and Lewis Grassic Gibbon (*A Scots Quair*, 1932–4). It is symptomatic of the centrality of Scots vernacular to Scottish literary identity that when the young Christopher Murray Grieve set out to renew Scottish poetry in the 1920s, he invented as his alter ego one 'Hugh MacDiarmid', an archetypal Scottish poet steeped in and reusing the language of early Scottish writing.[5] That the oldest continuing literary language in Scotland was not Scots, but Gaelic, did not have the same defining impact on Scottish literature and Scottish identity. Gaelic remained separate, almost self-contained, while Scots, through the influence of Burns and the huge popularity of Scottish magazines such as *Blackwood's*—founded in 1814 to compete with the international success of the *Edinburgh Review*, which, from its inception in 1802, set the model for magazine publication for the nineteenth century—became the second literary language of the British Empire.

Rather than being an alternative to English, Scots was, according to Allan Ramsay, an extension of it: English, 'of which we are Masters, by being taught it in our Schools, and daily reading it', was supplemented by 'all our own native Words, of eminent Significancy', these Scots expressions making 'our Tongue by far the completest'.[6] The potential 'completeness' of Scots-English meant that no matter how much English came to dominate the public life of Scotland, Scottish writers continually returned to it as the resource that established the distinctiveness of their work. From the 1930s to the 1970s poets such as Sydney Goodsir Smith, Robert Garioch, and Alexander Scott were following Hugh MacDiarmid down the path of a highly literary Scots; and dramatists such as Robert McLellan (*Jamie the Saxt*, 1937) and Donald Campbell (*The Jesuit*, 1976) were exploiting Scots through plays set in historical periods when Scots was still the normal speech of both upper and lower classes in Lowland Scotland. If the King James Bible, inspired by the first Scottish King of England, made a certain kind of English the language of religion in Scotland, and the foundation of the nation's linguistic anglicization, the publication in 1983 of Professor W. L. Lorimer's *New Testament in Scots*—which became an unexpected best-seller—was testimony to the ongoing desire of many Scottish readers

---

[5] For the pre-Scots literary traditions see Thomas Owen Clancy (ed.), *Triumph Tree : Scotland's Earliest Poetry* (Edinburgh, 1998); for the earlier Gaelic tradition, William Gillies, 'Gaelic Literature in the Later Middle Ages', in Clancy and Pittock (eds.), *The Edinburgh History of Scottish Literature*, vol.1 (Edinburgh, 2007).

[6] *Works of Allan Ramsay*, eds. B. Martin and J. W. Oliver, *Scottish Text Society*, 6 vols., 19 (Edinburgh, 1945), vol. i, xviii.

for a version of the Bible in what remained, despite two hundred and fifty years of anglicization, their own language.

In the 1850s David Masson, soon to be Professor of English Literature at the University of Edinburgh and one of the first professional literary critics, pondered 'The Scottish Influence in British Literature' and, listing how many influential Scottish writers overlapped with the life of Burns, declared that 'in reading the writings of such men, one is perpetually reminded, in the most direct manner, that these writings are to be regarded as belonging to a strictly national literature'.[7] And considering the achievement of Scottish writers, Masson reflected on how the rise of Scottish literature since Burns's Kilmarnock edition of 1786 was as remarkable as the rise of Scottish philosophy in the sixty years before that publication:

> Considering the amount of influence exerted by such men [Scott, Jeffrey, Campbell, Chalmers, Wilson, Carlyle] upon the whole spirit and substance of British literature, considering how disproportionate a share of the whole literary produce of Great Britain in the nineteenth century has come either from them or from other Scotchmen, and considering what a stamp of peculiarity marks all that portion of this produce which *is* of Scottish origin, it does not seem too much to say, that the rise and growth of Scottish literature is as notable a historical phenomenon as the rise and growth of Scottish philosophy.[8]

Much has been made in the last half-century of the achievements of the Scottish Enlightenment philosophers, who have come to be regarded as the glory of Scottish culture, while Burns and Scott have been steadily written out of the history of international literature in English. But Alexander Broadie's *A History of Scottish Philosophy* (2009) concludes in the 1960s, with little evidence of a powerful continuing influence, whereas Scottish literature remains as a flourishing element in contemporary Scottish life. Indeed, it is arguable that the thirty years from 1979 were among the most distinguished in the whole history of Scottish culture. The celebration of Burns may now have been reduced to a ritual in which literary value plays little part, but the sense of the significance of Scotland's writers to the nation's identity remains intense—as is manifest by the inscriptions chosen to decorate the new Scottish Parliament when it was opened in 2004.

## Collecting the Nation

For sixty years from the 1630s, Scotland was a country riven by civil and religious strife. By the 1690s, two courts claimed royal authority over Scotland. In London was the Williamite court, whose authority had been accepted in Scotland when William III

---

[7] David Masson, *Essays Biographical and Critical* (Cambridge, 1856), 399.

[8] Ibid., 408.

agreed to the abolition of prelacy in the Church of Scotland—a running sore that had provoked conflict from the time of Charles I's accession to the throne in 1625; and at Versailles in Paris there was the exiled Jacobite court, where James VII and, after 1701, James VIII were supported by Louis XIV in their claim to be the rightful kings both of Scotland and England. The cost of these seventy years of strife was enormous: many of the leading Scottish families were ruined by debt, towns such as Aberdeen and Dundee had been sacked, uncountable thousands had been killed (including hundreds accused of witchcraft), and many had died of the return of the plague in 1645. As power shifted, different religious groups were driven into exile. Scotland was a nation in ruins: many of its greatest buildings destroyed, its most powerful families impoverished, and the national coffers emptied by the disaster of the attempt in 1696 to set up a Scottish colony in Darien on the isthmus of Panama. (For a more optimistic appraisal see Chapter 15.)

The rebuilding of Scotland in the eighteenth century was to be given spectacular embodiment in the classicism of Edinburgh's New Town in the 1780s, which was designed to celebrate the peaceful Union of 1707 and, quite literally, to turn its back on Scotland's earlier history, as embodied in Edinburgh's Old Town. But even before the Union treaty was concluded, some were endeavouring to recover the remnants of an older Scotland from the ruins of the seventeenth century. In 1706 the Edinburgh printer James Watson, a man of Jacobite sympathies, published the first volume of his *Choice Collection of Comic and Serious Scots Poems Both Ancient and Modern* in order to make available the poetry of our 'own native Scots Dialect', poetry that had either been printed 'most uncorrectly' or 'never before printed'.[9] Watson's *Choice Collection*, containing some poems dating back to pre-Reformation Scotland, such as 'Christ's Kirk on the Green', attributed to King James V, was to inspire two collections by Allan Ramsay, both published in 1724. His *Tea Table Miscellany* was a collection of lyrics, mostly in Scots, intended for domestic performance: it went through more than twenty editions in the following three-quarters of a century, as well as through many imitations by other editors, and contributed to the fashion for 'national' songs that became part of the emerging 'British' culture of the eighteenth century. It was Ramsay's *Ever Green* of 1724, however, that seriously attempted to reconstitute the national past, through 'a collection of Scots Poems, wrote by the Ingenious before 1600'. The *Ever Green* made available for the first time a substantial number of poems by Dunbar, Henryson, and Montgomerie preserved in the Bannatyne manuscript.

Ramsay's effort to reconstitute the Scottish literary past and to collect Scottish popular song was in turn to be the inspiration for generations of Scottish writers and scholars: Bishop Percy's *Reliques of Ancient English Poetry* (1765) had much of its impact because of the twenty Scottish ballads and songs supplied by his Scottish correspondent, Lord Hailes, who himself re-edited material from the Bannatyne manuscript in *Ancient Scottish Songs* (1770); David Herd's *Ancient and Modern Scots Songs* (1769) claimed that the fragments of the past had at last been gathered into 'one body'—but the dismem-

---

[9]  *Watson's Choice Collection of Comic and Serious Scots Poems Both Ancient and Modern* (1706–11; Glasgow, 1869), Pt. 1.

bered past was to continue to give up new fragments to each succeeding generation: Burns at the end of his career in the songs he collected for James Johnson's *Scots Musical Museum* (1787–1803) and Walter Scott at the beginning of his, in *Minstrelsy of the Scottish Border* (1802), both confirmed the richness of the oral tradition of Scots, riches that were to be further excavated by William Motherwell in his *Minstrelsy, Ancient and Modern* (1827) and by William Aytoun's *Ballads of Scotland* (1858). The lore of Gaelic Scotland was collected in *Carmena Gadelica* (1900) by Alexander Carmichael, and the *Greig-Duncan Folk-Song Collection*, gathered in the north-east of Scotland in the decade before the First World War, required eight volumes for its publication in the 1970s and 1980s.

Recurrently, collecting the past was the founding basis of new Scottish writing. When Christopher Grieve set out to 'modernize' Scottish poetry after the First World War, it was under the banner of 'Back to Dunbar', and by means of the resources of John Jamieson's *Etymological Dictionary of the Scottish Language* (1808), which combined both medieval literary examples and folk materials to provide an account of the history of Scots words. After the Second World War, poet-scholars like Hamish Henderson would return to the collection of folk literature as the basis for a new revival of national culture. This drive to collect and reconstitute the fragments of the nation would be repeated in the 1960s and 1970s in relation to working-class writing, for example by the efforts of William Donaldson to recover Scots prose published in local newspapers in the nineteenth century and by Tom Leonard's edition of the working-class poets of Renfrew.[10] And women's writing would undergo a similar recuperation in the 1980s and 1990s, bringing back into the canon a host of forgotten writers from even relatively recent times. These included playwright Ena Lamont Stewart, whose dramatization of working-class life in *Men Should Weep* (1948) was revived to great effect by the 7:84 Theatre Company in the 1980s, and Helen Adam, who combined writing Scottish ballads with participating in the Beat poetry movement in San Francisco in the 1950s and 1960s.

Lurking in Ramsay's *Evergreen*, however, was a poem entitled 'The Vision', which he claimed to have been 'compylit in Latin be a most lernit Clerk in Tyme of our Hairship and Oppression, anno 1300, and translatit in 1524', and which is attributed to 'Ar. Scot.' This name might have implied the sixteenth-century Scottish poet Alexander Scott, but it in fact concealed 'Allan Ramsay Scotus', recalling the events of Scotland's suffering under the oppression of Edward I as an allegory of its suffering under the Hanoverians. Ramsay's creation of an 'original' ancient poem revealed how easily the editorial effort of reconstituting the body of the nation's literature could turn into the creative replenishment of the nation's past with modern productions. The editor as gatekeeper between the past and the present was also an aspirant poet recreating the past in his own image: Burns infused old songs with his own lyrical grace, while James Hogg's mother famously complained that Walter Scott had ruined her songs when he had them printed. The

---

[10] William Donaldson, *Popular Literature in Victorian Scotland: Language, Fiction and the Press* (Aberdeen, 1986); Tom Leonard, *Radical Renfrew: Poetry from the French Revolution to the First World War* (Edinburgh, 1990).

'fakesong' that imitated folksong for an audience of readers rather than listeners—as in the work of Lady Nairne—underlined how different was the finality of print from the fluidity of oral culture.

Such tensions underlay the most influential literary event of eighteenth-century Scotland—the publication, in 1760, of James Macpherson's *Fragments of Ancient Poetry*. Macpherson, a young schoolteacher with literary ambitions, was encouraged by the Edinburgh literati to extend the collecting activities of Lowland Scots by engaging in a similar venture in the Gaelic-speaking Highlands. He returned with translations into English of what were claimed to be fragments of Gaelic epics produced by the blind bard Ossian in the third century AD, epics that had been maintained by oral transmission for over a thousand years. The impact of Macpherson's work was sensational: it provided Britain with an alternative to classical mythology, one imbued with a wild nobility and heroic passion that was to shape much subsequent Romantic literature. The transition from classical to native mythology was to be dramatized through quotations from the *Fragments* in Goethe's influential *The Sorrows of Young Werther* (1774), which helped Macpherson's poetry to inspire the search for equivalent ancient epics in the upsurge of national self-expression that swept Europe from Finland to Galicia. In nineteenth-century Ireland the effort to reclaim Macpherson's Celtic heroes as Irish rather than Scots was to be the inspiration of W. B. Yeats's Irish Revival.

In Britain, doubts about the authenticity of Macpherson's collection were not assuaged when Macpherson rapidly published two complete epic poems—*Tamora* and *Fingal*—in 1762–3 while refusing to provide the Gaelic originals on which they were based. In Britain, *Ossian*'s reputation shifted from celebrated literary revolution to despised literary fraud but it continued to exert an international influence throughout the nineteenth century, and the transformation it had made in the international perception of Scotland would reshape Scottish identity forever. At the very moment when the traditional life of the Highlands of Scotland was being destroyed in the aftermath of the Jacobite Rebellion of 1745–6, Macpherson's translations transformed the Scottish Highlands from a place of social and economic backwardness into the homeland of a noble spirituality that retained values long lost to Western urban culture. 'There we find the fire and enthusiasm of the most early times,' Hugh Blair declared in his 'Critical Dissertation on the Poems of Ossian', 'combined with an amazing degree of regularity and art.'[11] Adam Ferguson, in his *Essay on the History of Civil Society* (1767), gave an account of what is lost in the transition to modernity: that loss was symbolically reversed in Macpherson's collection and re-presentation of the Gaelic past, which became, suddenly, the exemplar of modern national identity. The Highlands were transformed into the place where poetry and mythology had survived, a place where the imagination had retained a vigour that had been lost to more advanced societies, making what had been a barbarous and uncultivated—and unvisited—place into one of noble sublimity, lure to Johnson and Boswell on their tour of the Highlands in 1773, and thereafter to poet, musician, and artistic tourists from Wordsworth to Mendelssohn and Landseer.

---

[11]  Howard Gaskill, ed., *The Poems of Ossian and Related Works* (Edinburgh, 1996), 348.

# THE PLACE OF MEMORY

Macpherson's Ossianic poems are doubly poems of memory: the poems call back into the contemporary world a lost Gaelic past but do so through a poetic persona who is himself calling up the memory of the dead:

> Thou askest, fair daughter of the isles! whose memory is preserved in these tombs? The memory of Ronnan the bold, and Connan the chief of men; and of her, the fairest of maids, Rivine the lovely and the good. Why seek we our grief from afar? Or give our tears to those of other times? But thou commandest, and I obey...[12]

Macpherson's poetry commands a haunted world. As his eighteenth-century English is haunted by a Gaelic almost none of his readers could speak, so his landscape teems with ghosts to whom the living call out: 'Speak to me, hear my voice, sons of my love! But alas! They are silent...'.[13] This structure of double memory—a return to an ancient world in which a character recalls a world still more ancient—was to be regularly rehearsed by Scottish writers. James Beattie's *The Minstrel*, of 1774, intended as its subtitle declares to be a study of 'The Progress of Genius', is set in a primitive pastoral world:

> There lived in Gothic days, as legends tell,
> A shepherd-swain, a man of low degree;
> Whose sires, perchance, in Fairyland might dwell,
> But he, I ween, was of the north countrie:
> A nation famed for song, and beauty's charms;[14]

The protagonist, Edwin, has to learn his art from his 'Beldam', who can 'chant the old heroic ditty o'er' and tell tales of 'knights, and feats of arms' and the 'moonlight-revel of the fairy glade'.[15] And Walter Scott's first poetic success, 'The Lay of the Last Minstrel' (1802), has the same double structure, focusing on an old minstrel in the seventeenth century who sings a bardic tale of border conflict in the Middle Ages:

> His legendary song could tell –
> Of ancient deeds, so long forgot;
> Of feuds, whose memory was not;
> Of forests, now laid waste and bare;
> Of towers, which harbour now the hare;
> Of manners, long since chang'd and gone;
> Of chiefs, who under the grey stone
> So long had slept, that fickle Fame
> Had blotted from her rolls their name...[16]

---

[12] Howard Gaskill, ed., *Fragments of Ancient Poetry*, poem IX, 19.

[13] Ibid., 21.

[14] James Beattie, *The Minstrel* (1771), Bk. 1, xiii.

[15] Ibid., Bk. 1, xlvi.

[16] Walter Scott, *The Lay of the Last Minstrel* (1810), from J. Logie Robertson, ed., *The Poetical Works of Sir Walter Scott* (Oxford, 1894), 30, Canto IV, conclusion.

The need to collect the remnants of an almost forgotten past made Scotland peculiarly a place of memory, a place whose literature gained its power by evoking the past to which those scattered remnants pointed. So John Home's *Douglas* (1756) is set in the early Middle Ages, during the Viking invasions of Scotland, and has as its central character a woman—Lady Randolph—who is obsessed by the losses of the past:

> O Douglas! Douglas! If departed ghosts
> Are e'er permitted to review this world,
> Within the circle of that wood thou art,
> And with the passion of immortals hear'st
> My lamentation.[17]

Similarly, Joanna Baillie's drama, *The Family Legend*, which was staged in Edinburgh by Sir Walter Scott in 1812, is built around family memories of sixteenth-century Scotland. Such works invoke an almost forgotten historical era by focusing on a character who is, like the author, obsessed with reaffirming a connection with the past. Scotland becomes in these works, as Scott was to express it in *The Lay of the Last Minstrel*, a land where poetry 'still reflects to Memory's eye':[18]

> O Caledonia! stern and wild,
> Meet nurse for a poetic child!
> Land of brown heath and shaggy wood,
> Land of the mountain and the flood,
> Land of my sires! what mortal hand
> Can e'er untie that filial band,
> That knits me to thy rugged strand![19]

Poetry is the offspring of wildness and wilderness, and Scotland's wildernesses make it a natural home to the imagination. Even Jane Porter's novel *The Scottish Chiefs* (1805), written in celebration of the 'liberty' for which Britain was fighting against Napoleonic France, is an account of the struggle of William Wallace for national liberty in the fourteenth century.

This recollective dimension of Scottish writing encouraged the use of genres that were naturally suited to remembrance. Elegies are the distinctive mode of both Allan Ramsay's and Robert Fergusson's earliest poems in Scots, as though the poems elegize the passing of the language in which they are written as well as the Scots characters they celebrate, and Ramsay's most successful work was the pastoral comedy *The Gentle Shepherd* (1728), a play that transforms the era of the Restoration, some sixty years earlier, into an idyll in which sundered parents and children can be reunited and love fulfilled. Enacted in vernacular Scots and including songs which Ramsay had published in his anthologies, *The Gentle Shepherd* suggests not only that the fragments of the past can be recomposed by art but that a rediscovered past can provide a critical perspective on a degraded present.

---

[17] John Home, *Douglas* (Edinburgh, 1757), Act I, scene i, 7.
[18] Scott, *The Lay of the Last Minstrel*, Canto IV, ii.
[19] Ibid., Canto VI, ii.

Hugh Blair believed that Ramsay's play was a perfect modern version of pastoral but that its use of Scots would make the play unreadable to succeeding generations; in fact, however, it had a long history of successful stage production till the late nineteenth century, and its celebration of Scotland as a place of pastoral virtue would inspire identification of Scotland's social virtues with its rurality—as in Robert Fergusson's 'The Farmer's Ingle':

> Peace to the husbandman and a' his tribe,
>     Whase care fells a' our wants frae year to year!
> Lang may his sock and cou'ter turn the glybe,
>     And bauks o' corn bend down wi' laded ear!
> May Scotia's simmers ay look gay and green;
>     Her yellow har'sts frae scowry blasts decreed!
> May a' her tenants sit fu' snug and bien,
>     Frae the hard grip o' ails, and poortith freed;
> And a lang lasting train o' peacefu' hours succeed![20]

It is a theme taken up by Burns in 'The Cotter's Saturday Night', in which rural virtue becomes the spiritual essence of Scottish identity:

> The chearfu' supper done, wi' serious face,
>     They, round the ingle, form a circle wide;
> The sire turns o'er, wi' patriarchal grace,
>     The big *ha'-Bible*, ance his *Father's* pride.
>     His bonnet rev'rently is laid aside,
> His *lyart haffets* wearing thin and bare;
>     Those strains that once did sweet in ZION glide,
> He wales a portion with judicious care,
> '*And let us worship GOD!*' he says, with solemn air.[21]

If, for Fergusson and Burns, it was 'from scenes like these, old Scotia's grandeur springs', their identification of Scotland with an agricultural world would rapidly turn into nostalgia for a lost world as Scotland's peasantry were cleared from the land—a nostalgia that would not only dominate the writings of the late nineteenth-century 'Kailyard' school, which took its inspiration from J. M. Barrie's collection of stories 'Auld Licht Idylls' (1888) and became a byword for sentimental recollection, but would continue to shape Scottish writing into the twentieth century. In *Sunset Song*, the first volume of Lewis Grassic Gibbon's *A Scots Quair* (1932–4), for instance, the central character, Chris, lives through the destruction of the old agricultural world during the First World War. Despite its presentation of the raw and repressive nature of the agricultural community, and despite the trilogy's overall celebration of technological progress, *Sunset Song* is nonetheless a pastoral elegy:

---

[20] *The Works of Robert Fergusson to which is prefaced a Sketch of the Author's Life* (1807; Edinburgh, 1970), 290.

[21] Andrew Noble and Patrick Scott Hogg, eds., *The Canongate Burns* (Edinburgh, 2001), 90.

So, hurt and dazed, she turned to the land, close to it and the smell of it, kind and kind it was, it didn't rise up and torment your heart, you could keep at peace with the land if you gave it your heart and hands, tended it and slaved for it, it was wild and a tyrant, but it was not cruel.[22]

Chris is the embodiment of Scotland as memorial, each section of the novel made up of her recollections as she sits by ancient standing stones on top of the hill close to her farm, standing stones that represent the ancient memory of the folk and which will become at the novel's end a War Memorial, with her husband's name inscribed on it.

This centrality of memory to the Scottish muse is underlined by the development of a theory of aesthetics—of 'taste' as it was known in the eighteenth century—founded principally on memory. In his *Treatise of Human Nature* (1739), David Hume had argued that all our mental experience was shaped by the 'association of ideas', in which things were linked together by the recollection of their proximity to one another in space or time, or by their perceived similarities. From this, Hume developed a theory of art in which the effect of any work of art lay in the associations that it was able to inspire in the perceiving mind, associations which constituted the 'beauty' attributed to the artwork—the more powerful the associations, the more beautiful the work. It was an explanation taken up by Alexander Gerard in his *Essay on Taste* in 1759 and in Archibald Alison's *Essays on Taste* of 1793, which formed the basis of the critical theory of the *Edinburgh Review* under the editorship of Francis Jeffrey from 1802. The associationist conception of beauty as dependent entirely on memory linked literature and landscape in a mutual interdependence. A landscape could only be experienced *as* beautiful if it aroused associations, and those associations would be more powerful if they derived not from merely personal memories but from the common associations of shared literary experience; works of literature, equally, gained power by inspiring the recollection of particular places.

The effect can be seen in Tobias Smollett's *Humphry Clinker* (1771), in which a Welsh family, touring Britain, arrive in the Highlands:

We have had princely sport in hunting the stag on these mountains—These are the lonely hills of Morven, where Fingal and his heroes enjoyed the same pastime; I feel an enthusiastic pleasure when I survey the brown heath that Ossian wont to tread; and hear the wind whistle through the bending grass—When I enter our landlord's hall, I look for the suspended harp of that divine bard, and listen in hopes of hearing the aerial sound of his respected spirit.[23]

The landscape is experienced as a recollection of literature in a process that later writers would adapt by making the evocation of landscape and its associations central to their works: Scott's *The Lady of the Lake* (1810), for instance, invokes in its very title Arthurian mythology that will turn Loch Katrine, the setting of much of the poem, into a place of 'enchantment', where a disguised King can both encounter the alien Celtic culture with

---

[22] Lewis Grassic Gibbon, *A Scots Quair* (London, 1946), 174.
[23] Tobias Smollett, *Humphry Clinker* (1771; London, 1985), 277.

which he shares his kingdom and re-enact the earlier achievements of the heroes of romance:

> And thus an airy point he won,
> Where, gleaming with the setting sun,
> One burnish'd sheet of living gold,
> Loch Katrine lay beneath him roll'd,
> In all her length far winding lay,
> With promontory, creek and bay,
> And islands that, empurpled bright,
> Floated amid the livelier light,
> And mountains, that like giants stand,
> To sentinel enchanted land.[24]

Loch Katrine is the central character of Scott's *Lady of the Lake* (1810) because it is a place where nature echoes with minstrel songs and folk songs in imitation of Scott's own art, an art which, in its recall of the past, continues to people the landscape with story and enrich it with memory. The mutual empowerment of landscape and literature is also, however, a threatening dependence—the art of memory is enacted on the brink of its extinction, threatened always by a loss of memory that would be the loss not only of the landscape but of the nation it symbolizes. Scott's art, like that of many of his contemporaries, aimed to retain the memory of the nation against the forces that, he believed, were 'gradually destroying what remains of nationality and making the country *tabula rasa*.'[25]

## IN THE THEATRE OF HISTORY

In 1730 the London-based Scot James Thomson published a long poem entitled *The Seasons*, which was to be extended and embroidered until its final edition in 1746. Its celebration of the natural world introduced into anglophone poetry something that would later be identified as 'Romanticism', a term to whose implications Thomson's poem contributed:

> …And here a while the muse
> High hovering o'er the broad cerulean scene,
> Sees Caledonia in romantic view –
> Her airy mountains, from the waving main
> Invested with a keen diffusive sky,
> Breathing the soul acute; her forests huge,
> Incult, robust, and tall, by Nature's hand

---

[24] Walter Scott, 'The Lady of the Lake' (1810), Canto I, xiv, in *The Collected Poetical Works of Sir Walter Scott*, ed. J. Logie Robertson (Oxford, 1894), 211.

[25] W. E. K. Anderson, ed., *The Journal of Sir Walter Scott* (Edinburgh, 1998), 131 (14 March 1826).

> Planted of old; her azure lakes between,
> Poured out extensive, and of watery wealth
> Full; winding deep, and green, her fertile vales,[26]

Where later Romantic poets saw in nature redemption from the evils of society, Thomson saw the spirit of progress at work transforming the world: the life of the savage is:

> A waste of time! till Industry approached
> And roused him from his miserable sloth;
> His faculties unfolded; pointed out
> Where lavish Nature the directing hand
> Of Art demanded; showed him how to raise
> His feeble force by the mechanic powers,
> To dig the mineral from the vaulted earth
> …
> Nor stopped at barren bare necessity;
> But, still advancing bolder, led him on
> To pomp, to pleasure, elegance, and grace:
> And, breathing high ambition through his soul,
> Set science, wisdom, glory in his view.[27]

The structure of *The Seasons* would seem to imply a cyclic conception of human experience, such as Thomson would have learned in his training for the ministry at Edinburgh University. The poem, however, celebrates not only nature but the city as the place where:

> … every form of cultivated life
> In order set, protected, and inspired,
> Into perfection wrought …

and celebrates the 'Commerce' of 'the busy merchant' whose trading fills the country 'with foreign plenty'. 'All', Thomson concludes, 'is the gift of Industry'.[28] It is a vision of progress that would come to dominate Scottish thinking about society in the course of the eighteenth century and which would inspire Scottish writers to explore the forces that produced such progress. The arrival of the Jacobite army in Edinburgh in 1745—described by Walter Scott in *Waverley* (1814) as an event that 'conveyed to the South-Country Lowlanders as much surprise as if an invasion of African Negroes or Esquimaux Indians had issued forth from the northern mountains of their own native country'[29]—posed the question of what forces had shaped lowland society that made it so different from highland society, of what made 'progress' possible. It was a question which led Scottish writers into an investigation of history so intense that, in a now

---

[26] James Sambrook, ed., James Thomson, *The Seasons* and *The Castle of Indolence* (Oxford, 1989), 'Autumn', 112–13, ll. 876–7.

[27] Ibid., 91, ll. 72–8, 90–4.

[28] Ibid., 92, ll. 109–11, 119–21, 141.

[29] P. D. Garside, ed., Walter Scott, *Waverley* (Edinburgh, 2007), ch. 44, 229.

famous letter of 1770, David Hume claimed Scotland as 'the historical nation'—not for its national deeds but because of its fame in the writing of history.

Hume's *History of England* (1754–62), in particular, was acclaimed throughout Europe both for the quality of its research and standard of its writing, and Hume himself regarded it as his contribution to 'literature'. Scotland's foremost eighteenth-century novelist, Tobias Smollett, whose *Humphry Clinker* had been preceded by *Roderick Random* (published in 1748 and therefore among the earliest of novels in English), wrote a competing *Complete History of England* and also a continuation of Hume's history, covering the period after 1688 at which Hume had stopped. The 'continuation' of historian by novelist appropriately acknowledged how much the novel owed to the techniques of the historians in the construction of narrative and the description of character. Hume's history continually pauses to analyse the nature of the actors in his history and the underlying causes of their actions:

> Cromwell, by whose sagacity and insinuation Fairfax was entirely governed, is one of the most eminent and most singular personages, which occurs in history. The strokes of his character are as open and strongly marked, as the schemes of his conduct were, during the time, dark and impenetrable. His extensive capacity enabled him to form the most enlarged projects: his enterprising genius was not dismayed with the boldest and most dangerous. Carried by his natural temper, to magnanimity, to grandeur, and to an imperious and domineering policy; he yet knew, when necessary, to employ the most profound dissimulation, the most oblique and refined artifice, the semblance of the greatest moderation and simplicity.[30]

It is by such character drawing that Jane Porter introduces us to William Wallace in her *The Scottish Chiefs*:

> Checked at the opening of life in the career of glory that was his passion, secluded in the bloom of manhood from the social haunts of men, he repressed the eager aspiration of his mind; and strove to acquire that resignation to inevitable evils which could alone reconcile him to forego the promises of his youth; and enable him to view with patience that humiliation of Scotland which blighted her honour, menaced her existence, and consigned her sons to degradation or obscurity.[31]

But behind Hume's history was more than just techniques that would come to be identified with fiction: the Scottish historians of the Enlightenment subscribed to what Dugald Stewart described as 'conjectural history'—the assumption that, since human nature was everywhere the same, the historian could conjecturally interpolate what the actual records of history had lost. This allowed them to envisage how primitive societies might have been organized and allowed them, in turn, to propose that human beings had passed through several—usually four—different stages of development that led from

---

[30]  David Hume, *The History of England, from the Invasion of Julius Caesar to the Revolution in 1688*, 8 vols. (London, 1767), vol. 7, ch. lvii, 28–9.

[31]  Fiona Price, ed., Jane Porter, *The Scottish Chiefs* (1810; Peterborough, Ontario, 2007), 45.

primitive pastoralism to modern commercial society, and that in each of these stages only certain kinds of social organization were possible. History, therefore, was fundamentally the account of human beings' progress from one stage of society to another. In each of these stages only certain kinds of roles were available, with the result that each stage was also a kind of theatrical stage on which the historical actors could only adapt themselves to a limited number of roles. For David Hume 'the mind is a kind of theatre, where several perceptions successively make their appearance; pass, re-pass, glide away',[32] and for Adam Smith morality operates by virtue of the sympathy that links the individual to an 'impartial spectator' who regards life as a kind of theatre in which can be balanced the appropriate flows of emotion: if 'We weep even at the feigned representation of a tragedy',[33] then how much more will our sympathy go out to sufferers in real distress? History was theatre where 'impartial spectators' judged characters by the sympathy they provoked.

When Walter Scott, stung by the impact of Byron's *Childe Harold* (1812–18) and fearing the decline of his literary fortunes, turned secretly from writing verse romances to writing novels, what he produced was not a prose version of the historical romances that had been such a feature of previous Scottish writing, including his own, but something entirely new—a historical novel that dramatized the turning point of the stages of history. In *Waverley* (1814), Scott used the Jacobite rebellion of 1745–6 to present the conflict between a pastoral society based on family and clan loyalties and a modern commercial society based on property. The tragedy of the destruction of the earlier stage of society— a society endowed with the noble heroism celebrated by Macpherson—was balanced against the comedy of a progressive history that produces a new and more liberal social order. The protagonist, Edward Waverley, is an Englishman accidentally caught up in the rebellion and captivated by its glamour: he is on the stage of history at a decisive moment in history's progress between stages, and discovers himself to be an actor on the wrong side of the transition:

> It was at that instant, that looking around him, he saw the wild dress and appearance of his Highland associates, heard their whispers in an uncouth and unknown language, looked upon his own dress, so unlike that which he had worn from his infancy, and wished to awake from what seemed at the moment a dream, strange, horrible and unnatural.[34]

Waverley's realization that he is a man dressed for a part he does not want to play but from which he cannot escape is indicative of the inherent theatricality of Scott's novels, a theatricality which allowed them to be transferred easily to the stage. Consequently, dramatizations of Scott novels were the staple of Scottish theatre throughout the

[32] L. A. Selby-Bigge, ed., David Hume, *A Treatise of Human Nature* (1739; Oxford, 1888), Bk. I, pt. iv, sect. vi, 253.

[33] D. D. Raphael and A. L. Macfie, eds., Adam Smith, *The Theory of Moral Sentiments* (Indianapolis, 1984), I, ii, 5.4, 43.

[34] Walter Scott, *Waverley*, ch. 46, 236.

nineteenth century,[35] and some of the novels—most famously *The Bride of Lammermoor*, which was adapted by Donizetti—rapidly became part of the repertoire of European opera.[36]

The tension between Scott's dramatization of the real forces of history and his construction of theatrical narratives has dogged criticism of his works, which has been torn between praising the realism of his presentation of the historical past and bewailing the romantic theatricality of his plots. But Scott, concealed as the 'Author of Waverley', was intensely aware of the *artifice* of novel-writing: in the 'Introduction' to *Ivanhoe* he compares the author to 'an actor' who 'by possessing in a pre-eminent degree the external qualities necessary to give effect to comedy, may be deprived of the right to aspire to tragic excellence'. The novelist, like such an actor, must escape the expectations 'which confine him to a single course of subjects',[37] by switching not only from the Scottish history and manners with which Scott first made his reputation to the history of other countries and cultures, but between different generic constructions of the historical past—the tragedy of *The Bride of Lammermoor* of 1819 balanced by the 'romance' of *Ivanhoe* published in the same year.

Scott's experiments with the genres possible within the frame of the historical novel, and with the role of the narrator as intermediary between past and present, were to inspire a host of experimental Scottish novel-writing in the twenty years after 1814. Some, like James Hogg's *The Brownie of Bodsbeck* (1817) and John Galt's *Ringan Gilhaize* (1823), were direct responses to Scott—in both cases challenges to Scott's presentation of Covenanting Scotland in *Old Mortality* (1816); others, like Christian Johnstone's *Clan-Albin* (1815), Susan Ferrier's *Marriage* (1818), or John Gibson Lockhart's *Adam Blair* (1822) use the Highlands as the location for supernatural events, for escape from moral strictures, or as a touchstone of sensibility. The possibilities of the historical novel opened up by Scott were to continue to shape Scottish fiction for over a hundred years: Robert Louis Stevenson's *Kidnapped* (1886) and the unfinished *Weir of Hermiston* (1896) set their action in Scotland's dramatic history; John Buchan's first novel in the 1890s, *John Burnet of Barns* (1898), was a historical romance of the seventeenth century and his most successful novel, *Witch Wood* (1927), returned there to analyse the hypocrisies of Calvinism in the period of Scotland's witch-hunts; and, in 1948, Naomi Mitchison's *The Bull Calves* used the Scottish Highlands after Culloden (1746) as a parallel to the post-Second World War era of reconstruction.

But the issue with which Scott's fiction had confronted Scottish writers was the role of the historian-author himself or herself. Scott's concealment of his identity as author and his attribution of his narrative to various intermediaries foregrounded the issue of the text's relationship to the past which it reconstructed, and of the author's role in that

---

[35]  See Bill Findlay, ed., *A History of Scottish Theatre* (Edinburgh, 1998), ch. 4, Barbara Bell, 'The Nineteenth Century', 144 ff.

[36]  Scott himself saw Rossini's *Ivanhoe* in Paris in 1826, only seven years after its original publication: see John Sutherland, *The Life of Walter Scott* (Oxford, 1995), 310; and also Jerome Mitchell, *Walter Scott Operas* (Tuscaloosa, AL, 1977).

[37]  Ian Duncan, ed., Sir Walter Scott, *Ivanhoe* (Oxford, 1998), 'Introduction', 4.

reconstruction. In *Annals of the Parish* (1823), John Galt ironically explored the gap between individual memory and historical record through the accidental reminiscences of the Reverend Micah Balwhidder, whose tenure in the manse in the parish of Dalmailing exactly matches the period of George III's monarchy and makes him a local equivalent of the king who has lost control of his kingdom. Unlike the conjectural historian, Balwhidder has no organizing narrative structure for his history but relates it in a simple chronology, listing events for each of his fifty years as parish minister. He is surrounded by the technological and social transformation of Scottish society in the period of the American and French Revolutions, but when the great developments of the time force themselves on his awareness, his natural reaction is evasion: confronted with a mass of working people made unemployed, he hides in his closet; discovering the growth of Glasgow and the poverty of its working people, he returns to his parish to tell his wife that if 'we live within the narrow circle of ignorance, we are spared from the pain of knowing many an evil; and, surely, in much knowledge there is sadness of heart'.[38] Galt's text thus develops a double structure in which, through his central character's very evasion of history, the history of Scotland's transformation by industry and empire is made to appear. Even more radical is Hogg's *Confessions of a Justified Sinner* (1824), which presents us with a narrative from the early eighteenth century that has been discovered and reinterpreted by an 'Editor' who gives us his version of events before we read the text itself, thus encouraging us to prejudge its contents. For Hogg, the Editor represents the blinkered understanding by which those of a later time attempt to understand their predecessors, and the double text sets the world views of two historical epochs in conflict with one another. The same ironic structure is repeated by Thomas Carlyle in his *Sartor Resartus* (1833), in which an editor struggles to make sense of the works of a German philosopher, works that he nonetheless claims will have a transforming effect on his British public. Since the life of the German philosopher is clearly a fiction based on novellas such as Goethe's *The Sorrows of Young Werther*, we are caught in a dialectical interplay of competing fictions that at once mocks the possibility of uncovering the real while providing the context for Carlyle to put forward his own challenging interpretation of German idealism.

The radical uncertainty of such texts reveals the extent to which the historical novel actually put in doubt both the possibility of historical knowledge and a narrative realism that could truthfully represent the past. Their challenge to history and to realism were to be little appreciated by later nineteenth-century critics for whom realism was the norm for both historical narrative and novelistic representation, but in the latter part of the twentieth century, when the self-consciousness of fiction and the textuality of history came to dominate critical debate, these texts were seen as prescient of the era that came to be known as 'postmodernism'. What they reveal, however, is a complex literary culture of competing modes of writing, each struggling to maintain its own authority and, in the process, undermining the authority of other forms of discourse. Byron—who

---

[38]  James Kinsley, ed., John Galt, *Annals of the Parish* (1821; Oxford, 1967), ch. xxxii, '1791', 137.

acknowledged himself 'half a Scot by birth, and bred/A whole one'[39]—satirized Edinburgh's literary culture in 'English Bards and Scotch Reviewers', as run by 'young tyrants…/Combined usurpers on the throne of taste', and Edinburgh's publishing world as one in which the machinery of text has run mad:

> No dearth of bards can be complain'd of now,
> The loaded press beneath her labour groans,
> And printers' devils shake their weary bones
> …
> Behold! In various throngs the scribbling crew,
> For notice eager, pass in long review;
> Each spurs his jaded Pegasus apace,
> And rhyme and blank maintain an equal race;
> Sonnets on sonnets crowd, and ode on ode;
> And tales of terror jostle on the road;[40]

But Byron was himself a part of the destabilizing environment he criticized. When the London-based Scottish publisher John Murray published the first two Cantos of Byron's *Childe Harold's Pilgrimage* in 1812, the poem combined medieval romance, contemporary travelogue, confessional autobiography, and political satire in a disorienting—but exhilarating—combination that made the work, and its author, an overnight sensation. To Byron's sceptical eye, however, neither political nor literary power can make a significant mark on history:

> Ah! such alas! the hero's amplest fate!
> When granite moulders and when records fail,
> A peasant's plaint prolongs his dubious date.
> Pride! bend thine eye from heaven to thine estate,
> See how the Mighty shrink into a song!
> Can Volume, Pillar, Pile preserve thee great?
> Or must thou trust Tradition's simple tongue,
> When Flattery sleeps with thee, and History does thee wrong.[41]

The claims of History are as illusory as the enchantments of theatre.

## BEYOND HISTORY

Scotland's major eighteenth-century historians had presented England's history as the paradigmatic version of the narrative of progress, a narrative into which, after the Union, Scotland would be harmoniously incorporated. It is an expectation dramatized

---

[39] Frederic Page, ed., *Byron: Poetical Works*, a New Edition, corrected by John Jump (Oxford, 1970), 'Don Juan', Canto X, xvii, 781.

[40] Page, ed., *Byron: Poetical Works*, 'English Bards and Scotch Reviewers', 83–4, 124–6, 143–8.

[41] Page, ed., *Byron: Poetical Works*, *Childe Harold's Pilgrimage*, Canto I, xxxvi, 186.

in Scott's *Waverley* with the marriage of Edward Waverley, accidental English Jacobite, to Rose Bradwardine, daughter of a Scottish antiquarian. Each is allowed to escape the clutches of the past into a future no longer distorted by the nation's former conflicts. Ironically for a nation that had just created the historical novel, this made the Scottish past irrelevant to its national future (see also Chapter 1). As early as 1816, in *Old Mortality*, Scott presents a Scotland in which none of the competing factions can be the foundation for a modern nation, so that instead of benefiting from a happy marriage of past and present, the protagonist is forced into exile to await a change in the tenor of the national life. By 1818, in *The Heart of Midlothian*, Scott was creating a narrative structure in which the wild and savage are not tamed by civilization but, like the illegitimate son of Jeanie Deans's sister Effie, continually escape its claims: having unknowingly killed his own father before fleeing as an indentured servant to Virginia, the boy there kills his master and joins himself 'to the next tribe of wild Indians'.[42] The savage is not harmoniously integrated into progressive history but continually re-establishes itself outside of history's control. The historical novel becomes the medium not for the exploration of the turning points within the stages of history, but of the boundary between a world governed by history and another governed by forces over which history has no sway. Hogg's *Confessions* dramatizes these as a Devil who cannot be set aside by history, even though the 'Editor' believes that 'in this day, and with the present generation, it will not go down that a man should be daily tempted by the Devil, in the semblance of a fellow-creature'. To the generation that rediscovered Hogg's novel after the Second World War, the reality of diabolic evil in the semblance of a fellow creature had become, again, only too painfully real. Robert Louis Stevenson's *The Master of Ballantrae* (1889) similarly exposes the frailties of progressive history: Stevenson sets up his tale as though it were a traditional historical novel, with two brothers representing the Jacobite and Hanoverian sides in the Rebellion of 1745–6, but instead of a narrative about the orderly extension of civilization and progress across Britain's imperial territory, what we are given is a narrative in which characters from opposite extremities of the British Empire end up in a North American wilderness. The brothers cannot stand for successful and unsuccessful historical forces, for both are driven backwards from modernity towards its origins—one into infantile subjection, the other into primitive barbarism. The failure of history is underlined by the episodic structure of *The Master*, with its several narrators who disrupt the orderly progress of the narration, and by the role of the principal narrator, MacKellar, who is himself deeply engaged in undermining the very tale he claims to tell.

Such novels subvert the structure of progressive history to question the ultimacy of the values by which it is guided. It was a questioning intensified by the unfolding discoveries of Scottish geologists, such as James Hutton and Charles Lyell, which revealed how insignificant was the timescale of recorded history, and, in 1844, by Robert Chambers's early account of evolution in *Vestiges of the Natural History of Creation*,

---

[42] David Hewitt and Alison Lumsden, eds., Walter Scott, *The Heart of Mid-Lothian* (Edinburgh, 2004), ch. 53, 467.

which prefigured much of what Charles Darwin was to argue fifteen years later. In the same period Scottish scientists such as William Thomson (Lord Kelvin), Peter Guthrie Tait, and James Clerk Maxwell were revolutionizing the understanding of the universe through their studies of thermodynamics, electricity, and magnetism. The new consciousness that this produced was described in 1865 by David Masson, appointed that year as Professor of Rhetoric and English Literature at the University of Edinburgh, as one that required 'the notion of *Interplanetary*, or even *Interstellar, Reciprocity*. Imperceptibly, by the action of many suggestions from different quarters, men have of late contracted or recovered a habit of interplanetary recollectiveness in their thoughts about things—a habit of consciously extending their regards to the other bodies of our solar systems, and feeling as if somehow *they* were not to go for nothing in the calculation of the Earth's interests and fortunes…'.[43] A world of such enormities of space and time, and which, through the workings of entropy, was bound to end in dissolution, was a world that made human history insignificant; a universe that consisted only of energy, continually in transformation, was a universe which could not be portrayed within the conventions of representational realism, whether historical or novelistic. To Masson, the romance genre of Shakespeare's late plays was far superior to modern realism precisely because it conveyed how illusory was the world portrayed by realism.

In order to chart what was beyond history, Scottish writers took to exploring alternatives to realism. Amongst the earliest is George MacDonald's *Phantastes* (1856), which, through fantasy, creates an image of the world as revealed by thermodynamics, a world of energy, constantly changing shape:

> Looking out of bed, I saw that a large green marble basin, in which I was wont to wash, and which stood on a low pedestal of the same material in a corner of my room, was overflowing like a spring; and that a stream of clear water was running over the carpet, all the length of the room, finding its outlet I knew not where. And, stranger still, where this carpet, which I had myself designed to imitate a field of grass and daisies, bordered the course of the little stream, the grass-blades and daisies seemed to wave in a tiny breeze that followed the water's flow; while under the rivulet they bent and swayed with every motion of the changeful current, as if they were about to dissolve with it, and, forsaking their fixed form, become fluent as the waters.[44]

While MacDonald discovers in this world of shape-changing the possibilities of redemption, its dark alternative in relentless determinism was to be the focus of James 'B. V.' Thomson's *The City of Dreadful Night* (1874):

> All substance lives and struggles evermore
> Through countless shapes continually at war,
> By countless interactions interknit:
> If one is born a certain day on earth,

---

[43]  David Masson, *Recent British Philosophy* (London, 1865), 148.
[44]  George MacDonald, *Phantastes* (1858; London, 1983), ch. 2, 7.

> All times and forces tended to that birth,
> Not all the world could change or hinder it.[45]

This is a world to which 'realism' is utterly inadequate, and which adopts the tenor of biblical prophecy to deny the Bible's authority:

> As I came through the desert thus it was,
> As I came through the desert: On the left
> The sun arose and crowned a broad crag-cleft:
> There stopped and burned out black, except a rim
> A bleeding eyeless socket, red and dim.[46]

In this 'hell' Thomson's speaker finds that 'I was twain,/Two selves distinct that cannot join again',[47] a theme that was to be taken up by Robert Louis Stevenson in another 'fantasy' driven by the new energy physics of shape-changing, *The Strange Case of Jekyll and Hyde* (1886). Jekyll's discovery of his other self in the demonic Hyde seems to have allowed him to defeat the laws of thermodynamics, as well as those of morality, since he can expend energy on committing crimes as Hyde, while being able to return to an undiminished version of himself as Jekyll. But Hyde's dissipation of energy gradually turns Jekyll into 'a creature eaten up and emptied by fever, languidly weak in both body and mind'.[48] The complex sequence of narrators in Stevenson's tale, ending with Jekyll's own first-hand account of his destruction, dramatically underlines the overwhelming of enlightened modernity by an irresistible darkness: 'The dismal quarter of Soho seen under these changing glimpses, with its muddy ways, and slatternly passengers, and its lamps, which had never been extinguished or had been rekindled afresh to combat this mournful reinvasion of darkness, seemed, in the lawyer's eyes, like a district of some city in nightmare.'[49]

Stevenson theorized the significance of this anti-realist dimension of his art in his 'Humble Remonstrance', an essay that took issue with Henry James's conception of the novel in 'The Art of Fiction'. Stevenson wrote:

> Life is monstrous, infinite, illogical, abrupt and poignant; a work of art, in comparison, is neat, finite, self-contained, rational, flowing and emasculate. Life imposes by brute energy, like inarticulate thunder; art catches the ear, among the far louder noises of experience, like an air artificially made by a discreet musician. A proposition of geometry does not compete with life; and a proposition of geometry is a fair and luminous parallel for a work of art. Both are reasonable, both untrue to crude fact; both inhere in nature, neither represents it.[50]

---

[45] Ian Campbell, ed., James Thomson, *The City of Dreadful Night and Other Poems* (1874; Glasgow, 2008), 'XIV', 29–30.

[46] Ibid., 'IV', 12.

[47] Ibid.

[48] Robert Louis Stevenson, *Markheim, Jekyll and the Merry Men* (Edinburgh, 2004; 1886), 292.

[49] Ibid., 247.

[50] Glenda Norquay, ed., *R. L. Stevenson on Fiction: An Anthology of Literary and Critical Essays* (Edinburgh, 1999), Section I, 85.

This resistance to realism is as evident in the 'supernatural tales' of a writer such as Margaret Oliphant, much of whose massive output held itself within the limits of nineteenth-century realism, as in the self-conscious fictions of J. M. Barrie, such as *Sentimental Tommy* (1896) and *Tommy and Grizel* (1900). It was with *Peter Pan* (1906), however, that Barrie invented a style that could both mock the conventions of realism and reveal truths unimaginable within those conventions. Peter, as eternal as an atom and as forgetful of the history of its transformations, is a primitive force of energy that continually disrupts and undermines the order on which modern civilization believes itself to be based. The very fact that *Peter Pan* is a children's story represents a refusal of the teleologies of adulthood, as well as of the historical purposes of the imperial world mocked by the pirates and Indians of the Never Land.

Pan's name suggests, of course, that he belongs, at least in part, to the world of the primitive, a world that was being charted during the course of Barrie's career in J. G. Frazer's immense study of primitive mythology, *The Golden Bough*, first published in two volumes in 1890 and, by 1915, extending to twelve. Now that its anthropology has been discounted, Frazer's work stands as a great imaginative construction—a vast detective novel tracking down the key to humanity's most primitive instincts. And what it attests to is the power of forces that continually undermine progressive history: there is, Frazer insists:

> a solid layer of savagery beneath the surface of society … unaffected by the superficial changes of religion and culture.… The dispassionate observer, whose studies have led him to plumb its depths, can hardly regard it otherwise than as a standing menace to civilisation. We seem to move on a thin crust which may at any moment be rent by the subterranean forces slumbering below.[51]

The forces of savagery are massive, indeed almost geological, the forces of progressive history feeble, a fragile surface that will not sustain us. It is a juxtaposition that was to find literary form in the first major Scottish work of the twentieth century, George Douglas Brown's *The House with the Green Shutters* (1900), for it juxtaposes a 'realistic' narrative—indeed, a narrative designed to oppose the 'myths' of Kailyard fiction by the intensity of its realistic portrayal of the downfall of the Gourlay family—with a structure based on Greek tragedy, as though the earliest form through which humanity emerged from savagery continues to shape the lives of those who live within the modern savagery of capitalism. Frazer's juxtaposition of the ahistorical primitive with a feeble modern history become, in *House with the Green Shutters*, the juxtaposition of the ahistorical truth of primitive tragedy with the 'progressive' history of modern economic development in a small Scottish village. Scotland is a place where the forces from beyond the boundaries of history insistently reveal themselves to be more powerful than the history that people assume is the ultimate force reshaping their society: progressive history turns ineluctably into ancient tragedy. Frazer's vision of a modernity undermined by the primitive would continue to shape Scottish novelists' account of the world throughout

---

[51] J. G. Frazer, *The Golden Bough* (London, 1922), 56.

the twentieth century—as late as 1991, Allan Massie was to invoke it in *The Sins of the Father*, his novel of Nazi survivors in Argentina in the 1960s.

# GOING DOWN TO HELL

In Neil Gunn's *The Serpent* (1943), the central character, Tom, is sent to an apprenticeship in Glasgow, where he is introduced to the evolutionary theories that he had only ever heard mocked in his highland home. At a public meeting to which he goes with his room-mate Dougal, he listens to a speaker who extols the virtues of Robert Owen's socialism:

> The speaker had touched on 'what is called progress, the progress of the machine age, of capital, of world-wide expansion. When we come down to human essentials, what does this progress amount to?'
> 'Progress and poverty,' responded Dougal...[52]

Scotland in 1914 was one of the most industrialized countries in the world and if, as Marxism and socialism proclaimed, the world of the future was to belong to the working classes, then Scotland ought to have been in the vanguard of progress towards that goal. Many of its leading writers of the 1920s and 1930s certainly believed so, and adapted their art to communist and socialist purposes. 'Hugh MacDiarmid' moved from the literary Scots of his early poetry to a celebration of the demotic of factory workers:

> The haill shop's dumfoonderin'
>     To a stranger like me.
> Second nature to you: you're perfectly able
>     To think, speak and see
> Apairt frae the looms, tho' to some
> That doesna sae easily come.
>
> Lenin was like that wi' workin' class life,
>     At hame wi't a'.
> His fause movements couldna been fewer,
>     The best weaver Earth ever saw.
> A' he'd to dae wi' moved intact
>     Clean, clear, and exact.[53]

Lewis Grassic Gibbon Leslie Mitchell, too, reshaped his Scots to an urban vernacular that celebrated the revolutionary potential of the working classes:

> ...what was wrong up there, why had they stopped? Chaps cried *Get on with it, Jim, what's wrong?* Syne the news came down [...] the police were turning the procession

---

[52] Neil Gunn, *The Serpent* (London, 1978; 1943), 25.

[53] Hugh MacDiarmid, 'Seamless Garment', *Complete Poems*, 2 vols. (1931; London, 1978), vol. 1, 311–12. Reproduced with permission from Carcanet Press Ltd.

back down into Paldy by way of the wynds. It wasn't to be let near the Town Hall at all, the Provost had refused to see them or Trease.

And then you heard something rising about you that hadn't words, the queerest-like sound, you stared at your mates, a thing like a growl, low and savage, the same in your throat. And then you were thrusting forward like others—*Never mind the Bulgars, they can't stop our march!*[54]

And a working-class dramatist like Joe Corrie presented, in plays such as *In Time o' Strife* (1927), the conflicts of strike-torn working-class communities.

As the political impulse promised by socialism stalled, however, under the impact of the Depression of the 1930s, and the gradual ebbing away of Britain's imperial power, urban Scotland became a place seemingly abandoned by historical progress. In the imagination of its writers, Glasgow, once the workshop of the world and exemplar of municipal socialism, became a city without purpose. The transformation is traced by Edwin Muir in his *Autobiography* (1940; 1954): at the age of twenty-one, recovered from the illness that had first accompanied his family's transfer from Orkney to Glasgow, he is converted to socialism in an 'emotional transmutation' that was 'a recapitulation of my first conversion at fourteen';[55] after the First World War, however, Glasgow has become the antithesis of such spiritual transmutation:

> I was returning in a tramcar from my work; the tramcar was full and very hot; the sun burned through the glass on the backs of necks, shoulders, faces, trousers, skirts, hands, all stacked there impartially. Opposite me was sitting a man with a face like a pig's, and as I looked at him in the oppressive heat the words came into my mind, 'That is an animal.' I looked round me at the other people in the tramcar; I was conscious that something had fallen from them and from me; and with a sense of desolation I saw that they were all animals...my mind saw countless other tramcars where animals sat or got on or off with mechanical dexterity...and I realized that in all Glasgow, in all Scotland, in all the world, there was nothing but millions of such creatures living an animal life and moving towards an animal death as towards a great slaughter-house.[56]

Despite works that present the life of middle-class Glasgow, such as Catherine Carswell's *Open the Door!* (1920), and novels such as Dot Allan's *Hunger March* (1934) and George Blake's *The Shipbuilders* (1936), which juxtapose working-class life with the lives of middle-class Glaswegians, the slums of Glasgow come to be the intransigent image of the nation's decay. In *The Changeling* (1958) by Robin Jenkins, the world of the slums is one where:

> Newly-born babies in their prams, if washed, looked pathetically alien there; but in a short time, in two years or less, they had begun to acquire the characteristics which

---

[54] Lewis Grassic Gibbon, *Grey Granite*, third part of *A Scots Quair* (London, 1946), 395.
[55] Edwin Muir, *An Autobiography* (London, 1954), 113; the first six chapters were published as *The Story and the Fable* (London, 1940).
[56] Ibid., 43.

would enable them to survive amidst that dirt and savagery, but which naturally detracted a great deal from their original beauty. By manhood or womanhood they were as irretrievably adapted to their environment as the tiger to his.[57]

In Jenkins's *Fergus Lamont* (1979), the nation's delusions about its romantic identity are shown both to be born in the slums and to founder in them. Glasgow becomes an unchanging hell, the ironic endpoint of a nation that had believed itself possessed of a religion of the elect. It is the world in which Alasdair Gray was to enmesh Duncan Thaw in *Lanark* in 1981, with the revelation that 'Hell was the one truth and pain the one fact which nullified all others' and 'history was an infinitely diseased worm without head or tail, beginning or end'.[58]

To escape the dehumanization to which history had brought its cities, Scottish writers returned regularly to Scotland's countryside and to places where a sense of community could be rebuilt. In Nan Shepherd's *The Weatherhouse* (1930), Garry Forbes, back wounded from the hell of the Western Front, and considering returning there, looks out over the Aberdeenshire farmland where his aunt lives:

> Mrs Hunter sailed across the stackyard in a stream of hens. And on his steep, thin field Francie Ferguson walked, casting the seed. It was his moment of dignity. Clumsy, ridiculous, sport of a woman's caprice and a byword in men's jesting, as he cast the seed with the free ample movement of the sower Francie had a grandeur more than natural. The dead reached through him to the future. Continuity was in his gait. His thin upland soil, ending in stony crests of whin and heather, was transfigured by the faith that used it, he himself by the sower's poise that symbolised his faith.[59]

In *Magnus Merriman* (1934), Eric Linklater mocked the politics of the 1930s and the literary nationalism of his contemporaries before having his protagonist retreat to Orkney where he discovers 'that his life was kin to all the life around him, even to the beasts that grazed in the fields, and to the very fields themselves'.[60] The same act of return is undertaken by several of Neil Gunn's protagonists, most notably by Kenn in *Highland River* (1937), for whom the journey home is also the recovery of the memory of the folk that modernity had tried to erase:

> In the last few moments before he had risen he had seen himself walking towards the mountain, much as, in the last year or two, he had seen the little figure of the boy Kenn adventuring into the strath. What older mind, in this curious regress, was now the observer might be difficult to say, for its apprehension seemed profounder than individual thought. Pict, and Viking too, and Gael; the folk through immense eras of time...[61]

---

[57]  Robin Jenkins, *The Changeling* (Edinburgh, 1989; 1958), 17.
[58]  Alasdair Gray, *Lanark* (Edinburgh, 1981), 160.
[59]  Nan Shepherd, *The Weatherhouse* (Edinburgh, 1988; 1930), 172–3.
[60]  Eric Linklater, *Magnus Merriman* (Edinburgh, 1990; 1934), 299.
[61]  Neil Gunn, *Highland River* (Edinburgh, 1994; 1937), 241.

Since modernity has, seemingly, no future, recovery can only be by way of the past, and that return to the past as the beginning of recuperation from a failed present is typical of much Scottish writing from the 1920s to the 1950s. Edwin Muir himself began to overcome his Glasgow experiences by recollecting his childhood in Orkney and infusing its landscape with symbols made significant by his experience of psychoanalysis; Sorley Maclean's poetry in Gaelic, by its use of a language being steadily eroded by modernity, represented a recuperation of the past that parallels the content of poems such as 'Hallaig':[62]

| | |
|---|---|
| Tha iad fhathast ann a Hallaig. | They are still in Hallaig |
| Clann Ghill-Eain's Clann MhicLeòid, | MacLeans and MacLeods, |
| na bh' ann ri linn Mhic Ghille Chaluim: | all who were there in the time of Mac Gille Chaluim |
| chunnacas na mairbh beò. | the dead have been seen alive. |
| Na fir nan laighe air an lianaig | The men lying on the green |
| aig ceann gach taighe a bh' ann | at the end of every house that was, |
| na h-igheanin' nan coille bheithe, | the girls a wood of birches, |
| dìreach an druim, crom an ceann. | straight their backs, bent their heads. |

Similarly, the novels, stories, and poems of Iain Crichton Smith turn insistently on the recovery from the destructive impact of Calvinisim on both Gaelic culture and modern life, as do the works of George Mackay Brown, set on an Orkney whose traditional culture stands still in defiant opposition to modernity. Even as urbane a poet as Norman MacCaig discovers that poetry is insistently a return to rural, Gaelic-speaking Scotland: '... no need to invoke/That troublemaker, Memory, she's everywhere.'[63]

This profound distrust of the course taken by Scottish history had implications for the genres that Scottish writers could use: a 'realism' which could *document* Scotland's hell would also be submissive to it, so that those who wished to resist modernity required a style that could challenge accepted reality. J. M. Barrie's exploitation of the supernatural in plays such as *Mary Rose* (1920), in which the eponymous heroine disappears on a Scottish island to return twenty-five years later unchanged, and in his novella, *Farewell Miss Julie Logan* (1931), in which a nineteenth-century minister meets and falls in love with an eighteenth-century Jacobite woman, drew on a long tradition of Scottish writings about encounters with the supernatural, not to mention with the Devil—as in Burns's 'Tam O' Shanter'—and these were traditions that were to be regularly revisited by Scottish writers. James Bridie (Osborne Henry Mavor) drew on this tradition in *Mr Bolfry* (1943), a play in which the Devil (Mr Bolfry) is conjured up in the house of a minister of the Church (Mr McCrimmon); McCrimmon, tall and grey, and Bolfry, elfin, small, and dark, are distorted mirror images of one another:

---

[62] Sorley MacLean, 'Hallaig', *From Wood to Ridge* (Manchester, 1989), 229, Reproduced with permission from Carcanet Press Ltd.

[63] Norman MacCaig, 'Return to Scalpay', *Collected Poems* (London, 1990), 280.

| BOLFRY: | I have told you, Sir. My name is Bolfry. In the days of sanity and belief, it was a name not unknown to men of your cloth. |
| McCRIMMON: | You are dressed like a minister. Where is your Kirk? |
| BOLFRY: | In Hell. |
| McCRIMMON: | Are there Kirks in Hell? |
| BOLFRY: | Why not? Would you deny us the consolations of religion?[64] |

Hell is no longer the 'other place' but this place in the present. It is a theme taken up in Muriel Spark's *Hothouse by the East River* (1973), in which the ghosts of people killed in the Second World War continue to live on in New York in the 1960s, a hell of secular culture where 'there isn't any war and peace any more, no good and evil, no communism, no capitalism, no fascism,'[65] but where everyone 'missed out the mortality problem.'[66] Characters in Spark's novels are regularly visited by the supernatural—Mrs Hogg in *The Comforters* (1957), who disappears out of existence; the voice on the telephone informing the characters of *Momento Mori* (1959) 'remember you must die'; Margaret Mutchie in *Symposium* (1990), who is always close to suspicious deaths and whose Uncle Magnus is like a character out of an old ballad, suffering a 'divine affliction' that enables him to 'prognosticate and foreshadow.'[67]

Such supernatural intrusions into plots are echoed by characters who gain access to alternative dimensions of existence—like Art and Old Hector in Neil Gunn's *The Green Isle of the Great Deep* (1944), in which, having fallen in a river and nearly drowned, the two main characters arrive in a parallel universe dominated by a local version of the totalitarianism then threatening the world. Fantasy mirror images of, or alternatives to, Scotland's failed present allowed Scottish writers to create significant narratives from a history from which narrative seemed to have been evacuated: in Alasdair's Gray's *Lanark* (1981), Duncan Thaw's life in Glasgow in the 1950s is continued in fantasy form by the life of 'Lanark', who inhabits, first, a Glasgow full of creatures turning into dragons and then a Scotland being literally consumed and turned into energy for others' use by an international conspiracy of the supposedly enlightened; while in *Poor Things* (1992) nineteenth-century Glasgow becomes the scene of a double reworking of the Frankenstein myth, when a humanly engineered doctor revivifies a suicide by grafting into her body the brain of her own unborn child. These fantasy versions of the real reveal what realism itself cannot capture: the structure of a worldwide capitalism that deprives people of their humanity. As Scotland was overwhelmed in the 1980s by the effects of 'Thatcherite' policies that destroyed its traditional industries, such fantasies became the medium through which Scotland's incapacity to control its history could be envisaged: Iain Banks's *The Bridge* (1986) takes place in a city inhabiting a structure like the Forth Bridge, whose

[64] Cairns Craig and Randall Stevenson, eds., *Twentieth-Century Scottish Drama* (Edinburgh, 2001; 1943), 241.

[65] Muriel Spark, *The Hothouse by the East River* (Harmondsworth, 1975; 1973), 63.

[66] Ibid., 110.

[67] Muriel Spark, *Symposium* (Harmondsworth, 1991; 1990), 81.

ends are so distant they have never been seen; and in A. L. Kennedy's *So I am Glad* (1995) an unemployed drifter turns out to be Cyrano de Bergerac, returned to reinhabit the world and still carrying with him the consciousness of an earlier century. Alasdair Gray's *A History Maker* (1994) ironizes the whole tradition of the historical novel by envisaging a future society in which men are restricted to playing war games instead of making real war, and in which history has, effectively, been brought to an end, returning us to the cyclic world of oral culture from which the eighteenth-century literati had sought to escape.

## TYPES OF VOICE

In 1961 Ian Hamilton Finlay published a small collection of poems written in phonetic representation of Glasgow dialect, *Glasgow Beasts, an a Burd, haw, an Inseks, an aw, a Fush* (1961). The adoption of Glasgow dialect was a direct challenge to the principles of MacDiarmid's Scottish Renaissance movement, and to those who continued to develop its commitment to a highly literary Scots, such as Sydney Goodsir Smith, whose *Carotid Cornucopious* (1947) and *Under the Eildon Tree* (1948) represent the major achievements of the 'second generation' of the Scottish Renaissance. Despite the fact that there was no agreed standard for the representation of Scots in written form—efforts at agreement in the 1940s came to nothing—it was nonetheless accepted that Scots as a literary language was quite different from Scots as a spoken vernacular. Hamilton Finlay, however, chose to emphasize the phonetics of contemporary Glasgow speech, an example that was to be taken up decisively in the work of Tom Leonard:

> right inuff
> ma language is disgraceful
> ma maw tellt mi
> ma teacher tellt mi
> thi doactir tellt mi
> thi priest tellt mi
> ...
> jist aboot ivry book ah oapnd tellt mi
> even thi introduction tay the Scottish National Dictionary tellt mi[68]

The refusal to conform to the style of the Scottish National Dictionary and instead to put trust in the value of *contemporary* Scots went against the whole tradition of modern writing in Scots. Leonard's poem concludes:

> ach well
> all livin language is sacred
> fuck thi lohta thim

---

[68] Tom Leonard, *Intimate Voices: Selected Work 1965–1983* (Newcastle, 1984), 120.

The language we 'live in' (livin) is a living language: it is sacred even if it includes vocabulary ('fuck') that is unacceptable in 'educated' society. For Leonard this was a poetry that emphasized 'sound'—the cover of his *Intimate Voices* (1984) collection offers a poem which transforms 'in the beginning was the word' in ten lines into 'nthibiginninwuzthiwurd', before declaring 'in the beginning was the sound'—but its impact on the eye was just as crucial. Words became a physical presence sculpted onto the page, defying the ease with which the eye normally scans them and forcing the reader to explore their physical as well as their aural structure. It was a recognition that was to lead Hamilton Finlay towards concrete poetry—in which language was exploited for its visual potential—and then into the placement of language in a physical environment with which it would interact. At Stonypath, in the Pentlands, Finlay created a garden that celebrated the intersection of sculpted language and planned nature and which became one of the major achievements of Scottish culture in the last half of the twentieth century.

The interaction of vernacular language with its physical representation, however, was a key element in the innovations of Scottish writing in this period, exemplified in the huge variety of Edwin Morgan's experimental work, such as 'Canedolia':

> oa! hoy! awe! ba! mey!
> *who saw?*
> rhu saw rum. garve saw smoo. nigg saw tain. lairg saw lagg.
> rigg saw eigg. largs saw haggs. tongue saw luss. mull saw yell.[69]

The poem foregrounds Scotland as a soundscape rather than a landscape, one where sounds turn into perceptions ('tongue saw luss') and perceptions into sounds ('mull saw yell'). Scotland becomes in Morgan's poetry, as in Finlay's garden, a crossing place: a crossing place of languages, of cultures, of discourses, of real and unreal(ized) encounters.

The defamiliarization of an apparently banal world that these crossings produced was to inspire a generation of Scottish writers to experiment both with the physical representation of language and with the complexities produced by the interaction of a local culture with a globalized world. In James Kelman's novels, for instance, each of his central characters appears to create a unique linguistic world, operating by its own rules and in defiance of those of 'standard English':

> But it couldnay get worse than this. He was really fuckt now. This was the dregs; he was at it. He had fucking reached it now man the fucking dregs man the pits, the fucking black fucking limboland, purgatory; that's what it was like, purgatory, where all ye can do is think. Think. That's all ye can do. Ye just fucking think about what ye've done and what ye've no fucking done; ye cannay look at nothing ye cannay see nothing it's just a total fucking disaster area, yer mind, yer fucking memories, a disaster area.[70]

---

[69] Edwin Morgan, *Collected Poems* (Manchester, 1990), 156. Reproduced with permisson from Carcanet Press Ltd.
[70] James Kelman, *How late it was, how late* (London, 1994), 172.

This demotic declaration of independence was to unleash a torrent of writing in Scots, and an acceptance of the Scottish *voice*, the contemporary Scottish voice, as the appropriate literary medium for Scottish writers. Liz Lochhead's translations of Molière into Scots, together with plays such as *Mary Queen of Scots Got her Head Chopped Off* (1989), translate historical events and works into a contemporary idiom, while John Byrne's television dramas *Tutti Frutti* (1987) and *Your Cheatin' Heart* (1990) play similar games between the Scots of contemporary urban Scotland and the American culture which saturates its media, so that the American 'Gene' can be misheard as Scottish 'Jean':

> DORWOOD:    *(loudly)* There's my redundancy money off the rigs inside the Gene Autry wireless, tell her.
> *(Tamara leans down to the car again)*
> TAMARA:    *(to engineer)* Something about Jean, is that what you got?
> ENGINEER:    He's just after tellin' us the wife's name was Cissie, what one we supposed to bring back, the wife or the fancy wumman?
> DORWOOD:    *(loudly)* I was savin' up to take her an'...I was savin' up to take us to Nashville, if she asks you.[71]

Scotland has become a place where translation between cultures and languages is not an afterthought—it is fundamental to every linguistic act: Scotland is a place where language is so profuse that it continually mistakes its object, producing endless confusion but, at the same time, a chaotic creative vitality. The 'livin language' of the immediacy of the voice and the apparently permanent structures of type intersect to produce a unique linguistic environment, both contemporary and yet rooted in a long tradition of literary independence. No one would have predicted, in 1980, that a novel written in a series of Edinburgh dialects could have been a literary let alone a popular success, but Irvine Welsh's *Trainspotting* (1993), rendered in the language of Edinburgh's working-class drug culture, was to be, like the film based on it, an international best-seller.

## Endings and Beginnings

In the 1970s and 1980s the possibility that Scottish culture was facing a 'doomsday' annihilation seemed to some all too imminent.[72] An increasingly strident assertion of specifically English cultural values by influential magazines such as *P N Review*, and by English politicians who regarded the 'failure' of the devolution referendum of 1979 as an end to the issue of a separate Scottish Parliament, suggested that an identifiably Scottish culture was no longer one of the possibilities of the modern world. In 1984, however, in

---

[71] John Byrne, *Your Cheatin' Heart* in Cairns Craig and Randall Stevenson, eds., *Twentieth-Century Scottish Drama: An Anthology* (Edinburgh, 2001), 577.

[72] The 'doomsday scenario' was one in which the Conservatives had a permanent majority at Westminster on the basis of English votes, while Scotland and Wales voted consistently for Labour, and thus the majority of Scots and Welsh went unrepresented at a UK level.

his *Sonnets from Scotland*, Edwin Morgan began to envisage a series of alternative Scotlands, both past and future, that symbolized the persistence and vitality of the culture. One of them brings together Scotland's greatest geologist, James Hutton, and greatest poet, Robert Burns, by way of Burns's evocative folk lyric, 'A Red, Red Rose', with its strange temporal perspective: 'Till a' the seas gang dry, my Dear,/And the rocks melt wi' the sun':

> James Hutton that true son of fire who said
> to Burns 'Aye, man, the rocks melt wi the sun'
> was sure the age of reason's time was done:
> what but imagination could have read
> granite boulders back to their molten roots?
> And how far back was back, and how far on
> would basalt still be basalt, iron iron?
> would second seas re-drown the fossil brutes?
> 'We find no vestige of a beginning,
> no prospect of an end.'[73]

The final lines quote Hutton's conclusion to his account of the earth's geological processes in *Theory of the Earth* (1785), but in the context of the political failures of the 1970s and 1980s, their assertion became a reaffirmation of the value of the nation's literary history, a literary history to which Burns continued to be central and that refused to acknowledge the 'prospect of an end'.

## FURTHER READING

Brown, Ian, Clancy, Thomas Owen, Manning, Susan, and Pittock, Murray (eds.), *The Edinburgh History of Scottish Literature*, 3 vols. (Edinburgh, 2007).

Craig, Cairns, *The Modern Scottish Novel* (Edinburgh, 1999).

—— ed., *The History of Scottish Literature*, 4 vols. (Aberdeen, 1987–9).

Crawford, Robert, *Scotland's Books: The Penguin History of Scottish Literature* (London, 2007).

Duncan, Ian, *Scott's Shadow: The Novel in Romantic Edinburgh* (Princeton, 2007).

Findlay, Bill, ed., *A History of Scottish Theatre* (Edinburgh, 1998).

Hart, Francis Russell, *The Scottish Novel* (London, 1978).

Pittock, Murray G. H., *Scottish and Irish Romanticism* (Oxford, 2008).

Whyte, Christopher, *Modern Scottish Poetry* (Edinburgh, 2009).

[73] Morgan, *Collected Poems*, 443.

CHAPTER 6

........................................................................................

# THE CLEARANCES AND THE TRANSFORMATION OF THE SCOTTISH COUNTRYSIDE

........................................................................................

## ROBERT DODGSHON

UNDERPINNING the transformation of the Scottish countryside during the seventeenth–nineteenth centuries, and forming a vital precondition for the Improving Movement, were far-reaching changes in the structure and layout of farms and in the nature of the farm community. Initial discussion of these changes played on the contrasting experience of the Highlands and Lowlands. In the former, change was seen as achieved via the clearances, with traditional runrig touns[1] and their multiple tenants being swept away to form large sheep farms, whilst in the latter, traditional runrig touns were seen as transformed via a reorganization of runrig holdings into separate farms, with some claiming a significant role for the *1695 act anent lands lying runrig*. Subsequent research has greatly modified this picture. On the one hand, it has uncovered a greater diversity of means by which the traditional toun gave way to what essentially formed the modern farm landscape whilst, on the other, it revealed that what we can bundle together under the heading of this diversity played a role in all areas.

The cornerstone for this shift in perspective has been our better understanding of the term 'clearances'. When first coined as a description of the changes that swept across the Highlands and Islands over the second half of the eighteenth and first half of the nineteenth century, the meaning, chronology, and distribution of the clearances were all

[1] The term *toun* was used throughout Scotland to describe the standard farm unit, or unit of set, prior to improvement. Some were set to more than one tenant, or multiple tenants, whose different shares were laid out in the form of intermixed strips, that is, as a *runrig toun*.

clearly defined. It was seen as a term that best captured the sudden and socially disruptive way in which many traditional runrig communities in the Highlands were swept aside to make way for sheep. Yet too easily, we allowed the headline story to smother the detail and variety of change that actually took place. More recent research has revised our reading of what happened in two significant ways.

First, whilst the wholesale clearance of touns to make way for sheep is still rightly seen as the prime means by which many highland touns were restructured, it is clear that a significant number of touns did not experience a clearance. We have long known that many along the western seaboard were tidied up into newly configured crofting townships rather than cleared. Others experienced a clearance but via a gradual reduction of tenant numbers. Still others were reorganized or divided out into small consolidated farms. Finally, a sizeable number of highland touns did not undergo any form of fundamental structural change, other than enclosure, in their transition to modern forms since, even by the time they first appear in late seventeenth-century rentals, they were held and worked as single tenancies.

Second, there is now a case for seeing the clearances as a process that affected all parts of Scotland. This revision turns on how we interpret the abundant evidence that has been uncovered showing that many traditional runrig touns in the Lowlands were transformed through a gradual, drawn-out process of tenant reduction. The scale and rapidity of this reduction was generally more restrained when compared to the big clearance events of the Highlands, but the eventual outcome of even a gradual process of tenant reduction was still one of toun clearance. Alternative forms of reorganization, such as the restructuring of multiple-tenant touns through their division or reorganization into small consolidated farms, also had a role to play in the Lowlands but their overall contribution now needs a more measured view.

The fact that the same bundle of processes were at work across Scotland, transforming old toun structures into modern farm layouts, does not mean that a geographical approach to such change no longer has value. A key driver of change in the Scottish countryside over the seventeenth–nineteenth centuries was the shift towards more market-responsive and specialized systems of farm production. When seen at the outset of the seventeenth century, the field economy of pre-improvement touns everywhere would have shared much in common in that most were organized around a mixed output of grain and livestock. At this point, their guiding strategy and the reason why there would have been a degree of sameness about their field economy was their overriding need to secure basic subsistence plus rent and seed. These defined horizons of basic need limited their direct market engagement. This is not to say that grain and stock were not being marketed, but what we see being marketed largely comprised the surplus rents in kind gathered in by landlords. What most ordinary farmers traded on their own account at this point would have been modest.

Over the mid-late seventeenth century, this situation began slowly to change. Foremost amongst the changes that we can detect was the way in which growing urban demand and improvements in grain output combined to enable touns in the more fertile parts of the Lowlands, as well as those along the east coast whose access to the sea enabled produce to be traded at a distance, to market an increasing amount of grain.[2] Part of this increase undoubtedly represented the landlord's take on the increasing output of touns. However, there remain questions about how much of it can be attributed to a growing surplus left in the hands of those tenants who commanded larger and larger holdings and who engaged in costly land improvements (i.e. liming). Establishing the build-up of market responsiveness is important when we come to look at the restructuring of touns. Different farming systems had different thresholds as regards the holding size at which they became viable, thresholds that factored in the capital needed to equip or stock them, their labour needs, the scale at which particular husbandries were most effective, etcetera. As areal specialization developed, we can expect the restructuring of touns and the farm sizes produced by it to have had these thresholds in mind. It is for this reason that any review of restructuring still benefits from a geographical approach, one sensitive to the interrelated factors of resource endowment, market advantage, and emerging areal specialization. With this in mind, I want to arrange the discussion under the standard headings of the Lowlands, Southern Uplands, and Highlands and Islands.

# THE LOWLANDS

Early studies of how the pre-improvement touns of the Lowlands were transformed tended to deal with the problem in terms of how surveyors remapped the landscape so as to produce a layout pattern of consolidated, regularly enclosed farms. Few delved into the question of whether it was in any way rooted in processes that had long been under way, though John Lebon's early work on Ayrshire clearly highlighted some of the deeper processes that may have been at work, with the planned, regular forms created by eighteenth-century improvers being contrasted with an older (pre-1700) piecemeal process of transformation, one that reincorporated the lineaments of the old touns and their furlongs in the new farm structure.[3] Likewise, whilst some early studies referred to the importance of tenant reduction as a process for restructuring,[4] they did not expand on what it involved. Some discussions even complicated matters by referring to the division of touns, making blanket references to the general importance of the *1695 act anent lands lying runrig*,[5] but what such divisions involved was not specified. Yet

---

[2] *State of Certain Parishes in Scotland M.D.C.XXVII* (Edinburgh, 1835), 133–5; T. C. Smout and A. Fenton, 'Scottish Agriculture before the Improvers—An Exploration', *Agricultural History Review*, xiii (1965), 75–7 and 82–4; I. D. Whyte, *Agriculture and Society in Seventeenth-Century Scotland* (Edinburgh, 1979), 178–94, 223–34, and 246–7.

[3] J. H. G. Lebon, 'The Process of Enclosure in the Western Lowlands', *Scottish Geographical Magazine*, 62 (1946), 103–5.

[4] Ibid., 9; J. Tivy, 'Easter Ross: A Residual Crofting Area', *Scottish Studies*, 9, no. 1 (1965), 69; Smout and Fenton, 'Scottish Agriculture', 80.

[5] Acts of Parliament of Scotland, ix, 421; J. E. Handley, *The Agricultural Revolution in Scotland* (Glasgow, 1963), 17.

once these questions are confronted, our perspective on how farm structures changed in the Lowlands alters.

## The Clearance of Lowland Touns

We can approach this change in perspective by looking first at what late seventeenth century data can tell us about the structure of the toun community in the Lowlands prior to the Improving Movement. As well as tenants, and subtenants who held land off the former, there also existed crofters and cottars. The crofters mostly held service crofts, such as those attached to mills, brewseats, or ferries, or given to ploughmen. They could be quite sizeable holdings (5–10 acres) but their prime characteristic, and what ensured the continued use of the term into the modern age, was the fact that they were held as separate, consolidated smallholdings and not enmeshed within a toun's runrig. Cottars were a more diverse category. They provided essential labour for tenants (i.e. ploughing, sowing, harvesting, herding, shearing, etcetera) in return for what might have been a garden attached to a cot or a few rigs within the toun's runrig, plus the right to graze a cow or a few sheep. It was the fact that their contract was based on labour in return for housing and subsistence that helps distinguish them from subtenants, the latter simply being lessees of land from the main tenant or tenants. Frequently, those cottars less endowed broadened their subsistence base by also practising a craft or trade, like that of wheelwright or carter.

Looking at the way touns were structured around such groups, analyses of poll-tax data for the 1690s show that a significant number of lowland touns were already in the hands of single tenants even by this point, with the rest of the toun community being made up of cottars of various descriptions and, in the larger touns, crofters. Thus, using 1696 data for Aberdeenshire, Ian Whyte found that in the fertile low-ground arable areas (such as around Aberdeen itself, the Garioch, and in the valleys of the Ythan and Deveron), over 70 per cent of touns were already in the hands of single tenants. By comparison, less progress had been made in hillier, more pastoral areas like Buchan. The distinction was sufficiently clear for Whyte to conclude that 'there seems to have been a relationship between farm structure and the orientation of the economy towards arable or pastoral farming'.[6] This analysis of the poll-tax lists was subsequently broadened by Tom Devine. Again, his analysis revealed that in fertile counties like West Lothian, Midlothian, and Berwickshire, the proportion of single-tenant touns was already between 60 and 75 per cent, whilst high levels could also be found in Fife and Ayrshire but only in local pockets.[7] Whether long established or the product of recent changes, single tenancy was clearly well established by the 1690s. When we cross match the proportion of farms in the hands of single tenants at this point with their size, we are clearly

---

[6] Whyte, *Agriculture and Society*, 142.

[7] T. M. Devine, *The Transformation of Rural Scotland: Social Change and the Agrarian Economy 1660–1815* (Edinburgh, 1994), 9–11.

dealing with some holdings whose output must have exceeded their subsistence needs plus rent and seed. However, across the region as a whole, the larger number of tenants present in multiple-tenant touns compared to single-tenant touns meant that the majority of tenants still farmed within multiple-tenant touns. Further, the fact that multiple tenants were more numerous meant that overall average holding size per tenant was still only modest, so that the majority would still have been bound in both their thinking and practice by the pressing needs of subsistence.[8]

When we use rentals to probe more closely into the balance between multiple and single tenancy, it becomes clear that the shift from one to the other was achieved by means of a process of tenant reduction, a process which, if sustained, ultimately led to single tenancy and the removal of runrig. As a process of restructuring, it differed from that underpinning the Highland clearances only in its rate of tenant reduction, representing, as Devine put it, a 'clearance by stealth'.[9] That tenant reduction was in progress before the 1690s is supported by analyses of rental sequences for the second half of the seventeenth century.[10] How much change took place over the first half of the seventeenth century is less clear but it would be wrong to think that if we could push our perspective back still further, we would ultimately reach a point at which all touns were held by multiple tenants, thereby providing us with a *terminus post quem* for the start of the switch into single tenancy. Single-tenant touns had probably always had a presence. What happened from the 1690s onwards is more clearly defined. Tenant numbers shrank quickly over the first half of the eighteenth century, with any remaining multiple tenancies finally disappearing during the early decades of the Improving Movement. The scale of this shrinkage can be seen through rental data sampled by Devine from estates across the Lowlands. Two estates from those sampled illustrate the chronology and speed with which the rump of multiple tenancies disappeared over the first half of the century. On the Morton estate in Fife, 43 per cent of holdings were still held within multiple tenancies in the 1710s but only 3 per cent by the 1740s. Likewise, on the Douglas estate in Lanarkshire, 64 per cent were still held within multiple-tenant touns in the 1730s but this had fallen to 16 per cent by the 1750s.[11] However, unlike in Aberdeenshire, where the shift into single tenancy on the higher ground lagged behind its progress on the lower, there is a case for arguing that single tenancy may have developed sooner on the higher ground that fringed the central Lowlands or which lay in blocks across it (i.e. the Pentland Hills) than on the more fertile ground, due to the early spread of commercial sheep production.[12]

---

[8] Devine, *Transformation of Rural Scotland*, 7 and 11.

[9] Ibid., 122.

[10] Whyte, *Agriculture and Society*, 151–2.

[11] Devine, *Transformation of Rural Scotland*, 25; R. A. Dodgshon, 'The Removal of Runrig in Roxburghshire and Berwickshire 1680–1766', *Scottish Studies*, 16 (1972), 123–7.

[12] Sir John Clerk, for instance, talked about his 'wild sheep rooms' in the Penthills being in the hands of only one or two tenants from the late seventeenth century onwards, B. M. W. Third, 'The Significance of Scottish Estate Plans and Associated Documents', *Scottish Studies*, 1 (1957), 50. See also R. A. Dodgshon, 'Agricultural Change and its Social Consequences in the Southern Uplands of Scotland 1600–1780', in T. M. Devine and R. Mitchison, eds., *Ireland and Scotland 1600–1850* (Edinburgh, 1983), 46–59.

Patently, the eventual outcome of any sustained reduction in tenant numbers was a substantial increase in holding size per tenant and, ultimately, single tenancy. Where tenant reduction acted as the prime process for restructuring, it also meant that the traditional toun would have formed the basis for the farm structures that we see in the modern landscape. Admittedly, later adjustments tweaked the size of some farms either upwards through amalgamations or downwards via the detachment of blocks, so as to achieve a better size or balance of land qualities within a farm. Otherwise, amongst the larger farms that came to dominate farm structures in areas like the Merse and Lothians (2–300 acres) and Fife (1–200 acres)[13] were traditional touns recast in a modern guise, a carry-over that explains why some of the regional differences in holding size from the pre-improvement period were carried over into the post-improvement period.[14] As well as involving significant increases in farm size per tenant, the spread of single tenancy probably led to efficiency gains through the greater freedom that it afforded over decision making, especially when we add the increased private rate of return on investments in land improvement and better husbandry.

What is less clear is how the spread of single tenancy may have altered the relationship between farming and the marketplace. Prior to c.1700, many lowland tenants would have had some degree of insulation from the direct demands of the market since they paid the bulk of their rents in kind, including substantial quantities of meal, wheat, and bere (or barley). They would have been involved in the mechanics of marketing in so far as many were required to deliver their grain rents directly to a market specified by the estate,[15] and would have appreciated its price-fixing functions, but it does not follow that they were also engaged in marketing for their own profit. Devine has suggested that not only was their direct engagement with markets still modest by c.1700, but because the majority of holdings would still have been small, the typical farmer would have approached his day-to-day routines and decision making with a peasant mentality rather than as someone looking to seize market opportunities.[16] In effect, their behaviour would have been rent-responsive rather than market-responsive. His reading is persuasive, but we should keep in mind that it relies on the assumption that, beyond what was taken up for rent, used as seed or consumed as subsistence, few tenants would have had sufficient surplus left to engage in much direct marketing themselves. However, quite apart from the role played by householding, or selling what they had in surplus for what they were deficient in, we need to ask whether those tenants who were reported to have taken on significantly larger holdings, extended their arable, and borne the heavy cost of improving land with lime during the seventeenth century, would have had the incentive to do so if they did not reap some private gain from having a marketable surplus left in their own hands. That said, the low margins meant that there was still a debit

[13] J. Sinclair, *General Report of the Agricultural State, And Political Circumstances, of Scotland*, 5 vols. (Edinburgh, 1814), vol. i, 179–80.

[14] Devine, *Transformation of Rural Scotland*, 125.

[15] E.g. SRO, GD124/17/130/1, tack for oxgate land in Upper Dramalachie, 1725.

[16] Devine, *Transformation of Rural Scotland*, 15–16.

side for many tenants. Even as some were breaking out of the trinity of one to eat, one to saw, and one to pay the laird with by now adding 'and one to market', events turned against them, the poor harvests of the 1690s and early 1700s leaving many with insufficient grain for rent and subsistence, let alone profit.[17]

Whatever the degree of tenant marketing by *c.*1700, what is not in doubt is that this point saw the start of a critical shift, with lowland rents in kind undergoing a steady conversion into cash during the opening four or five decades of the eighteenth century.[18] What had previously been paid as rent in kind now had to be marketed by tenants, exposing them directly to market prices. The speed with which the shift took place suggests that it was linked to very specific changes in how landlords perceived the benefits of collecting and marketing rents in kind. One explanation may lie in the impact of poor harvests on rents during the closing years of the seventeenth and early years of the eighteenth century, harvests that left many tenants in heavy arrears. The repeated dearths that characterized the 1690s and early 1700s were as much crises of rent as they were crises of subsistence.[19] Levying rents in cash rather than kind may have been a way in which landlords could hold onto the book value of rents, at a time when harvests were low and prices high. For comparison, when prices fell sharply in the decade or so following the end of the Napoleonic Wars in 1815, some lowland landlords faced a reversed situation and responded by reintroducing grain rents.[20]

## The Divided Estate

The removal of multiple-tenant or runrig touns through a division of the various shares into separate farms has always been part of the debate, but its precise role and significance has lacked definition. In the first place, the fact that so much multiple tenancy disappeared before the 1690s should, in itself, make us wary about the part played by the *1695 act.* When we look closely at documented instances of its application, it is clear that its intended purpose was to facilitate the removal of examples involving heritors, enabling them to be divided at the instigation of any one of those involved. It had no bearing on other forms of runrig.[21] Scattered examples of these proprietary runrig touns existed across the Lowlands.

---

[17] K. J. Cullen, *Famine in Scotland—The 'ill years' of the 1690s* (Edinburgh, 2010), esp. 31–92.

[18] Devine, *Transformation of Rural Scotland*, 23–4; M. Johnstone, 'Farm Rents and Improvement: East Lothian and Lanarkshire, 1670–1830', *Agricultural History Review*, 57, Part I (2009), 45–6.

[19] K. J. Cullen, C. A. Whatley, and M. Young, 'King William's Ill Years: New Evidence on the Impact of Scarcity and Harvest Failure during the Crisis of the 1690s on Tayside', *Scottish Historical Review*, lxxxv, no. 2 (2006), 250–76.

[20] *Farmers Magazine*, xcv (1833), 365; C. Stevenson, 'On the Agriculture of the County of East Lothian', *Transactions of the Highland and Agricultural Society of Scotland*, xiv (1853), 275–324; R. S. Skirving, 'On the Agriculture of the County of East Lothian', *Transactions of the Highland and Agricultural Society of Scotland*, 4th series, vol. v (1873), 11.

[21] H. Hamilton, *An Economic History of Scotland in the Eighteenth Century* (Oxford, 1963), 57; Dodgshon, 'Removal of Runrig', 127–8; M. Gray, *The Highland Economy 1750–1850* (Edinburgh, 1957), vol. i, 66; Devine, *Transformation of Rural Scotland*, 122.

The majority were organized around feu tenure, a heritable tenure held in return for the payment of an annual feu-duty. Many originated through the feuing-out of land by the abbeys, such as those created by Paisley, Scone, Kinloss, and Inchaffray abbeys in the sixteenth century, or by border abbeys like Melrose.[22] At their foundation, some feuars agreed amongst themselves to divide these feu-touns out into separate holdings, but others elected for a runrig layout probably as a carry-over of earlier pre-feuing arrangements. Yet whether based on feuing or other forms of hereditary possession, we can find some proprietary runrig touns agreeing to a redivision out of runrig long before the *1695 act*. At Crail (Fife), the three proprietors of the farm of Boarhills, tired of the 'loss and inconvenience' of their runrig, decided in 1577 to redivide their land into consolidated shares,[23] though such early agreements were not always so straightforward.[24] The examples that survived down into the eighteenth century are likely to have been those whose occupiers could not agree over a division. Because they were executed through the local sheriff courts, those divided under the act are well documented.[25] However, we must not let this better documentation deceive us. When we compare the number of proprietary runrig touns to those based solely around tenants, they were a relatively minor subtype.

Discounting the role of the *1695 act* in the removal of runrig touns based solely around tenants does not mean that the latter were never removed by a division. It is just that the runrig intermixture of land between tenants did not require any legal process to change either the number of tenants involved or the layout of shares on the ground. Landlords were required to give notice of a tenant's removal via a summons in the local sheriff's court but, in most cases, this was merely a procedural step at the end of a tenant's tack (lease), or where they had fallen into arrears.[26] When a tenancy agreement expired, it was in the hands of the landlord to decide whether there should be a change in how a toun was laid out, though the choice over whether shares were to be divided out as runrig or as consolidated holdings was usually left to tenants.[27] In the same way, any decision to reduce tenant numbers was also in the hands of landlords. For most tenant touns, the process was bound up with normal routines for the resetting of touns. Few would even have had the pretence of ceremony that we see at Lichtnie (Angus), where the two tenants were required to choose between a fiddle and its bow in a simple lottery to decide who was to have the farm as a single tenancy.[28]

---

[22] M. H. B. Sanderson, *Scottish Rural Society in the 16th Century* (Edinburgh, 1973), 117; J. H. Romanes, 'The Kindly Tenants of the Abbey of Melrose', *Juridical Review*, li (1939), 201–16; Dodgshon, 'Removal of Runrig', 128–33.

[23] J. E. L. Murray, 'The Agriculture of Crail, 1550–1600', *Scottish Studies*, 8 (1964), 86.

[24] Whyte, *Agriculture and Society*, 149; B. M. W. Third, 'Changing Landscape and Social Structure in the Scottish Lowlands as Revealed by Eighteenth-Century Estate Plans', *Scottish Geographical Magazine*, 71 (1955), 83–93.

[25] Dodgshon, 'Removal of Runrig', 128–33.

[26] Devine, *Transformation of Rural Scotland*, 113.

[27] Whyte, *Agriculture and Society*, 149–50.

[28] F. Cruickshank, *Navar and Lethnot* (Brechin, 1899), 290. In fact, many farms around Lichtnie had been in the hands of single tenants since at least the 1720s, ibid., 338–40. For other examples, see C. Rogers, ed., *Register of Coupar Abbey*, 2 vols. (London, 1880), vol. i, 144, 188, and 200; NAS, GD225/269; Dodgshon, 'Removal of Runrig', 123 and 125.

Yet whilst the 1695 *act* played no role in the process, we can find examples of tenant runrig being removed by a division, but they were not processed through the local sheriff's court. Instead, the surveying, mapping, and evaluation of each tenant's runrig holding was carried out by the estate, though such rig-by-rig surveys of tenant runrig were relatively rare.[29] Those instances where it led to a division based on what tenants had earlier held in runrig probably involved tenants or families whose occupation had been long-standing and whose runrig shares had ceased to be subject to reallocation, the latter perhaps being in acknowledgement of the former. We know that some tenants claimed the enduring occupation of their holdings on the basis of kindly tenure, but few made such claims by the late seventeenth century. Margaret Sanderson's study of tenures during the sixteenth and early seventeenth centuries found families in possession of the same holding for over a century,[30] but a tenant finding favour because 'his father, grandfather, and forbears have been their [*sic*] since memory of man'[31] is more difficult to find by the latter part of the seventeenth century. A detailed study of tenant stability on the Panmure estate (Angus) during the second half of the seventeenth century showed that only 18 per cent of tenants had possession of their land for more than eighteen years.[32] Of course, some divisions of tenant runrig may have stemmed from the fact that wadsets (grants of land as security for a debt) were involved or, as on the Stobhall estate in Perthshire where runrig survived late into 1780s, parts may have been life-rented,[33] so that each tenant's right of claim had to be carefully accounted for in the new order. In fact, once long leases were involved, carrying out a detailed pro rata division of runrig shares into consolidated holdings may have been seen, whatever its cost, as a means by which new farm structures could be established quickly. Even so, as a means of removing tenant runrig touns, such divisions were the exception not the rule.

## The Persistence of Small Farms

Analyses of touns prior to improvement have shown that small tenant farmers dominated the Scottish countryside everywhere. The widespread role played by tenant reduction would suggest that the gradual disappearance of these small farmers was a predominant feature of the structural changes that took place in the decades prior to the Improving Movement and during its early stages. However, we must not usher the small lowland farmer offstage too quickly. Whilst the division of tenant runrig touns via a division process played only a small part in the structural changes of the seventeenth and

[29] For Dalmahoy, see SRO, RHP1021; Third, 'The Significance of Scottish Estate Plans', 51–3. For divisions, see Hamilton, *Economic History of Scotland*, 62–3.

[30] Sanderson, *Scottish Rural Society*, 131.

[31] A. Miller, ed., *The Glamis Book of Record*, 1st series, xi (Edinburgh, 1890), 98–9.

[32] D. Whyte and K. A. Whyte, 'Continuity and Change in a Seventeenth-Century Scottish Farming Community', *Agricultural History Review*, 32 (1984), 162.

[33] A. Wight, *Present State of Husbandry in Scotland*, 3 vols. (Edinburgh, 1778), vol. i, 24–9.

eighteenth centuries, estates did reorganize many such touns into small–medium consolidated farms, but with no attempt to match the number of new farms created to the
number of tenants who had shared the toun in runrig or to reaccommodate those who
had previously held land under runrig. It was a form of division but only in a generalized
way, the details of any earlier runrig layout being ignored in the creation of new farms.[34]
Such generalized divisions probably took place where landlords wanted to avoid the
large farm units produced by allowing entire touns to pass into the hands of a single tenant. This was especially the case in areas like the western Lowlands and north-east
Scotland, where specialized cattle breeding and rearing were important and where small
to medium-sized farms were deemed viable, enabling good tenants to draw on sufficient
capital to stock them.[35]

The creation of small to medium-sized farms via the generalized reorganization of
touns was similar in its effects to the laying out of small farms and smallholdings on
waste ground. Low-ground muirs were common across the Lowlands. Many were small,
irregular patches of moss or nutrient-poor soils that broke up the arable of most pre-
improvement touns and which became a target of land-reclamation schemes (i.e. draining, liming, marling) during the early stages of improvement, as farmers tried to create
more regular and uniform blocks of arable and pasture. Others were more extensive
areas of waste ground that had been used as common grazings, some positioned entirely
within an estate but others—the commonties—shared between different estates or landowners. Though we can find quite large farms being created out of these former grazings
as estates took steps to privatize them over the second half of the eighteenth and early
nineteenth centuries, many landowners and their agents saw them as an opportunity to
create regimented arrays of small farms or lots. Estates saw these smallholdings as a
cheap form of land improvement, one that substituted labour for capital. In some cases,
these schemes of muir or mossland colonization would have functioned as a form of
internal social budgeting for estates, with the colonization of reclaimable land being
seen as a way of absorbing some of those displaced by tenant reduction elsewhere on the
estate, thereby conserving some of the estate's social capital.

We need only look at the size and sheer number of muirs or mosses that were
reclaimed across the Lowlands over the eighteenth and early nineteenth centuries to
appreciate the extent to which they will have served to absorb some of those displaced
elsewhere. The muir at Cowie in Stirlingshire was typical. When divided out of commonty in 1760, all the large proprietors who received shares laid out their newly divided
portions in small lots.[36] Other landlords took advantage of mossland reclamation
schemes, like those who endowed the so-called 'moss-lairds' settled on mossland in

---

[34] References to 'divisions' of tenant runrig are mostly generalized divisions, e.g. A. Geddes,
'Changes in Rural Life and Landscape, 1500–1950', in *Scientific Survey of South-Eastern Scotland*
(Edinburgh, 1961), 127; I. H. Adams, *The Mapping of a Scottish Estate* (Edinburgh, 1971), 15–19.

[35] *Old Statistical Account of Scotland* [hereafter *OSA*], viii, 490; see also 263 and 403.

[36] J. Macdonald, 'On the Agriculture of the Counties of Forfar and Kincardine', *Transactions of the
Highland and Agricultural Society of Scotland*, 4th series, xiii (1881), 11.

Airth parish in Stirlingshire, most of whom possessed only a handful of acres.[37] The controlled creation of smallholdings on muir ground was a particular feature of eighteenth- and early nineteenth-century farm restructuring in the north-east.[38] Along with the smaller farms created by the generalized division of runrig touns, the eruption of smallholdings on muirs and mosses gave parts of the north-east as significant a presence of them as were to be found in what later became the so-called crofting counties.[39] Yet though their presence in the north-east increased markedly over the second half of the eighteenth century, smallholdings did not originate at this point. During the harvest failures that characterized King William's lean years in the 1690s and early 1700s, some tenants faced with accumulating rent arrears were said to have abandoned their holdings and to have solved their subsistence problems by squatting on muir ground. Extant surveys for the area suggest small farms or smallholdings continued to be 'newly taken in' from the waste ground throughout the eighteenth century.[40] Against this background, we can see the surge in their creation during the late eighteenth and early nineteenth centuries as replacing earlier uncoordinated efforts at the establishment of smallholdings with their controlled top-down creation by estates.

## The Social Consequences of Restructuring in the Lowlands

These different approaches to the restructuring of lowland touns clearly had different social consequences. Whilst we can find touns in which tenant numbers were reduced with some of the suddenness and manifest social collapse that were a feature of the Highland clearances, many single-tenant touns in the Lowlands appear to have been the product of a gradual, step-wise process of tenant reduction, whose conversion to single tenancy can be tracked across a number of rentals. Of course, the impact of even a gradual conversion was still one of fewer tenants. Some indication of just how fewer lies in the widespread references to the amalgamation of holdings and the shrinkage of the farming community in the parish reports of the *Old Statistical Account* (hereafter *OSA*).[41] However, the parish reporters were not the most reliable of witnesses to what had been happening.[42] Too often, they fail to make it clear to what type of occupier (tenants, sub-tenants, or cottars) they were referring and whether the amalgamation being referred to was brought about by tenant reduction within multiple-tenant touns or through the

---

[37] J. Tait, 'The Agriculture of the County of Stirling', *Transactions of the Highland and Agricultural Society of Scotland*, 4th series, xvi (1884), 150 and 172.

[38] Devine, *Transformation of Rural Scotland*, 133–4.

[39] D. Turnock, 'Small Farms in North Scotland: An Exploration in Historical Geography', *Scottish Geographical Magazine*, 91, no. 3 (1975), 164–81.

[40] G. S. Keith, *A General View of the Agriculture of Aberdeenshire* (Aberdeen, 1811), 143, 151–2, and 154; J. G. Mitchie, ed., *The Records of Invercauld* (Aberdeen: New Spalding club, 1901), 138; V. Gaffney, *The Lordship of Strathavon* (Aberdeen: Third Spalding club, 1960), 99, 130; NAS, RHP1824.

[41] Typical OSA references to farm amalgamations can be found in *OSA*, i, 1791, 163, 319–20; iii, 1792, 468 and 547; 1793, viii, 112–13.

[42] Devine, *Transformation of Rural Scotland*, 112.

amalgamation of small consolidated farms. Further, for many, the key structural changes would not have been within their living memory. In fact, what stands out about the whole process of tenant reduction within lowland areas is that despite being an ongoing feature of landholding across a century or more, there is a dearth of contemporary comment about it as opposed to retrospective comment, other than that provided by estate documentation. This dearth probably reflects the fact that as well as being only one—admittedly the most important—of a number of means by which the old order was transformed into the new, tenant reduction unfolded in a 'relatively painless' way,[43] occurring at a pace that enabled those displaced to be absorbed back into the farming community as cottars, labourers, tradesmen, and the like, some in the newly created estate villages; as smallholders on the many lots newly carved out of muir ground; or into nearby urban centres. Arguably, it was this combination, the gradual rather than sudden release of tenants en masse coupled with the presence of local opportunities for establishing new forms of subsistence, that explains why tenant reduction in the Lowlands, though socially challenging and disruptive, did not lead to unrest or any form of direct action.

Trying to explain what happened to those tenants and subtenants displaced by tenant reduction is only part of the problem. We also need to ask how processes like tenant reduction affected the cottar. If we look at the problem in the seventeenth century, when the switch into single tenancy still had some way to run, most multiple-tenant touns had cottars. The poll-tax returns for the 1690s enable us to see what was happening to them as multiple-tenant touns were reduced to single tenancy. The answer is that initially most appear to have been absorbed by the labour needs of the new single-tenant farm. In Aberdeenshire, for example, the number of cottars on single-tenant farms equalled those that had existed in multiple-tenant touns.[44] Analysis of the poll-tax returns elsewhere also suggests that cottars remained widespread in those areas that had made the greatest progress in the switch to single tenancy, accounting for between a quarter and one third of the total rural community.[45] In fact, given the extent to which multiple-tenant touns would have used family labour as well as that of their cottars, there is a case for arguing that single-tenant farms, with the labour of only a single family, needed more cottars. On the face of it, the shift from multiple to single tenancy does not appear, in itself, to have been sufficient to undermine the position of cottars.

If anything, the new husbandries that spread across the Lowlands from the 1750s onwards raised labour demands, adding new tasks like weeding, hoeing, hedging, and marling to farm routines and making more use of labour across the farming year. The point is well made by the fact that at the height of what one local writer called 'high pressure farming' in the 1840s, a farm like East Barns in east Lothian had a total on-the-farm population of 150, of whom 45 were farm servants occupying 24 cottages, making it a

[43] Ibid., 113–14.
[44] Whyte, *Agriculture and Society*, 139 and 145; Dodgshon, 'Agricultural Change and its Social Consequences', 56–7.
[45] Devine, *Transformation of Rural Scotland*, 13–14 and 140.

community as sizeable as any pre-improvement toun.[46] Yet despite this enlarged need for labour, late eighteenth- and early nineteenth-century commentators widely reported that cottar numbers fell sharply over the second half of the eighteenth century. Estate documents bear this out, with cottars disappearing from the rental record. Devine cites the example of Inverdovart on the Tayfield estate in Fife. With as many as thirteen cottars in the early seventeenth century, all trace of them had disappeared by the early nineteenth century.[47] For some, their disappearance was manifest through the way many of the cottages assigned to cottars now lay abandoned. What lay behind this apparent shrinkage were shifts in how farm labour was contracted rather than in the amount of farm labour needed. With the onset of the Improving Movement, farming increasingly relied on wage-based day labour, with the wider support traditionally provided for cottars (access to arable, grazing rights) being stripped out of the contract. At a time when innovation was changing the character of farming, the improving farmer sought close control over his arable and grass resources. Enclosure was part of that control, but removing the cottar's interest in a rig or two of arable and his or her right to contribute to the farm herd or flock was another. These were significant savings. In one estimate, that for the Rossie estate (Fife), cottars were said to have occupied 20 per cent of infield land.[48] Changes also took place in how labour was housed. The provision of cot-towns or cottages for cottars disappeared. At a time when many farmers moved out of their old ferm-toun clusters to more substantially built houses on their newly consolidated farms, shedding responsibility for the burden of cottar housing must have appealed. However, other solutions emerged. Former cottars, as well as former tenants and subtenants, were amongst those who settled in the planned estate villages that now emerged across the Lowlands.[49] The trade or servicing functions that lay behind their foundation made them attractive to cottars who had previously practised a trade or craft and who could still provide farm labour at peak times of the year. Some farms, however, clung to on-the-farm provision but in a way that reduced the scale of their obligation, as with the chaumer and bothy systems in Fife and Angus and the bothy system in the north-east. The former developed across both Fife and Angus and involved a separate accommodation block alongside the farm for unmarried male farm servants, with meals being provided within the farmhouse. The bothy system developed across the north-east and was based around an on-the-farm dormitory block, but the farm servants housed under it ate separately from the farmer and his family. Further, though the bothy system involved unmarried servants, married men were also present but forced to live away from their families.[50]

---

[46] H. M. Jenkins, 'Report on Some Features of Scottish Agriculture', *Journal of the Royal Agricultural Society of England*, 2nd series, vii (1871), 164.

[47] Devine, *Transformation of Rural Scotland*, 140–1.

[48] Wight, *Present State*, vol. i, 356.

[49] T. C. Smout, 'The Landowners and the Planned Village', in N. T. Philipson and R. Mitchison, *Scotland in the Age of Improvement* (Edinburgh, 1970), 73–106: D. G. Lockhart, 'The Planned Villages', in M. L. Parry and T. R. Slater, eds., *The Making of the Scottish Countryside* (London, 1980), 249–70.

[50] Keith, *General View of the Agriculture of Aberdeenshire*, 515; I. Carter, *Farm Life in Northeast Scotland, 1840–1914* (Edinburgh, 1979), 98–136.

# THE SOUTHERN UPLANDS

Like many toun economies elsewhere in Scotland prior to the mid-eighteenth century, those of the Southern Uplands were essentially mixed farm economies but, compared to the highly integrated farm economies that emerged later with the adoption of turnips and sown grasses, the arable and livestock sectors of the pre-improvement toun were only loosely coupled. Animals provided manure for arable but not on the scale that became possible with turnips and sown grasses. Likewise, from an arable perspective, no fodder crops were grown but autumn fodder was provided through stubble grazing. Figures compiled by the Buccleuch estate relating to touns in the central part of the Southern Uplands provide a glimpse of this mixed economy. The data was compiled to show farm losses following the bad harvests of the early 1680s. Revealingly, they show grain losses to be as much a factor as stock losses, even for areas like Ettrick and Teviotdalehead. Yet what also comes across from the data is the scale of the sheep-farming enterprises that had been established by the 1680s, with quite a number maintaining flocks of over five hundred sheep and some having over one thousand. As with contemporary rentals, the listings show around 50 per cent of farms as in the hands of single tenants.[51] The presence of large flocks and single tenancies measure how far the Southern Uplands had responded to growing market demand even by the 1680s. It was well primed to make such a response. Even whilst being maintained as a royal forest back in the sixteenth century, 'stedes' in Ettrick were used for farm stock alongside hunting.[52] Given this early involvement in stock farming, it is hardly surprising that following its deforestation and the setting of these 'stedes' to single tenants for a cash rent, specialist stock production was seen as the means for raising such cash. When we find Edinburgh lawyers buying local farms in the wake of the bankruptcies that followed the 1680s losses and then reorganizing them into specialist sheep-producing units,[53] it would not be unreasonable to suppose that they were following an example that had already been set by then. That said, the decades following the crises of the early 1680s undoubtedly saw a rising demand for sheep and wool from the area, and may have set off a new round of toun restructuring in response.

The rise of commercial sheep farming on the higher ground of southern Scotland can be matched by the rise of commercial cattle farming in the south-west. Initially, the flow of cattle across the border to English markets was as much about Irish cattle as about locally reared stock. Following the restrictions placed on Irish cattle imports in the 1680s, farmers in the south-west, from Carrick round to Galloway, appeared to have taken up the slack in supply. By the closing years of the seventeenth century,

---

[51] NAS, GD 224/243/7; GD224/283/1; GD224/937/15.

[52] J. M. Gilbert, *Hunting and Hunting Reserves in Medieval Scotland* (Edinburgh, 1979), 267.

[53] E. S. Richards, *A History of the Highland Clearances: Agrarian Transformation and the Evictions 1746–1886* (London, 1982), 165.

many were heavily involved in supplying cattle fattened for the English market, especially in Galloway. Two features stand out about involvement in this trade. The first
was the involvement of landowners in the development of the trade, including major
landowners like the Earl of Galloway. The second was the way it was developed around
the establishment of large enclosures or parks. Some were simply the parks around
mansions given an extra purpose. Others were custom-made. The park established by
Sir David Dunbar at Baldone in 1682, what one seventeenth-century source described
as 'the mother of all the rest', extended to over 1,800 acres.[54] This was cattle farming on
a ranch-like scale, one that must have led to the dispossession of many tenants and
cottars. In time, the development of cattle rearing in the area encouraged landowners
and their tenants also to enclose what had been open or common grazing ground. The
clearance of touns to create grazing farms, along with the growing restriction on what
could be grazed, fed into the violence of 1723–4, when 'levellers' in Galloway pulled
down some of the dykes that had been built in parishes like Keltony Buittle, Rerrick,
Twynholm, and Tongland.[55] Order was quickly restored, but this direct action against
dykes and farm restructuring raises questions about why such violent opposition to
restructuring erupted here. In comparison, there are no signs of unrest occurring to
the east, in the main body of the Southern Uplands, during the wave of tenant reductions and restructuring that occurred over the closing decades of the seventeenth century. Admittedly, there had been a significant presence of single tenancy since the
deforestation of Ettrick whilst the tenant reductions that followed the storms and
financial losses of the early 1680s, when single tenancies became even more widespread, were probably met with resignation over their misfortune rather than opposition to a landlord-driven process of dispossession. Further, by c.1700, the growth of
domestic industry in counties like Selkirkshire helped to ease some communities
through the transition. By comparison, if we are looking for those local factors that
helped to separate out the plight of the Levellers, then three stand out. First, prominent amongst those who imparked land and who farmed the parks created were landlords. Second, quite apart from the symbolism attached to the physical enclosure of
land at a time when enclosure was still a rarity, some of the cattle parks created took in
what had been common grazing lands, so that the resource base of local farms was
squeezed by their creation. Third, many of the local farmers who stood to lose vital
access to such grazings were small cattle farmers or drovers whose stock would have
involved considerable financial outlay and risk. Somewhere amidst the interplay
between these three factors probably lay the trigger for the destruction of the Galloway
park dykes.

[54] W. Macfarlane, *Geographical Collections Relating to Scotland. Made by W. Macfarlane, part ii*
(Edinburgh: Scottish History Society, 1907), lii, 107.

[55] T. MacLelland, 'On the Agriculture of the Stewartry of Kirkudbright and Wigtownshire,
*Transactions of the Highland and Agricultural Society of Scotland*, 4th series, xvii (1975), 33; Whyte,
*Agriculture and Society*, 125; I. L. Donnachie and I. MacLeod, eds., *Old Galloway* (Newton Abbott,
1974), 48–60.

# The Highlands and Islands

Whilst the Highlands no longer has exclusive claim to the clearances as the means by which traditional pre-improvement touns were transformed into what became the foundations of the modern farm layout, it still remains the part of Scotland where they had their most dramatic impact. Even here though, there are qualifications to be made. Some highland touns were already in the hands of single tenants by *c*.1700, long before specialized sheep farms developed.[56] Admittedly, in the Hebrides and along the western seaboard especially, a substantial proportion of touns were held by tacksmen, many of whom sublet the bulk of their holding to subtenants so that, on the ground, these appeared as typical multiple-tenant touns.[57] However, some touns were kept in hand by tacksmen and farmed using cottars. Change for these touns was simply about deciding when to switch to sheep, a relatively straightforward switch if they were already treated as 'grass rooms', or farms specializing in cattle.[58] Elsewhere, when restructuring was carried out, a clearance was the prime means used but, as Margaret Storrie demonstrated in her work on Islay, other forms of restructuring were also employed.[59] Further, as her work also demonstrated, restructuring was not always a singular point or moment of change. Many touns or farms passed through successive phases of restructuring as conditions and expectations changed.

## Sheep and the Clearances

Amongst those touns that were set directly to multiple tenants, the prime—if not the only—strategy chosen by estates was to reduce them to single tenancy via a clearance event, or what one writer has called an 'expulsive clearance',[60] so as to make way for sheep. The earliest of such clearances took place in the 1750s in the southern Highlands. They can be seen as the northwards extension of a process that had already been running for a century or more in the Southern Uplands, with the expansion of market demand for sheep now drawing in yet more suppliers. Seeing it as the continuation of an expansion that had earlier swept across the Southern Uplands is given added support by the fact

---

[56] R. A. Dodgshon, *From Chiefs to Landlords: Social and Economic Change in the Western Highlands and Islands c.1493–1820* (Edinburgh, 1998), 128–30 and 135.

[57] Ibid., 93–5; E. R. Cregeen, 'Tacksmen and their Successors: A Study of Tenurial Reorganization in Mull, Morvern and Tiree in the Early Eighteenth Century', *Scottish Studies*, 13 (1969), 94–102; F. J. Shaw, *The Northern and Western Islands of Scotland* (Edinburgh, 1980), 48–57.

[58] Examples of 'rooms' can be found in NAS, GD1129/1/3/45, a commentary on the set of farms in Netherlorn compiled in the 1730s.

[59] M. C. Storrie, 'Landholdings and Settlement Evolution in West Highland Scotland', *Geografiska Annaler*, 43 (1965), 138–61.

[60] F. McKichan, 'Lord Seaforth and Highland Estate Management in the First Phase of Clearance 1783–1815', *Scottish Historical Review*, 1, vol. lxxxvi (2007), 50.

that whilst some local tenants, especially in the south-east Highlands, did make the transition from being runrig tenants to sheep farmers, many of those who pioneered the spread of sheep farming in the Highlands were drawn from southern Scotland. John Campbell, the farmer who replaced four runrig tenants in the Dunbartonshire toun of Glenovoe in 1754 and who was reputed to be the first large-scale sheep farmer in the area, previously farmed in Annandale in Dumfries-shire.[61] His background was comparable to many others from the Southern Uplands who took sheep farms over the second half of the eighteenth century. In short, it was not just the demand for sheep that drove expansion, but also, the demand for land from would-be tenants whose experience in the Southern Uplands made them acutely aware of the burgeoning market opportunities. Their vision of the economic possibilities contrasted with that of commentators like Andrew Wight, who, in 1775, argued that 'very probably after doing mischief to themselves', those who converted the Highlands to sheep 'will return to black cattle'.[62]

Unlike the gradual reduction in tenant numbers that we see in many lowland touns, the Highland clearances generally involved a sudden collapse of tenant numbers and of the community fashioned around them, with touns being cleared and reset in a single act of restructuring. Heightening this sense of social collapse was the fact that many highland touns were fairly crowded affairs, developed around a bustling mix of tenants, subtenants, and cottars. A 1775 survey of Cromarty referred to 'a considerable Number of Sub-tennants, Maillers & Cottagers on this Estate and particularly in the Barony of Coigach',[63] but it was the same everywhere. Some were larger than their low-ground counterparts, as Ian Whyte found when he compared tenant numbers in touns in the upper part of Glen Muick (Aberdeenshire) with those in the lower part.[64] In addition, many appear pressed hard against their arable resources. Some highland landowners had long been happy to pack their estates with would-be followers, clansmen, and potential military recruits. For their part, highland communities had a tendency to consume rather than trade their surpluses, adding extra mouths rather than extra profit. In time, this became a critical factor in northern and north-western coastal areas where the extra subsistence per acre yielded by the spread of the potato, the extra income provided by the development of kelp manufacture, and the extra income and subsistence provided by fishing meant that many communities grew rapidly over the late eighteenth century and opening decades of the nineteenth. Even inland, use of the potato and the rising price of stock helped to release some of the constraints that had bound traditional toun economies, though growth was less than in coastal communities. By the end of the Napoleonic Wars in 1815, the collapse of the kelp trade plunged many coastal touns into crisis. In addition, falls in the price of stock and grain, poor harvests, and the first signs of the potato's vulnerability to disease not only deepened the subsistence problems of coastal areas but also spread the problems

[61] J. A. S. Watson, 'The Rise and Development of the Sheep Industry in the Highlands and North of Scotland', *Transactions of the Highland and Agricultural Society of Scotland*, 5th series, xliv (1932), 6–8.

[62] Wight, *Present State*, vol. ii, 40.

[63] NAS, E746/73; V. Wills, ed., *Statistics of the Annexed Estates 1755–1756* (Edinburgh, 1973), 30–75.

[64] Whyte, *Agriculture and Society*, 143.

inland.[65] Given the growth of extra numbers and development of acute subsistence problems ahead of the main wave of clearances, it is not surprising that what took place in the far north and north-west, much more so than what happened in the southern Highlands, came to define the clearances as a large-scale and draconian removal of tenants.

We can highlight some of these differences by comparing what happened in the southern Highlands, where the clearances were mostly concentrated before 1800, with what happened in the north and north-west Highlands, where the main clearances were largely if not entirely a post-1800 event. In the former, most multiple-tenant touns were modestly sized. Only the more favourably endowed could boast more than 30–40 acres plus access to more than 500 acres of hill ground. When cleared, these formed only small to medium-sized sheep farms and it is not surprising that we find estates joining farms together, not just to have a better balance between wintering and summering ground, but also so as to achieve a larger, more viable size. As runrig communities, most averaged no more than four to six tenants, plus subtenants and cottagers or cottars, though locally, we can find much larger communities.[66] In some cases, we can recover exact figures for groups that normally lie hidden, like cottars. Listing for Netherlorn in Argyll, for instance, reveals seventeen out of the twenty-five touns had cottars, averaging 2.78 per toun.[67] Yet even when we take the number of cottars present into account, they appear fewer in number when compared to those in touns to the north and north-west. Further, when we look at those that experienced a clearance event, the impact of change was lessened in one of three ways. First, some estates responded to the early opportunities for sheep farming by detaching hill pasture or shieling ground from touns and creating sheep farms out of them rather than by clearing the core of touns.[68] Second, we find some of the conversions to commercial sheep farms were initially held as a joint tenancy.[69] This ongoing presence of tenant partnerships probably reflected the considerable start-up costs involved in stocking such farms. Third, not only did some sheep farms maintain sizeable arable sectors, but many in the southern and central Highlands continued to maintain a fold of cattle (= herd of c.20 cows) down to the 1840–50s, when an increase in sheep and wool prices led to a renewed surge in sheep numbers.[70]

---

[65]  Gray, *Highland Economy 1750–1850*, 181–90.

[66]  Dodgshon, *From Chiefs to Landlords*, 128–30.

[67]  GD112/9/1/3/48; Dodgshon, *From Chiefs to Landlords*, 138 and 155. At the other extreme, Davoch of Clachan in Strathglass was reported to have eleven farmers plus twelve cottars when it was cleared in 1801–3; see *Evidence Taken by the Royal Commissioners of Inquiry on the Condition of Crofters and Cottars in the Highlands of Scotland*, Irish University Press, Parliamentary Series [hereafter IUP, PS], vol. 22 (1969; 1884), vol. 25, 2,768.

[68]  D. Turnock, *Patterns of Highland Development* (London, 1970), 25; Gaffney, *Lordship of Strathavon*, 29–31.

[69]  E.g. NAS, GD112/12/1/3/26. There was in fact a variant to this joint occupation of sheep farms. Some estates created sheep farms but set them to joint or multiple tenants who had previously held then in runrig. This happened in Glenshiel when the Seaforth estate created six sheep farms in 1801 and set them to former runrig tenants, grouping between two to four tenants back in each new farm, McKickan (2007), 53–4. See also P. Gaskell, *Morvern Transformed: A Highland Parish in the Nineteenth Century* (Cambridge, 1968), 51–2, 235–6.

[70]  R. A. Dodgshon, 'Livestock Production in the Scottish Highlands Before and After the Clearances', *Rural History*, Part I, 9 (1998), 30 and 32.

When we look at the experience of the northern and north-west Highlands, we can draw out a number of differences. Toun size here was more varied, but locally there were some very large toun communities. The presence of these larger touns had two consequences. It meant that when large-scale sheep production began to spread rapidly through the area in the 1800s, the clearances that ran ahead of it displaced large numbers of people. This can be illustrated by the 'several thousand' cleared, 1814–16, from the interior straths of Sutherland, including Strathnaver, followed by the 3,331 people removed from touns in the parishes of Kildonan, Lairg, and Rogart in 1819.[71] The organization of sheep farming in these northern Highlands emphasized this gap between what existed before and after. The sheep farms created were physically much larger than elsewhere. Many of the pre-clearance touns on which sheep farms were based were physically more extensive than those in the southern Highlands. Also, not only did they start off with larger base units, the sheep holdings created often embraced groups of former pre-clearance touns so as to create vast working units. Donald and William Mackay, for instance, built a holding of over 150,000 acres from an initial base at Melness in Sutherland. Others captured their sheer scale by computing them in ways that were thought more striking, so that Greig of Tulloch was described as having '100 square miles under sheep' whilst the Cameron of Corychvilly's holdings annually clipped 37,000 sheep.[72] As a list of shepherds and hirsels for part of the Sutherland estate makes clear, the organization of these vast multi-farm enterprises emphasized the depopulation brought about by sheep farming, since former touns were now grouped together into single continuous sheep farms; each one was subdivided into a small number of hirsels, with each hirsel being managed by a single shepherd and made up of an area of pasture to which a flock was attached, or hefted.[73] Where multiple tenancies were reduced to single tenancies in lowland touns, ongoing labour needs still meant that the farm community could be quite large. On the vast sheep holdings that emerged in the far north of the Highlands, however, whole touns could be replaced simply by a single shepherd and his family, except at shearing time. Without doubt, the scale and starkness of this social transition, with large thriving communities giving way to the solitude of the shepherd, helped to fuel the social tensions and confrontations that underpinned some of the clearances.

The events surrounding the clearances in Strathnaver were especially significant in publicizing what was happening and their social cost to a much wider audience. Though the Sutherland estate orchestrated its clearances in a planned way, with tenants offered

---

[71] E. S. Richards, 'Structural Change in a Regional Economy: Sutherland and the Industrial Revolution, 1780–1830', *Economic History Review*, xxvi (1973), 71.

[72] J. Macdonald, 'On the Agriculture of the County of Sutherland', *Transactions of the Highland and Agricultural Society of Scotland*, 4th series, xii (1880), 24 and 63; M. Bangor-Jones, 'Sheep Farming in Sutherland in the Eighteenth Century', *Agricultural History Review*, 50 (2002), 181–202. A good illustration of how former runrig touns were combined into a single working unit is provided by the Valamoss in Lochs parish, the first sheep farm on Lewis. It was created in 1803 by combining six former touns together; see McKickan (AQ), 'Lord Seaforth and Highland Estate Management', 60.

[73] NLS, Sutherland MSS, 313/993; NSA, xiv, 1845, 504.

crofts that had been newly laid out along the coast, most with facilities added to provide supplementary sources of income from fishing and other activities, the heavy-handed and brutal way in which some clearances in Strathnaver were executed in 1814 led one of the duke's agents or under-factors, Patrick Sellar, to be charged with culpable homicide.[74] He was, in the event, cleared of the charge, but the evidence presented, and the wider debate surrounding the trial, changed perceptions not just within the mind of the highland community but also within that of the public at large. As well as being an agent for the estate, responsible for collecting rents from the tenants in Strathnaver, Sellar was also the person who had bid successfully to convert the Strathnaver touns into a sheep farm. He was therefore, the person charged with issuing the orders of eviction when the tacks in placed expired in 1814 as well as being the beneficiary of those evictions. Though a self-interested man, he acted cautiously over the evictions, negotiating different times of removal for those who were to be given new lots on the coast according to their circumstances. In practice, the different arrangements put in place led to confusion over what precisely was happening. When we add in the estate's policy of excluding from new lots those whom it deemed to be troublesome, we can understand why some removals became moments of tension and confrontation. To those reading contemporary newspaper reports of the trial in Edinburgh and London, references to houses being pulled down would have seemed to confirm the brutality that surrounded the Strathnaver removals, even though tenants in the region had themselves routinely stripped out the roof timbers and doors on their removal from a tenancy.[75] The problem for Sellar was that the heavy-handedness with which some clearances in Strathnaver were carried out led to the death of an elderly woman. Yet arguably, what propelled Strathnaver into the headlines was the way in which this personal tragedy and the drama of a trial for a duke's agent were combined with circumstances that encapsulated the extremes of the clearances as a process, with a significant number of busy, well-settled touns being replaced by a single extensive sheep farm, the tack for which lay in the hands of the very person charged with managing their clearance!

## The Role of Division

Whilst the wholesale clearance of touns was the prime means by which highland touns were restructured, and certainly the means that generated most reaction and controversy, it was not the only means. As in the Lowlands, some highland touns were reorganized into small, compact farms using a generalized form of division. These had favour during the early stages of change in the Highlands. There was a good reason for this. When highland estates, including the commissioners for the forfeited estates, first began

[74] E. S. Richards, *The Highland Clearances* (Edinburgh, 2009), 178–89.

[75] See, for example, R. A. Dodgshon, 'West Highland and Hebridean Settlement Prior to Crofting and the Clearances: A Study in Stability or Change?', *Proceedings of the Society of Antiquaries of Scotland*, 123 (1993), 423.

to address the problem of how to restructure traditional touns in the mid-eighteenth century, excess numbers were not yet considered a pressing issue and small to medium-sized farms were still considered viable holdings when laid out as consolidated holdings. Such schemes produced farms that were much smaller than sheep farms.[76] In time, as market conditions changed and as numbers grew, their size proved their undoing. Some estates responded by carrying out a subsequent round of amalgamations, as happened on the Perthshire section of the Breadalbane estate in the 1830s.[77] The Argyll estate responded differently, at least as regards its Mull and Tiree farms. Its initial attempt to reorganize runrig touns into medium-sized, consolidated farms of a standard size, its so-called four-mail land policy, was designed to keep a reasonable number of tenants (roughly, four per toun) on the land.[78] However, increasing population, the growing problem of what the estate called its supernumeries, soon made the holdings created inadequate for the growing numbers on the estate, and a new reorganization was deemed necessary. Through this second reorganization, what emerged were smaller croft-sized holdings based on crofting townships. In effect, the initial reorganization had served as a stepping stone to the emergence of crofting townships.[79] Second thoughts on restructuring were also a feature of change in Morar in Inverness-shire. After the Earl of Moray, its owner, came of age in 1827, its various touns were quickly restructured into a graded mix of small and medium-sized farms as well as large sheep farms, the guiding principle being that such a grading enabled tenants with modest capital to progress up the farming ladder. In fact, this initial reorganization proved unsuccessful and the estate responded by carrying out a new restructuring in 1879, downsizing some and enlarging others so as to create a simple bimodal pattern of small crofts, as at Mallaig, and large sheep farms, like Kinlochmorar,[80] a pattern ultimately repeated throughout the western and northern Highlands.

Instances where estates carried out a full division of runrig, reallocating runrig shares into consolidated holdings on a pro rata basis, were not common in the Highlands and Islands. Even in the mid-eighteenth century, most of the smaller holdings, especially along the western seaboard and in the Hebrides, were still held on a year-to-year basis. If we add the fact that many touns still carried out an annual reallocation of runrig shares, then we can understand why formal divisions of tenant runrig were deemed unneces-sary when estates came to restructure them. Those subjected to formal divisions, includ-ing quite a number on the Gordon estate in Inverness-shire and the Lovat estate in

[76] M. Gray, 'The Abolition of Runrig in the Highlands of Scotland', *Economic History Review*, 2nd series, v (1952–3), 51; Gaffney, *Lordship of Strathavon*, 19; A. H. Millar, ed., *A Selection of Scottish Forfeited Estates Papers 1715:1745* (Edinburgh: Scottish History Society, 1909), lvii, 236; NAS, GD112/12/1/2/36 and 37; NAS, GD112/12/1/2/14; NAS, RHP972/2 and 5.

[77] Gray, 'Abolition of Runrig', 52. See also M. C. Storrie, 'Landholdings and Population in Arran from the Late Eighteenth Century', *Scottish Studies*, 11 (1967), 61.

[78] E. R. Cregeen, *Argyll Estate Instructions: Mull, Morvern, Tiree 1771–1805*, 4th series, i (Edinburgh: Scottish History Society), 1964), 23, 58–9, 197–8.

[79] Ibid., xxxi, 67–9 and esp. 73–4.

[80] D. Turnock, 'North Morar—The Improving Movement on a West Highland Estate', *Scottish Geographical Magazine*, 85 (1969), 17–30.

Inverness-shire and Ross and Cromarty, were the exception.[81] In normal circumstances, such divisions were carried out only where runrig had been underpinned by a long-term stability of layout, such as where it was based on feuars or heritors, like those to be found along the eastern side of the Highlands, for example, at Dingwall (Ross and Cromarty).[82] Taking the Highlands and Islands as a whole, most examples of proprietary runrig divided by legal process were in the Northern Isles, especially Shetland. They involved heritors of different sorts, including some who held their land heritably by odal or udal tenure, the law introduced by the Norse. Most were not divided until the nineteenth century and, in a few cases, not until the twentieth century.[83]

## The Genealogy of Crofting Townships

Crofts were an old-established unit of landholding, the term long being used to describe small, consolidated holdings that functioned as service holdings attached to mills, ale-houses, etcetera, or as holdings assigned to high-status farm servants like ploughmen. Their renewed creation from the late eighteenth century onwards did not alter their definition as a small, consolidated arable holding, with defined grazing rights, but it did rework the concept into a plural form by creating what became the crofting township. These township clusters were laid out in a planned grid-like fashion, some as narrow rectangular ladder farms and others in a square, block-like shape. During the closing decades of the eighteenth century, we can see three key strands being slowly intertwined in their evolving DNA.

The first was the widespread emergence of smallholdings on waste ground that from the outset were labelled as crofts. Initially, they were a prominent feature along the eastern edges of the Highlands, where many were established on extensive areas of marginal waste ground, including many on the privatized blocks of former commonty land created by mid-late eighteenth-century divisions, like that at Millbuie in the Black Isle.[84] Others were established by squatters, including many by tenants dispossessed by the clearances and tenant reductions now being implemented further west.[85] Second, and a point already noted, some small to medium-sized farms were created out of the restructuring of multiple-tenant touns. Examples of this can be found across the region. Those created on the Breadalbane and Argyll estates before 1800 have already been mentioned,

---

[81] G. Kay, 'The Landscape of Improvement: A Case Study of Agricultural Change in North East Scotland', *Scottish Geographical Magazine*, no. 2, 78 (1962), 100–11; SRO, RHP1783. See also Millar, ed., *A Selection of Scottish Forfeited Estates Papers 1715: 1745*, lxvii, 71; V. Wills, ed., *Reports on the Annexed Estates 1755–1769* (Edinburgh, 1973), 89–90.

[82] NAS, RHP 1474.

[83] W. P. L. Thomson, 'Township, House and Tenant-Holding: The Structure of Runrig Agriculture in Shetland', in V. Turner, ed., *The Shaping of Shetland* (Lerwick, 1998), 107–27, 333–4; A. Fenton, *The Northern Isles: Orkney and Shetland* (Edinburgh, 1978), 42–3.

[84] Tivy, 'Easter Ross', 72–3; see also *Evidence... Condition of Crofters and Cottars*, IUP, PS, vol. 25, 2,639–40.

[85] Tivy, 'Easter Ross', 69 and 72; Gaffney, *Lordship of Strathavon*, 99.

but other examples can be cited for areas both south and north of the Great Glen.[86] Third, during the 1780s, the British Fisheries Society added a vital strand when it laid out a number of planned villages on the west coast (i.e. Ullapool, Tobermory) as fishing stations. As well as providing the facilities needed for fishing (i.e. curing stations, boat building, cooperage), a prime feature of these villages was the fact that they were laid out around small crofts, whose occupiers were expected to balance fishing or related trades with small-scale farming. There were some areas where ad hoc forms of dual economy had long been evolving, such as on the Assynt coast, but the British Fisheries Society now set it down within a planned framework based on the croft.[87]

By the 1790s, these different inputs had become fused together in the concept of the crofting township. However, by this point, critical price changes precipitated by the Napoleonic Wars from 1793 onwards had also begun to play a part in their formation. On the one hand, the sharp inflation of sheep and wool prices added a still more powerful incentive to the clearance of those touns that possessed extensive grazing grounds. On the other, a sharp rise in kelp prices and the labour demands created by the production of kelp gave landlords a vested interest in packing their coastal touns. They were helped by the fact that by the closing decades of the eighteenth century, most highland touns were experiencing rapid population growth. They were also helped by the potential boost to subsistence now afforded by fishing and the growing use of the potato, both of which enabled more to live off less land.[88] In fact, where combined, kelp, fishing, and the potato, along with the willingness of crofters and cottars to spade difficult land, redefined the lower threshold of what was deemed a viable croft, leading some estates to distinguish between full and half-crofts, depending on whether supplementary income or subsistence was available in addition to arable.[89] In the north, the Sutherland estate provides a well-documented example of how the coming together of these various trends in restructuring and market conditions was used to develop a regional approach to restructuring, with the interior straths being depopulated and those displaced being resettled in new crofting settlements established along the coast, like Brora and Helmsdale.[90] The contrast that was created is captured by two statistics from James Macdonald's 1880 essay on the county of Sutherland: 95 per cent of farms there were by 1870 under 20 acres, the vast majority of which were on the coast, with the interior given over simply to 30–40 large sheep farms.[91] As elsewhere, the crofting townships planted on the coast were based on dual economies, with crofting being combined with fishing or even activities like mining or glass-working. On Skye, Lewis, Harris, and the Uists, the same contrast was played out

[86]  Tivy, 'Easter Ross', 69.

[87]  H. Home, ed., *Home's Survey of Assynt*, 3rd series, lii (Edinburgh: Scottish History Society, 1960), 11, 14, 15, 17, and 19.

[88]  Gray, *Highland Economy 1750–1850*, 105–41.

[89]  R. J. Adam (ed.), *Papers on Sutherland Estate Management 1802–1816*, vol. 1 (Edinburgh: Scottish History Society, 1972), 27. Skye examples on the MacLeod of MacLeod estate are provided by *Report of the Commissioners of Inquiry into the Condition of the Crofters and Cottars in the Highlands and Islands* (Edinburgh, 1884), 25.

[90]  Richards, 'Structural Change', 68.

[91]  Macdonald, 'Agriculture of the County of Sutherland', 49.

at a finer scale, with areas of sheep farming being locally interdigitated with areas given over to sheep and others to crofting townships, even along the coast. The creation of the latter on these islands during the early nineteenth century, many between 1810 and 1815, formed one of the most concentrated acts of toun restructuring anywhere in Scotland.[92] Some were laid out across part of the former multiple-tenant touns that they replaced, but others involved displacement, either from a site nearby or from a more distant part of the estate, so that crofters had to reclaim their arable afresh, a task made all the more demanding given that many of these displaced townships were on poorer land compared to the original toun, such as was the case with those settled in the bays areas of east Harris.

The conditions under which these crofting townships developed proved far from stable. When we read how John Blackadder, the surveyor charged with laying out crofts on the Macdonald estate both in Skye and North Uist in 1810–11, laid out crofts at a size that 'may answer for enclosures...should it be thought proper at any future period to let any of them [townships] to single tenants', it is clear that this temporariness was in mind from the outset.[93] As the Napoleonic Wars drew to a close in 1815, the price of kelp, along with that of stock and grain, fell. Poor harvests and the first signs of the potato's vulnerability to disease in 1816–17 added to the problems.[94] Whereas market conditions recovered for sheep and wool, they only worsened for the smallholder and crofter. As the problems of the latter deepened, a shift in attitude took place amongst landowners. So long as there was profit in kelp, landlords had not only been tolerant of the large, crowded communities to be found on the coast but had encouraged them. As income from kelp declined, as subsistence problems emerged and rents arrears accumulated, what had earlier been planned out as a solution, the crofting township, now came to be seen as a burden. From a landowner's perspective, declining income meant it was no longer about trying to keep a balance between the needs of their smallholders and those of the large sheep farmer, but about trying to maximize their returns from land. The sale of so many highland estates over the first half of the nineteenth century emphasized this shift in attitude.[95] With a background in commerce, banking, and industry, many of those now buying into the region were unencumbered by obligations to their smaller tenants, though even the attitude of traditional landlords tended to shift at this point. A. I. Allan Macinnes saw this shift from trying to accommodate smallholders in some numbers to a policy of rent maximization at all costs as so significant that he distinguished what happened before the 1820s and 1830s as constituting a first phase of clearance and what happened afterwards as a second phase.[96] His

[92] Gray, 'Abolition of Runrig', 50.

[93] NAS, GD221/116.

[94] J. Hunter, *The Making of the Crofting Community* (Edinburgh, 1976), 34–49.

[95] Gaskell, *Morvern Transformed*, 28–46; T. M. Devine, *Clearance and Improvement: Land, Power and People in Scotland 1700–1900* (Edinburgh, 2006), 187–217; T. M. Devine, *Clanship to Crofters' War: The Social Transformation of the Scottish Highlands* (Manchester, 1994), 63–83.

[96] A. I. Macinnes, 'Scottish Gaeldom', in T. M. Devine and R. Mitchison, eds., *People and Society in Scotland, vol. I, 1760–1830* (Edinburgh, 1988), 70–90; A. I. Macinnes, 'Commercial Landlordism and Clearance in the Scottish Highlands: The Case of Arichonan', in J. Pan-Montojo and K. Pedersen, eds., *Communities in European History* (Pisa, 2007), 49.

distinction is an important one, though there is a case for breaking down his first phase, separating out its initial stages, when estates thought that small to medium-sized farms might still be viable, from that which had unfolded by the 1790s, when laying out crofts and so-called fisher-crofts, or half-crofts, became the norm.

The diminished regard for the small tenant by the 1820s, whether those in surviving multiple-tenant touns or in newly founded crofting townships, manifested itself in different ways. To start with, we find less and less provision made for those still being cleared to make way for sheep. Whilst estates like the Sutherland estate continued to offer newly created lots on the coast for those displaced, we find an increasing number of instances, especially in the Hebrides, in which the absolute minimum or even no provision was made. Tenants and cottars affected by the comprehensive clearance of Rum in 1826 and 1827 and, later, the succession of removals from South Uist and Barra that culminated in the large-scale clearances of 1851, for example, were provided only with free passage to North America, a common solution at this point as landlords resorted to exporting their problems.[97] Those with long memories might have argued that whole touns of tenants and cottars had emigrated before, led en masse by their tacksmen during the crises of the 1740s and 1770s,[98] but there was a difference between an emigration of choice and the coercion that underpinned some of the removals from South Uist and Barra in the late 1840s and in 1851.

For those tenants and cottars who remained, conditions were not necessarily any better. Despite their planned, regulated appearance, crofting townships were not fixed, immutable affairs. Many were subject to an ongoing process of restructuring, as their resident numbers initially increased through further population growth, as more were moved into them from newly created sheep farms, and as the collapse of kelp production after 1815 left many who had depended wholly on kelp without adequate means of subsistence.[99] These problems reached crisis point during the 1840s potato famine.[100] Yet at a time when communities needed support, some landowners chose to restructure their property afresh. Not only were many of the surviving multiple-tenant touns swept away in the 1840s and 1850s with little or no provision for resettlement, but some estates—as John Blackadder had foreseen—now began to clear even their crofting townships to make way for sheep, a clear sign of how thinking had moved on. The island of Ulva was typical of these shifts in estate policy. As elsewhere, it was underpinned by a change in ownership. Those who occupied

---

[97] Probably because no crofters were present, the Napier Commission did not gather evidence for Rum. Most of its inhabitants were reportedly 'united in [a] general emigration to America' in 1826, *New Statistical Account of Scotland, County of Inverness, 1834–45*, vol. 14, 152–3. In his own 'commission', Mackenzie talked about the island's 'most melancholy cycle'. Its touns were cleared for a sheep farm, but when that enterprise failed, the island was put under deer; A. Mackenzie, *The History of the Highland Clearances* (Glasgow, 1883), 222–6. For North Uist and Barra, see Richards, *Highland Clearances*, 265–88; *Evidence... Condition of Crofters and Cottars*, IUP, PS, 22, 643–98 and 785–836.

[98] Dodgshon, *From Chiefs to Landlords*, 116.

[99] Gray, *Highland Economy 1750–1850*, 130–8.

[100] *Report... Condition of the Crofters and Cottars*, 143 and 162; Hunter, *Making of the Crofting Community*, 50–72; T. M. Devine, *The Great Highland Famine: Hunger, Emigration and the Scottish Highlands in the Nineteenth Century* (Edinburgh, 1988), 33–56.

the lots or crofts into which its touns were divided *c.*1810 were described in an 1825 sale advertisement for the island as engaged in cattle rearing and fishing, and to have made 'a very handsome profit' from the making of kelp. By the late 1840s, though, the new owner had already started clearing them for what, for him, was the greater profit of sheep.[101] The mid-late nineteenth-century surge in the creation of deer forests added still further pressure on the crofter, with some crofting townships (i.e. in the Park district of Lewis) no less than sheep farms (i.e. that on Rum) being emptied to make way for them.[102]

Those crofting townships that survived these late clearances faced their own problems, with new pressures that slowly squeezed their resource base. The growth in numbers alone meant that crofts were now routinely subdivided or split into smaller crofts, either because crofters themselves split their crofts between children (a practice that many estates tried to prevent) or because estates crowded more into the township as they continued to resettle some of those cleared from new sheep farms and deer forests.[103] The evidence submitted to the Crofters Commission provides many examples of this more crowded crofting landscape. For example, at Balemore in North Uist, the original eighteen crofts laid out in 1814 eventually became thirty-five; this also happened in most of the large townships that lay along the north-west coast of Lewis, like Upper Carloway, where what started out as nineteen crofts became forty-five, eighteen of which were new crofts created out of its common grazings and occupied by people 'who for the most part were from districts that were cleared in order to make way for sheep'.[104] In some cases, the numbers involved were such that estates eventually re-lotted the township, tidying up the effects of growth but making the new lots smaller.[105] A source of real grievance in a significant number of townships was the fact that blocks of vital common grazings were detached from them and annexed to adjacent sheep farms, deer forests, or

---

[101]  NLS, Plan of the Islands of Ulva, Gometra, Colonsay, Inch Kenneth, Staffa, etc., by John Leslie, 1812; NAS, GD174/1087/1, Particulars of the Estate of Ulva, 1825; Mackenzie, *History of the Highland Clearances*, 228–9. See also Richards, *Highland Clearances*, 162 and 303–8; *Evidence taken by the Royal Commission*, IUP, PS, vol. 22, 708–9; *Report ... by the Crofters Commission on the Social Condition of the People of Lewis in 1901, As Compared with Twenty Years Ago* (Glasgow, 1902), lxx.

[102]  The Park evictions are discussed in *Evidence ... Condition of Crofters and Cottars*, IUP, PS, vol. 23, 1,150. The switch from sheep to deer on Rum is detailed in Mackenzie, *The History of the Highland Clearances*, 222–6. For a review of deer forests generally at this point, see also W. Orr, *Deer Forests, Landlords and Crofters: The Western Highlands in Victorian and Edwardian Times* (Edinburgh, 1982), 28–70.

[103]  The way crofters subdivided crofts between children is illustrated by evidence for the Bays area of Harris by *Evidence ... Condition of Crofters and Cottars*, IUP, PS, vol. 23, 861. The way landlords used existing crofting townships as dumping grounds for those who had been dispossessed elsewhere on their estates during the mid-nineteenth century, without adding extra land, is illustrated by the actions of Sir James Matheson on Lewis, e.g. *Evidence ... Condition of Crofters and Cottars*, IUP PS, vol. 23, 997.

[104]  *Evidence ... Condition of Crofters and Cottars*, IUP, PS, vol. 22, 832; vol. 23, 954–5. See also ibid., 977, 989, 991, 1,026, and 1,133.

[105]  One of the more detailed examples of overcrowding and re-lotting is provided by that of Coll township on Lewis. Initially lotted out into twenty-two crofts, more were added in a piecemeal way until, about 1850, the entire township was formally re-lotted into forty-seven crofts. Between then and the point at which the Napier Commission collected its evidence, twenty more crofters were moved in; *Evidence ... Condition of Crofters and Cottars*, IUP, PS, vol. 23, 1,026.

sporting grounds,[106] or, as at Upper Carloway, were used to create new crofts.[107] To compound their resource problems, what also comes across from the evidence presented to the *Crofters Commission* is the number of cottars and others labelled as squatters and landless who were reported as still present in crofting townships, especially in the Hebrides. Thus, between them, the 11 townships in the parish of Knock (Lewis) had 173 individuals listed as cottars, or 15.7 per township.[108]

Whilst the shocks created by the potato famines of 1815–16 and the 1840s had exposed the endemic weakness of a subsistence farm economy now heavily reliant on potatoes, the different ways in which the resource base of crofting townships were progressively squeezed (i.e. splitting of crofts, addition of new ones, reduction of grazings) weakened the crofting economy still further. Yet when the hill grazings previously attached to townships in the Braes district on Skye were detached in 1865 and incorporated into sheep farms without any adjustment of rent for the crofters, few could have foreseen how it would help to trigger far-reaching change. How the change affected crofters' rights was never clarified and they continued to make use of the grazings. However, in 1881, when the tack of the sheep farm expired, they appealed to the estate for an adjustment of rent in lieu of what they had lost. After their case was rejected, they declared a rent strike in spring 1882. When the inevitable eviction notices were ignored, the authorities responded by sending in a force of Glasgow police, a deployment that led to a violent confrontation, the so-called Battle of the Braes.[109] This was not the first confrontation involving crofters to make the national press: those in Strathnaver in 1814 and on Barra in 1851 had received publicity far beyond the townships involved. However, neither provided the catalyst for wider change in the position of the small tenant or crofter. What was different about the confrontation at the Braes was the reinforcement that its impact quickly received from other events at this point. Before the year had ended, a rent strike by tenants in Glendale in north-western Skye over the way they were still burdened by old exactions, such as labour days on the landlord's farm, had also prompted tenants and cottars into direct confrontation with the authorities, though the police involved were always fewer than at the Braes.[110] On the wider political stage, the publicity surrounding these events offered powerful support to those who were working at this point to politicize the crofter's cause and to bring about highland land reform. Timely cross-connections were also made to a parallel debate, with the enactment of Irish land reform in Gladstone's Land Bill of 1881 providing powerful encouragement for those campaigning for a similar bill for the Highlands. The government response to such demands was to set up the Napier

---

[106] For examples, see *Report... Condition of the Crofters and Cottars* (1884), 117; *Evidence... Condition of Crofters and Cottars*, IUP, PS, vol. 23, 1,133.

[107] Ibid., 955.

[108] *Report... Condition of the Crofters and Cottars* (1884), 143.

[109] Hunter, *Making of the Crofting Community*, 133–7; Devine, *Clanship to Crofters' War*, 209–27; *Evidence... Condition of Crofters and Cottars*, IUP, PS, vol. 22, 1–37.

[110] Hunter, *Making of the Crofting Community*, 137–41; *Evidence... Condition of Crofters and Cottars*, IUP, PS, vol. 22, 362–438.

Commission in 1883 to look into the *Condition of the Crofters and Cottars in the Highlands and Islands of Scotland*. Informed by the Commission's collected evidence, which symbolically began with that for the Braes,[111] and by its published report (1884),[112] and pressed by the newly founded Highland Land Law Reform Association (1883),[113] the government somewhat tardily put together a Crofters Act that was eventually enacted in 1886. The Act formally defined what it saw as the Crofting Counties[114] and, within them, gave crofters security over tenure, enabled them to bequeath their holding to a person, provided compensation for improvements, established a procedure for the enlargement of crofts, and set up a permanent Commission to adjudicate on fair rents. Perhaps surprisingly, those MPs who now represented the crofters did not vote for it because, like the Highland Land Law Reform Association, they also wanted greater provision for the allocation of extra land for crofts and, bound up with that, some provision for cottars.[115] In time, provision for extra land and new crofts, including crofts for cottars and those who were landless, did come with the setting up of the Congested Districts Board by the Congested Districts (Scotland) Act of 1897, powers that the Board acted on quickly.[116] Between them, we can see these two legislative responses to the grievances of the crofters and cottars as effectively bringing to an end that phase of the region's history that can be labelled under 'the clearances'.

# CONCLUSION

The transformation of the pre-improvement toun into the consolidated farms of the modern Scottish countryside was a primary requisite for the Improving Movement and the spread of new husbandries, a change that, by its very nature, profoundly altered farm structures and the appearance of the rural landscape. It also had the less visible but no less vital effect of replacing the shared or negotiated space of the pre-improvement toun with the private space of the consolidated farm, thereby altering the context of decision making and releasing a new potential for how husbandry should develop, not least because it raised the rate of private returns on investment. Yet however beneficial it was to the progress of the Improving Movement, 1760–1815, the restructuring of touns must

---

[111] The submitted evidence was published separately from the report: *Evidence Taken by the Royal Commissioners of Inquiry on the Condition of Crofters and Cottars in the Highlands of Scotland*, IUP, PS, vols. 22–25.

[112] *Report . . . Condition of the Crofters and Cottars* (1884).

[113] Hunter, *Making of the Crofting Community*, 143–5.

[114] *Crofters Holdings (Scotland) Act* (1886), 49 and 50 Vict. C.29; *Crofters Common Grazings Regulation Act* (1891), 54 and 55, Vict. C.41; H. A. Moisley, 'The Highlands and Islands—A Crofting Region?', *Transactions and Papers. Institute of British Geographers*, 321 (1962), 83–95.

[115] Hunter, *Making of the Crofting Community*, 163. The disappointment over the lack of any provision for cottars was justified not just because of how many were still present, but because the Napier Commission was charged with enquiring into the '*Condition of Crofters and Cottars*'.

[116] *First report of the Congested Districts Board for Scotland, 1st October 1897 to 31st December 1898, to the Secretary for Scotland*, 1899 [C. 9165].

not be shoehorned into the same chronology. Restructuring was as much a feature of the century or so prior to 1760, and the three or four decades after 1815, as of the years between. Just as the chronology of restructuring has been extended, so also have the means by which it was accomplished. We now know that in one form or another many touns across the Lowlands no less than the Highlands were restructured via a process of tenant reduction, a process that could be fast-tracked or unfold slowly. Either way, the sum effect, often the violent effect, was that of a clearance. In many instances, such clearances fossilized an outline of the old toun structures within the modern landscape, recasting them as medium-large farms. Yet whilst a clearance was the prime means of restructuring across the whole of Scotland, other means were also used. Some runrig touns were divided out into small, consolidated farms. Different processes were employed here, but each had the effect of recreating in the modern landscape the pattern of small working units that had prevailed under runrig in the pre-improvement landscape. When we add the many small farms created *de novo* out of reclamation and drainage schemes and the crofts created out of highland and Hebridean touns over the eighteenth and nineteenth centuries, we can better appreciate how restructuring not only produced a landscape of consolidated holdings, but also reconfigured the farming ladder, leaving many areas with a pattern dichotomized between large and small farms.

## FURTHER READING

Devine, T. M., *Clanship to Crofters' War: The Social Transformation of the Scottish Highlands* (Manchester, 1994).
—— *The Transformation of Rural Scotland: Social Change and the Agrarian Economy 1660–1815* (Edinburgh, 1994).
—— *Clearance and Improvement: Land, Power and People in Scotland 1700–1900* (Edinburgh, 2006).
Dodgshon, R. A., 'Agricultural Change and its Social Consequences in the Southern Uplands of Scotland 1600–1780', in T. M. Devine and R. Mitchison, eds., *Ireland and Scotland 1600–1850* (Edinburgh, 1983), 46–59.
Hunter, J., *The Making of the Crofting Community* (Edinburgh, 1976).
Orr, W., *Deer Forests, Landlords and Crofters: The Western Highlands in Victorian and Edwardian Times* (Edinburgh, 1982).
Richards, E. S., *A History of the Highland Clearances: Agrarian Transformation and the Evictions 1746–1886* (London, 1982).
—— *The Highland Clearances* (Edinburgh, 2009).
Storrie, M. C., 'Landholdings and Settlement Evolution in West Highland Scotland', *Geografiska Annaler*, 43 (1965), 138–61.
Turnock, D., *Patterns of Highland Development* (London, 1970).
Whyte, I. D., *Agriculture and Society in Seventeenth-Century Scotland* (Edinburgh, 1979).

# CHAPTER 7

......................................................................................

# A GLOBAL DIASPORA

......................................................................................

## T. M. DEVINE

In 2010 the Scottish government announced a 'Diaspora Engagement Plan' outlining an ambitious strategy for connecting with Scots emigrants overseas. A few years earlier, the Scottish Centre for Diaspora Studies, generously funded by external endowment, had been established in the University of Edinburgh with a prime focus of study on the emigrations of the peoples of Scotland since medieval times.[1] Yet the use of the term 'diaspora' is not uncontentious. Purists in the social-science community lament the dilution of its original meaning, traditionally employed to describe the forced uprooting and resettlement of peoples outside their homelands.[2] The Jews were the classic case of that particular trauma, but the *Penguin Atlas of Diaspora* (1991) also includes Armenians, Gypsies, black Africans, Chinese, Palestinians, and Irish as other exemplars of diasporic peoples who have suffered the coercive experience.[3] The Scots, Welsh, and English, together with most other European nations, are notable by their absence from the list of the dispossessed.

Even if the term 'diaspora' can be used in the Scottish case, there are analytical dangers that need to be recognized. The original emphasis on 'uprooting' suggests the experience of the emigrant as victim, driven into enforced exile by state oppression or landlords' decision, a concept that might be very appropriate for certain periods in Scottish history, but on the whole is a distorting myth which does little justice to the complexity of the narrative of emigration over the centuries. In the modern era, in particular, it might serve simply to legitimize the widespread popular belief that most Scots left Scotland after 1700 because of the notorious Highland clearances. This is a perspective that some academic historians would reject root and branch, while others recognize that

---

[1] www.scotland.gov.uk/News/Releases/2010/09/14111014; www.shc.ed.ac.uk/Centres. This chapter draws on arguments presented in my recent book, *To the Ends of the Earth: Scotland's Global Diaspora, 1750–2010* (London, 2011).

[2] Paul Basu, *Highland Homecomings* (Abingdon, 2007), 10–11.

[3] G. Chaliand and J.-P. Rageau, *The Penguin Atlas of Diasporas* (New York, 1991), xix.

forced displacement of people in some parts of the country, including above all the Highlands, merits serious attention as an important part of the overall story.

Nevertheless, the use of 'diaspora' to describe dispersal of peoples outside their homeland is now well established in a number of contexts. The sociologist Robin Cohen has argued that returning to the Greek root of the word, to 'scatter' or 'sow', and also its early meaning to describe widespread Greek colonization of the Mediterranean, allows 'diaspora' to be used more extensively and meaningfully in emigration history. He goes further and outlines what he sees as the most common features of diasporic peoples: movement from the homeland either because of 'push' or 'pull' factors to several foreign destinations; a collective memory and myth about the old country; a sense of empathy with members of the same ethnic group in the new lands and also the incidence of return movements.[4] As this chapter and others will demonstrate (see Chapters 14, 16, 22, 27, 28), most of Cohen's categories do fit the Scottish experience of emigration remarkably well. This analysis will therefore consider that experience in three parts. Part one presents a general overview. Part two focuses on the great migrations between c.1830 and c.1939, with special emphasis on the reasons for movement. Finally, part three surveys the more recent outward movement between 1945 and the present day.

# 1

The Scottish diaspora of the last seven hundred years or more has had several distinctive features. While it has been suggested that by the later twentieth century an estimated 15 million people of Scottish descent lived outside Scotland, the longevity of Scottish emigration, stretching back to the thirteenth century, might indicate that the estimate could still err on the conservative side.[5] Considerable outward movement from Scotland, often on a substantial scale, has occurred from the 1400s through to the 1990s. Peaks and troughs of emigration did, of course, characterize that history. Much of the seventeenth century, the decades c.1840 to 1914, the 1920s, and again in the post-war years c.1950 to the 1980s, were phases of quite massive loss of population.[6] Again, in the second half of the twentieth century when UK emigration in general was in decline, the Scottish rate of outward movement persisted. Between 1500 and 1990, only in the first half of the sixteenth century, the early decades of the eighteenth century, and the years of global warfare during 1776–83, 1793–1815, 1914–18, and 1939–45 did Scottish emigration fall to more modest levels.[7]

---

[4] R. Cohen, *Global Diasporas: An Introduction* (London, 1997), 21–6.

[5] David Armitage, 'The Scottish Diaspora', in Jenny Wormald, ed., *Scotland: A History* (Oxford, 2005), 272.

[6] Isobel Lindsay, 'Migration and Motivation: A Twentieth-Century Perspective', in T. M. Devine, ed., *Scottish Emigration and Scottish Society* (Edinburgh, 1992), 156; Armitage, 'Scottish Diaspora', 282.

[7] Devine, *Scottish Emigration, passim.*

Another characteristic Scottish feature was the scale and volume of emigration. The best current estimates for 1600–50 suggest an annual average loss of two thousand people. Since most of those who left were young men aged fifteen to thirty, overwhelmingly engaged in military service and petty trading in Europe, it is reckoned that perhaps a fifth of that age group left Scotland at the time. This figure is very close to the more familiar rates of male Scottish emigration for the middle decades of the nineteenth century.[8] These early modern levels were matched by few other European countries and regions. The contrast, for instance, with the English pattern was striking. Over the entire seventeenth century a net annual migration of just over seven thousand individuals has been suggested for England. The estimated Scottish figures were between a quarter and a third of this annual rate, though England's population was around six times that of Scotland between 1600 and 1700.[9] It should be stressed, however, as Steve Murdoch and Esther Mijers make clear in Chapter 16, that there is now much more scholarly scepticism about some of the numerical estimates of early modern Scottish migration to Europe that have long been accepted. Eye-catching figures culled from literary sources could have been cited without due caution. First-generation migrants could easily be conflated with second- and third-generation offspring of earlier arrivals because of their Scottish-sounding surnames, so resulting in an artificial inflation of the total numbers of 'true' emigrants from Scotland in the period. Moreover, many migrant Scots moved to more than one locality, region, or state during their lifetimes. Both soldiers and merchants habitually travelled to those parts of Europe where the opportunities were greatest, thus making multiple shifts of residence and place of business inevitable and also perhaps encouraging double and treble counting of exiled Scots by the unwary scholar, again leading to inflated estimates. For Poland-Lithuania in particular, recent careful archival research has drastically cut back some of the numbers of Scots that were generally accepted in the past (see Chapter 16).

The evidence for diaspora becomes more robust in the later eighteenth century and thereafter. Once again the contrasting levels of out-migration from Scotland and the rest of mainland Britain were marked. Between 1701 and 1780 about 80,000 English left for America, a total that was more or less the same as the estimated loss from Scotland over those seven decades, though England's population at the time was nearly eight times greater.[10] In terms of absolute numbers, however, even higher levels were reached in the nineteenth and twentieth centuries. From 1825 to 1938, over 2.3 million Scots left for overseas destinations. When the estimated 600,000 who moved across the border to England between 1841 and 1911 are included in the total, it is little wonder that Scotland has come to be regarded as the European capital of emigration in that period.[11]

---

[8] T. C. Smout, N. C. Landsman, and T. M. Devine, 'Scottish Emigration in the Seventeenth and Eighteenth Centuries', in Nicholas Canny, ed., *Europeans on the Move* (Oxford, 1994), 85–90.

[9] Ibid., 90.

[10] J. Horn, 'British Diaspora: Emigration from Britain, 1680–1815', in Peter J. Marshall, ed., *The Oxford History of the British Empire. Volume 2: The Eighteenth Century* (Oxford, 1998), 31.

[11] M. W. Flinn, ed., *Scottish Population History from the Seventeenth Century to the 1930s* (Cambridge, 1977), 441–2.

The numbers are striking and the change in scale from the 1700s very marked—80,000 to 90,000 departures for overseas have been estimated between 1700 and 1815.

The exodus in the century after *c.*1840 was even greater in absolute terms. At its peak, in the 1920s, over 363,000 Scots left for the USA and Canada in a single decade, although many returned as employment prospects across the Atlantic became less attractive during the Great Depression of the 1930s.[12] These figures have to be set against a national Scottish population size of 4,472,103 at the census of 1901. Even before the huge losses of the interwar period, emigration was still immense. In the eight decades before the First World War, for every two babies born who survived past infancy, one was likely to leave Scotland in adulthood.[13]

Of sixteen western and central European countries considered, three—Ireland, Norway, and Scotland—consistently topped the league tables as the source of proportionately most emigrants. Ireland headed the table in most years. Norway and Scotland fluctuated in their relative positions. However, in three key decades, 1851–60, 1871–80, and 1901–10, Scotland was second only to Ireland in this unenviable championship.[14] The upward trajectory was temporarily interrupted by the five years of world conflict from 1914 and then by the short-lived post-war boom until 1921. But, thereafter, the dynamic of mass emigration reasserted itself. Between 1920 and 1929, those leaving Scotland averaged 46,876 per year, a figure that specifically excluded cross-border migration to England. Scots numbered one in ten of the UK population in that decade but accounted for 28 per cent of all British and Irish emigrants to the USA, 26 per cent of those to Canada, and 20 per cent of migrants to Australasia.[15] The nation now headed the international league table of European emigration to overseas destinations, a long way ahead of both Ireland and Norway. For the first time since the eighteenth century, Scottish population actually fell in the 1920s by over 40,000. The eminent Scottish writer Edwin Muir was the most eloquent of several commentators to voice deep disquiet: '... my main impression ... is that Scotland is gradually being emptied of its population, its spirit, its wealth, industry, art, intellect and innate character. If a country exports its most enterprising spirits and best minds year after year, for fifty or a hundred or two hundred years, some result will inevitably follow.'[16]

More emigrants came from mainland Britain as a whole per head of population between *c.*1850 and 1939 than from most other European countries. But Scottish emigration, at least from the 1860s, was significantly higher per head of population than that of England and Wales. From 1881 to 1931, England lost an average of fourteen inhabitants per thousand, Wales seventeen per thousand, but the Scottish figure was thirty-five per thousand.[17] Over the longer period, from the 1850s, the pattern was similar. Annual

---

[12] N. J. Evans, 'The Emigration of Skilled Male Workers from Clydeside during the Interwar Period, *International Journal of Maritime History*, xviii (2006), 255–80.

[13] T. M. Devine, 'The Paradox of Scottish Emigration', in Devine, ed., *Scottish Emigration*, 1.

[14] Dudley Baines, *Migration in a Mature Economy* (Cambridge, 1985), 10.

[15] Evans, 'Emigration of Skilled Male Workers', 255–79.

[16] Edwin Muir, *Scottish Journey* (London, 1935), 94.

[17] John Bodnar, *The Transplanted: History of Immigrants in Urban America* (Bloomington, IN, 1985), 4.

emigration from England and Wales in the second half of the nineteenth century was one per thousand, but for Scotland the figure was 1.4, and nearly two per thousand in some decades. Overall, England and Wales lost 9 per cent of natural population increase (i.e. births over deaths). In Scotland the fall was around 25 per cent.[18]

European migration in the nineteenth and first decade of the twentieth century, especially from Scandinavia, the German states, Spain, and Italy, was marked by visible differences within these countries, with regions of high loss existing alongside others where levels of out-migration were demonstrably less significant.[19] The evidence contained in the Poor Law Commission Report of 1844 suggests a different pattern in Scotland for the nineteenth century. Emigration was noted as being common throughout the country with over two-thirds of parishes reporting losses. As Michael Anderson has already noted in Chapter 2, later in the 1860s nine out of ten Scottish parishes experienced net out-migration.[20] Studies of emigration to New Zealand for the Victorian period confirm that the last place of residence of emigrants from Scotland was relatively evenly spread and representative of the broad demographic structure of the country.[21] Nevertheless, it is still true that the central Lowlands, and especially the towns and cities of the industrial areas, had disproportionate numbers of emigrants after c.1860, particularly so in the case of movement to the USA. But that concentration was primarily a result of changing population settlement within Scotland as urbanization and industrialization intensified and migration from rural counties to the towns and cities accelerated.[22]

Evidence from some regions of Belgium and France in the nineteenth century also suggests that higher per-capita incomes as a consequence of industrial growth could slow down emigration considerably.[23] Similarly, north-western Italy was a major source of emigration before 1900, but as it experienced the spread of industrial development the axis shifted to the poorer central and southern regions of the country. The same process has been described in Catalonia in Spain during this period.[24] Economic growth, so it is argued, provides alternatives to emigration and absorbs those who might have left if the onset of better times had not taken place. This model fits Scotland well in the early modern period when poverty, a fragile economy, and recurrent food shortages, sometimes resulting in famine crises in the 1620s and 1690s, were likely to impel large-scale outward movement. But it conflicts with the history of emigration from Scotland in more modern times. Certainly, in the later eighteenth century and possibly through

[18] Eric Richards, *Brittania's Children: Emigration from England, Scotland, Wales and Ireland since 1600* (London, 2004), 118, 180, 236.

[19] Walter Nugent, *Crossings: The Great Transatlantic Migrations, 1870–1914* (Bloomington, IN, 1992).

[20] I. R. Levitt and T. C. Smout, *The State of the Scottish Working Class in 1843* (Edinburgh, 1979), *passim*.

[21] Rosalind R. McClean, 'Scottish Emigrants to New Zealand 1840–1880' (unpublished PhD thesis, University of Edinburgh, 1990), 122, 157, 175–6, 436–7.

[22] Devine, 'Paradox of Scottish Emigration', 6–8.

[23] Charlotte Erickson, *Leaving England: Essays on British Emigration in the Nineteenth Century* (Ithaca, NY, 1994), 58.

[24] Nugent, *Crossings*, 95, 104. For Italian emigration see also Donna R. Gabaccia, *Italy's Many Diasporas* (Washington, 2000).

to the 1850s, the Highlands, the poorest region of all, had more emigrants per head of population than other parts of the country.[25] But, as the Scottish exodus reached unprecedented proportions, depopulation in the north and west inevitably meant a pro-portionate and absolute decline in the highland factor. So generally after *c*.1860, lowland emigration exceeded that from Gaeldom, normally by a factor of seventeen to one down to the First World War.[26] Industrialization had radically reshaped Scotland to a greater extent than most European countries, so that by 1910 only one in ten Scots were engaged in agriculture or related employment. At the census of 1911, 60 per cent of the Scottish people lived in towns and cities (as measured by settlements of 5,000 or above). But this economic and social revolution had not stemmed the tide of emigration.[27] (For a differ-ent perspective on the 'paradox' of Scottish emigration see Chapter 27.)

The great flood of Scots emigrants was paralleled by expansion and change in the regions of overseas settlement. In the popular imagination it is the diaspora to the British Empire and the United States that commands attention. Yet as one scholar has noted, 'in the perspective of the last 700 years, that two-century-long movement to the anglo-phone Empire was a historical aberration. For at least four centuries before 1707, and increasingly again from the Second World War the main destinations for Scottish migrants have been European.'[28] That was indeed the pattern until near the end of the seventeenth century. Fewer than 10,000 Scots had settled in America and the West Indies by then, compared with the many thousands who had left for the European conti-nent.[29] (See Chapter 14.)

But in the last quarter of the seventeenth century, the emigration axis started to shift towards the Atlantic world. It was arguably one of the most decisive developments in modern Scottish history, but also one of the least understood. The end of the Thirty Years War in 1648 was a factor, since for a time it closed down much of the earlier demand for soldiers in western Europe. Rich pickings for merchants and petty traders in Poland-Lithuania also became less abundant as that country degenerated into a series of internal struggles and foreign wars.[30] The new attractions emerging across the Irish Sea, in Ulster, with the distribution of Irish land to Protestant Scots and other settlers from mainland Britain, were also relevant. In this respect, the impact of the 'Lean Years' in the Scotland of the 1690s is striking. It was the worst Scottish subsistence crisis of modern times. Hunger and famine-related diseases caused an estimated fall in population of between 5 and 20 per cent between different areas of the country, a figure in the range of relative

[25]  T. M. Devine, *Scotland's Empire, 1600–1815* (London, 2003), 94–139; Levitt and Smout, *State of the Scottish Working Class*, 91–2.

[26]  Bodnar, *The Transplanted*, 4.

[27]  Nugent, *Crossings*, 47; Devine, 'Paradox of Scottish Emigration', 3–4; Charlotte Erickson, 'Who were the English and Scots Emigrants in the Late Nineteenth Century', in D. V. Glass and R. Revelle, eds., *Population and Social Change* (London, 1972).

[28]  Armitage, 'Scottish Diaspora', 276.

[29]  David Dobson, *Scottish Emigration to Colonial America 1607–1785* (Athens, GA, 1994).

[30]  Devine, *Scotland's Empire 1600–1815*, 26–48.

demographic decline suffered during the Great Irish Famine of the nineteenth century. Perhaps Scotland lost somewhere in the region of 160,000 people, about half of this number directly by hunger and disease, the rest by emigration. The most recent calculations suggest that about 40,000 to 50,000 emigrants left Scotland in these crisis years, though it is highly likely that some later returned to the homeland. Europe, England, and the Americas certainly accounted for some. But Scandinavia and Poland-Lithuania were no longer the favoured areas as they had been in former times. Ulster now attracted the overwhelming majority of Scots migrants. It was in the 1690s, even more so than in earlier decades, that the Scottish identity in whole areas of that province was established and confirmed.[31] (See Chapters 22, 27, and 28.)

The story in the eighteenth and nineteenth centuries is more familiar (and is covered in detail in Chapters 22, 27, and 28). The Scottish diaspora spread far and wide over this period: the thirteen colonies that constituted the United States of America from 1783; British North America (later Canada); the Caribbean Islands, India, Australasia, and South Africa. These were the main areas of settlement until the second half of the twentieth century, though the West Indies and India were essentially 'sojourning' colonies where the prime objective in the eighteenth century and later for most migrants was to make some money and then return to Britain to live in comfortable status in later life. But by *c*.1900 Scots were also to be found in significant pockets in the cattle estancias of Argentina and Uruguay, the trading towns of the River Plate estuary, as coffee and tea planters in Ceylon (Sri Lanka), and as physicians, teachers, engineers, traders, and missionaries throughout Africa, China, Japan, and South Asia.[32] The Scottish diaspora from the later eighteenth century now became global in range and impact.

## 2

The age of European migration across the globe in the nineteenth century was made possible by a series of related influences. As the populations of states increased and social tensions within them become more common, so governments became more interested in emigration as a potential safety-valve for emerging political problems. In Britain, the ideology of 'systematic colonization' became a fashionable set of ideas and theories in the views associated with Edward Gibbon Wakefield and others. Building on the theories of Thomas Malthus, it was argued by advocates such as Wakefield that emigration could be a blessing rather than a curse, creating markets abroad for British industry while, at the same time, easing demographic pressures at home. These views became widely influential. In 1837 the New Zealand Association was formed in London along

---

[31] Smout, Landsman, and Devine, 'Scottish Emigration', 86; Patrick Fitzgerald, ' "Black '97": Reconsidering Scottish Migration to Ireland in the Seventeenth Century, and the Scotch-Irish in America', in W. Kelly and John R. Young, eds., *Ulster and Scotland 1600–2000* (Dublin, 2004).

[32] Devine, *To the Ends of the Earth*.

the lines suggested by Wakefield to support emigration to the Antipodes. The new thinking also inspired government intervention in the emigrant trade, particularly to Australia, still thought too distant and unappealing to attract unsubsidized immigration. Between 1828 and 1842, 180,000 emigrants sailed for Australia.[33] Most were assisted by a scheme of bounties through which colonial governments paid ships' masters and merchants a fee to recruit potential settlers from Britain and Ireland.

However, these changes in elite attitudes to colonization were less significant than advances in communications: 'the physical links improved and thickened into virtual bridges—hundreds of large ships, sailing or steaming regularly; whole systems of long-range canals; whole systems of trunk railroads.'[34] The steamship is rightly regarded as a key development, but it is important that the earlier and parallel improvements to sailing-ship design are recognized too; bigger vessels, wooden hulls with iron all helped to prolong the age of sail, particularly for long-distance voyages until the 1880s.[35] Related developments in commerce were also deeply significant. During and after the Napoleonic Wars, British North America became the nation's main source of timber, accounting for 75 per cent of all such imports in 1819–23. This was a boon to the Atlantic emigrant traffic because empty timber ships took a human cargo on their return voyages.[36] It was a similar story as far as the importation of wool from Australia and New Zealand was concerned: 'On the long voyage out from the UK the clipper ships carried human beings; on arrival at ports in New Zealand and Australia, the steerage berths were cleared away and the 'tween decks filled with wool bales for the voyage home.'[37] Indeed, it was above all the profitability of the wool trade that made the long-distance emigration to New Zealand a lucrative enterprise over several decades.

Of course, the development of the ocean-going steamship was catalytic. Although the cost of steamship travel was actually about a third dearer than crossing by sailing ships, the new vessels soon radically increased speed, comfort, and safety. In the 1850s it took six weeks to cross the Atlantic from UK ports. By 1914 the average voyage time had fallen to around a week. By drastically cutting voyage times the steamship also removed one of the major costs of emigration: the time between embarkation and settlement during which there was no possibility of earning.[38] This was especially crucial for the skilled and semi-skilled urban tradesmen who comprised an increasing proportion of Scottish emigrants in the later nineteenth century. They were now able to move on a temporary basis in order to exploit high wages or labour scarcities at particular times in North America. This factor also explains the increasing scale of return emigration. By 1900 it is estimated

[33] Frank Broeze, 'Private Enterprise and the Peopling of Australia, 1831–1850', *Economic History Review*, 35 (1982), 235–53.

[34] James Belich, *Replenishing the Earth: The Settler Revolution and the Rise of the Anglo-World 1783–1939* (Oxford, 2001), 179.

[35] Richards, *Britannia's Children*, 122.

[36] Belich, *Replenishing the Earth*, 109.

[37] McClean, 'Scottish Emigrants to New Zealand', 22.

[38] C. K. Harley, 'Ocean, Freight Rates and Productivity, 1740–1913', *Journal of Economic History*, 48 (1988), 851–76.

that around one-third of those Scots who left their homeland came back sooner or later.[39] The evidence from New Zealand suggests that returns became more common over time. Returnees rose from 36 per cent of outward sailings between 1853 and 1880 to 82 per cent of the 1 million outward sailings between 1881 and 1920. The increases corresponded exactly with the impact of transport innovation on the New Zealand route.[40]

The most dramatic and decisive advance made possible by the steamship was paralleled by the railway and the canal, which ensured that emigrants could be quickly and easily transported from all areas through the national network to the port of embarkation. Agreements were commonly made between shipping and railway companies, allowing emigrants to be transported free to their port of departure. The expansion of the railroad in North America brought similar benefits. By the 1850s the completion of the Canadian canal network and the associated railway development facilitated access to the western USA by allowing emigrants to book their passage to Quebec and Hamilton and then by rail to Chicago. The links between steamships and railways led to the provision of the highly popular through-booking system by which emigrants could obtain a complete package, with a ticket purchased in Europe allowing travel to the final destination in America. *Chambers' Journal* in 1857 described it as a 'prodigious convenience' that would 'rob emigration of its terrors and must set hundreds of families wandering'.[41]

Scots emigrants had a particular advantage because the railway system existed alongside a number of major shipping lines operating from the Clyde, which by the 1850s had developed a worldwide network of services. The significant passenger companies were the Albion, Allan, Anchor, City, and Donaldson lines, sailing mainly on a number of routes across the Atlantic; the City Line to India; the Allan Line to South Africa, and, from the 1860s, the Albion Line to New Zealand. In addition, some of the major railway companies in Canada played a vigorous proactive role in the emigrant business. They recognized that the railway was not simply an easy and rapid mode of transport for new arrivals from Europe but was also the most effective way of opening up the wilderness and prairie territory to permanent settlement. The mighty Canadian Pacific Railway Company (CPR) became very active in the promotion of emigration as a result. In 1880 it had been allocated 25 million acres of land between Winnipeg and the Rocky Mountains by the Dominion government. In order to generate profit, the company had to increase traffic through expanding areas of settlement, and to achieve this goal it embarked on an aggressive marketing campaign in Britain designed to stimulate emigration to the prairies. Scotland was specifically targeted, and agents of the CPR toured rural areas, giving lectures and providing information. The CPR even sought to reduce the hardships of pioneering by providing ready-made farms in southern Alberta, with housing, barns, and fences included as part of the sale.[42]

---

[39] M. Anderson and D. J. Morse, 'The People', in W. H. Fraser and R. J. Morris, eds., *People and Society in Scotland, 1830–1914* (Edinburgh, 1990), 16.

[40] McClean, 'Scottish Emigrants to New Zealand'.

[41] Quoted in M. Harper, *Emigration from North-East Scotland*, 2 vols. (Aberdeen, 1988), vol. ii, 22.

[42] Ibid., *passim*.

These initiatives by a large organization in attracting settlement to the prairie provinces were but one manifestation of a wider revolution in communicating the attractions of emigration to the peoples of Europe. The letters of emigrants to their families at home had always been the most influential medium for spreading information about overseas conditions. With the steamship, railway, and telegraph, this traditional form of communication became even more effective as postal services became still more frequent, increasingly reliable, and speedier. Emigrant letters, written as they were by trusted family members, retained a great significance as the more credible source of information on overseas employment, prices, and wages. Letters were sometimes supplemented by remittances sent home to relatives.[43]

Returning migrants were also a key source of information. It is wrong, for instance, to assume that those who came back did so because they necessarily experienced failure and disillusion in the New World, although some were indeed in this category. The Scottish press printed articles from time to time about emigrants who had returned with 'blighted hopes and empty purses'. The steamship revolution was bound to mean that the number of emigrants returning could increase markedly when conditions in the receiving countries temporarily deteriorated. However, many returnees had originally left Scotland with no intention of settling permanently in America. This was especially the case with tradesmen and semi-skilled workers. In the north-east of Scotland, for instance, several hundred granite workers migrated annually to American yards each spring, before returning to Aberdeen for the winter. Coal miners from Lanarkshire also developed a tradition of temporary movement for work in the USA. Masons and other skilled building workers were in great demand on a seasonal basis. By the 1880s there seems to have been a willingness to go overseas at relatively short notice. In the latter part of that decade, for example, scores of Scottish building tradesmen who had responded to advertisements in the press descended on Austin, Texas, when work on the state capital was halted by a strike of American workers. Evidence from Scandinavia, Italy, Greece, and England suggests that the 'failed' returning migrants were usually in a minority. There seems no reason to suppose that the Scottish pattern was any different. 'Successful' returnees must indeed have been a potent source for spreading knowledge of overseas conditions in local communities and even a positive influence in encouraging further emigration.[44]

To these personal and family networks was added in the later nineteenth century a veritable explosion in the quality and quantity of information available to potential emigrants. The Emigrants' Information Office opened in 1886 as a source of impartial advice and information on land grants, wages, living costs, and passage rates. Circulars, handbooks, and pamphlets were made available in greater volume and were valued because of their avowed objectivity. Even more important were local newspapers. Advertisements

---

[43] Angela McCarthy, *Personal Narratives of Irish and Scottish Migration, 1921–65: 'For Spirit and Adventure'* (Manchester, 2007), and Angela McCarthy, ed., *A Global Clan: Scottish Migrant Networks and Identities Since the Eighteenth Century* (London and New York, 2006).

[44] Bodnar, *The Transplanted*, 53–4.

for ships' sailings, information on assisted passages, numerous letters from emigrants, and articles on North American life were very regular features as the Scottish population was relentlessly bombarded with all the facts of the emigration experience. Overseas governments and land companies also became more aggressive, professional, and sophisticated in promoting emigration. In 1892, for instance, the Canadian government appointed two full-time agents in Scotland who undertook a tour of markets hiring fairs, agricultural shows, and village halls. The illustrated lecture, using the magic lantern, was a favourite device. W. G. Stuart, the agent for the north, was even able to deliver his presentation in Gaelic if the audience required it.

From the 1870s to the First World War, the Canadian government's aim was to settle the Prairie West with immigrants who would establish an agricultural foundation for the Dominion. The key influence on the booster strategy was Clifford Sifton, the Minister of the Interior from 1896 to 1905. He pioneered the first emigration communications plan by flooding selected countries with appealing literature, advertisements in the press, tours for key journalists who then filed flattering copy on their return home, paying agents' fees on a commission basis for every immigrant who settled in Canada, and giving bonuses to steamship agents for promoting the country in the United Kingdom. The rural districts of Scotland were especially targeted because of their historic links with Canada and the country's reputation for experienced farmers and skilled agricultural workers.[45]

Yet even the revolution of communications and information would have been insufficient if it had not been for the gargantuan increase in demand from the industrializing countries of Europe for the raw materials and food produce of the new lands. It was the explosion in the export of timber, wool, meat, mutton, cotton, and other staples to feed the industries and rising populations of Europe that powered the new economies and so made them increasingly attractive places in which to settle and work. The transformation was fuelled by the massive export of capital from Britain after c.1850, a process in which Scotland had a leading part. Between 1865 and 1914, the UK invested over $5 billion in the USA alone, facilitating the construction of railways, the reclaiming of land, and the building of towns without which large-scale settlement from the Old World would have been impossible.[46]

In turn, the great immigrations were neither uniform nor persistent but were triggered intermittently by a series of booms that sucked in labour at different times, in different countries, and in diverse regions of each country. Some of these could last for several years, others were more short-lived. When they collapsed, return migration, especially in the later nineteenth century, tended to occur.[47] In essence, the combination of better communications, superior flows of information, and the huge rise in staple exports from the primary producers had created a new international labour market in which workers were no longer constrained by national frontiers. This pattern goes a long

[45]  Harper, *Emigration from North-East Scotland*, vol. ii, 1–41.
[46]  Devine, *To the Ends of the Earth*, 228–50.
[47]  Belich, *Replenishing the Earth, passim.*

way to explaining the changing attraction of different destinations, as the syncopation of boom and bust was often different in the various settler societies. The model helps us to understand why Scottish emigration shifted rapidly from the USA to Canada in the years before the First World War but back again to the USA in the 1920s.

This, then, was the new environment for mass international migration, which deeply influenced the Scottish exodus as well as that of other nations. What the context cannot explain, however, is why Scotland, by any standards a successful industrial economy in the vanguard of Victorian modernity, lost so many more of its people than the European or mainland British average before 1930. The puzzle is compounded by one additional feature. Unusually, like England, Scotland was also a country of substantial immigration as well as emigration. By 1901, around 205,000 Irish born had made their homes in Scotland. Indeed, Irish immigration was proportionately greater in Scotland than England. Only 2.9 per cent of the population of England and Wales were Irish in 1851. The Scottish figure was 7.2 per cent. To the Irish should be added about 40,000 Jews, Lithuanians, and Italians who mainly arrived between 1860 and 1914 in Scotland, together with an unknown number of English moving from south of the Border.[48] (See Chapter 26.)

Traditionally, and perhaps still in popular opinion, the conundrum could be resolved by consideration of the plight of the Highlands in Scottish history. Until the middle decades of the nineteenth century the region did indeed contribute disproportionately to the total Scottish outflow. In more precise terms the western Highlands and Islands did so; most of those who left the parishes of the southern, central, and eastern fringes, at least in the first instance, made for the lowland towns.[49] The factors explaining the highland exodus are far from simple. The far west was a poor, conservative peasant society where, through subdivision, the access to land, albeit in minute holdings, was still possible for the majority. The regional society most closely comparable within the British Isles was the west of Ireland, which was broadly similar in its poverty, social system, and tenacious attachment to peasant values. For these very reasons, however, emigration from that area was limited compared to Ulster and the eastern districts of Ireland.

In part, what made the western Highlands different from patterns in the Irish West was the incidence of soldier emigration from the region. It was probably the most recruited area of the British Isles in the period 1775 to 1783 and again between 1795 and 1815.[50] This not only established a tradition of mobility and spread knowledge of overseas destinations, but the military settlements created after the Seven Years War and the American War also acted as the foci of attraction for successive waves of highland emigrations. Scottish Gaeldom was also different because it was much more subject to

[48] T. M. Devine, *The Scottish Nation, 1700 to 2007* (London, 2006), 486–522.
[49] T. M. Devine, *Clanship to Crofters' War: The Social Transformation of the Scottish Highlands* (Manchester, 1994), 177–91, 241–50.
[50] Matthew P. Dziennik, '"The Fatal Land": War, Empire and the Highland Soldier in British America, 1756–1783' (unpublished PhD thesis, University of Edinburgh, 2010), 33–73; Andrew Mackillop, *'More Fruitful than the Soil': Army, Empire and the Scottish Highlands 1715–1815* (East Linton, 2000).

intense levels of commercialization than the communities of the west of Ireland. The rent inflation of the post-1760 period, the 'modernization' of the social system through the destruction of the old joint tenancies, the imposition of the croft system and the clearances for sheep, all represented the powerful impact of 'improving' ideology and lowland market forces on traditional society. Up to *c.*1820, the highland emigrations can be regarded as attempts to resist the forces that were transforming the old ways so painfully and rapidly. Internal protest was muted but the alternative of emigration was significant and preferred to migration to the south, perhaps because of the 'independence' that came from the possibility of holding land across the Atlantic.[51]

The mass outward movement of highlanders after 1820, and especially in the famine of the 1840s and 1850s, was deeply significant. That period between 1846 and 1856 saw particularly high levels of loss from the region, on one estimate accounting for about a third of the population of the western mainland and insular parishes from Ardnamurchan in the extreme west to Cape Wrath in the north. Several localities experienced even greater ouflows.[52] Thereafter, however, the highland share of overall Scottish emigration became much less.

It might reasonably be suggested, however, that the Gaels who moved to the Lowlands in the first instance and then eventually emigrated were concealed within the numbers of those who left directly from urban areas. Yet the proportion of first-generation highlanders in lowland towns and cities in the 1851 census was rarely more than 10 per cent, and in Glasgow, for instance, significantly lower than that.[53] Scots who gave a town or city as their last place of residence before departure, though born in rural districts, were much more likely to have originally moved from a lowland farm or village rather than a highland croft. The Highland clearances cannot then explain, either directly or indirectly, mass Scottish emigration after *c.*1860 even if they were important between the 1760s and the Famine. Therefore, if we are to reach any substantive conclusions on the origins of this national movement afterwards, the clues have to lie in the lowland countryside and the urban/industrial areas of the Central Belt.

To a significant extent the very nature of Scottish economic transformation in the period after *c.*1760 became the vital context for extensive emigration. Far from restraining outward movement by providing new employment and material improvement, as in some parts of Europe, the distinctive nature of Scottish industrialization may have actually stimulated a continuing exodus of people. Basic to the Industrial Revolution in Scotland was profound change in rural social and economic structures. In the Lowlands, farms were consolidated, subtenancies removed, and the terms of access to land became more rigid and regulated.[54] (See Chapter 6.) Over time, fewer and fewer had legal rights

[51] T. M. Devine, *Clearance and Improvement: Land, Power and People in Scotland 1700–1900* (Edinburgh, 2006), 175–86.

[52] T. M. Devine, *The Great Highland Famine* (Edinburgh, 1988), 192–211.

[53] Charles W. J. Withers, *Urban Highlanders: Highland-Lowland Migration and Urban Gaelic Culture, 1700–1900* (East Linton, 1998).

[54] T. M. Devine, *The Transformation of Rural Scotland: Social Change and the Agrarian Economy 1660–1815* (Edinburgh, 1994), 36–164.

to farms as consolidation accelerated and subdivision of holdings was outlawed. As numbers rose through natural increase, the mobility of people became inevitable. Peasant proprietorship in Scotland (commonplace throughout central and southern Europe) was unknown, and by 1840 most lowland rural Scots were non-inheriting children of farmers, farm servants, country tradesmen, textile weavers, and day labourers. The Scottish Poor Law before 1843 was also notoriously hostile to the provision of relief for the able-bodied unemployed, though, in practice, modest doles were often given. The majority of the population of the lowland countryside therefore relied mainly on selling their labour power in the market to survive. It was inevitable that the ebb and flow of demand for labour enforced movement upon them, not least because for farm servants accommodation and employment were limited. To be without a job was also to be without a place to stay. Even before 1800 such domestic mobility was already present, and some suggest this gave Scotland a higher incidence of internal migration than countries such as France or the German states.[55]

In the nineteenth century internal migration within Scotland certainly intensified. There were at least five reasons for this.[56] First, population was rising while both agricultural and industrial opportunities in rural areas were stagnant or, especially after c.1840, contracting rapidly. In consequence, the proportion of the natural population employed in agriculture declined markedly from 24 per cent in 1841 to 10 per cent in 1911. Second, most permanent agricultural workers on Scottish farms were 'servants' hired on annual or half-yearly contracts, who received accommodation as part of their labour contract. The unemployed farm worker, who inevitably had lost his home as a result, had no choice but to move to seek for a job. Third, Scottish urbanization was notable for its speed and scale. The proportion of Scots living in settlements of over 5,000 rose from 31 per cent in 1831 to almost 60 per cent in 1911. The vast majority of the new urban populations were from the farms, villages, and small towns of the lowland countryside. Fourth, the first phase of industrialization down to c.1830 had extended manufacturing employment, especially in textiles, in rural areas. During the coal, iron, and steel phase, production concentrated more intensively in the central Lowlands, the Border woollen towns, Dundee, Fife, and Midlothian. Indeed, one of the most striking features of Scottish industrial capitalism was its extraordinary concentration. This process ensured a rapid shedding of population from areas of crumbling employment to the regions of rapid growth in the Forth–Clyde valley. Fifth, in the last quarter of the nineteenth century, clear evidence emerged of a growing rejection by the younger generation of the drudgery, social constraints, and isolation of country life. The towns had always had an attraction but now they seduced the youth of rural society as never before.

The interaction of all these influences produced an unprecedented level of mobility. The 1851 census shows that no less than a third of the Scottish population had crossed at

---

[55] R. A. Houston, 'The Demographic Regime', in T. M. Devine and R. Mitchison, eds., *People and Society in Scotland, 1760–1830*, 2 vols. (Edinburgh, 1988), vol. i, 20.

[56] For these points see T. M. Devine, ed., *Farm Servants and Labour in Lowland Scotland, 1770–1914* (Edinburgh, 1984), *passim*.

least one county boundary. Demographic research has demonstrated also that in the 1860s the vast majority of parishes in all areas were experiencing net outward movement of population. Heavy losses in the Lowlands were especially pronounced in the south-west region and in many parts of the east from Berwick to Moray. The only areas attracting people were in the central zone and the textile towns of the Borders. As Michael Anderson and Donald Morse suggest: 'The conclusion must be that almost the whole of rural Scotland (and many of the more industrial and commercial areas also) were throughout our period, unable to provide enough opportunities at home to absorb even quite modest rates of population increase.'[57]

This demographic pattern is crucial to an understanding of the roots of Scottish emigration. Scots were mobile abroad in part because they were increasingly very mobile at home.[58] Emigration, then, could be seen as an extension of migration within Scotland, because it was much less challenging after 1860 with the revolution in transatlantic travel associated with the steamship and railways. Such a suggestion is entirely consistent with the point made earlier that most emigrants in the later nineteenth century were urban in origin, because almost certainly concealed within this category were many who had been born into an agricultural or industrial artisan background in the countryside and had moved to the towns before leaving Scotland altogether.

Equally, some evidence suggests that from the later nineteenth century the volume of emigration varied inversely with internal migration. People in country farms and villages searching for opportunities elsewhere seem to have been able to weigh the attractions of the Scottish towns against those of overseas destinations and come to a decision on the basis of these comparisons. In the decades 1881–90 and 1901–10, for instance, there was heavy emigration, with 43 and 47 per cent respectively of the natural increase leaving the country. In the same twenty-year period, movement to Glasgow and the surrounding suburbs fell to low levels, while there was actual net movement out of the western Lowlands. On the other hand, during the 1870s and 1890s emigration declined but larger numbers moved to the cities and towns of the west.[59] This pattern suggests an informed and mobile population that had access to sources of information such as newspapers, letters from relatives, and intelligence from returned migrants, which enabled judgements about emigration to be weighed and considered.

In essence, lowland rural emigration was not induced so much by the reality or the threat of destitution or deprivation as by the lure of opportunity. Throughout the nineteenth and early twentieth centuries, Canada and Australasia were the great magnets for those who wished to work the land, while rural tradesmen and industrial workers tended to opt more for the USA. From emigrant letters and newspaper articles one can piece together the attractions of emigration for both small tenants and farm servants. A

---

[57] Anderson and Morse, 'The People', 19, 22.

[58] R. H. Campbell, 'Scotland', in R. A. Cage, ed., *The Scots Abroad: Labour, Capital, Enterprise* (London, 1985), 10.

[59] Jeanette M. Brock, *The Mobile Scot: A Study of Emigration and Migration, 1861–1911* (Edinburgh, 1999), 178–209.

primary incentive was the possibility of owning a holding that was relatively cheap to acquire and increasingly made available for purchase in developed form by land companies and Dominion and provincial governments. In Canada and Australia, land was plentiful whereas in Scotland even wealthy farmers were dependent on their landlords, with tenure regulated by a detailed lease enforceable at law and other sanctions. The Scottish tenants' agitation of the 1870s showed the tensions that these relationships could sometimes generate. In the colonies, on the other hand, owner-occupation, the much desired 'independence', and the right to bequeath the hard-worked land to the family were all on offer and at reasonable rates. The strains imposed by the Agricultural Depression in the 1870s and early 1880s added to discontent in some areas and further increased the attractions of emigration. The Board of Agriculture in 1906 reviewed the reasons for the decline in the rural population and concluded with respect to Scotland that:

> Many correspondents refer to the absence of an incentive to remain on the land and of any reasonable prospect of advancement in life, and it is mentioned in some districts, particularly in Scotland, many of the best men have been attracted to the colonies, where their energies may find wider scope and where the road to independence and a competency is broader and more easy to access.[60]

This can be seen most vividly in the pages of the weekly *People's Journal*, Scotland's most popular periodical of the time, selling at a penny per issue. By 1890 its total circulation over a six-month period was reckoned to have reached 5 1/2 million at home and abroad with an average of 212,000 copies printed each week. The *Journal* proudly boasted that it 'enters more Scottish Households than any other Newspaper' and was 'sold by 10,000 newsagents'. Importantly, it was 'specially designed to promote the interests of the working classes' and crucially, virtually every issue had articles on emigration worldwide, providing comment, advice on changing employment conditions, and the opportunities available overseas for people from both town and country.

Ironically, the dynamic heart of the Scottish economy, the regions of advanced industrialism, were the main sources of emigrants after *c.*1860. But, when the nature of urban and industrial society is probed more deeply, key fault lines are revealed that make the exodus more comprehensible. For a start, huge social inequalities were entrenched in those manufacturing districts of the nation where armies of semi-skilled, unskilled, and casual labourers serviced the mighty industries of mining, shipbuilding, engineering, and textiles. Notoriously, west-central Scotland and the Dundee area in particular proportionately had relatively few professional, commercial, and managerial classes.[61] Some of the lower middle class might have had the chance to move up the social scale with energy, talent, and connections. But it was much more difficult and often impossible for those below to 'get on' and achieve advancement. The barriers, even to minimal social

[60] Quoted in Harper, *Emigration from North-East Scotland*, vol. ii, 55.
[61] T. C. Smout, *A Century of the Scottish People, 1830–1950* (London, 1986), 109–13.

mobility, for the vast majority of the population of Victorian Scotland, seem to have been granitic and enduring.

One telling indicator was the background of students in the Scottish universities. They did attract from a much broader social range than Oxford and Cambridge but, even so, the hard evidence does not entirely support the myth of the 'democratic intellect'. The Argyll Commission's analysis concluded that a third of students in the nation's universities came from professional families and over a half from the middle classes as a whole. The sons of skilled artisans with traditional skills—carpenters, shoemakers, and masons—were also represented. But the offspring of miners, farm servants, and factory workers were notable by their virtual absence. The leading historian of the Victorian universities has concluded that the son of a church minister was one hundred times more likely to go to a Scottish university than a miner's son, and that 'most working class students were drawn from the very top stratum of their class, while neither the rural poor or the factory workers, or the unskilled workers in the towns had more than a token representation'.[62] The celebrated 'lads o' pairts' (boys of talent) did exist but they were few and far between. Against this background, the aspirational attractions of the overseas territories, even if much exaggerated in the booster literature, must have struck a chord with many.

Another factor of considerable relevance was the reward to labour. Relative to England and Wales, industrial Scotland was a low-wage economy. Despite variation between sectors, Scottish wages were often up to 20 per cent below the equivalent in English trades before c.1860, though the evidence suggests a degree of convergence thereafter.[63] Yet when costs of living are taken into account, on the eve of the First World War in 1914, most earnings in Scottish manufacturing still lagged 10 to 12 per cent behind those in English industrial areas.[64] Of course, there is no inevitable correlation between low wages and emigration. What is critical is the relative differential between opportunities at home and overseas. In the second half of the nineteenth and early twentieth centuries that differential between western Europe and the New World became greater. Wages and opportunities were increasing at home, but they were doing so with even greater speed overseas because the American economies were very rich in resources but grossly underpopulated. Those with industrial skills and experience were especially in demand.[65] The scenario for mass emigration from societies such as Scotland was clearly emerging as the previous constraints on movement crumbled. Ignorance of conditions across the Atlantic and in Australasia diminished further as more and more information was disseminated through the press, government sources, emigration societies, and advice from previous emigrants. This was widely absorbed into Scottish society where

[62] R. D. Anderson, *Education and Opportunity in Victorian Scotland* (Edinburgh, 1983), 152.

[63] R. H. Campbell, *The Rise and Fall of Scottish Industry, 1707–1939* (Edinburgh, 1980), 76–101; Smout, *Century of the Scottish People*, 112.

[64] R. G. Rodger, 'The Invisible Hand: Market Forces, Housing and the Urban Form in Victorian Cities', in D. Fraser and A. Sutcliffe, eds., *The Pursuit of Urban History* (London, 1980), 190–211.

[65] J. D. Gould, 'European Intercontinental Emigration 1815–1914: Patterns and Causes', *Journal of European Economic History*, 8 (1979).

literacy levels by the standards of most countries in Europe were high. Emigration therefore became available to many more as income levels rose in the later nineteenth century. The sheer cost had been a significant obstacle to many in previous times. Detailed analysis of migration in Scottish rural society after 1870 has suggested a marked increase in social expectations, a change partly related to higher wages but also to further expansion in educational opportunities after the legislation of 1872 compelling higher levels of school attendance.[66] It may have been the case that there were similar attitudinal changes among many urban and industrial workers, which made more attractive the lure of greater opportunities overseas. This was where the transport revolution became of key importance, since now the essential infrastructure had emerged to define and shape a truly transatlantic labour market.

Thus, the habitual and historic internal mobility of the Scots could now be translated fully into global movement. In the same way as they had long compared wages and employment within Scotland, it was now easier than ever before to evaluate opportunities in New York, Toronto, Chicago, Johannesburg, and Melbourne in relation to those in Glasgow, Dundee, and Edinburgh. The income differentials were often so great and the skills shortage in the New World so acute that many thousands could not resist the temptation, especially since, in the event of failure, the return journey home was but the price of a steamship ticket. The chances were also there, of course, for the skilled of that other advanced economy, England. But it is hardly surprising that the Scots found emigration more irresistible. Scotland was still a poorer society than England and the difference between opportunities at home and abroad was greater for its people. Quite simply, they had more to gain by emigration.[67]

But it was not simply because the rewards of industry at home could not compete with those abroad or in England. Scottish emigration also attained such high levels *because* of the peculiar economic structure of the society. It had a higher proportion of its inhabitants employed in industrial work by 1871 than any other country in western Europe apart from England. But unlike England, the majority of the employed male population in Scotland were heavily concentrated in the capital-goods sector of shipbuilding, coal, metals, and engineering. To an unusual extent, many of these activities were heavily dependent on the export market. The Scottish economy lacked the cushion of a growing service sector and a range of industries catering for the domestic consumer that were emerging south of the border.[68] After 1830 the British economy as a whole became subject to more extreme fluctuations in the trade cycle, whereas in Scotland the amplitude and duration of cyclical change was more violent because of the tight interrelationships within the heavy industrial structure, the bias towards foreign markets, which were inherently fickle, and the relative weakness of domestic demand.

---

[66] Devine, ed., *Farm Servants and Labour*, 119–20, 251–3.

[67] Flinn ed., *Scottish Population History*, 442.

[68] C. H. Lee, 'Modern Economic Growth and Structural Change in Scotland: The Service Sector Reconsidered', *Scottish Economic and Social History*, 3 (1983), 5–35.

This economic insecurity was basic to emigration. Violent fluctuations in employment were integral to Scottish industrial 'prosperity' even in the heyday of Victorian and Edwardian expansion. Their scale and frequency can be seen in the building industry, which employed about 7 per cent of the occupied male labour force in the 1880s. Between 1881 and 1891 the numbers employed fell by 5.1 per cent, rose by 43.3 per cent from 1891 to 1901, and contracted again by a massive 21.4 per cent over the years 1901–11.[69] Not surprisingly, emigration was at its height at the bottom of these cycles. Because fluctuations were probably more savage and longer lasting in Scotland, it is reasonable to assume that the volume of outward movement would be greater than south of the border. The dramatic peaks in Scottish emigration, during the later 1840s and early 1850s, the mid-1880s, from 1906 to 1913, and in the 1920s, all took place in periods of serious industrial depression at home.

In the final analysis then, it would seem that most Scots left their native land in search of opportunity, 'independence', and an ambition to 'get on', aspirations which, for the reasons described above, could not easily be satisfied in the homeland itself. It is significant that the very poor and destitute of the towns and cities were not usually accounted among the emigrants in any great numbers. Most of those who left may have had few resources but normally had at least some modest means. Pressure to go was not irrelevant—as witnessed by the correlation of economic downturn at home and increased emigration abroad. But what comes through strongly from the evidence is the central importance of individual human choice and decision, even if these attributes were themselves powerfully influenced by the prevailing structural forces of society, ideology, and economy.

# 3

A few years after the end of the Second World War, a Scottish National Party pamphlet was published with the title *Beware of Emigration*. It argued that 'nothing has sapped the life of Scotland more in the last 150 years than mass emigration', and lamented that it was always the lifeblood of the nation, 'the young and enterprising, the skilled craftsmen and…the back-bone of industry' who were the first to leave.[70] Few took note of the warning. Scottish emigration, inevitably constrained by six years of global conflict, quickly returned to pre-war levels soon after 1945 and for some decades thereafter. Between 1951 and 1981, 753,000 Scots left the country, around 45 per cent of them for England and the rest for new lives overseas. As Table 7.1 demonstrates, there was fluctuation over time in outward movement, but emigration at high levels was sustained throughout the period, though with some signs of deceleration by the later 1980s.

---

[69] J. H. Treble, 'The Occupied Male Labour Force', in Fraser and Morris, eds., *People and Society in Scotland*, 195–6.

[70] Quoted in Catriona M. M. Macdonald, *Whaur Extremes Meet: Scotland's Twentieth Century* (Edinburgh, 2009), 115.

Table 7.1  Net Migration from Scotland, 1931–89 (thousands)

| Decades | UK | Overseas |
| --- | --- | --- |
| 1931–51 | 210 | 10 |
| 1951–61 | 140 | 142 |
| 1961–71 | 169 | 157 |
| 1971–81 | 52 | 99 |
| 1981–9 | 70 | 47 |

Source: Annual Reports of the Registrar General Scotland, 1931–89.

From 1951 to 2006 net migration loss, defined as the difference between the number of people moving to from those leaving a country, was about 825,000, described by one authority as 'a staggering amount' from a nation of little more than five million.[71] Most of this haemorrhage occurred before the 1990s, as in that decade there began a phase of relative balance with the number of immigrants coming to Scotland starting to equal the number of emigrants leaving the country. Once again, as in the past, the Scottish experience contrasted with that of England and Wales. Scots continued to supply a disproportionate number both of Britain's internal migrants and also its emigrants.[72] As a result, Scotland's share of the population of the United Kingdom fell from 11 per cent in 1914 to just over 9 per cent by 1981. Between 1921 and 1961 the population of England grew by nearly one-third; Scotland by only 5 per cent. Emigration on a substantial scale was sustained much longer north of the border. Historians of English emigration describe a post-war surge in the 1950s and 1960s, which started to wane by the 1970s. Not so in Scotland.[73]

As late as 2003 to 2006, over 217,000 Scots left for other parts of the United Kingdom or overseas. Those who went abroad numbered 82,200 over that four-year period. However, it should be borne in mind that the cumulative figure of annual outflows inflates 'real' emigration because it includes a substantial proportion of Scottish students, many of whom later returned home after completion of study, together with English-domiciled and overseas students going back after training in Scotland and hence not 'Scots' by any normal definition.[74]

Again, until near the end of the twentieth century, Scotland failed to attract enough immigrants to compensate for these large losses. The Irish once again moved in large numbers to England after 1950 but not to Scotland. Similarly, Asian migration to Britain tended to peter out as it approached the north of England. In 1966 a mere 2 of every 1,000 Scots were natives of the New Commonwealth. The figures for England and Wales

---

[71]  R. F. Wright, 'The Economics of New Immigration to Scotland', David Hume Institute Occasional Paper, no. 77 (2008), 13.

[72]  Richards, Britannia's Children, 205–6, 271.

[73]  Ibid.

[74]  Wright, 'Economics of New Immigration', 15–16. I am grateful to my colleague, Professor Michael Anderson, for advice on these data.

were over twelve times greater. The difference in order of magnitude was such that it suggests Scotland was not regarded as a land of opportunity from the immigrant perspective, as it had been in the nineteenth century.[75]

Eventually, however, it was the increase in immigration to Scotland that began to make for a more favourable migration balance. By 2004 total in- and out-migration was about 70,000 per year, in each direction, resulting in a net loss of just 2,000 people, a radical reduction compared to most years in the twentieth century and earlier. By 2004 this small loss had even turned into a favourable balance of over 27,000, then 19,800 in 2005, and 21,600 in 2006.[76] Two factors were influential. First, there was a significant growth in English immigration to Scotland, with 220,000 first-generation English in 1951 compared to 408,984 in 2001, an overall rate of increase of 84 per cent. The English-born are now by far Scotland's largest immigrant group.[77] Second, Scotland shared in the sharp rise in immigration to the United Kingdom from the countries that joined the European Union in May 2004. Poland was the prime though by no means the only source. The Polish Consulate in Edinburgh considered that the number of Polish immigrants to Scotland rose rapidly to around 50,000 by the end of 2006. Current (2010) estimates of the incomers vary between 75,000 and 85,000.[78]

It could perhaps be predicted that the acute austerity and rationing of necessities in the years after 1945 would have resulted in a new surge of emigration, especially for a generation that still had vivid memories of the profound poverty and insecurities of the 1930s.[79] More difficult to explain, and awaiting detailed research, was not only the continuation of outward movement for several decades after the 1950s but also its considerable increase in scale. After all, economic recovery and material improvement had proceeded apace in the 1950s. It was in 1957 that Harold Macmillan made his oft-quoted remark: 'Let's be frank about it, most of our people have never had it so good.' His comment had particular relevance to Scotland, which had endured a good deal of pain for much of the interwar period. Now unemployment, the curse of the 1930s, fell to historically low levels. Between 1947 and 1957, Scottish unemployment was remarkably stable and only varied between 2.4 per cent and 3 per cent of an insured labour force, even though that had actually increased significantly by over 690,000 between 1945 and 1960. There were now jobs for virtually everyone who wanted to work. Full employment also brought rising incomes. The average working-class household in 1953 was reckoned to be 2.5 to 3 times better-off than in 1938. For a time, even the gap in average wage levels between England and Scotland narrowed. The nation's health improved, not simply because of the new prosperity but also as a result of legislative changes and scientific advances. The National

[75]  Richard Finlay, *Modern Scotland 1914–2000* (London, 2004), 305.

[76]  'Demographic Trends in Scotland: A Shrinking and Ageing Population', *ESRC Seminar Series: Mapping the Public Policy Landscape* (2004), 1.

[77]  Murray Watson, *Being English in Scotland* (Edinburgh, 2003), 27.

[78]  Aleksander Dietkow, 'Poles in Scotland—before and after 2004', in T. M. Devine and David Hesse, eds., *Scotland and Poland: Historical Encounters, 1500–2010* (Edinburgh, 2011).

[79]  A. James Hammerton and Alistair Thomson, *Ten Pound Poms: Australia's Invisible Migrants* (Manchester, 2005), 52, 67.

Health Service from 1948 extended free treatment to all, while by the Education (Scotland) Acts of 1945 and 1947 local authorities could insist on the medical inspection of pupils and the provision of free treatment. Antibiotics were introduced for the first time on a large scale in the mid-1940s and soon wiped out tuberculosis, the killer disease of countless young adults in the past. By 1960, Scotland's infant mortality rate was the same as that of the USA and close to the figures for England and Wales. Rising living standards in the 1950s were confirmed by the steady increase in the range of new appliances, such as washing machines, vacuum cleaners, and electric cookers, which made homes easier to run. Leisure patterns were transformed by the television and, for a long time after its introduction, cinema audience figures tumbled. The number of TV sets grew from 41,000 in 1952 to well over 1 million 10 years later, an explosion that was fuelled partly by the huge demand for televisions at the time of the Queen's Coronation in 1953. The nation's long-term housing crisis was now also tackled for the first time on a large scale with an extraordinary total of over 564,000 new houses built in the two decades after 1945. As the urban slums came down, many thousands of Scots for the first time had decent houses, with inside toilets and equipped to modern standards.[80]

Yet these major gains in living standards failed to stem the flow of Scots emigrants. Wage levels and real incomes in the 1950s and 1960s, despite the better times, were indeed marginally behind those of England, but it is generally agreed that these small differences cannot convincingly explain why so many left.[81] The Toothill Committee Report on the Scottish Economy in 1960, for instance, was sceptical of any likely connection between economic vicissitudes at home and levels of emigration abroad. They 'could find no clear relationship between unemployment and emigration rates...no doubt whatever the conditions at home, many Scots still migrate as they have done even during the most prosperous period'.[82] Indeed, Scots emigrants in this period were on the whole more highly skilled and came from better social backgrounds than those who moved to England for work.[83]

Much more study of motivation is needed, but again, as in the past, the movement abroad seems to have been aspirational and therefore spurred on by the material improvements at home that engendered a new spirit of optimism and desire for even greater opportunities. The late twentieth-century communications revolution including television, the telephone, and air travel also made emigration easier than at any point in the past, as well as providing more immediate and appealing information on the higher quality of life that was possible abroad at the very time when rising incomes were making emigration more affordable. A vital factor was the enthusiastic commitment of Commonwealth governments to encourage white, and especially British, emigration from the late 1940s. The most elaborate and successful recruitment campaigns were mounted by Australia.[84] For the Australian people the nightmare scenario of Japanese invasion and occupation during the Second World War

---

[80] Devine, *Scottish Nation, 1700–2007*, 562–5.

[81] A. K. Cairncross, ed., *The Scottish Economy* (Glasgow, 1953), 1–8.

[82] *Report of the Committee of Enquiry into the Scottish Economy (Toothill Report), Scottish Council Development and Industry* (1961), paragraphs 14.16–14.18.

[83] Finlay, *Modern Scotland*, 307.

[84] Hammerton and Thomson, *Ten Pound Poms*, 40, 45, 68–70.

had almost become a horrendous reality. In the years of peace thereafter, 'populate or perish' therefore became the national mantra in an attempt to provide a demographic bulwark against future enemies. The result was legislation in 1947 promising subsidized fares of £10 for each adult emigrant and free passage for children under the age of fourteen. Additional migration offices were opened in British cities. Bureaucracy for potential migrants was cut, countless glossy brochures were distributed depicting sunny outdoor lifestyles in Australia, and information sheets were produced offering the British settlers special support for health and social security. In the 1960s and 1970s Scots made up between a quarter to a third of the British exodus to Australia. Only in 1973 was this 'White Australia Policy' abandoned and immigration targets reduced.[85]

Other countries also developed their own policies. In 1952 the USA eased immigration restrictions and in subsequent years Scots comprised over a quarter of all British emigrants there. Indeed, for a time, visa allocations to Britain were so generous they were never completely taken up. Canada until 1962 gave preference to immigrants from the United Kingdom, France, and the United States, while New Zealand offered £10 passages for key workers from 1947 until 1975. But by that decade, overseas immigration policies had become much more restrictive, with a consequent decline in the volume of emigration from Britain.[86]

# 4

. . . . . . . . . . . . . . . . . . . . . . . . . . . . . . . . . . . . . . . . . . . . . . . . . . . . . . . . . . . . . . . . . . . . . . . . . . . . . . . . . . . . . . . . . . . . . . . . . . . . . . . . . . . . . . . . . . . . . . . . . . . . . . . . . . .

Scotland is a nation that has experienced many generations of outward movement on an unusually large scale. This made for a 'greater Scotland' beyond the seas which, for better or worse, had a significant effect, not only on the countries of settlement in many parts of the world (as indicated in Chapters 14, 16, 22, 27, and 28) but also on the homeland itself: major demographic loss; the mass exodus of the young, resourceful, and energetic; repatriation of profits earned in foreign climes by Scottish adventurers; cultural and educational transfers from Europe, America, and Asia. All of these factors, and others, must have had a profound and complex impact on the moulding of the Scottish nation, and modern scholarship is only now beginning to unpick them. It is an important task for researchers of the future.

## FURTHER READING

Armitage, David, 'The Scottish Diaspora', in Jenny Wormald, ed., *Scotland: A History* (Oxford, 2005).
Cage, R. A., ed., *The Scots Abroad: Labour, Capital, Enterprise* (London, 1985).
Ditchburn, David, *Scotland and Europe* (East Linton, 2000).

[85] Timothy J. Hatton, 'Emigration from the UK, 1870–1913 and 1950–1998', *European Review of Economic History*, 8 (2004), 166.
[86] Ibid., 175–8.

Devine, T. M., *Scotland's Empire 1600–1815* (London, 2003).

—— *To the Ends of the Earth: Scotland's Global Diaspora 1750–2010* (London, 2011).

—— *Scottish Emigration and Scottish Society* (Edinburgh, 1992).

Gray, Malcolm, 'Scottish Emigration: The Social Impact of Agrarian Change in the Rural Lowlands 1775–1875', *Perspectives in American History*, vii, 1973.

Grosjean, A., and Murdoch, S., eds., *Scottish Communities Abroad in the Early Modern Period* (Leiden, 2005).

Harper, Marjory, *Adventurers and Exiles: The Great Scottish Exodus* (London, 2003).

—— and Constantine, Stephen, *Emigration and Empire* (Oxford, 2010).

McCarthy, Angela, *Personal Narratives of Irish and Scottish Migration, 1921–65: 'For Spirit and Adventure'* (Manchester, 2007).

—— ed., *A Global Clan: Scottish Migrant Networks and Identities Since the Eighteenth Century* (London and New York, 2006).

Mackenzie, John M., and Devine, T. M., eds., *Scotland and Empire* (Oxford, 2011).

Murdoch, Steve, *Network North: Scottish Kin, Commercial and Covert Associations in Northern Europe 1603–1746* (Leiden, 2006).

Smout, T. C., Landsman, Ned C., and Devine, T. M., 'Scottish Emigration in the Seventeenth and Eighteenth Centuries', in Nicholas Canny, ed., *Europeans on the Move* (Oxford, 1994).

Worthington, David, *Scots in Hapsburg Service 1618–1648* (Leiden, 2003).

# PART II

# REFORMATION, REGAL UNION, AND CIVIL WARS, 1500–*c*.1680

CHAPTER 8

········································································

# THE RENAISSANCE

········································································

## ANDREA THOMAS

FOR a long time it was assumed that Scotland did not participate in the Renaissance, but in the last twenty years this myth has been challenged. Specialists have focused on redis-covering specific aspects of Scotland's Renaissance heritage: major studies are listed in the Further Reading. Yet to be fully explored are the connections and interactions between the various strands of cultural activity, and the broader overview of the Renaissance in Scotland. The precise definitions, characteristics, and boundaries are also still open to some debate, with scholars offering different versions of what consti-tutes the Scottish Renaissance from one discipline to another. This essay attempts to explore some of these issues.

## WHAT WAS THE RENAISSANCE?

The term 'renaissance' simply means 'rebirth' and the concept has been applied to many creative periods. However, the original Renaissance was the pre-eminent intellectual and cultural movement of late-medieval and early-modern western Europe, straddling the notional boundaries between these two historical eras, and traditionally seen as lay-ing the foundations of the modern age. The Renaissance is so called because it involved a revival and reapplication of the cultural achievements of classical Greece and Rome, which were regarded as the pinnacle of civilization. The essential characteristics were identified in the mid-nineteenth century by the cultural historian Jacob Burckhardt, who focused on the Italian peninsula as its birthplace.[1]

Burckhardt developed a notion of historical self-awareness as a form of new individu-alism, which he applied to an examination of the prominent writers, scholars, artists,

---

[1] Jacob Burckhardt, *Die Kultur der Renaissance in Italien: ein Versuch* (Basel, 1860), also available in translation.

and architects of Renaissance Italy, who were the foremost practitioners of the revival of the antique and a humanist agenda of active engagement with public life and the rational, scientific investigation of the natural world. His analysis was magisterial and seminal and, like many such works, it came under attack in the twentieth century. Medievalists in particular challenged the view that the Middle Ages were culturally or intellectually 'dark', in contrast with the enlightened, 'modern' Renaissance.[2] An interest in classical literature and philosophy and a thriving intellectual culture have been detected at many points in medieval Europe, so that the Renaissance now looks more like a distinct evolution of late-medieval culture rather than a sharp reaction against it.

Yet, despite the caveats, the essence of Burckhardt's thesis still has value, not least because the ideas of a conscious break with the past and a revival of the antique were current in Italy at the time. In the mid-fourteenth century, Petrarch first described the centuries that separated his own time from the glories of ancient Rome as a 'dark age'. He promoted a revival of Latin literature in an attempt to resuscitate Italian culture. By the 1490s, the philosopher Marsilio Ficino could describe the humanist resurgence of Latin, and increasingly Greek, scholarship as the restoration of a golden age. In the 1550s and 1560s, Giorgio Vasari's monumental *Lives of the Artists* used the Italian term for rebirth, *rinascita*, to describe the achievements of the Italian painters, sculptors, and architects of his period.[3] However simplistic their views might have been, for Petrarch, Ficino, Vasari, and others, Italy was progressing from a medieval past into a modern future by emulating the culture of the ancients.

Again, the received view of the chronological and geographical spread of the Renaissance has been criticized in recent years. Traditionally, it is deemed to have started in Italy in the late fourteenth century and spread north and west during the fifteenth century, so that by the mid-sixteenth century it had influenced all of Europe. By the early seventeenth century, artistic and cultural styles in most places were mutating into the complex embellishment of the Baroque. This model is not entirely unsound but it also needs refining. The Renaissance spirit arrived in northern states at different times and with varying degrees of Italian influence. Likewise, at the end of the period, where Vasari detected the waning of the Italian Renaissance in the 1560s, the northern Renaissance is usually deemed to have ended around 1600–20, as the Renaissance gradually faded into the Baroque. The association of the Baroque with the militant Catholicism of the Counter-Reformation has also made the use of this term problematic in Protestant states. Whilst the northern Baroque style did develop in Scotland in the seventeenth century, it is often not identified as such, but instead termed 'the late Renaissance'. Thus it is common for the Scottish Baroque to be completely overlooked and 'the Renaissance' unjustifiably extended through the seventeenth century to meet the Enlightenment.[4]

---

[2] E.g. C. H. Haskins, *The Renaissance of the Twelfth Century* (Cambridge, MA, 1927).

[3] Theodore E. Mommsen, 'Petrarch's Conception of the "Dark Ages"', *Speculum*, 17 (1942), 226–42; M. Ficino, *Opera Omnia*, ed. S. Toussaint (Paris, 2000), 944; Giorgio Vasari, *Le Vite delle più eccellenti Pittori, Scultori et Architettori* (Florence, 1550; expanded edn., Florence, 1568), also available in translation.

[4] E.g. Charles McKean, 'Renaissance Architecture', in Bob Harris and Alan R. MacDonald, eds., *Scotland: The Making and Unmaking of the Nation, c.1100–1707*, 5 vols. (Dundee, 2006–7), vol. 2, 183–200.

The Italians were in many respects at the forefront of the Renaissance but not invariably the pioneers of every innovation. Cultural influences in some disciplines flowed instead from north to south and there was considerable cross-fertilization. Furthermore, the traditional view tends to evaluate the northern Renaissance according to the extent to which it imitated Italian models, which underestimates the importance of the varied local interpretations of the Renaissance in the north. The diversity of styles is now more commonly seen as a strength rather than a weakness. Thus the scarcity of direct Italian influences and the hybrid nature of the Scottish Renaissance are no longer deemed to signify an experience necessarily inferior to continental developments.

# The Scottish Context

Notwithstanding this reappraisal of the nature of the Scottish Renaissance, it is possible to demonstrate Scottish connections with Italy and other European states, which were more extensive than has often been imagined.[5] Although geographically at the margins of Europe, Scotland in the fifteenth and sixteenth centuries engaged vigorously with the ecclesiastical, academic, diplomatic, dynastic, military, and mercantile networks of the period. The Renaissance in Scotland was thus an amalgamation of influences, both foreign and domestic, some of which originated in Italy whilst others were rooted in northern Europe. Italian impulses that found resonance in Scotland included the notion of historical self-awareness and self-fashioning in pursuit of individual fame and glory. In northern Europe this was adopted enthusiastically by monarchs of the young nation-states, including the Stewarts, who used Roman imperial models to validate their authority, sought to present kingship as a unifying national force, and promoted the magnificence of courtly spectacles as evidence of their virtue and greatness. This was blended with an obsession with chivalry and heraldry that provided continuity with the medieval past.

Another important influence was the impact of humanism. This also had Italian roots, although the greatest humanist of the age was Desiderius Erasmus of Rotterdam. Humanism in this period meant the academic disciplines of the *studia humanitatis*: poetry, grammar, history, moral philosophy, and rhetoric, in Latin or Greek. Humanists believed that their studies could uncover universal truths of great moral force, so they promoted active engagement in public life by intellectuals, who could thus benefit wider society: the *res publica* or commonweal. The humanists also stressed the dignity and rationality of mankind, the value of studying the wisdom and eloquence of the ancients (preferably in the original languages or accurate translations), the importance of promoting literacy and education (utilizing printed texts and vernacular languages), and the scientific method of exploring the natural world by observation, deduction, and

---

[5] David Ditchburn, 'Scotland and Europe', in Harris and MacDonald, eds., *Scotland*, vol. 1, 103–20; Steve Murdoch, 'Scotland and Europe', in Harris and MacDonald, eds., *Scotland*, vol. 2, 126–44.

experimentation. The humanist programme was adopted enthusiastically in Scotland and adapted to local needs by public intellectuals such as William Elphinstone, Hector Boece, and George Buchanan.

The art and architecture of Renaissance Italy prioritized the imitation of Greek and Roman forms. The rules of harmony and proportion established by the architect and engineer Vitruvius influenced the construction of many buildings, whilst painters and sculptors focused on realism and naturalism, and developed new genres such as portraiture and landscape. Italian artists pioneered the use of artificial perspective, classical proportion, the manipulation of light and shade to create the illusion of solidity, and anatomical precision in representing the human form. Many of these ideas were adopted by the northern Renaissance, but there was also a persistent attachment to the magnificent decoration of the High Gothic style, so classical motifs were often incorporated as one element amongst others in an architectural, sculptural, or painted scheme. This was certainly true of Scotland where, in the fifteenth century, classical motifs were introduced alongside a revival of the native Romanesque, and in the sixteenth century, classicism was often projected through the lens of the French court style.

Many Scottish developments were focused on the royal court, which had the most prestigious continental connections, but cultural patronage was also exerted by the Church, the universities, the nobility, and the burgh communities. However, it is probably fair to say that the most influential prelates, academics, lords, and burgesses of the period also had strong ties to the royal court. From the reign of James III, Edinburgh was acknowledged as the nation's capital, and was therefore also the main centre where the court interacted with the wider community. The loss of artistic patronage by the Church after 1560 and by the court after 1603 were thus significant obstacles to the later development of the Scottish Renaissance, which, by the early seventeenth century, was concentrated in the country house, university, and professional classes. By this time, civic humanism, which stressed public service, was also giving way to an emphasis on private contemplation and retreat from the world advocated by stoicism.

## EARLY RENAISSANCE IMPULSES, 1424–1503

It is difficult to identify precisely when the first stirrings of the Renaissance were felt in Scotland, but if notions of historical self-awareness and individualistic self-fashioning are significant, then arguably the roots may be traced to the personal rule of James I (*r*.1406–37). James returned to Scotland after eighteen years in English captivity, where he had absorbed the culture of the English, French, and Burgundian courts. He had a steely determination to restore and extend royal authority, and he has famously been termed 'a king unleashed'.[6] He seems to have intended to make the Stewart monarchy

---

[6] Ranald G. Nicholson, *Scotland: The Later Middle Ages* (Edinburgh, 1974), 281.

the source of all justice and the guarantor of peace and prosperity for the whole nation. His political programme included removing magnatial threats to his power, developing the role of the nobles as servants of the Crown, and increasing the regularity and stability of royal income. He also sought to promote the prestige and dignity of his dynasty in Europe. Thus he set the agenda for the adult reigns of his successors.[7] The rising European profile stemmed from the marriage of James's eldest daughter, Margaret, to the dauphin in 1436. Through her connections, three of her sisters also married into grand continental houses, whilst her brother, James II, married a niece of the Duke of Burgundy, Mary of Gueldres, in 1449.[8] Both James III and James IV subsequently made significant foreign marriages and, through such prestigious alliances, the Stewarts were clearly asserting their parity with other princes.

Not only did James I have a novel approach to the dignity and power of the Crown, but he also initiated new cultural developments. He is believed to have been a significant poet in his own right, but only one work survives: *The Kingis Quair* (c.1424). This is usually categorized as a medieval rather than a Renaissance poem, since its main stylistic influences are Boethius, Chaucer, Gower, and Lydgate, but it is also the first surviving example of a long line of courtly love poems and dream-visions, which stretches well into the sixteenth century.[9] Furthermore, in its autobiographical nature, it has certainly caught an aspect of the Renaissance spirit. James was also aware that a resurgent monarchy needed an impressive architectural setting. His building work at Linlithgow was a significant new departure: the first royal residence described as a palace, and clearly built for comfort and display rather than defence. The east range was largely built for him, and it is also likely that the quadrangular plan of the palace dates from this period. Certainly, it had taken on this shape by the reign of James III and stylistically it has been regarded as innovative: combining a revival of the Scottish Romanesque (with classical overtones) within the form of an Italian seigneurial *palatium ad modum castri*.[10] By the end of the fifteenth century, similar quadrangular palaces for elegant, courtly living were also being developed at Holyrood, Falkland, Edinburgh, and Stirling. All were imposing structures embellished with assertive heraldic imagery. The ambitious Stewart monarchs thus provided the theatrical backdrop for the dramatic display of the Renaissance court.

This rather heterogeneous approach is characteristic of the architecture of the Renaissance in Scotland, which continued to use traditional medieval features such as crenellations, parapets, conical turrets, and machicolations as decorative, rather than

[7] Michael Brown, *James I* (Edinburgh, 1994), 201–8. See also Michael Brown and Roland Tanner, eds., *Scottish Kingship, 1306–1542: Essays in Honour of Norman Macdougall* (Edinburgh, 2008).

[8] Priscilla Bawcutt and Bridget Henisch, 'Scots Abroad in the Fifteenth Century: The Princesses Margaret, Isabella and Eleanor', in Elizabeth Ewen and Maureen M. Meikle, eds., *Women in Scotland, c.1100–c.1750* (East Linton, 1999), 45–55.

[9] John MacQueen, 'Poetry—James I to Henryson', in R. D. S. Jack, ed., *The History of Scottish Literature, Volume 1: Origins to 1660*, 4 vols. (Aberdeen, 1987–8), 55–60.

[10] John G. Dunbar, *Scottish Royal Palaces: The Architecture of the Royal Residences during the Late Medieval and Early Renaissance Periods* (East Linton, 1999), 5–10; Ian Campbell, 'A Romanesque Revival and the Early Renaissance in Scotland, c.1380–1513', *Journal of the Society of Architectural Historians*, 54 (1995), 302–25.

FIGURE 8.1 Renaissance piety: Hugo van der Goes, the Trinity College Altarpiece, c.1478–9, now in the National Galleries of Scotland. Reproduced by permission of The Royal Collection © 2011, Her Majesty Queen Elizabeth II.

defensive, elements throughout the period and beyond, alongside the revival of the Scottish Romanesque (in the fifteenth century) and the introduction of more Italianate, classical motifs (in the sixteenth century). The attachment to the castellated style reflected an enthusiasm for chivalry, whilst the Romanesque revival has been linked to a growing sense of national identity, in opposition to the English Perpendicular Gothic. This hybrid national style has much in common with the Renaissance in the Netherlands, the Baltic, Scandinavia, and northern France, and shows that Scotland was well integrated into European culture.[11] It can be seen not only in the development of the royal palaces but also in the foundation of collegiate churches.

About forty collegiate churches were established in Scotland in the period and several combined elements of the international Gothic and Renaissance styles. For example, Trinity College, Edinburgh, founded by Mary of Gueldres in about 1460, had Flemish influences on its architecture but, more importantly, was graced with a magnificent altarpiece of the late 1470s in the most fashionable Netherlandish style. Commissioned by Edward Bonkil, the provost, from Hugo van der Goes, it was probably originally a triptych but only the two 'wings' have survived (Fig. 8.1). When open, they depict James III and his queen kneeling at prayer and presented by saints to the subject of the missing central panel, presumably the Virgin. When they are closed, Bonkil is shown kneeling

[11] Aonghus MacKechnie, 'Court and Courtier Architecture, 1424–1660', in Richard D. Oram and Geoffrey P. Stell, eds., *Lordship and Architecture in Medieval and Renaissance Scotland* (Edinburgh, 2005), 294–9; Campbell, 'A Romanesque Revival', 302–11; Roger Mason, 'This Realm of Scotland is an Empire? Imperial Ideas and Iconography in Early Renaissance Scotland', in B. E. Crawford, ed., *Church, Chronicle and Learning in Medieval and Early Renaissance Scotland* (Edinburgh, 1999), 73–91.

before the Holy Trinity in a striking portrait, which was probably taken from life. This is a piece of northern Renaissance art of the highest quality and, although it was painted for a royal site, there is no reason to imagine that it was unique or even particularly unusual. Indeed, further chance survivals suggest that other churches were also fashionably furnished.[12]

The origins of Scottish Renaissance humanism may also be found in the fifteenth century. For example, in 1484 the royal secretary, Archibald Whitelaw, who had taught at St Andrews and Cologne, was sufficiently well versed in the classics to give an elegant Latin oration, incorporating references to Cicero, Vergil, Seneca, and Livy, before Richard III of England. Whitelaw also had a fine library, which included works by Lucan, Horace, and Sallust, and he was a tutor to the young James III.[13] The records of the fifteenth-century university libraries have survived only in fragments, but St Andrews (founded 1411), Glasgow (1451), and King's College, Aberdeen (1495) would surely have had considerable collections of humanist works, not least because Scottish students and teachers shuttled regularly to and from the continental universities. In 1496 the founder of King's College, Bishop Elphinstone, steered through Parliament an Education Act requiring all property holders to ensure that their heirs were schooled in Latin, the arts, and law: the humanist agenda had reached the public sphere.[14]

# CHIVALRIC GLORIES, 1503–1567

Between the marriage of 'the thistle and the rose' in 1503 and the deposition of Mary, Queen of Scots in 1567, the Renaissance in Scotland reached its apogee. The culture fostered at the royal courts of James IV, James V, and Mary promoted the chivalric, imperial, and humanist themes that had originated in the fifteenth century. However, there were also two long royal minorities when the cultural influence of the Crown was weak. Nevertheless, there is evidence of courtly culture spreading beyond the royal centres into the universities, burghs, and country houses, especially during the 1540s and 1550s, and so the Renaissance gathered momentum during this period.

James IV's marriage to Margaret Tudor in 1503 was considered to be a national and personal triumph, and the culture of the court became more confident and innovative as a result. The preparations for the marriage included an exchange of portraits with the English court, the commissioning of an exquisite Book of Hours from a Flemish

---

[12] Colin Thompson and Lorne Campbell, *Hugo van der Goes and the Trinity Panels in Edinburgh* (Edinburgh, 1974); Duncan Macmillan, *Scottish Art, 1460–2000* (Edinburgh, 2000), 18–25.

[13] J. Durkan, 'The Beginnings of Humanism in Scotland', *Innes Review*, 4 (1953), 5–24, 119–22; Norman Macdougall, *James III* (Edinburgh, 2009), 245–82.

[14] J. Durkan and A. Ross, 'Early Scottish Libraries', *Innes Review*, 9 (1958), 5–167; John Higgit, ed., *Scottish Libraries: Corpus of British Medieval Library Catalogues*, 12 (London, 2006), 44–74, 155–66, 375–85; L. J. MacFarlane, *William Elphinstone and the Kingdom of Scotland, 1431–1514* (Aberdeen, 1995), 236–7, 245, 290–402.

workshop, and the completion of a magnificent great hall and forework at Stirling Castle. The palace at Holyrood was also extensively rebuilt. James IV's later works included another great hall at Edinburgh Castle, which had elegant, Italianate roof corbels, provided by an Italian mason.[15] After a pause in the minority of James V, the adult king resumed a construction programme in a similarly chivalric style at Holyrood, Linlithgow, and Falkland. These buildings were all festooned with heraldic sculpture, weather vanes, and stained glass extolling the pedigree and prestige of the dynasty. It is notable that the first Scottish register of arms, David Lindsay's *Armorial* of *c*.1542, was compiled at this time, and the interest in chivalric display was also spreading out from the royal court. It can be seen, for example, in the heraldic ceiling of St Machar's Cathedral, Aberdeen (*c*.1520).[16]

By this time, the cult of chivalry was transforming from the practical, military purposes of medieval knighthood into the more ornamental and honorific interests of the Renaissance courtier. Moreover, there was a widespread belief in the classical origins of chivalry, and Hector of Troy, Alexander the Great, and Julius Caesar were often portrayed as prototype chivalric knights. The enthusiasm for jousting displayed by James IV and James V, along with many of their nobles, acted as a cohesive force. The most celebrated tournaments were those of the Wild Knight and the Black Lady of 1507 and 1508, but James V also staged jousts and tournaments more frequently than is usually recognized, and was proud of his membership of the most prestigious European chivalric orders. Their insignia were displayed on his Linlithgow gateway alongside a Scottish chivalric collar. However, despite popular tradition, and rather surprisingly, it seems that there was no formally established Scottish order of knighthood at this time.[17]

As a woman, Mary, Queen of Scots could not fully participate in a revival of the cult of chivalry during her brief adult reign, but as dowager Queen of France she was wealthy enough to afford grand court entertainments, spectacles, and rituals to promote a message of national reconciliation and royal revival. Her court is famous for its balls, masques, and celebrations, and these often had a purpose more political than frivolous. For instance, in February 1566 Mary's consort Henry Stuart, Lord Darnley, was admitted to the order of St Michael in an elaborate ceremony at Holyrood that was deliberately, but unsuccessfully, calculated to entice Scottish nobles back to the Mass.

However, the most spectacular Renaissance festival of the period was staged for the baptism of Mary's heir, Prince Charles James (later James VI), at Stirling Castle. There

[15] Macmillan, *Scottish Art*, 30–1; L. MacFarlane, 'The Book of Hours of James IV and Margaret Tudor', *Innes Review*, 11 (1960), 3–21; Richard Fawcett, 'The Architecture', in Fawcett, ed., *Stirling Castle: The Restoration of the Great Hall* (York, 2001), 1–14; Dunbar, *Scottish Royal Palaces*, 40–9, 56–61, 77–83.

[16] Andrea Thomas, *Princelie Majestie: The Court of James V of Scotland, 1528–1542* (Edinburgh, 2005), 59–72, 203–5; Helena M. Shire, 'The King in his House: Three Architectural Artefacts Belonging to the Reign of James V', in Janet Hadley Williams, ed., *Stewart Style, 1513–1542: Essays on the Court of James V* (East Linton, 1996), 63–72.

[17] Thomas, *Princelie Majestie*, 199–207; Katie Stevenson, 'The Unicorn, St Andrew and the Thistle: Was There an Order of Chivalry in Late-Medieval Scotland?', *Scottish Historical Review*, 83 (2004), 3–22.

was already a long tradition of Scottish royal pageantry focused on coronations, entries, weddings, christenings, and funerals, but the baptism of 1566 was extraordinary. Mary was promoting the message that her dynasty would bring the return of a golden age and was the only guarantor of peace and unity. The service in the Chapel Royal was followed by a lavish banquet, which stressed the unity of the nation in front of foreign ambassadors. Then there were hunts, feasts, poetry, dance, and theatre, with many French and Italian influences, culminating in a mock siege involving costumed combatants and fireworks. This was modelled on the Valois triumphs at Bayonne of 1565, which had celebrated peace and reconciliation after civil war, and it was the high point of Mary's reign.[18] The fact that her regime collapsed so spectacularly only months later has obscured the significance of this remarkable example of a Scottish Renaissance festival.

Amongst the many-layered imagery of the baptism at Stirling Castle were references to the Arthurian Round Table, the goddess Astraea, and the return of the classical golden age. All these motifs were conventionally associated with the theme of imperial monarchy, which was another significant feature of the Scottish Renaissance. By the sixteenth century this was a widespread feature of European political discourse, based on the Roman law doctrine that 'the king is emperor in his own kingdom'. This notion was embodied in the symbol of the 'closed', arched crown, which was worn by emperors, as opposed to the 'open' circlet worn by medieval kings. As early as 1469 Parliament had declared that James III possessed 'full jurisdiction and free empire within his realm', and in the 1480s the king's image on his silver groats wore an arched crown in 'probably the earliest Renaissance coin portrait outside Italy'.[19] Soon the symbol of the arched crown appeared on a wide range of images: seals, heraldic devices, manuscripts, and sculptures, even the steeples of churches with royal connections such as St Giles, Edinburgh. The first Scottish monarch to wear an arched crown was James V, whose diadem was reworked to include arches in the spring of 1532, at a point when he was consolidating his authority. It was adjusted again in 1540, with the arches of 1532 reattached, and this crown forms part of the modern Honours of Scotland.[20]

For James IV and James V the notion of imperial monarchy meant portraying Scottish kingship as a unifying national force, promoting independence from English claims to suzerainty, defending territorial integrity, pursuing a monopoly of the administration of justice, and encouraging the creation of a distinctive national Church within the Catholic communion. For Mary and her son James VI the imperial theme mutated to promoting their claims to the English succession, whilst still presenting themselves as the embodiment of national unity with sovereign jurisdiction. James IV and James V invested heavily in modern military technology to defend the realm: James IV is noted

---

[18] Michael Lynch, 'Queen Mary's Triumph: The Baptismal Celebrations at Stirling in December 1566', *Scottish Historical Review*, 69 (1990), 1–22; *idem.*, 'The Great Hall in the Reigns of Mary, Queen of Scots and James VI', in Fawcett, ed., *Stirling Castle*, 15–17.

[19] I. H. Stewart, *The Scottish Coinage* (London, 1955), 67.

[20] Andrea Thomas, 'Crown Imperial: Coronation Ritual and Regalia in the Reign of James V', in Julian Goodare and Alasdair A. MacDonald, eds., *Sixteenth-Century Scotland: Essays in Honour of Michael Lynch* (Leiden, 2008), 43–67.

for creating a royal navy that included the great warship *The Michael*; whilst James V rebuilt the navy in the 1530s, commissioned the first navigational guide to the Scottish coast, and undertook two voyages around Scotland, 'beating the bounds' of his kingdom.[21] Both kings also employed foreign armourers to manufacture modern artillery in Edinburgh.[22] The importance of the sovereignty of the Crown in Parliament was stressed by James IV in his plan to have parliamentary statutes printed by the newly established Edinburgh press of Chepman and Myllar in 1508. The proposed publication never appeared but the king's printer, Thomas Davidson, produced an edition of James V's laws in 1541. The first printed edition of all the Scottish Acts of Parliament was commissioned for Mary in 1566. James V had also enhanced his status as the fount of all justice by the foundation of the College of Justice under his patronage, and partly on an Italian model, in 1532.[23] Only after his death, and particularly after the removal of the clergy from the court, did the College of Justice start to assert more independence from royal control.

The systematic dissemination and application of the king's laws was complemented by the creation of a national Church under royal authority. Both James IV and James V made full use of the papal indult of 1487, which brought the major Scottish benefices under royal patronage. Also important was the publication of William Elphinstone's *Aberdeen Breviary* in 1509–10 by Chepman and Myllar. This was an attempt to supplant the English Sarum Use with a Scottish national liturgy. Because the first Scottish press was so short-lived, the Elphinstone plan was not fully realized, but the intention was clear. As a matter of prestige, James IV also founded the Chapel Royal in Stirling Castle as a collegiate establishment in 1501. The personnel were to be skilled in music, and elaborate Renaissance polyphony of the highest quality would have accompanied the royal devotions. The Reformation iconoclasts particularly targeted liturgical books, so almost all Scottish sacred music of this period has been lost, but the surviving works of Robert Carver, a canon of Scone with links to the Chapel Royal, indicate the presence of at least one master, and we have fragments of the works of others. The *Carver Choirbook* (1503–46) contains copies of pieces by English and Flemish composers as well as Carver's remarkable oeuvre, demonstrating the influences that inspired him.[24] By the 1530s, the Chapel Royal was at its height, and Crown control over the Scottish Church was such that the latter can be seen as 'not so much a department of state as a

---

[21] Roger Mason, 'Renaissance and Reformation: The Sixteenth Century', in Jenny Wormald, ed., *Scotland: A History* (Oxford, 2005), 119.

[22] Norman Macdougall, *James IV* (Edinburgh, 2006), 223–46, 308–9; Thomas, *Princelie Majestie*, 155–77.

[23] Thomas, *Princelie Majestie*, 12–14, 150–1; Michael Lynch, 'The Reassertion of Princely Power in Scotland: The Reigns of Mary, Queen of Scots and King James VI', in Martin Gosman, Alasdair MacDonald, and Arjo Vanderjagt, eds., *Princes and Princely Culture, 1450-1650*, 2 vols. (Leiden, 2003–5), vol. 1, 212, 216; Andrew Mark Godfrey, *Civil Justice in Renaissance Scotland: The Origins of a Central Court* (Leiden, 2009).

[24] Macdougall, *James IV*, 218–19; Thomas, *Princelie Majestie*, 104–12; D. James Ross, *Robert Carver and the Art of Music in Sixteenth-Century Scotland* (Edinburgh, 1993).

FIGURE 8.2 Renaissance flamboyance: the sculptural decoration of James V's palace at Stirling Castle, c.1540 (east facade). Reproduced by permission of Professor Richard Fawcett.

sub-department of the royal household'.[25] Ironically, considering the patriotic intentions of James IV and James V, royal control and exploitation of the Church reached a point where spiritual authority was undermined, which hugely inflamed the Reformers.

In 1536 James V sailed to France for his brief first marriage, to Madeleine of Valois, and he and his entourage enjoyed an extended stay at the court of Francis I. This visit, along with the arrival in Scotland of Mary of Guise in 1538 as James's second wife, provided a direct injection of the French courtly version of Italian Renaissance style into Scotland. This is most clearly displayed in the royal works at Falkland and Stirling. The Falkland courtyard facades, designed and built by French masons, represent the earliest wholly Renaissance architectural scheme in the British Isles, where classical motifs such as pilasters, consoles, pediments, and roundels are an integral part of the design rather than decorative details applied to a traditional form. The Stirling palace block is a more hybrid creation, with crenellations and crow-stepped gables placed above a vivid Renaissance sculptural scheme, which has strong French and Burgundian influences (Fig. 8.2). The most remarkable relic of James V's palace at Stirling is a collection of carved oak roundels from the ceiling of his presence chamber, known as the Stirling Heads. Derived

[25] Michael Lynch, *Scotland: A New History* (London, 1992), 155.

ultimately from Italian models via French sources, the carvings are a vigorous and mature example of Renaissance design in Scotland. French influence was also exerted on the portraits of the period: Corneille de Lyon painted James V and his two wives, and set a standard of lifelike realism for later artists to follow. In the 1540s and 1550s French Renaissance influence spread from the court into the architecture of noble residences, many of which adapted aspects of the designs of the Loire chateaux into a hybrid style that Charles McKean calls 'Marian'.[26]

The humanism of the Scottish Renaissance was also developing apace at this period and spreading out into wider society. An erudite Italian humanist, Giovanni Ferrerio, taught at the Abbey of Kinloss for several years in the 1530s and 1540s, established an impressive library there, and wrote several works of Scottish history and biography. Translations of the classics became more common: Gavin Douglas produced a fine and faithful rendition of Virgil's *Aeneid* in 1513, and John Bellenden made a freer translation of the first five books of Livy's *History of Rome* in 1533. There were also some very accomplished neo-Latin writers at this time: James Foulis, Hector Boece, and George Buchanan, among others, had all studied and taught abroad and were able to write highly polished Latin prose or poetry modelled on the classical authors. John Mair and Hector Boece published rival accounts of the history of Scotland in 1521 and 1527 respectively. Mair is often described as a scholastic rather than a humanist, although his work has some humanist overtones. Boece, who was the first principal of the new humanist university at Aberdeen, wrote elegant rhetoric, praising the determination of the Scots to preserve their independence under their hero kings. Thus Boece's *Scotorum Historia* struck a chord with James V, and the king commissioned Bellenden to translate it into Scots and Davidson to print it, so that it would be more widely known.[27]

The vernacular literature of the period also displays humanist influences and Franco-Italian inspiration, mixed with an attachment to the traditions of various genres: advice to princes, petitions, and dream visions. The most famous vernacular poets of the period were William Dunbar and Sir David Lindsay. They wrote poetry commemorating the spectacles of the courts of James IV and James V respectively, but after 1543 Lindsay retreated to his Fifeshire estates, where his verses took on a more humanistic and moral tone, focused on the theme of the commonweal: what has been termed 'vernacular humanism'. Here he took his courtly interlude of 1540 and developed it into one of the first surviving Scottish plays: *Ane Satyre of the Thrie Estatis*. This combines the traditional form of a morality play with influences from the English court poet, John Skelton, the French *sotie* genre, and the humanist moral agenda. It was first performed in the

---

[26] Thomas, *Princelie Majestie*, 72–9, 84–5; Dunbar, *Scottish Royal Palaces*, 27–37, 49–55, 165–6; Shire, 'The King in his House', 72–96; Charles McKean, *The Scottish Chateau: The Country House of Renaissance Scotland* (Stroud, 2001), 99–120.

[27] John MacQueen, 'Aspects of Humanism in Sixteenth- and Seventeenth-Century Literature' in *idem.*, ed., *Humanism in Renaissance Scotland* (Edinburgh, 1990), 10–26; John Durkan, 'Education: The Laying of Fresh Foundations', in ibid., 125–31, 153; Nicola Royan with Dauvit Broun, 'Versions of Scottish Nationhood, c.850–1707', in Ian Brown et al., eds., *The Edinburgh History of Scottish Literature, Volume One: From Columba to the Union (until 1707)* (Edinburgh, 2007), 177–80.

burgh of Cupar in 1552 and was revived for Mary of Guise in Edinburgh in 1554, demonstrating a clear connection between the court and the wider community. By the 1550s lay literacy and education had developed sufficiently to provide an audience for vernacular literature beyond the court in the urban professional and merchant classes, especially in Edinburgh. *Elégies* and *chansons* had been written for James V in France and were immediately imitated and popularized by Scots poets, who developed a versatile tradition of lyrical poetry. By the mid-1560s George Bannatyne was able to collect dozens of examples, many from the pen of Alexander Scot, in his eponymous manuscript.[28]

The establishment of a Scottish printing press in Edinburgh was very important to reinforce the growing lay literacy of Renaissance Scotland. The Chepman and Myllar press was short-lived, but Davidson's was active between 1528 and 1541, and the number of rival presses grew from the 1560s, yet many books were still imported as late as 1600. Significantly, the 'vernacular' Bibles of the Scottish Reformation were in English and, before 1579, all were printed abroad. This contributed to a creeping anglicization of Scottish culture, which accelerated after 1603. Wider access to education was also important for the growing laicization of Scottish culture, since university graduates increasingly took up professions such as the law or government administration. Wider educational opportunities were provided by new colleges at St Andrews, but most significant for lay education was the establishment at Edinburgh in the 1550s of town lectureships in law, Greek, Latin, and philosophy under the patronage of Mary of Guise. The idea probably came from Francis I's *lecteurs royaux* of 1530, and the initiative was driven by Robert Reid, Bishop of Orkney, who, as Abbot of Kinloss, had brought Ferrerio to Scotland. This project also formed the kernel of the 'Tounis College' of Edinburgh, opened in 1583 and partly funded by Reid's legacy, which became the university.[29]

# THE PROTESTANT RENAISSANCE, 1567–1625

The Reformation of 1560 and the deposition of Mary, Queen of Scots in 1567 brought great changes to the culture of Scotland. The Protestant Kirk took the Second Commandment against graven images very seriously, thus widespread, systematic destruction of liturgical books, stained glass, sculpture, and religious paintings took place, which erased almost all of the nation's Catholic heritage. Furthermore, native artists and craftsmen faced a crisis of patronage. For many painters, the solution was to decorate the walls, and especially the ceilings, of the houses of lords, lairds, and burgesses, which were increasingly provided with the comforts of refined living. Over a

[28] Thomas, *Princelie Majestie*, 101–2, 140–4, 148–50; Carol Edington, *Court and Culture in Renaissance Scotland: Sir David Lindsay of the Mount, 1486–1555* (East Linton, 1995) 45, 115–41; Theo van Heijnsbergen, 'Early Modern Literature', in Harris and MacDonald eds., *The Making and Unmaking of the Nation*, vol. 2, 232–4.

[29] Thomas, *Princelie Majestie*, 150–2; Durkan, 'Education: The Laying of Fresh Foundations', 150–6; Mason, 'Renaissance and Reformation', 114–16.

hundred examples of vibrant, robust, and inventive decorative schemes survive from the period. The most impressive include the ceiling at Prestongrange, painted in 1581 for Mark Kerr, commendator of Newbattle, and the long gallery at Pinkie House, painted for Alexander Seton, Earl of Dunfermline, in about 1613. These schemes give some indication of how the interiors of pre-Reformation churches might have looked. Although the paintings were executed by unnamed Scottish artists, the patrons were increasingly educated and cultivated men, who commissioned decoration derived from continental emblem and pattern books, encapsulating humanist moral and philosophical symbolism. Thus the schemes contain images of genealogy, heraldry, piety, classical myths, allegory, and moral fables. The styles range from the grotesque and arabesque decoration of the High Renaissance, through the more Mannerist designs of c.1600, into early Baroque forms dominated by the complex embellishment of cartouches, strapwork, *putti*, and *trompe l'oeil*. The inspiration was clearly continental, but the results were distinctively Scottish.[30]

The other aspect of painting that flourished after the Reformation was portraiture. Since Protestantism emphasizes the importance of an individual's direct relationship with God, great significance was attached to the strength of character and personality of each person, which artists attempted to capture. Again, the impetus owed much to foreign influences, mainly from the Netherlands. For instance, James VI employed two Flemings in succession as court portraitists: Arnold Bronckhorst in the early 1580s and Adrian Vanson, c.1584–1602. Collections of portraits could also have propaganda value: images of the first five kings James, omitting Mary, were displayed at James VI's Edinburgh entry in 1579, urging him to emulate his male forebears rather than his mother; whilst Theodore Beza published *Icones* in Geneva in 1580, to memorialize the heroes of the European Reformation. The book was dedicated to James VI and included his portrait, taken from a coin. The first significant native portraitist was George Jameson of Aberdeen, who flourished in the 1630s and painted in the Dutch Baroque style of Daniel Mytens and Frans Hals.[31]

The art of music suffered more severely than painting from the censure of the Kirk. Thomas Wode thought that 'musike sall pereische in this land alutterlye' but he managed to preserve one piece of Renaissance polyphony, David Peebles's *Si quis diligit me* (c.1530), amongst the psalm settings he collected in the 1560s (Fig. 8.3). The pre-Reformation cathedrals, collegiate churches, and abbeys had supported song-schools to train choristers in the art of sacred polyphony but they were all closed down. James VI started a revival of burgh song-schools in 1579, and managed to retain part-singing at the Chapel Royal. At the same time, an anonymous manuscript, *The Art of Music*, was prepared for one of the new song-schools and seems to have set high standards. Yet Church composers were largely restricted to simple, homophonic settings of metrical psalms, which

---

[30]  Michael Bath, *Renaissance Decorative Painting in Scotland* (Edinburgh, 2003), 79–121.

[31]  Macmillan, *Scottish Art*, 40–7, 58–63; Michael Lynch, 'Court Ceremony and Ritual during the Personal Reign of James VI', in Julian Goodare and Michael Lynch, eds., *The Reign of James VI* (East Linton, 2000), 76.

FIGURE 8.3 Renaissance harmony: a page from Thomas Wode's Psalter, 1562–6. Reproduced by permission of Edinburgh University Library.

Peebles, for one, found irksome. However, there was an outlet for musical creativity in the dance and chamber music performed at court and in the homes of the increasingly urbane and cultured laity. James VI's court musician, William Hudson, took 'extraordiner panis' teaching the king to dance, which was now an accomplishment essential for a gentleman, and collections of lively Scottish dance tunes, alongside foreign pieces, were made for Robert Gordon of Straloch (*c*.1620) and Sir John Skene (*c*.1625).[32]

The religious and political changes of the 1560s also impacted on civic and royal ceremonial. James VI's 'joyous entry' into Edinburgh in 1579 combined many traditional

[32] D. James Ross, *Musick Fyne: Robert Carver and the Art of Music in Sixteenth-Century Scotland* (Edinburgh, 1993), 87–97, 133–9; John Purser, 'Early Modern Music', in Harris and MacDonald, *The Making and Unmaking of the Nation*, vol. 2, 216–18; John Durkan, 'Early Song Schools in Scotland', in Gordon Munro et al., eds., *Notis Musycall: Essays on Music and Scottish Culture in Honour of Kenneth Elliott* (Glasgow, 2005), 125–32.

elements with strident Protestant didactics and highly intellectual humanist symbolism. The king cultivated his image as a philosopher king, ushering in a new golden age, acting as a new David, Solomon, and Constantine combined. He recast the earlier Stewart claims to imperial monarchy into an assertion of divine monarchy, stressing his God-given destiny to rule over a Great Britain of multiple realms. This was most fully expressed in the grandest set-piece ceremony of the period: the 1594 baptism of the heir, Prince Henry Frederick. This three-day festival centred on the Chapel Royal at Stirling, newly rebuilt to the proportions of Solomon's temple, and involved a theatrical tournament mimicking the Elizabethan Accession Day tilts. It climaxed with an English-style banquet and masque featuring a 'ship of state' crewed by classical deities and virtues. The extravagant spectacle was masterminded by William Fowler, whose pageant book was published in both Edinburgh and London. This was 'government by photo-opportunity'.[33]

In a rapidly changing cultural climate there were nevertheless elements of continuity. The pre-Reformation Scottish interest in lay education was adopted and expanded by the Kirk as part of the drive to create a godly people, which subsumed the earlier humanist goal of nurturing virtuous citizens. The *First Book of Discipline* envisaged a school in every parish, which was difficult to achieve for financial reasons, but some of the burgh grammar schools cultivated very high standards of Latin, and occasionally Greek, scholarship. Expansion of university provision included the foundation of Edinburgh in 1583 and Marischal College, Aberdeen, in 1593, and many Scots still finished their education abroad. By 1600, Scotland was one of the most literate societies in Europe.[34] In such a climate, it is hardly surprising that James VI was given a rigorously classical and godly education by his tutors, George Buchanan and Peter Young. The king remarked wryly that he was forced to speak Latin before he could speak Scots.

Today, George Buchanan is most famous as the chief detractor of Queen Mary and the man who did not spare the rod on his royal pupil. At the time, he was a towering figure of the European Renaissance. He taught at universities in France and Portugal, translated texts from Greek into Latin, and was a prolific Latin author, who employed the full range of neoclassical literary genres. His poetry is considered to be particularly accomplished and many of his poems and plays exerted considerable influence on French Renaissance literature. Buchanan wrote flattering courtly verses and masques for Queen Mary before her liaison with the Earl of Bothwell. After her deposition in 1567, he wrote *De Jure Regni apud Scotos* (1579) and *Rerum Scoticarum Historia* (1582), justifying the right of resistance to tyrants with passionate eloquence. For Buchanan as much as for John Knox, whose *History of the Reformation* (1587) was thoroughly self-justificatory, history was a branch of rhetoric. James VI was an apt pupil and owed much of his

---

[33] Lynch, 'Court Ceremony and Ritual', 71–92; *idem*., 'Reassertion of Princely Power', 220–7; *idem*., 'The Great Hall in the Reigns of Mary, Queen of Scots and James VI', 19–21.

[34] John Durkan, 'Schools and Schooling to 1696' and 'Universities to 1720', in Michael Lynch, ed., *The Oxford Companion to Scottish History* (Oxford, 2001), 561–3, 610–12.

intellectual development to Buchanan's influence, but he rejected his teacher's political philosophy outright.[35]

James VI was slow to take up the reins of government but swift to provide cultural leadership. As a young man in the 1580s he drew around him a group of inventive and versatile poets, traditionally known as the Castalian Band. James's *Essayes of a Prentise in the Diuine Arte of Poesie* (1584) was a manifesto for rejuvenating Scots literature by seeking inspiration in French and Italian rhetorical and metaphorical poetry. The Castalians responded enthusiastically, producing many stylish translations and fine lyric verse. As with decorative painting, it is possible to detect in Castalian poetry, especially that of Alexander Montgomerie, an awareness of the Mannerist aesthetic, which was rapidly developing abroad and would lead Renaissance culture into the Baroque of the seventeenth century.[36] In the 1590s James VI began to take more interest in theology and politics than poetry, publishing *The Trew Law of Free Monarchies* (1598), which expounds a philosophy of divine monarchy and rejects the resistance theories of Knox and Buchanan. He also wrote *Basilikon Doron* as a handbook on kingship for his eldest son, Henry, which is much more pragmatic about the realities of rule. These, and many other tracts, were the products of a studious, stoical *rex pacificus*, who in many ways embodied the virtues of Renaissance humanism, yet also exhibited the grandiose ambition of his Stewart forebears in his desire to rule united kingdoms as God's anointed. James VI also cultivated his European image, since he had ambitions to become a leader of Christendom: many of his prose works were translated for continental consumption with this in mind.[37]

Cultural continuities are also apparent in the architecture of this period. Although James V's wholehearted adoption of the French Renaissance style was not pursued systematically after his death, classical motifs still feature in the works of James VI. The 1594 Chapel Royal at Stirling has a strictly classical entrance, based on a design by Sebastiano Serlio, and the Linlithgow north wing of 1618 employs classical pediments in an elegant, balanced scheme. Beyond the royal works, similar themes were apparent in aristocratic architecture too. Mar's Wark, Stirling (*c.*1570), is now a shell but its symmetrical fenestration and fine string courses recall something of the classicism at Falkland; whilst Crichton Castle has a thoroughly Italianate diamanté facade with a classical loggia, built for the Earl of Bothwell in the 1580s. The chivalric impulse, which preserved the attachment to traditional castellated architecture, also continued into this period and beyond, with many noble residences becoming increasingly flamboyant, particularly in the north-east. The reasons for the persistence of the castellated style are unclear, but

---

[35] Jack MacQueen, 'From Rome to Ruddiman: The Scoto-Latin Tradition', in Brown et al., eds., *Edinburgh History of Scottish Literature*, vol. 1, 189–96; Bill Findlay, 'Performances and Plays' in ibid., 258; Royan with Broun, 'Versions of Scottish Nationhood', 180–1.

[36] Roderick J. Lyall, *Alexander Montgomerie: Poetry, Politics, and Cultural Change in Jacobean Scotland* (Tempe, AZ, 2005), 11–28, 344–7.

[37] Roderick J. Lyall, 'James VI and the Sixteenth-Century Cultural Crisis', in Goodare and Lynch, eds., *The Reign of James VI*, 55–70; *idem.*, 'The Marketing of James VI and I: Scotland, England and the Continental Book Trade', *Quaerendo*, 32 (2002), 204–17.

Charles McKean believes that it was a deliberate rejection of classical forms, influenced by the French baronial style. His hypothesis is still open to some debate. Also open to discussion is the classification of the architecture of the 1620s and 1630s. Buildings such as the Parliament House and Moray House in Edinburgh, or the Nithsdale wing at Caerlaverock Castle, are often described as part of the Scottish Renaissance, but many of their features could be interpreted differently. The combination of broken pediments, half-moon pediments, buckle quoins, obelisks, strapwork finials, and similar details in other European countries would indicate the Baroque. Aonghus MacKechnie concedes the term 'Mannerist', but 'Baroque' is conspicuously underused in the Scottish context and would merit investigation.[38]

# CONCLUSION

It is now readily apparent that the Scots participated fully in the northern Renaissance and this should become more widely acknowledged as further research continues. Much like the Dutch, French, and Scandinavians, the Scots were cultural magpies, who borrowed ideas and images from classical and continental sources and adapted them to local needs. They created a distinctive national style in some areas, the scholarly interpretation of which is still in its infancy. The cultural vandalism of the Reformers has made it easier to investigate literary and architectural developments than the history of music and painting, but there is still much to learn. In time, scholars will uncover more of the details of specific artists and artefacts, and the influences upon them, which will in turn allow a more nuanced understanding of the Renaissance to be shaped. It is to be hoped that a scholarly exploration of the Scottish Baroque will also emerge in due course.

## FURTHER READING

Bath, Michael, *Renaissance Decorative Painting in Scotland* (Edinburgh, 2003).

Dunbar, John G., *Scottish Royal Palaces: The Architecture of the Royal Residences during the Late Medieval and Early Renaissance Periods* (East Linton, 1999).

Durkan, John, numerous articles over many years, especially those in *Innes Review*.

Edington, Carol, *Court and Culture in Renaissance Scotland: Sir David Lindsay of the Mount, 1486–1555* (East Linton, 1995).

MacDonald, A. A., Lynch, Michael, and Cowan, Ian B., eds., *The Renaissance in Scotland: Studies in Literature, Religion, History and Culture Offered to John Durkan* (Leiden, 1994).

---

[38] Aonghus MacKechnie, 'James VI's Architects and their Architecture', in Goodare and Lynch, eds., *The Reign of James VI*, 162–5, 167–8; *idem.*, 'Court and Courtier Architecture', 306–14; Miles Glendinning and Aonghus MacKechnie, *Scottish Architecture* (London, 2004), 67–89; Alastair M. T. Maxwell-Irving, 'The Maxwells of Caerlaverock', in Oram and Stell, eds., *Lordship and Architecture*, 227–8; McKean, *The Scottish Chateau*.

MacQueen, John, *Humanism in Renaissance Scotland* (Edinburgh, 1990).

Mason, Roger A., *Kingship and the Commonweal: Political Thought in Renaissance and Reformation Scotland* (East Linton, 1998).

Oram, Richard D., and Stell, Geoffrey P., eds., *Lordship and Architecture in Medieval and Renaissance Scotland* (Edinburgh, 2005).

Ross, D. James, *Musick Fyne: Robert Carver and the Art of Music in Sixteenth-Century Scotland* (Edinburgh, 1993).

Thomas, Andrea, *Princelie Majestie: The Court of James V of Scotland, 1528–1542* (Edinburgh, 2005).

Thomas, Andrea, *Glory and Honour: The Renaissance in Scotland* (Edinburgh, forthcoming).

# CHAPTER 9

·············································

# REFORMED AND GODLY
# SCOTLAND?[*]

·············································

JENNY WORMALD

ON 16 September 2010 two notable religious figures came to Edinburgh. One was the Reverend Ian Paisley, leader of the Free Presbyterian Church of Ireland. The other was the Pope, Benedict XVI. Paisley and his supporters went to the Magdalen Chapel in the Cowgate, the church where, Paisley erroneously claimed, the Scottish Reformation of 1560 began its life, presided over by John Knox. The Reverend's doughty defence of that Reformation was somewhat weakened by the fact that Edinburgh exists on two levels, and geographically it was Paisley and his 60 followers who were at a disadvantage. They were tucked away out of sight in the depths of the Cowgate while some 125,000 people were out on the streets that soared above it to roar their welcome to the Pope after he had been formally and warmly received by the Queen at Holyrood. Thus Edinburgh on the 450th anniversary of the Reformation.

What has this to do with the sixteenth-century Reformation and its great reformer John Knox, who had identified the papacy with Antichrist? The differences between 1560 and 2010 are of course vast. But Paisley could undoubtedly regard himself as standing for reformation principles that only in the modern world were being rejected. He had, after all, interrupted John Paul II's speech to the European Parliament in 1988, shouting out that 'I denounce you as Antichrist'. Here, then, was one link between late sixteenth- and early twenty-first-century Scotland. Paisley, heir to Knox, was the representative of the long-held belief in the peculiarly godly nature of reformed Scotland; those who cheered the Pope were the destroyers of that Scottish godly Protestantism that from the sixteenth to the twentieth century had been the bedrock of the nation's identity and justifiable pride in itself.

But where were the Scottish heirs of Knox? The Moderator of the Kirk of Scotland was welcoming Pope Benedict and thereafter going to London to read the Gospel at the

* I am very grateful to Jane Dawson for her helpful comments on the first draft of this chapter.

ecumenical service at Westminster Abbey led by the Pope and the Archbishop of Canterbury. It did rather look as though Scotland had gone soft; as recently as 1961 there had been the clarion call of the godliness of the Kirk when J. S. McEwen, Professor of Theology at the University of Aberdeen, had depicted Knox as rescuing Scotland from the Whore of Babylon.[1]

To see it in this way is, however, to buy into the belief of the unusual godliness of reformed Scotland, a belief which began its life in the late sixteenth century and flowered with renewed vigour after the union of the parliaments in 1707. But it is possible that what was happening in September 2010 was evidence not so much of Scotland going soft on faith, but of a very different kind of link with the Reformation past; and this forces a fundamental question about the insistent and sometimes strident claims for an unusually high level of godliness by the Kirk, by those offshoots which set themselves up when the Kirk was not godly enough, and by historians who bought into these claims. In asking this question, there is no intention of seeking to deny or to disparage what could be a deeply moving and inspiring sense of a simple and disciplined relationship between man and his God. But it can hardly be denied that Scotland was a distinctly grimmer place to live as it put down its reformed roots. The delightful mid-sixteenth-century poet Richard Maitland of Lethington tells us so in his haunting poem beginning 'Quhair is the blyithnes that hes bene?'[2] He was not alone. And perhaps we should listen more closely to such voices. It may be time to move away from concentration on godly success and think rather about whether H. L. Mencken's famous definition of Puritanism, 'the haunting fear that someone, somewhere, may be happy', might have some relevance to the imposition of godliness in early-modern Scotland. Did sixteenth-century Scotsmen, unlike their early twenty-first-century descendants, really want to be grey, grim, and unhappy? Or does the difference lie more in the fact that they were unable to escape the shackles imposed on them by the ruling reforming elite with more or less backing from secular authority? Indeed, one might go further and ask whether, apart from the mid-seventeenth century, Scotland as a whole was really godly at all.

There is a problem here. Since McEwen wrote, reformation studies have, with a few lurid exceptions, been much more balanced, the product of the cooler eye of the historian than the passion of the godly. But the focus has been on the battle to establish and then maintain the Kirk fought out throughout the sixteenth and seventeenth centuries between the leaders of religious and secular society; simply because there are far fewer of them, Scottish historians have lagged behind their English counterparts in trying to look beyond top-level religious controversy. We know well enough that the ungodly King James VI had a long and vitriolic battle with the godly leaders of the Kirk, that in the short term he triumphed, more or less, but in the longer term godliness prevailed, becoming rampant under the Covenanters. But there has been far less attention paid to the ordinary parishioners who after 1560 found old certainties gone and new and much

---

[1]  J. S. McEwen, *The Faith of John Knox* (London, 1961).
[2]  W. A. Craigie, ed., *The Maitland Quarto Manuscript* (Edinburgh, 1920), 15.

more precise certainties imposed on them. They have not been wholly ignored; but they have tended to be viewed through the prism of the harsher discipline of the reformed Kirk. And it is certainly the case that, as the Kirk dug itself in, a whole new level of discipline was increasingly imposed on the population, successfully because it was imposed at parish level. The ungodly Stuart kings gave up summoning general assemblies, the national court of the Kirk, in 1618; none met again until Charles I was on the run in 1638, and that was a profoundly different assembly, which not only argued with secular authority but imposed its godly will on it. But presbyteries and kirk-sessions were still on the go. And that made it all too possible to view disciplined Scotland as godly Scotland, its sinners hounded and punished.

Such a view has been exceedingly prevalent; and the idea of the power of local discipline through the local courts of the Kirk does seem to make sense. And historians such as Michael Graham and Margo Todd, who have begun investigations that go far beyond the power struggle, have undoubtedly added very considerably to our understanding of the early-modern Kirk; Michael Lynch first argued for a longer timescale for the Kirk to establish itself than used to be thought, an argument recently reinforced by John McCallum's detailed study of Fife.[3] Yet Todd, whose book is a wonderful new approach to the subject, is far too nuanced and wide-ranging simply to reiterate the old view, but even she surely retreats into too much caution; her final chapter is entitled 'A Puritan Nation'. Certainly there were Puritans in Scotland, 'very pestes in the Churche & commonweale',[4] who, as far as King James was concerned, were a good deal noisier and nastier and more demanding than his sister monarch's in England. The difference before 1603 was that James was less paranoid about his Scottish Puritans than Elizabeth; when he met the English ones at Hampton Court after his accession in 1603 as James I of England, they seemed, by comparison, remarkably well mannered. But were these 'pestes' quite so dominant in James's mind as in the minds of later historians?

And is it possible to move further from the idea of Puritan-inspired and discipline-imposed godliness? Christopher Haigh has recently attacked 'kirk-session discipline' as an explanation for the Scottish Reformation because England had its discipline also.[5] This overstates the case, simply because English discipline was more patchy, less coherent, and less structured. But it raises a valid question. Moreover, there is a problem about the kirk-session records themselves, which are regarded as evidence for godly Scotland. But are they? Or is it that modern historians have still tended to play into what was

---

[3] Michael Graham, *The Uses of Reform: 'Godly Discipline' and Popular Behaviour in Scotland and Beyond, 1560–1610* (Leiden, 1996); Margo Todd, *The Culture of Protestantism in Early Modern Scotland* (New Haven, 2002); Michael Lynch, 'Preaching to the Converted?', in A. A. MacDonald, Michael Lynch, and Ian Cowan, eds., *The Renaissance in Scotland: Studies Offered to John Durkan* (Leiden, 1994), 31–43; John McCallum, *Reforming the Scottish Parish: The Reformation in Fife, 1560–1640* (Farnham, 2010).

[4] J. Craigie, ed., *The Basilikon Doron of King James VI*, 2 vols. (Edinburgh, 1944–50), vol. i, 79.

[5] Christopher Haigh, 'The Clergy and Parish Discipline in England, 1570–1640', in Bridget Heal and Ole Peter Grell, eds., *The Impact of the Reformation Movement: Princes, Clergy and People* (Aldershot, 2008), 141.

actually a powerful and prehensile myth, the myth of godliness created in the early-modern period, and sustained in differing forms ever since, and that it is time that more effort was made to unpick that myth?

There is good reason to do so. Going back to H. L. Mencken, it is surely troubling that the essence of godliness seems to be about excessive austerity and making people miserable. This is not, of course, simply a Scottish problem; one need only look at the great predestinarian theologians, going back to St Augustine, or consider Simon Stylites on his pillar. But Scotland does rank among the intensely miserable godly societies. While in the Scriptures Christ enjoins his followers to 'love thy neighbour as thyself', nowhere in the Bible, that fundamental handbook of reformed religion, does Christ enjoin his followers to 'shop thy neighbour to the local kirk session'; that was a man-made injunction. Individuals with an unusually high level of spirituality, with an ability to lead an unusually austere and godly life, can indeed provide immense inspiration to lesser mortals, and in the Catholic Church they have their rightful place; they are the saints, to whom people could look for intercession and help. It was a very different matter when austere and godly ministers insisted that *all* lesser mortals had to become saints and live austere and godly lives. But that is what Scotland has long prided itself on: its exceptional level of godliness since the days of John Knox.

Yet the local records of the Kirk, so consistently used to illustrate godly Scotland, actually tell us about the failure to make Scotland godly. They insistently tell the story of resistance to godliness. Of course, the Kirk recognized that all men were sinners—even if its leaders had an unpleasant tendency to exempt themselves—and that some were reprobates. What seems to have puzzled the Kirk is that it could not, try it ever so hard, eradicate sin, or at least drive it respectably underground and out of sight. The general assembly in 1596 set out in extensive detail the terrible backsliding of Scottish sinners, and what the ministers must do. Yet for all their efforts, and at the height of their apparent success, in 1649 they found 'the wholl Land [*still*] polluted with sin'. And this almost a century after the godly Reformation.[6] It was a very genuine perplexity, because the Scottish godly, unlike English divines, had seen the Reformation as an event, not an ongoing process. What we call *The First Book of Discipline* was actually entitled in 1560 *The Buik of Reformatioun and Discipline of the Kirk*; and in 1563 the Catholic apologist Ninian Winzet attacked 'the new impietie callit . . . the Reformatioun of the Protestantis'.[7]

But the answer is surely obvious: many people in post-Reformation Scotland hated the godly. They refused to be driven into welcome or unwelcome godliness by the discipline of the Kirk. Eradication of sin, the determination of the Kirk to stamp out the celebration of Christmas, its unsatisfactory and inconsistent change to the sacrament of

[6] David Calderwood, *The True History of the Church of Scotland*, 8 vols. (Edinburgh, 1842–9), vol. v, 394–411; T. Thomson and C. Innes, eds., *The Acts of the Parliaments of Scotland*, 12 vols. (Edinburgh, 1814–75), vol. iii, pt. 2, 173. [my italics]

[7] Jenny Wormald, 'Reformations, Unions and Civil Wars, 1485–1660', in Jonathan Clark, ed., *A World by Itself: A History of the British Isles* (London, 2010), 289.

baptism, its strict sabbatarianism, its attack on drinking, dancing, and play-acting, bon-fires at Beltane and midsummer: all these were strenuously resisted, and continued to be resisted throughout the seventeenth century, by those who were not persuaded of the advantages of the godly life, and were determined on their right to continue to enjoy themselves as they had done in the easier world of pre-Reformation Scotland.

Some—like Richard Maitland of Lethington—did not do so. But not all sank into depressed acceptance; far from it. They made life intolerable for that hard-working body, the presbytery of Stirling, whose records, especially if read without an undue concentra-tion on sexual sin, significantly redress the balance between the efforts of the godly to contain and punish sin and the more light-hearted determination of the sinners to with-stand these efforts. A few examples of this remarkably entertaining source will suffice to illustrate the point:

On 7 May 1583, 'The brethrein wndirstandand that on sonday last thair was ane drum strukin in the brugh of Stirling be ane certane of servand men & boyis & May playis usit quhairby the sabbothe day was prophainit and the kirke sclanderit.' So the town baillies were told to ensure that it did not happen again 'wndir the paine of the censures of the kirk to be excute againis thame', which is a pretty pathetic response.

On 21 May 1583, 'Johnne Wod & Johne broun schulmaisteris at the kirkis of Mwthill & Strogayth (Strageath)' were summoned 'for playing of clark playis on the sabboth day' and also using the same for unlawful administration of baptism and marriage. Wod turned up and was ordered to make public repentance and confess his fault immediately after the sermon. Broun, though often called, did not appear until 28 May, when he denied it all. On 11 June he was told to write a thesis in Latin on whether it was lawful to play clark plays[8] on the Sabbath or not, and whether it was lawful to make clark plays on any part of Scripture or not, and produce it before the brethren on 2 July. He did arrive on that day, and presented his thesis not only in the required prose but also in verse. It is anyone's guess how far the brethren understood the thesis, and the verse sounds like deliberate provocation. But it worked to Broun's advantage, for by that time the brethren were getting worked up over the amount of swearing and filthy bawdrie which was going on in his school. Broun was ordered to reappear for judgement on 6 August; and the story ends with another pathetic climbdown, when the brethren 'admittis him to teiche latein grammar at the kirk of Strogayth quhair he is presentlie or in any ythir place qwhair he may profit the kirk of god in teaching of the youthe'. Apparently, a schoolmas-ter who had proved that he could write Latin—prose and verse too—was the answer to swearing and bawdrie, especially if they could not understand the Latin themselves. Certainly it was a total victory for John Broun.

Then in January–February 1584 there was the mysterious case of the marriage of the laird of Tulliallan, which was performed by a disguised man. Was he the minister? The brethren decided yes, on the grounds that he was 'ane honest lyk man cled lyk ane

---

[8]  Clerk (Scots clark) plays were scripture-based plays; but after the Reformation, the term came to be used as one of opprobrium, to criticize anything disapproved of by the reformers.

minister with ane taffety hatt quhais name thai knew not....' Perhaps it was necessary to be circumspect about godliness in the case of a laird.

Finally, on 14 November 1592 the brethren were exercised by 'John qwhyt Pyper in Sawchie', who 'plait with his pyp in the grein of Allway on the Sonday befoir none immediatelie aftir he was forbidden to do the samin be the said Minister in the kirk forsaid and also minasit the said minister be outragiuss words'. John ignored several summons, but eventually turned up on 15 May 1593—which was hardly quick and rigorous discipline— when he admitted that he had indeed played his pipe before a bridegroom, but denied that he had threatened the minister; then on reflection he said that perhaps he had, because he was drunk at the time and could not remember. For this, the threat of excommunication was lifted and he was ordered to make one public repentance.[9]

This last case happened in the year when the godly were apparently jubilant and exultant because of the Golden Act of 1592 (the colour reflecting Presbyterian triumph), which effectively suspended episcopacy and legally underwrote presbyteries.[10] This is a very different side of the story. And it is worth noting that only one public repentance was demanded for profaning the Sabbath and, indeed, being drunk on the Sabbath. This contrasts with the hefty repeated public repentances imposed on fornicators and adulterers. The godly did appear to be obsessed with sexual sins. But perhaps there has been too much concentration on that obsession, as if the local courts thought of nothing else. It may be that the point which has been missed here is that far from being able to impose godly discipline generally, the authorities found adultery and fornication to be the easy bits to punish, often involving, as they did, jealousy and anger among the parties themselves or their slighted spouses. So presbyteries and sessions could look for a measure of local support. It seems to have been different on matters to which local society did not object, play-acting, pipe playing, swearing, and drunkenness, and different again on the matter of the sacraments of baptism and marriage, and the courts had therefore to tread much more carefully.

The difficulty for the Stirling presbytery in eradicating music and play-acting is very much reinforced by John McGavin's work on drama in sixteenth-century Haddington, East Lothian, which has shown that the presbytery could by no means count on other sources of authority, notably the council, which maintained its role as the provider of plays after the Reformation, or a local schoolmaster, John Brounsyde, who set up a successful school just outside the town to rival the unpopular burgh one. And the Kirk found it difficult in the extreme to eradicate Robin Hood, the Abbot of Unreason, and craft plays from the burghs of Scotland.[11] Possibly not every official of the Kirk wanted to. We have some way to go in searching out the reality of 'godly Scotland'; the next step is

---

[9] James Kirk, ed., *Stirling Presbytery Records 1581–1587* (Edinburgh, 1981), 114, 118–19, 122, 129–30, 163, 196–7, 199; NAS CH2/722/2.

[10] *Acts of the Parliaments of Scotland* [hereafter *APS*], vol. iii, 541–2.

[11] John J. McGavin, 'Drama in Sixteenth-Century Haddington', *European Medieval Drama*, 1 (1997), 147–59; 'The Kirk, the Burgh, and Fun', *Early Theatre*, 1 (1998), 13–26. I owe much to Professor McGavin's work and to the pleasure of discussions with him.

to find out whether those who imposed discipline can all be herded together in the ranks of the godly.

Meanwhile, it is possible to offer one speculation. A particular appeal of the reformed Kirk was, apparently, that it allowed the laity a much more participatory role in its services. One may certainly question how far the laity embraced with enthusiasm the new length of these services, and in particular the length of the sermons. And, subjective though it must ultimately be, one may also question the other form of participation, , music. The account of the two thousand who turned out on the Royal Mile in Edinburgh to sing 'Now Israel may say', when in 1582 the minister John Durie returned from exile, is a gripping invocation of the power of music. Significantly, the two hundred who began the psalm were singing in four parts.[12] But congregational singing in unison does not immediately and automatically inspire people. It is an art which has to be learned, as the immediate post-Vatican II dismal congregational caterwauling in Catholic churches demonstrated all too clearly. To be fair, Scottish psalm and hymn singing did come to create a very distinguished musical tradition; and thanks to the enchanting and delightfully illustrated Partbooks of the former Catholic musician Thomas Wode, who became a Reader in the reformed Kirk, we get a remarkable view of the beginnings of that tradition. Yet banning organs, where they existed, can hardly have helped it in its early days. That the Kirk was aware of the problem is reflected in the efforts made to revivify the pre-Reformation song-schools in the burghs to provide choristers to lead part-singing. But in the main the new musical experience was unison singing.[13] It is still possible to get a sense of its profound limitations from the CD accompanying Christopher Marsh, *Music and Society in Early Modern England*. The four-part psalm 'Blessed are they that perfect art' is lovely (no. 44); the unaccompanied psalm 29 with precentor and congregation (no. 45) is frankly grim, slow, and dragging (though sung by experienced singers).[14] In modern times, psalm singing in the Wee Free Church, which only in November 2010 removed the ban on organs and on the singing of hymns, still reflects something of the difficulty, though it is also moving testimony to the effect of long experience. It indicates, therefore, what the experience of those who first encountered reformed music must have been.[15]

If the appeal of the new music of the Kirk may be seriously doubted, an old appeal held firm. Just outside Stirling was a holy well—Christ's well—long believed to have healing powers. In the later sixteenth and first half of the seventeenth century, the Stirling presbytery records are stuffed with agonized complaints about people insisting on visiting the well; nothing would stop them 'passing in pilgrimage to chrystis woll and using of

---

[12] Calderwood, *True History*, vol. iii, 646–7.

[13] Gordon J. Munro, 'The Scottish Reformation and its Consequences', in Isobel Woods Preece, *Our awin Scottis use: Music in the Scottish Church up to 1603* (Glasgow and Aberdeen, 2000), 273–303; *APS*, vol. iii, 174.

[14] Christopher Marsh, *Music and Society* (Cambridge, 2010); see ch. 8.

[15] It is worth comparing the unaccompanied psalm in the Marsh CD with, for example, the CD *Gaelic Psalms from the Hebrides of Scotland* (Isle of Lewis, 2003).

superstitioun and idolatrie'. And why, from their point of view, should they stop? Hauled year in, year out, before the presbytery, they explained that they had gone to the well for healing, of headaches, pains in their sides, difficulty in walking, and so on. The most dramatic example was on 14 May 1595, when Helen Jameson, brought before the brethren, explained that she had gone the previous year to the well 'to gait her bairnis ein heallit quhilk was blind ane moneth befoir. She wash his ein thrys with the watir thairof and alledgis that the bairn saw er he come hame'; and so she had returned this year to give thanks. For this she and her husband were sentenced 'to mak public repentance in lining clathis the nixt thrie Sabboth dayes bairfuted'. It is rather pleasing that the husband was sentenced along with his wife, because he was sufficiently cowardly to try to distance himself, claiming that he had not been there. In any event, the presbytery's efforts, in this case and others, were futile. Even posting guards around the well failed to keep the faithful away; they said that they needed the water for healing, and seem to have been able to go and get it.[16] This has its parallels throughout Scotland, even in the very godly northern burgh of Elgin in Moray; as late as 1659, well into Scotland's excessively godly period, parishioners were brought before the Dunblane kirk-session for this offence, while the capital itself was beset with the problem in that very holy year of 1649, when the godly ministers appeared to reach their high point of control.[17] In an article on 'Sacred spas...in Britain', Alexandra Walsham does point out the difficulty of preventing visits to wells. But when she says that 'In Scotland a Calvinist church made more systematic efforts to stamp out such practices', we hear again the echo of the Scottish godly myth.[18] There were the local courts of the Kirk, and there was an Act of Parliament in 1581.[19] But the point is that the practices were not systematically stamped out. What was so marvellous about Scottish godly discipline if a century after the Reformation people were still going to holy wells? No wonder the godly in 1649 lamented about 'the wholl Land polluted by sin'.

One of the Stirling cases cited above brings up the wrongful administration of baptism and marriage, which brings us to the issue of the sacraments. It was one thing for reforming theologians to turn their intellectual minds to the question of the sacraments, and reduce them to two. It may have been quite another for ordinary parishioners, when their long-accustomed rites of passage were suddenly altered. Marriage, despite the confusion over whether it was a sacrament, was probably the least problematic. But baptism and care for the dying and the dead were a very different matter. And these take us firmly into the interplay between central and local, the conflict between King James and the really hardline Presbyterians, the Melvillians, and its impact on the parishes.

The struggle itself is a subject with plenty of enjoyment in its own right, because the king, unlike the Presbyterians, had a sense of humour, and a robust way with words, which gave him the power to tweak the tails of the godly and get his own way; hence the occasion

---

[16]  NAS CH2/722/2.

[17]  Todd, *Culture of Protestantism*, 219–20.

[18]  Alexandra Walsham, 'Sacred Spas? Healing Springs and Religion in Post-Reformation Britain', in Heal and Grell, *Impact of European Reformation*, 214.

[19]  *APS*, vol. iii, 212.

when the Kirk maliciously called a fast in Edinburgh on the day when the king proposed to hold a banquet for the departing French ambassador—the banquet, of course, going ahead.[20] But it was a long and grim struggle, even if James won in the end. And its high point came with the king's notorious Five Articles of Perth, long a subject of debate among historians, and recently revived when Alan MacDonald and Laura Stewart argued that so offensive were these articles—private baptism and Communion, Confirmation, the celebration of Christmas and Easter, and above all kneeling at Communion—that it was they, and not the accession of Charles I in 1625, which opened a 'high road' that would lead to the breakdown of the 1630s and 1640s.[21] I have engaged with their arguments elsewhere, and will not pursue the general theme here.[22] But there is a strong case for arguing that their unpopularity was less than is usually suggested, and certainly not uniform throughout the country. Thus, for example, the king's article only demanded preaching on Christmas Day, when in fact people in Perth and Aberdeen had long been going further, defying the Kirk's prohibition of Christmas by enjoying themselves as their predecessors had done; and in 1609 the Lords of Session went on strike for the right to have a Christmas holiday. Moreover, even where the Kirk did manage to impose its will, there was an all too effective ungodly answer: the celebration of the wholly pagan feast of Hogmanay. Hogmanay is a striking example of the difference between myth and reality. And when in 1958 the Kirk did finally recognize Christmas, it made no difference whatsoever to social practice, except that those who wanted could now go to church, and Christmas was officially recognized as a holiday. King James had his godly opponents; the first General Assembly which discussed the articles in 1617 rejected them, and it was only in 1618 that a rather differently constituted assembly at Perth accepted them—hence the name. But the king also had his supporters, not only among those who now felt freer to enjoy Christmas, but among those for whom, for example, the disciplinary load was now lightened on a matter that deeply touched the family: private baptism and private communion.

The Kirk's view of baptism was strikingly inconsistent. Although it had retained baptism as one of the two sacraments, and despite its insistence on reliance on the Scriptures, it departed from the text 'unless a man be born of water and of the Spirit he cannot enter into the kingdom of God' by saying that baptism was not strictly necessary because it was valid only if done in the face of the congregation; here is a good case of those godly who thought, in their desperation to uphold their godly principles, that they could

---

[20]  Calderwood, *True History*, vol. iii, 699–700.

[21]  A. R. MacDonald, 'James VI and I, the Church of Scotland, and British Ecclesiastical Convergence', *Historical Journal*, 48 (2005), 885–903; L. A. M. Stewart, ' "Brothers in treuth": Propaganda, Public Opinion and the Perth Articles Debate in Scotland', in R. Houlbrooke, ed., *James VI and I: Ideas, Authority and Government* (Aldershot, 2006), 151–68, and 'The Political Repercussions of the Five Articles of Perth: A Reassessment of James VI and I's Religious Policies in Scotland', *Sixteenth-Century Journal*, 38 (2007), 1,013–36.

[22]  Jenny Wormald, 'The Headaches of Monarchy: Kingship and the Kirk in the Early Seventeenth Century', in Julian Goodare and Alasdair A. Macdonald, eds., *Sixteenth-Century Scotland: Essays in Honour of Michael Lynch* (Leiden, 2008), 367–93.

actually do better than the Bible.[23] Ordinary parishioners were not well versed in the higher flights of theology. They knew, as their ancestors had known, the dangers to the soul of the unbaptized child. James's furious reply to a minister who asked him whether he thought that a child who died unbaptized was damned shows where his sympathies lay: 'No', he said, 'but if you, being called to baptize the child, though privately, should refuse to come, I thinke you shall be damned.'[24] This article, along with private communion for the sick and dying, offered spiritual consolation denied by the godly in the Kirk. Stubborn to the end, they gave way on the principle, but insisted that a certificate asserting terminal illness was needed for private communion, and that private baptism could be performed only during the day. No wonder the inhabitants of godly Scotland did not unite behind what looks like pernickety godly mean-mindedness. And some of these inhabitants continued to invoke the age-old consolation of praying for their dead, anathema as it might be to the protestant Kirk.

It is of course unarguable that Scotland became a Calvinist country, though at no time did those arch enemies (the Catholics) disappear. What is arguable is the emphasis on the success of godliness, at the expense of those, recognized by King James, who as time passed became increasingly accustomed to being members of a Protestant rather than a Catholic Kirk, yet strenuously objected to being godly. They are the people left out of the myth, or included only to enhance the role of the godly rather than being recognized in their own right. So who or what created the myth? The initial effort was made by the usual suspects: John Knox, Andrew Melville, James Melville, and the Presbyterian historians David Calderwood and John Row; then there was the inevitable scapegoat for anything that went wrong in the mid-seventeenth century, namely, Charles I, ably assisted by the fanatical Covenanter Archibald Johnston of Wariston and Archibald, Marquis of Argyll; there was the grisly and exaggerated period of the Killing Times; and then, giving the myth a new twist, came the union of parliaments in 1707, which sparked off a long-lasting debate about the sovereignty of Christ—or rather, the Kirk—in Scotland, complicated by the persistent lingering on of commitment to the Covenanting principle. And underpinning it all was fear: the fear of subordination to England. In the late thirteenth century, the Scots had thought up a distinguished origin myth in a hurry to meet the imperialist claims of Edward I. In 1603 there was the deep irony that the last act in the story was that a Scottish king united the kingdoms. But the very fact of coming closer to England in the later sixteenth century because of supposedly common ground in religion, and being dynastically tied to it from the beginning of the seventeenth, brought its own new fear, the fear of marginalization and neglect. What better way to reinforce Scottish identity, Scottish pride, than by asserting the special godliness of its Kirk, 'one of the purest kirks under heaven this day', as the 1616 confession said.[25] The other was Geneva; it was certainly not England.

---

[23] John 3:5, *APS*, vol. ii, 532–3; Calderwood, *True History*, vol. vii, 239.

[24] Quoted by Alan Cromartie, 'King James and the Hampton Court Conference', in Houlbrooke, ed., *James VI and I*, 71–2.

[25] Calderwood, *True History*, vol. vii, 241.

Despite the efforts of Knox, Melville, Calderwood, and Row, however, it was not in the first century of the Kirk's existence that the myth of godly Scotland really put down roots. Godliness was undoubtedy claimed, and with some success. The French Protestant theologian Theodore Beza preferred Scotland's Genevan model of Church courts to England's Episcopal Church. The English Bishop Bancroft was clearly terrified of the Scottish godly; Catholics, it seems, were in his eyes actually preferable to Knox and Buchanan.[26] On the other hand, English Puritans and Presbyterians were impressed by the godly. How they knew about them actually owes in some measure to Elizabeth I, who was terrified of her home-grown Puritans but quite happy to make life difficult for her fellow monarch James VI of Scotland by giving pulpit space in London to those godly preachers Andrew Melville, David Black, and others, when he booted them out of Scotland; and she gave a haven in the north of England to a Scottish Puritan cell plotting revolution, namely, the exiled Ruthven Raiders of 1583 with their attendant minister James Melville. That kind of royal game-playing was not, incidentally, all one way; when Robert Waldegrave was driven out of England for his part in printing the Marprelate Tracts in 1589, James openly welcomed him to Scotland and gave him the prestigious job of king's printer.

But claiming superior godliness did not make it real. Powerful though the prose may be of Knox's *History of the Reformation*,[27] thunder as he might from the pulpit of St Giles in Edinburgh, Knox was in fact marginalized in the first years of reformation, not just because of his disastrously timed *First Blast of the Trumpet*, for which Elizabeth never forgave him, but because his attacks on Mary, Queen of Scots, from whom the Protestants were getting support, were equally ill-timed. Calderwood, taking up the baton from Knox, also sought to portray Scotland as particularly godly; what he provides is in fact a description of failure. As Michael Lynch has pointed out, Calderwood's account of the year 1596 claims it to be the pinnacle of godly success; yet, as he has to admit, by the end of that glorious year, God's favour had given way to King James's ungodly success when his reaction to a particularly godly attack on him—threatening to move his capital away from Edinburgh—changed the minds of the godly citizens, merchants, and craftsmen, and turned them into slavish king's men.[28] Perhaps the unwittingly funniest part of Calderwood's *History of the Church of Scotland* is his own account of chasing after a hostile King James from Scotland as far as Carlisle in Cumbria in 1617, and writing him letters begging him for forgiveness and favour on the grounds that he had misunderstood His Majesty's command to keep silent, and would, of course, not preach now that it had been explained to him.[29]

Indeed, the failure to establish successful godliness led to a new problem, that sorting out myth from reality in this early period of reform created not one myth but two; and

---

[26] Richard Bancroft, *Daungerous Positions and Proceedings, published and practised with this Iland of Brytain* (London, 1593), 22–9.

[27] W. C. Dickinson, ed., *John Knox's History of the Reformation in Scotland*, 2 vols. (New York, 1950).

[28] Lynch, 'Preaching to the Converted?', 301; Calderwood, *True History*, vol. v, 387–8.

[29] Calderwood, *True History*, vol. vii, 273–5.

the two were mutually conflicting. For especially after 1596 a different note was more emphatically sounded: the note of persecution. Although it was in 1596 that Andrew Melville made his most outspoken claim for the separation of Crown and Kirk, when he famously told the king that 'thair is twa kings and twa kingdoms...thair is Chryst Jesus the King and his Kingdom the Kirk, whose subject King James the Saxt is, and of whose kingdome nocht a king, nor a lord, nor a heid but a member', the slide was on. In April 1597, when the General Assembly at St Andrews, the heartland of Presbyterian strength, proved ineffective, James Melville wrote that 'the court began to govern all' and the freedom of the kirk was subordinated to the 'polytic esteat of a frie monarchie'.[30] Worse was to follow, as James moved towards the restoration of episcopacy in Scotland, which was achieved, if as yet in a limited way, when three bishops were appointed in 1600. Leading and outspoken Presbyterian ministers such as David Black of St Andrews and Robert Bruce of Edinburgh were muzzled. And the Presbyterian attempt to hold a General Assembly in Aberdeen led to imprisonment for some of its members and accusations of high treason—a capital crime—and ultimately to their summons in 1606 to what could be called the second Hampton Court Conference, incarceration in the Tower of London, and exile. The new theme of the sufferings of the persecuted godly rather than the achievements of the successful godly was now heard. Here is Lady Culross, writing her *Ane Godlie Dreame* (1603):

> O Lord, how lang it is thy will,
> That thy puir Sanctis sall be afflictit still?...
> Thy sillie Sancts are tostit to and fro
> Awalk, O Lord, quhy sleipest thou sa lang
> ...
> The warld prevails, our enemies ar strang
> The wickit rage, bot wee ar puir and waik...

Moreover, this passage was rewritten as a sonnet of spiritual comfort for Andrew Melville in the Tower in 1607.[31] Persecution of the godly, so encapsulated here, is of course an eternal theme; Christ had told his followers what they would suffer and the Acts of the Apostles and the Letters of St Paul bear ample witness to what they did suffer. But the use of persecution by the early-modern Scottish godly simply underlines the fact that they were forced to turn to it, to seek spiritual consolation from it, when they were no longer able to trumpet the godliness they were imposing on their country. This universal theme was not simply a myth. But in Scotland it can be regarded as myth, not just because Scottish persecution was in fact neither severe nor long-lived, but because it had its own place in the developing belief in the particular godliness of Scotland.

One may question, therefore, how much the pictures painted by the Melvilles, Calderwood, and Row had to do with the state of the Kirk of their day; for those who

[30] Calderwood, *True History*, vol. v, 440; *Autobiography and Diary of James Melville* (Edinburgh, 1842), 412, 414.

[31] I am very grateful to Dr Jamie Reid-Baxter for the text of this poem and for discussion about it.

painted these pictures knew very well that they were imposing black and white on the ambivalent and grey. King James's greatest opponent, Andrew Melville, after all, wrote adulatory verse on the birth of Prince Henry in 1594. Moreover, they knew that unlike their English counterparts they were dealing with a Calvinist king, some of whose ecclesiastical policies they thoroughly agreed with: an educated clergy, decent stipends for the ministry. So their abiding influence does not relate to contemporary reality. It comes from the desire of later generations to believe in their picture.

We can take that hugely contentious issue, episcopacy, as an example. In 1957, in the course of discussions with the Church of England, the Kirk made the historically outrageous claim that it had never had bishops. In fact, had it not been for what happened after Charles I's accession in 1625, it is perfectly possible to contend that James's Church, that Episcopal-Presbyterian hybrid, might have survived. James's bishops were moderate men, dressed at the king's behest in plain black ministerial gowns, working in harmony with the Church courts.[32] Patrick Forbes of Aberdeen was rightly respected and popular. William Cowper, Bishop of Galloway and formerly second minister of Perth, was actually more godly than the first minister, John Malcolm, who pointed out that Cowper objected to Malcolm's refusal to prevent feasting at Yule, 'yet he accepted of a bishopric, and I continued minister at Perth'.[33] Amazingly, as late as 1637, the future ardent Covenanting minister Robert Baillie claimed that 'bishops I love', while his contemporary, the godly Earl of Rothes, objected to them only on the grounds of their lack of zeal in preaching.[34] But Baillie hit the nail squarely on the head. It was the Jacobean-style bishop that he loved; he went on to inveigh against the proud papistical type of bishop, the type that Charles I was intruding on the Kirk, and which would return with the restoration of Charles II. That was the death knell of episcopacy in the Kirk. Thus it was that Calderwood and Row were believed, while the royally commissioned account of John Spottiswoode, Archbishop of St Andrews, a man highly sensitive to the tensions in the Jacobean Kirk, an account written without the fire and vitriol of Calderwood and Row, was consigned to the dustheap.[35] But it should be remembered that, even when the Kirk was established in 1690 as Presbyterian and non-Episcopal, these hated bishops were not consigned to the dustheap; there has been an Episcopal Church in Scotland from that day to this.

What gave the myth its real foundation was that brief period of the appalling mistakes of Charles I, and the appalling zeal of the Covenanters. For less than a decade, between 1637 and the mid-1640s, the godly Scots could believe that they were determining events in the fight with Charles I. Charles, unlike James, had sought to Anglicanize the Kirk,

---

[32] *APS*, vol. iv, 435–6.

[33] Todd, *Culture of Protestantism*, 222–3.

[34] Robert Baillie, *The Letters and Journals* (Edinburgh, 1841–2), vol. i, 2; John, Earl of Rothes, *A Relation of Proceedings concerning the Affairs of the Kirk of Scotland from August 1637 to July 1638* (Edinburgh, 1830), 4.

[35] Calderwood, *True History*; John Row, *The History of the Kirk of Scotland* (Edinburgh, 1842); John Spottiswoode, *History of the Church of Scotland... to the end of the reign of James VI* (Edinburgh, 1847–51).

and suffered grievously for it. With the National Covenant of 1638, the godly triumphed in Scotland against their king. With the Solemn League and Covenant of 1643, they sought to Scotticize the English Church: the Covenant was made for the *preservation* of the Kirk, and the *reformation* of the Churches of England and Ireland.[36] How, despite the presence of the Presbyterians in England, the Scots actually managed to convince themselves that this was a realistic prospect—though they tried it again when negotiating with Charles I after the first Civil War—suggests godliness spiralling into a dream world.

Reality was a long inevitable decline. Charles II, the Covenanted king of 1651, understandably never went near Scotland again after the Restoration in 1660. The Covenanters dwindled into a small, extremist sect in south-west Scotland, the Cameronians. That created its own myth, of the heroic godly martyrs of the 'Killing Times', but in fact they were less popular then than they were to become, though they are still remembered in their mythical form in some of the parishes of Ayrshire. The Kirk itself was losing confidence in the Edinburgh of the 1690s; and a glance at the list of books on the shelves of Edinburgh University library suggests why: Hobbes, burned in Oxford in 1683; Spinoza; Descartes; the deist works of John Toland and Charles Blount; Richard Simon's *Critical Enquiries into the Various Editions of the Bible*, John Edwards's work on atheism. There the students sat, reading such works under the watchful eyes of portraits of Luther, Melanchthon, Zwingli, and Calvin, with the skull of George Buchanan to cheer them up. One of them, Thomas Aitkenhead, became the target of the Kirk's frantic need to regain control. He was brutally and probably illegally executed for blasphemy in 1697, the same year that over in the west, at Paisley, saw the last of Scotland's determined witch-hunts (if not the last actual execution).[37] Few outside Scotland recognized a Kirk sensing itself under threat and more than ever needing its myth; they saw the horrendous godliness of the Scottish Kirk, which in itself helped to reinforce the myth.

A new lease of life came with the Union of 1707, when Covenanting principles roared back into life: the union of parliaments would mean breaking the covenants, as Scots MPs were forced to sit in a Parliament that contained bishops. And in the longer term, among the many highly complex debates on the legal basis for the Union, especially in the nineteenth and twentieth centuries, the Kirk became highly assertive about its own position. The General Assembly, which represented the sovereignty of Christ, had an authority in ecclesiastical matters that no secular power could challenge.[38] And as the Kirk claimed a godly status unrivalled by any institution in England, so the myth revived and was now dramatically extended. The idea of Presbyterian democracy was born. Knox, Calderwood, and Row now came into their own—though in a form that they would not have recognized.

---

[36]  *APS*, vol. vi, part i, 41–3.

[37]  Michael Graham, *The Blasphemies of Thomas Aitkenhead: Boundaries of Belief on the Eve of the Enlightenment* (Edinburgh, 2008); for the contents of the library, see ch. 4.

[38]  Of the extensive literature on this subject, I pick out here Colin Kidd, *Union and Unionisms: Political Thought in Scotland, 1500–2000* (Cambridge, 2008); see especially ch. 6.

'Democracy' was in fact virtually unused, from the classical world—when Aristotle himself had consigned it to his three bad forms of government—until the American and French Revolutions, when it took off into all sorts of weird and wonderful forms, as we see today.[39] On the rare occasions it was used, 'democracy' was a dirty word; for both the ungodly King James and the godly Robert Baillie it was a term of condemnation. James, in his vitriolic attack on the Puritans in *Basilikon Doron* (1599), wrote of the tumultuous beginnings of the Reformation when there was no order from the Prince, and the Puritans 'begouth to fantasie to themselves a Democratick forme of government...[an] imagined Democracie'. Baillie, in 1643, asserted the need to 'eschew that democratic anarchy and independence of particular congregations which they knew to be opposite to the word of God and destructive wholly of that discipline'.[40]

But once democracy was in vogue, as the highest form of government, why should the Kirk not annex it? Hence the lurid claims of two godly luminaries of the Kirk, Professor Alexander Martin, Moderator of the United Free Church and influential in the union of the United Free Church and Church of Scotland, in 1929, and Archibald Main, Professor of Ecclesiastical History, University of Glasgow, 1922–42. In ringing tones, Martin claimed that 'It had been on the floor of the General Assemblies rather than in the corrupt estates (parliament) or Privy Council that the battle of the Scottish people for freedom had been fought and won. The burden of the poor was borne for centuries by the Church unaided and in her system of education she laid during the past ages the system of democracy in which all barriers were laid down, and the way was open and free for all.' Main asserted that 'Our country was not a nation, in any strict sense of the word, before the Reformation.... The refashioning of the medieval Church accomplished more for the unity of the Scottish race than the victory at Bannockburn or the defeat at Flodden. After the year 1560 the ordinary man gained what the extraordinary cleric had lost. No more was the layman a humble puppet of Mother Church. He could voice his views in Kirk sessions or General Assembly, he could take part in the election of his minister, he had the opportunity of influencing public opinion.'[41] It is a little difficult to believe that the sinners of the early-modern period would have recognized this luxury. But it was a wonderful theme to be pressed into the service of national pride.

So the myth is solid and enduring. It remains a source of pride, even in an increasingly secular and multicultural society, with the Kirk's membership steadily declining. It has its amusing side. It also has its terrifying one, in the sectarianism that in the modern period continues to cast its hideous shadow over the fundamental message of Christianity. Nevertheless, there are signs that this is beginning to diminish; in December 2010 the city fathers of Glasgow decided to restrict the Orange marches, to the fury of the Orangemen. That is not the only sign. The response to the papal visit, the

---

[39] See the fascinating discussion by John Dunn, *Setting the People Free: The Story of Democracy* (London, 2005).

[40] Craigie, ed., *Basilikon Doron*, vol. i, 75; Baillie, *Letters and Journals*, vol. ii, 115.

[41] Cited by Graham Walker, 'Varieties of Scottish Protestant Identity', in T. M. Devine and R. Finlay, eds., *Scotland in the Twentieth Century* (Edinburgh, 1996), 255–6.

fact that it was godly Irishmen who had to carry the godly flag, suggests that alongside the apparent triumph of the Scottish godly there has been a flourishing ability to serve the Lord in ungodly fashion. That ability, which can be traced back to those who asserted their right to do so in the early decades of the Reformation, merits attention.

## FURTHER READING

Graham, Michael, *The Uses of Reform: 'Godly Discipline' and Popular Behaviour in Scotland and Beyond* (Leiden, 1996).

—— *The Blasphemies of Thomas Aikenhead: Boundaries of Belief on the Eve of the Enlightenment* (Edinburgh, 2008).

Kidd, Colin, *Union and Unionisms: Political Thought in Scotland 1500–2000* (Cambridge, 2008).

Kirk, James, *Patterns of Reform: Continuity and Change in the Reformation Kirk* (Edinburgh, 1989).

McCallum, John, *Reforming the Scottish Parish: The Reformation in Fife, 1560–1640* (Farnham, 2010).

MacDonald, Alan R., *The Jacobean Kirk, 1567–1625: Sovereignty, Polity and Liturgy* (Aldershot, 1998).

Mullan, David G., *Episcopacy in Scotland: The History of an Idea, 1560–1638* (Edinburgh, 1986).

—— *Scottish Puritanism 1590–1638* (Oxford, 2000).

Todd, Margo, *The Culture of Protestantism in Early Modern Scotland* (New Haven, 2002).

Woods Preece, Isabel, *Our awin Scottish use: Music in the Scottish Church up to 1603* (Glasgow and Aberdeen, 2000).

# CHAPTER 10

## THE 'RISE' OF THE STATE?

### LAURA A. M. STEWART

HAS there ever been such a thing as the Scottish state? For some historians, the answer is 'no' and, if they are right, this could be a very short chapter. There was an ancient and sovereign kingdom of Scotland, with its own monarch, Parliament, and governing structures, but it never had the chance to develop into a modern state because government, in Keith Brown's phrase, was 'hijacked by London'. When the ruling house of Stewart acceded to the English throne in 1603, an 'embryonic British state' expanded at the expense of Scotland's 'fledgling' structures and poached its personnel. A Scottish state glimmered into existence during the 1640s, only to be 'blown away' by Oliver Cromwell's thoroughly English New Model Army. This was an experience from which the Scottish state never fully recovered. Although the regal union was not merely a 'halfway house' on a straight road leading to incorporating union, the erosion of political sovereignty that resulted means that the concept of a Scottish state is, at best, problematic.[1]

An alternative view has been proposed by Julian Goodare. Instead of regarding the Britannic union as the moment when Scottish political autonomy was fatally compromised, Goodare describes how Crown and Parliament worked together across the late sixteenth and early seventeenth centuries to forge an 'absolutist state'. The result was nothing less than a 'Stewart revolution in government', whereby the nobility and the Church opted to relinquish their private jurisdictions in favour of 'configuration' within a 'single matrix of power'. By these means, a unified, centralized state was operating by the precociously early date of 1625, the year of Charles I's accession.[2]

---

[1] Keith Brown, *Bloodfeud in Scotland, 1573–1625: Violence, Justice and Politics in an Early Modern Society* (Edinburgh, 1986), 272; Keith Brown, 'From Scottish Lords to British Officers: State Building, Elite Integration and the Army in the Seventeenth Century', in Norman Macdougall, ed., *Scotland and War AD 79–1918* (Edinburgh, 1991), 136 and n. 11; Keith Brown, *Kingdom or Province? Scotland and the Regal Union, 1603–1715* (Basingstoke, 1992), 2.

[2] Julian Goodare, *State and Society in Early Modern Scotland* (Oxford, 1999), 7, 8, 16, 286; Julian Goodare, *The Government of Scotland, 1560–1625* (Oxford, 2004), 4–6, 9, 299, 304. Goodare's work raises more questions than this survey can adequately address. See Keith Brown's reviews of Goodare's work in *Scottish Historical Review* [*SHR*], 80:209 (2001), 123–6; 86:221 (2007), 138–9.

These conflicting interpretations of the state do not hide an elephant in the room so much as reveal the elephant in the bed: Scotland sleeps with a partner that, on good days, takes up more than its fair share of space and, on less good days, has almost flattened its neighbour.[3] The ambiguities of Scotland's relationship with England have perhaps encouraged historians to concentrate on the indigenous ideas, institutions, and structures that fostered the creation of the independent medieval kingdom—and made it prickly enough to wake the elephant when a flattening was in the offing.[4] The question is whether the state can be used to understand Scottish society, rather than describe the response of Scottish society to English/British dominance. One historian is sceptical about this possibility. Allan Macinnes has suggested that the state-formation paradigm is an introspective one that cannot be anything other than Anglocentric. Almost paradoxically, it is by appreciating the extraordinary breadth of the horizons viewed by successive generations of Scots that we can better understand the polity that came to be known as the United Kingdom.[5]

The absence of agreement amongst these scholars reflects the wider problem of how we define a highly abstracted concept like the state. In its most common usage, it is taken to mean a territory where a people are organized into a political community under one government.[6] This is easy enough to understand, although we are conscious that some complicated processes must have been at work to enable 'a people' and 'a political community' to recognize themselves as such. Sometimes the definition is further truncated so that the state becomes secular government itself. In this form, it can often be found juxtaposed with the Church.[7] The state is rarely used in these instances as an investigative tool. Pioneers of the idea that the state could be used in this way were not historians but sociologists. 'Does Scottish politics exist?', they asked. The assumption that modern political communities had to be sovereign nation states was at odds with the reality of Scotland's 'lively and distinctive' post-1707 political culture. By exploring the meanings of 'state', 'nation', and 'society' more closely, sociologists enabled modern Scotland to emerge as a political entity possessing a high degree of stateness, despite incorporating union. One can now 'quibble' that modern Scotland 'is a semi-state'.[8]

Sociologists tend to see the state as an 'ineluctably modern' phenomenon, but can historians define the state in a way that gives it meaning across long time periods? Scholars who have sought to historicize the state have focused on its distinctiveness

---

[3] Paraphrasing the title of a publication by Ludovick Kennedy, who acknowledged an earlier work by Paul H. Scott, *Still in Bed with an Elephant* (Edinburgh, 1998), Introduction and p. 1.

[4] Significant studies include Jenny Wormald, *Court, Kirk and Community: Scotland, 1470–1625*, 2nd edn. (Edinburgh, 1991); Brown, *Bloodfeud*; Roger Mason, *Kingship and the Commonweal: Political Thought in Renaissance and Reformation Scotland* (East Linton, 1998).

[5] Allan Macinnes, *Union and Empire: The Making of the United Kingdom in 1707* (Cambridge, 2007), 4, 49.

[6] This is, broadly speaking, how Goodare defines the state in *State and Society*, 12. A later modification describes it as 'a system of institutions and personnel', Goodare, *Government*, 5.

[7] Brown, *Kingdom or Province?, passim*; Wormald, *Court, Kirk and Community, passim*.

[8] Alice Brown, David McCrone, and Lindsay Paterson, *Politics and Society in Scotland* (Basingstoke, 1998), 27, 36. See also David McCrone, *Understanding Scotland: The Sociology of a Stateless Nation* (London, 1992).

from other forms of political organization and suggested a combination of features that achieves this.[9] The state is a unified network of agencies that are centrally coordinated. It operates in a territorially demarcated area. It claims a monopoly over the making and implementation of authoritative and binding rules, which it alone has the legitimate right to effect, by force if necessary. Rules are made on a rational and open basis, rather than according to custom or the will of a powerful person. These features together enable the state to exercise a different kind of power from other political apparatuses. For the scholar, therefore, a broad working definition looks something like this: the state is a centrally coordinated network of agencies claiming a monopoly over binding rule-making and the exercise of legitimate force within a demarcated territory.[10]

For some historians, the emergence of the state as a political force helps to define the early modern period. In recent years, English scholars have been to the fore in advancing this way of thinking.[11] Traditional histories of the state portrayed its power as fundamentally coercive. A process of relentless centralization imposed unpalatable policies on a largely passive people. States were, first and foremost, war-making machines requiring a vast centralized bureaucracy to feed their insatiable appetite for men and money. In Charles Tilly's famous dictum, 'war made the state, and the state made war'.[12] John Brewer queried whether the pressures generated by sustained warfare were as likely to crush state structures as catalyse them into new forms. This implied that relatively sophisticated state structures would need to be 'well rooted' *before* sustained conflict occurred. Tilly was not wrong to see war as one of the foundations of state formation, but other factors now demanded consideration.[13]

Current histories of the English state emphasize processes of negotiation and brokerage. They argue that focusing on *power* has distracted scholars from asking questions about *authority*. As Steve Hindle has perceptively pointed out, the former 'can be maintained by force', but the latter requires 'some degree of reciprocity'. This point is important because most early modern governments lacked the means to control people effectively. Instead, the state had to develop an integrative relationship with civil society. Individuals and groups invited the state in when they found that it served their aims better than the alternatives, particularly in relation to issues such as poverty and property rights. At the same time, the actions and words of an expanding body of office-holders

---

[9]  Brown, McCrone, and Paterson, *Politics and Society*, 31. The pioneering works are Michael Braddick, *State Formation in Early Modern England, c.1550–1700* (Cambridge, 2000), 19; Steve Hindle, *The State and Social Change in Early Modern England* (Basingstoke, 2000), 232.

[10]  Braddick, *State Formation*, 17–19; Brown, McCrone, and Paterson, *Politics and Society*, 28–9.

[11]  Braddick, *State Formation*; John Brewer, *The Sinews of Power: War, Money and the English State, 1688–1783* (London, 1989); Hindle, *State and Social Change*.

[12]  Charles Tilly, 'Reflections on the History of European State-Making', in Charles Tilly and Gabriel Ardant, eds., *The Formation of National States in Western Europe* (Princeton, 1975), 42.

[13]  Brewer, *Sinews of Power*, 138–9. The state's unique organizational capability is discussed in Jan Glete, *War and the State in Early Modern Europe: Spain, the Dutch Republic and Sweden as Fiscal-Military States, 1500–1660* (London, 2002). See also Christopher Storrs, ed., *The Fiscal-Military State in Eighteenth-Century Europe: Essays in Honour of P. G. M. Dickinson* (Farnham, 2009); Richard Bonney, ed., *The Rise of the Fiscal State in Europe, c.1200–1815* (Oxford, 1999), 2.

acted as channels through which 'governmental will' could penetrate the nooks and crannies of society. These channels allowed the views of people from outside the political elite to shape the nature and extent of government activity. Although the expansion of the state was not a 'zero-sum game', where winners defeated losers, some individuals and groups were clearly in a better position than others to use state power to consolidate and enhance their status. Others found that they had little influence over the operation of a state that increasingly demarcated the bounds of their personal autonomy.[14]

At the dawn of the seventeenth century, England was probably amongst the most unified, centralized states in Europe. Its authority was derived, in part, from an unusual level of 'social depth', whereby quite humble people served in an extensive network of minor offices and resorted to law to resolve disputes.[15] Yet, even in England, the early modern state was not a totality. Its power was far from all-embracing and it had to contend with alternative power structures and sources of authority.[16] In the decentralized kingdom of Scotland, the alternatives were all the more potent. The continuing political and social relevance of lordship, and the semi-detached nature of governing structures in parish and burgh, posed serious challenges to the establishment of an effective network of public administration. The state undoubtedly required 'noble consent' to function, but it also needed some measure of engagement from middling and lower social groups. How state power was experienced by Scottish men and women of all social levels has received limited attention from historians. This chapter will attempt to suggest ways in which an understanding of the development of the state can lead us into questions about legitimacy, authority, and power in early modern societies.[17]

But what of that vexed matter of sovereignty? Does it matter whether state power emanates from London or Edinburgh? The fact of having to pay taxes, for example, is probably more important to most people than who's asking for them, but the latter point must surely affect whether a tax is regarded as legitimate. The removal of the pivot of executive power to a neighbouring state had political consequences, but His Britannic Majesty was not the sole will of government and his prerogatives had to be exercised, and were experienced, through Scottish offices, institutions, and practices.[18] There was no joint British council or representative assembly to coordinate policy across the archipelago.[19] Scottish

---

[14] Braddick, *State Formation*, 27, 93; Steve Hindle, *The State and Social Change in Early Modern England, 1550–1640*, 236; Steve Hindle, *On the Parish: The Micro-Politics of Poor Relief in Rural England, c.1550–1750* (Oxford, 2004), 95, 447; Keith Wrightson, 'Politics of the Parish', in Paul Griffiths, Adam Fox, and Steve Hindle, eds., *The Experience of Authority in Early Modern England* (Basingstoke, 1996), 27.

[15] Hindle, *State and Social Change*, 21.

[16] Braddick, *State Formation*, 19.

[17] Laura A. M. Stewart, *Urban Politics and the British Civil Wars: Edinburgh, 1617–53* (Leiden, 2006), 26–7, 59–66; Brown, *Bloodfeud*, 14–17, 44, 48–9, 270 [quotation]; Jenny Wormald, *Lords and Men in Scotland: Bonds of Manrent 1442–1603* (Edinburgh, 2003), ch. 3.

[18] Braddick, *State Formation*, 24, 27.

[19] The Committee of Both Kingdoms existed for about three years during the mid-1640s. It never had the final say in matters of war and peace. Allan Macinnes, *The British Revolution, 1629–1660* (Basingstoke, 2005), 162.

and English governing structures remained largely separate, with almost no shared juris-diction. Binding rule-making was made and interpreted by Scottish lawyers and admin-istrators. Scotland was not Ireland: neither the English Privy Council, nor its Parliament, had jurisdiction over Scottish affairs, although the king personally sought the advice of people who were not Scots and appointed a handful of them to the Scottish Privy Council. For most of the seventeenth century, the government dealt with violent Scots by deploy-ing other, more reliable, Scots to deal with them. Even Oliver Cromwell resorted to gov-erning Scotland through its own laws and many of its localized administrative structures. For all these reasons, it is meaningful to talk of a Scottish state in the seventeenth century.

# 1

Historians have travelled a long way from the assumption that Scotland had a 'problem' because its government was less unified and centralized than that of some of its neigh-bours.[20] Pioneering work by Jenny Wormald and Keith Brown revealed that 'anarchy and bloodshed' were not the obvious corollaries of central government's less than mus-cular presence across the kingdom. Private, particularist modes of regulating social rela-tions were not necessarily ineffective and may have been well suited to contemporary notions of what 'justice' meant. There are limitations to this argument: these forms of justice did not, perhaps, 'satisfy everyone' so much as everyone who mattered. History tends not to record the opinions of sisters and daughters who, as part of the settlement of feuds, were married to men who had visited violence upon their family.[21] The public, universalist type of justice available through legal systems staffed exclusively by men may not, of course, have served women, especially poor women, much better. This point is a reminder that state structures cannot be understood purely as ideal types, isolated from wider society. They develop because they are useful, especially to elites and rulers.

As a centrally coordinated network, the early modern Scottish state was small in scale and limited in its reach. Charles I's reconstructed Privy Council of 1626 was led by ten senior officers of state. These men directed a corps of secretaries, deputies, advocates, and other officials, who ran the central courts of session and justiciary (civil and crimi-nal law respectively), managed the government's records, and administered the Crown's finances.[22] Most of the routine business of government was carried out by the Privy Council. A wide-ranging and basically undifferentiated remit did not change in essen-tials after 1603. Its ethos, despite some moves towards independent decision making, remained largely reactive. Parliament, like the sixteenth-century monarchy, was peripa-tetic and had no permanent home of its own until 1639. Central government had no

---

[20]  Rosalind Mitchison, *Lordship to Patronage: Scotland, 1603–1745* (Edinburgh, 1990), 15.

[21]  Brown, *Bloodfeud*, 58, 234, 272. Wormald strikes a more cautious note in *Lords and Men*, 131–6.

[22]  *Register of the Privy Council of Scotland, 1625–27*, ed. David Masson (Edinburgh, 1899), 1st series, vol. i, pp. vii, l, lii.

standing forces, raised and paid for out of its own revenues, with the exception of a royal guard that was wound up in 1611 in order to save money. There was no militia until the 1660s and there were no lord lieutenants until the 1790s. When armed force was required, the Crown continued to rely on summoning lords with their retinues. Since there was no external aggressor that considered Scotland worth invading by the later sixteenth century (even if individual Scots were fighting other people's wars elsewhere), there was little call for a sophisticated fiscal infrastructure. The Scottish monarchy could neither levy the range of taxes available to its French counterpart nor do so without the consent of the Estates. Accordingly, there was no permanent office for the collection of taxes.

If conceived of as a network of offices and personnel, the state interacted with a collection of particularist jurisdictions, which possessed extensive and varied discretionary powers. The most important unit of local government was the sheriffdom. Most of the two dozen or so sheriffs, who were invariably titled landowners, held the office heritably. Central government could not threaten these people with removal or significantly influence the appointment of their subordinates. A number of sheriffdoms did pass into Crown hands during James's reign, and more were acquired by Charles, but they amounted to less than one-third of the total in 1625. In the fifty-plus royal burghs, which held their privileges directly from the Crown, there were more opportunities to ensure that the right people were elected annually to town councils. Periodic bursts of concern about urban elections on the part of central government did not, on the whole, encourage a wider interest in how the burghs ran their affairs. Moreover, when tested over the election of controversial figures to the magistracy or the enforcement of contentious religious policies, town councils could not always be relied on to comply or to convince the rest of the urban community to do likewise.[23]

Tenants-in-chief, including the royal burghs, could hold law courts that were not subject to direct oversight from central bodies and whose routine work rarely came to their attention. Whether the baron courts met contemporary expectations of justice amongst tenants and labourers, rather than landowners, remains to be seen, although the likelihood that they provided cheaper services and faster results than either the justice ayres[24] that periodically toured the country, or the central courts in Edinburgh, were surely points in their favour. Regalities were another localized jurisdiction that covered much of the country. Many were held heritably, their powers extended to trying serious crimes, and other Crown officials could be excluded from their bounds. It therefore seems highly unlikely, given the particularist nature of the local courts, that recourse to law became a meaningful way for Scottish people to become exposed to, and interact with, state authority.

One notable area of innovation in local government was the introduction of justices of the peace from 1609. Although this office was established on a national scale and made

---

[23] Laura A. M. Stewart, 'Politics and Government in the Scottish Burghs, 1603–38', in Julian Goodare and Alasdair A. MacDonald, eds., *Sixteenth-Century Scotland: Essays in Honour of Michael Lynch* (Leiden, 2008), 427–50; Stewart, *Urban Politics*, 156–66.

[24] An itinerant court of justice.

directly accountable to central government, its effectiveness as a conduit of state authority may have been minimal. Justices were always intended to carry out relatively menial
tasks, rather than the wide-ranging judicial and administrative work shouldered by their
centuries-old English counterparts.[25] Town councils attained the right to act as justices
within their sometimes quite extensive bounds, so the office did almost nothing to
enhance state authority there. Although James made considerable efforts to have justices
accepted, Privy Councillors seem to have allowed them to slip from view by the early
1620s. In 1629 Charles reminded his councillors that the peace commissions should have
been renewed on his accession. Little was done until Charles personally undertook a
more interventionist policy in the wake of his visit to Scotland in 1633. The remit of the
office was widened and justices were expected to report back on some of their activities.
Despite Charles's enthusiasm, it is likely that justices, in most areas, remained under the
shadow of the sheriffs. The Campbells of Glenorchy, a powerful cadet branch of the
house of Argyll, may have represented the general attitude of many of their peers in
the 1630s: if justices there must be, justices would at least be *their* people.[26]

Thus far, we have been considering the state in secular terms. When it came to organizational capability on a national scale, however, the ecclesiastical authorities, despite the
upheavals of Reformation, were arguably the exemplar. Historians have shown how the
secular powers in England allied themselves with the evolving structures of the post-
Reformation Church to create the 'civil parish'. This coalition facilitated not only a widening of the state's remit, but also a deepening of its reach.[27] It is more difficult to argue for a
Scottish equivalent. Even when kings claimed supremacy in religious affairs and allowed
the Kirk's policy-making body, the General Assembly, to fall into abeyance, the lower
Church courts continued to exist and they operated largely in parallel to the existing
structures of local government. Cooperation between the two occurred, but kirk-sessions
and presbyteries maintained a strong sense of institutional independence throughout the
seventeenth century, even when the episcopate was fully operational. It was the Church
courts that took responsibility for important but time-consuming social matters, such as
regulating morality, arbitrating when household relations broke down, and providing for
the poor. While they clearly expected the secular authorities to support their work, it
seems clear enough that the initiative on these issues lay with the Church.

Scotland's parishes were not units of secular government in the way that historians
have argued for early modern England. This is perhaps most apparent in an area of social
activity that was becoming a preoccupation for many local communities: poor relief. The
Church operated a national system (at least in theory) that allowed for a high degree of
local discretion. Despite being based on voluntary giving rather than compulsory rates, it
seems to have worked, in normal times, about as well as contemporary expectations and
prejudices would allow. As far as the poor were concerned, assistance came from the hand

---

[25] Goodare, *Government*, 190, 204–5, 217. For English justices, see Braddick, *State Formation*, 30–2.
[26] NAS, Breadalbane Muniments, GD112/39/56/1, Campbell of Glencarradale to Campbell of
Glenorchy, 5 July 1635.
[27] Hindle, *State and Social Change*.

of the kirk-sessioner. Legislation enacted in the late sixteenth century and refined in 1649 permitted secular officials in town and country to tax the inhabitants of a parish for the purpose of supporting their poor. However, there was no effective machinery for compelling officials to act and, with the exception of Edinburgh, the requirement to establish regular compulsory rates was 'widely ignored'. Crisis years in the mid-1620s and the 1690s revealed the shortcomings of the system. When parish provision either proved inadequate or failed altogether, there were no centrally coordinated agencies capable of forcing the necessary redistribution of resources.[28]

By the early seventeenth century, the Scottish state had undergone some significant developments in terms of the activities it encompassed and the way it was organized. Its accumulation of power in this period was, nonetheless, 'very gradual'. In key areas, such as fiscal and military capacity, the state's weaknesses were not exposed largely because the king and his advisers avoided doing things that might have antagonized the landed elite. A different situation prevailed with Charles's accession in 1625. That the new king thought it necessary to adopt such a comprehensive programme to enhance the power of the state implies very strongly that he, at least, was aware of its limitations: fiscal, military, legal, and administrative. But the state, as it appeared to be developing in the 1630s, was increasingly offensive to a broad and powerful coalition of nobles, lawyers, lairds, burgesses, and clerics. If the state was unable to rely on the voluntary consent of leading social groups, it had to possess the means to compel instead. Charles appears not to have understood this. As the Scottish elite withdrew support from the royal regime over the autumn and winter of 1637–8, a 'coercive vacuum' developed.[29] It would be filled, with astonishing speed, by the Covenanters.

## 2

If it was fear of a hyperactive state that helped to propel Scottish elites into rebellion, the ensuing decade must have come as a shock. At the centre, Parliament arrogated to itself the power to convene and dismiss its representatives, as well as control the procedures by which legislation was prepared and passed. When Parliament was not sitting, executive power transferred to a smaller body called the Committee of Estates, which would come into its own once crises in Ireland (1641) and England (1642) necessitated the remobilization of Scottish forces. A Privy Council that had been exhibiting suicidal tendencies since 1637 was now effectively killed off. As a final collective thumbing of the nose at Britannic majesty, the 1641 Parliament insisted that all legislation passed since

---

[28]  Rosalind Mitchison, *The Old Poor Law in Scotland: The Experience of Poverty, 1574–1845* (Edinburgh, 2000), chs. 1 and 2; Laura A. M. Stewart, 'Poor Relief in Edinburgh and the Famine of 1621–24', *International Review of Scottish Studies*, 30 (2005); Karen Cullen, *Famine in Scotland: The 'Ill Years' of the 1690s* (Edinburgh, 2010), 97 [quotation], 110–17.

[29]  Brown, *Bloodfeud*, 270.

1639 be published before it had been touched with the royal sceptre, thereby implying that its legality was not dependent on the king's assent. Technically speaking, the king-in-Parliament remained the supreme law-making authority, but Charles was not fooled into believing he was anything other than a figurehead.

When rebellion broke out in 1637, Charles's Scottish administration had no standing forces it could call upon to quell disorder. Within a year or so, an army was being used to stamp out resistance in the north and, from the mid-1640s, to help collect taxes. James and Charles had been able to do little more than tinker around the edges of an archaic taxation system that woefully underestimated the worth of the propertied. As early as 1639, with war looming, the new government embarked on an ambitious revaluation, which enabled taxation to tap more of the nation's wealth. In 1644 the first excise tax on staple goods was introduced. Although the extent of resistance and noncompliance still need to be considered, it is clear that the experiences of the 1640s were transforming the state's fiscal and military potential.

Parliamentary government relied on an elaborate network of committees, coordinated directly from the centre and linking every shire, burgh, and parish in the country. Justices of the peace must have seemed unassuming by comparison; the committees were intruded into every region of the country and given wide-ranging powers, although we know little about how they functioned in practice. Evidence from the only substantial local record to come to light shows that, as well as organizing the war effort in their communities and collaborating with centrally appointed local tax collectors, the committees were also able to 'sit upon civil effaires' and judge 'anie controversies' requiring resolution.[30] It is true that royal officials were not abolished, but this was because they were bypassed wherever it was deemed necessary.

One important source of continuity with the past was maintained. In the early days of the Covenanting regime's existence, when war committees had not yet been established, the presbyteries were employed to collect voluntary donations, mobilize opinion, and organize the sending of representatives to Edinburgh. The legitimization of shire war committees was almost certainly aided by association with a well-established Church court. If true, this might present an interesting Scottish variation on the English civil parish: the presbyterian shire, perhaps. This was a formidable alliance. For a time, it enabled the resources of Scottish society to be mobilized by central government more effectively than ever before. True to form, however, the presbytery remained emphatically the ally, not the tool, of secular government. When a faction led by James, third Marquis of Hamilton, gained the political initiative in 1647, it sought to use the state to raise an army for Charles I. Its opponents, headed by Archibald Campbell, first Marquis of Argyll, walked out of government, knowing that the many presbyteries that opposed the Engagement with the king would influence people in the localities and stymie the levy.

---

[30] *Minute Book kept by the War Committee of the Covenanters in the Stewartry of Kirkcudbright, 1640 and 1641*, ed. J. Nicholson (Kirkcudbright, 1855), 114–15.

Although the Covenanting state was undeniably under severe strain by the later 1640s, the assumption that it had been on an inevitable downward spiral from 1643 must be questioned.[31] Having survived the multiple crises of the mid-1640s, central government now sought to rehabilitate its relationship with local communities and revive its fiscal and administrative infrastructure. This activity was interrupted by the final crisis of Charles I's life. His execution in 1649 prompted the Scottish political leadership to invite his eldest son, Charles, to Scotland as a Covenanted king, but his presence in Scotland stretched their political legitimacy to its limits. As an English invading force approached the border in the summer of 1650, central government struggled to harness diminishing local resources and maintain control over the country's armed capability. Yet the regime did not collapse from within. It took the superior organizational capacity of a wealthier neighbour state, and one of England's most gifted military commanders, Oliver Cromwell, to destroy Covenanting government. Even then, it was a close-run thing.[32]

The Covenanting state was more powerful than its predecessors, but it could not have established itself unless it also commanded authority. The National Covenant of 1638 was the government's founding statement of its principles. This document, which was distributed all over Scotland to be sworn and signed by ordinary men and women, purported to band the people with one another and with God in defence of religion, kingdom, and king. The argument that the government was directing a war for national self-preservation seems ultimately to have been widely accepted, despite expressions of doubt about the legitimacy of what the Covenanters were doing. Supporters of the king asserted that, under the cloak of religion, a group of power-hungry nobles were trying to seize Charles's crown. The Covenanting leadership maintained that they merely wished to preserve and restore the ancient laws and liberties of the kingdom. This argument was undermined somewhat by the far-reaching changes made to the constitution, the extirpation of episcopacy, and the overhauling of the taxation system. We know a great deal about why there was opposition to Charles, but there is still more to say about how the Covenanters harnessed and directed discontent, while resisting the powerful appeals to custom and tradition made by Charles's supporters.

The people of Scotland, like their counterparts in many other early modern European countries, found that war made the state. In its determination to mobilize the country for conflict, the government erected a network of personnel that could be coordinated more effectively from the centre. New forms of government were validated, at least initially, by the active participation of a wider cross-section of the social elite than had been possible before 1638. Superior resource extraction enabled the state to exercise a more meaningful monopoly over the legitimate use of force. The state could now coerce where it failed to persuade. In the north-east, the existence of an army convinced many people there to conform to the new order. An assertively Protestantizing state with enhanced powers of compulsion must have made life particularly uncomfortable for Catholics. It

---

[31] David Stevenson, *Revolution and Counter-Revolution, 1644–51* (Edinburgh, 2003), xvi.

[32] Laura A. M. Stewart, 'Fiscal Revolution and State Formation in Mid Seventeenth-Century Scotland', *Historical Research*, 84: 225(2011), 443–69.

probably also furthered the polarization of highland society and widened the cultural divide between Gaelic- and Scots-speaking peoples.[33] Use of the state to support more effective regulation of sexual morality, delimit access to poor relief, or tax specific activities such as selling ale, may have particularly affected women. These are tentative suggestions: the social impact of state formation during this critical decade, for individuals, households, and communities, demands further investigation.

# 3

This chapter has focused on the first half of the seventeenth century because that is where scholarly research has been concentrated. Although some important studies have emerged recently on Restoration politics and on the 1707 Union, none of these works have explicitly been concerned with government, while the 1690s remain comparatively under-researched. Allan Macinnes is one of the few historians to have attempted a long perspective on the Union treaty, by considering commercial and economic activity across the seventeenth century.[34] There is no integrated and sustained thesis on the development of Scotland's fiscal, military, and governmental infrastructure between the civil wars and the 1707 Union.

Current work suggests that developments were small-scale when compared with England, Sweden, or the Dutch Republic, yet the implications for Scottish society must have been profound. New offices that were directly accountable to central government, regularized taxation, and the use of military personnel to bypass uncooperative civil governors, were innovations from the civil-war era that took on renewed significance in the decades of Restoration and Revolution. This raises two issues that await further research before they can be addressed with confidence. Elite expectations about the uses to which the state could and should be put almost certainly underwent significant change in this period. It seems likely that these expectations were increasingly incompatible with the political imperatives of monarchs who were involved in Continental European affairs in a way unparalleled since the reign of Henry VIII. Meanwhile, structures that were unable to project Scottish state power abroad were, nonetheless, developing an enhanced capability to exercise control over the population at home. The state was more powerful in the reigns of Charles I's sons than in his own time, but it was not necessarily more authoritative.

'I wold onley have arms in the King's hand with some money and then I feare neither rebellion nor a new warre.'[35] John Maitland, Duke of Lauderdale, who dominated Scottish politics for the best part of two decades, succinctly sums up policy-making in the Restoration era. Far away in London, this translated into keeping Scotland firmly

[33]  Allan Macinnes, *Clanship, Commerce and the House of Stuart, 1603–1788* (East Linton, 1996), ch. 4.
[34]  Macinnes, *Union and Empire*.
[35]  R. A. Lee, 'Government and Politics in Scotland, 1661–1681' (PhD thesis, University of Glasgow, 1995), 171, quoting NLS, Ms.7023/60.

under control, by any means deemed of least inconvenience to an English administration with many other things to worry about. The chances of being able to achieve this were greatly diminished by the reintroduction of the episcopal hierarchy, without making sufficient concessions to the many clerics and lay people who remained committed to the National Covenant and Presbyterianism. While the escalation of discord and violence, especially in the south-west, has been given considerable attention, the effects this had on the operation of local government are less well understood. Religious policy in the seventeenth century continually exposed the basic unreliability of local governors, who were prepared to turn a blind eye to activities such as conventicling in the interests of minimizing confrontation in their communities. Before the 1640s, the powers of compulsion that central government could exercise were limited, leaving them with little choice but to seek accommodation with local elites. From the civil-war era, the security of the state validated actions that would have been beyond the bounds of political credibility only a generation earlier.

Sending in the army was the obvious way to compel obedience from obdurate local governors. Tim Harris has argued that central government increasingly opted to use the military to bypass civil structures in the localities. Although his examples tend to be drawn from the most troubled, and troublesome, region of Scotland, the south-west, it is likely that the threat of quartering men on this town, or that estate, convinced many to do as they were told. Soldiers were used not only to assist a centrally-appointed network of tax collectors, known as commissioners of supply, but also to extract fines imposed on those who refused to conform to the new order. Granting special commissions of justiciary to military men in the pay of central government avoided reliance on potentially partial local elites or the snail-paced workings of the central justice system. Backed by the threat of force, central government agencies could afford to be less respectful of the particularist privileges held by many shires and burghs. A series of mandatory oaths and tests for all office-holders were used to purge local government. Town councils were remodelled by revoking charters and enabling the direct appointment of magistrates. Suspect behaviour became the excuse to remove heritable jurisdictions and bestow their powers on loyalists. Scots law seemed to offer little scope for redress. Without safeguards such as habeas corpus, which protected the accused from indefinite imprisonment, or stringent restrictions on the use of torture, the law increasingly appeared to serve, rather than regulate, the state.[36]

The vigorous activity of the Scottish military arguably belied both its small size and comparative underfunding. Standing forces reached around three thousand men in the 1680s, were added to during the war years of the 1690s, and reduced back to this figure in 1701. A militia was created after 1668 to provide more armed support at less expense. In theory, this gave the government a further twenty-two thousand men with at least some

---

[36] Tim Harris, *Restoration: Charles II and his Kingdoms, 1660–1685* (London, 2005), 112, 121–4, 355–6, 362, 365–7. Macinnes, 'Repression and Conciliation', 177–9. Commissioners of supply collected the cess. The excise was usually farmed out to private collectors. There were experiments with direct collection in the 1660s.

military training, although it is possible that nowhere near this number were ever mustered. The so-called 'Highland host', which was sent into the south-west in 1678 on free quarter, numbered around eight thousand men. Whatever its other shortcomings, the host was effective insofar as its deployment convinced the Estates to vote an unprecedentedly large tax of £1,800,000 Scots over five years.

Military needs created fiscal demands. Despite seemingly endemic corruption, mismanagement, and the ongoing problems of collection, it has nonetheless been estimated that, towards the end of his reign, Charles II's annual income from the ordinary revenues was about three times that of his father's. Some two-thirds of this money was being spent directly on the military establishment.[37] The restored monarchy initially sought to avoid recourse to the taxes associated with the civil-war era, but the administration was not in a position to abandon potentially lucrative sources of revenue. The excise and the cess (monthly maintenance), which had both been pioneered in the 1640s, were continued. Later, a hearth tax (1690) and a poll tax (1693, 1695, and twice in 1698) were temporarily introduced. There seems little doubt that these taxes greatly increased government revenues. However, they remained unable to meet rising public expenditure and, even in good years, officers of state were perpetually short of the ready cash required to oil the wheels of government. Although one historian has averred that Scotland's central administration 'evolved rapidly' in the Restoration era, it may have remained ill-equipped to cope with the increasing volume and sophistication of the revenue streams it was expected to handle. Charles II's financial officers expressed concern about the complexity of their work, while treasury accounts for the ordinary revenues were not audited after 1692. Whether central government was capable of providing adequate oversight of a mushrooming network of local collectors, preferably by individuals with knowledge of accounting procedures, has not been investigated.[38]

The second half of the century saw important changes in the fiscal regime, yet they were insufficient to create a Scottish force that decision-makers, in both Edinburgh and London, could have complete confidence in. When one of several rebellions in this period broke out in 1679, English troops, commanded by the king's illegitimate son, James, Duke of Monmouth, were brought into Scotland to suppress it. English money and troops were required even more urgently in the 1690s, to prop up a narrowly based Revolutionary government facing Jacobite insurrection and the possibility of a French invasion.[39] Memories of Scotland's decisive role in the destabilization of the British polity after 1637, and Charles II's personal memory of an acutely miserable year as a Covenanted king of Scots, undoubtedly shaped elite attitudes towards state power. Lauderdale's tactic of preying on fears that 1641 would come again may ultimately have provoked the rebellions that justified maintaining a military establishment. When they

---

[37] Lee, 'Government and Politics', 130, 137. Customs duties on certain imported goods were part of the king's ordinary revenues. The excise tax was later granted to Kings Charles and James for life.

[38] Athol L. Murray, 'The Scottish Treasury, 1667–1708', SHR, 45 (1966), 96, 98–9. Athol L. Murray, 'Administration and Law', in T. I. Rae, ed., The Union of 1707: Its Impact on Scotland (Glasgow, 1974), 33–4.

[39] Macinnes, 'Repression and Conciliation', 184–5. Monmouth's wife was the Scottish peer Anne Scott, Duchess of Buccleuch in her own right, whose name he took upon marriage.

occurred, perhaps some people decided that accepting assistance from London was better than being overrun by rebels and then overrun by an English army bent on restoring what it called order. These same people could have opted to pay more taxes to fund a reliable Scottish army. Past experience suggested that such forces would be commanded by powerful individuals over whom civil government exercised little practical control. It was not an attractive alternative.

At the end of the seventeenth century, the Scottish state was fragile, limited, and increasingly unable to guarantee its own security. Further research may reveal that it was not developing the wide-ranging competency, specialist administrative personnel, and comparative levels of accountability that made the attainment of long-term stability more likely. Although central government increasingly took a role in the advancement of economic ventures, the state was less capable of doing the same for Scottish interests abroad. Without a credible naval force of its own, Scotland had to rely on English or Dutch convoys to protect its merchant shipping in the North Sea. Should Scotland wish to trade further afield, or establish a colony, a navy would be essential. There were entrepreneurial Scots who established 'thriving and expansive' commercial networks overseas, but it is striking that they did so almost without reference to the state. Ironically, the entrepreneurs who became so skilled at evading customs and excise duties (as well as the English Navigation Acts) were also denying the state much-needed revenues. Without this fiscal infrastructure, the state was unable to provide Scottish international merchants with the military and diplomatic support that their English, Dutch, and Spanish rivals could call upon.[40]

All early modern states were used by rulers and elites to exercise control over territory, population, and trade routes. By these means, the state secured its own existence. At this most fundamental level, the Scottish state increasingly seemed incapable of performing the functions required of it. One obvious problem was that many of the responsibilities thrust upon the state were the product of policies driven by Britannic, not Scottish, imperatives. Many of these policies were not in tune with the interests of Scottish elites and, consequently, the state that was used to implement them could not claim universality. A fully autonomous Scottish state, for example, would never have gone to war with one of its leading trading partners, the Dutch Republic. Had Charles II found himself (much to his own horror) permanently resident in Scotland, his religious policies would necessarily have been more sympathetic to Presbyterian sensibilities. However, too much emphasis on the British dimension can distract us from looking more closely at indigenous power structures. Maarten Prak and Jan Luiten van Zanden have argued, with reference to the Dutch Republic, that 'the quality of public institutions' is a chief factor in determining how effectively states can raise taxes.[41] Late seventeenth-century Scotland

[40] Macinnes, *Empire and Union*, 205, 225. Christopher Whatley with Derek Patrick, *The Scots and the Union* (Edinburgh, 2006), 75, 116, 125, 165–6. Union did not solve the problem of tax evasion; Brown, *Kingdom or Province?*, 194.

[41] Maarten Prak and Jan Luiten van Zanden, 'Tax Morale and Citizenship in the Dutch Republic', in Oscar Gelderblom, *The Political Economy of the Dutch Republic* (Farnham, 2009), 144.

seems to have struggled to develop public institutions, especially in the fiscal sphere, that were seen to be relatively accessible, fair, and transparent according to the standards of the day.

The Covenanting state was different. To all intents and purposes, it was autonomous. The new regime's drive to attain legitimacy encouraged a heavy emphasis on conciliar, participatory, and comparatively transparent governing structures. Its relatively sophisticated military and fiscal infrastructure, for all its many problems, had been achieved with the consent and active involvement of a relatively wide cross-section of the lowland population. But it did not survive. One factor amongst many influencing this outcome, which still needs to be more fully researched, may have been elite disengagement from its governing structures after 1648. With the restoration of the Britannic monarchy, the features that had defined the Covenanting state were tarnished by association with rebellion, war, and conquest. With so much power vested in the person of the monarch, later incarnations of the state too obviously became the tool of narrow-interest groups, who sought to enhance its fiscal and military capability to pursue their own ends. During the second half of the century, the state's coercive and repressive aspects were not sufficiently balanced by a potentially more positive presence in the commonplace legal, economic, or social activities that dominated people's lives.

By the end of the seventeenth century, an autonomous Scottish state was faltering. A more competitive geopolitical environment had rendered a regal union between two unequally matched rivals virtually unworkable. Yet important and sometimes dramatic changes had occurred in the way that the state was organized, used, and thought about across the seventeenth century. What these changes meant for Scottish men and women at all levels of society demands further study, not least because much of the infrastructure of the post-1707 state was a product of many decades preceding the Treaty of Union. Although the Scottish Parliament and Privy Council disappeared in the early eighteenth century, the framework of local government, with its peculiar amalgam of heritable jurisdictions, centrally appointed officials, and semi-detached parishes, was not substantially altered for another forty years. Alexander Murdoch has observed that because Scotland enjoyed 'a state of "semi-independence" in the eighteenth century', British state power was mediated through institutions that remained 'largely separate and distinct'.[42] The state's coordinating agencies were Anglo-Britannic, but many Scots were cocooned within particularist governing structures, which isolated them from experiencing the British state in the same way as their English, Welsh, or Irish neighbours. The Union of 1707 did not create a single, unified entity called the British state any more than it forged a single, unified British identity.[43]

---

[42] Alexander Murdoch, *The People Above: Politics and Administration in Mid-Eighteenth-Century Scotland* (Edinburgh, 1980), 27.

[43] Bernard Crick, *Crossing Borders: Political Essays* (London and New York, 2001), 8–9, critiquing Linda Colley, *Britons: Forging the Nation, 1707–1837* (New Haven, 1992). See also Colin Kidd, *Subverting Scotland's Past: Scottish Whig Historians and the Creation of an Anglo-British Identity, 1689–c.1830* (Cambridge, 1993), Introduction.

## FURTHER READING

Bonney, Richard, ed., *The Rise of the Fiscal State in Europe, c.1200–1815* (Oxford, 1999).

Braddick, Michael, *State Formation in Early Modern England, c.1550–1700* (Cambridge, 2000).

Brown, Keith, *Bloodfeud in Scotland, 1573–1625: Violence, Justice and Politics in an Early Modern Society* (Edinburgh, 1986).

—— *Kingdom or Province? Scotland and the Regal Union, 1603–1715* (Basingstoke, 1992).

—— 'From Scottish Lords to British Officers: State Building, Elite Integration and the Army in the Seventeenth Century', in Norman Macdougall, ed., *Scotland and War AD 79–1918* (Edinburgh, 1991).

Goodare, Julian, *State and Society in Early Modern Scotland* (Oxford, 1999).

—— *The Government of Scotland, 1560–1625* (Oxford, 2004).

Hindle, Steve, *The State and Social Change in Early Modern England* (Basingstoke, 2000).

Lee, R. A., 'Government and Politics in Scotland, 1661–1681' (PhD thesis, University of Glasgow, PhD thesis, 1995).

Macinnes, Allan, *Union and Empire: The Making of the United Kingdom in 1707* (Cambridge, 2007).

McCrone, David, *Understanding Scotland: The Sociology of a Stateless Nation* (London, 1992).

Stevenson, David, 'The Financing of the Cause of the Covenants, 1638–51', *Scottish Historical Review*, 51 (1972).

—— ed., *The Government of the Covenanters, 1637–51* (Edinburgh, 1982).

Stewart, Laura A. M., 'Fiscal Revolution and State Formation in Mid Seventeenth-Century Scotland', *Historical Research*, 84:225 (2011).

Whatley, Christopher, with Patrick, Derek, *The Scots and the Union* (Edinburgh, 2006).

CHAPTER 11

································································

# REAPPRAISING THE EARLY MODERN ECONOMY, 1500–1650

································································

T. M. DEVINE

**1**

································································

This topic is one of the Cinderella themes of Scottish history. Lodged between the rich historiographies of the Reformation, Union, and Enlightenment, it has tended not only to suffer neglect in research terms but also from an unduly negative stereotyping of social and economic experience over the period of one hundred and fifty years. As one perceptive commentator has put it:

> Lack of concern meant lack of sustained investigation, and in the absence of evidence to the contrary the image of Scottish society in the early modern period became dominated by a stereotype which is only now breaking down. Among those few scholars who seriously addressed these issues prior to the late 1970s the dominant interpretative tone established was a distinctly negative variant of Scottish exceptionalism. Early modern Scotland was different all right; and the difference was held to lie in Scotland's poverty and backwardness; in the peripheral, archaic, largely static nature of Scotland's economy and society prior to the eighteenth century.[1]

The reasons for this pessimistic characterization were many. The comments of contemporary travellers, notably those from the south of England and invariably highly critical of Scottish conditions, were sometimes used incautiously by later historians. These

---

[1] K. E. Wrightson, 'Kindred Adjoining Kingdoms: An English Perspective on the Social and Economic History of Early Modern Scotland', in R. A. Houston and I. D. Whyte, eds., *Scottish Society 1500–1800* (Cambridge, 1989), 251.

reporters were forcibly struck by dire poverty, squalid housing conditions, and backwardness of agriculture. As late as 1705, Joseph Taylor Esq., 'Late of the Inner Temple', concluded as he headed north, after leaving Berwick, that he was 'going into the most barbarous country in the world'. He reported that 'everyone reckoned our journey extremely dangerous' and was warned that 'twoud be difficult to escape with our lives, much less without the distemper of the country'.[2] A hundred years before, after the Union of Crowns (1603), the fear of closer relationships with Scotland under a Scottish-born king, James I and VI, unleashed a venomous wave of Scotophobia in the Westminster Parliament. Sir Christopher Piggot, Knight, was one of several who entered into 'matter of invective against the Scotts', denouncing their country as 'the barrenest land in existence'.[3]

Scottish historians during the Enlightenment of the eighteenth century also contributed to the making of the caricature, for virtually all regarded pre-Union Scotland as a society mired in poverty, feudal backwardness, and intellectual intolerance.[4] The Improving writers of the same era were unequivocal in their condemnation of the archaic and wasteful nature of early modern agriculture. It was depicted as rigid in structure, primitive in technique, and uneconomic in both land cultivation and the employment of labour. These publicists were almost evangelical in their uncritical propagandizing on behalf of the emerging agrarian capitalist system. It was, therefore, inevitable that the old order, in which most families still produced for their own immediate needs within a broadly subsistence culture, would suffer by comparison with one increasingly geared to  massively expanding market demand. The Improving writers also enthusiastically favoured the separate, single holding under one master as the only means to liberate individual energies and initiative. Communalism, which was often at the root of many older practices, was despised as the enemy of progress and the irrational perpetuation of custom and conservatism.[5]

As Chapter 15 demonstrates, much work has now been done to partially rehabilitate the Scottish economy in the decades immediately before the Union of 1707. No longer can that period be simply dismissed as an era of profound darkness before the post-Union dawn. Ironically, however, this focus on the decades after *c.*1660 has suggested, often by implication, sometimes explicitly, that the period before was the real 'dark age', which had only started to come to an end by the later seventeenth century.[6] It is also ironical, therefore, that pessimistic perceptions of the early modern economy may have been buttressed rather than qualified by this important development in Scottish historical research into

[2] Joseph Taylor, *A Journey to Edenborough in Scotland (1705)*, ed. William Cowan (Edinburgh, 1903), 94–5.

[3] Quoted in S. G. E. Lythe, *The Economy of Scotland in its European Setting 1550–1625* (Edinburgh, 1960), 205.

[4] Colin Kidd, *Subverting Scotland's Past* (Cambridge, 1993).

[5] T. M. Devine, *The Transformation of Rural Scotland: Social Change and the Agrarian Economy 1660–1815* (Edinburgh, 1994), 2.

[6] Michael Lynch, 'Whatever Happened to the Medieval Burgh? Sound Guidelines for Sixteenth- and Seventeenth-Century Historians', *Scottish Economic and Social History*, 4 (1984), 5–20.

the post *c*.1660 era. The bias was likely to be fortified by the incidence of civil war, military occupation, and material distress in the years immediately before *c*.1660, which, nevertheless, were not at all typical of pre-Restoration society, especially before 1640. In addition, both contemporaries and some modern scholars tended too often to look to England as the external comparison against which the Scottish economy should be judged. But seventeenth-century England (like the Low Countries) was exceptional in Europe in the nature of its advanced economy, burgeoning trade, and the maturity of financial institutions.[7] More meaningful and typical analogies were with the Scandinavian countries, France, and the states of central and eastern Europe. In an era when regional differences, because of poorer transport, were more pronounced than in modern times, the question of Anglo-Scottish comparison itself becomes problematic. There were many Englands and many Scotlands, and generalization at the national level often becomes not only difficult but pointless. The Scottish population is sometimes described in this period as under-nourished and vulnerable to serious food shortage. However, in the sixteenth century perhaps a third of English peasantry are reckoned to have lived in extreme poverty and another third only in marginally better circumstances. As late as the 1620s, northern areas of England experienced widespread dearth. In this respect, any difference in the experience of Scotland and the north of England was one of degree rather than of kind.[8]

When all is said and done, nonetheless, there is no denying the fact that Scotland did face formidable climatic and environmental constraints in the sixteenth and early seventeenth centuries. Though as Christopher Smout has noted (see Chapter 1), there were extensive tracts of fertile low arable land, notably in the east, but also in significant pockets elsewhere, much of Scotland was hill country suited only to rough grazing. Even at the present day, after many generations of reclamation and improvement, some two-thirds of the total area of the country remains under rough grazing. At lower altitudes, clay soils and schists in the glaciated valleys meant that cultivation here was often inhibited by marsh, moss, and bog. The number of Scottish place names with '-bog' or '-moss' attached to them has long been noted,[9] and, as one writer has put it with memorable eloquence:

> Much of Scotland's soil is shallow and acid. The rock pokes through the worn sleeve of the turf; erosion gullies fan downwards from the ridges; the deciduous trees have short trunks and low, crouching canopies. This has been a hard country to live in … Scottish earth is in most places—even in the fertile south and east—a skin over bone, and like any taut face it never loses a line once acquired. Seen from the air, every trench dug and every dyke raised, every hut footing and post hole, fort bank and cattle path, tractor mark and chariot rut seems to have inscribed its trace.[10]

Climatic factors added to the challenges. The country's northerly position meant that it endured more wind and rain and shorter growing seasons than most of the rest of the

---

[7] J. A. Sharpe, 'The Economic and Social Context', in Jenny Wormald, ed., *The Seventeenth Century* (Oxford, 2008), 151–77.

[8] Ian Whyte, *Agriculture and Society in Seventeenth-Century Scotland* (Edinburgh, 1979), 11–12.

[9] Ibid., 7–8.

[10] Neal Ascherson, *Stone Voices: In Search of Scotland* (London, 2002), 27.

British archipelago. These adverse influences were experienced especially acutely in the early modern period because of the impact of the Little Ice Age, a sequence of particularly cold phases occurring between the late thirteenth and the end of the nineteenth centuries. Winter and summer mean temperatures fell to low levels in Britain between 1430 and 1480 and again from 1645 to 1715. In both cases, temperatures in Scotland were a degree or two lower than in the counties of central England.[11] These disadvantages were compounded by scarcity of wood resources. Woodland cover was reckoned to have fallen to 10 per cent of the available land area in 1500 and to 5 per cent by the Union of Parliaments in 1707. This did mark out Scotland from the other peasant societies of Scandinavia and northern Europe where extensive forests were a plentiful source of timber, tar, turpentine, and other woodland products.[12] It was hardly surprising then that doors, posts, and roof timbers were so prized in Scotland that they were written into tenurial agreements.[13] The country had to rely on imports from Norway for building and construction, with a consequent drain on scarce resources and balance of payments.[14]

The environmental dice were therefore heavily loaded against Scotland in this period. In 1682 one contemporary, who urged the London-based Hudson's Bay Company to recruit Scots, noted 'that countrie is a hard country to live in, and the poore-mens wages is cheap, they are hardy people both to endure hunger and cold…I am sure they will serve for six pound pr. yeare and be better content with their diet than Englishmen will be.'[15] The writer was saying in effect that Scots were so fashioned by the challenges of their natural environment that they would provide good servants in the wilds of North America. Against this background, it is not surprising to learn that dearth, shortage, and even famine were often experienced by the Scottish population, so seeming to confirm the lugubrious observations of travellers and the views of some later scholars. Scottish food supply was undoubtedly finely poised and bare sufficiency could easily become acute shortage when climatic conditions worsened. Thus between 1560 and 1600 there was perhaps harvest shortfall in some parts of Scotland in two years out of five. But really serious famines, such as that of 1623, which caused significant increases in mortality, were much less frequent.[16] We need to note also that in most years between 1500 and 1660 there was sufficiency and sometimes surplus. In the decades before the Reformation of 1560 food supply in most areas seemed reasonable. There were good years thereafter in the late 1560s and from 1573 to 1585, despite the general deterioration of the period before 1600. After the subsistence crisis of the mid-1590s food supply stabilized during

---

[11]   Robert A. Dodgshon, 'The Little Ice Age in the Scottish Highlands and Islands: Documenting its Human Impact', *Scottish Geographical Magazine*, 121 (2005), 322–3.

[12]   T. C. Smout, *Nature Contested* (Edinburgh, 2000), 46–9.

[13]   Richard Saville and Paul Auerbach, 'Education and Social Capital in the Development of Scotland to 1750', presented at the *Economic History Annual Conference, University of Reading, March/April, 2006*, 6.

[14]   Smout, *Nature Contested*, 49.

[15]   Quoted in Allan I. Macinnes, Marjory-Ann D. Harper, and Linda G. Fryer, eds., *Scotland and the Americas, c.1650–c.1939: A Documentary Source Book* (Edinburgh, 2002), 139.

[16]   T. M. Devine and S. G. E. Lythe, 'The Economy of Scotland under James VI', *Scottish Historical Review*, 50 (1971), 99–100.

the first twenty years of the seventeenth century.[17] Thereafter, there were mortality crises in the 1640s and at a regional level in the Northern Isles in 1634 and parts of western Scotland in 1634–5.[18] On the whole, therefore, the later sixteenth century stands out as the time of real difficulty (though not in every year). But for the remainder of the period Scotland enjoyed for the most part more favourable conditions.

Some perspective is also needed here. As already indicated, Scotland's main comparators are with Scandinavia and countries in central, southern, and eastern Europe. When set alongside these, the Scottish record of fluctuating food supply does not appear to be in any way exceptional. Those countries on the maritime periphery of north-west Europe were equally vulnerable to climatic deterioration. Indeed, both France and Scandinavia retained their vulnerability much longer than Scotland well into the eighteenth century.[19] In addition, it has been noted that the seven northern counties of England, the poorest south of the Border, while being better off than some parts of Scotland, were not so by much.[20] In that sense the Scottish rural economy can be considered typical rather than exceptional in the broader European context: 'A Scottish farmer would have found many differences in detail between the life he was accustomed to and that which existed in Brittany, Cornwall, Wales, Ireland, Northern England or Norway...these would often have been differences of degree rather than kind and he would possibly have found more overall similarity in the basic character of agriculture, the techniques employed and the season-to-season preoccupations of the rural year'.[21]

## 2

Though exact figures cannot of course be cited, Scottish population, like England's, started to grow from the later fifteenth century, continuing for much of the sixteenth century and only stabilizing again in the 1630s and 1640s. Estimates vary from 500,000 to 700,000 around 1500, while a figure of just over one million has been most favoured by historians for the later seventeenth century.[22] There is evidence that even modest increases in the numbers to be fed could put pressure on a fragile economy. One indicator was the expansion of settlement and cultivation area into more marginal land. Another was the evidence of splitting of townships as some reached greater sizes because of population growth, thus making the working of field systems less manageable. This helps to explain the number of farms on modern maps distinguished by such prefixes as

[17] Lythe, *Economy of Scotland*, 16–23.

[18] Michael Flinn et al., eds., *Scottish Population History from the Seventeenth Century to the 1930s* (Cambridge, 1977), 116–50.

[19] M. M. Flinn, 'The Stabilisation of Mortality in Pre-Industrial Europe', *Journal of European Economic History*, 3 (1974), 301.

[20] Smout, *Nature Contested*, 68.

[21] Whyte, *Agriculture and Society*, 22.

[22] Ian D. Whyte, *Scotland before the Industrial Revolution* (Harlow, 1995), 112–13, 133.

Easter, Mid, Wester, Over, and Nether.[23] Perhaps the most compelling proof of a labour surplus comes from the contemporary state's obsession with the problem of vagrancy and its potential threat to social order. The concern was a key factor in the passing of statutes in 1574, 1579, and 1592 designed to provide for those in need but also to control vagrancy. They laid down savage penalties for able-bodied masterful beggars, declaring that only 'cruikit folk seik impotent folk and waik folk' be allowed to beg. The impression was sometimes given, indeed, that the Scottish countryside was overrun by vagrants who menaced some settled communities.[24]

These demographic and economic pressures resulted in strategies to manage risk and reduce the impact of overpopulation on poor communities. By far the most significant of these was the remarkable scale and increase of emigration, which is considered in detail in Chapters 7 and 16. Throughout the seventeenth century the rate of movement out of Scotland may well have been the highest in Europe, at times in the 1630s and 1640s reaching perhaps one in five adult males. Again, precise figures cannot be known and recent research on emigrant communities in Poland-Lithuania and Scandinavia has qualified some of the wilder claims. Recent scholarship on Scottish migration to Scandinavia and Poland-Lithuania has considerably reduced the high estimated figures to be found in older writings (see Chapter 15).[25] But even the lower bounds of the estimates are impressive, with a suggested 70,000 to 85,000 Scots leaving primarily to trade across Europe and fight in Continental armies between 1600 and 1650. Equally remarkable was the geographical range of the exodus, into central and eastern Europe, Norway, Denmark, Sweden, the Low Countries, England, and increasingly to the north of Ireland as the axis of emigration started to swing to the west in the seventeenth century.[26] All in all, the diaspora must have helped to reduce resource pressures in several parts of the homeland, perhaps not so much in terms of scale (which modern scholarship is now recalibrating downwards) but because of the continuous nature of the exodus and the spread of its territorial origins in Scotland. The north-eastern counties were the main source areas of the European migrations, closely followed by Tayside, the Forth Valley, and the Lothians. In contrast, most Scots who sailed for Ulster were natives of the far south-west, western Renfrewshire, Lanarkshire, and southern Argyll. The movement to northern England and London still awaits its historian, but if the seventeenth century replicated the marginally better-document eighteenth then most of those who went south had probably come from the country districts and small towns of the Border region (see Chapters 7 and 16).

[23] R. A. Dodgshon, *Land and Society in Early Scotland* (Oxford, 1981), 195–204.

[24] R. Mitchison, 'North and South: The Development of the Gulf in Poor Law Practice', in Houston and Whyte, *Scottish Society*, 200–2.

[25] See W. Kowalski, 'Kraków Citizenship and the Local Scots', in R. Unger and J. Basista, eds., *Britain and Poland-Lithuania: Contact and Comparison from the Middle Ages to 1795* (Leiden, 2008), 264; Peter P. Bijer, 'Scots in the Kraków Reformed Parish in the Seventeenth Century', in T. M. Devine and David Hesse, eds., *Scotland and Poland: Historical Encounters, 1500–2010* (Edinburgh, 2011).

[26] T. C. Smout, N. C. Landsman, and T. M. Devine, 'Scottish Emigration in the Seventeenth and Eighteenth Centuries', in Nicholas Canny, ed., *Europeans on the Move* (Oxford, 1994), 76–90.

Another response was radical changes in the pattern of food consumption. In the later Middle Ages, meat, cheese, butter, and milk were commonly eaten. By the end of the sixteenth century, the Scots had adopted a new diet, principally founded on oatmeal and bere. The elites and middling sorts still had a great range of choice but for the majority a food revolution had taken place. People in more straitened times were going for a much more humble diet. On the face of it, it seemed to reflect increased poverty as pressure on food resources intensified. Scotland became 'The Land o' (Oat) Cakes' and occasionally invited the scorn of observers in the eighteenth century like Samuel Johnson with his famous remark that a food eaten by horses in England was the diet of the commonality of Scotland.[27] Ironically, however, since oatmeal is rich in vitamins, full of roughage, and contains calcium, together with a number of trace elements, it provided very healthy fare and ensured that the Scots suffered less from chronic malnutrition than others in the early modern world. Indeed, the diet has been hailed by modern nutritionists as much superior to that of the present day.[28] Recent work on recruits to the British Army in America in the middle decades of the eighteenth century show that those of Scottish birth stood almost an average of an inch and a half taller in height than their English-born counterparts. Scholars reckon that this differential can be mainly accounted for by better standards of nutrition, based on a monotonous but essentially healthy meal-based diet.[29]

This was but one confirmation of the early modern rural economy's capacity for change and rational response to long-term threat. There were others, several of which were designed to reduce risk in a country of uncertain climate and poor natural endowment. As one authoritative commentator has it, 'there are some clear parallels in the English and the Scottish experience of socio-economic change...more than enough to render absurd the old assertion that Scotland existed in a condition of virtual social and economic stasis'.[30] One crucial response was to exploit the comparative advantage in pastoral husbandry as opposed to arable farming where Scotland was, in most areas, at an obvious disadvantage. A clear trend has been identified in the course of the seventeenth century away from the old commerce in skins and hides towards a trade in live cattle to lowland towns and English cities. The peak export period for skins were the middle decades of the sixteenth century. By the 1660s, however, up to forty-eight thousand cattle were crossing the Border, a figure that continued to rise in subsequent decades: 'It must be presumed in the earlier period the Scots ate the original contents of the hides, but in the later one the animals were digested in English stomachs while the Scots ate something else'.[31] It was an economic change that ran in parallel with the transformation in national diet already described.

---

[27] Samuel Johnson, *A Dictionary of the English Language* (1773).

[28] A. J. S. Gibson and T. C. Smout, *Prices, Food and Wages in Scotland 1550–1780* (Cambridge, 1995), 226–43.

[29] R. Floud, K. Wachter, and A. Gregory, *Height, Health and History* (Cambridge, 1990), 193.

[30] Wrightson, 'Kindred Adjoining Kingdoms', 254.

[31] D. Woodward, 'A Comparative Study of the Irish and Scottish Livestock Traders in the Seventeenth Century', in L. M. Cullen and T. C. Smout, eds., *Comparative Aspects of Scottish and Irish Economic and Social History 1600–1900* (Edinburgh, 1977), 147–64; A. Gibson and T. C. Smout, 'Scottish Food and Scottish History, 1500–1800', in Houston and Whyte, eds., *Scottish Society*, 64.

A vital influence on this development was the growth of greater stability from the early seventeenth century in the Scottish Borders and, to a lesser extent, in the Western Highlands. The Border countryside was in 1603 still a frontier zone that had truculently resisted full incorporation into either England or Scotland. Indeed, the very week that King James travelled south to London, the Armstrongs, a leading Borders family, also moved into England bent on plundering the countryside as far as Penrith in Cumbria. The Regal Union was, however, a decisive watershed. The old problems of recalcitrance could now be dealt with by a single executive, especially after the establishment of a joint Anglo-Scottish Commission under the Earl of Dunbar in 1605–6. It was said that it quickly hung over 140 of 'the nimblest and most powerful thieves in all the borders' and (as the report continued ominously) 'fully reduced the other inhabitants to obedience'.[32] Members of the most lawless families were shipped to the Plantation of Ulster while others were exiled to service in the Dutch armies. The peel towers, architectural symbols of family military independence, were demolished in large numbers.[33] By the 1620s, therefore, though there may not yet have been a final solution to the Border problem, the territory had become more stable than at any period in its recent history. The time was ripe for the further development of sheep-farming in these more peaceful conditions.

Even before this, however, pastoral husbandry was already big business. In 1578 Bishop Leslie could write of Tweeddale that 'in this countrie...evin as with thaw nychbouris, that sum of thame ar knawen to have a fow or five hundir, utheris agane aucht or nyne hundir, and sum tyme thay ar knawen to have a thousind scheip'.[34] But the scale of the activity expanded further in the decades after 1603, with specialization growing in the export of mutton for the coalfields of north-east England as well as the traditional output of wool for the textile manufactures. By the 1640s, money rentals had become dominant on most Border estates, confirming the market orientation of the big sheep farms of the region.[35]

As in the Borders, the most successful and decisive initiatives by the Scottish state in Gaeldom took place after the Regal Union because the clans were then confronted by the awesome naval and military power of a unified and expansionist British state, which could coordinate strategy much more effectively against the two Gaelic societies of the Highlands and Ireland. The ruthlessly efficient annexation of native lands in the six counties of Ulster and the establishment of the colonial plantation there in the early seventeenth century forcibly brought home to the chiefs in the Western Highlands, who had strong kinship links with Irish landed families, the new overt danger of resisting the authority of the state. More directly, the end of rebellion in Ulster after c.1610 markedly reduced the opportunities for mercenary service by the highland *buannachan*, or household men, the warrior class who had long survived on the opportunities of booty and military employment across the Irish Sea.

---

[32] Lythe, *Economy of Scotland*, 197.

[33] Ibid., 198–9.

[34] Quoted in Robert A. Dodgshon, 'Agricultural Change and its Social Consequences in the Southern Uplands of Scotland, 1600–1780', in T. M. Devine and David Dickson, eds., *Ireland and Scotland 1600–1850* (Edinburgh, 1983), 48.

[35] Ibid., 49–52.

The government of James VI and I did not undertake the draconian policy of whole-sale annexation in the Highlands that it had initiated in Ireland. Instead, a variety of strategies were executed and partial expropriation of those clans that were considered to be especially delinquent was driven forward. The main victims were ClanDonald South, the ClanLeod of Lewis, the MacIains of Ardnamurchan, and ClanGregor. A policy of colonization was designed to drive a further wedge between Gaelic Ireland and Scotland, and plans were made to establish colonies of 'answerable inlands subjects' in Lewis, Lochaber, and Kintyre, although only the last settlement was even partially successful. Much more effective was the launching of military and naval expeditions along the western seaboard in 1596, 1599, 1605, 1607, and 1608. This direct intervention was paralleled by the award of judicial commissions to lieutenants, drawn mainly from 'trustworthy' magnate families on the highland–lowland frontier, such as the Gordon earls of Huntly and the Campbell earls of Argyll, to demand bands of surety from lawless clans.

These, however, were all traditional techniques that had long been employed in the Borders. The state also embarked on a novel attempt to produce a final solution to the highland problem by tackling what were seen as the social roots of disorder, the strategy of 'planting civilitie', which James himself had outlined in his *Basilikon Doran* and that was laid out in 1609 in the Statutes of Iona to which all the major chiefs in the Hebrides gave their consent. The nine statutes ranged from the suppression of beggars and vaga-bonds to the control of wine and whisky, from the limitation of the chief's retinue to the strengthening of the reformed Church, from sending the heirs of men of substance to the Lowlands for education to the prohibition of ordinary clansmen from carrying arms. Not only were the chiefs bound to observe the statutes but they were also enjoined to appear personally before the Privy Council at stated intervals. The statutes were a com-prehensive attempt to impose lowland values on Gaeldom, destroy the basis of lawless-ness, and control the perceived excesses of clanship.

There has been considerable historical debate about the actual impact of these initia-tives. Whatever their effects as a whole, it is plain that they did have a powerful influence on clan elites. The chiefs were expected to become partners with the state in the mainte-nance of order and were also held to account for the conduct of their clansmen. This was achieved through the exaction of substantial sureties and the demand from 1616 that chiefs appear annually before the Privy Council. Attendance at Edinburgh was rigor-ously enforced from then until the outbreak of the Scottish Revolution in 1638.

These strategies of political control resulted in substantial changes within clanship.[36] Heavy economic burdens were placed on the *fine* (clan gentry). For example, the sure-ties recommended in the Statutes of Iona varied in the 1610s from £3,000 to £18,000 sterling. The expenses of appearing before the Privy Council in Edinburgh on an annual

[36] The paragraphs that follow on the Western Highlands and Islands are based on A. I. Macinnes, 'Crown, Clans and *Fine*: The "Civilising" of Scottish Gaeldom', *Northern Scotland* 13 (1993); F. J. Shaw, *The Northern and Western Islands of Scotland: Their Economy and Society in the Seventeenth Century* (Edinburgh, 1980); R. A. Dodgshon, 'West Highland Chiefdoms, 1500–1745', in R. Mitchison and P. Roebuck, eds., *Economy and Society in Scotland and Ireland, 1500–1939* (Edinburgh, 1988).

basis were also considerable and those who attended could be detained for up to six months. Sir Rory MacLeod of Dunvegan complained to James VI in 1622 that his annual appearances meant that he was away from his estates for more than half the year, making it difficult for him to manage them effectively. Sojourns in Edinburgh also led to expenditure on lawyers and agents and an increased appetite for the more sophisticated lifestyle of the capital. The accounts of seventeenth-century highland families, such as the MacDonalds of Clanranald and the MacLeods of Dunvegan, indicate significant and growing outlays on expensive clothing, furniture, and exotic foods. They were becoming more assimilated into the mainstream of Scottish landed society. A vital consequence was that rentals in kind, formerly dispensed to ensure the social cohesion of clanship through communal feasting and collective hospitality, were increasingly marketed outside the Highlands to maximize elite incomes. Chiefs were still tribal leaders but were also now looking more to their lands as assets, a transition that would finally be completed in the eighteenth century. The droving trade in live cattle to the south now became ever more important to the economies of the north and west.

Recent scholarship has also shown how early modern rural society developed techniques and practices to reduce the threshold of risk at times of climatic threat and increasing demographic pressure.[37] The old world, contrary to the opinion of the Improving propagandists of later years, was inherently rational and pragmatic in attempts to preserve food supplies. Thus, bere, the drink crop of Scottish agriculture, was preferred to barley because it was better suited to acidic soil and, while it could be sown later, still ripened up to three weeks earlier than barley. The dominance of oats as Scotland's main food crop was easily explicable as, again, they ripened earlier than other grains, tolerated conditions of wind and rain, and produced reasonable yields even on poor soils.

Robert Dodgshon has demonstrated in detail how the Highlands and Islands coped with the perennial risks of cold, wet, flood, storm, and wind during the Little Ice Age.[38] The distribution of 'good' and 'bad' land among cultivators in the runrig system (perennially denounced by the eighteenth-century Improvers) was one approach. The widespread use of 'lazy beds' or raised sandwiches of earth, facilitated drainage and, at the same time, enabled grain to be sown on thin soils. It was also a custom of the region, and other parts of Scotland, for landowners to provide discounts (or 'eases') of rental in times of crisis, and 'rests' with rents being deferred to the following year. Since a major proportion of rental at this period was still often paid in grain, these adjustments allowed muchneeded food supplies to be channelled back into the peasant economy. Labour-intensive spade husbandry was also employed to raise grain yields, often to a surprising extent. In Islay, for instance, grain yields increased sevenfold, from 324 bolls of meal in 1542 to 2,193 bolls in 1614.[39] In the Lowlands, the increasing and lavish use of lime also helped

---

[37] Robert A. Dodgshon, 'Coping with Risk: Subsistence Crises in the Scottish Highlands and Islands, 1600–1800', *Rural History*, 15 (2004), 1–25.

[38] Ibid.

[39] Gibson and Smout, 'Scottish Food and Scottish History', 77.

much marginal land into more regular cultivation. An effective treatment for Scotland's vast acreages of acidic soils, it was regarded as 'the principal way of gooding the soil' in the seventeenth century.[40]

## 3

This rise in farm output not only helped to sustain the rise in national population but also the expansion of the non-food-producing urban areas of Scotland. If growing urbanism is an indicator of greater levels of economic sophistication and exchange, then the period c.1590 to c.1640 was one of impressive advance in Scotland. The proportion of population living in the five largest towns nearly doubled between 1500 and 1600, and doubled again by 1700. At the beginning of the sixteenth century one estimate suggests that under 2 per cent of the population lived in towns with more than ten thousand inhabitants. Manifestly, by this measure, Scotland was far behind highly urbanized countries like the Low Countries, England, and northern Italy. But that pattern began to change in the later sixteenth century, as Tables 11.1 to 11.3 reveal.

Thus, by the later seventeenth century, parts of the Lowlands were quite heavily urbanized compared to the European norm, although the Highlands were almost devoid of towns. The process seems to have been one of thickening in certain areas and much less activity in others where, for instance, much of the far south-west, Borders, and north-east had only a scattering of small burghs, essentially large villages rather than

Table 11.1 Urbanization in Scotland, England, and Wales, 1500–1700—percentage of total population in towns with over 10,000 inhabitants

|  | 1500 | 1550 | 1600 | 1650 | 1700 |
|---|---|---|---|---|---|
| Scotland | 1.6 | 1.4 | 3 | 3.5 | 5.3 |
| England and Wales | 3.1 | 3.5 | 5.8 | 8.8 | 13.3 |

Source: J. de Vries, European Urbanisation 1500–1800 (London, 1984), 39.

Table 11.2 Population in towns with over 10,000 inhabitants (thousands)

|  | 1500 | 1550 | 1600 | 1650 | 1700 |
|---|---|---|---|---|---|
| Scotland | 13 | 13 | 30 | 35 | 53 |
| England and Wales | 80 | 112 | 225 | 425 | 718 |

Source: J. de Vries, European Urbanisation 1500–1800 (London, 1984), 39.

[40] Smout, Nature Contested, 69. See also Devine, Transformation of Rural Scotland, 46, 54–5, 87.

Table 11.3 Percentage increase in urban population from previous date

|  | 1500 | 1550 | 1600 | 1650 | 1700 |
|---|---|---|---|---|---|
| Scotland | – | 0 | 130 | 17 | 51 |
| England and Wales | – | 40 | 128 | 94 | 45 |

Source: J. de Vries, *European Urbanisation 1500–1800* (London, 1984), 39.

towns.[41] But the area around the Firth of Forth was, even by the standards of advanced European countries, highly urbanized. One calculation has it that over 40 per cent of the population of that region lived in towns near the end of the seventeenth century. It was a figure higher than East Anglia and close to that of the Low Countries at the time.[42]

The vibrancy of some towns reflects the health of Scottish overseas trade in the 1590s to the 1620s, especially in the traditional exports of fish, grain, hides, and woollen cloth. The towns were commercial rather than industrial centres, nodal points for imports, internal trade, and the export of produce from the landed estates.[43] In 1611–14, for instance, over half of Scottish exports by value were agricultural. Here two positive trends can be identified. First, as noted earlier, skins, a major staple of Scottish trade for centuries, fell dramatically in volume in the course of the seventeenth century. Some two hundred thousand skins were shipped to the Baltic yearly in the early 1600s. By 1660, this had fallen by more than half, indicating the attempt by landowners and farmers to trade up to the more valuable droving economy in live cattle. Second, salt and coal exports, previously negligible, boomed in this period. One authority suggests a tenfold increase in coal exports from the 1550s to the 1630s, though that estimate remains somewhat speculative. Despite these developments, however, the range of burghal exports was still uncomfortably narrow and, because they were so tied into the rural economy, were likely to experience dramatic fluctuation as climatic conditions changed over time and affected outputs in the countryside.

In assessing the triggers of urban expansion, we should not forget the important insight from the distinguished Irish historian Louis Cullen. Conventional accounts tend to stress Scotland's peripheral geographic status on the edge of Europe, only marginally connected to the main arteries of international commerce. Not so Cullen; for him the Scots were at the centre of things:

> Scotland's location seems vital and beneficial for its history. Scotland not only had easy access to Ireland but shared a common land frontier with England, and had a long coastline on the North Sea. Thus Scotland faced three ways. Its long North Sea

[41] Michael Lynch, ed., *The Early Modern Town in Scotland* (London, 1987).

[42] T. M. Devine, 'Scotland', in Peter Clark, ed., *The Cambridge Urban History of Britain, Volume II, 1540–1840* (Cambridge, 2000), 151–2.

[43] M. Lynch, 'Continuity and Change in Urban Society, 1500–1700', in Houston and Whyte eds., *Scottish Society*, 85–117.

coastline gave it the benefit of access to what was in effect Europe's inland sea, at the heart of economic development in northern Europe well into the seventeenth century. The sea journey from Scotland to Scandinavia and the Baltic was shorter than from any of the more developed parts of eastern England. As a consequence, Scots were not only to the fore in the penetration from their islands of this region and its north German, Polish and Russian hinterland, but they assumed a dominant position in the English-speaking colonies there which they continued to hold in the seventeenth century.... All this helped to give an impetus to economic changes in the eastern Lowlands of Scotland. The small coastal towns of Fife were already well developed and numerous in the sixteenth century, and Scottish merchants, pedlars and mercenaries, though their numbers appear exaggerated in some contemporary accounts, had created a very real and far-flung establishment across the north of Europe.[44]

Throughout the period considered here the east-coast centre and especially Edinburgh–Leith retained their old dominance. Between 1460 and 1600, around 80 per cent of the Exchequer customs revenue was generated by Edinburgh, Dundee, and Aberdeen. The capital tightened its grip even further over these decades. By the last years of the sixteenth century, Edinburgh had virtually developed a monopoly over the nation's export trade. From Leith, for instance, 83 per cent of all skins and 73 per cent of all cloth left the country. Research into the merchant community that controlled this commerce is also revealing.[45] Rather than the traditional picture of a class hidebound by guild regulation and conservative practice, Edinburgh's elites were found to be energetic, entrepreneurial, and progressive, developing joint partnerships, ship ownership, pushing into new markets in Europe, and spending their capital on a remarkable series of domestic investments, including coal and lead mining, cloth-making, herring-curing, and small-scale manufactories.[46]

Equally significant is the evidence at the same period of increased vibrancy in Glasgow, the principal burgh of the west. The town tripled in population between 1560 and 1660 to 14,700, and moved from sixth place in the list of tax paid by the leading Scottish burghs in 1583 to third, just marginally behind Dundee and Aberdeen. The origins of one of the most momentous developments in Scottish commercial history, the change in the economic axis from the east to the west of the country, can be traced back to this period. It was not, however, the transatlantic factor that was the motor at this stage but rather the growth of trade across the North Channel to the newly established Scottish settlements in Ulster, 'Scotland's first colony', and the trafficking in linen cloth across the more stable Borders by a new breed of 'English merchants' in the western burgh. The platform was being built for the emergence of Glasgow in later decades as 'the boom town of the seventeenth century'.[47]

[44] L. M. Cullen, 'Scotland and Ireland, 1600–1800: Their Role in the Evolution of British Society', in Houston and Whyte eds., *Scottish Society*, 227.

[45] James J. Brown, 'Merchant Princes and Mercantile Investment in Early Seventeenth-Century Scotland', in Lynch ed., *Early Modern Town in Scotland*, 126.

[46] Ibid., 127–41.

[47] James McGrath, 'The Medieval and Early Modern Burgh', in T. M. Devine and G. Jackson, eds., *Glasgow. Volume I: Beginnings to 1830* (Manchester, 1995), 43–55.

The record therefore confirms that at least down to the 1620s the Scottish burghal and commercial economy was on an upward curve sustained in part by a more responsive system of food supply and a run of good harvests (*pace* 1623–4). Thereafter, as far as the 1640s, our knowledge became much more hazy. There is a pressing need for the scholarly gap to be addressed between the end date of *c.*1625 in S. G. E. Lythe's pioneering work and the years of revolution and English conquest from the late 1630s onwards. At the moment the consensus is that if the Scottish economy was indeed on the move in the early seventeenth century, the momentum came to an abrupt halt in the 1640s:

> …the outbreak of the Covenanting wars in 1638 heralded the start of a 15-year period of disaster for the Scottish economy. Both town and countryside suffered from attack, plundering, military occupation, heavy taxation, and the casual levying of additional funds. Trade was disrupted and vessels were seized.[48]

The great towns of Aberdeen and Dundee were both sacked and pillaged. The bloodiest fighting occurred in the central and south-western Highlands, with districts despoiled and townships laid waste by the marching and counter-marching of royalist and Covenanting armies.[49]

Scholars disagree, however, on the extent and speed of the recovery during the Cromwellian Union that followed. Some argue that it was patchy and lengthy. Another perspective, based on Clyde and Aberdeen trade and shipping data, indicates a quicker response in the south-west and north-east regions. It is yet another confirmation that the Scottish economy was a veritable mosaic in this period, with widely varied experiences in different localities over time.[50]

# 4

In the last generation or so, important reappraisals of the early modern Scottish economy have been published. The intrinsic rationality of much pre-modern agricultural practices and their capacity to evolve and adapt in order to attempt to reduce the threshold of risk in a country of uncertain climate and poor natural endowment is now well established. With that new awareness has come the need to compare Scotland not with precociously advanced nations but rather with the western and central European norm. Scotland was not simply a land of uniform and endemic backwardness. Phases of relative prosperity have been identified in addition to the more familiar bleaker times. The architectural glories of such gems as Fyvie Castle, Craigievar, the Bruce House at Culross, and Gladstone's Land in Edinburgh suggest that some members of the landed and urban

---

[48] Whyte, *Scotland before the Industrial Revolution*, 281.

[49] T. M. Devine, *Clanship to Crofters' War* (Manchester, 1994), 14.

[50] For a discussion see T. M. Devine, 'The Cromwellian Union of the Scottish Burghs: The Case of Aberdeen and Glasgow, 1652–1660', in John Butt and J. T. Ward, *Scottish Themes: Essays in Honour of S. G. E. Lythe* (Edinburgh, 1976), 1–16.

elites not only had impressive aesthetic taste but also possessed the capital to fund attractive architecture and pleasing internal decoration. Indeed, some scholars have seen Scotland as 'a dynamic and expansive society' before *c.*1640, developing trading communities in ports from Bergen in Norway to Gdansk in Poland and along the great river valleys of central Europe; then moving into Ulster; a growing town life; a developing system of schooling at the parish level able to support four universities, compared with one in Ireland and two in England. Nevertheless, the economy never achieved structural change: the advances were made within given parameters and stalled for a time in the maelstrom of the conflicts of the 1640s.

There remains much for new research to explore in this fascinating period. But two issues in particular stand out. The years from the 1630s to *c.*1660 have been worked over by historians of politics and religion. But, despite some glimmers, these three decades remain something of a dark age in terms of economic history. Then there is the intriguing question of the likely impact of the 'Greater Scotland' of emigration to Europe and the Scottish merchant communities there on the homeland itself.[51] Were the two mainly insulated from one another or was the connection so close that emigration need no longer simply be seen as a reflection of dire poverty but perhaps also at the commercial level as a route to national expansion in the manner of imperial adventuring in the eighteenth century and beyond. The answer to that question might well result in a further reappraisal of the early modern economy of Scotland at some point in the future.

## FURTHER READING

Dodgshon, R. A., *Land and Society in Early Scotland* (Oxford, 1981).

——— *From Chiefs to Landlords: Society and Economy in the Western Highlands and Islands c. 1493–1820* (Edinburgh, 1998).

Gibson, A. J. S., and Smout, T. C., *Prices, Food and Wages in Scotland 1550–1780* (Cambridge, 1995).

Grosjean, Alexia, and Murdoch, Steve, eds., *Scottish Communities Abroad in the Early Modern Period* (Leiden, 2005).

Houston, R. A., and Whyte, I. D., eds., *Scottish Society 1500–1800* (Cambridge, 1989).

Lynch, Michael, ed., *The Early Modern Town in Scotland* (London, 1987).

Lythe, S. G. E., *The Economy of Scotland in its European Setting 1550–1625* (Edinburgh, 1960).

Whyte, Ian D., *Agriculture and Society in Seventeenth-Century Scotland* (Edinburgh, 1979).

——— *Scotland before the Industrial Revolution* (Harlow, 1995).

---

[51] Alexia Grojean and Steve Murdoch, eds., *Scottish Communities Abroad in the Early Modern Period* (Leiden, 2005). One authority has argued that Scottish external mercantile networks in northern Europe 'resulted in a subtle transfer of capital, goods and cultural commodities back into Scotland'. Yet the hard evidence to support this statement remains elusive and sketchy. See Steve Murdoch, *Network North: Scottish Kin, Commercial and Covert Associations in Northern Europe 1603–1746* (Leiden, 2006), 248.

CHAPTER 12

. . . . . . . . . . . . . . . . . . . . . . . . . . . . . . . . . . . . . . . . . . . . . . . . . . . . . . . . . . . . . . . . . . . . . . . . . . . .

# SCOTLAND RESTORED AND RESHAPED: POLITICS AND RELIGION, *c*.1660–1712

. . . . . . . . . . . . . . . . . . . . . . . . . . . . . . . . . . . . . . . . . . . . . . . . . . . . . . . . . . . . . . . . . . . . . . . . . . . .

## ALASDAIR RAFFE

THE period between the Restoration of Charles II and the creation of the United Kingdom was a crucial phase in the formation of modern Scotland's political and religious cultures.[1] A time of sharp divisions and controversial political experimentation, the five decades after 1660 engaged the nation's rulers and thinkers in a search for answers to two sets of intertwined questions. The first concerned political authority: how, and from where, would Scotland be governed? What sort of monarchy should the nation have, and what other institutions were necessary? The second questions related to religious institutions and ideas. What would be the character of the national Church, and how could the rival claims of religious and political authority be reconciled? How could religious diversity—and ultimately a plurality of Churches—be accommodated within a stable society? These religious problems fundamentally influenced the context in which Scotland's monarchs attempted to rule. The two sets of questions had shaped Scottish politics since the sixteenth century, and had become especially problematic after the royal court moved to London in 1603. But the decades after 1660 are noteworthy for the divisive and often extreme solutions proposed. Moreover, tentative answers to the problems were in place by the end of the period, eventually allowing Scotland some respite from its early modern experience of religious and political turmoil.

Historians rarely study the five decades after 1660 as a unit. Justifiably, they often portray the Revolution of 1688–90 as a turning point. This chapter assesses the politics and religious debates of the Restoration period (1660–88), before considering the changes brought by the Revolution, and the character of post-Revolution Scotland. The chapter concludes that there are good reasons for seeing the 'Union

---

[1] For economic and social developments, see chs. 11, 13, and 16.

settlement'—the constitutional package combining regnal and parliamentary union in 1707, the abolition of the Scottish Privy Council in 1708, and the Toleration Act of 1712—as a more decisive set of changes than those of 1688–90. In terms of Scotland's major political and religious questions, the Revolution had made options available, but the Union settled on particular answers.

When distinguishing between the pre- and post-Revolution periods, historians have been influenced by several familiar narratives through which the history of these years has been told. For the period 1660–88, there are two especially well-worn interpretations. First, there is an account of Restoration politics in terms of the rise and fall of two dukes, Lauderdale and York. A second narrative concerns the Crown's religious policies in the Restoration period: its attempt to impose a uniform episcopalian settlement on the Church. For the years after the Revolution, two popular images can be identified, one broadly Whiggish in character, the other essentially Jacobite. The Whig tradition sees the period 1690–1707 as the last stage in the formation of Great Britain. Political trends and economic setbacks in the 1690s pointed towards a new relationship with England, and Scotland's elites argued about, but in most cases came to terms with, parliamentary union. The alternative account of the period characterizes the Revolution as a political betrayal, the first of a series of disasters that befell Scotland during, and as a result of, King William's 'ill years'.

# 1

The high political narrative of Restoration Scotland describes how John Maitland, Earl and later Duke of Lauderdale, and James, Duke of York and Albany and later King of Scots, made and broke alliances in pursuit of a monopoly of power. Lauderdale, who had been a prisoner of the Cromwellian Protectorate and became secretary to the restored Charles II, initially worked with John, Earl of Middleton, royal commissioner to Parliament in 1661 and 1662. Parliament passed an Act of Indemnity, pardoning most participants in the wars and governments of the 1640s and 1650s, but not until 1662. Thus potential opponents of the Restoration legislation enacted before the indemnity were reluctant to criticize Middleton's agenda for fear of being exempted from pardon. The 'billeting affair', Middleton's attempt to have Parliament exclude Lauderdale from the indemnity, forcing him from office, backfired, and Middleton himself fell from power. Lauderdale then allied with John Leslie, Duke of Rothes, letting him take the blame for administrative inefficiency, corruption, and religious coercion so severe that it provoked a Presbyterian rising in 1666. With Rothes discredited, Lauderdale himself assumed the office of royal commissioner to the parliaments and conventions of estates from 1669 to 1678. He remained in post as secretary, and also acted as one of the commissioners supervising the Scottish Treasury. But Lauderdale's allies became fewer and of lower status, and powerful opposition to him emerged within the political elite. Charles protected his secretary until the Presbyterian rising of 1679 made Lauderdale's position untenable. In late 1679, then, the king sent to Edinburgh his brother James, who took control of the Privy Council and served as commissioner in the Parliament of 1681. James briefly succeeded in recovering wide-ranging support for the Crown's government of Scotland, from which he benefited on his accession to the throne in 1685. But his political style and pro-Catholic religious agenda were divisive: by 1688, his government was narrowly based, and many of Scotland's nobles, lairds, and burgesses were ready to contemplate a revolution.[2]

These political events gripped contemporaries who were unfamiliar with, or had forgotten, royal government. In his *Memoirs*, Sir George Mackenzie of Rosehaugh described the change of government following the billeting affair as 'so great a surprisal, and being the first, [it] made such deep impressions upon us, who were unacquainted with such alterations'.[3] Gilbert Burnet, another contemporary observer who shared Mackenzie's fascination, laid down the outlines of the high political narrative in *Burnet's History of His Own Time* (1724–34), which he began writing in the mid-1680s.[4] Before departing for London in 1674, Burnet had been successively episcopalian minister of Saltoun in East Lothian and Professor of Divinity at Glasgow University. For a while, he was patronized by Lauderdale and Charles II; Burnet was acquainted with the Duke of York, and had been a close friend of James Drummond, later Earl of Perth, chancellor from 1684 and subsequently a Catholic convert. Thus Burnet's *History* was well informed about Scotland under Charles II. Moreover, Burnet's emphasis on political factions and manoeuvres was later complemented by other printed sources. One was Mackenzie's *Memoirs*; the most influential was the *Lauderdale Papers*, a selection of Lauderdale's correspondence edited by Osmund Airy in 1884–5.[5] Subsequent historians focused on the personality and chicanery of Lauderdale, often absorbing from Airy an ambivalent appraisal of the man, and a one-dimensional hostility towards his rivals, in particular James Sharp, Archbishop of St Andrews.[6] Meanwhile, the rise and fall of James VII was comparatively under-researched, not least because the king's archive was destroyed by

---

[2] From a wide literature, see especially Julia Buckroyd, *Church and State in Scotland, 1660–1681* (Edinburgh, 1980); Gillian H. MacIntosh, *The Scottish Parliament under Charles II, 1660–1685* (Edinburgh, 2007); Ronald A. Lee, 'Government and Politics in Scotland, 1661–1681' (unpublished PhD thesis, University of Glasgow, 1995); John Patrick, 'A Union Broken? Restoration Politics in Scotland', in Jenny Wormald, ed., *Scotland Revisited* (London, 1991); John Patrick, 'The Origins of the Opposition to Lauderdale in the Scottish Parliament of 1673', *Scottish Historical Review* [hereafter *SHR*], 53 (1974), 1–21; Kirsty F. McAlister, 'James VII and the Conduct of Scottish Politics, *c.*1679 to *c.*1686' (unpublished PhD thesis, University of Strathclyde, 2003); Tim Harris, *Revolution: The Great Crisis of the British Monarchy, 1685–1720* (London, 2006), chs. 2 and 4.

[3] George Mackenzie, *Memoirs of the Affairs of Scotland from the Restoration of Charles II* (Edinburgh, 1821), 115.

[4] Gilbert Burnet, *Burnet's History of His Own Time*, ed. Osmund Airy, 2 vols. (Oxford, 1897–1900), covers the period 1660–85.

[5] Osmund Airy, ed., *The Lauderdale Papers*, 3 vols, Camden Society, 2nd series (London, 1884–5).

[6] W. C. Mackenzie, *The Life and Times of John Maitland, Duke of Lauderdale (1616–1682)* (London, 1923). But see Julia Buckroyd, *The Life of James Sharp, Archbishop of St Andrews, 1618–1679: A Political Biography* (Edinburgh, 1987); Raymond Campbell Paterson, *King Lauderdale: The Corruption of Power* (Edinburgh, 2003).

French Revolutionaries in 1793. Nevertheless, historians found a suitably critical perspective on James's government of Scotland in the journals of Sir John Lauder of Fountainhall, a lawyer and parliamentarian in the 1680s, but a loyal adherent of William II from 1689.[7]

This traditional narrative dwells on factional politics, partly because there was broad agreement among the ruling elite on the need to uphold the Stuart monarchy, to preserve and even extend the royal prerogative. In recent years, historians have done much to examine the noble ethos and revived royalism of Restoration politics.[8] Scotland's magnates asserted their position of political leadership, which had been threatened in the 1640s and 1650s by radical clergy and lairds, by the greater significance given to moneyed merchants in a period of war and high government expenditure, and by English occupation. The struggles between Lauderdale and his rivals were largely about access to the king in London, the control of material resources, and minor matters of policy. Though major ideological differences concerning monarchical authority and Church government existed in Scottish society, most men who objected to the royalist consensus were excluded from power by oaths of allegiance to the king. James's success in Edinburgh in 1679–82 was based on a renewal of royal authority and patronage, brought geographically and emotionally closer to Scotland's political and professional elites.[9] The Test oath, enacted by Parliament in 1681, alienated some politicians and clergy from James, but their principal objection to the oath was its internal inconsistency, rather than its wide definition of royal authority.

Working with the story of the rise and fall of Lauderdale and York, historians have probed the nature of Scotland's government and its political institutions. Lauderdale's success, it is argued, depended on his proximity to Charles II at court, and his control of the flows of information between the king and Scotland. Lauderdale's weakness, which James was to replicate, was a growing isolation from the political nation, vividly illustrated by his hectoring confrontations with the Scottish Parliament. Making innovative use of the traditional Restoration sources, revisionist scholars of the pre-Union Parliament have demonstrated that while Parliament magnified the royal prerogative in numerous statutes, it was also a source of opposition to royal policies. This was apparent in 1669–70, when the Crown proposed Anglo-Scottish union, and more strikingly in 1686, when parliamentary opposition prevented the passage of an act repealing religious

[7] John Lauder, *Historical Observes of Memorable Occurrents in Church and State from October 1680 to April 1686*, eds. Adam Urquhart and David Laing, Bannatyne Club (Edinburgh, 1840); John Lauder, *Historical Notices of Scotish [sic] Affairs*, ed. David Laing, 2 vols, Bannatyne Club (Edinburgh, 1848). See the forthcoming biography of James VII by Alastair Mann.

[8] Julia M. Buckroyd, 'Bridging the Gap: Scotland, 1659–1660', *SHR*, 66 (1987), 1–25; Matthew Glozier, 'The Earl of Melfort, the Court Catholic Party and the Foundation of the Order of the Thistle, 1687', *SHR*, 79 (2000), 233–8; Clare Jackson, *Restoration Scotland, 1660–1690: Royalist Politics, Religion and Ideas* (Woodbridge, 2003).

[9] Hugh Ouston, 'York in Edinburgh: James VII and the Patronage of Learning in Scotland, 1679–1688', in John Dwyer, Roger A. Mason, and Alexander Murdoch, eds., *New Perspectives on the Politics and Culture of Early Modern Scotland* (Edinburgh, [1982]).

penal laws, despite its approval by government loyalists among the Lords of the Articles.[10]

The familiar narrative of politics fits well with another recent historiographical trend: the development of British perspectives on Restoration politics and culture. Lauderdale and York were political giants in England as well as Scotland. In the late 1670s, opposition to the Crown's ministers in the English Parliament drew on evidence of Lauderdale's supposedly tyrannical government of Scotland.[11] In 1679 James went to Edinburgh in part to remove himself physically from English politics at a time when the Westminster Parliament was agitating for his exclusion from the succession. While English Whigs condemned the Crown's record in Scotland, Tories applauded the Scots' loyalty to their kings. For historians of English political culture in this period, Scottish events have assumed a new significance.[12]

For all its value, the traditional interpretation of Restoration politics has had several negative consequences for Scottish historiography. It focuses excessively on short-term political changes, and though it assumes that politicians acted on materialist motives, little is known about the economic basis of their authority. Partly because of their expenditure in the civil wars, many nobles were highly indebted in the Restoration period. At root of much of the criticism of Middleton, Rothes, and Lauderdale were concerns that they maximized the profits of office (and of religious coercion) to pay back their debts and live in luxury. Yet there have been relatively few studies on the extent of noble indebtedness and the strategies landowners pursued to recover their finances. To date, most research on debts of the elite has concentrated on highland chiefs.[13] More generally, Restoration historians have defined politics too narrowly, focusing on the factional struggles of the political elite, and on relations between men in Edinburgh and London. There are few assessments of women's political activities, or of popular participation in politics, for long a dominant agenda in the history of Restoration England.[14]

To examine the resources and institutions of the state in late seventeenth-century Scotland, historians have had to break free from the confines of the traditional political narrative. As one scholar of the Treasury under Lauderdale complains, Airy's selection of the *Lauderdale Papers* was thematically narrow, directing research energies away from administrative themes. Various other studies of government and bureaucracy have

[10] MacIntosh, *Scottish Parliament under Charles II*; Alastair J. Mann, ' "James VII, King of the Articles": Political Management and Parliamentary Failure', in Keith M. Brown and Alastair J. Mann, eds., *Parliament and Politics in Scotland, 1567–1707* (Edinburgh, 2005).

[11] Tim Harris, *Restoration: Charles II and his Kingdoms* (London, 2005), 168–9.

[12] See Grant Tapsell, *The Personal Rule of Charles II, 1681–85* (Woodbridge, 2007), ch. 6; John Kerrigan, *Archipelagic English: Literature, History, and Politics, 1603–1707* (Oxford, 2008), ch. 9.

[13] Allan I. Macinnes, *Clanship, Commerce and the House of Stuart, 1603–1788* (East Linton, 1996); Douglas Watt, ' "The laberinth of thir difficulties": The Influence of Debt on the Highland Elite, c.1550–1700', *SHR*, 85 (2006), 28–51.

[14] But see Maurice Lee, *The Heiresses of Buccleuch: Marriage, Money and Politics in Seventeenth-Century Britain* (East Linton, 1996); R. A. Houston, *Social Change in the Age of Enlightenment: Edinburgh, 1660–1760* (Oxford, 1994), ch. 5; Harris, *Restoration*, 338–41; Harris, *Revolution*, 151–3.

yet to be synthesized into the general literature.[15] Political historians could do more to interrogate the consensus among legal scholars that the codification of Scots law in the Restoration period was the basis for the preservation of distinct legal arrangements after the Union.[16] And the revival of interest in Parliament could be balanced with more systematic research on the Privy Council.

Yet the most striking gaps in Restoration historiography lie in religious themes. The details of Restoration religious policy in Scotland form an even more entrenched narrative than that of high politics.[17] Following the restoration of bishops to the Church in 1661–2, the Crown attempted to enforce universal conformity with the Church of Scotland, imposing fines, imprisonment, exile, and execution on thousands of Presbyterian dissenters. The government's policy used to be written about chiefly from the dissenters' point of view, not least because theirs became the winning side of the argument with the re-establishment of Presbyterianism in 1690. The development of a Presbyterian bias in the historiography was ensured by the publication of the *History of the Sufferings of the Church of Scotland* (1721–2) by the minister Robert Wodrow. In opposition to the Restoration government's claim that the Presbyterians were politically seditious, and therefore justly punished, Wodrow argued that they had suffered persecution merely for their religious beliefs. Likewise, he interpreted acts of Presbyterian resistance, notably the risings of 1666 and 1679, as freedom fighting. Dedicating the *History* to George I, Wodrow characterized the Presbyterians' nonconformity as a struggle for 'revolution Principles'—the tenets of 1688–9—'even before the revolution was brought about'.[18]

As Colin Kidd has argued, the balance between early modern radicalism and polite eighteenth-century Whiggery in Wodrow's *History* was 'precarious'; it would be unacceptable to later, more conservative Presbyterian historians such as William Robertson.[19] Yet Wodrow's contribution has structured most subsequent histories of Restoration religion, including those hostile to Presbyterianism. Such was Wodrow's command of the sources that even the most recent scholarly accounts of religious policy repeat his narrative, if not his bias.[20] Furthermore, the resistance of the Restoration Presbyterians was a fruitful theme for nineteenth-century novelists, and remained appealing to a wide readership into the twentieth century. After Wodrow, historians of Restoration Presbyterianism such as John Howie paid disproportionate attention to the Cameronians, a small group of extremists who seemed to

[15]  Roy W. Lennox, 'Lauderdale and Scotland: A Study in Restoration Politics and Administration, 1660–1682' (unpublished PhD thesis, Columbia University, 1977), 25; Lee, 'Government and Politics'; Athol L. Murray, 'The Scottish Treasury, 1667–1708', *SHR*, 45 (1966), 89–104.

[16]  See J. D. Ford, *Law and Opinion in Scotland during the Seventeenth Century* (Oxford, 2007).

[17]  For earlier historiographical surveys see Ian B. Cowan, *The Scottish Covenanters, 1660–88* (London, 1976), 167–71; Buckroyd, *Church and State*, 164–71.

[18]  Robert Wodrow, *The History of the Sufferings of the Church of Scotland from the Restoration to the Revolution*, ed. Robert Burns, 4 vols. (1721–2; Glasgow, 1828–30), vol. i, xxxv.

[19]  Colin Kidd, *Subverting Scotland's Past: Scottish Whig Historians and the Creation of an Anglo-British Identity, 1689–c.1830* (Cambridge, 1993), 69.

[20]  Cowan, *Scottish Covenanters*; Buckroyd, *Church and State*; Elizabeth H. Hyman, 'A Church Militant: Scotland, 1661–1690', *Sixteenth Century Journal*, 26 (1995), 49–74.

represent Covenanting Presbyterianism in its most heroic and principled phase.[21] Wodrow's careful but partisan account was simplified and distorted. The Presbyterians had become the stuff of popular history, commemorative monuments and parochial folklore.

By the late twentieth century, it was common for historians to decry the dominance of the religious-policy narrative and its tendency to inhibit fresh thinking about Restoration Scotland.[22] Yet it is important not to misconstrue the place of religion in late seventeenth-century historiography. While the enforcement of uniformity has been analysed at length, religious life itself has generally been overlooked. Following Wodrow, historians have predominantly used government sources: proclamations, Privy Council registers, and politicians' correspondence. Less often studied are Restoration Presbyterians' writings on Church government, their sermons, diaries, and correspondence. Despite some fine discussions of resistance theory, much remains to be said about the ideas at stake in the controversy between Presbyterians and episcopalians.[23] Furthermore, the episcopalian Church—the supposed beneficiary of the government's policy—has hardly been studied. The only book-length appraisal draws solely on printed sources and is over fifty years old.[24] Recent improvements in the accessibility of manuscript ecclesiastical records should encourage new research on the Restoration Kirk as an institution, and on its social and cultural roles.

Government policy, cruelty, and violence have diverted historians' attentions from religious beliefs and worship. Yet a body of new research signals a change in emphasis. David Mullan's work on Presbyterian diaries and memoirs should encourage more studies of the religious lives of the clergy and laity. The present author argues that the years after 1660 saw the emergence of an episcopalian confessional culture, distinct in terms of theology, liturgy, and piety from the Presbyterian culture that would dominate post-Revolution Scotland. In an article on Sir Robert Moray, Frances Harris has suggested how the religious, intellectual, and political interests of a Restoration statesman can be reconciled.[25] Drawing on these insights, historians should seek to recast the place of religion in the

---

[21] Cameronian biographies feature disproportionately in John Howie, *Biographia Scoticana: or a Brief Historical Account of the Lives, Character and Memorable Transactions of the most Eminent Scots Worthies* (Glasgow, 1775).

[22] Lennox, 'Lauderdale and Scotland', 2; Lee, 'Government and Politics', iii, 4; Jackson, *Restoration Scotland*, 1–4.

[23] I. M. Smart, 'The Political Ideas of the Scottish Covenanters, 1638–88', *History of Political Thought*, 1 (1980), 167–93; Robert von Friedeburg, 'From Collective Representation to the Right to Individual Defence: James Steuart's *Ius Populi Vindicatum* and the Use of Johannes Althusius' *Politica* in Restoration Scotland', *History of European Ideas*, 24 (1998), 19–42; Colin Kidd, 'Religious Realignment Between the Restoration and Union', in John Robertson, ed., *A Union for Empire: Political Thought and the British Union of 1707* (Cambridge, 1995); Jackson, *Restoration Scotland*, chs. 5–7.

[24] Walter R. Foster, *Bishop and Presbytery: The Church of Scotland, 1661–1688* (London, 1958).

[25] David G. Mullan, ed., *Women's Life Writing in Early Modern Scotland: Writing the Evangelical Self, c.1670–c.1730* (Aldershot, 2003); David G. Mullan, ed., *Protestant Piety in Early-Modern Scotland: Letters, Lives and Covenants, 1650–1712*, Scottish History Society (Edinburgh, 2008); David G. Mullan, *Narratives of the Religious Self in Early-Modern Scotland* (Farnham, 2010); Alasdair Raffe, 'Presbyterians and Episcopalians: The Formation of Confessional Cultures in Scotland, 1660–1715', *English Historical Review*, 125 (2010), 570–98; Frances Harris, 'Lady Sophia's Visions: Sir Robert Moray, the Earl of Lauderdale and the Restoration Government of Scotland', *The Seventeenth Century*, 24 (2009), 129–55.

historiography, recovering its social and intellectual significance, and at the same time defining politics more broadly to encompass ideological disagreement. There is a need for international perspectives on Scottish religion after 1660, particularly research on the influence of the Church of England and of continental Protestants and Catholics. Intellectual continuities and traditions should be brought back into focus. By studying religious and political life across long time periods, historians will be able to break down the restrictive chronological barriers of 1660 and 1688, and with them the distortions of the standard narratives.

## 2

In the traditional interpretations examined in this chapter, the Revolution of 1688–90 stands either as a terminal moment or as a point of departure. There are important reasons for seeing the interval between William of Orange's invasion of England in November 1688 and the re-establishment of Presbyterianism in the summer of 1690 as a turning point. In politics, the Revolution brought a rapid reconfiguration of the governing elite, reviving the careers of opponents of James VII, including figures such as Sir James Dalrymple of Stair and Sir Patrick Hume of Polwarth who had spent parts of the 1680s in exile in the Netherlands.[26] Of greatest consequence—particularly for highland society— was the rehabilitation of Archibald Campbell, son of the executed ninth Earl of Argyll, who regained his father's title. For the Campbells, Dalrymples, and their peers, dynasties that shaped eighteenth-century politics and society, the Revolution was a rebirth.

In the shorter term, the Revolution was a milestone of institutional change. By comparison with the parliaments of 1661–2, the convention of estates that met in March 1689 asserted its own importance, adopting a Claim of Right designed to reconfigure the relationships between the monarchy, its subjects, and their parliaments. The Claim and the accompanying articles of grievances have always attracted much historical scrutiny. But it is important to remember how many of the innovations requested in these documents were the subject of continuing political struggles after William and Mary accepted the throne. The supposed right to address the Crown was highly ambiguous, as the Country Party's petitioning campaign of 1699–1700 proved. Presbyterianism was re-established as a result of parliamentary pressure, not because the king was obliged by the Claim of Right. The abolition of the parliamentary Lords of the Articles was also something of a chance event; and it was not the permanent setback for the Crown that historians used to describe.[27] Nevertheless, the Revolution's institutional changes altered the place of

---

[26] Ginny Gardner, *The Scottish Exile Community in the Netherlands, 1660–1690* (East Linton, 2004); Keith L. Sprunger, *Dutch Puritanism: A History of English and Scottish Churches of the Netherlands in the Sixteenth and Seventeenth Centuries* (Leiden, 1982), chs. 15 and 16.

[27] James Halliday, 'The Club and the Revolution in Scotland, 1689–90', *SHR*, 45 (1966), 143–59; Alastair J. Mann, 'Inglorious Revolution: Administrative Muddle and Constitutional Change in the Scottish Parliament of William and Mary', *Parliamentary History*, 22 (2003), 121–44.

Parliament in Scottish politics. Subsequent meetings required careful management by the government, and provided a more suitable platform for political opposition than had existed in the Restoration period. Moreover, the removal of the bishops from politics, and the revival of the General Assembly as the governing authority in the Kirk, introduced further complexity to political life. Institutional reforms brought by the Revolution ensured that in the period 1690–1707 Scotland would not be amenable to government by a single, pre-eminent minister of the nature of Lauderdale or York.

In a related way, the Revolution was a watershed for popular participation in politics. Historians used to suggest that the nobility were nearly as dominant in 1688–90 as they had been at the Restoration. Yet recent scholars have paid more attention to crowd violence in the Revolution, notably anti-Catholic demonstrations and the eviction of episcopalian ministers from parishes across southern Scotland. The so-called 'rabbling' of the clergy catalysed the resurgence of Presbyterianism, and helped to shape a Revolution settlement more radical than that achieved in England.[28] The survival of the Williamite regime in the 1690s depended on international war, and on support among Scotland's elites. But historians should remember that the Revolution had popular foundations, and that the violence of 1688–9 made politicians more aware of the destabilizing (and potentially counter-revolutionary) role of crowds.

More fundamentally still, the Revolution changed Scotland's menu of political options. In the Restoration period, as has been seen, royalism was a pervasive and unifying ideology, restricting the discussion of alternative visions. From 1689, support for the Revolution was the government's shibboleth, but political culture was more pluralist. Jacobitism had a rival ideological premise rooted in the political theology of indefeasible hereditary succession and divine-right monarchy. A few committed Jacobites served at James VII's court in exile, at St Germain-en-Laye to the west of Paris. Of those remaining in Scotland, the most principled refused oaths of allegiance to William and Mary and withdrew from politics, while less conscientious Jacobites remained in positions of influence under the new regime.[29] Meanwhile, the Revolution encouraged some Williamites to consider further change, ranging from union with England to Andrew Fletcher of Saltoun's radical schemes for social and political reconstitution. Much remained unsettled in the immediate post-Revolution years.

In religious terms, it might be said, 1688–90 was a decisive turning point. Conventionally, it is depicted as the 'triumph of Presbyterianism',[30] the conclusion of the Restoration narrative of persecution and resistance. This is a simplification: mainstream Presbyterians had enjoyed considerable freedoms to worship and organize since accepting James VII's second declaration of indulgence of June 1687. For their eighteenth-century descendants,

---

[28] Bruce Lenman, 'The Scottish Nobility and the Revolution of 1688–1690', in R. A. Beddard, ed., *The Revolutions of 1688* (Oxford, 1991); Tim Harris, 'The People, the Law, and the Constitution in Scotland and England: A Comparative Approach to the Glorious Revolution', *Journal of British Studies*, 38 (1999), 28–58; Neil Davidson, 'Popular Insurgency during the Glorious Revolution in Scotland', *Scottish Labour History*, 39 (2004), 14–31.

[29] See ch. 18 in this volume.

[30] Cowan, *Scottish Covenanters*, ch. 9.

however, it was William's invasion that 'delivered the Nation from Civil and Religious Oppression', and 'confirmed to' the Kirk 'all the Religious Rights and Privileges which she now enjoys'.[31] Rather than James's dubious prerogative indulgence, the statutes of 1689–90 in favour of Presbyterianism (and the Act of Security for the Church, passed with the Union in 1707) assumed symbolic importance. According to episcopalian historians, however, the Revolution began a century of prosecution, dispersal, and suppression, a narrative with parallels to the Presbyterian account of the Restoration, but with less historiographical prestige.[32] Both Presbyterian and episcopalian narratives presented the Revolution as a turning point, but historians increasingly question the assumptions behind these simplistic interpretations.

## 3

The Revolution, then, brought more diversity to Scotland's politics, expanding the range of options for the country's future. Yet if there is one issue that dominates the historiography of the reigns of William and Mary and Anne it is union with England.[33] As a result, political events of the period immediately preceding 1707 are far better understood than those of the 1690s. Historians of William's reign have often focused on short episodes, and the wider post-Revolution political culture has attracted few scholars. Moreover, frequent changes in office-holding ensured that there is no obvious political career around which to structure a coherent narrative of the years 1690–1707. Consequently, the traditional perspectives on the period were determined more by attitudes towards the Revolution and the Union than by the nature of politics in the intervening years. Two highly politicized narratives developed; reactions to them have shaped the subsequent historiography.

The first narrative focuses on the final twists and turns of the 'road to union'. By overturning the authoritarianism of Charles II and James VII, it suggests, the Revolution allowed for a more open and realistic assessment of Scotland's political trajectory. Greater union with England had been a possibility since 1603, but British unity had been postponed in the Restoration period by the willingness of Charles and James to take advantage of the rivalries between their kingdoms. Scotland's reactionary nobles had relished the opportunity to abandon the Cromwellian union, and to compete for monopoly of an autonomous political arena. With these anti-union forces weakened,

---

[31] 'Act appointing a national thanksgiving in commemoration of the revolution in 1688', in *The Principal Acts of the General Assembly of the Church of Scotland* (Edinburgh, 1788), 32.

[32] Frederick Goldie, *A Short History of the Episcopal Church in Scotland from the Restoration to the Present Time* (London, 1951). But see Gavin White, *The Scottish Episcopal Church: A New History* (Edinburgh, 1998).

[33] See ch. 17 in this volume.

the politicians of the 1690s could weigh up Scotland's options more objectively and produce, after several false starts, the parliamentary union of 1707.[34]

This tendentious account of post-Revolution politics was elaborated first by eighteenth-century Whigs, buoyed up by Scotland's intellectual and economic progress since the Union. For William Robertson, 1688–90 inaugurated a modernization of Scottish society, since it reacted against the destructive dominance of the nobility, and pointed towards integration with the country's more advanced southern neighbour. Parliamentary union was itself a product of the Revolution, which was thus the starting point of a story of Scottish liberty. The success of empire, and the 1801 parliamentary union with Ireland, gave historians other reasons to praise the achievements of 1707. Meanwhile, nineteenth-century Whigs further denigrated the pre-Union society from which modern Scotland had emerged.[35]

In practice, the road from revolution to union was far from smooth. Many English politicians, predominantly but not exclusively Tories, were opposed to union. In Scotland, anti-English sentiment increased, particularly when the government of William's southern kingdom obstructed Scottish attempts to settle a colony at Darien on the isthmus of Panama in 1698–1700. At times, the Scottish Parliament pursued projects that were seen as provocative or hostile in England, notably the Darien scheme and the Act of Security (1704). Yet Parliament's escape from the dominance of Crown and noble interests, which, it was assumed, shaped Restoration politics, was a necessary part of the Whig narrative. In its 'last six years', wrote William Law Mathieson in 1905, Parliament displayed 'most unexpected vigour', before the institution 'made a good end' by voting for its own abolition.[36] Politics in the years 1690–1707, though fractious and unseemly, appeared more liberal than in the Restoration period. But ultimately, Parliament's struggles were to usher in a better future.

By the 1970s, this narrative was under attack. William Ferguson and P. W. J. Riley refused to see the period preceding the Union as one of constructive debate and high-minded statesmanship, and instead emphasized cynical political manoeuvres, parliamentary management, and bribery.[37] The ascendancy of the Namierite historical

[34] For nuanced discussions, see T. C. Smout, 'The Road to Union', in Geoffrey Holmes, ed., *Britain after the Glorious Revolution, 1689–1714* (London, 1969); Maurice Lee, *The 'Inevitable' Union and other Essays on Early Modern Scotland* (East Linton, 2003), ch. 1.

[35] Colin Kidd, 'The Ideological Significance of Robertson's *History of Scotland*', in Stewart J. Brown, ed., *William Robertson and the Expansion of Empire* (Cambridge, 1997), 132–3; Richard B. Sher, '1688 and 1788: William Robertson on Revolution in Britain and France', in Paul Dukes and John Dunkley, eds., *Culture and Revolution* (London, 1990); Alexander Murdoch, 'The Legacy of the Revolution in Scotland', in Alexander Murdoch, ed., *The Scottish Nation: Identity and History* (Edinburgh, 2007), 39; Michael Fry, 'The Whig Interpretation of Scottish History', in Ian Donnachie and Christopher Whatley, eds., *The Manufacture of Scottish History* (Edinburgh, 1992).

[36] William Law Mathieson, *Scotland and the Union: A History of Scotland from 1695 to 1747* (Glasgow, 1905), 176.

[37] William Ferguson, 'The Making of the Treaty of Union of 1707', *SHR*, 43 (1964), 89–110; William Ferguson, *Scotland's Relations with England: A Survey to 1707* (Edinburgh, 1977), 180–272; P. W. J. Riley, *The Union of England and Scotland: A Study in Anglo-Scottish Politics of the Eighteenth Century* (Manchester, 1978).

approach, which questioned the importance of principles in politics, and the rise of Scottish nationalism, seriously undermined the 'road to union' perspective. In recent years, however, the elitist and materialist interpretation associated with Riley and Ferguson has itself been in retreat. The dominant approach in post-Revolution political history is shifting between post-Namierite and post-Habermasian modes.[38] Scottish historians are rightly wary of the specific characteristics of Jürgen Habermas's view of the public sphere, which draws particularly on evidence of post-Revolution London. Coffee houses and periodical publications played smaller roles in Scotland; the Privy Council continued to censor printed publications until its abolition in 1708. Broadly conceived, however, a post-Habermasian approach places politics in wide social and cultural contexts, assesses both institutions and practices, and recovers the ideologies behind political debates. In Karin Bowie's work, for example, the period's pamphlets point to political engagement by a wider section of Scottish society than either Riley or Ferguson acknowledged. For Allan Macinnes, pamphlet debates and commercial projects show how different attitudes to political economy informed discussions of Scotland's future.[39] But while these and other scholars suggest new agendas in post-Revolution political history, the historiographical gains have so far accrued more to the early years of Anne's reign at the beginning of the eighteenth century than to the 1690s, which still attract less interest.

One reason for this neglect of William's reign is its reputation for disaster. The narrative of 'King William's ill years' has a tenacious appeal in the popular history of Scotland. Originating in contemporary Jacobite polemic, the narrative sought to discredit the Revolution of 1688–90 by associating the Williamite regime it established with war, misgovernment, and economic calamity. The 'ill years' view was built on a selective and episodic survey of events, particularly the Massacre of Glencoe, the failure of the Darien scheme, and the famine of the late 1690s. The Glencoe Massacre of February 1692 was the most extreme outcome of the Crown's highland policy, which reversed the anti-Campbell drift of the 1680s and subjected the western Highlands to greater external military interference. By exposing the government's mismanagement and brutality, Parliament's 1695 investigation of the Massacre made Glencoe a symbol of William's failings. Later in the 1690s, further evidence of the king's malign influence emerged when, to avoid provoking Spain's rulers, who saw Darien as an imperial possession, he withdrew his support from the Company of

[38] For a discussion concentrating on English historiography, see Brian Cowan, 'Geoffrey Holmes and the Public Sphere: Augustan Historiography from Post-Namierite to the Post-Habermasian', *Parliamentary History*, 28 (2009), 166–78.

[39] Karin Bowie, *Scottish Public Opinion and the Anglo-Scottish Union, 1699–1707* (Woodbridge, 2007); Allan I. Macinnes, *Union and Empire: The Making of the United Kingdom in 1707* (Cambridge, 2007), ch. 8. For other ideological dimensions, see John Robertson, 'An Elusive Sovereignty: The Course of the Union Debate in Scotland, 1698–1707', in Robertson, ed., *Union for Empire*; Clare Jackson, 'Conceptions of Nationhood in the Anglo-Scottish Union Debates of 1707', in Stewart J. Brown and Christopher A. Whatley, eds., *The Union of 1707: New Dimensions* (Edinburgh, 2008). For the development of print culture, see Alastair J. Mann, *The Scottish Book Trade, 1500–1720: Print Commerce and Print Control in Early Modern Scotland* (East Linton, 2000).

Scotland's attempt to colonize the territory. Making William shoulder the blame for the failure was useful to Jacobite propagandists, to unionists seeking compensation from England, and to the Company of Scotland, keen to bury the evidence of its own mismanagement. Compounding the gloom at the end of the decade, famine caused a mortality crisis and serious economic disruption. Graphic tales of the poor's suffering coloured later negative accounts of the period. It is important to remember how readily contemporaries linked natural disasters to national sins. While the Presbyterian establishment blamed the famine on epidemic immorality, Jacobites could portray harvest failures as God's punishment for the illegitimate Revolution and the abolition of episcopacy.[40]

Twentieth-century historians abandoned the Jacobitism and providentialism of the 'ill years' interpretation, but few sought to rehabilitate William's government. Indeed, many scholars have found the king guilty of neglecting Scotland. Preoccupied with European wars, it is argued, William devoted insufficient time to Scotland, misconstruing its political divisions and exacerbating its difficulties. This undermined his Scottish ministers, and the resulting policies could exasperate opinion south of the border, notably when the formation of the Company of Scotland provoked a hostile reaction from the English East India Company. The Crown's financial demands meant that William was more responsive to pressure groups in the City of London and Westminster than in Edinburgh. Before Darien, the tightening of the English Navigation Acts had already shown the union of the Crowns working against Scottish economic interests. And while William came to recognize that some reconfiguration of the Anglo-Scottish relationship was necessary, his death in 1702 prevented him from implementing further union.[41]

William's agenda was undoubtedly dominated by European politics and the English fiscal–military state. But it is misleading to claim that Scotland's problems in the 1690s resulted from royal neglect. Recent research on Secretary James Johnston and the Earl of Portland discredits Riley's view that Scottish politics was without sure management before the rise of the Duke of Queensberry in the late 1690s.[42] Likewise, scholars have shown that the government was forced to devote energy to managing Presbyterian expectations and the politics of the General Assembly.[43] Aside from its adverse effects on

[40] Allan I. Macinnes, 'William of Orange—"Disaster for Scotland"?', in Esther Mijers and David Onnekink, eds., *Redefining William III: The Impact of the King-Stadholder in International Context* (Aldershot, 2007); Christopher A. Whatley with Derek J. Patrick, *The Scots and the Union* (Edinburgh, 2006), ch. 4; Paul Hopkins, *Glencoe and the End of the Highland War* (Edinburgh, 1998); Douglas Watt, *The Price of Scotland: Darien, Union and the Wealth of Nations* (Edinburgh, 2007); Karen J. Cullen, Christopher A. Whatley, and Mary Young, 'King William's Ill Years: New Evidence on the Impact of Scarcity and Harvest Failure during the Crisis of the 1690s on Tayside', *SHR*, 85 (2006), 250–76; Karen J. Cullen, *Famine in Scotland: The 'Ill Years' of the 1690s* (Edinburgh, 2010).

[41] P. W. J. Riley, *King William and the Scottish Politicians* (Edinburgh, 1979); Macinnes, 'William of Orange'.

[42] Riley, *King William*; Mann, 'Inglorious Revolution', 131–40; David Onnekink, 'The Earl of Portland and Scotland (1689–1699): A Re-Evaluation of Williamite Policy', *SHR*, 85 (2006), 231–49.

[43] Ryan K. Frace, 'Religious Toleration in the Wake of Revolution: Scotland on the Eve of Enlightenment (1688–1710s)', *History*, 93 (2008), 355–75, at 368–74; Michael F. Graham, *The Blasphemies of Thomas Aikenhead: Boundaries of Belief on the Eve of the Enlightenment* (Edinburgh, 2008); Alasdair Raffe, 'Presbyterianism, Secularization, and Scottish Politics after the Revolution of 1688–90', *Historical Journal*, 53 (2010), 317–37.

overseas trade, however, the impact of war on Scottish society remains to be examined in detail.[44] And while recent scholars have recovered the political and religious principles behind support for the Williamite regime,[45] the culture of monarchy in the changed post-Revolution context calls for further study.

By emphasizing the ideologies of politics, historians can recover the partisanship of the period.[46] The main opposition groups in Parliament, the Club of 1689–90, and the Country Party that emerged in the late 1690s, contained their share of opportunists, but both groups raised important ideological questions about the Church, monarchy, and subjects' rights. By comparison with England, where the oath of allegiance to the Crown was initially more inclusive, the Scottish regime was ideologically narrow. More attention needs to be paid to the strategies of opposition adopted by politicians and clergy in this cultural context, ranging from the formation of alliances in St Germain-en-Laye and England to passive disobedience to new institutions and requirements.

A more fundamental and challenging task for historians of post-Revolution political culture is bridging the gulf between religion and high politics seen in the works of Namierite historians and teleological accounts of secularization. Religious debates were of at least as much significance after 1690 as before. Moreover, the partisanship of William's governments is most clear in their support for a Kirk that sought to overcome its episcopalian rivals, manipulating an account of the recent past that radically disavowed the religious policy of Charles II and James VII. Yet hardliners among the Presbyterian laity and clergy articulated a destabilizing critique of the Church's compromises with the post-Revolution regime. The re-established Kirk was doctrinally united, but differences over its political strategy began to set the scene for the eighteenth-century fragmentation of Presbyterianism.[47]

The re-emergence of Presbyterianism from 1687 changed the relationship between the Kirk and Scottish society in various ways that call for fresh research. The Restoration Church had retained kirk-sessions, in which lay elders helped to enforce parochial discipline. But where episcopacy was unpopular, men of sufficient standing were reluctant to serve. In these areas, the post-1687 Presbyterian kirk-sessions may have had a moral authority their episcopalian predecessors lacked, allowing for a more severe policing of the population. The General Assembly and its commission worried about episcopalian nonconformity and Catholicism, and its clergy paid more attention than had the bishops to campaigns against immorality, blasphemy, and heterodoxy. It is unclear, however,

---

[44]  But see Keith M. Brown, 'From Scottish Lords to British Officers: State Building, Elite Integration and the Army in the Seventeenth Century' and Bruce P. Lenman, 'Militia, Fencible Men, and Home Defence, 1660–1797', in Norman Macdougall, ed., *Scotland and War, AD 79–1918* (Edinburgh, 1991).

[45]  Whatley with Patrick, *Scots and the Union*.

[46]  See Derek Patrick's forthcoming study of Scotland under William and Mary; David Hayton, 'Traces of Party Politics in Early Eighteenth-Century Scottish Elections', *Parliamentary History*, 15 (1996), 74–99.

[47]  Raffe, 'Presbyterianism, Secularization, and Scottish Politics'; Colin Kidd, 'Conditional Britons: The Scots Covenanting Tradition and the Eighteenth-Century British State', *English Historical Review*, 117 (2002), 1,147–76.

to what extent Scotland participated in the movement for the reformation of manners, so important to post-Revolution Whig culture in England. There has been research on how the 'immoral' responded to ecclesiastical discipline, but too little is known about the place of religious minorities such as Catholics and Quakers in local communities.[48] Scotland's religious links with Ulster, reconfigured by the 1690 settlement, also require more study.[49]

A theme of long-term importance is the appointment of parish ministers. In July 1690 Parliament abolished the right of lay patrons to nominate clergy to vacant parishes, instead allowing elders and owners of heritable property to select candidates. This innovation was an affront to the nobility, and a source of conflict in numerous localities before the restoration of lay patronage in 1712. Although it may have been intended to secure the settlement by allowing Presbyterian congregations to call ministers of their liking, some episcopalian parishes used the 1690 legislation to frustrate Presbyterian control. Others resorted to violence not unlike that seen in the rabblings. While the Revolution sought a new balance in religious life between popular energies, clerical, and elite authority, its religious outcomes were untidy.

# 4

Was the Union settlement of 1707–12 a more decisive turning point than the Revolution of 1688–90? Before suggesting an answer, it will be helpful to return to the major political and religious problems outlined at the start of this chapter. What sorts of institutions would govern Scotland? What would be its constitutional relationship with its monarchs and with England? To what extent would the government try to sustain a uniform national Church in a religiously pluralist society?

Whiggish historians gave a simplistic account of the institutional changes of 1688–90 and 1707, based on teleological assumptions about the inevitability of union. Since the 1960s, historians have highlighted contingencies in the negotiation of the Union and its passage through Parliament, emphasizing that the 1707 settlement, though it was a reaction to political developments since 1688, was only one of numerous possible reactions. This underlines the value of seeing 1690–1707 as a period of uncertainties and possibilities, rather than as a

---

[48] Bill Inglis, 'The Impact of Episcopacy and Presbyterianism, before and after 1690, on one Parish: A Case Study of the Dunblane Kirk Session Minutes', *Records of the Scottish Church History Society*, 33 (2003), 35–61; Rosalind Mitchison and Leah Leneman, *Sexuality and Social Control: Scotland, 1660–1780* (Oxford, 1989); Graham, *Blasphemies of Thomas Aikenhead*. On the reformation of manners, see Craig Rose, 'Providence, Protestant Union and Godly Reformation in the 1690s', *Transactions of the Royal Historical Society*, 6th series, 3 (1993), 151–69.

[49] See John R. Young, 'Scotland and Ulster in the Seventeenth Century: The Movement of Peoples over the North Channel', in William Kelly and John R. Young, eds., *Ulster and Scotland, 1600–2000: History, Language and Identity* (Dublin, 2004).

prologue to the formation of the United Kingdom. Thus the Revolution was a major event, but one without clear answers to Scotland's political dilemmas. Any sense of finality surrounding the Union is misleading, and a movement to have the Act repealed nearly succeeded in 1713. Yet the Union settlement was a radical answer to the institutional questions in Scottish politics, providing a full stop and a change of paragraph.

Presbyterian and episcopalian histories both called the Revolution a religious turning point. But like the 'road to union' narrative, these interpretations depend too much on hindsight, obscuring the real uncertainties of religious life after 1690. Far from triumphant, the re-established Kirk was opposed in many areas of Scotland, maligned in print, and fearful for the survival of its privileged status. The Church's claims to autonomous religious authority conflicted with the Crown's Erastian pretensions, sparking controversies that dissipated only gradually under the Hanoverians. Particular tension surrounded the legacy of the National Covenant (1638) and the Solemn League and Covenant (1643), played down by cautious clergy though central to popular Presbyterianism. Not even the hegemony of Calvinist doctrine—to modern commentators, a key element of Scottish culture—seemed certain while Anglican moral theology and deist heterodoxy gained converts.[50]

Beyond the 'denominational' perspectives of Presbyterian and episcopalian history, the Revolution settlement looks still less like a set of answers to Scotland's religious problems. Protestant nonconformity had existed since the Cromwellian occupation. The 1680s was the last decade in which violent suppression was tried as a solution to religious diversity. But no legal toleration of worship outwith the established Church was enacted before 1712. Aside from statutes against irregular marriage and baptism, episcopalian dissenters were not subject to penal laws until after the Jacobite rising of 1715. Episcopalians benefited from periods of de facto toleration from 1690, but the Presbyterian commitment to a uniform religious establishment ensured that the position of dissenters was uncertain. Union with Anglican England, in which Protestant nonconformists had gained toleration in 1689, finally brought a solution to Scotland's problems of religious diversity (but not to the benefit of Catholics). The creation of a biconfessional state in 1707 weakened the principle of national uniformity, though it was the British Parliament's often intolerant Anglican majority that passed an Act for episcopalian toleration in 1712. Perhaps that date, and not 1690 or 1707, should be seen as the symbolic starting point of Scotland's modern religious history.

This chapter has suggested various agendas for reshaping late seventeenth- and early eighteenth-century Scottish and English political and religious history. By assessing the traditional narratives, scholars can offer new conceptual frameworks and periodizations. In the history of political and religious institutions, the Revolution and the Union will remain as thresholds or turning points. If broader social and cultural approaches to religion and politics are adopted, however, continuities and long-term changes may prove more important.

---

[50] Raffe, 'Presbyterianism, Secularization, and Scottish Politics'; Graham, *Blasphemies of Thomas Aikenhead*.

# FURTHER READING

Bowie, Karin, *Scottish Public Opinion and the Anglo-Scottish Union, 1699–1707* (Woodbridge, 2007).

Cowan, Ian B., *The Scottish Covenanters, 1660–88* (London, 1976).

Harris, Tim, *Restoration: Charles II and his Kingdoms* (London, 2005).

—— *Revolution: The Great Crisis of the British Monarchy, 1685–1720* (London, 2006).

Jackson, Clare, *Restoration Scotland, 1660–1690: Royalist Politics, Religion and Ideas* (Woodbridge, 2003).

Kidd, Colin, 'Religious Realignment Between the Restoration and Union', in John Robertson, ed., *A Union for Empire: Political Thought and the British Union of 1707* (Cambridge, 1995).

MacInnes, Allan I., *Union and Empire: The Making of the United Kingdom in 1707* (Cambridge, 2007).

MacIntosh, Gillian H., *The Scottish Parliament under Charles II, 1660–1685* (Edinburgh, 2007).

Mullan, David G., *Narratives of the Religious Self in Early-Modern Scotland* (Farnham, 2010).

Raffe, Alasdair, 'Presbyterianism, Secularization, and Scottish Politics after the Revolution of 1688–90', *Historical Journal*, 53 (2010), 317–37.

—— 'Presbyterians and Episcopalians: The Formation of Confessional Cultures in Scotland, 1660–1715', *English Historical Review*, 125 (2010), 570–98.

Riley, P. W. J., *King William and the Scottish Politicians* (Edinburgh, 1979).

Whatley, Christopher A., with Patrick, Derek J., *The Scots and the Union* (Edinburgh, 2006).

# CHAPTER 13

......................................................................................

# THE EARLY MODERN
# FAMILY

......................................................................................

## ELIZABETH EWAN

ON 25 July 2009 roughly eight thousand people from Scotland and its diaspora marched up Edinburgh's Royal Mile in 'The Parade of the Clans', a signature event of Scotland's 'Year of Homecoming'. Each group strode behind a banner bearing the name of the family or clan to which they claimed ancestral links. Although one can question the relevance of such images to modern Scotland, there was no denying the overwhelming pride and sense of belonging that such links gave participants. Indeed, clan and family ties are among the most recognized aspects of 'Scottishness' around the world.

But what do we know about the historic Scottish family, as opposed to images largely based on nineteenth-century traditions. Perhaps because of the popularity of clan roots among modern diaspora Scots and the resulting association with 'tartanism', most historians have tended to focus their research elsewhere. While family history has flourished in those other areas since the 1980s, Scottish studies, especially of the pre-modern family, have only recently begun to appear, despite earlier calls for such work.[1]

The importance of studying the family lies not just in itself but in what it can reveal about society as a whole. The family is often seen as essentially private in contrast to the public world of politics, economics, religion, and culture. However, this sharp public–private divide does not work in practice. Families were critical in shaping people who participated in public life, as well as those with lives less visible to historians. It was in families that 'values were taught, learning initiated, spiritual well-being nourished, bodily health cared for and social order established'.[2]

---

[1] T. C. Smout, *A Century of the Scottish People* (London, 1986), 292. See now 'Introduction' and 'Guide to Further Reading' in E. Ewan and J. Nugent, eds., *Finding the Family in Medieval and Early Modern Scotland* (Aldershot, 2008), 1–8, 175–80; Women in Scottish History, www.womeninscottish history.org

[2] Ewan and Nugent, 'Introduction', 8. See also Eleanor Gordon, 'The Family', in L. Abrams et al., eds., *Gender in Scottish History Since 1700* (Edinburgh, 2006), 235–67.

This chapter surveys recent work, examines the current state of knowledge and some central debates, and suggests directions for future research. In the early modern period, most families were part of a larger household of co-residents, including parents, children, servants, apprentices, and sometimes other kin. The major focus here is on the nuclear family unit of parents and children, but the chapter will explore briefly the family's place in the wider context of kinship and society.

Although Scottish family history is a fairly new field, the tradition of histories of individual families goes back to medieval times. Genealogical histories have been an important source for the history of highland families in particular. Histories of noble families proliferated in the seventeenth century; the nineteenth century saw the lavish family histories produced by Sir William Fraser. Fraser's volumes, containing many primary sources, continue to be a rich mine for historians. Recently, studies of families such as the Campbells have placed them firmly in their contemporary context, while studies of monarchs have illuminated the workings of families at the very highest echelons of power.[3]

Much impetus for European family history came from the rise of social history. Studies of population and family reconstitution encouraged research into family history in the 1970s and 1980s. Demographic work in Scotland resulted in the 1977 *Scottish Population History*, still essential for early modern historians, although it begins in the seventeenth century.[4] One topic arising out of this work was illegitimacy. A description of Scotland as 'the classic country of illegitimacy' spurred research by Rosalind Mitchison and Leah Leneman, who pioneered the use of kirk-session records for such studies. Their work focused on the period after 1660, but recently earlier records have been used extensively for both quantitative and qualitative research.[5]

Related to illegitimacy studies were explorations of Scottish forms of marriage, including the prevalence of irregular marriage.[6] The darker aspects of illegitimacy were explored in studies of infanticide, although mainly after 1690.[7] Other aspects included divorce, marriage litigation, and domestic abuse. There has been debate over how much

[3] David Allan, '"What's in a Name"? Pedigree and Propaganda in Seventeenth-Century Scotland', in E. Cowan and R. J. Finlay, eds., *Scottish History: The Power of the Past* (Edinburgh, 2002), 147–8; Keith Brown, *Noble Society in Scotland* (Edinburgh, 2000); Steve Boardman, *The Campbells 1250–1513* (Edinburgh, 2006); *The Stewart Dynasty in Scotland* series, 7 vols. (Edinburgh, 1982–2006).

[4] M. Flinn et al., *Scottish Population History: From the Seventeenth Century to the 1930s* (Cambridge, 1977).

[5] Peter Laslett, 'Introduction', in P. Laslett et al., eds., *Bastardy and its Comparative History* (Cambridge, 1980), 41; R. Mitchison and L. Leneman, *Sexuality and Social Control* (Oxford, 1989); *Sin in the City* (Edinburgh, 1998); Michael Graham, *The Uses of Reform* (Leiden, 1996); Margo Todd, *The Culture of Protestantism in Early Modern Scotland* (New Haven, 2002); Janay Nugent, 'Marriage Matters: Evidence of the Kirk Session Records of Scotland, c.1560–1650' (unpublished PhD thesis, University of Guelph, 2004).

[6] T. C. Smout, 'Scottish Marriage, Regular and Irregular 1500–1940', in R. B. Outhwaite, ed., *Marriage and Society* (New York, 1981), 204–36; W. D. H. Sellar, 'Marriage, Divorce and the Forbidden Degrees', in W. N. Osborough, ed., *Explorations in Law and History* (Dublin, 1995), 59–82.

[7] Deborah Symonds, *Weep Not for Me* (University Park, 1997).

the Protestant Reformation of 1559–60 changed marriage practices and the extent to which Reformed Church teachings were accepted by the general population.

The 1980s saw a growing interest in women's history, with Rosalind Marshall's survey of women's lives, *Virgins and Viragos*, and Christina Larner's study of the witch-hunt, *Enemies of God*, which began the flourishing field of witch-hunt studies in Scotland.[8] Marshall's work, especially, had much to say about the family. The relationship between women's history and family history has sometimes been awkward as many early historians of women resisted the idea that women were primarily defined by their familial roles and focused on women's lives outside the family. However, recent work has recognized the significance of the patriarchal structure of the early modern family for both women's and men's lives and for the formation of gender identity, while work on the 'marital economy' has brought together insights into gender and family history.[9] Recognizing the family's importance to political life has further broken down barriers between the study of 'public' and 'private' life. The most extensive recent studies have been of the elite, but there has also been increasing interest in those comprising the majority of the population, both rural and urban.[10]

As the site of the most intimate of human relationships, the family leaves few written records. Rising to this challenge, historians have used a wide variety of traditional and less traditional sources, especially to learn more about non-elite families, people less likely to produce the documents and correspondence that have proven such a fertile source for the elite. Such sources include archaeological sources, ballads, material culture, tombstones, architecture, and literary works.[11]

In medieval Scotland, marriage was a sacrament, the only one always conferred by the laity rather than the clergy (baptism of infants by laypeople being allowed if death was imminent). The central element was the free consent of the parties involved. Marriage was created by the partners exchanging vows in the present tense ('I marry you'), or words in the future tense, if the relationship was later consummated. Although the Reformation ended the sacramental nature of marriage, the centrality of consent remained and many characteristics of medieval marriage continued. Partners could marry without a clergyman and without witnesses; although such marriages were considered irregular, and discouraged by the Kirk, they were recognized as valid

---

[8] Rosalind Marshall, *Virgins and Viragos: A History of Women in Scotland from 1080 to 1980* (London, 1983); Christina Larner, *Enemies of God: The Witch-Hunt in Scotland* (Baltimore, 1981); Julian Goodare, ed., *The Scottish Witch-Hunt in Context* (Manchester, 2002); Brian Levack, *Witch-Hunting in Scotland* (New York, 2008).

[9] Megan Doolittle, 'Close Relations? Bringing Together Gender and Family in English History', *Gender & History*, 11, no. 3 (November 1999), 542–54; Gordon, 'The Family', 235–7; Amy Erickson and Maria Ågren, eds., *The Marital Economy in Scandinavia and Britain 1400–1900* (Aldershot, 2005).

[10] Jenny Wormald, 'Bloodfeud, Kindred and Government in Early Modern Scotland', *Past and Present*, 87 (May 1980), 54–97; Keith Brown, *Bloodfeud in Scotland 1573–1625* (Edinburgh, 1986); Brown, *Noble Society*; Maureen M. Meikle, *A British Frontier?* (East Linton, 2004); Alison Cathcart, *Kinship and Clientage* (Leiden, 2006); Margaret H. B. Sanderson, *A Kindly Place?* (East Linton, 2002); *Scottish Rural Society in the Sixteenth Century* (Edinburgh, 1982).

[11] See essays in Ewan and Nugent, eds., *Finding the Family*.

until 1939. Problems arose if one partner contested the validity and there were no witnesses to swear to the marriage. In 1516 Jonet Mur attempted to block the marriage of Laurence Scot and Isabella Montgomery by arguing that she had already contracted with Laurence.[12]

Girls could legally marry at twelve, boys at fourteen. Many elite children, especially girls, married in their teens. Parents often arranged future marriages for underage children, especially in royal families. Recent work in Europe has suggested that actual child marriages were not as common as once thought, and were largely restricted to elite families, where marriages commonly sealed political or economic alliances. Although more research is needed, it appears most lowland Scots followed the north-west European family model of life-cycle service, relatively late marriage in the twenties, fairly close age of bride and groom, and the formation of nuclear households. Highland girls may have married earlier, and possibly more women remained unmarried, a reminder that demographic regimes could vary within Scotland.[13]

To marry legally, partners could not be already married or contracted and, in the pre-Reformation period, they could not be related within four or fewer degrees of consanguinity, that is, share a common great-great grandparent. The medieval Church also included relationships through affinity (marriage), spiritual affinity (godparentship), and previous sexual relationships, making it likely that potential partners would be related, especially among the small Scottish elite. Wealthy families purchased dispensations from Rome; an added advantage was that if a marriage was unsuccessful, it was often possible to discover a 'previously unrecognized' degree of consanguinity and have the marriage annulled. The Reformed Church reduced the forbidden degrees so that even first cousins could marry; however, incest laws were criminalized in 1567, and confusion over what precisely constituted 'incest' meant several people paid with their lives before the law was clarified in 1709.[14]

There is debate about the role of parents in making marriages. In Scotland, unlike many other countries, parental consent never became a legal requirement. In elite families, however, where property and political power were closely tied to marriage alliances, parents usually played a crucial role in arranging children's matches. If an elite child was orphaned, the king could grant wardship and right of marriage to a guardian. Some children rejected the choices of their parents or guardians. Margaret, daughter of Lord Ruthven, refused to marry John Oliphant, to whom her parents had betrothed her as a child, 'because she had no carnal affection for him'.[15] There may have been increasing freedom of choice by the later seventeenth century. The role of parents in other families

[12] Gavin Ros, *Protocol Book 1512–1532* (Edinburgh, 1907), no. 148; Sellar, 'Marriage and Forbidden Degrees', 59–70.

[13] Ewan and Nugent, 'Introduction', 1–2; R. A. Houston, *The Population History of Britain and Ireland, 1500–1750* (Cambridge, 1995), 2–3, 6.

[14] Sellar, 'Marriage and Forbidden Degrees', 72–82; B. Levack, 'The Prosecution of Sexual Crimes in Early Eighteenth-Century Scotland', *Scottish Historical Review*, 89, no. 2 (October 2010), 173–7, 186–90.

[15] H. Paton and G. Donaldson, eds., *The Protocol Book of James Young* (Edinburgh, 1941–52), no. 704.

is less clear; studies elsewhere have suggested that young people of the middling and lower social groups, who often left for work in their teens, exercised more independent choice as they were away from home, had accumulated goods of their own, and had a wider range of possible partners. Ballads show young people exercising such choice, although some tales emphasize the tragic consequences.[16] Not everyone took advantage of this freedom. In 1527 Alexander Black sold his right to choose a marriage partner to David Wedderburn in return for £20 and said he would accept any woman David chose, so long as she was free from disease, especially syphilis, and of honourable character, no matter how blind or lame she was.[17]

Regular marriage involved several steps. The first was betrothal, or handfasting. Often betrothal followed hard negotiations between the couple's parents (or sometimes the couple themselves) over the marriage contract. Although most common among the elite, where extensive property was involved, contracts were used quite far down the social scale. They stipulated the contribution made by the bride's family in goods and property, which constituted her tocher (dowry); many also set out the groom's contribution, which formed the wife's terce (dower) if she was widowed. If no provision was made for her, a widow was entitled to a third of her husband's goods. More study is needed, but work on noble marriages suggests that, as elsewhere in Europe, tochers were rising in this period, and that the relative value of the terce to the tocher was decreasing, implying that power lay increasingly with the groom's family.[18]

There has been controversy about handfasting, with some arguing it was a form of trial marriage. This idea is generally rejected, although some have argued for the existence of a form of trial marriage, at least in the highland areas.[19] Following betrothal, banns were proclaimed on three successive Sundays to ensure there were no known impediments. Before 1560 the wedding took place at the church door, after which the party entered the church for a nuptial Mass. After the Reformation, the wedding took place within the church. In both cases, the conclusion of the wedding ceremony was the signal for community celebration and feasting. Both Kirk and Parliament tried to limit these celebrations, but such attempts were generally unsuccessful.[20]

Most marriages ended with the death of one spouse. Under medieval Church law, marriages were indissoluble. They could only be annulled as invalid from the start. Some historians have argued that attitudes to the permanence of marriage were more relaxed in Scotland than elsewhere, perhaps as a result of Celtic influences, and that annulment

---

[16] Katie Barclay, ' "And Four Years Space, being Man and Wife, they Loveingly Agreed": Balladry and Early Modern Understandings of Marriage', in Ewan and Nugent, eds., *Finding the Family*, 23–34.

[17] Dundee City Archives, Dundee Protocol Book, fo. 92.

[18] Brown, *Noble Society*, 76–9. For negotiations, see J. Dawson, ed., *Campbell Letters 1559–1583* (Edinburgh, 1997), 28–34.

[19] Christine Peters, *Women in Early Modern Britain, 1450–1640* (Basingstoke, 2004), 8–10. See D. Sellar, 'The Family', in E. J. Cowan and L. Henderson, eds., *Everyday Life in Medieval Scotland* (Edinburgh, 2011), 96, 100, 103–4.

[20] J. Nugent and M. Clark, 'A Loaded Plate: Food Symbolism and the Early Modern Scottish Household', *Journal of Scottish Historical Studies*, 30, no. 1 (2010), 48–54.

was used more commonly than in many countries, but more research is needed.[21] Separation of bed and board was allowed in certain instances, primarily adultery, but neither partner could remarry until the death of the other spouse. Following the Reformation, divorce was allowed on the grounds of adultery or desertion (Scotland being one of the earliest countries to allow the latter as a ground for divorce); a new study reveals how the early commissary court dealt with such cases.[22] In Scotland, unlike England where formal divorce was the preserve of the elite, couples quite far down the social scale instigated divorce proceedings. Some spouses were quite determined. Margaret Millok of St Andrews attempted to have her marriage to John Gyb annulled on the ground of his impotency in April 1562; when this failed, she reversed her claims of impotency and successfully divorced him for adultery.[23] It is likely more informal divorces also occurred.

Upon marriage, a woman's legal status changed although a man's did not.[24] Although she kept her own surname, a wife lost her independent legal persona and came under her husband's authority. He decided where they lived. Under the *jus mariti*, he gained most of the moveable property a woman brought to marriage, except for her paraphernalia that included her personal clothing and jewellery. The *jus mariti* had both advantages and disadvantages for him, for he also became responsible for any debts his wife contracted before marriage.

A wife's heritable estate came under her husband's administration by the *jus administrationis*, although he did not own it. At her death it passed to her heir, although if she predeceased her husband but had borne a living child, even if it died shortly afterwards, her husband enjoyed the *courtesy*, rights to the rents of the property for life. Although he was not supposed to alienate such property without his wife's consent, if he did she could not reclaim it until after his death. A wife could not make a will without her husband's consent. However, contemporary jurists expected husbands to give consent and in practice many wives bequeathed the property that would have come to them as a widow. While wives' rights appear very limited, recent studies have stressed the difference between theory and practice, demonstrating how legal restrictions were frequently circumvented. It has also been argued that the courts, particularly the kirk-sessions, were

---

[21] Ishbel Barnes, *Janet Kennedy, Royal Mistress* (Edinburgh, 2007), 1–2, 85–6; Domhnaill Uilleam Stiubhart, 'Women and Gender in the Early Modern Western Gàidhealtachd', in E. Ewan and M. M. Meikle, eds., *Women in Scotland c.1100–c.1750* (East Linton, 1999), 236–7; Jane Dawson, 'The Noble and the Bastard: The Earl of Argyll and the Law of Divorce in Reformation Scotland', in J. Goodare and A. A. MacDonald, eds., *Sixteenth-Century Scotland* (Leiden, 2008), 152–3; Sellar, 'The Family', 95–6, 98–9.

[22] Thomas Green, 'The Court of the Commissaries of Edinburgh: Consistorial Law and Litigation, 1559–1576' (unpublished PhD thesis, University of Edinburgh, 2010).

[23] *Register of the Minister. Elder and Deacons of the Christian Congregation of St Andrews*, 2 vols. (Edinburgh, 1848–1931), vol. i, 153–6. See also J. Nugent, ' "None must meddle betuene man and wife": Assessing Family and the Fluidity of Public and Private in Early Modern Scotland', *Journal of Family History*, 35 no. 3 (2010), 221, 227; L. Leneman, *Alienated Affections* (Edinburgh, 1998).

[24] A. D. M. Forte, 'Some Aspects of the Law of Marriage in Scotland: 1500–1700', in E. Craik, ed., *Marriage and Property* (Aberdeen, 1985), 104–18.

regarded as allies by wives attempting to resolve domestic disputes, although the extent to which such courts were 'gender-blind' has been debated.[25]

The law supported the existence of a patriarchal household, but how did patriarchy work in practice? As elsewhere in Europe, advice literature and role models such as the virgin martyrs and Mary stressed that wives should be chaste and obedient and unquestioningly accept their husbands' authority.[26] The extent to which women followed this advice is debatable and the issue of power relations within the family requires further research. Literary sources suggest that assertive wives were well known, even if many figures have to be treated with caution as the creations of male authors. Travellers commented on the strong characters of Scottish wives, the Spanish ambassador to James IV's court stating that they were 'absolute mistresses of their houses, and even of their husbands'.[27] Moreover, patriarchy imposed restrictions on husbands as well as wives. An adult man's masculinity was defined by his ability to properly govern and provide for a household; a marriage contract for John Murray and Marion Loutfit in 1539 stated that it was John's responsibility 'to entertain her at board, bed and rightful requisites as becomes a husband to a wife'. The honour and reputation of both sexes were tied to family.[28]

Sometimes the household head's power of correction over family members was abused. As Alison Calland complained in 1561, her husband should 'not bear empire above me as a tyrant'.[29] The seventeenth-century Privy Council records included several complaints by women of domestic abuse, and kirk-sessions often mediated in such cases. Domestic abuse was often hidden behind the walls of the family home, and authorities were reluctant to interfere with a husband's authority within his own family; cases of abuse and discord appear in the records mainly when private behaviour became public, and disturbed the community beyond the household's walls, such as when a Stirling couple kept their neighbours awake all night with their quarrelling.[30]

Gauging affection between spouses is difficult, but there is evidence of real trust and affection in marriages. Some beautiful Gaelic women's verse spoke of the poet's love for her husband. Aithbhreac Inghean Coirceadaill lamented her husband's death: 'Oh rosary that woke my tears,/beloved the finger that on you did lie,/beloved the kindly

[25] Winifred Coutts, 'Wife and Widow: The Evidence of Testaments and Marriage Contracts', in Ewan and Meikle, eds., *Women in Scotland*, 176–86; Michael Graham, 'Women and the Church Courts in Reformation Era Scotland', in ibid., 187–8; Todd, *Culture of Protestantism*, 275–91. Cf. Gordon DesBrisay, 'Twisted by Definition: Women under Godly Discipline in Seventeenth-Century Scottish Towns', in Y. V. Galloway and R. Ferguson, eds., *Twisted Sisters: Women, Crime and Deviance in Scotland Since 1400* (East Linton, 2002), 137–55.

[26] Audrey-Beth Fitch, 'Power through Purity: The Virgin Martyrs and Women's Salvation in Pre-Reformation Scotland', in Ewan and Meikle, eds., *Women in Scotland*, 16–28.

[27] Pedro de Ayala in P. Hume Brown, ed., *Early Travellers in Scotland* (Edinburgh, 1891), 47.

[28] Robert Rollok, *Protocol Book 1534–1552* (Edinburgh, 1931), no. 141; E. Ewan, '"Many Injurious Words": Defamation and Gender in Late Medieval Scotland', in R. A. McDonald, ed., *History, Literature and Music in Scotland, 700–1560* (Toronto, 2002), 163–86.

[29] *Register of the Minister*, vol. i, 63–4.

[30] *Extracts from the Records of the Royal Burgh of Stirling AD 1519–1666* (Glasgow, 1887), 18. See also Nugent, "None must meddle", 223, 226.

generous heart/that you belonged to until tonight.'[31] Letters often included terms of endearment, as did even some more formal documents such as property transactions and testaments. In pre-Reformation Scotland, it was common to arrange prayers to be said for one's soul after death to decrease time in Purgatory, and these obit foundations often specified others, especially spouses, whom the donor wished to benefit as well. John Crummy, an Edinburgh burgess who had taken his family to Linlithgow in 1530 to escape the plague, paid £5 to arrange Masses for the souls of his wife and children, all of whom had succumbed.[32] The specification of burial place might also indicate affection for a spouse, especially if the person had married more than once. From the seventeenth century there are increasing numbers of surviving gravestone epitaphs; many indicate the attributes that spouses valued in each other.

A wife could not sell property, sue in courts, or make contracts without her husband's consent. She was only entitled to take independent actions where these involved providing necessities for the family, as manager of the household. However, women's frequent appearance in court and their active role in the economy suggest the husband's consent was usually forthcoming, not surprising as the wife's actions were generally for the spouses' joint benefit. Most marriages were very much partnerships. A family was crucial to supporting men's position in society. This was especially true in economic terms. Wives' economic contributions are obscured in records that identify only the male household head, but the emergence of widows carrying on their husband's occupations after their death suggests the role they played as wives. Wives were frequently executors for their husbands. In landowning families, wives managed estates while husbands were involved in politics, in exile, or at war. In merchant families, the wife's role was sometimes visible when a husband was absent.[33] As Bartholomew Glendunwyne said before going overseas, 'the goods that I have and the debts that are owing to me, the said Margaret [Gordon] my spouse knows'.[34] In peasant families, the gendered division of labour was suggested by the poem, 'The Wife of Auchtermuchty', in which the husband proved totally incapable in his efforts to take on his wife's tasks when the couple swapped duties, but the work of both was crucial to the household's survival.

By law, a husband was responsible for his wife's debts, but court records often cite the names of both spouses in debt cases, suggesting the debt was the woman's. In Aberdeen in the 1680s, the wife's name is sometimes recorded first. The practice of identifying wives helps elucidate the active role of married women in commerce, a role obscured in countries such as England where a wife's debt is almost always recorded under her husband's name.[35]

[31] C. Kerrigan, *An Anthology of Scottish Women Poets* (Edinburgh, 1991), 53.

[32] J. Beveridge and James Russell, eds., *Protocol Books of Dominus Thomas Johnsoun* (Edinburgh, 1920), no. 18.

[33] Helen Dingwall, 'The Power Behind the Merchant? Women and the Economy in Late Seventeenth-Century Edinburgh', in Ewan and Meikle, eds., *Women in Scotland*, 152–62.

[34] Paton and Donaldson, eds., *Protocol Book of James Young*, no. 1242.

[35] Gordon DesBrisay and Karen Sander Thomson, 'Crediting Wives: Married Women and Debt Litigation in the Seventeenth Century', in Ewan and Nugent, eds., *Finding the Family*, 85–98.

A late seventeenth-century Edinburgh gravestone recounts how Marjorie Brodie 'kept her shop' and 'did for her Husband's credit'; the latter perhaps referred to his reputation as much as his financial well-being, but the two are connected.[36] Urban women often acted as shopkeepers, looking after the retail part of the business. They were also involved in the production process in crafts such as bonnet-making. Many craft guilds recognized the role of wives and daughters in the craft and protected the employment of female family members, even when discriminating against other women in the trade.[37]

Women also contributed to the marital economy by undertaking supplementary work. Many jobs were related to skills learned in preparation for running a household, such as brewing ale, renting rooms, moneylending, wet-nursing, and providing child-care.[38] In some English towns, wives were legally able to carry on separate businesses from their husbands under 'femme sole' status. Although the term was apparently not used in Scotland, evidence exists of wives carrying on separate occupations from their husbands.

There is debate over the extent to which women's paid work was an extension of domestic duties. Possibly most wives carried on different work from their husbands in towns such as Edinburgh by the late seventeenth and eighteenth centuries, and their input should be seen as mutual rather than supplementary, but further research is needed, especially for the earlier period.[39] Women's training possibly suited them more than men to undertaking different activities, as they were less likely to have been trained through a specialized apprenticeship. Although a few were apprenticed, most spent their teenage years in domestic service and possibly learned something of the skills of various crafts, skills later used for a variety of wage-earning occupations. The marital economy relied on the work of all members of a household, married couple, servants, and children.

Both the Catholic and the Reformed Church taught that a primary purpose of marriage was the procreation of children. The history of childhood is a rapidly growing field,[40] although there is much to be done on Scotland. A recent study of the nobility included a section on children, and David Mullan's publications on religious autobiography have made available those sources in which seventeenth-century adults reflect on

---

[36] R. Monteith, *Theater of Mortality* (Edinburgh, 1704), 40.

[37] Marshall, *Virgins*, 52.

[38] N. Mayhew, 'The Status of Women and the Brewing of Ale in Medieval Aberdeen', *Review of Scottish Culture*, 10 (1996–7), 16–21; C. Spence, 'Women and Business in Sixteenth-Century Edinburgh', *Journal of Scottish Historical Studies*, 28, no. 1 (2008), 1–19.

[39] Elizabeth Sanderson, *Women and Work in Eighteenth-Century Edinburgh* (London, 1996), 74–6, 108–25; R. A Houston, *Social Change in the Age of Enlightenment* (Oxford, 1994), 78–91; E. Ewan, 'For Whatever Ales Ye: Women as Producers and Consumers in Late Medieval Scottish Towns', in Ewan and Meikle, eds., *Women in Scotland*, 125–36; R. A. Houston, 'Women in the Economy and Society of Scotland 1500–1800', in R. Houston and I. Whyte, eds., *Scottish Society 1500–1800* (Cambridge, 1989), 118–47.

[40] Margaret L. King, 'Concepts of Childhood: What We Know and Where We Might Go', *Renaissance Quarterly*, 60 (2007), 371–407.

their own experiences of childhood and those of their children.[41] The seventeenth century saw the publication of several accounts of pious children, perhaps due to a religious milieu that gave unusual attention to the words of the less powerful members of society. One does wonder, though, what the playmates of the Fife child Emilia Geddie thought when she rebuked them for breaking the Sabbath and reminded them that 'tho' we be but bairns, yet we must die.'[42]

Childbirth was fraught with dangers for mother and child. The trepidation mothers felt can be glimpsed in women's letters. Lilias Grant, writing to her mother of her pregnancy, hoped for a maternal visit before she was in danger of death.[43] The period was marked by high maternal and infant mortality. The law of courtesy encompassed the possibility of mother or child dying in childbirth, as it applied even if the child died shortly afterwards. The fact that the child had to be heard to cry suggests that men remained outside the birthing chamber and supports other evidence that childbirth was an all-female occasion, with the mother attended by a midwife and close female relatives and friends.[44]

A major debate has been the impact of the frequent loss of children on parent–child relations. Family historians have responded to earlier work that painted a picture of rather cold emotionless families in the medieval and early modern period, gradually giving way to more affectionate companionate marriages in the eighteenth century. The family's emotional life is its most hidden aspect, but recent work has revealed the deep affection parents and children could feel for each other, and the grief that parents felt over the loss of their offspring. Reverend James Melville's neighbour told him how when he was a child his father 'would ley me down on my back, pleying with me'. In 1596 the Stirling Presbytery acknowledged the devastating loss mothers felt on a child's death when it petitioned the General Assembly to let mothers who accidentally smothered their infants suffer a less public penalty of repentance than nurses, as it feared the mothers might 'be swallowed up with over great heaviness'.[45] Family correspondence also reveals real concern for children. Of course, not all families were happy. High levels of mortality meant it was common for children to experience the loss of at least one parent, and blended families, formed by the remarriage of a widowed parent, were perhaps as usual as today. The resulting tensions can be seen in testaments that tried to forestall any arguments over property between children of a first marriage and a second spouse and children from that marriage.

Following birth, it was common, especially in wealthier families, to employ wet-nurses, although some argued that mothers should nurse their own children. Live-in wet-nurses were commonly employed by the elite; for less wealthy families, wet-nursing

---

[41] Brown, *Noble Society*, ch. 7; David Mullan, *Narratives of the Religious Self in Early-Modern Scotland* (Aldershot, 2010); David Mullan, ed., *Women's Life-Writing in Early Modern Scotland* (Aldershot, 2003).

[42] Mullan, *Narratives*, 172.

[43] Marshall, *Virgins*, 106.

[44] My thanks to David Sellar for discussion of this point.

[45] Mullan, *Narratives*, 147–51; Rev. James Melville in J. G. Fyfe, ed., *Scottish Diaries and Memoirs 1550–1746* (Stirling, 1928), 83; NAS, Stirling Presbytery Records, CH2/722/3, fo. 4r.

might involve sending their children away to the wet-nurse's home, although recent research has suggested that at least some families brought wet-nurses to live with them. Single women in seventeenth-century Aberdeen, for example, fined by the kirk-session for bearing illegitimate children, paid their fines through employment as live-in wet-nurses for urban families.[46]

Shortly after birth the baby was baptized. If the child was in danger of imminent death, baptism could be carried out by the midwife. Baptism not only welcomed the child into the Christian community, but also extended family alliances and connections through the choice of godparents.[47] Mothers did not usually attend the baptism as it was so close to the birth, but there were celebrations of her first upsitting after the birth, and her churching, her first attendance at the kirk. The latter occasion especially could be the scene of much festivity and drinking, to the dismay of local kirk-sessions.

The early childhood years are the most obscure, perhaps because these were when mothers had the most responsibility for upbringing. Fathers in post-Reformation Scotland were expected to provide their offspring with religious education, leading family prayers every day, with the children being examined on religious doctrine by the kirk.[48] Sometimes children were fostered or boarded out. Fostering was quite common among the highland elite; many children and foster-parents formed strong bonds, the emotions of some foster-mothers being preserved in poetry.[49] It does not seem to have been so common to send children away in the Lowlands, although children might be boarded out if their own mothers were unable to care for them.

Parents' responsibilities included providing guidance to their children. While early modern Scotland did not produce the many conduct books offering advice on proper behaviour found elsewhere, literate audiences probably had access to some of these works. Some parents and guardians, including James VI, committed their advice to paper, providing evidence on how children were regarded and how their parents and guardians thought they ought to behave (as opposed to how they actually behaved). Others weighed in with advice to the young kings who came to the throne in the later fifteenth and sixteenth centuries—poets and theologians offered instruction on how to become both a good man and a good monarch.[50] Some writers, such as the minister James Kirkwood, author of *The True Interest of Families* (1690), offered advice to both parents and children.

---

[46] Gordon DesBrisay, 'Wet Nurses and Unwed Mothers in Seventeenth-Century Aberdeen', in Ewan and Meikle, eds., *Women in Scotland*, 210–20; Mullan, *Narratives*, 151–4.

[47] Jane E. A. Dawson, ' "There is Nothing Like a Good Gossip": Baptism, Kinship and Alliance in Early Modern Scotland', in C. J. Kay and M. A. MacKay, eds., *Perspectives on the Older Scottish Tongue* (Edinburgh, 2005), 38–47; Melissa Hollander, 'The Name of the Father: Baptism and the Social Construction of Fatherhood in Early Modern Edinburgh', in Ewan and Nugent, eds., *Finding the Family*, 63–72.

[48] Nugent, "None must meddle", 221–2.

[49] Alison Cathcart, *Kinship and Clientage*, 80–5; Anne C. Frater, 'Women of the Gaidhealtachd and their Songs to 1750', in Ewan and Meikle, eds., *Women in Scotland*, 74–6.

[50] Joanna Martin, *Kingship and Love in Scottish Poetry, 1424–1540* (Aldershot, 2008); Allan, 'Pedigree and Propaganda', 150–2.

There is debate over whether early modern individuals experienced adolescence; however, most historians recognize a period of transition between childhood and adulthood.[51] For many, the early teens were marked by moving away from home, with boys being apprenticed, attending school or university, or becoming agricultural servants, and girls going into domestic service. Apprenticeship contracts were occasionally recorded in town court registers. Apprentices, servants, and employers appeared in court to settle disputes over wages or conditions of service. University records and statutes shed some light on student life. A code of behaviour issued for Marischal College students in Aberdeen prohibited abusive language, frequenting taverns, and playing card games, although a student there in the 1650s remembered his student life involving most of these activities.[52]

University and apprenticeship were two ways in which boys were socialized into adult masculinity. For elite boys, military training was an important part of becoming an adult, although perhaps decreasingly so as military skills became less central to aristocratic identity. Other aspects of youthful masculinity were found where exuberance boiled over into disorder and resulted in miscreants coming before the local courts. Around Christmas 1586 Adam Elphinstoun and his young cronies kept Glasgow awake all night with riotous celebrations in the street, played with a horse's head, and were likely the culprits who placed the dead animal's bones at the minister's gate.[53] Recent studies of masculinity have discussed its two extreme forms, aggressiveness and self-control. Young men were socialized to control their passions and become responsible heads of households. While the Reformation, with its stress on the godly household, may have intensified this moral message, similar expectations existed in the late medieval period.[54]

For girls, records of servant contracts and testaments provide glimpses into the world of domestic service. Probably 10 per cent of girls were employed in service in the four largest towns in the later seventeenth century. The position of domestic servants needs more investigation; some studies have stressed the negative aspects, especially their vulnerability to sexual exploitation by males in the household (servants being a high proportion of those coming before the kirk-session for bearing illegitimate children), while others have pointed out the positive aspects of service, which could give girls some independence, allow them to build up dowries, and provide choice in the selection of spouses.[55]

---

[51] Konrad Eisenbichler, ed., *The Pre-Modern Teenager* (Toronto, 2002).

[52] Mullan, *Narratives*, 185.

[53] Glasgow City Archives, St Mungo's Kirk Session, CH2/550/1, 115–29 *passim*. See also the example in J. J. McGavin, 'The Kirk, The Burgh and Fun', *Early Theatre*, 1 (1998), 15–22.

[54] Alexandra Shepard, 'From Anxious Patriarch to Refined Gentleman? Manhood in Britain circa 1500–1700', *Journal of British Studies*, 44, no. 2 (April 2005), 281–95; Derek Neal, *The Masculine Self in Late Medieval England* (Chicago, 2008).

[55] DesBrisay, 'Wet Nurses and Unwed Mothers', 212–15; E. Ewan, 'Mistresses of Themselves: Domestic Servants and By-Employments in Sixteenth-Century Scottish Towns', in A. Fauve Chamoux, ed., *Domestic Service and the Formation of European Identity* (Bern, 2004), 411–14.

Families were not isolated units, but interacted with other parts of society. Some of their closest relationships were with kin. Scotland is traditionally seen as a country where kinship ties remained strong much later than in some other European countries (and indeed, in its modern manifestation of clan societies, remain strong, if in a more artificial form). Anthropological approaches have added much to the understanding of the role of kinship. The work of Jenny Wormald on bonds of manrent, Keith Brown on bloodfeud, and Robert Dodgshon on clanship has explored ties of blood and marriage, looking for comparisons to contemporary European as well as to anthropological evidence. Kinship ties have been explored for lairdly families in the Borders. Kinship could mean as much or as little as people wanted it to mean.[56] Kinship ties below the nobility have been less explored, but sources exist; for example, notaries' protocol books, registers of deeds, and testaments that record connections between kin have been relatively untapped.

Recent European work has pointed out that 'kinship' might mean different things in different aspects of life. For example, while inheritance practices may have become more patrilineal and restricted to the senior male line in the late medieval and early modern period, for political purposes kinship was often defined more broadly, bringing together all those of a surname who had normally had little practical contact with one another. The stress on 'surname' in documents suggests a similar pattern in Scotland. Alison Cathcart's work has highlighted how fictive as well as 'blood' kinship played an important role in the strategies of highland families. Cathcart and others have also demonstrated the importance of marital alliances in the long-term strategies of families, raising questions about the strength of marriage ties compared to other types of bonds between families.[57]

Scattered family branches might be brought together by forging a vision of a shared past. Genealogies and family histories were important tools in reinforcing links between family members distanced by migration or marriage. The production of such histories increased in the seventeenth century, partly as a result of the need to establish status in the wider aristocratic world that focused on the Scottish king's court in London after 1603, and also against new families coming to prominence through royal service. Families such as the Maitlands also cooperated to produce household books of poetry and other writings, which preserved their memory among their descendants.[58]

Was there a sense of lineage and family history below the elite? Cynthia Neville has shown how oral memory preserved medieval traditions of ancestral rights to property among even small landholders.[59] A similar study for the early modern period might

---

[56] Jenny Wormald, *Lords and Men in Scotland* (Edinburgh, 1985); Brown, *Bloodfeud*; R. Dodgshon, *From Chiefs to Landlords* (Edinburgh, 1998); Meikle, *A British Frontier?*, 25. See also Sellar, 'The Family', 91–5.

[57] D. W Sabean, S. Teuscher, and J. Mathieu, eds., *Kinship in Europe* (New York, 2007); Cathcart, *Kinship and Clientage*, 99–112.

[58] Allan, 'Pedigree and Propaganda', 147–67. My thanks to Joanna Martin for this point.

[59] C. J. Neville, 'Finding the Family in the Charters of Medieval Scotland, 1150–1350', in Ewan and Nugent, eds., *Finding the Family*, 11–22.

reveal whether the disruption to traditional landholding caused by the feuing movement of the later fifteenth and sixteenth centuries resulted in a diminution of such senses of ancestry. Patterns of medieval obit foundations reveal family connections with particular altars over the generations. In some, a sense of lineage and the importance of the wider family is shown in the request that the officiating priest be chosen from among those of the founder's surname or family.[60] Requests for burials in family vaults or burial plots also suggest a sense of continuity with the past.

Families existed within communities. Regarded by secular and religious authorities as the fundamental unit of society, they were subject to supervision and interference by their neighbours, Church, and State. Although the door and walls of the home symbolized a division between a private and a public world, in practice boundaries were very permeable. The Church recognized the home as a place of private worship led by the male household head, but occasionally attempted to replace a father as the family's leader of religious instruction if it regarded him as negligent. Kirk-sessions intervened in marital disputes and quarrels between families, while all community members were expected to maintain surveillance over their neighbours' behaviour. Court records, especially witch-hunt documents, have revealed tensions simmering both within families and between households.[61]

Families responded to external pressures and events, although individuals might react in different ways. Changing economic conditions saw members migrating elsewhere for employment; recent work has emphasized the mobility of the population, both within and outside Scotland. Such migration not only affected the host community but also the families left behind.[62] A family's prosperity could vary over the life course, depending on such variables as the number of dependent children. Rosalind Mitchison's work on poor relief has provided a basis for work on family strategies for coping with poverty. Recent studies have examined how families reacted to famine and to dislocations caused by the witch-hunt.[63] The early modern period, marked by frequent visitations of plague, food shortages, and warfare, provides an excellent context in which to examine how families reacted to crises.

[60] Mairi Cowan, 'The Spiritual Ties of Kinship in Pre-Reformation Scotland', in Ewan and Nugent, eds., *Finding the Family*, 120–1.

[61] Nugent, "None must meddle", 219–26; Lauren Martin, 'Witchcraft and Family: What Can Witchcraft Documents Tell Us About Early Modern Scottish Life' *Scottish Tradition*, 27 (2002), 7–22; L. Martin, 'The Witch, the Household and the Community' in J. Goodare, ed., *Scottish Witches and Witch-Hunters* (forthcoming); Scott Moir, 'The Crucible: Witchcraft and the Experience of Family in Early Modern Scotland', in Ewan and Nugent, eds., *Finding the Family*, 49–59; J. R. D. Falconer, 'A Family Affair: Households, Misbehaving and the Community in Sixteenth-Century Aberdeen', in ibid., 139–50.

[62] Ian D. Whyte and Kathleen A. Whyte, 'The Geographical Mobility of Women in Early Modern Scotland', in Leah Leneman, ed., *Perspectives in Scottish Social History* (Aberdeen, 1988), 83–106.

[63] Rosalind Mitchison, *The Old Poor Law in Scotland* (Edinburgh, 2000); Karen Cullen, 'The Famine of the 1690s and its Aftermath: Survival and Recovery of the Family', in Ewan and Nugent, eds., *Finding the Family*, 151–62; Moir, 'The Crucible'.

The family was central to people's understandings of their world. The family was used as a metaphor in the expression of political ideas and ambitions, from the Union of the Crowns of 1603 to the idea of the monarch as father of the realm. The family itself was a little commonwealth, with the father head of state. Marriage was central to politics, forging alliances between Scotland and other countries, ending (or attempting to end) feuds between warring families, being used to reward loyal service to a monarch, and influencing court factions and loyalties in wartime. The family fostered culture in all its forms. Elite families patronized artists, musicians, writers, and architects, while families at all levels passed on stories, songs, games, and pastimes, which made up the period's vibrant oral and traditional culture.[64]

Not everyone lived in families, although often substitutes for families existed. An unbalanced sex ratio in towns left many women unmarried; both secular and religious authorities attempted to ensure they entered domestic service and were included in a household. The Edinburgh authorities enacted laws against women living alone in the 1530s, and the kirk-sessions of Stirling and Glasgow similarly cracked down in the 1590s.[65] More research is needed on the experience of single women, including mothers of illegitimate children after their appearance on the penitent stool. Before the Reformation, secular clergy were required to be celibate (although in practice concubinage was widely practised). Did ideas about the masculinity of the clergy change when they, like their parishioners, could marry? Medieval monks, nuns, and friars lived apart from families, although the terminology of religious houses (mother prioress, father abbot) emphasized the nature of the institution as a substitute family. Many nuns continued contact with their natal families, and succession to religious offices was often a family affair.[66]

Where should the study of the family go from here? As the family intersects with every aspect of early modern society, there are many different directions in which research can proceed. The following are only a few suggestions.

Although family reconstitution is difficult because of patchy records, it is possible to reconstruct a good part of those local communities that have kirk-session records, court records, protocol books, and/or testaments. Such work explores how the web of family and kin connections affected community life. It sheds light on the relative importance of agnatic and cognatic kinship. Studies of families over several generations reveal changing strategies as they face new circumstances. Such local studies reveal regional differences, and they benefit from cooperation with the ranks of enthusiastic genealogists researching their family trees.

---

[64] Dolly MacKinnon, '"I have now a book of songs of her writing": Scottish Families, Orality, Literacy and the Transmission of Musical Culture c.1500–c.1800', in Ewan and Nugent, eds., *Finding the Family*, 35–48; Mark Hall, 'Playtime Everyday: The Material Culture of Medieval Gaming', in Cowan and Henderson, eds., *Everyday Life*, 145–68.

[65] *Extracts from the Records of the Burgh of Edinburgh 1528–1557* (Edinburgh, 1871), 27, 40; NAS, Holyrude Kirk Session CH2/1026/1/2, 3–31 *passim*; CH2/550/1, 347.

[66] Kimm Curran, 'Religious Women and their Communities in Late Medieval Scotland' (unpublished PhD thesis, University of Glasgow, 2006).

Studies of material culture through surviving objects, archaeological evidence, literary sources, and testaments can shed light on families' daily activities, gender roles, and standards of living. Recent work elsewhere has begun to examine the symbolic meanings of household items. How such articles were used or passed on casts light on their meaning to their owners. For example, food and its consumption often had ritualistic meaning.[67] Sumptuary laws showed how clothing indicated status. The ways in which families stamped their personalities on their homes, for example through the use of marriage lintels, can also be examined. House plans reveal how families functioned and the gendered use of space. Maps and cartographic evidence combined with archaeological and documentary evidence build up a picture of settlements and the environment in which people lived. The insights of environmental history can also contribute to such studies.

Many written sources can be re-examined for evidence by asking new questions. Women's writings, including autobiographies and biographies, commonplace books, correspondence, and poetry, could be particularly valuable.[68] Research has revealed the value of witchcraft depositions for the history of the family; other local and central court records can also shed light on family roles, expectations, and networks. Such sources can be interrogated for what they say about gender roles and expected behaviour, and how these intersect with the family. For example, witness testimony and insults provide insights into honour and reputation for men and women, and show how closely connected these were with family and household.

Finally, studies of the Scottish family should continue to engage with family history research elsewhere. Two recent syntheses of the current state of research on the early modern Scottish family have appeared in studies of women in Britain.[69] Both include some misconceptions about the nature of early modern Scottish society, especially about the ubiquity of clanship, but this should not detract from the value of their comparative research and the questions they raise. Scottish family history has much to contribute to the study of the early modern family throughout Europe. A good start has been made and the way forward looks promising indeed.

## FURTHER READING

Brown, Keith, *Noble Society in Scotland* (Edinburgh, 2000).

Cathcart, Alison, *Kinship and Clientage* (Leiden, 2006).

Ewan, E., and Meikle, M. M., eds., *Women in Scotland c.1100–c.1750* (East Linton, 1999).

—— and Nugent, J., eds., *Finding the Family in Medieval and Early Modern Scotland* (Aldershot, 2008).

[67] Nugent and Clark, 'A Loaded Plate', 43–63.

[68] Suzanne Trill, 'Early Modern Women's Writing in the Edinburgh Archives, *c.*1550–1740', in S. Dunnigan et al., eds., *Woman and the Feminine in Medieval and Early Modern Scottish Writing* (Basingstoke, 2004), 201–25; Mullan, *Women's Life-Writing*.

[69] Peters, *Women in Early Modern Britain*; Rosemary O'Day, *Women's Agency in Early Modern Britain and the American Colonies* (Harlow, 2007).

Forte, A. D. M., 'Some Aspects of the Law of Marriage in Scotland: 1500–1700', in E. Craik, ed., *Marriage and Property* (Aberdeen, 1985), 104–18.

Marshall, Rosalind, *Virgins and Viragos: A History of Women in Scotland 1080–1980* (London, 1983).

Martin, Lauren, 'Witchcraft and Family: What Can Witchcraft Documents Tell Us About Early Modern Scottish Life?', *Scottish Tradition*, 27 (2002), 7–22.

Meikle, Maureen M., *A British Frontier?* (East Linton, 2004).

Mitchison, Rosalind, and Leneman, Leah, *Sexuality and Social Control* (Oxford, 1989).

Mullan, David G., *Narratives of the Religious Self in Early-Modern Scotland* (Aldershot, 2010).

Nugent, Janay, '"None must meddle betueene man and wife": Assessing Family and the Fluidity of Public and Private in Early Modern Scotland', *Journal of Family History*, 35, no. 3 (2010), 219–31.

Sanderson, Margaret H. B., *A Kindly Place? Living in Sixteenth-Century Scotland* (East Linton, 2002).

Sellar, David, 'The Family', in E. J. Cowan and L. Henderson, eds., *Everyday Life in Medieval Scotland* (Edinburgh, 2011).

Smout, T. C., 'Scottish Marriage, Regular and Irregular 1500–1940', in R. B. Outhwaite, ed., *Marriage and Society* (Oxford, 1981), 204–36.

Todd, Margo, *The Culture of Protestantism in Early Modern Scotland* (New Haven, 2002).

# CHAPTER 14

·············································································

# THE SEVENTEENTH-CENTURY IRISH CONNECTION

·············································································

## PATRICK FITZGERALD

ANY exploration of the waves of migration and bonds of association that have characterized the historic relationship between Scotland and Ireland must begin with a consideration of the physical geographical context within which this human history was played
out. Firstly, let us consider the North Channel, the body of water, no more than 22 kilo-
metres at its narrowest point, that lies between the tip of the Kintyre peninsula and Torr
Head on the north Antrim coast. Even today those who regularly traverse this 'narrow
sea' talk in the vernacular idiom about going 'ower the sheugh', a sheugh in Irish meaning a field drainage ditch and thereby emphasizing the limited impediment to contact.
This perspective may be widened out to accommodate a view of the entire body of the
Irish Sea as acting over the *longue durée* as an inland sea or inland waterway, a bridge to
coastal cultural contact rather than a barrier.[1] Half a millennium ago travel by sea across
this channel could prove easier than the equivalent trip on land. As one recent historian
of Ulster and the Isles at this time observes, 'the culture of the region was a maritime
one; the sea was its plastic foundation in transport, livelihood, even poetic idiom'.[2]

In 1995 Graham Walker entitled a survey of political and cultural interaction between
Scotland and Ulster, *Intimate Strangers*. He reminds us at the outset, in an overview of
the longer-term historical relationship, of the problematic nature of Scottish settlement
in Ulster from the early seventeenth century.[3] The extent to which the Scots could
establish and sustain intimate relations in Ireland, with natives and other newcomers,
or find this 'new world' forever 'the land of the stranger', remains a central and unresolved question. Viewing the outcomes of migration as a three-element process, can we
determine over time the extent to which Scots in Ireland leant towards segregation,

---

[1] D. Brett, *A Book Around the Irish Sea: History Without Nations* (Dublin, 2009), 14–15.
[2] S. Kingston, *Ulster and the Isles in the Fifteenth Century: The Lordship of the Clann Domhnaill of
Antrim* (Dublin, 2004), 19.
[3] G. Walker, *Intimate Strangers: Political and Cultural Interaction Between Scotland and Ulster in
Modern Times* (Edinburgh, 1995), 1.

integration, or modulation between the two polarities? Could they, in other words, remain intimate yet strangers, living together and living apart, simultaneously?[4]

## 1600–10: A Decade of Transformation

The accession in March 1603 of James VI of Scotland to the English throne as James I served to affect a significant transformation in how Scottish migration to Ireland was viewed from London or Dublin. In short, what had consistently been regarded as part of the problem came to be seen as a potential part of the solution. In the opening years of his reign James was preoccupied with sustaining peace, keeping expenditure down, exercising patronage, and promoting a real constitutional union. We should not, however, underestimate the new king's conservative inclinations.[5] If, looking forward, we can discern how Plantation Ulster might come to be viewed as 'a laboratory for Empire', we can also, with a contemporary eye, see how colonization in the Scottish Isles in the preceding decade had served as 'a laboratory for Ulster'.[6]

The 'wisest fool in christendom' was sufficiently canny to learn from the Scottish experience that the private enterprise of gentlemen adventurers might progress his agenda most efficiently. The murky negotiations surrounding Conn O'Neill's release from imprisonment in Carrickfergus Castle, under pardon in the summer of 1604, opened an early door for experimentation in Ulster. Hugh Montgomery (1560–1636) and James Hamilton (c.1560–1644), two Scottish favourites of the king, with roots in the same area of south-west Scotland, gained sizeable landed footholds in north Down.[7] From 1605 on, their endeavours, in close conjunction with the king, amply demonstrated how two men with means and ability could draw upon accessible estates in the Scottish Lowlands to develop and people what Michael Perceval-Maxwell describes as 'a sort of Scottish Pale'.[8] These initiatives would come to represent both a key precedent and practical bridgehead for later, more ambitious colonization.

---

[4]  P. Fitzgerald and B. Lambkin, *Migration in Irish History, 1607–2007* (Basingstoke, 2008), 62–8; A. Ford, 'Living Together, Living Apart: Sectarianism in Early Modern Ireland', in A. Ford and J. McCafferty, eds., *The Origins of Sectarianism in Early Modern Ireland* (Cambridge, 2005), 13.

[5]  J. Wormald, 'High Politics: A Very British Problem: The Stuart Crown and the Plantation of Ulster', in *History Ireland*, 17 (2009), no. 3, 20–3.

[6]  J. H. Ohlmeyer, '"Civilizinge of those Rude Partes": Colonization within Britain and Ireland, 1580s–1640s', in N. Canny, ed., *The Origins of Empire: The Oxford History of the British Empire*, 5 vols. (Oxford, 1998), vol. 1, 124–47. 'Laboratory for Empire' was the subtitle deployed for a series of three academic conferences held in London, Derry, and Dublin in 2009 to mark the 400th anniversary of the Ulster Plantation.

[7]  M. Perceval-Maxwell, *The Scottish Migration to Ulster in the Reign of James I* (London, 1973), 46–60. A comprehensive entry relating to James Hamilton can be found in the *Dictionary of Irish Biography* (Cambridge, 2009), vol. 4, 397–9. Somewhat surprisingly, there is no equivalent entry for Hugh Montgomery.

[8]  Ibid., 56.

In north Antrim, Randall MacDonnell, son and heir to Sorley Boy MacDonnell and future first Earl of Antrim, was also actively engaged in sponsoring the migration and settlement of lowland Scots. Here, an individual fulfilling a role much closer to that of the traditional Gaelic chieftain and retaining personal allegiance to Catholicism, sought to attract Protestant Scots as tenants to his Ulster estate.[9] Recent archaeological excavations in the vicinity of MacDonnell's primary seat at Dunluce Castle, on the north Antrim coast, cast a fascinating fresh light on the precocious efforts of one native landholder to avoid debt and embrace urbanization, a commercial market economy, and estate improvement.[10] Here Lord Deputy Chichester and the Dublin government were more directly engaged in developments, and new Scottish migrants tended to occupy fortified posts, mixing in amongst their former native inhabitants.[11] The different patterns of colonization described above dominated the debate that presaged the Official Plantation of the six escheated counties, which would follow in the wake of the flight of the earls of Tyrone and Tyrconnell in 1607.

# 1610–50

If the year 1603 altered the context of relations between the three kingdoms, the year 1607 and the departure of the earls of Tyrone and Tyrconnell for the Continent confirmed the potential for dramatic acceleration in the pace and scope of British colonization in Ulster. By 1610 the way had been clearly marked for the Crown's direct involvement in the most ambitious Plantation scheme yet undertaken in Ireland, indeed one might add, anywhere in the early modern world. The records of the Privy Council in London, as the body that did most to shape the scheme, have not survived for this period, which makes it difficult for historians to reconstruct the planning process confidently. We know that the king himself came to take a very direct personal interest in the project, and it has been suggested that it may have been Chichester, once so implacably opposed to any Scottish involvement in Ulster, who stimulated the king's enthusiasm by signalling the potential inclusion of Scots alongside English planters.[12] There is insufficient space here to rehearse the precise mechanisms by which over half a million acres in the six escheated counties of Armagh, Cavan, Coleraine (renamed

[9] J. H. Ohlmeyer, *Civil War and Restoration in the Three Stuart Kingdoms: The Career of Randal MacDonnell, Marquis of Antrim* (Dublin, 2001), 18–48; *Dictionary of Irish National Biography* (Cambridge, 2009), vol. 5, 959–63.

[10] A summary of the excavation findings is available at www.science.ulster.ac.uk/esri/Excavations-at-Dunluce-Castle.html

[11] Perceval-Maxwell, *Scottish Migration*, 67.

[12] R. Gillespie, 'Planned Migration to Ireland in the Seventeenth Century', in P. J. Duffy, ed., *To and From Ireland: Planned Migration Schemes c.1600–2000* (Dublin, 2004), 24; N. Canny, *Making Ireland British, 1580–1650* (Oxford, 2001), 192.

Londonderry), Donegal, Fermanagh, and Tyrone came by 1640 to hold a British population of more than twenty thousand souls.[13] The involvement of the Scots gave the
Plantation of Ulster a distinctive character in comparison with previous plantation
schemes outside Ulster, such as those in the counties of Leix and Offaly in the Irish
Midlands, embarked upon in the 1540s, and the larger-scale effort to plant the province
of Munster after 1583 and the defeat of the Desmond rebellion. Rather than migrants
from Scotland merely supplementing migrants from England and Wales in Ulster after
1610, the Scots came to predominate within the settler population. By 1640 settlers from
Scotland probably made up something like two-thirds of the British population within
the six escheated counties. Within the eastern counties of Antrim and Down, with its
firm pre-1610 base for development, the Scots proportion was more likely to be three-
quarters or more.[14]

In the initial stages of the Plantation scheme the mass of Scots migrants crossing to
Ulster to take up leases tended to be drawn to those 'undertakers' allotted estates, with
baronies reserved for Scottish grantees. Over time, however, the agency exercised by
individual migrants within Ulster became clear, as tenants moved in search of the most
favourable lease or economic opportunity. The phenomenon of 'colonial spread', by
which settlers penetrated inland from the ports of entry, particularly along river valleys,
did not respect official boundaries, and soon the counties bordering Ulster were becoming subject to plantation or simply informal migration and settlement by speculators
and tenants. In this sense, for Scots settlers the idea of an expanding frontier, moving
gradually south and west, must have seemed real enough. Counties such as Louth,
Monaghan, Longford, and Leitrim, and the western province of Connacht, were soon
open to planters moving in from the north and east.[15] Thus, the port town of Sligo with
its strong medieval tradition of maritime trade and surrounded by significant timber
resources, was an obvious magnet to Scots settlers who had been granted less fertile and
more remote land in west Ulster. Therefore, during the course of the seventeenth century, Sligo town in Connacht rather than Ulster, became one of the most Scottish urban
centres in Ireland.[16]

---

[13]  Population estimates offered here are based on those presented by W. MacAfee, 'The Population of
Ulster, 1630–1841: Evidence from Mid-Ulster' (unpublished D.Phil. thesis, University of Ulster, 1987),
vol. 2, 344. Detailed accounts of the Plantation in Ulster include P. Robinson, *The Plantation of Ulster:
British Settlement in an Irish Landscape, 1600–1670* (Dublin, 1984); R. Gillespie, *Colonial Ulster: The
Settlement of East Ulster, 1600–1641* (Cork, 1985); Perceval-Maxwell, *Scottish Migration*; Canny, *Making
Ireland British*.

[14]  S. J. Connolly, *Contested Island: Ireland 1460–1630* (Oxford, 2007), 302.

[15]  Robinson, *The Plantation of Ulster*, 116–19; Canny, *Making Ireland British*, 362–89; L. Kennedy, K. A.
Miller, and M. Graham, 'The Long Retreat: Protestants, Economy and Society, 1660–1926', in R. Gillespie
and G. Moran, eds., *Longford: Essays in County History* (Dublin, 1991), 31–61; B. MacCuarta, 'The
Plantation of Leitrim, 1620–41', in *Irish Historical Studies*, xxxii, no. 27, 2001, 297–320.

[16]  M. O'Dowd, *Power, Politics & Land: Early Modern Sligo, 1568–1688* (Belfast, 1991), 152, 160–4;
P. Fitzgerald, 'Scottish Migration to Ireland in the Seventeenth Century', in A. Grosjean and S.
Murdoch, eds., *Scottish Communities Abroad in the Early Modern Period* (Leiden, 2005), 43–8.

Before progressing much further it is important to return across the North Channel in order to view developments from a Scottish rather than an Irish perspective. In adopting this approach it is worth noting two contemporary trends, which have served to place greater emphasis upon migrants' Scottish origins and to recognize the role of plantation in Ulster within the context of early modern Scottish history and the emergence of a Scottish diaspora. In relation to the former, we should acknowledge the large body of research undertaken by individuals in pursuit of family history. Increasing numbers of those who may see themselves as being of Ulster-Scots or Scotch-Irish lineage have pursued their genealogies back across the North Channel.[17] The extent to which any of this research has so far influenced academic history is debatable, but the increasing digitization of records and the pursuit of an essentially prosopographical or collective biographical approach by historians may allow all of this data to bear fruit in the future. One specific yet central issue upon which such research could cumulatively shed light is the issue of 'to and fro' migration, particularly attempting to establish the proportion of Scots migrants in the 1650s or 1690s, in particular, who were earlier refugees from Ireland now returning west.[18] In relation to the second of these trends we can point to an increasing awareness of developments in Ulster within Scottish historiography. Two publications from the 1960s, J. D. Mackie's *History of Scotland* (1964) and T. C. Smout's *History of the Scottish People, 1560–1830* (1969), reveal single fleeting references to the Ulster Plantation in both instances. Although only beginning in 1700, T. M. Devine's *Scottish Nation* (1999) acknowledges the significance of seventeenth-century migration to Ireland in the Foreword and reveals the relevance of the ongoing relationship throughout the volume. The same author's *Scottish Empire, 1600–1815* (2003) devotes an entire chapter to migration to Ulster and subsequent transatlantic migration by Ulster Scots.[19] Finally, we should acknowledge as a further marker in this direction a conference organized by Dr John Young at the University of Strathclyde in September 2010, which specifically explored Scotland and the Ulster Plantation on the occasion of its 400th anniversary.

In considering the specific geographical origins of migrants from Scotland to Ulster in the reign of James I and VI, the obvious contrast to be drawn with what had gone before was the reorientation away from the Western Isles and Highlands and towards the Scottish Lowlands. Whilst some have sought to nuance this characterization of the

---

[17] See for example W. J. Roulston, *Researching Scots-Irish Ancestors: The Essential Genealogical Guide to Early Modern Ulster, 1600–1800* (Belfast, 2005); D. Dobson, *Scotland During the Plantation of Ulster: The Peoples of Dumfries and Galloway, 1600–1699* (Baltimore, MD, 2008).

[18] J. Agnew, *Belfast Merchant Families in the Seventeenth Century* (Dublin, 1996); J. Ohlmeyer, 'Scottish Peers in Seventeenth-Century Ireland'—I am grateful to Prof. Ohlmeyer for providing me with a copy of this paper prior to its publication in D. Edwards and M. Ó Siochrú, eds., *Scots in Early Modern Ireland* (Manchester, forthcoming). Note also The Irish in Europe Project, which may be consulted at www.irishineurope.com.

[19] J. D. Mackie, *A History of Scotland* (Harmondsworth, 1964), 190; T. C. Smout, *A History of the Scottish People, 1560–1830* (Bungay, Suffolk, 1969); T. M Devine, *The Scottish Nation, 1700–2000* (London, 1999), xxi; T. M. Devine, *Scotland's Empire, 1600–1815* (London, 2003), 140–63.

migration and highlight successful highland planters, there can be no denying the pre-dominance of those drawn from south-west Scotland and the Border counties within the migration stream to Ulster after 1603.[20] Not surprisingly, the great majority of such migrants were Protestant and this fact was obviously central to the civilizing and security imperative behind the scheme and the Crown's promotion of it. However, there were exceptions such as occurred within the barony of Strabane in County Tyrone, where the Hamiltons (of Renfrewshire) oversaw the settlement of sizeable numbers of Scots tenantry who shared their Catholicism. In County Cavan, Sir Alexander Gordon, on a somewhat smaller scale, established a Catholic Scots enclave in the vicinity of Kilmore.[21] The plantation theory that the native Irish could be converted to Protestantism and 'civilized' by following the example set by model planters was most glaringly flouted by the migration, both forced and voluntary, which brought members of the notorious riding clans of the lawless Anglo-Scottish Borders to Ulster. Here, the desire to establish order in the Scottish Borders took precedence over any reform agenda in Plantation Ireland and added into the mix of British settlers taking up lands in western counties such as Fermanagh, nominally Catholic and notoriously violent members of border reiving families such as Armstrong, Graham, Johnston, and Elliott.[22]

From a contemporary popular perspective, of course, the predominant result of the Plantation of Ulster was religious transformation, making Ulster the only Irish province with a genuinely substantial Protestant population and more distinctively still a substantial Presbyterian community, largely but not exclusively associated with Scottish ethnicity. In Ulster from 1610, however, we are confronted by what Sean Connolly describes as a 'hybrid ecclesiastical structure', which sustained a 'distinctive Scottish enclave' including four Scottish bishops and over sixty ministers within the pre-1640 Church of Ireland in Ulster.[23] During the reign of James I and VI the space and latitude that permitted such accommodation began gradually to decline, and events in 1625, following James's death in March and Charles I's accession, exposed the growing tensions. In the summer of that year a spirit of religious revival convulsed the area of the Six Mile Water river valley in south Antrim, with significant numbers of settlers coming to hear the preaching of the Scots minister James Glendinning.[24] More liturgically conservative

[20]   J. M. Hill, 'The Scottish Plantations in Ulster to 1625: A Reinterpretation', in *Journal of British Studies*, xxxii (1993), 24–43; Perceval-Maxwell, *Scottish Migration*, 252–89.

[21]   B. MacCuarta, *Catholic Revival in the North of Ireland, 1603–41* (Dublin, 2007), 100–7; R. J. Hunter, *The Plantation in Ulster in Strabane Barony, Co Tyrone, 1600–41* (Coleraine, 1982); J. Dooher and M. Kennedy, eds., *The Fair River Valley: Strabane Through the Ages* (Belfast, 2000), 57–80, 317–18; B. MacCuarta, 'Catholic Revival in Kilmore Diocese, 1603–41', in B. Scott, ed., *Culture and Society in Early Modern Breifne/Cavan* (Dublin, 2009), 168; D. Edwards, 'A Haven of Popery: English Catholic Migration to Ireland in the Age of Plantations', in A. Ford and J. MacCafferty, eds., *The Origins of Sectarianism in Early Modern Ireland* (Cambridge, 2005), 119.

[22]   Perceval-Maxwell, *Scottish Migration*, 284–5; R. Bell, 'Sheep Stealers from the North of England: The Riding Clans in Ulster', in *History Ireland* (1994), vol. 2, no. 4, 25–9.

[23]   Connolly, *Contested Island*, 355–6.

[24]   M. J. Westerkamp, *Triumph of the Laity: Scots-Irish Piety and the Great Awakening, 1625–1760* (New York, 1988), 23–6.

elements within the Church of Ireland reacted negatively to these open-air communions and the display of religious enthusiasm. The succession of Charles had only served
to stoke the fires of faction as he sought to augment the powers of the episcopate, and
promote Laudianism and Arminian doctrines, which were anathema to many clergy
and laity in Ulster and Scotland. The conflict culminated in 1638 when the Lord Deputy,
Thomas Wentworth, introduced the so-called 'Black Oath' to secure obedience to the
king and denounce the principles of the national Covenant drawn up in Scotland and
signed by thousands earlier that year. Rather than sign, significant numbers of Scots settlers departed Ulster and returned to Scotland. At this juncture Wentworth may well
have reflected upon the initial caution his predecessor Chichester had expressed at the
beginning of the century with respect to Scottish migration into Ulster.[25] In 1640 there
thus remained significant distance between English and Scots settlers in Ulster, and not
only on issues of religion. Marianne Elliott concludes that 'the early Scots settlers were
closer to their Irish counterparts, in dress, work practices and housing, than to the
English'.[26]

The extent to which the particular migration stream towards Ulster is appreciated as
an integral part of the early modern Scottish diaspora and understood is significantly
more advanced than was the case a generation ago. This appreciation, however, remains
greater in Scotland itself than in Ulster. One fragmentary piece of material evidence,
from recent excavations conducted at the MacDonnell seat of Dunluce Castle on the
north Antrim coast, serves to illustrate the point.[27] Here archaeologists unearthed a late
sixteenth-century Polish coin, which signposts the significantly greater flow of migrants
from early seventeenth-century Scotland directed east across the North Sea towards
Scandinavia, the Baltic states, and beyond. A pioneering essay by Smout, Landsman,
and Devine in the early 1990s estimated that the number of migrants leaving Scotland
for Scandinavia and Poland-Lithuania during the first half of the century (between fifty-
five thousand and seventy thousand) was more than double the total moving from
Scotland to Ireland (between twenty thousand and thirty thousand).[28] As might be
anticipated, migrants from eastern Scotland were more strongly oriented towards
northern and eastern Europe than those from the west, but Steve Murdoch, who has
developed research in this area, has pointed to diasporic interconnections. Malcolm
Hamilton, born at Kilbirnie in north Ayrshire in the 1570s, was allotted two thousand
acres at Monea, in County Fermanagh, during the Ulster Plantation. Two of his sons,
Hugh and Lewis, went on in the 1620s to serve as officers in the Swedish Army. Enobled
as barons Hamilton of Deserf, they ultimately returned to Fermanagh with their

---

[25] J. Bardon, *A History of Ulster* (Belfast, 1992), 132–4, provides a narrative account of events, whilst
J. McCafferty, *The Reconstruction of the Church of Ireland; Bishop Bramhall and the Laudian Reforms,
1633–1641* (Cambridge, 2007), fleshes out the broader context.

[26] M. Elliott, *The Catholics of Ulster: A History* (London, 2000), 128.

[27] See www.science.ulster.ac.uk/esri/Excavations-at-Dunluce-Castle.html.

[28] T. C. Smout, N. C. Landsman, and T. M. Devine, 'Scottish Emigration in the Seventeenth and
Eighteenth Centuries', in N. Canny, ed., *Europeans on the Move: Studies in European Migration,
1500–1800* (Oxford, 1994), 85.

Swedish families in 1662 and one of Lewis's sons, Gustavus, distinguished himself as Governor of Enniskillen during the Williamite war of 1689–91.[29]

Comparison between the Scottish migration flows to Ireland and northern Europe during this half-century also throws into relief a critically important factor in terms of the endurance of any immigrant ethnic community—the gender balance of the migration flow. Whilst there were women amongst the migration flow to Europe, the preponderance of pedlars and military recruits fashioned a predominantly male migration, which intermarried into the host societies frequently and integrated relatively easily. This served to promote a significant level of 'ethnic fade' within second and third generations.[30] It remains difficult to be precise about the gender balance within the migration flow to Ireland. Nicholas Canny, in relation to the Scots, suggests that there were 'probably three women for every four men who made the journey to Ulster'. It certainly seems likely that women were more strongly represented within the settler population as time progressed, and we know that the short crossing allowed some men to return to their homeland to secure a wife.[31]

One historian, in pursuing a prosopographical study of the Scottish peers in seventeenth-century Ireland, was able to probe the issue of ethnicity in relation to the choice of marriage partner. Jane Ohlmeyer, in examining thirty-four marriages where the geographical origin of the bride was known, found that whereas Irish and English brides were taken in the early decades of the seventeenth century, Scottish women predominated. However, after mid-century, peers of Scottish origin came to show a marked preference for Irish or English brides, indicating a second- and third-generation preference for establishing marriage alliances in Ireland rather than looking back to Scotland. In addition, Scottish peers in Ulster were increasingly, as the century wore on, selecting their own estates in Ireland as their place of burial rather than choosing a final resting place in Scotland. Intermarriage between Scottish settlers and the native Irish also occurred further down the social scale, particularly in those areas where the newcomers were most densely concentrated and, perhaps, more frequently after the initial phase of settlement. The original conception by those who planned Plantation, that Irish and British populations should be segregated from each other as far as possible, proved impossible to enforce. Certainly the majority of male deponents who testified to their losses after the rising of October 1641 recorded their marriage to wives who also originated in Britain.[32] As the new society in Plantation Ulster bedded down, more Scots

---

[29]  S. Murdoch, 'The Scots and Ulster in the Seventeenth Century: A Scandinavian Perspective', in W. Kelly and J. R. Young, eds., *Ulster and Scotland, 1600–2000: History, Heritage and Identity* (Dublin, 2004), 85–104; S. Murdoch, 'Irish Entrepreneurs and Sweden in the First Half of the Eighteenth Century', in T. O'Connor and M. A. Lyons, eds., *Irish Communities in Early-Modern Europe* (Dublin, 2006), 353.

[30]  Devine, *Scotland's Empire*, 23–4; Grosjean and Murdoch eds., *Scottish Communities Abroad*.

[31]  Canny, *Making Ireland British*, 211–12; M. O'Dowd, *A History of Women in Ireland, 1500–1800* (Harlow, 2005), 94–6.

[32]  Ohlmeyer, 'Scottish Peers in Seventeenth-Century Ireland', in Edwards and Ó Siochrú, eds., *Scots in Early Modern Ireland*; Elliott, *The Catholics of Ulster*, 130–1; Robinson, *The Plantation of Ulster*, 186–8; O'Dowd, *History of Women in Ireland*, 94–6.

married partners whose origins lay in England or Wales, but there is little evidence to challenge the view that most married within the Scots ethnic group. Even allowing for peaceful cultural transfer and mixing in Ireland, some contrast with Scots military and mercantile migrants integrating into largely urban environments in the towns of northern and eastern Europe is evident. The 1641 depositions serve to confirm the impression of Scots settlers forging fairly tight-knit communities of pastoral farming families, regularly modulating between the polarities of segregation from and integration with their new neighbours.[33]

In October 2010 a major exhibition entitled 'Ireland in Turmoil: The 1641 Depositions' was opened at Trinity College Dublin in order to make available to a wider public the evidence drawn from the manuscript witness testimonies of more than eight thousand British settlers in Ireland who had suffered as a result of the rising. Earlier in the year digitized transcriptions of the same material were made available online.[34] Prior to this, Canny had promoted the use of these unique records in order to shed light on the economic and social history of pre-1641 Ireland, and particularly the British settler community. His analysis of the depositions, particularly those from Ulster counties, points to the difficulties of applying any simple native-versus-newcomer dichotomy to the events of the autumn of 1641. Deponents alleged that Scots in different parts of Ulster not only did little to protect English settlers from attack but actually assisted the Irish in attacking them.[35] The problems concerning any simple ascriptions of loyalty and identity in relation to Scots in Ulster only become greater during the war-torn, highly-factional decade that followed the rising of October 1641. The still strong sense of Scotland as 'motherland' became all too evident during the course of the months following the rising. As the popular rebellion increasingly ran out of control, thousands of Scots fled as refugees to the west coast of Scotland. In the presbyteries of Ayr and Irvine alone there were estimated to be four thousand such refugees by the middle of 1642.[36] In April 1642 Major General Robert Monro landed in Ulster with a Scots army, and despite the many twists and turns in allegiance and strategy evident over the course of the subsequent eight years, some consistency is apparent. This force remained focused upon Ulster, drawing logistical support and direction from Edinburgh rather than London, and sought to recoup Scots property acquired since 1605 and lost during the rising.[37] In the summer of 1642 the regimental chaplains and office elders in Monro's army formed a presbytery at

[33] O'Dowd, *History of Women in Ireland*, 96; C. Thomas, 'The City of Londonderry: Demographic Trends and Socio-Economic Characteristics, 1650–1900', in G. O'Brien, ed., *Londonderry: History & Society* (Dublin, 1999), 367–8.

[34] See www.1641.tcd.ie.

[35] Canny, *Making Ireland British*, 480; N. Canny, 'The 1641 Depositions as a Source for the Writing of Social and Economic History: County Cork as a Case Study', in P. O'Flanagan and C. Buttimer, eds., *Cork: History & Society* (Dublin, 1993), 249–308.

[36] J. R. Young, 'Scotland and Ulster in the Seventeenth Century: The Movement of Peoples over the North Channel', in W. Kelly and J. R. Young, eds., *Ulster & Scotland, 1600–2000: History, Heritage and Identity* (Dublin, 2004), 17–20.

[37] Canny, *Making Ireland British*, 562–3.

Carrickfergus in County Antrim, and in the course of the following decade east Ulster witnessed the intensive formation of Presbyterian congregations. As noted by Patrick Adair, who arrived in Ireland in 1646 and became the first historian of Irish Presbyterianism, 'there began a little appearance of a formed church in the country'.[38] Although one should not exaggerate the pace at which a Scottish-style model of Church government took shape after 1642, there can be no denying its significance as a transitional marker of Presbyterianism becoming a parallel and rival structure to the Episcopalian Church of Ireland and acting as the primary badge of identity for the Ulster Scots.[39] The extent to which these settlers in the 1640s looked back towards Scotland should not, perhaps, surprise us. The degree to which they remained, in the preceding half-century, a people apart from both London and Dublin narrowed opportunities for fuller integration and promoted the backward glance to the old country.

## 1650–90

The Cromwellian reconquest of Ireland, complete by 1653, re-established a sense of security for the Protestant interest in Ireland and initiated a re-peopling process that drew on Scotland as well as England and Wales. However, it also served to highlight the extent to which Scots in Ulster, particularly those who had supported the royalist cause, continued to be viewed from London as a potential threat. In May 1653 a proclamation by the Commonwealth regime proposed transplanting southwards a group of leading Scots from counties Antrim and Down to Tipperary, in Munster. The initiative was never pursued in practice, as the threat to Oliver Cromwell from Scotland receded, but it serves to remind us of the perceived potential strategic threat that proximity to the Scottish Highlands and Isles continued to pose to centralized authority in London or Dublin.[40] Despite continuing doubts in Westminster about the loyalty of Scots, it is clear that the years after 1653 witnessed a very significant wave of Scottish migration into east Ulster, in particular. The depredations of a decade of warfare, and heavy excess mortality brought about by plague in the opening years of the 1650s, created the circumstances by which tenants in search of a generous lease, or artisans looking for a decent wage, were likely to be attracted across the North Channel. There were also, of course, push factors, and we should bear in mind that the oft-quoted summation of British planters in Ulster as 'the scum of both nations' is most likely to have applied to immigrants of this era. Estimating with any precision the volume of such migration is challenging, and figures

---

[38] A. Gailey, 'The Scots Element in North Irish Popular Culture: Some Problems in the Interpretation of Historical Acculturation', in *Ethnologia Europa*, vol. 8 (1975), 2–21; P. Adair, *A True Narrative of the Rise and Progress of the Presbyterian Church in Ireland, 1623–70* (Belfast, 1886), 99.

[39] R. Gillespie, 'The Presbyterian Revolution in Ulster, 1660–90', in W. J. Sheils and D. Woods, eds., *The Churches, Ireland and the Irish* (Oxford, 1989), 159–60.

[40] R. F. G. Holmes, *Our Presbyterian Heritage* (Belfast, 1985), 37.

proposed range from as high as eighty thousand to as low as ten thousand. Louis Cullen's estimate of between forty thousand and fifty thousand migrants, in the absence of strong evidence within Scotland itself of a mass exodus, has been judged liberal and a figure of twenty-four thousand migrants proposed by Rab Houston seems a more reasonable guestimate. The acceptance of this lower figure still suggests that movement was more intensive during the Cromwellian period than at any point in the three decades before 1640.[41] Clearly some of those entering Ulster after 1653 were returnees who had departed in the preceding decade and a half. In west Ulster, for example, 'Old Protestants', including many Scots settled before 1641, proved well placed in the 1650s to buy up land from English soldiers eager to return 'home', but such continuity may be less evident further down the social scale. The crucial point to appreciate here is the high level of turnover experienced by the Scots population in Ulster during the decades between 1640 and 1660. One comparison between British surnames recorded in the Muster Rolls of the 1630s with those listed in the Hearth Money Returns of the 1660s, in the baronies of north and west Ulster, regularly demonstrates continuity of below 50 per cent and occasionally as low as 20 per cent.[42] It might be argued that older histories, particularly those shaped in the later nineteenth century, tended to stress continuity between the Jacobean Ulster Plantation settlement and nineteenth-century Presbyterianism. Thus John Harrison, writing on the history of *The Scot in Ulster*, two years after the first Home Rule Bill of 1886, moves almost seamlessly from a consideration of 1641 to a treatment of Ulster after 1660. Where the immigration of the 1650s is referred to briefly, it is suggested that being feared, it tended to be exaggerated.[43] In light of recent research relating to Scottish migration to Ireland later in the century and renewed interest in the early Stuart Plantation era, it might be concluded that the migration of the middle decades of the seventeenth century now represents a very live issue on the historical research agenda for the early twenty-first century.

Although a sense of pragmatism served to fashion a good deal of unity amongst Irish Protestants intent upon retaining their lands at the restoration of Charles II in 1660, there were early signals of difficulties ahead for Ulster's Presbyterians. Two northern ministers sent to England to demand that their 'Covenanted King' should uphold the covenant received short shrift. By the time sixty-one of seventy serving

[41] The Rev. Andrew Stewart, the source of the quotation, was born in County Antrim in the mid-1620s and ordained at Donaghadee, County Down, in 1646. In 1649 he fled to Scotland but returned in 1652; *Dictionary of Irish Biography* (Cambridge, 2009), vol. 9, 62–3; Smout, Landsman, and Devine, 'Scottish Emigration in the Seventeenth and Eighteenth Centuries', in Canny, ed., *Europeans on the Move*, 87; L. M. Cullen, 'Population Trends in Seventeenth-Century Ireland', in *Economic and Social Review*, 6 (1975), 154; R. A. Houston, *The Population history of Britain and Ireland, 1500–1750* (Basingstoke, 1992), 62.

[42] K. McKenny, 'The Seventeenth-Century Land Settlement in Ireland: Towards a Statistical Interpretation', in J. H. Ohlmeyer, ed., *Ireland from Independence to Occupation, 1641–1660* (Cambridge, 1995), 198; W. MacAfee and V. Morgan, 'Population in Ulster, 1660–1760', in P. Roebuck, ed., *Plantation to Partition: Essays in Ulster History in Honour of J. L. McCracken* (Belfast, 1981), 47.

[43] J. Harrison, *The Scot in Ulster: Sketch of the History of the Scottish Population of Ulster* (Edinburgh, 1888), 79–80, 84.

ministers in Ulster had rejected the restored episcopal order and were expelled from their Church of Ireland livings, the proverbial writing was on the wall.[44] Nonetheless the intense persecution of the early 1660s did recede somewhat and some Covenanting Presbyterians from the south-west of Scotland who came to Ulster in the 1660s may have seen Ireland as a relative haven of toleration. A stagnant economy served to reduce immigration until the later 1660s, then a renewed influx of Scots was sustained until the severe subsistence crisis of 1674–5.[45] Throughout the later 1670s and particularly the early 1680s, the so-called 'Killing Times' created the conditions in south-west Scotland for numbers of those drawn from the radical Covenanting tradition to seek refuge in Ulster. This created its own tensions amongst Presbyterians there, keen to prove their loyalty to the Crown, and many of the most radical tended to move back and forth across the narrow sea in response to fluctuations in the levels of toleration or persecution. The impact of fresh migration was being detected in west Ulster as increasing numbers of migrants entered Ulster through the port of Derry. It was reported in 1683 from Donegal that land was 'plentifully planted with Protestant inhabitants, especially with great numbers out of Scotland'.[46] After 1685, economic depression and political instability following the accession of James II caused a brake to be applied to immigration and may indeed have sponsored net migration in the opposite direction. Finally, in 1689–90 the outbreak of the Williamite war in Ireland witnessed a substantial return migration of Scottish migrants and those of Scottish descent.[47]

We may conclude that immigration from Scotland to Ireland in the generation between the Restoration and the Williamite war was likely to have been similar in scale to that during the 1650s (between twenty thousand and thirty thousand), but that many of these individuals moved regularly backwards and forwards between Ulster and south-west Scotland. It is also important to recognize that this migration occurred against a backdrop of declining movement from England and Wales, so that Ulster's settler population was becoming increasingly Scots in complexion during these decades. Furthermore, the migrants of this era were more regularly free agents rather than individuals whose relocation was sponsored by landowners acting in the interests of the Crown, as had tended to be the case in the early part of the century. Southern and western Scotland continued to act as the primary feeder region for migration, and this tended to consolidate the predominance of a pastoral-based agricultural economy and a sense

---

[44] A. Clarke, *Prelude to Restoration in Ireland: The End of the Commonwealth, 1659–1660* (Cambridge, 1999), 315; S. J. Connolly, *Divided Kingdom: Ireland, 1630–1800* (Oxford, 2008), 140.

[45] MacAfee and Morgan, 'Population in Ulster', in Roebuck, ed., *Plantation to Partition*, 50–53; Cullen, 'Population Trends in Seventeenth-Century Ireland', 155.

[46] Young, 'Scotland and Ulster in the Seventeenth Century', in Kelly and Young, eds., *Ulster and Scotland*, 20–2; B. Vann, *In Search of Ulster-Scots Land: The Birth and Geotheological Imaginings of a Transatlantic People, 1603–1703* (Columbia, 2008), 130–1; Roulston, *Researching Scots-Irish Ancestors*, 8.

[47] R. Gillespie, *The Transformation of the Irish Economy, 1550–1700* (Dundalgen, 1991), 18; Young, 'Scotland and Ulster in the Seventeenth Century', in Kelly and Young, eds., *Ulster and Scotland, 1600–2000*, 24.

of dissenting independence. Whilst the government in London and Dublin viewed this phenomenon with real reservations concerning the ultimate loyalty of migrants, governors in Edinburgh openly worried about the disappearance of tenants and servants leaving farms in Scotland underpopulated and unprofitable.[48] Although we can observe Ulster becoming more Scottish, there remains little contemporary comment concerning changes in a sense of belonging in the 'new world' of Ireland.

# 1690–1715

Despite some three generations of migration, predominantly from the Scottish Lowlands into Ulster, we should be wary of exaggerating the firmness of the hold that the 'Protestant Interest' enjoyed before 1690. The thousands of refugees who filtered into Derry prior to the famous siege of 1689 had no doubt strong memories of the rising of October 1641, and here in the west, outside core areas of British settlement, Ulster Scots could retain feelings of frontier isolation.[49] The phase of heaviest migration from Scotland to Ireland was only to come after peace had been re-established by the Treaty of Limerick in October 1691, and this final migration was to prove critical in confirming Presbyterian and Scots demographic predominance in eighteenth-century Ulster. Acknowledgement of the importance of this *fin-de-siècle* Scots reinforcement is well established. Harrison's *The Scot in Ulster* (1888) referred to a contemporary estimate, which described fifty thousand Scotch Presbyterian families pouring into Ulster since the Revolution. What Harrison, like several other late nineteenth-century historians, failed to indicate was the fact that the strength of migration in this decade derived not only from strong pull factors in Ulster, particularly post-war generous leasing terms, but a major push in Scotland, namely, devastating famine.[50] The work on demographic history in the 1970s, in both Ireland and Scotland, reinforced the significance of the famine and the westward migration that resulted from it.[51] Only in recent years, however, has focused research been applied to the issue of the impact of the 1690s famine at a national level and specifically related to migration patterns, including those to Ireland. Karen Cullen's work suggests that an estimate of fifty thousand migrants from Scotland to Ireland in the course of the decade is 'not unreasonable' and that such migration drew disproportionately, as it had before 1690, upon western and south-western Scottish counties. Detailed exploration of both kirk and municipal records from the port town of

---

[48] R. Gillespie, *Settlement and Survival on an Ulster Estate: The Brownlow Leasebook, 1667–1711* (Belfast, 1988), xviii; L. M. Cullen, *The Emergence of Modern Ireland, 1600–1900* (London, 1981), 57, 87.

[49] MacAfee and Morgan, 'Population in Ulster, 1660–1760', in Roebuck, ed., *Plantation to Partition*, 58–9.

[50] Harrison, *The Scot in Ulster: Sketch of the Scottish Population of Ulster*, 87.

[51] M. W. Flinn et al., *Scottish Population History from the Seventeenth Century to the 1930s* (Cambridge, 1977), 164–86; MacAfee and Morgan, 'Population in Ulster, 1660–1760', in Roebuck, ed., *Plantation to Partition*, 57–60.

Ayr revealed subsistence migrants, including women and children, receiving charity on their way to Ulster, as well as some evidence of Scottish parishes sponsoring migration of potential long-term drains on poor-relief funds. The absence of famine conditions in Ulster added to its magnetism in these years, but as the best deals in the land market were snapped up and the limitations of charity in the Ulster congregations exposed, there is evidence of return migration. Overall, Cullen concludes that migration during this period was 'slightly more fluid and less of a one-way process than previously thought'. Finally, she suggests that in these crisis conditions, patterns of migration to Ulster were more closely linked to patterns of internal subsistence migration in Scotland than previous movements to Ireland, which tended to be more permanent in nature.[52] Firm conclusions on these points may await fuller exploration of pre-1690 migration patterns.

Undoubtedly, recent research has served to reveal the complex and heterogeneous character of this substantial Scottish migration to Ireland at the end of the seventeenth century. Nonetheless, a number of common themes may be discerned. Viewed historiographically, particularly from an Ulster perspective, we can see how the depiction of large numbers of Scots coming to Ireland as famine refugees would serve to challenge or disturb the dominant popular construction of such migrants as sturdy planters coming to take up land or set up in trade. The nationalist and unionist versions of history that took shape in the decades after Ireland's Great Famine (1845–51) were ill-inclined to look for parallels between Irish and Scottish migrants or Catholic and Protestant migrants from different eras. The reaction to Scots immigrants by Ulster's Anglican elite could be particularly hostile, and a further rapid acceleration in the establishment of Presbyterian congregations set off something of a panic amongst those now feeling outnumbered by dissenters and looking across to Scotland where episcopacy had recently been supplanted as the established religion. Contemporary Church of Ireland polemicists, sensing their authority under threat, feared those importing the contagion of nonconformist ideas as they may have feared poorer famine refugees carrying plague.[53] Ulster's Catholics were also clearly sensitive to the reinforcement of Presbyterianism, and even as late as the second decade of the eighteenth century, the Catholic Bishop of Clogher, Hugh McMahon, wrote of Scots Calvinists 'coming over here daily … seizing the farms in the richer parts of the country and expelling the natives'.[54] Much of what McMahon observed was likely the consequence of secondary internal migration as Presbyterian farming families pushed out south and west towards the settlement frontier established in the course of the preceding century. Even a full century on from the commencement of plantation this frontier was less fertile ground for the establishment of intimate relations, and further onward migration would prove an option for some.

[52] K. J. Cullen, *Famine in Scotland: The 'Ill Years' of the 1690s* (Edinburgh, 2010), 157–86.
[53] P. Fitzgerald, " 'Black' 47' ": Reconsidering Scottish Migration to Ireland in the Seventeenth Century and the Scotch-Irish in America', in Kelly and Young, eds., *Ulster and Scotland, 1600–2000*, 71–84.
[54] P. Livingstone, *The Monaghan Story* (Enniskillen, 1980), 132.

## FURTHER READING

Canny, Nicholas, *Making Ireland British, 1580–1650* (Oxford, 2001).

Cullen, Karen J., *Famine in Scotland: The 'Ill Years' of the 1690s* (Edinburgh, 2010).

Devine, T. M., *Scotland's Empire, 1600–1815* (London, 2003).

Fitzgerald, Patrick, 'Scottish Migration to Ireland in the Seventeenth Century', in A. Grosjean and S. Murdoch, eds., *Scottish Communities Abroad in the Early Modern Period* (Leiden, 2005), 27–52.

Gillespie, Raymond, *Colonial Ulster: The Settlement of East Ulster, 1600–1641* (Cork, 1985).

MacAfee, William, and Morgan, V., 'Population in Ulster, 1660–1760', in P. Roebuck, ed., *Plantation to Partition: Essays in Ulster History in Honour of J. L. McCracken* (Belfast, 1981), 46–63.

Ohlmeyer, Jane H., "'Civilizinge of those Rude Partes": Colonization within Britain and Ireland, 1580s–1640s', in N. Canny, ed., *The Origins of Empire: The Oxford History of the British Empire*, 5 vols. (Oxford, 1998), vol. i, 124–47.

Perceval-Maxwell, M., *The Scottish Migration to Ulster in the Reign of James I* (London, 1973).

Robinson, Philip, *The Plantation of Ulster: British Settlement in an Irish Landscape, 1600–1670* (Dublin, 1984).

Roulston, William J., *The Essential Genealogical Guide to Early Modern Ulster, 1600–1800* (Belfast, 2005).

Smout, T. C., Landsman, Ned C., and Devine, T. M., 'Scottish Emigration in the Seventeenth and Eighteenth Centuries', in N. Canny, ed., *Europeans on the Move: Studies in European Migration, 1500–1800* (Oxford, 1994), 76–112.

Walker, Graham, *Intimate Strangers: Political and Cultural Interaction Between Scotland and Ulster in Modern Times* (Edinburgh, 1995).

Young, John R., 'Scotland and Ulster in the Seventeenth Century: The Movement of Peoples over the North Channel', in W. Kelly and J. R. Young, eds., *Ulster and Scotland, 1600–2000: History, Heritage and Identity* (Dublin, 2004), 11–32.

# PART III

## UNION AND ENLIGHTENMENT, *c.*1680–1760

CHAPTER 15

....................................................................

# NEW PERSPECTIVES ON PRE-UNION SCOTLAND

....................................................................

## KARIN BOWIE

SCOTLAND before the Union of 1707 can be difficult to assess, for three reasons. Firstly, views of the century before 1707 have been shaped by attitudes towards the Union itself. Most historians writing between 1707 and the mid-twentieth century saw the Union in a positive light. In their minds, the Union had rescued Scotland from difficult circumstances and enabled social, political, intellectual, and economic progress. The resulting histories contrasted the more objectionable aspects of the seventeenth century with improvements after 1707. This perspective was renewed in the 1970s by the Oxford historian Hugh Trevor-Roper (later Lord Dacre), who sought to defend the Union against rising interest in Scottish devolution. Trevor-Roper insisted that the seventeenth century represented 'the darkest age of Scottish history', marked by the 'feudal power of the nobility', the 'fanaticism of the clergy', and an 'arrested economy'. By 1707, he argued, the Scots' desperate situation gave them no choice but to sacrifice their 'feeble' Parliament and embrace incorporating union with England.[1]

This negative view of pre-Union Scotland has been reinforced by historiographical comparison with seventeenth-century England. For social, political, cultural, and economic historians, England has been seen as the birthplace of modernity. Against exceptionalist accounts of England, with its coffee-house clubs, leading-edge theorists, and sophisticated financiers, Scotland has seemed backwards. This has reinforced periodization conventions that tend to fragment perspectives on Scotland's pre-Union era. The decades of the seventeenth century slip out of focus as historians foreground the earlier Renaissance and Reformation periods or the later Enlightenment and Empire phases. Studies of the long sixteenth century tend to stop at 1625 (the end of the reign of James VI and I) or 1638 (the National Covenant), while studies of the long eighteenth century

---

[1] Hugh Trevor-Roper, 'The Anglo-Scottish Union', in *From Counter-Reformation to Glorious Revolution* (London, 1992).

begin with the 1660 Restoration, the 1688–9 Revolution, or even the 1707 Union. General histories usually offer chapters on the seventeenth century or the period 1560–1707, but more specialized studies prefer to focus on reigns or crisis points.

These historiographical issues have begun to be addressed in recent decades. Since the 1960s, debate over the formation of the Union has made historians more alert to the way in which attitudes towards Anglo-Scottish union have shaped histories of the pre-1707 period. A trend towards multiple-kingdoms British history has improved our understanding of the Union of Crowns era (1603–1707), though there is still no modern monograph-length study of this period from a Scottish perspective. The negative view of Scotland in comparison to England has been undermined as historians question England's distinctiveness and identify multiple forms of modernity within and beyond Europe.[2] In studying Scottish history, scholars have assessed a broader range of European comparators and have sought to describe change in Scottish, rather than English, terms. At the same time, the new British history has drawn attention to the interconnectedness of England and Scotland in the Union of Crowns. Together these trends have challenged the notion of a static Scotland while pointing to English as well as European influence on change in Scotland.

This chapter will draw together a range of recent work to provide a fresh appraisal of the pre-Union century. It will focus on three areas of supposed backwardness highlighted by Trevor-Roper: Scotland's society and political practices; its intellectual culture; and its economy and trade. While a more positive consensus will be identified across these topics, the chapter will highlight points of debate on the extent of Scottish development in these areas.

## Society and Politics

Older accounts have stressed the medieval nature of Scotland's noble-led society and political systems. In comparison to early modern England's broadening electorate, emerging public sphere, and vigorous parliamentary culture, Scottish society and politics seemed embedded in older patterns. This view, however, has been eroded. Key areas of debate have emerged around three interlocking issues: the degree to which a politically significant 'middling sort' appeared in Scotland; the extent to which the state expanded its influence over localities; and how far the nobility experienced a decrease in power and influence as a consequence.

Compared to England's yeoman farmer, gentry, and financier classes, Scotland's middling sorts have seemed a pale reflection, dominated by nobles who were given licence by a weak state to retain a militarized power base well into the eighteenth century.

---

[2] For example, J. C. D. Clark, *English Society, 1688–1832: Ideology, Social Structure and Political Practice during the Ancien Régime* (Cambridge, 1985), and Björn Wittrock, 'Early Modernities: Varieties and Transitions', *Daedalus*, 127, no. 3, 19–40.

Vigorous empirical research into Scottish society and politics, however, has begun to outline patterns of internal development in Scottish terms. Scotland's middling sorts now appear in the form of smaller proprietors, educated professionals, and prosperous tenant farmers, merchants and artisans. Though Rab Houston and Ian Whyte stress that the middling ranks were 'less prominent' than in England, these growing ranks were literate and possessed property or affluence, which gave them some degree of political responsibility and independence.[3]

In rural society, proprietorship rose through feuing (payment of a large upfront sum to the feudal superior, followed by a small annual duty) and wadsetting (loans made by tenants or tacksmen to landowners). Margaret Sanderson and Walter Makey have emphasized the significance of the sixteenth-century feuing movement in creating many smaller landholders in lowland Scotland. Tenants with savings, or speculators with capital, could use feuing to secure a heritable estate. Allan Macinnes has shown how wadsetting led to a similar outcome in the Highlands from the mid-seventeenth century.[4] Here the tacksmen loaned money upwards to the clan elite, securing heritable control of their farms until the loan was repaid or, more often, title was awarded on cancellation of the debt. In the Lowlands, rising inflation transferred effective control to feuars, while burgeoning debt held by highland chiefs gave leverage to wadsetters. The proliferation of proprietorship through feuing and wadsetting can be seen in the rise of a new term, the 'heritor', which encompassed all heritable landholders, noble or not, in a parish. Alongside the smaller heritors, agricultural improvement (described below) and the spread of parish schooling brought more lowland tenant farmers into the ranks of the literate middling sort.

Political engagement for this stratum came through office-holding and participation in an expanding public sphere. The lesser heritors shared responsibility with the nobility for the maintenance of the parish church and school. Many served alongside tenant farmers as elders in the kirk-session. Smaller proprietors did not qualify to vote for a shire representative to Parliament, and many retained strong links to the territorial nobility through feudal superiorities, kinship, or commercial relations, but they still had more political independence than a tenant who remained subject to a landlord for the renewal of leases. Even tenant farmers could participate in political discourse: in 1705 a Scottish periodical featured a tenant farmer as an archetypal 'Country Man' in dialogue with his local schoolmaster on political matters.[5]

As the schoolmaster figure suggests, educated professionals became more socially and politically significant before the Union. After the Reformation, the clergy emerged as a university-educated social group, comfortably provided with generous stipends by the

---

[3] R. A. Houston and I. D. Whyte, 'Introduction: Scottish Society in Perspective', in R. A. Houston and I. D. Whyte, eds., *Scottish Society 1500–1800* (Cambridge, 1989), 3.

[4] Margaret Sanderson, *Scottish Rural Society in the Sixteenth Century* (Edinburgh, 1982); Walter Makey, *The Church of the Covenant 1637–1651* (Edinburgh, 1979); Allan I. Macinnes, *Clanship, Commerce and the House of Stuart, 1603–1788* (East Linton, 1996), 142–4.

[5] [John Pierce?], *A dialogue between a Country-Man and a Landwart School-Master, concerning the proceedings of the Parliament of England, in Relation to SCOTS Affairs* (Edinburgh, 1705).

1630s. Graduates aiming for a parish post often served first as schoolmasters in the expanding parish school system, doubling as precentors and kirk-session clerks. Law and medicine became increasingly attractive careers for younger sons of landowners. By 1672, lawyers acting in the central courts had been incorporated as the Faculty of Advocates. The physicians formed a Royal College, after several earlier attempts, in 1681. Hugh Ouston and Roger Emerson have shown how, by the Restoration period, lawyers and physicians in Edinburgh had joined Scottish nobles in the role of the learned virtuoso. These educated professionals were to become a bastion of the Scottish middling sorts, wielding increasing political and cultural power despite their official absence as a social group from traditional systems of representation in parliamentary and burgh politics. Parish ministers, like church elders, might have close relationships with territorial lords, but clerics also had links to central authorities and could exert independent leadership at the community level through the pulpit and kirk-session.

In the burghs, rising affluence and urban populations brought more merchants and craftsmen into a middling level over the long term. This process was most notable in the increasingly stratified society of Edinburgh, Scotland's burgeoning capital city. While literacy levels rose across the century in Scotland, they rose fastest in the burghs, through a combination of occupational demand and educational availability. Rab Houston's research has shown that the vast bulk of the literacy gains of the pre-Union century were enjoyed by the middling sorts, with urban craftsmen and tradesmen reaching a level of 85 per cent literacy by the 1690s.[6] Literate burgesses served as church elders, constables, and town-guard officers, while the greater availability of news and print in the towns fed political awareness.

Scholars generally agree that literate middling sorts, particularly lairds, lawyers, and clergy, provided the administrative manpower for a slowly expanding state. More controversial is the question of how far they contributed to a transfer of power from the traditional devolved jurisdictions of the nobility to state-based institutions. Though Whig histories celebrate the 1747 abolition of heritable jurisdictions in Scotland as a benchmark of post-Union modernization, the pre-Union period saw significant erosion of these bailiwicks. If the kirk-session is interpreted as an extension of central authority, as in Julian Goodare's work on state formation, then the development of the session's disciplinary jurisdiction can be seen in this light. Though kirk-sessions usually worked cooperatively with local barony courts, their growth coincided with the declining remit of these secular courts and the rise of the parish as a political unit. The new parish courts had strong connections to the centre through Scotland's unique network of regional presbyteries, which remained in place throughout the century despite changes in episcopal government.

Centralized systems impinged in other ways on local authority over time. The Justices of the Peace, though not considered successful, presented a challenge to traditional courts and managed in some areas to carve out a meaningful role. Perhaps more significant on an ad hoc basis were judicial commissions issued by the Privy Council. Goodare

---

[6] R. A. Houston, *Scottish Literacy and the Scottish Identity: Illiteracy and Society in Scotland and Northern England 1600–1800* (Cambridge, 1985), 35, 47.

has stressed the extent to which Commissions of Justiciary issued to lairds for witch trials represented an extension of state control into localities through the role played by the Privy Council as a kind of grand jury.[7] In the Restoration period, commissions of discipline allowed central authorities to leapfrog uncooperative sheriffs to prosecute conventiclers. More directly, the Jacobean and Caroline episcopate reached into the parishes through a redeveloped Court of High Commission, pursuing laymen and clergy for nonconformity. Under Charles II, the High Court of Justiciary was reconstituted with circuit courts in 1672 to regularize the prosecution of criminal cases.

The long-term development of state judicial systems went hand in hand with a reduction in the military power of the Scottish nobility. Jenny Wormald and Keith Brown have documented a decline in lowland practices of armed feud by the early seventeenth century, corresponding with a greater pursuit of justice at law.[8] The need to maintain armed followings declined as the use of the king's courts proved more effective in the settlement of disputes. Though James VI had demonstrated a commitment to reducing blood-feud from the 1590s, the Union of Crowns gave a further impetus to this with the pacification of the Anglo-Scottish border. In contrast to the Lowlands, the Highlands remained more militarized, but Allan Macinnes has shown how economic forces as well as lowland cultural example encouraged highland chiefs to begin to shed expensive military retainers by mid-century.[9]

The early modern Scottish state sought to monopolize the making of war by moving, as in other European realms, away from a feudal common army raised by territorial nobles towards standing regiments led by professional officers. Informed by the experiences of Scottish officers serving in Swedish regiments, the Covenanting state adopted the latest military methods to march against Charles I in 1639.[10] The Restoration Parliament declared the making of war to be the king's right alone and authorized in 1661 a new militia under Privy Council control. After the Revolution, William II and III and Anne raised regiments from Scotland for British service in continental wars. Militarism remained part of noble culture, with young nobles receiving training in the arts of war; but for most, military service became a career choice as younger sons officered royal or mercenary regiments.

This demilitarization of the Scottish nobility indicated a transition in the nature of lordship in the pre-Union period, though historians disagree how far this signalled a decline in the power and influence of the titled nobility in personal terms. While nobles may have

[7] Julian Goodare, 'Witch-Hunting and the Scottish State', in Julian Goodare, ed., *The Scottish Witch-Hunt in Context* (Manchester, 2002).

[8] Jenny Wormald, 'Bloodfeud, Kindred and Government in Early Modern Scotland', *Past & Present*, 87 (May 1980), 54–97; Keith Brown, *Bloodfeud in Scotland 1573–1625: Violence, Justice and Politics in an Early Modern Society* (Edinburgh, 1986).

[9] Alan I. Macinnes, 'The Impact of the Civil Wars and Interregnum: Political Disruption and Social Change within Scottish Gaeldom', in Rosalind Mitchison and Peter Roebuck, eds., *Economy and Society in Scotland and Ireland 1500–1939* (Edinburgh, 1988).

[10] Edward M. Furgol, 'Scotland Turned Sweden: The Scottish Covenanters and the Military Revolution, 1638–1651', in John Morrill, ed., *The Scottish National Covenant in its British Context* (Edinburgh, 1990).

shifted 'from lordship to patronage', there is uncertainty over the extent to which the middling (or lower) sorts became more significant in early modern Scottish political practices. Traditionally, the sociopolitical radicalism of the Covenanting period has been understood to have vanished with the conservative backlash of the Restoration. Noble dominance continued after the 'unrevolutionary' Williamite Revolution of 1688–9, with P. W. J. Riley portraying the pre-Union Parliament as a sordid arena for nobles on the make.[11]

More recent perspectives have highlighted the vigour of parliamentary and popular politics across the pre-Union century, while acknowledging the continuing importance of noble leadership in Scottish political culture. Faced with an absentee monarch, oppositional nobles turned to popular opinion as a means of resisting Crown policy in the name of the commonwealth. Having opened this Pandora's box with the Covenanting rebellion of 1637–9, they found it difficult to close again. Allan Macinnes has described the mobilization of grassroots resistance in this rebellion, while Walter Makey and John Young have stressed the social and political radicalism of the ensuing Covenanting revolution.[12] Popular resistance continued to disrupt Restoration politics, fuelling the emergence of a more organized parliamentary opposition.[13] Derek Patrick and Tim Harris have indicated the influence of popular politics in the making of the 1688–9 Revolution in Scotland; and other work has investigated this in the events leading to the Union of 1707.[14] New research has stressed the extent to which the Crown struggled to manage Parliament between the Revolution and the Union, faced with oppositional factions, active lobbying, and mass petitioning.[15]

These reassessments of political culture have been aided by a reinterpretation of Scottish religious culture. Margo Todd's groundbreaking study of the making of Protestant culture in Scotland has highlighted the power of religious ideology within Scottish society while avoiding the judgemental baggage of sectarian history or the institutional focus of traditional Kirk–State studies. Interest in the culture of the clergy and laity has created a better appreciation of the patriotic and political nature of Scottish

---

[11] P. W. J. Riley, *King William and the Scottish Politicians* (Edinburgh, 1979); P. W. J. Riley, *The Union of England and Scotland* (Manchester, 1978).

[12] Allan Macinnes, *Charles I and the Making of the Covenanting Movement* (Edinburgh, 1991); Makey, *The Church of the Covenant*; John R. Young, 'The Scottish Parliament and the Covenanting Revolution: The Emergence of a Scottish Commons', in John R. Young, ed., *Celtic Dimensions of the British Civil Wars* (Edinburgh, 1997).

[13] Gillian H. Macintosh, *The Scottish Parliament under Charles II, 1660–1685* (Edinburgh, 2007).

[14] Derek J. Patrick, 'Unconventional Procedure: Scottish Electoral Politics after the Revolution', in Keith M. Brown and Alastair J. Mann, eds., *Parliament and Politics in Scotland, 1567–1707* (Edinburgh, 2005); Tim Harris, *Revolution: The Great Crisis of the British Monarchy, 1685–1720* (London, 2006), 364–421; Karin Bowie, *Scottish Public Opinion and the Anglo-Scottish Union, 1699–1707* (Woodbridge, 2007).

[15] Keith M. Brown, 'Party Politics and Parliament: Scotland's Last Election and its Aftermath, 1702–3', in Brown and Mann, *Parliament and Politics in Scotland*; Karin Bowie, 'Publicity, Parties and Patronage: Parliamentary Management and the Ratification of the Anglo-Scottish Union', *Scottish Historical Review*, 87, supplement (2008), 78–93; Jeffrey Stephen, 'Defending the Revolution: The Church of Scotland and the Scottish Parliament, 1689–95', *Scottish Historical Review*, 89:1, no. 227 (April 2010), 19–53.

piety and the fierce desire of many to preserve what they saw as Scottish forms of worship, discipline, and Church government. The story of the bifurcation of Scottish Protestant culture into Presbyterian and Episcopalian forms, linked to radical and royalist or, later, Whig and Jacobite political aims, has begun to be outlined through new work on Covenanting, Episcopalian, and Jacobite cultures.

This cultural approach has allowed historians to take a wider view of political systems, looking beyond the institutions of Kirk, State, and Parliament to identify an emerging public sphere accessed by the growing middling sort outlined above. Alistair Mann's work on the Scottish book trade has given us a better appreciation of the rising, if uneven, availability of political print in this period, while British work on pamphleteering has begun to indicate how Scottish print intersected with a London-based public sphere in the Anglo-Scottish union.[16] The Scottish public sphere may not have boasted as many coffee houses as London's, but historians have begun to recognize the significance of public discourse in shaping Scottish opinions and enabling political participation.

It seems clear that historians can no longer view the pre-Union period as one of social and political stagnation. Scotland, like other European kingdoms at the time, continued to be led by its nobility, but religious controversy encouraged wider social engagement in politics. This was enabled by long-term trends in social change, state formation, and lordship similar to those seen across Europe. Scotland's experience of the seventeenth century, on this evidence, was not medieval but distinctly early modern. Because the patterns of change seen in Scotland do not match those of England, they have been seen as inferior by generations of scholars. In more recent work, Scottish modes of early modernity have been found, shaped by the realm's unique circumstances and traditions, though scholars still debate the extent of social and political change.

## INTELLECTUAL CULTURE

Commentators have tended to see Scottish intellectual culture in the pre-Union period as moribund, held back by Calvinist intolerance and the 1603 departure of the monarch's court to London. For literary scholars, the loss of royal patronage and the Kirk's distrust of imaginative literature, especially drama, have been seen to have doomed Scottish culture to a period of inertia. Among historians for whom religious toleration is a marker of modernity, the pre-Union Scottish Kirk has been condemned for its bigotry. Trevor-Roper believed that while the Scottish north-east may have harboured a degree of Arminian moderation within the Stuart Episcopalian Kirk, only English influence after 1707, starting with the Westminster Toleration Act of 1712, could curb the excesses of Scotland's fanatical Presbyterians.

[16] Alastair J. Mann, *The Scottish Book Trade 1500–1720* (East Linton, 2000); Joad Raymond, *Pamphlets and Pamphleteering in Early Modern Britain* (Cambridge, 2002); Alastair Raffe, 'Episcopalian Polemic, the London Printing Press and Anglo-Scottish Divergence in the 1690s', *Journal of Scottish Historical Studies*, 26 (2006), 23–41.

As with studies of society and politics, however, more recent work has challenged these negative views. Explorations of the 'early Enlightenment' have pushed the frontiers of intellectual dynamism into the Restoration period, while work on Renaissance and Reformation culture has traced continuities across the 1603 watershed. By connecting these studies, patterns can be discerned across the pre-Union period in law, science, literature, and theology. Scottish thinking continued between 1603 and 1707, adapted to the particular circumstances of the century. These activities reveal continuing intellectual exchange with Europe, especially Protestant France and the Netherlands, and rising interaction with England in the Union of Crowns.

In pointing to a relative lack of new Scottish philosophical works in the seventeenth century, Alexander Brodie has suggested that the Renaissance humanists' return to classical texts discouraged, for a time, the philosophical innovation that would emerge in the next century.[17] Instead, intellectual dynamism in Scotland, as elsewhere in Europe, appeared in writings on the law and science. The Union of Crowns, for example, spurred the legal humanist Sir Thomas Craig of Riccarton to investigate English and Scottish feudal law (*Jus Feudale*, 1603) and assess the feasibility of legal union between the two kingdoms (*De Unione Regnorum Britanniae*, 1605). After several decades of monarchical union, later jurists sought to document the distinctiveness of Scottish law in the *Institutions* of James Dalrymple, Viscount Stair (1681), and Sir George Mackenzie of Rosehaugh (1684).

In the sciences, Roger Emerson has highlighted the medical and geographical projects of Sir Robert Sibbald, Geographer Royal, physician to the king and founder of the Royal College of Physicians in Scotland. Though Sibbald may not have been at the cutting edge of medicine, he embodied an increasing orientation in educated Scottish culture towards scientific debate and improvement. Sibbald acted as a hub within the Scottish virtuosi, with correspondence links to like-minded gentlemen in England, Paris, and the Netherlands. Michael Hunter has shown how even Robert Kirk, a minister from the remote Gaelic-speaking parish of Aberfoyle, could contribute an ethnological study of Scottish fairies to British discussions on the nature of matter and the reality of spirits.[18]

In literature, scholars have tended to dismiss the outpouring of vernacular prose in this period as turgid or overenthusiastic, while romanticizing ballads as the surviving expression of a pre-Reformation oral culture. Two shifts in scholarly attention have begun to revise this view of the literary corpus. By tracing continuities in Renaissance culture into the seventeenth century, scholars are recovering the diversity of Scottish intellectual life in the pre-Union period. The vitality of Scottish neo-Latin poetry has been rediscovered, though progress is handicapped by the need for specialist language skills.[19] As well, the turn to religious culture, noted above, has highlighted the significance

---

[17] Alexander Brodie, *A History of Scottish Philosophy* (Edinburgh, 2010), 99–103.

[18] Michael Hunter, *The Occult Laboratory: Magic, Science and Second Sight in Late Seventeenth-Century Scotland* (Woodbridge, 2001).

[19] James Macqueen, 'Scottish Latin Poetry', in R. D. S. Jack, ed., *The History of Scottish Literature*, 4 vols. (Aberdeen, 1987–8), vol. i.

of vernacular religious texts. David Mullan's editions of spiritual autobiographies, for example, have provided new material for the reconstruction of Calvinist piety.[20] Fresh readings of Scottish ballads, combined with witch-trial evidence, have helped to reconstruct the nature of post-Reformation magical beliefs.[21] Work on popular entertainment has revealed a greater variety of public performance in post-Reformation Scotland, despite clerical disapproval of formal drama.[22] Together these various projects are helping to reconstruct a clearer picture of the cultural life of this period.

Perhaps the most tenacious complaint about pre-Union Scotland remains the notion of the fanatical, intolerant Kirk. Many modern historians continue to see the stern Calvinist discipline of this period as repugnant and the Kirk's attack on popular beliefs and festive practices as regrettable. Yet here too a cultural approach has turned historians' attention to the slow processes of negotiation and adaptation by which most Scots came to accept, and even embrace, Protestant culture, though further research is needed to unpick regional differences in the pace and nature of Scottish Protestantization.[23]

While there remains no doubt that many in the Kirk embraced the values of a confessional age in which there was little room for dissent, scholars have sought to complicate simple notions of Calvinist 'fanaticism' by demonstrating the continuous presence of intellectual inquiry, forms of moderation, and even notions of toleration within Scottish church culture. Studies of Presbyterian intellectuals have highlighted thinkers like Samuel Rutherford and James Steuart of Goodtrees, who wrote relatively moderate and well-informed political theory for a learned audience, while acknowledging the less cosmopolitan nature of more radical Covenanting writers.[24] Setting aside the monolithic notion of 'the Kirk', these and other studies have looked instead at the range of beliefs and practices articulated by clergy and laity, influenced by British and European intellectual contexts.

David Allan has indicated how exposure to neo-Stoic philosophy encouraged latitude in the Kirk, particularly among senior episcopalian clerics trained at universities abroad.[25] In the Jacobean Church, episcopalian figures like Andrew Boyd, Bishop of Argyll, urged toleration of Presbyterian practices at the parish level in order to maintain unity in the Scottish Church.[26] Later in the Restoration period, Colin Kidd has identified

---

[20] David Mullan, ed., *Women's Life Writing in Early Modern Scotland, c.1670–c.1730* (Aldershot, 2003); David Mullan, ed., *Protestant Piety in Early-Modern Scotland: Letters, Lives and Covenants, 1650–1712* (Edinburgh, 2008).

[21] Edward J. Cowan and Lizanne Henderson, *Scottish Fairy Belief: A History* (East Linton, 2001).

[22] Bill Findlay, 'Beginnings to 1700', in Bill Findlay, ed., *A History of Scottish Theatre* (Edinburgh, 1998).

[23] John McCallum, *Reforming the Scottish Parish: The Reformation in Fife, 1560–1640* (Farnham, 2010).

[24] Caroline Erskine, 'The Political Thought of the Restoration Covenanters', in Julian Goodare and Sharon Adams, eds., *Scotland in the Age of Two Revolutions* (forthcoming). I am grateful to Caroline Erskine for sharing her typescript of this paper.

[25] David Allan, *Philosophy and Politics in Later Stuart Scotland: Neo-Stoicism, Culture and Ideology in an Age of Crisis, 1540–1690* (East Linton, 2000).

[26] Jamie Reid-Baxter, 'Mr Andrew Boyd (1567–1636): A Neo-Stoic Bishop of Argyll and his Writings', in Julian Goodare and Alasdair A. Macdonald, *Sixteenth-Century Scotland* (Leiden and Boston, 2008).

a 'Scottish school of latitudinarian theology' centred on Robert Leighton, Bishop of Dunblane and Archbishop of Glasgow under Charles II. Leighton's moderation owed much to his postgraduate continental education in civil law and neo-Stoic philosophy, as well as his close links with Anglicans through his official posts. Leighton's sponsorship of talks with Presbyterian dissenters between 1669 and 1672 reflected a British intellectual framework in echoing the published ideas of James Ussher, Archbishop of Armagh, on a minimalist episcopate. Leighton's latitudinarian associates included Gilbert Burnet, whose moderate views were also shaped by an international education and milieu.

In a similar vein, Clare Jackson has indicated how the circumstances of the Restoration led the Stuart episcopate to avoid stringent *jure divino* claims for government by bishops in order to encourage Presbyterian reconciliation. Moderate clergy like Burnet urged cooperation among Scottish Protestants against greater external dangers such as Catholicism, atheism, and ungodliness. These arguments succeeded with relatively temperate Presbyterians, such as George Meldrum, who complied with the new regime despite personal doubts about prelacy. Like other moderates, Meldrum accepted the Restoration settlement until the Test Act of 1681 and then returned to the national Church via the indulgence of 1687.

Though the Revolution of 1688–9 brought hardline Presbyterians back into the national Church, political conditions encouraged moderation among leading clerics as they sought to steer a course between an unsympathetic monarch and their more enthusiastic colleagues. These included figures like Meldrum, who had complied with prelacy or accepted indulgences in the Restoration; and others, like William Carstares, whose British intrigues and continental exile had inculcated a more *politique* perspective. These individuals cooperated with like-minded Presbyterian lay elites, including the political theorist turned Lord Advocate, Sir James Steuart of Goodtrees. Tristram Clarke's research indicates how the Presbyterian Church after 1690 came to accommodate Williamite episcopalians such as John Robertson, formerly of Greyfriars Kirk in Edinburgh, and Laurence Charteris, formerly Professor of Divinity at Edinburgh University.[27] Other episcopalian moderates accepted into the Kirk included James Gordon, a minister in Banchory who had advocated accommodation in a 1679 tract, *The Reformed Bishop*.

Some parishioners as well as clergy turned towards moderation in response to the disorders of the century. Clare Jackson and Julia Buckroyd have noted the rise of anti-clericalism among Restoration elites, marked by disdain for religious enthusiasm.[28] On a more intellectual plane, British and European print and correspondence encouraged movement among the educated towards deism. As Michael Graham's micro-history shows, rising panic among clerics about deism found an outlet in the pursuit of Edinburgh University student Thomas Aikenhead, leading to his execution for blasphemy in 1697.

[27] Tristram Clarke, 'The Williamite Episcopalians and the Glorious Revolution in Scotland', *Records of the Scottish Church History Society*, 24, no. 1 (1992), 33–51.
[28] Julia Buckroyd, 'Anti-Clericalism in Scotland during the Restoration', in Norman Macdougall, ed., *Church, Politics and Society: Scotland 1408–1929* (Edinburgh, 1983).

Frequently cited as the ultimate example of the fanatical intolerance of the Scottish Kirk, Aikenhead's execution must also be seen, in light of Graham's study, as evidence of a counter-current of lay abstraction from the teachings of the Kirk.[29] Though Presbyterian authorities expected the laity to attend church and restrict their activities on the Sabbath, limited cooperation spurred the passage of Sabbatarian legislation in Parliament, town councils, and the General Assembly after 1690. R. Douglas Brackenridge has suggested that the ineffectiveness of these laws can be seen in their frequent repetition.[30]

Not all scholars agree with the new emphasis on moderation in pre-Union religious culture. Alasdair Raffe and C. D. A. Leighton have provided reminders of the uncompromising nature of much post-Revolution Presbyterian and non-jurant episcopalian thought.[31] Still, though the extent of moderation before 1707 remains debatable, recent scholarship has eroded simplistic notions of a fanatical and intolerant Kirk. Scholars have begun to recover the diversity of pre-Union Scottish religious culture, including irreligion and irenicism as well as orthodoxy. Rather than stagnating, Scottish intellectual culture continued to reflect European influences while interacting more with English discourse. Findings in theology, science, literature, and law point to forms of dynamism and moderation that complicate the stereotypically negative picture of a benighted century. More research remains to be done in order to delineate fully the indigenous cultural dynamics of the pre-Union age, but it seems that this period cannot be dismissed as the darkness before the dawn of the Enlightenment.

# ECONOMY AND TRADE

As in society, politics, and culture, new research has developed a different understanding of the Scottish economy before the Union. A recent assessment concludes that it is 'no longer acceptable to write off seventeenth-century Scotland'.[32] Nevertheless, sharp debate continues on whether the notorious disasters of the 1690s reveal short-term or more fundamental weaknesses in the Scottish economy before 1707. The debate arises in part from competing historiographical aims: some historians highlight the catastrophic conditions of the century's end in order to explain contemporary economic pressures towards incorporation, while others focus on countervailing trends in an attempt to

---

[29] Michael Graham, *The Blasphemies of Thomas Aikenhead: Boundaries of Belief on the Eve of the Enlightenment* (Edinburgh, 2008).

[30] R. Douglas Brackenridge, 'The Enforcement of Sunday Observance in Post-Revolution Scotland 1689–1733', *Records of the Scottish Church History Society*, 17 (1972), 33–45.

[31] Alasdair Raffe, 'Presbyterianism, Secularisation, and Scottish Politics after the Revolution of 1688–90', *The Historical Journal*, 53, no. 2 (2010), 317–37; C. D. A. Leighton, 'Scottish Jacobitism, Episcopacy, and Counter-Enlightenment', *History of European Ideas*, 35 (2009), 1–35.

[32] Christopher Whatley, 'Taking Stock: Scotland at the End of the Seventeenth Century', in T. C. Smout, ed., *Anglo-Scottish Relations from 1603 to 1900* (Oxford, 2005), 104.

explain the roots of post-Union growth. Either way, new studies have challenged any simple explanation for the Union or economic development thereafter. As in culture, society, and politics, the aim now is to reconstruct Scottish economic dynamics on their own terms in order to appreciate the rationality and, in some sectors, vitality of Scottish responses to British and European contexts.

Countering older accounts of a declining agrarian sector, Ian Whyte's work suggests slow improvement disrupted by periods of war. By the 1640s, new ideas for the improvement of agriculture were spreading to Scotland from England and the Continent, but the disorders of the Wars of the Three Kingdoms and the Cromwellian occupation hampered change. With the return of peace, Acts of Parliament in the 1660s encouraged the protection of crops by enclosure, the planting of trees, and the use of legumes for fertility. A set of three Acts in 1695 included a measure enabling the consolidation of runrig strips. With parliamentary Acts indicating an interest in change, estate papers demonstrate actual alterations in agrarian practices. Rising market orientation can be seen in a long-term trend towards the payment of rents in cash and the issuing of written leases. The growing market demands of Edinburgh encouraged the improvement of properties around the capital, with prosperous tenants running larger holdings in Lothian and Berwickshire by the end of the century. Whyte's analysis is supported by comparative studies that stress the positive effect of rising urban demand and the negative effect of war on agricultural productivity in early modern Europe.[33]

Gains over the Restoration period allowed tenants to accumulate savings in good years, often loaning these out to lairds to finance estate expansion.[34] The commercial development of estates by landholders in both the Lowlands and the Highlands reflected a need to reduce huge debts incurred in wartime, as well as a fashionable desire to display status through conspicuous consumption. Rosalind Marshall's study of the third Duchess of Hamilton shows how the proceeds from an intense redevelopment of Duchess Anne's estates funded the rebuilding of Hamilton Palace according to French and English models, complete with continental-style sash windows.[35] Similar efforts on other home farms contributed to rising arable productivity, with larger grain surpluses exported in good years. In the Highlands, proprietors profited by droving beef on the hoof to the Lowlands as an already flourishing domestic cattle trade expanded into larger English markets by the 1680s. Highland landholders also used steelbow, a form of sharecropping, to help tenants establish or expand farms. Rural industry developed among proprietors with natural resources, most notably in coal mining for export to English markets and the linked manufacture of salt for the domestic market.

These developments on landed estates accompanied an associated expansion in marketing networks. John Harrison's Perthshire study has shown how improving local

---

[33] Philip T. Hoffman, *Growth in a Traditional Society: The French Countryside 1450–1815* (Princeton, 1996).

[34] I. D. Whyte and K. A. Whyte, 'Debt and Credit, Poverty and Prosperity in a Seventeenth-Century Scottish Rural Community', in Rosalind Mitchison and Peter Roebuck, eds., *Economy and Society in Scotland and Ireland 1500–1989* (Edinburgh, 1988).

[35] Rosalind K. Marshall, *The Days of Duchess Anne* (London, 1973).

administration of road-maintenance laws enhanced transport infrastructures, aiding the movement of grain to market and lime to fields.[36] Larger traders began to operate across multiple burghs while smaller traders proliferated in new burghs of barony and regality and local markets and fairs. By 1672, rising pressure on the restrictive privileges of the royal burghs led to an Act of Parliament allowing the export of agricultural produce from burghs of barony and regality.

Alongside these changes, manufacturing expanded across the century. Gordon Marshall's attempt to use Scottish manufacturing as a Weberian case study may have been met with scepticism, but his research outlines the growth of this sector. As in agriculture, an improving spirit can be seen in a series of parliamentary Acts designed to encourage manufacturing. Legislation between 1641 and 1681 sought to develop the weaving of cloth from native wool by offering tax incentives to joint-stock entrepreneurs and erecting tariff barriers to English cloth. Ventures in woollen cloth, as well as glass, soap, iron, and paper, were established before 1660, followed by projects in linen, rope, pins, and sugar.[37] At the same time, T. C. Smout has shown how less capital-intensive systems of rural part-time spinning and weaving supplied increasing exports of woollen and linen textiles, most notably linen from Perthshire and Renfrewshire and woollen plaiding and stockings from Aberdeenshire. Tariff pressures on selling prices squeezed margins and pushed quality towards the low end of the market, but by the end of the century, linen cloth had become a significant export sector, with much of it sold to England and its colonies.

These areas of growth and improvement are now better understood for the pre-Union period, but this does not change the fact that Scotland's position in the Union of Crowns created difficulties for economic development in this period. Historians agree that the 1603 Union created tension between Scottish and English interests, with English imperatives in diplomacy, war, and political economy taking precedence in the multiple monarchy. While Scots were naturalized in England from 1608, they were still treated as aliens and barred from the carrying trade to the English colonies through a series of Navigation Acts (although clandestine activity by Scottish merchants was prevalent). English influence in foreign policy led to repeated wars with Scotland's traditional trading partners, the Netherlands and France. The Anglo-Dutch wars of the 1650s, 1660s, and 1670s, and the French wars of the 1690s and early 1700s, disrupted Scottish trade and triggered the imposition of punitive tariffs and outright prohibitions on Scottish goods.

Scottish exports to England rose as these political circumstances closed off continental markets and fuelled the development of the cattle, coal, and linen exports noted above. Traditionally, this shift towards English markets has been seen as presaging the economic union of 1707. T. C. Smout provided a modern empirical base for this view with an influential 1963 study of Scottish overseas trade. This combined new research

---

[36] John G. Harrison, 'East Flanders Moss, Perthshire, a Documentary Study', *Landscape History*, 30 (2008–9), 7–8.

[37] Gordon Marshall, *Presbyteries and Profits: Calvinism and the Development of Capitalism in Scotland 1560–1707* (Edinburgh, 1980).

into Scottish exports with an analysis of the pamphlet literature on incorporating union, concluding that the better arguments lay with those writers who saw incorporating union as the only way out for a failed economy. Resistance to these conclusions offered by political historians like William Ferguson and P. W. J. Riley created a major battleground in Union historiography over the significance of economics in the making of the Union. This has resulted in two historiographical views of the pre-Union economy: a pessimistic interpretation based on Smout and elaborated by Christopher Whatley; and a more optimistic view advanced by T. M. Devine and Allan Macinnes.

The pessimistic view updates the traditionally negative view of the pre-Union economy. It acknowledges evidence for internal development but still emphasizes the underlying constraints of the Union of Crowns in a mercantilist world. In this view, the benefits achieved by improvers and entrepreneurs were destroyed by a combination of blows in the 1690s, revealing fundamental weaknesses in the post-1603 Scottish economy. These blows started as the Revolution ushered in the long Nine Years War with France (1688–97), which disrupted trade and created extraordinary tax demands on the Scottish economy. Though the Scots' commercial privileges in France had been eroded since 1603, France nonetheless remained a key trading partner for Scotland. British war with France thus had a disproportionate effect on Scotland, not least because a massive expansion of the English navy supplied convoys for English, but not Scottish, shipping. This allowed French privateers to take Scottish prizes while at the same time the English navy intercepted Scottish ships caught trading with the enemy. Scottish traders sailing for French wine and salt had less to offer, as the French government placed heavy tariffs on Scottish coal and prohibited woollen cloth and fish even after the peace treaty of 1697. At home, the demands of war led to a 50 per cent increase in the land tax in 1690, and the imposition of new forms of taxation with a 1690 hearth tax followed by poll taxes in 1693, 1695, and 1698.

At the same time, a spasm of the Little Ice Age hit agricultural yields in Scotland. New research has stressed the seriousness of the harvest failures of the 1690s, with climate change adversely affecting upland areas from the early years of the decade.[38] While the largest tenants and landowners may have prospered by selling surpluses at higher prices, the consecutive bad years left smaller players with a dearth of seed, breeding stock, and ploughing animals. This, combined with the out-migration or death by famine of agricultural workers, left land lying unused for years. Not only did this undermine earlier gains in agricultural productivity, but in monetary terms the collapse of agrarian income short-circuited the chains of credit on which the Scottish economy depended. A growing credit crisis was intensified from 1696 by emergency taxation and borrowing to fund unprecedented levels of spending by local and national authorities on imported victual to relieve the poor. Rural income was further hit by English protectionism as a result of the raising of English tariffs on Scottish linen in 1698.

---

[38] Karen J. Cullen, Christopher A. Whatley, and Mary Young, 'King William's Ill Years: New Evidence on the Impact of Scarcity and Harvest Failure during the Crisis of the 1690s on Tayside', *Scottish Historical Review*, 85:2, no. 220 (October 2006), 250–76.

Just as agricultural returns began to collapse, Scotland's investors sank their capital into a patriotic venture that directly challenged powerful English commercial interests. Launched in 1695, the initial aim of the Company of Scotland Trading to Africa and the Indies was to create new markets for Scottish wool in Africa. Investors in the English East Indian trade saw the company as a threat to their monopoly, sparking concerted efforts to block the company's fund-raising efforts in London and continental money markets. In response, a patriotic stir in Scotland attracted not just a wealthy elite to the Company's 1696 subscriptions but also a large number of small and institutional investors, from widows to royal burghs. As Douglas Watt's history of the Company shows, these investors saw no returns in the short term as the Company shifted to a high-risk American colonization strategy that clashed with the diplomatic interests of the Crown and the economic interests of English Caribbean colonies.[39] The tying-up of capital in the Company, falling agrarian returns, and a European shortage of specie combined to produce a major recession in the late 1690s, leading some contemporaries to conclude that Scotland's position in the Union of Crowns was untenable.

This assessment of Scotland's economic problems helps to explain contemporary support for incorporating union, but some historians feel that it underplays the potential for the Scottish economy to recover from a short-term combination of external difficulties. They have emphasized the continuing vitality of Scottish trade in certain sectors, most notably with North American colonies. This alternative view stresses the resilience and entrepreneurial spirit of Scottish merchants in the pre-Union period, suggesting that, given time, the economy could have recovered from the extreme circumstances of the 1690s. Reinforced by Steve Murdoch's reconstruction of Scottish trading networks in northern Europe, T. M. Devine's study of 'Scotland's empire' points to the success of seventeenth-century Scots as emigrant traders in Continental Europe, particularly Poland-Lithuania, Sweden, and Norway-Denmark; and as colonists and traders in Ulster and the North American plantations.[40] From mid-century, Scottish trade to the English plantations in particular offered a means of exploiting Scotland's position in the Union of Crowns. With support from the Duke of York, Scotland's commercial elites formed an explicit strategy to build exports via colonial trade, leading to Scottish ventures in South Carolina (1684) and East New Jersey (1685). As well, Allan Macinnes's recent study of the Union notes the many loopholes by which Scottish traders sold coarse Scottish linen and other exports to North America. Macinnes has argued that Scottish evasion of the Navigation Acts had reached sufficient heights by 1705 to motivate English, as opposed to Scottish, desires for economic union in order to regularize Scottish colonial trade.

These optimistic and pessimistic views of Scottish trade on the eve of Union are, of course, not mutually exclusive. In revising more simple explanations for the making of the Union, together they indicate the responsiveness of the Scottish economy in

---

[39] Douglas Watt, *The Price of Scotland: Darien, Union and the Wealth of Nations* (Edinburgh, 2007).

[40] Steve Murdoch, *Network North: Scottish Kin, Commercial and Covert Associations in Northern Europe 1603–1746* (Leiden and Boston, 2006); T. M. Devine, *Scotland's Empire, 1600–1815* (London, 2003).

the pre-Union period as it changed according to European, Atlantic, and British circumstances. As with assessments of culture, society, and politics, historians may not agree on the overall health of the pre-Union economy, but they understand that it was not static.

\*\*\*

There is little doubt that pre-Union Scotland had its problems. Since the 1960s, though, historians have become uncomfortable with the notion that modernity arrived in Scotland with the Anglo-Scottish Union of 1707. Hugh Trevor-Roper's trenchant restatement of this in the 1970s, in the context of arguments over devolution, has impelled a new generation of historians to challenge older interpretations of society, politics, culture, and trade in pre-Union Scotland. Recent scholarship has featured broader comparative frameworks and a willingness to take Scottish development on its own terms. A historiographical shift towards cultural studies has prompted new perspectives on political, religious, and intellectual culture. The result is a fertile field of inquiry with significant areas of debate inviting further research. Periodization conventions still truncate our sense of the pre-Union period, highlighting the need for works of synthesis cutting across the early modern period. Indisputably, however, there is a new consensus which suggests that Scotland did not simply leapfrog to modernity on the back of the Union. There was something we can call 'early modern' Scotland, though the shape of this transitional period still remains the subject of robust discussion.

## FURTHER READING

Devine, T. M., 'The Union of 1707 and Scottish Development', *Scottish Economic & Social History*, 5 (1985), 23–7.
—— *The Transformation of Rural Scotland* (Edinburgh, 1996).
Emerson, Roger L., 'Sir Robert Sibbald Kt, the Royal Society of Scotland and the Origins of the Scottish Enlightenment', *Annals of Science*, 45 (1988), 41–72.
Goodare, Julian, *State and Society in Early Modern Scotland* (Oxford, 1999).
Houston, R. A., and Whyte, I. D., eds., 'Introduction: Scottish Society in Perspective', in *Scottish Society 1500–1800* (Cambridge, 1989).
Jackson, Clare, *Restoration Scotland 1660–1690: Royalist Politics, Religion and Ideas* (Woodbridge, 2003).
Kidd, Colin, 'Religious Realignment Between the Revolution and the Union', in John Robertson, *A Union for Empire: Political Thought and the Union of 1707* (Cambridge, 1995).
Macinnes, Allan I., *Clanship, Commerce and the House of Stuart, 1603–1788* (East Linton, 1996).
—— *Union and Empire: The Making of the United Kingdom in 1707* (Cambridge, 2007).
Ouston, Hugh, 'York in Edinburgh: James VII and the Patronage of Learning in Scotland 1679–1688', in John Dwyer, Roger A. Mason, and Alexander Murdoch, eds., *New Perspectives on the Politics and Culture of Early Modern Scotland* (Edinburgh, 1982).
Smout, T. C., *Scottish Trade on the Eve of Union, 1660–1707* (Edinburgh and London, 1963).

Stevenson, David, 'Twilight before Night or Darkness before Dawn? Interpreting Seventeenth-Century Scotland', in Rosalind Mitchison, ed., *Why Scottish History Matters* (Edinburgh, 1991).

Todd, Margo, *The Culture of Protestantism in Early Modern Scotland* (New Haven and London, 2002).

Trevor-Roper, Hugh, 'The Religious Origins of the Enlightenment' and 'Scotland and the Puritan Revolution', in *Religion, the Reformation and Social Change* (London and Basingstoke, 1972), and 'The Anglo-Scottish Union', in *From Counter-Reformation to Glorious Revolution* (London, 1992).

Whatley, Christopher, 'Taking Stock: Scotland at the End of the Seventeenth Century', in T. C. Smout, ed., *Anglo-Scottish Relations from 1603 to 1900* (Oxford, 2005).

Whyte, Ian D., *Agriculture and Society in Seventeenth-Century Scotland* (Edinburgh, 1979).

CHAPTER 16

# MIGRANT DESTINATIONS, 1500–1750

## STEVE MURDOCH AND ESTHER MIJERS

Scholars of early modern Scotland have long mused over the plethora of migrant destinations utilized by those tens of thousands of Scots who, for a number of reasons, either chose or were forced to leave their homeland.[1] Their push and pull factors have long been discussed and include economic opportunity or necessity, political considerations, coercion, conflict, and, as Christopher Smout alludes to in this volume, climate change. Taken together these migration triggers have led to claims that Scotland was the country with the highest levels of migration in Europe.[2] This in turn has implications for our understanding of the state of the Scottish economy and society, as the more inflated the migration figures are compared to the notoriously inaccurate population statistics, the more significance is attached to such problems of economy and society.[3]

Scottish population movement overseas, the role and place of the Treaty of Union of 1707 in determining the destination of Scottish migrants, and other issues are much-debated topics.[4] The non-specialist might be lured into thinking that an alteration to the principal migrant destinations followed immediately after 1 May 1707. This is due, in

[1] T. C. Smout, N. C. Landsman, and T. M. Devine, 'Scottish Emigration in the Seventeenth and Eighteenth Centuries', in N. Canny, ed., *Europeans on the Move: Studies on European Migration, 1500–1800* (Oxford, 1994), 76–112.
[2] Smout, Landsman, and Devine, 'Scottish Emigration', 76; Jelle van Lottum, *Across the North Sea: The Impact of the Dutch Republic on International Labour Migration, c.1550–1850* (Amsterdam, 2007), 26, 52, 163.
[3] Reliable statistical data for the Scottish population in the seventeenth century is scarce. See for instance Smout, Landsman, and Devine, 'Scottish Emigration', 85; Michael W. Flinn, ed., *Scottish Population History from the Seventeenth Century to the 1930s* (Cambridge, 1977).
[4] Christopher A. Whatley, *The Scots and the Union* (Edinburgh, 2006), 361; L. Fontaine, *History of Pedlars in Europe* (Oxford, 1996), 36–7, 119–20; T. M. Devine, *Scotland's Empire, 1600–1815* (London, 2003), chs. 2 and 3; Van Lottum, *Across the North Sea*, 27; Peter J. Bajer, 'Scots in the Polish-Lithuanian Commonwealth, XVIth–XVIIth Centuries: Formation and Disappearance of an Ethnic Group' (unpublished PhD thesis, University of Monash, 2009), 101.

part, to the historians' short-hand term 'post-1707 period' or similar derivations used as markers to cover extensive periods of time, often without either qualification of a start or an end date. Therefore, there remain questions to be answered as to where Scottish migrants actually went and at what junctures. The Dutch demographer Jelle van Lottum has argued, for instance, that after the Union 'the number of southward migrating Scots...increased', not so much to England but especially to North America and the Caribbean as well.[5]

Van Lottum's observation is factually correct but does not give qualification to show that this migration followed on from earlier expeditions into the Americas. As Tom Devine points out, Scottish colonial schemes in the Americas in the seventeenth century had ended in disaster at Darien in Panama during the mid to late 1690s, while 'penetration of the English empire by stealth after 1707 turned out to be much more effective and profitable'.[6] From then on the movement of people out of Scotland and into the Americas grew to be one of the largest out-migrations Scotland has ever known. Thus the non-specialist may be left with a feeling that there was a changing axis of migration from Europe in the east to the Americas in the west, or, put more bluntly, that one dynamic replaced another. However, this transatlantic shift does not fully assess the often long periods between the end of phases of larger-scale migration to Europe and the Union of 1707, nor the time it took after the Union for a meaningfully great westward migration to take place. Indeed, it fails completely to consider an end point (if there was one) for migration to Europe post-1707. There are other problems too. We need to take care not to confuse qualitative data with quantitative information. Small groups of successful migrants can skew the picture of migration significantly. Likewise substantial but less visible groups run the risk of being downplayed owing to their lack of discernible impact in their new host societies. Here we need only think of the numbers of often nameless female migrants who barely register in the historical record.[7] But that does not make them unimportant in terms of the history of Scottish migration nor of that of their host destination.

In this chapter we consider significant episodic migrations to given locations, and ask whether such waves to one place were actually a supplement to, or a replacement of, migrations to another. As the works of numerous scholars have previously shown, Scots had been sojourning or migrating to Europe in ever-increasing numbers from the early medieval period.[8] Several main locations emerge as host destinations for Scottish populations and, depending on what one believes, the nations and locations that bene-fited from significant Scottish immigration even by the sixteenth century might include France, Poland-Lithuania, Ireland, the Low Countries, and England—though

---

[5] Van Lottum, *Across the North Sea*, 27. Cf. Smout, Landsman, and Devine, 'Scottish Emigration', 76, 86, 89, 90.

[6] Devine, *Scotland's Empire*, xxvii.

[7] See for instance Siobhan Talbott, 'Scottish Women and the Scandinavian Wars of the Seventeenth Century', in *Northern Studies*, 40 (2007), 102–27.

[8] For an excellent and concise review of the main scholarship see T. C. Smout's foreword in A. Grosjean and S. Murdoch, eds., *Scottish Communities Abroad in the Early Modern Period* (Leiden, 2005), ix–xiii; For specific works, see the Further Reading.

migration to the latter has been woefully under-researched.[9] The reasons for the movement of people to each of these areas varied and could be determined by close cultural ties, military alliances, or simply commercial necessity—a feature that reveals itself in many of the destinations concerned. Of the greatest importance here is that we must be extremely careful not to bulk all these European migrations together to suggest a steady and continuous outward flow of Scots to the Continent. We have to view each wave of migration on its own merits to establish the origins of the movement, its limitations, and assess the reasons why it either came to an end or at least declined from a perceptible flow to a more limited trickle.

This chapter aims to provide an overview of Scottish migrant destinations from the Reformation until the middle of the eighteenth century. It establishes general chronological and geographical patterns that will allow future assessment of the impact of the British Union, rather than to assume that it was a watershed in Scotland's migration history.

# MIGRATION IN THE POST-REFORMATION PERIOD

Although Scottish migration to Europe can be dated back much further, the religious changes of the mid-sixteenth century provided a fresh and powerful impetus, opening new destinations while altering existing relations with others, such as France, Scotland's main ally until 1560. Jane Ohlmeyer has claimed that 'the onset of the Protestant Reformation shattered Scotland's close relationship with France (enshrined in the "Auld Alliance")', although that epoch-defining perspective has recently been challenged in the most comprehensive research into the subject.[10] For sure the once substantive Garde Écossais entered into a period of decline after 1560, reducing it from a full regiment to a symbolic guard of around one hundred men.[11] Subsequently, many Scottish troops sought out alternative overseas service in places where their new-found Protestantism (if that was their main motive) could be best served. That said, it would be quite wrong to

[9] Smout, Landsman, and Devine, 'Scottish Emigration', 84; I. D. Whyte, *Migration and Society in Britain, 1530–1830* (Basingstoke, 2000), 27; S. Murdoch, 'Scotland, Europe and the English Missing Link', in *History Compass*, 5/3 (2007), 890–913; Van Lottum, *Across the North Sea*, 27. See also John H. McCulloch, *The Scot in England* (London, 1935); Justine Taylor, *A Cup of Kindness: A History of the Royal Scottish Corporation, a London Charity, 1603–2003* (East Linton, 2003); G. Cameron, *The Scots Kirk in London* (Oxford, 1979); Stana Nenadic, ed., *Scots in London in the Eighteenth Century* (Cranbury, 2010).

[10] J. Ohlmeyer, 'Seventeenth-Century Ireland and Scotland and their Wider Worlds', in T. O'Connor and M. Lyons, *Irish Communities in Early Modern Europe* (Dublin, 2006), 459. This notion is challenged in Siobhan Talbott, 'An Alliance Ended? Franco-Scottish Commercial Relations, 1560–1714' (unpublished PhD thesis, University of St Andrews, 2010).

[11] W. Forbes-Leith, *The Scots Men-at-Arms and Life Guards in France, 1458–1830*, 2 vols. (Edinburgh, 1882); E. A. Bonner, 'Continuing the "Auld Alliance" in the Sixteenth Century: Scots in France and French in Scotland', in G. G. Simpson, ed., *The Scottish Soldier Abroad, 1247–1967* (Edinburgh, 1992).

think that Scottish Protestants did not also seek service under Catholic monarchs, or that Catholics would not also serve the Protestant powers.[12]

Motives and rationale for migration were not static. Thus while France had become an unpopular choice for Scottish soldiers in 1560, it became popular for Catholic refugees, scholars, priests, and merchants. Furthermore, under her Protestant King Henri IV, a new levy of Protestant Scots was undertaken in 1589.[13] While this support is less than surprising given Henri's Protestant sympathies (he only converted to Catholicism in 1593), sanctioned levies were, occasionally, also allowed to countries often more hostile to Britain.[14]

Without doubt 1560 changed certain aspects of Scotland's relations to Europe, though not always as thoroughly as one might expect. As contemporary recruitments show, military contacts between Scotland and the Catholic powers did not cease with the Reformation. Nor can we simply refer to Protestant or Catholic countries. England and the Dutch Republic harboured substantial Catholic populations while France had many Protestant enclaves.[15] Enforced exile was experienced by Scottish religious and political refugees after regime-changing events in 1639, 1651, 1660, 1689, 1715, and 1745. At each traumatic episode individuals were either exiled, fled, or were forced by circumstance to leave Scotland in fear of persecution by a regime they opposed. Often the simplest way for migrants to find employment was through military enlistment, but the service chosen was seldom random or motivated simply by financial inducements.

# SEVENTEENTH-CENTURY MILITARY MIGRATIONS

The religious upheaval of the post-1560 period informed the choice of destination for the military Scot. With the outbreak of the Dutch Revolt against Spain in 1568, thousands of Scots joined the struggle in support of their Calvinist brethren.[16] The Scots Brigade remained as a permanent part of the Dutch military structure until the outbreak of the

---

[12] For Scottish Catholics serving in Lutheran Sweden and Orthodox Russia see S. Murdoch, *Network North: Scottish Kin, Commercial and Covert Associations in Northern Europe, 1603–1746* (Leiden, 2006), 99–103, 120. For Scottish Protestants entering French service see M. Avenel, ed., *Lettres, Instructions Diplomatiques et Papiers d'État du Cardinal Richelieu*, 8 vols. (Paris, 1855–77), vol. vi, 211–13, 238–40.

[13] A. H. Williamson, 'Sir James Colville of Easter Wemyss', in the *Oxford DNB*; For the permission for the French to recruit three thousand men see *Calendar of State Papers* [hereafter CSP] *Relating to Scotland and Mary, Queen of Scots, 1589–1593* (Edinburgh, 1936), 441. Robert Bowes to Lord Burghley, Edinburgh, 26 December 1590.

[14] See for instance David Worthington, *Scots in Habsburg Service, 1618–1648* (Leiden, 2004), 67–73.

[15] Siobhan Talbott, '"*My Heart is a Scotch Heart*": Scottish Calvinist Exiles in France in their Continental Context, 1605–1638', in David Worthington, ed., *British and Irish Emigrants and Exiles in Europe, 1603–1688* (Leiden, 2010), 197–214.

[16] M. Glozier, 'Scots in the French and Dutch Armies during the Thirty Years' War', in S. Murdoch, ed., *Scotland and the Thirty Years' War 1618–1648* (Leiden, 2001), 126.

Fourth Anglo-Dutch War in 1780, having early on earned their collective soubriquet as 'the Bulwark of the Republic'.[17] There is no doubt that these soldiers earned their pay in foreign service, but the loyalty of the Scots Brigade was ultimately to their British monarch, as evidenced by the British Crown's right to prioritize their deployment when required. This was demonstrated in a number of campaigns where the Brigade was flagged as 'British' and moved out of the Netherlands into Germany, Bohemia, or back to Britain on behalf of the House of Stuart.[18] That the soldiers could equally prioritize their confessional concerns over dynastic loyalty was demonstrated during the Glorious Revolution of 1688. Scots in the 1690s were also serving in increasing numbers in the Protestant (albeit Lutheran) armies of Denmark-Norway and Sweden. In the 1570s, 1,600 Scots were levied for Sweden, after which a regular and unbroken stream of companies and regiments enlisted into Swedish service.[19] The ever-growing Scottish presence in Sweden was complicated by the re-establishment of the Scottish-Danish alliance in 1589, for that treaty stipulated mutual support in all wars. The numbers of Scots in European armies, particularly the Danish and Swedish, increased dramatically after the Bohemian Revolt in 1619, albeit not immediately. Rather, numbers in these armies were maintained, while volunteers also enlisted in the various contestant armies of the Thirty Years War that were more immediately engaged in the conflict—the Bohemians, the Dutch, and, for a minority, the Spanish Habsburgs.[20] By the war's end in 1648, some thirty thousand had fought in Germany on behalf of Sweden, although high rates of attrition meant the actual numbers in Swedish service at any one time were far smaller than this figure suggests. As a result, recruiting for Sweden continued until the supply of soldiers all but dried up in 1638. However, several thousand Scottish troops remained in Swedish service rather than return home. They formed a main migrant pool of soldiers on the Continent along with the Dutch Brigade in the Netherlands and the Régiment de Douglas in France, which itself was composed of the remnants of the ten thousand Scots who enlisted in that country in the 1630s and 1640s.[21]

The Cromwellian conquest of Scotland in 1651 made it hard for many to return, and significant numbers of refugee Scottish soldiers remained abroad. Scots of all persuasions

[17] The most complete survey of this unit remains J. Ferguson, ed., *Papers Illustrating the History of the Scots Brigade in the Service of the United Netherlands*, 3 vols. (Edinburgh, 1899). Cf. Hugh Dunthorne, 'Scots in the Wars of the Low Countries, 1572–1648', in G. G. Simpson, ed., *Scotland and the Low Countries, 1124–1994* (East Linton, 1996).

[18] Steve Murdoch, 'James VI and the Formation of a Stuart British Military Identity', in Steve Murdoch and A. Mackillop, eds., *Fighting for Identity: Scottish Military Experience, c.1550–1900* (Leiden, 2002), 12–15, 19.

[19] For the specifics of the origins of the Scottish-Swedish levy see Alexia Grosjean, *An Unofficial Alliance: Scotland and Sweden 1569–1654* (Leiden, 3003), 14–24.

[20] Murdoch, *Scotland and the Thirty Years' War*, 14; Thomas Brochard, 'Exile and Return from the Far North of Scotland from the Reformation to the Revolution', in *Études écossaises: Exil et Retour*, no. 13 (2010), 21; Worthington, *Scots in Habsburg Service, passim*.

[21] Avenel, *Lettres*, vol. vi, 211–13, 238–40; Matthew Glozier, *Scottish Soldiers in France in the Reign of the Sun King: Nursery for Men of Honour* (Leiden, 2004), 41–7.

looked to escape the 'Cromwellian Usurpation', and indeed the option of foreign service over imprisonment was offered by the English authorities to those Scots still in arms as an enticement to end their uprising. So it was that another Scandinavian enlistment occurred in 1655–6.[22] The Anglo-Dutch wars also saw Scottish numbers in Dutch service swell. An in-depth study of the Scottish presence in Dutch service has warned against overplaying their numbers in the seventeenth century. However, by the beginning of the eighteenth century, the total increased dramatically and during 'Queen Anne's time' some two thousand Scots appear to have been in Dutch maritime service.[23] At the same time, the Scots Brigade in the Dutch Republic remained at full strength. There were also some individuals who put themselves up for hire to whomever would pay them.[24]

A significant military and political migration occurred after William of Orange gained the 'vacant' Scottish throne in 1689, leading to an exodus of Stuart supporters to the Continent. The Scots among these and the subsequent exoduses of 1716 and 1746 enlisted in armed forces as far afield as Russia, Ukraine, Prussia, Finland, Sweden, and France, though final numbers have yet to be established.[25] Nonetheless, in France, Scots could still be found serving in military units until the 1770s.[26] While those loyal to the House of Stuart found refuge in sympathetic countries, others could also find service abroad so that, for example, the navy of Russia could host both Jacobites and pro-Hanoverians, sometimes simultaneously.[27] Nonetheless it was fitting that the last regular Scottish military force in Continental Europe was one of the first established, the Scots Brigade, finally 'nationalized' as a Dutch regiment in 1782.[28] Importantly, Scottish military migrants overseas could serve as ethnic anchors, encouraging or supporting civilian contacts between

[22] A. Grosjean, 'Royalist Soldiers and Cromwellian Allies? The Cranstoun Regiment in Sweden, 1655–1658', in Murdoch and Mackillop, *Fighting for Identity*, 61–82.

[23] A. Little, 'A Comparative Survey of Scottish Service in the English and Dutch Maritime Communities, 1650–1707', in Grosjean and Murdoch, eds., *Scottish Communities Abroad*, 367, 369.

[24] See for example B. Botfield, ed., *Passages from the Diary of General Patrick Gordon of Auchleuchries, 1635–1699* (Aberdeen, 1859); T. Ameer-Ali, ed., *Memoirs of Sir Andrew Melvill* (London, 1918).

[25] Bruce Lenman, 'The Jacobite Diaspora, 1688–1746: From Despair to Integration', in *History Today*, vol. 50, issue 5, April 1990; G. Behre, 'Gothenburg in Stuart War Strategy 1649–1760', in G. G. Simpson, ed., *Scotland and Scandinavia 800–1800* (Edinburgh, 1990), 109–13; Rebecca Wills, *The Jacobites and Russia, 1715–1750* (East Linton, 2002); Murdoch, *Network North*, 313–54; Steve Murdoch, 'The French Connection: Bordeaux's Scottish Networks in Context, 1670–1720', in G. Leydier, ed., *Scotland and Europe, Scotland in Europe* (Cambridge, 2007), 26–55; Siobhan Talbott, 'Jacobites, Anti-Jacobites and the Ambivalent: Scottish Identities in France, 1680–1720', in B. Sellin, P. Carboni, and A. Thiec, eds., *Écosse: l'identité nationale en question* (Nantes, 2009), 73–88; A. L. K. Nihtinen, 'Field-Marshal James Keith: Governor of the Ukraine and Finland, 1740–1743', in A. Mackillop and S. Murdoch, eds., *Military Governors and Imperial Frontiers c.1600–1800: A Study of Scotland and Empires* (Leiden, 2003), 99–117.

[26] André Pagès, 'Les Lys et le Chardon: Les Écossais de la Maison du Roi', in *Académie des Sciences et Lettres de Montpellier*, Séance du 22/05/2006, Conf. n° 3942, Bull. 37 (2007), 109–20.

[27] A. G. Cross, 'Scoto-Russian Contacts in the Reign of Catherine the Great (1762–1796)' in National Library of Scotland, *The Caledonian Phalanx* (Edinburgh, 1987), 24–46; S. Murdoch, 'Soldier, Sailor, Jacobite Spy; Russo-Jacobite Relations 1688–1750', in *Slavonica*, no. 3, vol. 1 (Spring 1996/7), 7–27.

[28] Jochem Miggelbrink, 'The End of the Scots-Dutch Brigade', in Murdoch and Mackillop, *Fighting for Identity*, 83–103.

Scotland and the Continent.[29] However, in the post-1707 period, the majority of Scottish servicemen who fought across the globe did so as part of the British Army, Royal Navy, or the private forces of the East India Company.

## CIVILIAN CONSIDERATIONS

Commercial developments pre-1707 were arguably as significant as the martial migrations to Scotland and Europe. A case study of Bordeaux reveals that commercial interaction was undertaken by a small group of successful commercial agents rather than a large established community such as was found at the same time in Rotterdam, Bergen, Gothenburg, or Stockholm.[30] Recent research confirms that Franco-Scottish commerce did not rely so heavily on the establishment of large communities centred on guilds, brotherhoods, or stranger churches. Rather the numbers of Scottish agents were lower, albeit the trade they conducted was in many cases far more substantive, particularly in French wine.[31]

The difference in commercial methods between the northern and southern migrant communities is interesting, particularly when we consider the pedlars thought to have flooded into the Baltic countries. Several contemporary estimates claimed that some thirty thousand Scottish families lived within the commonwealth in 1620–1 alone, with the number rising to fifty thousand by the middle of the century.[32] Regardless of the truth of such statistics, the mere belief in their accuracy has drawn the attention of scholars ever since.[33] Yet, the most recent scholarship by Peter Bajer has revised the figure of actual

---

[29]  Paul K. Monod, Murray Pittock, and Daniel Szechi, eds., *Loyalty and Identity: Jacobites at Home and Abroad* (Basingstoke, 2010).

[30]  For the Bordeaux case study see Steve Murdoch, 'The French Connection: Bordeaux's Scottish Networks in Context, 1670–1720', 26–55. For the Scottish community in Rotterdam see D. Catterall, *Community Without Borders: Scots Migrants and the Changing Face of Power in the Dutch Republic, c.1600–1700* (Leiden, 2002); For the Scots in Bergen see N. Pedersen, 'Scottish Immigration to Bergen in the Sixteenth and Seventeenth Centuries', in Grosjean and Murdoch eds., *Scottish Communities Abroad*, 135–65. For the Gothenburg Scots see in the same volume A. Grosjean and S. Murdoch, 'The Scottish Community in Seventeenth-Century Gothenburg', 191–223. For the Scots in Stockholm see Steve Murdoch, 'Community, Commodity and Commerce: The Stockholm-Scots in the Seventeenth Century', in Worthington, *Emigrants and Exiles*, 31–66.

[31]  Talbott, 'An Alliance Ended?', *passim*.

[32]  There are at least two contemporary sources for this piece of information. See *CSPD*, 1619–1623, 237. Chamberlain to Carleton, 24 March 1621; William Lithgow, *The Totall Discourse of the Rare Adventures and Painefull Peregrinations of long Nineteene Yeares Travayles from Scotland to the most famous Kingdomes in Europe, Asia and Affrica* (Glasgow, 1906), 368. Lithgow actually says thirty thousand Scottish families. For the fifty thousand reference see Robert Frost, 'Scottish Soldiers, Poland-Lithuania and the Thirty Years' War', in Murdoch, *Scotland and the Thirty Years' War*, 192; Anna Biegańska, 'A Note on the Scots in Poland, 1550–1800', in T. C. Smout, *Scotland and Europe 1200–1850* (Edinburgh, 1986), 159.

[33]  See for example Smout, Landsman, and Devine, 'Scottish Emigration', 81; Devine, *Scotland's Empire*, 11; Waldemar Kowalski, 'The Placement of the Urbanised Scots in the Polish Crown during the Sixteenth and Seventeenth Centuries', in Alexia Grosjean and Steve Murdoch, eds., *Scottish Communities Abroad in the Early Modern Period* (Leiden, 2005), 63.

migrants downwards to five or six thousand in total throughout the period 1600–1800.[34] Despite a wealth of scholarship in both English and Polish highlighting the lower numbers, some scholars cling to the inflated statistic of thirty thousand and even suggest 'it is a slightly conservative estimate'.[35] The simple, but fundamental mistake made here is failing to separate the native-born Scottish migrants from their progeny; confusing born-Scots who moved away with ethnic-Scots growing up in the host-country of their birth, and in the process clouding issues of population history and Scottish demography.[36] Moreover, Maria Bogucka has argued that the numbers of pedlars have been grossly exaggerated and that records from Danzig suggest a more sophisticated, higher-status merchant was more common than traditionally understood; a conclusion endorsed by Bajer.[37] With both many fewer migrants and of higher status, new appraisals are required about the conditions both in the native and host societies that produced and received these migrants. The commercial opportunity afforded to these migrants is self-evident, but surprisingly religion could also be a factor. The mixed confessional nature of the migration allowed Scots to choose parts of the commonwealth as appropriate to their faith. Nowhere was that more evident than in the Lithuanian town of Kedainiai.

In the 1630s, some Scottish Calvinists feared that the Kirk in Scotland was 'backsliding' towards Rome under the direction of an autocratic monarch who had made his contempt for royal challenge quite explicit during his 1633 Scottish Parliament.[38] It is interesting to note that contemporaneously with events in Scotland the town of Kedainiai in Lithuania witnessed a small 'plantation' of Protestant Scots followed by a more sustained chain migration.[39] Crucially here, the creation of a Scottish oligarchy in Kedainiai in the second half of the seventeenth century masks the fact that immigration had actually reduced dramatically; instead second-generation Scots were coming to the fore.[40] This was a trend across the commonwealth. There is consensus among scholars of the subject that the Scottish brotherhoods and guilds were in decline by the

---

[34] Peter J. Bajer, 'Scots in the Polish-Lithuanian Commonwealth, XVIth–XVIIth Centuries: Formation and Disappearance of an Ethnic Group' (unpublished PhD thesis, University of Monash, 2009), 100–1. Bajer puts the figure for Scots *and their descendants* at no more than five to six thousand souls in the mid-1640s and is scathing of the larger figures. See also Kowalski, 'The Placement of the Urbanised Scots', 64. Previous scholars have also noted figures in this region. See A. Biegańska, 'Andrew Davidson (1591–1660) and his Descendants', in *Scottish Slavonic Review*, 10 (1988), 7.

[35] Van Lottum, *Across the North Sea*, 26.

[36] Biegańska, 'A Note on the Scots in Poland', 158.

[37] Maria Bogucka, 'Scots in Gdansk (Danzig) in the Seventeenth Century', in A. I. Macinnes, T. Riis, and F. G. Pedersen, eds., *Ships, Guns and Bibles in the North Sea and the Baltic States, c.1350–c.1700* (East Linton, 2000), 41.

[38] Anon., *The grievances given in by the Ministers before the Parliament holden in June 1633* (1635); J. R. Young, 'Charles I and the 1633 Parliament', in K. M. Brown and A. J. Mann, *Parliament and Politics in Scotland, 1567–1707* (Edinburgh, 2005), 101–37.

[39] R. Žirgulis, 'The Scottish Community in Kėdainiai c.1630–c.1750', in Grosjean and Murdoch, eds., *Scottish Communities Abroad*, 225–45; S. Murdoch, 'The Scottish Community in Kedainiai (Kiejdany) in its Scandinavian and Baltic Context', in *Almanach Historyczny*, 1/9 (Kielce, 2007), 47–61.

[40] Žirgulis, 'The Scottish Community in Kėdainiai', 237; Bajer, 'Scots in the Polish-Lithuanian Commonwealth', 233.

1640s.[41] Waldemar Kowalski has determined that 'Scottish mass migration to the Polish Crown seems to have come to an end by the 1660s', while Bajer has observed that the Lublin-Scots were last mentioned as an identifiable 'nation' in the commonwealth in 1681.[42] Migration to Poland-Lithuania did not cease at this time, but it did slow considerably in comparison to the late sixteenth and first half of the seventeenth century, leaving a substantial community of ethnic, if not native-born Scots.

At the same time migration to Poland-Lithuania peaked, locations closer to home also saw an influx of migrants. The notorious 'Plantation of Ulster' saw the arrival of as many as thirty thousand Scots between 1609 and 1641 with a mission to 'plant civility' through Scottish enclaves.[43] The Scots chose not to limit themselves to the official settlements that the monarch had set aside for them in the north of Ireland.[44] Indeed, these settlements were treated effectively as points of entry, undermining their very existence as Scottish enclaves. Many Scots quickly moved to the more commercially lucrative centres in Ireland, especially Dublin and Cork. Many others dissipated into the wider diaspora beyond the Stuart kingdoms; thousands arrived in Scandinavia with Scottish regiments in the first half of the seventeenth century and many more moved on to the Americas in the eighteenth.[45] A large Scottish community did survive in Ulster, though neither in the form nor with the results envisaged either by the king or presumably by the original planters themselves; at least some of the civilizing 'Planters' turned out to be Scottish Catholics.[46]

The establishment of trade networks was a fundamental feature in the migration process. Scotland produced a variety of products including coal, fish, salt, and leather, goods all previously dealt with by scholars of commerce in great detail. In order to exchange them the Scots developed a factoring network across Europe. Officially, the most important Scottish commercial agent in Europe throughout the early modern period remained the Conservator of the Scottish staple at Veere in the Dutch Republic.[47] Since the mid-sixteenth century a Scottish Conservator had remained there, and all Scottish trade in staple goods was theoretically targeted to that city exclusively.

---

[41]   Bajer, 'Scots in the Polish-Lithuanian Commonwealth', 228.

[42]   Kowalski, 'The Placement of Urbanised Scots', 85; Bajer, 'Scots in the Polish-Lithuanian Commonwealth', 187, 228.

[43]   Smout, Landsman, and Devine, 'Scottish Emigration', 78; Alexander Murdoch, British Emigration, 1603–1914 (Basingstoke, 2004), 13–23; Patrick Fitzgerald, 'Scottish Migration to Ireland in the Seventeenth Century', in Grosjean and Murdoch eds., Scottish Communities Abroad, 28.

[44]   Fitzgerald, 'Scottish Migration to Ireland', 28. See also Fitzgerald in this present volume, ch. 14.

[45]   Steve Murdoch, 'The Northern Flight: Irish Soldiers in Seventeenth-Century Scandinavia', in T. O'Connor and M. A. Lyons, eds., The Ulster Earls and Baroque Europe: Refashioning Irish Identities, 1600–1800 (Dublin, 2010), 88–109. David Noel Doyle, 'Scots-Irish or Scotch-Irish', in Michael Glazier, ed., The Encyclopedia of the Irish in America (Indiana, 1999).

[46]   Calendar of State Papers Ireland, 1525–1632, 203, 207; Murdoch, 'The Northern Flight', 95–6.

[47]   M. P. Rooseboom, The Scottish Staple in the Netherlands an account of the trade relations between Scotland and the Low Countries from 1292 till 1676, with a calendar of illustrative documents (The Hague, 1910); T. C. Smout, 'Scottish Commercial Factors in the Baltic at the End of the Seventeenth Century', in Scottish Historical Review, xxxix (1960), 122–8; T. C. Smout, Scottish Trade on the Eve of Union (Edinburgh, 1963), 15, 67, 90–9, 107, 189; V. Enthoven, 'The Last Straw: Trade Contacts along the North Sea Coast: The Scottish Staple at Veere', in Juliette Roding and Lex Heerma van Voss, eds., The North Sea and Culture, 1550–1800 (Hilversum, 1996), 209–21; Murdoch, Network North, 148–52.

Throughout the seventeenth century a small but vibrant Scottish community remained in the town with their own social and religious institutions, and the last Conservator did not leave office until 1799.[48] However, to focus only on the staple goods being exchanged at Veere would be to miss the important commercial developments being made by Scottish entrepreneurs elsewhere in the Dutch Provinces, especially in Rotterdam, and elsewhere on the Continent. For example, the second half of the century saw the Scots achieve their greatest influence in Swedish commerce.

Networks with Scandinavia, the Baltic, the Dutch Republic, and France continued long after the 1707 Union, albeit much diminished, and were not immediately replaced by Scots trying to grab a share of England's economic wealth or any dramatic shift west across the Atlantic.[49] It should be stressed that in terms of numbers, commercial migrants are dwarfed by the military ones. Some perspective is provided when we consider that there were probably twice as many Scottish soldiers in Scandinavian military service in a five-year period (1627–30) as there were commercial migrants in the Americas and Poland-Lithuania combined throughout the entire seventeenth century.[50] And that was even before the largest of the recruiting drives for the Thirty Years War had begun (1630–8). This is not to say that commercial migrants were less important. In terms of repatriation of capital and the continuance of lifeline commerce, that is certainly not the case. But in terms of simple migration statistics, the evidence speaks for itself.

# Educational Migrations

Following the 1560 Reformation, Scottish exiles became involved with running or establishing religious houses across the Continent, to train and support a Scottish Catholic clergy. The most important of the French colleges were those at Douai and Paris, while others were situated in Rome, Ratisbon (Regensburg), Madrid, and Valladolid.[51] Some Scots also moved to the Italian Peninsula to study, either at the Scots College at Rome

---

[48] Enthoven, 'The Last Straw', 209, 219.

[49] W. Mackay, ed., *The Letter-Book of Baillie John Steuart of Inverness, 1715–1752* (Edinburgh, 1915). For the British commercial nation in Danzig in the eighteenth century (including Scots) see Almut Hillebrand, *Danzig und die Kaufmannschaft grossbritannischer Nation* (Frankfurt am Main, 2009). Scottish migration to Poland continued even throughout the nineteenth century. See Mona McLeod, *Agents of Change: Scots in Poland 1800–1918* (East Linton, 2000). For the presence of Scots in France post-1707 (and the fact that not all Scots in France were Jacobites) see Talbott, 'Jacobites, Anti-Jacobites and the Ambivalent', 73–88.

[50] Steve Murdoch, *Britain, Denmark-Norway and the House of Stuart* (East Linton, 2003), 201–25; Grosjean, *An Unofficial Alliance*, 55–73.

[51] J. H. Burton, *The Scot Abroad* (Edinburgh, 1864), 190–8; W. Forbes Leith et al., eds., *Records of the Scots Colleges at Douai, Rome, Madrid, Valladolid and Ratisbon*, 2 vols. (Aberdeen, 1906); W. Forbes Leith, ed., *Memoirs of Scottish Catholics during the XVIIth and XVIIIth Centuries*, 2 vols. (London, 1909); A. Mirot, *Souvenirs du Collège des Écossais* (Paris, 1962); J. L. Carr, *Le Collège des Écossais à Paris, 1662–1962* (Paris, 1962); Brian M. Halloran, *The Scots College, Paris, 1603–1792* (Edinburgh, 1997); Tom McInally, 'Scottish Catholics Abroad, 1603–88: Evidence Derived from the Archives of the Scots Colleges', in Worthington, *Emigrants and Exiles*, 261–79.

(founded 1600) for theological reasons, or to study medicine at the University of Padua.[52] In addition to training Scottish priests, the Scots Colleges also offered university education to those denied it at home through the enforcement of oaths designed to exclude Catholics. However, it was not only the exiles who chose to go abroad for higher education. Again here, France is instructive: the issue of religion was not always that straightforward in France, as Henri IV's conversion of convenience demonstrated. The country hosted many Protestant institutions, which Scots both attended as students or worked at as academics.[53] Furthermore, the Scots College in Paris would admit Protestant students, as they did even in 1638 at a time when religion was once more at the forefront of the Scottish mind. Recent scholarship has clearly shown that religion would not necessarily inhibit such enrolments, commercial contacts, or continued friendships.[54] Similarly, Leiden, although originally founded in 1575 as a Protestant institution, attracted significant numbers of Scots from a variety of religious backgrounds.[55]

The Thirty Years War proved to be a devastating conflict in educational terms as well. As Howard Hotson has argued, the death and destruction of the war impacted on academia by diverting students away from the Baltic and German universities towards those in Scandinavia, Poland-Lithuania, and especially to the newly established University of Leiden in the Netherlands. It would be the end of the golden era for the universities of the Holy Roman Empire and resulted in a dramatic and lasting change in the direction of Scottish educational migration.[56] A new type of student also emerged in this period. Perhaps surprisingly, opportunities presented themselves for children of Scottish soldiers during the Thirty Years War. Some would follow their fathers to the Continent and gain an education as part of their parent's participation in a specific army. In Sweden their numbers certainly account for many of those ethnic Scots who ended up in Swedish institutions either during or after the war. But one has to look further south in Europe to find Scots actively seeking out an educational institution rather than simply attending one close to hand.

Leiden particularly benefited from the redirection of international students in the first half of the sixteenth century. Scottish students, although among the first to arrive after the university's foundation in 1575, only began to appear in great numbers in the middle of the seventeenth century.[57] From the 1650s onwards, the Scottish presence at the four

---

[52] R. A. Marks, 'The Scots in the Italian Peninsula in the Thirty Years' War', in O'Connor and Lyons, eds., *The Ulster Earls*, 334–46.

[53] M. Tucker, *Maîtres et étudiants écossais à la Faculté de Droit de l'Université de Bourges 1480–1703* (Paris, 2001); M. Tucker, 'Scottish Students and Masters at the Faculty of Law of the University of Bourges in the Sixteenth and Seventeenth Centuries', in T. van Heijnsbergen and Nicola Royan, eds., *Literature, Letters and the Canonical in Early Modern Scotland* (East Linton, 2002).

[54] Murdoch, *Network North*, ch. 3 and *passim*.

[55] James K. Cameron, 'Some Scottish Students and Teachers at the University of Leiden in the late Sixteenth and Early Seventeenth Centuries', in Simpson, *Scotland and the Low Countries*, 122–36.

[56] Howard Hotson, 'A Dark Golden Age: The Thirty Years' War and the Universities of Northern Europe', in Macinnes, Riis, and Pedersen, eds., *Ships, Guns and Bibles*, 235–70.

[57] Cameron, 'Some Scottish Students', 124.

Dutch universities grew exponentially, aided by the establishment of Protestant exile communities that sprang up in the wake of the Stuart Restoration of 1660.[58] These joined the existing Scottish–Dutch community made up of merchants, soldiers, sailors, and their families.[59] Many exiles took the opportunity to improve their education, while enjoying the legal protection of their student status at the same time. A second wave of Scottish exiles arrived in the 1680s, coinciding with a first peak in Scottish student numbers.[60]

After the Glorious Revolution, the Dutch universities continued to attract substantial numbers of Scottish students. A Dutch degree was often no longer the main reason; instead time spent at a Dutch university became the starting point of a Grand Tour of Europe. Between 1680 and 1730, Scottish student presence at the Dutch universities reached its peak.[61] In the context of the number of matriculations at the five universities in Scotland— Edinburgh, Glasgow, St Andrews, and King's College and Marischal College in Aberdeen— around the same time, the Dutch universities were effectively a sixth Scottish university, especially when it is borne in mind that many more Scots studied there without ever matriculating.[62] It is clear then that the 1707 British Union had a negligible effect on student matriculations, either for the Scottish Catholics who continued to go to their colleges abroad or to those scholars of medicine and law for whom the Dutch universities proved so enticing. When the numbers did begin to reduce, it was reflective of more opportunities within Scotland rather than through any direct consequence of Union.

## A TRANSATLANTIC SHIFT?

If the Williamite period of British history saw an increase in Scottish student migration to Europe and the continued participation of Scots in the military and civilian spheres on the Continent, although at more realistic numbers than previously suggested, what then

---

[58]  For the Netherlands-based religious exiles see Ginny Gardner, 'A Haven for Intrigue: The Scottish Exile Community in the Netherlands, 1660–1690', in Grosjean and Murdoch, eds., *Scottish Communities Abroad*, 277–99; Ginny Gardner, *The Scottish Exile Community in the Netherlands, 1660–1690* (East Linton, 2004); for the Elbe–Weser-based Scottish exiles see Kathrin Zickermann, 'Across the German Sea: Scottish Commodity Exchange, Network Building and Communities in the Wider Elbe-Weser Region' (unpublished PhD thesis, University of St Andrews, 2009).

[59]  For these see variously Rooseboom, *The Scottish Staple*; Catterall, *Community Without Borders*; A. Little, 'A Comparative Survey of Scottish Service in the English and Dutch Maritime Communities, c.1650–1707', in Grosjean and Murdoch, eds., *Scottish Communities Abroad*, 333–73.

[60]  Gardner, 'A Haven for Intrigue', 286. For a breakdown of Scottish student numbers, see Esther Mijers, 'Scottish Students in the Netherlands, 1680–1730', in Grosjean and Murdoch, eds., *Scottish Communities Abroad*, 301–31.

[61]  Mijers, 'Scottish Students in the Netherlands', 301–31.

[62]  Esther Mijers, 'Scotland and the United Provinces: A Study in Educational and Intellectual Relations, 1680–1730' (unpublished PhD thesis, University of St Andrews, 2002), ch. 3. Cf. See Roger L. Emerson, *Academic Patronage in the Scottish Enlightenment: Glasgow, Edinburgh and St Andrews Universities* (Edinburgh, 2008), 212.

can be said for any supposed 'Transatlantic Shift' around 1700 or 1707? Certainly the post-1689 period saw Scottish migration to the Americas develop into a more substantial stream. However, Scots had been leaving for the New World since the beginning of the seventeenth century. Benefiting from James VI and I's British aspirations and his legal policy of post-nati citizenship, the first colonial venture was the short-lived settlement of Nova Scotia. In 1621 James had issued a charter covering the area from the St Croix to the St Lawrence rivers (henceforth known as Nova Scotia) and a year later on Cape Breton.[63] Plans were drawn up for the establishment of a series of plantations that were to attract Scottish migrants, though none of these were executed until 1629. The settlement on Cape Breton Island came to a premature end when it was destroyed in a French attack later that same year. A second settlement at Port Royal survived but was forced to be given up in 1632 at the Treaty of St-Germain-en-Laye between Charles I and France. Attempts at reviving the claim came to little, although the name Nova Scotia survived.[64] Scots also took an active interest in the Caribbean at around the same juncture. James Hay, the first Earl of Carlisle, was granted proprietorship of Barbados and other Leeward Islands in 1625. Scots soon became instrumental in the development of the island and were recruited as both administrators and planters, although their numbers remained very small. Much larger numbers appeared in the Caribbean as (forced) indentured servants during the Cromwellian and Restoration periods.[65] Others left of their own volition and settled across the Caribbean and North America after their period of indentured servitude. In comparison to the larger settlements previously discussed, these initial ventures involved much smaller numbers, though it should be noted that they could either represent independent attempts at transatlantic settlement or be part of multinational endeavours.

Scottish activity in the Americas often arose as part of British or joint Anglo-Scottish ventures. David Dobson has demonstrated that from the earliest attempts to establish communities in Nova Scotia in the 1620s, there was never *intended* to be a mono-ethnic Scottish community in the Americas, although particularly Scottish institutions like the Scots' Charitable Society of Boston Massachusetts were established to support them.[66] He confirms the findings of previous studies which have highlighted that the English were an integral part of the Nova Scotia scheme from the outset, and were also initially

---

[63] John G. Reid, *Acadia, Maine and New Scotland: Marginal Colonies in the Seventeenth Century* (Toronto and Buffalo, 1981); D. Dobson, *Scottish Emigration to Colonial America, 1607–1785* (Athens and London, 1994, 2004), 39.

[64] A. I. Macinnes, *Union and Empire: The Making of the United Kingdom in 1707* (Cambridge, 2007), 145; John G. Reid, 'The Conquest of "Nova Scotia": Cartographic Imperialism and the Echoes of a Scottish Past', in Ned C. Landsman, ed., *Nation and Province in the First British Empire: Scotland and the Americas, 1600–1800* (Cranbury, London, and Mississauga, 2001), 39–59. For Scottish activity in Newfoundland as late as 1701, see David Dobson, 'Seventeenth-Century Scottish Communities in the Americas', in Grosjean and Murdoch, eds., *Scottish Communities Abroad*, 115.

[65] Dobson, 'Seventeenth-Century Scottish Communities', *passim*; Mark Jardine, 'The United Societies: Militancy Martyrdom and the Presbyterian Movement in Late-Restoration Scotland, 1679–1688 (unpublished PhD thesis, University of Edinburgh, 2009).

[66] See Dobson, 'Seventeenth-Century Scottish Communities', 108–12; W. Budde, 'The Scots' Charitable Society of Boston Massachusetts', appendix 5 in Taylor, *A Cup of Kindness*, 255–7.

intended to be involved in any plantation scheme to be undertaken by the Company of Scotland in the 1690s as well.[67] Similarly, most English schemes involved numerous Scots and Irish—such as for instance the settlements along the Chesapeake—while members of these nations also found their way into other European colonies. Even Oliver Cromwell hoped to develop mixed colonies such as that on Pulau Run in the East Indies, which he ordered should be composed of sixty men 'English, Scotch or Irish'.[68] There were often sound reasons why Scots were included in these schemes; the English authorities in both the Americas, as well as in Ireland, saw the Scots in terms of a defensive barrier between them and the 'savages'.[69]

Opportunities for Scots continued to develop in the second half of the seventeenth century regardless of a Stuart regime that is sometimes presented as hostile to Scottish involvement in transatlantic schemes. Thus Scottish interest in American colonial activities was given a new lease of life in the late 1660s as a result of the patronage of James, Duke of York (later James VII and II). They featured in his plans for his newly-acquired proprietary colony of New York.[70] The well-documented 'Darien Scheme' in the mid-1690s to settle the isthmus of Panama was an even bigger fiasco, ending in the untimely deaths of several thousand Scots and the humiliation of many investors of the Company of Scotland.[71] The settlement and eventual demise of this colony in the 1690s occurred almost contemporaneously with the establishment of the most successful Scottish colony in the Americas. This was the Quaker colony of East New Jersey, which enjoyed the encouragement and the protection of the English government. Between 1683 and 1685 several hundred Scots settled in Perth Amboy.[72] They would eventually challenge the land patents of older English towns and appoint a Scottish governor, resulting in a  counterclaim, after the Navigation Acts of 1696, which questioned the legitimacy of their status. The Scots won their case and the post-nati debate of the early 1600s had come full circle.

Historians agree that over the course of the seventeenth century some 7,000 Scots left for the Americas.[73] Some 4,500 of those went to the Caribbean in various capacities.[74] Their numbers need to be adjusted when we take into account those present in other

[67] Previous works have suggested that the Scots were even in the minority among the settlers. See N. E. S. Griffiths and J. G. Reid, 'New Evidence on New Scotland, 1629', in *The William and Mary Quarterly*, 49, no. 3 (July 1992), 497.

[68] *The Court Minutes of the East India Company, 1650–1654*, ed. E. B. Sainsbury (Oxford, 1913), 373.

[69] Griffiths and Reid, 'New Evidence on New Scotland, 1629', 492; Smout, Landsman, and Devine, 'Scottish Emigration', 80; N. Canny, 'The Origins of Empire', in N. Canny, ed., *The Origins of Empire* (Oxford, 1998), 13.

[70] Dobson, 'Seventeenth-Century Scottish Communities', 119, P. Goldesborough, 'An Attempted Scottish Voyage to New York in 1669', *Scottish Historical Review*, 40 (1961), 56–9.

[71] G. P. Insh, *Scottish Colonial Schemes* (Glasgow, 1922); Devine, *Scotland's Empire*, 44–54; Douglas Watt, *The Price of Scotland* (Edinburgh, 2007).

[72] N. C. Landsman, *Scotland and its First American Colony, 1683–1765* (Princeton, 1985); Dobson, 'Seventeenth-Century Scottish Communities', 124–35.

[73] Smout, Landsman, and Devine, 'Scottish Emigration', 87; A. I. Macinnes, M. Harper, and L. Fryer, eds., *Scotland and the Americas, c.1680–1939* (Edinburgh, 2002), 13.

[74] D. Hamilton, *Scotland, the Caribbean and the Atlantic World, 1750–1820* (Manchester, 2005), 3.

European colonies, most notably the Dutch. It is important to stress that the Dutch Republic relied on foreign employment for its imperial ventures. Scots certainly served in Brazil and were active along the Wild Coast and in the Caribbean, where they played a role of significance in the early years of Dutch activity, in particular in the various attempts to settle in Tobago.[75] They also served in the Dutch East Company (VOC).[76]

Scots were also among the first settlers to arrive in New Netherlands in the 1620s and 1630s. Like their counterparts in the Old World, they obtained trading rights and were effective in joining Dutch society. By the time the colony was conquered by the English, a number of successful Scots were living in New Netherlands and held important positions in its administration. They often arrived indirectly, but could find countrymen in whichever part of the North American continent they travelled. But that they arrived there from locations already playing host to more substantial Scottish enclaves should serve to remind us that Europe still had a role to play as the major recipient of Scottish migrants both up to and beyond the Union of 1707.

Bearing the above caveats in mind, and the consensus of historians who study the topic, it is abundantly clear that the British Union of 1707 did not immediately impact upon the numbers of Scottish migrants either leaving for the European continent or arriving in the Americas. T. C. Smout and Ian Whyte, among others, have previously argued that the Union of 1707 was an important episode in Scotland's history but not decisive and 'economically marginal'.[77] The same appears to be true with regard to the impact of Union on emigration. The first post-Union venture in the Americas, the re-conquest of Nova Scotia, occurred in 1712, followed a year later by the taking of St Kitts.[78] However, large-scale Scottish migration to Nova Scotia did not really begin until the later eighteenth century, while the massive migration to Cape Breton only took place a century later.[79] Douglas Hamilton has observed that migration to any part of North America only significantly began to increase in the mid-1730s when the first highland settlements began to appear in Georgia (New Inverness, later Darien) in 1735. These were followed by settlements in New York in 1738; Cape Fear, North Carolina, in 1739; and the Chesapeake from the 1740s. In the Caribbean the real change was brought about by the acquisition of the Windward Islands in 1763, leading to further migration and settlement.[80] However, as Christian Auer has demonstrated, the same trigger of 'political exile' as observed in several migrations of the seventeenth

---

[75] Esther Mijers, 'A Natural Partnership? Scotland and Zeeland in the Early Seventeenth Century', in A. I. Macinnes and A. H. Williamson, eds, *Shaping the Stuart World, 1603–1714: The Atlantic Connection* (Leiden, 2006), 248–9.

[76] Victor Enthoven, Steve Murdoch, and Eila Williamson, eds., *The Navigator: The Log of Captain John Anderson, VOC Pilot-Major, 1640–1643* (Leiden, 2010), 87–115.

[77] I. D, Whyte, *Scotland's Society and Economy in Transition, c.1500–c.1760* (Basingstoke, 1997), 159–60; T. C. Smout, *A History of the Scottish People, 1560–1830* (London, 1969), 226.

[78] Michael Fry, *The Scottish Empire* (Edinburgh, 2001), 97.

[79] C.W. Dunn, *Highland Settler: A Portrait of the Scottish Gael in Cape Breton and Eastern Nova Scotia* (Wreck Cove, 1991); S. Murdoch, 'Cape Breton, Canada's "Highland" Island?', in *Northern Scotland*, 18 (1998), 31–42.

[80] Hamilton, *Scotland, the Caribbean and the Atlantic World*, 4.

century found currency again in the eighteenth century after the passing of the Transportation Act of 1718.[81]

# CONCLUSION

One of the problems raised in compiling a survey essay like this is how to manage the information and particularly how to address the 'numbers game' which underpins some of the basic assumptions suggested in the introduction. We have been careful throughout this essay to avoid speculative statistics, but only draw on figures that have been reasonably well verified. Previously, benchmark research studies have tabulated numbers of Scots thought to have migrated to a particular location and added these together to give a total estimate of Scottish migrant numbers.[82] Not only has recent scholarship challenged the statistics for some particular locations, but the historians concerned have failed to consider the sheer mobility of the migrants themselves between migrant destinations. The same Scots could and did turn up in more than one location and in several different capacities, leading to the possibility that they can be counted several times over. Complicating matters further, the foreign-born Scots appear to have been just as mobile as their native-born countrymen and find their way into migrant statistics for the wrong reasons. Closer scrutiny of the actual place of birth of self-identifying Scots suggests that fewer individuals left Scotland than was previously believed, while the Scottish communities abroad had a larger foreign-born, ethnic Scottish component.

Here, we have been able to show that particular periods witnessed episodic outflows of Scotland's population and that some of these at least can be tied in with specific events. There was a relative decline in migration to Europe, which was not paralleled by a significant transatlantic movement until after 1760.[83] It is hard to distinguish patterns, however, other than to note that some of the migrations were enduring (Scottish Catholics to the European Colleges) or disproportionally large (participation in the Thirty Years War), while the importance of others (Scottish students in the Netherlands) have been overplayed due to their relative impact. This was both in terms of their scale relative to Scotland's population and compared to migrations by other ethnic groups, such as for instance English or German migrants to the New World. That said, the process of systematically documenting migration from Scotland to particular locations has been dramatically advanced in recent years. For the pre-Union period, rigorous research in European archives has altered perceptions of the scale of the migrations. In some cases (Sweden), we

---

[81] Christian Auer, 'The Transportation of the "Scottish Martyrs" in 1793: A Particular Form of Exile?', in *Études écossaises: Exil et Retour*, no. 13 (2010), 80. For more on the transportation and exile of the Scottish Martyrs in the 1790s see in the same volume Gordon Pentland, 'Radical Returns in an Age of Revolutions?', 91–102.

[82] Smout, Landsman, and Devine, 'Scottish Migration', 85, 90.

[83] This point has been previously made in Smout, Landsman, and Devine, 'Scottish Migration'. See also Tom Devine's chapter in this volume, T. M. Devine, 'A Global Diaspora', ch. 7.

have to revise figures up after research has demonstrated it was Stockholm and not Gothenburg that proved the main commercial magnet, although the numerical adjustment, from sixty to three hundred Scots, is less impressive than the percentile increase of 500 per cent. In others (Poland-Lithuania), we have now to considerably revise statistics down—perhaps up to 85 per cent. And as this particular exodus has given rise to speculation over the condition of Scotland, a new evaluation of the social issues at home is required as clearly there was not the great 'push' out of migrants that was once believed.

Within this reassessment, regional differences within Scotland must be examined next. A first analysis from the Scotland, Scandinavia, and Northern Europe (SSNE) Biographical Database shows the North East (from the River Tay to the Moray Coast) as the largest migrant-producing region, followed by the Northern Isles.[84] An additional analysis of Scottish testaments kept in the Gemeentearchief Rotterdam confirms the status of the North East followed by Edinburgh, the Lothians, and Fife, while the Northern Isles virtually drop off the radar.[85] What little is known about student statistics for the Netherlands show Fife as the most important migrant-producing region, followed closely by Aberdeenshire.[86] In the west, the majority of migrants to Ulster were natives of Galloway, Ayrshire, and southern Argyllshire, including the islands of that county. Few areas of the country, therefore, did not have experience of some emigration, though further and systematic research is required before any suggestions can be made regarding the regional economic and social influences in Scotland.

Whilst older migrant destinations have attracted fresh research, 'new' locations are being treated with more scholarly considerations than previously. Research into the Scots in Spain and Portugal is ongoing, while pilot studies have now been completed and published for Scottish migration into locations as diverse as the Italian Peninsula and South and South East Asia.[87] We can now look to a number of these host locations in turn and find some interesting comparisons and contrasts with other groups; the Scots with the Jews in Poland-Lithuania, or between the Scots and the Germans in Sweden. Some interesting comments have already been made on the general similarities and differences between the Scots and their Irish, Norwegian, and Dutch contemporaries in the early modern period.[88] There are still some important gaps that need filling: England is deserving of several studies, with London alone presenting a willing scholar an enormous undertaking. Similarly, we know that Hungary played host to a vibrant Scottish community in the early modern period, though to date the challenge of mapping the Scottish–Hungarian diaspora has not been met.[89] Furthermore,

---

[84]    Scotland, Scandinavia and Northern Europe (SSNE Biographical Database): www.st-andrews.ac.uk/history/ssne. Data consulted 1 November 2010.

[85]    Gemeentearchief Rotterdam: http://www.gemeentearchief.rotterdam.nl/content/index.php?option=com_wrapper&Itemid=21. Data consulted 1 November 2010.

[86]    Mijers, 'Scotland and the United Provinces', appendix II.

[87]    Marks, 'The Scots in the Italian Peninsula', 336–48.

[88]    T. O'Connor, S. Soger, and L. H. van Voss, 'Scottish Communities Abroad: Some Concluding Remarks', in Grosjean and Murdoch, eds., *Scottish Communities Abroad*, 375–91.

[89]    Their presence is recorded in such documents as *An Exhortation of the Generall Assembly of the Kirk of Scotland unto the Scots Merchants and others our Country-people Scattered in Poleland, Swedeland, Denmark, and Hungary* (Edinburgh, 1647). See also A. B. Pernal and R. P. Gasse, *The 1651 Polish Subsidy to the exiled Charles II, Oxford Slavonic Papers*, xxxii (Oxford, 1999), 28.

while it is clear that there is an advanced understanding of the numbers and locations of Scottish migrants to the Americas on either side of 1707, the same is not true for many European destinations. While we do have some interesting and general contributions, the scholarship on Europe as a Scottish migrant destination in the eighteenth century has not been covered in the same depth as for the century before. To fully contextualize when the European destinations ceased to be attractive and actually gave way to the Americas, this will have to be a necessary task. Europe, it appears, is ripe for a series of fresh archival challenges.

## FURTHER READING

Burton, J. H., *The Scot Abroad* (Edinburgh, 1864).

Devine, T. M., *Scotland's Empire, 1600–1815* (London, 2003).

Fedosov, D., *The Caledonian Connection: Scotland-Russia Ties, Middle Ages to Early Twentieth Century. A Concise Biographical List* (Aberdeen, 1996).

Ferguson, J., ed., *Papers Illustrating the History of the Scots Brigade in the Service of the United Netherlands*, 3 vols. (Edinburgh, 1899).

Forbes Leith, W. et al., eds., *Records of the Scots Colleges at Douai, Rome, Madrid, Valladolid and Ratisbon*, 2 vols. (Aberdeen, 1906); W. Forbes Leith, ed., *Memoirs of Scottish Catholics during the XVIIth and XVIIIth Centuries*, 2 vols. (London, 1909).

Grosjean, Alexia, *An Unofficial Alliance: Scotland and Sweden 1569-1654* (Leiden, 3003).

—— and Murdoch, Steve, eds., *Scottish Communities Abroad in the Early Modern Period* (Leiden, 2005).

Landsman, N. C., *Scotland and its First American Colony, 1683-1765* (Princeton, 1985).

Leydier, G., ed., *Scotland and Europe, Scotland in Europe* (Cambridge, 2007).

McLeod, Mona, *Agents of Change: Scots in Poland 1800-1918* (East Linton, 2000).

Monod, Paul K., Pittock, Murray, and Szechi, Daniel, eds., *Loyalty and Identity: Jacobites at Home and Abroad* (Basingstoke, 2010).

Murdoch, S., *Network North: Scottish Kin, Commercial and Covert Associations in Northern Europe, 1603-1746* (Leiden, 2006).

—— and Mackillop, A., eds., *Fighting for Identity: Scottish Military Experience, c.1550-1900* (Leiden, 2002).

Nenadic, Stana, ed., *Scots in London in the Eighteenth Century* (Cranbury, 2010).

Simpson, G. G., ed., *The Scottish Soldier Abroad, 1247-1967* (Edinburgh, 1992).

—— ed., *Scotland and the Low Countries, 1124-1994* (East Linton, 1996).

Smout, T. C., ed., *Scotland and Europe 1200-1850* (Edinburgh, 1986).

—— Landsman, N. C., Devine, T. M., 'Scottish Emigration in the Seventeenth and Eighteenth Centuries', in N. Canny, ed., *Europeans on the Move: Studies on European Migration, 1500-1800* (Oxford, 1994).

Worthington, David, ed., *British and Irish Emigrants and Exiles in Europe, 1603-1688* (Leiden, 2010).

# CHAPTER 17

......................................................................................................

# UNION HISTORIOGRAPHIES

......................................................................................................

## CLARE JACKSON

THE tercentenary of the Scottish Parliament's approval of the Treaty of Union on 16 January 2007 coincided with a regular monthly press conference at 10 Downing Street. Asked why no major celebrations of the anniversary were being held, the prime minister, Tony Blair, replied that 'the most important thing is not fireworks but... giving a good reason as to why the union of England and Scotland is good for today's world and the future'.[1] Several months later, the tercentenary of the Union coming into force on 1 May was overshadowed in Edinburgh by elections, the following day, to the devolved Scottish Parliament, which—aptly perhaps—returned a minority Scottish National Party administration. Seven and a half years previously, on 1 July 1999, the state opening of the new Parliament was choreographed to incorporate resonant echoes of the ceremonial 'riding of Parliament' before 1707, appealing to nostalgic notions that the Parliament was being reconvened, rather than created anew.

Alongside politicians and pundits, historians have been drawn to proposing and refuting 'good reasons' for Anglo-Scottish union in 1707 and subsequently. For the Union of 1707 remains the canonical moment in modern Scottish history: an event that 'casts a long shadow... both backwards and forwards'.[2] It is also a uniquely emotive subject, largely due to the irresistible temptation to identify, in circumstances surrounding its eighteenth-century enactment, factors conferring or denying the legitimacy of Scotland's continued connections with England. Controversial when framed in 1707, the Union has provoked Manichean divisions among eighteenth-century politicians and subsequent critics alike. Accordingly, whilst Allan Macinnes identifies three distinctive features of union historiography—'its longevity, its partisanship and its ideological fragmentation'—Christopher Whatley regrets Scotland having 'a historiography of the Union which is scarred by bias', and has attacked com-

---

[1] 'Blair Backs Anglo-Scottish Union', *Press Association National Newswire* (Press Association, 2007).
[2] Bruce Lenman, 'Union, Jacobitism and Enlightenment', in Rosalind Mitchison, ed., *Why Scottish History Matters* (Edinburgh, 1991), 48.

mentators 'whose error-strewn accounts have followed tortuously illogical paths to their preordained conclusions'.[3]

Since its enactment, inspiration has been drawn from the rhetoric of contemporary Union commissioners, such as James Douglas, Duke of Queensberry, who confidently reassured parliamentary colleagues in 1707 that 'we and our posterity will reap the benefit'.[4] Another commissioner, Sir John Clerk of Penicuik, recorded that Scotland had thereby 'been led from the political wilderness on to the only true road to happiness and prosperity'.[5] Panegyrical paeans thereafter assimilated the Union within a Whiggish trajectory of political liberty and commercial prosperity, informing Hugh Trevor-Roper's admiration in 1977 for 'that great, unique and irreversible act of statesmanship, as it has generally seemed'.[6] As Tony Claydon has observed, 'the Union stood as a shining beacon' for Whig historians, deemed 'nearly as significant as the Magna Carta, the Protestant Reformation, the 1688 revolution or the 1832 Reform Act'.[7]

By contrast, however, equally tenacious support has attached to the private regrets of another union commissioner, Sir George Lockhart of Carnwath, that measures deployed to secure its enactment involved 'bribing a nation to undo themselves', ensuring that the Union 'sold and betrayed the sovereignty, liberty, trade, wealth and everything that is esteemed dear and sacred by a free people'.[8] Published anonymously by his political enemies, Lockhart's *Memoirs* (1714) included allegations regarding sums secretly paid to some of his parliamentary colleagues from Queen Anne's ministry, which fuelled enduring depictions of the Union negotiations as sordidly corrupt, whereby the Scots were, as Robert Burns memorably claimed, 'bought and sold for English gold'.[9] To explain the Union's 'almost miraculous' enactment, charges of venality, together with claims of threatened English invasion, remain vociferously upheld by the Scottish nationalist Paul Scott, whose strenuous denunciations of the Union explain his inclusion amongst 'those for whom scholarship comes second to national piety'.[10]

---

[3]  Allan Macinnes, *Union and Empire: The Making of the United Kingdom in 1707* (Cambridge, 2007), 12; Christopher Whatley, *Bought and Sold for English Gold?* (Edinburgh, 2001), 14, 21.

[4]  Thomas Thomson and Cosmo Innes, eds., *The Acts of the Parliament of Scotland* [hereafter *APS*], 12 vols. (Edinburgh, 1814–75), vol. xi, 491.

[5]  Sir John Clerk of Penicuik, *History of the Union of England and Scotland*, ed. Douglas Duncan (Edinburgh, 1993), 174.

[6]  Hugh Trevor-Roper, 'The Anglo-Scottish Union', in *From Counter-Reformation to Glorious Revolution* (London, 1993), 287.

[7]  Tony Claydon, ' "British" History in the Post-Revolutionary World, 1690–1715', in Glenn Burgess, ed., *The New British History: Founding a Modern State 1603–1715* (London, 1999), 118.

[8]  Sir George Lockhart of Carnwath, '*Scotland's ruine*': *Lockhart of Carnwath's Memoirs of the Union*, ed. Daniel Szechi (Aberdeen, 1995), 172, 171.

[9]  James Kinsley, ed., *Burns: Poems and Songs* (Oxford, 1969), 512.

[10]  John Robertson, ed., *A Union for Empire: Political Thought and the British Union of 1707* (Cambridge, 1995), xiv; see Paul Scott, 'The "almost miraculous passage" of the Union of 1707', *History Scotland*, 7 (July/August 2007), 30–5.

Whilst the Union's tercentenary 'occurred to almost no rejoicing and public ceremonial', it stimulated 'a bumper period for the publication of Union-related' research.[11] Nascent consensus was even detected among 'Scots of all stripes' that, if nothing else, the Union's enactment in 1707 was 'controversial, contingent and ironic'.[12] In 1907, by contrast, Peter Hume Brown compiled an essay collection to commemorate the Union's bicentenary, marvelling that, despite the eight contributors' different fields of expertise, their articles all 'converge to one conclusion—that the Union was inevitable, and at the same time, desirable'.[13] Until the mid-twentieth century, as Richard Finlay observed, Scotland 'followed its own peculiar historiographical *Sonderweg* which has emphasised the inevitability and durability of the Union with England'.[14] In the 1960s, however, the 'inevitability thesis' was attacked by William Ferguson, who emphasized the unpredictable outcome of negotiations in the 1700s, caustically objecting that few events had been more 'abused by subjectivity and determinist interpretations'. Viewing English financial inducements as tools of effective patronage, Ferguson's oft-quoted characterization of the Union as 'probably the greatest "political job" of the eighteenth century' articulated a prevalent Namierite tendency to accord primacy to high-political machinations, which was expanded in the 1970s by Patrick Riley, for whom the Union was endorsed 'by men of limited vision for very short-term and comparatively petty, if not squalid, aims'.[15] By the Union's tercentenary, however, there was broad support for Whatley's contention that, over the previous generation, 'the pendulum of historiographical fortune' had 'swung excessively in the direction of cynicism and contempt for Scotland's pre-union politicians'.[16]

Seeking to steer between the extremes of teleological determinism and short-term opportunism, this chapter supplies a conspectus of Union historiographies three centuries after the Treaty's enactment. Following a brief account of significant factors influencing events in 1706–7, this chapter first identifies a discernible impetus towards interpreting Anglo-Scottish Union as a rational and principled decision, irrespective of the terms of the actual settlement. Examining lineages of support for closer union, particularly from 1689 onwards, revisionist accounts have emphasized the sheer complexity and interrelated nature of events in 1707, seeking to restore a rationale to the actions of eighteenth-century contemporaries, implicitly denied by derisive denunciations of cynical self-interest. Thereafter, the chapter explores the energetic extent to which parochial preoccupations with domestic considerations have been displaced by scholars keen to contextualize the Union's enactment in terms of English, Irish, continental, and imperial imperatives.

---

[11] Michael Keating, *The Independence of Scotland: Self-Government and the Shifting Politics of Union* (Oxford, 2009), 45; Stewart Brown, Colin Kidd, and Christopher Whatley, Supplement to *Scottish Historical Review* [hereafter *SHR*], 87 (2008), v.

[12] Colin Kidd, 'Hard Men of the North', *Times Literary Supplement*, 12 October 2007, 12.

[13] P. Hume Brown, ed., *The Union of 1707* (Glasgow, 1907), 1.

[14] Richard Finlay, 'New Britain, New Scotland, New History? The Impact of Devolution on the Development of Scottish Historiography', *Journal of Contemporary History*, 36 (2001), 384.

[15] William Ferguson, 'The Making of the Treaty of Union', *SHR*, 43 (1964), 89, 110; Patrick Riley, *The Union of England and Scotland: A Study in Anglo-Scottish Politics of the Eighteenth Century* (Manchester, 1978), xvi.

[16] Christopher Whatley with Derek Patrick, *The Scots and the Union* (Edinburgh, 2006), 25.

# 1

At the start of the eighteenth century, closer political union with England represented one possible means of addressing serious and interrelated concerns facing Scotland. Following the Williamite Revolution of 1688, the dynamics of Stuart multiple monarchy had altered decisively, as ecclesiastical pluralism within Britain was created by the re-establishment of Presbyterianism, whilst the abolition of the Lords of the Articles removed royal control over the Scottish Parliament's proceedings. From the mid-1690s, domestic economic conditions deteriorated amidst harvest failures and famine, while Scottish mercantile networks were disrupted by English involvement in the Nine Years War (1688–97). Frustrated by restrictive English trade tariffs and export prohibitions, an attempt to establish a separate Scottish trading colony at Darien, on the Panamian isthmus, dramatically failed, involving the loss of up to one-quarter of Scotland's liquid capital. In 1700 the death of Queen Anne's last surviving child, the Duke of Gloucester, provoked dynastic insecurity, to which the English Parliament's Act of Settlement (1701), entailing the succession in the House of Hanover, was regarded by the Scots as an unacceptably unilateral response. Further afield, the death in 1700 of the last Spanish Habsburg monarch, Charles II, prompted the War of the Spanish Succession (1701–14), which unleashed the alarming spectre not only of a Franco-Spanish global hegemony but potentially also a British War of Succession, since Louis XIV favoured restoration of the Catholic Jacobite dynasty to the British thrones. Abortive discussions regarding possible renegotiation of the Anglo-Scottish regal union of 1603 were convened at Whitehall between November 1702 and February 1703. The Scottish Parliament's Act of Security (1704), defending Scotland's right to choose an alternative monarchical successor unless Anglo-Scottish trade inequities were redressed, provoked retaliatory legislation by the English Parliament in March 1705 stipulating that, unless the Scots confirmed the Hanoverian succession, they would be declared aliens in England, and their coal, cattle, and linen exports prohibited. Pending repeal of the 'Aliens Act', the Scottish Parliament voted in autumn 1705 to invite Queen Anne to nominate commissioners to enter renewed negotiations for closer Anglo-Scottish union. A Treaty of Union was agreed by Scottish and English commissioners between April and July 1706, and debated by the Scottish Parliament between October 1706 and January 1707. It was approved, with minor amendments, by 110 votes to 67 with 46 abstentions, before debate and ratification by the English Parliament in February, receiving royal assent on 6 March, to take effect from 1 May 1707.

Contextualizing the Union in terms of the intensity and longevity of Anglo-Scottish interactions need not denote resurrection of discredited Whig shibboleths. Rather, it explores the experiences of two independent early modern kingdoms sharing a discrete geographical space within which rich amounts of argumentation and constitutional experimentation occurred. Whilst early modern Scottish authors were predominantly concerned to defend the nation's autonomy as a sovereign and independent kingdom, Colin Kidd has nevertheless insisted that 'unionism also has an impeccably Scottish pedigree' and should not be axiomatically discredited as a 'lap-dog ideology' that is 'un-Scottish and inauthentic, a form of false consciousness which is passively derivative of English values, aims and interests'.[17]

For early modern Scots, some form of peaceful, negotiated alliance with their southern neighbour remained a long-standing option, however attractive or repulsive. As Roger Mason has shown, visions sporadically mooted included expansionist English imperialism during Henry VIII's 'Rough Wooing' in the 1540s and a language of godly concord and Protestant providentialism following the Scottish Reformation in the 1560s.[18] Meanwhile, James VI's accession as James I of England in 1603 was accompanied by ambitions to achieve closer political, ecclesiastical, and economic union. Although James's aspirations were frustrated by English antagonism, Jenny Wormald has suggested that, by elevating the rhetoric of Anglo-Scottish amity over precise practicalities, royal union plans may have been intended to provoke 'a subtle shift in mental perceptions which in the long term would have its effect'.[19] During the mid-century civil wars, the ecclesiastical export of Presbyterianism also underpinned the Solemn League and Covenant (1643) concluded between Scottish Covenanters and English Parliamentarians, which did not involve explicit political incorporation, but undertook to bring Scotland, England, and Ireland into the 'nearest coniunction and [u]niformitie in religione' and to maintain a 'firm peace and union'.[20] Whilst visions of negotiated settlements foundered amidst the brutal realities of Cromwellian military occupation and enforced union during the 1650s, renewed discussions regarding incorporating Anglo-Scottish union in 1670 were more pragmatic and circumscribed. Prompted by pressures to remove mutually hostile trade restrictions, the constitutional proposals discussed in 1670 bear a striking similarity to those eventually concluded in 1707.[21]

Whilst the experience of regal union entailed diverse, contingent, and often short-lived expedients, historians increasingly regard the Williamite Revolution of 1688-9 as a watershed in focusing debate about its future feasibility. With hindsight, Clerk of Penicuik claimed that the Revolution conferred on 'Scotland its best chance ever for an agreed union with England'.[22] Following James VII and II's flight to France, the Convention of Estates drafted legislation insisting that, without a union of 'the bodys politick of the [two] nations', Scotland would revert to its previously 'deplorable condition', and it optimistically appointed union commissioners, three of whom would

[17] Colin Kidd, *Union and Unionisms: Political Thought in Scotland 1500-2000* (Cambridge, 2008), 39, 2.

[18] See Roger Mason, 'The Scottish Reformation and the Origins of Anglo-British Imperialism', in Mason, ed., *Scots and Briton: Scottish Political Thought and the Union of 1603* (Cambridge, 1994), 161-86.

[19] Jenny Wormald, 'James VI, James I and the Identity of Britain', in Brendan Bradshaw and John Morrill, eds., *The British Problem, c.1534-1707: State Formation in the Atlantic Archipelago* (Basingstoke, 1996), 148.

[20] *APS*, vol. vi, 42.

[21] Clare Jackson, 'The Anglo-Scottish Union Negotiations of 1670', in Tony Claydon and Thomas Corns, eds., *Religion, Culture and National Community in the 1670s* (Cardiff, 2011), 35-65.

[22] Clerk of Penicuik, *History*, 81.

later serve in the same capacity in 1706–7.[23] Despite vigorously opposing Union in 1706–7, Andrew Fletcher of Saltoun admitted in January 1689 that he could not conceive 'any true settlement but by uniting with England in Parliaments', while recognizing that closer religious and legal union remained unfeasible.[24] Although the Scots' decision to settle the Crown on William and Mary eclipsed demands for union, Whatley and Derek Patrick have argued that its subsequent enactment in 1707 derived as much from 'persistence and principle as patronage and prostitution'.[25] Some form of renegotiated union with England was thus perceived to offer the most effective means of guaranteeing the Revolution's gains: a Protestant monarchy, the re-establishment of Presbyterianism, and legislative independence in the Scottish Parliament.

If substantial numbers regarded Anglo-Scottish union as a way of securing the 'Revolution interest', reconsideration of perceived alternatives is also required. In Scotland, both the replacement of James VII and II as monarch with his daughter and son-in-law and Presbyterianism's re-establishment were opposed by the former king's adherents. Historiographically, Macinnes has argued that Jacobitism's political potency has often been 'presumed rather than substantiated', arising from disproportionate interest in its literary, symbolic, and cultural resonances, and international diplomacy surrounding the Jacobite courts-in-exile, reinforced by credulous acceptance of Whig propaganda. He nevertheless acknowledges Jacobitism's capacity 'to represent an alternative national interest' in Scottish politics from 1689 onwards, combining *ancien régime* attachments to dynastic legitimacy, divine-right monarchy, religious confessionalism, and patriotic independence. Since the Stuarts' unswerving adherence to Catholicism deterred most Scots from supporting their cause, securing the 'Revolution interest' thereby rendered attractive measures that would constitute a bulwark against a Jacobite restoration, such as closer Anglo-Scottish union.

'Revolution interest' was not, however, necessarily synonymous with 'national interest'. Closer Anglo-Scottish union might prevent a Jacobite restoration and preserve Presbyterianism, but material conditions also demanded attention. Historiographically, the significance attached to economic factors in enacting Union has fluctuated. Older Whiggish accounts emphasized the fact that fifteen of the Treaty's twenty-five articles related to economic provisions which, together with Scotland's commercial prosperity during the eighteenth and nineteenth centuries, seemingly rendered the economic rationale for union axiomatic. In 1907, for example, Hume Brown claimed that, throughout the seventeenth century, Scotland was 'a severed and withered branch, and her people knew it'.[26] Accounts acknowledging a case for closer Anglo-Scottish union still attract criticism as 'a sort of Marxist determination without the Marxism, in other words, a reiteration of the idea that Scotland's economic woes made Union inevitable'.[27] Yet such

[23] Quoted by Whatley, *Scots and the Union*, 29.

[24] Quoted by T. C. Smout, 'The Road to Union', in Geoffrey Holmes, ed., *Britain after the Glorious Revolution* (London, 1969), 183–4.

[25] Whatley, *Scots and the Union*, 29.

[26] Hume Brown, *Union of 1707*, 4.

[27] Michael Fry, *The Union: England, Scotland and the Treaty of 1707* (Edinburgh, 2006), 3.

censure is undeserved. For while there is broad acceptance that 'the economy and economic issues lay at the heart of contemporary thinking and debates about union', historiographical fissures remain concerning the 'condition of Scotland' in the 1690s and 1700s and the extent to which increasingly qualified assessments of the actual economic benefits derived from Union, especially in the pre-1750 period, may illogically have deflected attention away from the optimistic aspirations of contemporaries regarding anticipated gains.

Whilst the economic case for union was once a casualty of a preference for high-political interpretations, Whatley has rehabilitated arguments advanced by Christopher Smout and Roy Campbell in the 1960s and 1970s.[28] Structural economic weaknesses, including an adverse trade balance with every nation except England, a lack of manufacturing capacity, limited domestic demand, and an endemic shortage of specie, combined with short-term pressures such as international warfare, extensive famine, and the Darien scheme's failure in the mid-1690s, 'tipped Scotland over the edge of an economic abyss' and, psychologically, unleashed a 'near chiliastic language of despair' amongst its inhabitants.[29] The extent to which Scots were intent on remedying their plight was reflected in the centrality accorded to economic incentives by pamphleteers and the fact that Article IV of the Treaty, guaranteeing limited free trade, secured the highest majority of votes of any article in 1706 (154 to 19). Such an interpretation has, however, been criticized as unduly pessimistic. T. M. Devine, for example, has termed the so-called 'ill' or 'lean' years of the 1690s 'an aberration, a reflection of an especially severe but essentially short-lived spell of climatic deterioration' that should not obscure Scotland's fundamental economic resilience, entrepreneurship, and keenness to develop new trading networks and colonial ventures from the 1680s onwards.[30] Claiming that 'a nationwide recovery was well under way' by 1702,[31] Macinnes has likewise queried the attractiveness of union for Scottish merchants with extensive continental networks, a lucrative trade in carrying goods between countries, and effective stratagems for evading the English Navigation Acts.

Whereas older analyses of the Union's enactment emphasized high political machinations, the role of religion has recently been rehabilitated, with increased prominence placed on the severity of Presbyterian opposition to union. In the 1970s, by contrast, Riley contended of Scotland's statesmen that 'their professed religious affiliations could be modified' and were easily eclipsed by ambition and avarice.[32] Sectarian divisions gen-

---

[28] See T. C. Smout, *Scottish Trade on the Eve of Union, 1660–1707* (London, 1963), and 'The Anglo Scottish Union of 1707. I: The Economic Background', and R. H. Campbell, 'The Anglo-Scottish Union of 1707. II: The Economic Consequences', in *Economic History Review*, new series, 16 (1964), 498–527 and 468–77.

[29] Whatley, *Scots and the Union*, 139, 140.

[30] T. M. Devine, 'The Union of 1707 and Scottish Development', *Scottish Economic and Social History*, 5 (1985), 25.

[31] Allan Macinnes, 'The Treaty of Union: Made in England', in T. M. Devine, ed., *Scotland and the Union 1707–2007* (Edinburgh, 2008), 65.

[32] P. W. J. Riley, *King William and the Scottish Politicians* (Edinburgh, 1979), 7.

erated in 1690 by episcopacy's disestablishment and Presbyterianism's re-establishment nevertheless remained so sensitive that ecclesiastical and theological matters were specifically excluded from the bilateral union commissioners' remit in summer 1706. An 'intrusion into the voting agenda' on the Articles of Union occurred, however, when the Scottish Parliament was obliged to respond to pressure from the Kirk's Commission of the General Assembly and pass the Act for Securing the Protestant Religion and Presbyterian Church Government on 12 November 1706.[33] As Clerk of Penicuik recalled, 'the trumpets of sedition began to fall silent' as the Act allayed most Presbyterian fears, despite residual concerns including the presence of twenty-six Anglican bishops in the English House of Lords.[34] Although Devine described the Act as 'a master stroke which immensely weakened one of the key elements in the anti-union campaign', Jeffrey Stephen disagrees, claiming that its belated inclusion into the union debates was 'an attempt to rectify the major blunder' in having originally omitted ecclesiastical discussion from the Treaty negotiations; the Act was therefore 'a master stroke of the church not the political ministry'.[35] In forming a stance on union, both Presbyterians and Episcopalians thus needed to adjudicate between securing Protestantism through Anglo-Scottish union or risk encouraging a French-sponsored pro-Catholic Jacobite restoration. Presbyterians particularly needed to judge whether Protestant security with ecclesiastical pluralism justified jettisoning mid-seventeenth-century visions of a pan-Britannic Presbyterian union as outlined in the Solemn League and Covenant of 1643. A united British Parliament, especially under an English Tory majority, might not only grant religious toleration to Scottish Episcopalians but also jeopardize the Presbyterian establishment. Ultimately, however, legislative provision to protect Presbyterianism's establishment revealed irreconcilable aspirations of Episcopalian Jacobites and radical Cameronian and Hebronite Presbyterians. Addressing his Jacobite colleagues in opposing the Treaty, Robert Wodrow acknowledged it to be 'a lamentation that our road and y[ou]rs lyes now together, but I am persuaded we will not go far together'.[36]

## 2

Since principled support for the Treaty within Parliament House contrasted starkly with hostile crowds assembled outside, historians have become interested in calibrating the effects of public opinion on the Treaty's enactment. In 1714 Lockhart of Carnwath's *Memoirs* recalled an atmosphere in 1706–7 wherein travellers would 'find everybody enraged and displeased', sporadic acts of mob violence serving to remind parliamentary

---

[33]  Macinnes, *Union and Empire*, 302.

[34]  Clerk, *History*, 121.

[35]  T. M. Devine, *Scotland's Empire* (London, 2003), 57; Jeffrey Stephen, *Scottish Presbyterians and the Act of Union 1707* (Edinburgh, 2007), 70, and 'The Kirk and the Union, 1706–7', *Records of the Scottish Church History Society*, 31 (2002), 95.

[36]  Quoted by Stephen, *Scottish Presbyterians*, 201.

colleagues that 'the union was crammed down Scotland's throat'.[37] Amidst interest in emerging 'public spheres' in early modern England and Continental Europe, Karin Bowie has denied the making of the Union to be 'a simple story of coercion, betrayal and Scottish impotence' by examining instances of collective resistance to the Treaty, such as crowds, demonstrations, and bonfires alongside a burgeoning print media of pamphlets, periodicals, broadsheets, songs, and verse. Insisting that 'public opinion helped to create the union crisis', Bowie has examined petitions submitted to Parliament—mostly opposing the Treaty—from national institutions such as the Commission of the General Assembly and the Convention of Royal Burghs, alongside 79 petitions from 116 individual shires, burghs, parishes, and presbyteries, bearing the signatures of over twenty thousand Scots.[38] Whilst the scale of external pressure might justify earlier interpretations that focused on the stratagems deployed to secure the Treaty's legislative approval, it also explains significant amendments and concessions, including Article XXIV, confirming that the national regalia and public records would remain in Scotland.

Renewed interest at events in Parliament House has partly arisen in response to stimulating research findings by the Scottish Parliament project, established at St Andrews University in 1997. Whatley and Patrick's prosopographical and psephological studies of voting patterns among members of the post-Revolution Parliament revealed considerable correlation between a 'Revolution interest' and supporters of the Union in 1706–7, including not only a 'court' interest of around ninety politicians, but another group of around twenty-five, known as the *squadrone volante*, whose conversion to the pro-union parliamentary lobby proved critical.[39] Elsewhere, Ian McLean and Alistair McMillan found that anti-union petitions were more likely to be submitted from constituencies whose parliamentary representatives consistently opposed the Union, suggesting that 'petitions reflected rather than induced voting behaviour'. Assessing the potential influence of pecuniary incentives, they detected 'surprisingly little direct association' between support for the Union and ownership of stock in the failed Darien venture, but nevertheless acknowledged more compelling potential for inducements to have influenced support for Article XXII determining Scotland's parliamentary representation in a united Britain. With 112 out of 157 burgh and shire commissioners voting to have their representation reduced from 157 members to 45, and 144 out of 166 noble members likewise supporting their representation falling from 166 to just 16 peers in a united House of Lords, McLean and McMillan observed 'an early case of…turkeys voting for Christmas (albeit with many receiving a huge stuffing)'.[40]

Revisiting the influence of public opinion in the Union's enactment has also opened up intriguing avenues for future research, some of which may prove intractable, given

---

[37] Lockhart of Carnwath, 'Scotland's ruine', 177, 144.

[38] Karin Bowie, *Scottish Public Opinion and the Anglo-Scottish Union, 1699–1707* (Woodbridge, 2007), 8, 162.

[39] See Derek Patrick and Christopher Whatley, 'Persistence, Principle and Patriotism in the Making of the Union of 1707: The Revolution, Scottish Parliament and the *squadrone volante*', *History*, 92 (2007), 162–86.

[40] Ian McLean and Alistair McMillan, *State of the Union: Unionism and the Alternatives in the United Kingdom since 1707* (Oxford, 2005), 33, 45, 58.

the vagaries of source survival. As Bowie acknowledges, she focuses on lowland opinion, having found little surviving evidence of petitioning or crowd activity in Gaelic-speaking areas. Nevertheless, room remains for more systematic investigations of the social composition of those featuring in anti-union crowd agitation, whilst regrettably little is known about female involvement, since women were often barred from signing addresses and petitions, despite featuring prominently in contemporary anecdotes. Observing anti-union opposition among devout Presbyterians, for example, Daniel Defoe surmised that 'the women are the instructers and the men are meer machin[e]s wound up'.[41] We also lack detailed quantitative information indicating the size of pamphlet print runs, numbers of editions, estimated readership, and sale prices.

Such considerations matter, since the reinstatement of principle in union historiographies has simultaneously depended on rehabilitating ideological argumentation. A bibliography of publications concerning Anglo-Scottish relations during Queen Anne's reign, compiled in the late 1970s, enumerated over five hundred items, whilst essays edited by John Robertson in the mid-1990s attested to the qualitative and cosmopolitan richness of constitutional theorizing prompted by debates surrounding the Union of 1707.[42] Whilst Robertson accorded Fletcher of Saltoun primary credit for the sophistication of the debates over union, Fletcher is no longer lionized as a lone authority. Rich insights have been gleaned from reconsidering the writings of numerous authors including Lord Belhaven, Francis Grant, James Hodges, George Mackenzie (Earl of Cromarty), William Paterson, George Ridpath, and William Seton of Pitmedden, whilst John Kerrigan regards Defoe's contribution to the union debates as 'drastically underrated'.[43]

One striking aspect of these discussions was the sheer heterogeneity of constitutional futures mooted, which supplied 'a genuine alternative to the offer of incorporation emanating from London'. Fletcher, for example, held the optimum outcome of a renegotiation of the existing regal union to be a confederal union of equal partners which, by creating 'a sort of United Provinces of Great Britain', would necessarily require the division of England and other parts of the British Isles into smaller entities, potentially supplying an attractive model for imitation throughout Continental Europe.[44] In the *Rights and interests of the two British monarchies* (1703), James Hodges addressed the merits and demerits of incorporating union, but also discussed alternative arrangements, including the 'Auld Alliance' between Scotland and France and versions derived from the federal union between Lithuania and Poland, and unions among the Dutch states, thirteen Swiss cantons, and ancient Greek republics. Far from falling simply into rival pro-union and anti-union constituencies, the diversity of deliberations has led Kidd to allege 'the discreet irony that the Union debates of 1698–1707...largely took the form of an intra-unionist conversation'.[45]

---

[41]  Quoted by Whatley, *Scots and the Union*, 288.

[42]  W. R. and V. B. McLeod, *Anglo-Scottish Tracts, 1701–1714: A Descriptive Checklist* (Lawrence, KA, 1979); Robertson, ed., *Union for Empire*.

[43]  John Kerrigan, *Archipelagic English: Literature, History, and Politics 1603–1707* (Oxford, 2008), 326.

[44]  Robertson, 'Empire and Union: Two Concepts of the Early Modern European Political Order', in Robertson, ed., *Union for Empire*, 33.

[45]  Kidd, *Union and Unionisms*, 68.

Whilst the Treaty's eventual form may not have attracted universal acclaim, a principled intellectual case for supporting union gained increasing ground, drawing on combinations of arguments outlined above. Interestingly, despite the significance Ferguson attached to magnate strategies, coalition politics, and financial inducements in securing the Union's enactment, he also drew attention to the 'imperial crowns debate' that emerged during the 1690s amidst English attempts to revive medieval claims to suzerainty over Scotland.[46] Whilst the Scots constructed convincing counter-arguments, dynastic uncertainty provoked by the English Act of Settlement rendered it difficult for Scottish sovereignty to be defended in terms of unbroken dynastic continuity without admitting the Jacobites' hereditary claim. Hence Robertson has emphasized 'the elusiveness of Scotland's sovereignty, understood as the kingdom's historic independence', recognizing that, for early eighteenth-century writers, it was 'a sovereignty almost impossible to put into a viable constitutional form'.[47]

Moreover, the extent to which loss of a separate Parliament necessarily entailed abandonment of Scottish nationhood resurfaced in 1706 when English union commissioners insisted on incorporating union, categorically refusing to countenance federal or confederal alternatives. As the Earl of Cromarty had asked in *Parainesis Pacifica* (1702), 'Doth the Change of Governments, or Form of Constitutions of Government, annihilate the People or the Nation?'[48] Patriotism did not thereby become an exclusively anti-Union preserve, since supporters and opponents alike predicated their positions on calculations of long-term utility and how best to preserve the *salus patriae*.[49] With the Kirk's establishment secured by separate legislation, a committed Presbyterian, such as Francis Grant, Lord Cullen, could style himself *The Patriot resolved* (1707) and support the Union since it protected Presbyterian Protestantism and promised prosperity.

Indeed, Grant's confident characterization of the Treaty of Union as 'an unchangeable contract'[50] was not only disputed by contemporaries but also illustrates the extent to which, as Kidd has shown, the 'constitutional dilemmas which arose out of the Union of 1707 ... remain a matter of intense debate'.[51] Alongside uncertainty as to whether the Union was actually a treaty, justiciable in international and/or domestic law, divisions of opinion have long subsisted as to whether its provisions were fundamentally constitutive of a new British state or whether they were open to reversal by a majority vote in a united British Parliament. At the Treaty's enactment, arguments advanced by the Earl of Cromarty's cousin, and former Lord Advocate, Sir George Mackenzie of Rosehaugh, were posthumously revived by Presbyterian opponents of union to deny that the Scottish Parliament had the right to vote itself out of existence by a simple majority vote.[52] In the

---

[46]  William Ferguson, 'Imperial Crowns: A Neglected Facet of the Background to the Treaty of Union', *SHR*, 53 (1974), 22–44.

[47]  Robertson, 'Preface', *Union for Empire*, xvii.

[48]  Sir George Mackenzie, Earl of Cromarty, *Parainesis pacifica* (London, 1702), 4.

[49]  Clare Jackson, 'Conceptions of Nationhood in the Anglo-Scottish Union Debates of 1707', *SHR*, 87 (2008) supplement, 61–77.

[50]  [Francis Grant], *The patriot resolved* (n.p., 1707), 10.

[51]  Kidd, *Unions and Unionism*, 85.

[52]  [Robert Wylie], *A letter concerning the union &c.* ([Edinburgh], 1706).

1670s Mackenzie had insisted that 'parliaments cannot overturn fundamentals'; indeed, the commissions entrusted to Members of Parliament 'presupposeth, that there must be a Parliament, and consequentlie, that they cannot extinguish, or innovate the Constitution of the Parliament of Scotland'.[53] Nearly three centuries later, the jurist T. B. Smith invoked similar language to describe the Union as a 'fundamental law' of the British state and thus of greater authority than individual acts of the British Parliament.[54] Smith's opinion was directed towards a rival constitutional orthodoxy, associated with the English jurist A. V. Dicey, who strenuously defended the doctrine of unlimited parliamentary sovereignty at Westminster and famously claimed that 'neither the Act of Union with Scotland, nor the Dentists Act, 1878, has more claim than the other to be considered a supreme law'.[55] The Union's constitutional status thus remains a fertile subject for deliberation, not only in courts of law, as in cases such as *MacCormick v. Lord Advocate* (1953), *Gibson v. Lord Advocate* (1975), and *Robbie the Pict v. Hingston* (1998), but also among constitutional lawyers keen to revisit the Treaty's provisions amidst subsequent constraints on the Westminster Parliament's untrammelled sovereignty, most notably those arising from British membership of the European Community.

## 3

If incorporating union was a contingent matter for Scottish contemporaries, it was not an issue of exclusively domestic preoccupation. Across Europe, unions were a ubiquitous feature of early modern politics as the number of independent polities fell from just under 500 in the early sixteenth century to fewer than 350 by 1800. Whilst pamphleteers invoked a rich range of different constitutional types of union, Macinnes has shown how broader concerns about French and Dutch views of Anglo-Scottish union prompted the Scottish Privy Council to authorize the translation and publication of excerpts from the *Paris Gazette* and *Haarlem Courant* at the beginning of 1706.[56]

Historiographically, the tercentenary of the Williamite Revolution in 1988 saw a discernible shift away from Whiggish narratives of domestic Providential Protestant rescue to evaluating events from a European perspective.[57] A similar historiographical adjustment has informed analyses of events in 1707 with Robertson claiming that, in 'its principles as well as in its circumstances, British union was a thoroughly European event'.[58] In an explicitly comparative investigation, Robertson juxtaposed the experiences of early eighteenth-century Scots with those of contemporary Neapolitans who found themselves unexpectedly

---

[53]  Quoted by Jackson, 'Anglo-Scottish Union', 54–5.

[54]  T. B. Smith, 'The Union of 1707 as Fundamental Law', *Public Law* (1957), 99–121.

[55]  Quoted by Kidd, *Union and Unionisms*, 83–4.

[56]  Macinnes, *Union and Empire*, 238.

[57]  See, for example, Jonathan Israel, ed., *The Anglo-Dutch Moment: Essays on the Glorious Revolution and its World Impact* (Cambridge, 1991).

[58]  Robertson, 'Empire and Union', 35.

subsumed within the Habsburg monarchy in July 1707 and thereafter ruled from Barcelona by Archduke Charles of Austria. Recognizing that, by 1700, 'the Scottish elite had every reason to feel frustrated, both economically and politically', Robertson described the dilemma posed to Scots and Neapolitans alike as subjects of ancient monarchies which had now become absentee monarchies.[59] As Fletcher of Saltoun had lamented in 1703, Scotland 'was totally neglected, like a farm managed by servants, and not under the eye of the master'.[60]

Three years later, however, the farm master had certainly taken an interest in his northern kingdom, even if Fletcher himself opposed the Treaty. A tercentenary after its formulation, historians are increasingly interested in establishing whether, as Macinnes argues, 'England became the driving force for the Treaty of Union'.[61] Endorsing claims for a reservoir of pro-union support within Scotland, David Hayton also suggested that, after the Williamite Revolution, 'the Scots could probably have been brought to agree to a treaty at any time'.[62] If so, attention needs to be directed towards discovering why the English suddenly became converts by 1706.

Whilst the War of the Spanish Succession provided a catalyst for substantive constitutional reorganization throughout Europe, its exigencies also rendered security of England's northern border a key military priority. Whilst historians disagree over whether deteriorating Anglo-Scottish relations between 1703 and 1705 raised a realistic spectre of armed hostilities, the English would clearly have been reluctant to withdraw troops fighting in Flanders and Spain to quell Scotland by force.[63] Threatened English invasion has been cited as crucial in securing the Treaty's parliamentary passage in Scotland by those nationalists who steadfastly deny any domestic support for union.[64] Adverse memories of the Cromwellian version of union imposed on Scotland during the 1650s certainly meant that latent fears of armed conquest remained 'an unavoidable, intrinsic dimension of Anglo-Scottish relations' thereafter.[65] As diplomatic relations deteriorated in 1705, the English Treasurer, the Earl of Godolphin, warned the Earl of Mar that, unless the situation improved, England had 'the power, and you may give us the will' to impose a forcible solution at a time when the Scots would be unable to rely on French military assistance.[66] The following year, English troops were mobilized northwards to Berwick and the north of Ireland as the Treaty was debated in Edinburgh.

---

[59] John Robertson, *The Case for the Enlightenment: Scotland and Naples 1680–1760* (Cambridge, 2005), 56.

[60] Andrew Fletcher, 'An account of a conversation &c.', in *Political Works*, ed. John Robertson (Cambridge, 1997), 186.

[61] Macinnes, 'Treaty of Union', 54.

[62] David Hayton, 'Constitutional Expedients and Political Expediency, 1689–1725', in Steven Ellis and Sarah Barber, eds., *Conquest and Union: Fashioning a British State, 1485–1725* (Harlow, 1995), 277.

[63] See Christopher Storrs, 'The Union of 1707 and the War of the Spanish Succession', in *SHR*, 87 (2008) supplement, 31–44.

[64] For example, Paul Scott, 'An English Invasion would have been Worse: Why the Scottish Parliament Accepted the Union', *Scottish Studies Review*, 3 (2003), 9–16.

[65] Robertson, 'Empire and Union', 34.

[66] Historical Manuscripts Commission, *Fourteenth Report, Appendix Part III. The Manuscripts of the Duke of Roxburghe...and the Countess Dowager of Seafield* (London, 1894), 207.

From a different perspective, Macinnes has identified principles of political economy as influential in reversing traditionally indifferent or antagonistic English attitudes towards closer Anglo-Scottish union. Insisting that the Scots regarded the 'targeted pursuit of colonies as the commercial alternative to union' from 1660 onwards, Macinnes has shown how Scottish commercial networks succeeded in circumventing the English Navigation Acts via legal loopholes, specific exemptions, smuggling, collusion, the disguised ownership of vessels, and other stratagems that an overstretched imperial infrastructure was unable to prevent. Such activities severely depleted English colonial customs returns at a time when the Treasury relied heavily on such revenue to fund the country's emergence as a fiscal–military state. Fears of domestic demographic stagnation simultaneously challenged England's ability to resource both its continental military activities and its global imperial ambitions. Accordingly, Macinnes argues that Scottish commercial networks were 'transformed from being viewed as significant disruptors of trade to a new role as potential pillars of Empire' while, more generally, 'Scotland came into the position of favoured nation'.[67]

Accession to the Treaty of Union was not, however, universally popular in England, and nor did the manner of its negotiation imply spontaneous Anglo-Scottish accord. Indeed, the extent to which the Treaty's provisions reproduced terms agreed during earlier rounds of union negotiations was reflected in the fact that, in 1706, the Scottish and English commissioners required only one plenary meeting in the Cockpit at Westminster to discuss the extent of Scottish parliamentary representation in a united Britain. As one Scottish commissioner rued, 'none of the English during the Treaty had one of the Scots so much as to dine or drink a glass of wine with them'.[68] Inevitable resentment surfaced in England that terms of ostensible equality had been agreed between two parties who were, economically at least, conspicuously unequal. For although Scotland's allocation of forty-five MPs in the House of Commons (one-twelfth of the total) was denounced as a demographic under-representation, alternative calculations confirmed that Scotland's land-tax assessment was one forty-fifth the size of England's. Meanwhile, although parallel legislation to that agreed for the Presbyterian Kirk in Scotland was also passed confirming the established status of the Episcopalian Anglican Church, fears arose regarding the possible insinuation of Presbyterianism through union. During debates in the House of Lords in February 1707, Lord Hailsham insisted that the Union would join 'such jarring incongruous Ingredients' that he deemed necessary 'a standing Power and Force, to keep us from falling asunder and breaking in pieces every Moment'.[69]

Albeit refreshingly counter-intuitive, Macinnes's inference that 'England was as much if not more in need of a stable political association' as Scotland in 1707 remains

---

[67] Allan Macinnes, 'Union Failed, Union Accomplished: The Irish Union of 1703 and the Scottish Union of 1707', in Dáire Keogh and Kevin Whelan, eds., *Acts of Union: The Causes, Contexts and Consequences of the Act of Union* (Dublin, 2001), 74, 61, 63.

[68] Historical Manuscripts Commission, *Report on the Manuscripts of the Earl of Mar and Kellie* (London, 1904), 271.

[69] [Abel Boyer], *The history of the reign of Queen Anne, digested into annals. Year the fifth* (London, 1707), 443.

debatable.[70] Increased attention to England's instrumental role as the regal union's stronger partner does, however, resonate with arguments of political scientists pondering the Union's future. Drawing potential parallels with the 'velvet divorce' between the Czech Republic and Slovakia in 1993, McLean and McMillan envisage a possible 'tartan divorce' wherein the weaker partner in a union 'has routinely and noisily complained for decades' about its subordinate status, 'only to be taken by surprise when the larger partner suddenly offers' independence.[71]

Reappraising English motivations for incorporating union in 1707 has, in turn, ignited interest in Irish dimensions to Anglo-Scottish union as Irish parallels were regularly invoked by eighteenth-century Scots, whilst 'the Anglo-Scottish union constitutes an event in Irish history' in stimulating simultaneous alterations in attitudes regarding possible Anglo-Irish union.[72] Examining the emergence of unionist ideology in Ireland from the 1690s onwards raises the counter-factual question of why Anglo-Scottish union was concluded in 1707, whereas concurrent calls for Anglo-Irish union went unheeded.

Following the Williamite Revolution, Ireland faced a similar predicament to Scotland. English legislation directed towards eliminating economic competition included two Irish Cattle Acts in the 1660s, but intensified with the Irish Woollen Act (1690), banning the export of Irish wool, and the Resumption Act (1700). Although no Irish Parliament convened between 1666 and 1689, its legislative subordination to the English Privy Council thereafter ensured that 'the constitutional fiction that [Ireland] was an autonomous kingdom...appeared increasingly threadbare; the colonial dependency more naked'.[73] Nevertheless, the demographic imbalance in favour of Catholics explained the markedly more propitiary response to the English Act of Settlement from the Irish Parliament than that of its Scottish counterpart. Within a broader ancient constitutionalist rhetoric demanding restoration of Irish legislative independence, William Molyneux's *Case of Ireland* (1698) contained a quiet allusion to incorporating Anglo-Irish union as an outcome 'we should be willing enough to embrace; but this is an Happiness we can hardly hope for'.[74] Thereafter, abortive negotiations for incorporating Anglo-Scottish union, starting in 1702, prompted both Houses of the Irish Parliament to submit addresses to Queen Anne requesting 'a more firm and strict union' with England, while the Parliament's formal congratulations on the Anglo-Scottish union of 1707 were accompanied by subtle appeals for 'a yet more comprehensive union' to encompass all her kingdoms.[75]

---

[70]   Macinnes, 'Treaty of Union', 69.

[71]   McLean and McMillan, *State of the Union*, 255.

[72]   Jim Smyth, ' "No remedy more proper": Anglo-Irish Unionism before 1707', in Brendan Bradshaw and Peter Roberts, eds., *British Consciousness and Identity: The Making of Britain, 1533–1707* (Cambridge, 1998), 301.

[73]   Jim Smyth, 'The Communities of Ireland and the British State, 1660–1707', in Bradshaw and Morrill, eds., *The British Problem*, 261.

[74]   William Molyneux, *The Case of Ireland Stated*, ed. J. G. Simms (Dublin, 1977), 84.

[75]   Quoted by James Kelly, 'The Act of Union: Its Origins and Background', in Keogh and Whelan, eds., *Acts of Union*, 53.

Among early eighteenth-century Scots, attitudes towards Anglo-Scottish union were thus conditioned by the essential need to differentiate Scotland's sovereign independence from Ireland's provincial relegation and 'slavery'. As the failed Darien venture's chief promoter, William Paterson, insisted in 1706, 'nothing in the world can be a greater argument for the Union of this Kingdom, than the present practise [*sic*], sense and disposition of Ireland'.[76] Moreover, the model of Anglo-Scottish union was thereafter regularly invoked as the most satisfactory means to defuse destabilizing tensions in eighteenth-century Anglo-Irish relations. Convinced of the rationale for Irish incorporation in the 1790s, the British government commissioned the Keeper of the Records in Scotland, John Bruce, to publish records outlining various Anglo-Scottish union initiatives between 1603 and 1707. Ironically, however, the unstable nineteenth- and twentieth-century legacies of the Irish Act of Union of 1801 generated 'the historiographical eclipse of unionism with Unionism'. As Kidd has argued, most analyses of unionist argumentation in Scotland hitherto had 'relatively little to say about the Anglo-Scottish Union of 1707 compared to the British-Irish union of 1800 and the problems of Irish home rule'.[77]

As the Irish parallel implies, recognizing English motivations for Anglo-Scottish union involves reappraising imperial ramifications of the seventeenth-century regal union and qualifying the credence axiomatically attached to the deceptively attractive claim that, through Anglo-Scottish union, the Scots abandoned hope of founding independent colonies, but gained a global empire. Whilst revisionist accounts of the Union have seen 'a marked reduction in the perceived importance of empire',[78] the rationale that overseas colonies could stimulate Scottish economic regeneration and also offset the adverse effects of English mercantilism was nevertheless logical. Colonial possessions and commercial profits had assisted both the Dutch United Provinces and Portugal in attaining, or retaining, independence from the Spanish Habsburgs.[79] Moreover, the Darien settlement was—ironically—first envisaged as a joint-stock venture, equally open to English and Scottish investors seeking to evade the East India Company's monopoly before resistance from the latter Company rendered it a solely Scottish project. Although £400,000 was successfully raised in domestic subscriptions between February and August 1696, untrammelled excitement was converted into equally acute despair by the project's failure, traditionally blamed on English sabotage, deliberately sanctioned by King William. Recent accounts have, however, instead emphasized the misguided confidence and broader incompetence of the Company of Scotland's directors in seeking to settle a radically inhospitable environment that remained strategically important to Spain.

In psephological terms, McLean and McMillan deemed the lack of correlation between investment in the Company of Scotland and parliamentary support for union

---

[76] Quoted by Macinnes, *Union and Empire*, 131.

[77] Kidd, *Union and Unionisms*, 11, 10.

[78] Andrew Mackillop, 'A Union for Empire? Scotland, the English East India Company and the British Union', *SHR*, 87 (2008) supplement, 117.

[79] John Robertson, 'Union, State and Empire: The Union of 1707 in its European Setting', in Lawrence Stone, ed., *An Imperial State at War: Britain from 1689 to 1815* (London, 1994), 234.

significant since 'it destroys the Namierites' central contention' that those who had lost large amounts of money in the failed venture would invariably support the Treaty.[80] For within the Treaty's provisions, Article XV supplied an undertaking that the English would pay the Scots an 'Equivalent' of £398,085—representing around £55.5 million in current values—as compensation, inter alia, for the Company's dissolution, with an accrued interest rate of 5 per cent. Rather than representing a cynical inducement to secure support for union, historians now emphasize the payment's unexpected and curious character, with Douglas Watt deeming it 'an unusual departure in corporate history: a shareholder bail-out with cash provided by a foreign government'.[81]

As discussions concerning its imperial parallels illustrate, the Anglo-Scottish Union of 1707 remains an enduringly resonant reference point, endowed with what Kerrigan has termed 'terminal-inaugurative status' in determining not only how historians choose to characterize the pre-1707 Scottish past, but also Scotland's experiences thereafter.[82] Discussions of how and why Anglo-Scottish Union occurred in 1707 must therefore be separated from analysis of its subsequent effects, both beneficial and deleterious. As Sir Walter Scott confessed to Maria Edgeworth in 1825, for example, had he been alive in 1707, he 'would have resigned my life to have prevented' its enactment, but since it was 'done before my day, I am sensible [it] was a wise scheme'.[83] Divorcing studies of the Union's eighteenth-century enactment from informing discussions about Scotland's modern constitutional destiny should, however, denude the subject's capacity to divide future generations of historians into mutually exclusive nationalist or unionist constituencies. As Bernard Crick has insisted, 'There is no logical connection between the cause of union in 1707 and where one can stand today. Times change.'[84]

## FURTHER READING

Brown, Stewart J., and Whatley, Christopher A., eds., *The Union of 1707: New Dimensions*, Supplement to *Scottish Historical Review*, 87 (2008).
Devine, T. M., ed., *Scotland and the Union 1707–2007* (Edinburgh, 2008).
Kidd, Colin, *Union and Unionisms: Political Thought in Scotland 1500–2000* (Cambridge, 2008).
Macinnes, Allan I., *Union and Empire: The Making of the United Kingdom in 1707* (Cambridge, 2007).
Robertson, John, ed., *A Union for Empire: Political Thought and the British Union of 1707* (Cambridge, 1995).
Whatley, Christopher A., with Patrick, Derek J., *The Scots and the Union* (Edinburgh, 2006).

---

[80]  McLean and McMillan, *State of the Union*, 60.
[81]  Douglas Watt, *The Price of Scotland: Darien, Union and the Wealth of Nations* (Edinburgh, 2007), 220.
[82]  Kerrigan, *Archipelagic English*, 353.
[83]  David Douglas, ed., *Familiar Letters of Sir Walter Scott*, 2 vols. (Edinburgh, 1894), vol. ii, 312.
[84]  Bernard Crick, 'Scotching the Scots', *The Political Quarterly*, 79 (2008), 240.

....................................................................................................

# CHAPTER 18

# SCOTTISH JACOBITISM IN ITS INTERNATIONAL CONTEXT

....................................................................................................

## DANIEL SZECHI

FROM its very inception Scottish Jacobitism was an intrinsically international phenomenon. At its core lay a network of supporters at home who plotted and planned for the great day, but these men and women were always connected to an exterior network of overseas exiles who lobbied foreign governments and smuggled arms, money, and propaganda into Scotland to promote the cause. Between them they created a revolutionary underground movement dedicated to overthrowing the existing order.[1]

But Scotland was far from unique in this respect. There were Jacobite movements in the other kingdoms of the British Isles, and elsewhere in Europe (and beyond) there were similarly clandestine organizations violently opposing imperial states. Scottish Jacobitism is thus a striking example of a much larger phenomenon, and we can in consequence learn a great deal by studying it.[2]

First, however, we need to understand what it was. Scottish Jacobitism had its own particular structures, internal dynamics, identity, objectives, and potential. These shaped its history as a political movement, and in turn form the basis for understanding Scottish Jacobitism in a wider context.

---

[1] Bruce Lenman, *The Jacobite Risings in Britain 1689–1746* (London, 1980), 20–2, 24–6; Colin Kidd, *Subverting Scotland's Past: Scottish Whig Historians and the Creation of an Anglo-British Identity, 1689–c. 1830* (Cambridge, 1993), 18–19, 26–7; Allan I. Macinnes, *Clanship, Commerce and the House of Stuart, 1603–1788* (East Linton, 1996), 1–24. Though Jacobitism was not a modern political movement, it shared many characteristics with such organizations. These include: acknowledged and generally recognized leaders, broad-based mass adherence, an understood and accepted ideological position, a programmatic agenda stemming from that ideology, and a propaganda output designed to win support in the public sphere.

[2] Paul Kléber Monod, *Jacobitism and the English People, 1688–1788* (Cambridge, 1989); Éamonn Ó Ciardha, *Ireland and the Jacobite Cause, 1685–1766: A Fatal Attachment* (Dublin, 2002). For examples of ideological resistance beyond Europe, see Jonathan D. Spence on the White Lotus and Heaven and Earth Societies (Triads) in China, the latter of which was specifically pledged to the restoration of the Ming dynasty: *The Search for Modern China* (London, 1990), 51, 61, 63–4, 112–14.

# THE MAINSTREAM OF SCOTTISH JACOBITISM

The structure of Scottish Jacobitism reflected the structure of Scottish society. The leaders of the movement correspondingly came from the highland and lowland social elite. Noblemen like James Maule, Earl of Panmure, thus assumed a leading role in Forfarshire because he was the wealthiest, most respected Jacobite aristocrat in the region. In 1715 he accordingly instructed his tenants to join his regiment, selected suitable officers from heritor families tied to his house and marched off to war at the head of his men in a way that would not have been out of place four centuries earlier.[3]

Yet such instances of the social power of the Jacobite elite can be deceptive. Scotland's noble and heritor dynasties (and their highland counterparts) certainly played a major role in mobilizing and directing Jacobite (and Whig) Scotland. But there was more to the Jacobite (and Whig) cause than imperious aristocrats and dumbly obedient commoners. Ideology and interest lay at the heart of the great majority of Jacobites' commitment to the cause. Thus their best recruiting sergeant was the Episcopal Church. This, eighteenth-century Scotland's most influential dissenting Protestant Church, drew the allegiance of approximately 30 per cent of the population for at least two generations after 1688, and its ministers regularly exhorted their congregations to be loyal to the Stuarts for nearly a century.[4] The net effect was to make support for the Stuarts little less than a bounden religious duty for many Scots. The underground Catholic Church, too, had a strong commitment to the Stuarts because of the dynasty's diehard Catholicism, and produced a similar effect on the tiny Catholic community. Both Churches acted as institutional engines producing generation upon generation of Jacobites until the late 1740s. Thereafter the grip of the Episcopal Church was broken by sustained persecution, and the Catholic Church in Scotland was obliged to desist when the Vatican formally abandoned the Stuarts in 1768.[5]

Yet religion was far from being the sole motivation for Scottish Jacobites. At least equally important in many cases was the conviction after 1707 that the Stuart cause was Scotland's cause. Without doubt many Whigs were genuinely patriotic 'North Britons', but if you dreamed of re-establishing an independent Scotland, proudly free of English

---

[3] Ian D. Whyte, *Scotland before the Industrial Revolution: An Economic and Social History c. 1050–c.1750* (London, 1995), 155–8, 254–9; National Archives of Scotland [henceforth NAS], GD 45/1/201: Panmure regiment official return, c. October 1715; Daniel Szechi, *1715: The Great Jacobite Rebellion* (London, 2006), 96, 123.

[4] British Library [henceforth BL], Add. MS 37993 (Polwarth Letterbook), 10 September–27 December 1715; Bruce Lenman, 'The Scottish Episcopal Clergy and the Ideology of Jacobitism', in Eveline Cruickshanks, ed., *Ideology and Conspiracy: Aspects of Jacobitism, 1689–1759* (Edinburgh, 1982), 36–47; Murray Pittock, *The Myth of the Jacobite Clans* (Edinburgh, 1997), 47.

[5] Daniel Szechi, *George Lockhart of Carnwath, 1681–1731: A Study in Jacobitism* (East Linton, 2002), 201–2; Callum G. Brown, *Religion and Society in Scotland Since 1707* (Edinburgh, 1997), 31; Murray Pittock, *Jacobitism* (Basingstoke, 1998), 128–9; Daniel Szechi, *The Jacobites: Britain and Europe 1688–1788* (Manchester, 1994), 120, 130–1.

influence and values, you really had nowhere else to go than Jacobitism.[6] The Union thus opened the way for the Jacobites to become the standard-bearers of the national cause. Indeed it is clear that many Jacobites saw themselves as patriotic Scots first and Stuart loyalists only second.[7] Neither landlords nor ministers inspired the small party of plebeian Scots whom the English clergyman Robert Patten encountered in Northumberland making their way north in 1715. When he asked them what they were about, they boldly told him, 'We are Scotsmen, going to our homes to join our country-men that are in arms for King James.'[8]

There were also those who turned to Jacobitism for want of a better option. Asked why he had turned out to fight for Charles Edward Stuart in 1745, William Boyd, Earl of Kilmarnock, replied: 'for the two kings and their rights, I cared not a farthing which pre-vailed; but I was starving, and, by God, if Mahommed had set up his standard in the Highlands I had been a good Mussulman for bread'.[9] There were probably not many Jacobites as materialistic as Kilmarnock (the prospects were better on the Whig side), but his case drives home a central truth about the Scottish Jacobites: as well as being patriotic idealists and faithful believers they were just like other Scots in most respects, and in their ranks were to be found malcontents, chancers, *bon vivants*, and religious bigots of all kinds.[10] Thus in 1715 crowds of humble Jacobites displayed their feelings about Catholicism by greeting the proclamation of King James in towns like Kelso with cries of: 'No Hannoverian! No Popery! No Union!' And in 1745 David Wemyss, Lord Elcho, specifically blamed Charles Edward's Catholicism and the Catholic Irish officers who joined him for the failure of the rebellion.[11] There was likewise a vein of anti-high-lander feeling among the lowland Jacobites.[12]

[6] NAS, GD 259/2/31: William Scott to [Patrick, jr] Scott of Ancrum, Marshalsea Prison, 27 December 1715; Macinnes, *Clanship*, 193, 194; NAS, GD 220/5/624/2: [Stair to Montrose], Paris, 18/29 February 1716.

[7] John Sibbald Gibson, *Lochiel of the '45: The Jacobite Chief and the Prince* (Edinburgh, [1994], 1995), 'Mémoire d'un Écossais', 176; Daniel Szechi, *Jacobitism and Tory Politics, 1710–14* (Edinburgh, 1984), 85, 102, 130–1; David Laing and Thomas Macknight, eds., *Memoirs of the Insurrection in Scotland in 1715. By John, Master of Sinclair. With Notes by Sir Walter Scott, Bart* (Edinburgh: Abbotsford Club, 1858), 1–2, 372.

[8] Robert Patten, *The History of the Rebellion in the Year 1715. With Original Papers, and the Characters of the Principal Noblemen and Gentlemen Concern'd in it* (London, 1745), 29.

[9] Lenman, *Jacobite Risings*, 256–7.

[10] Daniel Szechi, 'The Image of the Court: Idealism, Politics and the Evolution of the Stuart Court 1689–1730', in Edward Corp, ed., *The Stuart Court in Rome: The Legacy of Exile* (Aldershot, 2003), 53–5; W. D. Macray, ed., *Correspondence of Colonel N. Hooke, Agent From the Court of France to the Scottish Jacobites, in the Years 1703–7*, 2 vols. (London: Roxburghe Club, 1870), vol. ii, 333–4: terms concerted by Anne Drummond, Dowager Countess of Erroll and others in 1705, passed to Colonel Nathaniel Hooke, June 1707; vol. ii, 335: Heads of the Instrument of Government, [June 1707?]; Szechi, *Lockhart of Carnwath*, 141–5, 175–6.

[11] Laing and Macknight eds., *Memoirs of the Insurrection*, 158, 160; SP 54/8/74c: intelligence from Perth, Stirling, 18 September 1715; Evan Charteris, ed., *A Short Account of the Affairs of Scotland in the Years 1744, 1745, 1746. By David, Lord Elcho* (Edinburgh, 1907), 417–18.

[12] Laing and Macknight eds., *Memoirs of the Insurrection*, 26, 88, 128, 136.

The corollary of which is that despite the very real ideological division between Jacobites and Whigs, and its episodically vicious expression in events like the harrying of the Highlands after the '45, the Jacobites never separated from the rest of Scottish society. Kinship, friendship, and business complicated political commitments on both sides, and intermarriage never ceased.[13] Hence Jacobite and Whig merchants in Aberdeen regularly cooperated to further their commercial interests, and scions of Jacobite families secured lucrative posts policing and exploiting the British Empire courtesy of Whig patrons who well knew they would be 'out' as Jacobites if they had the opportunity to show their mettle. Likewise, Whig Scots who had connections in London worked hard to obtain pardons for friends, neighbours, and kinsmen in the aftermath of the '15 and the '45.[14] It is not amiss to observe that the Jacobites probably would have done the same for them if the shoe had been on the other foot.

What lay at the root of these interconnections as much as the simple business of life was a low-key, shared Scottish identity. In 1716 an estimated one thousand primarily Presbyterian, Whig denizens of Edinburgh launched a bloody attack on a party of drunken Dutch soldiers who publicly bragged about killing a Jacobite highlander and cutting off his head. In the same vein, and despite the fact that she was either neutral or a Whig, Flora Macdonald famously helped Charles Edward escape in 1746.[15] She was far from alone in stepping out of her way to help someone from the other side who was in trouble with the authorities, and, indeed, there are so many similar instances that they are clearly part of a pattern of mutual responses to the enduring connections between Scots of otherwise diametrically opposed political convictions.

The Jacobites, then, were and continued to be an integral part of Scottish society despite their theoretical exclusion from the new order. This gave the movement a deep resilience, such that it was able, by rebuilding within its core areas and exploiting enduring connections with the Scottish Whigs, to survive two catastrophic defeats before succumbing to a third. In the context of the Jacobite movement as a whole, this effectively turned the Scottish Jacobites into the vanguard of the Stuart cause. The Jacobite Irish were politically toxic in the rest of the British Isles because they were overwhelmingly Catholic in religion, and however much they promised the English Jacobites always proved faint hearts.[16] The exiled monarchs' only usable, and only willing, military asset in the British Isles lay in Scotland.

---

[13]  Macinnes, *Clanship*, 213; Margaret Sankey and Daniel Szechi, 'Elite Culture and the Decline of Scottish Jacobitism 1716–1745', *Past and Present*, 173 (2001), 103–5.

[14]  Kieran German, 'Jacobite Politics in Aberdeen and the '15', in Paul Kléber Monod, Murray Pittock, and Daniel Szechi, eds., *Loyalty and Identity: Jacobites at Home and Abroad* (Basingstoke, 2009), 88, 94; Bruce Lenman, *The Jacobite Clans of the Great Glen 1650–1784* (London, 1984), 181–210; Frederick A. Pottle, ed., *Boswell's London Journal 1762–1763* (London, [1950], 1951), 29, 41, 199; Sankey and Szechi, 'Elite Culture', 103–24.

[15]  Daniel Szechi, 'Retrieving Captain Le Cocq's Plunder: Plebeian Scots and the Aftermath of the 1715 Rebellion', in *Loyalty and Identity*, 98–119; Frank McLynn, *Charles Edward Stuart: A Tragedy in Many Acts* (London, 1988), 280–7, 290.

[16]  Szechi, *1715*, 93–4; Eveline Cruickshanks, *Political Untouchables: The Tories and the '45* (London, 1979), 36–65.

The lingering military traditions of clanship, the inaccessibility of large parts of the country, and the Protestant credentials of the great majority of Scottish Jacobites further cemented their military importance within the Jacobite underground. This is not to say that the military potential of the Scottish Jacobites was in reality more than skin deep. Most of the Scottish population, even in the Highlands, was completely unused to handling military-calibre weapons of any kind. Even if they had been, there were nowhere near enough such weapons in civilian hands properly to equip a rebel army, which is why Jacobite regiments like the Macgregors went into action at Prestonpans in September 1745 with the rank-and-file armed with nothing more than sharpened scythes.[17] Their appreciation of the scale of this problem restrained the movement's leaders from being as militant as they otherwise might have been, as did the memory of their defeats, but ultimately it did not stop them embracing the chance to fight for the cause. Hence when Charles Edward decided to sail from France for the British Isles in 1745, he did not consider landing in Yorkshire or Galway. He gambled that even if he turned up at Moidart without anything like adequate quantities of weapons (or troops, or money) enough local Jacobites would come out in arms to get the rebellion off the ground, and he was proven right.[18]

But there was another branch of Scottish Jacobitism that was directly relevant to the viability of the cause: the Scottish Jacobite diaspora in Europe. And it was there, in many ways, that the dream of a Stuart restoration and the rebirth of an independent Scotland were irretrievably damaged.

## The Scottish Jacobite Diaspora

Long before there was Jacobitism there was a European Scottish diaspora. The Scottish Jacobite diaspora was thus only the latest surge in a long-running stream of human beings moving out of Scotland, and it directly benefited from the connections created by migrant communities long before it arrived, and often blended in with those same communities. In this the Jacobites were helped by the fact that migrants specifically driven to leave by Jacobitism probably only numbered four to five thousand. They were correspondingly only a small part of the mass migration of perhaps as many as two hundred thousand Scots over the same period.[19]

---

[17] Szechi, *1715*, 54–7; Macray, ed., *Correspondence of Colonel N. Hooke*, vol. ii, 260–1: 'Memorial of the Scotch for the King of France', 7 May 1707; Chevalier [James] de Johnstone, *Memoirs of the Rebellion in 1745 and 1746 (1820)*, 34.

[18] Daniel Szechi, ed., *The Letters of George Lockhart of Carnwath 1698–1732* (Edinburgh: Scottish History Society, 1989)' 5th series, vol. ii, 93: Lockhart to the Old Pretender, [Dryden?], 8 August 1726; McLynn, *Charles Edward Stuart*, 111–12, 129–34.

[19] Ian D. Whyte, *Migration and Society in Britain 1550–1830* (Basingstoke, 2000), 113–14, 116–17; Steve Murdoch, *Network North: Scottish Kin, Commercial and Covert Associations in Northern Europe 1603–1746* (Leiden, 2006); Historical Manuscripts Commission, *Calendar of the Stuart Papers Belonging*

Where the Jacobite diaspora did stand out was in the status of the emigrants involved. Whereas most Scottish migrants tended to have quite humble origins, the Jacobites came disproportionately from the upper ranks of the social elite.[20] Scots of such high status normally only travelled overseas for the purposes of education and tourism, the better to fit them to be urbane gentlemen at home. Instead they found themselves stranded abroad seemingly indefinitely.

This came as a shock, and one to which many proved incapable of adapting. There were two possible responses. One was to make the best of it and try to find a new life overseas. George Keith, Earl Marischal, took this route and was spectacularly successful. Marischal rose to high rank in Spanish and French service before becoming a trusted adviser to Frederick the Great of Prussia. In similar vein, James Drummond, the Jacobite Duke of Perth, became chamberlain for Queen Mary of Modena and dedicated himself to the service of the exiled dynasty.[21]

This subgroup of Scottish exiles could lose interest in the cause and instead turn their energies to fostering their new careers. Marischal took this path arguably before, and certainly after, the '45. From being one of the key assets the Jacobite cause possessed, Marischal effectively became its enemy, discouraging others from becoming Jacobites and blocking Charles Edward's attempts to engineer a new rising in the British Isles. In general, however, Scottish servants of the European great powers and the Stuart court in exile continued to be strongly activist and did their best to promote the Jacobite cause. During the '45, for example, Scottish exiles in Sweden persuaded the Swedish government to send about six hundred Swedish officers and soldiers to Scotland to help provide the professional military expertise the Jacobites so desperately needed.[22] The rebellion was defeated before they could get there, but it is a striking example of the positive impact the exile lobby could have. The second option for the Jacobite exiles was to focus all their efforts on getting home by any means possible. This was the option favoured by many Jacobite exiles and profoundly affected the vitality of the movement. Sometimes this was in obvious ways, as when John Erskine, Earl of Mar, deliberately

---

*to His Majesty the King Preserved at Windsor Castle* [henceforth HMC Stuart], 8 vols. (London, 1902–20), vol. ii, 105: Lieutenant-Colonel Nathaniel Forbes to John Erskine, Earl of Mar, Paris, 11/22 April 1716; vol. ii, 128–9: Sir Hugh Paterson of Bannockburn to Mar, Leyden, 18/29 April 1716. This is assuming the outflow noted by Whyte for the period 1650–1700, *c.* 2,500 *per annum* (Whyte, *Migration and Society*, 115; and n.b.: Whyte's figures do not even include migration to Europe and England) continued into the eighteenth century. Scotland's population was approximately one million at the time.

   [20]   T. C. Smout, *A History of the Scottish People 1560–1830* (London, 1985), 154–5; Daniel Szechi, ' "Cam Ye O'er Frae France?"': Defeat, Exile and the Mind of Scottish Jacobitism, 1716–27', *Journal of British Studies*, 37 (1998) 363–4.

   [21]   Edward Furgol, 'Keith, George, styled tenth Earl Marischal' (Oxford online *Dictionary of National Biography* entry [henceforth *ODNB*]: http://www.oxforddnb.com/view/article/15265?docPos=2; accessed 30 March 2009); Edward Corp, 'Drummond, James, fourth Earl of Perth' (*ODNB*: http://www .oxforddnb.com/view/article/8070?docPos=2; accessed 30 March 2009).

   [22]   McLynn, *Charles Edward Stuart*, 94–7, 429–31; Stuart Handley, 'Butler, James, second Duke of Ormond' (*ODNB*: http://www.oxforddnb.com/view/article/4193?docPos=10; accessed 30 March 2009); Goran Behre, 'Sweden and the Rising of 1745', *Scottish Historical Review*, li (1972), 148–71.

betrayed Francis Atterbury, Bishop of Rochester and the leader of the English Jacobites, to the rising Whig minister Robert Walpole, in the hope of a pardon.[23] Usually, however, the effect was more subtle but nearly as pernicious. In order to get home, exiles like George Lockhart of Carnwath had to ask their Whig kith and kin to intercede for them with the government. In London, Whig intercessors, such as James Graham, Duke of Montrose, and Archibald Campbell, Earl of Islay, would lobby English ministers and pledge their political credit that their Jacobite friends would henceforth behave themselves if allowed to come home. And in most cases the government at Westminster would eventually, grudgingly, grant them leave to do so. Once home, the former exiles were expected to stay out of Jacobite intrigues and give no further trouble. To breach these terms would have been dishonourable, and, in addition, would embarrass the Whig friends who had got them leave to return in the first place.[24] When subsequently forced to choose between the Stuart cause and their obligations to Whig family and friends, some returned exiles, most famously Lord George Murray in 1745, disregarded their social commitments and took up arms again, but most did not and neither did their families. Thus the majority of the Scottish exiles who negotiated their way home became part of a great network of elite ex-Jacobites slipping insensibly, year by year, into the embrace of the Whig regime. When Charles Edward raised his standard in 1745, they were as a group definitely sympathetic. Yet they did nothing substantial to help him and those who did rally to the Stuart cause.[25]

The diaspora was, then, a mixed blessing for the Scottish Jacobite community. Those who made a new life overseas could provide vital support in a crisis, but could also become indifferent or even hostile as their careers abroad prospered. Those who found they could not cope with life in exile and asked their Whig kith and kin to find them a way home usually de facto neutralized themselves and their families. The net effect was the weakening of the Scottish movement as a whole.

# THE EUROPEAN CONTEXT

Until the French Revolution of 1789, eighteenth-century Europe may not have been as turbulent as the two preceding centuries, but it nonetheless saw plenty of major political upheavals. Rebel movements defied the state from the Ukraine to Catalonia and each was, of course, peculiar to its time and place, so that prima facie their differences are more significant than their similarities. What, for example, could the Russian

---

[23] Szechi, '"Cam Ye O'er Frae France?"', 387–8, 389–90; Alistair and Henrietta Tayler, *A Jacobite Exile* (London, 1937), 21, 32, 41, 60; Edward Gregg, 'The Jacobite Career of John, Earl of Mar', in E. Cruickshanks, ed., *Ideology and Conspiracy: Aspects of Jacobitism, 1689–1759* (Edinburgh, 1982), 184–92.
[24] Szechi, *Lockhart of Carnwath*, 150; Sankey and Szechi, 'Elite Culture', 116–24, 124–5.
[25] See, for example, the Chevalier Johnstone's encounters with Robert Rollo, Lord Rollo, and his family, and with Grant of Rothiemurcus: Johnstone, *Memoirs of the Rebellion*, 218, 235, 236–7; Sankey and Szechi, 'Elite Culture', 125–7.

Orthodox communities of Cossack warriors of the Zaporozhian Sich have in common with the likes of the Earl of Panmure and Lord George Murray? Yet there are some striking affinities. To take just the Ukrainians, Hungarians, and Catalans, they were all trying, like the Scottish Jacobites, to preserve a traditional autonomy, guaranteed by the terms of their affiliation in times past with a more powerful state. In each case success would undoubtedly have preserved the power and authority of the native elite, but the appeal of the proto-national cause was still broad enough to inspire support among the common people. All three movements were opposed by elements within their own community, who for reasons ranging from their own patriotic take on the best course of action to personal cupidity, adhered to the imperial power. Finally, all the rebel groups tried to trade on their military–strategic usefulness in the epic wars of the era to solicit military support from the great powers. And, like the Jacobites, they were all comprehensively defeated.[26]

For reasons of space, one example must stand for many, and for the purposes of this essay it will be Habsburg Hungary. The Ottoman vassal state of Transylvania and Royal (Habsburg) Hungary were ethnically and historically part of the kingdom of Hungary, and both had long enjoyed semi-autonomy in consequence of being contested between the Habsburg and Ottoman empires. By the late seventeenth century, though, the balance of power began to shift decisively in favour of the Habsburgs, as may be seen from the increasing pressure that the militantly Catholic dynasty began putting on the Hungarians (many of whom were Calvinist Protestants) to convert to Catholicism. The traditional Magyar response to such measures had always been rebellion, an appeal to their brethren in Transylvania and the Turks for support, and a war of raids up to the gates of Vienna, which usually persuaded the Habsburgs to back down.[27]

The Hungarians' circumstances now, however, changed for the worse. In the late seventeenth century new, more effective Habsburg armies were deployed into the region and drove the Turks out of Royal Hungary and Transylvania, rolling back the Ottoman Empire as far as Serbia and Romania. The Hungarians were left with no natural allies, and when the Habsburgs recommenced their Catholicization drive (and the general extension of imperial authority that went with it) and Prince Ferenc Rákóczi rebelled in 1703 in the name of Hungarian liberties, the only ally he could find was Louis XIV. Louis

---

[26] For the Ukraine, see Zenon E. Kohut, 'Ukraine: From Autonomy to Integration (1654–1830s)', in Mark Greengrass, ed., *Conquest and Coalescence: The Shaping of the State in Early Modern Europe* (London, 1991), 182–7; O. Subtelny, *The Mazepists: Ukrainian Separatism in the Early Eighteenth Century* (New York, 1981), 21–2, 24, 25, 31, 40–52, 90–104, 140–57, 172–7. For Catalonia, see John H. Elliott, *Imperial Spain 1469–1716* (London, [1963], 1965), 371–3; Henry Kamen, *Spain 1469–1714: A Society of Conflict* (Harlow, [1983], 1986), 268–9; Henry Kamen, *The War of Succession in Spain 1700–15* (London, 1969), 242–68, 384–5. Hungary is dealt with below.

[27] Michael Hochedlinger, *Austria's Wars of Emergence: War, State and Society in the Habsburg Monarchy 1683–1797* (Harlow, 2003), 82–3, 154, 160; Ágnes Várkonyi, 'Rákóczi's War of Independence and the Peasantry', in Janos M. Bak and Bela K. Király, eds., *From Hunyadi to Rákóczi: War and Society in Late Medieval and Early Modern Hungary* (New York, 1982), 369–70; Béla Köpeczi, 'The Hungarian Wars of Independence of the Seventeenth and Eighteenth Centuries in their European Context', in *Hunyadi to Rákóczi*, 446–9.

cared nothing for Hungarian liberties, but he was interested in hampering the Habsburg war effort in the War of the Spanish Succession (1701–14), so he despatched a few French officers to help direct the rebels' efforts, and provided a small trickle of military supplies and money. This was never, though, on a scale to match the support that the Ottoman Empire had once been able to provide.[28]

Rákóczi, the dissident nobility, and the broad range of ethnic and social groups who cleaved to them nonetheless showed considerable resilience, at least in part inspired by the summary of their cause expressed on the banner that Rákóczi himself handed to the peasant rebels who persuaded him to come out of Polish exile to lead them against the Habsburgs: '*cum Deo pro patria et libertate*' ('with God, for the homeland and liberty'). His explicitly patriotic agenda included independence, religious toleration, and the emancipation of all serfs, and their families, who joined the rebel cause. It was to be expected that this latter would be unpopular with Hungary's landowners; it is consequently interesting that to promote the cause many noblemen accepted the Rákóczi government's increasingly broad programme of peasant emancipation. Those members of the nobility who would not join were rhetorically deracinated as unpatriotic and 'German'.[29] This platform generated widespread support for the rebellion, and gave it such a good start in terms of controlling territory that Rákóczi's forces were able to survive eight years of largely unsuccessful warfare. By 1711, however, they had been so comprehensively defeated by a combination of Habsburg regulars and pro-Habsburg Hungarians that further resistance was no longer practical. Rákóczi was forced into exile, and eventually found a refuge in the Ottoman Empire. The final end came when his faithful follower Count Miklós Bercsényi tried raiding Hungary from there in 1717 and found no support for further resistance. Though serf culture in parts of Hungary had apparently developed a stubborn belief in Rákóczi's imminent, redeeming return, the surviving rebels, both noble and serf, made the best peace they could and thereafter, like the negotiator of their surrender, Baron Sándor Károlyi, concentrated on working their way back with the Habsburgs.[30]

The Hungarian experience was both very different from, and tantalizingly similar to, that of the Scottish Jacobites, Ukrainians, and others. In effect, they were all radicalized by their circumstances (thus laying down a usable history for the nationalist future) and defeated by them.

---

[28] Hochedlinger, *Austria's Wars of Emergence*, 101–11, 156–66; Kálmán Benda, 'The Rákóczi War of Independence and the European Powers', in *Hunyadi to Rákóczi*, 433–4, 436–7, 438.

[29] Várkonyi, 'Rákóczi's War of Independence and the Peasantry', 369, 371–82; Lothar Höbelt, 'The Impact of the Rákóczi Rebellion on Habsburg Strategy: Incentives and Opportunity Costs', *War in History*, 13 (2006) 2, 4; Köpeczi, 'The Hungarian Wars of Independence', 449.

[30] Höbelt, 'Rákóczi Rebellion', 4, 5–7, 12; Ágnes Várkonyi, 'Rákóczi, Ferenc II' and 'Transylvania' in Linda Frey and Marsha Frey, eds., *The Treaties of the War of the Spanish Succession: An Historical and Critical Dictionary* (Westport, CN, 1995), 368–70, 443–5, and 'Rákóczi's War of Independence and the Peasantry', 385–6; Peter F. Sugar, 'Bercsényi, Gróf Miklós', 'Károlyi, Nagy-Károlyi Baró (later Gróf), Sándor', and 'Szatmár, Peace of', in *Treaties of the War of the Spanish Succession*, 41–2, 229–30, 428–30.

There are many more examples of (unsuccessful) resistance to the centralizing drive of Europe's great powers contemporaneous with the Scottish Jacobite movement. What makes the Scottish (and Irish) Jacobites stand out is that they were the outliers. Four decades after their peers were subdued the Jacobites were still resisting. Indeed, some at least of the Scottish Jacobites were still plotting another insurrection in the early 1750s, and the last French invasion attempt predicated upon coordination with a Jacobite uprising was set to go off in 1759.[31] The deep resilience of the Scottish Jacobite movement probably lay at the heart of this long survival, but it is not a sufficient explanation. For that we must turn to the geopolitical strategy of the European great powers.

## SCOTTISH JACOBITISM AND THE EUROPEAN GREAT POWERS

Early modern European great-power politics were spectacularly lethal. At the beginning of the sixteenth century there were approximately sixteen major powers; by the late eighteenth century there were about six (Britain, France, Spain, the Habsburg Empire, Russia, and Prussia). The others were either subsumed or broken and ended the period as, at best, minor players in the great power game. In a grand strategic sense, this was Scotland's fate. For the aggressive English, then British, state, however, Scottish Jacobitism created a major extra complication. Scottish Jacobitism was dangerous because it had a powerful, patriotic purchase in Scotland. But just as importantly, because it was part of a broader movement touching all three kingdoms, Scottish Jacobite success held the potential to destabilize English/British control of Ireland and even open the way for civil war in England. Rebellions on such a scale had previously knocked great powers such as France, Spain, and Russia out of the game for some time, and in the case of Poland, so damaged one as to lead to its terminal decline.[32] In contemporary geopolitical terms, if Jacobitism was a potential nuclear weapon with respect to the English/British polity, the Scottish Jacobites were the trigger. All that a rival great power needed to do to throw the English/British state into chaos was set off the Jacobite bomb.

---

[31]  For a review of the theories of the advancing early modern state and the problems this engendered, see Jack A. Goldstone, *Revolution and Rebellion in the Early Modern World* (London, 1991), 12–23; Charles Tilly, 'Reflections on the History of European State-Making', in Charles Tilly and Gabriel Ardant, eds., *The Formation of National States in Western Europe* (London, 1975), 6, 15, 18, 20–3, 24–30, 37, 38–46, 71–80.

[32]  Richard Bonney, *The European Dynastic States 1494–1660* (Oxford, 1991) 163–79; Elliott, *Imperial Spain*, 346–54; Roland Mousnier, *Peasant Uprisings in Seventeenth-Century France, Russia and China*, trans. Brian Pearce (London, 1971), 179–95; Norman Davies, *God's Playground: A History of Poland. Volume I: The Origins to 1795*, 2 vols. (Oxford, 1981), 467. The sum total of European states fell from approximately 500 in 1500 to fewer than 350 by 1789, and shrank to only 25 by 1900 (Greengrass, 'Introduction: Conquest and Coalescence', in *Conquest and Coalescence*, 1–2).

This, of course, was more difficult than might appear at first sight. The Stuart court in exile was always looking for support from the great powers, and taking the period as a whole it showed energy and diligence in developing every possible opportunity. It was not, however, about to throw away its best asset, the Scottish Jacobite underground, for a mess of pottage. As the Stuarts' faithful minister, Charles Middleton, Earl of Middleton, pointedly told a French government agent in 1705 they were: 'l'unique ressource qui reste pour le Roy d'Angleterre [James III and VIII]'. Correspondingly, though they could occasionally be seized by over-optimism or desperation, the exiled Stuarts wanted concrete commitments by European great powers before they would ask their supporters to take the potentially fatal step of rebelling.[33] The one occasion on which matters slipped out of the exiled dynasty's control, the great Jacobite rebellion of 1715, was an object lesson in the need to make sure such a rising was coordinated with unequivocal support from a European great power. But even the '15 was not a total loss, for it also demonstrated that the Scots could, as they had repeatedly promised, mobilize tens of thousands of men. And subsequently, when Sweden, Spain, Russia, France, and Prussia came into conflict with Britain, they all scouted the Jacobite option, and two, Spain and France, made serious attempts to exploit it.[34]

The dynamics of the working relationship between the great powers and their Jacobite clients, moreover, sheds considerable light on the strengths and weaknesses of Scottish Jacobitism in the international arena. Again, one example must stand for many, and the best for our purposes is France and the '45.

To secure a revolution in the British Isles the Jacobites calculated that they needed an invasion by a regular armed force to provide professional military support for the Jacobite rebellion that would be the heart of the operation. But such an invasion was always liable to use a lot of resources and be militarily difficult. Which meant that Jacobite proposals were only likely to be taken up when they looked like the best, or least bad, strategic option. Thus the Jacobites had first to find a moment when France was in military trouble, then convince the French government that such an operation would best serve France's needs, and furthermore maintain that conviction in the face of the multiplicity of other attractive targets that were bound to arise while the invasion was pending, expenses multiplied, and doubts developed. The first two of these came together in 1743 when Louis XV and his ministers seized on Jacobite suggestions that they invade England in the wake of French defeats in Germany. Decisions taken in such crises are, however, inherently volatile. Delays, or the easing of the crisis, tend to produce a rapid turn to more promising, or at least less risky, strategic prospects on the part of military

---

[33] Macray ed., *Correspondence of Colonel N. Hooke*, vol. i, 197: Hooke to Torcy, St Germain, 30 May/10 June 1705; vol. ii, 172–3: Queen Mary to Anne Drummond, Countess of Erroll, 15/26 March 1707; Szechi, *Lockhart of Carnwath*, 148–9; Frank McLynn, *France and the Jacobite Rising of 1745* (Edinburgh, 1981), 29–34; McLynn, *Charles Edward Stuart*, 78.

[34] Szechi, *1715*, 51–76, 125; Macray ed., *Correspondence of Colonel N. Hooke*, vol. ii, 257: 'Memorial of the Scotch for the King of France', 7 May 1707; Szechi, *Jacobites*, 90–116.

institutions and their ministerial protagonists.[35] And this was exactly how matters played out in 1743–4. The invasion of England and a rising in Scotland were systematically prepared. But then the English Jacobites (as usual) got cold feet and asked for more time to prepare, the weather turned foul, and the Royal Navy interposed itself between the French invasion ports and southern England. The French government was accordingly obliged to postpone the operation. Louis and his ministers then lost interest, the troops and materiel were redeployed to other theatres, and the whole project was shelved.[36] That should have been the end of the affair, but the relationship between great powers and their clients was, and is, not straightforwardly utilitarian. Great-power decision-makers can be swayed by an emotional reaction to their clients' conduct, and this was the case eighteen months later, in 1745, when, in effect, the Scottish Jacobites briefly took control of the French agenda.

Analyses of France's part in the '45 all acknowledge the unearned strategic gains it made as a result of the rebellion. The rebellion broke out virtually free of charge, as far as France was concerned, because Charles Edward Stuart raised his initial funding by tapping the Scottish and Irish Jacobite diasporas, and the first costs of the rising in Scotland were met primarily from Scottish, and then English, resources. The Jacobite victory at Prestonpans in September 1745 also cost France nothing, but prompted the withdrawal of the bulk of the British contingent from the Allied army in Flanders and thus guaranteed that the French army commanded by Maurice de Saxe would continue, and accelerate, its conquests in the region. By the time the British government felt able to despatch William, Duke of Cumberland, and his forces back to the Low Countries in 1746, the Allied position there was in a virtual state of collapse, and do what he could the militarily mediocre Cumberland was incapable of retrieving the situation. Given that France's armies were doing badly in Italy and overseas, this was a lifeline. It is generally agreed that the War of the Austrian Succession ended in a draw stemming from the mutual exhaustion of the warring powers.[37] In large part the reason France was able to extract itself even that successfully was owing to the Scottish distraction.

But the impact of the Scottish rebellion on the course of the war was not just a matter of cold realpolitik for Louis and his ministers. The Scottish Jacobites' successes up to the spring of 1746 in effect tied the French king and his ministers to them emotionally. In all our cold, detached analyses of the military events of 1745–6 it is easy to lose sight of the way Charles Edward and the Scottish Jacobites dazzled contemporaries for the best part of a year. As a direct consequence Louis XV developed an almost chivalric inclination to

---

[35]  Reed Browning, *The War of the Austrian Succession* (New York, 1993), 134–7, 139–40, 149–50; Claude Nordmann, 'Louis XIV and the Jacobites', in Ragnhild Hatton, ed., *Louis XIV and Europe* (London, 1976), 96; McLynn, *France and the Jacobite Rising of 1745*, 143–63.

[36]  Cruickshanks, *Political Untouchables*, 53, 63–5; Browning, *The War of the Austrian Succession*, 156–8, 172; McLynn, *Charles Edward Stuart*, 89–95.

[37]  McLynn, *Charles Edward Stuart*, 117–18; Rupert C. Jarvis, *Collected Papers on the Jacobite Risings*, 2 vols. (Manchester, 1971), vol. i, 175–97; Christopher Duffy, *The '45* (London, 2003), 100; Daniel Szechi, 'Culloden and the '45 in European Context', in Tony Pollard, ed., *Culloden: The History and Archaeology of the Last Clan Battle* (Barnsley, 2009), 221–6.

back his bold allies to the best of his ability. Hence the piecemeal despatch of French regiments and military supplies direct to Scotland, where they significantly bolstered the shaky Jacobite state, and, far more importantly, Louis's attempt in December 1745 to throw together another invasion of southern England to back up the Scots and rescue them from the threat posed by Cumberland's army.[38] The Scottish Jacobites were in effect shifting France's strategic priorities, and it was fortunate that Louis had appointed a really good general like Maurice de Saxe to command in the southern Netherlands. Despite the fact that the Scottish Jacobite tail was busily wagging the French dog, and the consequent diversion of desperately needed troops from his forces, de Saxe was able to continue his conquest of the Austrian Netherlands.[39]

That the French response to the '45 was, moreover, principally a response to the Scottish Jacobites rather than Charles Edward per se, is apparent from the aftermath of the rising. Many, if not most, of the Jacobite commanders who arrived in France on French ships specifically sent on Louis XV's orders to save them and their prince did not consider the affair to be at an end. Nor did Louis XV. In December 1746 he offered to send the exiles and the newly arrived Charles Edward back to Scotland with a six thousand-strong invasion force, plus ample supplies of arms and money. When Charles Edward made it clear that he wanted nothing to do with such an expedition, and preposterously and unrealistically demanded eighteen to twenty thousand men for an invasion of England, a key group of Scottish exiles headed by Donald Cameron of Locheil attempted to take Louis up on his offer on their own account. The French were open to this idea, but still hoped for Charles Edward's cooperation, and peace came before there was a break in the impasse.[40] We can only speculate as to the consequences and outcome if the Scottish exiles had had their way.

The Scottish Jacobites were thus more than simply pawns in the great-power game. Their manifest ability to dislocate Britain's strategic plans drew the great powers to them as a potentially useful tool, but it did not stop there. Their brave performance in the field could draw the admiration and, crucially, the emotional commitment, of powerful European statesmen. But only for short periods. For most of the Jacobite era it was hardnosed geopolitics that dictated the conduct of the great powers towards the Scottish Jacobites. Even in that context, though, the potential threat they posed had useful consequences for the movement as a whole. In particular, it led to various great powers offering surreptitious encouragement and secret subventions. These kept the cause alive into the mid-eighteenth century and sustained the Jacobites' hopes as late as the Seven Years War.[41] It is not going too far to say that Britain's great-power rivals thereby effectively

[38] McLynn, *France and the Jacobite Rising of 1745*, 75, 86–7, 87, 99, 110–11, 117–63, and *Charles Edward Stuart*, 308–9.

[39] McLynn, *France and the Jacobite Rising of 1745*, 110, 130, 135, 152; Browning, *War of Austrian Succession*, 259–60, 268–9.

[40] McLynn, *France and the Jacobite Rising of 1745*, 221; Doron Zimmerman, *The Jacobite Movement in Scotland and in Exile, 1746–1759* (Basingstoke, 2003), 56–7, 58–70; Gibson, *Lochiel*, 156–66, 173–7.

[41] Zimmerman, *Jacobite Movement in Scotland and in Exile*, 123; Szechi ed., *Letters of George Lockhart*, 233–4: Lockhart to the Old Pretender, [Edinburgh?], 25 July 1725.

(and at minimal cost to themselves) kept Jacobitism going—and Britain correspondingly constrained—far longer than might otherwise have been the case.

# CONCLUSION

Scottish Jacobitism was inspired by a blend of dynastic loyalty and proto-nationalism, with the balance of power probably lying on the patriotic/nationalist side. Albeit that Dr Johnson had a good point when he described patriotism as the last refuge of the scoundrel, and that there were few greater scoundrels than Simon Fraser, Lord Lovat, it is nonetheless significant that the old villain nonetheless died for the cause in 1747 quoting Horace: *dulce et decorum est pro patria mori* ('sweet and seemly it is to die for one's country'). Scottish Jacobitism was also the most usable, though not necessarily the most powerful, component of the movement as a whole. Moreover, it was sufficiently alienated from the new order in Scotland to be able episodically to stand opposed to it for three generations, while at the same time sufficiently connected to Whig Scotland economically and socially to be able to survive the long years of peace. For in many ways keeping the faith when nothing was happening was just as important in sustaining the Jacobite cause as turning out to fight when the royal standard was raised at Kirkmichael or Glenfinnan. All these features of the Scottish Jacobite movement made it the vital component of the Jacobite movement. It is no coincidence that despite the raw power of the Irish Jacobites they could not sustain the cause alone. Once the Scots (and to a much lesser degree, the English) had fallen away, the Stuart cause was on a fast track to oblivion. Charles Edward's degeneration into a violent, drunken brute in the 1750s implicitly stemmed from his despair as he helplessly witnessed this process unfolding.[42]

In terms of European power politics, the Scottish Jacobites in many respects began as just one of a number of ethnic, patriotic movements resisting the imperial drive of the European great powers. But they kept going far longer, and always posed a greater danger to their target polity, than their peers. Initially at least, the Ukrainians, Hungarians, and Catalans endorsed the status quo. Indeed, what they principally objected to were changes in the accustomed state of affairs. By contrast, the Scottish Jacobites always sought the overthrow of the entire post-Revolutionary order in the British Isles. They also had unchallengeable leaders (in that all Jacobites recognized the exiled Stuarts as their legitimate monarchs), resident safely beyond the frontiers of the British state and able to give their cause a respectability and resonance that the others simply could not match. Louis XIV and Cardinal Giulio Alberoni (in 1718, on behalf of Philip V of Spain) might pose as noble defenders of Hungarian liberties, but no one was under any illusion

---

[42]   Edward Furgol, 'Fraser, Simon, eleventh Lord Lovat' (*ODNB*: http://www.oxforddnb.com/view/article/10122?docPos=5; accessed 1 April 2009); McLynn, *Charles Edward Stuart*, 308–454. It is worth remembering that in the sixty-nine years between 1691 and 1760 the Scots Jacobites (and never all of them) were 'out' for only about seventeen months.

about their fundamental motivation for supporting Rákóczi and the rebel cause. By contrast, Louis XIV and Louis XV were far more sincere in taking up the legitimist, Catholic cause of the Stuarts. Likewise, by maintaining the image of legitimate monarchy at the exiled court, James II and VII and his son were able to put themselves in the position of being able to communicate as one monarch to another when dealing with princes such as Charles XII and Peter the Great.[43]

The Stuart court in exile also provided legitimation for everything its followers believed in and aspired to. Most Scottish Jacobites were loyalists as well as patriots. And therein they revealed a central truth about the Scottish Jacobite movement. It was a bipolar phenomenon, and hence a bridge between old and new ideologies of resistance to the imperial states of Europe. On the one hand it drew on 'ancient' traditions of Scottish dynastic fealty; on the other it looked to create a national political revolution in Scotland regardless of what the Stuarts wanted. We should correspondingly understand it as a Janus-like movement, one that drew strength from the past, but looked to a very different future. Scottish Jacobitism was not a modern nationalist movement, but it may have been on the verge of becoming one.

## FURTHER READING

Black, Jeremy, *Culloden and the '45* (Stroud, 1990/2000).
Corp, Edward T., with Gregg, Edward, Erskine-Hill, Howard, and Scott, Geoffrey, *A Court in Exile: The Stuarts in France, 1689–1718* (Cambridge, 2004).
Duffy, Christopher, *The '45* (London, 2003).
Hopkins, Paul, *Glencoe and the End of the Highland War*, rev. repr. (Edinburgh, 1998).
McLynn, Frank, *France and the Jacobite Rising of 1745* (Edinburgh, 1981).
—— *Charles Edward Stuart. A Tragedy in Many Acts* (London, 1988).
Macinnes, Allan I., *Clanship, Commerce and the House of Stuart, 1603–1788* (East Linton, 1996).
Pittock, Murray, *Poetry and Jacobite Politics in Eighteenth-Century Britain and Ireland* (Cambridge, 1994).
—— *The Myth of the Jacobite Clans*, 2nd edn. (Edinburgh, 2009).
Szechi, Daniel, *The Jacobites: Britain and Europe 1688–1788* (Manchester, 1994).
—— *George Lockhart of Carnwath, 1681–1731: A Study in Jacobitism* (East Linton, 2002).
—— *1715: The Great Jacobite Rebellion* (London, 2006).
Zimmerman, Doron, *The Jacobite Movement in Scotland and in Exile, 1746–1759* (Basingstoke, 2003).

---

[43] Arthur McCandless Wilson, *French Foreign Policy During the Administration of Cardinal Fleury 1726–1743: A Study in Diplomacy and Commercial Development* (Westport, CN, [1936], 1972), 10; Edward Corp with Edward Gregg, Howard Erskine-Hill and Geoffrey Scott, *A Court in Exile: The Stuarts in France, 1689–1718* (Cambridge, 2004), 158–80; Cruickshanks, *Political Untouchables*, 52; Jeremy Black, *Culloden and the '45* (Stroud, [1990], 2000), 31; Maurice W. Bruce, 'Jacobite Relations with Peter the Great', *Slavonic Review*, xiv (1935–6), 360–1.

# CHAPTER 19

................................................................

# THE RISE (AND FALL?) OF THE SCOTTISH ENLIGHTENMENT

................................................................

## ALEXANDER BROADIE

## THE CONCEPT OF AN ENLIGHTENMENT

THE eighteenth-century cultural movement known as the European Enlightenment contained a specifically Scottish Enlightenment which was recognized as a powerhouse of ideas in fields as diverse as philosophy, political economy, physics, chemistry, and geology. In this introductory section I shall first identify some of the luminaries (or 'literati') of the Scottish Enlightenment and then give a brief account of what it is that makes something an 'Enlightenment'.

First, the people. They included the philosophers Francis Hutcheson, David Hume, Dugald Stewart, and Thomas Reid; the political economists Adam Smith and Sir James Steuart; the historian William Robertson; the sociologists John Millar and Adam Ferguson; the jurisprudential thinkers John Erskine of Carnock and Henry Home (Lord Kames); the mathematicians Colin Maclaurin, Matthew Stewart, and Robert Simson; the physicist John Robison; the chemists William Cullen and Joseph Black; the engineer James Watt; and the geologist James Hutton. Others also could have been named, and behind those of the first rank there was a considerable hinterland of enlightened activity.

As to the question of what an Enlightenment is, I shall base my account on the answer given by the German philosopher Immanuel Kant. He argued that an Enlightenment has two principal features: first, the presence of people willing and able to think for themselves rather than simply accepting ideas on the authority of others; and secondly, a society that has a sufficient level of tolerance to enable its creative, independent-minded individuals to put their ideas into the public domain in relative safety, that is, without fear of retribution. Where tolerance has a sufficient foothold, high-cultural activity is likely to flourish, and to do so in respect of at least most of its disciplines.[1] In eighteenth-century Scotland there were many who were willing and able to think for themselves, and the level of tolerance in the country was sufficient to enable thinkers to discuss their ideas in public with relative safety, at which moment there arose geniuses such as Hume, Smith, Reid, Black, and Hutton.

However, the concept of the Scottish Enlightenment is contested. William Robert Scott, who appears to have coined the term 'Scottish Enlightenment', referred to the Glasgow philosopher Francis Hutcheson as 'the prototype of the Scottish Enlightenment, that is, the diffusion of philosophic ideas in Scotland and the encouragement of speculative tastes among the men of culture of the generation following his [Francis Hutcheson's] own'.[2] Some commentators, perhaps influenced by the idea that Hutcheson was the prototype, have held that the disciplines of the Scottish Enlightenment were moral philosophy, political economy, and history, as contrasted with others who have noted the place of mathematics and the natural sciences in the Scottish Enlightenment. But my concept of the Scottish Enlightenment does not involve a privileging of any set of disciplines, since it is defined in terms of the flourishing of creative, high-cultural activity, in whatever disciplines.[3]

The Scottish Enlightenment was not parochial; its participants belonged to the Republic of Letters whose citizens published their ideas, thereby conversing with thinkers from the wider European Enlightenment, from England, France, Germany, the Netherlands, Italy, and elsewhere. Scotland's Enlightenment not only began at around the start of the wider movement but also both nourished and was nourished by it; for the Scots read thinkers such as Montesquieu, Etienne Bonnot de Condillac, George-Louis Leclerc de Buffon, Denis Diderot, Jean le Rond d'Alembert, Voltaire, Antoine Laurent Lavoisier, Cesare Beccaria, Immanuel Kant, Johann Gottfried Herder, David Hartley, Joseph Priestley, and Edward Gibbon, and almost all, if not all, of these latter figures read the Scots.

It has been held by some that the 1707 Union of Scotland and England is a major element in the explanation of how Scotland came to have an Enlightenment. The Acts of Union were indeed followed a decade or so later by the beginnings of the Scottish Enlightenment, but we should avoid the fallacy of confusing temporal sequence with causal. While the Union was probably a causal factor, it may have been of rather minor significance as compared with another, namely Scotland's own cultural resources. In the

---

[1] See Immanuel Kant, 'What is Enlightenment?', in *Kant: Political Writings*, ed. Hans Reiss (Cambridge, 1996), 54–60.

[2] William Robert Scott, *Francis Hutcheson: His Life, Teaching and Position in the History of Philosophy* (Cambridge, 1900), 265.

[3] For the account focused on moral philosophy, political economy, and history see Hugh Trevor-Roper, 'The Scottish Enlightenment', *Studies on Voltaire and the Eighteenth Century*, 58 (1967), 1,635–58, and John Robertson, 'The Scottish Contribution to the Enlightenment', in Paul Wood, ed., *The Scottish Enlightenment: Essays in Reinterpretation* (Rochester, NY, 2000), 37–62. For emphasis on the role of science, see Roger Emerson, 'Science and the Origins and Concerns of the Scottish Enlightenment', *History of Science*, 26 (1988), 333–66; C. W. J. Withers and P. Wood, eds., *Science and Medicine in the Scottish Enlightenment* (East Linton, 2002); and D. B. Wilson, *Seeking Nature's Logic: Natural Philosophy in the Scottish Enlightenment* (Pennsylvania, 2009).

second part I shall seek to demonstrate that Scotland had the resources necessary for an Enlightenment; their absence from some accounts enhances the view that the occurrence of the Scottish Enlightenment requires explanation in terms of something extraneous to Scotland, such as an English culture that came to shape Scotland's after the Union.

My aim is not to argue for the proposition that there was a seventeenth-century Enlightenment in Scotland—for by modern standards seventeenth-century Scotland, like all countries in Europe during that century, was grievously intolerant. Instead, my proposition is that Scotland of the pre-Enlightenment period had many significant intellectual achievements to its name, and that these achievements make the Enlightenment far less surprising than it would have been had it arisen after a period of intellectual poverty.

Following the discussion of the intellectual life of pre-Enlightenment Scotland in the second part, the third part contains a brief account of some of the writings that emanated from the Scottish Enlightenment itself. Finally, in the fourth part I raise the question of when the Scottish Enlightenment ended.

## SCOTTISH HIGH CULTURE, 1500–1700

During the three centuries that preceded the Union, Scotland had more than its fair share of intellectually strong scholars. They had a natural home in the Church and the universities, operated at the cutting-edge of research, and published works that were widely recognized as of the highest intellectual level. They taught in the Scottish universities, of which three were founded during the fifteenth century, in St Andrews, Glasgow, and Aberdeen, and they were also prominent among the teaching staff in universities of Continental Europe. During the pre-Reformation period Scotland's line-up of formidable scholars included John Mair (c.1467–1550), from the farm town of Gleghornie near Haddington. He rose to be Professor of Philosophy at the University of Paris, then became Principal of Glasgow University (1518–23), and spent his last sixteen years as Provost of St Salvator's College, St Andrews. Amongst those who were students at Paris while he was teaching there were Ignatius Loyola, John Calvin, Francisco de Vitoria, George Buchanan, and François Rabelais, and it is probable that all of them attended his lectures. His circle of Scottish friends included George Lokert, who was Rector of St Andrews University and Dean of Glasgow after many years teaching Arts at Paris; the moralist and logician William Manderston, who likewise was Rector of St Andrews; and Robert Galbraith, who became a senator of the College of Justice at Edinburgh after years spent as Professor of Roman Law at Paris.[4]

During the century and a half between the Reformation and the Enlightenment the intellectual productivity of Scotland gathered momentum. Duncan Liddel (1561–1613)

[4] Alexander Broadie, *A History of Scottish Philosophy*, rev. edn. (Edinburgh, 2010), 47–86.

from Aberdeen was a mathematician and astronomer who studied at Frankfurt under the Scot John Craig (later James VI's physician), and then moved to Rostock, where he expounded Copernicus's theories to leading German astronomers. Liddel endowed the first Chair of Mathematics at Marischal College, Aberdeen, in 1613. The astronomer Thomas Seget of Seton knew both Galileo Galilei and Johannes Kepler, and indeed gave a copy of Galileo's *Siderius Nuncius* to Kepler, who had not till then known Galileo's work. Kepler and Seget worked conjointly on their astronomical investigations. The mathematician John Wedderburn (1583–*c*.1645) from Dundee, a friend of Kepler, produced mathematical support for Galileo when the latter came under attack from Martin Horky. John Napier (1550–1617) from Merchiston, near Edinburgh, invented logarithms. His book *Mirifici logarithmorum canonis descriptio* (*Description of the Wonderful Canon of Logarithms*, 1614) was transformative for mathematicians, physicists, and astronomers, and his invention of the slide-rule was likewise a boon for scientists. James Gregory (1638–1675) from Aberdeenshire, the first Professor of Mathematics at Edinburgh, gave the initial comprehensive mathematical account of the reflecting telescope.[5] His brother David Gregory (1661–1708), who was likewise Professor of Mathematics at Edinburgh, taught Newtonian mechanics at Edinburgh before the teaching of it was undertaken in Newton's home university of Cambridge. The fact that, during the century prior to the Union, chairs of mathematics were founded or refounded in St Andrews, Edinburgh, Glasgow, and in King's College and Marischal College, Aberdeen, and that during that same period observatories were built at St Andrews, and at both King's College and Marischal College, indicates the extent to which mathematical and astronomical studies received institutional recognition in Scotland during the period leading up to the Enlightenment.

Among the virtuosi active during the latter part of the seventeenth century was Robert Sibbald (1641–1723). From 1685 he was the first Professor of Medicine at Edinburgh University and was in addition a co-founder, with Dr Andrew Balfour (1630–1694), of the Physic Garden (later the Royal Botanic Gardens) at Edinburgh, whose purpose was to provide a steady supply of herbs for the burgeoning medical school. Sibbald was also a founder, in 1681, of the Royal College of Physicians of Edinburgh. Its other founders included Archibald Pitcairne (1652–1713), a Professor of Medicine at Leiden before returning to Edinburgh, where he practised medicine and published treatises on his medical research.

These facts are important for an understanding of the origins of the Scottish Enlightenment, for during the eighteenth century Scotland was famed for the quality of its teaching and research in medicine; and the eighteenth-century pre-eminence of the Edinburgh medical school had roots deep within seventeenth-century Scotland. Hence by the time Alexander Munro *primus* began lecturing on anatomy and surgery at Edinburgh in 1719, the university had long been laying the foundations for its development, during the Age of Enlightenment, into perhaps the greatest centre in Europe for medical education.

Scotland was active in other areas also. In the fields of philosophy, political theory, theology, and ecclesiology there were, among many others, the Aristotelian scholar

---

[5] Alex Keller, 'The Physical Nature of Man: Science, Medicine, Mathematics', in John MacQueen, ed., *Humanism in Renaissance Scotland* (Edinburgh, 1990), 97–122.

Robert Balfour (d. *c*.1625); Samuel Rutherford (1600–1661), who was Professor of Latin at Edinburgh and Rector of St Andrews University, and whose *Lex Rex* (1644) has been described as 'the most influential Scottish work on political theory';[6] Robert Boyd of Trochrague (1579–1627), who was head of the Protestant College at Saumur and Principal of Glasgow University; Gilbert Burnet (1643–1715), who authored *Vindication of the Authority, Constitution, and Laws of the Church and State of Scotland* (1673); and Henry Scougal (1650–1678), Professor of Divinity at King's College, Aberdeen, and author of *The Life of God in the Soul of Man* (1678), a work in the genre of personal piety, which went through many editions and established itself as a classic of Protestant devotion. There were also major contributions in the field of law by Sir George Mackenzie of Rosehaugh (1636–1691), and James Dalrymple, first Viscount Stair, whose *Institutions of the Law of Scotland* (1681) is one of Scotland's greatest legal texts.

These many achievements demonstrate that by the start of the Scottish Enlightenment the country was already operating at a high level across a wide range of academic disciplines. There is, therefore, evidence for the claim that early in the eighteenth century the country was well placed to develop an Enlightenment from within its own intellectual resources and in conjunction with the intellectual communities of Europe. At this moment something special, and unaccountable, happened—geniuses arose. The cultural space within which geniuses could arise and flourish was in place, but, as always with the emergence of such men, good fortune was also required. I am thinking of Hume, Smith, Reid, Black, Hutton, and others, whose presence in eighteenth-century Scotland ensured that it was a golden century of Scottish high culture. For one feature of geniuses who are free to put their ideas into the public domain is that they set the agenda for the thinking of others. For example, once Hume had published his *Treatise of Human Nature* (1739–40) it was difficult, almost impossible, for philosophers in Scotland, or indeed elsewhere in Europe, to write as if Hume had not existed. His sceptical theses were so powerfully argued that almost all philosophers felt the need to attend to them. Reid acknowledged the centrality of Hume for his own development, and was the central figure in one of the great philosophical schools of the Enlightenment, the Scottish school of common sense philosophy.

# INTO AND THROUGH THE AGE
# OF ENLIGHTENMENT

Continuities from the pre-Enlightenment to the Enlightenment in Scotland are to be found within both the arts and the sciences, and I shall now comment briefly on both, while indicating some prominent doctrines of the Scottish Enlightenment.[7]

---

[6] David Stevenson, *Revolution and Counter-Revolution in Scotland, 1644–51* (London, 1977), 235.
[7] For detailed discussion of the Scottish Enlightenment see Alexander Broadie, ed., *The Cambridge Companion to the Scottish Enlightenment* (Cambridge, 2003).

On the arts side the continuity is well symbolized by the relation between Gershom Carmichael (1672–1729) and Francis Hutcheson (1694–1746). Carmichael, the son of a Scottish Presbyterian minister, was a student at Edinburgh, spent a year at St Andrews, and thereafter taught at Glasgow, as a regent and then, from 1727, as first occupant of the Chair of Moral Philosophy. Carmichael more than any other person was responsible for the introduction of the European tradition of natural law into the Scottish universities, where it flourished throughout the eighteenth century. Perhaps the three greatest natural law theorists of the seventeenth century were Hugo Grotius (1583–1645), Samuel Pufendorf (1632–1694), and John Locke (1632–1704). Carmichael studied them all, and by the 1702–3 session was lecturing on Pufendorf's *De officio hominis et civis* (*On the Duty of Man and Citizen*). His commentary on it was published some years later.[8]

Natural-law theory investigates human nature, draws conclusions concerning what constitutes our well-functioning, and proposes morally-binding precepts that we must embody if we are to function well. Natural-law theorists have taken different views on how secular a theory of natural law should be. Grotius's was strongly secular whereas Pufendorf's had some religious content, though Carmichael, who paid especial attention to our duties to God, thought Pufendorf's account inadequate in this area.

Francis Hutcheson studied moral philosophy at Glasgow at a time when Carmichael was lecturing there on natural-law theory. Hutcheson's family were Ulster Scots, his father and grandfather were Presbyterian ministers, and before entering Glasgow University in 1711 he had received his schooling in Ireland from a Glasgow graduate who had based the school syllabus on the teaching programme at Glasgow. Hutcheson must have been familiar with the Glasgow teaching of moral philosophy even before he arrived as a student. Thereafter he worked on Carmichael's ideas, adding new elements, particularly regarding the notion of a moral sense, a receptor that enables us to draw the distinction between virtue and vice and to apply these categories appropriately, and he also emphasized more than Carmichael the role of benevolence in our moral lives. In addition he took a softer line than Carmichael on the question of the place of God in the moral dimension of our lives, and though Hutcheson held that the concept of God has a role in the moral narrative, he was not logically committed to the view that only a believer can be virtuous.

The two greatest moralists of the Scottish Enlightenment, David Hume and Adam Smith, were indebted to Hutcheson in various ways. Smith, a student of Hutcheson's at Glasgow, referred affectionately to 'the never to be forgotten Hutcheson', and though, like Hume, Smith appears not to have accepted that moral philosophy needs to assume the existence of God, he took Hutcheson's moral philosophy very seriously, as witness the fact that in discussing systems emphasizing the moral motive of benevolence, Smith affirmed 'of all the patrons of this system, ancient or modern, the late Dr Hutcheson was undoubtedly, beyond all comparison, the most acute, the most distinct, the most

---

[8] Gershom Carmichael, *Supplementa et observationes ad clarissimi viri Samuelis Pufendorfii libros duos De Officio Hominis et Civis* (Glasgow, 1718).

philosophical, and what is of the greatest consequence of all, the soberest and most judicious'.[9]

All three philosophers, Hutcheson, Hume, and Smith, helped to advance the great European project of natural law, a project that is focused on the concept of human nature. Natural-law theory requires an account of human nature because our morality is a morality for humans, not for any other order of being. Hume's greatest philosophical work, *A Treatise of Human Nature* (1739–40), which culminates in a theory of morality, presents a detailed account of human nature; and Thomas Reid moved in this direction also, with a detailed account of human nature preceding the exposition of a moral philosophy appropriate to his concept of human nature.[10]

There was general agreement among the literati that the study of human nature had to be conducted with the aid of a methodology appropriate to the natural sciences. In a word, what Hume termed 'the science of man'[11] had to be based on observation and experiment.

Reid's work in this field led him to a set of 'principles of common sense', principles that cannot be proved, do not require proof, and must be presupposed if we are to prove anything. Among his principles are these. First, that we really do perform all the mental operations of which we are conscious—where 'consciousness' refers to our awareness of internal acts and events, such as rememberings and reasonings, and not to our awareness of external ones. Secondly, we know our past experiences by memory as we know our present mental operations by consciousness. Our memory can deceive us, but nevertheless we find ourselves, by nature, believing what memory tells us. To deny either of these principles (and many more are proposed by Reid) is to reject a principle that is part of the original constitution of our nature and through which we have characteristically human experience.

All this is 'common sense', something to which almost all human beings would sign up. But why say things that receive almost universal assent? It is because some philosophers were thought to have denied them. Hume was believed to have argued for a scepticism so widespread that it encompassed the external world, personal identity, objective moral standards, and God,[12] and it was thought necessary to develop countervailing arguments. It is this that Reid does on the basis of his principles of common sense.

---

[9] Adam Smith, *The Theory of Moral Sentiments*, eds. D. D. Raphael and A. L. Macfie (Indianapolis, 1984), VII, ii, 3.3.

[10] See Reid, *An Inquiry into the Human Mind on the Principles of Common Sense* (1764; critical edition ed. Derek R. Brookes, Edinburgh, 1997); *Essays on the Intellectual Powers of Man* (1785; critical edition ed. Derek R. Brookes and Knud Haakonssen, Edinburgh, 2002); *Essays on the Active Powers of Man* (1788; critical edition, eds. Knud Haakonssen, James Harris, and Edinburgh, 2010).

[11] David Hume, *A Treatise of Human Nature*, ed. P. H. Nidditch, 2nd edn. (Oxford, 1978), xv.

[12] For Hume's scepticism regarding causality, the external world, and the senses, see his *Treatise of Human Nature*, ed. L. A. Selby-Bigge, 2nd edn., rev. P. H. Nidditch (Oxford, 1978), Book One. His doctrine that the virtue of justice is purely conventional is argued for in his *Treatise*, Book Three; and his alleged scepticism about the existence of God was thought to have been argued for in his *Dialogues Concerning Natural Religion*, for which see Hume, *Principal Writings on Religion including Dialogues Concerning Natural Religion and The Natural History of Religion*, ed. J. C. A. Gaskin (Oxford, 1993).

Another way to advance the science of man is to do history. Hume writes:

Mankind are so much the same, in all times and places, that history informs us of nothing new or strange in this particular. Its chief use is only to discover the constant and universal principles of human nature, by showing men in all varieties of circumstances and situations, and furnishing us with materials, from which we may form our observations, and become acquainted with the regular springs of human action and behaviour. These records of wars, intrigues, factions, and revolutions, are so many collections of experiments, by which the politician or moral philosopher fixes the principles of his science...[13]

Hume's prescription for moral philosophy calls for deployment of the kind of empirical evidence that is the substance of historical research. Nevertheless, a particular form of historical enquiry that developed in the Scottish Enlightenment was a genre that Dugald Stewart qualified as 'conjecture'. He mentions two examples, Adam Smith's account of the origin of language and David Hume's of the origin of religion, and his purpose is to emphasize the fact that the two philosophers proceed as empirical scientists even though they are conjecturing about a period of human history for which there is little or no detailed evidence whether documentary or even archaeological. His thesis was that there is evidence, not direct but indirect, which permits progress on questions concerning distantly past origins.

Stewart held that on the basis of a scientific account of human nature it is possible to calculate how humans would behave in a given set of circumstances. Though the resultant historical narrative is conjecture it is scientifically well grounded, since the account of human nature on which it is based is scientific and the extrapolation from that account is a rational exercise.[14] So this form of historical writing, which the Scottish Enlightenment produced in abundance, is part of natural science.

Adam Smith regards property law as a function of the state of development of society and so, as a conjectural historian, he produces an account of the social stages, indicates when property appears on the scene, and shows how laws governing it become more complex and sophisticated. The four stages, of the hunter-gatherer, herdsman, farmer, and finally citizen in a modern commercial society, are described in the *Wealth of Nations* and also in the lectures on jurisprudence that Smith delivered as Professor of Moral Philosophy at Glasgow University.[15] It is in terms of the historical realities of the commercial stage of society that Smith develops the characteristic doctrines of the *Wealth of Nations*, such as the importance of international free trade and the need for a relatively big government.

---

[13] David Hume, *An Enquiry Concerning Human Understanding*, ed. Tom L. Beauchamp (Oxford, 1999), 150.

[14] Dugald Stewart, *Account of the Life and Writings of Adam Smith LLD*, in Adam Smith, *Essays on Philosophical Subjects*, eds. W. P. D. Wightman and J. C. Bryce (Oxford, 1980), 293.

[15] Adam Smith, *An Inquiry into the Nature and Causes of the Wealth of Nations*, eds. R. H. Campbell and A. S. Skinner (Indianapolis, 1982); Adam Smith, *Lectures on Jurisprudence*, eds. R. L. Meek, D. D. Raphael, and P. G. Stein (Indianapolis, 1982).

Some postulated a 'state of nature' antecedent to the social state. The postulate is investigated by Adam Ferguson, Professor of Moral Philosophy at Edinburgh, who notes two
prominent accounts of it, by Thomas Hobbes and Jean-Jacques Rousseau. On Hobbes's
account the state of nature, lacking law-enforcement agencies and law makers, is a miserable state whose inhabitants' lives are 'solitary, poor, nasty, brutish and short',[16] a state
from which people have to escape if they are to lead a full and comfortable life. Rousseau,
in contrast, argues that the state of nature is a state of innocence, and that society brings
corruption. Ferguson rejects both accounts because their conjectures about the state of
nature are not supported by the empirical evidence. He points out that the available evidence represents people as living in society and therefore supports the conclusion that
social living is natural for us. For Ferguson the state of nature *is* social.[17]

The scientific spirit of men such as Hume, Smith, and Ferguson, manifest in their
study of human nature, makes them heirs of Scotland's seventeenth-century scientific
culture. I shall turn now briefly to consider the place of the natural sciences in the
Scottish Enlightenment and to note a significant continuity between pre-Enlightenment
and Enlightenment science. Reference was made earlier to the fact that the Edinburgh
medical school was pre-eminent in Europe. Among those who contributed to its reputation was William Cullen (1710–1790), a student at Glasgow University from which he
graduated first as Master of Arts and then as Doctor of Medicine. He taught chemistry
and medicine at Glasgow, taking up a Chair of Medicine in 1751, before transferring to
Edinburgh, becoming Professor of Chemistry and eventually Professor of the Practice
of Medicine there. Now known for his introduction into medicine of the term 'neurosis',
he carried out ground-breaking researches into the nervous system and devised an
influential principle for the classification of diseases.[18] His four-volume work, *First Lines
of the Practice of Physic* (1777–84), provided a detailed and comprehensive view of medical practice. It was translated into many languages and confirmed his reputation as one
of the great medical teachers of the Enlightenment.

Yet more distinguished than Cullen was Joseph Black (1728–1799), who studied under
Cullen at Glasgow and taught at Glasgow before taking up the Chair of Medicine and
Chemistry at Edinburgh. He is now known chiefly for a series of discoveries he made in
his late twenties and early thirties. Experiments on magnesia alba led him to the discovery of carbon dioxide, or 'fixed air', as he termed it, the first time ever that a gas was characterized by a chemical process. He then demonstrated that carbon dioxide was different
from the air in the atmosphere. Next by a series of observations and experiments he discovered the phenomena of latent heat and specific heat.

Among Black's close friends and colleagues was James Watt (1736–1819). Watt, who
spent some years as Glasgow University's mathematical instrument maker, was thinking

---

[16]  Thomas Hobbes, *The Leviathan*, ed. Richard Tuck (Cambridge, 1991), Book 1, ch. 13.

[17]  Adam Ferguson, *An Essay on the History of Civil Society*, ed. Fania Oz-Salzberger (Cambridge,
1995), 9.

[18]  A. L. Donovan, *Philosophical Chemistry in the Scottish Enlightenment: The Doctrines and
Discourses of William Cullen and Joseph Black* (Edinburgh, 1975).

about steam engines from the latter 1750s, a time when John Robison (1739–1805), lecturer in chemistry at Glasgow, and author of a paper (1757) on a way to improve the Newcomen steam engine, was having discussions with him on the practical applications of steam. It was in 1765 that Watt hit upon the idea of employing a separate condenser as a way of overcoming the considerable wastage of power in Newcomen's engine. He duly patented his 'Watt engine', an invention that would impact on the development of the Industrial Revolution. He was involved in a vast array of engineering works, such as the survey that he did preparatory to the building, by Thomas Telford, of the Caledonian Canal between Inverness and Fort William (1801–23). Robison, who was no less interested in electricity than in steam engines, is perhaps best known today for his discovery of the inverse-square law of electrical force.

A further scientific discipline in which a major advance was made from within the Scottish Enlightenment is geology. James Hutton studied at Edinburgh University under the mathematician Colin Maclaurin, and subsequently transferred to Leiden, where he studied medicine and was awarded an MD for a thesis on the circulation of the blood. It was, however, for his researches into recycling on a planetary scale that he is remembered. In 1685 Archbishop James Ussher of Armagh had declared, on biblical grounds, that the world was created at the start of the night preceding the twenty-third day of October in the year 4004 BC. But Hutton seems early to have become convinced both that rocks on the Earth's surface are formed from particles from earlier bodies and also that forces of erosion are a permanent feature of the surface of the planet. He identified five stages in the recycling process, and argued that the surface of the planet is the effect of an endlessly dynamic process, whose products include minerals embedded in other minerals, and fossilized sea creatures on tops of mountains. This led him to the conclusion that 'with respect to human observation, this world has neither a beginning nor an end'.[19] Hutton's 'theory of the earth' was demonstrated in the course of geological field trips, often undertaken with friends such as John Clerk of Eldin and John's brother George Clerk Maxwell. No geologist thereafter could ignore Hutton's findings.

His theory was attacked by some members of the Kirk, but others were not disturbed by the theory's implications for religion. The Kirk was not monolithic and while part of it was hostile to aspects of the Scottish Enlightenment, another part, the 'moderate party', was not. At the start of the Scottish Enlightenment proto-moderates fought hard to square intellectual demands with Church doctrine, and within a short period three professors at Glasgow University, Francis Hutcheson, William Leechman, and John Simson, faced Kirk opposition. Hutcheson was criticized because of his doctrines that we are naturally benevolent and that a person can be virtuous even if he does not believe in God; Leechman was charged with heresy (though his reputation survived intact and indeed he was later appointed principal of the university); and Simson, who taught that the Christian revelation has to be able to pass the test of

---

[19] *The 1785 Abstract of James Hutton's Theory of the Earth*, intr. G. Y. Craig (Edinburgh, 1987), 28.

rationality, faced an ecclesiastical court that forbade him to teach though he was allowed to retain his academic chair. These men demonstrated that Christian values and Enlightenment values were not incompatible, and though the writings of Hume on religion, principally *The Natural History of Religion* (1757) and *Dialogues Concerning Natural Religion* (published posthumously in 1779), provide room for dispute as to whether he was an atheist, a deist, a sceptic, or at least a non-Christian, Hume was the exception. Most of the literati were dedicated Calvinists.

This last point is pertinent to the question of whether there was anything Scottish about the Scottish Enlightenment. In reply it is helpful to compare Scotland and France, for many think, or thought, that the French Enlightenment was *the* great manifestation of Enlightenment values. The character of the movement was certainly different in the two countries. Two differences may be observed. First, though some of the leading literati were not professors, many were. These latter include Hutcheson, Smith, Hugh Blair, Reid, Maclaurin, Cullen, Robison, Black, Robertson, Dugald Stewart, and John Playfair. By contrast, in the French Enlightenment, no first-, second-, or even third-rank figure was a professor. France's universities were under the control of the Catholic Church, and the Church sanctioned whatever was taught. In consequence the great *lumières*, the French literati, such as Montesquieu, Voltaire, Diderot, d'Alembert, Claude-Adrien Helvétius, Baron d'Holbach, and Lavoisier did not hold university chairs. Secondly, whereas Leechman, Blair, Reid, George Campbell, Robertson, Ferguson, and others were Calvinists and Kirk ministers, in France most of the *lumières* were deists, religious sceptics, or even atheists.

The literati wrote on politics, political economy, social institutions, law, religion, and education, and their thinking could not be uninfluenced by their experience, especially their experience of the great national institutions of religion, education, and the law. These institutions formed or informed the minds of those brought up in them, and since all those institutions were distinctively Scottish, the three great classes of contributors to the Scottish Enlightenment, the professors, lawyers, and preachers, were bound to reflect the institutions in their writings. The outcome was a cultural movement whose Scottishness ran deep, even as the movement produced writings of universal significance.

# WHEN DID THE SCOTTISH ENLIGHTENMENT END?

The term 'Enlightenment' has two uses, one as a name to pick out a period lasting for approximately most of the eighteenth century. The period is distinguished because of its intellectual or more broadly cultural ferment. As regards the Scottish part of the European Enlightenment, some might say that it began in the 1720s with the publication of Hutcheson's first major works and ended perhaps in the 1790s with the death of Reid.

Others would say it ended later. George Elder Davie, a noted historian of eighteenth-and nineteenth-century Scottish intellectual life, dates the demise at around the 1840s.[20]

But 'Enlightenment' can also be understood as a general term to pick out a period (and there could be many such, and in many places) marked by tolerance and by the presence of people willing and able to think for themselves. On this basis there was a Scottish Enlightenment during the eighteenth century, but not a seventeenth-century version. There were enlightened people in that earlier century, but the period was marked, in Scotland as across Europe, by high levels of intolerance. But some decades after Thomas Aikenhead was hanged for blasphemy in 1697,[21] the emergence of the moderate party in the Kirk was a sign of the heightened respect for the virtue of tolerance.

There is significant continuity in Scottish intellectual life from the eighteenth century to the nineteenth, measured not only in terms of the survival of major players—Adam Ferguson died in 1816, James Watt in 1819, and Dugald Stewart in 1828. Some of these (as well as others of their generation) continued to be influential more or less to the end of their days. But a new generation was arising. One of the new guard was William Hamilton (1788–1856), a student at Glasgow University who, for twenty years until his death, was Professor of Logic and Metaphysics at Edinburgh. Hamilton's philosophy was a synthesis of the common sense philosophy of Thomas Reid and the idealist metaphysics of Immanuel Kant, with Hamilton supporting both philosophers in their rejection of Hume's global scepticism, and supporting Reid rather than Kant at certain crucial points where the two philosophers were in disagreement.

Hamilton's use of Kant is important. Hamilton was the first in a long line of significant Scottish philosophers to make extensive use of Kant's thought. Thereafter others, such as James Frederick Ferrier, Andrew Seth (also known as Andrew Seth Pringle-Pattison), Edward Caird, and R. B. Haldane, attended to German thinkers, especially Fichte, Schelling, and Hegel, who themselves were writing in Kant's shadow. Some have spoken of the Germanizing of Scottish philosophy, but a major part of the German thinkers' agenda was set by Hume's global scepticism, and indeed Kant himself explicitly acknowledged that his philosophy was motivated in part by the need to answer Hume. Towards the end of the nineteenth century and into the twentieth, philosophers saw Reid as presenting at least as strong a case against Hume as the German thinkers had done.

In the course of these discussions, some brilliant philosophy was published, such as Ferrier's *An Introduction to the Philosophy of Consciousness*, which originally appeared as a series of seven papers in *Blackwood's Magazine* (1838–9), Pringle-Pattison's *The Scottish Philosophy: A Comparison of the Scottish and German Answers to Hume* (1885) and his *Hegelianism and Personality* (1887). There were not philosophical geniuses in nineteenth-century Scotland to match Hume, Smith, and Reid in the eighteenth, but there was still a great deal of philosophy of wonderfully high quality being done. No sign

---

[20] George Elder Davie, *Ferrier and the Blackout of the Scottish Enlightenment* (Edinburgh, 2003).

[21] Michael Hunter, ' "Aikenhead the atheist": The Context and Consequences of Articulate Irreligion in the Late Seventeenth Century', in Michael Hunter and David Wootton, eds., *Atheism from the Reformation to the Enlightenment* (Oxford, 1992), 221–54.

here of an end to the Scottish Enlightenment, if Enlightenment be measured in terms of people thinking for themselves in a context in which they can put their ideas into the public domain without risking retribution. Furthermore, the works just mentioned, as well as many others of the period, demonstrate a commitment throughout the nineteenth century to the study of Hume, Reid, and other Scottish philosophers of the preceding century. To the end of the nineteenth century in Scotland there was a continuity of ideas at the heart of the philosophical discourse, and the discourse remained of outstandingly high quality.

Nevertheless, George Davie has argued that the Scottish Enlightenment ended in the 1840s, and that it did so mainly as a result of the adoption by Ferrier of an account of consciousness that contradicted the Scottish Enlightenment's naturalistic thinking.[22] But against Davie's argument two points may be noted. First, there is a good deal more to philosophy than the philosophy of consciousness and a good deal more to Scottish discussion of the philosophy of consciousness than just Ferrier's discussion. Secondly, there is a good deal more to the Scottish Enlightenment than philosophy, and in particular there is science and, as we shall observe, science of a world-beating sort is also part of the achievement of nineteenth-century Scotland.

To turn therefore to science, it may be recalled that among those who went on field trips with James Hutton was George Clerk Maxwell. His great-grandson James Clerk Maxwell (1831–1879) was a pupil at Edinburgh Academy, and then a student at Edinburgh University, where he read logic and metaphysics under Sir William Hamilton. He also attended classes in moral philosophy, physics, and chemistry. The broad cultural formation, a characteristically Scottish education, that he received was a matter of permanent satisfaction to him. The breadth of this formation surfaced in several of his writings, including his inaugural lecture as Professor of Natural Philosophy at Marischal College, Aberdeen (1856), and in an essay on the philosophy of action in which he argued that determinism is not supported by particle physics.

Among the greatest achievements of James Clerk Maxwell was his work on thermodynamics and the kinetic theory of gases. He discovered during this work that the second law of thermodynamics (that heat generally cannot flow spontaneously from a material at a lower temperature to a material at a higher temperature) is a statistical probability but not an inviolable law. This insight of Maxwell's, christened 'Maxwell's demon' by William Thomson, Lord Kelvin, was a permanent worry to Kelvin as implying a statistical view of physical reality that seemed to him unacceptable, even though he did not succeed in overturning Maxwell's argument.

Maxwell's work on field theory likewise led to unsettling conclusions. He it was who discovered that light and electromagnetism are two different forms of the same energy. His *Treatise on Electricity and Magnetism* (1873) was transformative. Physics would not be the same again; relativity, as Albert Einstein later acknowledged, was implicit in Maxwell's equations. Our modern world, its microwave ovens, electron microscopes, and television sets, are a consequence.

[22] Davie, *Ferrier*.

Lord Kelvin himself made hardly less impact in his day, and the *Treatise on Natural Philosophy* (1867), which he wrote with Peter Guthrie Tait, Professor of Physics at Edinburgh, made as much of an impression at the time as Maxwell's own *Treatise*. From Lord Kelvin's theories there were developed the first transatlantic cable and a compass usable in boats with iron hulls. The Kelvin temperature scale, starting at $0°$ Kelvin, the lowest possible temperature in the universe, is now in regular use.

Much else was happening in Scottish high culture during the second half of the nineteenth century, and the overall picture is of intellectual activity at the highest level and across a wide range of disciplines. To which I wish to add that this tremendous activity was continuous with the period known as the Scottish Enlightenment. Why not conclude, therefore, that the Scottish Enlightenment did not end at approximately the end of the eighteenth century but instead continued on its way and was still in good fettle at the end of the nineteenth century and into the twentieth?

But there is a different narrative, one proposed by Cairns Craig, namely that in the nineteenth century there arose a Scottish Enlightenment of a different kind from that of the eighteenth. What emerged was a 'second Scottish Enlightenment', characterized by 'Scotland's *self*-enlightenment as to the nature and development of its own history and of its own past cultural achievements, and also a *self*-enlightenment as to the relevance of those national traditions to the issues confronting a modern society'.[23] Craig produces persuasive evidence to support his position, including the founding of the Scottish Text Society (1882) and the Scottish History Society (1886), the building of the Scottish National Portrait Gallery (1885–1900), and the publication of many explicitly Scottish works such as *Scottish History and Literature to the Period of the Reformation* by John Merry Ross (1884). To this list (and I have mentioned only a fraction of the examples given by Craig), there could be added a significant number of philosophy books whose titles refer to Scottish philosophy, such as Ferrier's *Scottish Philosophy, the Old and the New* (1856) and Pringle-Pattison's *Scottish Philosophy* (1885).

The national self-awareness implicit in these titles of institutions and of books is a crucial part of the ethos of Scottish high culture during the latter part of the nineteenth century. It is, however, a sign not of a new Enlightenment but of an intensification of the Scottishness that was already a feature of the Enlightenment in Scotland in the previous century. I accept Cairns Craig's premises but not his conclusion. In a word, the Scottish Enlightenment continued into the nineteenth century with its Scottishness intact and, if anything, even more robust and more explicit. Far from the Scottish Enlightenment ceasing at the end of the eighteenth century, it had still not ceased a century later.

To this it may be added that in a way different to that so far discussed the Scottish Enlightenment may be said to have continued into and through the nineteenth century, for it was one of Scotland's greatest invisible exports. To take brief note of two examples, ideas of the literati were taken up, developed, and became dominant in both France and America.

---

[23] Cairns Craig, *Intending Scotland: Explorations in Scottish Culture since the Enlightenment* (Edinburgh, 2009), 84.

Pierre-Paul Royer-Collard (1763–1845), Professor of the History of Modern Philosophy at the Sorbonne, was committed to the Scottish common sense philosophy and lectured on it, especially on Reid and Dugald Stewart. Amongst those who heard Royer-Collard lecturing on the Scottish philosophy was Victor Cousin (1792–1867), who in 1815 was appointed to the academic chair vacated by Royer-Collard. Not only did Cousin use his lectures as a vehicle for the dissemination of Reid's philosophy, but also, as Minister of Public Education, he ensured that Reid's ideas had a significant status in philosophical education in France, a status they retained until at least the end of the nineteenth century.

In America also we find that the Scottish school of common sense philosophy played a role throughout the nineteenth century. For example, Charles Sanders Peirce embraced a version of Reidian philosophy that he termed 'critical common-sensism'.[24] Certainly there were differences, but my point here is only to indicate that Peirce's version of the Scottish school of philosophy was written by a man familiar with, and largely in sympathy with, the earlier version.

Some varieties of American pragmatism might seem to leave little room for the common sense philosophy since they allow for the possibility of an evolutionary process at work even among our most deeply embedded beliefs, beliefs such as those the school of common sense philosophy identified as principles of common sense. William James, who subscribed to such a process, nonetheless found space in his philosophy for a role for common sense principles and he kept a close eye on the accomplishments of his Scottish philosophical predecessors.[25]

Today Scottish Enlightenment philosophy plays a perceptible role in America in the rich field of reformed epistemology, in which notions of warrant and testimony are developed that are conceptually and causally in close touch with the eighteenth-century school.[26] This new appropriation indicates the robustness and sheer persuasiveness of the Scottish school.

There is, therefore, substantial evidence that the Scottish Enlightenment continued with its character and vigour intact throughout the nineteenth century in Scotland and also that it maintained a form of existence furth of Scotland in other national cultures that had appropriated the ideas of the eighteenth-century literati. It should be added that the sorts of reasons I have adduced for the claim that the Scottish Enlightenment continued through the nineteenth century apply no less to the period since then. Understanding the concept of enlightenment in terms of people thinking for themselves and able to publish their thoughts without fear of retribution by the intolerant, the Scottish Enlightenment is still with us. Of course things could be better, but that is not to imply

---

[24] See for example, 'Six Characters of Critical Common-Sensism', in *Collected Papers of Charles Sanders Peirce*, eds. Charles Hartshorne and Paul Weiss, vol. 5, *Pragmatism and Pragmaticism* (Cambridge, MA, 1934; reprint, Bristol, 1998), 293–305.

[25] See Charlene Haddock Siegfried, 'The Philosopher's "license": William James and Common Sense', *Transactions of the Charles Sanders Peirce Society*, 19 (1983), 273–90.

[26] Nicholas Wolterstorff, *Thomas Reid and the Story of Epistemology* (Cambridge, 2001).

that the Scottish Enlightenment has ceased. The Scottish Enlightenment should be seen as a Scottish project to enhance our exercise of the virtues of toleration and autonomous reason. Since the arrival of Scottish devolution in 1999, there have been many calls for a second Scottish Enlightenment. They are premature. The second cannot start until the first has run its course.

## FURTHER READING

Allan, David, *Virtue, Learning and the Scottish Enlightenment* (Edinburgh, 1993).
—— *Scotland in the Eighteenth Century: Union and Enlightenment* (London, 2001).
Berry, Christopher, *Social Theory in the Scottish Enlightenment* (Edinburgh, 1997).
Broadie, Alexander, *The Scottish Enlightenment: The Historical Age of the Historical Nation*, 2nd edn. (Edinburgh, 2007).
—— *A History of Scottish Philosophy*, rev. edn. (Edinburgh, 2010).
—— ed., *The Scottish Enlightenment: An Anthology* (Edinburgh, 1997).
—— ed., *The Cambridge Companion to the Scottish Enlightenment* (Cambridge, 2003).
Craig, Cairns, *Intending Scotland: Explorations in Scottish Culture since the Enlightenment* (Edinburgh, 2009).
Lenman, Bruce, *Enlightenment and Change: Scotland 1746–1832*, 2nd rev. edn. (Edinburgh, 2009).
Phillipson, Nicholas, *Adam Smith: An Enlightened Life* (London, 2010).
Wilson, David B., *Seeking Nature's Logic: Natural Philosophy in the Scottish Enlightenment* (Pennsylvania, 2009).
Withers, Charles W. J., and Wood, Paul, eds., *Science and Medicine in the Scottish Enlightenment* (East Linton, 2002).
Wood, Paul, ed., *The Scottish Enlightenment: Essays in Reinterpretation* (Rochester, NY, 2000).

CHAPTER 20

......................................................................................................................

# THE BARBAROUS NORTH? CRIMINALITY IN EARLY MODERN SCOTLAND

......................................................................................................................

## ANNE-MARIE KILDAY

THE notion that Scotland has long been depicted as a lawless, 'uncivilized' nation by its more 'civilized' southern counterpart is a historical red herring. Rather, it was not until the nineteenth century, when a general moral panic regarding crime and criminal activity took hold across Britain as a whole, that Scotland, in particular, was portrayed as a bad example to its neighbours south of the Tweed. For instance in 1844, the Tory Sheriff of Lanarkshire, Archibald Alison, declared that 'in Scotland, destitution, profligacy, sensuality and crime advance with unheard-of rapidity in the manufacturing districts. And in these areas throughout the country as a whole, the dangerous classes massed together, combine every three of four years in some general strike or alarming insurrection, which, while it lasts, excites universal terror.'[1] By the mid-nineteenth century then, the link between rising crime and social disintegration was strongly felt in a Scottish context.

In the earlier period, however, the criminal condition of Scotland is harder to establish in general terms. For instance, the collection and publication of nationwide crime statistics did not begin in earnest until the middle of the nineteenth century.[2] Moreover, social commentators and pressmen alike paid little attention to the illegal exploits of individuals in the pre-modern era, preferring instead to concentrate on matters of state or economy. This makes it difficult to analyse the range and extent of felonious activity in Scotland before 1850. In addition, little historical scholarship has been undertaken thus far on Scottish criminal enterprise in the early modern period, so we are faced with

---

[1] Archibald Alison, 'Causes of the Increase of Crime', *Blackwood's Edinburgh Magazine*, lvi (1844), 1–14 at 1–3.

[2] See Robert Sindall, 'The Criminal Statistics of Nineteenth-Century Cities: A New Approach', *Urban History Yearbook*, 13 (1986), 28–36 at 29.

a variety of research questions that need to be addressed in this chapter. What type of criminality prevailed in early modern Scotland, and how does this compare with that elsewhere? Was there a gendered difference in the criminality on display during this time? Were there regional variations in criminal activity evident during the early modern period? Is there evidence of change over time in the types of crimes committed and the levels of violence employed? In other words, can we see evidence of a 'civilizing process' where more violent crimes were tamed and the perpetration of more commercial crimes increased? What factors influenced criminal activity in Scotland and did these differ from motives elsewhere? And finally, to what extent was the nineteenth-century concept of the 'Barbarous North' applicable to Scotland during the early modern era?

This chapter is based on evidence of serious criminality across Scotland between 1700 and 1830. As well as utilizing broadside material and popular literature, the chapter will base its conclusions on nearly 6,500 criminal prosecutions brought before the Scottish Justiciary Court during the period under review. The Justiciary Court was the supreme jurisdiction dealing with criminal matters in Scotland.[3] The High Court of Justiciary was established in 1672 and based in Edinburgh. Three associated Circuit Courts were also organized at this time to extend the reach of the court's jurisdiction across Scotland. The North Circuit related to courts held in Aberdeen, Inverness, and Perth. The West Circuit managed the courts held in Glasgow, Inverary, and Stirling, and the South Circuit dealt with the courts held in Ayr, Dumfries, and Jedburgh. After 1747, an increase in the volume of business brought before the Justiciary Court, due to its assimilation of defunct local jurisdictions, meant that the court went on circuit twice a year, usually in the spring and autumn.

The Justiciary Court had a wide remit when dealing with criminal offences. In the early modern period it dealt with moral crimes and petty offences from time to time, but these were increasingly assigned to the more 'inferior' jurisdictions (such as the Sheriff Court and the Justice of the Peace Court) over the course of the eighteenth century. In the main, therefore, the Justiciary Court dealt with 'serious' offences such as political and treasonous crimes, the four pleas of the Crown (murder, rape, robbery, and arson), and other felonious activities. These included assault, bestiality, counterfeiting and fraud, infanticide, riot, sodomy, theft, and the sale of stolen goods (known in Scotland as resett), as well as a variety of other misdemeanours.

In the management of these offences, the court also had a wide range of punishments at its disposal. However, from the end of the seventeenth century onwards, the punishments meted out by the Justiciary Court became more fixed and prescribed. Sentences of death by hanging or banishment overseas were the most common punishments received by those convicted of political crimes or serious offences, especially those which had involved the use of violence. For lesser offences heavy fines, corporal punishment, and

---

[3] For further discussion of Scottish jurisdictions see Anne-Marie Kilday, *Women and Violent Crime in Enlightenment Scotland* (Woodbridge, 2007), ch. 2, and also Stephen J. Davies, 'The Courts and the Scottish Legal System, 1600–1747: The Case of Stirlingshire', in Victor Gatrell, Bruce Lenman, and Geoffrey Parker, eds., *Crime and the Law: The Social History of Crime in Western Europe Since 1500* (London, 1980), 120–54.

imprisonment (or even a combination of the three) were more regularly meted out by judges of the Justiciary Court.[4]

It should be remembered from the outset that any study of criminal activity that is largely based on court indictments will only ever provide a snapshot of the illegality that took place. Indictment evidence tends to reflect the amount of crime reported rather than the amount of crime actually committed, since the real incidence of crime can never fully be known. Thus, in any study where court records predominate over other source materials, the picture of criminal behaviour will be incomplete. Just as many variables affected the reporting of crime as its perpetration. Furthermore, indictment records in themselves cannot tell the whole story of crime and those who perpetrated it. For instance, little evidence is provided about the backgrounds of the suspects accused of serious crime. A further complication associated with Justiciary Court evidence in particular is that it will provide a relatively unbalanced picture of Scottish criminality. As that court only dealt with the most serious offences, an analysis of its records might exaggerate the picture of serious crime in early modern Scotland and downplay more general, everyday acts of petty illegality. Thus subsequent studies using other court records or alternative source material might eventually qualify some of the findings of this chapter. Ultimately, it can be said that this work analyses a significant proportion of the serious crimes indicted in Scotland between 1700 and 1830.

The chapter will start with a brief review of the limited historiography we have relating to early modern criminality in Scotland. The piece will then move on to examine the nature of Scottish crime in the period 1700–1830. To do this, four categories of serious crime will be examined: property crime, fatal violence, harmful violence, and crimes of protest. Within each of these categories the relative incidence of criminality, the offenders involved, the methodology employed, and the motive behind the criminality will each be addressed in turn. Through this type of detailed analysis, the chapter will address the research questions outlined above with a view to determining whether Scotland could be considered a 'barbarous' nation during the early modern period.

## THE HISTORIOGRAPHY OF SCOTTISH CRIME

The Scottish experience of deviant behaviour has been largely neglected by scholars until relatively recently. This has led one historian to describe Scotland as a nation without a criminal record.[5] Certainly, by comparison, historians south of the border (and

---

[4] The punishment of Scottish offenders will not be specifically addressed in this chapter, but will be referred to where pertinent. For further discussion of this topic see Anne-Marie Kilday, 'Women and Crime in South-west Scotland: A Study of the Justiciary Court Records 1750–1815' (unpublished PhD thesis, University of Strathclyde, 1998), ch. 6.

[5] Margaret A. Crowther, 'Scotland: A Country With No Criminal Record', *Scottish Economic and Social History*, 12 (1992), 82–6 at 82. I am grateful to Dr Bill Knox (University of St Andrews) for alerting me to this reference.

arguably those elsewhere) have gone much further in dealing with the issue of crime across historical periods.[6] Interestingly, however, much of the work that has been carried out on crime north of the border has tended to focus on female criminality during the early modern period. Scholars have gone little further than this in either chronological terms or in relation to gender, and save for a few articles on punishment practices and general survey pieces that emphasize the potential of studying Scottish crime in the period after 1747, little has as yet been achieved.[7]

Arguably, the only real exception to this historiographical void is the work that has been carried out on popular disturbance and protest in Scotland. This type of illegality has been examined over a longer period of time and has included reference to both male and female participants. 'Traditional' scholarship has highlighted what has been termed an 'orthodoxy of passivity' amongst the Scottish populace.[8] Writers like Christopher Smout maintain that one of the most notable elements of lowland Scottish society, especially in relation to the early modern period, is the almost total absence of overt social discontent amongst the Scottish people.[9] This notion of the 'uninflammability' of the Scots has more recently been challenged, however, chiefly by the work of Christopher Whatley.[10] Although at first glance the Scots might appear more quiescent in comparison to their English counterparts, there is compelling evidence emerging which suggests that they were far less 'tame' than had previously been supposed.

From the blood-feud and clan wranglings of the sixteenth century, the Covenanting rebellions of the mid-seventeenth century, the Levellers' revolt in Galloway in 1724 and the various Jacobite risings most prominent in the eighteenth century, through to the anti-clearance protests in the Highlands which began in the mid-nineteenth century and escalated thereafter, there appears to have been something of a tradition of

---

[6]  See for instance James A. Sharpe, *Crime in Early Modern England 1550–1750* (London, 1999); Julius R. Ruff, *Violence in Early Modern Europe 1500–1800* (Cambridge, 2001); Clive Emsley, *Crime and Society in England, 1750–1900* (London, 1996); Ted R. Gurr, ed., *Violence in America: The History of Crime* (Newbury Park, CA, 1989), and Anne-Marie Kilday and David S. Nash, eds., *Histories of Crime: Britain 1600–2000* (Basingstoke, 2010). For further discussion of the dearth of scholarship on Scottish crime history see Kilday, *Women and Violent Crime in Enlightenment Scotland*, ch. 1.

[7]  For examples of scholarship that demonstrate the potential of studying Scottish crime see Marion M. Stewart, 'In Durance Vile: Crime and Punishment in Seventeenth and Eighteenth Century Records of Dumfries', *Scottish Archives: The Journal of the Scottish Records Association*, i (1995), 63–74; John G. Harrison, 'Women and the Branks in Stirling c.1600–c.1730', *Scottish Economic and Social History*, xviii (1998), 114–31; Ian Donnachie, ' "The Darker Side": A Speculative Survey of Scottish Crime during the First Half of the Nineteenth Century', *Scottish Economic and Social History*, xv (1995), 5–24, and Margaret A. Crowther, 'Criminal Precognitions and their Value for the Historian', *Scottish Archives: The Journal of the Scottish Records Association*, i (1995), 75–84.

[8]  This orthodoxy is outlined in Christopher A. Whatley, 'How Tame were the Scottish Lowlanders during the Eighteenth Century?', in Thomas M. Devine, ed., *Conflict and Stability in Scottish Society 1700–1850* (Edinburgh, 1990), 3.

[9]  See for instance T. Christopher Smout, *A History of the Scottish People 1560–1830*, (London, 1969), 303–10 and 417.

[10]  See Whatley, 'How Tame were the Scottish Lowlanders?', 1–30, and Christopher A. Whatley, *Scottish Society 1707–1820: Beyond Jacobitism, Towards Industrialisation* (Manchester, 2000), chs. 4 and 5.

'collective action' in Scotland.[11] This seems to have been largely ignored by proponents of the 'passivity' thesis. Further evidence relating to the first half of the eighteenth century cites incidents such as the anti-Union and malt-tax riots of the early 1700s, the Porteous riot of 1736, as well as a variety of anti-customs scuffles, food riots, religious-based revolts, and numerous forms of 'everyday' protest.[12] This suggests that traditional thinking regarding popular disturbances in Scotland is in need of revision, particularly with reference to the eighteenth-century experience. This present chapter extends and develops the emerging revisionist historiography of Scottish protest by providing a detailed analysis of the range of collective action that men and women were engaged in between 1700 and 1830.

Much of the remaining scholarship around early modern Scottish criminality has been limited to discussion of the types of crimes traditionally associated with women, namely witchcraft and infanticide.[13] My own earlier work, *Women and Violent Crime in Enlightenment Scotland*, advanced this orthodox analysis to include the investigation of female participation in more mainstream forms of criminal activity. The piece concluded that Scottish women were involved in a range of violent offences during the long eighteenth-century period, and owing to the fact that they had betrayed the notional qualities of their sex when they had behaved in an overtly felonious manner; the Scottish authorities were keen to apprehend and punish them through public displays of judicial authority.[14] Clearly, the Scottish courts recognized the potential for female deviancy. This contrasts with the English experience, where the criminality of women was largely ignored as anomalous and unusual. South of the Tweed during the early modern period, women were not considered independent, autonomous actors in criminal activity. Rather, it was believed that they only ever perpetrated illegal acts at the behest of men.

Despite advancing our knowledge of Scottish crime and the reaction to its committal in the early modern period, this earlier analysis was restricted to the Lowlands of the country and only effectively examined the history of crime in Scotland over a sixty-five-year period. Whilst it is certainly refreshing to see that the history of female criminality

---

[11]  For further discussion see Kilday, *Women and Violent Crime in Enlightenment Scotland*, ch. 6.

[12]  See for instance Whatley, 'How Tame were the Scottish Lowlanders?', 1–30; Whatley, *Scottish Society*, chs. 4 and 5; and especially K. J. Logue, *Popular Disturbances in Scotland 1780–1815* (Edinburgh, 1979).

[13]  As indictments for witchcraft were rare amongst the Justiciary Court material between 1700 and 1830, the offence will not be analysed in this chapter. For relevant works on witchcraft see Christina Larner, *Enemies of God: The Witch-hunt in Scotland* (London, 1981), and Julian Goodare, ed., *The Scottish Witch-Hunt in Context* (Manchester, 2002). For relevant works on infanticide see Deborah A. Symonds, *Weep Not for Me: Women, Ballads and Infanticide in Early Modern Scotland* (University Park, PA, 1997); Anne-Marie Kilday, ' "Monsters of the Vilest Kind": Infanticidal Women and Attitudes to their Criminality in Eighteenth-Century Scotland', *Family and Community History*, 11, no. 2 (2008), 100–15, and the essays by Anne-Marie Kilday, 'Maternal Monsters: Murdering Mothers in South-west Scotland, 1750–1815', and Lynn Abrams, 'From Demon to Victim: The Infanticidal Mother in Shetland, 1699–1802', in Yvonne G. Brown and Rona Ferguson, eds., *Twisted Sisters: Women, Crime and Deviance in Scotland since 1400* (East Linton, 2002), 156–79 and 180–203 respectively.

[14]  For further discussion see Kilday, *Women and Violent Crime in Enlightenment Scotland, passim*.

in the pre-modern era has received the attention of scholars before that of men, it is nonetheless remarkable that as yet there is no scholarship of male criminality, in a country traditionally associated with aggression, confrontation, and displays of masculine authority. This chapter will go some way to address this evident historiographical lacuna by looking at the crimes of Scottish men alongside those of Scottish women between 1700 and 1830.

# INVESTIGATING SCOTTISH CRIMINALITY

## Property Crime

As was the case elsewhere in Britain and Europe during the early modern period, crimes against property made up the vast majority of business brought before the courts.[15] The preponderance of property offences undoubtedly relates to the fact that these crimes were relatively easy to commit and were likely to bring some form of material or personal gain. Although, in general, theftuous offences were less likely to be reported than other types of crime, since the cost of bringing a prosecution often meant that legal action was not worthwhile, this type of crime still dominated legal proceedings. Indeed, indictments for theft predominated over all other categories of crime brought before the Justiciary Court and involved a significant number of male and female participants.[16]

For instance, during the middle decade of the eighteenth century, Colin Martin, Betty McIntosh, Margaret Wilsone, and Christian McGichan were indicted at the West Circuit Court of Glasgow for 'stealing and carrying away a certain quantity of silk and yarn, twelve spindles of linen thread, a webb of handkerchiefs, four table napkins and eight silver candlesticks' from two houses in Kirkintilloch. Angus McIntosh, an excise officer, was indicted at the High Court in Edinburgh for stealing bank notes 'to the value of thirty pounds sterling and upwards' from the pocket of Thomas Gray whilst they drank together at an Ayrshire inn. Agnes Bishop was charged with the theft of several bottles of wine, some cheese, and an iron bucket from her master's shop in Dundee. In the same period Walter Graham was accused at the South Circuit of Dumfries of stealing a watch from the person of Alexander Constable, his landlord.[17]

From the recorded evidence, we can see that although daring on occasion, the crimes committed by Scottish thieves tended to be fairly mundane rather than ambitious or elaborate. Most of the indicted individuals could not be considered 'professional' or career criminals, as their activities were largely a result of opportunity rather than prior

---

[15] For discussion of the predominance of property crimes in Europe during the early modern period see Michael R. Weisser, *Crime and Punishment in Early Modern Europe* (Hassocks, 1979), 16.

[16] See Kilday, 'Women and Crime in South-west Scotland', chs. 4, 5, and 7.

[17] See respectively National Records of Scotland (NRS), Justiciary Court (JC) 13/11; JC3/31; JC26/144; JC12/9.

planning, and on the whole, recidivism was rare. Having said this, however, there is evidence to suggest that a criminal network existed in early modern Scotland, in both rural and urban areas. There was an obvious market for stolen goods at this time, and the range of items stolen by Scottish thieves reflects that greed, as well as need, was a motivational factor in this type of criminal endeavour. Rather than being stolen for immediate use, goods were commonly sold on to black marketeers for profit. Receiving stolen goods, or resett, was frequently indicted at the Scottish Justiciary Court. Overwhelmingly, it was the preserve of female offenders, in part because, traditionally, pawn-broking was a female concern.[18]

Aside from varieties of theft, fraud and forgery offences were evident amongst the property crimes indicted at the Justiciary Court. However, they were relatively uncommon until the latter decades of the eighteenth century when the cash nexus had developed sufficiently enough to merit exploitation. Far more commonly seen in the records of the Scottish courts throughout the early modern period was the crime of robbery.

Robbery, or stouthrief, was the crime most feared by the Scottish populace, principally because it involved the violent subduing of the victim. For this reason, indictments for robbery regularly resulted in a conviction, and it was common for perpetrators to be executed with bodily mutilation inflicted pre- and post-mortem. Criminal historians of pre-modern England have described how robbers there would typically use only *enough* violence to make the victim part with their belongings. This meant a great deal of variety was involved in terms of the amount of violence perpetrated and, indeed, it seems that in many instances mere verbal intimidation was all that was required.[19] In Scotland, however, some 79 per cent of those accused between 1700 and 1830 were additionally charged with aggravated assault as well as robbery, reflecting the severity of their actions.

In addition, where in England the vast majority of robbers did not carry violent or lethal weapons, preferring instead, where violence was indeed employed, to use fists or temporary strangulation, from witness evidence in Scotland it is clear that most robberies were carried out using knives, razors, pistols, or cudgels. In these respects, the actions of Scottish robbers bear direct comparison with those of the 'footpad' robbers prevalent in eighteenth-century London. As Frank McLynn describes it: 'The species of London criminal feared most was the footpad, the armed robber operating on foot, usually in gangs'. Due to the fact that footpads could not leave the crime scene very quickly, they regularly attempted to lower their chances of apprehension by rendering their victim incapacitated through extreme acts of violence. As a result, McLynn argues, 'the footpad was regarded with loathing and horror'.[20]

---

[18] For further discussion of this crime see Anne-Marie Kilday, 'Women and Crime', in Hannah Barker and Elaine Chalus, eds., *Women's History: Britain 1750–1800—An Introduction* (Abingdon, 2005), 174–93 at 178.

[19] For further discussion see for instance David Taylor, *Crime, Policing and Punishment in England, 1750–1914* (Basingstoke, 1998), 32–3, and David Philips, *Crime and Authority in Victorian England: The Black Country 1835–1860* (London, 1977), 246–8.

[20] Frank McLynn, *Crime and Punishment in Eighteenth-Century England* (London, 1989), 5–6. See also David Brandon, *Stand and Deliver: A History of Highway Robbery* (Stroud, 2001), 158–71.

A typical example would be the case of Mary McGhie, who was indicted for robbery at the North Circuit Court in Inverness in 1765. The jury heard how the pannel (the accused) crept up behind Alexander McWilliam, struck him over the head with an iron pipe and repeatedly beat him to the ground, stabbing him about the legs with a razor. McGhie then took hold of her victim by the throat and almost strangled him with his necktie whilst ordering him to yield his purse. When McWilliam refused to do this, McGhie grabbed her victim by the hair and dragged him to a nearby burn where she 'sat upon the victim's head whilst it was underwater rendering him quite insensible; he thereafter vomited and started to cry.' McWilliam was latterly rescued by some passersby, but not before McGhie had made off with more than seven pounds in gold and silver sterling.[21]

As the above example illustrates, Scottish women clearly played their part in this type of crime, and were not merely there to make up the numbers, or to act as lookouts, as historians have often supposed.[22] Rather, Scottish women were active participants in criminal activity in their own right, and this was arguably most evident when it came to robbery. Scottish women made up a third of those indicted for this offence at the Justiciary Court. This proportion is markedly higher than that found elsewhere in Britain during the early modern period,[23] and suggests not only a predilection for violence amongst Scottish women, but also a determination on the part of the Scottish authorities to bring violent female offenders to justice.

The most infamous criminals in eighteenth-century Scotland were robbers who killed their victims. Individuals like Robert Dun and John Key, who shot and killed James Hutchison while robbing him of his saddlebags and a watch in Ayr in 1781, or Alexander Martin, who used an axe to bludgeon his victim to death in Aberdeen in 1824 before making off with various items of jewellery, were vilified in both the courtroom and in the press.[24] Despite the expression of universal horror at this type of crime, Scottish society was nonetheless fascinated by murderous robbers. The growth of popular interest in crime and criminality, which largely began in the post-Enlightenment era in Scotland, was seemingly initiated by the actions of felons like Dun, Key, and Martin as well as their criminal successors.

## Fatal Violence

Unlike many other crimes, homicide was unlikely to contribute much to the 'dark figure' of unreported crime in early modern Scotland. This was not only due to the seriousness

---

[21] NRS JC11/25.

[22] See for instance John M. Beattie, 'The Criminality of Women in Eighteenth-Century England', *The Journal of Social History*, 8 (1975), 80–116 at 90; Ruff, *Violence in Early Modern Europe*, 235; Sharpe, *Crime in Early Modern England*, 109.

[23] See the comparisons drawn in Kilday, *Women and Violent Crime in Enlightenment Scotland*, 134.

[24] NRS JC12/17 and National Library of Scotland (NLS) L.C. Fol. 73 (076).

of the offence but also to the difficulties associated with the disposal of evidence. Between 1700 and 1830, men predominated in indictments for homicide across Britain. In Scotland they outnumbered women by nearly three to one. However, if we broaden our definition of homicide to include killings more generally, then the gender difference is not as substantive, due to women's predominance in instances of infanticide or newborn child killing.[25]

Scottish men were more likely to kill outside the home as a consequence of drunken brawls or heated arguments. It was very rare for a man to be involved in a premeditated act of murder. One curiosity from the recorded evidence is the extent to which soldiers were indicted for homicide, particularly in urban areas. This was probably a reflection of the fact that they were regularly armed but often unoccupied, which seems to have been something of a deadly combination. Men also killed within the domestic sphere, but this was fairly unusual and was typically limited to attacks on spouses or paramours. There is little evidence of other familial murders or the killing of domestic servants, which appears to have been more common south of the Tweed during the early modern period.[26]

The following examples are typical of the range of homicide indictments charged against Scottish men in the pre-modern era. James Day was indicted in Edinburgh in 1724 for the murder of James Park, whom he bludgeoned to death with a poker after a dispute about money. Day tried to cover up his crime by cutting Park's body into pieces with a view to burning the remains, but he was caught by the authorities while doing this. In 1758 David Edwards (a sergeant in the Regiment of Foot) was indicted at the South Circuit in Ayr for the murder of a fellow soldier. A witness reported that the victim had not only been wounded by the marks of a bayonet, but he had also been strangled. The murder had taken place after a drunken altercation involving a prostitute. Later in the eighteenth century, James Henderson was indicted for the murder of Alexander Gillespie in Aberdeen. In the middle of the night in October 1790, a drunken Gillespie had been throwing stones at Henderson's house and had broken a window. Henderson was incensed by the damage to his property. He ran outside and using an axe, hit Gillespie over the head with such force that it took three men to remove the murder weapon from the victim's skull. John Wilson was similarly accused of homicide in 1827. In the midst of a heated argument, where Wilson had accused his wife of having an affair, he stabbed her repeatedly in the chest and shoulder with a clasp knife while endeavouring to extort a confession of her infidelity. When none was forthcoming, Wilson grabbed his wife by the hair and slit her throat from ear to ear with a large carving knife. Realizing what he had done, Wilson then tried to take his own life, but was prevented from doing so by a neighbour.[27]

---

[25] For further discussion see Kilday, *Women and Violent Crime in Enlightenment Scotland*, 43–4 and 63–6.

[26] See James A. Sharpe, 'Domestic Homicide in Early Modern England', *Historical Journal*, 24 (1981), 29–48.

[27] See respectively NRS JC26/108, JC12/9, NLS 6.365 (104), and Ry. III. a 2 (78).

The Scottish women accused of killing in the early modern period, in contrast to their male counterparts, almost exclusively killed within the domestic sphere. Lovers and spouses were often the victims (sometimes in retaliation for abuse of one kind or another), but women could also kill their servants and other relations on occasion. Most commonly, however, Scottish women killed their children, particularly newborns. Infanticide was a particular concern of the Scottish Judiciary, as it was a blatant example of overt deviance amongst women that went directly against the notional qualities of their sex. Moreover, there is evidence to suggest that Scottish women who perpetrated infanticide committed their crime in a much more violent manner than has been depicted elsewhere. Blood was commonly shed in episodes of infanticide across early modern Scotland. Although the exact reasons for this heightened aggression remain unclear, the murder of newborn children in Scotland goes a long way to explain the unsympathetic attitude of the Scottish authorities towards women convicted of this crime.[28]

The following examples are typical of the acute level of violence employed by Scottish infanticidal women. In 1708, in Kinghorn, Fife, Margaret Selkirk was indicted for 'using her bare hands to rip the jaws of her newborn infant down to its throat'. In Jedburgh seven years later, Jean Stourie bludgeoned her baby to death with a smoothing iron, 'by which one if its eyes popped out'. Catharine Gray used a garden rake to bludgeon her child to death in Blairgowrie, Perthshire, in 1732. In 1765 Kathrine Finlay was indicted for an infanticide where she had dismembered her son with a kitchen knife, placed the pieces in a large jug, and boiled the contents on the fire. Then in 1803 Catherine Chalmers was brought to court for having slit her newborn infant's throat 'from ear to ear' with a razor.[29]

Fatal violence of any sort could certainly excite interest from the general populace, even in a pre-sensationalist era. The authorities regarded homicide and infanticide as serious crimes and convictions, for either offence commonly resulted in execution. Yet, perhaps because most of the murders were committed in hot blood, or lacked premeditation, robbery was considered the more heinous offence by judicial officials. Although instances of fatal violence are often used as a barometer of how violent a country is over time, there is no real evidence of change over time in terms of incidence, weaponry, methodology, or motive in recorded Scottish killings, save for a slight increase in poisonings towards the end of the century. Indictment material suggests that in relation to serious interpersonal violence at least, the notion of a 'civilizing process' had only a limited part to play in early modern Scottish society.[30] Killings in post-Enlightenment Scotland largely mirrored those of the century before.

---

[28]  For further discussion of this offence in a Scottish context see the references in note 13 above as well as Kilday, *Women and Violent Crime in Enlightenment Scotland*, ch. 4, and David S. Nash and Anne-Marie Kilday, *Cultures of Shame: Exploring Crime and Morality in Britain 1600–1900* (Basingstoke, 2010), ch. 3.

[29]  See respectively NRS JC3/2, JC12/4, JC11/8, JC13/14, and JC11/47. Supplementary material on these cases can be found in the relevant process papers (JC26).

[30]  For further discussion of Norbert Elias's theory of the 'civilizing process' in relation to Scottish society see Kilday, *Women and Violent Crime in Enlightenment Scotland*, Conclusion.

## Harmful Violence

The Scottish judicial attitude to more everyday types of violent activity differed to that of its southern counterpart in the way offences were categorized. In England the term 'assault' was used in a blanket fashion to describe all types of non-fatal skirmishes and misbehaviour.[31] In Scotland, by contrast, a broad palette of specific offences existed by which to indict belligerent individuals. Attempted murder, aggravated assault, hamesucken (an attack on a person within their own dwelling place), abuse, or ordinary assault, as well as violent threatening, are just a few examples of the offences charged against Scottish men and women during the early modern period. One interesting thing to note is the relative absence of sexual violence from Scottish court proceedings. Between 1700 and 1830, only a handful of rapes and other forms of sexual assault were indicted at the Justiciary Court. Indeed the number of bestiality cases far outnumbers those of interpersonal sexual violence, but this disparity is most likely due to under-reporting than limited perpetration.[32]

Due to the nature of the remit of the Justiciary Court, the types of harmful violence indicted there were relatively 'serious' in nature. Although the Justiciary evidence offers us a glimpse of *some* of the types of everyday violence committed in early modern Scotland, a survey of offences brought before the more minor Scottish courts would tell us more. From the evidence we do have to date, it is clear nonetheless that instances of harmful violence were regularly brought to the court's attention. This is evident not only from the official trial papers, but also from the thousands of applications made to the Justiciary Court for bonds to keep the peace, where individuals craved personal protection from the authorities in the midst of disputes between family members, neighbours, and acquaintances.[33]

From the recorded evidence and the examples below, we can see that on the whole, the acts of harmful violence perpetrated in early modern Scotland were unplanned and unpremeditated. They often simply occurred as part of a drunken altercation, but other episodes were more specifically to do with defending honour and reputation, financial disputes of one sort or another, or were the culmination of long-running tensions between neighbours. There are only a few instances of domestic violence on record from the period. This is largely due to the fact that at the time, the physical chastisement of a

---

[31] See, for instance John M. Beattie, *Crime and the Courts in England, 1660–1800* (Oxford, 1986), 75–6, and James A. Sharpe, *Crime in Seventeenth-Century England: A County Study* (Cambridge, 1983), 117–19.

[32] For further discussion on the problems with investigating sexual violence historically see Anna Clark, *Women's Silence, Men's Violence: Sexual Assault in England 1770–1845* (London, 1987), and Kim Stevenson, ' "Most Intimate Violations": Contextualising the Crime of Rape', in David S. Nash and Anne-Marie Kilday, eds., *Histories of Crime: Britain 1600–2000* (Basingstoke, 2010), ch. 4.

[33] These bills are called Letters of Lawburrows and can be found in the Justiciary Court Process Papers (JC26). See for example NRS JC26/579/92 brought by John Campbell (Argyll).

wife by her husband was permitted, and thus, only on the most grievous of occasions did this type of abuse come to light.[34]

At Stirling in October 1708 John Foyar was indicted for the assault and battery of Sir James Stewart, whom he had attacked with a poker after a game of cards went sour. Stewart escaped with his life, but was badly beaten and bruised by his assailant. In 1736 Elizabeth Lynch was indicted for invading, assaulting, beating, and wounding Hugh Lawson upon the High Street of Perth. In carrying out the attack, Elizabeth had 'used a whip to the great effusion of Lawson's blood and danger of his life'. Elizabeth claimed that she had received abusive language from Lawson and that 'she had taught him a lesson in how to behave'. John Fulton was indicted at the South Circuit of Ayr in 1774, charged with violently assaulting, beating, wounding, and bruising one Neil Finnie. The court heard that Fulton 'had reason to suspect that liberties had been taken with his character by Mr Finnie', through correspondence which Fulton had seen. In revenge for this slur on his reputation, Fulton attacked Finnie with a broken bottle, cutting one of his ears off and disfiguring his facial features so that he was barely recognizable to his family. Felix McLaughlin and his wife Alice were indicted in 1815, charged with assaulting, maiming, and wounding various individuals on Glasgow Green. Alice McLaughlin was drunk and had become very aggressive. To her husband's amusement and her neighbours' dismay, she began to attack random men and women with a garden fork, stabbing them in the buttocks and legs 'whilst shouting all manner of profanities at the top of her lungs'.[35]

Acts of harmful violence happened across Scotland between 1700 and 1830 anywhere people came together. There was no obvious rural or urban predilection for this type of criminality and, in general, no significant change in perpetration over time. As we have seen, both men and women perpetrated brutal types of assault in early modern Scotland. Unlike instances of fatal violence, however, female assailants who committed assault were not wholly restricted to the domestic sphere. Rather, they were often involved in violent altercations outside the home involving neighbours or individuals from the local community. Although there are some discernible trends regarding motive, most of the reasons that lay behind the recorded episodes of aggression brought before the Justiciary Court were typically idiosyncratic and dependent on personal circumstances and individual attitudes on specific occasions.

## Crimes of Protest

Grievances of a more popular nature lay at the heart of the crimes of protest indicted in early modern Scotland. It has already been acknowledged that historically, the Scots

---

[34] For further discussion of domestic assault in early modern Scotland see Kilday, *Women and Violent Crime in Enlightenment Scotland*, 87–92. For further discussion of this offence in the early modern period more widely see Joanne Bailey, *Unquiet Lives: Marriage and Marriage Breakdown in England, 1660–1800* (Cambridge, 2003), and Elizabeth Foyster, *Marital Violence: An English Family History 1660–1850* (Cambridge, 2005).

[35] See respectively NRS JC13/1 (I am very grateful to Dr Katherine D. Watson for alerting me to this reference), JC11/9, JC12/14, and JC26/371.

were not shy in coming forward about things with which they disagreed. It is clear that on relatively regular occasions this recalcitrance could escalate into criminal activity of one type or another, and could involve both male and female participants. Although it could be argued that there was a diminishing sense of 'community' as commercialism occurred over the course of the eighteenth century, there is still incontrovertible evidence of a 'popular spirit' rallying in the face of more centralized authority across Scotland during the pre-modern period.

A variety of factors caused Scottish individuals to protest. Commonly, however, popular disturbances related to the imposition of some sort of authoritative change that the public considered unfair or unjust. Offences such as riot, mobbing, tumult, or convocation of the lieges could often result nationwide, in the wake of various pieces of legislation being passed that directly affected the lives of the Scottish populace. The widespread nature of Union riots, malt-tax riots, militia riots, patronage riots, and an assortment of industrial disputes are all good examples of this in the early modern Scottish context.[36] Protest could also be more localized in nature and regularly occurred in reaction to perceived unjust practices by local officials. For example, food riots were commonplace across eighteenth-century Scotland in times of dearth, when foodstuffs were forestalled or prices were set at an unreasonable level. A typical example of this occurred at Greenock in Renfrewshire in February 1764. On that occasion David Kerr, Thomas Orr, John Hair, Alexander Boag, Thomas Reid, Robert Hyndman, John Hunter, Elizabeth Harris, Anne Flood, Catherine Bradley, and Margaret Ferguson came together after hearing that grain was being transported out of the harbour to be sold elsewhere, despite the fact that the last harvest had been poor. The court heard that upon learning this news the pannels tore down some of the ship's rigging and then proceeded to use this material as weaponry by which to assault members of the ship's crew. Eight crew members were attacked 'to the great effusion of their blood and the danger of their lives'. One of them lost an eye in the incident, one had his bottom lip torn off, and others found 'several of their tuith [teeth] to be missing'.[37]

From the recorded evidence, it is clear that instances of popular disturbance could be violent and injurious. Multiple participants were involved and they were regularly armed with weapons of one sort or another. The aggressive nature of Scottish protest did not particularly escalate or shrink over time, but rather it was relatively consistent and commonplace. The degree of violence used by Scottish rioters was not necessarily anarchic or unrestrained, but was often calculated and measured in order to achieve a specific end. Protest occurred throughout the country during the early modern period, but was more likely to occur in populous areas, where it was easier for like-minded individuals to come together.

At a more local level, another form of protest was the crime labelled the 'assault of authority'. Usually this was less of a protest against centralized change, and more of a protection measure employed to guard against an arrest or the imposition of a legal

[36]  For further discussion of these protests see the references in notes 11–12 above.
[37]  See NRS JC3/33.

sanction such as the payment of excise duty. For instance, at the South Circuit in Ayr in 1765, John Thomson, Robert Thomson, and James Miller were indicted and charged with 'invading, assaulting, beating and wounding some officers of His Majesty's Revenue and their assistants'. The court heard that the three men were caught with smuggled liquor on their persons by the excise men. In an attempt to escape, the pannels violently attacked two of the officers with the liquor bottles, breaking the jaw of one of the excise men in the process. In the fracas that then ensued, there was much bloodshed and multiple injuries were received on both sides. Similarly, in 1779 Margaret Tait from Paisley was indicted for an assault on William Gordon, a sheriff officer who had come to deliver an arrest warrant against her husband. Margaret repeatedly hit Gordon over the head with a smoothing iron and while he was unconscious, she stripped him naked, rubbed manure in his hair and over his torso, forced the arrest warrant into his mouth to act like a gag, and then dragged him by the hair to a ditch situated outside her house, where he remained for several days until he was rescued by a passing traveller.[38]

As can be seen from one of the above examples, women were often involved in this form of protest. Indeed, they narrowly outnumbered their male counterparts in indictments for this offence at the Justiciary Court. The reasons for the enhanced involvement of women in this type of crime remain as yet unclear, but part of the explanation may be that men were more likely to be engaged in work and thus absent from the household when the authority figures came to call. Even if this description is accurate, as the evidence shows, we should not underestimate the strength and determination of Scottish women when faced with the defence of their families and the protection of their livelihoods. Clearly, when provoked, Scottish women were a force to be reckoned with.

# CONCLUSION

The Scots do not appear to be that different from peoples elsewhere, in terms of the range and incidence of the types of criminality they perpetrated. On the whole, serious offences were not commonplace amongst Scottish society, and instead the courts were filled with business that related to more everyday types of violence and petty theft. The recorded evidence does not indicate a substantive change in criminal behaviour between 1700 and 1830. Violent offences occurred at a relatively static rate over the eighteenth century, and although property offences increased during that time, much of this escalation can be explained by a substantive increase in population. In addition, there is little evidence to support the notion of a favoured *locus operandi* for criminal activity during the early modern period, although over time, the more populous urban areas of the country came to dominate criminal proceedings.[39]

---

[38] See respectively NRS JC12/11 and JC26/220.
[39] For further discussion of trends in Scottish criminality over the course of the eighteenth century, see Kilday, 'Women and Crime in South-west Scotland', ch. 7.

The explanations that Scottish men and women gave for their participation in criminal activity were individualistic and multifarious, but not particularly unexpected or necessarily revealing. The defence of honour, of reputation, or of livelihood were familiar excuses heard during the proceedings of the Justiciary Court. Moreover, although it could be argued that the Scots were more likely to stand up for their rights than their counterparts elsewhere in Europe during the early modern period, more generally, their criminal motives related to their personal circumstances, rather than any sense of a common grievance or common purpose.

These conclusions should not lead to the impression that Scotland was a timid nation. Although we must remember that this chapter has exclusively analysed crimes that were more serious in nature, the evidence presented here indicates nonetheless that the Scots were not afraid to use violence to achieve their desired ends. As we have seen, both Scottish men and Scottish women were capable of committing brutal, bloodthirsty, and injurious acts on their family, their friends, and their neighbours. Yet their behaviour was not necessarily more violent or barbarous than that of individuals elsewhere in early modern Europe. Moreover, the Scots were more likely to commit an offence against property rather than an offence against a person during the period before 1830.[40]

The notion of Scotland as a barbarous nation, which came so strongly to the fore in the nineteenth century, appears to be unfounded, at least in an early modern context and based on the evidence presented here.[41] Perhaps the idea was first planted by pro-Unionists hungry to exert authority over the 'chaotic' and 'backward' Scottish populace in the early 1700s? It is more likely, however, that the notion of Scotland as a wayward and unlawful nation derived from within. In Scotland religious influence operated closely with judicial authority in the period before 1850. For instance, ministers from the Kirk Session (Scotland's ecclesiastical court) not only acted as the upholders of religious observance across the country, but they and the Church elders functioned as a type of public law-enforcement agency prior to the instalment of a professional police system. Kirk-session ministers often interviewed criminal suspects in attempts to extract confessions; they regularly made arrests and turned individuals over to state prosecutors; and they commonly testified in trial proceedings against their own parishioners. Then, in order to justify their actions, the same ministers gave impassioned sermons that decried the widespread wickedness of the Scottish populace. Many of these sermons were published, as were newspaper accounts of court proceedings and broadsides containing the confessions of convicts

[40] For further discussion see Kilday, *Women and Violent Crime in Enlightenment Scotland*, Conclusion.

[41] As indicated above, studies of more 'regular' criminality in other jurisdictions may provide different conclusions to the ones presented here. This kind of analysis is inadequate at present, but examples of the limited work that has been done include Frank Bigwood, 'The Courts of Argyll, 1664–1825', *Scottish Archives*, 10 (2004), 26–38; Christopher A. Whatley, 'The Union of 1707, Integration and the Scottish Burghs: The Case of the 1720s Food Riots', *Scottish Historical Review*, 78 (1999), 192–218, and J. R. D. Falconer, 'Mony Utheris Divars Odious Crymes': Women, Petty Crime and Power in Later Sixteenth-Century Aberdeen', *Crimes and Misdemeanours: Deviance and the Law in Historical Perspective* [SOLON On-line Journal], 4, no. 1 (2010), 7–36.

waiting to be executed. The long reach of this dual level of scrutiny, where the judiciary effectively worked in partnership with the Church, must have gone some way to create and promote the idea of Scotland as a lawless, uncontrollable nation.[42]

Yet, perhaps this unique context of scrutiny also suggests something else about the nature of Scottish justice between 1700 and 1830. The effect of both religious and legal authorities working together to curb bad behaviour implies that the Scottish criminal-justice system was regularly more intrusive and thus more effective. Although this may have resulted in Scotland attaining a false reputation as a barbarous nation, in reality it suggests that the Scots were proficient at managing criminality in the early modern period. Along with normal criminal investigations, religious surveillance operated on the ground to maximize local cooperation in gleaning information about suspected offences and suspected offenders. Certainly, it is clear from trial papers that parishioners regularly informed on each other under examination. From this, it is difficult to see how criminals would have been able to evade capture in early modern Scotland, and as a result, the level of unrecorded crime may well be lower in a Scottish context compared to elsewhere. This suggests that far from being a barbarous nation, Scotland's system of justice was more regulated, checked, and effective than its English equivalent. Moreover, if the ability to control personal and individual behaviour successfully is seen as a key marker of a 'modern' society, does this evidence not suggest that the Scots were in fact more 'modern' and thus more 'civilized' than either they or indeed their southern counterparts realized?

## FURTHER READING

Bigwood, Frank, 'The Courts of Argyll, 1664–1825', *Scottish Archives*, 10 (2004), 26–38.

Crowther, Margaret A., 'Scotland: A Country With No Criminal Record', *Scottish Economic and Social History*, 12 (1992), 82–6.

Emsley, Clive, *Crime and Society in England, 1750–1900* (London, 1996).

Falconer, J. R. D., 'Mony Utheris Divars Odious Crymes': Women, Petty Crime and Power in Later Sixteenth-Century Aberdeen', *Crimes and Misdemeanours: Deviance and the Law in Historical Perspective* [SOLON On-line Journal], 4, no. 1 (2010), 7–36.

Kilday, Anne-Marie, 'Women and Crime', in Hannah Barker and Elaine Chalus, eds., *Women's History: Britain 1750–1800—An Introduction* (Abingdon, 2005), 174–93.

—— *Women and Violent Crime in Enlightenment Scotland* (Woodbridge, 2007).

Nash, David S., and Kilday, Anne-Marie, *Cultures of Shame: Exploring Crime and Morality in Britain 1600–1900* (Basingstoke, 2010).

Ruff, Julius R., *Violence in Early Modern Europe 1500–1800* (Cambridge, 2001).

Sharpe, James A., *Crime in Early Modern England 1550–1750* (London, 1999).

Whatley, Christopher A., 'The Union of 1707, Integration and the Scottish Burghs: The Case of the 1720s Food Riots', *Scottish Historical Review*, 78 (1999), 192–218.

---

[42]  For further discussion of the influence of the Church on matters of Scottish criminality see Nash and Kilday, *Cultures of Shame*, ch. 3.

# PART IV

## THE NATION TRANSFORMED, 1760–1914

# CHAPTER 21

# INDUSTRIALIZATION AND THE SCOTTISH PEOPLE

STANA NENADIC

## AN INDUSTRIAL REVOLUTION?

SCOTLAND in the nineteenth century had an economy and a society subject to one of the most rapid early transformations in industrial experience of any country in the Western world.[1] Unique among the smaller European countries with peasant-based local economies surviving well into the nineteenth century, though as yet subject to little comparative analysis, Scotland's dramatic shift from a mostly underdeveloped, rural backwater in the mid-eighteenth century to one of the key industrial hubs of the British empire by the mid-nineteenth century, was largely orchestrated from above, by government and its agencies, and by wealthy landowners.[2] The impact of rapid industrialization on the workplace, on conditions of life, and on Scottish culture was profound, though not as profound, sudden, or damaging as late nineteenth-century changes in Germany or Russia, or even in smaller industrial regions such as Catalonia in northern Spain, a comparison with Scotland that would merit further scrutiny.

There is a popular characterization of nineteenth-century Scotland as a country defined by heavy industry. It arises out of end-of-century structural change and the politicization of sectors such as shipbuilding that employed well paid and vociferous male workers in large workplace units. It is also a consequence of economic data, such as output figures.[3] Yet industrial output as a technical measure tells us little about the actual

---

[1] See T. M. Devine, C. H. Lee, and G. C. Peden, eds., *The Transformation of Scotland: The Economy Since 1700* (Edinburgh, 2005); W. W. Knox, *Industrial Nation: Work, Culture and Society in Scotland, 1800–Present* (Edinburgh, 1999).

[2] Roy Campbell, *The Rise and Fall of Scottish Industry, 1707–1939* (Edinburgh, 1980).

[3] C. H. Lee, *Scotland and the United Kingdom: The Economy and the Union in the Twentieth Century* (Manchester, 1995), 28.

lives of people. In Glasgow, that most industrial of cities, with over two-thirds of its male and female workforce employed in industry through much of the century, the numbers engaged in engineering, tool making and metal working only exceeded those in textiles and clothing in 1911. Shipbuilding around 1900, at just 2 per cent of the employed work-force in Glasgow, was equalled by printing and publishing and was about half the size, in terms of numbers employed, of furniture making and woodworking, a flourishing industry here as in Edinburgh or Aberdeen, associated with skilled male workers based in numerous small workshops.[4] Industrial employment was shaped by the manufacture of consumer goods, much of it undertaken using craft techniques to supply local demand. Family-based production flourished in nineteenth-century Scotland, but some consumer-oriented family firms, such as Keiller of Dundee, were major undertakings.[5] The Keiller family firm was founded in the early nineteenth century in an area of Scotland that then as now produced outstanding soft fruits. Soft fruit does not travel well, but sugar does and hence a jam-making industry developed close to the source of the fruit. Turning raspberries into jam was a seasonal, kitchen-stove enterprise that expanded into confectionery and then marmalade using imported raw materials. By mid-century, Keiller had factories in the Channel Islands to avoid sugar duties and facili-tate access to Mediterranean oranges, and by 1890 it owned a massive manufacturing complex close to the Victoria Docks in London. London and Empire were Keiller's main markets. It was a bigger company than Rowntree's of York or Cadbury's of Birmingham, whose importance for Dundee is still celebrated in the aphorism 'city of jam, jute and journalism'.

Urban history has shaped our understanding of Scottish industry and its often nega-tive social consequences.[6] Yet the big-city perspective obscures the fact that many of those who worked in industry were found in villages and small towns the length of the country, from the fish-processing, coalmining, and quarrying centres of Caithness to the Borders tweed burghs. Moreover, engagement in industrial entrepreneurship was not just the preserve of the self-made businessmen of Glasgow or Dundee who attract scholarly attention.[7] In Scotland, more than in England, much rural industrial employ-ment was promoted by aristocrats, such as the Dukes of Sutherland with their flourish-ing coal and textile village at Brora in the far north-east; or the Earls of Breadalbane, who owned and developed slate quarries at Easdale in Argyll; or the Dukes of Buccleuch and Lords Lothian, who owned much of the extensive coal industry south of Edinburgh, a large part of the so-called 'eastern district' which by mid-century employed more min-ers and produced more coal than the better-known 'western district' focused on

    [4] Richard Rodger, 'The Labour Force', in W. Hamish Fraser and Irene Maver, eds., *Glasgow, Volume 11: 1830–1912* (Manchester, 1996), 167–8.

    [5] W. M. Mathew, 'Animus, Absenteeism, and Succession in the Keiller Marmalade Dynasty, 1839–1919', *Journal of Scottish Historical Studies*, 28 (2008), 44–61.

    [6] See, in particular, Fraser and Maver, *Glasgow, Volume 11*.

    [7] A. Slaven and S. Checkland, eds., *A Dictionary of Scottish Business Biography*, 2 vols. (Aberdeen, 1986, 1990).

Lanarkshire.[8] The impact of Scotland's great aristocratic estates on Scottish industrial experience is still little known, though research on the Sutherland estates offers insights.[9]

Industrial employment only exceeded agriculture in the second half of the century, but industry touched most lives. It was a more intensely present phenomenon in Scotland than in England, because the small size of the country and the wide distribution of industry meant that even those parts of the population that were not involved in industrial work saw it close at hand. There was no such phenomenon in Scotland, even in remote areas, of disconnection from the experience of industry—as there was in England, where industry and its attendant problems were in the 'north' and alien to much of the rich and powerful in the 'south'. In Scotland, the rich and the powerful, and they did not come more rich or powerful than the great Scottish aristocrats, were intimately connected with industry. And even in Edinburgh, with its 'douce' professional and gentrified culture, the bulk of the working population was industrial by the mid-nineteenth century.[10]

So what lay behind the rapid transformation of Scotland's industrial sector, and how were these forces connected to the social and cultural experience of Scotland's people? Geography was clearly important, for it allowed merchants in the west to take advantage of Atlantic trading routes to develop a flourishing cotton industry, the driving force behind the 'first' industrial revolution. Geological endowments were also fortunate, for it was cheap and easily accessed coal and iron that shaped the rise of the heavy industries which formed the 'second' industrial revolution of the later nineteenth century.[11] Geography and geology were significant in another sense, for they determined the character of agriculture, forcing men and women off an abundance of unproductive land to seek opportunities elsewhere, thereby providing a steady supply of cheap labour, which was one of Scotland's key competitive advantages. When connected with the politics of Empire, population movement also ensured the supply from overseas of crucial raw materials and the government-protected markets on which much of Scotland's industry relied. But of equal importance was the impact of the Enlightenment in Scotland, which witnessed a transformation in ways of thinking that underpinned the transformation of industry.[12] Focused on what has been termed the 'rich-country: poor-country debate'— that is, why are some countries rich, and what do poor countries have to do to become rich in their turn—there were three key themes in Scotland's Enlightenment.[13] How does

---

[8] David Bremner, *The Industries of Scotland: Their Rise, Progress and Present Condition* (Edinburgh, 1869), 18.

[9] Eric Richards, *The Leviathan of Wealth: The Sutherland Fortune in the Industrial Revolution* (London, 1973); Annie Tindley, *The Sutherland Estate, 1850–1920: Aristocratic Decline, Estate Management and Land Reform* (Edinburgh, 2010).

[10] Richard Rodger, *The Transformation of Edinburgh: Land, Property and Trust in the Nineteenth Century* (Cambridge, 2001), 22.

[11] See Joel Mokyr, *The Lever of Riches: Technological Creativity and Economic Progress* (Oxford, 1990).

[12] See Bruce Lenman, *Integration and Enlightenment: Scotland 1746–1832* (Edinburgh, 1992).

[13] I. Hont and M. Ignatieff, 'Needs and Justice in the Wealth of Nations: An Introductory Essay', in I. Hont and M. Ignatieff, eds., *Wealth and Virtue* (Cambridge, 1983).

trade operate and how can it be encouraged? How can ingenuity and invention be stimulated? And what role should governments take in the management of commerce and invention? Change was embraced, and in an age when economic, moral, and social concerns were viewed as a whole, some cautioned against the damaging social effects of modernization. It was a warning, famously illustrated by Adam Smith in the 1770s, that many seemed to forget in the nineteenth century.

The pace of change was swift in Scotland when compared with other places, but in lived experience it was charted more slowly, as illustrated in John Galt's novel *Annals of the Parish*, first published in 1821 and thought by many early readers to be fact not fiction.[14] Set in rural Ayrshire between 1760 and 1810, and described through the experience and opinions of the local minister, the *Annals* shows the transformation of a community as agriculture and the rhythm of the seasons give way to industry and commerce. New coalmines are established from the 1760s, and 'truly, it is very wonderful to see how things come round; when the talk was about the shanking of thir heughs, and a paper to get folk to take shares in them ...'.[15] Itinerant Irishmen drift through the parish in the 1780s, looking for work but soon moving on to Glasgow, to the relief of local housewives mindful of their vegetable gardens and chickens. Old gentry families die out, or move to Edinburgh, and their property is bought by the new commercial elites, chief among them Mr Cayenne, a Virginia merchant, who with business partners from Glasgow builds a cotton mill in the parish and a new town for the workers and gets a community of muslin weavers established there, and 'brought women all the way from the neighbourhood of Manchester in England, to tech the lassie bairns in our old clachan tamouring [embroidering fine muslin]'.[16]

Industrial expansion impressed but troubled the local observers in this fictional distillation of experiences that were echoed in fact, parish by parish, in the *Statistical Accounts of Scotland*. For Galt's minister, 'the minds of men were excited to new enterprizes; a new genius, as it were, had descended upon the earth.' But there were problems threatening in the 'signs of decay in the wonted simplicity of our country ways' and in the broken health and psychological dislocation of the industrial workers, who were mostly poor migrants from other parts of the country.[17] Radical politics, workplace protests, and the tragic suicide of a factory overseer and his wife, ruined in the cotton bankruptcies of 1808, illustrated for a popular audience some of the social consequences of industrialization. Gains in wealth, expanded horizons, and new opportunities were contrasted with the plight of the victims of change. Indeed, the sense of cultural loss that came with modernization remained a theme of commentaries on the subject, be they fiction or fact, throughout the century.

[14]   Christopher Whatley, ed., *John Galt 1779–1989* (Edinburgh, 1979).
[15]   John Galt, *Annals of the Parish* (Oxford, 1986), 30.
[16]   Ibid., 127–8.
[17]   Ibid., 197.

# CHANGES IN THE WORKPLACE
# AND IN LABOUR MARKETS

One of the immediate impacts of industrialization in Scotland, and the subject of many historical studies since the first flowering of Scottish economic and social history in the 1960s, was seen in changes in the workplace, as work moved indoors and towards geographies of concentration, initially in industrial villages and then gravitating towards the bigger towns and cities. On the surface, indoor manufacturing seems preferable to outdoor farming in Scotland's often harsh climate. But indoor work was associated with new and punishing employment regimes defined by the clock and facilitated by new sources of artificial lighting—gas was used for lighting in factories long before it was domesticated—that led to longer hours, shift systems, and night-time working.

Early industrial workplaces in cottages or workshops were better, particularly for those such as the fine handloom weavers of Paisley, who worked relatively short hours for good pay during the 'golden age' and had time for leisure and a rich cultural life. But domestic weaving frames got bigger and noisier, and the handloom weavers' hours of work grew as their rates of pay fell with competitive undercutting by merchants and skill displacement, first by home-based female and child labour and then by factory weaving.[18] Manufacturing processes ultimately compromised the homes of hand-based industrial workers and family life suffered. Family finances were also compromised by the need of home-based workers to pay for their own machinery, be it the weaving frames which locked them into punitive loan or rental arrangements with the merchants they supplied, or the later sewing machines that from the 1860s were 'hire purchased' in their tens of thousands by home-based female workers engaged in the sweated clothing industries.

By 1850, industry was decisively separated from the domestic sphere for most workers, and some of the best paid in the later nineteenth century could support comfortable homes in new model tenements in industrial suburbs like Dalry in Edinburgh or Partick in Glasgow.[19] But in the early phase of rural industrialization, when factory workers, often youths and children, were brought in from elsewhere, accommodation was part of the deal, and it was subject to overseer scrutiny and policing on a scale unseen in previous work regimes. Food provision also commonly came through shops run by early factory owners, offering significant scope for exploitation of the workforce. These problems, which were particularly acute in smaller and remote factories and in the mining and quarrying industry, were not unique to Scotland; but in Scotland compared with the north of England, work opportunities were fewer and factory workers, including many Gaelic-speaking highlanders and Irish poor, were often compliant.

---

[18]  T. C. Smout, *A Century of the Scottish People 1830–1950* (London, 1986), ch. 4.
[19]  Rodgers, *Transformation*, ch. 7.

Arising out of these concerns and informed by late Enlightenment debates, the imposition of factory regulation, focused on hours of work, particularly for children, and the parallel provision of factory-based education, was a cornerstone of growing government intervention in the industrial economy. In Scotland, however, with its abundant cheap labour, when the rules were applied, factory owners often simply dismissed their child workers rather than support the costs of a time-restricted workforce to be educated at the employer's expense, and the system of factory inspection seems to have favoured business. Indeed, Leonard Horner, the Factory Inspector for Scotland in the 1830s, declared himself 'against the proposed introduction of a minimum working week of 48 hours for children between twelve and thirteen years of age as he thought it would cause hardship and inconvenience to both workers and owners'.[20] And of Horner's successor, James Stuart, it was said, 'during his inspections he had found under age children concealed in the mills, one behind baskets and another in a privy, but these and other offences Mr Stuart had failed to prosecute'.[21]

The movement of the Scottish population towards industrial employment, which was also characterized by a growing bias in the occupied workforce towards male workers (the male to female worker ratio was 2/1 in 1841 and 2.5/1 in 1911), was accompanied by a general increase in hours of work. It is difficult to estimate the hours of work of the agricultural workforce, and farming often disguised structural underemployment, which contributed to low incomes. Attempts were made to restrict the hours of vulnerable industrial workers, but the forty-eight-hour minimum working week suggested for twelve-year-olds in the 1830s textile industry, normally worked over six days with Sunday free, is telling. In 1834, a time of full employment but low pay, Glasgow handloom weavers reported a thirteen-hour working day.[22] Hours of work continued high to the 1890s, when the introduction of the half-day Saturday holiday heralded the start of a fall. Yet there was massive variation. Of the well paid and skilled male workforce, such as those in the closely regulated gas industry, it was reported in the 1890s that over the previous sixty years, wages had risen by 125 per cent and working hours had fallen by an average of one hour per day.[23] But skilled male workers still worked an average week of over fifty-four hours.[24] These adult men were mostly involved in full-time, regular employment. Many industrial workers were not so lucky. In Glasgow's late nineteenth-century female unskilled labour market, the working day was shorter, but payments, earned by the hour or piece, were commensurately low, and underemployment and poverty were commonplace.[25]

---

[20] 'Reports made to the Secretary of State by the Inspectors of Factories, in pursuance of the 45th section of the Factories Regulation Act', *Parliamentary Accounts and Papers*, vol. xlv, 156 (1836), 14.

[21] 'Mills and factories. Second report from the Select Committee', *Parliamentary Papers* [hereafter *PP*], vol. x, 227 (1840), 108–12.

[22] 'Handloom weavers' petitions. Report from the Select Committee', *PP*, vol. x, 556 (1834), 72–84.

[23] *The Scotsman*, 27 August 1892, 2.

[24] Knox, *Industrial Nation*, 8.

[25] J. H. Treble, 'The Characterisation of the Female Unskilled Market and the Formation of the Female Casual Labour Market in Glasgow, 1891–1914', *Scottish Economic and Social History*, 6 (1986), 33–46.

Changes in work regimes and payment were paralleled by changes in the gendering of work, which was also shaped by technological innovation. Industrial ingenuity, another key theme of Scotland's practical Enlightenment, was applied to production processes to increase efficiency and profit for entrepreneurs, and one of the primary mechanisms whereby this was achieved was through reducing the skill of the workers involved.[26] Unskilled or semi-skilled factory work, and in particular that associated with the textile industry, was dominated by women and girls. Commercial specialization meant that certain towns, such as Dundee or Dunfermline, had remarkable concentrations of female industrial workers by mid-century, a phenomenon that has been well described by historians, though the mechanisms whereby these localized labour markets operated are, as yet, little understood.[27] Other places, dominated by skilled men, such as the Clyde shipbuilding towns of the later nineteenth century, had less employment for women. Sectoral concentration inevitably introduced another new phenomenon, the experience of mass unemployment arising out of the fluctuations in the international economy, to which Scottish industry was increasingly vulnerable. Yet concentration, in good times or bad, also generated a sense of popular unity and fuelled calls for industrial reform.

The Scottish labour movement was powerful where skills and wages were high, and it is not surprising that calls for reform were related to the physical dangers that industry represented. Iron making was a dangerous employment and so too was coalmining. The journalist David Bremner, in the first comprehensive survey of Scottish industry undertaken initially for *The Scotsman* newspaper and published as a book in 1869, provided details on the dangers of coalmining, an area of intense cultural unity and workplace power. Yet Scottish mines were not as dangerous as those in England, mainly due to the absence of 'fire-damp', which caused explosions, and most of the men and boys who died in Scottish mines were killed by falls of coal.[28] The lead industry, which had major works in and around Glasgow to supply the growing demand for lead roofs, pipes for water and gas, and type for the printing industry, was particularly damaging to health.[29] By the late nineteenth century, industrial inspectors had made detailed recommendations on protective clothing, respirators, prescribed drinks, and regular medical inspection, and there was legislation prohibiting women under the age of twenty from working with white lead, which was known to damage female fertility.[30] Explosives were also manufactured in Scotland for use in the building and railway industries, both famously dangerous to life and limb. Explosives factories were hazardous places for the mainly female workforces, as was recorded in a report to the Secretary of State for the Home Department in 1884 following an accident in a cartridge factory owned by the Nobel Explosive Company at Ardeer in Ayrshire, which killed ten teenage girls and injured

[26] R. H. Campbell, *Carron Company* (Edinburgh, 1961); John Butt and Kenneth Ponting, eds., *The Scottish Textile Industry* (Aberdeen, 1987).

[27] Eleanor Gordon, *Women and the Labour Movement in Scotland, 1850–1914* (Oxford, 1991).

[28] Bremner, *Industries*, 18–19.

[29] Ibid., 139.

[30] 'Various Lead Industries: Report from the Departmental Committee', *PP*, vol. xvii, 7239 (1894).

four others.[31] Moreover, visitors to industrial sites, attracted by the spectacle and excitement of industry, were sometimes the unfortunate victims of the noxious materials that industry employed, as in September 1886 in the picturesque setting of Inverary in Argyll, as recorded by the Scottish Inspector of Explosives, a government post usually held by retired military men:

> Messrs. William Sim and Co., who leased Crarae Quarry, were contractors for supplying paving stones for the city of Glasgow. The streets were paved under the direction of the Police and Statue Labour Committee of the Town Council. In 1886, the Committee had been in existence for 50 years, so a 'monster blast' was undertaken at Crarae in commemoration of the foundation of the Committee. The steamer 'Lord of the Isles', which sailed each day from the Clyde to Inveraray, brought visitors to Loch Fyne to see the 'monster blast'. Any visitors who wished to do so were invited to land at Crarae pier and inspect the quarry after the explosion. Many of the visitors were overcome by the fumes of the gunpowder and seven people died from the effects of the poisonous gases.[32]

# Conditions of Life

Some areas of work were injurious to health, but the greater threat, resulting in significant rises in the death rate and a fall in life expectancy in Scotland, was born out of overcrowding in industrial cities.[33] Contemporary statistics revealed Glasgow housing to be among the worst in Britain, though no British city could match the horrors of industrial northern Europe, in St Petersburg or Berlin, and Glasgow's problems also stimulated local-government intervention. But the impact of housing and sanitation reform on the experience of industrial Scots was limited before 1914. The urban industrial workforce was one in which harsh work regimes, low or irregular wages, and poor housing were painfully obvious in the physical appearance of children and adults. The stunted growth of children meant that the poorer classes of industrial workers were three inches shorter than those of the better paid, and Scots, on average, were smaller in the nineteenth century than in the century before.[34] Textile workers were notoriously unhealthy in appearance, the result of often impoverished rural backgrounds and long hours from childhood spent bent over machinery, causing deformities of the spine. Home-based female industrial workers, again due to hours spent in fixed positions, suffered badly in their health and also in their capability to undertake the other types of unpaid work on which their

---

[31] 'Report to the Secretary of State for the Home Department by Col. A. Ford, H. M. Inspector of Explosives', *PP*, vol. xvii, 4075 (1884), 26.

[32] Ibid., vol. xvii, 4928, 13.

[33] Charles Withers, 'The Demographic History of the City, 1831–1911', in Fraser and Maver, eds., *Glasgow*, 141–62.

[34] R. Floud, K. Wachter, and A. Gregory, *Height, Health, and History: Nutritional Status in the United Kingdom, 1750–1980* (Cambridge, 1990).

families relied. The embroidered muslin industry, employing about ten thousand women in the Glasgow area through much of the nineteenth century, was typical. It was described in the 1830s as 'an employment which, in most instances, unfits women for other occupations, and, besides, it frequently injures their health, and leaves them very helpless, when they get houses of their own, as to the management of their domestic concerns'.[35] This highlights one of the common characteristics of the Scottish industrial scene, and a cause of growing concern among social commentators and reformers at the time, and among historians subsequently—the impact of industry on families.

Men and youths dominated industrial work in the late nineteenth century. Legislation and regulation, family pressures, and employer preferences had gradually driven out adult women. Early industrial workplaces commonly employed whole families in mutually dependent units that reproduced some aspects of what was traditionally seen in agriculture. But changes in business organization towards larger, specialized units—and Scotland was particularly associated with very large industrial workplaces—coupled with employment regulation to exclude women from physically dangerous or morally problematic working situations, as seen, for instance, in the mining industry where heat underground resulted in the near-nakedness of workers, undermined this early family dimension. There was a trend towards gender and age segregation in industry that reinforced the patriarchal character of family relations in working-class communities. The more skilled an industrial male worker, the less likely it was that his wife and adult daughters worked outside the home. Moreover, in those workforces that were dominated by adult women, as in the Dundee or Dunfermline textile industries of the later nineteenth century, there was considerable philanthropic effort to 'domesticate' the women involved into the traditional home-focused skills of cooking, sewing, and childcare.[36]

Working-class status hierarchies, the subject of critical scrutiny by historians of class in the 1980s, were reinforced among skilled workers in western Scotland's metal and engineering sector by privilege systems of apprenticeship and employment that favoured the sons of men already established in the industry.[37] Industrial-worker patriarchy, which mirrored the lives and rhetoric of many of the great industrialists themselves, was reproduced in conservative patterns of marriage and family formation. Men mostly married women with similar family backgrounds to their own and skilled men did not choose their marriage partners from among women who had worked in industry. One of the consequences of this structuring of the industrial workforce by mid-century was that working-class men and women lived entirely separate lives, with men outside the home and in male company, either at work or in work-related leisure facilities such as the pub or football ground, for most of their waking hours. Women were based in the home with their large families, for couples of this sort did not engage in the family-limitation practices seen in other groups of Scots from the later decades of the nineteenth century, and lived narrow and culturally

---

[35] Bremner, *Industries*, 310.
[36] Gordon, *Women and the Labour Movement*.
[37] Knox, *Industrial Nation*.

impoverished existences.[38] Some industries were dominated by a female workforce, and women in some towns brought in the largest share of the family wage, but in these areas of manufacturing, seen typically in the linen, jute, and woollen districts, patriarchy was reproduced in employee hierarchies, with male overseers and foremen controlling the work regimes of even the most skilled of women. It was difficult for single adult women to get by on their own, so in towns like Dundee, there were many all-female households composed of unmarried sisters, or mother and daughters, who remained together for mutual support. In these communities, marriage opportunities for women were few in a country where high male emigration had also generated a 'spinster problem'. The separation of the sexes, the financial dependence of women, and conflict over family access to male-earned wages resulted in high levels of domestic violence in Scotland, a subject noted by a few but, as with many areas of women's history, still awaiting detailed comparative study.[39]

The social consequences of industrial work were deleterious to many conditions of life in Scotland, but the movement of a mostly rural population from low-paid agricultural employment to better-paid industrial and urban work had, on balance, a positive impact on the circumstances of many people's lives, a fact that econometricians have demonstrated, but which runs counter to much popular history and many scholarly studies of industrial suffering.[40] The impact of better industrial earnings was accentuated by the changing character of industrial work with the growth of the new working-class elite and the expansion of industrial bureaucracies towards the end of the century, which saw the well-educated sons and sometimes the daughters of the labour aristocracy move from manual work to white-collar office work.[41] Industrialization made Scotland richer than ever before, as economists and business historians have shown, and was for many ordinary families a real opportunity for upward social mobility.

## SIGHTS, SOUNDS, AND SMELLS OF INDUSTRY

Industrial expansion was relentless in Scotland and it was commonly resisted because of its encroachment on the environment, a subject that exercised many contemporaries but, other than in the work of T. C. Smout, has been little studied.[42] Attempts by Glasgow manufacturers to colonize the open spaces of Glasgow Green for their bleach fields, or to block the public footpaths along the banks of the Clyde with their factory buildings,

---

[38] M. Anderson and D. J. Morse, 'The People', in W. Hamish Fraser and R. J. Morris, eds., *People and Society in Scotland, Volume 11: 1830–1914* (Edinburgh, 1990).

[39] Knox, *Industrial Nation*, ch. 9.

[40] C. H. Lee, 'Economic Progress: Wealth and Poverty', in Devine, Lee, and Peden, eds., *Transformation*, 128–58.

[41] R. Guerriero Wilson, *Disillusionment or New Opportunities? The Changing Nature of Work in Offices, Glasgow 1880–1914* (Aldershot, 1998).

[42] T. C. Smout, *Exploring Environmental History: Selected Essays* (Edinburgh, 2009).

were vigorously resisted from the early nineteenth century. Moves in the 1820s to develop coalmining in central Glasgow were also overturned by those elements of the community who sought to protect the fast-vanishing amenity of a city that had boasted, as late as 1800, of its salmon fishing at Glasgow Bridge and the great crops of honey from beehives on the roofs of tenement buildings.

One of the major polluters was the paper-making industry of rural eastern Scotland, whose waste chemicals and refuse discharged into rivers killed fish and were 'unpleasant to the nostrils, if not pernicious to the health of the people dwelling on the banks of the polluted waters'.[43] Cases in law, particularly those taken by local proprietors against the paper-makers on the River Esk—which forced the introduction of waste recycling—Acts of Parliament, and newspaper campaigns were frequent by the 1870s as industry spread to new locations. A *Scotsman* editorial of 1880, prompted by attempts from manufacturers to revoke anti-pollution legislation, captured the popular mood in a country where many still had rural roots:

> Contemplation of the Clyde or the Kelvin at Glasgow, the Cart at Paisley, or the Irwell at Manchester, is sufficient to make any observer possessed of the sense of smell resolve to do all in his power to prevent other rivers, such as the Tweed, the Ness, and the Tay, from being brought into the same abominable state. People who have had the good fortune to have been brought up in the country beside a running stream are apt, without being at all sentimental, to take up the matter much more keenly. It is a personal injury that the burn which has been their friend and companion should be soiled and polluted almost beyond recognition; and for its sake they are sharply set against the fouling of streams anywhere and for anything.[44]

Attempts to protect the countryside were shaped by revulsion at the impact of intensive industry on the urban environment. Francis Groome, author of one of the finest gazetteers of late nineteenth-century Scotland, describing the Bridgeton area of east Glasgow, was struck by the elegance of Bridgeton Cross, 'a decagonal, cast-iron pavilion, with surmounting clock tower 50 feet high' which had been erected in 1875, but also remarked that the area 'contains many cotton factories and other public works [and] presents, in general, a dingy, murky appearance'.[45] Even the private houses of the business elite were compromised by industrial expansion. These included the house of Cowlairs, a fine detached mansion in extensive grounds about two miles north of central Glasgow, built as a 'charming country retreat' in the second half of the eighteenth century and considerably extended in 1824 by John Gourlay, a Glasgow distiller. But though still in Gourlay family ownership when the house was described in 1878, it was long abandoned as a family residence since 'the N. B. Railway cut the property in two between the house and the offices, and what amenity was left has been destroyed by their great engine works and by the spread of the city'.[46]

[43]  Bremner, *Industries*, 335.
[44]  *The Scotsman*, 27 August 1880, 4.
[45]  Frances H. Groome, *Ordnance Gazetteer of Scotland* (Edinburgh, 1885).
[46]  John Guthrie Smith and John Oswald Mitchell, *Old Country Houses of the Old Glasgow Gentry*, xxv, Cowlairs (Glasgow, 1878).

Yet despite the well-known negative impact of industry through water pollution and noise and choking atmospheres, it was also associated with spectacle and entertainment, a subject that historians of tourism have explored. The Carron Ironworks near Falkirk was a visitor attraction from its first foundation in the late eighteenth century, the great blazing furnaces at night being an awesome sight for those seekers after the sublime who found within the Scottish landscape evidence of both the might of God in the mountains and torrents, and of man and science through industry. Armchair tourists were aware of this spectacle through the popular guides to Scotland. Even Robert Burns was moved by the infernal reputation of the place to write the following verse on the window at an inn at Carron, having tried and failed to be admitted to view the ironworks as a tourist:

> We cam na here to view your warks
> In hopes to be mair wise,
> But only, lest we gang to hell,
> It may be nae surprise...[47]

A visit to Carron en route to the Highlands featured in all tourist itineraries around 1800. Another famous 'must do' was a visit to Robert Owen's New Lanark, which had vast machinery and buildings, the beautiful Falls of Clyde nearby, and the spectacle of large numbers of children engaged in industrial work and education in a model regime. Visits to notable factories remained popular and, as the century advanced, many industrialists sought to represent the spectacle and achievement of industry not only through machines and power and size, but also through spectacular architecture and design. So the Bridgeton area of Glasgow might have struck the visitor with its 'dingy' and 'murky' appearance, but it was also where James Templeton & Sons chose to build their iconic carpet factory in the late 1880s, designed in a Venetian Gothic style based on the Doge's Palace in Venice, and grafted onto an older cotton works on the same site. Employing many hundreds of workers making carpets using the chenille Axminster process (patented by Templeton in 1839), the facade of red, green, and yellow glazed brick was a marvellous sight.[48]

Templeton's sense of style was also displayed for a mass audience through a series of international exhibitions held in Glasgow. At the first in 1888, which ran for six months and was attended by almost six million visitors, James Templeton & Sons mounted a vast display of woollen upholstery and carpets in the Grand Hall, where, alongside a giant statue of Burns, there were daily concerts and organ recitals. At the second exhibition in 1901, the firm constructed a colourful 'mosque-style' pavilion between the Industrial Hall and the Art Galleries, which featured considerably in the photographic record and tourist memorabilia that marked the event.[49] The second exhibition, held, like the first one, in Glasgow's Kelvingrove Park, was attended by over eleven million visitors, and as

---

[47] Ian Donnachie, 'A Tour of the Works: Early Scottish Industry Observed, 1790–1825', in A. J. G. Cummings and T. M. Devine, eds., *Industry, Business and Society in Scotland since 1700* (Edinburgh, 1994), 43.

[48] G. D. Hay and G. P. Stell, *Monuments of Industry and Illustrated Historical Record* (Glasgow, 1986), 68.

[49] Perilla Kinchin and Juliet Kinchin, *Glasgow's Great Exhibitions* (Bicester, 1990), 31, 86.

with the Great Exhibition of 1851 in London on which it was modelled—whose profits were invested in the creation of the Victoria and Albert Museum—it led to the founding of a permanent art gallery and museum for Glasgow. Edinburgh also had a publicly funded museum of science and industry.

The relationship between industry and art, science and design, was celebrated and rewarded (for prizes were normally given for the best-manufactured items on display) through highly visible and popular spectacles both large and small. Dundee had an 'Exhibition of Industry' in the town's Drill Hall, the largest available indoor space, between December 1887 and January 1888. It was sponsored by the Dundee and District United Trades Council, with patrons including the local Members of Parliament and the Earl of Strathmore. The exhibits, for which prizes were awarded for workmen, apprentices, and scholars, were divided into three sections—'industrial and domestic work, hand done', 'trades and manufactures', and 'art'. There was also an exhibition of local natural history—indeed, the Dundee Naturalist's Society was one of the event's sponsors, an incongruous relationship perhaps given the damage inflicted by industry on nature, but not unexpected since naturalist societies flourished in industrial places because they offered working men an avenue for study and leisure away from the environments in which they worked.[50] The presence of hand-worked goods at the Dundee exhibition is a telling inclusion, for the making of fine, predominantly textile goods by highly skilled women was still a major employment in the town. However, the largest section was the second, which incorporated twenty-two distinct classes of manufacture and design ranging from 'scientific and mechanical inventions' to 'baking and confectionery work'. One category, reflecting the reforming purposes of the exhibition, was for 'architectural drawings; plans for working men's houses etc'. Profits from the event, which proved a popular success, were donated to Dundee's Royal Infirmary.[51]

# INDUSTRIAL HEROES

Industry had a further impact, for it gave rise to a new pantheon of national heroes, celebrated through popular biography and iconography.[52] The first to achieve recognition were the inventors, particularly James Watt (1736–1819), scientist and developer of the steam engine, who was also a mathematical instrument maker and surveyor. Indeed, the William Wallace National Monument near Stirling, opened in 1869 with an audience of over seventy thousand in attendance, included a 'Hall of Heroes' comprising sixteen busts of well-known modern Scots, three of them inventors—Sir David Brewster (1781–1868),

---

[50] Diarmid A. Finnegan, 'Natural History Societies in Late Victorian Scotland and the Pursuit of Local Civic Science', *British Journal for the History of Science*, 38 (2005), 53–72.

[51] *Dundee Exhibition of Industry* [Exhibition Catalogue] (Dundee, 1887).

[52] Christine MacLeod, *Heroes of Invention: Technology, Liberalism and British Identity, 1750–1914* (Cambridge, 2007).

scientist and optical innovator; William Murdock (1754–1839), pioneer of gas lighting; and, of course, James Watt. Watt also dominated a popular engraving and accompanying volume of memoirs titled 'Distinguished Men of Science of Great Britain living in 1807–8', which was published in London in the 1860s by William Walker, son of a Musselburgh salt manufacturer. The imaginary scene, set in the library of the Royal Institution and dominated by Scots, marked the centenary of the Act of Union and was a celebration of the 'inestimable benefits which have resulted to mankind from the labours of these gifted men ... the Grand Main-Springs of our National Wealth and Enterprise'.[53]

Not only the wonders of industry in the hands of inventors but the popular evocation of the celebrated businessman as social benefactor came to mark this new industrial hagiography. Schools, public libraries, and art galleries, concert halls and parks, were all endowed by industrialists, some of them, like Andrew Carnegie, having made their industrial fortunes overseas. In most cases, the buildings that housed these institutions preserved the names of the benefactors long after the demise of the industries from which they took their wealth. Who, for instance, in the streets of Kirkcaldy today could tell you anything of the three men called Michael Nairn, father, son, and grandson, whose wealth generated through the manufacture of floor cloths and linoleum—with factories in Fife, the United States, France, and Germany, and warehouses in London and Paris as well as Glasgow and Manchester—was gifted to the town to build a hospital in 1890, a new high school in 1894, a YMCA in 1895, and a public park in 1927? The monumental buildings and open spaces bequeathed to local communities such as those in Kirkcaldy, where Michael Nairn & Co. was the largest employer, made a lasting contribution to the Scottish townscape.

A popular narrative that suggested public-spirited men of industry and invention were role models for the working population was widely articulated through magazines like *The British Workman* (first published in 1855) and through the pen of Samuel Smiles (1812–1906), doctor and newspaper editor from Haddington (present-day East Lothian), who made his career in Leeds, and specialized in industrial biographies with such edifying titles as *Self-Help* (1859), *Character* (1871), and *Thrift* (1875). An account of Britain and of Scotland that privileged the contributions of industrialists was also sealed at the end of the century with the first publication of the *Dictionary of National Biography*, in which big science and heavy engineering dominated and men associated with the 'technological icons of imperialism'—railways, shipping, and the arms industry—were disproportionately represented. Through Crown-bestowed honours, the state, in a mirror to popular culture, created a new national elite of its industrialists, though many of the richest had left Scotland and day-to-day involvement in businesses to enter national political life in London by the turn of the century. We know much about the lives and achievements of such men, though less about their failures or comparative performance with business elites in other industrial regions of Britain or Europe.

[53] MacLeod, 'Distinguished Men of Science of Great Britain', Feature Essay, *Oxford Dictionary of National Biography* Online 2004. www.oxforddnb.com.ezproxy.webfeat.lib.ed.ac.uk/view/theme/97115? backToResults=list=|group=|feature=yes|aor=8|orderField=chrono

Some industrial workers were elevated to national celebrity status. The Paisley weaver poet and songwriter Robert Tannahill (1774–1810), who reputedly composed at his hand-loom, was one of the sixteen Scots whose busts were placed in the William Wallace National Monument 'Hall of Heroes'. Working men who made their mark through the labour movement were famous by the end of the nineteenth century, such as miner James Keir Hardie (1856–1915), who honed his skills in the temperance movement and in popular journalism before winning a seat in Parliament in 1892, where he caused a sensation by deliberately wearing working men's clothing.[54] There were even a few working women from industrial backgrounds who mainly through local politics achieved popular distinction in the eyes of fellow Scots. They include Mary Barbour (1878–1958), the daughter of a Renfrewshire carpet weaver, who worked as a carpet printer, before marrying an engineer at Fairfield's shipyards and settling to married life in Govan. Though her celebrity was forged during the Glasgow rent strikes of 1915 and she was the first woman to serve on Glasgow's town council following election in 1920, her political career in the Labour Party and commitment to social reform was schooled in the 1890s through the Kinning Park Co-Operative Guild, the first such organization in Scotland.[55]

## INDUSTRY IN SCOTTISH CULTURE

The growing presence of industrial entrepreneurs and workers in national affairs was a mirror to the role of industry in shaping Scottish cultural life and identity. There was celebration to be sure, but there was also an inevitable rejection by many of an industrial reality that was brutal in its impacts. From the Owenite socialists of the 1820s, who sought to recreate a pastoral and moral ideal in utopian communities, to the arts and crafts movement of the later nineteenth century, which focused on hand-crafted manufacture and backward-referencing, organic ideals of modernism, Scots were locked into an ambiguous relationship with their own experience of rapid economic change.[56] The basic problem was that industrial life and industrial organization ran counter to the fundamental nature of Scottish moral community. Galt had highlighted this in his novel, *Annals of the Parish*, and it was echoed in powerful but backward-looking Victorian highlandism. The dislocation caused by industry was condemned by evangelical religious leaders such as Thomas Chalmers, with his experiments in parish poor-law reform in 1820s Glasgow, and by numerous city and factory missionary groups.[57] It was reflected in the movement for factory schooling and in later nineteenth-century endeavours to

[54] Kenneth O. Morgan, 'James Keir Hardie', *ODNB* Online. www.oxforddnb.com.ezproxy.webfeat.lib. ed.ac.uk/view/article/33696?docPos=5
[55] Audrey Canning, 'Mary Barbour', *ODNB* Online. www.oxforddnb.com.ezproxy.webfeat.lib.ed.ac. uk/view/article/54393?docPos=5
[56] Elizabeth Cumming, *Hand, Heart and Soul: The Arts and Crafts Movement in Scotland* (Edinburgh, 2006).
[57] Stewart J. Brown, *Thomas Chalmers and the Godly Commonwealth in Scotland* (Oxford, 1982).

create rational leisure facilities for industrial workers. Scottish clergy were vigorously engaged with industrial problems, often mediating in workplace disputes. Yet popular religious magazines, such as the Reverend Norman Macleod's *Good Words*, hardly ever mentioned Scotland's industrial reality.

The ambiguous nature of Scottish industrial experience, a product of the collective psychological trauma inflicted by rapid change, is striking and merits further study. And yet there is still further ambiguity in the characterization of Scotland as a country of coal and iron, metal and engineering, which masks that other side of Scottish cultural and creative endeavour that was given over to consumer and fashion goods, where beauty and design were the primary considerations. Design was initially sponsored by the Board of Trustees for Manufactures through prizes offered for the best-manufactured items and through the founding of schools of drawing and design, initially in Edinburgh from the 1760s, with a branch in Dunfermline by the 1830s, and in Glasgow from 1845, with a branch in Paisley. The intention of these schools, which were open to talented youths and later girls, was to produce designers for industry.[58] In 1849 there were 362 students at the Glasgow School of Design, with many finding employment in calico printing and fine-muslin manufacture.[59] The later development of this school as a centre of arts and crafts design particularly associated with Charles Rennie Macintosh, who represents a peculiarly Scottish, organic, and iconic response to modernism, could not have happened without the earlier foundation in industry.

The uniting of art and industry was seen particularly strongly in Dunfermline, where there was an early design school serving linen manufacture in the production of fine-patterned damask tableware. Initially a hand-based industry, steam-driven Jacquard looms were introduced from 1849 and by the 1870s there were eleven factories in the town employing a workforce of over six thousand. One of the largest works, built in 1851 and employing fifteen hundred women by 1870, was owned by Erskine Beveridge, who began his career as a draper's apprentice and was later a major sponsor of the direct railway link between Edinburgh and Dunfermline.[60] Beveridge commissioned the finest designers for his fashionable napery, including such local talent as Joseph Paton, father of Sir Noel Paton the artist, and the celebrated Italian artist and designer Agostino Aglio, who mainly worked for the Manchester textile industry.[61] One of the factories in Dunfermline was that of Messrs D. Dewar & Sons of London, which, with an eye to the contemporary fashion market, produced the celebrated 'Crimean Hero Tablecloth', 'inspected and greatly admired by the Queen and Prince Albert at Balmoral' and a best-seller. It comprised a border of twenty-four 'faithful portraits' of national and international military heroes and royals, with armorial bearings and leafy scrollwork.[62] It was

[58] J. Mason, 'The Edinburgh School of Design', *Book of the Old Edinburgh Club*, 27 (1949), 67–97.

[59] 'Schools of Design. Reports Made to the Board of Trade Since 1849', *PP*, vol. xlii, 730 (1850), 41–4.

[60] Lesley Fergusson, *Wanderings with a Camera in Scotland: The Photography of Erskine Beveridge* (Edinburgh, 2009), 1–3.

[61] Valerie Hunter, *Designs of Desire: Architectural and Ornamental Prints and Drawings, 1500–1850* (Edinburgh, 1999).

[62] Bremner, *Industries*, 256.

prize-winning artefacts like this, for a prosperous consumer market, that dominated the output of much of Scottish industry, yet the Dunfermline fine-damask industry, like many others which fell victim to changing fashions, disappeared with barely a whimper after the First World War and has never been studied.

The son of Erskine Beveridge was a pioneer in industrial and engineering design and expanded his business in the 1890s to new factories in Cowdenbeath, Ladybank, and Dunshalt. But for Erskine Beveridge junior, like many second- and third-generation manufacturers, his principal love lay elsewhere. A notable antiquarian collector, he is remembered today as a photographer of quaint rural scenes, an heir to those many cultural commentators who in words or images saw the essence of Scotland in small, traditional communities. From Allan Ramsay's verse play *The Gentle Shepherd*, published in 1725 and popular through the eighteenth century and beyond, to J. M. Barrie's best-selling novel and play *The Little Minister*, published in 1891, Scottish poets and novelists viewed rural simplicity as exemplifying a moral ideal. These vastly influential writers, the Edinburgh-based pastoral poet and the London-based leader of the sentimental 'kailyard' school, were born into industrial communities, the first in the mining village of Leadhills, the second to a family of Kirriemuir weavers, but their creative impulse came from the land and nature and tradition, real or invented. Industry, during the age when Scotland was a great industrial country, offered nothing equivalent other than through industrial design, an area that is barely recognized today. Indeed, it is one of the paradoxes of Scottish cultural life that the flowering of creativity in literature or art in response to this greatest of transformations in the history of the country, only took place in the twentieth century when industry began its slow and painful decline.[63]

## FURTHER READING

Bremner, David, *The Industries of Scotland: Their Rise, Progress and Present Condition* (Edinburgh, 1869).

Campbell, Roy, *The Rise and Fall of Scottish Industry, 1707–1939* (Edinburgh, 1980).

Devine, T. M., Lee, C. H., and Peden, G. C., eds., *The Transformation of Scotland: The Economy Since 1700* (Edinburgh, 2005).

Fraser, W. Hamish, and Maver, Irene, eds., *Glasgow, Volume 11: 1830–1912* (Manchester, 1996).

—— and Morris, R. J., eds., *People and Society in Scotland, Volume 11: 1830–1914* (Edinburgh, 1990).

Gordon, Eleanor, *Women and the Labour Movement in Scotland, 1850–1914* (Oxford, 1991).

Knox, W. W., *Industrial Nation: Work, Culture and Society in Scotland, 1800–Present* (Edinburgh, 1999).

[63]  Ian A. Bell, 'Work as if you Live in the Early Days of a Better Nation: Scottish Fiction and the Experience of Industry', in H. Gustav Klas and Stephen Knight, eds., *British Industrial Fictions* (Cardiff, 2000).

Lee, C. H., *Scotland and the United Kingdom: The Economy and the Union in the Twentieth Century* (Manchester, 1995).

MacLeod, Christine, *Heroes of Invention: Technology, Liberalism and British Identity, 1750–1914* (Cambridge, 2007).

Mokyr, Joel, *The Lever of Riches: Technological Creativity and Economic Progress* (Oxford, 1990).

Richards, Eric, *The Leviathan of Wealth: The Sutherland Fortune in the Industrial Revolution* (London, 1973).

Rodger, Richard, *The Transformation of Edinburgh: Land, Property and Trust in the Nineteenth Century* (Cambridge, 2001).

Slaven, A., and Checkland, S., eds., *A Dictionary of Scottish Business Biography*, 2 vols. (Aberdeen, 1986, 1990).

Smout, T. C., *A Century of the Scottish People 1830–1950* (London, 1986).

CHAPTER 22

.....................................................................................................................

# SCOTLAND AND THE EIGHTEENTH-CENTURY EMPIRE

.....................................................................................................................

## DOUGLAS HAMILTON

THE revitalization of Scottish history in the 1960s reawakened scholarly interest in over-seas connections that had lain more or less dormant since the 1930s. As a result, eighteenth-century Scots have appeared as Virginian tobacco merchants, Jamaican planters, American scholars, African explorers and slave traders, Indian nabobs, and sol-diers and doctors seemingly everywhere.[1] With a few notable exceptions, however, these studies of Scots overseas have often been region-specific rather than offering a broader imperial or global perspective. This 'Scotland and...' approach reflects the great diversity of Scottish experiences overseas, as well as the shifting imperial foci that determined which Scots went where, with what intentions, and with what results.

Part of the difficulty with a more global perspective lies in the nature of 'British Empire', which remained a congeries of disparate territories rather than a unified and coherent whole. Boston, Barbados, and Bengal were all key centres of British power, but empire looked very different in each of them. By the same token, not all imperial loca-tions were equally important at all times; nor were all territories constantly part of the Empire throughout the century. The clearest example is in North America, where the Thirteen Colonies broke away from the Empire in 1776.

[1] Francis Russell Hart, *The Disaster of Darien* (Boston and New York, 1929); George Pratt Insh, *The Company of Scotland Trading to Africa and the Indies* (London and New York, 1932); Andrew Dewar Gibb, *Scottish Empire* (London, 1937). Later work includes: T. M. Devine, *The Tobacco Lords* (Edinburgh, 1975); Ned C. Landsman, *Scotland and its First American Colony 1683–1765* (Princeton, 1985); David Hancock, *Citizens of the World* (Cambridge, 1995); T. M. Devine, *Scotland's Empire, 1600–1815* (London, 2003); Douglas J. Hamilton, *Scotland, the Caribbean and the Atlantic World, 1750–1820* (Manchester, 2005); John M. MacKenzie with Nigel R. Dalziel, *The Scots in South Africa: Ethnicity, Identity, Gender and Race, 1772–1914* (Manchester, 2007); George K. McGilvary, *East India Patronage and the British State: The Scottish Elite and Politics in the Eighteenth Century* (London and New York, 2008).

This chapter suggests that despite this background of diversity and instability some Scots were able nonetheless to focus a coherent global imperial vision. Imperial Scots created global portfolios of myriad overseas enterprises and opportunities that shifted seamlessly between the 'first' and 'second' empires. By so doing, rather than 'swinging to the east' they facilitated the global circulation of people, resources, and capital. This global enterprise is explored through Scottish activities in the Empire.

As well as locating the Scottish experience at the heart of the Empire, this chapter notes that eighteenth-century Scots did not feel themselves confined to British imperial endeavour, but sought advantage in other European empires. This facility to work through alternative imperial traditions had its roots in long-standing personal and mercantile relationships between Scots and northern Europe and Scandinavia, and in the particular circumstances of the demise of Scotland's own independent empire at Darien on the isthmus of Panama.[2]

The imperial relationship was not simply about the outward projection of Scottish people, capital, and ideas, however. Scots also brought empire home. While the profitability of empire and the extent of its impact on industrialization remains a matter of historical debate, it is now clear that eighteenth-century Scotland was influenced in many and sometimes surprising ways by overseas engagements.

# THE DAWNING OF A NEW CENTURY

The eighteenth century had an inauspicious beginning for imperial Scots. The national euphoria surrounding the Darien scheme in 1695 dissipated rapidly as the Company of Scotland breathed its last, leaving resentment and vindictiveness in its wake. Darien is sometimes regarded as the desperate denouement of independent Scottish imperial ambitions. The failure of the Caledonia colony to secure Scotland's place as a global player appeared to rush it into Union in 1707, after which Scots redirected their efforts into a new British Empire.

This notion of 1707 as a watershed is problematic for considerations of the Empire, however. There were Scots in the Americas—not counting Darien—long before the Act of Union. Perhaps 4,500 Scots went to the Caribbean before 1707, while there were Scottish settlements in East New Jersey and Carolina by the 1680s.[3] Most Scots were there with English consent, but others were involved in illegal trading, frequently with the connivance of local officials. English authorities were notably irritated by Scottish smuggling, often through the Dutch Caribbean, from and to Virginia, Maryland, Pennsylvania, and New York in the later 1690s. The Governor of New York noted in

---

[2] The classic study of the 'Darien' scheme is Insh, *The Company of Scotland*. See also Douglas Watt, *The Price of Scotland: Darien, Union and the Wealth of Nations* (Edinburgh, 2007).

[3] Hamilton, *Scotland, the Caribbean and the Atlantic World*, 3; Landsman, *Scotland and its First American Colony*.

May 1698: 'There has been a most licentious trade with pirates, Scotland and Curaçao.'[4]

Moreover, as Andrew Mackillop has pointed out, the effects of Union and, in particular, of the terms of the post-Darien 'Equivalent', varied dramatically across different imperial spheres. While it is perfectly credible to regard 1707 as a fillip to pre-existing Scottish ambitions in the Atlantic, the Union effectively barred large-scale Scottish imperial activity in India and the East. In this formulation, the Equivalent was a pay-off brokered by the East India Company to compensate Scotland for giving up its aspirations to an eastern empire. One important result of the closure of this British route to the east was the redirection of Scottish enterprise to companies formed in Trieste, France, Ostend, and Sweden.[5]

That Scots sought opportunities in the imperial domains of European powers is unsurprising. Scots, as Chapter 16 in this volume makes clear, had long-standing connections with a series of European nations that were not immediately severed following the Act of Union. Nor did they necessarily turn to them only because access to the East India Company seemed restricted. For some Scots, these seemed like perfectly natural (and perhaps preferable) routes to an eastern empire. British India therefore remained a predominantly English empire run by the United Company of Merchants of England trading to the Indies. Between 1700 and 1730, only 17 of the 547 merchants and factors (agents) in its overseas stations were Scots.[6]

The blockage in the East began to ease in the 1720s, largely as a result of domestic British political wrangling. Under Robert Walpole's administration, Indian patronage became part of the political management of Scotland, orchestrated at first by the Dukes of Argyll. Through the Argethalians and their managers in Scotland, a succession of young Scots found opportunities in East India Company service in return for political and electoral loyalty at home.[7] At the same time, other Scots found their way to India and beyond under the cover of foreign companies. Jacobites in particular held little hope of advancement in Hanoverian Britain, especially after 1715 and 1745, and so found alternative avenues in European concerns. And once in India, as George McGilvary notes, 'permanent residence was usually allowed in the English company's settlements upon desertion from a rival company'.[8]

If control of the British Empire in the East remained (by and large) in the hands of the East India Company until the 1780s, in the West the situation was different. There, the shipment of sugar and tobacco was controlled by private entrepreneurs, as was the increasingly lucrative trade in enslaved Africans following the end of the Royal African

---

[4] *Calendar of State Papers, Colonial Series, America and the West Indies* (London, 1904) [hereafter CSP] 1696–7, 'An account of several things whereby illegal trade is encouraged…', 71–4; Quote from CSP 1697–8, Governor the Earl of Bellomont to the Lords of the Treasury, 239–40.

[5] Andrew Mackillop, 'Accessing Empire: Scotland, Europe, Britain and the Asia Trade, 1695-c.1750', *Itinerario*, 29, 3 (2005), 14–17; idem., 'A Union for Empire? Scotland, the East India Company and the British Union', *Scottish Historical Review*, 87 (2008) supplement, 122; McGilvary, *East India Patronage*, 20–1.

[6] Mackillop, 'A Union for Empire?', 133.

[7] McGilvary, *East India Patronage*, 13–15.

[8] Ibid., 21.

Company's monopoly.[9] Individual migrants could flourish provided they could make it across the Atlantic, as could merchants with the goods and means to trade.

With Union and the ending of formal institutional barriers to empire in the Atlantic after 1707, Scots moved quickly to seize their new opportunities as migrants, merchants, doctors, soldiers, slave traders, plantation owners, and, significantly, as appointed imperial officials and governors. In addition to the relative freedom of access in the Atlantic, a series of other reasons help explain why 1707 had a more immediate impact on westbound enterprise. The Americas offered a wider range of opportunities for a broader spectrum of Scots. The colonies of settlement to the north—in what are now Canada and the United States—held out at least the prospect of land and prosperity for Scots of all classes. The southern tobacco-producing states of Virginia and the Carolinas offered opportunities for Scots as merchants, factors, and clerks. And further south, in the Caribbean, there was a whole range of vacancies for predominantly young male Scots managing and profiting from the plantation system and the enslavement of Africans.

For Scots not in the Empire, though, the immediate benefits of 1707 were unclear. The promised wealth of overseas enterprise was not apparent until a generation after Union. India remained relatively inaccessible, while even the might of the Tobacco Lords was not entirely evident until about the 1740s.[10]

In both East and West, the Empire itself also remained insecure. The vision of Britain bestriding the world as an imperial colossus was far from established in the first half of the century, nor was it something that might reasonably have been predicted at that time. As well as European imperial rivalries around the world, powerful non-European forces in North America, India, and Africa ensured that all European empires remained contingent on their political and economic support. By the 1760s, however, a series of profound shifts at home and overseas reshaped Scotland's relationship with empire.

# A MILITARY EMPIRE

The period of the Seven Years War, between 1756 (or 1754 in North America) and 1763, witnessed a transformation in the scale of the British Empire and of Scottish activity in it. Coupled with major changes at home, this period, and far more so than 1707, ought to be regarded as a pivotal moment in the history of Scotland and the Empire. The scale of this global conflict, and the resulting extension of the Empire, demanded an expansion of the armed forces.[11]

---

[9] David Eltis, 'The Volume and Structure of the Atlantic Slave Trade: A Reassessment', *William and Mary Quarterly*, 58, 1 (2001), 43. See the data at www.slavevoyages.org

[10] Devine, *Tobacco Lords*, vi.

[11] Fred Anderson, *The Crucible of War: The Seven Years War and the Fate of Empire in British North America, 1754–1766* (London, 2001); Bruce Lenman, *Britain's Colonial Wars, 1688–1783* (Harlow, 2001); Brendan Simms, *Three Victories and a Defeat* (London, 2008), 387–500; John Brewer, *The Sinews of Power: War, Money and the English state 1688–1783* (London, 1987); Jonathan R. Dull, *The French Navy and the Seven Years War* (Lincoln, NE, 2006).

The East India Company army grew from three thousand regular troops in 1749 to twenty-six thousand at the end of the Seven Years War, and by 1778 it numbered sixty-seven thousand. The vast majority were sepoy troops, complemented by around four thousand European soldiers and officers. It was in the officer corps that Scots were especially prominent, with as many as one in three Europeans being Scots, compared to one in eleven among the European ranks.[12]

In North America and the Caribbean the threat from French and Indian forces required the stationing of British Army regulars. Scottish regiments played prominent roles in many of the major set-piece battles on American soil.[13] Scots were also prominent as military commanders, in both the British Army and Navy, in the American and Caribbean theatres of war.

The real significance of high-ranking Scots in an imperial context lies in their assumption of the civilian commands in colonial territories once peace returned. Across the Empire, civilian authority was increasingly vested in the hands of military commanders. In 1763 the new governments in Quebec, East and West Florida, and the Ceded Islands were handed to four Scottish governors, all of whom had recently held military commands. These particular posts relied in part on the patronage of Lord Bute, but they also represented a general trend in British thinking about the role of military men in the civilian governance of empire.[14]

Officers were mobile throughout the Empire and it was common for them to serve in different parts of the Empire. The trajectory of Sir Archibald Campbell of Inverneil's career serves to illustrate the point. Inverneil is perhaps best known as the Governor of Madras between 1786 and 1789. But he began his career in the Caribbean when he served on the captured French island of Guadeloupe under another Scottish commander, Robert Melville, during the Seven Years War, before being stationed in Bengal in 1768. He then went back to the Americas, this time at the head of a 3,500-strong expedition to Georgia during the American War, before being promoted to Lieutenant Governor then Governor of Jamaica between 1781 and 1784.[15] For Scots officers military service brought a global sense of their empire.

For most regular troops and especially those drafted to serve, any overseas posting was unpopular: financial considerations, separation from families, capture, and the risk of death from disease as well as war, all acted as significant demoralizing elements.[16] There is evidence that highlanders signed up for the army believing that they would not

---

[12]  Gerald Bryant, 'Officers of the East India Company's Army in the Days of Clive and Hastings', *Journal of Imperial and Commonwealth History*, 6, 3 (1978), 203; *idem.*, 'Scots in India in the Eighteenth Century', *Scottish Historical Review*, 64, 177 (1985), 23.

[13]  Lenman, *Britain's Colonial Wars*, 144, 234–5.

[14]  Douglas Hamilton, 'Robert Melville and the Frontiers of Empire in the British West Indies, 1763–1771', and Andrew Mackillop, 'Fashioning a "British" Empire: Sir Archibald Campbell of Inverneil and Madras, 1785–9', in A. Mackillop and S. Murdoch, eds., *Military Governors and Imperial Frontiers c.1600–1800* (Leiden, 2003), 181–204, 205–31.

[15]  Mackillop, 'Fashioning a "British" Empire', 205–31.

[16]  Linda Colley, *Britons: Forging the Nation* (London, 1994), 283–319.

be forced to serve overseas. In January 1783, just as the American War ended, the 77th Regiment, the Athol Highlanders, were told they were going to India. They mutinied at Portsmouth, refusing to be 'like bullocks to be sold' to the East India Company. When it transpired that another highland regiment, the 78th Seaforths, had been sent to India and then disbanded there in 1784, rather than in Scotland, it fostered a deep distrust towards military service. By the 1790s, when recruitment drives were made across Scotland, recruiters were at pains to explain that military service would be confined to Scotland, unless England was invaded. But the experience of the Athols and Seaforths remained in the popular memory. When Lord Seaforth tried to raise a new fencible regiment in the Western Isles in spring 1793, he faced serious popular opposition. In 1797, after the introduction of the Scottish Militia Act, there was widespread civil disobedience and rumours circulated in Perthshire and Stirlingshire that recruits were to be drafted into regiments for the East and West Indies, or even to be sold into slavery.[17]

This general anxiety was heightened by the very real dangers of military service overseas. If death and disease were constant threats, then the risk of capture by enemy forces and the accounts of it that filtered back represented both personal trauma and the continued insecurity of the Empire. Robert Gordon, a Scottish ensign, wrote of his maltreatment after being captured by the forces of Mysore in India: 'they tore off our clothes and behaved in a most indecent manner'. Meanwhile in North America, captivity narratives by Scots officers tended to highlight the brutality of their captors in ways that were likely to frighten further potential recruits. Accusations of cannibalism—'While they were feasting on poor Capt Robson's body'—intentionally marked non-Europeans as 'savage'.[18]

In India, the Scottish military relationship with empire was not straightforward or a wholly successful one. The growing number of Scottish officers and troops, for example, did not always cover themselves in glory. At Pollilur in September 1780, Colonel William Baillie of Dunain and his men presided over a defeat so ignominious that Indians disparaged them and Britons feared for their empire in the East.[19] In the Americas, the defeats inflicted during the early years of the Seven Years War and then in the American Revolutionary War, with the loss at Yorktown in 1781 coming hard on the heels of the reverse at Pollilur, likewise resulted in heavy casualties among the disproportionately large Scottish contingents among British forces.

To the rank and file, then, imperial endeavour was not something to be welcomed uncritically by the century's end. But for officers, imperial service in India, North America, or the Caribbean remained attractive as long as it held out the prospect of

---

[17] Kenneth J. Logue, *Popular Disturbances in Scotland, 1780–1815* (Edinburgh, 1979), 107–8, 116–18; Bryant, 'Scots in India in the Eighteenth Century', 25–6.

[18] Linda Colley, *Captives: Britain, Empire and the World, 1600–1800* (London, 2002), 137–307; National Army Museum, London, NAM 6409–67–3, Robert Gordon, 'Narrative or Journal of the Misfortunes of the Army captured at Bedanore by Tippo-Saheb, Sultan', 21; NAM 6003/117, 'Relation of a captivity among the Indians of North America by Major John Rutherfurd, AD 1763', fol. 9v.

[19] Colley, *Captives*, 269–73; Lenman, *Britain's Colonial Wars*, 256.

advancement. In this sense, for them the Empire was a means to an end, and in this officers had much in common with other Scots in the expanding British Empire.

# A POPULAR EMPIRE

Scots had long been a mobile people who looked to overseas residence, as well as soldiering or trading, as a way of progressing. Before the eighteenth century their destinations had been predominantly European, and while these locations were not altogether abandoned, the British Empire became the principal outlet for aspiring Scots. Although emigration appears largely to have been classless, particular destinations attracted Scots of different status.

By the second half of the eighteenth century, the sugar colonies of the Caribbean had become the most important parts of the British Empire. It was here, especially in Jamaica and, after 1763, Dominica, Grenada, St Vincent, and Tobago, that Scots flocked in their thousands.[20] This movement of people was eclipsed by those going to North America, but the relative numbers in the Caribbean is especially striking. The planter and historian Edward Long's belief that as many as a third of the white population in Jamaica was of Scottish descent by the 1770s is often cited; and in the southern Caribbean, the land sales after the acquisition of the Windward Islands in 1763 suggest Scottish landownership amounted to between 30 and 40 per cent. Political representation was even higher. Scots were the largest national group in the Grenada Assembly for much of the final third of the eighteenth century, while Tobago saw meetings of the assembly attended only by Scots.[21]

That Scots were highly visible in the local affairs of the island assemblies and councils was a reflection of their position in the white communities in the Caribbean. They were to be found as plantation owners and merchants, and their employees: clerks, bookkeepers, and overseers. The proposition that Scots were prominent in medicine is now almost axiomatic, but new research has established the prominence of Scots as attorneys (i.e. those managing estates for absentee landowners, not attorneys-at-law). In these positions, Scots held positions of great responsibility, with implications not only for the owners and their sugar output, but also for the thousands of enslaved Africans over whom they wielded enormous power.[22] In securing these jobs, Scots often relied on patronage extended through family and local connections.

---

[20] Alan L. Karras, *Sojourners in the Sun: Scottish Migrants in Jamaica and the Chesapeake, 1740–1800* (Ithaca, NY, 1992); Hamilton, *Scotland, the Caribbean and the Atlantic World*; Devine, *Scotland's Empire*, 221–49. Perhaps seventeen thousand Scots went to the Caribbean between 1750 and 1800, Hamilton, *Scotland, the Caribbean and the Atlantic World*, 23–4.

[21] Edward Long, *The History of Jamaica*, vol. 2 ([1774], London, 1970), 286–7, 316–19; Hamilton, *Scotland, the Caribbean and the Atlantic World*, 143–6.

[22] For doctors see Richard B. Sheridan, *Doctors and Slaves: A Medical and Demographic History of Slavery in the West Indies* (Cambridge, 1984), and Hamilton, *Scotland, the Caribbean and the Atlantic World*, 112–39; for attorneys, see B. W. Higman, *Plantation Jamaica, 1750–1850: Capital and Control in a Colonial Economy* (Kingston, Jamaica, 2005), 67–8, 77.

The nature of Caribbean slave society determined which Europeans ventured to the Caribbean. The presence of hundreds of thousands of slaves, an increasing number of whom developed artisan skills, ensured that there was little demand for white labour in the eighteenth-century West Indies. The existence of slavery, allied to an absence of cheap and available land, curtailed Caribbean opportunities for Scots of artisan, labouring, and agricultural backgrounds. This was a destination for well-capitalized Scots, or for those who were literate, numerate, and with connections to potential employers. Furthermore, the Caribbean was not regarded as a place to bring up families, nor was it a healthy place to live. As a result, the vast majority of Scottish migrants to the Caribbean were young, single, and male. It is also certain that most of them had no intention of settling permanently in the West Indies: they went to the Caribbean to make money and then return.[23] The West Indies were also regarded as an important investment opportunity for Scots. This was true for the merchant class, some of whom integrated their mercantile activities with plantation ownership. The gentry and aristocracy regarded the potential revenues from the Caribbean as essential to the invigoration of their fortunes at home.

It was not until the abolition campaigns of the 1780s and 1790s that widespread concern was expressed about the nature of Caribbean fortunes. In the 1760s and 1770s, in the context of anxieties about how money was being made in India, the Caribbean had been regarded as a place where 'genteel fortunes' could be made.[24] The landed basis of plantation profits in the Caribbean elevated the perception of West Indian wealth above that derived from 'shaking the pagoda tree' in India. The morality of Caribbean wealth was rarely debated, and Scots who made money from the Caribbean displayed no more remorse about the abuse of African lives than any other ethnic group.

The success of Scottish activity in the Caribbean depended (as did all others) on the regularity of the supply of labour from Africa. Its importance meant that there was money to be made in slave trading. Scottish investors, captains, merchants, surgeons, and crew all worked to make the slave trade profitable. Relatively few voyages originated from Scottish ports, and many Scottish merchants chose to base their slave-trading operations in the English ports of Liverpool, Bristol, and London. These operations were also active on the African coast, where they appeared in key slaving centres. One of the best known is Bance Island, in the mouth of the Sierra Leone River.[25] If anything, West Africa was even less hospitable a place than the Caribbean, and the presence of powerful African rulers ensured that European traders failed to establish anything other than toeholds along the coast. Elsewhere in eighteenth-century Africa, the numbers of Scots were similarly limited. Some Scots in Dutch service had been at the Cape since the

---

[23] Karras, *Sojourners in the Sun*, 3–6.

[24] *Scots Magazine*, 28 August 1766, 443.

[25] Hancock, *Citizens of the World*, 172–220; Daniel L. Schafer, 'Family Ties that Bind: Anglo-African Slave Traders in Africa and Florida, John Fraser and his Descendants', in G. Heuman and J. Walvin, eds., *The Slavery Reader* (London, 2005), 778–95.

seventeenth century; still more arrived with and in the wake of the British military during the Napoleonic Wars.[26]

For those Scots who went to India and the East, too, sojourns in the Empire were meant to be temporary and opportunities for large-scale migration to India were limited. Even if Scots had wanted to move there and take their chances with the climate and disease, India was never regarded as a colony of settlement, nor even, like the Caribbean, as a colony of plantations. As a result, for those not in the military the main opportunities came in either the civil administration of the East India Company, as free merchants, or as captains or crews of merchant ships. The promise of great riches—even more than the Caribbean, India was regarded as a place where vast fortunes could be acquired—lured Scots, usually well connected and often from Scotland's gentry and even aristocratic families.[27]

While the ambition of Scots in the Caribbean, Africa, and India was almost uniformly to make money and to return, it did not always work out that way. Not all Scots who went into the Empire were successful; indeed for all the promised riches of an imperial career, it often turned out to be an activity fraught with risk. Profits from trade were vulnerable to fluctuations in climate, production, price, and geopolitical circumstances. For migrants in tropical locations, in particular, disease was a constant threat and mortality rates were often ruinously high. Many who went out never came home. At the same time, though, there were some who decided to stay longer, sometimes because garnering their fortune took longer than planned, and sometimes because they settled and raised families with indigenous peoples.

This general perception of Scots seeing the Empire as a temporary situation in the eighteenth century did not apply to migrants to North America, however. The demographics of Scottish emigration there suggest the movement of people determined to carve out new lives overseas. Like many other aspects of eighteenth-century empire, large-scale Scottish involvement emerged fully in the second half of the century. There were, of course, significant movements before then, but the period immediately after 1763 was marked by what some historians regard as an 'emigration mania' that lasted until the American War. In this period perhaps forty-five thousand Scots went to North America, out of a total of one hundred thousand across the whole century.[28]

Unlike to the Caribbean, emigration to North America was quite democratic. People of all social groups emigrated, as a study based on a 'Register of Emigration' from 1773 to 1776 noted. Among the 3,872 Scots listed in the Register, most were drawn from agricultural backgrounds, or were artisans or labourers, but some were of gentle birth while others were involved in trade. Compared to English migrants, relatively few Scots went as indentured servants and most of them came from the industrializing central belt. Highlanders, on the other hand, tended to travel in family groups and to pay their own

---

[26] MacKenzie with Dalziel, *The Scots in South Africa*, 29–39.

[27] Bryant, 'Scots in India in the Eighteenth Century', 22–41.

[28] Devine, *Scotland's Empire*, 108–9.

passage. By far the most common destinations were New York, North Carolina, and Pennsylvania. These colonies were served by major ports, but they all also offered huge swathes of territory into which Scots would fan out, the 1763 Proclamation Line notwithstanding.[29]

This period coincided with fundamental transformations in Scottish economic and political life, which recast social relationships across the country. In addition, a series of short-term economic shocks in the 1760s and 1770s undermined the positions of many Scots. All the passengers on the *Commerce*, which sailed from Greenock for New York in February 1774, cited 'Poverty and to get Bread' as their reasons for leaving.[30] North America, to them, appeared as a vast system of outdoor relief. At the same time, however, many highlanders and lowlanders were highly organized and motivated when it came to emigration to a continent that held out the promises of land and liberty. This was not yet the desperate flight of destitute highlanders fleeing rapacious landowners: most landlords and the government were appalled by the ebb tide of people and tried to prevent it. In this period, Scots were not necessarily forced from their homes, but saw emigration as a 'rational choice' in the face of fundamental and unpopular change at home.[31]

British territory in Canada had been increased by the retention of Quebec in 1763, but before the 1780s, Scots seemed drawn only to Nova Scotia, and even then, in comparatively small numbers. After American independence, however, Canada became the principal North American destination for Scots for the remainder of the century, taking more than five times the number of immigrants compared with its now-independent neighbour. The Scottish population there was swollen, not only by migrants directly from Scotland, but also by American Loyalists of Scottish descent, who moved north back into British-owned territory.[32]

Across North America, Scottish arrivals found themselves in polyglot societies, where they mixed with other Europeans and, importantly, Native Americans. It is difficult to ascribe a 'Scottish' response to the encounter between them. For those Scots who first met Native Americans in the Seven Years War, they encountered some as allies and some as enemies aligned with the French. Against the latter, 'Highlanders who had seen scorched-earth tactics applied to their homelands in 1746 applied them in Cherokee country in 1760 and 1761.'[33] To Scots like this, William Robertson's Eurocentric view of Native American society as 'savage' seemed familiar. Indeed, Scots were much like any other European settlers and traders in their racialized and superior attitudes to Native

---

[29] Bernard Bailyn, *Voyagers to the West: A Passage in the Peopling of America on the Eve of the Revolution* (New York, 1986). See especially 89–240.

[30] 'List of passengers from 3d February. excl. to the 10th of February 1774 inclusive', in V. R. Cameron, ed., *Emigrants from Scotland to America 1774–1775* (Baltimore, 1965), 1–5.

[31] Devine, *Scotland's Empire*, 138–9.

[32] J. M. Bumsted, 'The Scottish Diaspora: Emigration to British North America, 1763–1815', in Ned C. Landsman, ed., *Nation and Province in the First British Empire: Scotland and the Americas, 1600–1800* (Lewisburg, PA, 2001), 136–7.

[33] Colin Calloway, *White People, Indians and Highlanders: Tribal Peoples and Colonial Encounters in Scotland and America* (Oxford, 2008), 38.

Americans. Fur traders often took little account of Native American ritual custom and practice, while land-hungry settlers apparently felt little remorse (nor saw any irony) in clearing Native Americans from their traditional homelands. Civilians taken captive by Native Americans were equally as unsympathetic as their military counterparts.[34]

These examples serve as a useful corrective against any romanticized notions of a particular empathy between Scots colonists and the colonized Native Americans, but they do not tell the whole story. Some Scots, and highlanders in particular, engaged in cultural practices that if not necessarily familiar to Native Americans were at least comprehensible to them. In areas dominated by the fur trades and in the colonial back country, encounters between some Scots and Native Americans resulted in the emergence of new cultural forms and Metis (mixed-descent) populations. Among the latter were some significant players, not the least of whom was Alexander McGillivray, leader of the Creek Indians in colonial Georgia during the American War, who was the son of Lachlan McGillivary, a Scottish trader, and a Metis woman of French and Creek descent.[35]

# A Global Empire

For many Scots, as indeed for other Britons, the Empire was about commerce and, bolstered by the protection of Navigation Acts and the British military, they set about accumulating wealth. Merchants are often associated with particular colonial commodities, whether tobacco, sugar, or slaves. Houstoun and Company of Glasgow, for example, dominated the importation of sugar using a series of agents in a number of Caribbean islands, while the 'Tobacco Lords' of Glasgow have been the subject of meticulous scholarship. There were strong connections between them, with Glasgow's increasingly powerful mercantile community sharing experience and intelligence, as well as joint-financing and intermarrying, which in some respects allowed (at least in the Atlantic) a 'Glasgow style' of trading to emerge. This was based on 'store' rather than 'commission' trading, and utilized carefully selected agents in the colonies, while control remained located on the Clyde. In this way, Glasgow merchants grew rich on colonial trade, and in so doing provided employment opportunities for hundreds of other Scots in the American south and the Caribbean.[36] Other Scots, instead of basing their operations in Scotland, moved to positions of advantage in England, with Liverpool, Bristol, and London being the major destinations. From these ports, they embarked on trading

---

[34] Calloway, *White People, Indians and Highlanders*; Stewart J. Brown, 'William Robertson, Early Orientalism and the Historical Disquisition on India of 1791', *Scottish Historical Review*, 88, 2 (2009), 289–312.

[35] The best study of the relationship between Scots and Native Americans is Calloway, *White People, Indians and Highlanders*, on which this section is based.

[36] Douglas Hamilton, 'Scottish Trading in the Caribbean: The Rise and Fall of Houstoun and Company', in Landsman, ed., *Nation and Province*, 94–126; Devine, *Tobacco Lords*.

ventures to the Americas, Africa, and Asia, facilitating the movement of colonial commodities, British manufactures, and the enforced displacement of Africans.

Yet while merchants can be identified as Indian merchants, 'tobacco lords', or sugar merchants, many of them had a far more global sense of their activities. The Baillies of Dochfour, for example, are associated with the Atlantic, and were renowned as traders in sugar and slaves. They were based originally in the Caribbean but shifted to Bristol and London by the 1780s as their operations expanded. At the same time, their near relations, the Baillies of Dunain, ventured east, to India and to the African coast. When James Baillie wrote suggesting India 'for a change' in 1775, it did not mark a shift but a widening in his imperial vision. This idea of a global, familial empire was not unique to the Baillies. Countless Scottish families developed interests that implied a global understanding of empire and transcended what historians have since regarded as shifts from west to east. Among the most important families were six of the seven sons of Sir James Johnstone of Westerhall. In the Atlantic world, George Johnstone became Governor of East Florida in 1763, William acquired Caribbean interests through his marriage into the Pulteney family, and Alexander acquired the 1,000-acre Baccaye plantation in Grenada, which he renamed Westerhall, and which was valued at over £54,000 sterling in 1770. In India, meanwhile, John Johnstone amassed a fortune of £300,000, his brother Gideon also went there, while the youngest brother, Patrick, died in the 'Black Hole' at Calcutta in 1756. Six sons of this noble family thus made their ways in the Empire concurrently in the East and West. The career of Alexander Johnstone is particularly revealing. He started out in India before being dismissed from Company service in 1767.[37] Did he know this was coming? Perhaps his acquisition of the Grenadian plantation in December 1766 suggests he did. In any event, his imperial movement was a swing to the West not the East.

## THE EMPIRE IN SCOTLAND

It is clear that thousands of Scots seized one or more of the myriad opportunities overseas. Yet these prospects were open to all Britons. Why were Scots, in particular, so well positioned and so willing to seize them in the years after the Seven Years War? By the 1760s, the prospect of wealth in the Empire was apparent: Glasgow was being transformed by the tobacco lords, while the riches of the East seemed inexhaustible. To a people with education and aspiration, but relatively few domestic opportunities, empire appeared to be a panacea. For their English counterparts, patronage systems created more chances at home and this fostered a greater reluctance among them to take a chance on an imperial career. This should not be overplayed: the Empire was

---

[37] Hamilton, *Scotland, the Caribbean and the Atlantic World*, 74; McGilvary, *East India Patronage*, 339–45.

not short of English adventurers; but empire was more important to a greater proportion of Scots.

In essence, this is what Walpole had realized as early the 1720s when his use of Indian patronage became central to the political management of Scotland. In luring Scottish politicians with the wealth of the Indies, the Hanoverian regime also drew the Scottish elite closer to it.[38] In this sense India, along with visible incomes from the sugar, cotton, and tobacco trades, helped unite a British elite. It did not, of course, do it completely or immediately: the Jacobite rising of 1745, if nothing else, signalled that Union was not to be taken for granted. By the 1760s, however, the Jacobite threat to the stability of Britain had diminished and the performance of Scottish (and especially highland) troops in the Seven Years War went some way to reducing the distrust of Scots. Scottophobia lingered, but triumphs like Quebec, with the very visible presence of highland soldiers, suggested that overseas endeavours were becoming British. For some Jacobites, empires (including those of other European powers) were significant in their 'rehabilitation' as Britons. Stints as officers, or planters, or merchants overseas allowed them to leave Scotland as dangerous, seditious Jacobites and to return as wealthy, imperial Britons. Empire profoundly reshaped the relationship of Scots with Britain: in some cases it made being British worthwhile; in others it enabled a mobility in mainland Britain, through which many more Scots settled in England than English people did in Scotland. Over time, the wealth and influence accruing to imperial Scots created a cycle (which Scottophobic satirists regarded as venial rather than virtuous) in which imperial standing enhanced positions in British civic, political, and economic life, which in turn enabled more and more Scots to seek advancement overseas.

The Empire had practical and visible effects in all parts of Scotland and across all walks of life. The wealth of empire and the impact of its profits have long been debated. Adam Smith, in an early salvo, argued that 'under the present system of management... Great Britain derives nothing but loss from the dominion which she assumes over her colonies'.[39] In the twentieth century, successive generations debated this point, with Eric Williams proclaiming that profits from slavery bankrolled British industrialization, and others claiming that money invested in empire produced a lower return than it would have done at home.[40] That said, and for all Smith's misgivings, the authors of the 1791 account of Inverness in the *Statistical Account of Scotland* noted the 'great influx of money from the East and West Indies' that contributed to 'the increasing prosperity of the burgh'.[41] Indeed, while more scholarship is needed in this area, there is a growing

---

[38]  McGilvary, *East India Patronage*, 18.

[39]  Adam Smith, *An Inquiry into the Nature and Causes of the Wealth of Nations* (1776), ed. K. Sutherland (Oxford, 1993), 355, 361.

[40]  Eric Williams, *Capitalism and Slavery* (Chapel Hill, NC, 1944). For an example of the debate, see R. B. Sheridan, 'The Wealth of Jamaica in the Eighteenth Century', *Economic History Review*, 18 (1965), 292–311; Robert Paul Thomas, 'The Sugar Colonies of the Old Empire: Profit or Loss for Great Britain', *Economic History Review*, 21, 1 (1968), 30–45; R. B. Sheridan, 'The Wealth of Jamaica in the Eighteenth Century: A Rejoinder', *Economic History Review*, 21, 1 (1968), 46–61.

[41]  Sir John Sinclair, *The Statistical Account of Scotland, 1791–99*, eds. D. J. Withrington and I. R. Grant, 20 vols. (Wakefield, 1975–83), vol. 17, 96.

corpus of evidence suggesting that powerful causal links can be made between imperial enterprise and economic, social, and cultural change in Scotland.[42]

Atlantic merchants invested in industry and often in ways that related to the commodities they imported. This integration of activities meant that sugar merchants were often investors in sugar refiners, while those importing cotton had interests in manufacturers in west-central Scotland. By investing in this way, some imperial Scots were quite explicit about what they hoped to achieve by linking Scottish and overseas interests. In 1766 James Stirling of Keir considered making the enslaved on his Jamaican estate wear tartan because 'it will help encourage our Woollen manufactory'.[43]

The Empire was important not just for what was imported: long before the extraordinary industrial output of the later nineteenth century, the Empire provided an important export market for Scottish commodities. Between 1765 and 1795 there was a tenfold increase in exports of linen to Jamaica, where coarse cloth was in demand as clothing for enslaved Africans. By 1796, almost two-thirds of all Scottish linen exports went to Jamaica.[44] The slave economies also fuelled demand for Scottish herring. The overseas markets drove further industrial development. Industries ancillary to textiles—kelp and chemicals, for example—grew with them. At the same time, new investments were proposed. John Campbell's suggestion in 1774 of a canal linking Inverness to the west through the Great Glen was inspired explicitly by a desire to facilitate exports of Moray Firth fish and imports of colonial commodities.[45]

For all these industrial developments, investment in land remained a prime concern for imperial Scots. Gentility did not come instantly with the acquisition of land, but without it, was even less likely to be conferred on West India merchants and Indian nabobs. Imperial revenue was also important for those who already owned estates. For the latter group, the shifts in Scottish agricultural practice and the desire to construct and remodel country houses required wealth that only empire could bring.

Making these investments possible were significant capital flows, both in terms of revenue coming into Scotland and in the generation of credit for overseas ventures. George McGilvary has highlighted the injection of eighteenth-century Indian wealth into land, industry, and finance, and has estimated, albeit tentatively, that between £500,000 and £750,000 was invested annually. Similar patterns are apparent for Caribbean and North American revenue, as merchants and planters reinvested their imperial wealth. Many arguments about the impact of investment are based on case studies, from which wider macro-economic arguments are made. In this they remain—as

[42]  Devine, *Tobacco Lords*, 18–51; Bryant, 'Scots in India in the Eighteenth Century', 37–41; Hamilton, *Scotland, the Caribbean and the Atlantic World*, 195–221. Devine, *Scotland's Empire*, 320–45, offers a broad survey.

[43]  Glasgow City Archives T-SK 22/2, Stirling of Keir Papers, James Stirling to William Stirling, 5 September 1766.

[44]  A. J. Durie, *The Scottish Linen Industry* (Edinburgh, 1979), 88, 152–3.

[45]  J. Campbell, *A Political Survey of Britain*, 2 vols. (London, 1774), vol. 1, 213–15.

McGilvary puts it—'largely conjectural'.[46] The general contours of the thesis are never-theless convincing: the challenge for historians is to quantify accurately these capital injections.

Just as imperial wealth came into Scotland, so too did Scottish finance support over-seas ventures. It is clear from the activities of Glasgow sugar and tobacco merchants, two of the most dynamic imperial sectors, that the generation of capital was a local affair. The emphasis on London as a financial centre is well known, and there is evidence of Amsterdam providing imperial capital, especially after 1772, but for Scottish Atlantic merchants, west-central Scotland remained the primary source of finance until the French Revolutionary War. Even more significantly, it was not banks to which merchants turned, but to investors from among the mercantile and manufacturing classes. In this way Scots without an otherwise direct link developed a stake in empire.[47]

It is easier to suggest some of the social and cultural resonances of imperial invest-ment than to measure its economic impact. Imperial wealth clearly affected the nature of the Scottish elite. The emergence of Scottish imperial and industrial ventures as part-nerships between merchants, manufacturers, and landowners indicates a growing coalescence within, and reshaping, of Scottish elites. One effect of imperial wealth, and the prominence of the mercantile class among Scottish politicians, was to enhance their standing in the Scottish elite, previously the preserve of the legal and intellectual establishment.

This process was felt throughout society. The 'improvement' of Scottish estates was significant not just for the elite, but for the tenantry whose lives were materially affected. The increasingly commercialized view of land—and the desire for profit—led not just to clearances but to a recasting of relationships and demands across the agricultural sector.

Other walks of Scottish society were reshaped too. Education in the new Scottish academies wore a distinctly imperial aspect, both in terms of investments in their con-struction and the curricula they offered.[48] These schools, like the rest of Scotland, were also home to black people of Scottish descent. The immigration of (particularly) non-Europeans is now, of course, a matter of public controversy. The history of Scotland and the Empire suggests that notions of a previously 'white' country are misplaced. As well as a series of well-known Black Scots—the radical Robert Wedderburn, son of a Jacobite Scot in Jamaica being perhaps the most high profile—many ordinary people of African, Indian, and Scottish descent lived and worked and were educated across the country.[49] Their presence challenges historians to think carefully about who they regard as 'Scottish' in late eighteenth-century Scotland.

---

[46] McGilvary, *East India Patronage*, 184–202; Hamilton, *Scotland, the Caribbean and the Atlantic World*, 195–220; Devine, *Scotland's Empire*, 320–45.

[47] Hamilton, *Scotland, the Caribbean and the Atlantic World*, 104–5; T. M. Devine, 'Sources of Capital for the Glasgow Tobacco Trade, c. 1740–1780', *Business History*, 16, 2 (1974), 124–5.

[48] Hamilton, *Scotland, the Caribbean and the Atlantic World*, 207–9.

[49] Wedderburn was voted as one of the 100 Great Black Britons in 2007: www.100greatblackbritons.com/list.html

# CONCLUSION

The burgeoning scholarship in this field has illuminated as never before the range and vitality of connections between Scotland and the Empire. There is the promise of future research on India, the fur trade, and a host of other themes. Yet the real challenge is not just to explore the sectors in which Scots operated overseas, but to consider how Scottish practices and experiences explain how empires worked. There are a series of opportunities for meaningful comparisons with key English imperial regions that mirror Scotland's mercantile connections and industrial or financial hinterlands, like the north-west or the south-west. This would also answer some occasional queries by non-Scottish historians about the typicality of the Scottish experience.[50] But if we are properly to understand Scotland and empire (and not just the British iteration), and to consider Scotland as an exemplar of overseas entrepreneurialism, more detailed comparisons of the role of Scots in the British and other empires might allow a clearer sense of the precise ways in which Scots shaped empires. Moreover, comparisons with regions of other countries—notably in France and Spain—offer real opportunities to extend the notion of empire as a creator of new identities and thereby to contextualize the emergence of coherent European states marked by significant regional divergence.

## FURTHER READING

Calloway, Colin, *White People, Indians and Highlanders: Tribal Peoples and Colonial Encounters in Scotland and America* (Oxford, 2008).

Devine, T. M., *Scotland's Empire, 1600–1815* (London, 2003).

Hamilton, Douglas J., *Scotland, the Caribbean and the Atlantic World, 1750–1820* (Manchester, 2005).

Hancock, David, *Citizens of the World* (Cambridge, 1995).

Harper, Marjory, *Adventurers and Exiles: The Great Scottish Exodus* (London, 2004).

Landsman, Ned C., ed., *Nation and Province in the First British Empire: Scotland and the Americas, 1600–1800* (Lewisburg, PA, 2001).

McGilvary, George K., *East India Patronage and the British State: The Scottish Elite and Politics in the Eighteenth Century* (London and New York, 2008).

MacKenzie, John M., with Dalziel, Nigel R., *The Scots in South Africa: Ethnicity, Identity, Gender and Race, 1772–1914* (Manchester, 2007).

Watt, Douglas, *The Price of Scotland: Darien, Union and the Wealth of Nations* (Edinburgh, 2007).

Whyte, Iain, *Scotland and the Abolition of Black Slavery, 1756–1838* (Edinburgh, 2006).

---

[50] For example, Trevor Burnard, 'Review of Hamilton, *Scotland the Caribbean and the Atlantic World, 1750–1820*', *Slavery and Abolition*, 27, 2 (2006), 309.

CHAPTER 23

......................................................................................

# THE CHALLENGE OF RADICALISM TO 1832

......................................................................................

GORDON PENTLAND

HINDSIGHT tends to impose an artificial coherence on political movements. In April 1831, in the midst of intense agitation in favour of parliamentary reform throughout the United Kingdom, *The Scotsman* (founded in 1817 as the mouthpiece of Edinburgh's increasingly liberal middle classes) called for an end to 'the Forty Years' War' between the people outside of Parliament and a corrupt oligarchy denying them their rights.[1] This Whig history of parliamentary reform was born in tandem with the passage of the Reform Acts themselves. These were seen to be the fruits of a long campaign beginning, in England, with John Wilkes in the 1760s and accelerated everywhere by the galvanizing effect of the French Revolution. Pre-reform political arrangements across the United Kingdom, but in Scotland more than anywhere else, were damned both by radical polemic and by Whig hagiography.

There was, of course, some substance to these condemnations of pre-reform politics and to the optimistic narrative of how they came to be amended. One coherent story can be told of the entire period from the 1770s to the 1830s. At the start, Scottish politics was an intimate, face-to-face affair. Political structures ensured a restricted electorate in both urban and rural contexts and a system that ran smoothly with the grease of patronage, while it entailed reciprocal obligations and chains of interdependence.[2] By 1832 Scotland had well-developed traditions of extra-parliamentary activity, sustained by meetings, petitions, associations, and a wide press, and had spawned large and diverse movements in support of the reform of many Scottish and United Kingdom institutions.[3]

---

[1] *The Scotsman*, 27 April 1831.

[2] William Ferguson, 'The Electoral System in the Scottish Counties before 1832', *Stair Society Miscellany*, 2 (1984), 261–94; Ronald M. Sunter, *Patronage and Politics in Scotland 1707–1832* (Edinburgh, 1986).

[3] For an influential thesis concerning the 'modernization' of politics in Britain see Charles Tilly, *Popular Contention in Great Britain, 1758–1834* (Cambridge, MA, 1995).

Such a trajectory would seem to align Scotland neatly with three broad models of political change: first, an older model of 'Atlantic Revolution', whereby economic and social factors such as the rise of the 'middling sort' and the traumatic and disruptive nature of industrialization and urbanization, coupled with the political earthquakes of the French and American revolutions, were the crucial motors; second, a more recent model, where the explanation for this transformative change is cultural and is found in a revolution in print and its expanding audiences; and finally, an ambitiously globalized 'Age of Reform'.[4]

Like any grand narrative, these ones have their difficulties. Applied unreflectively, they can mask discontinuities and disunity, periods of inaction and reaction. They can also support the tendency of historians to explore oppositional politics and to pit apparently 'progressive' movements against an 'establishment' or *ancien régime*, which can be caricatured as immobile and static and whose dynamism and adaptability are all too often ignored. Confident narratives are thus matched by more qualified accounts of an 'Age of Uncertainty' as 'what was once a teleologist's dream...has lately been turning into a post-modernist's nightmare'.[5]

Indeed, this uncertainty has destabilized radicalism as one of the central organizing concepts for the period. As a distinctive ideology and programme encompassing political, social, economic, and moral reform, it was only after 1819 that both hostile and friendly contemporaries began to refer consistently to 'radicalism' (and, indeed, to 'radicals'). This has led some scholars to condemn its use before this reification as anachronistic and ahistorical.[6] More constructive have been approaches that remain sensitive to these difficulties, but nevertheless treat radicalism before the 1820s as a meaningful description for a fluid body of ideas and strategies regarding the state, society, religion, and human relations to these. Certainly, such criticisms have established that radicalism must be described, explained, and defined contextually.[7] Only by an investigation of events, personalities, structures, groups, and the rapidly shifting contexts in which politics were practised can we begin to achieve an accurate description of the developing political culture of Scotland across these years.

Principally, the concerns of Scottish historians have been shaped by three groups of questions. First, they have been exercised by the question of class: to what extent were

---

[4] Highlights of this literature include: R. R. Palmer, *The Age of the Democratic Revolution*, 2 vols. (Princeton, 1959–64); Roger Chartier, *The Cultural Origins of the French Revolution*, trans. Lydia G. Cochrane (Durham, N. C., 1991); C. A. Bayly, *The Birth of the Modern World 1780–1914* (Oxford, 2004), part i.

[5] David Eastwood, 'The Age of Uncertainty: Britain in the Early Nineteenth Century', *Transactions of the Royal Historical Society*, 6th ser., 8 (1998), 91–115; David Cannadine, *Class in Britain* (New Haven, 1998), 57.

[6] The most sceptical treatment can be found in J. C. D. Clark, 'Religion and the Origins of Radicalism in Nineteenth-Century Britain', in Glenn Burgess and Matthew Festenstein, eds., *English Radicalism, 1550–1850* (Cambridge, 2007), 241–84.

[7] See for example John Brewer, *Party Ideology and Popular Politics at the Accession of George III* (Cambridge, 1976), 18–21; Mark Philp, 'The Fragmented Ideology of Reform', in Mark Philp, ed., *The French Revolution and British Popular Politics* (Cambridge, 1991), 50–77.

popular politics, and radicalism in particular, a reflection of Scotland's experiences of industrialization and demographic expansion across this period; and how far do they provide a key to the exploration of class formation and inter-class relations?[8] A second and related set of questions revolve around the issue of 'stability': was Scotland *relatively* more stable a society across this period, especially in comparison to England and Ireland; and, if so, what factors would explain this?[9] A final set of questions run throughout modern Scottish historiography: what do the politics of the period reveal about the relationship between England and Scotland, and the position of Scotland within the imperial state?[10]

This essay will follow the existing historiography and bisect the 'Age of Reform' along the line provided by the Napoleonic Wars. It will suggest what was distinctive about popular political developments in Scotland in each of these periods. In attempting to synthesize historical approaches it will highlight questions specific to each period as well as those more generally applicable ones outlined above. Throughout, the essay will endeavour to identify areas of research and lines of inquiry that might fruitfully be developed by historians, and it will end by summarizing what might be done to expand further our knowledge of Scottish politics and society during this dynamic but problematic period.

## 1

One of the more venerable questions surrounding popular politics concerns origins. It tends to be conceptualized as a search for the 'roots' of the popular radicalism of the 1790s. Implicit in this search for origins is a challenge to reconcile pre-existing or 'indigenous' political traditions and languages and their role in shaping radicalism in the 1790s with a long-held notion that Scotland was somehow 'awakened' from a deep and largely apolitical slumber by the transformative events in France. With some notable exceptions there has been little sustained work on popular politics during the first two-thirds of the eighteenth century.[11] Nevertheless, plausible episodes of 'politicization' that demonstrate the interplay of internal and external stimuli can be identified during the period of the American Revolution.

---

[8] For example, J. D. Young, *The Rousing of the Scottish Working Class* (London, 1979), ch. 2.

[9] For example, T. M. Devine, 'The Failure of Radical Reform in Scotland in the Late Eighteenth Century', in T. M. Devine, ed., *Conflict and Stability in Scottish Society 1700–1850* (Edinburgh, 1990), 51–64. These concerns speak to the agenda outlined in Ian R. Christie, *Stress and Stability in Late Eighteenth-Century Britain: Reflections on the British Avoidance of Revolution* (Oxford, 1984).

[10] For example, John Brims, 'The Scottish "Jacobins", Scottish Nationalism and the British Union', in R. Mason, ed., *Scotland and England, 1286–1815* (Edinburgh, 1987), 247–65.

[11] H. T. Dickinson and Kenneth J. Logue, 'The Porteous Riot: A Study of the Breakdown of Law and Order in Edinburgh, 1736–1737', *Journal of the Scottish Labour History Society*, 10 (1976), 21–40; Bob Harris and Christopher A. Whatley, ' "To solemnize His Majesty's birthday": New Perspectives on Loyalism in George II's Britain', *History*, 83, no. 271 (July 1998), 397–419; Valerie Wallace, 'Presbyterian Moral Economy: The Covenanting Tradition and Popular Protest in Lowland Scotland, 1707–c. 1746', *Scottish Historical Review*, 89, no. 1 (April 2010), 54–72.

In particular, historians have highlighted the significance of the agitation against a modest proposed measure of Catholic relief after 1778 and the movements for burgh and county reform during the 1780s. The first of these, according to R. K. Donovan, brought 'active, long-lived political awareness to large numbers of Scotsmen for the first time', although the ideas and language that framed the agitation—defence of the liberties secured by the Revolution and a politicized anti-Catholicism—underpinned the well-established 'master narrative' of eighteenth-century politics in Scotland and England.[12] Both the no-popery agitation and the burgh and county reform movements, however, evinced a conscious appeal to a national public and the exploration of new political organizations and technologies. These examples can be joined by evidence for extensive Scottish involvement in pan-British movements and, in particular, in the innovative and ultimately successful campaign for the abolition of the slave trade from the late 1780s.[13]

All of these developments point to more general contexts for popular politics as well. An increasing volume of scholarship has pushed a model of the public sphere shorn of its original secularism and constituted by religion instead. There has been some treatment of just how religion in Scotland informed and shaped popular politics, but far more could be done to uncover the political dimensions of Scottish religious and ecclesiological disputes in the late eighteenth century, especially in light of recent arguments identifying religion as the taproot of radical politics.[14] Similarly, scholars might challenge more effectively those orthodoxies surrounding the politically conservative nature of Scottish enlightenment thought. This might be done partly by determining the scale and content of 'popular enlightenment' in late eighteenth-century Scotland.[15] In short, while the roots of Scottish 'Jacobin' politics are certainly discernible during the first eighty years of the eighteenth century, far more might be done to discover how deep they went and of what they consisted.

However substantial these foundations for Scottish popular politics were, the French Revolution will always hold centre stage as an event of crucial importance (as it does in many other 'national' historiographies). Perhaps the best place to begin any analysis of

---

[12] R. K. Donovan, *No Popery and Radicalism: Opposition to Roman Catholic Relief in Scotland, 1778–1782* (New York, 1982), 7; Kathleen Wilson, 'Inventing Revolution: 1688 and Eighteenth-Century Popular Politics', *Journal of British Studies*, 28, no. 4 (October 1989), 349–86. The burgh reform movement still awaits its modern historian, but see John Brims, 'The Scottish Democratic Movement in the Age of the French Revolution' (unpublished PhD thesis, University of Edinburgh, 1983), 45–54.

[13] Iain Whyte, *Scotland and the Abolition of Black Slavery* (Edinburgh, 2006).

[14] See for examples Terry Brotherstone, ed., *Covenant, Charter and Party: Traditions of Revolt and Protest in Modern Scottish History* (Aberdeen, 1989); Ned. C. Landsman, 'Liberty, Piety and Patronage: The Social Context of Contested Clerical Calls in Eighteenth-Century Glasgow', in Andrew Hook and Richard B. Sher, ed., *The Glasgow Enlightenment* (Edinburgh, 1995), 214–26. For excellent explorations of these issues in other contexts, see I. R. McBride, *Scripture Politics: Ulster Presbyterians and Irish Radicalism in the Late Eighteenth Century* (Oxford, 1998); James E. Bradley, 'The Religious Origins of Radical Politics in England, Scotland and Ireland, 1662–1800', in James E. Bradley and Dale K. Van Kley, eds., *Religion and Politics in Enlightenment Europe* (Notre Dame, 2001), 187–253.

[15] Bob Harris, *The Scottish People and the French Revolution* (London, 2008), 25–40.

the 1790s is to think in terms of *politicization* rather than the *growth of radicalism*. If one telling criticism levelled at the dominant idea of the 'public sphere' is that it has erroneously been conceptualized as a secular space, another is that it has been seen as necessarily an oppositional one. The best scholarship would now regard this emerging public sphere as both 'socially heterogeneous' and 'politically multi-directional'.[16] Growing numbers of people from the 1790s were interested in domestic and international politics and had access to an exponentially increasing volume of printed matter as 'the audience for political debate...decisively widened during the 1790s'.[17] There was no direct correlation, however, between an expanding press and the growth of reform movements. The public sphere was a space for the development of arguments for and defences of 'things as they are' as well as for coruscating critiques of the status quo. It seems far more fruitful to begin with an idea of the 1790s as witnessing a process of politicization, without making facile conclusions about the direction and content of that politicization.

From within this sphere of competing levels of discourse and arguments, however, it is popular radicalism that has attracted the lion's share of historical attention. Historians can tell a fairly straightforward story: of how the French Revolution was initially welcomed by most people in Scotland, but developed in such a way as to galvanize a radical politics which reached the artisan classes; of how this spawned reform societies, whose middle-class members abandoned them in the face of war and a radicalizing French Revolution; of how this further polarized opinion and created a vigorous loyalist reaction that made life very difficult for radicals; and of how the movement reached its apogee in a dramatic series of conventions, which were met by government with legal repression. This climactic period was followed by a couple of insurrectionary death spasms, before radicalism disappeared until 1815. What is very marked and has recently been underlined as distinctive in the Scottish context was the rapidity of the expansion of Scottish radicalism and its equally rapid contraction.[18]

'Radicalism' itself, however, is an anachronistic term that needs to be used with considerable caution. Once historians begin to explore the sinews of this 'movement', its coherence rapidly disappears. In terms of political discourse and ideas there is no simple answer to whether these were 'homegrown' or 'imported': instead radicals appealed to an eclectic mix of political languages, positioning themselves rhetorically depending on the political context.[19] So too, we are only beginning to uncover the diversity of

---

[16] T. C. W. Blanning, *The Culture of Power and the Power of Culture: Old Regime Europe 1660–1789* (Oxford, 2002), 12.

[17] John Stevenson, 'Scotland and the French Revolution: An Overview', and Bob Harris, 'Print and Politics', in Bob Harris, ed., *Scotland in the Age of the French Revolution* (Edinburgh, 2005), 262, 164–95; Bob Harris, 'Scotland's Newspapers, the French Revolution and Domestic Radicalism (*c.* 1789–1794)', *Scottish Historical Review*, 84, no. 1 (April 2005), 38–62.

[18] Harris, *Scottish People*, 80–92.

[19] Gordon Pentland, 'Patriotism, Universalism and the Scottish Conventions 1792–1794', *History*, 89, no. 295 (July 2004), 340–60; Mark Philp, 'Disconcerting Ideas: Explaining Popular Radicalism and Popular Loyalism in the 1790s', in Burgess and Festenstein, eds., *English Radicalism*, 157–89.

experiences across Scotland, as scholars have moved away from a concentration on the dramatic events in Edinburgh.[20]

Even at the level of individuals, while there are good biographies of some major figures, such as the Scottish 'martyr' Thomas Muir and the transatlantic propagandist James Thomson Callender, there are many more whose roles in popular politics have gone unexplored.[21] It seems likely, for example, that further work on William Skirving, who was transported to New South Wales in 1794 for his involvement in the British Convention, could reveal interesting material on the ideological underpinnings of Scottish radicalism. Educated for the Burgher ministry and with an enduring interest in improvement and 'agrarian patriotism', Skirving occupies an interesting juncture between religion, Enlightenment thought, and popular radicalism. Literary historians (some of them too enthusiastically) have gone a considerable distance in trying to return the towering figure of Robert Burns to his appropriate ideological and political contexts.[22] The potentially more revealing project of rescuing other less celebrated radical poets from his shadow and from the condescension of posterity has scarcely begun.[23] Similarly, while scholarly work has charted how those who governed Scotland responded to the challenges of the 1790s, material on the experiences of opposition Whigs—including towering 'British' figures, such as the Earl of Lauderdale—is virtually non-existent.[24] These are just some 'gaps' in the scholarship, which demonstrate the potential for further research on Scotland in the 1790s.

What is clear from the recent historiography of popular politics in both England and Scotland is the importance of remaining sensitive to rapidly changing national and international contexts. A crucial part of these was the development of an organized loyalism in Scotland and its attempts both to repress radical activity and to present a convincing rhetoric in defence of the status quo. For a considerable time this was a major absence from the historiography as historians tended to rely on a rather caricatured idea

---

[20] Bob Harris, 'Popular Politics in Angus and Perthshire in the 1790s', *Historical Research*, 80, no. 210 (November 2007), 518–44; Val Honeyman, ' "A Very Dangerous Place"? Radicalism in Perth in the 1790s', *Scottish Historical Review*, 87, no. 2 (October 2008), 278–305. It should be noted, however, that the possibilities for similar studies in the future are limited by the paucity of the available historical sources for most areas during this period.

[21] Christina Bewley, *Muir of Huntershill* (Oxford, 1981); Michael Durey, *'With the Hammer of Truth': James Thomson Callender and America's Early National Heroes* (Charlottesville, VA, 1990).

[22] Liam McIlvanney, *Burns the Radical: Poetry and Politics in Late Eighteenth-Century Scotland* (East Linton, 2002). For a brief discussion of the controversy surrounding *The Canongate Burns* see Robert Crawford, *The Bard: Robert Burns, a Biography* (Princeton, 2008), 9–10.

[23] Tom Leonard, ed., *Radical Renfrew: Poetry from the French Revolution to the First World War* (Edinburgh, 1990); Andrew Noble, 'Displaced Persons: Burns and the Renfrew Radicals', in Harris, ed., *Scotland in the Age of the French Revolution*, 196–225.

[24] David J. Brown, 'Henry Dundas and the Government of Scotland' (unpublished PhD thesis, University of Edinburgh, 1989); *idem.*, 'The Government of Scotland under Henry Dundas and William Pitt', *History*, 83, no. 270 (April 1998), 265–79. The exception to the neglect of the Whigs, which demonstrates the potential for research, is Emma Vincent Macleod, 'The Scottish Opposition Whigs and the French Revolution', in Harris, ed., *Scotland in the Age of the French Revolution*, 79–98.

of the 'establishment' or 'Pitt's Terror'. Some seminal historical work has demonstrated, in different ways, the importance of recovering histories of popular loyalism and of phenomena such as the mass volunteer movement.[25] This is not simply a question of filling in a blank to complete a picture of Scotland in the 1790s. Radicalism cannot be seen in isolation from its proper context, which is provided by loyalism. Mark Philp's influential formulation, that we examine radicalism as a 'developing political practice whose principles and ideological commitments are as much forged in the struggle as they are fetched from the arsenal and brought to it', implies that even attempting to look at 'loyalism' and 'radicalism' apart from one another inhibits our ability to discuss either.[26]

If historians have abandoned linear histories of radicalism as a narrative of heroic resistance and inevitable progress, so too the developing historiography of 'loyalism' is more than just about putting flesh on the bogeyman story of King Harry and Lord Braxfield, spy systems, and repression. While there is, of course, evidence of repression at both local and national levels, historians also need to take seriously loyalist attempts to persuade and the willingness of many Scots to be persuaded. What historians are beginning to reveal is a distinctive Scottish loyalism, one that relied on the sponsorship of clerical and lay elites far more extensively than its English counterpart, could make effective use of the unique nature of the Scottish courts, and was marked by considerable experimentation in methods of political communication.[27] Similar sensitivity needs to be shown in exploring the Scottish contribution to military mobilization and national defence during these years. A number of scholars have shown how a disproportionately large Scottish involvement can provide a crude index of Scottish loyalty for the period. It must also provide a central plank to any explanation of Scotland's relative stability as well as to explorations of Scottish and British identities. The same scholars have demonstrated, however, that loyalism and volunteering (let alone other forms of mobilization) were not synonymous.[28] In short, 'loyalist' and 'patriotic' politics are emerging as phenomena that are every bit as complex and multivalent as radicalism.

It is understanding these contexts that allows for more sophisticated approaches to some of the big questions historians have asked of radicalism. Many of these questions have either implicitly or explicitly been concerned with revolution and its avoidance. This shapes much of the historiography in England and Ireland as well, in both helpful and unhelpful ways. Economistic and structural explanations for Scotland's relative 'stability' and its imperviousness to revolution have formed an important part of a revived

[25] H. T. Dickinson, 'Popular Loyalism in Britain in the 1790s', in Eckhart Hellmuth, ed., *The Transformation of Political Culture: England and Germany in the Late Eighteenth Century* (Oxford, 1990), 503–33; Linda Colley, *Britons: Forging the Nation, 1707–1837* (New Haven, 1992), chs. 5–7; J. E. Cookson, *The British Armed Nation, 1793–1815* (Oxford, 1997).

[26] Philp, 'The Fragmented Ideology of Reform', 53.

[27] The best published account of Scottish loyalism to date is Harris, *Scottish People*, ch. 4. See also Atle Libaek Wold, 'The Scottish Government and the French Threat, 1792–1802' (unpublished PhD thesis, University of Edinburgh, 2003); Emma Vincent, 'The Responses of Scottish Churchmen to the French Revolution, 1789–1802', *Scottish Historical Review* 73, no. 2 (October 1994), 191–215.

[28] Harris, *Scottish People*, 135–9; Atle Libaek Wold, 'Scottish Attitudes to Military Mobilization and War in the 1790s', in Harris, ed., *Scotland in the Age of the French Revolution*, 140–63.

historiography of modern Scotland. Simple questions about radical 'failure' or the 'success' of the status quo, however, tend to mask the fluidity and contingencies created by rapidly changing contexts. Radicalism declined spectacularly quickly after 1793—but how do we explain a partial revival of oppositional politics from 1796? To talk of elites as 'robust' or stable is to paint them as static, whereas in reality the 1790s was a period of dramatic transformative change for political and religious elites as much as for anyone.[29]

We might, for example, count as a 'success' the fact that there was no revolution in late eighteenth-century Scotland, but elites achieved this at the expense of sponsoring a popular loyalism, or a 'vulgar conservatism', which invited growing numbers into political debate.[30] They had to think about creative ways of doing this, but one outcome was clear after 1815: the genie of popular mobilization could not be put back in the bottle. It is by not only exploring political structures but by attempting to look at the political culture as a whole that historians can begin to ask different questions of this problematic period. Historians should continue to eschew facile characterizations of 'the growth of radicalism' or the 'triumph of reaction' and instead attempt to describe and analyse the interactions between a wide variety of different groups and individuals—Whigs, Tories, patriots, radicals, loyalists—and their contested and often innovative attempts to appeal for support among the people.

## 2

One major blind spot for political historians of Scotland is the years between the Peace of Amiens (1802) and the end of the Napoleonic Wars (1815). This is also partly true for the English context, though much more has been done to explore both metropolitan and regional popular politics in England during the period.[31] The implications of this lacuna for the history of radicalism are important. The mass reform movement that emerged after 1815 has perhaps been characterized as more 'explosive' than the facts warrant. Scotland certainly took some part in the revived reform campaign that coalesced around issues of wartime corruption, while the possible political content of events such as the great weavers' strike of 1812 has yet to be studied in the same creative manner as Luddism.[32] It seems likely that close attention to local contexts might reveal networks of

[29] See, for example, the exploration of the Revolution's impact on Scotland's Church leaders in Colin Kidd, 'The Kirk, the French Revolution, and the Burden of Scottish Whiggery', in Nigel Aston, ed., *Religious Change in Europe 1650–1914: Essays for John McManners* (Oxford, 1997), 213–34.

[30] Mark Philp, 'Vulgar Conservatism, 1792–3', *English Historical Review*, 110, no. 435 (February 1995), 42–69.

[31] J. Ann Hone, *For the Cause of Truth: Radicalism in London, 1796–1821* (Oxford, 1982); Peter Spence, *The Birth of Romantic Radicalism: War, Popular Politics and English Radical Reformism, 1800–1815* (Aldershot, 1996); Katrina Navickas, *Loyalism and Radicalism in Lancashire, 1798–1815* (Oxford, 2009).

[32] Spence, *Birth of Romantic Radicalism*, 123–4; N. Murray, *The Scottish Handloom Weavers, 1790–1850: A Social History* (Edinburgh, 1978), chs. 8–9.

individuals and groups who kept reformist and radical politics alive and reshaped them during the long war years. The Scottish tour undertaken by the veteran English radical leader and activist Major Cartwright—which is seen as an 'external' stimulus to the revival of reform after 1815—was prearranged and it seems likely that he was, at least to a certain degree, pushing at open doors.[33] This is not the place to assess whether popular political activity in Scotland *did* persist and adapt after 1800: the point is that we simply do not know and assiduous research might well prove capable of providing a valuable hinge between the popular politics of the 1790s and those after 1815.

In any event the politics of E. P. Thompson's 'heroic age of popular radicalism' in Scotland were different in several key respects from those of the 1790s.[34] Many of these differences are traceable to the end of the Napoleonic Wars and the radically altered social and political contexts that followed.[35] First, there were the social and economic ramifications of the war itself. The year 1816 witnessed both a poor harvest and a trade depression, which was to return in 1819. Into an already struggling labour market were thrust some three hundred thousand demobbed soldiers—a large number of whom were Scots returning to their homes to establish themselves as labourers or weavers and who thus exacerbated downward pressure on wages—as well as an accelerating number of Irish immigrants.[36]

It was a volatile situation, and a government that was only slowly coming under the sway of economic liberalism could never have met it entirely successfully. Even before the end of the Napoleonic Wars it had passed a new corn law, which had been intended to insulate farmers and landowners from falling prices. Facing interest payments on a national debt that was two times the size of the national income, the government had to resort to the expedient of maintaining wartime taxes. The result after 1816 was a regressive tax regime, whose legitimacy remained in question until the 1840s.[37] It was a volatile mix which threatened to alienate a number of different groups.

Any tendency to see politics after 1816 as characterized only by the development of a working-class reform movement would again view radicalism outside of its proper contexts. In concert with Whigs, for example, it was the essentially middle-class campaign to repeal the wartime property tax that provided the focus for the first national petitioning campaign after 1815 and, for the advocate Henry Cockburn, the first meetings 'for the avowed purpose of controlling Government on a political matter'.[38] Later, burgh reform

[33] William M. Roach, 'Radical Reform Movements in Scotland from 1815 to 1822: With Particular Reference to Events in the West of Scotland' (unpublished PhD thesis, University of Glasgow, 1970), 17–25; F. D. Cartwright, *Life and Correspondence of Major Cartwright*, 2 vols (London, 1826), vol. ii, 110–17.

[34] See Gordon Pentland, *The Spirit of the Union: Popular Politics in Scotland, 1815–1820* (London, 2011).

[35] Norman Gash, 'After Waterloo: British Society and the Legacy of the Napoleonic Wars', *Transactions of the Royal Historical Society*, 5th ser., 28 (1978), 145–57.

[36] J. E. Cookson, 'Early Nineteenth-Century Scottish Military Pensioners as Homecoming Soldiers', *Historical Journal*, 52, no. 2 (June 2009), 319–41.

[37] Martin Daunton, *Trusting Leviathan: The Politics of Taxation in Britain, 1799–1914* (Cambridge, 2001), chs. 1 and 2.

[38] Henry Cockburn, *Memorials of His Time* (Edinburgh, 1856), 302.

would revive, recycling arguments from the 1780s and prosecuted by a broad coalition of radicals, moderate reformers, and opposition Whigs.

The success of the campaign against the property tax and the mobilization of a new radical campaign were testament in themselves to how the end of the wars had opened up spaces for politics. Crucially, it had also removed some of the key rhetorical props of a patriotic status quo. The fit between loyalism and patriotism had never been exact during the war years, but the distance between the two expanded dramatically after 1815, while the very rationale for armed loyalism was all but removed. Ministers consistently voiced 'strong objections' to embodying armed volunteers in Scotland after 1815, and the grandiose plans of men like Walter Scott, who sought to raise a force from around his home at Abbotsford in the Borders, were treated cautiously.[39] If the study of loyalism in the 1790s is underdeveloped, it is all but non-existent for the period following the end of the wars, when radicalism successfully recaptured the rhetoric of 'patriotism', which had been lost to reformers during the 1790s.[40]

It was in this dramatically altered context that the mass-platform agitation was forged. Its main features demonstrate something that had been apparent during the 1790s: Scottish and English radicals were operating within an increasingly common and Parliament-centred political culture, pursuing the same goals, communicating with one another, and reading the same newspapers.[41] There were also some continuities in the rhetoric that drove post-war radicalism. The 1790s had seen the development of a critique of governmental corruption and its impact in inflating the national debt and placing unbearable burdens on society. What was marked about the post-war platform was how this message was simplified and repeated relentlessly as a critique of 'old corruption', which sought to politicize post-war dearth and economic and social dislocation.[42] Many other elements from the 1790s were apparent: there was an internationalist strand that criticized the new holy alliance and the retrogressive agreement at Vienna, which was finalized in June 1815 and redrew the political map of Europe; there was condemnation of slavery; and there was an optimistic belief in the perfectibility of the people. These other concerns, however, took a back seat to a stark diagnosis of the political causes of distress and an equally stark solution comprising a radical reform of Parliament based on the achievement of universal suffrage and annual parliaments.

An equally significant departure lay in the strategies and organization of this reform campaign. Mass meetings had been essayed in the 1790s (1795, for example, had seen such meetings in London and Sheffield) but had been a dangerous political strategy,

---

[39] National Archives, Home Office Correspondence (Scotland), HO 102/26, f. 665, William Rae to Lord Sidmouth, 15 December 1816; Edgar Johnson, *Sir Walter Scott: The Great Unknown*, 2 vols. (New York, 1970), vol. i, 693–5.

[40] Though see Pentland, *Spirit of the Union*, chs. 2 and 3. For an excellent study of loyalism in this period in England see Jonathan C. S. J. Fulcher, 'Contests over Constitutionalism: The Faltering of Reform in England, 1816–1824' (unpublished PhD thesis, University of Cambridge, 1993).

[41] Bob Harris, 'Scottish-English Connections in British Radicalism in the 1790s', *Proceedings of the British Academy*, 127 (2005), 189–212.

[42] John Belchem, *Popular Radicalism in Nineteenth-Century Britain* (London, 1996), chs. 2–3.

always liable to see reformers branded as a 'mob'.[43] This fear remained 'the spectre haunting the radical movement', but after 1815 radicals sought to exorcize it through an emphasis on the orderly and constitutional nature of the mass platform.[44] The huge meeting in October 1816 at Thrushgrove in Glasgow was only the most famous of hundreds of mass, orderly, open-air meetings in Scotland across this period.[45]

The emphasis on 'mass' and on inclusiveness in pursuit of a single object entailed other strategic changes. For example, the rhetoric and practice of petitioning focused on the number of names subscribed to repeated petitions. The recalibrated reform critique and the emphasis on numbers also opened up political spaces for women, who had been less welcome in the masculine tavern- and club-oriented politics of the 1790s. The politicization of subsistence issues, such as bread prices and the impact of corn laws, helped to create these spaces. Women played a crucial and highly visible role in the ritualistic aspects of radicalism by, for example, embroidering and giving caps of liberty to orators or wearing white at mass meetings.[46]

Part of what facilitated this mass mobilization and the diffusion of a simple and repetitive message of union was the expansion of the realm of print and, especially, the development of a cheap press. The crucial turning point here was William Cobbett's decision to release the leading article of his *Political Register* in London in an unstamped twopenny format, which won a large readership among both Scottish and English radicals. There was a similar expansion in the Scottish press, which again articulated both radical and loyalist positions. Attempts by Scottish elites to launch distinctive loyalist newspapers and the political propagandizing of men like Scott, whose anti-reform dystopia *The Visionary* appeared as letters in the *Edinburgh Weekly Journal* before being published in pamphlet form in 1819, suggest that print sources might form a good basis for an examination of Scottish loyalism during this period.[47]

The reform movement reached its apogee in August 1819 with the infamous events surrounding the Peterloo massacre in Manchester.[48] The response to this butchery saw protests from many groups in Scotland, including many members of the middle classes and qualified condemnation from bolder Whigs. Indeed, the reaction to Peterloo further emphasizes the integrative nature of popular politics in Britain during this period.

---

[43]  Michael T. Davis, 'The Mob Club? The London Corresponding Society and the Politics of Civility in the 1790s', in Michael T. Davis and Paul A. Pickering, eds., *Unrespectable Radicals? Popular Politics in the Age of Reform* (Aldershot, 2008), 21–40.

[44]  Ian Haywood, *Bloody Romanticism: Spectacular Violence and the Politics of Representation, 1776–1832* (London, 2006), 196; Gordon Pentland, 'Militarization and Collective Action in Great Britain, 1815–1820', in Michael T. Davis and Brett Bowden, eds., *Disturbing the Peace: Collective Action in Britain and France, 1381 to the Present* (Basingstoke, 2012).

[45]  For a detailed account of this meeting see J. Smith, ed., *Life and Recollections of James Turner of Thrushgrove* (Glasgow, 1854), 25–38.

[46]  Anna Clark, *Struggle for the Breeches: Gender and the Making of the British Working Class* (Berkeley, 1995), chs. 8 and 9.

[47]  Roach, 'Radical Reform Movements', 300–45; R. M. W. Cowan, *The Newspaper in Scotland: A Study of its First Expansion 1815–1860* (Glasgow, 1946), ch. 1.

[48]  For which see Donald Read, *Peterloo: The 'Massacre' and its Background* (Manchester, 1958).

Radicals in Scotland (many of whom subscribed to the *Manchester Observer*, the *Black Dwarf*, and other English publications) responded to the events at Peterloo with another series of mass meetings and carefully followed the massacre's aftermath in the courts and in Parliament. As a movement premised on a radicalized constitutionalism, however, it faced considerable strategic difficulties when constitutional rights to meet and organize were savaged by the Six Acts of 1819.[49]

As in the 1790s, there had been an insurrectionary current running alongside and sometimes merging with the constitutionalist mass-platform agitation after 1816. In 1816–17, whatever the role of the Scot Alexander Richmond, a reputed government spy, an insurrectionary network around Glasgow had clearly been plotting, apparently using the model of the United Irishmen to fashion cells.[50] Throughout the period any such plans were susceptible to government interference and to structural weaknesses within popular radicalism itself. Radical movements were strongest at their local bases and weakest in any attempt to mobilize nationally, where their only legitimate means of organization was the press. Aspirations to spark a general rising really came to fruition with the so-called 'Radical War' of 1820. This followed the posting of an anonymous proclamation in places throughout the west of Scotland and resulted in a number of violent incidents, notably at Bonnymuir, Strathaven, and Greenock.

There is no historical agreement as to the scope or significance of this attempted general rising. Assessments range from seeing it as, first, 'the futile revolt of a tiny minority' and a pathetic death spasm of the constitutional movement; second, as an attempt at a coordinated rising with elements in the north of England and perhaps even the Cato Street conspirators in London, the strength of which will never be known because the rising was aborted; finally, as a doomed attempt at a nationalist republican uprising, precipitated by the machinations of English *agents provocateurs* and their elite handlers.[51] What is clear is that the instability in Scotland did represent a significant threat and that both the authorities and the participants took it very seriously indeed.[52] It proved, in the long run, to be most important as a source of heroes and villains, lessons and warnings, and provided a politically 'usable' event that helped to shape the language and actions of future activists.[53]

[49] For this legislation see J. E. Cookson, *Lord Liverpool's Administration: The Crucial Years, 1815–1822* (Edinburgh, 1975), 102–16, 178–99.

[50] Roach, 'Radical Reform Movements', ch. 3; *idem.*, 'Alexander Richmond and the Radical Reform Movements in Glasgow in 1816–17', *Scottish Historical Review*, 51, no. 1 (April 1972), 1–19; Martin J. Mitchell, *The Irish in the West of Scotland, 1797–1848: Trade Unions, Strikes and Political Movements* (Edinburgh, 1998), ch. 3.

[51] Broadly the interpretations of, respectively, Malcolm I. Thomis and Peter Holt, *Threats of Revolution in Britain, 1789–1848* (London, 1977), ch. 3; F. K. Donnelly, 'The Scottish Rising of 1820: A Re-Interpretation', *Scottish Tradition*, 6 (1976), 27–37; Peter Berresford Ellis and Seamus Mac a'Ghobhainn, *The Scottish Insurrection of 1820* (London, 1970).

[52] Good accounts and analysis of the Radical War can be found in Christopher A. Whatley, *Scottish Society 1707–1830: Beyond Jacobitism, Towards Industrialization* (Manchester, 2000), 307–27; Pentland, *Spirit of the Union*, ch. 4.

[53] Gordon Pentland, ' "Betrayed by infamous spies"? The Commemoration of Scotland's Radical War of 1820', *Past & Present*, 201, no. 1 (November 2008), 141–73.

If the Radical War was not a successful model spawning republican imitators, it was followed by an event that, in the short term, was far more influential: the Queen Caroline Agitation of 1820. The attempt of George IV to deprive his estranged wife of her titles and, ideally, achieve a divorce, electrified British politics and spawned a large movement in defence of Caroline's 'cause'. It provided what one historian has seen as a kind of healing of the body politic after the violence of 1819–20, but has received little attention in the Scottish context.[54] It provided a populist issue, which could bind a large number of different groups across Scotland—working-class radicals, bourgeois reformers, members of the Whig opposition and women—in the pursuit of a single cause. In one interpretation, the Caroline agitation marks the point at which 'Radicalism' became a kind of third party in the state, and the political culture shifted from one that could admit of no reform to one where it at least seemed possible.[55] Crucial in this was the rehabilitation and reshaping of the Whig Party in Scotland, which had begun with the establishment of the *Edinburgh Review* in 1802 and was to have profound implications for the conduct of parliamentary and popular politics into the 1830s.[56]

The 1820s, like the early 1800s, are something of a blind spot for historians of Scotland. The broad contours are clear enough. The decade witnessed a 'middling' sort growing in confidence and increasingly being identified and identifying themselves as a coherent body and the repository of political and social virtues. Such a narrative fits well with a wider historiographical shift from thinking about social class as an objective and explanatory category to exploring the political sources of social perception and description.[57] The varied reforming activity of the 1820s, across a broad range of secular, religious, and moral issues, played a crucial role in facilitating the crystallization of a 'middle-class' identity. Labour historiography, on the other hand, has tended to view the 1820s as a period of retreat and soul-searching. A more buoyant economy and the 'defeats' of 1815–20 stimulated an exploration of alternatives, more especially the growing culture of self-improvement and an apolitical early socialism.

The divisions between these two historiographies can be overstated. The 1820s was a decade during which the technologies and strategies of modern political organization—the meeting, the press, the national association—were refined and applied to a bewildering diversity of projects. Again, it is not helpful to look at this period solely in terms of class conflict and formation. Instead the period from 1815 to 1830 might be viewed as another intense period of politicization in Scotland. When the 'reform crisis' arrived it

---

[54] Dror Wahrman, 'Public Opinion, Violence and the Limits of Constitutional Politics', in James Vernon, ed., *Re-reading the Constitution: New Narratives in the Political History of England's Long Nineteenth Century* (Cambridge, 1996), 83–122; Catriona M. M. Macdonald, 'Abandoned and Beastly? The Queen Caroline Affair in Scotland', in Yvonne Galloway Brown and Rona Ferguson, eds., *Twisted Sisters: Women, Crime and Deviance in Scotland since 1400* (East Linton, 2002), 101–13.

[55] Fulcher, 'Contests over Constitutionalism', ch. 4.

[56] Gordon Pentland, *Radicalism, Reform and National Identity in Scotland, 1820–1833* (Woodbridge, 2008), ch. 1.

[57] See especially Dror Wahrman, *Imagining the Middle Class: The Political Representation of Class in Britain, c.1780–1840* (Cambridge, 1995).

was created by a unique constellation of circumstances. The response—from a broad-based 'national' reform movement, exploiting a range of techniques to ensure 'union' and organization and encompassing activists from among the Scottish Whigs, local elites, and the middle and working classes—had been rather longer in the making.[58]

# 3

Across this perplexing period new directions can be sought by expanding the content of the political culture that historians seek to describe and analyse, diversifying those concepts we employ to do so, and multiplying the contexts in which we explore Scottish political history. First, in terms of expanding the range of study it should be clear that it is no longer possible to explain phenomena such as 'radicalism' simply by attempting to identify either their social constituency or their ideological content. The very best work examines political culture as a whole and asks questions about the shifting discourses and strategies of different groups, while sensitively examining their complex social and ideological characters. One recent path-breaking account of Scotland in the 1790s has shown the fruits of this approach, by analysing radicals and loyalists, Foxites and ministerialists, women, rioters, and soldiers as constituents of a single political culture.[59]

Nevertheless, some political groups and political positions remain woefully understudied. For example, loyalism (especially after 1816), the Whig opposition, and middle-class liberalism would all benefit from close historical attention. While Scottish source material thankfully loomed large in Anna Clark's landmark study of women in popular politics, *Struggle for the Breeches: Gender and the Making of the British Working Class* (1995), as yet there has been no answer to Catriona Macdonald's eloquent plea that we uncover the specific history of women's involvement in radical politics during this period.[60] Linda Colley's claims about the impact of the French Wars in opening loyalist and patriotic political spaces to women could fruitfully be tested in the Scottish context.[61] Without some attention to the diverse groups and voices that comprise any political culture, we risk an impoverished account of this period.

Secondly, in terms of concepts, Scottish political history remains under-theorized and greater efforts might be made to engage with and produce work that is self-consciously interdisciplinary. As a period, the 'Age of Revolutions' has been one of considerable historical creativity and, indeed, the Scottish context has provided fruitful soil for some

---

[58] Pentland, *Radicalism*, passim; idem., 'Scotland and the Creation of a National Reform Movement, 1830–32', *Historical Journal*, 48, no. 4 (December 2005), 999–1,023.

[59] Harris, *Scottish People*, passim.

[60] Clark, *Struggle for the Breeches*; Catriona M. M. Macdonald, '"Their laurels wither'd, and their name forgot": Women and the Scottish Radical Tradition', in Edward J. Cowan and Richard J. Finlay, eds., *Scottish History: The Power of the Past* (Edinburgh, 2002), 225–52.

[61] Colley, *Britons*, 250–62.

extremely influential work on popular politics. The drama of the sedition trials of the 1790s, for example, has spawned its own mini-historiography, exploring contests over political language and the nature of the courtroom as a political and contested space.[62] In particular, work over the last two decades has vastly expanded our perceptions of what constitutes the 'political': symbolic practices and what might broadly be called the political culture of popular movements have become crucial and fruitful areas of inquiry.[63] The disciplinary borrowings on which this expansion rests might be taken further. Cultural geography, for example, might have a great deal to tell historians about how to interrogate the 'spaces' in which popular politics were practised.[64] A recent study of the 'folk memory' of the 'Year of the French' in Ireland might inspire historians of Scotland to consider how political events are remembered in a multitude of different ways.[65]

Finally, in terms of contexts, historians might think on both bigger and smaller scales. Local and regional studies across this period remain thin on the ground. More of them, where such studies are possible, might afford greater texture to our understanding of events outside Edinburgh and Glasgow. Such studies are crucial, because they allow historians to interrogate apparent 'silences' by identifying networks of activists, but they might also serve to lay bare the complex processes of politicization.

In terms of wider contexts, while Irish-Scottish comparisons have proved fruitful, it is remarkable that serious consideration of the Scottish-English context of popular politics has emerged only recently.[66] Similarly, the 'Atlantic World' setting of Scottish radicalism demands more attention. Michael Durey's pioneering work on James Thomson Callender is not only virtually the only good biography of a prominent Scottish radical, but is also unique in its careful delineation of the contours of the Atlantic print culture in which he moved.[67] Additionally, very recent work on Canada suggests that the recent flowering of imperial history could provide instructive contexts and comparisons for

---

[62] John Barell, *Imagining the King's Death: Figurative Treason, Fantasies of Regicide 1793–1796* (Oxford, 2000), ch. 4; James Epstein, ' "Our real constitution": Trial Defence and Radical Memory in the Age of Revolution', in Vernon, ed., *Re-reading*, 22–51; Michael T. Davis, 'Prosecution and Radical Discourse during the 1790s: The Case of the Scottish Sedition Trials', *International Journal of the Sociology of Law*, 33, no. 3 (September 2005), 148–58; Nolan Marchand, 'Reading Dress, Reading Culture: The Trial of Joseph Gerrald, 1794', in Jessica Munns and Penny Richards, eds., *The Clothes that Wear Us: Essays on Dressing and Transgressing in Eighteenth-Century Culture* (Newark, 1999), 320–35.

[63] Paul Pickering, 'Class without Words: Symbolic Communication in the Chartist Movement', *Past & Present*, 112, no. 1 (August 1986), 144–62; James Epstein, *Radical Expression: Political Language, Ritual and Symbol in England, 1790–1850* (Oxford, 1994); Robert Poole, 'The March to Peterloo: Politics and Festivity in Late Georgian England', *Past & Present*, 192, no. 1 (August 2006), 109–53.

[64] For a recent example see Katrina Navickas, 'Moors, Fields, and Popular Protest in South Lancashire and the West Riding of Yorkshire, 1800–1848', *Northern History*, 46, no. 1 (March 2009), 93–111.

[65] Guy Beiner, *Remembering the Year of the French: Irish Folk History and Social Memory* (Madison, 2007).

[66] See especially E. W. McFarland, *Ireland and Scotland in the Age of Revolution: Planting the Green Bough* (Edinburgh, 1994).

[67] Durey, 'With the Hammer of Truth'.

the history of domestic popular politics.[68] Thinking along such lines and identifying new content, concepts, and contexts might not serve to rehabilitate a unified 'Age of Reform', but it will certainly help to ensure that the period remains one of creative uncertainties for historians of modern Scotland.

## FURTHER READING

Devine, T. M., ed., *Conflict and Stability in Scottish Society 1700–1850* (Edinburgh, 1990).

Donovan, R. K., *No Popery and Radicalism: Opposition to Roman Catholic Relief in Scotland, 1778–1782* (New York, 1982).

Epstein, James, *Radical Expression: Political Language, Ritual and Symbol in England, 1790–1850* (Oxford, 1994).

Harris, Bob, *The Scottish People and the French Revolution* (London, 2008).

—— ed., *Scotland in the Age of the French Revolution* (Edinburgh, 2005).

McFarland, E. W., *Ireland and Scotland in the Age of Revolution: Planting the Green Bough* (Edinburgh, 1994).

Meikle, Henry W., *Scotland and the French Revolution* (Glasgow, 1912).

Pentland, Gordon, *Radicalism, Reform and National Identity in Scotland, 1820–1833* (Woodbridge, 2008).

—— *The Spirit of the Union: Popular Politics in Scotland, 1815–1820* (London, 2011).

Whatley, Christopher A., *Scottish Society 1707–1830: Beyond Jacobitism, Towards Industrialization* (Manchester, 2000).

[68] Michael Gauvreau, 'Covenanter Democracy: Scottish Popular Religion, Ethnicity, and the Varieties of Politico-Religious Dissent in Upper Canada, 1815–1841', *Histoire Sociale*, 36, no. 71 (May 2003), 55–83; Valerie Wallace, 'Exporting Radicalism within the Empire: Scots Presbyterian Political Values in Scotland and British North America, c. 1815–c. 1850' (unpublished PhD thesis, University of Glasgow, 2009).

# CHAPTER 24

...................................................................................................

# THE SCOTTISH CITIES[1]

...................................................................................................

## RICHARD RODGER

ON Hogmanay 1811, the activities of gangs of 'ferocious banditti' resulted in muggings and the death of a police officer in Edinburgh.[2] The shock waves that reverberated through the City Chambers on New Year's Day 1812 were the catalyst for a prompt response from the Town Council and Magistrates. They concluded that the 'present system of police is totally inadequate' and 'a new bill [should be] brought into parliament, with every possible despatch' to ensure 'a more efficient police force'. Sixty-eight persons were arrested in conjunction with the murder; subsequently, three men were executed and five transported for their offences.

For the ruling elite of the capital, the episode captured the instability of an urban system, and no doubt many drew some personal comfort from their decision to quit the congested closes and wynds of the Old Town for the more spacious and regular streets of the first New Town, begun in 1767. If this pattern of social and residential segregation was most pronounced in Edinburgh, it was also evident in streets formed on Glasgow's Blythswood estate and that of Bon Accord in Aberdeen. Elsewhere in Scotland, the reorientation of trade and industry in the eighteenth century towards the Atlantic and colonial trades reinvigorated the west of Scotland burghs, and Glasgow particularly. The pace of economic growth, although a generation behind that of England, assumed a sufficient momentum in the early nineteenth century to attract to the Scottish cities significant numbers of migrants from highland and lowland Scotland, as well as from Ulster and the southern Irish provinces.[3] Consequently, the population of Glasgow quadrupled between 1801 and 1841; in Edinburgh, the increase in population in these four decades was itself greater than the entire city in 1800. Whereas in 1800, 20 per cent of Scots lived

---

[1] Originally there were three cities—Edinburgh, Glasgow, and Aberdeen. Dundee acquired that status in 1899. These are the cities considered in this chapter. Inverness acquired city status in 2001 and Stirling in 2002. The case of Perth is ambiguous. Though a royal burgh styling itself a 'city', it did not possess this status in a formal sense. Since 2009 it has pressed for city status.

[2] *The Edinburgh Annual Register*, January 1812, 1–3.

[3] M. Gray, *Scots on the Move: Scots Migrants 1750–1914* (Dundee, 1990).

in towns of 5,000 or more inhabitants, 40 per cent did so by 1861, and 60 per cent by 1911. Though many smaller towns were also transformed by the influx of population, predictably it was the cities that were most affected. In 1851, one in five Scots lived in the four cities—Glasgow, Edinburgh, Dundee and Aberdeen—and by 1911 the ratio was one in three. By 1911, Scots were a more urbanized nation than any other in the world, except for England (Figures 24.1 and 24.2).

The unprecedented pace of expansion in the first half of the nineteenth century put the Scottish urban system under immense pressure as the cities and major burghs were fundamentally reshaped by the interrelated processes of mercantile and industrial growth. The Ordinance Survey maps for the late 1840s and 1890s reveal the remarkable spatial and functional changes in Scottish cities. Space became more specialized as home and work were decoupled under the advancing mode of factory production; the circulation of people and products required new thoroughfares; leisure and sport acquired

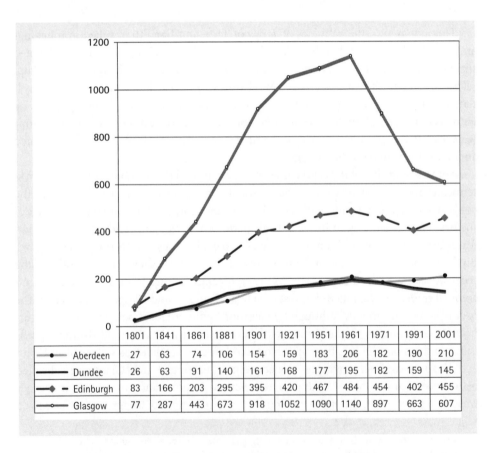

| | 1801 | 1841 | 1861 | 1881 | 1901 | 1921 | 1951 | 1961 | 1971 | 1991 | 2001 |
|---|---|---|---|---|---|---|---|---|---|---|---|
| Aberdeen | 27 | 63 | 74 | 106 | 154 | 159 | 183 | 206 | 182 | 190 | 210 |
| Dundee | 26 | 63 | 91 | 140 | 161 | 168 | 177 | 195 | 182 | 159 | 145 |
| Edinburgh | 83 | 166 | 203 | 295 | 395 | 420 | 467 | 484 | 454 | 402 | 455 |
| Glasgow | 77 | 287 | 443 | 673 | 918 | 1052 | 1090 | 1140 | 897 | 663 | 607 |

FIGURE 24.1 The population of the four cities, 1801–2001 (in thousands).
        Notes:  i. Endinburgh includes leith; Glasgow includes environs later incorported.
                                ii. Local government boundaries changed in 1975.
    Source:  B. R. Mitchell and P. Deane, Abstract or British Historical Statics (Cambridge 1962)

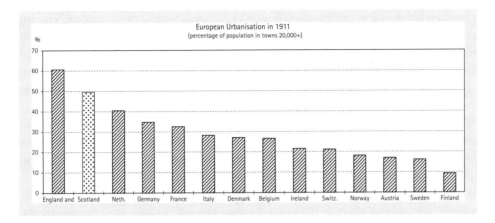

European Urbanisation in 1911
(percentage of population in towns 20,000+)

FIGURE 24.2  Scottish urbanization in a European setting.
*Source:* J. De Vries, *European Urbanisation 1500–1800* (London, 1984), 39–48.

areas exclusively dedicated to them; the department store and shopping arcade revised spaces of consumption; the reach of city governance became more widespread; and the physical extent of the city engulfed peripheral villages and small burghs as greenfield sites became the future brownfield sites. The city ingested neighbouring settlements for industrial and residential purposes, as well as for public utilities such as gasworks. Private-enterprise jute factories, chemical plants, rubber factories, shipyards, printers and publishers, railway workshops, marine engineering and boiler-making firms clearly needed larger sites, but so too did the numerous bakeries, foundries, and breweries as economies of scale were delivered by advancing technological change. Annexation, a topic in urgent need of further research, extended the urban area of the city appreciably, so that it was no longer possible to cross the built-up area on foot. The jurisdictional reach of the new city boundaries was extended, and the responsibility for the management and administration of the city increasingly resided with a few powerful elected committee chairmen and a salaried executive group of municipal professionals—the town clerk, burgh chamberlain, burgh engineer, burgh surveyor, and medical officer of health. Their administrative fiefdoms also merit further research.

# SCALE, MASS, DENSITY, AND COMPLEXITY

Scale, mass, density, and complexity were key characteristics of urban change in the nineteenth-century Scottish city, and if, as the photographic record shows, the crowd was symbolic of the intense energy associated with the factory gate, sports fixtures, political meetings, and ceremonial events, this took place in an increasingly regulated environment. Social control was never far away from the actions of authority; disorder, instability, and uncertainty increased risk and were anathema to a middle class with considerable investments in property, public positions, and political power. Under conditions of rapid urbanization, not to manage urban space was to invite social disintegration, and the middle classes were not likely to accede to that when their hard-fought fortunes and family legacies were at stake. Managing the urban environment was central to their continuing prosperity.[4]

How, then, did the Scottish city of 1800 differ to that of 1900? To a resident of Aberdeen, Dundee, Edinburgh, or Glasgow in 1800 who was miraculously resurrected in 1900, their city would have appeared fundamentally different. They might recognize the street layout and topographical features such as hills and harbours, though these, too, changed appreciably with new docks and quays, and even a makeover to the castle rock in Edinburgh.[5] The skyline, with its new post-Disruption church building and numerous phallic industrial chimneys, also registered a fundamental change; derricks and gantries populated the quayside and railway yards of the cities; landmark public buildings, subsequently the subject of the heritage industry and the listing process, began to populate the Scottish Victorian city; and infrastructural investment in transport and utilities were among the most dramatic changes in the city townscape. The railway age with its stations and sidings, its cuttings and bridges, its hotels and concourses, changed the city, and they warrant further research. Approaching or leaving a station through the bowels of the earth or astride the silvery Tay were engineering feats destined to impress passengers.

The reality of the railway was its transformative impact on the city and its built environment as the companies displayed an insatiable hunger for land.[6] By 1873, the Great North of Scotland and the Caledonian Railway were respectively the fifth and eighth largest landowners in Aberdeen; in Edinburgh, the North British was fourth largest; and in Glasgow, the Caledonian Railway was only just pushed into second place behind Glasgow Corporation as the largest landowner, while the North British was the third and the Glasgow Union Railway the eighth largest landowner.[7] The companies defined the parameters of the land market and their activities affected the functioning of the city and its inhabitants. The spaghetti junctions of the nineteenth century were south Laurieston in Glasgow and Dalry in Edinburgh. Deep cuttings and highly visible viaducts were built to reach docksides and new industrial estates. Even before tenements were built, neighbourhoods were zoned, development was blighted, and future communities were already divided and stigmatized. For the resident the railway was noisy, dirty, and an obstruction on the way to work or worship; for the traveller within and between cities, however, it was liberating. These were fundamental and distinctive changes, and the urban impact was all the greater since earlier transport changes associated with canals were much less significant in the Scottish cities than in Birmingham, Manchester, or Leeds.

---

[4] W. H. Fraser, 'Municipal Socialism and Social Policy', in R. J. Morris and R. Rodger, eds., *The Victorian City: A Reader in British Urban History* (Harlow, 1993), 258–80.

[5] R. J. Morris, 'The Capitalist, the Professor and the Soldier: The Re-making of Edinburgh Castle, 1850–1900', *Planning Perspectives*, 21 (2007), 55–78.

[6] J. R. Kellett, *The Impact of Railways on Victorian Cities* (London, 1969), 208–43.

[7] *Parliamentary Papers* [hereafter *PP*], *1874*, lxxii, Owners of Lands and Heritages 1872–73, Part iii. The railway companies owned 582 acres within Glasgow's boundaries in 1872 compared to 291 owned by the City Council.

Railway engines and, more significantly, stationary steam engines produced another transformative impact on Scottish cities, namely, smoke pollution; as factory-based manufacturing production expanded exponentially, so did coal consumption.[8] Soon the newly constructed, honey-coloured stone tenements of the Central Belt were soot-stained through industrial, and increasingly household, consumption of coal. By 1860, 67 per cent of the male workforce in Dundee was employed in manufacturing; in Glasgow, it was 56 per cent; among working women, 85 per cent in Dundee and 67 per cent in Glasgow worked in manufacturing.[9] This reflected the growth both of the scale of production and technological complexity in mid-Victorian industry, as well as the contribution of the cities to Scottish industrial development. A unique survey of employers in the four cities and five other burghs—Greenock, Inverness, Leith, Paisley, and Perth—shows that the 35 largest firms employed on average 662 workers, and that firms with more than 75 people on their payroll constituted 3.2 per cent of all employers and 50 per cent of the total workforce.[10] Dualism in the industrial structure of the Scottish cities—three-quarters of all firms employed fewer than ten workers—meant that small workshops and craft-based skills generally continued to be located in the older parts of the cities; new manufacturing giants found greenfield sites on the urban fringe suitable for the expanded scale of operations necessary to compete in national and world markets. This was the case at Parkhead and Springburn in Glasgow, or Fountainbridge in Edinburgh, or Lochee in Dundee, where Cox Brothers developed the largest jute factory in the world between 1849 and 1864, with its 282-foot chimney symbolizing the productive power of 820 power looms, 150 handlooms, and 5,000 employees.[11]

As the population and economic activity of the cities developed, pressure on land increased, encouraging the gentry to quit their homes and sell the modest estates that ringed the eighteenth-century cities. The inclination of landowners to part with all or some of their estates depended on the price offered, the position of their land in relation to the drift of development, the financial position of the family itself and their assessment of the long-term prospects for their property. This varied both within and between cities, though the concentration of ownership in relatively few hands (Table 24.1) meant a substantial amount of land might suddenly become available; alternatively, it might be 'hoarded' in the expectation of better returns in the future, thus limiting the supply of building land in the short term. Absenteeism often figured in the decision too. In Edinburgh, 18 per cent of the acreage of the city and 8 per cent of its annual rental value was in the hands of powerful figures such as Sir Thomas Dick

[8] These environmental impacts on the Scottish city deserve further research.

[9] D. Reeder and R. Rodger, 'Industrialisation and the City Economy', in M. J. Daunton, ed., *Cambridge Urban History of Britain*, 3 vols. (Cambridge, 2000), vol. 3, 553–92.

[10] R. Rodger, 'Concentration and Fragmentation: Capital, Labor, and the Structure of mid-Victorian Scottish Industry', *Journal of Urban History*, 14:2 (1988), 187–9, tables 1 and 2.

[11] Gazetteer for Scotland, Lochee, http://www.scottish-places.info/towns/townfirst407.html

Table 24.1  Concentration of landownership in Scottish cities, 1872

| | Landowners with 1 acre or more | | |
| --- | --- | --- | --- |
| | Owners (%) | Acreage (%) | Annual Value (%) |
| Aberdeen | 2.1 | 68.4 | 19.5 |
| Dundee | 3.5 | 72.1 | 28.6 |
| Edinburgh | 3.7 | 42.9 | 27.3 |
| Glasgow | 2.8 | 62.4 | 26.8 |

Source: PP 1874, lxxii, Owners of Lands and Heritages 1872–3, Part iii.

Lauder and Lieutenant Colonel Alexander Learmonth, both of whom lived in London on the proceeds of, respectively, their 68 and 86 acres in Edinburgh.[12]

The centrifugal expansion of the city and the emigration of the four-storey Scottish Victorian tenement form to new peripheral industrial settlements and middle-class suburbs was influenced by financial crises at home and abroad. First, the stock-market crash and the collapse of the English banking system (1825), then the City of Glasgow Bank failure (1878), and latterly the Baring crisis (1890), together with local factors concerning the maturity of loans, affected builders and rendered the building industry in the Scottish cities subject to fluctuations on a scale far more volatile than those in any other industry. Glasgow and Dundee house-builders were more susceptible to this instability than those in Edinburgh and Aberdeen.[13]

The pulse of construction activity left its mark in other ways. Building development crabbed its way outwards unevenly; rarely was this in a concentric pattern since the direction of expansion depended on landowners' preferences and the proximity to nodes of industrial or residential development. Consequently, particular neighbourhoods were clothed in new building at the same time and the physical features reflected this as dormer or bay windows became fashionable and WCs essential. 'Greek' Thomson remained influential in Glasgow in contrast to the surge of neo-Gothic in Edinburgh; thus the tone and architectural texture of the cities differed.[14] Similarly, red sandstone tenements in Glasgow featured prominently from the 1860s, but in Edinburgh this material was mainly confined to fin-de-siècle ornamentation.[15] Swathes of Victorian tenements

[12] R. Rodger, The Transformation of Edinburgh: Land, Property and Trust in the Nineteenth Century (Cambridge, 2001), 114–17.

[13] R. Rodger, 'The Victorian Building Industry and the Housing of the Scottish Working Class', in M. Doughty, ed., Building the Industrial City (Leicester, 1986), 151–206. The City of Glasgow bank failure resulted in 80 per cent of shareholders losing their money, and about two-thirds of Glasgow builders going out of business.

[14] M. Glendinning, R. MacInnes, and A. MacKechnie, A History of Scottish Architecture: From the Renaissance to the Present Day (Edinburgh, 1996), 243–84.

[15] M. Macnicol and M. Devlin, The Red Sandstone Buildings of Edinburgh (Grantown-on-Spey, 2009).

presented a degree of homogenization in their outward appearance because street after neighbouring street was built within the space of a few years and, as importantly, because basic no-frills building was all that a manual labouring class could afford. Monotony in the built environment was not the monopoly of the twentieth-century housing estate.

What the resurrected visitor of 1900 would have noticed was the loss of informality in the built environment. Improvement projects straightened out streets, removed courts and wynds, and rendered the interstices of the city redundant. The secret city of pends and vennels[16] was gradually demolished or diminished either as part of the initiatives of city councils to improve surveillance by illuminating and thus regulating confined spaces within their jurisdictions, or to generate development opportunities as a means of enhancing the local taxation potential of dilapidated and insanitary sites. Gone were many of the informal stalls with their dues payable to the council; moved on or fined were the itinerant street-sellers. Newly created in the late nineteenth century were spaces for specialist wholesale markets for vegetables, meat, fish, and corn that required land-extensive premises, as did indoor retail spaces and arcades, arenas for exhibitions, meetings, and parades. Space became less promiscuous; increasingly it was dedicated to specific uses. Tax, an overlooked research topic, and tighter regulatory controls regarding public behaviour, were uppermost in municipal minds.

These initiatives in the public sphere developed first in Glasgow in 1800 through the introduction of a local police act and spread to Edinburgh in 1805.[17] Initially concerned with amenities—mainly lighting, paving, and cleansing—and with public-order responsibilities that were beyond the scope of a voluntary constabulary, the police commissioners' autonomy led them to embrace increasingly complex services. In the first half of the nineteenth century these included buildings in a dangerous state, street obstructions, and the loading and even parking of vehicles. Police powers defined the weights and measures applicable to sales of coal and grain; they fixed charges for hackney carriages, required the registration of dealers in second-hand goods, and of pawnbrokers. Where pollution either by smoke or where tar or acid leeched into water courses, the offending businesses were named and shamed and a schedule of fines applied; stricter controls were placed on slaughterhouses and meat quality, and on butter, meal and bread, fish and poultry; and gambling was discouraged in a system of regulation that required the Superintendent of Police to act 'for the public Interest, for the removal of all nuisances within the Limits of Police'.[18] As an example of the fine grain of Police Commission control, and of the public-interest principle, fines applied where flowerpots were precariously positioned on tenement windowsills. Micro-management is not a new creature of public administration.

What was new was that the cities forged a system of public administration between 1800 and 1850 based around the political dualism of elected police commissioners and

---

[16] Wynds, vennels, pends, and closes were arrow alleys that gave access to the 'backlands' of tenements from which flats, commercial premises, and workshops were accessed.

[17] D. G. Barrie, *Police in the Age of Improvement: Police Development and the Civic Tradition in Scotland 1775–1865* (Cullompton, 2008), 33–7, 81. Between 1812 and 1854 twenty Edinburgh improvement acts with over eleven hundred sections were approved by Parliament.

[18] Edinburgh Police Act 1817, *57 Geo. 3, cap. 33*, sections 21, 26–30.

town councillors. This evolving and complex system of Scottish urban administration was highly significant because the passage of so many local acts signalled the precedence of municipal interests over national legislation. Just as Edinburgh had aped Glasgow, as had Aberdeen, so Greenock, Port Glasgow, Dumfries, Leith, Paisley, Inverness, Kilmarnock, Perth, Kirkcaldy, Dunfermline, Peterhead, Airdrie, Alloa, Bathgate, Dingwall, and Dalkeith followed suit.[19] These local regulatory powers were not a top-down innovation from Westminster. It was the experience of Police Commissions in the Scottish burghs that moulded the clauses in national legislation—the Burgh Police (Scotland) Acts of 1833 and 1848, and even that much-lauded act of 1862, the Lindsay Burgh Police (Scotland) Act.[20] Indeed, the cities had little need of clauses in national statutes; they possessed them already, and only occasionally needed to adopt individual clauses in national legislation to avoid the expense of returning to Parliament for a revised local act. Ultimately, the dual system of civic administration in which Town Council and Police Commission participated was bureaucratic, expensive, and inefficient. Successively, in Glasgow (1846), Dundee (1851), Edinburgh, (1856), and Aberdeen (1871) the Police Commissions were disbanded as Town Councils reasserted their control over municipal affairs.

It is difficult to stress sufficiently the significance of the early nineteenth-century administrative machinery to the trajectory of city development in Scotland, and this warrants further investigation. The police commissioners acknowledged from the outset that the vulnerable in society were in need of protection, and that the actions of property owners legitimated public intervention in the private sphere. Property rights, then, were at the heart of public administration in nineteenth-century Scottish cities.

## PROPERTY, DENSITY, AND MORTALITY

In 1818 the House of Lords delivered a watershed judgement that fundamentally influenced the character of city development and, indeed, that of all subsequent Scottish building.[21] Lord Eldon's judgement insisted that a feuing[22] plan was not a sound basis on which to define property rights and thereafter all restrictions (burdens) pertaining to a property had to be included in the feu charter, i.e. at the time of conveyance. Thus, an individual could not change the use of his property and adversely affect the amenity of his neighbour. Another distinctive feature of Scottish urban tenure, sub-infeudation or feu-farming, was also boosted by the legal clarification given to property values in 1818.

---

[19] Barrie, *Police*, 284.

[20] P. Laxton and R. Rodger, *Insanitary City: H. D. Littlejohn and the Report on the Sanitary Condition of Edinburgh (1865)* (forthcoming).

[21] R. Rodger, *The Transformation of Edinburgh*, 62–6.

[22] Feuing is a form of land tenure, specific to Scotland, in which land is granted 'in feu' by the superior to the vassal on condition of the payment of an annual sum of money (feu-duty) and other occasional payments.

The way sub-infeudation worked to finance the building of Scottish cities was explained by James Gowans, an Edinburgh contractor in the 1860s and 1870s:

> A builder looks forward to the town increasing, and he takes up a lot of land from the superior at £50 an acre, and then by re-feuing or building himself he works it up to £200 an acre. That has been done with this city and large fortunes have been made out of it.[23]

On a given footprint, piling properties high, storey upon storey, was a spatial device peculiar to Scotland that maximized feuing income, increased rentals, and improved rateable values and local taxation. In conjunction with the Scottish legal system, the tenement was a brilliant device that unlocked sums from small savers for assured returns. Consequently, as a Royal Commission in 1917 reported, tenements were:

> to be found from Dumfries in the South to Lerwick on the far North...in small county burghs immediately surrounded by open fields...from county hamlet to the great cities.[24]

Changes in the law in the early nineteenth century served their purpose: Scottish urban development flourished and the tenement was instrumental in that process.

The downside was that with land and building costs higher in Scotland, affordable living space was diminished.[25] City dwellers, and Scots generally, paid a high price for their housing, and not simply in monetary terms since overcrowding meant mortality and morbidity were higher in urban Scotland. This was a concern that even fractured the Church of Scotland in 1843. The triangle of poverty, housing, and health was central to medical thinking, as William Alison, Professor of Medical Jurisprudence at Edinburgh University, explained:

> in the two greatest cities in Scotland, where the science and civilization of the country might be supposed to have attained their highest development, and where medical schools exist...the annual proportions of deaths to the population is not only much beyond the average in Britain, but very considerably greater than that of London.

Alison continued:

> Let us look to the closes of Edinburgh, and the wynds of Glasgow, and thoroughly understand the character and habits, the diseases and mortality, of the unemployed poor, unprotected by the law...let us study the condition of the aged and disabled poor...so far from priding ourselves on the smallness of the sums which are applied to this purpose in Scotland we must honestly and candidly confess, that our

---

[23] *PP 1884–85*, xxx, Royal Commission on Housing of the Working Classes, Scotland, Evidence of Gowans, Q.18893.

[24] *PP 1917–18*, xiv, Royal Commission on the Housing of the Industrial Population of Scotland, Rural and Urban, Report, 2232.

[25] R. Rodger, 'The "Invisible Hand"—Market Forces, Housing and the Urban Form in Victorian Cities', in D. Fraser and A. Sutcliffe, eds., *The Pursuit of Urban History* (London, 1983), 190–211.

parsimony in this particular is equally injurious to the poor and discreditable to the rich in Scotland.[26]

In fundamental opposition to this viewpoint, Dr Thomas Chalmers, evangelical minister and subsequent Free Church founder, was convinced that a reinvigorated parish system based on home visits and religious instruction was the most effective and compassionate way to improve the spiritual, moral, and material condition of the country in general and the cities in particular.[27]

The causes of deficient housing conditions were many. On the supply side, land, legal, and building costs were higher in Scotland than elsewhere in Britain. Rents were correspondingly higher, as was recognized in the twentieth century through rent-control arrangements. On the demand side, real wages were low, bouts of unemployment frequent, particularly in Glasgow and Dundee, and poor relief less generous than under the English system. Pound for pound, Scots' real wages bought less space than those of their English relations.

City authorities faced deteriorating environmental health conditions until the 1870s. Until mid-century, the basis of local taxation was unclear and simple statistical data on births and deaths was crude before civil registration was established in 1855.[28] Turf wars between the various committees and subcommittees of council, and between the multiple jurisdictions of the city, meant an issue such as defective drains might be registered as a nuisance but involve the deliberations of several council committees—finance, cleansing, works, and drainage, as well as the Dean of Guild court, the roads authority, and the parochial board.

Statistical evidence, in the form of civil registration in 1855 and the reform of local taxation in 1854, permitted a more robust city management to emerge from mid-century. Influential medical figures, Drs William Gairdner (Glasgow) and Henry Littlejohn (Edinburgh), provided knowledge of best practice in public hygiene, identified particular causes of ill-health in the city, and contributed thoughtfully to city policies on epidemics, occupational diseases, drainage arrangements, public cemeteries, and water supply and disposal. Both men were their city's first medical officer of health, Gairdner from 1863 to 1872, and Littlejohn from 1862 to 1908, and their national reputations gave them influence at the city level, with Littlejohn's meticulously researched *Report on the Sanitary Condition of the City of Edinburgh* (1865) universally praised.

In the last third of the nineteenth century, efforts to introduce piped water to the cities, build isolation hospitals, monitor food, air and water quality, and demolish insanitary housing each improved the city environment.[29] Yet in 1911, despite the positive

---

[26] W. P. Alison, *Observations on the Management of the Poor in Scotland* (Edinburgh, 1840), iv–v; C. Hamlin, 'William Pulteney Alison, the Scottish Philosophy, and the Making of a Political Medicine', *Journal of the History of Medicine and Allied Sciences*, 61 (2006), 144–86.

[27] S. J. Brown, *Thomas Chalmers and the Godly Commonwealth in Scotland* (Oxford, 1982), 91–151.

[28] A. Cameron, 'The Establishment of Civil Registration in Scotland', *Historical Journal*, 50 (2007), 378–95.

[29] C. M. Allan, 'The Genesis of Urban Redevelopment with Reference to Glasgow', *Economic History Review*, 18 (1965), 589–613; P. J. Smith, 'Slum Clearance as an Instrument of Sanitary Reform: The Flawed Vision of Edinburgh's First Slum Clearance Scheme', *Planning Perspectives*, 9 (1994), 1–27.

results of public-health policies, 8.7 per cent of the Scottish urban population still lived in one-room houses, and 39.2 per cent in two-room accommodation; in England, one- and two-roomed houses constituted 7.1 per cent of the housing stock.[30] Using the English Registrar General's definition of overcrowding, 55.7 per cent of Glasgow inhabitants were overcrowded, with Dundee 48.2 per cent, Aberdeen 37.8 per cent, and Edinburgh with 32.6 per cent overcrowded—approximately four to six times more densely packed than the average Englishman.[31] On the eve of the First World War, mortality rates in one-room Glasgow flats were double those in four-room properties, and infant mortal- ity was four times higher.[32] One indicator above all others stands out in terms of ameni- ties: shared toilets. In 1915, 62 per cent of inhabitants in Glasgow and 35 per cent in Edinburgh shared a toilet in two-room flats—the most common type.[33]

It mattered little what the indicators were—height, weight, skin condition, dental car- ies, skeletal deformities, or life expectancy—all pointed to the effects of adverse living conditions in a tenement world.[34] Environmental deficiencies in Dundee, Glasgow, and Edinburgh were correlated with tenement life: 'foul air to breathe, impure water to drink...cramped space and cradled in dirt' meant that children 'must grow up through sickly and unhappy adolescence into weak and stunted manhood'.[35] Undoubtedly, over the course of several generations there was a complicated relationship between nature and nurture, but the undeniable conclusions of a study of 72,000 Glasgow school- children was that living in a small house was injurious to health.

Living in congested space, in a room that was multifunctional, brought stresses and strains. Tall buildings, dark stairs, narrow closes, and box beds had adverse psycho- logical effects, and the demands of fetching and carrying water, disposing of slops and human waste, cleaning and cooking, childbirth and child-minding were arduous every- day routines in a multi-storey tenement world. Space was far from private. The rituals of laying out the dead and giving birth were undertaken among the rhythms and routines of daily life. The communal life of the stair, the wash house, and drying green had some benefits to offset the humdrum of everyday city life for the manual working classes and their families, though it was the dramatic fall in prices between 1870 and 1914 that did more to improve the lot of working and middle classes, as food and commodity prices tumbled by an average of about 1 per cent per annum.

---

[30] *PP 1912–13*, cxi, Census of England and Wales, 1911, vol. ii, tables xlvi and xlvii.

[31] *PP 1912–13*, cxix, Census of Scotland, 1911, parts 1–4.

[32] A. K. Chalmers, 'The Death Rate in One-Apartment Houses: An Enquiry Based on the Census Returns of 1901', *Proceedings of the Royal Philosophical Society of Glasgow*, 34 (1902–3), 131; *PP 1917–18*, xiv, Royal Commission, Report, para 658; Scottish Land Enquiry Committee, *Report* (Edinburgh, 1914), 371.

[33] *PP 1917–18*, xiv, Royal Commission, Report, 77.

[34] R. Rodger, 'Wages, Employment and Poverty in the Scottish Cities 1841–1914', in G. Gordon, ed., *Perspectives of the Scottish City* (Aberdeen, 1985), 25–63.

[35] J. B. Russell, 'The Children of the City: What Can We Do For Them?', *Edinburgh Health Society Lectures* (Edinburgh, 1886), 92–3.

# THE CITY AS SPECTACLE

The noise, bustle, and smell contributed to the sensescape of the city. Brewery, bonded warehouse, jute and rubber mill, steam boilers, railway engines, fish processing, bonemeal, and catgut, and a host of deafening weaving, smelting, and forging activities each gave a recognizable odour and colour to individual Scottish cities. Sound, sight, and smell were each assaulted, and occasionally appeased.

A pleasurable aspect of the nineteenth-century Scottish city was the music and entertainment that filled the bandstands, parks, and public spaces. The detachments of army and navy personnel garrisoned in the city meant it was they who regularly played in city parks, and were also on parade when members of the royal family and foreign delegations visited. Indeed, the durability of the military in the modern city seems to have escaped notice. When the freedom of the city was conveyed upon political and industrial figures, and heads of state were awarded honorary degrees, a military pomp and circumstance accompanied these rituals. Similarly, civic ceremonies were increasingly evident with foundation stones laid and buildings opened by royalty and aristocracy with increasing frequency as the tentacles of the municipal mission reached ever outwards into the suburbs. Even a councillor's funeral involved a deputation of fellow councillors in flowing robes and chains of office. So frequent were these late-Victorian civic occasions that Edinburgh councillors had to renew their robes and regalia.[36] Ceremonies were invented and expanded: war memorials appeared; vessels were launched; the Church of Scotland ministers processed annually; and the Battle of the Boyne was recalled as it had been since 1690. International Exhibitions in Edinburgh (1886) and Glasgow (1888, 1901) provided the stage for thousands of visitors, and several national and international conferences of industrialists and scientists held their annual conferences in Scottish cities every year.

The city itself was part of the performative element of Scottish society. Royal occasions brought people, all classes of people, onto the streets, whether in public celebration or mourning. These were not exclusively events for the titled or officialdom. Judged by contemporary photographs and newspapers, the general public joined in as participants, cheering physical prowess and horsemanship, and enjoying public music, bell-ringing, and fireworks displays. There were highland games, fetes for children, coronation mugs, and, significantly, 'dinners for poor persons'. Far from being in retreat before 1914, as claimed for English civic rituals,[37] the Scottish city enjoyed a flowering of colourful pageant and ceremony.

---

[36] 'The "Common Good" and Civic Promotion: Edinburgh 1860–1914', in R. Colls and R. Rodger, eds., *Cities of Ideas: Civil Society and Urban Governance in Britain 1800–2000* (Aldershot, 2004), 144–77.

[37] S. Gunn, *The Public Culture of the Victorian Middle Class: Ritual and Authority and the English Industrial City, 1840–1914* (Manchester, 2000).

# Space and the Reinvention of the Twentieth-Century City

Enquiries in Dundee, Edinburgh, and Glasgow (1904–7), a national investigation into Scottish land by the Liberal Party (1911), various Departmental Committees and a Royal Commission (the Bannatyne Commission 1911–17), each identified adverse living conditions associated with the physique of Scottish city dwellers. At the dawn of the twentieth century there was little sign that City Improvement Trusts, civic societies, company and philanthropic housing initiatives, the Charity Organisation Society, Social Union, cooperative workmen's efforts, or early social housing were making an impact on housing quality. Living conditions needed more than palliative care. The First World War brought its own difficulties: escalating city rents in the wake of rapid price inflation; rent strikes on Clydeside and rent control; direct political action; and disequilibrium in land and property markets.[38] The government's pledge 'Homes Fit for Heroes' was adopted as an 'insurance premium' to counteract national strikes and anxiety over political stability.[39] Council housing was the result. The landscape of the Scottish city was never the same again.

The nineteenth-century tenement with its communal stair, shared amenities, and social dramas was a design of the past. 'Four-in-a-block' maisonettes and two- or three-storey council housing mass-produced on an industrial scale on the periphery of the cities represented the future in the 1920s and 1930s. A new centrifugal impetus dominated the interwar years and altered the internal socio-economic structure of the Scottish cities. In parallel, bungalow development satisfied middle-class demand and ensured the permanence of the socially segregated twentieth-century city.

Whereas the concentration of the Victorian poor in central city districts provided access to casual labour markets, credit networks through pawnbrokers and shopkeepers, and family support systems through kinship links, these essential elements in the social fabric were jettisoned in the twentieth century—in favour of volume housing on peripheral estates lacking social facilities, frequent bus links, and the social capital of clubs and organizations that were critical to a functional civil society. At Kennyhill, Riddrie, and other Glasgow locations, 50,277 council houses were built between 1919 and 1939 on 4,735 acres; like others in Aberdeen, Dundee, and Edinburgh, these estates were labelled as 'problematic'.[40] Council-house designs, authorized by the Scottish Department of Home and Health and approved by the Treasury, came in pattern-books and, since

---

[38] J. Melling, *Rent Strikes: People's Struggle for Housing in West Scotland 1890–1916* (London, 1983), 18–26.

[39] M. Swenarton, *Homes Fit for Heroes: The Politics and Architecture of Early State Housing in Britain* (London, 1981), 78–9.

[40] S. Damer, *From Moorepark to 'Wine Alley'* (Edinburgh, 1989), 1–22; N. J. Morgan, '£8 "Cottages for Glasgow Citizens": Innovations in Municipal Housebuilding in the Inter-war Years', in R. Rodger, ed., *Scottish Housing in the Twentieth Century* (Leicester, 1989), 125–54.

70 per cent of all interwar housing in Scotland was built by local authorities, added a further dimension to homogenization in the built environment.[41] Monotonous, tree-less estates for social housing and mass-produced bungalows for owner-occupiers reinforced social segregation and introduced a high degree of cloning in the physical fabric of the Scottish city.[42]

Yet more fundamental changes to city spaces were encountered as regional planning gained momentum after 1945. Housing policy was no longer considered in isolation to work, transport, public services, education, and communities. Integrated or comprehen-sive planning represented the way forward, as was evident after 1946 in the path-breaking Clyde Valley Regional Plan, and those for other Scottish cities.[43] The Clyde Valley plan placed the revival of Glasgow in a regional setting; recommendation 34 stated: 'In the City of Glasgow, additional peripheral growth... should be limited to 250,000.' Another recommendation baldly stated that 'three new towns are recommended'.[44] This report established an enduring tension between region and city, between the Scottish Office, as the arm of government with its town-planning advisers, and the city councils as the rep-resentatives of local people. Intervention from government constrained local autonomy and reopened political sores.

The decision by the government to establish the East Kilbride Development Corporation in 1946 was taken against Glasgow's wishes.[45] Planners were less concerned with local issues and nurtured a grander vision of centrally directed reconstruction that relocated factories and workers from congested cities to New Towns conceived as eco-nomically and socially efficient. The planners' vision was one of rationality, predicated on the basis of decentralization and the merits of a reduced city scale.

The political agenda was simple: to restrain the political power of Glasgow.[46] Tom Johnston, Secretary of State for Scotland, appointed Patrick Abercrombie to draw up the Clyde Valley Regional Plan in the knowledge that the decentralizing principles of city management were enshrined in Abercrombie's pre-war work and Garden City prin-ciples. Abercrombie's regional framework was simple: to remove 500,000 tenement dwellers, rehouse half within a newly designated Green Belt that encroached on the exist-ing city boundaries, and rehouse the other 250,000 'overspill' in four New Towns. A further agency in this political power play was the Scottish Special Housing Association (SSHA),

---

[41] This was in stark contrast to English boroughs where 70 per cent of interwar housing was built for owner-occupiers.

[42] M. Glendinning and D. Watters, eds., *Homebuilders: MacTaggart and Mickel and the Scottish Housebuilding Industry* (Edinburgh, 1999).

[43] P. Abercrombie and R. H. Matthew, *The Clyde Valley Regional Plan 1946* (Edinburgh, 1946); R. Lyle and G. Payne, *The Tay Valley Plan* (Dundee, 1950); P. Abercrombie and D. Plumstead, *A Civic Survey and Plan for the City and Royal Burgh of Edinburgh* (Edinburgh, 1949); W. D. Chapman, *The City and Royal Burgh of Aberdeen: Survey and Plan* (Aberdeen, 1949).

[44] Abercrombie and Matthew *Clyde Valley Regional Plan*, 340–4, recommendations 21, 35.

[45] New Towns were established at Glenrothes (1948), Cumbernauld (1955), Livingstone (1962), and Irvine (1966).

[46] M. Pacione, *Glasgow: The Socio-Spatial Development of the City* (Chichester, 1991); M. Keating, *The City that Refused to Die* (Aberdeen, 1988).

a government quango that built 100,000 houses in the period 1937 to 1987, and was used tactically by the Scottish Office to influence housing policy in Glasgow through Treasury support for overspill policies.[47]

Within this regional planning framework, Glasgow Corporation sought to develop its own policies and priorities through local plans. These centred on the demolition of 172,000 unfit houses, equivalent to 58 per cent of the housing stock, replaced by flats at lower densities. Work at Pollok, Drumchapel, and Easterhouse increased supply by about 6,000 units annually in four-storey tenements that were diametrically opposed in design and density to the proposals in the Clyde Valley Plan.[48] Glasgow Council allocated flats on the basis of defined guidelines and sectarian quotas, and higher rents for SSHA and New Town accommodation resulted in a social filtering process by providing housing primarily for skilled workers and leaving the city centre with greater levels of social deprivation.

Another policy approach, based on twenty-nine Comprehensive Development Areas (CDAs) within Glasgow in 1957, involved substantial demolitions and rehousing on the peripheral estates. In one of the CDAs, Huthesontown-Gorbals (population 26,860; density 1,133 persons/acre), 91 per cent of the dwellings were considered incapable of improvement.[49] The CDAs could not arrest the abrupt decline in manufacturing employment, though they were successful, in conjunction with Glasgow Corporation's Department of Architecture and Planning, in building mixed developments along the lines of those by London County Council, where four-storey flats and maisonettes were interspersed with a number of sixteen-storey tower blocks.[50] This was significant because through the experience of tower-block construction within the city, the Glasgow Housing Committee flexed its muscles and, in direct opposition to the regional plan, 'unleashed the most concentrated multi-story building drive experienced by any British city, with high flats accounting for nearly three-quarters of all completions' between 1961 and 1968.[51] The city skyline changed fundamentally (Figures 24.3 and 24.4).

Though city land use altered fundamentally under local and regional planning decisions, structural changes in the Scottish economy were also at work. While the manufacturing base of the cities held up reasonably well until 1950, thereafter it went into a tailspin. In the 1950s, 53 per cent of all jobs in the four Scottish cities were in manufacturing; the percentage fell rapidly in the 1960s to 43 per cent in 1970, and then to 36 per cent in the early 1980s.[52] More surprisingly, between 1981 and 1996 there was the almost

[47] R. Rodger and H. Al-Qaddo, 'The Scottish Special Housing Association and the Implementation of Housing Policy 1937–87', in R. Rodger, ed., Scottish Housing, 184–213.

[48] By 1954, 95 per cent of Glasgow Council's new housing was in tenements.

[49] M. J. Miller, The Representation of Place: Urban Planning and Protest in France and Great Britain 1950–1980 (Aldershot, 2003), 189–98, 209–14.

[50] P. J. Bull, 'The Effects of Redevelopment Schemes of Inner-City Manufacturing Activity in Glasgow', Environment and Planning A, 13 (1981), 991–1,000.

[51] M. Glendinning, Tenements and Towers: Glasgow Working-Class Housing 1890–1990 (Edinburgh, 1990), 48; M. Pacione, 'Housing Policies in Glasgow since 1880', Geographical Review, 69:4 (1979), 395–412.

[52] J. Macinnes, 'Why Nothing Much Has Changed', Employment Relations, 9:1 (1987), 51.

**FIGURE 24.3** Aerial view *c.*1950 of the Canongate, Holyrood Palace, Holyrood Park, and the sites of the Scottish Parliament building, Edinburgh, and showing the gasometers and a mixed industrial and residential use in part of the medieval city. © RCAHMS. Aerofilms Collection. Licensor www.rcahms.gov.uk DP 065085.

identical loss of manufacturing employment in Edinburgh (−49 per cent) and Glasgow (−47 per cent).[53] But whereas overall employment in Edinburgh increased by 10 per cent in these years due to rapid growth in tertiary-sector jobs, drastic reductions of about 35 per cent in unskilled and semi-skilled work in Glasgow were not offset by modest professional employment gains, and so total employment in Glasgow fell by about 15 per cent between 1981 and 1996. Though the outlook for Scottish manufacturing seemed

[53]  I. Turok and N. Edge, *The Jobs Gap in Britain's Cities: Employment Loss and Labour Market Consequences* (Bristol, 1999), 43.

**FIGURE 24.4** Aerial view (1991) of West Pilton and Muirhouse flats, Edinburgh. © Crown Copyright: RCAHMS. Licensor www.rcahms.gov.uk SC 418272.

bleak overall, there were bright spots, as with the biomedical and technological industries that migrated in the 1980s to Dundee and accounted for 10 per cent of the United Kingdom's digital-entertainment industry in 2010, and petroleum and gas industries which sustained the Aberdeen economy from the 1970s.

Fundamental changes in manufacturing meant industrial sites lay vacant and buildings derelict. Prompted by the Thatcher Conservative government, the land holdings of nationalized industries were released as part of privatization and deregulation policies. Simultaneously, in the effort to restrain public expenditure, central government rate-capped local authorities, thus encouraging Scottish cities to release some of their property holdings to fund social and cultural activities. The relationship between council and developers remains unclear but it represented a nexus of power that deserves further investigation. City-centre land became relatively abundant for the first time in generations, and redevelopment followed as cities sought to increase their tax revenues by encouraging office developments, shopping malls, waterfront projects, and leisure parks. Private-enterprise initiatives materialized in the form of cinema complexes, nightclubs, wine bars, and coffee shops, as the city centre was transformed from a site of production to a centre of consumption. Encouraged by financial sweeteners and planning permissions, the multiples and multinationals invaded both high streets and 'edge city' malls. Moneylenders were welcomed into churches to finance conversions; student flats, loft-living, and apartments for 'twinkies' occupied the sites of former warehouses, some of which were refurbished, and others newly constructed on sites that had previously provided local employment. So where chimneys and warehouses once stood, glass, steel, and chrome replaced them with entirely new shapes and materials, and the navigational aids by which citizens had moved around the city for decades were demolished as one distinctive building after another conceded its footprint to glistening new offices and flats.[54]

The most conspicuous of the public-renewal initiatives was the Glasgow Eastern Area Renewal (GEAR) project (1976–90), which was responsible for the coordination of social, environmental, and industrial activity in an area of 1,600 hectares, or 8 per cent of the city.[55] GEAR was significant in a national context by anticipating both the London and Merseyside Docklands initiatives and because up to 20 per cent of properties could be held in private ownership, thus heralding in 1980 another seismic change in Scottish cities with the 'right-to-buy' legislation introduced by the Conservative government under Thatcher. As GEAR came to a conclusion, the Scottish Office announced in 1988 'New Life for Urban Scotland'. Considered a 'landmark in the history of urban regeneration in Scotland',[56] four peripheral housing estates—Castlemilk (Glasgow), Ferguslie Park (Paisley), Wester Hailes (Edinburgh), and Whitfield (Dundee)—were selected for new ten-year urban-regeneration partnerships coordinated through the Scottish Development Agency. These projects provided valuable lessons on how to tackle urban regeneration.

De-urbanization and its consequences remains an underexplored feature of urban Scotland in the late twentieth century.[57] All four cities lost population in the 1960s and 1970s; Glasgow and Dundee continued to lose population, and only from the 1990s did Aberdeen rebound, as did Edinburgh in the 2000s (see Fig. 24.1). Whereas overspill and New Town Development were deliberate policies to decant Glaswegians, city shrinkage was the product of complex factors. The construction of improved dual-carriageway roads and prefabricated tin sheds as distribution centres and locations for light

---

[54] U. Wannop, 'The Glasgow Eastern Area Renewal (GEAR) Project: A Perspective on the Management of Urban Regeneration', *Town Planning Review*, 61 (1990), 455–74; R. Leclerc and D. Draffan, 'The Glasgow Eastern Area Renewal Project', *Town Planning Review*, 55 (1984), 335–52.

[55] Keating, *The City that Refused to Die*.

[56] The Scottish Office, *Progress in Partnership* (HMSO, 1993).

[57] R. Rodger, 'Urbanisation in Twentieth-Century Scotland', in T. M. Devine and R. J. Finlay, eds., *Scotland in the Twentieth Century* (Edinburgh, 1996), 122–53.

manufacturing around the periphery of each of Scotland's cities contributed to a gradual but steady move of workers and families to small towns within commuting distance of the cities. Glitzy glass-fronted offices continued to recruit workers from beyond the city limits, and they added to the flow of daily commuters. High land values and property prices in the Scottish cities meant that commuting, lemming-like by car and packed public transport, was the travel-to-work experience for the majority. Demographics also played a part. The popularity of smaller satellite towns flourished due to cheaper housing costs, educational provisions, and the perception of a safer urban environment for families. For flat-sharing young adults, the city centre increasingly became a social space with an appealing night life, as it was for cut-price airline weekenders, and stag and hen parties.

Whereas Victorian industry could be found in the historic core of Scottish cities, by the end of the twentieth century the city had been turned inside out. The mobile city had arrived. Manufacturing and distribution had been dispatched to the periphery to take advantage of open space and road-transport connections; a major modern communications hub—the airport and its support activities—was outside the city limits, Dundee excepted; stone tenements had been torn down and turned into hard core for road developments; retail activities retained a toehold in the city centre but were also a dominant out-of-town activity; the corner shop and the local pub were fighting rearguard actions as their 'regulars' were relocated to fringe estates; moneylenders were anonymous distant institutions; and parish churches were no longer used exclusively for worship. A sense of continuity, of belonging to a locality, of community engagement and the accumulated social capital associated with it, could no longer be taken for granted in the late twentieth-century city. Social-networking websites, internet shopping, and electronic banking gained the ascendancy. The Scottish city had mutated, as it always had and always will, for better and for worse.

## FURTHER READING

Abercrombie, P., and Plumstead, D., *A Civic Survey and Plan for the City and Royal Burgh of Edinburgh* (Edinburgh, 1949).

Blaikie, A., *The Scots Imagination and Modern Memory* (Edinburgh, 2010).

Fraser, W. H., and Lee, C. H., eds., *Aberdeen 1800–2000: A New History* (East Linton, 2000).

Fraser, W. H., and Maver, I., eds., *Glasgow. Vol. 2, 1830 to 1912* (Manchester 1996).

Glendinning, M., MacInnes, R., and MacKechnie, A., *A History of Scottish Architecture: From the Renaissance to the Present Day* (Edinburgh, 1996).

Maver, I., *Glasgow* (Edinburgh, 2000).

Miskell, L., et al., eds., *Victorian Dundee: Image and Realities* (East Linton, 2000).

Rodger, R., *The Transformation of Edinburgh: Land, Property and Trust in the Nineteenth Century* (Cambridge, 2001).

CHAPTER 25

········································································································

# IDENTITY WITHIN THE UNION STATE, 1800–1900

········································································································

## GRAEME MORTON

## THE UNION STATE

FOR good reason contemporary reflection on the Union state in 1800 was scarce. The state was geographically distant, being for most Scots an irrelevance to their daily life. With no national newspaper or periodical in circulation, parliamentary discussion was dated, variable, or simply unknown. Originating in 1783, *The Glasgow Herald* did not publish daily until 1859; *The Scotsman* would not appear until 1817; and it was not until the 1830s that provincial newspapers came to the fore. At the century's start, chapbooks and broadsides told tales of monarchs and the constitution, the army and the navy, William Wallace, the Stuarts, and the Covenanters. *The Scots Magazine* (1739), the *Edinburgh Review* (1802), and the early periodicals dissected culture, religion, sedition, foreign governments, the constitution, and politics. But the state, as a structure of bureaucratic government, was detached from household debate.

This lack of contemporary interaction with the nineteenth-century Union state—which to a lesser or greater extent lasted throughout the century—was reflected upon by the Royal Commission on the Constitution in 1973. It described that state as 'mostly passive and non-interventionist' to the extent that '[t]he individual one hundred years ago hardly needed to know that the central government existed'.[1] With a curtailed franchise pre-1832, around forty-five hundred Scots voted; they were all men. The state in the first half of the century did not record Scots' birth, marriage, or death. Few paid any tax, and even fewer paid it to the Treasury. It was 1799 when national taxation was imposed upon those with an income over £60, lasting until 1816 when the emphasis shifted to taxing commodities. Even a decade

---

[1] *Royal Commission on the Constitution, 1969–1973*, vol. 1, Report (Cmnd. 5460) (Chairmen, Lord Crowther, Lord Kilbrandon), 75 (para 227), 76 (para 232).

after its reintroduction, income tax produced only one-tenth of the state's revenue in 1853, with fewer Scots than English earning sufficiently to precipitate a contribution.[2] Constitutionally, the Union state was the stable reality. The adult generation who had blazed the trail of the Jacobite cause at the '45 had all but passed away, and those that followed had the stories and promptings from their elders, but no direct experience. For many the Union state was as much about monarchy as it was about law makers. The Hanoverian line had passed through its third coronation. The monarch had yet to be seen north of the border but loyalty held sway. Radicalism peaked in the 1790s, and would continue to rumble into the 1820s and beyond that into Chartism and suffrage disputes. Where the Scots understood the role of the state most clearly, and where it fashioned an identity that was shared, was in matters overseas. Coming out of the eighteenth century, the Scots found common cause as Britons facing down the upheavals of American independence, war with France, the United Irishmen's challenge to British rule, and union with Ireland. Tales of great men, especially military men, marked Scotland's impact in its Empire role. The regiments and the (often brutal) successes of the Scottish soldier were strong narratives at home, evidence that has been charted by T. M. Devine.[3] Similarly, accounts of Scottish overseas missionaries coupled firmly nation and Empire across the genders.[4] These were identities of the Union state. In John M. Mackenzie's terms, the British Empire, for the Scots, reflected English institutions imbued with a Scottish ethos. Importantly, he argues, it gave Scotland a platform through which it could counter its large southern neighbour.[5]

## EMPIRE AND HOME IDENTITIES

Nationalist campaigning throughout the second half of the century pointed to the Union state being an Empire state, to the detriment of domestic affairs. The nationalists of the 1850s worried that each and every question of Empire was dominating parliamentary time. In the 1880s and 1890s these grievances were growing. To show how the Imperial Parliament might better manage its affairs, Australian Theodore Napier distributed his pamphlet 'Scotland's Demand for Home Rule' (1892), outlining plans for a local national parliament.[6] Attending a committee meeting of the Scottish Home Rule Association in Edinburgh in June 1895, Napier heard it was the Australian colonies that were the most

---

[2] W. Farr, 'The Income and Property Tax', *Journal of the Statistical Society of London*, vol. 16, no. 1 (March 1853), 4. Income tax was reintroduced in 1842.

[3] T. M. Devine, 'Imperial Scotland', in T. M. Devine, ed., *Scotland and the Union, 1707–2007* (Edinburgh, 2008), 112.

[4] E. Breitenbach, *Empire and Scottish Society: The Impact of Foreign Missions at Home, c.1800 to c.1914* (Edinburgh, 2009).

[5] J. M. Mackenzie, 'Essay and Reflection: On Scotland and the Empire', *The International History Review*, vol. 15, no. 4 (November 1993), 732–9.

[6] *The West Australian*, 25 August 1892, 4; *Northern Territory Times and Gazette*, 23 September 1892, 2, 3; *The Queenslander*, 10 September 1892, 499.

active supporters of state reform. Letters were read from Sydney and Melbourne, and acknowledgement made of a parcel of pamphlets received by the Imperial Federation League of Victoria. The campaign to mould the Union state into a federation of Greater Britain sought support in England, with the Liverpool branch campaigning in the north as well as posting a short statement to political associations throughout the United Kingdom.[7] The colonial nationalists claimed the clarity of distance to explain the detrimental force of centralized imperial government upon Scotland and themselves:

> We believe that nothing less than a wisely devised and comprehensive scheme of Imperial Federation will meet the case, and preserve the Colonies from drifting from Britain. At the present moment almost all the Colonies are enjoying the blessing of local autonomy or Home Rule. In this respect they have the advantage over the mother country, which, in its incorporate Union, subjects the will and voice of the smaller nationalities of Scotland and Ireland to the will of the largest one, England.[8]

Combining state and ethnicity, Napier identified the relationship of Britain to its colonies as a flow of trade under the Union flag linked by blood.[9] And it was the blood relationship—to the grandfather if not closer—that St Andrews Societies overseas sought when administering succour to the colonial Scot. Throughout the year, the boards in these societies gathered information on those they might help. They held their festivities each November with their governors instructed to wear a cross of St Andrew or a thistle on their left breast. These and related Caledonian societies helped sustain business, social, and religious communities of Scots within the British colonies, as studies of India, South Africa, North and South America, and Australasia have shown. Robert Burns, of course, was also celebrated, most especially leading up to, during, and immediately after the centenary celebrations in 1859. In the Burns Club of New York, the St Andrew's cross was displayed alongside the flag of St George and the Stars and Stripes.[10] Toasts were called for 'the birth day of Nature's own poet'; 'the genius of Burns'; 'Scotland, the land of our fathers'; and 'America, the land we live in'. In the same city that year, the Burns Anniversary Association met in Mozart Hall on Broadway, declaring there had been but two great kings of Scotland: John Knox and Robert Burns. These were customarily gatherings of men before equality was sought later in the century; until then, women were invited to admire the table settings and room decor, and to parade in their gowns, but to do so in advance of the revelry. Later, in 1880, New York's Central Park welcomed a statue of Burns alongside an earlier monument honouring Walter Scott. Scots, it would appear, were never alone in Empire. And through the use of the electrical telegraph mid-century, there were a good deal of fraternal greetings—in Scots—exchanged between suppers and balls alike.

---

[7]  *The Glasgow Herald*, 10 June 1895, 6.
[8]  T. Napier, *The Arrogance of Englishmen, a bar to Imperial Federation: Also Remarks on the Apathy of Scotsmen* (Edinburgh, 1895), 4.
[9]  Napier, *Arrogance of Englishmen*, 3.
[10]  *The New York Times*, 26 January 1858.

Scottish identity within Empire employed a standard set of ethnic markers to bring Scots together in the clubs, societies, and associations characteristic of civil society. Being part of the Union state's colonial endeavour brought a heightened Britishness alongside a version of Scottish national identity embedded in new communities. The familiar toast to the 'twa lands' at Burns suppers is suggestive of this. Scots at home also looked to Burns to hear and read their own language. With local and national administration underlining the dominance of English, Scots was more likely to be heard and read outside of the state. Janet Little (1759–1813), the Scotch Milkmaid, and the often-anonymous Carolina Oliphant (1766–1845), better known as Lady Nairne, followed Burns in producing popular verse in Scots. Coming from contrasting social worlds, addressing different audiences, Little and Oliphant brought folk memories into their writing, linking contemporary and historical life. Furthermore, it was Walter Scott, the anonymous creator of the Waverley series from 1814, who established the genre of the historical novel. From an initial print run of one thousand, *Waverley*'s success blossomed tenfold before the year was out. The Scottish historical novel was a literature that reflected the ancient nation now in its Union state. Scott's sentimental Jacobitism allied to a strong political unionism came out in his novels, diaries, and letters as it did throughout the gathering of the clans he organized for George IV in 1822, the first visit of a Hanoverian monarch to Scotland. Scott's childhood friend Jane Porter (1776–1850) had projected an earlier claim to the creation of the historical novel with *Thaddeus of Warsaw* (1803) and *The Scottish Chiefs* (1810), a novel about William Wallace, although the lack of temporal sensitivity compromised both romances. Like Scott, her novels mixed Jacobite romanticism with monarchical and military loyalty that was singularly British. Porter was an Anglo-Scot, born in Durham, raised in Edinburgh, who didn't write her seminal romance on Wallace until she returned south. Her most renowned brother, Sir Robert Ker Porter, made his name first as an artist of the epic *Storming of Seringapatam* (1800) in London, later becoming British consul to Venezuela (1825–40). Jane believed her writings embodied the stories of Scotland's Jacobite widows living on in Edinburgh after the '45 and the 'wholesome knowledge in the country, pervading all ranks'.[11] Continually reprinted by publishing houses in England, Ireland, and North America, *The Scottish Chiefs* sold steadily throughout the century, gaining the author plaudits but not wealth. Its success above all other tales of Wallace in this period, or of anything else she wrote, came from its rootedness in the social memory of the Scots within Union. Porter rejected the darker claims of nationalism, but insisted Scotland, like England, should celebrate its heroes lest her people 'sink in the estimation of nations abroad'.[12]

Translated into German, Hungarian, and French, Porter wrote in English not Scots. But the use of Scots under the Union state was part of a wide and varied canon that grappled with constitutional and economic variation alongside fears of social dislocation.

---

[11] J. Porter, *The Scottish Chiefs* (London, 1831), iii–iv.
[12] G. Morton, 'The Scottish Nation of Jane Porter in her International Setting', in J. A. Campbell, E. Ewan, and H. Parker, eds., *The Shaping of Scottish Identities: Family, Nation, and the Worlds Beyond* (Guelph, 2011), 228–9.

Dialects were different throughout the country. Gaelic in the north-west of Scotland struggled to engage the new society, but did so with some success. The inexorable progress of English was not simply linear. Words popped up that marked a Scoticizing of English. The most obvious would appear in broadsides where lassies were always 'bonnie' or, as in *Scotland Yet* (c.1860), past stories were best: 'Gae bring my guid auld harp ance mair'. Perhaps after Burns's death the *Harp of Caledonia* (c.1831) was no more, 'yet still his song f'rae shore to shore/Lives bright in Caledonia'. The Kailyard literature would turn this further into a pawky (crafty) appeal, stingingly sentimental, and non-political, but it would also be a sign of Scottish customs persisting within English literature. For Tom Nairn this genre was symptomatic of Scotland's failed political nationalism, but that is a hasty judgement. Having identified the disconnection between Scottish civil society and its Union state, Nairn idealizes a nationalism based on a unitary nation-state axis.[13] But identity flowed from an amalgam of structures that sustained nineteenth-century nationalism, favouring more Union, not less. The concept of Unionist-nationalism, as I have shown elsewhere, explains this identity.[14] Kailyard fitted such a world, where the language of Scots was employed as an ethnic marker in the works of Scott and John Galt, but used without discrimination in provincial newspapers and periodicals discussing the political and philosophical issues of the day, an important argument from William Donaldson.[15] English was dominating, but older tongues were wagging in the homes, and perhaps even in the afterlife: one prescient old widow from Sutherlandshire met with a United Presbyterian missionary in Edinburgh just days before she died in a tenement collapse. She spoke of her life soon ending and her Saviour's love, looking forward to her heavenly inheritance, speaking the 139th psalm from the Gaelic psalm-book 'which was read with true pathos'.[16]

## THE UNION STATE IDENTITY

The Union state, as it projected an identity of itself and for itself to the Scottish people, was one of constitutional defence against a foreign threat and the protection and promotion of Empire. It was an identity where the independence of the Presbyterian Church within a broader defence of Protestantism was central, although not exclusive. The Scots language was buffeted between nation and state, and Scottish culture and literature reflected this reality just as English confirmed its position as the lingua franca of bureaucracy. While the key features of identity-formation might be so rooted, and the increasing solidity of the Hanoverian line upon the throne recognized, the contemporary experience of the state was far from straightforward. Colin Kidd contends that the ideology of

[13] T. Nairn, *The Break-up of Britain* (London, 1981), 148–69.

[14] G. Morton, *Unionist-Nationalism: Governing Urban Scotland, 1830–1860* (East Linton, 1999), 54–7.

[15] W. Donaldson, *Popular Fiction in Victorian Literature: Language, Fiction and the Press* (Aberdeen, 1986).

[16] *History of Broughton Place United Presbyterian Church* (Edinburgh, 1872), 305, 314.

Unionism can be equated to cross-party support for the British state, but that it was encountered in many different ways.[17] However much we can date the making of Scots and their fellow islanders as Britons by the time the eighteen-year-old Victoria took the throne of her uncle in 1837, and no matter how much the Scots at various times throughout the century believed their national identity and languages were on the way out, resilience not fragility has been the reality. Scottish identity was corralled into political union before the ideology of nationalism of the late eighteenth century. From 1800 not only did these political ideas circulate, and were read about in their revolutionary reality, but the state was to expand its reach into society both administratively and through the electoral franchise. Mercantilism receded as free trade overcame the Corn Laws and other excise restrictions to stimulate economic growth through the bounty of Empire. In the philosophical view of John Stuart Mill, writing in the revolutionary year of 1848, international trade would substitute confrontation for mutual interdependence among nations.[18] The imperatives of free trade prioritized economic growth over statist ideology, and held back centrist impulses. Despite all the developments in central government that restructured society, from mid-century the British public expenditure per head of population remained substantially unchanged up to 1880.[19]

Where the Scots did experience greater transformation in their Union state was with their social institutions. Appointed to the Regius Chair of Medical Jurisprudence at Edinburgh University in 1820, and after two decades of further advocacy, W. P. Alison condemned the smallness of sums the poor law was distributing. He debated with Reverend Thomas Chalmers whether the state or the individual (or parish) should take on an increased burden. Reform in 1845 favoured Alison, moving the administration of poor relief from the Church of Scotland to the newly created Board of Supervision in Edinburgh. Compulsory legal assessment—rather than the voluntary system employed under the Church—central inspection, and institutional accommodation followed tenets first established in England, but were no mirror image. The Scots wanted to augment, not restrict help, and their costs inevitably increased: they were not compelled to build poorhouses and were generally more favourable to outdoor relief. The new parochial boards were elective bodies, although older property owners still dominated. The Board of Supervision was staffed with Scots—Lord Provosts of Edinburgh and Glasgow, the Solicitor General for Scotland, and various county sheriffs. And while giving credence to the centralization of Scotland's administration, the Board still worked within the handshakes and procedures of earlier more ad hoc times.[20] The reform of public health would similarly come under reforming pressure from methodologies and imperatives first applied south of the border, but the independence of the Edinburgh medical profession, and the dependence on the localities to put in place the sanitary and infrastructural reforms, again meant any solutions were later than in England and indigenous to Scotland.

[17] C. Kidd, *Union and Unionisms: Political Thought in Scotland, 1500–2000* (Cambridge, 2008), 19.
[18] J. S. Mill, *Principles of Political Economy* (London, 1848), 25–6.
[19] E. J. Hobsbawm, *Industry and Empire* (London, 1968), 233.
[20] J. Mitchell, *Governing Scotland: The Invention of Administrative Devolution* (London, 2003), 12–13.

# THE LOCAL STATE AND THE UNION

That the Scots had a Union not a unitary state is crucial to the national identity that formed, a point emphasized by James Mitchell.[21] Conglomerate states such as this were not unknown in early modern Europe, but the persistence of the Anglo-Scottish Union has been remarkable.[22] The state did centralize over the nineteenth century, but resistance was met at each stage, and rather than having its role diminished, the local state maintained and gained governance. By 1911, instructively, still there were only 944 civil servants or government officials in Scotland.[23]

Scholars have given attention to the boards and departments that gave Scotland its administrative structure in the eighteenth century: arguments that can be extended onwards even with the local/central government balance in flux. Being close to those they governed was a tension that sustained county and burgh reform. Scotland gained improved powers to administer its urban areas with burgh police legislation: Aberdeen (1795), Glasgow (1800), Greenock (1801), Port Glasgow (1803), Edinburgh (1805), Leith and Paisley (both 1806), Kirkcaldy, (1811), and Dundee (1824) each took on powers, and then on various occasions thereafter further capabilities, to protect and enhance the built environment.[24] The towns and cities were reinforced by Scotland-wide police legislation in 1847, 1850, 1857, 1862, and 1892. Hurried by past and impending town-hall bankruptcies—Aberdeen in 1817, Edinburgh in 1833—local government was reformed in 1833 (two years before reform of the boroughs in England). Introducing a similar but not identical franchise to that passed a year earlier for Westminster, the legislation left intact the police system to sit alongside the town councils. The resulting administrative duplication was sometimes problematic—as were the Joint Trusts created to deal with cross-boundary utilities from the 1870s—but both were preferable to the frustrations of guiding local legislation through Westminster. The outcome of the Town Councils (Scotland) Act of 1900 was a regular structure applied to the administrative running of the towns, which established a standard constitution of provost supported by bailies, and councillors elected from a system of adult male suffrage, later expanded in 1907 to include some women, removing the Police Boards and many of the Joint Trusts by 1929.[25]

Local administration also gained volume from the Union state passing down powers of intervention that were increasingly bureaucratic and systematic. A regular account of births, deaths, and marriages began in 1855 with the General Registrar Office for Scotland admin-

---

[21] J. Mitchell, *Strategies for Self-Government: The Campaigns for a Scottish Parliament* (Edinburgh, 1996), 38–9.

[22] S. Murdoch and J. R. Young, 'Union and Identity: Scotland in a Social and International Context', in *Angles on the English-Speaking World*, new series, vol. 7, 'The State of the Union: Scotland, 1707–2007', eds. J. Sevaldsen and J. Rahbek Rasmussen (Copenhagen, 2007), 35–6.

[23] T. C. Smout, *A Century of the Scottish People, 1830–1950* (London, 1986), 110.

[24] D. G. Barrie, *Police in the Age of Improvement: Police Development and the Civic Tradition in Scotland, 1775–1865* (Cullompton, 2008), 92, 106–9.

[25] Qualification of Women (County and Town Councils) (Scotland) Act 1907 (c. 48).

istering what had previously been left to the parish minister.[26] The equivalent office had begun registrations in England in 1837. Westminster channelled the hitherto large local legislation through the Local Government Board in 1870, rivalling the Poor Law Boards as the outwards sign of centralized government. The creation of the Scottish Education Department in 1872 and the Scottish Office in 1885, located in London, were part of the delayed and irregular recalibration of government north of the border. The Scottish Office started off with Charles Gordon-Lennox, Duke of Richmond and Gordon, as Scottish Secretary, despite him having argued there was no need for the post. The department was no more than a secretariat to support the decision making of the Local Government and Health Boards in Edinburgh, but would gain responsibility, size, and budget to structure Scottishness after the 1930s. As Mitchell makes clear, the Scottish Office paved the administrative path to devolution—a route too often ignored by scholars. In the Scots' experience of the Union state, local administration mattered to their lives; and it didn't always matter—despite what contemporary nationalists proclaimed—that Westminster's attention was directed elsewhere.

The final element of local administration took place in civil society: not directly part of the Union state, Morton contends, but empowered, enshrined, and legitimated by it. The Union state set the parameters and registration for a range of friendly societies and voluntary associations. Often framed in moral and religious terms, these actions confirmed a temperate, industrious, and pious life as an idealized Scottish identity, sustaining religiosity inside and outside the Kirk.[27] Help for the fallen, the poor, the disabled, the intemperate, the irreligious, the mad, and the criminal, along with a span of gender-specific, class, worker, and fraternal fellowships, were part of society's governance. Not by the Union state directly, but in its midnight shadow—its legal, administrative, and ideological framework.[28] In a significant supplement to this argument, S. Karly Kehoe identifies civil society as the locale in which Scottish Catholics secured their culture within a confirmed loyalty to the (Protestant) British constitution after 1840. As she explains, alongside the provision of education by women religious and a range of philanthropic and cultural associations, Scottish Catholic groups appropriated St Andrew and other symbols to display their Scottishness within the Union state.[29]

In a note of caution, Krishan Kumar argues that the concept of civil society is undermined by its elasticity. The interaction between state and society is crucial to the nation, he confirms, but wonders whether theorists are better advised exploring this through concepts of democracy, citizenship, and constitutionalism.[30] He further recommends

[26] Registration of Births, Deaths, and Marriages (Scotland) Act 1854 17 and 18, Vict., cap. 80.

[27] G. Morton, 'Identity out of Place', in T. Griffiths and G. Morton, eds., *A History of Everyday Life in Scotland, 1800–1900* (Edinburgh, 2010), 263–70, 279–80.

[28] G. Morton and R. J. Morris, 'Civil Society, Governance and Nation: 1832–1914', in R. A. Houston and W. W. J. Knox, eds., *The New Penguin History of Scotland: From the Earliest Times to the Present Day* (London, 2001), 356–7, 380–9, 398ff.

[29] S. K. Kehoe, *Creating a Scottish Church: Catholicism, Gender and Ethnicity in Nineteenth-Century Scotland* (Manchester, 2010), *passim*.

[30] K. Kumar, 'Civil Society Again: A Reply to Christopher Bryant's "Social Self-Organization, Civility and Sociology"', *The British Journal of Sociology*, vol. 45, no. 1 (March 1994), 130.

reflection upon the adaption of Britishness along with the Union state's evolution, and here perhaps these alternative concepts are employed more fittingly. Britishness was fluid, not static, not a cultural, not an ethnic nationalism, but a civic one. Or, in Kidd's view, Britishness was a utilitarian identity related to state not nation.[31] But while Scottishness is defaulted to nation, neither, it can be countered, was it excluded from state: civil society directs attention to its local and national tiers, whereas democracy, citizenship, and constitutionalism point to a necessary Britishness.

The term 'local government' did not supplant 'local administration' in the language of statute for Scotland until 1889. Local-government reform in England and Wales evolved from democratization of local affairs—rather than decentralization—and carried overtones of 'government'. In Scotland, although not wholly the case, much of what became local government trickled down from the centre and was named 'administration'.[32] Two routes, two nomenclatures, but in each experience national identity was based on the state's multidirectional relationship with society: reflecting Scottishness and Britishness.

# PARLIAMENTARY REFORM
# AND POLITICAL IDENTITY

There were no fireworks, or even much awareness, to greet the centenary of the Union in 1807; the abolition of slavery under the lead of William Wilberforce dominated public as well as parliamentary debate. Yet, in the years ahead the Union would be invoked as Scots politicians debated the structures within which their government operated.[33] William Dundas, nephew of the first Viscount Melville, summoned the Treaty's articles against the Sinecure Offices Bill of 1812, legislation that would alter how pensions and sinecures were proffered to those in public office. Fearing his argument might be regarded as 'invidious', still he could not 'suffer the rights of the Scottish people'.[34] Along with the other institutions to survive 1707, Dundas described the Sinecures Office as being 'the son of remuneration' to the Scottish people and no 'act of grace and favour'. He accused his opponents of never even thinking about the implication for the Union in proposing abolition. Here greater transparency was an assault upon the Union state that undermined the office of an independent monarchy lost a century more distant. The debate continued on unprincipled favouritism—but by choosing not to delve further into the

---

[31]  K. Kumar, *The Making of English National Identity* (Cambridge, 2003), 142, 147–9; C. Kidd, *Subverting Scotland's Past: Scottish Whig Historians and the Creation of an Anglo-British Identity, c.1689–c.1830* (Cambridge, 1993), 206–7, 214–15.

[32]  *The Laws of Scotland. Stair Memorial Encyclopaedia (SME) Reissue.* Local Government—Jean McFadden (Edinburgh, 1999), para vii, 11, para 10.

[33]  G. Pentland, *Radicalism, Reform and National Identity in Scotland, 1820–1833* (Woodbridge, 2008).

[34]  Sinecure Offices Bill. HC Deb 4 May 1812, vol. 22, cc. 1,159–78.

claims of loyalty, one opponent withdrew 'lest the headless ghosts of a Charles and a Montrose should be conjured up in the imaginations of the members for North Britain'.[35] The impetus had been to reduce costs, to reward talent, and to remove sinecures, but it was inimical to the Scottish nation because it weakened the influence of the Crown in the constitution.

This debate on the Union state highlights an element of trust that marked these pre-reform years: a belief that England would not be so disingenuous as to bring harm to the interests of the Scottish nation. On a discussion of heritable jurisdictions in 1826, Dundas again bemoaned that 'after these articles of Union, so solemnly ratified, was England now to violate them? Was the richer country to turn upon the poorer? The stronger upon the weaker?'[36] He could not believe England would be guilty of such injustice. It was the kind of faith that nationalists later in the century doubted could ever be possible. But at times it was difficult for the Scottish parliamentarians to maintain the moral high ground when so distant from their nation. Continuing the debate on Edinburgh's franchise, James Abercromby, first Baron Dunfermline, felt he could be counted a Scottish MP while representing an English constituency; others felt differently.[37] As the elements of franchise reforms and democratization were debated, comment was made that much of this was taking place in London, not Edinburgh. Legislation passed from Westminster had obvious implications for Scottish identity, being both the source of change and the obstacle to that change. Scottish parliamentarians were caught in this flux, alternating from praise to disapprobation in the press and broadside printings.[38]

Critiques of the political process began in earnest in the lead up to franchise reform. *The Loyal Reformers Gazette* first roared into print on 7 May 1831 from its offices in Glasgow, promoting the case of parliamentary reform while doing its best to avoid the attentions of the stamp office in Edinburgh. Its editors observed the path of legislation for England and especially for Scotland, their biggest fear being that the House of Lords—where 'the last stand of bigotry in antiquity is to be made'—would reject the will of the Commons.[39] Their loyalty was to William IV for the pressure he put on the peers to back reform. The newspaper's banner proclaimed: 'The King and the People/Stand and surround the King!/Through peril at home and abroad!/Close to the patriot Monarch cling/Who will not be led or awed/To do or to suffer wrong!'[40] But when William seemed not to provide the action they demanded, his title was blacked out from their front page. And while the paper was loyal to the Hanoverian constitution, it would willingly summon memories of Wallace to fight its cause.[41]

[35] Ibid., cc. 1,162.
[36] Representation of Edinburgh. HC Deb 13 April 1826, vol. 15, cc. 163–91 (c. 170).
[37] Ibid., cc. 188–9.
[38] *Anither New Sang* (c.1830–1840).
[39] *The Loyal Reformers' Gazette*, 11 November 1831, 289. My thanks go to Mark Dorsey for this reference.
[40] *The Loyal Reformers' Gazette*, 24 March 1832, 273.
[41] *The Loyal Reformers' Gazette*, 7 April 1832, 309.

Still there were protests after franchise reform that too much time was given to the interests of Irish over Scotch members, even with 1,270 hours allocated to debate Scotland in the 1832 session of Parliament compared to 918 hours in 1831.[42] Scottish business, it seemed obvious to those who took an interest, was suppressed, or abridged. Before the franchise was further expanded to include the skilled worker—in 1867 for England, 1868 for Scotland—it was much easier to manipulate parliamentary representatives, as had been the case before 1832. On the eve of the 1852 general election, the influence of faction was blamed in Edinburgh for not making the Protestant religion central to Parliament's decision making: 'a small but noisy and determined band of Papists in the House of Commons arrest the whole business of Parliament'. And as the nationalists argued for Scotland's rights to be treated equally with those of England, so the defenders of the Protestant faith wanted their own coterie, 'a resolute band of men in the House of Commons who understand, value, and are determined to defend the principles of the Reformation'.[43] The ten years of strife that led up to the Disruption in the Church of Scotland in 1843 had demonstrated in the most volatile terms the seriousness with which Scots took Presbyterianism to their hearts and minds. Along with the highland land crisis of the 1880s, I. G. C. Hutchison identifies the Disruption as the only other Scottish issue of sufficient importance to warrant extended discussion in Westminster, despite the presence of four Scottish prime ministers over the century. Even then, Parliament's concern was with its impact upon the Church of England than the finer details of Presbyterian theology.[44] To some, the Disruption was the single most significant nationalist event in the period. The decision by the House of Lords to uphold heritable authority over the presbytery led over 40 per cent of ministers to leave their manses and take nearly half of Scotland's national Church with them. The rhetoric of Union, Wallace, and Bruce was only occasionally combined with ecclesiastical arguments, yet it was a national and an international movement.[45] John M. Mackenzie claims its impact to have been extraordinary throughout the empire.[46] The Reverend Dr Cunningham travelled to New York in 1844 to raise awareness and funds for the newly created Free Church, a tour that was reported as far afield as in the New Zealand newspapers.[47] It is perhaps one of the most insular of debates within Presbyterianism's history, yet it was incomplete without the support of Scots around the globe, a feature that George Shepperson examined with evidence of donations amounting to around £3,000 coming from the southern slave-owning states of America.[48]

[42] 'The Reform Ministry and the Reformed Parliament', in *The Edinburgh Review*, 5th ed. (London, 1833), vol. 8.

[43] *General Election. Address of the Scottish Reformation to the Electors of Scotland* (Edinburgh, 1852), 1–2.

[44] I. G. C. Hutchison, 'Anglo-Scottish Political Relations in the Nineteenth Century, c.1815–1914', in T. C. Smout, ed., *Anglo-Scottish Relations from 1603 to 1900* (London, 2005), 261–2.

[45] S. J. Brown and M. Fry, eds., *Scotland in the Age of the Disruption* (Edinburgh, 1993).

[46] Mackenzie, 'On Scotland and the Empire', 727.

[47] *The Southern Cross*, 31 August 1844, 4.

[48] G. Shepperson, 'The Free Church and American Slavery', *The Scottish Historical Review*, vol. 30, no. 110, Part 2 (October 1951), 126.

# NATIONALISM WITHIN THE UNION STATE

The radical newspapers framed the franchise fight in constitutional terms of Union and Crown, and it was not too dissimilar to arguments found in the urban and provincial press. Free from the newspaper stamp tax in 1855 to publish daily, these organs of debate facilitated greater focus on the operation of the central state. The electrical telegraph allowed London news to be more quickly incorporated into the provincial papers; the rail journey from Edinburgh to London was nine hours (in 1888, in competition, the *Flying Scotsman* reduced this to under seven and a half hours). The queen could take the train all the way to Royal Deeside by 1862 and there conduct the business of state, much to the chagrin both of her ministers and *The Times*. Greater immediacy and familiarity with Westminster meant the state's operation came increasingly to reflect Scotland's national identity. There were two attempts to organize this identity into associational form. The home-rule decades of the 1880s and 1890s found the closest link between party politics and the rationale for a devolved legislative Parliament. The earlier phase was in the 1850s and centred on the National Association for the Vindication of Scottish Rights. Its figurehead was the Tory peer Archibald William Montgomerie, thirteenth Earl of Eglinton and first Earl of Winton. Like the Association's co-secretaries James and John Grant, who toyed with the Jacobite sympathies of their grandfather, Montgomerie was an intellectual romantic who flitted between causes. His public renown rested on the organization of a medieval spectacle on his family estate in 1839, drawing one hundred thousand (subsequently rather wet) spectators; in 1852 he was Lord Lieutenant of Ireland.[49] For this group of nationalists, Union came to be framed as the nation's future. This developed from an argument that administrative centralization was undermining the otherwise beneficial local independence established upon institutional separateness. The provosts and councillors from burgh and county councils bulked out its office-bearers, arguing for greater administrative powers of operation to come to them.[50] If the principle of union was right, but its operation undermined, then there was common cause between the localities. But if the principle of union were flawed, then it would be uncertain that local government benefited from legislative power returning to Edinburgh—that, after all, was centralization, too. In one of a series of letters sent to the Home Secretary, Lord Palmerston, the Glasgow lawyer and later Wallace monument campaigner William Burns argued that he favoured local not central government, while comrades feared the 'crushing policy of centralization' that only a 'just observance of the Treaty of Union' could prevent.[51] Their objection was that public business in the northern

---

[49] M. S. Millar, 'Montgomerie, Archibald William, thirteenth earl of Eglinton and first earl of Winton (1812–1861)', *Oxford Dictionary of National Biography* (Oxford, 2004).

[50] 'Address to the People' (Edinburgh, 1855), 8–18.

[51] 'A North Briton's Reply to Lord Palmerston', in *A Tract for the Times. Scottish Rights and Honour Vindicated, in letters to Viscount Palmerston, 'The Times', and 'Caledonian Mercury'* (Glasgow, 1854), 29; Red Lion [John Grant sen.], *Scotland and 'The Times'* (Edinburgh, 1853).

part of the United Kingdom was being ignored, that Scotland was subjugated to the will of English courts, and that a gradual dissolution of the Scottish character was the result. Campaigning took place through the press, with a series of articles sent to the Glasgow and Edinburgh newspapers, *The Times*, and to Scotland's provincial press. This, the clearest statement of the Unionist-nationalist position, came from an analysis of the Union state being overburdened and thus forced to gather in more power: 'the dreaded system of imperial centralization—the appointment, by the *state*, in the different localities, of government officials to manage *local* affairs'.[52]

The movement was short lived, breaking up as British engagement in the Crimea in the mid-1850s became more burdensome. Its members scattered, some into the committee charged with raising subscriptions for a national monument to William Wallace (beginning 1856, built 1869), the councillors to engage with administering an increasingly bureaucratic set of structures either devolved or empowered from the centre. Wallace was commemorated with statues throughout lowland Scotland: from Dryburgh (1814) to Aberdeen (1888), from Ayr (1819, 1831, and 1837) to Robroyston (1900). Burns would be first commemorated in stone in Edinburgh in 1831 and much more so overseas. The nationalists and the cultural movement that followed mixed Liberal progression with Tory preservation, the argument of Lindsay Paterson.[53] Burns and Wallace were modern democratic heroes who also personified the unchanging humanity of the Scottish character and the nation's social structure. When the Union was next invoked by a political cause, it was pushed along by a central government trying to impose a national Parliament on one part of the kingdom; but it was Ireland not Scotland being favoured.

## THE SCOTTISH HOME RULE ASSOCIATION

In January 1884 there had gathered an impressive array of Scotland's nobility, Conservative and Liberal MPs, plus representatives of the parochial boards, town councils, and public bodies, all packing the Free Assembly Hall in Edinburgh under the banner of a 'National Meeting'.[54] Their aim was to create a separate Department of State for Scotland. Edinburgh's Lord Provost, Sir George Harrison, argued there ought to be more than one national life in the British nation. He was prompted to action by concern that it was difficult to pass a Scottish Bill without £10,000 being spent on it, and the Scots were proud of their separate institutions from England. Playing to the crowd, he added that the English were welcome to their own institutions, those that suited them better. The

---

[52] Morton, *Unionist-Nationalism*, 133–54 (quotation at p. 150, original emphasis).

[53] L. Paterson, *The Autonomy of Modern Scotland* (Edinburgh, 1994), 65.

[54] *Convention of Royal Burghs of Scotland. The National Meeting in Favour of the Creation of a Separate Department of State for Scotland Held Within the Free Assembly Hall, Edinburgh, On 16th January 1884* (Edinburgh, 1900).

future Scottish Secretary and British Prime Minister A. J. Balfour supported the need for more satisfactory arrangements for the better administration of Scotland. He answered the charge that the inevitable ending of their arguments would be something akin to Home Rule, declaring 'all in this room, like him, were at one in thinking that no legislative act had been so fruitful of good consequences to the countries concerned, as the act of Union between Scotland and England'.[55] Prime Minister Gladstone made noises in favour of Scotland's government during the campaign, in order to secure his parliamentary seat in Midlothian (1879–1880, 1885, and 1890), but was reluctant to follow through lest he jeopardize his dealings with Ireland. In frustration, the Scottish Home Rule Association was formed by a group of disaffected Liberals in 1886.

In introducing the Government of Ireland Bill on 7 June that year, Gladstone asked his opponents to consider just who the Unionists were and who were the Separatists. He likened the debates in the popular press to those that circled the 1832 franchise reform when 'it was conscientiously and honestly believed by great masses of men, and intelligent men, too, that the Bill absolutely involved the destruction of the Monarchy'.[56] As with the Scottish rights society in the 1850s, home rulers at the end of the century aimed to resist rather than encourage separation. Much debate in 1890 focused on the cost and challenges of obtaining passage for Scotland's private legislation. Dr Gavin Clark, the Crofter MP for Caithness, saw the process as affecting the welfare of the Scottish people, with decisions often made against the wishes of the Scottish representatives. The desire was there to keep the Imperial Parliament, but so too to devolve Scotland's domestic affairs.[57] When Dr Donald MacGregor, the MP for Inverness-shire, requested of Gladstone in 1893 that he consider home rule all round as a means of taking local affairs out from the purview of the imperial Parliament, while supporting devolution as a good thing when a 'practical shape' can be obtained, the prime minister was unconvinced there was sufficient information for all parts of Great Britain to enable a decision to be made.[58] MacGregor's impetus was on learning that Burgh Police and Public Health Bills were unable to be debated in the current parliamentary session, warning that the unreformed legislation was accounting for thousands of preventable deaths.[59] He claimed Scotland was at least a quarter of a century behind England as a result. Liquor, grocers' licences, land tenure, reform of the recent Crofter's Act (1886), a Scotch Allotment Bill to match the rights of agricultural labourers in England, access to mountains and native heath, were all being neglected. It was estimated that with two hundred Private Bills allotted only ten days in the current parliamentary session, not more than 5 per cent would have a fair chance of being put before the House.[60] Even discussion of the Indian budget, Britain's imperial showpiece, was once delayed until the

[55]  Ibid., 24.
[56]  Government of Ireland Bill, Introduced into the House by Gladstone on 7 June 1886.
[57]  Adjourned Debate. HC Deb 19 February 1890, vol. 341, cc. 677–724.
[58]  Gladstone's debate on Home Rule from House of Commons, 19 December 1893, vol. 19.
[59]  HC Deb 19 February 1890, vol. 341, cc. 677–724 (678).
[60]  Ibid. (679).

end of an already busy session, and thus 'while the Anglo-Saxon race will dominate the world', MacGregor insisted:

> I feel that unless something is done to draw the bond closer, by and by in the race of nationalities, we may find ourselves in the background, unless something is done to give to every portion of the kingdom the management of its own domestic affairs.[61]

Loyalty to Britain was a familiar cry. The challenge was never to persuade Gladstone to forget Ireland, but to include Scotland's needs upon something approaching equal footing: 'Shame! Scotland Shame! to be the slave/of every canting English knave.'[62]

## The 'Member for Scotland'

The nationalists never had the membership numbers or sufficient representatives at Westminster to succeed by the ballot box or the division lobby, but this did not mean a politicized identity was silent. However ordinary Scots, local or national politicians, or nationalist associations interacted with their state, identity was forged in the complexities that flowed from the Union formation. To replicate this relationship, scholars have extended their examination to all its aspects: Empire, Whitehall, the Scottish Office, local administration, the local and national boards, civil society, and the spiritual challenge to temporal authority. All are unions within the Union state; and it is to this variation that analysis has turned to discern Scotland's 'missing' nationalism.

Building on this multidirectional approach, one possible means to further nuance an understanding of identity is to direct analysis to the level of the individual. A. P. Cohen conceives of national identity as a personal claim to 'my identity' and to 'my view of the world'.[63] It is a method that may guide scholars away from a current quandary, for while H. J. Hanham, Nicolas Phillipson, and Christopher Harvie have published pioneering work on the characters that peopled the nationalist movements of the nineteenth century, their analysis pre-dates how the Union state is now conceived.[64] Not only has the concept of 'personal nationalism' the potential to reinvigorate some benchmark evidence, the scope to include all, irrespective of party or affiliation, foregrounds the individual in Scotland's political identity.

Singling out one person who lived long enough and was involved sufficiently with Scotland's politics to exemplify personal nationalism, then Duncan McLaren makes a suitable choice. Born in Dunbartonshire in 1800, he spent his adult life in

---

[61] HC Deb 19 February 1890, vol. 341, cc. 677–724 (682).

[62] 'Is Scotland to get Home Rule?' (c.1870–1890).

[63] A. P. Cohen, 'Personal Nationalism: A Scottish View of Some Rites, Rights, and Wrongs', *American Ethnologist*, 23, 4 (1996), 803.

[64] H. J. Hanham, *Scottish Nationalism* (London, 1969); N. T. Phillipson, 'Nationalism and Ideology', in J. N. Wolfe, ed., *Government and Nationalism in Scotland* (Edinburgh, 1969); C. Harvie, *Scotland and Nationalism* (London, 1977; 4th edn., 2004).

Edinburgh, starting out as a draper. He was elected to Edinburgh's Town Council in the first post-reform election (1833), rising to become provost in 1851 until 1854. He first tried for election to Westminster in 1852, eventually succeeding in 1865, remaining incumbent until retiring in 1881. For his extensive knowledge of his country and the British Parliament, he was known as the 'Member for Scotland'.

McLaren has been described as an energetic Free Churchman, who was anti-drink, anti-establishment, anti-trade union, and anti-home rule.[65] His biographer makes much of McLaren's civic-mindedness. Even after leaving Edinburgh City Council, he continued to be active in the city's Chamber of Commerce, the Royal Infirmary, the Trade Protection Society, and his long-standing concern the Merchant Company.

McLaren used statistics not rhetoric to make his case for better parliamentary representation, comparing Scotland's share of taxation with that in 1707, asking 'why should Scotland have one-twelfth of the members when she pays for one-eighth of the taxes?'[66] Since 1868, Scotland had sent sixty representatives to Westminster, with three urban constituencies—Glasgow (three), Edinburgh (two), and Dundee (two)—returning more than one member. McLaren calculated that if determined by relative taxation, Scotland should send seventy-eight representatives, or by population figures it should be sixty-eight. His support for reform stemmed from a speech made to the National Convention in 1853 when he pushed for the re-creation of the office of Secretary for Scotland. He noted that Scotland had had its great Officer of State before the Union and her Secretary of State after the Union, and now it should be restored. His biographer J. B. Mackie claimed that McLaren joined the movement not out of patriotism, but because he had studied the issued 'historically and practically'. Later, having been consulted on the matter by the Scottish Boards inquiry in 1869, McLaren confirmed and then maintained his position until the post was created in 1885.[67]

Where we especially see nuance in this civic-minded proponent of local national administration was in the advance of governmental boards. These, he warned Gladstone, were 'giving birth to well-paid offices that were more or less sinecures beyond public control'. McLaren bemoaned the fact that the boards were overstaffed—identifying the Lunacy and the Prison Boards in particular—and that public opinion was never able to penetrate their workings. The efforts of the Fishery Board he branded 'the last fragment of monopolist and Anti-Free Trade principles in Scotland'. He suggested Scotland had outgrown such nursing. And while supporting the Register General Office, he did not understand why the work required three highly paid officials, a chief at £1,000 per annum, a Secretary at £500, and a chief clerk at £337. Similarly, he estimated the Office of Queen's Remembrancer could be done for £900 per annum rather than £1,250 with a clerk at £610 per annum alongside.[68]

[65]  G. C. Boase, 'McLaren, Duncan (1800–1886)', rev. H. C. G. Matthew, *Oxford Dictionary of National Biography* (Oxford, 2004).

[66]  J. B. Mackie, *The Life and Work of Duncan McLaren*, 2 vols. (London, 1888), vol. ii, 59, 61, 118–19.

[67]  Mackie, *Duncan McLaren*, vol. ii, 122; Mitchell, *Governing Scotland*, 21.

[68]  Mackie, *Duncan McLaren*, vol. ii, 123–4, 128–9.

Despite retirement, McLaren found sufficient energy in 1884 to join the deputation from the National Convention that visited Gladstone to make their case.[69] He had followed a principled life to the end; death came on 26 April 1886, the year the Scottish Home Rule Association pushed the politicization of their arguments firmly toward Scotland's agenda. This individual projected a version of nationalism that was historically based. It was enacted first in civil society and city hall before coming to the fore in the chamber at Westminster. The value he saw in administrative boards was qualified by their tendency toward centralization and functionaryism. His convictions on identity and character had little to do with party policy or compliance with the Whips office or even patriotism. Yet, the Member for Scotland was not about to give the Member for Midlothian a free hand to grant home rule for Ireland, while giving nothing of a similar stature to Scotland. His politics privileged the Scottish Secretary, a pre-Union office that would benefit the late-Victorian Imperial Parliament. This was McLaren's personal nationalism. Despite fears raised by an assortment of contemporaries, his personal identity in the Union state did not call out for more.

## FURTHER READING

Devine, T. M., ed., *Scotland and the Union, 1707–2007* (Edinburgh, 2008).

Kidd, C., *Subverting Scotland's Past: Scottish Whig Historians and the Creation of an Anglo-British identity, c.1689–c.1830* (Cambridge, 1993).

Kidd, C., *Union and Unionisms: Political Thought in Scotland, 1500–2000* (Cambridge, 2008).

Mackenzie, J. M., 'Empire and National Identities: The Case of Scotland', *Transactions of the Royal Historical Society*, 6th series, 8 (1998), 215–32.

McCrone, D., *Understanding Scotland: The Sociology of a Nation*, 2nd edn. (London, 2001).

McLean, I., and McMillan, A., *State of the Union: Unionism and the Alternatives in the United Kingdom since 1707* (Oxford, 2005).

Mitchell, J., *Strategies for Self-Government: The Campaigns for a Scottish Parliament* (Edinburgh, 1996).

—— *Governing Scotland: The Invention of Administrative Devolution* (London, 2003).

Morton, G., *Unionist-Nationalism: Governing Urban Scotland, 1830–1860* (East Linton, 1999).

—— 'Identity out of Place', in T. Griffiths and G. Morton, eds., *A History of Everyday Life in Scotland, 1800–1900* (Edinburgh, 2010).

—— and Morris, R. J., 'Civil Society, Governance and Nation: 1832–1914', in R. A. Houston and W. W. J. Knox, eds., *The New Penguin History of Scotland* (London, 2001).

Nairn, T., *The Break-up of Britain* (London, 1981).

Pentland, G., *Radicalism, Reform and National Identity in Scotland, 1820–1833* (Woodbridge, 2008).

Smout, T. C., ed., *Anglo-Scottish Relations from 1603 to 1900* (London, 2005).

---

[69]  Mackie, *Duncan McLaren*, vol. ii, 132–3.

# CHAPTER 26

........................................................................

# IMMIGRANTS

........................................................................

## BEN BRABER

As the nation transformed between 1760 and 1914, large numbers of immigrants settled in Scotland. Several hundred thousand came from Ireland and England. Smaller but still significant groups arrived from India, the British colonies and dependencies, the German and Italian states, and the Russian Empire. The 1911 Census recorded the presence in Scotland of almost four hundred thousand persons born outside the country—about 9 per cent of the total population (Table 26.1).[1]

No comprehensive study has been made of the history of immigrants and their descendants in Scotland. Some groups have been research subjects, mostly at local and regional level. However, English migrants, people from India, British colonies and dependencies, Africans, and Americans have largely escaped the attention of historians.[2] Few studies have made comparisons, involving different groups or contrasting developments in Scotland with what happened elsewhere, which would enable us to determine what were typically Scottish phenomena. This chapter therefore advances an approach that compares experiences of immigrants. It deals with four of the largest groups in the main settlement area before and during the First World War: the Irish, Germans, Russians, and Italians in central Scotland.[3]

---

[1] Population figures are derived from *Census of Great Britain, 1841* (London, 1843); *Census of Great Britain, 1851* (London, 1852); *Census of Scotland, 1861* (Edinburgh, 1864); *Eight Decennial Census of the population of Scotland taken 3rd April 1871* (Edinburgh, 1872); *Ninth Decennial Census of the population of Scotland taken 4th April 1881* (Edinburgh, 1883); *Tenth Decennial Census of the population of Scotland taken 5th April 1891* (Edinburgh, 1893); *Eleventh Decennial Census of the population of Scotland taken 31st March 1901* (Glasgow, 1902–3); *Census of Scotland, 1911: Report on the twelfth decennial census of Scotland* (Edinburgh, 1913). I am grateful to Nico Hampton for his research assistance.

[2] M. Watson, *Being English in Scotland* (Edinburgh, 2003), and M. Watson, R. Harris, and D. Kemp, *Being English in Scotland: A Guide* (Edinburgh, 2004), focus on the second half of the twentieth century. B. Maan, *The New Scots: The Story of Asians in Scotland* (Edinburgh, 1992), reviews individual Asians and a relatively small group of people recorded by the *Census of Scotland, 1911*, vol. ii, xvi, 504, as 'non-Europeans' from India (636 males and 10 females).

[3] The second largest group in 1911, formed by 161,650 English migrants, and the third largest group, made up of 17,890 persons from India, British colonies and dependencies, have to be omitted here because of insufficient evidence.

Table 26.1 Census figures on persons present in Scotland in 1911 who were born outside Scotland

| Birthplace | Total | Males | Females |
|---|---|---|---|
| Ireland | 174,715 | 99,992 | 74,723 |
| England | 161,650 | 82,487 | 79,163 |
| Wales | 3,452 | 1,805 | 1,647 |
| Isle of Man and Channel Islands | 1,105 | 550 | 555 |
| India, British colonies, and dependencies | 17,890 | 8,851 | 9,039 |
| Russia and Poland | 11,032 | 6,520 | 4,512 |
| Italy | 4,594 | 3,103 | 1,491 |
| Germany | 2,362 | 1,509 | 853 |
| USA | 1,176 | 618 | 558 |
| Norway | 996 | 766 | 230 |
| France | 720 | 314 | 406 |
| Denmark | 712 | 554 | 158 |
| Sweden | 711 | 380 | 131 |
| Austria and Hungary | 528 | 386 | 142 |

Smaller groups came from the Netherlands (407: 298 m, 109 f), Switzerland (369: 190 m, 179 f), Spain (300: 227 m, 73 f), and Belgium (137: 87 m, 50 f). Fewer than one hundred persons per country came from Portugal, Turkey, Serbia, Romania, and Bulgaria. The Census also recorded 263 Asians, including 171 from China and 21 from Japan. Fewer than one hundred persons had a birthplace in Africa. The total Scottish population was recorded at 4,365,855.

The Irish, subject of James Handley's pioneering studies, complemented by Brenda Collins and Martin Mitchell,[4] had been traditional migrants in Scotland, but they settled here in large numbers during the nineteenth century, notably in the 1840s—the Famine period—when the migratory swell turned into a wave. The Irish-born population of Scotland as recorded by the Census increased from 126,321 in 1841 to 207,367 persons in 1851 (from 4.8 to 7.1 per cent of the total population). By 1881 the figure had risen to 218,745 (5.9 per cent of the total and generally growing population) (Table 26.2).

Three-quarters of the Irish went to the west of central Scotland, foremost Lanarkshire and Renfrewshire (where in 1841 they already formed 13.1 and 13.2 per cent of the total population). By 1851, 59,801 Irish-born persons, or 28.8 per cent of all the Irish-born in Scotland, constituted 18.2 per cent of the total population of Glasgow. Some nearby towns had smaller, but relatively large and often fluctuating Irish settlements.

[4] J. E. Handley, *The Irish in Modern Scotland* (Cork, 1947); *idem.*, *The Irish in Scotland 1798–1845* (Cork, 1945); B. Collins, 'The Origins of Irish Immigration to Scotland in the Nineteenth and Twentieth Centuries', in T. M. Devine, ed., *Irish Immigrants and Scottish Society in the Nineteenth and Twentieth Centuries* (Edinburgh, 1991), 1–18; M. J. Mitchell, *The Irish in the West of Scotland 1797–1848: Trade Unions, Strikes and Political Movements* (Edinburgh, 1998).

Table 26.2 Census figures on Irish-born persons present in Scotland, 1841–1911

| Year | Total born in Ireland | Percentage of the total population | Males | Females |
|------|------|------|------|------|
| 1841 | 126,321 | 4.8 | 66,502 | 59,819 |
| 1851 | 207,367 | 7.1 | | |
| 1861 | 204,083 | 6.6 | 103,222 | 100,861 |
| 1871 | 207,770 | 6.2 | 108,234 | 99,536 |
| 1881 | 218,745 | 5.9 | 117,251 | 101,494 |
| 1891 | 194,807 | 4.8 | 105,760 | 89,047 |
| 1901 | 205,064 | 4.6 | 119,045 | 86,019 |
| 1911 | 174,715 | 3.7 | 99,992 | 74,723 |

Proportionally the largest Irish population was recorded in Port Glasgow; in 1881, 30.1 per cent of the 10,872 residents of its Parliamentary Burgh were born in Ireland. Elsewhere, numerous Irish settled in Dundee and West and Mid Lothian. In 1851, 14,889 Irish-born persons formed 18.9 per cent of the population of Dundee. During the same year the recorded Irish-born figure in Edinburgh and Leith peaked at 12,514, representing 6.5 per cent of the total population. Between 1861 and 1901 increasingly more Irish males than females came to Scotland, notably men aged twenty and over. However, local gender ratios varied. Dundee had about five Irishwomen for every three Irishmen in 1881.

The three groups of foreign immigrants, studied by scholars such as Kenneth Collins, Terri Colpi, Stefan Manz, Ellen O'Donnell, and me,[5] were much smaller (Table 26.3). In 1841, 1,303 Germans formed the largest group. It grew to 3,232 in 1901 but declined to 2,362 persons ten years later. By that time, the Russians had overtaken the Germans as the largest group with 11,032 persons, while there were 4,594 Italians in Scotland—both groups arrived largely after 1891. Most of these migrants formed part of a large population movement, which eventually took millions of people away from Continental Europe. Underlying the mass migration were the pressures of fast-growing populations and the apparently better economic prospects in the West. Persecution was an additional motive for Jews among the Russians and Germans. Jews formed a very large group among the people from the Russian Empire in Scotland, and they did so to a lesser extent among the Germans. During the period under review a large area of Poland and the Baltic countries were part of the Russian Empire. Another large group of people

---

[5] K. E. Collins, *Be Well! Jewish Health and Welfare in Glasgow, 1860–1914* (East Linton, 2001); T. Colpi, *The Italian Factor: The Italian Community in Great Britain* (Edinburgh, 1991); S. Manz, *Migranten und Internierte Deutsche in Glasgow, 1864–1918* (Stuttgart, 2003); E. O'Donnell, 'Clergy Ministering to Lithuanian Immigrants in Scotland, 1889–1989', *Innes Review*, 51 (2000), 166–87; *idem.*, ' "To keep our fathers' faith…": Lithuanian Immigrant Religious Aspirations and the Policy of West of Scotland Clergy, 1889–1914', *Innes Review*, 49 (1998), 168–83; B. Braber, *Jews in Glasgow 1879–1939: Immigration and Integration* (London, 2007).

Table 26.3 Census figures on German, Russian, and Italian-born persons present in Scotland, 1861–1911

| Year | Germans | Males | Females | Russians | Males | Females | Italians | Males | Females |
|------|---------|-------|---------|----------|-------|---------|----------|-------|---------|
| 1861 | 1,303 | | | 131 | | | 119 | | |
| 1871 | 1,531 | | | 260 | | | 268 | | |
| 1881 | 2,143 | 1,497 | 646 | 536 | 377 | 159 | 328 | 281 | 47 |
| 1891 | 2,052 | 1,459 | 593 | 1,475 | 1,017 | 458 | 749 | 541 | 208 |
| 1901 | 3,232 | 2,014 | 1,218 | 10,373 | 6,287 | 4,086 | 4,051 | 2,795 | 1,256 |
| 1911 | 2,362 | 1,509 | 853 | 11,032 | 6,520 | 4,512 | 4,594 | 3,103 | 1,491 |

recorded by the Census as Russians was formed by non-Jewish Lithuanians. In Scotland, Germans, Russians, and Italians were concentrated in Lanarkshire, notably Glasgow (on the eve of the First World War more than 1 per cent of the city's residents had a foreign nationality), but individual migrants and families settled in towns across Scotland.[6]

To review immigrant experiences, this chapter is divided in sections. The first deals with the Irish and has three subdivisions: the Irish in general, Irish Catholics, and Irish Protestants. While their large numbers warrant separate treatment of the Irish, the other migrants are grouped together in the second section. The final section compares their experiences. To make this comparison, aspects of the integration of immigrants into Scottish society are examined. Integration of immigrants is usually a long-term, non-linear and multifaceted process.[7] Within the scope of this chapter, it is impossible to review the entire process. Instead, the appraisal is limited to two aspects of integration: the reactions of the native population to the newcomers, and the participation of immigrants in the wider economy and politics.

# Irish Immigrants

## General

The background of the migrants affected attitudes of native Scots towards Irish immigrants, and feelings changed over time. From the end of the eighteenth century, observers complained about Irish beggars. The minister of the Established Church of Scotland in Newton-upon-Ayr wrote in his contribution to the first *Statistical Account of Scotland* (1791) that 930 of its 1,689 inhabitants originated outside the parish, including 60 born in Ireland, adding: 'It is suspected, that many more of the inhabitants have been born in Ireland . . . several of them being unwilling to tell the place of their birth, being poor, and afraid of being turned out of the town'.[8] However, several employers were said to welcome Irish workers. In 1836 William Dixon told the Select Committee on the State of the Irish Poor that Irish miners were 'fully more obedient and tractable' than Scottish colliers.[9]

Anti-Irish attitudes hardened during the period of the Famine when the influx of Irish migrants coincided with the economic depression of 1847–8 in Scotland and local

---

[6] *Census of Scotland, 1861*, vol. i, lx, 330–1; *Census of Scotland, 1891*, vol. ii, xliii–xliv, 344–9; *Census of Scotland, 1901*, vol. i, 316–21, vol. ii, xxviii–xxix; *Census of Scotland, 1911*, vol. ii, xcii, 505–6.

[7] Braber, *Jews in Glasgow*, xvi.

[8] *Statistical Accounts of Scotland (1791–1799)*, vol. ii, 580.

[9] *Evidence to the Select Committee on the State of the Irish Poor in Great Britain* (London, 1836), Appendix G, 114.

outbreaks of cholera in 1848. On 11 June 1847 the *Glasgow Herald* stated 'the streets of Glasgow are at present literally swarming with vagrants from the sister Kingdom'. It was believed they spread disease. Another aspect of their image was their unruliness, especially under the influence of alcohol. Reports about quarrelsome Irish navvies, Irish participation in violent labour disputes, and troubles between Irish religious factions reinforced this perception.[10]

In some middle-class eyes the presence of Irish immigrants had prejudicial effects on Scottish morality. From early on, the Irish were associated with petty theft and resetting. This was extended to other crimes. *The Scotsman* wrote on 27 December 1828 that the revelations about the body-snatchers Burke and Hare 'will strengthen the Scottish prejudices against the natives of the Emerald Isle', and stated 'that as there are more ignorance, degradation and misery in Ireland than in Scotland, the Irish are likely to fall more easily into the habit of committing crime'. Later it was feared that the native population would be infected by Irish vice. The 1871 Census reported 'an invasion…of the Irish race' that had created a 'body of labourers of the lowest class with scarcely any education', who 'do not seem to have improved by residence among us', concluding it was 'quite certain that the native Scot who has associated with them has most certainly deteriorated'.[11]

During the first decades of the nineteenth century the Irish also gained a reputation as strike-breakers in mining disputes. Some Scottish working-class leaders regarded the immigrants as competitors who depressed wages and working conditions. The negative perception persisted in the 1880s when the future Labour leader Keir Hardie said the Irish miner had 'a big shovel, a strong back and a weak brain', came straight from 'a peat bog or tattie field', and produced 'coal enough for a man and a half'.[12] Here Hardie also referred to another aspect of the stereotype of the begging, disease-ridden, drunken, and violent Paddy, namely his stupidity.

As Mitchell has pointed out, anti-Irish bias was tempered by the participation of immigrants in trade-union and political activity. After their involvement in early weavers' unions, Irishmen formed the driving force behind the Glasgow Cotton Spinners Association and represented textile workers on the local trades' committees of the 1820s and 1830s. They took part in the radical United Scotsmen, Chartist, and Suffrage movements of the 1790s, 1830s, and 1840s. Later, Irish workers were prominent in the rank and file of organizations such as the Lanarkshire Miners Union and the National Iron and Steelworkers Union. They formed independent associations such as the United Labourers in the 1850s, but increasingly these unions were absorbed into the general labour movement. By 1892 the United Labourers had been re-established as the National

---

[10]   *Glasgow Courier*, 15 December 1840, *Glasgow Herald*, 14 December 1840, 26 April 1841.
[11]   *Census of Scotland, 1871*, vol. i, xix; vol. ii, xxxiv.
[12]   Quoted in D. Howell, *British Workers and the Independent Labour Party, 1886–1906* (Manchester, 1983), 142.

Labourers Union, the largest subscriber to the Glasgow Trades Council. Irishmen also represented other trades such as tailors and cabinetmakers.[13]

In terms of occupations, economic participation followed distinctive patterns. From the end of the eighteenth century, Irish seasonal migrants worked as harvesters in the developing Scottish agriculture or as labourers in the booming construction sector, where they built canals, docks, and railways. Many early migrants were weavers and textile workers. They left the struggling, often farm-based industry in north-east Ireland, meeting the fluctuating but generally rising demand for labour in the newly mechanized textile industries of Scotland. Dundee's textile industry drew in many women from south Ulster with experience in producing linen. Mining and iron manufacture too attracted the Irish. During the second half of the nineteenth century the rapid and massive industrial expansion in west-central Scotland provided new employment opportunities, for example in docks and shipyards along the Clyde. The earlier noted urban concentration of the Irish in the west of central Scotland and the varying gender ratio can be partly explained by the rise of local industries. Relatively few Irish established themselves as hawkers and shopkeepers.

The new Scottish economy offered chances for social mobility from casual work towards skilled jobs, but progress was disrupted by prolonged economic slumps, which caused unemployment and loss of status. In 1911 the Census recorded 88,809 Irish-born males in Scotland with an occupation (out of a total of 99,992 Irish-born men), of whom 24,813 were engaged in the manufacture of iron and other metals, 11,909 in mining, 6,019 in general labour, 4,963 in building, 3,492 in road transport, 3,071 in railway service, 2,985 in docks services, and 2,924 in local-government services. There were also 884 navvies. Apart from in the building industry, they were over-represented in all these sectors; Irish-born males constituted 17 per cent of all general labourers in Scotland. They were under-represented in agriculture and fishery, civil and post office services, the legal and medical professions, teaching, and commerce.

The 1911 Census also recorded 15,459 Irish-born females in Scotland with an occupation (out of a total of 74,723 Irish-born women), of whom 5,604 were engaged in domestic service, 2,794 in textile manufacture, and 1,923 in the making and selling of clothing. They were over-represented in domestic service, but slightly under-represented in textile manufacture. Smaller numbers of Irish-born women were recorded in clerical professions and services, medical services, and teaching, where they were over-represented, but they were behind in civil and post office services, art, music and drama, commerce, and agriculture.[14] The Census did not separately list occupations of immigrant descendants born in Britain. Nevertheless, these figures give an impression of a mainly working-class group, concentrated in some industries, often in unskilled or unpopular

---

[13] Handley, *The Irish in Scotland*, 314–15; Mitchell, *The Irish in the West of Scotland*, 21–41; *idem.*, 'Irish Catholics in the West of Scotland in the Nineteenth Century: Despised by Scottish Workers and Controlled by the Church?', in M. J. Mitchell, ed., *New Perspectives on the Irish in Scotland* (Edinburgh, 2008), 1–19.

[14] *Census of Scotland, 1911*, vol. iii, v–ix.

occupations, but moving into other areas such as railway and local government services, which apart from sanitary work also offered more desirable jobs in public transport.

## Irish Catholics

Negative attitudes towards Irish Catholics in Scotland were fed by existing religious intolerance that flared up at the end of the eighteenth century as steps were taken towards the emancipation of Catholics in the United Kingdom. The emotions were reignited just before the re-establishment of the Catholic hierarchy in England in 1851 and Scotland in 1878, and fuelled by the animosity between Protestants and Catholics that immigrants brought over from Ireland. On 15 January 1849 the Edinburgh newspaper *The Witness* wrote in an editorial that Catholicism was 'the author of Ireland's ruin':

> Popery lays an arrest on [the] mind, and is a complete barrier to social progress and happiness.... Wherever we find swarms of priests, we find, too, swarms of beggars.... Wherever we meet the shrining priest, there we are sure to meet the thief and the murderer in his wake.... In short, where Popery flourishes, nothing else can; for it is a moral vampire, which sucks the blood of nations...

The paper predicted calamitous results if the rise of Catholicism in Britain remained unchecked. *The Witness* represented extreme anti-Catholic tendencies among a minority of Protestants in Scotland during the Famine influx, but similar feelings were expressed in mainstream churches, where they lasted well into the twentieth century.

Occasionally, negative attitudes towards Irish Catholics were expressed violently. In 1850 the native population of Dunfermline drove Irish residents out of their town after drunken Irish navvies picked a fight with locals. Sporadically, riots broke out when religious factions clashed, often involving both Irish Catholics and Irish Protestants. In 1835 Protestants marched through the streets of Airdrie and wrecked a Catholic chapel, school, and houses. Twelve years later Catholics routed a Protestant march. In 1851 religious groups clashed in Greenock when Catholics protested against Protestant preachers speaking publicly about the dangers of growing Catholicism. Although occasional violence between Irish factions continued, clashes with the native population diminished in the later years of the nineteenth century.[15]

The hostility reinforced an Irish Catholic sense of communal identity, and the Roman Catholic Church in Scotland became an integrating force for Irish Catholics. With increasingly more immigrant clergy—in 1902 John Maguire became the first archbishop in Scotland from Irish descent—the Church created institutions that guided people from the cradle to the grave and strengthened ethnic cohesiveness in the face of prejudice. In addition, Irish Catholics set up mutual-benefit societies such as the Ancient

---

[15] National Archives, HO 45/3472; Handley, *The Irish in Scotland*, 43, 73, 290, 310–11; idem., *The Irish in Modern Scotland*, 95–9, 113–14.

Order of Hibernians (originally Hibernian Funeral Society, formed in 1836). This also resulted in segregation, but Bernard Aspinwall and Mitchell have argued that Catholic isolation should not be overestimated. Irish Catholics shared workplace, trade union, and political experiences with Irish Protestants and natives. Although often concentrated in specific areas and neighbourhoods, they lived next to people of other denominations, and intermarriage blurred the distinctions between Protestants and Catholics and between native and immigrant groups.[16]

Participation by descendants of Irish Catholics in the wider society was also influenced by Scottish education. Since 1816 Catholics in Scotland had been building their voluntary schools, outside the main system that was dominated by Protestants. Catholic schools often lagged behind in terms of resources, quality of buildings, and teacher numbers. However, by the turn of the century priests had improved teaching. After 1918, with their incorporation into the public system, Catholic schools became better resourced. Catholic children increasingly made use of bursary competitions and scholarships. The career of the eminent Catholic author and historian Denis Brogan, born in Glasgow in 1900, was an example of what could be achieved.

Although the number of pupils at Catholic schools rose from some forty-seven thousand in 1883 to about eighty-five thousand in 1908, many Catholic children went to general institutions because of the limited number of places at Catholic schools, the lack of Catholic schools in their neighbourhood, parental choice or indifference. On the eve of the First World War public-school children in Scotland generally enjoyed a wide choice of subjects, modern buildings, good equipment, new education methods, and able teachers. Scotland compared favourably with other countries in the relatively open structure of its educational hierarchy, with marginally more opportunities for upward social mobility. Some descendants of Irish immigrants profited from the limited openings that public education offered. However, their numbers remained small—people like Brogan were an exception and Irish Catholic upward mobility remained notoriously slow until the final quarter of the twentieth century.[17]

At the end of the nineteenth century, individual Irish Catholics began participating in Scottish politics. Earlier, Irishmen had been elected on local police, parish, and school boards, but now they entered county and municipal councils. One of the first elections of an Irish Catholic occurred in 1890 when John Torley was selected as county councillor in Dumbarton. Seven years later Patrick O'Hare became the first Irish Catholic town

---

[16] B. Aspinwall, 'Baptisms, Marriages and Lithuanians; or "Ghetto? What Ghetto?" Some Reflections on Modern Catholic Historical Assumptions', *Innes Review*, 51 (2000), 55–67; *idem.*, 'Catholic Devotion in Victorian Scotland', in Mitchell, ed., *New Perspectives*, 31–43; Mitchell, 'Irish Catholics in the West of Scotland in the Nineteenth Century', 10, 12.

[17] R. D. Anderson, *Education and the Scottish People 1750–1918* (Oxford, 1995), 75, 78, 89, 93–7, 138, 147–8, 308–9; B. Aspinwall, 'The Formation of a British Identity within Scottish Catholicism, 1830–1914', in R. Pope, ed., *Religion and National Identity: Wales and Scotland c. 1700–2000* (Cardiff, 2001), 268–306; *idem.*, 'The Catholic Irish and Wealth in Glasgow', in Devine ed., *Irish Immigrants and Scottish Society*, 91–115; T. M. Devine. 'The End of Disadvantage? The Descendants of Irish-Catholic Immigrants in Modern Scotland since 1945', in Mitchell, ed., *New Perspectives*, 191–207; Handley, *The Irish in Modern Scotland*, 191–227.

councillor in Glasgow. In 1912 the Catholic Socialist John Wheatley won a Glasgow council seat, followed a year later by Patrick Dollan (in 1938 Dollan became the first Lord Provost in Glasgow of Irish descent). In national politics Irish Catholics were not elected in Scotland until 1922 when Wheatley captured the Glasgow Shettleston parliamentary seat for Labour (in 1924 he became Minister of Health).

Before the First World War the Irish electorate in Scotland remained small; immigrants generally lacked the required qualifications. Nevertheless, Irish issues played a role in local and national elections. The general upsurge in Irish nationalism during the second half of the nineteenth century affected Irish immigrants in Scotland and their descendants. In 1870 this took the form of the Irish Home Rule movement. It included organizations such as the Glasgow Home Rule Association (founded in 1871) and local branches of the Irish National League of Great Britain (1883). The Home Rulers supported or opposed election candidates, depending on their position on the Irish question. This brought them into an alliance with the Liberals who introduced Home Rule bills. Labour also won Irish support. However, John McCaffrey and Elaine McFarland have contended that electors did not necessarily vote according to their ethnic origins, and it would be incorrect to assume that an 'Irish vote' went automatically to a specific candidate or party.[18]

## Irish Protestants

McFarland and Ian Meredith have calculated that during the middle decades of the nineteenth century up to a quarter of the Irish immigrants in Scotland were Protestant, including Episcopalians and Presbyterians. By 1914 this proportion had risen to about a third.[19] What differentiated Irish Protestants from Irish Catholics was their prominence in skilled jobs, while they suffered less from negative attitudes in the native population and had fewer incentives to develop a separate group identity. However, these differences should not be pressed too far.

Traditionally, Ulstermen came to work and study in Scotland. At the end of the eighteenth century, Irish Protestants provided instruction in the Scottish linen industry. At the same time, one in ten students at the universities of Glasgow and Edinburgh was Irish, most of them Protestant. When, during the first half of the nineteenth century, Scotland's industries attracted Irish workers, some large employers such as Bairds allocated skilled jobs and apprenticeships to Scottish and Irish Protestants, with unskilled positions going to Catholics. Later, skilled Protestant workers were recruited in Ireland

---

[18]  J. F. McCaffrey, 'Irish Issues in the Nineteenth and Twentieth Century: Radicalism in a Scottish Context', in Devine ed., *Irish Immigrants and Scottish Society*, 116–37; E. W. McFarland, *John Ferguson 1836–1906: Irish Issues in Scottish Politics* (East Linton, 2003), 50, 222.

[19]  E. W. McFarland, *Protestants First: Orangeism in Nineteenth-Century Scotland* (Edinburgh, 1990), 104–5; I. Meredith, 'Irish Migrants in the Scottish Episcopal Church in the Nineteenth Century', in Mitchell ed., *New Perspectives*, 44–64.

for employment in the shipbuilding industry on the Clyde, culminating in the establishment of the Harland & Wolff shipyard at Govan in 1912, for which the firm brought over a large contingent of its Belfast workforce.

The outcome was that among the Irish male immigrants relatively more Protestants than Catholics held skilled positions. However, there was considerable diversity in the Irish Protestant workforce. During the 1880s a majority of the Irish Protestant workers in Greenock were general labourers employed in the port. Case studies by John Foster, Muir Houston, Chris Madigan, and Graham Walker have indicated that most immigrants remained poor despite working hard all their life. They shared the deprivation with native Scots. Irish immigrants made up one-fifth to a quarter of all the applicants in Glasgow Poor Law records between 1867 and 1899, with Catholics only just outnumbering Protestants.[20]

A few Irishmen were very successful. They included Thomas Lipton, the son of Protestant working-class immigrants, who after 1871 applied American marketing techniques to build his grocery empire. Another Irish entrepreneur was John Ferguson. By 1860 this Protestant Ulsterman had settled in Glasgow, where he conducted a wholesale stationery and printers' business. However, as McFarland has described, it was his political career that made Ferguson stand out. He became one of the leaders of the Irish Home Rule movement. As a Home Ruler, Ferguson aligned himself with the Liberal and the Labour parties. He was an Honorary Vice President of the Scottish Parliamentary Labour Party, formed in 1888. In 1893 Ferguson was elected as a Liberal candidate on the Glasgow Town Council. But his interests went beyond the Home Rule issue. Three years after his election, Ferguson became a pivotal figure in the Workers' Municipal Electors Committee, formed under the auspices of the Glasgow Trades Council by local branches of organizations such as the Independent Labour Party and the Irish National League to campaign for Labour candidates on issues such as housing and working conditions.[21]

Ferguson was unrepresentative of the Irish Protestants in Scotland. Eric Kaufmann and McFarland[22] have demonstrated that many Protestants opposed Home Rule and a large number of them joined the Orange lodges. The Orange Order had been set up in Ireland at the end of the eighteenth century to defend Protestants against aggression from secret Catholic societies. Irish weavers introduced the order in Scotland. In Glasgow a lodge was formed in 1813. The movement grew during the second half of the nineteenth century, with the influx of Irish Protestant workers. At the end of the century, the main Orange organization in Scotland—the Loyal Orange Institution—had some twenty-five thousand members, of whom eight thousand lived in Glasgow.

The lodges had a bad reputation in the Scottish middle classes, who associated the Orangemen with violence and drunkenness and regarded their struggle as an alien

[20] J. Foster, M. Houston, and C. Madigan, 'Sectarianism, Segregation and Politics on Clydeside in the Later Nineteenth Century', in Mitchell ed., *New Perspectives*, 65–96; G. Walker, 'The Protestant Irish in Scotland', in Devine ed., *Irish Immigrants and Scottish Society*, 44–66.

[21] McFarland, *John Ferguson*, 4–21, 247–82.

[22] E. Kaufmann, 'The Orange Order in Scotland since 1860: A Social Analysis', in Mitchell ed., *New Perspectives*, 159–90; McFarland, *Protestants First*, 49–52, 66, 72, 105, 165–9.

import. Nevertheless, Orangemen were instrumental in the formation of the Glasgow Working Men's Conservative Association in 1865. They were involved in canvassing and served as constituency officials in working-class districts, but no Irish Protestants stood as Tory candidates before 1914. In general, the Orange lodges in Scotland served as reference points for Protestant immigrants in their new country at times of economic problems and social dislocation. Membership became a family tradition. The lodges shaped their members' identity and provided status for their office-bearers, helping them participate in the wider society.

# Germans, Jews, Lithuanians, and Italians

## Germans

German migration to Scotland followed a tradition of continental merchants operating in Scottish towns since the Middle Ages. As the Scottish economy expanded, the country attracted German manufacturers and brokers as well as engineers and clerks. Family ties often facilitated entry into the local economy and job market. Numerous retailers followed, including tailors, hairdressers, bakers, and butchers, who catered for the developing taste in the growing urban middle classes for luxury clothing, coiffure, and food. By 1911 many Scottish towns had a local German shopkeeper, and the German *Oberkellner* (head waiter) was a recognized figure in restaurants. German females mainly worked as servants and teachers.

In commerce, several Germans led the way. Among them was the chemicals broker Paul Rottenburg, who arrived in Glasgow as a twenty-one-year-old in the 1860s and became President of the Glasgow Chamber of Commerce in 1896. In his obituary of 4 February 1929 the *Glasgow Herald* praised Rottenburg as 'one of the most devoted and loyal of citizens'. Manz has shown that other Germans played leading roles too. An outstanding individual was Otto Ernst Philippi of thread-maker J. & P. Coats in Paisley. He helped bring about new management techniques and cartels in British clothing. In 1864 Henry Dubs founded his Glasgow ironworks, which by 1900 was the second largest locomotive producer in Britain. The Scottish demand for light beer, an alternative to heavy ale, was met by J. & R. Tennent in Glasgow, a British firm, which bought an entire brewery in Augsburg, had it shipped over, and brought in German brewers to produce what became popularly known as 'lager'.[23]

Despite having been well respected, during the First World War, German immigrants were interned, deported, and repatriated. They also became targets of violence when on 7 May 1915 a German submarine sank the *Lusitania*, a passenger ship that had been built by John Brown & Co. Ltd. in Clydebank. The major disturbances in Scotland took place

[23] Manz, *Migranten und Internierte*, 45–148.

in smaller towns such as Greenock, where on 12 May 1915 bottles were thrown through the windows of a naturalized German hairdresser. The following night a crowd of several hundred persons gathered outside the grocer's shop of another naturalized German. His windows were smashed and a young man attempted to burst in the door with a clothes pole. The police dispersed the crowd but later that night could not prevent rioters attacking the licensed premises of a German woman. As a result of the deportation, repatriation, and violence, the German communities in Scotland were virtually destroyed.[24]

## Jews

Among the Germans and Russians were many Jews, notably adherents of Orthodox Judaism. In 1914 some seven thousand Jews resided in Glasgow and about one thousand in Edinburgh. Many early Jewish settlers in Scotland were retailers and small manufacturers. One of the most successful Jewish entrepreneurs was Benjamin Simons. His wholesale fruit-trading company, established during the 1840s in Glasgow, profited from a combination of growing incomes that stimulated the demand for fruit, new cold-storage technology, and the availability of cheaper and faster means of transport. The Jewish occupational structure changed dramatically with the influx of Russian Jews towards the end of the nineteenth century. The newcomers concentrated on the clothing, furniture, and tobacco trades, where thousands of men and women operated as low-paid workers, with smaller numbers of independent workshop owners and retailers. A relatively high number of Jewish men—over three hundred in 1911—were occupied in hawking and Jews formed a large percentage of the total number of hawkers in Scotland.[25]

Through Jewish welfare the early settlers helped newcomers and unemployed workers gain an independent status, for example as a workshop owner or hawker. In addition, Jews created a network of mutual-benefit societies. Occupational change was achieved as Jews rose into the Scottish professions. This resulted partly from the participation of almost all Jewish children in general Scottish education. Relatively many Jewish children profited from the available openings. This created a high number of Jewish university students during the first half of the twentieth century, particularly in Medicine, where, as Kenneth Collins has illustrated, they continued a lineage of Jewish students coming to Scotland that was established in the early eighteenth century.[26]

The native attitudes towards Jews were ambivalent. There was admiration for successful individuals. On 29 December 1880 the popular Glasgow weekly *The Bailie* paid homage to Benjamin Simons: 'Fruit is no longer a luxury to our city [thanks to] a gentleman…living unobtrusively among us [who built up] this industry, which gives a new

---

[24] B. Braber, 'Within Our Gates: A New Perspective on Germans in Glasgow during the First World War', *Journal of Scottish Historical Studies*, 29 (2009), 87–105.

[25] Braber, *Jews in Glasgow*, 78–107.

[26] K. Collins, *Go and Learn: The International Story of Jews and Medicine in Scotland* (Aberdeen, 1988), 81–97.

means of livelihood to thousands.' However, Jews were also stereotyped as cunning scoundrels. This prejudice acquired a sinister dimension. In 1909 Oscar Slater, a German Jew, was wrongly convicted for the brutal murder of Glasgow spinster Marion Gilchrist—mostly because it was assumed he was a violent pimp.[27] The *Edinburgh Evening News* commented on 7 May 1909: 'The trial has cast a lurid light on the dark places of our great cities, in which such wretches [Slater and his associates] ply their calling. It shows a brood of alien vampires, lost to conscience, crawling in black depths at the basement of civilised society.' Despite this language, which was unusual and extreme in a Scottish context, Jews in Scotland were not subjected to large-scale violence until 1947, when events in Palestine sparked anti-Jewish riots in Glasgow.[28]

The Jewish responses to prejudice were generally subdued. The establishment sought the unobtrusiveness that *The Bailie* had ascribed to Benjamin Simons. During the Slater trial Jewish leaders decided to remain silent. When one of their ministers joined a campaign in support of Slater, they reprimanded him, but the rebuke took place behind closed doors 'in order not to attract further attention'.[29] However, the Jews also established the Glasgow Jewish Representative Council, an umbrella organization that appealed successfully to the authorities on behalf of the Jews among the German internees during the First World War.

Individual Jews got involved in local politics and trade-union activity. In 1883 Michael Simons, son and successor of Benjamin Simons, won a seat on the Glasgow Town Council, beating Reverend Robert Thomson, one of the founders of the Scottish Protestant Alliance. According to the *Jewish Chronicle*, Thomson went to the poll with the cry of 'No Jews and no Jesuits'. In reply, Simons stated that appeals were made to 'base prejudices... quite unworthy of this enlightened age'. He claimed 'to be able to take, and... was justified in taking as deep an interest in the welfare and progress of this city as any member of the community'.[30] Simons was the first Glasgow councillor of immigrant descent. The most outstanding Jewish trade unionist was Emmanuel Shinwell, initially a representative of the Jewish tailors on the Glasgow Trades Council. In 1910 he was appointed as Vice President of the Council (in 1922 Shinwell became MP for West Lothian and in 1924 he was appointed as Secretary for Mines).

## Lithuanians

From the 1870s Scottish coal- and iron-masters recruited young men from Poland and the Baltic lands for unskilled work in pits and blast furnaces. Some of the men brought their families. According to Tom Devine and Kenneth Lunn, by 1914 nearly eight thousand of

---

[27] B. Braber, 'The Trial of Oscar Slater (1909) and Anti-Jewish Prejudices in Edwardian Glasgow', *History*, 88 (2003), 262–79.

[28] Braber, *Jews in Glasgow*, 177.

[29] Scottish Jewish Archives Centre, Minute Book Glasgow Hebrew Congregation, 16 May 1909.

[30] *Jewish Chronicle*, 9 November 1883; *Glasgow Herald*, 19, 23, and 25 October 1883, 2 and 3 November 1883.

what came to be regarded as Lithuanians lived in Lanarkshire, Ayrshire, Fife, and West Lothian.[31] The first reaction of native and Irish workers to the influx of Lithuanians was one of hostility, as the newcomers were accused of accepting work at low wages and poor working conditions. This negative view persisted. In 1905 Father Charles Webb, a priest in Carfin, Lanarkshire, wrote that his flock regarded Lithuanian incomers as a threat to their livelihood: '[The Lithuanians] are looked upon with but little favour by the Irish people here, from a work point of view.'[32] These views were formed against the background of agitation across Britain that was mainly directed towards Russian Jews but also affected groups such as the Lithuanians, resulting in the Aliens Act of 1905, the first major legal attempt to stem foreign migration to the United Kingdom.

Tensions were somewhat defused as Lithuanians joined trade unions and participated in industrial actions such as the national miners' strike of 1912. The Catholic Church also extended its mission to these immigrants. In 1899 Reverend Vincent Warnagaris, based at St John the Evangelist in Glasgow, helped establish the Lithuanian Co-operative Society *Sandara* (Harmony). The Lithuanians were often Catholic, but some left the faith, while others combined religiousness with Socialism. Individually, Lithuanians were not active in Scottish politics before 1914. Instead, they formed their own organizations such as the Bellshill branch of the Marxist Lithuanian Social Democratic Party (1903).[33]

The First World War had repercussions for the entire Russian population of Scotland, but Lithuanians suffered most. Under the Anglo-Russian Military Convention of March 1917, male Russian nationals in Britain aged between eighteen and forty-one were compelled to join the British Army or return to Russia for military service. Many Russian immigrants were eligible for military duty or repatriation. The Glasgow Jewish Representative Council took up the case for the Jews among the Russians, but the Lithuanians lacked a similar organization. About one thousand of the eligible Lithuanian men chose to return to Russia. Only a third of them came back to Scotland after the war.[34] According to the *Glasgow Herald* of 12 March 1920, some six hundred dependants of the men who had decided to go back to Russia were forcefully repatriated.

# Italians

Before the nineteenth century, individual Italians worked in Scotland as bankers, merchants, artists, musicians, and priests. Between 1790 and 1820 skilled artisans arrived,

[31] T. M. Devine, *The Scottish Nation, 1700–2000* (London, 2000), 507–12; K. Lunn, 'Reactions and Responses: Lithuanian and Polish Immigrants in the Lanarkshire Coalfield, 1880–1914', *Journal of the Scottish Labour History Society*, 1 (1979), 23–38.
[32] Quoted in O'Donnell, 'To keep our fathers' faith…', 177.
[33] National Archives of Scotland, FS.5/197; B. Aspinwall, 'Baptisms, Marriages and Lithuanians; or "Ghetto? What Ghetto?" Some Reflections on Modern Catholic Historical Assumptions', *Innes Review*, 51 (2000), 55–67; O'Donnell, 'Clergy Ministering to Lithuanian Immigrants in Scotland', 174.
[34] S. Kadish, *Bolsheviks and British Jews: The Anglo-Jewish Community, Britain and the Russian Revolution* (London, 1992), 209–10, 228; M. Rodgers, 'The Anglo-Russian Convention and the Lithuanian Immigrant Community in Lanarkshire', *Immigrants & Minorities*, 1 (1982), 60–88.

followed by small numbers of political refugees and itinerant craftsmen. They were over-whelmed by new arrivals after the 1880s. Many Italians went into hawking, often selling figurines, while others made a living as wandering musicians or sold chestnuts and ice cream from barrows. Smaller numbers worked in mining and transport. At the turn of the twentieth century, Italians began making a transition to catering, shopkeeping, and hairdressing.

Terri Colpi has portrayed Leopold Giuliani as one of the outstanding Italian business-men in Scotland. Giuliani settled in Glasgow in the 1880s and less than twenty years later he owned sixty catering shops. He brought in boys and young men from Italy to work in his establishments. They often subsequently left to start their own business. This group specialized in confectionery, ice-cream making, and fish frying. Many Italian women worked in the small establishments, which were usually family-owned. They often cooperated, for example to buy supplies in bulk. In 1911 there were hundreds of Italian enterprises in this industry in Scotland, which employed almost two thousand Italian immigrants.[35] In the age of the temperance movement the Italian café became a respect-able Scottish institution as it catered, unlike public houses, for women and children.

Not everyone regarded the Italians as respectable. Speaking to the Glasgow Municipal Commission on the Housing of the Poor (1902–4), Matthew Gilmour, a long-serving house factor, said Italians (and Jews) had created places that had 'become hot-beds of gambling and everything else that is bad'.[36] Almost fifteen years later, the Town Clerk of Glasgow, J. Lindsay, wrote to the Scottish Office about applications for licences for refreshment shops from aliens, whom he called an 'undesirable class' to run such shops because he associated them with Sunday trading, the sale of alcohol, gambling, and bad language.[37] Despite such sentiments Italians were spared large-scale violence until Italy declared war on Britain in 1940, after which rioters attacked Italians and their businesses in Glasgow, Edinburgh, Gourock, and Greenock.[38]

# A COMPARISON OF IMMIGRANT EXPERIENCES

The examination of immigrant experiences raises several questions. This section aims to answer two of them: Why did the Italians and Jews for so long escape the violence that befell the Irish and Germans? And why were Germans, Jews, and Italians remarkable in terms of business success and social mobility?

---

[35]  *Census of Scotland, 1911*, vol. iii, 43–51; Colpi, *The Italian Factor*, 28–66.
[36]  Glasgow City Archives, Glasgow Municipal Commission on the Housing of the Poor, Evidence, 4793, 7401, and *Report and Recommendations Glasgow Municipal Commission on Housing of the Poor* (Glasgow, 1904), 19.
[37]  G. R. Rubin, 'Race, Retailing and Wartime Regulation: The Retail Business (Licensing) Order 1918', *Immigrants and Minorities*, 7 (1988), 184–205.
[38]  *Glasgow Herald*, 11 June 1940.

Throughout the nineteenth century the Irish suffered from negative stereotypes, which portrayed them as stupid, poor, diseased, drunken, violent, and criminal. Towards the end of the century and later on Jews and Italians were also associated with disease and crime, but in general Scottish hostility towards these two groups appeared to be more guarded. Stereotyping was sporadically accompanied by violence. Catholic immigrants were also victims of religious bigotry, which notably affected the Irish at the time of the Famine influx and re-establishment of the Catholic hierarchy in England. However, much of the anti-Catholic violence came from Irish Protestants, who themselves fell prey to maltreatment by Scots and Irish Catholics.

In contrast to the Irish, the Germans were well respected, but they suffered from wartime hostility. The demise of the German community was caused by a combination of numerical decline, government policy, and anti-German attitudes, which were extensions of existing anti-alien bias. The ability of the Germans to counter official measures, prejudice, and violence was hampered by a lack of political influence. Lithuanians also lacked political power, which contributed to their suffering during and shortly after the First World War. Jews were less severely affected by official measures and bigotry. They were more organized, and in Michael Simons the Jews had an influential leader who could present their case to the authorities. In addition, Jews and Italians were able to contribute to the war effort, which gave them a shared feeling of destination with the wider population and improved their reputation.

With the exception of the anti-German riots in 1915, hostile reactions to immigrants were related to the increasing size of the immigrant populations. When the Irish came to Scotland during the period of the Famine, coinciding with a Scottish economic recession and local outbreaks of disease, their influx was considered a danger to Scottish society and anti-Irish violence increased. When Russian immigration rose sharply at the end of the nineteenth century, a similarly perceived menace contributed to the anti-alien agitation. This suggests that hostility was caused by fear about unusually large influxes of people or anger about external events. However, as I have argued elsewhere,[39] hostile reactions to immigrants at the turn of the century were also expressions of feelings of uncertainty in the native population about general changes in Scottish society. So it was a combination of factors rather than a single factor that unleashed hatred.

The native population was also concerned about the participation of immigrants in the economy. The Irish were seen as strike-breakers and competitors in the labour market, a perception that also affected Lithuanians and, to a lesser extent, Jews. Germans and Italians were not perceived as a labour threat. However, the growing Scottish economy was able to absorb all groups. Through trade union and political activity, specialization in specific trades and occupations, or by filling vacancies in the labour market that were vital to the economy but unpopular with Scottish workers, immigrants could avoid or overcome competition with the native population, which somewhat eased the tension between Scots and immigrants. So in turn, attitudes about immigrants helped determine their participation in the wider economy. Irish and Lithuanian Catholics fell foul

---

[39] Braber, *Jews in Glasgow*, 26–8.

of discrimination in the labour market. The biased allocation of apprenticeships for skilled work hampered Irish Catholic social mobility. German, Jewish, and Italian successes in business resulted from reliance on kinship ties and specialization in niche trades and markets, as well as from traditional activities and roles in commerce and industry. That Jews were socially more mobile than other groups was mainly due to the participation of almost all Jewish children in public education, the Jewish tradition of learning, their communal welfare system, and the self-help groups that assisted individuals and families.

Conclusions from this comparison can only have a provisional character. More work remains to be done. As stated earlier, many groups have not yet been studied, research has often had a limited local or regional character, and few historians have attempted a comparison of immigrant experiences. A major omission in historical study concerns the English migrants in Scotland before the final decades of the twentieth century. When this oversight is corrected, it would also be useful to compare experiences of the English in Scotland at the end of the twentieth century with those of earlier generations and other groups. To identify specifically Scottish aspects of immigrant history, this comparative approach should also adopt a cross-border character, contrasting Scottish developments and events with what occurred in other locations, within the United Kingdom as well as abroad.

Despite the gaps in our knowledge, we can conclude that on the whole modern Scotland was able to integrate immigrants, but with temporary problems caused by sudden and large rises in the number of newcomers, events during the First World War, and factors such as anxiety about the direction of general developments in Scottish society. Some groups and individuals fared better than others because of specific qualities, circumstances, or coincidence. In general, immigrants had a powerful and complex impact on the development of the changing Scottish society. They contributed to Scotland's population growth, making up some of the losses arising from emigration. The migrants added to the membership of religious congregations, including the Protestant churches, but more notably the Catholic Church in Scotland. Meanwhile, their settlement increased bigotry and pressures on all newcomers to conform to the Scottish norm, which in itself contributed to shaping Catholicism and Judaism in Scotland.

An abundant supply of labour was crucial to Scotland's industrial success. The migrants strengthened the Scottish labour force with manpower, skills, and experience, which aided the modernization of the transport system and the mechanization of industrial production that contributed to making Scotland one of the most advanced industrial nations on the eve of the First World War. As immigrants were prepared to work for wages and in conditions that native Scots often found unacceptable, employers were able to keep production costs down, which may also help explain why a large section of the population of one the most prosperous countries in the world remained desperately poor. Meanwhile, enterprising individuals played their part in the international success of the Scottish economy through their introduction or use of new production methods, management techniques, or general business models. They assisted in changing the distribution, wholesale, and retail trades. They also catered for new tastes and introduced new products. Finally, they lent a hand to trade unionism, and in politics they supported the Liberals, played a role in the Conservative Party, and aided Labour in achieving its electoral breakthrough.

## Further Reading

Braber, B., *Jews in Glasgow 1879–1939: Immigration and Integration* (London, 2007).

Collins, K. E., *Be Well! Jewish Health and Welfare in Glasgow, 1860–1914* (East Linton, 2001).

Colpi, T., *The Italian Factor: The Italian Community in Great Britain* (Edinburgh, 1991).

Handley, J. E., *The Irish in Scotland 1798–1845* (Cork, 1945).

—— *The Irish in Modern Scotland* (Cork, 1947).

Manz, S., *Migranten und Internierte Deutsche in Glasgow, 1864–1918* (Stuttgart, 2003).

McFarland, E. W., *Protestants First: Orangeism in Nineteenth-Century Scotland* (Edinburgh, 1990).

Mitchell, M. J., *The Irish in the West of Scotland 1797–1848: Trade Unions, Strikes and Political Movements* (Edinburgh, 1998).

—— ed., *New Perspectives on the Irish in Scotland*, (Edinburgh, 2008).

# CHAPTER 27

## THE SCOTTISH DIASPORA SINCE 1815

### ANGELA McCARTHY

DURING the nineteenth and twentieth centuries an estimated 3.25 million Scots left their homeland.[1] Teasing out the volume, chronology, and profile of Scottish emigration, along with the causes of this movement, characterizes the work of many historians based in Scotland. Typically emphasizing a grim Scottish economy, such works have spawned overarching depictions of Scottish migrants as adventurers or exiles.[2] These interpretations also appear in the countries where Scots settled and are connected to issues of migrant adjustment, including ethnic retention, assimilation, and contribution histories. Notably, much of this work focuses on a particular nation or region.[3] Although a few studies incorporate the experiences of Scottish migrants in several destinations, these efforts are rarely explicitly comparative and fail to explicate differences between the countries of settlement.[4] Indeed, the general impression of the historiography of the Scottish diaspora is that it is lacklustre, under-developed, and under-theorized. Some

---

[1] Marjory Harper, *Adventurers and Exiles: The Great Scottish Exodus* (London, 2003), 3; R. J. Finlay, *Modern Scotland, 1914–2000* (London, 2004), 302.

[2] See, for instance, Harper, *Adventurers and Exiles.*

[3] J. M. Bumsted, *The Scots in Canada* (Ottawa, 1982); Marjory Harper and Michael E. Vance, eds., *Myth, Migration and the Making of Memory: Scotia and Nova Scotia, c.1700–1990* (Halifax, 1999); Tom Brooking and Jennie Coleman, eds., *The Heather and the Fern: Scottish Migration and New Zealand Settlement* (Dunedin, 2003); Peter E. Rider and Heather McNabb, eds., *A Kingdom of the Mind: How the Scots Helped Make Canada* (Montreal and Kingston, 2006); John M. MacKenzie with Nigel R. Dalziel, *The Scots in South Africa: Ethnicity, Identity, Gender and Race, 1772–1914* (Manchester, 2007).

[4] Gordon Donaldson, *The Scots Overseas* (London, 1966); R. A. Cage, ed., *The Scots Abroad: Labour, Capital, Enterprise, 1750–1914* (Beckenham, 1985); T. M. Devine, ed., *Scottish Emigration and Scottish Society: Proceedings of the Scottish Historical Studies Seminar, University of Strathclyde, 1990–91* (Edinburgh, 1992); Tanja Bueltmann, Andrew Hinson, and Graeme Morton, eds., *Ties of Bluid, Kin and Countrie: Scottish Associational Culture in the Diaspora* (Markham, Ont., 2009).

exceptions exist. Whereas early accounts of Scottish migration typically contained biographical or anecdotal portraits with little analysis, or used individual stories to supply colour, more recent work explicitly situates individual experiences within frameworks of ethnic networking, identity formation, and issues of history and memory.[5] Studies of British emigration also offer fruitful comparative insights between the Scots and other ethnic groups.[6]

This chapter surveys the literature according to three overarching concerns evident from the extant historiography: the profile and pattern of emigration; its causes; and its consequences. Comparison is made with emigration from Ireland, not because the Irish diaspora offers the only fruitful means of contrast, but because much of the extant comparative work involving the Scots incorporates the Irish.[7] Suggestions for further research appear throughout the chapter, while the conclusion meditates on promising methodological avenues of research and assesses the significance of the Scottish diaspora. A word of definition is required at the outset. Despite the politically loaded terms 'emigration' and 'immigration', in light of the strong flow of internal movement within Scotland, 'emigration' rather than 'migration' is used throughout this chapter to refer to movement to other countries. 'Migrant' rather than 'emigrant' or 'immigrant', meanwhile, is the preferred term utilized for the individuals emigrating and embraces those who moved on a temporary, permanent, or multiple basis. 'Diaspora' is likewise a contested term but is used in recognition of the many places to which Scots travelled and the ties that continued to link them to home.

# THE PROFILE, PATTERN, AND PARADOX OF SCOTTISH EMIGRATION

Vague and inconclusive emigration statistics hinder attempts to establish the exact numbers of Scottish migrants in the nineteenth and twentieth centuries. Furthermore, the extant data fails to incorporate the flow from Scotland to England, does not account for

---

[5] Angela McCarthy, ed., *A Global Clan: Scottish Migrant Networks and Identities Since the Eighteenth Century* (London, 2006); Angela McCarthy, *Personal Narratives of Irish and Scottish Migration, 1921–65: 'For Spirit and Adventure'* (Manchester, 2007).

[6] Rowland Tappan Berthoff, *British Immigrants in Industrial America, 1790–1950* (New York, 1953); Charlotte Erikson, *Invisible Immigrants: The Adaptation of English and Scottish Immigrants in Nineteenth-Century America* (London, 1972); Eric Richards, *Britannia's Children: Emigration from England, Scotland, Wales and Ireland Since 1600* (London and New York, 2004); A. James Hammerton and Alistair Thomson, *Ten Pound Poms: Australia's Invisible Migrants: A Life History of Postwar British Emigration to Australia* (Manchester and New York, 2005); Jock Philips and Terry Hearn, *Settlers: New Zealand Immigrants from England, Ireland and Scotland, 1800–1945* (Auckland, 2008).

[7] T. M. Devine, 'Making the Caledonian Connection: The Development of Irish and Scottish Studies', in Liam McIlvanney and Ray Ryan, eds., *Ireland and Scotland: Culture and Society, 1700–2000* (Dublin, 2005), 248–57.

return migration, and excludes Scots leaving from English ports.[8] Nevertheless, there is general consensus on the broad characteristics of the volume, chronology, and direction of the outflow. In sheer numbers, at the very least an estimated 2 million departed from Scotland between 1825 and 1914 for non-European destinations, while 1.25 million left in the period after 1914. Several peaks can be discerned including 1881–90, 1901–10, and 1911–20 (with more than 200,000 emigrating), and 1921–30 when more than 400,000 departed.[9] Between 1951 and 1981, 753,000 Scots (15 per cent of the total population) left their homeland. This latter figure comprised 398,000 venturing overseas, while emigration to England reached almost 45 per cent of the outflow.[10] These statistics not only reveal an urgent requirement for a study of the Scottish diaspora in the period after the Second World War, but also the need for a scholarly investigation of the Scots in England.[11]

In sheer numbers the United States proved the most popular destination for Scots, followed by Canada, Australia, and New Zealand. The appeal of certain destinations, however, varied over time, with Canada receiving a greater percentage of the outflow in the period before the 1850s and between 1910 and 1929. How many Scots strategically entered Canada to gain access to the United States, however, is unknown. Australia and New Zealand were also periodically important, particularly during the gold rushes in the mid-nineteenth century (1853–64), while South Africa became more alluring towards the later nineteenth century and in 1935–8.[12] Scottish migrants also moved to other countries, including England, during this era of mass emigration, but their experiences remain largely uncharted. Indeed, the manifest neglect of the Scottish experience in England and the United States is curious. A possible explanation is the attention given to more 'exotic' Continental European migrant groups. But also important are the proportions involved. For instance, the number of recorded Scottish-born migrants peaked numerically in the United States at 354,323 in the 1930 Census, but they never supplied more than 1 per cent of the total population. In New Zealand, by contrast, the Scots-born peaked in 1886 at 54,810, but contributed 9.5 and 19.7 per cent respectively of the total and foreign-born population at that time.[13]

Generalizations about the socio-economic profile of the Scottish migrant flow are also tentative. Yet despite divergences according to destination, such as unskilled labourers veering to Canada and Australasia and skilled artisans to the United States and South

[8]   Michael Flinn, ed., *Scottish Population History from the 17th Century to the 1930s* (Cambridge, 1977), 447; Harper, *Adventurers and Exiles*, 3.

[9]   Flinn ed., *Scottish Population History*, 101.

[10]   Finlay, *Modern Scotland*, 306, 302.

[11]   Two popular studies are Alasdair Munro and Duncan Sim, *The Merseyside Scots: A Study of an Expatriate Community* (Birkenhead, 2001), and David Stenhouse, *On the Make: How the Scots Took Over London* (Edinburgh, 2004).

[12]   Flinn ed., *Scottish Population History*, 450–1.

[13]   For further figures, see appendix in Angela McCarthy, 'Scottish Migrant Ethnic Identities in the British Empire since the Nineteenth Century', in John M. MacKenzie and T. M. Devine, eds., *Scotland and the British Empire* (Oxford, 2011), 144–6.

Africa, the overarching profile is of a flow from Scotland that was male dominated until the First World War, generally skilled, and literate, and mainly from the Lowlands.[14] The broad profile of Irish emigration during this period, meanwhile, is characterized by gender parity, fewer marketable skills, and more illiteracy.[15] These broad approaches, however, hide various deviations. Looking at Scottish emigration regionally reveals that highlanders were more likely to move en masse whereas lowlanders moved in small family groups or as individuals.[16] By the mid-twentieth century, about one-quarter to one-third of Scots left in family groups and a disproportionate number continued to be skilled.[17]

This movement from Scotland took place during an era of mass European emigration. Between 1815 and 1930, central and western Europe experienced unprecedented mobility with an estimated 60 million people leaving for overseas shores. By contrast with countries such as Italy and Ireland, which respectively lost a recorded 9.9 and 7.3 million between 1815 and 1930, numerically Scotland was a minor player in the outflow. Per head of population, however, Scotland was regularly placed in the top three countries experiencing substantial emigration, and by the time of the interwar period, topped this emigration league table (Table 27.1).[18]

Comparison of these statistics has led to Scottish emigration being portrayed as a paradox. While other factors have been put forward to deepen this alleged puzzle, the central conundrum surrounds the movement of Scots from an urban industrial economy rather than an agrarian one: 'Heavy outward movement from backward and poor rural societies such as Ireland and Italy was not unexpected.'[19] There are, however, problems with this interpretation. First, the paradox assumes that Scots in the immediate decades after the mid-nineteenth century should be satisfied residing in the world's second most urban, industrial country. This, however, elides the more personal reasons that individuals had for moving, and the pressures of critical problems such as overcrowding in urban districts which were associated with Scotland's booming industrialization and urbanization, and which provoked some Scots to seek better lifestyles elsewhere.

Second, we need to consider such figures comparatively. Taking Dudley Baines's emigration league table and comparing it with Tom Devine's rates of urbanization (indicative of industrialization) for 1850, it is indeed apparent that Ireland's high emigration per head of population occurred from a country with low urbanization. Yet Switzerland and Austria, with lower rates of urbanization than Ireland, had low emigration rates.

---

[14] Flinn ed., *Scottish Population History*, 452–4.

[15] David Fitzpatrick, *Irish Emigration, 1801–1921* (Dublin, 1984), 7–9.

[16] Eric Richards, 'Varieties of Scottish Emigration in the Nineteenth Century', *Historical Studies*, 21, no. 85 (1985), 476.

[17] Finlay, *Modern Scotland*, 303.

[18] Dudley Baines, *Emigration from Europe, 1815–1930* (Basingstoke, 1991), 9, 7.

[19] T. M. Devine, 'The Paradox of Scottish Emigration', in Devine ed., *Scottish Emigration and Scottish Society*, 2.

Table 27.1 Annual average overseas emigration rate per 1,000 population

| | 1851–60 | 1861–70 | 1871–80 | 1881–90 | 1891–00 | 1901–10 | 1913 | 1921–30 |
|---|---|---|---|---|---|---|---|---|
| Ireland | 14.0 | 14.6 | 6.6 | 14.2 | 8.9 | 7.0 | 6.8 | 5.9 |
| Norway | 2.4 | 5.8 | 4.7 | 9.5 | 4.5 | 8.3 | 4.2 | 3.1 |
| Scotland | 5.0 | 4.6 | 4.7 | 7.1 | 4.4 | 9.9 | 14.4 | 9.2 |
| Italy | | | 1.1 | 3.4 | 5.0 | 10.8 | 16.3 | 3.4 |
| England | 2.6 | 2.8 | 4.0 | 5.6 | 3.6 | 5.5 | 7.6 | 2.7 |
| Sweden | 0.5 | 3.1 | 2.4 | 7.0 | 4.1 | 4.2 | 3.1 | 1.8 |
| Portugal | | 1.9 | 2.9 | 3.8 | 5.1 | 5.7 | 13.0 | 3.2 |
| Spain | | | | 3.6 | 4.4 | 5.7 | 10.5 | 6.3 |
| Denmark | | | 2.1 | 3.9 | 2.2 | 2.8 | 3.2 | 1.7 |
| Finland | | | | 1.3 | 2.3 | 5.5 | 6.4 | 2.1 |
| Austria–Hungary | | | 0.3 | 1.1 | 1.6 | 4.8 | 6.1 | 1.4 |
| Switzerland | | | 1.3 | 3.2 | 1.4 | 1.4 | 1.7 | 1.4 |
| Germany | | | 1.5 | 2.9 | 1.0 | 0.5 | 0.4 | 1.0 |
| Netherlands | 0.5 | 0.6 | 0.5 | 1.2 | 0.5 | 0.5 | 0.4 | 0.5 |
| Belgium | | | | 0.9 | 0.4 | 0.6 | 1.0 | 0.3 |
| France | 0.1 | 0.2 | 0.2 | 0.3 | 0.1 | 0.1 | 0.2 | 0.3 |

*Source:* Dudley Baines, *Emigration from Europe, 1815–1930* (Basingstoke, 1991), 10.

Table 27.2  European urbanization, 1910–11, and emigration rate, 1901–10

| Country | Urbanization (% in towns and cities with 20,000+) | Emigration rate per 1,000 population |
|---|---|---|
| England and Wales | 60.6 | 5.5 |
| Scotland | 49.5 | 9.9 |
| Netherlands | 40.4 | 0.5 |
| Germany | 34.7 | 0.5 |
| France | 32.5 | 0.1 |
| Italy | 28.2 | 10.8 |
| Denmark | 27.0 | 2.8 |
| Belgium | 26.6 | 0.6 |
| Ireland | 21.5 | 7.0 |
| Switzerland | 21.1 | 1.4 |
| Norway | 18.1 | 8.3 |
| Austria | 16.9 | 4.8 |
| Sweden | 16.1 | 4.2 |
| Finland | 9.3 | 5.5 |

*Source*: R. J. Morris, 'Urbanisation and Scotland', in W. Hamish Fraser and R. J. Morris, eds., *People and Society in Scotland II, 1830–1914* (Edinburgh, 1990), 74; Baines, *Emigration from Europe*, 10.

Meanwhile, Italy in 1850 was a middling urbanized country, yet its emigration figures for 1871–80 are low.[20] It is also instructive to compare an urbanization table for 1910 with Baines's table (see Table 27.2). Certainly some countries with low urbanization, such as Finland, Sweden, Austria, Norway, and Ireland, had moderate to high emigration rates, but other countries with low to moderate urbanization had low emigration rates, such as Switzerland, Belgium, and Denmark. Most instructive is Italy, which tops the emigration league table in 1901–10 but is more urbanized by 1910 than many other countries, including Ireland and Norway which also feature in the top four countries of emigration in Baines's table.

Further demonstrating the idea that emigration was not the preserve of agrarian-oriented economies (and urban-industrial Scotland according to the 'paradox') is comparison with England, the most industrialized country in the world in the mid-nineteenth century. Regularly found among the top five countries losing their population to emigration (until 1891 onwards), England's presence in Baines's league table also shows that urban industrial Scotland, the world's second most industrialized nation at this time (as noted above), is not an anomaly in this regard. Certainly, when aggregating data over the long run Scotland's proportional loss of people was substantially

[20]  T. M. Devine, 'Urbanisation', in T. M. Devine and Rosalind Mitchison (eds), *People and Society in Scotland I, 1760–1830* (Edinburgh, 1988), 28.

more than England's, but this was primarily due to heavy emigration in the twentieth century. An alternative impression arises when analysing statistics by decade (see Table 27.1). For instance, in the decades prior to 1901, apart from 1851–60, England's population loss was not wildly dissimilar from Scotland's; indeed between 1871 and 1880 for every 1,000 people England lost 4.0 to Scotland's 4.7. These figures are not as extreme as when compared with Ireland's loss of population. Yet just as problematically these conflations create distortions, and more intriguing are the comparisons evident each year. As Table 27.3 shows, Scotland's rate was higher for the period before the early 1860s, but stark differences only arise from 1905 onwards, at which point for every 1,000 people Scotland's rate is double or more that of England (and Wales).

Using simplistic industrial/agricultural divides to posit the idea that Scottish emigration is a paradox therefore becomes problematic. As Baines earlier argued in relation to European emigration more broadly, 'The general view that emigration was related to a lack of industrial development in a particular country is also not necessarily true.'[21] Indeed, it is more likely that transport innovations, the spread of information, and recourse to finances, among other factors associated with industrialization, were more likely to facilitate emigration. In Continental Europe, for instance, expansion of the railway and access to ports made emigration more practical, features common to Scotland.[22] Indeed, future research might compare emigration from certain districts in Scotland with the expansion of the rail network from the 1840s to see whether the penetration of the railway into certain districts generated peaks in emigration. We also need to identify those features that are distinctive about emigration from Scotland. One potential difference, though again not as striking when compared with Ireland, is that the flow from Scotland before 1900 was disproportionately skilled compared with a stronger flow of labourers from England.[23] In the absence of extensive statistical data, however, even this suggestion is speculative, but it does highlight the need for studies that examine the occupations of those leaving. Also vital to consider are the regions and specific localities that migrants left and the timing of those outflows.[24] Indeed, fine-grained longitudinal studies of migrants from particular localities would offer immense insight into such issues, particularly if undertaken within a comparative context with migrants from other nations. Just as critical, however, is to consider why so many Scots did not emigrate, for even at its peak in the interwar period Scotland only lost an average of 9.2 people for every 1,000.

---

[21]   Dudley Baines, *Migration in a Mature Economy: Emigration and Internal Migration in England and Wales, 1861–1900* (Cambridge, 1985), 15.

[22]   Nicholas J. Evans, ' "Aliens en route": Transmigration through U.K. ports, 1836–1914' (PhD thesis, University of Hull, 2006), 109.

[23]   Brinley Thomas, *Migration and Economic Growth: A Study of Great Britain and the Atlantic Economy* (Cambridge, 1973, first pub. 1954), 65–6.

[24]   See, for instance, Nicholas J. Evans, 'The Emigration of Skilled Male Workers from Clydeside during the Interwar Period', *International Journal of Maritime History*, 18:1 (2006), 255–80.

## Table 27.3  Total emigration per 1,000 people, 1853–1930

| Year | English and Welsh | Scottish |
|------|-------------------|----------|
| 1853 | 3.4 | 7.5 |
| 1854 | 4.9 | 8.8 |
| 1855 | 3 | 4.7 |
| 1856 | 3.4 | 4 |
| 1857 | 4.1 | 5.4 |
| 1858 | 2.1 | 3.9 |
| 1859 | 1.7 | 3.4 |
| 1860 | 1.3 | 2.8 |
| 1861 | 1.1 | 2.2 |
| 1862 | 1.7 | 4.1 |
| 1863 | 3 | 4.9 |
| 1864 | 2.7 | 4.8 |
| 1865 | 2.9 | 4.1 |
| 1866 | 2.8 | 3.8 |
| 1867 | 2.6 | 4 |
| 1868 | 2.7 | 4.6 |
| 1869 | 4.1 | 6.8 |
| 1870 | 4.7 | 6.9 |
| 1871 | 4.5 | 5.7 |
| 1872 | 5.2 | 5.7 |
| 1873 | 5.3 | 6.2 |
| 1874 | 4.9 | 5.8 |
| 1875 | 3.5 | 4.2 |
| 1876 | 3 | 2.8 |
| 1877 | 2.6 | 2.4 |
| 1878 | 2.9 | 3.1 |
| 1879 | 4.1 | 5.1 |
| 1880 | 4.4 | 6 |
| 1881 | 5.4 | 7.2 |
| 1882 | 6.2 | 7.2 |
| 1883 | 6.9 | 8.2 |
| 1884 | 5.5 | 5.7 |
| 1885 | 4.7 | 5.5 |
| 1886 | 5.3 | 6.5 |
| 1887 | 6.1 | 8.8 |
| 1888 | 6.1 | 9.1 |
| 1889 | 5.8 | 6.4 |
| 1890 | 4.9 | 5.2 |
| 1891 | 4.8 | 5.5 |

(continued)

| Year | English and Welsh | Scottish |
|------|-------------------|----------|
| 1892 | 4.6 | 5.7 |
| 1893 | 4.5 | 5.5 |
| 1894 | 3.3 | 3.5 |
| 1895 | 3.7 | 4.3 |
| 1896 | 3.3 | 4 |
| 1897 | 3 | 3.7 |
| 1898 | 2.9 | 3.6 |
| 1899 | 2.7 | 3.7 |
| 1900 | 3.2 | 4.6 |
| 1901 | 3.4 | 4.7 |
| 1902 | 4.2 | 5.8 |
| 1903 | 5.3 | 8.1 |
| 1904 | 5.2 | 8.2 |
| 1905 | 5 | 9 |
| 1906 | 6.4 | 11.5 |
| 1907 | 7.7 | 14.3 |
| 1908 | 5.1 | 9 |
| 1909 | 5.3 | 11.2 |
| 1910 | 7.2 | 16.8 |
| 1911 | 8.4 | 18.7 |
| 1912 | 8.7 | 15.3 |
| 1913 | 7.6 | 14.4 |
| 1914 | 4.1 | 7.2 |
| 1915 | 1.5 | 2.1 |
| 1916 | 1 | 1.7 |
| 1917 | 0.2 | 0.2 |
| 1918 | 0.3 | 0.2 |
| 1919 | 3.6 | 3.5 |
| 1920 | 5.5 | 10 |
| 1921 | 3.5 | 8.5 |
| 1922 | 3 | 8.1 |
| 1923 | 3.8 | 18.1 |
| 1924 | 2.8 | 8.1 |
| 1925 | 2.4 | 7.8 |
| 1926 | 2.7 | 10 |
| 1927 | 2.5 | 9 |
| 1928 | 2.2 | 7.9 |
| 1929 | 2.2 | 8.9 |
| 1930 | 1.4 | 5.4 |

*Source*: Compiled from Dudley Baines, *Migration in a Mature Economy: Emigration and Internal Migration in England and Wales, 1861–1900* (Cambridge, 1985), 301–6.

# CAUSES

In explaining Scottish emigration, the extant historiography typically emphasizes expulsion and grim domestic conditions. Movement from the Highlands, for instance, is frequently located in a context of overpopulation, few resources, pressure on the land, little demand for labour, and the sheep economy. Agricultural restructuring in the Lowlands in the nineteenth century also created dislocation.[25] Scottish emigration in the twentieth century is likewise situated in an economic framework characterized by the decline of heavy industry, the imposition of foreign tariffs, low wages, rife unemployment, the collapse of international markets, and the failure of industry to diversify.[26] Much of the historiography, then, has focused on a mono-causal interpretation of gloomy economic forces in Scotland inducing emigration, in which the 'journey from Scotland often began with failure at home'.[27] If emigration from Scotland is largely associated with a lack of economic opportunities, in Ireland, by contrast, mass emigration was seen as a damning indictment of British government policy. Yet the extent to which specific structural factors influenced particular individuals remains unknown.

Despite this bleak portrait of Scotland, it was a land sought by other diasporic groups such as the Irish and Italians whose experiences are among those covered in Chapter 26. Yet the numbers who were seasonal migrants or sojourners before moving overseas remains unknown. Key here also is that ethnicities such as the Irish counted among the migrant flow from Scotland, a feature which requires greater investigation. Moreover, groups such as the Irish, particularly those bound for North America after the Great Famine of the 1840s, are portrayed as exiles, a term also used of some of Scotland's migrants, particularly those associated with the Highland clearances.[28] Further examples of movement from Scotland fitting this conceptualization of forced migration include the transportation of convicts to Australia and the migration of handloom weavers.[29] Scottish emigration in the twentieth century is also viewed in dark terms. Nationalists considered that a lack of self-government caused emigration and blamed England. The inflow of Irish and English migrants to Scotland further strained opinion.[30]

An alternative but equally sweeping evaluation surrounding the determinants of Scottish emigration is found at the other extreme, that of adventurers, or 'Scots on the make', with its emphasis on successful, entrepreneurial Scots, many of whom were governors, administrators, politicians, and explorers. This approach arises predominantly

---

[25] Richards, 'Varieties of Scottish Emigration', 480–1, 477.

[26] Finlay, *Modern Scotland*, chs. 2–3; Chris Harvie, *No Gods and Precious Few Heroes: Twentieth-Century Scotland* (1981; Edinburgh, 2000), ch. 2.

[27] R. H. Campbell, 'Scotland', in Cage, ed., *The Scots Abroad*, 2.

[28] Kerby A. Miller, *Emigrants and Exiles: Ireland and the Irish Exodus to North America* (Oxford, 1985).

[29] Harper, *Adventurers and Exiles*, ch. 2.

[30] McCarthy, *Personal Narratives*, 18–19.

from a focus on the 'contribution' history that Scots made in their new lands, allegedly aided by their clannishness and Protestant work ethic.[31] It is an interpretation that continues to dominate much of the historiography of the Scots abroad, with a recent contribution claiming 'the story of enterprising Scots remains one of the absolutely central narratives of Canadian history.'[32]

As well as conditions in Scotland, several other broad factors help explain Scottish emigration: a culture of mobility built on movement in preceding centuries; high rates of internal migration that extended to emigration; greater awareness of overseas destinations through letters and propaganda; and the transport revolution.[33] Scotland's political position in the Union with England also facilitated the lengthy Scottish engagement with and settlement throughout the British Empire. Although most Scots self-financed the move to their new homelands, also influential in shaping some emigration from Scotland were immigration subsidies and incentives. Those moving to the British Empire, for instance, could avail themselves of many inducements including colonization schemes, predominant in the nineteenth century, and assisted and nominated passages that spanned both centuries. Assistance continued into the twentieth century with the Empire Settlement Act of 1922 and a £10 assisted passage after the Second World War proving particularly influential. Those moving to the United States, by contrast, were unable to avail themselves of such subsidies and made their own way, sometimes financially aided by friends and family already settled abroad. Cheaper and shorter voyages over time facilitated such journeys. The lures of gold and land grants likewise attracted numerous Scots—as well as migrants of other ethnicities—to various countries, particularly New Zealand, Australia, and Canada. Immigration policies enacted in potential destinations in the twentieth century saw the destinations to which Scots gravitated alter; an assessment of the changing character of these varied policies might assist in explaining the attraction of Scots to particular destinations during certain periods. In 1924, for instance, the Johnson-Reed Immigration Act was implemented which restricted the entry of migrants to the United States according to a quota system.

The role played by emigration agents in facilitating intending migrants with access to various inducements and the circulation of information about potential destinations throughout the nineteenth and twentieth centuries was also influential. In the nineteenth century this involved giving lectures, distributing pamphlets, displaying posters, and interviewing migrants. Similar tactics characterized the following century, with agents continuing to disseminate leaflets and booklets, place advertisements in newspapers, and prepare articles in newspapers.[34] Agent activity likewise operated in conjunction with other forms of propaganda, and debate surrounds the importance of boosterism versus

---

[31] Ian Donnachie, 'The Making of "Scots on the Make": Scottish Settlement and Enterprise in Australia, 1830–1900', in *Scottish Emigration*, 135–53.

[32] Douglas McCalla, 'Sojourners in the Snow? The Scots in Business in Nineteenth-Century Canada', in Rider and McNabb, eds., *A Kingdom of the Mind*, 77.

[33] Campbell, 'Scotland', in Cage, ed., *The Scots Abroad*, 1–28.

[34] Harper, *Adventurers and Exiles*, ch. 4; Marjory Harper, *Emigration from Scotland Between the Wars: Opportunity or Exile?* (Manchester, 1998), ch. 2.

personal letters and contact in spurring emigration.[35] Future research assessing variation in agent activity throughout the homelands and different forms of boosterism according to the target population would be illuminating. How various settlement countries were portrayed in such literature and how it varied in the European homelands would offer an interesting exercise.

Scottish migrants have also been grouped according to broad categories that seemingly explain their emigration, such as military men, administrators, explorers, gentlemen, and missionaries. The more extensive flow of non-professional migrants included the poor and agriculturalists as well as reluctant and female migrants. Indeed, a key area of future investigation is the extent to which personal decisions to emigrate were shaped by gender, a heavily under-researched aspect of the Scottish diaspora and Scottish history more generally. Scottish women moving to New Zealand, for instance, have been termed reluctant migrants, subject to decisions made by husbands and fathers. Fear of the voyage, apprehension about their destination, and the sadness of leaving kin also seemingly added to their aversion. Such unwillingness, however, was apparently more evident in the early years of settlement in New Zealand, with an inclination to emigrate more significant by the 1880s due to recognition that emigration improved the marital chances of a Scottish girl.[36] Future research in this sphere may establish to what degree Scottish women's emigration reflects competing explanations of their Irish counterparts: for marriage or work.[37] The apparently larger flow of married Scottish women, and a comparison of the destinations to which they gravitated, however, might generate more alternative satisfying explanations.

Conceptualized as 'helping the helpless', the emigration of children from Scotland, and Britain and Ireland more generally, as well as their experiences in the homelands, is a further avenue of exploration needed. Extant work has focused predominantly on orphan emigration, generating polarized debates about the effect of emigration on the children as well as their countries of origin and destination. On the one hand, the children were seen to be leaving dysfunctional and desolate physical surroundings for healthy environments, yet they came to be disparaged and despised in their new homelands.[38] Their emigration was also deemed to solve labour problems abroad, but was similarly criticized as 'a cynical strategy to delay state welfare provision at home'.[39] This focus on orphan emigration, however, excludes the dominant flow of child migrants: those who voyaged with or to their parents; an area of emigration that requires analysis.

---

[35] James Belich, *Making Peoples: A History of the New Zealanders from Polynesian Settlement to the End of the Nineteenth Century* (Auckland, 1996), 279 and ch. 12.

[36] Rosalind McClean, 'Reluctant Leavers? Scottish Women and Emigration in the Mid-Nineteenth Century', in Brooking and Coleman, eds., *The Heather and the Fern*, 103–16.

[37] Hasia Diner, *Erin's Daughters in America: Irish Immigrant Women in the Nineteenth Century* (Baltimore, 1983); Janet Nolan, *Ourselves Alone: Women's Emigration from Ireland, 1885–1920* (Lexington, 1989).

[38] Stephen Constantine, 'Children as Ancestors: Child Migrants and Identity in Canada', *British Journal of Canadian Studies*, 16, no. 1 (2003), 150–1.

[39] Harper, *Adventurers and Exiles*, 160.

More recently, theoretical and methodological developments in the social sciences, including a focus on concepts such as transnationalism and migrant networks, have influenced historical explanations of Scottish emigration. Highlighting the linkages between countries of origin and settlement, these transnational 'social spaces' include familial, economic, political, and religious ties that transcend the borders of nation states. Communication exchanges, flows of information and remittances, and the role of social networks are all fundamental areas of analysis.[40] Personal connections frequently proved essential in the decision to migrate, with evidence that the Scots, like some other nationalities undergoing profound emigration, had robust formal and informal networks which provided intending migrants with advice, funds, and information before and after emigration.[41] These potential migrants secured advice about various destinations from their contacts already settled abroad or those who had returned. Those connections could similarly act as sponsors of further emigration, though there is less evidence that the Scots sent remittances back home as with their Irish counterparts. The presence abroad of family and friends also lessened the emotions surrounding a migrant's departure.[42] Yet the extent to which more formal Scottish associational networks sought to promote emigration, as in the case of members of the Orange Order in Ireland who were encouraged to settle at Katikati in New Zealand, requires investigation.[43]

Greater emphasis on alternative methodologies such as comparative investigations and more systematic deployment of personal testimonies enhance efforts to explain emigration beyond the utilization of official sources, propaganda, and ephemera. We still await, however, sustained analyses of the correspondence exchanged between Scots during the nineteenth century, as undertaken for their Irish counterparts.[44] The twentieth-century Scottish flow, meanwhile, is illuminated by the deployment of oral testimony, which reveals a range of reasons prompting emigration including demographic pressure in households, economic conditions, health concerns, better lifestyle, climate, discrimination, the search for adventure, and wanderlust. While some analysts remain sceptical of the validity of such reminiscences, oral histories offer an important insight into the migration experience, with migrants retrospectively attributing a number of reasons for which the decision to leave was made.[45] Whether personal letters from the

[40] McCarthy, *Personal Narratives*, 3.

[41] McCarthy ed., *A Global Clan*.

[42] McCarthy, *Personal Narratives*, chs. 2–4.

[43] Donald Harman Akenson, *Half the World from Home: Perspectives on the Irish in New Zealand, 1860–1950* (Wellington, 1990).

[44] David Fitzpatrick, *Oceans of Consolation: Personal Accounts of Irish Migrants to Australia* (Cork, 1994); Angela McCarthy, *Irish Migrants in New Zealand, 1840–1937: 'The Desired Haven'* (Woodbridge, 2005). See, however, the examples from Scottish correspondents in Erickson, *Invisible Immigrants*, and extracts from letters (and other forms of personal testimony) in Allan I. Macinnes, Marjory-Ann D. Harper, and Linda G. Fryer, eds., *Scotland and the Americas, c.1650–c.1939: A Documentary Source Book* (Edinburgh, 2002).

[45] Harper, *Emigration from Scotland*; McCarthy, *Personal Narratives*, ch. 2. Other works utilizing interviews with Scottish migrants include Hammerton and Thomson, *Ten Pound Poms*, and Megan Hutching, *Long Journey for Sevenpence: Assisted Immigration to New Zealand from the United Kingdom, 1947–1975* (Wellington, 1999).

nineteenth century offer similar insight into these reasons remains to be seen. Regardless, recourse to such material demonstrates the complexities associated with the decision to emigrate. Comparative studies of Scottish and Irish migrants in the twentieth century, meanwhile, reveal that the most striking contrast surrounding motivation was a greater attribution by the Irish to political factors in spurring their departures.[46] Transnational and comparative approaches may help illuminate a fundamental, but little explored, question in diaspora studies more generally: why more people stay rather than move. Exploring this issue also promises to enhance our knowledge of Scotland's domestic history considerably, throwing light on such topics as fertility, nationalism, and culture.

A key puzzle, however, remains. Given that studies of migrants from many other countries identify similar explanations for emigration, why did Scots leave home? The answer likely lies in studies that move beyond broad explanations to focus on emigration during specific time periods in particular localities, taking into account individual movements and motivations in the context of a range of socio-economic, cultural, and political conditions at home *and* abroad. Conditions and connections with particular destinations are also critical and facilitate a more complex and nuanced interpretation of emigration from Scotland. Indeed, such accounts must recognize that decisions to emigrate were not made immediately or spontaneously, and that considerable planning and organization was necessary. As such, we need to identify conditions in the months or years prior to departure which may have influenced decisions. As Lorna Carter reminisced of her decision to leave Scotland in the mid-twentieth century, 'It was a bad winter the winter before, just months before, and I thought I've had enough of this.' Having elected to leave, though, there was an element of spontaneity in the selection of her destination: 'I wrote to New Zealand House and Australia House and whichever one was going to answer me first I was going.'[47] The reasons behind the final choice of destination, with so many competing options to choose from, is an ongoing critical avenue of enquiry. More detailed work on the profile and patterns of Scottish emigration, conditions at home, attractions in the new lands, and a range of facilitating factors would help illuminate the determinants of the outflow more fully.

# CONSEQUENCES AND IMPACT

Two central themes to date characterize studies of Scottish migrant settlement: assimilation and ethnic retention; and contribution history. Proponents of the assimilationist view of Scottish migrants typically perceive Scots as 'invisible ethnics' who assimilated to their new lands because of their Protestant faith and support for Empire.[48] As an early

---

[46]  McCarthy, *Personal Narratives*, ch. 2.

[47]  Angela McCarthy, 'Personal letters, oral testimony, and Scottish migration to New Zealand in the 1950s: The case of Lorna Carter', *Immigrants and Minorities* 23, no. 1 (2005), 70–1.

[48]  David Armitage, 'The Scottish Diaspora', in Jenny Wormald, ed., *Scotland: A History* (Oxford, 2005), 297.

scholar of Scottish emigration put it, the Scots 'always had a great gift for assimilation'.[49] This is partly attributed to the Scots not needing to defensively assert their ethnic identity, as did the Irish.[50] The assimilation view also arises from a focus on settlers rather than sojourners, emphasis on the decline of visible signs of ethnic retention, and concentration on the assimilative policies of white settler colonies of the British Empire, even though Scots moved globally. The appropriation of Scottish ethnic symbols by others also contributes to this interpretation.

The Scottish presence in varied occupational groupings similarly suggests that they infiltrated and assimilated into their new homelands, connecting migrants with a further key element of the assimilation historiography: that of contribution history. In Australia, Scots were disproportionately found in commerce and industry, and in politics, law, and journalism.[51] Scots in New Zealand were likewise considered to be over-represented as entrepreneurs, bankers, manufacturers, engineers, and large landowners, with a Scottish contribution seemingly found in several spheres: economic, cultural, literary, educational and religious, and political.[52] So too in the United States it is claimed that the Scots 'had an impact that often extended far beyond their numbers'.[53] The disproportion is also evident when comparing Scottish participation in Empire compared to their share of the British population, as Esther Breitenbach indicates in this volume (see Chapter 28). Yet the general lack of comparative work with other ethnic groups leaves us unaware of the depth of this Scottish influence in particular regions and countries, rather than in the Empire as a whole.

If, however, such disproportionate contributions are validated, the question remains as to why the Scots had such an impact. In a study of the American West, a Scottish emphasis on education is stressed in conjunction with other factors: 'A sense of adventure, a self-confidence, a familiarity with harsh landscape, a work ethic, an individualism that combined nicely with group loyalties, and, often, a set of industrial or agricultural skills set Scots apart from many of the other immigrants.'[54] Scottish over-representation in government in Australia, meanwhile, is attributed to a Scottish education, civic-mindedness, Presbyterian ethos, prior success, and national characteristics.[55] In the absence of comparative studies, there are problems with such explanations, as Mary C. Waters indicates in a chapter on social, psychological, and character traits in her influential *Ethnic Options*. The respondents to her questionnaires, she reveals, believed that certain characteristics, traits, and behaviours could be found among specific ethnic groups. What Waters divulged was that general values and beliefs were highlighted, such as family, education, hard work, and loyalty to God and country, but respondents felt these were

[49]  Donaldson, *Scots Overseas*, 124.
[50]  Harper, *Adventurers and Exiles*, 372.
[51]  Malcolm D. Prentis, *The Scottish in Australia* (Melbourne, 1987).
[52]  Tom Brooking, 'Sharing out the Haggis: The Special Scottish Contribution to New Zealand History', in Brooking and Coleman eds., *The Heather and the Fern*, 49–65.
[53]  Ferenc Morton Szasz, *Scots in the North American West, 1790–1917* (Norman, 2000), 12.
[54]  Ibid., 210–11.
[55]  Prentis, *The Scottish in Australia*, 65–6.

confined to their ethnic group. By adopting a comparative approach, Waters points to such values being universal and concludes: 'Researchers who concentrate or study one ethnic group at a time do not see how widespread and common such values are.'[56] While transnational linkages are found among other migrant groups, they perhaps offer a more useful explanation for Scottish adjustment. The time at which the Scots arrived and their size and proportion compared with other migrant groups would equally have played a part.

Perceptions of ethnic retention, meanwhile, are often associated with community studies of highlanders abroad, their presence being easier to trace due to the concentrated and isolated nature of much of their settlement, the continuing use of the Gaelic language, and the myths generated by highland migration. A sociological study of the relocation of around eight hundred migrants who followed disenchanted preacher Norman McLeod from the Highlands to Nova Scotia to Australia, and finally to Waipu and its environs in New Zealand, is a striking, if unrepresentative, example of such work, which largely focuses on highlanders in Canada.[57] Apart from the visibility of the highlander, some scholars suggest that the manner in which the Scots left home and the stories surrounding their collective departures played a decisive role in the formation of their ethnic identities abroad, with exiles (usually highlanders) more inclined than adventurers (generally lowlanders) 'to cling to their Scottish roots'.[58] Furthermore, when lowlanders did express their identity it was seemingly for economic advancement rather than the cultural solidarity sought by highlanders.[59]

Yet recent research, drawing on the example of New Zealand, suggests otherwise. Incorporating personal as well as public expressions of identity and blending insider and outsider accounts, it argues that Scottishness was expressed just as robustly by lowlanders and was not solely of cultural or economic significance but also of emotional value.[60] Language and accent, for instance, were as important for lowlanders as highlanders, while various national characteristics comprising clannishness, frugality, and caution were attributed to the Scots abroad irrespective of regional origin. Scottish material tokens included dancing and music (particularly the pipes), festivals (especially New Year), dress (bonnets, kilt, and tartan), and food and drink (particularly whisky, haggis, oatmeal, and porridge). Indeed, Scottish migrants in New Zealand shared a preoccupation with their distinctive fare as exhibited by Gaels in Quebec and their counterparts voyaging to

[56] Mary C. Waters, *Ethnic Options: Choosing Identities in America* (Berkeley and Los Angeles, 1990), 134, 138.

[57] Maureen Molloy, *Those who Speak to the Heart: The Nova Scotian Scots at Waipu, 1854–1920* (Palmerston North, 1991); Margaret Bennett, *Oatmeal and the Catechism: Scottish Gaelic Settlers in Quebec* (1998; Edinburgh, 2003).

[58] Marjory Harper, 'Exiles or Entrepreneurs? Snapshots of the Scots in Canada', in Rider and McNabb, eds., *A Kingdom of the Mind*, 34.

[59] Harper, *Adventurers and Exiles*, 371.

[60] McCarthy, *Personal Narratives*; Angela McCarthy, *Scottishness and Irishness in New Zealand since 1840* (Manchester, 2011).

Australia.[61] Yet the extent to which local conditions influenced similar or different constructions of Scottishness throughout the diaspora remains uncertain given the absence of comparative work.

Important here are studies of non-Gaelic-speaking Scots such as those who settled at Swan River in Australia. While this study is narrowly conceived, it indicates that Scots preferred to employ their fellow ethnics, work with them, and authorize them to tend to their affairs. It was, therefore, their overarching Scottishness as much as local ties that bound them together.[62] The social dimension of ethnic networks among Scots, both highlanders and lowlanders, is also striking, and was often just as important as the practical and financial benefits provided by family and friends.[63] These informal contacts frequently assisted newcomers with accommodation, employment, and money, and resemble those of other groups including the Irish.[64] Whether other ethnic groups operated in similar ways or whether they were more inclined to prioritize closer connections rather than the broader ethnic group is an unresolved area of analysis.

Not all Scots relied on ethnic networks, and some, such as Mary Ann Archbald in the United States, deliberately avoided creating and nurturing such linkages, seeking instead interaction with native-born Americans descended from other ethnic groups. Yet Mary Ann sustained an ongoing correspondence with her old friend in Scotland, Margaret Wodrow, a network of two that fulfilled emotional and sentimental, rather than practical, needs.[65] Scots in isolated settlements also operated without the support of such ethnic connections, although they too maintained contact with close connections living elsewhere.[66] Whether or not Scots without such ties were more inclined to suffer mental stresses or be apprehended for crimes would also be a fascinating research agenda.

While commercial networks between Scotland and the destinations of diaspora have been highlighted,[67] more formal networks included religious connections, and clubs and societies. Such contacts could be charitable or an entry into business and political spheres. Further research into the ways these networks differed according to their origins, development, function, and operation promises illuminating insight. A particular type of formal ethnic networking attracting attention throughout the Scottish diaspora

[61] McCarthy, *Scottishness and Irishness*, chs. 3, 4, 6; Bennett, *Oatmeal and the Catechism*; Malcolm Prentis, 'Haggis on the High Seas: Shipboard Experiences of Scottish Emigrants to Australia, 1821–1897', *Australian Historical Studies*, 36, no. 124 (2004), 299.

[62] Leigh S. L. Straw, *A Semblance of Scotland: Scottish Identity in Colonial Western Australia* (Glasgow, 2006), ch. 3, 103.

[63] McCarthy ed., *A Global Clan*.

[64] Enda Delaney and Donald M. MacRaild, eds., *Irish Migration, Networks and Ethnic Identities Since 1750* (London and New York, 2007).

[65] David Gerber, 'A Network of Two: Personal Friendship and Scottish Identification in the Correspondence of Mary Ann Archbald and Margaret Wodrow, 1807–1840', in McCarthy, ed., *A Global Clan*, 95–126.

[66] Eric Richards, 'Scottish Networks and Voices in Colonial Australia', in McCarthy ed., *A Global Clan*, 150–82.

[67] David S. Macmillan, *Scotland and Australia, 1788–1850: Emigration, Commerce and Investment* (Oxford, 1967).

is that of ethnic societies. While early histories were frequently undertaken by members to commemorate anniversaries, professional historians are pursuing more rigorous, analytical investigations. Such explorations highlight the divergent objectives, including a sense of Scottishness, among ethnic societies including St Andrews Societies and Gaelic Societies, as well as Burns Clubs and Caledonian Societies in various destinations. Membership has also been analysed, with some associations confined to Scots or particular elements of a Scottish ethnicity (such as the highland-born) while others were more open in their membership criteria.[68] The absence of many membership rolls, however, hampers consideration of how widespread membership was as well as the ethnic origins of members. By contrast, the Orange Order, one of the major Irish ethnic societies to receive sustained analysis, was generally open to all ethnicities, though there were membership variations according to time and place. In some parts of the Irish diaspora, for instance, the Irish-born and their descendants dominated whereas elsewhere other ethnic groups were prominent among Orangemen.[69] A key contrast of the ethnic societies of the Scots and the Irish, mirrored also in their ethnic periodicals, is the emphasis on cultural objectives among the Scots while Irish objectives were predominantly political.[70] Still outstanding, however, is a global study of such institutions and periodicals to determine the extent of the difference as well as presence or absence of diasporic and transnational linkages.

Another formal institution requiring investigation are the Churches to which Scots belonged, along with the internal religious life of migrants. Studies of the Irish diaspora emphasize this theme, and intriguing insights might be found in comparing the Scots with the English, particularly given the differences identified between Scottish and English forms of worship during the voyage to new settlements.[71]

Other avenues illuminating Scottishness abroad include analysis of Scottish material culture, with studies of the kilt revealing that it took on different aspects in distinct locations.[72] Scottish influence on colonial and indigenous material cultures has also received attention.[73] The naming of places, homes, businesses, public houses, animals, and individuals are also seen as expressions of Scottishness.[74] A recent exploration of such features in Western Australia claims that Scots were not alone in these practices, with Irish, English, and Welsh settlers similarly adopting naming practices. Yet the Scottish names

---

[68] Bueltmann, Hinson, and Morton, *Ties of Bluid, Kin and Countrie.*

[69] Delaney and MacRaild, eds., *Irish Migration*, xvii.

[70] McCarthy, *Scottishness and Irishness*, ch. 5.

[71] Ibid., 118–25.

[72] Heather Streets, *Martial Races: The Military, Race and Masculinity in British Imperial Culture, 1857–1914* (Manchester, 2004); Katie Pickles, 'Kilts as Costumes: Identity, Resistance and Tradition', in Bronwyn Labrum, Fiona McKergow, and Stephanie Gibson, eds., *Looking Flash: Clothing in Aotearoa New Zealand* (Auckland, 2007), 41–58.

[73] George R. Dalgleish, 'Aspects of Scottish-Canadian Material Culture: Heart Brooches and Scottish Pottery', 122–36, and Cath Oberholtzer, 'Thistles in the North: The Direct and Indirect Scottish Influence on James Bay Cree Material Culture', 99–121, both in Rider and McNabb, eds., *A Kingdom of the Mind.*

[74] MacKenzie, *Scots in South Africa*, 240–1; Straw, *Semblance of Scotland*, 113–15.

given to horses were more nationalistic than other ethnicities while Scottish clothing was distinctive with tartan and glengarrys. Some highland Scots expressed pleasure at encountering those speaking Gaelic.[75] Similar evidence that clothing and language conveyed an ethnic identity for English migrants is seemingly absent. The naming of colonial landscapes, meanwhile, is linked to broader ideas about colonization and ownership, with Scots possessing 'the land by naming it'. In other words, such naming was a symbol of possession by whites and dispossession of blacks.[76]

Interaction with and perceptions of other peoples is a further element of the consequences and impact of Scottish emigration requiring investigation. Where such studies have been undertaken, the focus is on highland engagement with indigenous peoples, often highlighting violence and brutality or parallel experiences of cross-cultural encounters.[77] Highland encounters with the Kurnai of Gippsland, Australia, for instance, underscore issues of dispossession: 'The heart of the tragedy is that these previously dispossessed Scots should come to inflict dispossession on others.'[78] It is a theme echoed in respect of the Irish: 'One of the fundamental stories of the Irish diaspora is of Irish emigrants choosing to do unto others what others had already done unto them.'[79] Recent research on Scottish (and Irish) perceptions of Maori in New Zealand provides a more nuanced perspective, showing that Scottish perceptions of Maori were influenced by the time of writing, as well as the effect of place and occupation of the migrant. It also raises questions as to whether Scots were more likely to compare and be compared with Maori than English migrants, and if so why.[80] This exploration is important in light of claims that a British assumption of cultural superiority and desire to civilize characterized Scottish attitudes towards Aborigines in Australia.[81] As well as further investigation of Scottish migrants mixing with indigenous peoples, other cross-cultural engagement is needed, including encounters and interactions with Irish and English migrants.

Indeed, the issue of Scots identifying as British is frequently assumed rather than tested, often arising from a focus on elites and propagandists. In Canada, for instance, there was a distinct 'paucity of the use of the term "British" to refer to customs, culture or the nationality of one's friends and neighbours'.[82] Missionary literature also privileged a Scottish identity over a British one.[83] Recent research on the Scots in New Zealand suggests that Britishness among Scots was generally only fleetingly identified in connection

---

[75] Straw, *Semblance of Scotland*, ch. 4.

[76] Straw, *Semblance of Scotland*, 112; MacKenzie, *Scots in South Africa*, 152.

[77] Don Watson, *Caledonia Australis: Scottish Highlanders on the Frontier of Australia* (1984; Sydney, 1997); Colin G. Calloway, *White People, Indians, and Highlanders: Tribal Peoples and Colonial Encounters in Scotland and America* (Oxford, 2008).

[78] Rodney Hall, 'Preface', in Watson, *Caledonia Australis*, xii.

[79] Donald Harman Akenson, *If the Irish Ran the World: Montserrat, 1630–1730* (Liverpool, 1997), 175.

[80] McCarthy, *Scottishness and Irishness*, ch. 7.

[81] Straw, *Semblance of Scotland*, 188.

[82] J. M. Bumsted, 'Scottishness and Britishness in Canada, 1790–1914', in Harper and Vance eds., *Myth, Migration and the Making of Memory*, 102.

[83] Esther Breitenbach, *Empire and Scottish Society: The Impact of Foreign Missions at Home, c.1790 to c. 1914* (Edinburgh, 2009), 182.

with toasts at Scottish ethnic gatherings, during international conflicts, or visits by royalty.[84] As imperial historian John MacKenzie contends, the British Empire, rather than
'creating an overall national identity [Britishness]...enabled the sub-nationalism of the
United Kingdom to survive and flourish'.[85] This national Scottish identity could at times
take priority over more regional, county, and local attachments.[86]

Less evident in the historiography is the sense of Scottishness articulated by the
Scottish descent group, although Waipu's highland settlement provides an interesting
insight. While the original settlers expressed their identity through religion, language,
and a desire to live as a community, it was only with later generations from the 1870s on
that 'a self-conscious acquisition and assertion' of Scottishness came to be expressed
through Scottish names, interest in Scottish writings, visible displays of Scottishness,
and the establishment of the Caledonian Games.[87] These visible displays of Scottishness
were also appropriated by those without Scottish connections.[88] In other cases, descent
identity connects to alternative identities such as the popularity of the Scottish heritage
movement in the American south being linked to a southern regional identity. In this
association, emphasis is given to the lost cause of Bonnie Prince Charlie to mirror the
military defeats of the American south.[89] Given the propensity of intermarriage, consideration of why descendant attachments to certain ethnicities are chosen over others also
requires investigation.

Return visits made to the homeland of their ancestors similarly provides insight into
the sense of Scottishness held by the descent group. One of the most well-known episodes of descendant (and Scots-born) return migration to Scotland in the twentieth
century concerned the return visits made by Scottish Americans throughout the 1920s
and early 1930s in connection with the Order of Scottish Clans in America. The tourists
spent about a month travelling through Scotland before returning to the United States.
Similar trips home were made by Australian Scots and Scots in England.[90] This roots
tourism continues with more recent descendants attributing their return to Scotland to
factors such as a romanticized landscape and culture, and a sense of homelessness.[91]

While developments in travel and technology as well as access to resources facilitate
descendant visits, Scottish migrants also returned home temporarily or permanently.
Yet return migration is a little-studied aspect of the Scottish diaspora, in part because
the historiography focuses on successful migrants while return implies disappointment
and a lack of success. There is also a problem with statistics, as it is difficult to quantify

[84] McCarthy, *Scottishness and Irishness*, 52–5.

[85] John M. MacKenzie, 'Empire and National Identities: The Case of Scotland', *Transactions of the Royal Historical Society*, 6th ser., vol. 8. (1998), 230.

[86] MacKenzie, *Scots in South Africa*, ch. 1; Straw, *Semblance of Scotland*, 103.

[87] Molloy, *Those who Speak to the Heart*, 125, 135.

[88] Berthoff, *British Immigrants in Industrial America*, 24–6.

[89] Celeste Ray, *Highland Heritage: Scottish Americans in the American South* (Chapel Hill, NC, and London, 2001), 18, 160.

[90] McCarthy, *Personal Narratives*, 204–5.

[91] Paul Basu, *Highland Homecomings: Genealogy and Heritage Tourism in the Scottish Diaspora* (Abingdon, 2007), 218.

who is returning. Nevertheless, it is estimated that around one-third of Scots returned home.[92] Other countries also experienced a rate of return of 20–40 per cent, though the return of Irish migrants was less common, estimated at only 10 per cent. Yet some groups who had strong rates of return migration also had strong rates of re-migration, that is, returning home and then moving on again. A focus on statistics, however, fails to incorporate those longing to return but who are unable to; nor does it distinguish between temporary, permanent, and multiple returns.

Twentieth-century Scottish migrants cite diverse reasons for return including illness and death; collective obligations; homesickness; and a desire to be home.[93] These replicate some of the explanations put forward by those returning from Australia to Britain in the twentieth century: the responsibilities, needs, and desires of family relationships in Britain; economic and job-related factors; and homesickness. Such explanations fit with other European migrant groups who returned during the nineteenth century including failure; success in the new home; homesickness; a call to return to take over the farm; and rejection of life overseas.[94] Further comparative work again has much to offer in this respect, as does the impact of returnees on the homeland. Not only would such comparative work embrace the impact of other ethnic groups on their homelands, but comparisons across time in Scotland would prove instructive. Did Scots returning in the nineteenth and twentieth centuries resemble or diverge from their counterparts who returned from other destinations in earlier time periods? To what extent would their experiences in diverse settlements, such as differing farming practices, have also influenced their impact back home?

# Conclusion

Throughout this chapter various avenues for future research were raised; here, some broader methodological and conceptual points are offered. First, in order to explain divergences from one country or region to another and formulate a more integrated interpretation of the Scottish diaspora, comparative work across settlements is urgently required. Such comparison likewise needs to contrast the experiences of the Scots with other ethnic groups. Consideration of the benefit of comparing old and new migrations from the homelands and in places of settlement also has much to offer. Can we identify similar motivations across time? To what extent did Scottishness differ in the early years of settlement compared to more recent years, and how do the identities of new arrivals fit with the articulation of Scottishness and other identities by the multigenerational

---

[92]   Baines, *Emigration from Europe*, 39; Armitage, 'The Scottish Diaspora', in Wormald, ed., *Scotland*, 282.

[93]   McCarthy, *Personal Narratives*, 208–12.

[94]   Mark Wyman, 'Emigrants Returning: The Evolution of a Tradition', in Marjory Harper, ed., *Emigrant Homecomings: The Return Movement of Emigrants, 1600–2000* (Manchester and New York, 2005), 21.

descent group? How different were the experiences of Scottish male and female migrants? Second, unlike the study of many other diasporas, investigation of the Scottish scattering is primarily the domain of historians. Yet contributions from sociologists and anthropologists, among others, and engagement with theoretical and conceptual concerns arising from the social sciences, will deepen analyses, particularly in examining Scottish emigration in the later twentieth century. Engagement with concepts such as colonialism, modernity, and the new imperial history may not only invigorate and give greater analytical vigour to studies of Scottish emigration, but will situate Scottish emigration in a broader, less introspective historiography. These avenues of enquiry seem necessary if scholarship of the Scottish diaspora is to escape accusations of relative insularity and under-theorization, and engage with scholarship on transnationalism and diaspora.

In the final analysis such explorations need to keep in mind a broader question: what is the comparative significance of the Scottish diaspora? In terms of the disproportionate outflow from Europe, Scotland was a key player, and further research is required into the quantitative character of emigration, the social composition of the migrant flow, and the causes of emigration across time and place to establish the ways they differed from or resembled those factors sparking emigration from other countries. The extant literature also suggests that the Scots were significant in the countries in which they settled, in some cases being disproportionately represented in a number of fields. Yet urgently required is ongoing research into the experiences of Scots in the destinations to which they gravitated, especially in those areas of settlement where academic accounts are required to balance extant popular studies, as in the case of England, or where most of the extant historiography is confined to the period before 1800, as with the United States. Assessing in what ways Scots were distinctive from other ethnic groups in their experience of migration would also illuminate their importance. Emigration is also significant to other themes in Scottish history including studies of gender, class, religion, politics, and cultural life. The current vibrancy of Scottish diaspora studies may therefore in due course provide answers to some of the key questions set out in this chapter.

## FURTHER READING

Brooking, Tom, and Coleman, Jennie, eds., *The Heather and the Fern: Scottish Migration and New Zealand Settlement* (Dunedin, 2003).

Cage, R. A., ed., *The Scots Abroad: Labour, Capital, Enterprise, 1750–1914* (Beckenham, 1985).

Devine, T. M., *To the Ends of the Earth: Scotland's Global Diaspora, 1750–2010* (London, 2011).

—— ed., *Scottish Emigration and Scottish Society: Proceedings of the Scottish Historical Studies Seminar, University of Strathclyde, 1990–1* (Edinburgh, 1992).

Harper, Marjory, *Adventurers and Exiles: The Great Scottish Exodus* (London, 2003).

—— and Vance, Michael E., eds., *Myth, Migration and the Making of Memory: Scotia and Nova Scotia, c.1700–1990* (Halifax, 1999).

MacKenzie, John M., with Dalziel, N. R., *The Scots in South Africa: Ethnicity, Identity, Gender and Race, 1772–1914* (Manchester, 2007).

McCarthy, Angela, *Personal Narratives of Irish and Scottish Migration, 1921–65: 'For Spirit and Adventure'* (Manchester, 2007).

—— ed., *A Global Clan: Scottish Migrant Networks and Identities Since the Eighteenth Century* (London and New York, 2006).

Prentis, M. D., *The Scottish in Australia* (Melbourne, 1987).

Ray, Celeste, ed., *Transatlantic Scots* (Tuscaloosa, 2005).

Rider, Peter E., and McNabb, Heather, eds., *A Kingdom of the Mind: How the Scots Helped Make Canada* (Montreal and Kingston, 2006).

CHAPTER 28

·······························································································

# THE IMPACT OF THE VICTORIAN EMPIRE

·······························································································

## ESTHER BREITENBACH

IF we look for evidence of the impact of Empire on Victorian Scotland, we can find it everywhere: in offering economic opportunities and imperial careers; in patterns of migration from Scotland; in changing patterns of consumption and in advertising; in the military contribution of Scots and the iconic imagery of the highland soldier; in the commitment of churches to foreign missions; in the achievements of famous Scots whether as colonial administrators, generals, or missionaries; in commercial, industrial, and business connections; in the press, periodicals, and literature; and in politics. Home and Empire exerted mutual influences on one another, as Scottish culture informed the practice of Scots abroad, and they in turn transmitted their images of Empire back home. This interconnectedness is central to understanding the impact of Empire on Scotland in the Victorian period, and how multifaceted this impact was, manifesting itself within economic, political, military, religious, social, and cultural spheres.

## EMPIRE AND ECONOMY

·······························································································

Debates on the economics of the British Empire in the nineteenth century have been preoccupied with the extent to which economic motives fuelled imperial expansion, whether there were distinct phases of imperialism driven by different economic imperatives, and whether the costs of Empire outweighed the economic benefits to Britain.[1] While many of these questions remain unresolved, at a general level there is a consensus

---

[1] P. J. Cain, 'Economics and Empire: The Metropolitan Context', in Andrew Porter, ed., *The Oxford History of the British Empire*, 5 vols. (Oxford, 1999), vol. iii, 31–52; A. R. Dilley, 'The Economics of Empire', in Sarah Stockwell, ed., *The British Empire: Themes and Perspectives* (Oxford, 2008), 101–30.

that Empire was significant to Britain's economic development in the nineteenth century, but not dominant given the advantages conferred on Britain by early industrialization and by pursuit of a free-trade regime from the 1840s. Historians of Scotland have tended to accord Empire a more central role in the country's economic fortunes in this period, although limitations of data prevent any fully systematic comparison.

Scotland's post-Union engagement with the 'first' British Empire facilitated its transformation into an industrial economy, since 'colonial profits helped prime the engines of Scottish industrialization',[2] most notably via the American tobacco and Caribbean sugar trades, and Scottish involvement in the East India Company. The empire provided markets for Scottish products, while the Caribbean was a source of cheap cotton for the growing Scottish textile industry, which dominated the first phase of industrialization. Some of the profits from the tobacco and sugar trades were invested in domestic production, and also went into the acquisition of landed estates, where landlords were often active 'improvers' of agriculture. By the 1830s, Scotland was entering a period of rapid industrialization, dominated by the heavy industries in the west of the country. Its natural resources of coal and iron ore were central to this phase of industrialization, aided by technological innovation, urbanization, and availability of labour, and improving communication and transport networks. The expanding engineering and shipbuilding industries served both imperial and wider international markets, as well as providing much of the transportation for those markets in the form of locomotives and ships. By 1913, Glasgow and its hinterland manufactured a substantial share of British-produced locomotives, rolling stock, shipping tonnage, and steel, with many of these products being exported to the empire.[3]

Textiles continued to play a role in the Scottish economy. The cotton industry suffered a long period of decline, effectively disappearing by the First World War, with the exception of more specialized products such as the cotton thread of which the Paisley firm of Coats became a major international producer.[4] The textile success story of nineteenth-century Scotland was the Dundee-based jute industry, which arose from the combination of Bengal-grown jute and whale oil from Dundee whalers, allowing the fibre to be spun in factory conditions.[5] Phenomenally successful though this industry was, becoming the major source of employment in the city and generating high profits for the owners, it reached its peak relatively quickly. Factory production of jute in Dundee had begun in 1838, while the first jute mill in Calcutta was set up in 1855. By the 1890s Calcutta had become the dominant centre of production of jute sacking and hessian cloth. Calcutta mills were able to meet the world demand for jute at lower prices than elsewhere. Dundee manufacturers turned to the production of finer and more specialized lines of jute, but the industry as a whole had begun its decline. The manufacturers' hope

---

[2] T. M. Devine, *Scotland's Empire, 1600–1815* (London, 2003), 93.

[3] T. M. Devine, 'Industrialisation', in T. M. Devine, C. H. Lee, and G. C. Peden, eds., *The Transformation of Scotland: The Economy Since 1700* (Edinburgh, 2005), 34–70.

[4] W. W. Knox, *Hanging by a Thread* (Preston, 1995).

[5] Gordon Stewart, *Jute and Empire* (Manchester, 1998).

that the British government would intervene to protect them from Indian competition was never realized.

Trade with the empire was important to the Scottish economy throughout the period, and increasingly so towards the end of the century. As a proportion of tonnage shipped from the Clyde, exports to the empire accounted for about 39 per cent between the mid-1880s and the first decade of the twentieth century, while the share of imports from the empire for the same period was around 31 per cent.[6] This would certainly have been higher than for the Scottish economy as a whole. Although not comparing like with like, it can be set against British figures, showing that the share of exports going to the empire for the period 1909–13 was 35.4 per cent, while the share of imports coming from the empire for the same period was 24.9 per cent.[7] Glasgow, 'deeply concerned with the trade side of imperialism',[8] saw trade to India and the Far East increase after mid-century. Further expansion of trade followed the opening of the Suez Canal in 1869, with India becoming ever more important as a shipping destination. Trade to Australia and New Zealand increased from the 1850s, while the discovery of gold in South Africa in the 1880s led to a rise in shipping traffic. As well as locomotives and other products of the steel and engineering industries, goods such as beer and whiskies also enjoyed an increasing share of imperial markets. MacEwans were exporting beer to Australia, New Zealand, India, Canada, and South America by the 1860s. Tennents also had large colonial sales, and in 1876 registered the Tennents' Red 'T' trademark for sole use throughout the British Empire.[9]

The major export-oriented industries of Victorian Scotland were only part of its economy, and other spheres of economic activity also had many interconnections with the empire. Scottish financial services extended into colonial operations, such as investments in colonial banks. Furthermore, Scotland supplied many trained personnel to staff the imperial banking system.[10] By the 1880s, 'Indian and colonial banks had established a network of branches and agencies throughout Scotland'.[11] Standard Life's operations throughout the empire were initiated in the 1850s, while other Edinburgh-based insurance companies also operated on a global scale.

Economic growth from the 1830s onwards generated surpluses of profits and savings that were available for investment. Several companies formed in Aberdeen in the 1830s for investments in Australia provide an early example of colonial investment. However, this was to really take off from the 1870s. North America was the major destination of Scottish capital, with heavy investment in US and Canadian railways, but Australia,

---

[6] T. M. Devine and John M. MacKenzie, 'Scots in the Imperial Economy', in T. M. Devine and John M. MacKenzie, eds., *Scotland and the British Empire* (Oxford, 2011).

[7] Cain, 'Economics and Empire'.

[8] Gordon Jackson and Charles Munn, 'Trade, Commerce and Finance', in W. H. Fraser and Irene Maver, eds,. *Glasgow. Vol. 2, 1830 to 1912* (Manchester, 1996), 52–95, 65.

[9] Anthony Slaven and Sydney Checkland, *Dictionary of Scottish Business Biography*, 2 vols. (Aberdeen, 1990), vol. 2.

[10] S. G. Checkland, *Scottish Banking: A History, 1695–1973* (Glasgow, 1975).

[11] R. C. Michie, *Money, Mania and Markets* (Edinburgh, 1981), 132.

New Zealand, South Africa, India, and Ceylon were also of interest to investors. As well as railways, money was invested in agricultural concerns such as stock-raising in Australia and New Zealand, mining ventures in India and South Africa, and tea plantations in India, promoted, for example, by Finlay, Muir, and Co. Estimates of Scottish foreign investment have put this as rising from around £60 million in 1870 to about £500 million in 1914, which would have represented a disproportionate share of total UK foreign lending.[12] More recent research by Christopher Schmitz has provided lower estimates for the total volume of overseas investment by Scottish residents, directly from Scotland and through intermediaries in London, suggesting that this rose from around £20 million in 1867 to £85 million in 1890 and £223 million by 1913, although he recognizes that the volume could have been higher.[13] Investment activity was not restricted to wealthy entrepreneurs. The Dundee investment trusts launched by Robert Fleming in 1873, for example, were a successful mechanism for small investors, channelling significant sums of capital for the construction of railways, primarily in the USA, but also in Canada, Cuba, and Argentina.[14] In Edinburgh substantial amounts of capital were similarly raised from small investors, through the establishment and management of investment trusts by Edinburgh legal firms.[15] While the majority of small investors were middle class, they were not exclusively male professionals, as there were also female and working-class investors. Such patterns of investment were often facilitated by the links of Scottish emigrant communities to Scots at home.

Imperial trade also had an impact on patterns of consumption in nineteenth-century Scotland, a topic as yet little investigated. Tea became a drink of mass consumption during the century, aided by the popularity of the temperance movement and its demand for alternatives to alcohol. Access to tea from China had been one of the motives leading to British aggression against China in the Opium Wars of 1839–42 and 1856–60, although continuing anxiety about access to Chinese markets led to the development of tea plantations in India and Ceylon from the 1860s. Scottish entrepreneurs were active in this field, from Finlay's tea plantations in India and Ceylon, established in the 1870s and 1880s, to Thomas Lipton's retail empire started in Glasgow in 1871, at the centre of which were his innovations in the marketing of tea.[16] The invention of refrigeration for long-distance shipping of goods brought Australian and New Zealand meat and dairy products to Scots' dinner tables—the first cargo of meat from New Zealand arrived in an Albion line ship in 1882.[17] Advertising of imperial commodities frequently stressed their colonial origins, for example, Camp Coffee. This product, produced by Campbell

[12] S. G. E. Lythe and J. Butt, *An Economic History of Scotland 1100–1939* (Glasgow, 1975); Bruce Lenman, *An Economic History of Modern Scotland* (London, 1977).

[13] Christopher Schmitz, 'The Nature and Dimensions of Scottish Foreign Investment, 1860–1914', *Business History*, vol. 39, no. 2 (1997), 42–68.

[14] Michael Fry, *Scottish Empire* (Edinburgh, 2001); Bill Smith, *Robert Fleming, 1845–1933* (Haddington, 2000).

[15] J. D. Bailey, 'Australian Borrowing in Scotland in the Nineteenth Century', *Economic History Review*, New Series, vol. 12, no. 2 (1959), 268–79.

[16] Slaven and Checkland, *Dictionary of Scottish Business Biography*, vol. 2.

[17] Jackson and Munn, 'Trade, Commerce and Finance'.

Paterson, was given a distinctive logo of a Sikh soldier serving 'his master the British army officer', a kilted Gordon Highlander.[18] Furthermore, imperial experience informed fashion and material culture. Paisley became a major centre of production of the eponymous patterned shawls in the first half of the nineteenth century, the popular design being copied from Kashmir silks and shawls.[19] Such habits of consumption were no doubt very similar to those elsewhere in Britain, but it would be of interest to investigate how Scottish importers, retailers, and commentators on consumption and fashion represented the imperial connection.

The imperial dimension of Scottish economic growth brought many benefits to the Scottish business class, and the empire increased in importance for both markets and investment towards the turn of the century. This no doubt consolidated the growing enthusiasm for imperialism, manifested also in militarism and missionary support. Yet much remains to be done to investigate how the entrepreneurs, merchants, and financiers who were most active in imperial spheres thought about Empire or whether they were influential in shaping public opinion in favour of imperialism. As is true of Britain generally, the empire played only a part in wider international economic relations, and the interests of industrialists and investors were often not tied exclusively to the notion of Empire. Some companies and individuals, however, have come to be particularly associated with imperialism, whether the 'imperialism of free trade' or the 'scramble for Africa'. The entrepreneurs William Jardine and James Matheson, for example, operating on the boundaries of the formal empire to extend British economic influence in China, were instrumental in pushing the British government into the First Opium War and acquisition of Hong Kong.[20] William Mackinnon, with his shipping and other commercial operations in East Africa, lobbied for British acquisition of territories in the region, thus participating in the 'processes of "informal imperialism"'.[21]

Mackinnon's career also adds weight to critiques of Peter Cain and Antony Hopkins's 'gentlemanly capitalism' thesis, which seeks to explain the character of late nineteenth-century British imperialism through the political and economic influence of a specific class of financiers based in the south-east of England.[22] As Forbes Munro has argued, Mackinnon fostered a business network that sustained British political influence both within and beyond imperial frontiers, through its presence in Calcutta, as well as Glasgow and London, with London 'merely one link in a chain of commercial cities across the world'.[23] The question of the political influence of Scottish businessmen with imperial interests thus deserves further scrutiny. Gordon Stewart has argued that

---

[18]  Slaven and Checkland, *Dictionary of Scottish Business Biography*, vol. 2, 8. This logo was replaced in 2006 by the image of Sikh and highland soldiers seated side by side. The older logo had been subject to criticism by race-equality organizations.

[19]  Valerie Reilly, *The Paisley Pattern: The Official Illustrated History* (Glasgow, 1987).

[20]  Robert Blake, *Jardine Matheson* (London, 1999).

[21]  J. Forbes Munro, *Maritime Enterprise and Empire* (Woodbridge, 2003), 499.

[22]  P. J. Cain and A. G. Hopkins, *British Imperialism, 1688–2000*, 2nd edn. (Harlow, 2001). For critiques, see Martin Daunton, '"Gentlemanly Capitalism" and British Industry 1820–1914', *Past and Present*, 122 (1989), 119–58, and Dilley, 'The Economics of Empire'.

[23]  Munro, *Maritime Enterprise and Empire*, 505.

Dundee jute interests lacked the political backing that Lancashire cotton magnates could drum up, but commercial, industrial, and financial interests in Glasgow and Edinburgh were likely to have been better placed. It is notable that successful entrepreneurs often had political ambitions, albeit less frequently in Parliament than within civic government, and many successful businessmen carried influence within political parties whether or not they held political office. A number of cases of imperial entrepreneurs entering the House of Commons can be cited, however, including Jardine, Matheson, and Kirkman Finlay.[24] The latter, for example, subsequent to his parliamentary career, played a leading role as a member of the Glasgow East India Association in campaigning for free trade and an end to the East India Company's monopoly in trade with China in the early 1830s.[25]

Scotland's form of industrial development in the nineteenth century has in retrospect been criticized for its narrow base and export-led character.[26] It has been argued that too little was done with the capital accumulated through industrial enterprises to diversify into home-based industries, or even to reinvest at home. One factor contributing to this was the potential for higher rates of profit to be generated by the export of capital overseas. Another factor was the limited production of consumer goods for home consumption, as the low wages of Scotland's unskilled working classes led to insufficient capacity in domestic consumption. This low-wage economy also reinforced Scotland's tradition of migration, as many Scots went south, or overseas to the USA and British colonies in search of higher wages and better opportunities, constituting a movement of labour on an unprecedented scale.[27] There were costs associated with this pattern of development as well as benefits. The narrow economic base was to prove disastrous in the long run, and the wealth generated was neither evenly distributed nor utilized productively at home. While industrialists, including those whose fortunes were owed to Empire, contributed some of their wealth to philanthropy, to founding schools, hospitals, or amenities such as parks, or to support for foreign missions, they showed little interest in the improvement of working-class conditions. Lack of investment in housing, for example, has been seen as an indictment of the industrial class in nineteenth-century Scotland.[28]

[24] For Dundee politicians' attempts to protect the local jute industry, see Stewart, *Jute and Empire*. Kirkman Finlay was MP for Glasgow Burghs and Lord Provost of Glasgow from 1812. See *Oxford Dictionary of National Biography* online: www.oxforddnb.com (accessed 17 December 2010). William Jardine served as MP for Ashburton in Devon from July 1841 until his death in February 1843. James Matheson succeeded his partner in this parliamentary seat, where he served until 1847, when he was returned as MP for Ross and Cromarty. See Robert Blake, *Jardine Matheson*.

[25] Yukihisa Kumagai, 'Kirkman Finlay and John Crawfurd: Two Scots in the Campaign of the Glasgow East India Association for the Opening of China to Trade, 1829–1833', *Journal of Scottish Historical Studies*, vol. 30, no. 2 (2010), 175–99.

[26] See, for example, T. M. Devine, *The Scottish Nation 1700–2007* (London, 2006).

[27] See Chapter 27 on emigration by Angela McCarthy.

[28] Bruce Lenman and Kathleen Donaldson, 'Partners' Incomes, Investment and Diversification in the Scottish Linen Area 1850–1921', *Business History*, vol. 21 (1971), 1–18; C. H. Lee, 'Economic Progress: Wealth and Poverty', in Devine, Lee, and Peden, eds., *The Transformation of Scotland: The Economy since 1700*, 128–56.

In this sense the profitability of empire-generated industries contributed to a very uneven distribution of wealth in Scotland, and to a high social cost to the labour without which such wealth could not have been created.

# THE MILITARY CONTRIBUTION TO EMPIRE

The British Empire provided employment for many Scots, whether as migrants to colonial territories or as part of the apparatus of imperial governance. Not least among these in numerical importance was service in the imperial army.[29] Scots had a tradition of serving as mercenaries in European armies—in Sweden, Poland, Russia, and the Netherlands—although there had been a reorientation away from northern Europe to military service across the Atlantic by the late seventeenth century.[30] Increasing engagement with the English military-fiscal state provided greater opportunities for Scots in the army.[31] This had already been facilitated by the 1603 Union of the Crowns and the Union of 1707, but it was the post-1745 period that witnessed a substantial increase in the number of Scots in the British Army. Among other things this served as a means whereby former Jacobites could rehabilitate themselves, while the incorporation of highland Scots in the British Army was seen as crucial to the maintenance of the Union and to internal security within the British state.

Scots were contributing disproportionately to the ranks of the British and East India Company armies by the late eighteenth century, and in the earlier part of the nineteenth century were still contributing disproportionately to the British Army. In 1830 Scotland contributed 13.5 per cent of the forces of the British Army, with only 10 per cent of Britain's population.[32] However, by 1886 the proportion of men contributed by Scotland to the British Army had declined to 8.1 per cent.[33] Indeed, by the 1830s and 1840s Scottish regiments had started recruiting outside Scotland.[34] By 1878, of nineteen 'nominally Scottish' regiments, only three, all highland, recruited as many as 60 per cent of their officers and men from Scotland.[35] Thus highland regiments recruited from the Lowlands and elsewhere, and lowland regiments recruited from England and Ireland.

Despite declining levels of recruitment to the army from Scotland in the nineteenth century, paradoxically Scottish regiments came to enjoy an ever higher public profile and popular acclaim. This was a consequence of the prominent role played by Scottish

[29]   Scots also served in the Royal Navy, but not on the same scale. See Brian Lavery, *Shield of Empire: The Royal Navy and Scotland* (Edinburgh, 2007).

[30]   T. M. Devine, 'Setting the Scene: Before the British Empire', Symposium on Scotland and Empire, University of Edinburgh, 18 November 2009.

[31]   Hew Strachan, 'Scotland's Military Identity', *Scottish Historical Review*, 85 (2) (2006), 315–32.

[32]   Stephen Wood, *The Scottish Soldier* (Manchester, 1987), 55.

[33]   Victor Kiernan, 'Scottish Soldiers and the Conquest of India', in Grant G. Simpson, ed., *The Scottish Soldier Abroad, 1247–1967* (Edinburgh, 1992), 97–110.

[34]   Wood, *The Scottish Soldier*.

[35]   Kiernan, 'Scottish Soldiers and the Conquest of India', 104.

regiments in conflicts in the Victorian era, from the Crimean War in Europe in the 1850s to several colonial conflicts, for example, the suppression of the Indian 'Mutiny' (1857–8), the Asante war in West Africa (1873–4), the Second Anglo-Afghan War (1878–81), Tel-el-Kebir in Egypt (1882), and the South African War of 1899–1902.[36] Regiments such as the Gordon Highlanders, the Black Watch, and the Seaforth Highlanders were praised for their bravery in combat, though the corollary of such fighting spirit was often a ruthlessness in punitive reprisals. But it was not only their military prowess that made Scots stand out. Highland uniforms drew the attention of war artists and photographers, while the newly developing practice of war reporting from the front in the newspaper press added to the glamour of the highland warrior. So entrenched was this image to become that at the time of the army reorganization of 1881 lowland regiments were also ordered to wear 'tartan "trews" and highland-style doublets'.[37]

If levels of recruitment to the army did not tally with the popularity of the image of the soldier, the popular militarism of nineteenth-century Scotland did ultimately generate a more enthusiastic response to enlistment. In 1914 Scots signed up to fight more readily than did the English, Welsh, or Irish.[38] One factor contributing to this response was the strength of the volunteer movement in Victorian Scotland. Launched in 1859, the volunteer movement produced twice as many volunteers per head of the population in Scotland than any other part of the United Kingdom.[39] In Edinburgh, for example, this included separate Rifle Volunteer Companies of advocates, solicitors, bankers, merchants, and university staff, while in Glasgow accountants and journalists also formed separate companies.

The volunteer movement played its part in the South African War, which involved not only regular army regiments but also auxiliary forces such as the Militia, Volunteers, and Imperial Yeomanry, resulting in an 'extensive involvement' of 'citizen soldiers' from Scotland.[40] As elsewhere in Britain, the South African War polarized political opinion in Scotland, leading to bitter divisions and public demonstrations by supporters on both sides of the pro-government and pro-Boer divide, which on occasion deteriorated into riots.[41] The troops themselves, however, were not a target of protest, often being welcomed home by enthusiastic crowds. Indeed, the South African War came to be memorialized the length and breadth of Scotland. This continued to feed imperialist sentiment, which contributed to the levels of enlistment in 1914 and 1915. The success of the volunteer movement, reorganized into the Territorial Force by 1914, resulted in many middle-class, white-collar, and skilled working-class men signing up, groups that had not previously responded to appeals for recruits.

---

[36] Edward M. Spiers, *The Scottish Soldier and Empire, 1854–1902* (Edinburgh, 2006).

[37] Charles Withers, 'The Historical Creation of the Scottish Highlands', in Ian Donnachie and Chris Whatley, eds., *The Manufacture of Scottish History* (Edinburgh, 1992), 143–56, 150.

[38] Strachan, 'Scotland's Military Identity'.

[39] Wood, *The Scottish Soldier*.

[40] Spiers, *The Scottish Soldier and Empire*, 157.

[41] Stewart J. Brown, ' "Echoes of Midlothian": Scottish Liberalism and the South African War, 1899–1902', *Scottish Historical Review*, lxxi (1992), 156–206.

In the nineteenth century the popular militarism of Scottish society was not so much reflected in consistently high levels of recruitment to the army but in participation in the volunteer movement and uniformed youth organizations, and by celebrations of Scottish military success within the empire. This resulted from the growing links of army to community, and from the circulation and reproduction of the imagery of Scottish military valour. The volunteer movement, for example, served to link the army to the largely urban communities from which it was drawn. At the same time the army reforms of the 1880s strengthened the local and regional identities of regiments. Furthermore, while military service itself was an exclusively masculine pursuit, soldiers often had wives and families, some of whom accompanied them in their postings to colonial territories,[42] or with whom they communicated by letter if they remained at home, while there were various veterans' and welfare organizations providing support to ex-servicemen and their families. Women could also take pride in Scottish military success,[43] and find attractions in the image of the soldier hero, and they turned out to see troops off or welcome them home.

While the conflicts being fought occurred in places remote from Scotland, the general public at home were well supplied with accounts of the actions of Scottish soldiers within the empire. As Edward Spiers makes evident, this was achieved by a variety of means, from the direct communications of soldiers to family and friends at home, the publication of memoirs, newspaper accounts, artistic representations in the form of paintings and prints, and in popular forms of entertainment such as song, music hall, and theatre.[44] For example, Piper Findlater, the hero of the storming of the Dargai Heights on the North-West Frontier (1897), became a music-hall celebrity, touring England, Ireland, and Scotland. This widespread consciousness of the army's role in Empire was reinforced through the links of regiments to communities at home, through the volunteer movement, and through uniformed youth organizations such as the Boys' Brigade and Boy Scouts. In this sense militarism came to be embedded in communities across Scotland, and ultimately evoked the ready response to enlistment in the First World War. Thus by the beginning of the twentieth century the identification of Scots with the British Empire and its defence had come to assume a prominent role in the national consciousness.

# IMPERIAL CAREERS

If the army was, numerically, the most significant source of employment for Scots in the British Empire, several other occupations offered the possibility of imperial careers, particularly for the educated professionals graduating from Scottish universities. Across a

---

[42] Diana M. Henderson, *The Scottish Regiments*, 2nd edn. (Glasgow, 1996). Henderson notes that sources reflecting women's experiences of military life appear to be very rare.

[43] See, for example, Katharine, Duchess of Atholl, *Working Partnership* (London, 1958).

[44] Spiers, *The Scottish Soldier and Empire*.

range of occupations Scots played a part in shaping the life of the empire, whether as emigrants in colonies of settlement or as 'sojourners' in colonial territories in the service of the imperial state, in the armed forces, colonial administration, or in medical service, or building the infrastructure of the empire as engineers and technicians. For some imperial careers, the significance lay not so much in the numbers pursuing them but rather in the capacity to achieve distinction on the imperial stage, and in the position individuals occupied within social and political networks connecting Empire to metropole. From the ranks of colonial administrators, explorers, and missionaries, for example, emerged prominent and celebrated personalities, whose high public profile further contributed to the idea that Scotland was making a notable contribution to the empire.

By the late eighteenth century, Scots had gained a direct route of access to positions in the East India Company through the system of patronage, within which the most powerful patron was Henry Dundas. Subsequently, Scots' share of positions within the Indian Civil Service (following the end of East India Company rule in 1858) was lower, but remained substantial. In mid-century a system of competitive examination for entry to the Indian Civil Service (and to other branches of the civil service) was introduced. While the Northcote Trevelyan reforms were intended to increase the proportion of civilians who had an Oxbridge background, this effect took some time to achieve, and both Scots and Irish continued to perform well within the competitive system.[45]

Scots achieved prominence as senior colonial administrators, making up a third of colonial Governors General between 1850 and 1939.[46] Family dynasties were apparent in such careers, for example, the Elgins, father and son, who served, among other things, as viceroys in India, with the latter subsequently being appointed as Colonial Secretary in Campbell-Bannerman's government in 1905. The Mintos, great-grandfather and great-grandson, were Governors General in Bengal and Canada respectively, with the latter also serving as Viceroy of India.[47] Movement between senior postings in different territories was a common pattern in administrators' careers, for example between Governor Generalship of Canada and Viceroyship of India, the latter recognized as the most important appointment within the empire. The empire thus helped to shore up the position of the Scots landed gentry. From the mid-eighteenth century, when access to positions in London was limited, colonial careers helped to incorporate the aristocracy into the British state as army officers and as colonial civil servants.[48] This pattern persisted throughout the nineteenth century, maintaining the status of the aristocracy as their power at home declined both economically and politically. The imperial careers of

[45]  C. J. Dewey, 'The Education of a Ruling Caste: The Indian Civil Service in the Era of Competitive Examination', *English Historical Review*, vol. 88, no. 347 (1973), 262–85.

[46]  Anthony Kirk-Greene, *Britain's Imperial Administrators, 1858–1966* (London, 2000).

[47]  Kirk-Greene, *Britain's Imperial Administrators, 1858–1966*; *Oxford Dictionary of National Biography* online, www.oxforddnb.com (accessed 22 January 2010).

[48]  Linda Colley, *Britons: Forging the Nation 1707–1837* (New Haven and London, 1992).

Scottish peers were a source of pride to many Scots, and 'the rising sentiment of popular imperialism stamped the role of the peerage in the consciousness of many'.[49]

One group of Scottish professionals with a highly visible role in Empire was missionaries. Foreign-mission societies appeared in Scotland with the establishment in 1796 of the Glasgow Missionary Society and the Edinburgh-based Scottish Missionary Society.[50] Following endorsement of foreign missions by the Church of Scotland in 1824, and the subsequent energetic take-up of missions by the Free Church of Scotland and the United Presbyterian Church in the 1840s, foreign missions came to be of perennial interest among churchgoers. The number of missionaries in the field grew from a tiny handful at the beginning of the nineteenth century to several hundred by the end of the century. Scottish missionary figures were celebrated not just in Scotland but across the Protestant and English-speaking world, for example, Alexander Duff, James Stewart, Mary Slessor, and Robert Laws. David Livingstone, the best known of all Scots missionaries, was an employee of the London Missionary Society, like his celebrated Scottish father-in-law, Robert Moffat. Both were nonetheless acclaimed in Scotland as missionary heroes, located within a missionary tradition seen as fulfilling the spirit of John Knox's reformation. Livingstone owed his fame as much to his explorations as to his missionary work, though he himself always stressed his missionary aims. While his achievements in exploration were exceptional, his qualifications as both minister and doctor, and his scientific interests, were less so. Several missionaries undertook expeditions to territories as yet unknown to Europeans, and their findings on geographical phenomena, geological formations, flora and fauna, and so on, were presented to scientific gatherings or published as scientific papers.

Missionaries were the emissaries of the churches at home, and in this sense enjoyed a special relationship to communities there. Supported by donations from Scottish churchgoers, and managed by foreign-mission boards of the Presbyterian churches, they were answerable to the Scottish churches and contractually obliged to send information for dissemination at home and to address congregations and public meetings when on furlough. The ultimate consequence of this was the acclamation of individual missionaries as heroic figures and the representation of the Presbyterian foreign-mission movement as a specifically Scottish contribution to the empire's 'civilizing mission'. Missionaries thus played a key role in shaping the perceptions of Empire and of colonial peoples among Scots at home throughout the nineteenth and well into the twentieth century.

The scientific activities of missionaries and others contributed to the imperial project of mapping, cataloguing, and codifying the territories, flora and fauna, and peoples of the empire. While the creation of this 'imperial archive' can be seen as a technique of management and control, it also acted as a catalyst for the flowering of scientific

---

[49]  I. G. C. Hutchison, 'The Nobility and Politics in Scotland, c.1880–1939', in T. M. Devine, ed., *Scottish Elites* (Edinburgh, 1994), 131–51, 144.

[50]  Esther Breitenbach, *Empire and Scottish Society: The Impact of Foreign Missions at Home, c.1790–c.1914* (Edinburgh, 2009).

endeavour and for the application of technical skills across the empire. Scots played a notable part in this, as explorers, cartographers, doctors, botanists, geologists, linguists, and so on.[51] Scottish universities were central to this, both through the volume of graduates being produced—which necessitated a proportion seeking careers outside Scotland—and through having a curriculum that provided the knowledge and skills relevant to the pursuit of scientific research and codification. John Hargreaves has indicated the extent to which graduates of Aberdeen University made their mark on the empire, though we still await detailed studies of other Scottish universities' links to it.[52] Over time the education of overseas students from British colonies was to become an additional vehicle for transmission of Scottish intellectual values to the empire. The strength of such links was not lost on contemporary observers. Edinburgh University, as the former prime minister the Earl of Rosebery declared in 1908, 'was the assiduous mother and foster-mother of the builders of the Empire'.[53]

## CIVIL SOCIETY AND EMPIRE

It was not only through economic activities, political, military, or other imperial careers that Scots demonstrated their engagement with Empire in the Victorian period. Civil society in Scotland also manifested a lively interest in the empire, through a variety of forms of organization, events, and cultural phenomena. Indeed the first significant civil-society movement that arose as a response to Empire, the abolitionist movement, had emerged in Scotland, as elsewhere in Britain, in the late eighteenth century. Following abolition of the slave trade throughout the empire in 1807, the anti-slavery movement in Scotland experienced two further phases of intense activity—firstly, from the 1820s onwards the campaign for abolition of slavery throughout the British Empire gained in strength, while subsequently Scots mobilized in support of the abolition of slavery in the USA.[54] There were many overlaps in membership between anti-slavery societies and foreign-mission committees, and continuing opposition to slavery was manifested in the aim of eradicating slave trading by Arabs in Africa, which contributed to enthusiasm for missions in East and Central Africa. A particularly significant dimension of the foreign-mission movement was its capacity actively to engage people across Scotland. For some churchgoers their interest in missions would have consisted of little more than passive consumption of sermons or addresses. Others, however, participated in

---

[51] John M. MacKenzie, *Empires of Nature and the Nature of Empires: Imperialism, Scotland and the Environment* (East Linton, 1997); Charles Withers, *Geography, Science and National Identity* (Cambridge, 2001).

[52] John D. Hargreaves, *Academe and Empire: Some Overseas Connections of Aberdeen University, 1860–1970* (Aberdeen, 1994).

[53] *Souvenir of the Scottish National Exhibition, Edinburgh Today* (Edinburgh, 1908), 56.

[54] Iain Whyte, *Scotland and the Abolition of Black Slavery, 1756–1838* (Edinburgh, 2006); C. Duncan Rice, *The Scots Abolitionists* (Baton Rouge, LO, 1981).

organizational networks across Scotland, through systems of church organization for mission support, or through Ladies' Associations and non-denominational societies such as the Edinburgh Medical Missionary Society. They showed a keen interest in developments within the mission field, put great efforts into fund-raising, attended public meetings to hear missionaries speak about their work, and took part in campaigns, such as the lobbying of the government in 1888 to make Nyasaland [Malawi] a Protectorate, in order to ensure the security of the Scottish missions there.[55]

Philanthropic and religious impulses proved capable of sustaining organizations over the longer term, and represented the most significant organized forms of engagement with Empire by Scots at home. However, other organizations also demonstrated an interest in Empire, imperial affairs, and imperialism itself—ranging from learned societies to imperial propaganda organizations. The impact that the experience of Empire had on the development of scientific knowledge met a ready audience at home, though how extensively this was the case remains a matter for investigation. The Edinburgh Botanical Society founded in 1836, for example, had members in imperial territories and collected specimens from abroad. The Royal Scottish Geographical Society (RSGS) was founded in 1884 at time of rising imperialist sentiment, and in its early decades was actively interested in imperial advance, especially in Africa, where the role of Scots in exploration was prominent.[56] The society had branches in Edinburgh, Glasgow, Dundee, and Aberdeen, and rapidly built up a substantial membership. Its objects were, however, to promote the utility of geography and not confined to imperial interests as such. Empire and imperialism were more specifically promoted by imperial propaganda organizations and through events such as exhibitions. The Imperial Federation League, the Unity of the Empire Association, the United Empire Trade League, the Primrose League, and the Victoria League all had branches in Scotland in the late nineteenth and early twentieth century.[57] The Edinburgh Unity of the Empire Association, for example, provided to a range of clubs and societies free lectures that aimed 'to bring home to all minds the importance of the British empire'.[58]

International exhibitions, initiated in Scotland with the 1886 Edinburgh exhibition, provided a platform for promotion of both Scotland and Empire. In the major Glasgow exhibitions of 1888, 1901, and 1911, 'empire and Scottishness predominated', while the imperial emphasis was to reach its apogee in the Glasgow Empire Exhibition of 1938.[59] The Edinburgh exhibitions of 1886, 1890, and 1908 also celebrated imperial connections,

---

[55] John McCracken, *Politics and Christianity in Malawi 1875–1940* (Cambridge, 1977); Andrew C. Ross, 'Scotland and Malawi, 1859–1964', in Stewart J. Brown and George Newlands, eds., *Scottish Christianity in the Modern World* (Edinburgh, 2000), 283–309.

[56] John M. Mackenzie, 'The Provincial Geographical Societies in Britain 1884–1914', in Morag Bell, Robin Butlin, and Michael Hefferman, eds., *Geography and Imperialism, 1820–1940* (Manchester, 1995), 93–124.

[57] Breitenbach, *Empire and Scottish Society*.

[58] Edinburgh Unity of the Empire Association, *Report of Fourth Session*, 1898–9.

[59] John M. MacKenzie, ' "The Second City of Empire": Glasgow—Imperial Municipality', in Felix Driver and David Gilbert, eds., *Imperial Cities* (Manchester, 1992), 215–37.

with Edinburgh acclaimed as an imperial city in 1908. Organizing committees of international exhibitions brought together landed gentry, civic elites, and political leaders, leading lights in the churches, business, and commercial life, the universities and other professional circles. Like many of the explicitly imperialist organizations and societies such as the RSGS, with a similar composition of leading members, they thus represented a nexus of political, civic, and social interests within Scottish society, committed, among other things, to the promotion of the British Empire.

Leadership of such organizations was dominated by the middle classes, though landed gentry often had high profiles as patrons or patronesses of organizations. Nonetheless, some also attracted working-class interest. This was perhaps most obvious in the case of foreign missions, which through the churches had access to an audience that included sections of the working classes. The iconic missionary figures of humble origins, David Livingstone and Mary Slessor, were certainly held up as aspirational models for the lower classes. Their backgrounds indicated a dedicated involvement in church life, which though not unique in Scottish life was not likely to have been typical, since this was a period when industrialization and urbanization contributed to the rapid rise of the 'unchurched poor'. The involvement of women, however, was characteristic of such civil-society interest in Empire, both in the earlier phase of philanthropic and religious organization and in the later development of scientific interest and imperial propagandist organizations.[60] Whilst women's participation often took the form of membership of auxiliary or separate women's organizations, they saw themselves as having an active role to play, whether fund-raising for foreign missions, promoting emigration to the colonies of settlement, or lobbying for schools to celebrate Empire Day. Such evidence of interest in Empire through the churches and other forms of voluntary organization in Scotland is crucial in challenging the view that Empire was only of interest to those who ran it or gained directly from it. Furthermore, it demonstrates that Empire had an appeal across gender and across class, that Scottish participation in Empire exerted a fascination for many, and that the accounts of Scottish contributions to 'civilizing' the peoples of the empire, whether through bringing European forms of scientific knowledge or through Christianity, contributed to a sense of national pride.

# THE PRESS AND EMPIRE

As might be expected, the press and publishing industries were crucial to the dissemination of imperial imagery and ideologies within nineteenth-century Scottish society, whether through the newspaper and periodical press, specialist publications such as those of the churches or the Royal Scottish Geographical Society, the production of

---

[60] Clare Midgley, *Women against Slavery: The British Campaigns, 1780–1870* (London, 1992); Lesley Orr Macdonald, *A Unique and Glorious Mission: Women and Presbyterianism in Scotland* (Edinburgh, 2000); Breitenbach, *Empire and Scottish Society*.

imperial maps and atlases by firms such as Bartholomews, or through literary responses to Empire. Writers such as Tobias Smollett, John Galt, Walter Scott, and Robert Louis Stevenson reflected in their fiction on the meaning of Empire, while poets and other writers took emigration as their theme.[61] The travel writing of Scots also embraced the empire, from 'Tom Cringle's Log' of Jamaican experiences to the African explorations of Mungo Park and Livingstone. The periodical press was a vehicle both for travellers' accounts and commentary on imperial affairs. Particularly significant in this respect was *Blackwood's Magazine*. Founded in 1817 as the Tory alternative to the *Edinburgh Review*, *Blackwood's* was to become increasingly 'identified as an official promulgator of conservative establishment views of the British imperial presence'.[62] As well as reportage from imperial locations and poetry and fiction on imperial topics, the journal carried much commentary on the conduct of imperial affairs, particularly on military matters, and was read throughout the empire as well as at home. *Blackwood's* was the vehicle for publication of early works by writers such as Joseph Conrad and John Buchan. Conrad's *Heart of Darkness* first saw the light of day in the pages of *Blackwood's*, a context which, David Finkelstein argues, has too frequently been ignored in interpretations of this text.

Although there is a growing literature on Scottish writing about Empire and on its audiences, there remains much scope for further work. Most seriously neglected here has been the coverage of Empire in Scottish newspapers. Robert Cowan's study *The Newspaper in Scotland*, published in 1946, has demonstrated how wide a range of newspapers existed in the period 1815–1860.[63] At this time much coverage of imperial affairs was reprinted from London-based newspapers, though editorializing and correspondence provided a clear flavour of Scottish opinion. For example, the emancipation of slaves in the West Indies was widely supported in Scotland by the 1820s. *The Glasgow Courier*, however, spoke up in defence of West Indian interests and 'fought the slave question to the last ditch'.[64] In the mid-nineteenth century, when the repeal of the Corn Laws and Navigation Acts 'had opened new vistas of free-trade prosperity', the press in Scotland reflected the view that colonies were a 'fiscal encumbrance' and should become 'financially and politically autonomous'—a reaction to rebellions and other tensions in Canada, Australia, and New Zealand. By the early 1850s, however, there was an awareness of the economic benefits arising from large-scale emigration, such as agricultural developments in Canada, while the discovery of gold in Australia persuaded many 'that the Empire might have a profitable future'.[65] Events in the East also attracted the attention

[61] Nigel Leask, 'Scotland's Literature of Empire and Emigration, 1707–1918', in Ian Brown, Thomas Owen Clancy, Murray Pittock, and Susan Manning, eds., *Enlightenment, Britain and Empire (1707–1918)* (Edinburgh, 2007); Angela Smith, 'Scottish Literature and the British Empire', in Devine and MacKenzie, eds., *Scotland and the British Empire*.

[62] David Finkelstein, 'Imperial Self-Representation: Constructions of Empire in *Blackwood's Magazine*, 1880–1900', in Julie F. Codell, ed., *Imperial Co-Histories: National Identities and the British and Colonial Press* (Madison, NJ, 2003), 95–108.

[63] R. M. W. Cowan, *The Newspaper in Scotland* (Glasgow, 1946).

[64] Cowan, *Newspaper in Scotland*, 374.

[65] Ibid., 385.

of the press, with the Opium War of 1839–42 occasioning much anti-Chinese sentiment. Ambivalence in the 1840s towards the expense of ruling India appears to have been swept away by reactions to the Indian uprising of 1857–8. The coverage of the 'Mutiny' was extensive, reflecting not only the momentousness of events, but also the changes in communication technology, such as the use of the telegraph, and the opportunities created for increasing circulation by the abolition of stamp duties. Graphic accounts of 'atrocities' of course did much to expand newspaper readerships at this time.

From around the 1860s electric telegraphy and the foundation of specialist press agencies transformed the process of news gathering, making it possible to incorporate news on national and international affairs in local newspapers, such as, in William Donaldson's example, the *Peterhead Sentinel*.[66] Furthermore, the late nineteenth century witnessed the development of an imperial press network that resulted in increased coverage in the British press of the white Dominions.[67] While much international coverage in Scottish papers still continued to be 'cribbed' from the London press, there was a range of ways in which a specific Scottish dimension might be manifested. As Richard Finlay has indicated, letters from soldiers gave direct accounts of imperial conflicts, the rhetoric of a superior Scottish contribution to Empire was used to disparage Irish aspirations to Home Rule, the imperialistic Volunteer movement was much covered in the local press, and Scottish papers were 'an important conduit for the promotion of emigration' through adverts, emigrants' letters, and favourable images of Scots as migrants.[68] Like Donaldson, Finlay stresses the importance of the local press. Furthermore, he questions the extent to which *The Scotsman* and *The Glasgow Herald* were representative of national opinion, given differences in political sympathies compared to the majority of local papers that tended to be liberal or independent.

If, as John MacKenzie has argued, study of the British press and the British Empire is underdeveloped, study of the Scottish press and Empire is even more so.[69] Although coverage of imperial affairs was unlikely to have predominated over domestic concerns, Empire and imperial affairs became more visible in the Scottish press during the nineteenth century, and in the later decades was a constant presence as well as occasionally providing the major focus of debate. Investigation of press coverage is essential for a more effective assessment of the place the empire occupied in public consciousness, as well as illuminating changing attitudes to Empire, and local and regional differences in interconnections with it. Furthermore, the scrutiny of press coverage and readership has some potential to shed light on working-class responses to Empire, such as the

---

[66] William Donaldson, *Popular Literature in Victorian Scotland: Language, Fiction and the Press* (Aberdeen, 1986).

[67] Simon J. Potter, *News and the British World* (Oxford, 2003). Potter does not cite any Scottish newspapers in his study, but it is likely that this would hold good for the Scottish press.

[68] Richard J. Finlay, 'The Scottish Press and Empire, 1850–1914', in Simon J. Potter, ed., *Newspapers and Empire in Ireland and Britain* (Dublin, 2004), 62–74, 66.

[69] John M. MacKenzie, 'The Press and the Dominant Ideology of Empire', in Potter, ed., *Newspapers and Empire*, 23–38.

shipyard workers' celebrations of the relief of Mafeking covered in *The Glasgow Herald* in 1900.[70]

# CONCLUSION

Scottish participation in the British Empire and its impact on Scotland have emerged as important fields of historical study relatively recently. There are many parallels with experience elsewhere in Britain, yet as Andrew Thompson has argued, both Empire and its impacts were diverse and pluralistic.[71] Certain impacts of Empire appear to have been intensified in the Scottish context, and there is already much evidence to indicate this. There remains scope, however, for further quantification of impacts, for example, more investigation of economic data, not just at a macro level or that of large-scale enterprises, but at the level of small investors, family firms, and of retailing and consumption. And while evidence reviewed here suggests extensive direct economic interests in Empire by the late Victorian period, there were asymmetries of region, class, and gender in the magnitude and meaning of such interests, which are not yet necessarily well defined.

The mobility of nineteenth-century Scots has already been well attested to through quantitative data, especially on emigration, Scots' share of the armed forces, and in colonial administration, but as yet the various groups of professionals who enjoyed colonial careers have not been afforded comparable attention. There is, however, a need to move beyond crude numbers and the reinforcement of 'disproportionate' Scottish participation, and to enquire further into motivations for and pathways to imperial careers, and how these shaped understandings of Empire in both colony and metropole. Such patterns of movement within and across the empire were, like other circuits of Empire, differentiated by class and gender.

Evidence considered in this chapter supports the view that Scotland's participation in the British Empire was influential in shaping Scottish society and identity in the Victorian period, and that recognition of an imperial role was embedded in Scottish society. This was not only because of the numbers of people who gained direct benefits from Empire, but also because of the range of social strata touched by Empire, and the appeal that the vision of Scotland's contribution to it exerted across boundaries of region, class, and gender. Furthermore, the networks of interests that bound people to Empire often overlapped and intersected in ways that reinforced its significance—for example, industrialists' support for foreign missions, the channelling of investments between Scottish communities at home and abroad, or the transmission of imperial 'knowledge' by returning administrators and missionaries to educational and religious institutions. The repeated interactions of such groups, often inhabiting the same political, social, and

---

[70] MacKenzie, 'The Press and the Dominant Ideology of Empire'.

[71] Andrew Thompson, *The Empire Strikes Back? The Impact of Imperialism on Britain from the Mid-Nineteenth Century* (Harlow, 2005).

cultural arenas, represented a mutual reaffirmation of the importance of their role in Empire. Nonetheless, attachment to Empire was conditioned by different interests. While in the Victorian and Edwardian eras these appear to have coalesced in celebration of an imperial identity, a deeper understanding of the asymmetries of imperial ties is likely to illuminate the emergence of the more fragmented and contested attitudes to Empire that were to emerge in the twentieth century.

## FURTHER READING

Breitenbach, Esther, *Empire and Scottish Society: The Impact of Foreign Missions at Home, c.1790–c.1914* (Edinburgh, 2009).

Devine, T. M., *Scotland's Empire, 1600–1815* (London, 2003).

—— *To the Ends of the Earth: Scotland's Global Diaspora, 1750–2010* (London, 2011).

—— and MacKenzie, John M., eds., *Scotland and the British Empire* (Oxford, 2011).

Finlay, Richard J., 'The Scottish Press and Empire, 1850–1914', in Simon J. Potter, ed., *Newspapers and Empire in Ireland and Britain* (Dublin, 2004), 62–74.

Leask, Nigel, 'Scotland's Literature of Empire and Emigration, 1707–1918', in Ian Brown et al., eds., *Enlightenment, Britain and Empire (1707–1918)* (Edinburgh, 2007).

MacKenzie, John M., '"The Second City of Empire": Glasgow—Imperial Municipality', in Felix Driver and David Gilbert, eds., *Imperial Cities* (Manchester, 1992), 215–37.

Munro, J. Forbes, *Maritime Enterprise and Empire* (Woodbridge, 2003).

Schmitz, Christopher, 'The Nature and Dimensions of Scottish Foreign Investment, 1860–1914', *Business History*, vol. 39, no. 2 (1997), 42–68.

Spiers, Edward M., *The Scottish Soldier and Empire, 1854–1902* (Edinburgh, 2006).

Stewart, Gordon, *Jute and Empire* (Manchester, 1998).

PART V

THE GREAT WAR
TO THE NEW
MILLENNIUM,
1914–2010

CHAPTER 29

..............................................................

# THE GREAT WAR

..............................................................

## E. W. McFARLAND

THE themes of tragedy and futility have come to dominate the popular memory of the Great War. In Scotland, its legacy is overlaid with a sense of inordinate sacrifice: a small nation, with a historic martial tradition, drawn into a global conflict of unprecedented destructive power. The emotional hold of this portrayal remains so powerful that the historian often struggles to confront the gap between memory and actual experience. Indeed, one of the most compelling aspects of the conflict is precisely how its meaning has changed over time. The sense of waste, disillusionment, and moral bankruptcy that came to surround it originally drew strength from the continuing evolution of survivors' memories in the interwar period, but also reflected the anti-heroic sensibilities of later decades. Yet, this unrelievedly negative interpretation would have surprised the many Scots in November 1918 who emerged from four years of struggle on both the home and fighting fronts, acutely conscious of the scale of loss, yet proud of and thankful for their contribution to an epic British victory.

Scotland has shared in the 'boom in memory' that has gathered ground since the 1990s. Popular historical treatments of the Great War have certainly flourished. Of varying quality, the best of these studies are capable of transcending military antiquarianism and the all-enveloping pathos of the 'mud and misery' genre to produce work that is well crafted and evocative.[1] Unfortunately, attempts to stimulate the growth of a more critical scholarship on the impact of the conflict among the professional historical community have proved less successful. Elsewhere in Western Europe and in the UK, historians have probed the war's dominant collective memory, notably through a reconsideration of issues of private and public remembrance. This has encouraged new perspectives on the war's cultural and material legacy, evidenced not least in the desire of revisionist military historians to strip away the layers of mythology that still surrounds

---

[1] Note for example: J. Alexander, *McCrae's Battalion: The Story of the Sixteenth Royal Scots* (Edinburgh, 2003); A. Weir, *Come on Highlanders! Glasgow Territorials and the Great War* (Stroud, 2005).

its conduct.[2] In contrast, scholarly interest in Scotland during this period has remained largely located within an older social and labour-history framework, overwhelmingly concentrated on the wave of industrial disputes and rent strikes in the west of Scotland between 1915 and 1919.[3] The latter have been recognized as some of the very few Scottish events in the twentieth century that 'mattered *vitally* to the history of mainland Britain', yet despite this ticket of entry to the historical mainstream, the impact of the preoccupation with 'Red Clydeside' has been curiously insular and restrictive.[4] Even if newer, focused studies operating within the tradition have added to our knowledge of previously neglected social groups, such as women factory workers, the new emphasis on 'those who cooked, transported and laboured' has arguably marginalized other vital areas of the Scottish Great War experience, notably including the contours of military service and popular commemorative culture.[5]

The impact of the familiar contours of primary research can also be traced through the Great War's treatment in the classic scholarly histories of Scotland. Appealing to a broad non-academic readership, these works are significant in their own right in helping anchor some of the most powerful 'truths' about the conflict in the popular consciousness. Not surprisingly, the first of these is that the war's real significance for Scotland stems from the battles on the home front, which served to 'raise the class consciousness of the workers by several degrees.'[6] Unfortunately, this concentration on domestic tensions has encouraged a more broad brushstroke approach to Scotland's military contribution; this is typically hailed as 'unique', although the precise scale of the associated 'rush to the colours' is seldom quantified or evidenced.[7] Similarly, great emphasis is placed on the 'disproportionate' severity of Scottish casualties, with losses so catastrophic that 'few working-class families escaped'.[8] The conflict's destructive power has in turn encouraged many commentators to frame the Great War as a turning point in Scotland's historic development, leading to an inevitable loss of 'mass innocence' and the sapping of national confidence.[9] Indeed, this sense of rupture and discontinuity has

---

[2] S. Heathorn, 'The Mnemonic Turn in the Cultural Historiography of Britain's Great War', *Historical Journal*, 48, no. 4 (2005), 1,103–24; S. Goebel, 'Beyond Discourse? Bodies and Memory of Two World Wars', *Journal of Contemporary History*, 142, no. 2 (2007), 377–85.

[3] For a recent and accessible overview of these developments see T. Royle, *Flowers of the Forest* (Edinburgh, 2006), 230–55. Examples of the 'Red Clydeside' debate include J. Foster, 'Strike Action and Working-Class Politics on Clydeside, 1914–1919', *International Review of Social History*, 35 (1990), 33–70; I. Maclean, *The Legend of Red Clydeside* (Edinburgh, 1999).

[4] J. Stevenson, 'Writing Scotland's History in the Twentieth Century: Thoughts from Across the Border', *Scottish Historical Review*, lxxvi, no. 1 (1997), 111.

[5] See K. Blackwell, 'Women on Red Clydeside: The Invisible Workforce Debate', *Scottish Social and Economic History*, 21, no. 2 (2002), 140–62; C. Moriarty, 'The Material Culture of Great War Remembrance', *Journal of Contemporary History*, 34, no. 4 (1999), 654.

[6] T. C. Smout, *A Century of the Scottish People 1830–1950* (London, 1984), 267.

[7] C. Harvie, *No Gods and Precious Few Heroes: Scotland since 1914* (Edinburgh, 1981), 24; M. Lynch, *A New History of Scotland* (London, 1991), 103.

[8] Harvie, *No Gods*, 24. See also R. Findlay, *Modern Scotland, 1914–2000* (London, 2004), 2–4; T. M. Devine, *The Scottish Nation, 1707–2007* (Harmondsworth, 2006), 309.

[9] Lynch, *New History*, 423; Findlay, *Modern Scotland*, 2–4; Devine, *The Scottish Nation*, 309.

been recently carried over into the first comprehensive account of the Scottish war experience, with its dramatized image of a country turned from a productive powerhouse into a stagnant backwater through four years of extraordinary effort.[10]

Against this background, it becomes important for the present discussion to examine what was genuinely new, distinctive, and transforming about the Great War's impact on Scotland. To this end, it takes a deliberately unbalanced approach by substituting the conventional debates on labour relations and class consciousness with an alternative focus on how the war was actually waged, won, and remembered. Here it is necessary to draw not only on new and unpublished doctoral research, but also on a more creative and outward-looking approach to Scottish history generally, characterized by increasing critical attention on Scotland's military role in the imperial project.[11] The picture that emerges is much more complex than any single dramatic watershed. On one hand, it was economic and demographic patterns rooted in Scotland's historic engagement with the international economy prior to 1914 that maximized the national contribution to the British war effort. Meanwhile, the emotional and cultural resources on which people drew to make sense of this most disorientating of modern wars were equally shaped by a powerful pre-existing martial tradition. Conversely, it was not simply the war's malign impact that dictated Scotland's immediate future, but rather the uncertainty and failed hopes of the post-war decades, which ensured that the Great War would be remembered and represented for future generations as a national tragedy rather than as an achievement.

1

...........................................................................................................

The sweeping scale of the Great War has often encouraged historians to identify great aggregations of experience at the expense of more subtle patterns of response. This is particularly the case in capturing the dynamics of volunteering, where one of the first difficulties is in penetrating the emotional layers of reinterpretation later elaborated by participants themselves. The post-war histories of individual Scottish 'Pals' battalions, such as the 16th Highland Light Infantry (HLI), characteristically emphasize the speed, spontaneity, and selflessness of the enlistment process.[12] Although only seven of these units were actually raised in Scotland, their mythology has become emblematic of the wider national response to the call to arms in 1914.

In contrast, recent studies drawing on a detailed accumulation of official statistics, cross-referenced with local economic and demographic data, offer a much more nuanced understanding of the 'distinctiveness' of the Scottish manpower contribution. Scotland raised a total of 320,589 men during the period of voluntary enlistment—one in four of Scottish

---

[10]  Royle, *Flowers of the Forest*, xxxi–ii.

[11]  See T. M. Devine, 'The Break-up of Britain? Scotland and the End of Empire', *Transactions of the Royal Historical Society*, 16 (2006), 163–80.

[12]  T. Chalmers, *A Saga of Scotland: The History of the 16th Battalion HLI* (Glasgow, n.d.), 4–5.

males between fifteen and forty-nine, and 13 per cent of the UK total.[13] Despite recruiting rates which were only slightly (2.3 per cent) above the UK average for the period of voluntary enlistment as a whole, it was during the opening months of the war that Scotland made its largest proportionate contribution to the new mass army, with the surge of 9,657 enlistments in a single week in August, constituting a striking 19.32 per cent of the UK total.[14] Although Scottish recruitment did not reach its highest volume until September 1914, this disproportionate contribution could not be maintained, as volunteering in England and Wales at last began to rise sharply from the end of the previous month.

Why were so many of the Scottish male population in a position to enlist immediately? The explanation seems to operate at two levels. In the first place, Scotland's export-oriented economy was initially badly destabilized by the outbreak of war, with its industrial sector contracting by 11 per cent by October 1914. The fear of unemployment was a powerful recruitment driver among urban industrial workers, evidenced most clearly in the high enlistment rates for those practising particularly vulnerable trades, like building and mining.[15] Lacking this immediate stimulant, agricultural workers and the middle classes were more measured in their response, balancing family security with national loyalty. Ultimately, however, the existence of this available manpower pool can best be understood as the product of long-term structural forces, in that it also contained the natural component of 'excess' labour which in peacetime had been absorbed by very high levels of emigration and internal migration. Disturbing the delicate balance between emigration and employment, the war had now conveniently released a potentially mobile population of young males for military service. The effects could be particularly felt in Scotland's rural counties: official percentage figures for county recruitment of men of military age between August 1914 and April 1915 reveal that the seven UK counties with the highest rates were all in Scotland, with five of these in the Highlands, where the historic lack of employment opportunities had already had a profound demographic impact.[16] Indeed, these records also reveal disparities in recruitment patterns within Scotland, with the highland region contributing an average of 57.8 per cent of males of military age, compared with the Central Belt's 32.3 per cent.

Rather than representing a brutal form of economic conscription these material realities are best interpreted as a predisposing framework within which subjective forces and communal pressures could also shape individual enlistment decisions. Volunteering should indeed be situated in the context of a more widespread psychological mobilization behind the war effort. French historians of the Great War have been perhaps the most influential in bridging the gulf between current meanings of the conflict and those of the generation of 1914 who actually made an emotional investment in its

[13] E. Spiers, 'The Scottish Soldier at War', in H. Cecil and P. H. Liddle, eds., *Facing Armageddon: The First World War Experienced* (London, 1996), 315.

[14] D. Young, 'Voluntary Enlistment in Scotland 1914–16' (PhD thesis, University of Glasgow, 2001), 255.

[15] Young, 'Voluntary Enlistment', 101–4.

[16] D. Coetzee, 'A Life or Death Decision: The Influence of Trends in Fertility, Nuptiality and Family Economies on Voluntary Enlistment in Scotland, August 1914 to December 1915', *Family and Community History*, 8, no. 2 (November 2005), 78, 87–8.

outcome.[17] In Scotland the keynote of this 'investment' was defensive patriotism. For many Scots, the war was a just and necessary crusade against an aggressor who threatened the very survival of the British Empire. At stake was not only the commercial self-interest expected of a free-trade economy, but the very ideals of 'liberty' and 'progress' that had long given popular imperialism its distinct local expression.

The opportunities that 'the common fight for freedom' promised for community advancement also mobilized marginalized groups within Scottish society, like the Catholic Irish, who, their leaders claimed, raised an estimated 24.4 per cent of the local volunteer total in Glasgow.[18] Yet such contributions were seldom acknowledged by contemporaries. Instead, the war would be hailed as an explicitly *Scottish* project—the work of a 'warrior nation'. The use of enlistment as a temporary shelter from economic hardship was indeed already deeply rooted in Scottish society, the Scottish military tradition having emerged during the later eighteenth century as a cultural rejoinder to exactly this type of practical expediency.[19] While population erosion during the later nineteenth century had progressively undermined traditional highland recruiting grounds, Scottish martial aspirations had nevertheless been exported in line with migration patterns, resulting in prestigious 'Scottish' territorial battalions in English cities and a host of 'Highland'-branded Canadian regiments.[20] The Great War now intensified this capacity for inclusion and adaptation—indeed, as J. G. Fuller suggests, at one stage in the conflict 143 Scottish battalions were included in the active list, with 86 of these alone bearing the appellation 'Highland'.[21] Although martial race ideology was hardly unique in 1914, the Scottish variant was particularly effective not only as a practical junction point between local patriotism, national identity, and imperial destiny, but also as a bond between the various disparate components of a rapidly expanding military establishment. Those joining the territorial and service battalions of historic Scottish regiments were now able to embrace the visible symbols of a heroic past despite suspicions over their own lack of military experience.[22] Meanwhile, the territorial force itself had long proved attractive to recruits precisely because of its ability to associate military service with social networks and local loyalties—indeed 'Pals' units with their own hastily constructed 'civic' identities proved much less central to the recruiting effort in Scotland than elsewhere in the UK.[23]

[17] See S. Audoin-Rouzeau and A. Becker, *Understanding the Great War* (London, 2002).
[18] E. W. McFarland, '"How the Irish Paid Their Debt": Irish Catholics in Scotland and Voluntary Enlistment, August 1914–July 1915', *Scottish Historical Review*, lxxxiii, no. 214 (October 2003), 261–84.
[19] S. Allen and A. Carswell, *The Thin Red Line: War, Empire and Visions of Scotland* (Edinburgh, 2004), 44.
[20] B. McEvoy, *History of the 72nd Canadian Infantry Battalion Seaforth Highlanders of Canada* (Vancouver, 1920); C. R. MacKinnon, *The Scottish Highlanders* (New York, 1995).
[21] J. G. Fuller, *Troop Morale and Popular Culture in the British and Dominion Armies 1914–1918* (Oxford, 1990), 164. At this point the Highlands contributed only around 8 per cent of Scotland's total population.
[22] W. A. Andrews, *Haunting Years: The Commentaries of a War Territorial* (London, 1930), 249.
[23] On the eve of war Scotland contributed 20 per cent of UK Territorial infantry: D. Duff, *Scotland's War Losses* (Glasgow, 1947), 35. In contrast, Young suggests that Scotland raised only 5.3 per cent of the total number of Pals battalions raised in the UK (Wales contributed 12.8 per cent), 'Voluntary Enlistment', 289. See also David Martin, ed., *The Fifth Battalion The Cameronians (Scottish Rifles)* (Glasgow, 1936).

Yet, regimental pride and the endorsement of tradition had their limits as well as uses. With industrial recovery ending Scotland's manpower surplus by the end of 1914, the rallying call of collective solidarity became even more strident, with middle-class youth as a particular target for recruiters. The rhetoric of Scottish martial prowess was now fully exploited, but despite the persistent mythology of battalions being created 'overnight' or 'in sixteen hours', the process of recruitment had now become increasingly protracted. Nor did all volunteers wish to join the Scottish infantry battalions that had absorbed the initial recruitment surge. Far from displaying the gullibility with which they have been associated, many Scots chose the relative safety of engineering and technical corps, where their skills could earn extra pay and allowances.[24]

## 2

Where the fate of those who enlisted is concerned, the popular memory of the Great War has a definite end point: the doomed battalions of high-spirited youth who joined together and trained together during 1914 and 1915 were also wiped out in often less than half an hour, amid the mechanized slaughter of the modern battlefield. There is great truth in this grievous human narrative. The first two years of the war represented the most costly test for the new mass army. Repeated daylight frontal attacks at Gallipoli between June and July 1915 cost the 52nd (Lowland) Division over 4,800 killed and wounded—a disaster mourned as a 'Second Flodden' in small communities across central Scotland.[25] Worse was to come. The Battle of Loos in September 1915, where forty-five Scottish battalions participated, is now recognized by military historians as the most lethal encounter of the war in terms of the percentage of combatant casualties: here the 15th (Scottish) Division lost 1,595 men killed, the highest number of any division engaged.[26] At the Somme the total volume of casualties was even greater, with the 51st (Highland) Division suffering 3,500 casualties in two single assaults in July 1916.[27]

Yet the *military* narrative that emerges from war diaries and operational histories is instead one of continuity and survival. The idea of the regiment as a 'living' entity, greater than the sum of men who served and died in its ranks, was a cornerstone of the Scottish military tradition. This concept was challenged by the scale of loss in the Great War, but by no means negated. For, although increasing UK manpower exhaustion meant some depleted formations were eventually composited, even the most shattered battalions were generally withdrawn from the line, rested, and after receiving reinforcements, were often able to continue as effective fighting units. The 17th HLI, for example, which

---

[24] Young, 'Voluntary Enlistment', 262.

[25] R. R. Thompson, *The Fifty-Second (Lowland) Division, 1914–1918* (Glasgow, 1923), 42–102.

[26] N. Lloyd, *Loos 1915* (Stroud, 2006), 156–8; F. T. Macleod, D. Macritchie, and W. G. Burn Murdoch, eds., *The Book of the Feill* (Edinburgh, 1917), 15 [letter from Ian Hay Beith].

[27] F. W. Brewsher, *The History of the 51st (Highland) Division 1914–1918* (Edinburgh, 1921), 80–5.

suffered 22 officer and 447 other-rank casualties on the opening day of the Somme, went on to regroup and pursue successful operations in the Hulluch-Cambrai sector: by 1917 it was reported to be 'in the highest spirits, battle scarred and with a glorious record of great achievements established'.[28] Indeed, the sanguinary reputation of this type of Scottish assault battalion on the Western Front has tended to eclipse the more varied experiences of Scots serving in line-holding units, technical arms, as well as in the Royal Navy and Air Force, or those involved in more distant campaigns, such as Salonika and Palestine.

Amid the new realities of combat, it is important to consider how far morale and performance were sustained by the survival of a distinctive Scottish military identity. While the dangers and hardships facing soldiers serving in Scottish battalions may not have diverged dramatically from their UK counterparts, their collective motivation was often underpinned by a highly positive self-image.[29] This in itself was enough to encourage robust responses from rival units. As Captain Owen of the Royal Welsh Fusiliers commented: 'The Jocks are all the same; both the trousered kind and the bare arsed kind: they're dirty in the trenches, they skite too much, and they charge like hell—both ways.'[30]

New research on the operational history of one of the most famous Scottish divisions illuminates the complex and fluid process through which corporate identity evolved.[31] The 51st (Highland) Division was a territorial unit, whose strong sense of 'Scottishness' was achieved through a fusion of subformation loyalties, based on local and regimental allegiances. Corporate unity among its formerly geographically dispersed battalions was consciously fostered by the adoption of the familiar motivational symbols of pipes and tartan, but was further reinforced during training and initial deployment through contact with other national groups and military formations. Ultimately, however, it was the division's battlefield success that bred a shared identity and self-belief, with the dramatic assault on Beaumont Hamel in November 1916 redeeming its earlier failures on the Somme. Continuing success also shaped public perceptions of the division, with positive press comment eagerly monitored and disseminated among its battalions—although there was little new in this desire for external validation, as Scottish soldiers had long played an active role in the creation of their own image.[32]

Good morale was, of course, also a reflection of features common to other British units, such as strong officer–men relationships, but there is evidence that the High Command recognized the importance of local, regional, and national homogeneity by particularly channelling Scots to the 'Scottish' divisions, where manpower demands permitted. Although recruitment to the 51st Division from its traditional local areas

---

[28] J. W. Arthur and I. S. Munro, eds., *The 17th Highland Light Infantry (Glasgow Chamber of Commerce Battalion): Record of War Service* (Glasgow, 1920), 58.

[29] Spiers, 'Scottish Soldier', 328. For individual testimony from Scottish participants see D. Young, *Forgotten Voices of the Great War* (Stroud, 2005).

[30] R. Graves, *Goodbye to All That* (London, 1961), 138.

[31] C. F. French, 'The 51st Division during the First World War' (PhD thesis, University of Glasgow, 2006).

[32] French, 'The 51st Division', 53; E. Spiers. *The Scottish Soldier and Empire, 1954–1902* (Edinburgh, 2006).

decreased markedly during 1916, locality was still an important focus even after conscription, and it was not until 1918 that the impact of dilution became critical. This official confidence was not misplaced, albeit the issue was less that of bolstering an innate Scottish 'martial spirit' than the maintenance of the type of powerful internal identity vital for any effective fighting unit. Combined with greater sophistication in tactical deployment, training, and preparation in successive campaigns, this would lay the basis for the reputation of the 51st as a crack 'storming' division.

# 3

Front-line soldiers were not only sustained by comradeship and unit solidarity but also through the eager continuation of links with families, workplaces, and the social and civic organizations of which they had been members in peacetime. Recent UK scholarship has increasingly emphasized the closeness of the home and fighting fronts, challenging the traditional image of the powerless, victimized soldier, alienated from civilian society. Instead, as Helen McCartney's study suggests, men turned to the traditional and the familiar in order to survive.[33] Through letters, leave, and the local press they presented accounts of their front-line experience that were often realistic and unmediated; in return they received practical and emotional support through gifts and written correspondence. This two-way contact may have helped produce a shared appreciation of the hardships experienced both at home and in the trenches, fostering a common perspective on the conflict.

Similar studies systematically probing the encounter between military and civilian society are sadly lacking for Scotland, constraining our understanding of how and why public commitment to the war effort endured over four years. However, the subtle, integrative account of the British home-front experience offered by Adrian Gregory does provide a valuable starting point for grasping the distinctive contours of civilian mobilization in Scotland.[34] Overlaid with the familiar rhetoric of shared 'sacrifice', civilian commitment to the war effort kept pace with levels of military participation. Gregory notes that eight out of ten counties with the largest number of War Savings Associations were in Scotland; Glasgow exemplified the very high rate of Scottish subscription, raising a record-breaking £14 million during 'Tank Week', January 1918.

Beyond solidarity with Scots in uniform, engagement on this scale drew on more diffuse patterns of cultural mobilization. Catriona Macdonald, for example, has highlighted the important role played by the Scottish provincial in this respect.[35] Drama, history, and mythology, she argues, were all deployed by editors to make a terrifying

---

[33] H. B. McCartney, *Citizen Soldiers: The Liverpool Territorials in the Great War* (Cambridge, 2005), 3.

[34] A. Gregory, *The Last Great War: British Society and the First World War* (Cambridge, 2008), 221–2.

[35] C. M. M. Macdonald, 'Race, Riot and Representations of War', in C. M. M. Macdonald and E. W McFarland, *Scotland and the Great War* (East Linton, 1999), 145–72.

conflict intelligible for local audiences, with Scotland's martial heritage used to frame even the most severe reversals in the familiar iconography of heroic last stands and 'death or glory' charges. Whilst promoting the sense of a larger common struggle to defend the British Empire, these 'imagined battlefields' may also have been instrumental in reinforcing and legitimating a singular Scottish vision of a global war.

Scotland's spiritual mobilization during the Great War has also received recent historical attention. As Michael Snape suggests, the religiosity of Scottish soldiers attracted favourable comment from army chaplains, when compared to their UK counterparts, albeit that attrition would claim many of those who had entered the war in a crusading spirit.[36] The Church of Scotland's own investigations suggested that 30 per cent of Scottish soldiers had 'vital' church connections, but even the 20 per cent figure presented in the 1919 Army and Religion report, which focused on the battered post-conscription army, was still double that for English troops.

While the war may have strengthened the 'diffuse Christianity' of citizen soldiers, the situation for institutional religion on the home front was rather more complex. As national Churches, claiming the adherence of the majority of Scots, both the Church of Scotland and the United Free Church had been enthusiastic supporters of the war from its outbreak.[37] However, although religious belief constituted a further potential source of emotional solidarity and national identity, institutional religion throughout Europe was severely tested by the demands of rationalizing mortality on a previously unimaginable scale.[38] Whereas the Roman Catholic Church already had clear rituals for dealing with sudden death, the Scottish Presbyterian denominations, already divided, struggled to develop controversial new liturgical and theological positions, such as prayers for the dead and salvation through death on the battlefield, to meet the needs of grieving congregations. The challenges that these denominations faced, suggests James McLeod, would circumscribe their impact on Scottish culture and society at a time of exceptional personal and national crisis.[39] Indeed, the war was also a searing personal experience for many ministers, challenging the optimistic theological liberalism that had underpinned earlier enthusiasm for the 'Social Gospel'.[40]

---

[36] M. Snape, *God and the British Soldier: Religion in the British Army in the First and Second World Wars* (London, 2005), 159–60.

[37] F. Douglas, 'Ritual and Remembrance: The Church of Scotland and National Services of Thanksgiving and Remembrance after Four Wars in the Twentieth Century' (PhD thesis, University of Edinburgh, 2006).

[38] See A. J. Hoover, *God, Germany, and Britain in the Great War: A Study in Clerical Nationalism* (New York, 1989); A. Becker, *War and Faith: The Religious Imagination in France 1914–1930* (Oxford, 1998).

[39] J. L. McLeod, ' "Greater Love Hath No Man Than This": Scotland's Conflicting Religious Response to Death in the Great War', *Scottish Historical Review*, lxxxi, no. 211, April 2002, 70–96; see also S. J. Brown, " 'A Solemn Purification by Fire": Responses to the Great War in the Scottish Presbyterian Churches, 1914–1919', *Journal of Ecclesiastical History*, 45, 1 (January, 1994), 82–104.

[40] *Reports to the General Assembly, 1921* (Edinburgh, 1921): Report of the Committee on Social Problems, 77–8. See J. Stewart, ' "Christ's Kingdom in Scotland": Scottish Presbyterianism, Social Reform and the Edwardian Crisis', *Twentieth Century British History*, 12:1 (2001), 1–22.

Naturally, it is industrial mobilization that has become the most fully documented aspect of the Scottish home front. This reflects the scale and significance of the phenomenon, but is also coherent with the prevailing socio-economic paradigm which has shaped Scottish historical writing on the war. After an initial period of dislocation, the highly specialized Scottish economy became increasingly directed towards war production, resulting in a massive increase in its productive capacity. The resultant concentration of reserved occupations meant that the conscription rate was much lower for Scotland than for England and Wales—14.6 per cent compared with 22.1 per cent. However, with 47 per cent of the male workforce already lost to the services, women's employment also dramatically expanded, with 31,500 women employed in munitions alone by October 1918.[41] Indeed, overlapping notions of 'work' and 'service' would grow to structure women's participation in a range of wartime tasks in Scotland, as elsewhere in the UK, including the uniformed auxiliary services. The breadth of this contribution is vividly captured in the various 'records of service' in which Scottish communities in the immediate aftermath of war sought to demonstrate how the bonds of 'civic unity' and 'common sacrifice' had underpinned the local civilian war effort.[42]

This image of a collective, communal effort in itself may have heightened the sense of a truly national consensus for victory, yet in reality the boundaries of 'the nation' were also constantly being drawn and redrawn amid the strains of war. Naturally, industrial relations ensured a major flashpoint—again, as Gregory suggests, illustrating limitations of the discourse of 'sacrifice'.[43] Here it is important to place the Scottish experience in its larger British context. Both South Wales and the Clyde stood out as exceptions to the relative social harmony that prevailed during the early phase of the war, each with a distinctive local mix of pre-war bitterness and wartime pressure. By 1917, however, both were already being overtaken by the north of England in terms of the scale and intensity of industrial unrest. In the Clydeside case, although disputes were essentially related to state intervention and war production, the actual aims of the antagonists proved to be more complex and disparate, dividing both the employer and trade-union camps.

Unfortunately, the extensive attempts made to unpick these 'class' dynamics have tended to divert attention away from the other internal tensions heightened by war. These were by no means confined to the workplace, but also reflected historic ethnic and religious divisions. Even the high initial enlistment rates among the Irish Catholic community in the west of Scotland were insufficient to prevent the reappearance of serious sectarian disturbances from autumn 1915 onwards in areas like Lanarkshire, where manpower shortages in munitions production had resulted in new migration and settlement from Ireland. In these cases, the timing of local military casualties also coincided with

---

[41]  C. Lee, 'The Scottish Economy and the First World War', in Macdonald and McFarland, *Scotland and the Great War*, 20–1.

[42]  These commemorative volumes are a much underused source for studying the Scottish home front. See, for example: *Peace Souvenir: Motherwell's Part in the Fight for Freedom* (Motherwell, 1919); J. Minto Robertson, ed., *The War Book of Turriff and Twelve Miles Around* (Banff and Turriff, 1926); S. Lindsay, ed., *Coatbridge and the Great War* (Glasgow, 1919).

[43]  Gregory, *Last Great War*, 187–91.

the highly publicized failure of recruitment drives in Ireland, casting the Irish as 'a race apart' from the imagined national community and rendering their war service invisible.[44] Such instances should remind us of the powerful local dynamics shaping the experience of 'total war', despite the greater control and compulsion from the national state which it also imposed.

# 4

It is perhaps in the area of commemoration and remembrance that the limitations of the traditional class-based template for understanding the Scottish Great War experience appear most exposed. In contrast to the communal frictions produced by the onset of war-weariness, Jay Winter has written eloquently of the 'bond of bereavement' which overlaid that of nation, rank, or class; the great divide in post-war society, he argues, was between those who had lost someone and those who had not.[45] The fact that Scotland's war casualties provided the basis for such a bond is evident, although unlike enlistment figures, their extent still defies precise calculation. Indeed, this has led to wildly differing estimates among commentators, with a figure of 174,000, or even 26.4 per cent of enlisted Scots suggested at the upper limits; the result is that ambitious international comparisons of Scotland's relative losses tend to rest on rather flimsy foundations.[46] Crucially, these contemporary debates neglect the way in which both the naming and the numbering of the dead were intertwined as part of the commemorative process. Attempts at quantifying the extent of the national military contribution within the empire, for example, reasserted a more inclusive definition of 'Scottishness', which said much about how the war was handled in cultural terms. Thus the official figure of 74,000 war dead was almost immediately scaled up to 100,000 (13 per cent of the British total) and would continue to rise during subsequent decades, through the inclusion of those serving in the Scottish regiments, regardless of their country of origin, and also by drawing in those of Scottish birth or descent serving in UK regiments or in the dominion forces.[47] Indeed a similar process of 'acquisition' also took place in constructing individual Rolls of Honour. In the case of the University of Glasgow, for example, the inclusion of casualties who had served in the officer-training battalion located at the university boosted its losses beyond that of other regional universities, enabling it to claim a contribution on a par with Oxford and Cambridge.[48]

---

[44]  E. W. McFarland, ' "Our Country's Heroes": Irish Catholics in Scotland and the Great War', in M. Mitchell, ed., *New Perspectives on Irish Migration in Scotland* (Edinburgh, 2008), 127–44.

[45]  J. Winter, *Sites of Memory: Sites of Mourning* (Cambridge, 1995), 102–8.

[46]  S. Wood, *The Scottish Soldier* (Manchester, 1987), 88; N. Ferguson, *The Pity of War* (Harmondsworth, 2006), 298–9.

[47]  See Royle, *Flowers of the Forrest*, 284, on this point.

[48]  *The Glasgow University Roll of Honour 1914–1919* (Glasgow, 1922); G. A. C. Hughes, 'Glasgow University and World War One' (MPhil thesis, University of Glasgow, 2006).

Great War commemoration across the combatant nations was a massive creative endeavour, addressing a basic need for death to be given meaning through memorialization. Yet, the making and interpretation of symbols of remembrance would also be shaped by the self-representation of 'the nation' and by the collective identities and public values embedded in different societies.[49] This fusion of the universal and the particular was given full expression as Scotland turned to grieve for its dead. Undoubtedly, the commemorative process was fuelled by vital spiritual and ethical imperatives that followed the broader European pattern.[50] Yet, in keeping with Scottish popular culture, their expression was rather less emotive and grandiloquent than elsewhere in Europe, with a focus on the service of real regiments rather than the trappings of mythical heroes and allegorical symbolism. The concept of individual sacrifice as a crucial component of victory had gained ground during the war, but the process of remembrance would also be driven by an acute sense that Scotland as a nation had made a distinctive contribution within the empire. Reflecting the confluence of Scottish values and war memories, two main commemorative themes emerged during the 'hurricane season of memorials' between 1919 and 1922.[51] The first was a sense of inconsolable sorrow, with the pain of survivors representing the ultimate homage to those who had been lost, while the second expressed sober pride in Scotland's military achievements and celebrated these as grounded in a unique 'national character'. Together these produced a powerful narrative of stoicism, survival, and deliverance which structured remembrance at both the national and the local level.

To date, scholarly attention in this area has largely focused on the Scottish National War Memorial at Edinburgh Castle.[52] In constructing a truly national tribute, the memorial was also remarkable for its inclusivity, attempting to reconcile the tensions of wartime through a new, shared expression of solidarity. Here Scotland's sacrifice was presented as the cement of imperial unity, with the memorial reaching out to audiences in the Scottish emigrant communities by representing their contribution in words and images, such as 'The Tree of Empire'.[53] With the initial disputes over its design and location almost forgotten by the time of the memorial's inauguration in 1927, it became a site of mass pilgrimage for thousands of bereaved Scots.

While grief was given an impressively stylized expression at a national level, its local dynamics were more personal and immediate. War losses were perhaps felt most keenly in those highland communities already stripped by emigration, where the largest

[49]  See G. L. Mosse, *Fallen Soldiers: Reshaping the Memory of the World Wars* (Oxford, 1990); A. King, *Memorials of the Great War in Britain: The Symbolism and Politics of Remembrance* (Oxford, 1998).

[50]  L. van Ypersele, 'Making the Great War Great: 1914–18 Memorials in Wallonia', in W. Kidd and B. Murdoch, eds., *Memory and Memorials: The Commemorative Century* (Aldershot, 2004), 30–1.

[51]  *The Scotsman*, 20 February 1919. The term is Lord Rosebery's.

[52]  A. Petrie, 'Scottish Culture and the First World War' (PhD thesis, University of Dundee, 2006), 174. For the memorial see F. W. Deas, *The Scottish National War Memorial Official Guide* (Edinburgh, 1928), 26–7. See also Ian Hay Beith, *Their Name Liveth: The Book of the Scottish National War Memorial* (London, 1931); Sir Lawrence Weaver, *The Scottish National War Memorial* (London, 1927).

[53]  J. Macleod, ' "By Scottish Hands, with Scottish Money, on Scottish Soil": The Scottish National War Memorial and National Identity', *Journal of British Studies*, 49 (January 2010), 73–96.

percentages of men of military age had enlisted in the opening months of the war. These volunteers had also pursued their front-line service in the critical first two years—often in the ranks of local territorial battalions where casualty rates were particularly high.[54]

The wave of local commemoration in Scotland that followed the war has been slow to generate detailed research. Yet Great War memorials remain Scotland's most widespread public monument, with a total of 1,545 currently listed in the *UK National War Memorials Inventory*.[55] Their total cost has been estimated at £652,000—equivalent to an expenditure of £6 per head of the fallen.[56] Most followed traditional commemorative styles. The commonest commemorative type was the simple memorial tablet, remembering individuals or groups of workmates, classmates, or fellow parishioners. It was, however, through the more visible town and village memorials, and the ceremonies which came to surround them, that civic Scotland attempted to come to terms with the destructiveness of war. Here the dead were symbolically cast as 'ideal citizens' whose sacrifice had imposed duties on survivors.[57] Therefore, while memorials functioned as sites for personal mourning, they also served as conduits for ethical and political ideas of community loyalty and disinterested service, leaving a space where a variety of different meanings of 'citizenship' and 'responsibility' could flourish, as long as these did not deny the basic affirmative purpose of commemoration.[58]

The mechanics of monument building did not differ from elsewhere in Britain. Local memorial committees featured municipal leaders, businessmen, and other interest groups; designs were frequently chosen by competition, usually from among the local Scottish architectural community, or commissioned from pattern books and supplied direct from the Aberdeen granite yards. However, the iconography that emerged from Scottish commemoration also reflected the struggle to give Scotland's wartime contribution a distinctive physical expression. The most common monument was the cross, often in its Celtic variant. Despite lingering suspicions over its pre-Reformation antecedents, this form actually proved more popular than in the UK as a whole.[59] The shortcomings of conventional religion during the war had clearly not damaged popular identification with Christian ideals, and through this familiar symbolism the recent struggle was presented as an ethical triumph of good over evil rather than a simple military victory, an emphasis strengthened by frequent references to 'peace' in inaugurating the memorials.[60]

---

[54] In Ross-shire official statistics suggested 58.6 per cent of men of military age had enlisted by April 1915. Here men served in a variety of front-line and reserve units, including the 4th Seaforth Highlanders, the county territorial battalion, which was first engaged with heavy losses at Aubers Ridge and Festubert in May 1915. In his discussion of the county's contribution, Duff estimates 28 per cent of the battalion in total died in the war: *Scotland's War Losses*, 43–6.

[55] www.ukniwm.org.uk

[56] G. Bell, 'Monuments to the Fallen: Scottish War Memorials of the Great War' (PhD thesis, University of Strathclyde, 1993), 463.

[57] For a local example see *Irvine Times*, 19 August 1921.

[58] King, *Memorials of the Great War*, 209.

[59] There are 283 crosses listed on the UK database, 18 per cent of total Scottish memorials, compared with 14 per cent for the UK as a whole.

[60] For examples see *Glasgow Herald*, 22 February 1921 (Govanhill Parish Church); 29 March 1921 (Montrose); 16 September 1921 (Caithness).

Other abstract forms, such as obelisks and columns, also proved popular in Scotland, again reflecting the popular taste for simplicity and reticence.[61] However, where figurative memorials were selected, these were also tangibly linked into national sentiment, with iconic visualizations of Scottish servicemen in their distinctive modern service dress predominating. Portrayals like the 'rugged, elemental soldier' created by Alexander Carrick for the Killin war memorial reassured audiences of the survival of pre-war ideals of Scottishness and masculinity, while providing a literal and metaphorical replacement for those who had fallen.[62]

# 5

To conclude, the Great War demonstrated both the strength and limits of Scotland's historic role as a military manpower reserve. Distinctive issues of national identity mediated Scottish engagement with the conflict, not least its traditional identification with the British imperial system. Yet, an introspective analysis, which remains at the level of particularity and excludes wider European comparisons, risks overstating the extent to which the conflict was really a key turning point in Scottish history.

In terms of Scottish politics, the evidence at first sight seems stark. In August 1914 there were fifty-four Liberal MPs, but ten years later only eight, while the number of Conservative and Unionist MPs rose over the same period from thirteen to thirty-six, and Labour from three to twenty-six.[63] However, the terminal decline of Liberalism both as a 'living faith' and an electoral force hardly approached the cataclysm which in Ireland swept away the old politics of constitutional nationalism and substituted a new revolutionary order.[64] Nor did the growing vitality of Scottish Unionism create corrosive faultlines of the type that would come to haunt French and German society in the interwar years, for in this instance the party at the heart of the 'anti-Labour front' was sustained by a non-ideological, interventionist approach to social and economic problems. Indeed, local studies also question how direct and deterministic the link actually is between these developments and the effects of war.[65]

[61] The totals are 108 obelisks and 99 columns; 13 per cent of Scottish memorials consist of these abstract types compared with 3 per cent nationally; 95 figurative memorials are listed (6 per cent of the Scottish total), of which 67 are of servicemen.

[62] J. A. Black, 'Ordeal and Affirmation: Masculinity and the Construction of Scottish and English National Identity in Great War Memorial Sculpture 1919–30', in Kidd and Murdoch, eds., *Memory and Memorials*, 75–91. In this case the model was a local casualty who had been killed at the Somme.

[63] I. G. C. Hutchison, *Scottish Politics in the Twentieth Century* (London, 2001), 29.

[64] K. Jeffery, *Ireland and the Great War* (Cambridge, 2000); A. Gregory and S. Paseta, *Ireland and the Great War: 'A War to Unite Us All'?* (Manchester, 2002).

[65] C. M. M. Macdonald, *The Radical Thread: Political Change in Scotland, Paisley Politics 1885–1924* (East Linton, 2000).

There is no doubt, however, that the crisis of the world economy did come to dominate and defeat the reconstruction of post-war Scotland. Here the role of the Great War was again a complex one, accelerating an already established pattern of decline rather than initiating it. The demands of war had extended productive capacity and encouraged immediate technological and social gains, such as the enhanced participation of women in the workplace. Yet these proved all too easily reversible, as the subsequent destabilization and restructuring of international trade and finance would prove disastrous for a vulnerable, export-oriented economy. The implications of failing overseas competitiveness would also become increasingly pressing for many individual Scots during the 1920s. The regular Scottish battalions may have quickly resumed the business of imperial soldiering, but returning 'citizen soldiers' soon discovered that they faced a new battle to secure employment—particularly the large and visible ex-service population who had suffered physical and mental injury as a result of the war.

It was against the background of industrial decline and ebbing national self-confidence that some survivors began to create a new popular memory of the war in which the solemn evocation of its moral purpose was replaced by a sense of waste and disappointment. Here national pride in a unique sacrifice for the empire gave way to resentment over casualties that were considered to be 'disproportionate', and which, for nationalists like Duncan Duff, reflected the exploitation and exhaustion of Scottish manpower and an unfair allocation of front-line risks.[66] In this analysis Scotland's war losses became in themselves part of the explanation of economic decline. In a Scottish variant of the 'lost generation' myth, it was the death of university students as junior officers that was believed to have robbed Scottish industry of its future leaders. This was despite an actual increase in graduate numbers at Scottish universities during the 1920s, reflecting the admission of women and the growth of undergraduate capacity to meet the demand from those returning from the war.[67]

Most veterans did not disclaim their own war service, nor did they repudiate their former leaders: when Douglas Haig died in 1928, his body lay in state in Edinburgh, and one hundred thousand people filed past his coffin.[68] Yet, they did struggle to reconcile the magnitude of the conflict with the shrinking hopes of the post-war decades. This growing sense of disenchantment is captured eloquently in two commemorative volumes dedicated to Glasgow's volunteer battalions. The 17th HLI's history was published in 1920, and presented a simple and direct account of its war service. Confident that the meaning and significance of this contribution would be shared by their audience, little more than a tense dedication was necessary: 'They ask a better Britain as their monument'. By 1934, when a further volume commemorating the 15th HLI eventually appeared, survivors had taken time to re-evaluate their experiences of both war and peace. The result was a much more self-consciously 'literary' production, where

---

[66] Duff, *Scotland's War Losses*, 44.

[67] Hughes, 'Glasgow University', 131. See also J. M. Winter, 'Britain's "Lost Generation" of the First World War', *Population Studies*, vol. 31, no. 3 (November 1977), 449–66.

[68] *The Scotsman*, 2, 4 February 1928.

the battalion's service is represented as a tragic journey—*An Epic of Glasgow*. The tone is also more contemplative, insisting that personal sacrifice should be remembered for its own sake, rather than for the nobility of its purpose—indeed the cause for which the war was fought is nowhere elaborated. Instead, reflected its author: 'The most wonderful memory which has survived the Great Disillusion is the memory of the greatness and grandeur of ordinary men…who faced unflinchingly all the hellish devices of modern war'.[69] Tragically, there could no longer be any guarantee that this sacrifice would be appreciated by wider society. A new generation was growing up without any direct experience of war, and for whom the conflict had to be 'imagined' before it could be remembered.

## FURTHER READING

Brown, S. J., ' "A Solemn Purification by Fire": Responses to the Great War in the Scottish Presbyterian Churches, 1914-1919', *Journal of Ecclesiastical History*, 45, 1 (January 1994), 82–104.

Fussell, P., *The Great War and Modern Memory* (Oxford, 1977).

Gregory, A., *The Last Great War: British Society and the First World War* (Cambridge, 2008).

King, A., *Memorials of the Great War in Britain: The Symbolism and Politics of Remembrance* (Oxford, 1998).

Macdonald, C. M. M., and McFarland, E. W., *Scotland and the Great War* (East Linton, 1999).

Macleod, J. L., ' "By Scottish Hands, with Scottish Money, on Scottish Soil": The Scottish National War Memorial and National Identity', *Journal of British Studies*, 49 (January 2010), 73–96.

—— ' "Greater Love Hath No Man Than This": Scotland's Conflicting Religious Response to Death in the Great War', *Scottish Historical Review*, lxxxi, no. 211 (April 2002), 70–96.

Royle, T., *Flowers of the Forest* (Edinburgh, 2006).

Spiers, E., 'The Scottish Soldier at War', in H. Cecil and P. H. Liddle, eds., *Facing Armageddon: The First World War Experienced* (London, 1996), 314–35.

Winter, J., *Sites of Memory: Sites of Mourning* (Cambridge, 1995).

---

[69]  T. Chalmers, *An Epic of Glasgow: History of the 15th Battalion HLI* (Glasgow, 1934). Note also the companion volume published by the same author in 1936, *A Saga of Scotland: The History of the 16th Battalion HLI* (Glasgow). The 5th (Territorial) Battalion also produced its own privately published account: F. L. Morrison, *The Fifth Battalion Highland Light Infantry* (Glasgow, 1921).

# CHAPTER 30

························································································

# THE INTERWAR CRISIS: THE
# FAILURE OF EXTREMISM

························································································

## RICHARD J. FINLAY

To assess the extent of the crisis that affected interwar Scottish society, it is necessary to place the discussion within a comparative context to give meaning and measurement to its severity. The consequences of the First World War had unleashed a torrent of political, social, and economic change across the world. The growth of political extremism and instability, made worse by fundamental changes in the global economy, were the hallmarks of much of contemporary European history in which politics on the Continent became increasingly polarized between far-right nationalism and Fascism and left-wing socialism and communism.[1] Liberal democracy struggled hard to put down roots after the Versailles Treaty of 1919 and found it difficult to grow in the shadows of both Joseph Stalin and Adolf Hitler. The enormity of the Second World War and all the horrors that it entailed has meant that historians find it difficult to look at the period without reference to the fact that it was then that the seeds were sown which would grow into the bloodiest war in human history. Historians of seventeenth-century Europe have identified a 'general crisis' in that period and historians of the twentieth century could take a leaf out of their book and focus more on the common experiences of the interwar period, rather than examine the same phenomena from the 'national' perspective.

---

[1] Giovanni Capoccia, *Defending Democracy: Reactions to Extremism in Interwar Europe* (Baltimore, MD, 2007); Martin Blinkhorn, *Fascism and the Right in Europe, 1919–1945* (London, 2000); Gregory M. Luebbert, *Liberalism, Fascism or Social Democracy: Social Classes and the Political Origins of Regimes in Interwar Europe* (New York, 1991); Roland I. Kowalski, *European Communism: 1848–1991* (Basingstoke, 2006); Peter Davies, *The Extreme Right in France, 1789 to the Present* (London, 2002), 79–100; Erik Hansen, 'Fascism and Nazism in the Netherlands, 1929–39', *European Studies Review*, 11 (1981), 355–85, and Martin Conway, 'The Extreme Right in Interwar Francophone Belgium: Explanations of a Failure', *European History Quarterly*, 26 (1996), 267–94.

One of the key objectives of this chapter is to relate the interwar Scottish experience to a wider British and European historiography. Firstly, the main contours of the crisis will be explored to demonstrate how politics and economics became enmeshed as Scottish society was polarized by class divisions. Although the political and cultural debates were heated, they took place in a context of social and economic stagnation in which unemployment and poverty showed no signs of disappearing, and indeed seemed to become solidified during the Great Depression. The sense of crisis was born out of a seeming impotence by the political mainstream to solve the nation's problems. Salvation only came as a result of preparation for war. The second part of the chapter will examine the question of why similar traumas of socio-economic dislocation that engulfed other political systems in Europe did not have the same effect in Scotland. Indeed, while there is a tendency to emphasize the degree of Scottish dislocation, what has received less attention is the remarkable stability with which Scotland weathered the interwar storm.

# 1

With splendid insularity, the historical debate in Britain has tended to point out the ways in which the United Kingdom diverted from the European norm and avoided the worst of the pitfalls of economic and political instability.[2] The 'mother' of democracy survived and emerged stronger from the experience.[3] Financial prudence, the balanced budget, and an overvalued sterling had helped to put the brakes on economic expansion in the period after the war relative to North America and Western Europe. As a result, British economic growth was sluggish and when the Great Depression arrived in 1929, its consequences were not as severe, because the economy had less far to fall. The impact of the Depression did not have the same disastrous social and economic consequences that led to political instability and extremism in some parts of Europe.[4] Although the popular image of the interwar period is associated with mass unemployment, poverty, hunger marches, and the dole queue, historians have revised this negative picture into one that was more positive. The historiography of the interwar era in Britain can be summed up as follows; in the era after the Second World War when Keynesian economics and state planning were the political orthodoxy, the 'Devil's Decade' was portrayed as one of failure on both the domestic and foreign-policy front. The 'Guilty Men' of the Tory-dominated

---

[2]  Arthur Bryant, *The Years of Endurance, 1793–1802* (London, 1942), and *Years of Victory, 1802–1812* (London, 1943). Also Julia Stapleton, *Sir Arthur Bryant and National History in Twentieth-Century Britain* (Lanham, MD, 2005).

[3]  Malcolm Smith, *Britain and 1940: History, Myth and Popular Memory* (London, 2000), 111–30.

[4]  Derek Aldcroft, *The British Economy: The Years of Turmoil, 1920–1951* (London, 1986), 44–84; B. W. E. Alford, *Depression and Recovery? British Economic Growth 1918–1939* (London, 1972), 13–15, 80–3; I. M. Drummond, *The Gold Standard and the International Monetary System, 1900–39* (Basingstoke, 1987), and Martin Daunton, *Wealth and Welfare: An Economic and Social History of Britain 1851–1951* (Oxford, 2007), 274–98.

national government presided over inaction regarding mass unemployment, while 'appeasing' the Fascist dictatorships.[5] As post-war optimism in the ability of the state to deliver prosperity began to wane, historians increasingly began to recast their assessments of the interwar era. The era of low inflation, low interest rates, limited trade-union power, and a revolution in consumerism and home ownership supplanted the image of regional unemployment, decaying heavy industry, and the problems of the 'North'. After all, average living standards rose faster than at any time in British history. Although it might be stretching the point, British historiography of the interwar era has tended to reflect the dominant ideological mores of the post-war period.[6] As the ideological gravity shifted from the corporate consensus towards the free market, and electoral significance tilted to the south-east, so this was reflected in changing attitudes to the record of the interwar government. The national government's economic policy was portrayed as a sensible reaction to the international turmoil, and the failure of political extremism to take root was also cited as evidence of the stability of the British state.[7]

Such an overview of the interwar situation in Britain, however, does not reveal the regional disparities that existed and downplays the fact that the process of social and economic disruption was not even. The contrasting experiences of the prosperous south and the poor north were a hallmark of interwar Britain, as indeed they were of the Thatcher era.[8] This was especially the case in Scotland, and for many contemporary observers there was a profound sense of dislocation and a pessimism. Arguably, unlike the North of England, and to a lesser extent Wales and Northern Ireland, the Scots had a fairly clear sense of national consciousness, which added an extra dimension to the experience of the interwar period that was different from other parts of the United Kingdom.[9] In some respects, Scotland was similar to mainland Europe in that the dislocation could be seen as a distinctive 'national' and not a 'regional' phenomenon. Furthermore, a comparison between a range of socio-economic indicators demonstrates that Scotland featured towards the top end of the negative spectrum.[10] Like the rest of

---

[5] Cato (Michael Foot), *The Guilty Men* (London, 1957).

[6] For pessimists: Charles Loch Mowat, *Britain between the Wars* (London, 1955), A. J. P. Taylor, *English History, 1914–1945* (London, 1965), and Robert Skidelsky, *Politicians and the Slump* (London, 1967). For 'optimists': J. Stevenson and C. Cook, *The Slump: Politics and Society During the Depression* (London, 1977), and J. Stevenson, *British Society, 1914–1945* (Harmondsworth, 1984). The debate is reviewed in A. Thorpe, *Britain in the 1930s* (Oxford, 1992).

[7] Andrew J. Thorpe, ed., *The Failure of Political Extremism in Interwar Britain* (Exeter, 1988), 1–10; Richard C. Thurlow, *Fascism in Modern Britain* (Stroud, 2000), and Martin Pugh, *Hurrah for the Blackshirts: Fascism and Fascists in Britain Between the Wars* (London, 2005).

[8] Stephen V. Ward, *The Geography of Interwar Britain: The State and Uneven Development* (London, 1988).

[9] R. J. Finlay, 'National Identity in Crisis: Politicians, Intellectuals and the "End of Scotland"', *History*, 79 (1994), 242–59.

[10] League of Nations, unemployment at the end of 1933: Germany 22.6%, Belgium 19.9%, Canada 21%, Denmark 37.5%, USA 22.6%, the Netherlands 40%, and the United Kingdom 15.1%, *Statistical Yearbook 1934–35*, 57–78. The Scottish figure for March 1934 was 24%, HC Debs, 22 March 1934, vol. 278, cc. 1,392–528. See also J. B. Orr, *Food, Health and Income* (London, 1936).

Britain, there was a desire to return to 'normalcy' after 1918, and to reverse the more disturbing trends that had emerged during the conflict. The traditional values of domesticity, deference, paternalism, individual independence, and the like, which formed what were imagined to be the quintessential characteristics of pre-war Scottish society, had all come under threat from new forces such as greater state intervention, organized labour, and the widespread acceptance of socialism. The rise of the trade-union movement and the Labour Party gave the working class political teeth, which were used to force a rent freeze, improve wages and conditions, and posit an alternative future in which the workers received a greater share of national wealth.[11] Socialism alarmed the imagination of the middle classes, and they seemed to have their fears confirmed by the results of the 1922 General Election when Labour became the largest single party in Scotland. Even the prospective Conservative prime minister, Andrew Bonar Law, was in fear for his political career as the Labour Party claimed ten of the fifteen Glasgow seats.[12] The sudden rise of Labour in Scotland, which went from minority to almost majority within the space of four years, gave the threat of socialism an urgency in Scotland that had few parallels within the United Kingdom. Local Tories and Liberals cooperated informally after the ending of the coalition government in 1922 just to keep Labour out. This ended after the Liberals supported the minority Labour government in 1924, which allowed the Tories to claim that they were weak in stopping socialism. The Liberal Party increasingly found itself squeezed out as politics became polarized around class interests and by 1924 was firmly relegated to the touchline. It is also worth stressing the role of political geography in contributing to the class polarization of Scotland in the 1920s. Given that the majority of Scots were squeezed into the Central Belt, it meant that the heartlands of socialism were never physically far away from the middle-class suburbs. This was unlike England, which had a political geography that largely separated Labour north from the Tory south and arguably added to a sense of physical remoteness, and possibly a degree of insulation, from the issue of class division.

Scottish politics in the interwar era were shaped by economic uncertainty. The onset of the First World War led to an unsustainable boom in the heavy industries that had been at the vanguard of the Victorian and Edwardian economy. The Clyde conurbation was the most important centre of armaments production in the United Kingdom and its productive capacity increased by a fifth to accommodate the insatiable demand for the staples of war. The easy profits of war meant that diversification into other sectors of the economy, such as consumer and electrical goods, was stopped in its tracks. If the Scottish economy had been unbalanced before 1914, the wartime boom pushed it into an unsustainable trajectory. After a short period of restocking, demand for the staples of the Scottish economy dried up. The uncertainty of the post-war global economy meant that

[11]  I. G. C. Hutchison, *A Political History of Scotland: Parties, Elections, Issues, 1832–1924* (Edinburgh, 1986), 277–309; J. J. Smyth, *Labour in Glasgow 1896–1936: Socialism, Suffrage, Sectarianism* (East Linton, 2000), 70–125, and William Kenefick, *Red Scotland: The Rise and Fall of the Radical Left, c. 1872–1932* (Edinburgh, 2007), 159–84.

[12]  Hutchison, *Political History*, 284, 314.

there was a reluctance to buy capital-investment goods such as ships or heavy-engineering plant. This in turn had a knock-on effect on coal and steel and demonstrated the tight industrial interdependency that had lain at the heart of Scottish economic success before 1914.[13] Reliance on wartime government orders had meant that pre-war markets, particularly in textiles and jute, were lost to overseas competitors. Political change in the form of the Russian Revolution of 1917 and the Versailles Treaty meant that Eastern European markets for fish and coal were also lost, with significant consequences for Scotland's east-coast mining and fishing communities. By the early 1920s, some one hundred thousand Scottish men were permanently 'superfluous' to economic requirements.

In a determined effort to return to 'normalcy', public spending was cut to balance the budget and the objective of returning sterling to the Gold Standard was achieved in 1926.[14] This had a number of important consequences for the Scottish economy. Firstly, it overvalued sterling, which meant that buying British goods became relatively expensive, putting export industries at a competitive disadvantage.[15] Secondly, it meant that the primary means to become competitive was to reduce wages, as labour was the single biggest cost determinant in most of Scottish industry. This in turn meant that diversification into the consumer industry was unlikely, because of low demand and a depressed domestic market. When the British economy began to expand in the interwar years, it was confined to those areas in the south led by consumer demand. Also, the business community was dogged by a 'wait-and-see' mentality, no doubt shaped by the experience of the pre-war cyclical economy when bad times had been followed by good ones, which led to an expectation that things would eventually turn right. This conservative approach placed a premium on survival and promoted the tendency of defensive amalgamations in order to beat the downturn. Often, this meant the sacrifice of more modern plant and machinery in order to keep inefficient and out-of-date units going. The fact that the economic problems seemed intractable, with no solution in sight, simply added to a sense of doom. The emphasis on low wages as the primary means to restore competitiveness in the economy did little to smooth troubled industrial relations, and a turbulent labour force further acted as a disincentive for investment in new branches of industry and manufacturing.

The troubles of the economy dovetailed with political change. The rise of organized labour and socialism certainly contributed to the conservative outlook of Scottish business leaders, and the primacy of wage reduction as a means of ensuring competitiveness was held as a fundamental tenant of belief. On the whole, rather than accommodate the trade-union movement, Scottish business was notorious for its class-confrontational outlook.[16] The Economic League, for example, was a shadowy organization funded by

---

[13] R. H. Campbell, *The Rise and Fall of Scottish Industry 1707–1939* (Edinburgh, 1980), 56–75.
[14] Daunton, *Wealth and Welfare*, 286–90.
[15] B. W. E. Alford, *Britain in the World Economy Since 1880* (Harlow, 1996), 72–80.
[16] Ronald Johnston, *Clydeside Capital, 1870–1920: A Social History of Employers* (East Linton, 2000), 169–210.

business to take on socialism because, as the group's leading industrialists believed, it perverted the laws of economics. Information on socialist activists was shared and blacklists were compiled of known agitators. Scottish class conflict does not sit easy with the representations of England by Prime Minister Stanley Baldwin and George Orwell as a gentle place of evensong and spinsters bicycling to church.[17] Anti-socialism was the defining political idea of the 1920s and the polarization of class was responsible for the rise of both the Labour and Conservative Party. By 1924, the Liberal consensus that seemed to be an essential hallmark of pre-war society was at an end. Class tensions were constantly reinforced by the prospects of industrial militancy. The 'spectre' of 'Red Clydeside' haunted the middle-class imagination, even though working-class militancy was in evidence in Edinburgh, Dundee, Aberdeen, and other towns and cities. The 1919 '8 hour day strike' was a prelude to the General Strike of 1926 when both left and right squared up to one another. One feature of the 1926 Strike in Scotland was the widespread use of police and arrest powers, which were used more extensively than in other parts of the United Kingdom.[18] In 1919 and 1926 middle-class volunteers were every bit as militant as strikers. The defeat of the strike in 1926 was significant in that it settled middle-class fears about revolution, while dampening working-class confidence in direct action. As was evidenced in other parts of Europe, the early and mid-1920s in Scotland was a period of deep and resentful class confrontation. While it is important not to over-emphasize the impact of class warriors on the development of Scottish politics in the interwar period, the fact remains that both the far left and far right were well represented in Scotland. While much class warfare was rhetorical, its impact on the public imagination should not be underestimated, whether it be the fiery revolutionary denunciations of the socialist politician James Maxton, who claimed that both Liberals and Tories were 'murderers of children', or the slash-and-burn attitude to state welfare of the industrialist Sir James Lithgow.[19]

The growth of class conflict was fuelled by the inheritance of nineteenth-century poverty and poor social conditions. Many of these, particularly housing, came to a head during the First World War because there was an immediate need to rehouse a quarter of a million people as a result of overcrowding in the existing slums. Growing expectations among the working class were heightened by the power of collective action which had squeezed concessions from the government. Wartime slaughter had led many workers to question their relationship with the state. If the nation could ask its citizens to lay down their lives in defence of the country, was it fair to expect them to put up with appalling social conditions and poverty? The number of ex-servicemen protesting in

---

[17]  Arthur McIvor, 'A Crusade for Capitalism: The Economic League, 1919–39', *Journal of Contemporary History*, 23 (1988), 631–55; Robert Colls, *Identity of England* (Oxford, 2002), 59–61; Stefan Collini, *Absent Minds: Intellectuals in Britain* (Oxford, 2006), 350–75.

[18]  Ian MacDougall, 'Some Aspects of the General Strike in Scotland', in I. MacDougall, ed., *Essays in Labour History* (Edinburgh, 1978), 170–207.

[19]  HC Deb. 27 June 1923, vol. 165, c. 2,382; while Lithgow told the Engineers Congress in Glasgow June 1938 that state expenditure on education for the working class beyond a certain level was a waste of money.

1919 was particularly alarming to the authorities. Yet, the strained public finances following the war meant that 'homes for heroes' was its first casualty. According to J. W. Pratt, MP, the vice president of the Scottish Board of Health, there was a paramount 'need for public and private economy'.[20] Made worse by mounting unemployment, there was no prospect of an immediate solution to the deep-seated problems of poverty and poor social conditions. The pre-war system of poor relief, dependent on local rating, likewise increased class tension as middle-class ratepayers wanted it cut back, while the unemployed working class wanted it implemented in full. In the early 1920s the courts were used as a means by the middle class to restrain generous poor relief.[21] The improvement of social legislation during the war also had an impact on middle-class property owners who let out slum housing. Property was a staple of middle-class *rentier* income, and many were reeling under the impact of what they believed to be intrusive state interference. About the same value of Scotland's national income was based on both property and wages (a higher proportion than England), and the impact of new legislation can be seen in the fact that some 12 per cent of Scotland's housing stock was simply abandoned.[22] The cost of maintenance was simply not economic. A key factor that has been identified in contributing to the European political crisis of the interwar years was the radicalization of the middle classes, whose fears of economic change and the growth of socialism drove them into the arms of the extreme right. In Scotland, this process is clearly visible. Wartime inflation devalued savings and salaries, growth of trade-union power threatened status, government regulation threatened business, and paternalism and deference declined. In other small European nations during the interwar era, the middle class increasingly surged to the extreme right and embraced nationalism and Fascism.

The limited stability of the late 1920s was ended by the Great Depression in 1929. Any prospect of economic recovery was dashed and in terms of the regional impact on Britain, Scotland was one of the worst affected. Credit dried up and the growth of protectionism hurt those parts of the British economy that were dependent on international trade, especially in the traditional heavy industries. The statistics for Scotland make for grim reading as the course of the Depression peaked in the early 1930s. Factory closures were higher, unemployment was greater, and recovery was slower.[23] When improvement came it was in the late 1930s as a result of rearmament, but this was slow and haphazard.

Unlike other parts of Europe, the crisis did not lead to political disintegration or crisis in Scotland, nor did it fuel the growth of extremist parties. The left suffered more than the right, and it is fair to say that there was a remarkable degree of consensus regarding the political course to be steered through the crisis. Labour, which had been in power when the Great Crash began, found itself ideologically ill-equipped to deal with the

---

[20] *The Rotarian*, January 1920, vol. xvl (1), 32.

[21] Ian Levitt, *Poverty and Welfare in Scotland 1890–1948* (Edinburgh, 1988), 118–41.

[22] A. D. Campbell, ' "Income" and Robert Baird "Housing" ', in A. K. Cairncross, ed., *The Scottish Economy: A Statistical Account of Scottish Life* (Cambridge, 1954), 52–4, 200–6.

[23] Finlay, 'National Identity in Crisis', 45–6.

crisis.[24] In essence, the party was caught between two competing visions of itself; namely a socialist party committed to an ideological programme and a party that sought to protect the interests of its working-class electoral constituency. It proved impossible for the party to marry these two objectives together. Scottish Labour was not a hothouse of intellectual socialism, especially after the death of its one original thinker, John Wheatley, in 1930.[25] Socialism was a rhetorical device that appealed to social justice and fairness, rather than a coherent and carefully articulated programme of political and economic change. Scottish Labour shared the mainstream British view that socialism was an evolutionary process that would grow organically out of the capitalist system as it collapsed under the weight of its own contradictions. What this meant and when this would happen had not been addressed and it bound the party to work within the parameters of the existing capitalist system until some unspecified event in the future. In short, this meant that the party had no answers to the problems of the Great Depression other than orthodox economic thinking.[26]

Yet, the impact of the Crash was felt with greatest consequence among traditional working-class Labour voters, particularly in the west Central Belt of Scotland. The decision of the Labour leadership to back financial orthodoxy, cut public expenditure, and balance the budget caused a split as the bulk of the trade-union movement and the rank and file rejected this course of action. The Labour leader, Ramsay MacDonald, had support from the Liberal and Tory parties because unpalatable economic cuts had to take place, and it was agreed to form a 'national government' so that no single party would take the blame.[27] Also, politicians did not know how far and deep the recession would travel. In the general election of 1931, the national government candidates romped home with a landslide, while those Labour MPs and candidates who refused to support the cuts were wiped out. This trouncing of the left was exacerbated by schism in the 1930s as the Independent Labour Party, under Maxton and particularly strong in Scotland, broke away from the official Labour Party.[28] Similar schismatic tendencies were in evidence among the broader Labour and trade-union movement as a result of growing communist influence.[29] Those Labour MPs who survived were not the most

[24] Philip Williamson, *National Crisis and National Government: British Politics, the Economy and Empire, 1926–1932* (Cambridge, 2003), 308–20.

[25] On Wheatley see David Howell, *A Lost Left: Three Studies in Socialism and Nationalism* (Manchester, 1986), 229–65.

[26] Williamson, *National Crisis*, 308–20, and Duncan Tanner, 'Political Leadership, Intellectual Debate and Economic Policy during the Second Labour Government', in E. H. H. Green and D. M. Tanner, eds., *The Strange Survival of Liberal England: Political Leaders, Moral Values and the Reception of Economic Debate* (Cambridge, 2007), 113–53.

[27] Nick Smart, *The National Government, 1931–40* (Basingstoke, 1999), 1–15.

[28] Gidon Cohen, *The Failure of a Dream: The Independent Labour Party from Disaffiliation to World War Two* (London, 2007), 15–29, and Ben Pimlott, *Labour and the Left in the 1930s* (Cambridge, 1977), 9–35, 89–98.

[29] Matthew Worley, *Class against Class: The Communist Party in Britain Between the Wars* (London, 2002), 44.

inspiring and when the working class needed a clear and articulate political voice, none was to be had. The first-past-the-post system meant that the use of one preferred 'national' candidate retarded Labour's progress in terms of MPs in the 1935 General Election, even though its share of the vote went up.[30]

The fact that the national government was able to command such electoral support in Scotland suggests that there was a degree of political stability, and though unemployment and poverty levels were high, they were not of such magnitudes to trigger a political crisis.[31] That said, however, there was considerable disquiet at the disproportionate effect the economic crisis had in Scotland compared to the rest of the United Kingdom, in particular the south of England.[32] Government policies received considerable criticism as being tailored to shore up economic development in the south through the imposition of tariff barriers to protect consumer-goods industries, which arguably harmed traditional heavy-export industries in the north. The policy of cheap money and credit created a market for consumer goods and helped fuel a house-building boom. Although coming off the Gold Standard in 1931 devalued sterling and should have helped exports, the reality of the depressed international markets and foreign tariffs meant that there was little upturn. For many it seemed that the key economic policies of the national government did little to address the problems of the depressed areas and traditional heavy industry.[33] Lanarkshire still had an unemployment rate of 27 per cent in the late 1930s.[34] In the press there were frequent comments on the state of Scotland, reflecting a wider concern that the nation was in decline. Books, pamphlets, and articles all chimed in to produce a chorus of doom. The south appeared to be draining the economic lifeblood as companies relocated to more prosperous markets in England. Economic recovery north of the border was slower and unemployment remained stubbornly higher. Some even talked about a conspiracy to drain Scotland of all its assets. Attention focused on high emigration rates and prompted fears that the best of the nation had left, while rabid anti-Catholic polemics talked about widespread Irish immigration replacing the best with the worst.[35] This debate took on a racist perspective and reinforced the idea that the Scots were dying out.[36] Like other parts of Europe, Scottish politics were tainted with cultural despair and pessimism.[37]

---

[30] Tom Stannage, *Baldwin Thwarts the Opposition: The British General Election of 1935* (London, 1980), 62–83, 247–72.

[31] David Powell, *British Politics, 1910–1935: The Crisis of the Party System* (London, 2004), 184.

[32] G. M. Thomson, *Scotland: That Distressed Area* (Edinburgh, 1935).

[33] Wal Hannington, *The Problem of the Distressed Areas: An Examination of Poverty and Unemployment* (London, 1935), 218.

[34] Clydesdale Bank, *Sixth Annual Survey of Economic Conditions* (Glasgow, 1939), 7.

[35] John Torrence, *Scotland's Dilemma* (Edinburgh, 1938).

[36] G. M. Thomson, *Caledonia: or the Future of the Scots* (Edinburgh, 1926), and Andrew Dewar Gibb, *Scotland in Eclipse* (Glasgow, 1932).

[37] Fritz Stern, *The Politics of Cultural Despair* (London, 1965); see R. J. Overy, *The Inter-War Crisis, 1919–1939* (London, 2007), 38–46, and R. J. Overy, *The Morbid Age: Britain and the Crisis of Civilization* (London, 2009), 93–136. For Scotland, HC Deb 22 November 1932, vol. 272.

It is worth commenting on the intellectual reaction to this 'crisis' as it chimed in with similar tendencies on the European mainland. The 'politics of cultural despair' looked for radical solutions to the failure of liberal capitalism. Industrial capitalism came in for a great deal of criticism. Hugh MacDiarmid, Edwin Muir, and Lewis Grassic Gibbon, for example, all extolled the virtues of rural life and believed that industrialization had blighted the nation. Gibbon and Muir veered to the left, arguing that socialism was the answer, whereas MacDiarmid tended to oscillate between the extremes of the left and right. The Scottish renaissance, although politically disparate, did have a unifying objective in believing that Scotland required a new sense of national culture and that the old one was flawed and deformed.[38] Scottish writers and intellectuals looked to Europe and beyond for their influence, and pointed with envy to the way in which 'culture' was supported and endorsed elsewhere. Just as the 'crisis' of the interwar era undermined many of the economic certainties of the old order, it had an equally dramatic impact in the way that it forced a reassessment of Scottish culture. The politicization of Scottish culture in this period is again something which shows that the experience was more similar to the European mainland than the rest of the United Kingdom.

Given the travails of Scottish society, it is not surprising that political nationalism emerged in this period in its modern guise. Many of the traditional bolts of Unionism were shaken as a result of the crisis. Although the realities of everyday bread-and-butter politics pushed the politics of identity way down the political agenda, for a vocal minority, however, the answer was nationalism.[39] Yet a major problem for the embryonic nationalist movement was an inability to find a consensus. Some wanted devolution, others independence, some wanted a separate political party, others a pressure group, and some were left wing whereas others were right wing. The history of the nationalist movement during this time was one of changing direction and strategy as one clique ousted the other. Although the nationalist movement failed to build up significant political momentum, its existence was believed to be the pinnacle of a wider sense of unease as to the state of the Scottish nation. It represented the extreme end of a spectrum of public thought that believed the Scots were being treated unfairly and that something drastic ought to be done. Government politicians were aware that the sense of national unease had the potential to crystallize into a more significant movement and took steps in the mid-1930s to address this national 'disquiet'.[40] After all, nationalism was the ascendant force in Europe and this might be a Scottish variant of the same phenomenon. Administrative devolution was instituted as a palliative, though with varying degrees of success.[41] Greater acknowledgement was made of Scottish nationhood within the Union.

---

[38] Marjery McCulloch, *Modernism and Nationalism: Literature and Society in Scotland 1918–1939* (Edinburgh, 2004).

[39] Richard J. Finlay, *Independent and Free: Scottish Politics and the Origins of the Scottish National Party, 1918–1945* (Edinburgh, 1994), 71–126.

[40] James Mitchell, *Governing Scotland: The Invention of Administrative Devolution* (Basingstoke, 2003), 117–49.

[41] James Mitchell, *Conservatism and the Union: A Survey of Conservative Party Attitudes to Scotland* (Edinburgh, 1990), 17–26.

Government reform, appeasement of a sense of national grievance, and the nationalist tendency to secessionism and ideological incoherence ensured that the Scottish National Party remained on the fringes of politics during the 1930s. Although Labour flirted with home rule in the late 1930s, this was more as a result of the growth in the powers of the Scottish Office, and a Parliament in Edinburgh was seen as an option to curtail the growth of central government, especially one that was dominated by the Conservative Party.[42] The growth of corporatism and the increasing role of business in government made many in the Labour Party feel that they were being frozen out of the political process and that political devolution would make the system more democratic. Also, nationalism was no longer perceived as a threat.

## 2

By the late 1930s, the worse of the Depression was over. Employment was growing slowly and events in Europe were concentrating minds away from domestic problems. The Second World War was to initiate a political revolution that would ensure greater state intervention in government policy and lay the foundations for the solution to Scotland's endemic socio-economic problems that had plagued the interwar era. In some respects the story is one of 'all's well that ends well'. Yet it is worth stepping back and looking at the era in isolation for a moment. In comparison with other European countries, it is also worth commenting on why Scotland had not faced a crisis of the magnitude that tipped the political balance towards extremism. After all, on the surface, Scotland looked to have all the necessary ingredients. There was a prolonged economic downturn with its concomitant effects of social dislocation and long-term, mass unemployment. Racism and nationalism were in the air with growing anti-Irish sentiment and the formation of a separatist nationalist political party. The middle class was becoming radicalized—a key factor explaining the growth of right-wing parties in Europe at the time. A huge reservoir of unemployed provided a suitable breeding ground for the politics of discontent.[43] As has been shown, there were elements of crisis, and Scottish society showed manifestations of this phenomenon that were commonplace in Europe but less pronounced in the United Kingdom. Any examination of the impact of the interwar crisis in Scotland must take into account the ways in which the Union seemed to exacerbate the problems, or at least not help, as was noted by contemporaries and many historians. But what tends to receive less attention are the ways in which the British connection ameliorated the worst aspects of the crisis.

To address the question why Scotland avoided a crisis, it needs to be borne in mind that the decision to return to the Gold Standard in 1926 put the brakes on much of the

---

[42] Tom Burns, *Self-Government for Scotland* (Edinburgh, 1939).

[43] Barry Eichengreen and T. J. Hatton, eds., *Interwar Unemployment in International Perspective* (Dordrecht, 1987), 1–51.

Scottish economy, especially in terms of its export market. The structural problems that dogged the 1920s were not solved by the time the Great Crash arrived in 1929, and as such it meant that, comparatively, the Scottish economy had not been built up to the heights that other economies achieved in the same period.[44] So rather than a 'Crash' as was experienced elsewhere, in Scotland it was more like a bump, albeit a heavy and pain-ful one. Although the Depression was deep and sustained, it was not as sharp and as traumatic there as was experienced by the heavy industries of Germany and the United States, for example. Furthermore, the fact that the Depression was region-specific in the United Kingdom meant that resources could be diverted from more prosperous parts to those in greatest need. According to the politician Sir Robert Horne, proportionately more was spent on Scottish unemployment benefit, education, and roads.[45] Some in the House of Lords advocated the abolition of the Scottish Office. because it would be more efficient if all government services in Scotland were absorbed into the 'great branches of the public service' to make it more efficient.[46] Although the 'hungry thirties' depict the iniquities of the means test, social-security payments in the United Kingdom were com-paratively generous compared to those elsewhere.[47] Also, the national government stood firm in maintaining payments in the face of relentless middle-class criticism against 'spongers and the work-shy'.[48] Indeed, the Scottish middle class was not averse to joining in with this tirade. Greater state regulation ensured equal provision throughout the United Kingdom and took power away from local agencies to prevent middle-class rate-payers limiting the amount of relief granted.[49] This comparative security prevented the emergence of greater political activism. Many contemporary observers pointed out the passivity, hopelessness, and apathy, rather than anger and a will to change or challenge things.[50]

Undoubtedly, the growth of political extremism forms a chain reaction in which the growth of the extreme left or right acts as a catalyst for an equally vigorous growth at the opposite end of the political spectrum. The defeat of the General Strike in 1926 and the trouncing of Labour in 1931, together with the fact that communism remained firmly on the fringes, helped to keep the middle class within the pale of traditional politics. The British first-past-the-post electoral system militated against the growth of minority par-ties, while at the same time guaranteeing the integrity of the larger ones. In spite of the existence of nationalist, Protestant, and communist groups, Scottish politics did not fragment. Further factors helped keep the radical propensities of the middle class in check. The social structure of Scotland did not have as prominent a number of the petty

[44]  Neil K. Buxton, 'Economic Growth in Scotland between the Wars: The Role of Production Structure and Rationalization', *Economic History Review*, 33, 4 (November 1980), 538–55.

[45]  HC Deb 24 November 1932, vol. 272, c. 242–3.

[46]  Ibid., vol. 85, c. 1,349.

[47]  Stevenson, *British Society*, 276–99, and Peter Baldwin, *The Politics of Social Solidarity: Class Bases of the European Welfare State, 1875–1975* (Cambridge, 1992), 107–47.

[48]  Stevenson, *British Society*, 315–17.

[49]  G. C. Peden, *British Economic and Social Policy: Lloyd George to Thatcher* (London, 1991), 105–13.

[50]  Edwin Muir, *Scottish Journey* (London, 1935), 110.

bourgeoisie compared with much of mainland Europe, a group that has traditionally been identified as the bedrock of far-right support. Most of Scotland's skilled artisans in heavy industry accepted their place within the proletariat and played an active role in the trade-union and labour movement. The underdevelopment of a domestic economy in the late-nineteenth and early twentieth century left Scotland with comparatively fewer shopkeepers and self-employed.[51] The extensive flow of middle-class and skilled working-class emigration during the 1920s had arguably removed a further reservoir of potential recruits to more radical politics.[52] The farming community was also structurally different, with fewer, but larger farms, than was to be found on the Continent, and although the rural community suffered during the Depression, the comparatively efficient nature of Scottish agriculture and its smaller proportion of the total workforce meant that it did not experience the same degree of dislocation as was felt in the European mainland or America. It is worth remembering that it was in the rural constituencies where the extreme right made its breakthrough in Europe.[53] 'Back to the land' solutions to the Depression were mooted fairly extensively, but a lack of support illustrates that it was more of a rhetorical device than a serious policy option.

Scottish politics were firmly rooted within British politics, which limited the scope for radical deviation. Indeed, the term 'Scottish politics' is somewhat of a misnomer in that it was more of a 'British politics' in Scotland. While Scotland did have its prominent class warriors on both the left and right, they were marginal within the British political sphere. Indeed, both the Labour and Conservative leaderships in Scotland were firmly moderate. The Red Clydesiders who survived into the 1930s were not ideologues, but pragmatists.[54] Maxton's secession of the Independent Labour Party in 1932 had the effect of marginalizing him, and those MPs elected under the ILP banner owed their success to personal followings in their respective constituencies rather that popular endorsement of the Cooke-Maxton Manifesto. Similarly, the Tory Party was firmly associated with moderates such as Walter Elliot and John Gilmour.[55] The Scottish Secretaries of State in the 1930s were fairly dull, pragmatic, and moderate, and although they drew attention to the plight of the nation, they did not disaggregate Scotland from the wider British context. Both the Tory and Labour Party addressed the solution of Scottish problems from a British perspective. Furthermore, they often reminded electors that unemployment and poverty were not just Scottish issues.[56] So long as British politics was immune to extremism, there was little chance of it taking off in Scotland because the organizations, the

---

[51] The number of self-employed decreased from 132,000 to 94,000 between 1921 and 1939; C. E. V. Leser, 'Manpower', in Cairncross, ed., *Scottish Economy*, 40.

[52] T. M. Devine, *The Scottish Nation 1700–2007* (London, 2006), 479–85.

[53] J. M. MacDiarmid, *The Deer Forests and How They Are Bleeding Scotland White* (Edinburgh, 1926), and see E. Cameron, *Land for the People: The British Government and the Scottish Highlands 1880–1925* (East Linton, 1996), 166–91.

[54] T. Brotherstone, 'Does Red Clydeside Matter Any More', in R. Duncan and A. McIvor, eds., *Militant Workers: Labour and Class Conflict on the Clyde, 1900–1950* (Edinburgh, 1997), 52–81.

[55] R. H. Campbell, 'The Committee of the Ex-Secretaries of State for Scotland and Industrial Policy, 1941–45', *Scottish Industrial History*, 2 (1981).

[56] HC Deb 22 November 1932, vol. 272, cc. 262–92.

issues, the personnel, and the debate north of the border were dominated by an agenda that was set in London. The British idiom had the effect of watering down any extremist tendencies that may have arisen as a result of a purely Scottish political agenda.

Europe after 1919 was dominated by the growth of irredentist nationalism that was dedicated to reclaiming territories and people displaced or lost as a result of Versailles.[57] It was a key issue in German and Eastern and Central European politics. The politics of nationalist grievance that plagued interwar Europe did not have a similar resonance in Scotland because it did not travel in one direction. There were no tensions or contradictions in holding both Scottish and British identities that were mutually self-reinforcing. Although a sense of Scottish identity increasingly became posited in opposition to a British identity, it did not displace it. For John Buchan, among others, there was a fear that an exclusive Scottish nationalism might become mainstream, as had an 'appeal to the professional and middle classes'.[58] But lawyers and doctors were not the stuff of revolution and revolt. It was more a politics of nationalist complaint. Also, while many might believe that Scotland was being treated unfairly, it did not follow that the solution was to abandon Britain and the Union. An exclusive Scottish nationalism that preached separatism found the ground barren among the middle class whose conception of patriotism was based on Britain. Throughout Europe nationalism found support among the middle class who saw it as an ideology that would stave off the threat from the left and restore conservative and traditional values.[59] Although many in the Scottish middle class felt that traditional notions of Scottishness were under threat, the same could not be said for Britishness, as witnessed by support for the Empire Exhibition in Glasgow in 1938. Indeed, Scottish nationalism was banded in with those things that posed a threat to traditional values, and its association with Irish nationalism and political radicalism further alienated potential support.[60] Furthermore, many mainstream nationalists recognized that the movement had to water down its message and moderate its ambitions in order to attract potential support.[61] Fascists in Scotland fared even worse and tied themselves up on the question of what nationalism to support.[62]

The growth of racism in the interwar period is another issue that seems to take the Scottish experience closer to the European mainland. Although anti-Irishness and anti-Catholicism were rampant in nineteenth-century Scotland, the phenomenon was morphing in the 1920s towards racism. Among many polemicists, Catholicism became more of a racial categorization than a religious one. According to the Church of Scotland: 'There are only two explanations of the great racial problem that has arisen in Scotland—the

[57] Oliver Zimmer, *Nationalism in Europe: 1890–1940* (Basingstoke, 2003), 59–72.

[58] HC Deb 22 November 1932, vol. 272, c. 262.

[59] Michael Mann, 'A Political Theory of Nationalism and Its Excess', in Sukumar Periwal and Ernest Gellner, eds., *Notions of Nationalism* (Budapest, 1995), 44–64.

[60] For claims of 'Rome Rule', Sir Robert Horne in HC Deb 22 November 1932, vol. 272, c. 261.

[61] Finlay, *Independent and Free*, 162–206.

[62] Stephen M. Cullen, 'The Fasces and the Saltire: The Failure of the British Union of Fascists in Scotland, 1932–1940', *Scottish Historical Review*, 87, 2 (2008), 306–31.

emigration of the Scots and the immigration of the Irish people.'[63] Catholics of Irish descent were portrayed as having innate racial tendencies towards colonization, crime, drunkenness, sexual deviance, squalor, and parasitic existence.[64] In looking through many of these polemics, it is hard to differentiate their intention and scope from the rabid anti-Semitism found in Europe. The following would not be out of place in *Der Stuermer*: 'disloyal to all the finest ideals and ambitions of the Scottish race; distinguished by a veritable will to squalor which is mainly responsible for Scottish slumdom; squatting and breeding in such numbers as to threaten in another hundred years to gain actual predominance in the country.'[65] Although produced in the main by cranks on the fringes of mainstream society, such ideas did have adherents who were highly placed and respectable individuals, such as the moderator of the reunited Church of Scotland and the Regius Professor of Law at Glasgow University. These pernicious sentiments were percolating into the mainstream of society, as the incidents of an official government inquiry in 1929 showed.[66] Official figures showed that Irish immigration had all but stopped, but that did little to quell the outlandish claims that every fifth child born in Scotland was 'Irish', nor abate the flood of anti-Catholic sentiment in the columns of newspapers and magazines. Outbreaks of sectarian violence showed that sectarianism had its followers who were prepared to take direct action. A number of proletarian Protestant groups and the winning of some seats in local-government elections demonstrated a potential pool of populist support, but no middle-class leadership emerged to direct it. In a British context, anti-Catholicism was meaningless and would be seen as a source of embarrassment. Indeed, Scottish interference with the passage of the English Common Prayer Book Bill in the House of Commons in December 1927, because of its 'Catholicism', was a good case in point.

While Scotland did manifest some of the characteristics associated with the general interwar crisis, the fact that it was located within a British political and economic sphere acted as a buffer against some of the worst of the effects. As many commentators at the time pointed out, the resources of the Scots were inadequate to deal with the full social consequences of mass unemployment. Indeed, the experience of economic dislocation in the interwar period was fundamental in establishing a unionist consensus that an independent Scotland would lose a transfer of resources from the United Kingdom necessary to meets its requirements. Certainly the experience of the British welfare provisions blunted the sharpness of trauma that might have been the case. The emphasis of government policy on the service sector was criticized for not doing enough for heavy industry, but parts of Scotland, especially in the Edinburgh environs, escaped lightly. The British political system acted as an effective buffer against the growth of political extremism. The Scottish dimension of the interwar crisis lacked the political weight to dent the

---

[63] *Reports on the Schemes of the Church of Scotland, 1927* (Edinburgh, 1927), 1,220.

[64] R. J. Finlay, 'Nationalism, Race and Religion: The "Irish Question in Interwar Scotland" ', *Innes Review*, xlii (Spring 1991), 46–67.

[65] Gibb, *Scotland in Eclipse*, 56–7.

[66] *Glasgow Herald*, 25 March 1929, and HC Deb 22 November 1932, vol. 272, c. 261.

dominance of British politics in Scotland. In short, a separate Scottish agenda never built up enough momentum to displace the wider British priorities that dominated Scottish politics at this time, and the potential growth of extremism was kept in check.

## FURTHER READING

Cameron, Ewen A., *Impaled Upon a Thistle: Scotland Since 1880* (Edinburgh, 2010).

Devine, T. M., *The Scottish Nation 1700–2007* (London, 2006).

Finlay, Richard J., *Modern Scotland, 1914–2000* (London, 2004).

MacDonald, Catriona M. M., *Whaur Extremes Meet: Scotland's Twentieth Century* (Edinburgh, 2009).

Orlow, Dietrich, *The Lure of Fascism in Western Europe: German Nazis, Dutch and French Fascists, 1933–1939* (Basingstoke, 2009).

Overy, R. J., *The Interwar Crisis, 1919–1939* (London, 2007).

Pugh, Martin, *Hurrah for the Blackshirts: Fascism and Fascists in Britain Between the Wars* (London, 2005).

Thorpe, Andrew J., ed., *The Failure of Political Extremism in Interwar Britain* (Exeter, 1988).

# CHAPTER 31

......................................................................................................

# THE RELIGIOUS FACTOR

......................................................................................................

## GRAHAM WALKER

SCOTLAND began the twentieth century as a profoundly religious country, at least if measured in terms of adherence to Churches; this reached an all-time peak in 1905.[1] By the end of the century, however, the country was implicated in what a leading scholar in the area has termed 'The Death of Christian Britain'.[2] Clearly, there is a lot to explain around the role of the religious factor in Scotland over the last century. Equally, it should be acknowledged that the decline of the Churches does not necessarily oblige us to discount the salience of religion as a notable issue in Scottish life as the twenty-first century takes its course. This chapter seeks to comprehend both the significance of religious institutions from 1900 to our own times and the various social and cultural effects of religion as a controversial subject or form of identity.

<br>

## 1

......................................................................................................

The century began with a highly important and symbolical reorganization of Scotland's dominant religious tradition of Presbyterianism. The coming together in 1900 of the Free Church and the United Presbyterians into the United Free Church signalled the cooling of the intra-Presbyterian conflict that had embittered much of the nineteenth century. The formal rift between the established Church of Scotland, still deferring to the United Kingdom practice of patronage in appointing parish clergy, and the various Presbyterian 'dissenters', still demanding disestablishment, remained; nevertheless, the fusion of the great majority of Presbyterianism's dissenters into one body foreshadowed moves to reunion with the 'national' Kirk. This eventually transpired in 1929 and was greatly facilitated by the 1921 Act of the Westminster Parliament, which was broadly interpreted as confirming the established Church's independence from the State. Indeed, one commentator has

---

[1] Callum Brown, *Religion and Society in Modern Scotland* (Edinburgh, 1997), 62–3.
[2] Callum Brown, *The Death of Christian Britain* (London, 2001).

pointed out that this made the constitutional position of the Church of Scotland 'unique in Britain' and was 'an abrogation of parliamentary sovereignty'.[3] The dissenters dropped their campaign to disestablish the Kirk after 1921. A further Act of Parliament in 1925 regarding Church property and finances then removed the final impediments to union between the Church of Scotland and the great majority of the United Free Church.

The 1921 Act was not unambiguous. Colin Kidd has pointed out that concessions to the Church of Scotland may have been at the cost of weakening its protections of the 1707 Act of Union, and he notes the absence in the 1921 Act of the 'language of establishment'.[4] The attention paid to such debating points rapidly diminished over the coming years, yet it is important to recognize the matter's wider connection to the relationship between Scottish Presbyterianism and the Anglo-Scottish Union. Kidd, along with other scholars, has highlighted the centrality of religion to the national question in Scotland and the manner in which ecclesiastical controversies more than any other kind had, by the early twentieth century, brought tensions between Scotland and England to the surface. As Kidd argues, the fundamental fault line within the Union for most of its history has been religious rather than political.[5] The twentieth century was to provide several notable instances of the intersection between Scottish religious identities and the question of the nature and desirability of political union, notwithstanding the sharp decline in strength and influence on the part of the established Church by the latter decades of the period. More thought, perhaps, needs to be given to how British identity and institutions served the interests of Scottish Protestantism rather than the other way round.

In the years leading up to the First World War, however, pan-Presbyterian Scotland gave every appearance of being geared to the cause of the British Empire. The imperial context was distinguished by much Scottish missionary activity and, arguably, the conspicuously vigorous promotion of moral and social visions. The exploits of David Livingstone in particular inspired heroic myths regularly reworked to fit the needs of the times.[6] In the Edwardian era Scottish Protestantism evinced a self-confidence that was substantially the result of its global reach. David McCrone sees this as the high point of the social power and influence of the Presbyterian bourgeoisie.[7] Notions of civic responsibility ran deep and the Presbyterian churches cherished what they saw as their character-forming contribution to the life of the nation. Although subject to gradual erosion from the growth of the State, Presbyterianism continued to exercise a role in the local provision of such services as education and welfare through to 1929, when the local-government system was re-organized and the old parish councils were abolished.

[3] George Rosie, 'Religion', in Magnus Linklater and Robin Denniston, eds., *Anatomy of Scotland* (Edinburgh, 1992), 80.

[4] Colin Kidd, *Union and Unionisms* (Cambridge, 2008), 243.

[5] Kidd, *Union*, 7.

[6] John Mackenzie, 'David Livingstone: The Construction of the Myth', in Graham Walker and Tom Gallagher, eds., *Sermons and Battle Hymns: Protestant Popular Culture in Modern Scotland* (Edinburgh, 1990), 24–42; also John Mackenzie, 'Scotland and the British Empire', *International History Review*, 4 (1993), 714–39.

[7] David McCrone, *Understanding Scotland: The Sociology of a Stateless Nation* (London, 1992), 132–3.

In relation to education in particular, Presbyterianism, in and out of the established Church, was linked in the popular mind with the pursuit of virtue, the profusion of 'lads o' pairts' equipped for the world's challenges, and the remarkable achievements of Scottish inventors and Scottish educational institutions.[8]

Yet amid self-congratulation and a measure of confidence, historians have found evidence of anxieties and alarm. The unsettling effects of industrialization and urbanization had long concerned Church leaders, fearful especially of 'the masses' drifting away from organized religion. In the Edwardian era suburbanization gathered pace and the Churches' contacts with the inner cities were stretched; there was also the competing attraction of organized leisure pursuits. Callum Brown has cautioned against losing sight of what he calls 'the religiosity of the common people' in this period, manifest in Church-related organizations and evangelical bodies like the Sunday schools and the Band of Hope.[9] Nevertheless, worries about 'the condition of the people' and the appeal of the growing Labour movement produced significant engagement with social problems on the part of the Churches and, in some cases, the radical politicization of clerics.[10]

Many of the poor and disadvantaged belonged to the Roman Catholic faith, particularly in Glasgow and the west of Scotland and in Dundee. Overwhelmingly the product of emigration from Ireland during the previous century, especially from the Great Famine of the late 1840s, this community—some 10 per cent of the population by the early twentieth century—in many ways looked to its church first and foremost for succour and guidance. As such some historians have tended to perceive a tendency towards insularity, occasioned or reinforced by anti-Catholic attitudes in Scottish society; this raised questions about the process of assimilation and the limits to it.[11] On the other hand, recent scholarship has revealed a more complex picture of greater Catholic participation in many aspects of Scottish public life and the emergence of a 'viable' Catholic community in the early twentieth century out of hitherto unappreciated social and economic improvements and the rise of a Catholic professional class.[12]

---

[8] See Graham Walker, 'Varieties of Scottish Protestant Identity', in Tom Devine and Richard Finlay, eds., *Scotland in the Twentieth Century* (Edinburgh, 1996).

[9] Brown, *Religion and Society*, 8–11; also Brown, *Death*, Introduction. The Band of Hope, formed in 1847, was a temperance organization set up to influence working-class children.

[10] See John Stewart, ' "Christ's Kingdom in Scotland": Scottish Presbyterianism, Social Reform, and the Edwardian Crisis', *Twentieth Century British History*, 12, no. 1 (2001), 1–22.

[11] Scholarly debate in this area derives from the pioneering work of James E. Handley, whose books *The Irish in Scotland 1798–1845* (Cork, 1943) and *The Irish in Modern Scotland* (Cork, 1947) have provided rich quarry for later scholars such as Tom Gallagher, *Glasgow: The Uneasy Peace* (Manchester, 1987). See discussion of Hanley's influence in Irene Maver, 'The Catholic Community', in Devine and Finlay, eds., *Scotland*; also T. M. Devine, *The Scottish Nation 1700–2000* (London, 1999), 486–500.

[12] See Martin J. Mitchell, ed., *New Perspectives on the Irish in Scotland* (Edinburgh, 2008), especially Chapter 1; Bernard Aspinwall, 'Catholic Realities and Pastoral Strategies: Another Look at the Historiography of Scottish Catholicism, 1878–1920', *Innes Review*, 59, no. 1 (Spring 2008), 77–112. It should also be noted that a significant indigenous Catholic community retained a presence in areas like the Gaelic-speaking west Highlands. The scholarly literature is slight but see Ray Burnett, ' "The Long Nineteenth Century": Scotland's Catholic Gaidhealtachd', in Raymond Boyle and Peter Lynch, eds., *Out of the Ghetto? The Catholic Community in Modern Scotland* (Edinburgh, 1998).

The Roman Catholic Church, whose hierarchy was restored in 1878, prioritized control over the education of its adherents and directed efforts in the political arena to this end. The struggles and sacrifices involved in providing a Catholic education outside the mainstream abated with the 1918 Education Act, which guaranteed full State support for a separate Catholic schools sector. Some Protestants regarded this concession as unduly favourable to the Catholic Church at a time when the Presbyterian Churches' educational influence was waning and soon to be marginalized, and the issue fuelled sectarian tensions off and on for the rest of the century. A distinguished historian of Catholicism in Scotland wrote: 'The feeling that the 1918 Act had brought the by now largely Scoto-Irish Catholic community into the life of the nation while preserving its ethos lies behind its defensive reactions in the twentieth century to any proposals to change what is seen as something of a constitutional symbol.'[13]

The 1918 Act was passed by a coalition government under a Liberal Prime Minister, David Lloyd George. The Catholics in Scotland had until this point largely backed the Liberals, chiefly on account of their policy of Home Rule for Ireland. However, with the coming of near-universal (male) franchise in 1918 and the inability of the Liberal Party to heal its divisions to assume the role of the major force for socially progressive politics, Catholics swung towards the Labour Party. Such a development was by no means inevitable: during the early years of the century the hierarchy was firmly anti-Labour, fearing the spread of socialist doctrines to the socially deprived mass of Catholics. The Labour Party's willingness to defend the new educational legislation softened the hostility of the Catholic Church after 1918, and it was clear that the Catholic–Labour electoral alliance which then developed in the west of Scotland was predicated heavily on the party not offending the Church's teachings on other, mainly moral, matters.

The Episcopalian Church in Scotland also provided schools at its own expense until 1918, after which most disappeared through mergers. This Church enjoyed significant support in the north-east, and to an extent grew in the late nineteenth century in the Central Belt and south of the country through Protestant Irish immigration. But the Episcopal Church's 'English' image, notwithstanding its colourful Jacobite history, weakened its claims to a share in national discourse and symbolism. Its role in Scottish public life was often a marginal one throughout the twentieth century.[14]

Completing the religious patchwork of the early twentieth century, the small Jewish community, based largely in and around Glasgow, grew to around 13,500 by 1914. Jews were prominent in certain trades like tailoring and made their presence felt in mercantile circles.[15] Edinburgh Jews, such as the Daiches family, played a significant intellectual role in that city and in the early life of the novelist Muriel Spark.

---

[13] John McCaffrey, 'Roman Catholics in Scotland: Nineteenth and Twentieth Centuries', in C. MacLean and K. Veitch, eds., *Scottish Life and Society: A Compendium of Scottish Ethnology. Volume 12: Religion* (Edinburgh, 2006).

[14] See Allan Maclean, 'Episcopalians', in MacLean and Veitch, *Scottish Life.*

[15] See Kenneth Collins, 'The Jews in Scotland', in MacLean and Veitch, *Scottish Life.*

## 2

All the main religious denominations in Scotland shared in the patriotic response to war in 1914. A year later it was estimated that around 90 per cent of the 'sons of the manse' had joined up for service, and Presbyterians rejoiced in Earl Haig, their co-religionist, ultimately taking charge of the British troops. Catholic Church leaders also supported the war effort and Catholics volunteered in large numbers. In its early stages the war tended to be viewed in terms of a religious crusade and an exercise in catharsis.[16]

As the war became one of attrition and the casualties mounted, doubts set in and the Churches' upbeat message of national spiritual renewal lost some credibility. Scholars of the Churches and the Great War have argued that the conflagration revealed how little influence the Churches had with the soldiers at the front.[17] The most popular religious support group in the trenches may have been the Salvation Army. Reports from army chaplains bemoaned the ignorance revealed by ordinary infantrymen of the essentials of the Christian faith, and their tendency to find spiritual comfort in 'pagan' ways. The sexual licentiousness of the men on the Western Front was deplored, and this was to an extent compounded by the perception that females at home—traditionally the moral backbone of the Churches and the community—were also falling into male habits of alcohol abuse and sexual misconduct. Before the end of the war the Presbyterian Churches were calling for a revival of puritan values, and were anxiously seeking to reposition themselves as central to the project of post-war social reconstruction.

The changed context of a country trying to come to terms with the losses suffered in the war, and a social and economic order in some flux, saw the Churches struggle to give direction and guidance. Firstly, much emotional energy was absorbed in grieving: the need to honour the dead in memorials and with pulpit panegyrics was urgent and compelling. The same impulse increased faith in spiritualism, evangelized by a famous Scot, Sir Arthur Conan Doyle. Then there was, for the Churches, the alarming spectre of revolutionary politics and a lurch to the left, as presaged during the war in the violent clashes between workers and authorities. On the part of the majority Presbyterian tradition, preoccupied also with progress towards unity between its main Churches, there was a conservative turn away from the 'social gospel' that marked the pre-war period. Leading figures such as the Reverend John White now personified the Kirk's fears of the political left and the perceived progress made by the Catholic Church as its main 'competitor'.[18]

---

[16] Robert Kernohan, *Scotland's Life and Work* (Edinburgh, 1979), 96–7; Elaine McFarland, ' "Our Country's Heroes": Irish Catholics and the Great War', in Mitchell, ed., *New Perspectives*, 127–44; Stewart J. Brown, ' "A Solemn Purification by Fire": Responses to the Great War in the Scottish Presbyterian Churches, 1914–19', *Journal of Ecclesiastical History*, 45, no. 1 (1994), 82–104.

[17] Brown, ' "Solemn Purification" '; Callum Brown, 'Piety, Gender and War in Scotland in the 1910s', in Catriona M. M. Macdonald and Elaine McFarland, eds., *Scotland and the Great War* (East Linton, 1999), 173–91.

[18] See Keith Robbins, *England, Ireland, Scotland, Wales: The Christian Church 1900–2000* (Oxford, 2008), 210–16.

The recent historiography of the religious factor in Scotland during the interwar period has indeed tended to focus on the sectarian tensions between Protestants and Catholics above all else.[19] The impact of the 1918 Education Act was a significant part of this; local-authority elections after the war often heard militant Protestant candidates denounce what they called 'Rome on the Rates'. Some of these candidates were sponsored by the Orange Order, a Protestant organization imported from Ireland during the nineteenth century and still largely directed by Protestant Irish immigrants to Scotland and their descendants well into the twentieth.[20] The Order, influential also at grassroots level in the Unionist (Conservative) Party in the west of the country, appealed increasingly to Protestant working-class Scots, and grew in strength after the war around the education controversy and the fear of Bolshevism. It also strengthened its popular cultural credentials with its colourful Battle of the Boyne celebrations and parades—the carnivalesque equivalent in Protestant circles to the Catholic Irish tradition of St Patrick's Day and Hibernian occasions. Riotous scenes had accompanied such factional dates on the calendar in areas of high Irish immigration in Lanarkshire, Renfrewshire, and Ayrshire as well as Glasgow from the mid-nineteenth century. However, community relations were put under even greater strain in the 1920s and 1930s against the austere economic background and the social scourge of unemployment.

In this context the Presbyterian Churches' involvement in the public controversy over the extent and impact of Irish immigration was highly divisive; the campaign carried on by leading figures of both the Church of Scotland and the United Free Church, and then by the re-united Church after 1929, repeatedly denounced Irish Catholics as 'alien' to Scottish values and culture and damaging to the country's social and economic welfare. Stewart J. Brown has demonstrated how dogged the Presbyterian campaigners were over a fifteen-year period in trying to bring about legislative change to curb specifically Irish Catholic immigration and even to repatriate Irish Catholics in Scotland.[21] Fears of the erosion of Presbyterian influence through the changes to the education system and the local-government reforms, combined with dismay over the extent of emigration— almost four hundred thousand Scots left the country during the decade 1921–31—led the Churches down this confrontational route, although it should be remembered that opinion within Presbyterianism was divided and anti-sectarian and conciliatory voices were also heard.[22]

---

[19]  See, for example, Stewart J. Brown, '"Outside the Covenant": The Scottish Presbyterian Churches and Irish Immigration, 1922–1938', *Innes Review*, 42, no. 1 (Spring 1991), 19–45; Richard J. Finlay, 'Nationalism, Race, Religion and The Irish Question in Inter-War Scotland', *Innes Review*, 42, no. 1 (Spring 1991), 46–67; Gallagher, *Glasgow*, Chapter 4; Brown, *Religion*, 191–6; Stewart J. Brown, 'Presbyterians and Catholics in Twentieth-Century Scotland', in Stewart J. Brown and George Newlands, eds., *Scottish Christianity in the Modern World* (Edinburgh, 2000).

[20]  See Elaine McFarland, *Protestants First: Orangeism in 19th-Century Scotland* (Edinburgh, 1990); Graham Walker, 'The Orange Order in Scotland Between the Wars', *International Review of Social History*, 37, no. 2 (1992), 177–206; Eric Kaufman, 'The Orange Order in Scotland since 1860: A Social Analysis', in Mitchell, *New Perspectives*, 159–90.

[21]  Stewart J. Brown, '"Outside the Covenant"'.

[22]  See Michael Rosie, *The Sectarian Myth in Scotland* (Basingstoke, 2004), 140–2.

For all the inflammatory rhetoric of the era, and the local electoral impact of Protestant parties in Glasgow and Edinburgh, the Education Act was left untouched, and successive Secretaries of State for Scotland refused to be pressured into anti-Irish Catholic legislation. Moreover, Michael Rosie's recent research reveals the extent to which Catholic propagandists waged their own campaign against Protestantism, and the way the Catholic Church pursued a policy of 'separatism' in various social and cultural areas.[23] The Catholic Church's insistence on a Catholic upbringing for all children of mixed marriages—following the guidelines of the 'Ne Temere' decree of 1907—aroused much resentment. The electoral impact of the Protestant parties proved ephemeral: as Steve Bruce has argued, the Scottish political world, subsumed as it was within the broader British party system, did not provide the opportunities for sectarian politics to thrive in the contemporary manner of the introverted and closed-off political unit of nearby Northern Ireland.[24] Catholics in Scotland could regard the Labour Party as a plausible vehicle for the pursuit of their interests in stark contrast to the political marginalization of their co-religionists in Ulster.[25]

Militant Protestantism found no support at the elite level in politics; while the press, when it intervened in the Irish immigration issue, did so to explode the myth that the country was being overrun.[26] The Scottish Office also disputed the claims of the Presbyterian Churches about immigrant numbers and contended that in the period 1921–31 more Irish emigrated from Scotland than entered it. On the other hand, a memorandum by a Scottish Office official did concede that even a small number of immigrants could aggravate the situation in areas of acute deprivation and unemployment, suggesting that sectarian animosities, whether genuine or cultivated and encouraged by some for their own ends, were always likely to emerge in straitened economic times.[27]

The Church of Scotland, especially after the reunion of 1929, was desperate to reassert itself as the national Church. In this its aspirations probably mirrored those of the Catholic Church in Ireland or Spain or Poland, and the Church of England south of the border, at the time. It was a self-conscious desire to make the nation and the Church appear intertwined, with the Church responsible for the nation's values and character. It was perceived as a worthy mission in a modernist world where old certainties were under cultural attack.[28] Such sentiments and claims were a notable feature of the ceremony attending the reunion of 1929, and certainly it is important to record that the Kirk membership following reunion stood at 1,300,000, some 27 per cent of the total population; as the novelist and politician John Buchan (son of a Free Church minister) put it in a book celebrating the event, the Church of Scotland was now truly 'of' Scotland and not

[23] Rosie, *Sectarian Myth*, ch. 7.

[24] Steve Bruce, *Conservative Protestant Politics* (Oxford, 1998), ch. 4.

[25] See Graham Walker, *Intimate Strangers: Political and Cultural Interaction Between Scotland and Ulster in Modern Times* (Edinburgh, 1995), ch. 4.

[26] Gallagher, *Uneasy Peace*, 167.

[27] Scottish Record Office (SRO), 37110/1. Scottish Office Report on the Irish in Scotland.

[28] See discussion in Robbins, *England*, ch. 4.

merely 'in' Scotland.[29] Around 90 per cent of Presbyterians now belonged to the 'national' Church, with outside of it only small congregations of dissenters in the Lowlands and the 'Wee Free' Free Presbyterian Church in the Highlands and Western Isles. Indeed, the latter congregations, drawn from the crofting community, were the most committed churchgoers and the most steadfast in defence of sabbatarian principles.[30] The Kirk, largely through its annual General Assembly and its 'Church and Nation' Committee, considered itself the voice of the nation and as such deserving of a hearing at the highest level of State.

# 3

Although mainly a period of retrenchment and conservatism, the 1930s witnessed the emergence of more liberal and indeed socially radical tendencies within Presbyterianism which were given momentum by the Second World War. George MacLeod's Church of Scotland ministry in the parish of Govan in Glasgow genuinely sparked a broad-based community activism and devalued sectarian divisions. MacLeod strove to reconnect Presbyterianism to earlier strands of Scottish Christianity, invoking the example of St Columba and proceeding to found the spiritual community of Iona in homage to him. MacLeod's willingness to embrace Catholic forms of worship while critical of the papacy earned him the suspicion of many Kirk traditionalists, but foreshadowed a more ecumenical era to come. His pacifism was to lead him to take a prominent part in the campaign for nuclear disarmament in the 1960s.[31]

Perhaps even more influential in his time, John Baillie provided a more expansive social and theological vision during the Second World War. The Baillie Commission, which highlighted the social problems faced by the nation, sought to bolster community spirit and advocated more public control of economic resources.[32] Baillie was Moderator of the General Assembly of the Kirk for 1943. By the time the London Labour government applied itself to the task of post-war reconstruction, the Churches in Scotland were more oriented towards a collectivist view of social and economic policy than in the period following the First World War. Recent scholarly work has revealed the vigour of the Kirk's industrial mission from wartime through to the late 1950s, and the constructive critique of communism that often accompanied it.[33] The advent of the Welfare State also caused fewer ripples of disaffection given the reduced role of the Churches in such areas since the 1920s.

[29]  Walker, 'Varieties'; John Buchan, *The Kirk in Scotland* (1930; Dunbar, 1985), 132.
[30]  Brown, *Religion and Society*, 153.
[31]  Ronald Ferguson, *George MacLeod* (London, 1990); Ian Bradley, *Believing in Britain: The Spiritual Identity of Britishness* (Oxford, 2008), 172–3.
[32]  Robbins, *England*, 284–5; also Tom Gallagher, *The Illusion of Freedom* (London, 2009), 51.
[33]  Elaine McFarland and Ronnie Johnston, 'Faith in the Factory: The Church of Scotland's Industrial Mission, 1942–58', *Historical Research*, 83, no. 221 (August 2010), 539–64.

The post-war era saw the Churches increase their membership. A full 46 cent of Scots had a formal Church connection in 1956, only 5 per cent lower than the all-time peak of 1905. The growth after the war was most striking in the Protestant churches while the Catholic peak came later in the mid-1960s. Figures regarding baptisms, marriages, and membership of church-related organizations indicate a significant surge until the end of the 1950s.[34] A burst of evangelical activity, most famously the revivalist rallies conducted by the American preacher Billy Graham, fuelled a particularly Protestant form of religious commitment in these years. It was in this era too that a group of young preachers and scholars founded the Scottish Church Theology Society and took forward work in biblical theology.[35] William Barclay began to establish his reputation as a popular communicator and Bible teacher and to give notice of his claim to be one of the most internationally renowned Christian leaders of the twentieth century.[36] Scots, and Britons more widely, were a 'believing people',[37] if not to Irish levels; church membership and attendance appear to have reflected strong religious convictions and, in the majority of cases, not merely a social obligation.

The Church of Scotland did not shirk from entering the political arena during the post-war agitation for a Scottish Home Rule Parliament. It was prominent in the broad-based 'Covenant' movement which feared that the new Labour government's centralizing creed placed Scotland's national distinctiveness within the UK at risk. Would Labour's pursuit of central economic planning lock Scotland into the British economy with little or no room for special Scottish needs and Scottish control of her own industry? The Kirk's defence of a national interest, perceived to be under threat from a London government heedless of the reciprocal obligations involved in making the political Union work, indeed foreshadowed its later opposition to much of the governing philosophy of Margaret Thatcher's Conservatives in the 1980s. It was well observed by the Scottish Secretary of State after the 'Stone of Destiny' episode in 1951 that the Labour government might expect 'continuing agitation' not only from the Nationalist movement but also the Church of Scotland.[38]

Nationalistic sensitivities were also evident around the issue of 'bishops in the Kirk'. Before the war there had been some suggestion that a reunited Church of Scotland might then pursue unity with Episcopal tradition. Strong opposition had been voiced, and when the matter resurfaced in the 1950s and 1960s a populist campaign denouncing the idea was conducted by the *Scottish Daily Express*.[39] The notion of a national Church distinctive in structures and form of worship, and drawing on a history of struggle and sacrifice, mobilized opinion emphatically in favour of the status quo.

[34] Brown, *Religion and Society*, 158–61.
[35] See the obituary of Professor Ronald Wallace in *The Herald*, 4 March 2006.
[36] Clive Rawlins, *William Barclay* (London, 1998).
[37] Grace Davie, *Religion in Britain since 1945* (Oxford, 1994), 77.
[38] Hector McNeil, quoted in Richard Weight, *Patriots* (London, 2002), 134.
[39] See Tom Gallagher, 'The Press and Protestant Popular Culture: A Case Study of the Scottish Daily Express', in Walker and Gallagher, eds., *Sermons and Battle Hymns*.

Callum Brown views the post-war period until the early 1960s as distinguished by a national or public culture shaped by and oriented to organized religion. From 1963, the sharp statistical fall in Church membership, attendance, and association revealed that Scotland, and Britain overall, turned more secular, 'a remarkably sudden and culturally violent event'.[40] The decline in Kirk membership was rapid and inexorable from this point to the end of the century when the proportion of Church of Scotland communicants relative to the Scottish population stood at less than 15 per cent.[41] The Roman Catholic Church in Scotland appeared less severely weakened by the new trends, although decline here was merely delayed until the 1980s, and the changes of Vatican II caused some uncertainty and confusion. Writing in the 1990s, Brown commented that Scots were 'forsaking their churches for worship, adherence, marriage, baptism and the religious education of their children'.[42]

The debate over the timing, pace, and nature of the secularization process has engaged many of the finest scholars of the social history and sociology of religion.[43] Callum Brown's criticisms of other scholars in the field of religion in Scotland have centred largely on what he sees as their failure to appreciate the suddenness and the singularity of the process from the 1960s. For Brown, the emergence of a counter-culture and especially the refashioning of gender roles challenged the moral authority of the Churches, and brought about fundamental change to the identity of the nation. Notwithstanding the persistence of a strong fundamentalist Calvinism in the Western Isles, and the sectarian tensions between Protestants and Catholics, Brown has placed the late twentieth-century experience of Scotland in the context of Britain's development as a pluralist and secular state and a 'post-Christian' country.

Churchgoing, in a new age of rival attractions such as television, simply became less fashionable, especially to those from a Protestant upbringing. This was in spite of the Church of Scotland appearing to move with the times in its landmark decision to permit the ordination of women ministers in 1969, and, in the views of one historian, becoming 'the last redoubt' of Scottish liberalism.[44] Indeed, the Kirk had taken some radical positions on African matters since the 1950s in the context of decolonization and civil rights, and the subject of foreign missions in the twentieth century is deserving of more scholarly inquiry.[45] Nevertheless, the Kirk's popular image tended to remain one of stern and censorious Calvinist joylessness. In a new televisual world of coruscating satire, it found

---

[40]   Brown, *Death*, 175–6; Robbins, *England*, 349.

[41]   Brown, *Death*, 165.

[42]   Brown, *Religion and Society*, 160–1; for Vatican II see McCaffrey, 'Roman Catholics'.

[43]   For example, Brown, *Death*; Steve Bruce, ed., *Religion and Modernization: Sociologists and Historians Debate the Secularization Thesis* (Oxford, 1992); Hugh McLeod, *The Religious Crisis of the 1960s* (Oxford, 2007); Davie, *Religion in Britain since 1945*.

[44]   Christopher Harvie, *No Gods and Precious Few Heroes* (London, 1981), 83.

[45]   Robbins, *England*, 329–30. For a rare academic treatment of the foreign missions theme see Andrew C. Ross, *The Blantyre Mission and the Making of Modern Malawi* (Lanham, MD, 1996). Ross was one of a distinguished group of Church historians during the 1960s in the Divinity Faculty at New College under the leadership of Professor Alec Cheyne. They adopted a more global perspective on the history of the Church of Scotland.

itself mercilessly lampooned, much in the way the Catholic Church was to be made fun of in late twentieth-century Ireland, while the critical attacks by many intellectuals on Calvinism's impact on Scottish life and culture also intensified. Scotland's Presbyterian heritage in this view was a dam against the creative and imaginative flow of the nation. It is only in recent times that effective challenges have been served to what many associated with the Kirk have long regarded as an unfair caricature.[46] Certainly, there seems little doubt that Calvinism, in common with theological matters more generally, has been little studied or understood by many who have been culturally shaped by the 1960s and later decades.

On the other hand, there have been scholarly re-evaluations of Calvinism's intellectual legacy in Scotland, and Will Storrar, an outstanding Presbyterian scholar, has pointed to the role played by Calvinist theology in 'Scotland's intellectual internationalism'.[47] The philosopher George Elder Davie stressed the significance of Presbyterianism to what he defined as Scotland's 'democratic intellect'.[48] Notwithstanding the formal separation of Protestantism from the education system, there remains a popular inclination to link educational achievements to the time-honoured Presbyterian stress on rigorous schooling.

As the Church of Scotland shrank so did it become even more emphatically middle class in membership. The loss of working-class adherents was vividly demonstrated by the decline of the Church-related bodies that once embraced them: by 1987 only 90,000 children attended Sunday school in comparison with a figure of 325,000 in 1956; while the Boys Brigade, which boasted 32,000 members in Scotland in 1950, was down to 9,000 by the end of the century.[49] In some contrast the Catholic Church in the later decades of the century could still claim a significant working-class membership.

Much of the Kirk's energy was invested in trying, in vain, to steady its membership. Shrinking numbers in the pews did not prevent it continuing to speak for the nation, increasingly presumptuously in a religiously pluralist and secular age, most notably at the annual General Assembly. The Church of Scotland also took an active part in the public debate over a Scottish Parliament during the 1970s, its interventions in favour of devolution irritating Conservatives. The decade, indeed, saw the spectacular rise of the Scottish National Party (SNP), a phenomenon fuelled in part by disillusioned Protestant Conservative voters. It has been shown that the SNP derived the great bulk of its support from Protestants in this period, despite two of its eleven MPs returned in the October 1974 election being Roman Catholic.[50] Only a last-minute intervention by senior Churchman Andrew Herron prevented a letter being read out from every Kirk pulpit ahead of the referendum on devolution in 1979, urging people to vote 'Yes'.[51]

[46] See discussion in Harry Reid, *Reformation* (Edinburgh, 2009), 359–70.
[47] For example, C. Beveridge and R. Turnbull, *The Eclipse of Scottish Culture* (Edinburgh, 1989); Will Storrar, 'Three Portraits of Scottish Calvinism', in Robert D. Kernohan, ed., *The Realm of Reform* (Edinburgh, 1999).
[48] George Elder Davie, *The Democratic Intellect* (Edinburgh, 1961).
[49] Johnston McKay, 'The Church Social', in MacLean and Veitch, *Scottish Life*.
[50] Jack Brand, *The National Movement in Scotland* (London, 1978), 150–4.
[51] See Rosie, 'Religion'.

The insufficiently affirmative referendum verdict followed by the election of Margaret Thatcher's Conservative government in 1979 radically altered the political context of the 1980s. In this era the Kirk was to be found voicing strident criticisms of the Thatcher government's 'laissez-faire' and individualistic policies and their effects on the less well-off in society. This culminated in the public rebuke delivered by the General Assembly to Thatcher after she had addressed it in 1989. It was no surprise, therefore, that the Kirk should join with the other Scottish Churches in campaigning again for a Scottish Parliament in the 1990s, and welcoming its implementation, finally, in 1999.[52] Indeed, the temporary home of the Parliament until the completion of the building at the foot of the Royal Mile in Edinburgh was the General Assembly Hall, a not inappropriate development, symbolically, in view of the Church's involvement in campaigns for Home Rule through the years and the General Assembly's claims to have acted as a surrogate Parliament in the past.

# 4

Prior to the opening of the new Scottish Parliament in September 1999, the Scottish classical composer James MacMillan delivered a keynote address to the Edinburgh Festival alleging 'endemic' religious bigotry in Scotland against Catholics.[53] One historian has judged the speech as 'a determination to break the link between Scotland and Presbyterianism'.[54] At the very least the speech had the effect of triggering an intense public debate over the nature and extent of sectarianism in Scotland at the dawn of a new century.

In a sense the ground had been prepared for MacMillan's intervention by the work of scholars, mainly historians, in bringing to light those episodes from the interwar period that had been largely forgotten or deliberately obscured in accordance with the new ecumenical spirit which dated at least from the 1960s. In 1963 the Moderator of the General Assembly of the Church of Scotland had paid an historic visit to the Vatican, while in 1975 Cardinal Thomas Winning became the first Catholic prelate to address the General Assembly. Most strikingly, the visit of Pope John Paul II to Scotland in 1982 produced conciliatory set-piece events and passed off without any major protest or disruption.

However, such civilities, while a marked change to the tense and acerbic atmosphere of the pre-war era, could not conceal the persistence of much prejudice. The open sectarian hostility of the Rangers versus Celtic football rivalry in Glasgow was only the most

---

[52] The role played by Canon Kenyon Wright (Scottish Episcopal Church) in the campaign for a parliament and in the Constitutional Convention 1989–95 should be noted. See also the reflections on the Kirk's role in the Convention in 'Submission by the Church of Scotland to the Commission on Scottish Devolution' (Calman Commission), 13 June 2008.

[53] For the text of the speech and commentaries on it both supportive and critical see T. M. Devine, ed., *Scotland's Shame?* (Edinburgh, 2000).

[54] Robbins, *England*, 462.

obvious sign of a continuing problem. Nor had the education question been emptied of its potential to cause resentments and foster misunderstandings and suspicion.

The new political context of devolution was crucial to the greater scrutiny given to sectarianism by the end of the century. Whereas in the past Scottish religious questions had been marginalized in the broader context of British politics—and it should not be forgotten that the Church of Scotland wished to be left to deal with its own affairs free from State interference—they were highlighted in the new Parliament. Moreover, members of the legislature, of all parties and none, had an incentive to be seen to be tackling specifically Scottish problems in the spirit of a 'new politics' and a new beginning for the nation. Shortly after becoming First Minister of a Labour–Liberal Democrat coalition government, Jack McConnell declared it his intention to rid Scotland of the 'shame' of religious sectarianism. A measure adding an additional penalty to crimes committed for sectarian motives was proposed by Liberal Democrat Donald Gorrie and passed by Parliament, notwithstanding the difficulties of proving such a motivation, and more generally, of defining the concept of sectarianism itself.[55]

Of all the faiths, it was the Catholic Church that seemed to adapt most readily to devolution and the sense of a new beginning. The Church's figurehead in Scotland, Cardinal Winning, soon proved himself an astute political operator; his combative style made life difficult for Scottish Executive ministers, particularly over the issue of the teaching of homosexuality in schools.[56] After that bruising encounter there was no likelihood of any Scottish government minister or party taking on the Church over the position of Catholic schools. The Church hierarchy indeed organized a formidable 'pressure group' campaign to lobby for what it took to be Catholic educational interests.[57]

Winning died in 2001, but his successor, Archbishop Mario Conti, also proved uncompromising. In December 2002 he claimed that calls for the abolition, or even amalgamation, of Catholic schools were 'tantamount to asking for the repatriation of the Irish, and just as offensive'.[58] Conti was unlikely to have been unaware of the significance of the 'repatriation' charge, echoing as it did the interwar campaign conducted by the Church of Scotland. The Kirk publicly apologized for this episode in 2001.

The media debate and the political activity around the issue of sectarianism have been accompanied by scholarly interventions. These have, in effect, fallen into two categories: those, first, which take the view that sectarianism is still deep-rooted and that it essentially amounts to anti-Catholicism; and, second, those scholars who question how serious a problem it now is in Scottish society and consider that equating it simply with anti-Catholicism is overly reductionist. In relation to the former category there has been

---

[55] For McConnell's campaign see Gallagher, *Illusion*, 105–7, 138; for Gorrie and his admission of the 'complex' nature of the issue see *The Herald*, 8 January 2005.

[56] On what became known as 'The Section 28 Controversy' see Stephen McGinty, *This Turbulent Priest: A Life of Cardinal Winning* (London, 2003); also David Evans, 'The Lesson of Section 28', in Gerry Hassan and Chris Warhurst, eds., *The New Scottish Politics* (Edinburgh, 2001).

[57] See Martin Steven, 'The Place of Religion in Devolved Scottish Politics', *Scottish Affairs*, 58 (Winter 2007).

[58] Quoted in Steve Bruce et al., *Sectarianism in Scotland* (Edinburgh, 2004), 113.

a tendency to detect prejudice lying behind criticisms of separate Catholic schools and the ethno-religious identity of Celtic football club. In addition it is claimed that anti-Catholic attitudes and stereotypes are still widely entertained and, at some level in society, influential.[59]

The opposing school of thought, most cogently expressed by scholars such as Steve Bruce, is concerned to show that Catholic communal distinctiveness and disadvantage have diminished within Scotland to the point where those who wish to prop up a model of a society riven with sectarian antagonisms have to resort to football to do so. Such scholars point to the widespread nature of intermarriage between Catholics and Protestants in contemporary Scotland; a recent survey revealed that more than half of the marriages of people under the age of thirty-five were 'mixed'.[60] Additionally, no significant differences between the economic opportunities of Protestants and Catholics were discerned, nor any divisive effects of political attitudes and voting behaviour.

For scholars like Steve Bruce the notion of Scotland as a society bearing a close resemblance to Northern Ireland is wrong-headed. Factors such as the rate of intermarriage and a political culture oriented historically towards social class issues question the kind of facile comparisons employed by MacMillan in his speech in 1999. Moreover, those sceptical of the extent of sectarianism in Scotland would also point to the country's resistance to contamination by the troubles which raged in Northern Ireland for close to thirty years from the late 1960s. For Bruce and others there is a tendency on the part of those alleging rampant sectarianism to present as typical what is now better regarded as exotic. Thus, fundamentalist Calvinist denunciations of Catholicism are read as representative of the nation's views when in fact it is the Free Church of Scotland, with its base in the Western Isles, which is currently marginalized and indeed routinely disparaged in Scotland.[61]

It might be added that the debate over sectarianism in Scotland of the late twentieth- and early twenty-first-century period has done little to put the issue in the context of a nation now much less religiously homogeneous, or indeed Christian. The contemporary realities of a multi-ethnic and multi-faith Scotland have tended to be obscured by an exclusive concern with Protestant–Catholic divisions and historical grievances. The sectarianism debate has only demonstrated the extent to which time-worn Protestant–Catholic tensions inhibit the kind of dialogue required to accommodate a variety of religious and other identities. By the end of the century Glasgow and Edinburgh together possessed thirty mosques and the Muslim community numbered close to fifty thousand.[62] Controversial matters such as faith schools can no longer be debated with reference only to Catholics and Protestants.

---

[59]  See Joseph M. Bradley, ed., *Celtic-Minded: Essays on Football, Culture and Identity*, vols. 1 and 2 (Argyll, 2004 and 2006); also T. M. Devine, 'The End of Disadvantage?', in Mitchell, *New Perspectives*; and Gallagher, *Illusion*, 138–9.

[60]  Bruce et al., *Sectarianism*, 97.

[61]  See John MacLeod, *Banner in the West* (Edinburgh, 2008).

[62]  Robbins, *England*, 399.

Furthermore, it is not clear from the sectarianism controversy whether it is actually religion that is being debated. As Callum Brown has put it: 'What precisely does "religion" contribute to religious identity?'[63] Is religious identity really a form of tribalism with little or no religious substance? As the debate develops, such conceptual disentanglement and clarification will be necessary if light is to be shed on the subject.

# 5

The challenges facing the Churches in the new century seem daunting. Continuing membership decline, institutional decay, an often inhospitable media, a cultural climate in which secular assumptions prevail: such would be the sort of problems regularly identified by embattled clergy and Church spokespersons. 'Modern Scotland is a secular state. The land of reformers and covenanters is as much a myth as the land of heather and highlander.'[64] So wrote a commentator in 2002 before going on to call for positive Christian engagement with contemporary society. The question of effective leadership thus emerges, and as the new century takes its course it remains to be seen whether the question will be convincingly answered. In this respect the Church of Scotland is still somewhat disadvantaged by its own democratic traditions. As Moderators must change each year there is less likelihood of an individual acquiring the value of public recognition so vital in an age of mass communications. The Kirk badly needs another William Barclay, but of such a figure there is little sign. The death of Cardinal Winning and the retirement of Episcopal Bishop Richard Holloway have left both Roman Catholic and Episcopal Churches with large spaces to fill. What all the Christian Churches have in common is the need to do more than simply manage decline.

Yet in Scotland, as in Britain more generally, the apparent dominance of secularism may conceal a greater religious sensibility and concern with religious matters than is often assumed. In the sociologist Grace Davie's words, many are still 'believing while not belonging'.[65] Modern science may have contributed hugely to the secularization process, yet the ethical questions surrounding scientific developments such as cloning and stem-cell research, in addition to the morality of much new technology and of modern weaponry, have given rise to debates in which religious interests can press their claims.[66] It is difficult not to conclude that, with Kirk membership down to some 650,000 in the early years of the twenty-first century, Scotland is 'post-Presbyterian' in the sense that the country's dominant tradition for so long is now just one of several faiths.

---

[63] Callum Brown, 'Review of Boyle and Lynch, *Out of the Ghetto?*', in *Scottish Historical Review*, 79, no. 4 (October 2000).

[64] Alwyn Thomson, 'Introduction', in Megan Halteman and Alwyn Thomson, eds., *Seek the Welfare of the City: Church and Society in Scotland and Northern Ireland* (Belfast, 2002).

[65] Davie, *Religion*; for discussion see Robbins, *England*, 464–75.

[66] See William Ferguson, 'Christian Faith and Unbelief in Modern Scotland', in Brown and Newlands, eds., *Scottish Christianity*.

However, it is less straightforward to speak of 'post-Christian' Scotland; the evidence here is much more ambiguous if the diversity of the country's Christian expressions and the advent of 'New Age' spirituality are taken into account.[67] The enthusiasm displayed by Catholics, and many non-Catholics, on the occasion of the visit of Pope Benedict XVI to Scotland in 2010 provided evidence that the appeal of what some refer to as 'militant secularism' is more limited than is often suggested.

For the period that is the concern of this essay scholars have tended to research religion in relation to political and social developments and to matters of ethnic or cultural identity. Those—often church ministers and priests—who have focused on theology and public worship have done so for their church audiences. It might be suggested that the two streams need to converge more tellingly, and that, in particular, historians and other scholars who write for a broader public should be more cognizant of questions of actual religious belief and practice, and be wary of making assumptions about what large groups of people think. Such studies will certainly have to be placed in the context of the different groups within religious communities as defined by such variables as geography, gender, and social background.[68]

Finally, there would appear still to be a widespread desire for the Churches and clergy to play a significant role in society. Gilleasbuig MacMillan has put the point in the following terms: 'The wish to have good theatre, links with the past, and language fit for the high purpose of worship is not a snobbish elitism, but a recognition of the nature of the event.'[69] Rituals, ceremonies, symbols, and institutional solidity are valued as part of the nation's heritage, and perhaps assume an even greater importance at a time when the country is entering a new phase of its history.

## FURTHER READING

Brown, Callum, *Religion and Society in Modern Scotland* (Edinburgh, 1997).

—— *The Death of Christian Britain* (London, 2001).

Brown, Stewart J., and Newlands, George, eds., *Scottish Christianity in the Modern World* (Edinburgh, 2000).

Bruce, Steve et al., eds., *Sectarianism in Scotland* (Edinburgh, 2004).

Davie, Grace, *Religion in Britain since 1945* (Oxford, 1994).

Devine, Tom M., ed., *Scotland's Shame?* (Edinburgh, 2000).

—— and Finlay, R. J. eds., *Scotland in the 20th Century* (Edinburgh, 1996).

Kernohan, Robert, ed., *The Realm of Reform* (Edinburgh, 1999).

MacLean, Colin, and Veitch, Kenneth, eds., *Scottish Life and Society: A Compendium of Scottish Ethnology*. Volume 12 Religion (Edinburgh, 2006).

[67] See Steven J. Sutcliffe, 'Alternative Beliefs and Practices', in MacLean and Veitch, *Scottish Life*.

[68] I am indebted to Dr Andrew Holmes regarding this point and his expertise on the study of religion in general.

[69] Gilleasbuig MacMillan, 'A Matter of Faith', in Gordon Graham, ed., *Talking Scots* (Aberdeen, 2000).

McRoberts, David, ed., *Modern Scottish Catholicism 1878–1978* (Glasgow, 1978).

Mitchell, Martin, ed., *New Perspectives on the Irish in Scotland* (Edinburgh, 2008).

Reid, Harry, *Reformation* (Edinburgh, 2009).

Robbins, Keith, *England, Ireland, Scotland, Wales. The Christian Church 1900–2000* (Oxford, 2008).

Rosie, Michael, *The Sectarian Myth in Scotland* (Basingstoke, 2004).

CHAPTER 32

......................................................................................

# GENDER AND NATIONHOOD
# IN MODERN SCOTTISH
# HISTORIOGRAPHY

......................................................................................

## CATRIONA M. M. MACDONALD

WOMEN'S role in the making of Scotland's past has been a recognizable feature of our historiography and public history for many generations although, waxing and waning with the priorities of each age, it has admittedly neither been a constant nor dominating presence. Nevertheless—while they may not have used the word itself—'gender' has played a role in the stories told by historians for at least one hundred years. That its role may not match the intellectual and methodological sophistication of our postmodern times, or be quite how some historians may have wished it to be, is only part of the story, and perhaps a rather distracting part.[1] To accept our historiography on anything but its own terms is risky. Such an approach threatens to impose anachronistic value judgements that may serve the interests of a particular historical genre or cause (women's history and feminism are the most obvious examples here), but it will tend to undervalue or at least misrepresent the achievements of previous generations about which we still remain somewhat ignorant.

Women's history, as conceived since the 1970s, was not the first and has not been the sole avenue through which gender concerns have intruded upon comfortable historical conventions, nor has it always offered the most successful or most obvious approach to gendering the Scottish past. The second half of the twentieth century certainly witnessed a reawakening of interest in women's history, but this period does not mark its beginning, nor—alternatively—its coming of age.[2] Spatial and temporal dynamics are important here. Unlike other historical disciplines, women's history has been too apt to sketch its

---

[1] E. Gordon, *Women and the Labour Movement in Scotland, 1850–1914* (Oxford, 1991), 3.
[2] D. Beddoe, *Discovering Women's History* (London, 1998), 5.

lineage across national boundaries, as if the universality of sexual differences inevitably yields a shared historiography, and has generally styled the lineage in a surprisingly Whiggish manner, presuming unrelenting progress and improvement in each generation. From the biographies of 'women worthies' in the late nineteenth century, through the 'her story' approaches of the 1960s to the challenges of postmodernism since the 1980s, such rites of passage in women's historiography are widely acknowledged to hold good across many national traditions, although their precise timing might vary a little.[3] In part as a consequence of this state of affairs, to date the development of gendered approaches to history in Scotland has been too readily considered within a British context in which any awareness of the development of Scottish historiography generally has been absent, or at least lacking nuance.[4] As a corollary to this, it will also perhaps not come as a surprise that, when measured against the English model, the historiography of women's history in Scotland has typically been considered backward or immature.[5] Writing in 1999, Terry Brotherstone is typical in this regard when he notes: 'English historiography in the late 1960s was at a different stage of development from that of Scotland.'[6] Three years later, the editors of *Twisted Sisters* were bold enough to suggest that the 'first two significant works on Scottish women's history' appeared just twenty years before.[7]

Current historiographical accounts of women's history in Scotland have tended to undervalue the contribution of other historical genres and of mainstream historical works to the study of women in the past, thus establishing for women's history an alternative historiography at one remove from standard accounts of Scottish history.[8] This needs to be readdressed. It is the aim of this chapter to consider the ways in which women's histories (as opposed to women's history) have informed Scottish historiography in the last hundred years, and to identify the extent to which gender perspectives (no matter how crude, no matter how old-fashioned) infused writings on Scotland's past in this period. Typically, women's history and gender history have been formally distinguished in historiographical critiques. Women's history—an attempt to uncover previously neglected narratives of female achievement and oppression—is typically seen as the precursor to a more sophisticated gender history in which female and male ideals, roles, and

---

[3] J. Purvis, 'From "Women Worthies" to Poststructuralism? Debate and Controversy in Women's History in Britain', in J. Purvis, ed., *Women's History: Britain, 1850–1945: An Introduction* (London, 1998), 1–22; J. W. Scott, *Gender and the Politics of History* (New York, 1999).

[4] E. Breitenbach, A. Brown, and F. Myers, 'Understanding Women in Scotland', *Feminist Review*, 58 (1998), 54–6.

[5] Elizabeth Ewan and Maureen M. Meikle, 'Introduction', in E. Ewan and M. M. Meikle, eds., *Women in Scotland c.1100–c.1750* (East Linton, 1999), xx.

[6] T. Brotherstone, 'Women's History, Scottish History, Historical Theory', in T. Brotherstone, D. Simonton, O. Walsh, eds., *Gendering Scottish History: An International Approach* (Glasgow, 1999), 257.

[7] Y. G. Brown and R. Ferguson, eds., *Twisted Sisters: Women, Crime and Deviance in Scotland Since 1400* (East Linton, 2002), 2. Here they are referring to Christina Larner, *Enemies of God: The Witch-Hunt in Scotland* (London, 1981), and Rosalind Marshall, *Virgins and Viragos: A History of Women in Scotland 1080–1980* (London, 1983).

[8] L. Abrams, 'Introduction', in L. Abrams, E. Gordon, D. Simonton, and E. J. Yeo, eds., *Gender in Scottish History Since 1707* (Edinburgh, 2006), 1.

experiences are identified as socially constructed and resting on particular epistemologies. While this is appropriate for contemporary circumstances, the use of such prescriptive categories is less appropriate when considering the limited scholarship in Scotland before the 1980s. For this earlier period, it would be anachronistic to distinguish schools of women's and gender history, and so more fluid terms are used here which—though they might frustrate a neat periodization and exacting terminology—reflect more accurately the level of maturity in approaches to gender in these years and the absence of a critical mass of material from which to draw definitive conclusions. In the process it will become apparent that the shifting socio-economic and political contexts of the times proved influential in the writing of Scotland's history (in this is included the history of Scottish women), and that the dynamic accommodation of Scotland within the UK state has had implications for how Scottish historians have written that history and what aspects of the past they have chosen to write about.

# 1899–1969

The memoirs of writers such as Henry Cockburn and Hugh Miller are well known, and yet in the hinterland of Scottish letters stand a multitude of authors whose recollections of lives lived and changes wrought might be identified as some of our earliest social histories. Elizabeth Grant's *Memoirs of a Highland Lady* (1897), alongside the autobiography of the Victorian novelist Margaret Oliphant, are notable exemplars of this form from the pen of female authors, but there were many more besides for whom women's contribution to the history of the nation, or at least a particular locality, was of interest.

Indeed, in keeping with the antiquarian interests of the times, many authors went beyond simple reflections and into serious historical research in order to ground their claims to voice the past with authenticity and legitimacy. In doing so, they gathered and recorded valuable insights into erstwhile neglected worlds. Worthy of comment in this regard are the works of Scotland's most prolific travel writer (and historian) of these years, George Eyre Todd, who, in books such as *Scotland: Picturesque and Traditional* (1895), did much to establish a historic sense of the Scottish landscape and environment.[9] Samuel Carment's *Glimpses of the Olden Time* (1897), however, is more typical of this school. He wrote:

> In the preparation of this work the compiler had for his aim, the desire to see the people of a former time not so much engaged in the great affairs of their nation's history...but rather to see them in the more retired and humble walks of life.[10]

In exploring the 'customs and manners of the past' such authors sought to preserve the knowledge of lifestyles that had already been eroded by industrialization, urbanization,

[9]  G. Eyre-Todd, *Scotland: Picturesque and Traditional* (London, 1895).
[10]  S. Carment, *Glimpses of the Olden Time* (Edinburgh, 1893), vi.

and the very print medium that, paradoxically, was their conduit to memorialization.[11] Given their focus on domestic life they might have proved a valuable route for the more thoroughgoing investigation of the pasts of Scotland's women. However, making little contribution (beyond adding a bit of local colour) to the history of the nation itself and laying no claims for accommodation in popular narratives of the past, they hardly impacted upon the formal historiography of the nation itself. If the first few editions of the *Scottish Historical Review* (*SHR*, established 1903) are to be our guide, women continued to enter the historiography in predictable ways. The editors appeared content to perpetuate the popular allure of Mary, Queen of Scots—no fewer than three articles about this most unfortunate monarch appeared in Volume Two alone—and the courage and self-sacrifice of Jacobite women were acknowledged in a piece in 1907 on Margaret Nairne.[12]

A book first published in 1899 would eventually point the way forward, although from first appraisal it appeared to reinforce rather than challenge many historiographical orthodoxies. In the preface to the first edition of *The Social Life of Scotland in the Eighteenth Century*, Henry Grey Graham noted:

> In Scotland during the eighteenth century there were only two outstanding events which, after the Union, specially belong to its history—the Rebellion of '15 and the Rebellion of '45.[13]

Scotland's history after 1707, therefore, needed a new approach. In this book, Graham would address:

> The social condition of the country—chiefly in the Lowlands—and the internal changes through which it passed during a hundred years, with details which the historian dismisses with impatience as unconsidered trifles marring the dignity of his theme and disturbing the flow of his narrative.[14]

In defensive mode, he asserted that it was, after all, 'in the inner life of a community that its real history is to be found'.[15] It seemed that only a new perspective on Scotland's past would allow it to live in history as it had not lived in politics after 1707. If any doubts remained, the agenda was reinforced in the first paragraphs of the first chapter:

> Feelings and usages had become part of life and character which were peculiarly Scottish, forming the undefinable quality of nationality.... This contrast and this separation continued very long after the Union of 1707, which united the governments, but could not unite the two peoples.[16]

---

[11]  Ibid., v.

[12]  D. Murray Rose, 'Mary Queen of Scots and her Brother'; Andrew Lang, 'The Household of Mary Queen of Scots in 1573'; Thomas Duncan, 'The Queen's Maries', in *Scottish Historical Review* [*SHR*], 2 (1905), 150–62, 345–55, 363–71. E. Maxtone Graham, 'Margaret Nairne: A Bundle of Jacobite Letters', *SHR*, 4 (1907).

[13]  H. Grey Graham, *The Social Life of Scotland in the Eighteenth Century* (London, 1969), ix.

[14]  Ibid., x.

[15]  Ibid., x.

[16]  Ibid., 1.

As Scotland shared a state apparatus with a more powerful neighbour, Graham eschewed the constitutional obsessions of the Whig historiographical tradition and went one step further when he concluded his study by reinforcing the false promise of Anglo-Britishness evident in the 'political and civic thraldom' under which the people of Scotland 'abided' until the Reform Acts of the nineteenth century.[17] Instead, he identified a national history for Scotland inherent in the very fabric of life, thus evidencing a historical confidence in these years somewhat underestimated by Colin Kidd in his groundbreaking study, *Subverting Scotland's Past* (1993).[18] Furthermore, this was not a crude racial determinism: Graham deliberately avoided the familiar and easier route of restyling North Britain as a Celtic periphery.[19] This undoubtedly made his approach all the more potent for those who would come after him, although few historians in the short term at least chose to follow in the wake of Scotland's first social historian, and his next work, *Scottish Men of Letters in the Eighteenth Century* (1908) did not appear to bode well for any reassessment of women's role in the national history of Scotland.

Graham's account of female lyricists, corralled in an awkward chapter entitled 'Women of Letters', bears the hallmarks of the times in which it was written:

> In the eighteenth century Scotswomen did not indeed take that position in literature which…members of their sex assumed in England.…But if they wrote little…[i]t lived on the lips and lingered in the ears of the people, when the works of more formidable and learned women stood forgotten on the shelves.

Graham must be excused for lacking the insights into the female intellectual culture of the Scottish elite researched by contemporary scholars such as Jane Rendall: it is only in recent years that women's role in the Scottish Enlightenment has been sensitively addressed, and attempts made to *incorporate* the works of female writers into the Enlightenment canon as well as draw attention to the gendered nature of aspects of Enlightenment scholarship and philosophy.[20] But Graham must be given credit for shifting attention from the 'high born dames' of Edinburgh to women such as Jean Adams, Jean Glover, and Isabel Pagan, and their contribution to the popular ballad tradition, and for imaginatively placing in their social context the writers of the Scottish Enlightenment. What is important in Graham's text is not that women are integrated into his narrative in a manner distinct from men—that is obvious—but the ways in which they do appear and the extent to which Scottish society *as a whole* looms large in his understanding of the literature of the times.

---

[17]  H. G. Graham, *Social Life of Scotland*, 538.

[18]  C. Kidd, *Subverting Scotland's Past* (Cambridge, 1993), 7.

[19]  C. Kidd, 'Race, Empire, and the Limits of Nineteenth-Century Scottish Nationhood', *Historical Journal*, 46:4 (2003), 873–92.

[20]  See J. Rendall, 'Clio, Mars and Minerva: The Scottish Enlightenment and the Writing of Women's History', in T. M. Devine and J. R. Young, eds., *Eighteenth-Century Scotland: New Perspectives* (East Linton, 1999); 'Women and the Enlightenment in Britain c. 1690–1800', in H. Barker and E. Chalus, eds., *Women's History: Britain, 1700–1850* (London, 2005), 9–32; '"Women that would plague me with rational conversation": Aspiring Women and Scottish Whigs c.1790–1830', in Sarah Knott and Barbara Taylor, eds., *Women, Gender and Enlightenment* (London, 2005), 326–48.

Scottish history was only just emerging as a distinct academic discipline as Graham's works appeared. In 1901 Peter Hume Brown was appointed the first Sir William Fraser Chair of Scottish History and Palaeography at the University of Edinburgh. Two years later the *SHR* was founded, and in 1913 the Chair of Scottish History and Literature at the University of Glasgow was established with the proceeds of the Scottish Exhibition, held at Kelvingrove in 1911. Outside the universities, though intimately associated with the nation's leading historical scholars, the Scottish History Society had been established in 1886 following a letter to *The Scotsman* that February from Lord Rosebery, then Foreign Secretary (he would become the Society's first president), in which he recorded his support for 'a Society in Scotland for printing the manuscript materials for Scottish history, especially social history'.[21]

Rosebery, British Prime Minister between 1894 and 1895, had been Under Secretary at the Home Office with special responsibility for Scotland between 1881 and 1883, and was to the fore in the years preceding the foundation of the Secretaryship for Scotland in 1885 in highlighting the restricted time available in the House of Commons and in government for the consideration of Scottish matters. His enthusiasm for Scotland's history, in similar terms, expressed a desire to correct an imbalance in the historiographical state of the nation.

There is a reforming zeal evident in *fin-de-siècle* scholarship and cultural activism in Scotland that was in keeping with a renewed interest from government in the particular political challenges facing the component nations of the Union state. Establishing the case for Scottish history, however, involved not just challenging the overlordship of English historiographical practices (many of them owing their potency to Scottish scholars),[22] but simultaneously changing the rules of engagement altogether. What constituted history had to be reconsidered. For historians of the late-modern period in particular, social history appeared to offer the way forward. But this was social history in the service of a higher ideal—a new national historiography—and sacrifices were inevitably made. Among these, one might argue, was a more thoroughgoing appreciation of women's role in the life of the nation. But one wonders whether there really was a choice. Some battles simply have to wait, and in any case, there is scant evidence that many voices were raised in protest.

When women *did* contribute to ongoing debates in the discipline, they tended to follow the imperatives of the time in ways that did not suggest that the feminization of Scottish historiography was a priority to them at least, or indeed to journal editors. This is most evident in the works of female contributors to the *SHR*. Between 1918 and 1928 female scholars such as Margaret Adam and Marguerite Wood respectively contributed articles on highland poverty and emigration, and the latter stages of the reign of Mary, Queen of Scots. Thereafter, while women were to the fore in contributing to the relaunched *SHR* from 1948 to 1950, their contributions in the 1950s and 1960s were few

---

[22] David Hume and Thomas Babbington Macaulay are, of course, most notable in this regard.

and far between and were largely made up of reviews. Again, there is little evidence of any urgent gender agenda. The radicalizing potential of Graham's social-history insights appeared to have been lost.

Evidence from monographs in these years, whilst somewhat more encouraging, is still ambiguous. Harry Graham's 1908 work, *A Group of Scottish Women*, foregrounded seventeen Scottish women notable for their 'heroism, courage, piety or wit'.[23] Yet he stopped short of challenging gender conventions:

> ...whatever views one may hold on the subject of woman's capacity to govern or achieve, it cannot be denied that she has always been the most fruitful source of inspiration for genius or eminence of any kind; that the noblest actions (and the greatest crimes) have been inspired by women.[24]

This image of woman as catalyst rather than creator was selective and in part disempowering. And yet, what there was of an alternative feminized narrative hardly recast woman's role more sympathetically. Some twenty-two years later, Eunice Murray's *Scottish Women of Bygone Days* (1930) offered a more strident appreciation of women's role in the past, but even then women were identified as much by what they could not do as by what they actually achieved. Reflecting on the women of the eighteenth century, Murray—a lifelong suffrage campaigner—noted:

> No wonder they were, in the main, anaemic women, who left little mark upon the history of their time; the wonder is they survived at all, and that any were fit to lead or take a place in the world of art and letters.[25]

While Murray's campaigning perspective was novel in the historiography of the nation, her methodology and focus followed convention: Mary, Queen of Scots, witchcraft, rites of passage, education, dress, and social life occupied her attention in this rather unsystematic volume. Little had changed, it appeared, since the days of H. H. Graham. Indeed, in Marion Lochhead's 1948 volume, *The Scots Household in the Eighteenth Century*, the author goes over much ground already covered by Graham some fifty years before. Change and progress, she asserts, 'are as apparent in domestic chronicles as in narratives of war or statesmanship'.[26] The case had been made already.

Indeed, many of the works that followed Lochhead, including Marjory Plant's *The Domestic Life of Scotland in the Eighteenth Century* (1952), refute any notion that there was incremental progress in the development of women's history, and social history for that matter, in Scotland. Whilst notably an early publication of the Edinburgh University Press, Plant's work added little to established historiographical conventions and might for that reason even be considered a step backwards.

---

[23] H. Graham, *A Group of Scottish Women* (London, 1908), viii.

[24] Ibid., vii.

[25] E. Murray, *Scottish Women in Bygone Days* (London, 1930), 29.

[26] M. Lochhead, *The Scots Household in the Eighteenth Century: A Century of Scottish Domestic and Social Life* (Edinburgh, 1948), 13.

With few openings in Scotland's universities for Scottish historians, one ought not to be surprised to find that the most significant contribution made by a female scholar to Scotland's history in these years came from a woman outside the Scottish 'academy', such as it was. The early career of Agnes Mure Mackenzie boded well for women's history in Scotland. Mackenzie's first work of non-fiction examined *The Women in Shakespeare's Plays* (1924), in which she reflected on previous female scholars' treatment of the same theme:

> in the nineteenth century as in the eighteenth, the opinions of women upon themselves were derived in the main not from their own direct observation of the subject, but from the attitude towards it of the opposite and more articulate sex, which whether colouring their minds by the insidious influence of suggestion or the more overt but more turbid one of contra-suggestion, was not altogether adapted to produce the dry light, nor always the sweet reasonableness, that best informs the truly discriminating critique.[27]

Even the *Aberdeen Press and Journal* felt compelled to acknowledge that Mackenzie 'emphasise[d] the modernness of Shakespeare's women': 'They are not heroines of plays written about 1600, but living women with the sort of feeling and impulses of women of to-day.'[28]

Turning to history, after a period of novel writing in the 1920s and early 1930s, it might have been hoped that Mackenzie, whose style was described by *The Scotsman* as 'frank and independent', would infuse Scottish historiography with the insights of such feminized literary criticism.[29] Indeed, aspects of her first novel, *Without Conditions* (1923), suggested Mackenzie's literary approach was one in which gender would be to the fore. The female protagonist, Miss Broadie, is not one for complying with convention: 'Miss Broadie of Balcairn had more than once challenged the Daurside gossips by her impetuous lack of heed for the restrictions it should have set about a well-brought-up young gentlewoman.'[30] Again, in *The Quiet Lady* (1926) reflections on gender are close to the surface. And in similar fashion we have (tongue in cheek) the following observation from Mackenzie's novel of the following year, *Lost Kinellan*: 'there was no New Woman about Bertha. She was good and gentle and domesticated—no Women's Rights nonsense about her.'[31]

Mackenzie's histories, however, show very little of the gendered insights evident in her fiction. In *Scotland in Modern Times* (1941) we are invited to consider the author's own position as a woman when she writes as follows:

> The present writer, as a young girl, attended a Cabinet Minister's meeting in Glasgow in 1914, and it gave her nightmares for many months thereafter. As was the usual

[27] A. M. Mackenzie, *The Women in Shakespeare's Plays* (London, 1924), xii.
[28] *Aberdeen Press and Journal*, 19 June 1924.
[29] *The Scotsman*, 8 September 1924.
[30] Ibid., 16.
[31] A. M. Mackenzie, *Lost Kinellan* (London, 1927), 19.

tactic at that time, a number of women rose and cried their slogan. She recalls one delicate-looking old lady with white hair, whose wrists had been grasped by a couple of powerful stewards, who were pulling hard in opposite directions; and a girl being carried feet first up a flight of stairs, while a respectable elderly gentleman marched alongside flogging her with a gold-topped umbrella. And though she was too young then to read their meaning, the faces of some of the men have stayed in her mind, and returned again vividly to her memory when she came to deal with the witchcraft prosecutions of the sixteenth and seventeenth centuries.[32]

Yet extracts like this one are the exception rather than the rule in Mackenzie's histories, and it is worth noting that this reflection is presented as a footnote, detached from the main narrative and in the third person—at one remove from the author herself. As a literary critic in her own right and a writer sensitive to the processes of both writing and reading, it is also of importance that Mackenzie consistently used the male pronoun without qualification in her writings, although she was only too apt to use the female pronoun with reference to the nation.[33]

Nationhood rather than gender offered the dominant perspective in Mackenzie's histories. It was history with a purpose. As a nationalist, she sought to ground claims for Scottish home rule in historic precedent, and to establish history as the means by which nationalism would be graced with antiquity. In the wartime pamphlet *Scottish Principles of Statecraft and Government*, Mackenzie noted: 'A nation is an idea, a pattern of living, a community that has a common tradition. It is a group of people shaped by a thought. That thought of Scotland has very ancient roots.'[34] Her emphasis on community echoes Graham's social focus fifty years before, as does her insistence on meaningful nationhood extending beyond 1707. Yet the presentism in her work is far more explicit. In contrast to the footnote on female suffrage, Mackenzie repeatedly foregrounds her politics in prefaces and conclusions. Consider this, the last lines of her wartime publication, *The Kingdom of Scotland: A Short History* (1940):

> As soon as peace has been secured in Europe, we must begin again, those who are left. For Scotland is not dead yet, nor will she die, 'so long as only a hundred of us stand'.[35]

One might conjecture that Mackenzie made a conscious choice between her feminism and her nationalism: there is scant evidence on which to ground such a conclusion, however.[36] Nevertheless, the explicit political intent of her writings is undeniable, and the

[32] A. M. Mackenzie, *Scotland in Modern Times, 1720–1939* (London, 1941), 229.
[33] A. M. Mackenzie, *The Process of Literature: An Essay Towards Some Reconsiderations* (London, 1929).
[34] A. M. Mackenzie, *Scottish Principles of Statecraft and Government* (Glasgow, n.d.), 7.
[35] A. M. Mackenzie, *The Kingdom of Scotland: A Short History* (London, 1940), 374.
[36] There is little evidence to suggest a parallel here with the experience of Irish suffrage campaigners, as discussed by Cliona Murphy, 'A Problematic Relationship: European Women and Nationalism, 1870–1915', in M. Gialanella and M O'Dowd, eds., *Women and Irish History: Essays in Honour of Margaret MacCurtain* (Dublin, 1997), 144–58.

historiographic consequences of that are clear. For Mackenzie—Honorary President of the Saltire Society in 1942—Scotland's history in the mid-twentieth century was fundamental to grounding claims for home rule, and—vice versa—history suggested that only home rule would be the natural outcome of historical processes which established Scotland's 'organic' nation status. Making these connections visible and raising them above the abstract was central to Mackenzie's work, making other concerns subordinate.

Between 1899 and 1969, establishing Scottish history's place within a resistant academic environment, challenging Whig perspectives on Scotland's past, and achieving both within a political context in which Scottish nationalism was regularly treated as an incidental and faintly comic distraction, proved to be the principal and most distinctive motivating factors in Scottish historical scholarship. Certainly, many other influences informed and infused the approaches of practitioners—here, one thinks of the influence of ethnography, cultural studies, and anthropology, for example, on the work carried out by Isabel Grant on the Scottish Highlands.[37] Nevertheless, one gets a sense of a discipline still struggling to establish its identity, still endeavouring to identify both its antecedents and its future, still unsettled about its purpose in a nation that did not boast a state. Gender perspectives in Scotland's historiography were certainly not absent, yet were subordinate to what were probably seen as more urgent imperatives, and were placed firmly within the context of social history and shorn for the most part of their radicalizing potential.

# 1969–2009

Agnes Mure Mackenzie died five years before a young academic, T. C. Smout, took up a post as assistant lecturer in the Department of Economic History at the University of Edinburgh. Reflecting on his early introduction to Scottish history in the north, Smout has recalled:

> Perhaps the whole corpus of professional Scottish research historians amounted to fewer than twenty individuals, of whom possibly fifteen worked in the universities. Their main concerns were political narrative, though the outlines of a national economic history were being sketched as well.[38]

The 1960s and 1970s, however, would see the transformation of Scottish historical studies, with Smout to the fore in establishing social history's contribution to this revival. His publication of 1969, *A History of the Scottish People, 1560–1830*, is one of the few texts in Scottish historiography that can clearly be identified as a turning point in the fortunes

---

[37] I. Grant, *Everyday Life of an Old Highland Farm* (London, 1924); *Highland Folk Ways* (London, 1961).

[38] T. C. Smout, 'Scottish History in the Universities since the 1950s', *History Scotland*, 7 (September/October 2007), 45–6.

and direction of the discipline, and its contribution to the gendering of Scottish history was fundamental if not immediately obvious.

In this particular regard, Smout's volume is as important for what it did not do as for what it did achieve. He does not offer a call to arms, and does not make the case for Scottish history. One might suggest that this silence, indeed, creates the impression that, by the late 1960s, there was no case to answer. (Smout's preface refers to 'the growing army of Scottish historical scholars' at the time of writing.) Instead, it is 'the ill-defined character of social history', rather than Scottish history, that appears to tax him. He writes:

> As to the problem of what social history is, I have resolved this in a way unlikely to satisfy the purists. Several chapters of the book are basically about politics.... Other chapters of the book are about cultural history.... The remainder of the book is mainly about the social organisation and material conditions of life for the Scottish people between the Reformation and the eve of the Great Reform Bill.[39]

Smout appeared to feel no compunction to justify a focus on Scotland that reached beyond 1707, and qualified the influence of the Union of the Parliaments. What seemed to matter to Smout was the dearth of scholarship on the history of Scottish society, not the arguments that could be used to justify addressing this.

For these reasons Smout's scholarship was liberated from an enforced engagement with the Whiggish tendencies of established English historiographical practice, which had in any case come under attack following E. P. Thompson's seminal study, *The Making of the English Working Class* (1963). This was a moment in time when Scottish history had an opportunity to free itself, like Thompson's artisans and hand-loom weavers, from the 'enormous condescension of posterity', and in the process Scottish voices (some of them female) heretofore unheard would be listened to more keenly. In *A History of the Scottish People* the role of women per se is somewhat masked by Smout's more explicit and deliberate focus on family and community. And yet, even here he draws attention to, for example, the influence of property-owning women in seventeenth-century Edinburgh, the living conditions of eighteenth-century craftswomen in the capital's Old Town, and the interface between fashion and class in the etiquette of the nineteenth century. In Smout's *A Century of the Scottish People 1830–1950*, published seventeen years later, the gendered nature of Scottish society is more to the fore with, for example, an entire chapter of this volume devoted to 'Sex, Love and Getting Married'.[40]

Scottish history, it appears, had to be peopled before it was gendered, and the times facilitated this. By 1969 the Union state as originally conceived no longer appeared the only legitimate constitutional arrangement for the UK: the Whig story had lost its happy ending, indeed, any ending seemed up for grabs. In 1967 Winnie Ewing won the Hamilton by-election for the Scottish National Party and a year later her party secured around 40 per cent of the vote in the local-council elections. The Scottish Unionists were even

---

[39]  T. C. Smout, *A History of the Scottish People, 1560–1830* (London, 1989), 11–12.
[40]  T. C. Smout, *A Century of the Scottish People, 1830–1950* (London, 1986), 159–80.

moving with the times: at the party conference in Perth in 1968, Ted Heath announced that, if elected prime minister, he would deliver a Scottish Assembly. Labour in power, meanwhile, established the Kilbrandon Commission (1969–73) to investigate the governance of the constituent nations of the UK. There was less need than ever before for Scottish historians to justify their existence, and every reason for them to inform public debate.

Rosalind Mitchison's *A History of Scotland* was published a year after Smout's *History*. Her 'Author's Note' is revealing:

> This book...has been finished at a time of considerable debate on the future government of the country. Within a few years the epilogue may be in need of revision. I ask the reader to bear in mind that in its own way this is a historical document, to be viewed in the light of changing events.[41]

The confluence of fresh academic interest in 'history from below' and the constitutional debates of these years revealed the latent potential in Scottish social history to recast and reinvigorate Scottish historiography by opening it up to new influences, new possibilities, and new priorities. The further concurrence with the second wave of feminism also meant that the history of women in Scotland would seek to assert itself. This grafting of feminism onto another compatible tradition reveals nothing new. Joan Wallach Scott has explored how in the USA social history 'offered important support for women's history' in these years, and later England's *History Workshop Journal* (established 1976) became 'a journal of socialist *and feminist* historians' from 1982.[42] How such processes have been made manifest in a Scottish context in the last forty years is instructive, if hardly distinctive.

The potential of women's history, whether feminist or otherwise, to consider lives below the level of the collectivities of class and/or nation meant that traditional interests in biography persisted beyond the 1960s, and continue even now to act as a lingering point of contact with past historiographical traditions. Of particular note in this regard has been the work of Rosalind Marshall. In works such as *The Days of Duchess Anne* (1973), *Virgins and Viragos* (1983), *Scottish Queens, 1034–1714* (2003), and *Queen Mary's Women* (2006), biography has been at the core of what she has offered Scottish historiography. Yet established methodologies could challenge commonly held notions of where power rested in Scottish society. Marshall concluded in 1983, for example, that 'throughout Scottish history women have enjoyed an unusual degree of influence despite the constraints of law and convention'.[43] Her focus on the world of the Scottish elite makes this assessment more convincing and less surprising than it may at first appear. Indeed, even in recent years, biographical studies have tended to focus on women whose status, class, or celebrity make it easier to identify relevant sources and convince reluctant publishers.[44] All in all it has been an approach which—despite innovative treatments

[41]  R. Mitchison, *A History of Scotland* (London, 1970), ix.
[42]  J. W. Scott, *Gender and the Politics of History* (New York, 1999), 21.
[43]  Marshall, *Virgins and Viragos*, 315.
[44]  Notoriety has also ensured the longevity of other biographical interests. See E. Gordon and G. Nair, *Murder and Morality in Victorian Britain: The Story of Madeleine Smith* (Manchester, 2009).

and extravagant claims to the contrary—remains limiting, being as it is constrained by just how far one can prove the representative or exceptional quality of individual lives.[45]

Despite the impetus of the late 1960s and 1970s, it took time for a recognizable 'women's history' in Scotland to assert its influence within the new social history. Still, of the writers of the time, two stand out. Leah Leneman and Rosalind Mitchison were instrumental in releasing social history's potential to tell women's stories in Scotland. This does not mean that they can be easily pigeon-holed as women's or feminist historians. Towards the end of her life in 1999, Leneman noted:

> What I have said all along, and would still say now, is that I am a feminist and a historian, but I am not a feminist historian. It is true that I am not interested in what might be termed masculine history, i.e. power and politics; I am interested in the lives of people in the past—of the interplay between the experiences and emotions that are common throughout the centuries with the particular state of knowledge and attitudes of the period I am studying—and since women make up half or more of the population, I am interested in them.[46]

In their single- and joint-authored publications, Leneman and Mitchison were instrumental in identifying the gendered voices of authority in Scotland, the potential for women to alter their spectrum of expectations and desires, and the insights that gender might afford Scottish history more broadly. So, for example, in *A Guid Cause* (1991) Leneman addressed the struggle for women's suffrage in Scotland as, in part, an expression of a far older and largely neglected women's movement in the late Victorian period, coinciding with whilst distinct from the 'struggle for democracy'—a theme that had by then been well covered in Scottish historiography, although its treatment had for the most part been gender blind. Together with Mitchison, in *Sexuality and Social Control* (1989), and the associated volumes, *Girls in Trouble* (1998) and *Sin in the City* (1998), the role of the Kirk and the legal establishment in shaping and, in turn, being shaped by sexual and gender conventions was brought to the fore. It is telling that it was Mitchison, along with Tom Devine in 1988, who edited the first volume of the significant People and Society in Scotland series, supported by the Economic and Social History Society of Scotland, which did so much to affirm the arrival of a new and more confident Scottish history, and prepare the foundations for further undergraduate and postgraduate study in the discipline in the last decade of the century. For our purposes here, however, what is of particular interest is that both Mitchison and Leneman came to women's history through their commitment to Scottish history.[47] Mitchison's first monograph in 1962 addressed the 'improving' exploits of Sir John Sinclair of Ulbster, and in the decades

---

[45]  W. W. J. Knox has sought to reinvigorate biography as a means by which the 'dynamic relationship between individual women and…patriarchal society' might be explored. His study of the lives of ten Scottish women, however, focuses on women whose exceptionalism makes general conclusions tentative at best. See W. W. J. Knox, *Lives of Scottish Women: Women and Scottish Society, 1800–1980* (Edinburgh, 2006).

[46]  L. Leneman, 'A Personal History', *Women's History Review*, 9:3 (2000), 453–81.

[47]  R. J. Morris, 'Obituary', *The Guardian*, 4 October 2002.

thereafter, preceding her death in 2002, her reputation was established as an economic, political, and social historian of Scotland with works such as *Life in Scotland* (1978), *Lordship to Patronage* (1983), and *The Old Poor Law in Scotland* (2000). Leneman, meanwhile, first earned academic acclaim for her 1986 study of the social history of the Atholl estates.[48]

It would be misleading, therefore, to style Leneman and Mitchison as the pioneers of women's history in late twentieth-century Scotland. Yet their seniority and established interests in more 'mainstream' Scottish history distinguish them as important transitional figures, perhaps alongside Olive Checkland, in the historiography of that genre in these years.[49] It would also be too neat to ignore the fact that a more explicitly feminist history was being written at much the same time as (and long before) they collaborated. Their lives overlapped with the next generation: the periodization is not straightforward.

While few might have appreciated it at the time, the birth of a new generation of women's historians in Scotland was anticipated by the publication of two starkly different texts—Elspeth King's *History of the Scottish Women's Suffrage Movement* in 1978, and Christine Larner's study of witch-hunting, *Enemies of God* (1981)—and ultimately heralded by the publication in 1983 of *Unchartered Lives: Extracts from Scottish Women's Experience, 1850–1982* by the Glasgow Women's Studies Group. Among the first publications clearly informed by a feminist perspective, this collection of essays presaged the left-leaning reforming impulse that would provide the momentum in the short term at least for the next stage in women's scholarship. In the foreword to this volume, Barbara Littlewood noted that 'debates between and among Marxists, socialist feminists, and radical feminists' were an important influence on the contributors.[50] Resting heavily on established interests in labour history in Scotland in a period when many of the established icons of Scottish industrialization were under threat, it is not surprising that among the first themes to benefit from such radicalizing tendencies was the world of work. In 1990 Eleanor Gordon and Esther Breitenbach co-edited *The World is Ill Divided: Women's Work in Scotland in the Nineteenth and Early Twentieth Centuries*, and a year later Gordon published *Women and the Labour Movement in Scotland, 1850–1914*. Both publications were from university presses and drew attention to the limitations of established traditions and conventional sources in addressing the history of Scottish women. It appeared that Scottish women's history had 'arrived', and had acquired the establishment status it had long laboured without.

There followed further edited collections, the most important being Gordon and Breitenbach's *Out of Bounds* (1992). Hindsight lends an air of prophecy to the themes

[48]  L. Leneman, *Living in Atholl: A Social History of the Estates, 1685–1785* (Edinburgh, 1986).

[49]  Checkland's valuable studies in health care and social history, and *Industry and Ethos: Scotland 1832–1914* (Edinburgh, 1984), co-authored with her husband, Sydney Checkland, suggest a similar career, yet her later work specialized in Anglo-Japanese studies, not women's history or, indeed, Scottish history.

[50]  B. Littlewood, 'Foreword', in Glasgow Women's Studies Group, *Unchartered Lives: Extracts from Scottish Women's Experiences, 1850–1982* (Glasgow, 1983), 1.

explored by contributors to this volume: these were to influence the trajectory of women's history in the next ten years. Education, sexuality, political and workplace activism, criminality, religion: all these proved to be themes that would drive forward the gender agenda in Scottish historiography in those *fin-de-siècle* years when women's historians themselves consolidated their collective achievements in the Scottish Women's History Network (established 1995, renamed Women's History Scotland from 2004) and interests became increasingly international in scope. Working together, members of Women's History Scotland thereafter did much to galvanize interest in the genre in the north, particularly with their landmark publications, *The Biographical Dictionary of Scottish Women* (2006) and the edited volume, *Gender in Scottish History Since 1700* (2006). In this latter volume, in part eschewing women's history in favour of more explicit gender approaches, new concerns with identity, medicine, and the body, arts and culture, and the family highlighted that women's history in Scotland was no longer 'snug in the asylum of taciturnity'.[51]

Developing interests in masculinity and innovative approaches to local history, particularly in the work of Lynn Abrams, confirm that the gendering of Scottish history is now a fully formed and conscious project for a discrete discipline.[52] This discipline—having broken through Whiggish constraints in the company of a new social history—is not just sufficiently confident to 'go it alone', but ambitious enough to eschew the national frame as the most appropriate context within which to address gender in Scotland and to do so through multi-disciplinary initiatives, as proved by the foundation of the International Centre for Gender and Women's Studies at the University of Glasgow.

Since 1969 a greater focus on the history of Scottish women, and emergent interests in gendered social and cultural conventions, have made a valuable contribution to the historiography of this northern nation. The association of women's history with Marxist history and the close relationship between gender and postmodern histories have also encouraged an engagement with historical theory at best muted in much conventional research in the north. This has facilitated robust critiques of the much-vaunted and somewhat unapologetic empiricism at the core of earlier historical scholarship, more sophisticated and searching readings of primary sources, and a broader definition of 'evidence' to include material objects and fictional narratives.

But what is the way forward? Three immediate areas of development suggest themselves to this Scottish historian at least. While the first two address how gender history might further inform Scottish history, the third suggests how gender history might more fully realize its potential in the current academic environment in Scotland.

Paradoxically, one might suggest that women's history has had its greatest impact on the history of the Scottish nation when it has problematized the notion of nationhood itself, largely—though by no means exclusively—by asserting the primacy of a collective

---

[51] J. Hendry, 'Snug in the Asylum of Taciturnity: Women's History in Scotland', in I. Donnachie and C. Whatley, eds., *The Manufacture of Scottish History* (Edinburgh, 1992), 125–42.

[52] L. Abrams, '"There was Nobody like my Daddy": Fathers, the Family and the Marginalisation of Men in Modern Scotland', *Scottish Historical Review* (1999); *Myth and Materiality in a Women's World: Shetland 1800–2000* (Manchester, 2005).

identity below and within and overwhelming national identity itself. In this manner, women's history has reaffirmed the complex nature of Scottish nationhood and notions of belonging in ways that have questioned essentializing tendencies in popular history and asserted the importance of change over time. This can and ought to be taken further. The interface between national and gender identities and their expression in mutually sustaining *and* contradictory tropes offers the researcher access to the very essence of what it is to *be* Scottish. To date too great an emphasis has been placed on Scottish identity in relation to English and/or British identity, with scant regard for how these are actually constituted in the lived experience of citizens. Gender certainly offers one way of exploring how national identity must find its way in bodies, beliefs, customs, laws, and economies inherently shaped by sexual norms and practices. And, of course, the opposite is true: gendered practices have no meaning beyond the societies that are infused with and subject to their influence, and—in the modern period at least—such societies have typically (though not exclusively) expressed themselves within national and/or ethnic parameters.

The narrativization of the pasts of nations and the communication of such histories through time and space—heritage—is the second area in which gender might inform future Scottish historiography. How gender has shaped the historical sense and sensitivities of each age ought to be central to historiographical studies in Scotland. If the foregoing discussion is anything to go by, much is to be learned in identifying how gender has shaped historiographical legacies. The ballad tradition, music, oral history, poetry, and art more generally—as much as history—all have something to contribute in this regard.

Only through more interdisciplinary, culturally aware, and theory-rich study will such potential be realized, however. And many scholars are already pursuing such agendas. By embracing insights from other disciplines; moving beyond social history into new avenues of cultural history; consciously critiquing established political histories (rather than lamenting their gender-blindness) via complex appreciations of nationhood, constitutionalism, and politics, and embracing the liberating tendencies of poststructural methods, gender history in Scotland will certainly continue to enliven and enrich our historiography and move beyond the dichotomies (e.g. public/private, feminist/Marxist, patriarchy/capitalism, social reform/social control) and stereotypes (e.g. 'The Angel of the House', 'blue stockings') that have tended to limit and, in turn, caricature its contribution to history so far.

# CONCLUSION

The coincidence of new constitutional and gender interests, and the flowering of a new social history in the late 1960s, brought together in a singular historical moment influences which—while extant—had previously had neither the power, the longevity, nor the correct environment to necessitate a fundamental change in Scottish historiography. That having been said, one would rest too much on serendipity to suggest that mere

coincidence or chance dictated the timing or indeed the trajectory of the historiographical changes that were consolidated in the last three decades of the twentieth century.
There were important economic, academic, political, and constitutional reasons why
Scotland needed its history in these years, and why that need could only be met by asking different questions of the past. A nation whose industrial identity was destroyed in
these years was investing more than ever before in the education of its young adults.
Shifting political fortunes, as after 1979 the Conservatives consolidated their hold on the
sentiments of middle England while simultaneously destroying any vestige of sympathy
they had enjoyed north of Carter Bar, also dictated that history would loom large in
popular appreciations of the state. The Border—as Graham had styled it in 1899, 'an
invisible march here and a narrow river there'—began to reassert itself in constitutional
discussions now emotively charged with the pain of long-term unemployment and a
feeling that somewhere along the line something important had been lost. Women's history chimed with the passions and pains of the moment: history showed that women did
not need lessons in disempowerment, or disenfranchisement, and had always understood that in marriages of apparent equals power was never equitably shared. Such
national preoccupations set within a global context of a communications revolution
relatively unhampered by state control, and the evolution of trans-national politics relating to gender, race, and environmentalism dictated that in contrast to the academic environment of one hundred years before, conditions supportive of new scholarship were in
place to an extent never before realized.

Yet women's history did not commence in Scotland with the second wave of feminism, nor does it owe more to that ideology (or to the sentiments galvanized at the
millennium's end by devolution) than it does to a century of empirical research.
Suggestions that sub-state status or a stunted intellectual environment held back the
genre in Scotland must be questioned when it is realized that the momentum challenging Whiggish conventions was also the motor of a new Scottish history in which
the female voice eventually would be heard. We might wish it was otherwise; we might
envisage an alternative lineage, or a shorter gestation. But it is a story worth telling in
its own voice and on its own terms, and it is the story past and present historians have
gifted to us now.

## FURTHER READING

Abrams, L., Gordon, E., Simonton, D., and Yeo, E. J., eds., *Gender in Scottish History from 1700*
(Edinburgh, 2006).
Breitenbach, E., and Gordon, E., eds., *Out of Bounds: Women in Scottish Society 1800–1945*
(Edinburgh, 1992).
Breitenbach, E., Brown, A., and Myers, F., 'Understanding Women in Scotland', *Feminist Review*,
58 (1998).
Brotherstone, T., Simonton, D., and Walsh, O., eds., *Gendering Scottish History: An International
Approach* (Glasgow, 1999).
Ewan, E. and Meikle, M. M., eds., *Women in Scotland c.1100–c.1750* (East Linton, 1999).

Ewan, E., Innes, S., Pipes, R., and Reynolds, S., eds., *The Biographical Dictionary of Scottish Women: From Earliest Times to 2004* (Edinburgh, 2006).

Gordon, E., *Women and the Labour Movement in Scotland, 1850–1914* (Oxford, 1991).

—— and Breitenbach, E., eds., *The World is Ill-Divided: Women's Work in Scotland in the Nineteenth and Twentieth Centuries* (Edinburgh, 1990).

Graham, H. G., *The Social Life of Scotland in the Eighteenth Century* (London, 1899).

Knott, S., and Taylor, B., eds., *Women, Gender and Enlightenment* (London, 2005).

Leneman, L., *A Guid Cause: The Women's Suffrage Movement in Scotland* (Aberdeen, 1991).

——, and Mitchison, R., *Girls in Trouble: Sexuality and Social Control in Rural Scotland 1660–1780* (Edinburgh, 1998).

—— —— *Sex in the City: Sexuality and Social Control in Urban Scotland, 1660–1780* (Edinburgh, 1998).

Mackenzie, A. M., *Scotland in Modern Times, 1720–1939* (London, 1941).

Marshall, R., *Virgins and Viragoes: A History of Women in Scotland 1080–1980* (London, 1983).

Mitchison, R., *A History of Scotland* (London, 1970).

Smout, T. C., *A History of the Scottish People, 1560–1830* (London, 1989).

CHAPTER 33

·····················································································

# THE STATELESS NATION AND THE BRITISH STATE SINCE 1918[1]

·····················································································

EWEN A. CAMERON

THE public discussion of this subject is imbued with moral dimensions and refers to disparate views of Scottish historical development over the course of the twentieth century.[2] Indeed, this theme contains a central question of modern Scottish history: how do we explain the apparent demise of the empire-leading, economic success story of the late nineteenth century and its replacement by a society and economy seemingly dependent on the state and unable to diversify or demonstrate the flexibility necessary to prosper in the economic conditions of the early twenty-first century.[3] There is, however, an alternative view which emphasizes that the Victorian success story was accompanied by cheap labour, appalling working conditions and, especially prominent in Scotland, poor housing. These conditions spawned social indicators that hardly made Scotland the envy of the world—the very high levels of infant mortality being one of the most noticeable.[4] The conquest of these historic problems in the post-war period through the National Health Service and the provision of public housing was the primary achievement of the

[1] Research for this chapter was funded by the Strathmartine Trust and the British Academy.
[2] Anthony Browne, 'Jocks Away', *Daily Mail*, 27 October 2007; David Leask and Douglas Fraser, 'Scotching the Myth', *The Herald*, 2 November 2007; Iain Macwhirter, 'Time to Stop the Subsidy', *The Guardian*, 8 February 2007; John Curtice, 'Offering an Alternative to the "Subsidy Junky" Jibe', *The Scotsman*, 16 June 2009; Magnus Linklater, 'Before you Start Laying into those Subsidy Junkies…Defending the Scots against English Bile', *The Times*, 27 June 2007.

[3] T. M. Devine, 'The Break-up of Britain? Scotland and the End of Empire', *Transactions of the Royal Historical Society*, 6th series, 16 (2006), 163–80.

[4] C. H. Lee, 'Regional Inequalities in Infant Mortality in Britain, 1861–1971: Patterns and Hypotheses', *Population Studies*, 45 (1991), 55–65; R. A. Cage, 'Infant Mortality and Housing: Twentieth-Century Glasgow', *Scottish Economic and Social History*, 14 (1994), 77–92.

state, as was the realization of a measure of prosperity through full employment in the post-1945 period.[5] So, the important role of the state in Scottish history since 1918 can partly be explained by historical forces arising from the speed of Scotland's economic development in the nineteenth century and the twentieth-century attempts to deal with the legacies of this process. These problems were too profound to be dealt with by private enterprise; only the mobilization of the resources of the state could eradicate the slums or improve the health of the nation.

There is, however, a problem in attempting to understand the state in a Scottish context. There is no doubt that sovereignty and authority are located at a United Kingdom level, even in a post-devolution context. Suggestions of Scottish autonomy or semi-independence are cultural or political, rather than constitutional or legal. Indeed, it might be argued that since the passage of the Scotland Act of 1998, with its definition of reserved powers and its necessary emphasis that the devolved Parliament does not affect the sovereignty of the Westminster Parliament, this point is explicit in the relationship between Scotland and the United Kingdom. Thus any attempt to explore the relationship between Scotland and 'the state' must deal with two separate but related issues: the extent to which a 'Scottish' state exists and the relationship between Scottish society and the United Kingdom state.

The political context to the debate over state intervention in Scotland is also an important consideration. Much of the moral tone of the debate was generated in the 1980s when Conservative governments deprecated government intervention, sought to reduce public expenditure, and berated the Scots for their apparent dependence on the state. There was, however, a paradoxical element to much of this comment. High levels of per-capita public expenditure were criticized and identified as a reason for the persistence of an old-fashioned economic and social structure in Scotland. This worked against one of the key policies of the government: economic transformation. Another central objective of the same government, however, was the maintenance of the Anglo-Scottish Union and the same evidence of high levels of state intervention in Scotland was capable of being repackaged as a key benefit of the Union.[6]

Although moral criticism of the Scots for dependence on the state were heard less vociferously in the period of Labour government from 1997, there was an undercurrent of suspicion about the method of calculating the block grant to the Scottish Office from 1979 to 1999 and the Scottish Parliament, which was funded by the same method, after 1999. Labour MPs and local newspapers in the north of England were particularly vocal in this line of argument, an extension of their traditional suspicion of the effects of devolution to Scotland.[7] Herein lies an interesting tension. The relatively high levels of public expenditure that have supported state intervention in Scotland help to shore up the

[5] C. H. Lee, 'Unbalanced Growth: Prosperity and Deprivation', in T. M. Devine, C. H. Lee, and G. C. Peden, eds., *The Transformation of Scotland: The Economy Since 1700* (Edinburgh, 2005), 220–2.

[6] Scotland in the Union: A Partnership for Good, Cm 2225, 1993, p. 15.

[7] Adrian Pearson, 'A Big Fat Zero for North Transport', *Newcastle Journal*, 24 June 2008; Anushka Asthana and Christopher Khadem, 'North of England Fears Public-Sector Axe in a Return to Divided Britain', *The Observer*, 23 May 2010.

Union, but the same factors have the capacity to cause resentment in areas with a similar economic structure and thereby potentially weaken the same Union.

This negative view of public-sector activity has not gone away with the demise of Thatcherism. In 2005 the chairman of Scottish Enterprise argued that the scale of government spending in Scotland 'crowded out' private-sector activity. Although there is no clear relationship between low levels of public spending and corporate taxation and economic growth, there is a negative perception of state activity in the Scottish media and in political debate. In Scotland public spending was just under 50 per cent of GDP in 2005 (the UK figure was 44 per cent), higher than Ireland (34 per cent) but lower than Sweden and Denmark at 56 and 57 per cent respectively. This data suggests that there is no necessary link between growth and public spending.[8]

The current economic crisis is also relevant as a context for this discussion, both in the intellectual responses to the downturn and in the policies that governments have adopted in their attempts to deal with the difficulties. This evidence may provide some support for those who wish to defend the extent of state intervention in Scotland over the period since 1945, or at least for those who wish to take the edge off the criticism of interventionist policy. The intellectual response contains a broad defence of interventionist policy, Keynesian economics, and considerable scepticism about shrinking the state and cutting public expenditure. The idea of an active state can be defended as a means of social and economic recalibration around ideas of fairness, equality, and collectivism; as opposed to the excessive individualism and market failures that have been identified as drivers of the crisis.[9]

The history of the development of state intervention in Scotland over the period since 1918 also contributes a legacy to the current devolved government in Edinburgh. In November 2010 Scottish Finance Secretary John Swinney implicitly noted that he was constrained by the extent of state activity in Scottish economic and social life as much as by the limited fiscal powers contained in the Scotland Act of 1998. He reminded the Scottish Parliament that approximately 55 per cent of his resource budget (as opposed to his budget for capital projects), or around £14 billion, went on public-sector pay.[10] This allowed the devolved government to argue that pressure to depart from the Scottish consensus on an active state was being driven by London and that if the Scottish Parliament had sharper fiscal tools at its disposal different routes through the crisis would have been available. An alternative point of view would see the Scottish government limited not so much by the nature of recent constitutional change but by the legacy of

    [8]  K. Birch and A. Cumbers, 'Public-Sector Spending and the Scottish Economy: Crowding Out or Adding Value', *Scottish Affairs*, 58 (Winter 2007), 36–56; *Scottish Economic Report* (December 2005), 85–6, 88.
    [9]  Robert Skidelsky, *The Return of the Master* (London, 2009), 168–93; Tony Judt, *Ill Fares the Land: A Treatise on our Present Discontents* (London, 2010), 198–237; Will Hutton, *Them and Us: Changing Britain—Why We Need a Fair Society* (London, 2010); Stuart Sim, *The End of Modernity: What the Financial and Environmental Crisis is Really Telling Us* (Edinburgh, 2010); Gordon Brown, *Beyond the Crash: Overcoming the First Crisis of Globalisation* (London, 2010).
    [10]  Official Report of the Scottish Parliament, 17 November 2010, col. 30463.

Scottish political and economic development over a much longer period. It is to this subject that we must turn.

Even before parliamentary devolution, the extent to which extensive areas of Scottish life were governed through autonomous or semi-autonomous institutions seemed to indicate that the Union of 1707, unlike the Anglo-Irish Union of 1801, was sufficiently flexible to permit a degree of Scottish autonomy.[11] This can be emphasized in a benign explanation of the seemingly extensive role of the state in Scotland since 1918. In the educational field, for example, the combination of Scottish autonomy and the small private sector, compared to other areas of the UK, has seen an increase in public expenditure in this area by a factor of ten since 1918.[12] Perhaps less benign was the distinctive organization and relatively high spending in the area of health services since 1945. The organizational distinctiveness was a product of building the NHS in Scotland from the pre-1945 Scottish welfare, hospital, and medical-education systems, pushing it down a different route from England.[13] The high levels of expenditure come from Scotland's unenviable health record in the post-1945 period. In the early part of this period the legacy of rapid industrialization and urbanization in the nineteenth century could be conscripted as an explanation. As the state conquered the classic problems of this legacy—such as infant mortality or tuberculosis—it began to face other seemingly intractable problems arising from poverty, poor diet, high levels of alcohol consumption, and heavy smoking. These factors ensure that this remains a key concern of the state in Scotland.[14]

The third prominent theme in the discussion of the relationship between Scotland and the state is rather different. It focuses not so much on political relationships as on economic conditions. This point of view suggests that far from being in a semi-autonomous position Scotland has, in fact, been dependent on the British state for much of the twentieth century and that this has inhibited Scottish economic development in the late twentieth century. In part, this view stems from the 1980s when the government in the United Kingdom sought to roll back the frontiers of the state. Through a combination of voting patterns and social conditions Scotland, with its 'culture of dependency', was perceived to be an obstacle in the way of such a project.[15] The Prime Minister, Margaret Thatcher, was puzzled by the unwillingness of the Scots to embrace her political philosophy. She implied that the condition of semi-independence or autonomy was at the heart of this problem. The Scottish Office structure captured her ministers and made them advocates for Scotland in the government rather than advocates of government policy in Scotland. Scottish civil society, including the media, the Churches, and the trade unions, were part of a political conspiracy devoted to defeating the objectives

[11] Lindsay Paterson, *The Autonomy of Modern Scotland* (Edinburgh, 1994).

[12] Lindsay Paterson, *Scottish Education in the Twentieth Century* (Edinburgh, 2003), 13.

[13] John Stewart, 'The National Health Service in Scotland, 1947–74: Scottish or British', *Historical Research*, 76 (2003), 389–410; Morrice McCrae, *The National Health Service in Scotland: Origins and Ideals, 1900–1950* (East Linton, 2003).

[14] Vera Carstairs and Russell Morris, *Deprivation and Health in Scotland* (Aberdeen, 1991).

[15] *Glasgow Herald*, 24 November 1987.

of her government.[16] Recent historians have argued that the matter does not rest there but has to take into account reactions to clumsy attempts at economic and social restructuring in the 1980s.[17]

Lying in the background to this discussion is a perception that Scotland is treated with excessive generosity by the Exchequer. This point can even be elevated into an explanation of the extensive state activity in Scotland. There is a history of public expenditure in Scotland being based on apparently generous formulae rather than an objective assessment of basic need. A formula of limited application and named after the then Chancellor of the Exchequer, G. J. Goschen, was developed in the 1880s and lingered until the 1950s.[18] This was not the means of general allocation of Scotland's share of public expenditure, but it was most often deployed in education spending.[19] In the 1970s, during the fractious debate over devolution, it was recognized that a new arrangement was required to find the size of the block grant to the putative Scottish Assembly and to make marginal changes to Scottish expenditure across a wider spectrum than Goschen had covered. This led to the Treasury undertaking an assessment of Scotland's public expenditure needs and coming up with another formula, designed to be temporary, based on population shares, which identified Scotland's share of any changes to public expenditure in England at 10/85ths: the 'Barnett Formula', after Chief Secretary to the Treasury Joel Barnett. This was the sole survival of the failure of the 1978 devolution scheme and has been altered from time to time to take account of population changes.[20] It means that any change to government spending in England and Wales on a particular area, such as health or education, devolved to the Scottish Office or, since 1999, the Scottish Parliament, will be reflected by a change to the grant to Scotland according to the formulaic proportion. Given that the period since the formula was introduced has been one of growing public expenditure, this has delivered relatively high levels of spending to Scotland.[21]

This is relevant but is far from the whole explanation for the distinctive role of the state in Scotland. Scottish government expenditure covers only about 60 per cent of public money spent in Scotland. The remaining 40 per cent comes from UK government spending on areas that have not been devolved—social-security payments and defence

---

[16]   Margaret Thatcher, *The Downing Street Years* (London, 1993), 618.

[17]   Richard Finlay, 'Thatcherism and the Union', in T. M. Devine, ed., *Scotland and the Union, 1700–2007* (Edinburgh, 2008), 157–74.

[18]   Iain Levitt, 'The Scottish Secretary, the Treasury and the Scottish Grant Equivalent, 1888–1970', *Scottish Affairs*, 28 (Summer 1999), 93–116, esp. 95; National Library of Scotland, Woodburn MSS, Acc. 7656/16/2, W. G. Pottinger to Arthur Woodburn, 13 August 1957; National Archives of Scotland, ED26/1323.

[19]   James Mitchell, *Governing Scotland: The Invention of Administrative Devolution* (Basingstoke, 2003), 149–81, 236–40.

[20]   Gavin McCrone, 'Scotland's Public Finances from Goschen to Barnett', *Quarterly Economic Commentary*, 24(2) (1999), 34–7.

[21]   David Heald and Alasdair McLeod, 'Scotland's Fiscal Relationships with England and the United Kingdom', and Iain McLean, 'Financing the Union: Goschen, Barnett, and Beyond', both in William Miller, ed., *Anglo-Scottish Relations from 1900 to Devolution* (Oxford, 2005), 81–94 and 95–112.

spending being two notable examples. The UK government's share of expenditure includes non-identifiable spending—spending that benefits the UK as a whole and cannot be allocated to any particular territory or region. Disputes over the measurement of this element of spending have dogged all attempts to find a definitive answer to the questions about the territorial allocation of spending in the United Kingdom, from the Catto Committee of the 1950s that investigated whether it would be possible to identify Scotland's share of revenue and expenditure and, more ambitiously, imports and exports.[22] Most investigations of the balance between revenue and expenditure relating to Scotland have concluded that the latter exceeds the former as a result of a relatively low base of taxation and relatively high levels of expenditure. That much of this material was motivated by the anti-nationalist politics of demonstrating that the Scottish economy was in deficit should be noted. This was certainly true of the inception of *Government Expenditure and Revenue Scotland*, which, despite its shortcomings, is regarded as the best source of information on the topic.[23] By the 1970s there was a widespread awareness that per-capita public expenditure in Scotland was higher than in England, and this has continued. This should not be seen, pejoratively, as 'subsidy', nor as evidence that Scotland was 'dependent' on England or the state. This view was widely held among English politicians and Treasury civil servants.[24] Despite the prejudice there was a rational basis to this state of affairs. It was the product of political decisions made by governments of both parties to spend money on particular problems, such as housing or transport, which had Scottish peculiarities, and which helped to create a large state sector in Scotland.[25] The existence of large, sparsely populated areas made Scotland a more expensive country to service. A rational argument could be made that if social and economic equity across the UK was the objective of government, then that required varying levels of public expenditure in its different parts. The alternative was to say that the underlying principle was flat levels of public expenditure across the country and to accept the political consequences, among them likely strain on the Anglo-Scottish Union. The Calman Commission on Scottish Devolution, which was established by the Scottish and UK governments in 2008 to examine the experience of devolution, has emphasized the extent to which the Barnett Formula has provided stability in the funding arrangements, and is an important part of the social and economic elements of the Anglo-Scottish Union. The same Commission has also noted that the reliance of the devolved government on grants from Westminster compromises the accountability of the Scottish Parliament in matters of revenue raising.[26] Clearly the matter of public

[22] Report on Scottish Financial and Trade Statistics, Cmd 8609, 1952.

[23] *First Evidence from the Independent Expert Group to the Commission on Scottish Devolution* (Edinburgh, 2008), 20–8. This and other documents from the work of the Commission are available at http://www.commissiononscottishdevolution.org.uk/

[24] Stewart, 'National Health Service in Scotland', 404.

[25] R. J. Finlay, 'Unionism and the Dependency Culture: Politics and State Intervention in Scotland, 1918–1997', in C. M. M. Macdonald, ed., *Unionist Scotland, 1800–1997* (Edinburgh, 1998), 100–16.

[26] Commission on Scottish Devolution, *Serving Scotland Better: Scotland and the United Kingdom in the 21st Century* (Edinburgh, 2009), 4–9, 70–4.

expenditure is central to the extensive activities of the state in Scotland, but the allocation of expenditure by formula to Scotland (and Wales and Northern Ireland) means that it is relatively easy to focus on the levels of state activity there and to make political points arising from it. Information on levels of spending on English regions is more obscure, a point made less frequently.[27] Thus the activities of the state in Scotland are a combination of the funding of areas of Scottish life that can be seen as the operation of Scottish civil society—the tangible elements of the 'stateless nation' version of Scottish development—and the working of the UK state.

Thus far we have examined the way in which the union has operated to expand the role of the state in Scotland in the post-1918 period. The issue, however, has other dimensions. A key element is the way in which the task faced by the state was conditioned by its inheritance from the pre-1914 period. As noted earlier, private enterprise was dominant in Scotland in the nineteenth century, a period in which the economy had undergone successive phases of industrialization and society had been transformed by migration and, particularly, urbanization. The state expanded in the twentieth century in an attempt to deal with the consequences of this pattern of development. This can be seen very clearly in the field of housing policy. In the nineteenth century, Scotland's housing was not only a byword for overcrowding and poor amenity but also for the dominant role of the private landlord; both factors were legacies of the particular pattern of Scottish urbanization in the nineteenth century. Although in 1915 the government recognized that the exigencies of wartime necessitated unconventional action in order to deal with the symptoms and consequences of the rent strikes of that year, there was a degree of political discomfort in contemplating even this minimal level of intervention.[28] The beginnings of a new housing market in Scotland were established in the interwar period, especially with legislation passed by Labour governments in 1924 and 1929, the latter emphasizing slum clearance. These Acts placed considerable power in the hands of local authorities as builders and landlords of vastly increased numbers of houses in the public sector in Scotland.[29] Conservative politicians were also active in this area, evidenced by legislation of the early 1920s and the establishment in 1938 of a central-government agency, the Scottish Special Housing Association, to address the housing issue in the 'Special Areas' and to provide a counterweight to the way in which housing gave enormous social and political influence to local government.[30] By 1944, however, after nearly a generation of effort by the state, 23 per cent of the Scottish housing stock was overcrowded and 44 per cent was of one or two

[27] Gavin Cameron, Iain McLean and Christopher Wlezien, 'Public Expenditure in the English Regions: Measurement Problems and (Partial) Solutions', *Political Quarterly* (2004), 121–31.

[28] The National Archives: Public Record Office [PRO], CAB 37/137/29, The Increase of Rents of Workmen's Dwellings, 17 November 1915.

[29] TNA: PRO, CAB 24/42/228, Housing of the Working Classes After the War, 19th February 1918; CAB 24/126/380, Dundee and the Housing Situation, 20 July 1921; CAB 24/180/625–6, Housing. Reconsideration of Subsidy, 30 July 1926; CAB 24/193/70–2, Reconsideration of Housing Subsidy, 5 March 1928.

[30] R. Rodger and H. Al-Quaddo, 'The Scottish Special Housing Association and the Implementation of Housing Policy, 1937–87', in Richard Rodger, ed, *Scottish Housing in the Twentieth Century* (Leicester, 1989), 186–8.

rooms: the figures in England and Wales were 3.8 per cent and 4.6 per cent.[31] This fact laid the foundations for a concentrated assault on this deep-seated problem in the post-war years. This is the area where the state had its greatest impact on modern Scotland. In the thirty years after the Second World War there was a bipartisan consensus and a confidence that investment in replacing old housing stock would eradicate historic problems. From the early 1950s to the mid-1970s, twenty-five thousand to forty thousand new houses were built each year, the majority in the public sector.[32] This reshaped urban Scotland, even in Edinburgh, a bastion of private building in the interwar years.[33] The new Conservative government in 1979 interpreted this as evidence of a stultifying dependency culture, but only the state had the resources and will to tackle Scotland's housing problems. In the mid-1970s the Labour government cut subsidies for building, public-sector completions fell, and owner occupation advanced as 450,000 council houses were, under Conservative legislation, sold to sitting tenants. By 1981 the public rented sector—with 54.6 per cent of Scotland's housing (26 per cent in England)—dominated the Scottish housing market. Concomitantly, relatively few Scots owned their own houses: only 34.7 per cent of Scottish households compared to 58 per cent of English and Welsh households in 1981.[34] In the twenty-year period to 1999, however, owner occupation grew from 35 per cent to 62 per cent of housing stock.[35] There can be few geographical or policy areas in the United Kingdom in which the state has developed so far and placed such a profound stamp on society, or retreated so markedly over a relatively short period, as in the field of Scottish housing.

Housing, however, might be seen as a symptom of a wider problem: the essential structure of the Scottish economy. Discussion of this area combines the themes of inheritance from the nineteenth century as well the importance of the role of the central British state. The key area of state intervention in Scotland in the period since 1918 has been in the management of the economy. This provides the biggest distinction from the period before the Great War when governments did not perceive this to be part of their duty. This area of state activity is manifestly not part of 'Scottish autonomy': throughout the period covered by this chapter it has been the Treasury and the Board of Trade in Whitehall that have made economic policy.[36] Consideration of this area takes us back to

---

[31] PP 1943–4 IV, Report on the Distribution of New Houses in Scotland, 11–12.

[32] Kevin Morgan, 'The Problem of the Epoch? Labour and Housing, 1918–51', *Twentieth Century British History*, 16 (2005), 227–55; Harriet Jones, ' "This is magnificent!": 300,000 Houses a Year and the Tory Revival after 1945', *Contemporary British History*, 14 (2000), 99–121.

[33] Annette O'Carroll, 'Tenements to Bungalows: Class and the Growth of Home Ownership before World War Two', *Urban History*, 24 (1997), 221–41.

[34] Thatcher, *Downing Street Years*, 623–4; A. Gibb, 'Policy and Politics in Scottish Housing since 1945', in Rodger, ed, *Scottish Housing in the Twentieth Century*, 177–80.

[35] Duncan MacLennan, 'Public Cuts and Private-Sector Slump: Scottish Housing Policy in the 1980s', in M. Cuthbert, ed., *Government Spending in Scotland* (Edinburgh, 1982), 171–97; Lindsay Paterson, Frank Bechofer, and David McCrone, *Living in Scotland: Social and Economic Change since 1980* (Edinburgh, 2004), 131, 197.

[36] G. C. Peden, 'The Managed Economy: Scotland, 1919–2000', in Devine, Lee, and Peden, eds., *The Transformation of Scotland*, 233–65.

some of the definitional points raised in the introduction, most notably the way in which the state worked closely with groups of businessmen in pursuit of shared economic objectives.[37] Indeed, one might argue that herein lie some of the fundamental reasons for the extent of state activity in Scotland in the period since 1918. There are two broad points here: the first concerns the economic structure that was inherited in the aftermath of the Second World War; and the second relates to the relationship between the state and the business community in Scotland. These points will be examined in what follows.

The experience of war in the twentieth century helped to draw the state into interventionist activity, but since the experience of war was not distinctively Scottish the particularity of the way in which this influenced Scottish life has to be explained. There had been extensive state intervention during the Great War, especially in the realms of control of industrial production and fiscal policy.[38] More significant in a Scottish context, however, were the compromises that were reached between private industry and the state in the form of the Munitions of War Act in 1915 and the creation of the Dilution Commission in 1916. The objective of these novel policies was to secure an environment in which industrial relations could be managed in a way that would not compromise the production of munitions and other war materials.[39] These innovations brought government into a close relationship with the employers and their supporters, some of whom felt that workers should be conscripted by the state in order to reduce friction with private employers.[40] These views capture the sense that state intervention in the Great War was conceived in the immediate context of the conflict and not as a precedent for long-term action. Another example of this outlook would be the 1915 legislation that restricted the power of house owners to increase rents in areas of munitions production.[41] Indeed, partnership between government and private enterprise during the Great War was weighted towards the latter to a greater extent than during the Second World War and later periods.

The legacy of the Second World War was entirely different and more important in an analysis of the long-term growth of the state. Although the Scottish economy had been much more geared to the demands of the war in 1914 than in 1939, there were several additional factors that elevate its importance in an analysis of this theme. The first is the legacy of the interwar period when the repercussions of the economic depressions had a

[37] This is a strong theme in Jim Phillips, *The Industrial Politics of Devolution: Scotland in the 1960s and 1970s* (Manchester, 2008).
[38] C. H. Lee, 'The Scottish Economy and the First World War', in C. M. M. Macdonald and E. W. McFarland, eds., *Scotland and the Great War* (East Linton, 1999), 29–30.
[39] Iain McLean, *The Legend of Red Clydeside* (Edinburgh, 1983), 28–37; Gerry R. Rubin, *War, Law and Labour: The Munitions Acts, State Regulation and the Unions, 1915–1921* (Oxford, 1987), 20–9.
[40] Keith Middlemas, *Politics in Industrial Society: The Experience of the British System since 1911* (London, 1979), 68–93; Richard Davenport-Hines, 'Weir, William Douglas, first Viscount Weir (1877–1959)', *Oxford Dictionary of National Biography*, 2004; online edn., May 2009. [http://www.oxforddnb.com/view/article/36818]; Oxford, Bodleian Library, MS Addison, dep.c.87, f. 247, Memorandum on Proposed Scheme for Establishment of Efficient Relationship between the Government and Controlled Establishments by Lynden Macassey, 1 May 1916.
[41] See the justification for such legislation at *Parliamentary Debates*, lxxxvi, 42, 25 November 1915.

very severe effect on the Scottish economy, which was still dominated by heavy industry. The principal manifestation of this was very high levels of unemployment, a problem that increasingly came to be seen as a fitting case for government intervention. In the 1920s the response to regional unemployment was to move the workers to the jobs. This was not successful and an additional approach, one that was retained in 'regional policy' until the 1980s, was tried in the 1930s. The Special Areas legislation of 1934, 1936, and 1937 sought to provide indirect assistance to areas with high levels of unemployment.[42] The National government (1931–40) in London had to be dragged towards these initiatives but, although Scottish Unionist enthusiasm was greater, they made only a marginal difference to unemployment.[43] The deep-seated nature of these problems, however, seemed clear to contemporaries, across the political spectrum, in the 1930s.[44] The Scottish Economic Committee, an offshoot of the Scottish National Development Council and composed of businessmen, trade-unionists, and academics, published a number of analyses in this decade. They identified structural problems, and argued for diversification and stimulation of the home market for consumer goods through government planning.[45] The Scottish Economic Committee (SEC), although composed of individual businessmen, was taken so seriously by the government that it can be regarded virtually as part of the state. This concern with unemployment was an important element of continuity in attempts by British governments to use the resources of the state to iron out regional economic disparities, something that remained a concern until the 1980s. A second important legacy of the interwar period, more particularly the 1930s, was the contribution of rearmament, especially warship building, to the recovery of the Scottish economy in the five years before the outbreak of the Second World War.[46] Thus, as Scotland entered the Second World War it had an economic structure inherited from the Victorian period that had not undergone significant modernization, despite the arguments of the SEC. The Second World War saw some isolated initiatives that brought new industrial enterprises to Scotland, such as the expansion of the Rolls Royce factory at Hillington in Glasgow or the establishment in 1944, with the help of funds from the Ministry of Aircraft Production, of Ferranti's Edinburgh factory.[47] These developments did not amount to a reorientation of the Scottish economy and with other wartime developments, such as the establishment of the North of Scotland Hydro Electric Board and the expansion of the

[42] NAS, DD15/12, Undated [but late 1938 or early 1939] memo concerning the Highland Development Commissioner.

[43] C. E. Heim, 'Industrial Organization and Regional Development in Interwar Britain', *Journal of Economic History*, 43 (1983), 931–52; W. R. Garside, *British Unemployment, 1919–1939: A Study in Public Policy* (Cambridge, 1990), 240–77.

[44] R. H. Campbell, 'The Scottish Office and the Special Areas in the 1930s', *Historical Journal*, 22 (1979), 167–83; Richard Saville, 'The Industrial Background to the Post-War Scottish Economy', in Richard Saville, ed., *The Economic Development of Modern Scotland, 1950–1980* (Edinburgh, 1985), 1–18.

[45] Scottish Economic Committee [SEC], *Scotland's Industrial Future: The Case for Planned Development* (1939); SEC, *Light industries in Scotland: A Case for Economic Development* (1939).

[46] M. Thomas, 'Rearmament and Economic Recovery in the Late 1930s', *Economic History Review*, 36 (1983), 552–79.

[47] W. Hornby, *Factories and Plant*, History of the Second World War, UK civil series (London, 1958), 290.

shipbuilding industry, the Second World War helped to embed the state in the Scottish economy and confirm the problematic economic structure of the 1930s. The level of employment in shipbuilding in 1947, for example, was 136 per cent of what it had been in 1939, and other industries that expanded their share of the workforce included the railways (240 per cent), engineering (136 per cent), the metal industries (140 per cent), and in a reminder that wartime tends to expand the bureaucracy of the state, the number of employees in government service in 1947 was 298 per cent of the total in 1939.[48] In addition, Scotland was more heavily represented in those areas of the economy that were nationalized in the late 1940s, especially industries such as coal and iron and steel (although it was privatized in the 1950s and renationalized in the 1960s). This, it has been argued, acted as a drag on innovation in the Scottish economy, making key sectors less amenable to adventure in times of plenty and inflexible in more difficult times.[49]

There is a great deal of evidence for the existence of a close relationship between business and government in Scotland, and frequent suggestions that this has created a cosy relationship which has sustained a comfortable reliance on the state.[50] Marxist theorists have argued that it is difficult to find another group in society which is able not only to wield influence by placing pressure on government but to enter into a partnership with the state and even to subvert the objectives of the state in its own interests.[51] Nevertheless, the cosiness and complacency of this approach can be overemphasized. There were persistent efforts by the business community and government to try to find ways to shift the economic structure onto a different and more diverse footing that would be less reliant on the state. This was attempted, as we have seen, in the 1930s by the Scottish Economic Committee. Perhaps the businessmen of that generation were drawn closer to government by the experience of wartime cooperation. Sir James Lithgow, the shipbuilder who had presided over the rationalization of that industry in the 1930s, had also been active in the Scottish Economic Committee and had acted as controller of merchant shipping during the Second World War.[52] Lithgow was well aware, through his ruthless implementation of rationalization in the 1930s, that wartime expansion was not a recipe for peacetime prosperity. Ill-health minimized his role in the industry in the post-war period, however. Steven Bilsland, the banker and son of Sir William Bilsland, whose fortune had been made in the food industry, proposed a Scottish Development Finance Corporation with the aim of working with the Scottish banks to provide funds for innovative business ideas, but this idea was not supported by his fellow bankers.[53]

Perhaps the most important effort by the business community in partnership with the state to provide suggestions for the reorientation of the economy came in the early 1960s.

[48] Saville, 'The Industrial Background to the Post-War Scottish Economy', 31.
[49] Peden, 'The Managed Economy', 247.
[50] I. G. C. Hutchison, 'Government', 48.
[51] Ralph Miliband, *The State in Capitalist Society* (London, 1969).
[52] Anthony Slaven, 'Lithgow family (*per. c.*1870–1952)', *Oxford Dictionary of National Biography*, 2004; online edn., May 2006 [http://www.oxforddnb.com/view/article/51878]
[53] T. A. B. Corley, 'Bilsland, Sir William, first baronet (1847–1921)', *Oxford Dictionary of National Biography*, 2004 [http://www.oxforddnb.com/view/article/50407]; *The Scotsman*, 10 August 1938, 8.

The Scottish Council (Development and Industry) appointed a committee that investigated the condition of the Scottish economy and produced an influential report. The latter committee, chaired by Sir John Toothill, the chairman of Ferranti, argued for a fundamental reorganization of the Scottish economy away from heavy industry, and also suggested a greater emphasis on identifying sectors and spaces for growth rather than targeting areas with high rates of unemployment.[54] Toothill was an interesting character. He did not have the same baggage as many of those we have already considered. He came north with Ferranti in 1944 and was aware of the practical as well as the business dimensions of his trade through his training in both engineering and accountancy. His was a challenging prospectus and one that was greeted with some enthusiasm in business circles in Scotland and within the Scottish Office, with whom his committee had a close relationship. This might be taken as further evidence for the incorporation into the state of this group of leaders within light industry, but the matter may not be as simple as it appears. Government departments such as the Board of Trade and the Scottish Office were very keen to have a report that would not be perceived to be partisan, and they were also willing to second civil servants to bolster the secretariat that would support Toothill: evidence, perhaps, of a close link between the formal state and the business interests in the Scottish Council.[55] Indeed, the point might be taken further in that one of the results of the publication of Toothill's report was the reorganization of the Scottish Office and the establishment of a new Scottish Development Department.[56] At a wide British level, however, there was much less enthusiasm for Toothill's ideas, which would have required a fundamental reordering of economic policy were they to be implemented.

This episode demonstrates a number of important points about state intervention, above all the fact that the state was not a monolithic entity. It provides some evidence for the autonomy of Scotland in that business interests and the Scottish Office were able to cooperate to produce a plan for the Scottish economy which was implicitly critical of central-government policy, as had been the Scottish Economic Committee in the 1930s. Nevertheless, it also hints at the circumscribed nature of such autonomy, in that beyond bureaucratic reorganization Toothill's investigation was to have little effect in terms of policy in the short term. Nevertheless, the episode provides evidence for the close relationship between the state and business leaders in Scotland. Business leaders made further efforts to persuade Conservative governments of the need for a fundamental shift in the economy in the late 1960s and 1970s with their 'Oceanspan' project. This was an attempt to make central Scotland a bridge for trade between the USA and Europe. The economic aim was to import raw materials on the west coast, feed manufacturing

---

[54] Phillips, *Industrial Politics of Devolution*, 19–27; James N. Toothill, *Report on the Scottish Economy* (Edinburgh, 1961).

[55] TNA: PRO, BT177/1791 contains many documents from 1959 and 1960 that demonstrate the close relationship between the Scottish Council and government departments in the establishment of this inquiry.

[56] I. Levitt, 'The Origins of the Scottish Development Department, 1943–62', *Scottish Affairs*, 14 (1996), 42–63.

industry and export finished goods from the east coast. The political aim was to provide an alternative to Labour's regional and nationalization policies.[57] Many of the same organizations and leading figures whose ideas we have traced since the 1930s were involved: the Scottish Council (Development and Industry) and businessmen from the Lithgow and Colville families. Oceanspan, like the Toothill Report, failed to achieve its objectives, but it provides evidence that the Scottish business community were prepared not only to engage with but also challenge the outlook of the state. Of course this was partly political. In 1968 Sir William Lithgow (son of Sir James) wrote to *The Times* from his shipyard in Port Glasgow arguing in favour of what he called 'social capitalism', which involved lower taxation on wealth-creating activities with the objective of greater individual self-reliance and less reliance on the state.[58] This would allow the state to invest in facilities, such as modern hospitals, for the really needy. Harold Wilson's Labour government of the day, however, had different priorities.

In part, the failure of these radical suggestions for economic restructuring of the Scottish economy was due to the commitment of governments to dealing with regional imbalances in economic indicators, especially unemployment. The heyday of regional policy came in the 1960s and 1970s with governments of both parties committed to the idea, although using different tactics.[59] This policy is particularly associated with Wilson's Labour government between 1964 and 1970, but it has been suggested that much of the intellectual architecture that supported Labour policy after 1964 had been put in place by the Conservative government which preceded it, although that government was less active in implementation of policy than its successor.[60] In a specifically Scottish context, however, landmarks from this period include a massive loan from the government to the Scottish steel industry, then in private hands, to build a strip mill at Ravenscraig in Lanarkshire, as well as support for vehicle- production plants at Linwood in Renfrewshire and Bathgate in West Lothian.[61] Indeed, it might be argued that these initiatives were barometers of the rise and fall of regional policy and the determination of government to implement them against the wishes of the private enterprises concerned. The withdrawal of support in the early 1980s and lack of political concern, with the consequential additions to the ranks of the unemployed—in contrast to earlier periods—condemned these plants to closure and signified the move away from state intervention to plan the economy. This presaged a period in which government would adopt the rhetoric of hostility towards the active and expansive state. This would have the effect of separating the task of economic restructuring, through policies such as privatization, from its Scottish political and constitutional consequences.

[57] Phillips, *Industrial Politics of Devolution*, 52–75; Jim Phillips, 'Oceanspan: Deindustrialisation and Devolution in Scotland, c.1960–1974', *Scottish Historical Review*, 84 (2005), 63–84.

[58] *The Times*, 28 March 1968, 11; Phillips, *Industrial Politics of Devolution*, 53.

[59] J. B. Parr, 'Growth-Pole Strategies in Regional Economic Planning: A Retrospective View', *Urban Studies*, 36 (1999), 1,195–215, 1,247–68.

[60] J. Tomlinson, 'Conservative Modernisation, 1960–64: Too Little, too Late?', *Contemporary British History*, 11 (1997), 18–38.

[61] Phillips, *Industrial Politics of Devolution*, 12–45.

This essay has explored the links between the role of the state and the operation of the Union in Scotland in the period since 1918. Although aspects of this topic—housing, economic development, the regeneration of the Highlands, education—have attracted a great deal of attention, there are big questions that remain to be examined by new research. It would be constructive if discussions of public expenditure in Scotland moved on from ritual denunciations of 'subsidy junkies' to a more considered approach to the impact of state activity on Scottish economic and social history. This cannot be done if Scotland's relationship with the state is treated in isolation from the impact of the state on other regions and nations of the United Kingdom, and much further work on this wider theme remains to be done. Attempts to link the role of the state into newer debates about Scottish history would also be helpful. One example would be the role of the state as an actor in the environmental changes that have taken place over the course of the century. This would involve detailed work on the generation of energy, the management of resources, the use of the landscape, the development of transport, and the history of pollution. The consequences of environmental change are a huge challenge for politicians at all levels and may provide a positive role for the state to play in a regulatory and activist role. The historical contextualization of these issues would be a signal contribution to understanding these problems.

The chapter has noted how the operation of the Union for much of the period delivered conditions where there was a consensus over the role of the state. For most of the period since 1918 there has been a recognition that many areas of Scottish society—education, health, rural society—were run by semi-autonomous institutions resourced by the British state. Through a variety of mechanisms, including explicit formulae, as well as physical conditions and political choices at all levels of government, relatively high levels of public expenditure have been a feature of the role of the British government in Scotland. This has persisted, until very recently, through a variety of different political contexts, even in the 1980s when the aspiration of government was to reverse this process. The extensive role of the state in Scotland was also developed as a response to massive social and economic problems which were, in the realm of housing, for example, legacies of earlier periods of development. Through this process the state stamped its mark on the social landscape of twentieth-century Scotland. The extreme difficulty of dealing with the problems posed by Scotland's industrial structure in the post-1945 period has had important long-term consequences. The ultimate failure of both the British and Scottish dimensions of the state in this area left Scotland particularly exposed to the economic conditions and Conservative ideology that characterized the 1980s. This produced a rapid and politically insensitive reorientation of economic structures which, in turn, helped to pave the way for devolution in the late 1990s and the revival of conditions where an expansive role for the state could once again be considered. Current economic conditions and the response of another government determined—even more so than its predecessor—to shrink the state, revive the prospects of polarization of Scottish and British political outlooks over the role of the state in society, and prompt continuing debate over the nature of the Union.

## FURTHER READING

Birch, K., and Cumbers, A., 'Public Sector Spending and the Scottish Economy: Crowding Out or Adding Value', *Scottish Affairs*, 58 (Winter 2007), 36–56.

Campbell, R. H., 'The Scottish Office and the Special Areas in the 1930s', *Historical Journal*, 22 (1979), 167–83.

Finlay, R. J., 'Unionism and the Dependency Culture: Politics and State Intervention in Scotland, 1918–1997', in C. M. M. Macdonald, ed., *Unionist Scotland, 1800–1997* (Edinburgh, 1998), 100–16.

Hutchison, I. G. C., 'Government', in T. M. Devine and R. J. Finlay, eds., *Scotland in the Twentieth Century* (Edinburgh, 1996).

Judt, Tony, *Ill Fares the Land: A Treatise on our Present Discontents* (London, 2010).

McCrone, Gavin, 'Scotland's Public Finances from Goschen to Barnett', *Quarterly Economic Commentary*, 24(2) (1999).

Mitchell, James, *Governing Scotland: The Invention of Administrative Devolution* (Basingstoke, 2003).

Peden, G. C., 'The Managed Economy: Scotland, 1919–2000', in T. M. Devine, C. H. Lee, and G. C. Peden, eds., *The Transformation of Scotland: The Economy Since 1700* (Edinburgh, 2005), 233–65.

Phillips, Jim, *The Industrial Politics of Devolution: Scotland in the 1960s and 1970s* (Manchester, 2008).

Rodger, Richard, ed., *Scottish Housing in the Twentieth Century* (Leicester, 1989).

Stewart, John, 'The National Health Service in Scotland, 1947–74: Scottish or British', *Historical Research*, 76 (2003), 389–410.

# CHAPTER 34

································································································

# CHALLENGING THE UNION

································································································

### IAIN McLEAN

## KILLING HOME RULE BY KINDNESS, 1885–1924

································································································

THE existential challenge to the Union began with the election of a disciplined cadre of MPs from the Irish Party in 1880. It culminated with the election of an SNP majority government in 2011. Scottish challenges to the Union, and government responses to them, from 1880 until 1922 were shaped by Irish challenges to the Union and government responses to those. Scottish challenges changed after the UK government accepted the independence of the Irish Free State in 1922.

The years from 1885 to 1921 have been described as the high age of *primordial unionism*.[1] For a primordial unionist, the Union of Great Britain and Ireland, passed by an Act of Parliament in 1800 and taking effect in January 1801, was to be defended at all costs. Why? *Because it was there.* King George III had vetoed Catholic emancipation in 1800; therefore the Union was never legitimate for Irish Catholics—about 7/8ths of the Irish population in the 1840s. Only with the franchise reforms of 1868 and 1885 did many of them get the vote. When they did, they voted en bloc for the Irish Party, whose sole legislative demand was for Irish Home Rule—what would now be called devolution. From 1885 to 1921 primordial unionists resisted this (to modern eyes) mild demand with unparalleled bitterness. The violent side of unionism reached its apex in 1913–14, when the party's leaders encouraged the Curragh 'contingent mutiny'[2] and the Larne gun-running of spring 1914. This *coup d'état* made unworkable Home Rule, the policy of the thrice-elected Liberal government and its Irish allies.

---

[1] Iain McLean and Alistair McMillan, *State of the Union: Unionism and the Alternatives in the United Kingdom since 1707* (Oxford, 2005), 122–34; Iain McLean, *What's Wrong with the British Constitution?* (Oxford, 2010), 142–7.

[2] So labelled by *The Manchester Guardian*, leader, 24 March 1914.

Prime Minister Gladstone's conversion to Home Rule in 1885 splintered the party systems throughout the British Isles. In Scotland, it created the Unionist Party, the dominant party until the 1950s. Confusingly, the 'Union' in its title was that with Ireland, not the Union of 1707, which remained unquestioned in the background. This Unionism created a competitive party system in Scotland. It united several strands. Some were overtly anti-Irish: or at least anti-Catholic Irish. As described in other chapters, mass migration of both Catholic and Protestant Irish people to the west of Scotland, and the long-standing links between Scots and Ulster Presbyterianism, brought Irish politics to Scotland. In 1923 the General Assembly of the Church of Scotland approved a report entitled 'The menace of the Irish race to our Scottish nationality'.[3]

Another strand of primordial unionism linked Union and Empire.[4] Scotland did disproportionately well out of the British Empire. The Scottish education system supplied doctors, engineers, and administrators that the English system was ill-equipped to do. To a primordial unionist, granting Home Rule to Ireland was the first step on a slippery slope to the disintegration of the British Empire. Thus, as long as the empire remained popular, Scottish nationalism would not be.

There was a kinder side to (Irish) Unionism. In fact, 'killing Home Rule by kindness' was one of the slogans of the Unionist governments of the UK from 1886 to 1905. To them, the Irish Question was a land question. If Irish peasants could be turned into smallholding proprietors by buying out their landlords with funds from the UK taxpayer, then Home Rule might go away. The unexpected success of the Crofters' Party in the highland seats in 1885 led Scottish land reform to be killed with kindness too. The Crofters' Commission was created in 1886 and has protected the highly distinctive crofting tenure ever since.[5] In Scotland as in Ireland, property rights were bought out in the interests of public order.

Administrative devolution to Scotland was bipartisan in that era. The office of Secretary for Scotland was created in 1885; it became a Secretaryship of State in 1926. Since 1707, Scotland had mostly been administered by Scots in any case, initially by the Lord Advocate, the government's Scots law officer. The Scotch Education Department was created in 1870, the Scottish Office in 1885; they were merged in 1918. The merged office became the place where Scottish home rule was killed by kindness. In the 1888 Budget the Unionist Chancellor G. J. Goschen provided the first block grant to fund Scottish and Irish administration. The proportions he set, for the tax revenues to be assigned, were 80, 11, 9 respectively for England and Wales, Scotland, and Ireland. This Goschen formula, or Goschen proportion, continued to dominate Scottish public finances until it was superseded by the Barnett Formula in the 1970s.

[3] S. J. Brown, 'Outside the Covenant: The Scottish Presbyterian Churches and Irish Immigration, 1922–38', *Innes Review*, 42 (1991) 19–45.

[4] T. M. Devine, *The Scottish Nation 1700–2000* (London, 1999), e.g. at 308; and his *Scotland's Empire 1600–1815* (London, 2003), *passim*.

[5] D. W. Crowley, 'The "Crofters' Party", 1885–1892', *Scottish Historical Review*, 35 (1956), 110–26; Ewen A. Cameron, *Land for the People? The British Government and the Scottish Highlands, c. 1880–1925* (East Linton, 1996), 10–12, 56–9.

From the outset Goschen was generous to Ireland, which contributed less than 9 per cent to UK GDP; therefore it always represented a redistributive transfer to Ireland. In 1888, however, Scotland was an average, or perhaps above-average, part of the UK in terms of GDP per head. Therefore its 11 per cent Goschen share was not redistributive. Redistribution was to the poorest part of Scotland, the Highlands, by the Crofters' Commission and similar measures. However, with the long decline of the Scottish capital-goods industrial base after 1918, and the relative decline of Scotland's population share, Goschen *became* redistributive, as successive (mostly Conservative) prime ministers and secretaries of state were well aware.

On the political left, Scottish Home Rule seemed a logical corollary to Irish Home Rule. Even Mr Gladstone nodded in that direction, although he did not do anything about it. Ramsay MacDonald, the future leader of the Labour Party, entered politics in 1886 as the London secretary of the Scottish Home Rule Association. In 1888 he wrote to his compatriot Keir Hardie, who was running as an Independent Labour candidate in the Mid-Lanark by-election, to praise Hardie's stand in 'the cause of Labour and of Scottish Nationality'.[6] Labour and Scottish nationality were for MacDonald the same cause.

Challenges to the Union in Scotland thus combined cultural nationalism with political unionism, as characterized by Colin Kidd.[7] A key figure was Sir Walter Scott, described elsewhere in this *Handbook*. A Tory who owed his baronetcy to the government of Lord Liverpool, Scott nevertheless unleashed fierce cultural nationalism in the *Letters of Malachi Malagrowther* (1826): his successful campaign to preserve Scottish banknotes (with us yet).[8] The politics of Malachi Malagrowther had another fling in the 1920s, this time around the Church of Scotland—another of the protected institutions of 1707. The independence guaranteed in 1707 was breached by the Patronage Act 1711/12. This breach was not remedied until the Disruption of 1843 and the final abolition of patronage in 1874.[9] However, a mischievous House of Lords legal judgement in 1904 awarded the entire property of the Free Church of Scotland to a tiny highland fragment, the 'Wee Frees'. The House of Lords (now the Supreme Court) is the only non-Scottish court in the Scottish legal system. Church establishment needed a domestic settlement, crafted by Scots in Scotland. This came in the form of the Church of Scotland Act 1921, which removes the theology of the Church from parliamentary or judicial interference.

---

[6] J. R. MacDonald to J. K. Hardie, 1888 (exact date not given in source). In W. Stewart, *J. Keir Hardie: A Biography* (London, 1921), 40.

[7] Rosalind Mitchison, 'Materials for the Study of Scottish History', in *A History of Scotland* (London, 1970), 430–42; Colin Kidd, *Subverting Scotland's Past: Scottish Whig Historians and the Creation of an Anglo-British Identity, 1689-c.1830* (Cambridge, 1993); his 'William Wallace, Unionist' [a review of McLean and McMillan, *State of the Union*], *The London Review of Books*, 28, no. 6 (23 March 2006), 17–18; and his *Union and Unionisms: Political Thought in Scotland, 1500-2000* (Cambridge, 2008). I assume that 'William Wallace, Unionist' is a mischievous subeditor's headline: nothing in the review warrants the claim.

[8] Sir Walter Scott, *The Letters of Malachi Malagrowther*, ed. P. H. Scott (Edinburgh, 1981). Originally published in 1826.

[9] A. Rodger (Lord Rodger of Earlsferry), *The Courts, the Church, and the Constitution: Aspects of the Disruption of 1843* (Edinburgh, 2008); McLean, *What's Wrong?*, 309–10.

Scottish Home Rule bills were drafted by Labour MPs in 1924 and 1928, although neither made any progress in Parliament. George Buchanan, promoter of the 1924 bill, said of the Church of Scotland Act:

> on a purely Scottish question, a question dealing with the religious feeling and aspirations of the Scottish people, members largely alien to our views should not be called upon in the main to decide a question of which they have no knowledge or thoughts.[10]

## UNIONISM UNCHALLENGED, 1924–66

However, by this time Unionism had a new basis: the welfare state. The traditional basis for spending on social protection was the poor law, which made local authorities responsible. But at times of structural unemployment, this was hopeless. The local authorities which had most need to offer social protection had the weakest tax base. All participants in the creation of the Edwardian welfare state knew this. From the first, Old Age Pensions (1908) were established on a UK national scale and financed out of national taxation. So was the National Insurance scheme (1911) of the Chancellor of the Exchequer, David Lloyd George. Sickness and unemployment insurance revealed the spatial dimension of social protection. People in poor areas (which are also areas of high unemployment) are more likely to be sick or unemployed than people in rich areas. Like pensions, National Insurance was financed out of national—not local—taxation. Under pressure from the Irish Party, whose votes were needed to enact National Insurance, Lloyd George had to concede a separate set of Irish Commissioners. This led to demands, also conceded, for separate Scots and Welsh Commissioners. The main civil-service architect of the bill, W. J. Braithwaite, complained that the Irish, Scottish, and Welsh lobbies 'wrecked the bill, splitting it up into four separate parts, but this was not because they were not given full consideration; it arose simply out of the nationalist position'.[11]

Braithwaite's fears might have had some substance if there had been any divergence between the four countries on the tax or the expenditure side of social protection. There never has been. In Northern Ireland, where social protection has supposedly been devolved since 1920, rates march in lock-step with those in Great Britain, and the Northern Ireland administration requests a transfer to make up the difference between payouts in Northern Ireland and National Insurance contributions paid in Northern Ireland. As part of killing Home Rule with kindness, it has always received these transfers without question.

So has Scotland. Although Scottish GDP per head was close to the UK average in the days of Lord Goschen, and is again now, for much of the twentieth century it was well

---

[10] *Parliamentary Debates*, House of Commons, 9 May 1924: http://hansard.millbanksystems.com (accessed 19 May 2010).

[11] W. J. Braithwaite, *Lloyd George's Ambulance Wagon: Being the Memoirs of William J. Braithwaite 1911–1912*, ed. by H. Bunbury (London, 1957), 148.

below. As purveyor of coal, ships, and locomotives to the empire, Scotland was badly hit in the 1920s and 1930s. Sickness and unemployment payments from the UK taxpayer softened the blow. So did the Goschen proportion, which protected the domestic spending controlled by the Scottish Office (i.e. everything except social protection). Under the Goschen proportion, Scotland was to receive 11/80 of what was spent in England and Wales on programmes it covered. But Scotland's relative population declined continuously below 11/80 of the population of England and Wales. Yet Scottish civil servants, backed by the Secretary of State, always treated Goschen as a floor, and never as a ceiling. If a case could be made for spending more than 11/80 of English and Welsh spending on a service (based on, for example, sparsity, cold, or the separate state-funded Catholic education system created by the Education [Scotland] Act 1918), then it was the job of officials and ministers to argue it. In 1926 Prime Minister Stanley Baldwin, who had earlier as Chancellor fought against Scottish spending rising above Goschen, allowed it to do just that, on the grounds that cutting spending would provoke nationalist sentiment. All Secretaries of State in Unionist governments have made that argument since then, the supreme exponent being Tom Johnston, the Labour Scottish Secretary in the Churchill wartime coalition government. By the 1970s, when the Treasury decided to replace Goschen by a formula that would cut down what they saw as overspending in Scotland and Northern Ireland, public spending per capita in Scotland was some 20 per cent above that in England.[12]

Thus, from 1911 onwards, the United Kingdom was an explicitly redistributive state. The redistribution was spatial as well as interpersonal. The old left-wing arguments for Home Rule lost their appeal. George Buchanan's Bill of 1924 already seemed an anachronism. Buchanan ended his career as the chairman (1949–53) of the National Assistance Board, the body in charge of distributing the non-insurance-backed component of social-protection spending.[13] National Assistance was paid at a uniform rate throughout Britain, and was financed out of general taxation.

# From Primordial Unionism to the Claim of Right

The foundation of the Scottish National Party (SNP) in 1934 by the merger of two smaller groups was therefore a sideshow in parliamentary terms. Its political space was already occupied by the Labour and Unionist parties. The Scottish leaders Walter Elliot (Unionist; Secretary of State 1936–8) and Tom Johnston (Labour; Secretary of State

---

[12] James Mitchell, *Governing Scotland: The Invention of Administrative Devolution*, (Basingstoke, 2003), 149–81; Iain McLean, *The Fiscal Crisis of the United Kingdom* (Basingstoke, 2005), 45–61.

[13] James J. Smyth, 'Buchanan, George (1890–1955)', in *Oxford Dictionary of National Biography*, edited by H. C. G. Matthew and Brian Harrison (Oxford, 2006). Online edn., ed. Lawrence Goldman. http://www.oxforddnb.com/view/article/32147 (accessed 27 December 2009).

1941–5) were true sons of Malachi Malagrowther. They protected Goschen. Elliot protected the Scottish film industry and advanced the career of its greatest ornament, John Grierson. Johnston created the North of Scotland Hydro-Electric Board: his revenge on *Our Scots Noble Families*, his sweeping 1909 attack on the aristocratic landlords whom he held responsible for the depopulation of the Highlands at the time of the Clearances.[14] The SNP won a by-election in Motherwell during the wartime truce in 1945, but lost the seat again in the general election a few weeks later.

Elliot and Johnston had to pass from the political scene before the SNP could make an impression. It scored decently in by-elections at Glasgow Bridgeton (1961) and West Lothian (1962). But its political space depended on the election of a Labour government in 1964. Out of office since 1951, Labour then captured more of the vote in both Scotland and Wales than in England. Its majority initially depended on its Scottish and Welsh seats. When it ran into economic trouble in 1966, it was therefore more vulnerable in Scotland and Wales than elsewhere. Cultural nationalism then took a hand. Labour faced a by-election in Welsh-speaking Carmarthen in 1966. It was won by Gwynfor Evans, giving Plaid Cymru its first parliamentary seat. In Scotland, the fortune of the Unionists had declined rapidly from a peak in 1955,[15] despite their rebadging as the Conservative and Unionist Party in 1965. The empire had gone; Irish sectarian conflict in the Glasgow area had declined; the Church of Scotland no longer talked of the menace of the Irish race. Although the much-maligned Conservative leader, Sir Alec Douglas-Home, was a Scot, his party failed to regain the Malagrowther vote. It never has; for instance, in the general election of 2010, there was a swing against the Conservatives in Scotland, where they retained only one seat. Focus-group research commissioned by the party in 1968 reported:

> The Scottish Conservative Party has got an exceedingly bad image. It is thought to be out of touch, a bastion of 'Foreign' (English) privilege ... associated with recalcitrant landowners. ... The Scottish Conservative Party was the only Scottish Party which, on mention, often elicited mirthful or mirthless laughter.[16]

Space was therefore available for Winifred Ewing of the SNP to make a sensational gain in one of Labour's safest seats at the Hamilton by-election in 1967. In 1970 the SNP lost Hamilton but made its first general-election gain, in the Western Isles. By then it also had a solid base in local government. It won seven Commons seats in the next general election, in February 1974, and eleven in October 1974. In that election it won over 30 per cent of the Scottish vote—more votes, but fewer seats, than the Conservatives.

---

[14] Gordon F. Millar, 'Elliot, Walter Elliot (1888–1958)', in *Oxford Dictionary of National Biography*, ed. H. C. G. Matthew and Brian Harrison (Oxford, 2004). Online edn., ed. Lawrence Goldman, January 2008, http://www.oxforddnb.com/view/article/33003 (accessed 19 May 2010); Graham Walker, *Thomas Johnston* (Manchester, 1989), 176; Thomas Johnston, *Our Scots Noble Families*, with preface by J. Ramsay MacDonald, 12th edn. (Glasgow, 1925). Originally published in 1909.

[15] When the Unionists won thirty-six of the seventy-one Scottish seats and a plurality of the vote. David and Gareth Butler, *British Political Facts 1900–1994* (Basingstoke, 1994), 216.

[16] ORC report, Conservative Party Archives, CA CCO 180/29/1/2, 4, cited by I. McLean and A. McMillan, 'How We Got Here', in J. Curtice and B. Seyd ed., *Has Devolution Worked? The Verdict from Policy Makers and the Public* (Manchester, 2009), 17–43, at 21.

Devolution was reborn in the summer of 1974. It was not a throwback to the Victorian campaigns for Home Rule, and it drew nothing from Northern Ireland, where direct Westminster rule had been imposed in 1972. Rather, Prime Minister Harold Wilson imposed it on a sceptical Labour Party in Scotland—it has been argued for reasons of statecraft.[17] He was aware that if the SNP surge continued, the electoral system would flip from punishing them to rewarding them. At around 35 per cent of the vote, evenly spread, the SNP will win more than half the seats in Scotland in a first-past-the-post election. In the wake of losing Hamilton, Wilson had appointed a Royal Commission on the Constitution, to put the problem of responding to the SNP off until after the 1970 election. The Commission had reported in favour of Scottish devolution in 1973.[18] Its report was initially ignored. But the SNP had already begun its second surge on the back of its most successful campaign slogan ever: *It's Scotland's Oil*. North Sea oil was beginning to flow and the SNP's credibility soared with it.

The Scotland and Wales Bills of the 1974–9 Labour governments failed, initially because of a Labour backbench revolt originating in Newcastle-upon-Tyne.[19] To the rebels, the Scots were richer than the Geordies but were already getting more public spending per head. Devolution would only widen that inequality. Why did the Scots deserve this, from a Labour government? Because they voted SNP, whereas the Geordies had only the Labour Party to vote for. The Geordie revolt was treated with some derision in Scotland, when it was noticed at all. But it was the key event in Scottish (non-)devolution in the 1970s. It signalled that a future devolution scheme would have to be fair to the English as well as to the Scots. A further Labour backbench revolt imposed a referendum, with a 40 per cent (of the electorate) threshold for a *Yes* vote, before the Scotland and Wales Acts 1978 could be brought into force. The Welsh vote threw out the scheme overwhelmingly. The Scottish vote approved it narrowly but did not reach the threshold. The SNP and the Conservatives forced the vote of no confidence that brought down the Labour government in March 1979.

And then—nothing happened. No Malagrowther roared at the rigged referendum result. (No post-war UK government, it could have been pointed out, had been elected on as many of the votes as 40 per cent of the electorate.) The SNP vote dropped back. Margaret Thatcher's government shelved devolution, reversing the Conservatives' previous policy (the 'Declaration of Perth', 1968). Harold Wilson had been wrong, it seemed, to assume that the Scots cared deeply about devolution. They cared deeply about protecting their share of UK public spending. To all the old arguments, they added a new one: it's Scotland's oil, and Scotland should get the benefit. Scottish support for that view spread far beyond the SNP. However, Scottish support for independence did not.[20]

For the first ten years of Conservative governments that held few Commons seats in Scotland or Wales, the pro-devolution elite of Scottish civil society remained silent. The SNP

[17] McLean and McMillan, *State of the Union*, 159–70.
[18] Royal Commission on the Constitution 1969–1973, *Report*, vol. I (HMSO: Cmnd 5460/1973).
[19] McLean and McMillan, 'How We Got Here'; the ultimate source was the author's observations as the committee vice-chair, later chair, on the Tyne & Wear Metropolitan County Council, 1973–9.
[20] Curtice and Seyd, *Has Devolution Worked?*, Table 5.1.

turned to infighting over the causes of its poor performance in the 1979 election. However, by 1988, when the Conservatives had introduced the poll tax ('Community Charge') in Scotland a year ahead of England,[21] the SNP revived sharply, winning the Glasgow Govan by-election by denouncing Scottish Labour MPs as the 'Feeble Fifty' who had failed to block it. This galvanized Labour, the Liberal Democrats, and some civil society organizations to create a Scottish Constitutional Convention. The SNP and Conservatives did not take part. The Convention opened in 1989 with a 'Claim of Right', whose title recalls documents of the same title in 1689 and 1842. Like both of the earlier documents, the 1989 Claim asserts the right of the Scottish people to determine policy in Scotland. The 1689 Claim had offered the Scottish throne to William and Mary, on condition (which they accepted) of maintaining Presbyterian establishment.[22] The 1842 Claim had objected to parliamentary and judicial interference in the self-government of the Church of Scotland.[23]

The Constitutional Convention reported in 1995, laying the groundwork for the Scotland Act 1998.[24] Its members thought carefully about the design of the new institutions. They failed to think about the two most difficult issues, that if discussed would have thrown up internal divisions. These were representation at Westminster, and finance: in shorthand, the 'West Lothian Question' and the 'Barnett Formula'.

# THE SCOTLAND ACT 1998 AND THE STATE OF THE UNION

The Labour government elected in 1997 picked up the proposals of the Constitutional Convention; but Prime Minister Tony Blair insisted on having a referendum first. The 1997 referendum had two questions: should there be a Scottish Parliament? And should it have the power to tax? Both were approved, the power to tax by a slimmer but still comfortable margin.

The Act, enacted in 1998 and coming into force in 1999, therefore adopted the proposals of the Constitutional Convention in every material detail. There were three important changes from the abortive scheme of 1978. First, ministers believed in the scheme. Blair himself was perhaps the most sceptical, but once the proposals had been approved in a referendum, there was no further doubt that in the words of his predecessor John Smith, they represented the 'settled will of the Scottish people'. Ministers' belief in the scheme prevented any repetition of the sullen departmental resistance that had made the 1978

---

[21] D. Butler, A. Adonis, and T. Travers, *Failure in British Government: The Politics of the Poll Tax* (Oxford, 1994), 85–136.

[22] Claim of Right Act 1689, *Acts of the Parliament of Scotland*, ix, 38, c.28, at http://www.rps.ac.uk/trans/1689/3/108 (accessed 19 May 2010).

[23] C. S. Parker, *Life and Letters of Sir James Graham, 1792–1861*, 2 vols. (London, 1907), vol. 1, 389.

[24] *Scotland's Parliament Scotland's Right: Report of the Scottish Constitutional Convention* (Edinburgh, 1995), at http://www.almac.co.uk/business_park/scc/scc-rep.htm (accessed 19 May 2010).

scheme unworkable. Second, whereas the 1978 scheme had listed the powers to be devolved, the 1998 scheme listed the powers to be reserved. This was a shorter and clearer list than its predecessor. Third and most important, the Scottish Parliament was to be elected by proportional representation, using an Additional Member scheme. Of its 129 members, 73 were to be elected from Scotland's Westminster territorial seats, and the remainder were to top those up in a way that would improve the overall proportionality of the result. Donald Dewar, sponsor of the bill and later the first First Minister, called its PR provisions 'the best example of charitable giving this century in politics'.[25] They would deprive Labour of a majority in the Scottish Parliament—hence Dewar's remark. But, more important, they would also deprive the SNP of such a majority unless, he thought, it were to get more than 50 per cent of the votes cast in a Scottish Parliament election. Dewar thought that this move killed separatism. He got one crucial sum wrong.

The first and second Scottish Parliament elections (1999 and 2003) both led to Labour–Liberal Democrat coalition administrations. On becoming First Minister in May 1999, Dewar wrote, 'The people of Scotland rightly have high hopes and expectations for their Parliament; they already feel a sense of ownership and of connection to it and we must not let them down.' But within eighteen months Dewar was dead.[26]

The second First Minister, Henry McLeish, was forced out over a dubious claim for office expenses. The administration stabilized under Jack McConnell. At the third Scottish Parliament election in 2007, the SNP formed an administration under the highly accomplished Alex Salmond, with Green support; however, the two parties together commanded only 50 of the 129 seats. The fourth election in 2011 produced a sensational result. Salmond's SNP won 69 seats—a majority—with 45.4 per cent of the constituency vote and 44 per cent of the list vote.

Many assessments of the achievements of the Scottish Parliament are coloured by party preferences. Labour-inclined commentators liked it at first; nationalists like it now; Conservatives have always been the most sceptical. The report of the Calman Commission on Scottish Devolution attempted a non-partisan evaluation. Calman thought that the Parliament's committees 'are more open and accessible than their UK Parliament counterparts. One of those who was particularly positive about the role of committees was the Auditor General for Scotland, who...[made] the interesting suggestion that there should be "an arrangement whereby each of the major portfolios of spend is subjected to planned scrutiny [perhaps] once a parliamentary session" by the Parliament's subject committees (with some backing from Audit Scotland).'[27]

---

[25] *Parliamentary Debates*, House of Commons, 6 May 1998: http://hansard.millbanksystems.com (accessed 19 May 2010).

[26] Iain McLean, 'Dewar, Donald Campbell (1937–2000)', *Oxford Dictionary of National Biography*, eds. H. C. G. Matthew and Brian Harrison (Oxford, 2008), Online edn., ed. Lawrence Goldman, http://www.oxforddnb.com/view/article/74700 (accessed 28 December 2009) (source of quotation); Wendy Alexander, ed., *Donald Dewar: Scotland's first First Minister* (Edinburgh, 2005).

[27] Calman, Sir Kenneth (chair) (2009). *Serving Scotland Better: Scotland and the United Kingdom in the 21st Century*. The Final Report of the Commission on Scottish Devolution is at http://www.commissiononscottishdevolution.org.uk/uploads/2009-06-12-csd-final-report-2009fbookmarked.pdf (accessed 28 December 2009).

To win the approval of the Auditor General for Scotland is a rare accolade. Audit Scotland combines what in England are two separate roles, that of the National Audit Office and the Audit Commission.

Calman went on to commend the committees of the Parliament, which combine the functions of Bill Committees and Select Committees at Westminster. Other procedures that have been widely commended include 'Decision Time', where all votes are taken at the end of a day's sitting, in contrast to the very slow Commons procedure; and the greater openness of the Scottish than the Westminster Parliament to receiving petitions.

Disputes between the Scottish and Westminster Parliaments about the powers of the former have, up to 2011, not tested the machinery created in the 1998 Act. For the first two Scottish Parliaments they were settled among politicians of the same party. The Joint Ministerial Committee envisaged in the Scotland Act never met between 2002 and 2008.[28] Since 2007, dispute resolution has remained unexpectedly informal, although the Parliaments are now controlled by different parties. For instance, the mechanism to ask the Supreme Court whether the Scottish Parliament had acted outwith its powers has never been invoked.

The most practical lubricant has been the non-statutory 'Sewel convention':

> the parliamentary convention whereby the UK Parliament will not normally legislate with regard to devolved matters in Scotland without the consent of the Scottish Parliament.[29]

Up to 2009, it had been invoked 101 times. Lord Sewel, in his evidence to Calman, suggested that the convention give an opportunity for Scottish ministers to pass the buck upwards rather than deal with devolved, but controversial, matters.[30] He may have been thinking of the Civil Partnerships Act 2004, which was entirely handled at Westminster, although its Scottish provisions were drafted by Scots lawyers working for the Scottish Executive. In the early years of the Parliament, Scottish ministers were bruised by some encounters with social conservatives on matters of morality, and may have quietly welcomed the opportunity not to be exposed to debate about civil partnerships.

The outstanding problems have been representation and finance, for which the short-hand has been 'West Lothian Question', or WLQ, and 'Barnett Formula', or Barnett. The WLQ is so called because it was constantly posed in the 1970s by Tam Dalyell, a fierce opponent of devolution who was then MP for West Lothian. Why should he, as MP for West Lothian under devolution, have the power to discuss education in Blackburn, Lancashire, but not education in Blackburn, West Lothian?[31] The shortest answer is 'Because that is what asymmetric devolution entails'. It has been said that the WLQ is not truly a question at all, but a rhetorical device to illustrate the problem of devolution. But

---

[28]  Calman Report, 4.28.

[29]  Calman Report, Glossary.

[30]  Calman Report, 1.162 and 4.88.

[31]  Tam Dalyell, *Devolution: The End of Britain?* (London, 1977). Dalyell continued to pose it for the rest of his career, e.g. in *Parliamentary Debates*, 14 November 1977: http://hansard.millbanksystems.com (accessed 19 May 2010).

there is a real issue here. Dalyell posed the question as an anti-devolution Scot. But it has more traction when posed by English opponents of devolution in the form, 'Why should *Scottish* MPs have the right to discuss education in Blackburn, Lancashire, when *English* MPs have no right to discuss education in Blackburn, West Lothian?'

The WLQ, as posed by Dalyell, is *not* about the right of a government that does not hold a majority of seats in territory X to legislate in territory X. This occurs in any country where the spatial patterns of voting vary across the country. The Conservatives have not had a majority of seats in Scotland since 1955, and have never had a majority of seats in Wales or (Northern) Ireland since universal suffrage. But all Conservative governments make laws affecting Scotland and Wales. The true WLQ is about the right of a government that is a minority in territory X to make laws affecting *only* territory X. Thus, most Conservative legislation affecting Scotland between 1979 and 1997 did not involve the true WLQ; but the Scottish poll-tax legislation did. It affected only Scotland, opposed by the majority of Scottish MPs. All the Scottish Conservative MPs involved in steering it through Parliament lost their seats at the 1987 general election.[32]

In bygone days, the true WLQ affected all parts of the UK. Cases include Irish coercion acts in the nineteenth century; Welsh Church disestablishment, blocked by the House of Lords until 1920; the Scottish Episcopalians Act 1711,[33] and the Scottish poll-tax legislation. None of these can now happen. Each, if it arose now, would be a devolved matter under the relevant legislation. So the true WLQ can only affect England. This issue has revived with the general election of 2010.

There used to be little England-only legislation, and therefore few English WLQs. But one was the Commons' double rejection of the proposed Church of England prayer book in 1927–8. That was no business of the Scots, Welsh, or Ulstermen; yet it was they who formed the Commons majority against the book. (They may have been taking their revenge for the English blocking of Welsh disestablishment, or the Law Lords' meddling with the Church of Scotland.) The majority of English MPs voting supported it.

Under asymmetric devolution, however, the UK government doubles as the government of England. Therefore, an English WLQ may arise whenever the parliamentary majority in England differs from the parliamentary majority in the UK, as with the Liberal governments of 1886, 1892–5, and 1910–18. The fury directed at them by the primordial unionists sprang perhaps from their majority of seats in England, whereas the Liberals, with their Labour and Irish allies, held a majority of seats in the UK. The WLQ would have arisen very sharply had the rainbow coalition of Liberal, Labour, Plaid Cymru, Green Party, and SNP, which appeared and vanished again on 10 May 2010, come to pass.

Prime Minister Gladstone wrestled with this problem in 1886 and 1893. He failed to solve it. He toyed with, but dropped, an 'in and out solution', recently revived under the label 'English votes on English laws' (EVOEL). Under EVOEL, MPs from outside

---

[32]  Butler et al., *Failure in British Government*, 129.
[33]  Carried by a majority in the Union Parliament, although the Scots MPs divided 14–13 against. Edinburgh, National Library of Scotland [NLS], Wodrow MSS, Wodrow Lett.Qu.VI f.65.

England would not be allowed to vote on England-only legislation. As set out in the Conservative general election manifesto for 2010:

> A Conservative government will introduce new rules so that legislation referring specifically to England, or to England and Wales, cannot be enacted without the consent of MPs representing constituencies of those countries.[34]

Consistently, majorities in England, and about half of Scottish respondents, agree that Scottish MPs should not be allowed to vote on English laws.[35] Unfortunately, EVOEL, even in the Conservatives' detailed implementation,[36] faces two probably insuperable problems:

1. That it is impossible to certify what is an England-only clause, especially as long as devolution finance keeps its present tangled format;
2. That EVOEL would lead to one party, or coalition, winning the votes on all-UK legislation, while another party would win the votes on England-only legislation. Which would then be the UK government?

It follows that the most dangerous situation for the WLQ remains a Parliament where Labour (and allies) have a majority of seats in the UK, while the Conservatives have the majority of seats in England. The 2010 Parliament came close. In England, the Conservatives won 297 of the 533 seats; in the rest of the UK, they won only 9 out of 117. It is therefore no surprise that the Liberal-Conservative governing coalition promised, on its formation, to address both the WLQ and the Barnett Formula.

The easiest solution for the WLQ (and Barnett) is of course Scottish independence. If enacted after the 2011 triumph of the SNP, that will come at a painful cost given the structural deficit in Scottish public finance,[37] and the likely tough negotiations over the liabilities of the Royal Bank of Scotland and the former HBOS. But it will mark the culmination of a century's challenge to the Union.

Unlike the WLQ, Barnett is technically easy to 'solve' within the Union, but the solution would inevitably involve a great deal of political pain. By the mid-1970s, HM Treasury had decided to trim public expenditure per head in Scotland and Northern Ireland, which they deemed to be unreasonably high. They hit on two cunning plans. One was an assessment of relative needs. The other was the so-called Barnett Formula.

The Needs Assessment was started in 1976, to cover the services proposed for devolution in the Scotland and Wales Bill. It was fiercely contested, especially by the Scottish

---

[34] Conservative Party, *Invitation to Join the Government of Britain* (London, 2010), 84.

[35] Curtice and Seyd, *Has Devolution Worked?*, Table 6.11.

[36] Report of the Democracy Task Force July 2008, see 'Tories Consider MP Voting Changes' at http://news.bbc.co.uk/1/hi/uk_politics/7481906.stm (accessed 21 April 2010). It proposed that non-English MPs should be barred from voting only at the Committee stages of an England-only bill, and not formally prohibited from voting at the Second or Third Reading. At the Third Reading, however, they would be unable to undo changes agreed at Committee stage.

[37] Scottish Government, *Government Expenditure and Revenue Scotland 2007–2008* (Edinburgh, 2009), Tables 4.1 and 6.1: http://www.scotland.gov.uk/Resource/Doc/276248/0082927.pdf (accessed 21 April 2010).

Office. Only meagre results were published, after the change of government and the dropping of devolution in 1979.[38] They show that Scotland and Northern Ireland were getting more per head to spend on domestic public services than their 'needs' seemed to warrant, and Wales less. No interdepartmental needs assessment has been conducted since then, although the Treasury has held some of its own. The three territorial departments have all made their own assessments, which show the same thing: that Scotland would suffer, and Wales would benefit, were the UK to move from Barnett to a 'needs-based' block-grant system. This has been confirmed by the Welsh equivalent of the Calman Commission.[39]

The Barnett Formula was designed to cut down Scots and Northern Irish 'overspending' gradually. The details are complicated.[40] But, if allowed to run without political interference, it would in due course have led to equal spending per head in the four countries of the UK. That would obviously be inappropriate, as Scotland, Wales, and Northern Ireland have higher spending needs than England. Wales and Northern Ireland are relatively poor. Scotland is not; but it has a cold climate, inhabited islands, and midges. The Treasury intended Barnett to run until relative spending matched relative needs, and then switch to needs assessment. That has never happened; and Barnett has been bypassed in various ways. Scotland still has higher public spending per head than Wales, or the north of England, although it is richer than both.

Because the Constitutional Convention had no incentive to enquire into a system under which Scotland did well, it did not consider the future of the block grant. Nor, obviously, did the SNP or its academic supporters. The White Paper introducing the Scotland Bill said that Barnett would continue. But it is not in the Act: it remains non-statutory. However, it now has almost no friends. The Calman Commission was created by a vote of the Unionist majority in the Scottish Parliament—the Conservative, Labour, and Liberal parties outvoting the 2007 SNP administration. It received logistical support from the UK government. All of these parties wished to see a replacement of Barnett. So does the SNP government, as it seeks an independent Scotland. All four parties (even the SNP) signalled support of Calman in their 2010 manifestos, Labour and the Liberal Democrats in identical wording.[41] The Liberal Democrats would replace Barnett by a needs assessment; the SNP would like it to be 'fairer' (i.e. to give Scotland more); Labour and the Conservatives say nothing explicit.

[38]  HM Treasury, *Needs Assessment Study—Report* (London, 1979); McLean, *Fiscal Crisis*, Table 4.2.

[39]  ICFFW (Independent Commission on Funding & Finance for Wales, 2009). *Working Paper: Replacing Barnett with a Needs-Based Formula.* Cardiff: ICFFW: http://wales.gov.uk/docs/icffw/news/091204needsworkingpaperen.pdf (accessed 21 April 2010).

[40]  But see McLean, *Fiscal Crisis*, 87–92; Iain McLean, Guy Lodge, and Katie Schmuecker, *Fair Shares? Barnett and the Politics of Public Expenditure* (London/Newcastle, 2008), Box 3.1.

[41]  *Invitation to Join*, 83; Labour Party, *A Future Fair to All* (London, 2010), 94: http://www.labour.org.uk/manifesto (accessed 19 May 2010). Liberal Democrats, *Liberal Democrat Manifesto 2010* (London, 2010), 92: http://network.libdems.org.uk/manifesto2010/libdem_manifesto_2010.pdf (accessed 21 April 2010). Scottish National Party, *Elect a Local Champion: Manifesto 2010* (Edinburgh, 2010), 17: http://www.snp.org/manifestos/westminster/2010 (accessed 21 April 2010).

One debilitating consequence of Barnett is that the Scottish Parliament has no fiscal responsibility. Almost everything it spends is raised by the UK government, out of UK taxation, and handed to it as a block grant. Therefore it has very weak incentives to consider whether spending gives good value for money, even with the Auditor General for Scotland at its back. Under the Calman plan, now enshrined in the Scotland Bill 2011, the UK's block grant to Scotland would be cut by half, as would the standard rate of income tax chargeable in Scotland (from 20p in the pound to 10p in the pound, at 2009 rates). It would then be for the Scottish Parliament to set a tax (say 9p, 10p, or 11p in the pound). Doing nothing would lead to a savage grant cut; so at the margin the Parliament's decisions on taxing and spending would be aligned.[42]

## CONCLUSION: A NATION OF MALAGROWTHERS?

Colin Kidd has argued for some years that most of what historians have taken as evidence for Scottish nationalism is actually a form of nationalist unionism.[43] I think that he takes this paradox too far, but it is certainly well grounded in history. Malachi Malagrowther and his family reappear frequently in Scottish history since 1707. Malachi grumbles about English ignorance of Scotland, and about unthinking English measures. But, deep down, he is content with the Union. Are the Scots truly a nation of Malagrowthers?

Before devolution, politicians differed. Nationalists, and opponents of devolution such as Tam Dalyell,[44] both expected a slippery slope: that devolution would lead to independence. The SNP welcomed this (expected) outcome; Dalyell deplored it; but their analysis was the same. Proponents of devolution believed not only that it was the settled will of the Scottish people, but that it would stay that way. Tables 34.1 and 34.2 help us judge.

The first block of figures (Table 34.1) shows a time series of Scots' constitutional preferences. It is remarkably stable. Really, there is only one movement: the near-halving of those opposed to any devolution between 1997 (when the new government promised it) and 1999 (when the Scottish Parliament came into existence). The election of an SNP government in 2007 neither resulted from, nor immediately caused, an upsurge in support for independence. The second block (Table 34.2) shows the time series of answers to the 'Moreno question', which is regularly used to tap feelings of subnational identity. It offers the respondent five choices. In Scotland these are 'Scottish not British', 'more Scottish than British', 'equally Scottish and British', 'more British than Scottish', and 'British not Scottish'. Table 34.2 groups these five responses into three. The Moreno series

---

[42] Independent Expert Group (IEG). *First Evidence from the Independent Expert Group to the Commission on Scottish Devolution* (Edinburgh, 2008).

[43] Kidd, *Subverting Scotland's Past*; Kidd, *Union and Unionisms*; 'William Wallace, Unionist'.

[44] Dalyell, *End of Britain?*, 305–7.

Table 34.1  Constitutional preference for Scotland, 1999–2007%

|  | 1992 | 1997 | 1999 | 2000 | 2001 | 2002 | 2003 | 2004 | 2005 | 2006 | 2007 |
|---|---|---|---|---|---|---|---|---|---|---|---|
| Independence |  | 28 | 28 | 30 | 27 | 30 | 26 | 32 | 35 | 30 | 24 |
| Devolution with tax powers |  | 44 | 50 | 47 | 54 | 44 | 48 | 40 | 38 | 47 | 54 |
| Devolution without tax powers |  | 10 | 8 | 8 | 6 | 8 | 7 | 5 | 6 | 7 | 8 |
| No devolution |  | 18 | 10 | 12 | 9 | 12 | 13 | 17 | 14 | 9 | 9 |

Table 34.2  'Moreno' national identity in Scotland, 1992–2007%

|  | 1992 | 1997 | 1999 | 2000 | 2001 | 2002 | 2003 | 2004 | 2005 | 2006 | 2007 |
|---|---|---|---|---|---|---|---|---|---|---|---|
| Scottish > British | 59 | 61 | 67 | 68 | 66 |  | 65 |  | 64 | 65 | 57 |
| Scottish = British | 33 | 27 | 22 | 21 | 24 |  | 22 |  | 22 | 22 | 28 |
| Scottish < British | 6 | 8 | 7 | 7 | 7 |  | 8 |  | 9 | 9 | 11 |

*Source*: Scottish Election Studies (1992–7); Scottish Social Attitudes (other data points). For question wording see Curtice and Seyd, *Has Devolution Worked?*, 119–21. The 2007 data was collected between May and November, after the election of the SNP government.

is also remarkably stable; again, the biggest movement occurred before devolution, with 'more Scottish' responses going up before 1999. In 2007, after the election of the SNP-led government, there is actually a shift the other way.

Combining the two blocks of figures, we can see that the Scots are indeed a nation of Malagrowthers. The median Scot favours the post-1999 status quo—devolution with tax powers—over both independence and a return to direct rule. At the same time, the median Scot thinks of herself as more Scottish than British. That is the legacy of a three-century mixture of cultural nationalism and political unionism.

This is not to predict that the SNP government would necessarily lose a referendum on independence, which they propose to hold in the lifetime of the 2011–16 Scottish Parliament. The WLQ continues to irritate the English (more than it does the Scots). Any replacement for Barnett will be less favourable to Scotland. Therefore a referendum could be held in an atmosphere of mutual recrimination, perhaps under a future Conservative government that had a material incentive to go against its historic Unionism and welcome the secession of Scotland (which would guarantee Conservative hegemony in the rest of the UK). Perhaps the nearest parallel would turn out to be, not the Quebec referenda of 1980 and 1995, but the velvet divorce of Slovakia and the Czech Republic in 1993, which occurred although only a minority in both countries favoured separation.[45]

[45] Iain McLean, 'Scotland: Towards Quebec—or Slovakia?', *Regional Studies*, 35 (2001), 637–44; Neal Ascherson, 'Future of an Unloved Union', in T. M. Devine, ed, *Scotland and the Union 1707–2007* (Edinburgh, 2008), 228–39, at 237–9.

In the UK general election of 2010, the SNP did poorly, gaining no seats; and its attempts to join a rainbow coalition were spurned by its potential red, green, and yellow partners. Nevertheless, the coalition parties agreed 'to establish a commission to consider the "West Lothian question"...[and] to the implementation of the Calman Commission proposals and the offer of a referendum on further Welsh devolution.'[46]

The coalition parties acknowledge both that the WLQ is a serious constitutional problem and that EVOEL is not the answer to it. The coalition took up Calman's scheme to reduce UK income tax in Scotland, in order to force the Scottish Parliament to set a tax. Although it does not eliminate the Barnett Formula, it reduces its importance in the funding block. The Calman plan was supported in the 2007–11 Scottish Parliament by 121 votes to 3, with even the reluctant SNP voting in favour. If the 2010 UK coalition survives, the nation of Malagrowthers will have to decide how to pay for their banknotes, as well as how to print them.

Does the sensational success of the SNP in 2011 change everything? It proves that Donald Dewar got his sums wrong. The SNP could win a majority of seats on a minority vote because 12 per cent of the regional vote was spread among small parties. It does not of itself lead to independence. Consider Quebec and Slovakia once more.

In the Canadian federal election held in the same week in 2011, the Bloc Québécois was almost wiped out, although the Parti Québécois remains very strong in Quebec elections. That is consistent with the SNP's doing badly in 2010 and spectacularly in 2011. Scots, like Quebeckers, are becoming used to voting differently in elections to different bodies. Support for independence may not rise much from the levels in Tables 34.1 and 34.2, and the SNP may lose its independence referendum.

Slovak independence was driven by Czechs who thought that Slovakia was doing too well. That is why the WLQ and Barnett remain central. In its submissions to Calman and the Scotland Bill, the SNP demanded, as it must, more fiscal autonomy for Scotland. But more fiscal autonomy means more fiscal responsibility. All parties fought the 2011 election as if the known cuts in UK public expenditure were not happening. Every party would spend, spend, spend. None would raise taxes. In the face of identical manifestos, the voters chose the team they liked the best—this is known as 'valence politics'.

When forced to make cuts, the 2011 government will of course blame the English. The end of the blame game is unpredictable. But if the English blame the Scots more than vice versa, the Slovak Republic of Scotland becomes a possibility—except that it will be a monarchy.

## Further Reading

Calman, Sir Kenneth (chair), *Serving Scotland Better: Scotland and the United Kingdom in the 21st Century* (Edinburgh/London, 2009).

---

[46] *Conservative Liberal Democrat Coalition Negotiations: Agreements Reached 11 May 2010:* http://www.conservatives.com/News/News_stories/2010/05/Coalition_Agreement_published.aspx (accessed 19 May 2010).

Curtice, J., and Seyd, B., eds., *Has Devolution Worked? The Verdict from Policy Makers and the Public* (Manchester, 2009).

Devine, T. M., *The Scottish Nation 1700–2000* (London, 1999).

—— *Scotland's Empire 1600–1815* (London, 2003).

Hazell, Robert, ed., *Constitutional Futures Revisited* (Basingstoke, 2008).

Keating, Michael, *The Independence of Scotland* (Oxford, 2009).

Kidd, Colin, *Union and Unionisms: Political Thought in Scotland, 1500–2000* (Cambridge, 2008).

McLean, Iain, and McMillan, Alistair, *State of the Union: Unionism and the Alternatives in the United Kingdom since 1707* (Oxford, 2005).

Mitchell, James, *Governing Scotland: The Invention of Administrative Devolution* (Basingstoke, 2003).

Murkens, Jo Eric, Jones, Peter, and Keating, Michael, *Scottish Independence: A Practical Guide* (Edinburgh, 2002).

Paterson, Lindsay, *The Autonomy of Modern Scotland* (Edinburgh, 1994).

Royal Commission on the Constitution 1969–1973 (Kilbrandon Commission), *Report*, Cmnd 5460.

*Scotland's Parliament Scotland's Right: Report of the Scottish Constitutional Convention* (Edinburgh, 1995).

Scott, Sir Walter, *The Letters of Malachi Malagrowther*, ed. P. H. Scott (Edinburgh, 1981). Originally published in 1826.

Walker, Graham, *Thomas Johnston* (Manchester, 1989).

# CHAPTER 35

.....................................................................

# A NEW SCOTLAND?
# THE ECONOMY[1]

.....................................................................

## G. C. PEDEN

IN the late twentieth century the Scottish economy underwent restructuring no less radical than in the Industrial Revolution. Whereas almost one in three Scots was in industrial employment in 1979, by 1986 fewer than one in four were.[2] On the other hand, Christopher Harvie's characterization of the Scottish experience under Margaret Thatcher's government of 1979–90 as 'instant post-industrialisation'[3] is open to two modifications: first, economists were discussing what they already called de-industrialization before she became prime minister;[4] second, the decline in industrial employment continued long after she resigned. Industrial employment peaked in the mid-1960s, and industry's share of total employment had already fallen from 39.3 per cent in 1965 to 32.3 per cent by 1979 (Fig. 35.1). There was a marked acceleration in the trend thereafter, with industry's share falling to 17.7 per cent over the next fourteen years to 1993, but there was a further fall to 11.1 per cent over the following fourteen years to 2007. In contrast, employment in services increased from 48.7 per cent of total employment in 1965 to 81.5 per cent in 2007.

This chapter addresses three questions. First, what is the nature of de-industrialization and how does it fit into long-term trends in Scottish history? Second, how have Scottish industries and services fared since 1965? Third, how did restructuring of the economy impact upon different regions of Scotland?

---

[1] I am grateful to Gavin McCrone for commenting on an earlier draft.

[2] Throughout this chapter industrial employment is defined to include mining, quarrying, oil and gas extraction, and electricity, gas, and water utilities as well as manufacturing.

[3] Christopher Harvie, *No Gods and Precious Few Heroes: Twentieth-Century Scotland*, 3rd edn. (Edinburgh, 1998), 164.

[4] Frank Blackaby, ed., *De-industrialisation* (London, 1979).

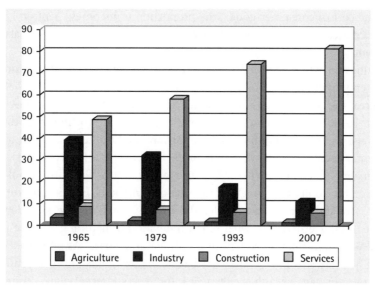

**FIGURE 35.1** Percentage shares of total employment in Scotland. Note: Agriculture includes fishing and forestry.

*Sources: Abstract of Regional Statistics* (London, 1966), table 4; *Regional Trends* (London, 1984), table 7.5; *Scottish Economic Statistics* (Edinburgh, 2000), table 3.11; Employee jobs—Scotland 1998–2008, http://www.scotland.gov.uk/Topics/Statistics/Browse/Labour-Market/DatasetsEmployment

# THE NATURE OF DE-INDUSTRIALIZATION

De-industrialization is an ambiguous term. Sometimes it is used to refer to employment and sometimes to industrial output. Whereas the numbers employed in industry fell sharply after 1979, the absolute value of industrial output fell by much less (Fig. 35.2). Indeed, industrial output was on a modestly rising trend from the late 1980s to the end of the century, even though its share of gross domestic product (GDP) was falling. In contrast, industrial employment tended to fall even when the value of industrial output was increasing. In all advanced economies in the last fifty years labour productivity has risen more rapidly in manufacturing than in services, with the result that increasing numbers of workers have been drawn into services.[5] Mass production of goods required greater transport, and financial, wholesale, and retail services. Employment in catering, hotels, and entertainment rose in response to changing patterns of consumer spending: as people became more prosperous, they spent smaller proportions of their incomes on food, and larger proportions on consumer goods or services. As mass production

---

[5] Robert Rowthorn and Ramana Ramaswamy, 'Deindustrialisation: Causes and Implications', in *Staff Studies for the World Economic Outlook* (Washington, DC, 1997), 61–77.

lowered the cost of consumer goods, the proportion of incomes spent on leisure and tourism increased. The expansion of education, health, and social services also created employment.

The timing and extent of de-industrialization varied between countries. For example, industrial employment in Scotland in 2000 was less than half of what it had been in 1970, whereas the absolute size of the manufacturing labour force in the USA remained fairly stable between these dates, even if it was a declining proportion of the total labour force. As regards industrial output as a proportion of GDP, the Scottish figure in 1996, 27.8 per cent, was rather higher than that for the UK as a whole (25.2 per cent), but lower than Germany (33.4 per cent) or Norway (32 per cent). The fortunes of industry depended on the ability to compete in international markets. In common with the rest of the UK, Scotland seems to have suffered from the 'Dutch disease', so called after the experience of the Netherlands, where the exploitation of natural gas in the 1960s was associated with high unemployment in traditional industries. As oil flowed ashore in increasing quantities from 1977, the UK's balance of payments improved and sterling's exchange rate rose against other currencies. Industry's international competitiveness was partly determined by the exchange rate, since a higher rate made exports more expensive, and imports cheaper. In these circumstances firms had either to reduce costs, which usually meant shedding labour, or go out of business. Figure 35.3 suggests there was a relationship between the rate of change in industrial employment and movements in the exchange rate. The rise of almost 20 per cent in the exchange rate between 1977 and 1981 was followed (with a two-year lag) by a 28.5 per cent fall in industrial

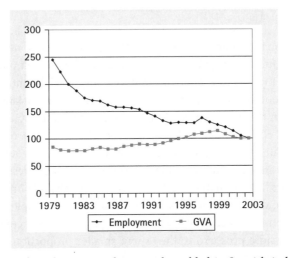

FIGURE 35.2 Indices of employment and gross value added in Scottish industry (2004=100). Note: Gross value added (GVA) is also known as GDP at constant basic prices.

*Sources*: Employment: Employee Jobs by Detailed Industry, Scotland, 1982–2009, Office for National Statistics; GVA: Gross Value Added chained volume measures at basic prices, 1963–2009, table 7, Office of the Chief Economic Adviser, The Scottish Government.

employment between 1979 and 1983. The downward trend of the exchange rate between 1981 and 1996 was associated first with a slackening of the decline in industrial employment until 1994, and a brief rise thereafter to 1998. Sterling rose again from 1997 and the downward trend in industrial employment resumed from 1999.

The exchange rate was not, however, the only factor shaping Scotland's industrial experience. At the end of 1973 and again in 1979 the Organization of Petroleum Exporting Countries (OPEC) engineered increases in the price of oil by restricting output. Between 1972 and 1974 the price quadrupled, and in 1979–80 it increased $2\frac{1}{4}$ times. Scotland benefited in so far as the exploitation of North Sea oil became more profitable. On the other hand, the long boom in the international economy since 1945 ended as most

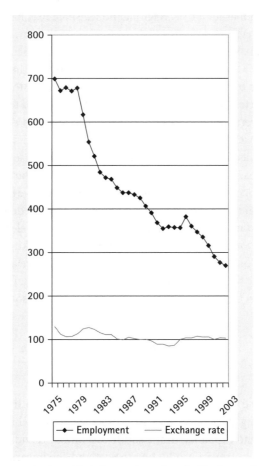

FIGURE 35.3 Employment in Scottish industry (000s) and effective exchange rate (1990=100). Note: The effective exchange rate is a trade-weighted average, with the scale of all currencies set so that the average 1990 value is 100.

Sources: Employment: *Abstract of Regional Statistics* and *Regional Statistics* (various issues 1966–84); Employee jobs by detailed industry, Scotland, 1982–2009, Office for National Statistics; Exchange rate: Bank of England's Statistical Interactive Database, http://www.bankofengland.co.uk code http://www.bankofengland.co.uk, series code XUAAGB.

oil-importing countries responded to a sharp deterioration in their balance of payments with deflationary policies. Down to 1976, British governments tried to maintain full employment with expansionary fiscal and monetary policies, but the resulting inflation saw retail prices rising at over 26 per cent in 1975. The Thatcher government came to power in 1979 determined to curb inflation, and bank rate was held at 14 per cent or more for twenty-one months from June 1979 and again in the winter of 1981–2. High interest rates hit business investment and were the principal reason why the UK's GDP fell by 4.6 per cent between 1979 and 1981, and the 1979 level of output was not reached again until 1983. High interest rates also attracted an inflow of foreign funds, increasing the demand for sterling, and adding to the balance-of-payments effect of North Sea oil on the exchange rate.

The Thatcher government also aimed to make the British economy more competitive by relying more upon market forces. Regional policy since 1945 had encouraged industrial investment in development areas where unemployment was above the national average, first with tax allowances, and later with grants. Since Scottish unemployment was higher than the UK average, the effect had been to subsidize industrial employment in Scotland. However, by the early 1990s government assistance to industry in Scotland was only about a quarter (in constant prices) of what it had been ten years earlier. Loss-making industries were allowed to fail, and enterprise zones set up in Clydebank, Dundee, and Motherwell had a fairly minor impact.

On the other hand, as Clive Lee points out, once the worst phase of industrial closures was over by late 1980s, GDP rose faster in Scotland than in the industrial regions of England and Wales.[6] Scotland's growth rate also improved relative to other mature economies, including Belgium, Denmark, the Netherlands, and Sweden.[7] Indeed, the effect of the reduced importance of loss-making industries, a rise in electronics production, and the increased importance of profitable services such as banking and finance, was to raise Scotland's GDP per head to the UK average in 1995. That relative position was not sustained, but in 2007 Scotland's GDP per head, at 96 per cent of the UK average, was higher than that of any other region apart from London and the south-east of England.

# INDUSTRY

Scotland's dependence on its Victorian staples continued into the second half of the twentieth century, long after newer industries, such as motor vehicles, electronics, and consumer durables, had expanded in the south-east and Midlands of England. Despite wartime dispersal of electronics production to Scotland and inward movement from the

[6] C. H. Lee, *Scotland and the United Kingdom: The Economy and the Union in the Twentieth Century* (Manchester, 1995), 52–7.

[7] John McLaren, 'Scotland's Improving Economic Performance: A Long-Term Comparative Study', in Fraser of Allander, *Quarterly Economic Commentary*, 28, no. 2 (2003), 42–8.

later 1940s of American light-engineering firms, a study by Glasgow University's Department of Applied Economics in 1954 found that the country's industrial structure was very much the same as it had been at the beginning of the century.[8] This was a serious disadvantage, as the industries in which Scotland specialized tended to be those for which there was increasing competition abroad. The need for structural change was recognized in 1961 by the Toothill Report, which called for the development of science-based industries, newer capital-goods industries, and engineering-based consumer industries.[9] The development of petrochemicals at Grangemouth in the 1950s and 1960s encouraged a belief in Whitehall and the Scottish Office that modern industries could be successfully located in central Scotland.

The discovery of North Sea oil in 1969 appeared to offer an opportunity for the regeneration of Scottish heavy industry, but outcomes fell short of early hopes. William Pike estimates that the Scottish content of expenditure on exploration, development, and production of oil in the Scottish sector of the North Sea down to 1989 was less than 23 per cent.[10] Scottish firms lacked experience of making the specialist equipment required. For example, the shipbuilding firm of Scott Lithgow took on contracts for the oil industry, but built only three semi-submersible rigs and two drill ships, all of them behind schedule and without making a profit on any of them. The John Brown yard, which was taken over by the American firm Marathon in 1972, and then by the French firm Union Industrielle d'Enterprise (UIE) in 1980, enjoyed only moderate success constructing rigs and, later, production platforms.[11] Most Scottish heavy industry was located in the west of the country, but the best sites for rig construction were on the east coast. Pike argues that had North Sea oil development been slower and subject to greater government control, as in Norway, Scottish firms would have had more time in which to adjust to oil-industry standards. However, successive London governments in the 1970s and 1980s looked to rapid development of the North Sea as a means of ending the UK's hitherto chronic balance-of-payments problems, as well as of bringing in revenue. In the event, rapidly growing unemployment after 1979 meant that much of the additional revenue had to be expended on social security. International oil companies were anxious to exploit the North Sea quickly in the wake of the OPEC price hike in 1973, and preferred to place orders with experienced suppliers abroad rather than wait for Scottish firms to acquire the necessary knowledge and skills. In 1985 the OPEC cartel broke and the price

---

[8] A. K. Cairncross, ed., *The Scottish Economy: A Statistical Account of Scottish Life* (Cambridge, 1954).

[9] Scottish Council (Development and Industry), *Inquiry into the Scottish Economy, 1960–61* (1961).

[10] William Pike, 'The Development of the North Sea Oil Industry to 1989, with Special Reference to Scotland's Contribution' (PhD thesis, Aberdeen University, 1991), 263, and 'The Oil Price Crisis and its Impact on Scottish North Sea Development, 1986–1988', *Scottish Economic and Social History*, 13 (1993), 56–71. Pending publication of Alex Kemp, *The Official History of North Sea Oil and Gas*, the best general account is Christopher Harvie, *Fool's Gold: The Story of North Sea Oil* (London, 1994), which has been described by its author as 'an interim and necessarily somewhat journalistic account'—'The Development of North Sea Oil and Gas', witness seminar held on 11 December 1999 (Institute of Contemporary British History, 2002, www.icbh.ac.uk/witness/northsea), 37.

[11] Sam McKinstry, 'Transforming John Brown's Shipyard: The Drilling Rig and Offshore Fabrication Businesses of Marathon and UIE, 1972–1997', *Scottish Economic and Social History*, 18 (1998), 33–60.

of oil fell, ending the North Sea boom. Some Scottish firms established a permanent presence in the oil and gas industry, but mainly as suppliers of onshore and offshore logistic, engineering, and drilling services. Of these the most successful was the Aberdeen-based John Wood Group, which has developed into an international energy-services company operating in fifty countries. However, the opportunity to develop indigenous technology and manufacturing capacity had been largely lost.

Scotland's traditional source of energy, coal, was affected by changes in oil prices. Coal had long been losing market share to oil, and employment in mining in 1973 was only a third of what it had been in 1957. The actions of the OPEC cartel in 1973 gave coal a price advantage, but the industry still faced competition from natural gas and imported coal. Moreover, years of retrenchment had left the industry with no capacity to respond to market expansion. In 1977, in an attempt to reduce heavy losses incurred in deep mining in Scotland, the Labour government brokered a five-year agreement between the National Coal Board (NCB) and the electricity industry in Scotland, whereby Scottish power stations guaranteed minimum purchases of coal at reduced prices. The reduction in prices was made possible partly by a government subsidy and partly by the closure of some uneconomic pits. The National Union of Mineworkers agreed to the latter in return for NCB undertakings to invest in other Scottish pits. Seven pits were closed but in the fifth year of the agreement (1981–2) all the remaining twelve pits were making operating losses. Meanwhile the Conservatives' Coal industry Act of 1980 had set the goal of a self-funding, unsubsidized industry by 1983/4, something that was almost impossible to achieve while the post-1979 recession was reducing demand for coal.[12] The implications were particularly serious for the Scottish Area of the NCB, given that, according to NCB figures in 1984, it incurred more than half of the UK industry's current loss on deep mining although it was responsible for little more than 5 per cent of UK output of coal. The government eased the industry's cash limits when confronted with the prospect of a miners' strike in Scotland in 1981, and used the breathing space to make preparations that enabled it to defeat the national (UK) miners' strike in 1984–5.[13] With the fall in the price of oil in 1985 any hope of the Scottish Area meeting the requirements of the 1980 Act disappeared, and by the end of the decade only two pits were active. With the failure of an attempted miners' buyout at Monktonhall in 1997, only Longannet in Fife remained, dependent on a contract to supply an adjacent electricity-generating station, and after that pit was flooded in 2002 an industry that had employed twenty-seven thousand men thirty years earlier became extinct, apart from open-cast mining.

Shipbuilding in Scotland, in common with the rest of the UK, had also lapsed into a state of dependency on the state before the Thatcher government took office in 1979. Failure to modernize in the post-war period meant that, once an initial boom ended in the late 1950s, Scottish yards were unable to match competition from Germany, the

---

[12] William Ashworth, *The History of the British Coal Industry*, vol. 5: *The Nationalized Industry* (Oxford, 1986), 236–7, 330–1, 381–2, 414–16.
[13] Jim Phillips, 'Workplace Conflict and the Origins of the 1984–85 Miners' Strike in Scotland', *Twentieth Century British History*, 20 (2009), 152–72.

Netherlands, Sweden, and Japan, where credit arrangements or subsidies encouraged investment in more modern techniques, and where industrial relations were better. In return for financial assistance, the shipbuilding firms agreed in 1967 to the Clyde yards being rationalized into two groups and the east-coast yards into one group. The Conservative government attempted to stop support for the industry in 1971, prompting a famous work-in organized by the shop stewards at the Upper Clyde Shipbuilders, which led in 1972 to the retention of two of UCS's yards, Yarrow and Fairfield, renamed Govan Shipbuilders. Demand for ships fell in the post-1973 recession, and in 1977 shipbuilding was nationalized. In 1979/80 Scottish yards were responsible for half of British Shipbuilders' losses, and closures and redundancies were inevitable. The nationalized corporation was privatized and its assets disposed of. Yarrows, which specialized in warships, was purchased in 1985 by a major defence contractor, GEC, who sold it to BAE Systems in 1999–2000. Fairfields was bought in 1988 by the Norwegian group Kvaerner Industrier, which modernized the yard to specialize in the construction of liquefied natural gas and chemical tankers, but by the later 1990s the market for such vessels was depressed and in 2000 the yard was also sold to BAE Systems. With the tailing off of orders for oil rigs and production platforms, and the closure of UIE's former John Brown's yard in 2001, the industry became heavily dependent upon warship construction. By 2009 shipbuilding provided work for 5,400 Scots, compared with 40,600 in 1971.

In the early 1960s considerable hopes were vested in motor-vehicle production as an alternative to shipbuilding as a market for steel, and as a stimulus to light engineering. However, the British Motor Corporation (BMC) and the Rootes group agreed to come to Scotland only because of government pressure, including both financial inducements and the withholding of industrial development certificates from sites closer to areas where the industry was concentrated. BMC invested in 1961 in a factory at Bathgate in West Lothian to make trucks, and Rootes followed in 1963 with a car factory at Linwood. The Linwood project was handicapped by the mediocrity of its products, initially the Hillman Imp, and plagued by poor industrial relations. Workers accustomed to the craft labour and work group autonomy embodied in the shipbuilding trades were alienated by the deskilling involved in working on automated assembly lines, and strikes and other forms of protest were frequent. Remote location from suppliers and markets, and the weak financial position of the factory's owners, were further factors that ensured that Linwood did not flourish even when the economy was buoyant. The American Chrysler Corporation took control of Rootes in 1967 as part of a rescue plan involving a government subsidy. Employment at Linwood rose from 7,600 in that year to 8,400 in the early 1970s. However, profits were elusive. In 1978, only two years after receiving a further government subsidy, Chrysler UK was acquired by the French firm Peugeot Citroën, which showed little interest in Linwood. The end came in the post-1979 recession, Linwood closing in 1981, and two years later the BMC factory at Bathgate also ceased production.[14]

---

[14] Alison Gilmour, 'The Trouble with Linwood: Compliance and Coercion in the Car Plant, 1963–1981', *Journal of Scottish Historical Studies*, 27 (2007), 75–93; Jim Phillips, *The Industrial Politics of Devolution: Scotland in the 1960s and 1970s* (Manchester, 2008), 13–15, 27–35, 41–4, 169, 180–1.

The decline first of shipbuilding and then motor-vehicle manufacture was bound to impact unfavourably on the steel industry. Indeed, the political decision in 1958 to erect Colvilles' steel-strip mill at Ravenscraig near Motherwell was taken in the belief that the high-quality light strip and sheet steel it would produce was a prerequisite for the development of motor-vehicle production and light engineering in Scotland. Prime Minister Harold Macmillan was concerned that unemployment was higher in Scotland than the UK average, and wanted jobs taken to the workers. As a result, an opportunity to relocate the steel industry to the Clyde coast, to minimize transport costs of imported ores, was missed. Sir Andrew McCance, the chairman of Colvilles, the company that built the mill, predicted it would be a financial disaster, but, granted a government loan facility, he gave way to political pressure. In the event, there was insufficient demand for the mill's products to make it profitable, and by the time Colvilles was nationalized in 1967 the company was close to bankruptcy.[15] When the Linwood car factory closed in 1981, Ravenscraig lost its major customer. It remained open only because Scottish Conservatives were reluctant to incur the opprobrium of closing what was still a nationalized enterprise. However, following the privatization of the British Steel Corporation in 1988, Ravenscraig had to pay its way and, despite improvements in labour productivity, production finally ceased in 1992.[16] The industry is not extinct in Scotland, however: there is a steel mill at Dalzell in Motherwell, and in 2010 its owner, the multinational Corus, announced that it would invest £8 million to help meet rising demand for heavy-plate products, creating sixty jobs there and at the neighbouring Clydebridge site.

Attempts to establish industrial growth points with the aid of government subsidies in the Highlands were likewise unsuccessful. A wood-pulp and paper mill was built between 1963 and 1965 by Wiggins Teape at Corpach near Fort William, with a view to providing a market for highland forestry. However, there were technical problems with the process chosen for producing pulp, which proved not to be particularly suitable for the type of paper most in demand. The decision to close the mill was taken in April 1979 and production ceased in 1981. An aluminium smelter was constructed between 1969 and 1972 at Invergordon, but there were technical problems with the supply of electricity, and the effects on demand for aluminium of the recession of 1980–81, allied to the strength of sterling, led to the smelter's closure in 1981.

The decline in employment in textiles began well before 1979. The jute industry, centred on Dundee, had been protected since the Second World War by a government Jute Control that fixed prices of imported goods. However, higher prices encouraged substitution: for example, paper instead of hessian for sacks, or man-made fibres for carpet backing. Employment in jute fell from a peak of twenty-one thousand in the mid-1950s to sixteen thousand by 1969, when the Jute Control was replaced by a system of quotas, and to seven thousand by 1979. The quota agreements were allowed to lapse in 1984 and production ceased in 1998. Polypropylene, a synthetic fibre, was adopted as an alternative to

---

[15]  Peter Payne, *Colvilles and the Scottish Steel Industry* (Oxford, 1979), 374–83, 393–405, 424.

[16]  David Stewart, 'Fighting for Survival: The 1980s Campaign to Save Ravenscraig Steelworks', *Journal of Scottish Historical Studies*, 25 (2005), 40–57.

jute by some firms from the late 1960s, but polypropylene required only about one-sixth of the labour per yard required in jute. Moreover, polypropylene production came to be dominated by the producers of the raw material, multinational petrochemical firms that organized the industry on a global scale. Don and Low of Forfar, a highly profitable firm in the 1980s, became a wholly owned subsidiary of Shell in 1986, thereby gaining access to the multinational's research and development facilities and financial resources for investment at the cost of loss of independence.[17] Of the old Dundee textile firms, Low and Bonar maintain a presence in the city, producing carpet yarn and polyethylene grass yarns, but the firm is now an international group and its headquarters were moved to London in 2000. The dominant firm in the Paisley thread industry, J & P Coates, amalgamated with Vantona Viyella in 1967 to form Coates Viyella, registered in Uxbridge, Middlesex. Despite diversification into synthetic fabrics in the 1950s, the Paisley mills found it difficult to compete with cheap foreign imports. Coates established mills in India and Brazil, and the last mill in Paisley closed in 1993. Between 1965 and 1979 output in the Border knitwear industry fell by 38 per cent and the labour force from 20,400 to 14,700; rationalization in the 1980s saw a further loss of over 60 per cent of manufacturing capacity. In Ayrshire the US chemical company Monsanto closed its nylon factories at Dundonald and Cumnock in 1979, but a remnant of the cotton industry—about one in five of the mills that had been active in the 1950s—survived into the twenty-first century by specializing in high-quality goods. Harris tweed was protected by statute, in that it must be handwoven in the Outer Hebrides, but following changes in fashion towards lighter materials, and an ill-conceived attempt in 2007 to standardize production by reducing the range of designs, an industry that had employed up to two thousand weavers in the 1970s was on the verge of extinction in 2009, with only 130 weavers in work. The importance of entrepreneurship and an eye for fashion was shown elsewhere in the clothing industry by the example of Michelle Mone, whose lingerie company MJM International, which started in Glasgow in 1996, was valued at £48 million in 2008.

No industry was more dependent on international markets than whisky, with about 80 per cent of output being exported. Consequently the rise of sterling in 1980 led to a sharp decline of sales. For most of the period, however, whisky was sufficiently profitable to attract takeover bids from outside Scotland, with the multinational Diageo becoming the dominant firm in 1997. The industry was protected in so far as Scotch whisky could only be distilled in Scotland (although there has been an increase since the 1970s in the proportion of bulk-blended whisky bottled and packaged overseas), but rationalization led to a decline in direct employment from 23,600 in 1978 to 9,500 in 2000. Elsewhere in the food and drinks sector there were signs that Scottish firms could expand. A. G. Barr, the makers of Irn-Bru, a carbonated soft drink dating from 1901, increased production in the 1990s by moving from Glasgow to a new plant in Cumbernauld, and using innovative marketing campaigns to make the brand the third most popular in the UK after

Coca-Cola and Pepsi. Irn-Bru is also manufactured under licence in North America, Russia, and South Africa. Another success story concerns Baxters of Fochabers, a family firm dating back to 1868, which expanded output of its range of soups and other food products in the 1980s by responding to changing consumer tastes and improving marketing and distribution, and went on to acquire ownership of food companies in Canada in 2007 and Australia in 2009.

The most successful industrial sector in the late twentieth century was electronics, a category including avionics, computers, semiconductors, and electrical components. Major American multinationals created branch factories in the post-war period, attracted by cheap female labour and the chance to exploit the potentially large European market, as well as by government financial incentives. Further overseas firms followed from the 1960s, and by the late 1970s electronics was the manufacturing sector attracting most inward investment. Employment rose from about thirty thousand in 1970 to forty-six thousand by 1997. Productivity growth was striking: output rose by 556 per cent between 1980 and 1992, while employment rose by only 12 per cent. Had it not been for electronics, industrial output in Scotland would have fallen instead of rising in the 1990s. On the other hand, 'Silicon Glen', stretching from Ayrshire to Dundee, was then overly dependent on multinationals interested in low-cost assembly, with only 12 per cent of material inputs sourced locally in 1993. Output fell by over 40 per cent between 2000 and 2003 as a result of a worldwide downturn in information and computer technologies, and there was an exodus of assembly work to low-cost locations. Since then there has been an increased emphasis on research and development, with links being established between universities and the industry in such fields as microelectronics, nanotechnology, optoelectronics, and digital media.

Overall, Scottish industry became more competitive after 1979 as labour-intensive industries were replaced by more capital-intensive ones. Whereas productivity growth in manufacturing in Scotland had lagged behind the G7 average in the 1960s and 1970s, in the 1980s the average annual change, 5.2 per cent, was higher than the G7 average (3.5 per cent) and a striking improvement on the Scottish figure for the 1970s (2 per cent).[18] Improvement was not confined to new industries, like electronics. Innovation and an eye for market opportunities could bring success even in older sectors, such as food and drink, and textiles and clothing.

# SERVICES

Financial services provide a remarkable example of an old-established sector innovating and expanding. For example, in 1959 the Bank of Scotland became the first British bank to install a computer to process accounts centrally, and in the 1970s the Clydesdale was a

---

[18] Gavin McCrone, 'European Challenges to Scotland', *Scotland Europa Centre*, paper no. 7 (Brussels, 1996), 20–1.

pioneer of automated banking. Despite increasing use of labour-saving information technology, employment in financial services increased from 63,400 in 1985 to 112,700 in 2005. Scottish banks, insurance companies, and investment trusts, with associated accountancy and legal services, had accumulated experience which, combined with an educated and numerate labour force, and low costs compared with London, gave them a comparative advantage. In the seven years following deregulation of British financial markets in 1986, the funds under management by Scottish life offices and independent fund managers increased threefold, placing Edinburgh in fourth place among European financial centres after London, Frankfurt, and Paris in terms of equity assets. In 2008 financial services accounted for over 7 per cent of Scotland's GDP.

Scottish clearing banks had long been open to takeovers by their English equivalents: the British Linen Bank, the Clydesdale, and the National Bank of Scotland had lost their independence in 1918–19, and Barclays acquired a substantial stake in the Bank of Scotland when a merger between the latter and the British Linen Bank was completed in 1971. In 1979 Lloyds Bank made a takeover approach to the Royal Bank of Scotland (RBS), which the latter's board rejected. In response to this pressure, RBS began talks in 1980 with Standard Chartered Bank that resulted in a bid. A counter-bid was made by the Hongkong and Shanghai Banking Corporation (now HSBC). There followed a campaign to preserve RBS's independence. It was argued that Scotland derived major benefit from having two independent banks, not only in terms of employment but also by providing services for Scottish business. Among the people who gave evidence to the Monopolies and Mergers Commission to this effect was George Matthewson, then chief executive of the Scottish Development Agency, who subsequently as chief executive of RBS built it up into one of the UK's biggest banks.[19] In 1999 the usual direction of takeovers was reversed when the Bank of Scotland and RBS competed in making hostile bids for the National Westminster, a London clearing bank twice the size of either. RBS won, making it the UK's second-largest banking group; considerable efficiency savings were made, largely south of the border, and back-office functions were concentrated in a new £350-million headquarters in Edinburgh. The Bank of Scotland, fearing a hostile takeover during a period of consolidation in the financial-services sector, sought security in a merger in 2001 with Halifax plc to form HBOS. However, HBOS was British rather Scottish, having its operational headquarters in West Yorkshire, although its corporate headquarters were in Edinburgh.

The survival of the Scottish banks down to the 1990s was attributed by the Bank of Scotland's official historian to a tradition of knowing borrowers' ability to repay and carefully working out the limits of risk.[20] These were not conspicuous characteristics of HBOS or RBS in the period 2001–8. The ready availability of funds on international money markets prior to the 'credit crunch' of September 2008 encouraged banks to borrow in order to increase their lending, while falling interest rates led to greater risk-taking in order to maximize profits. Such behaviour was common among the world's

---

[19]  Cmnd. 8472.
[20]  Richard Saville, *Bank of Scotland: A History 1695–1995* (Edinburgh, 1996), 812–13.

bankers, who believed, wrongly as it turned out, that risk could be minimized by being diversified through new forms of paper assets, collateralized debt obligations, and credit-default swaps, which obscured who the ultimate borrower was. All major banks suffered losses when it became apparent that many of the ultimate sources of the income for these assets, often poor people who had taken out 'sub-prime' mortgages on houses in the USA, could not maintain payments. HBOS and RBS, however, made mistakes that led to a loss of their independence. The Halifax component of HBOS, having previously been a building society, was heavily exposed to residential property, and a policy of diversifying risk would have pointed to a decrease in the proportion of lending secured against property; instead HBOS lent extensively to building firms or to commercial-property companies that proved to be unable to service loans once the credit-fuelled boom was over. On 17 September 2008, following the failure of the American bank Lehman Brothers and the freezing of money markets, there was intense speculation in HBOS shares and the government agreed that a takeover bid by Lloyds TSB would not be referred to the Competition Commission. Although the arguments in favour of Scotland having two independent banks were no less compelling in 2008 than in 1980, attempts to maintain HBOS's independence were brushed aside by the Treasury, and the takeover took effect in January 2009.

Meanwhile RBS had undertaken a huge expansion of its balance sheet relative to its capital base since Sir Fred Goodwin succeeded Matthewson as chief executive in 2001. RBS's vulnerability was increased by participation in a consortium with a Belgian and a Spanish bank to take over the Dutch bank ABN Amro in October 2007, whereby it acquired more sub-prime assets at a price above what Barclays had been willing to offer in a rival bid. In the next eleven months RBS shares fell from 402.47p to 71.7p. On 13 October 2008 the government moved to recapitalize the banks, giving it stakes of 43 per cent in the Lloyds TSB/HBOS bank and 57 per cent in RBS. On 19 January 2009 RBS shares fell by two-thirds to 11.6p, following the announcement of a £28 billion loss for 2008—the biggest in UK corporate history (the corresponding loss by HBOS was £10.8 billion). Further government assistance raised the state's holding in RBS in November 2009 to 84 per cent.

Consolidation and loss of independence were characteristics of other Scottish financial services. Perth-based General Accident acquired Yorkshire Insurance in 1967, becoming one of the largest composite insurance companies; in 1998 it merged with Commercial Union, and two years later there was a further merger with Norwich Union to form what is now Aviva. At the beginning of the 1990s Scotland had three powerful mutual life-insurance companies: Standard Life, Scottish Widows, and Stirling-based Scottish Amicable. Following demutualization, Scottish Amicable was taken over by Prudential in 1997 and Scottish Widows by Lloyds Bank in 2000. Standard Life demutualized in 2006 but retains its independence and headquarters in Edinburgh. Aberdeen Asset Management, established in 1983 by way of a management buyout, expanded in 2000–9 by acquiring a number of Scottish fund managers and parts of Deutsche Asset Management and Credit Suisse Asset Management to become the UK's largest listed fund manager. A formal merger in 2006 of Alliance Trust with Second Alliance Trust, two companies that had long shared the same headquarters in Dundee, made it the largest investment trust in the UK. There was much more, then, to Scottish financial services than two failed banks. Even so, employment in financial services peaked in 2005 (Fig. 35.4), before the credit crunch, and it seems a limit to the size of the sector has been reached.

Tourism is one of Scotland's largest business sectors, providing direct employment for 218,200 people in 2006 according to Visit Scotland. It was not clear how many of these jobs were part-time or seasonal. There is no tourism category in the annual official statistics, but trends are probably mirrored in the category of hotels and catering. Employment in hotels and catering was static at less than 110,000 for most of the 1980s, but rose thereafter to 180,400 in 2006 (see Fig. 35.4). Tourism became big business, with major improvements in the quality of accommodation. In the early post-war years tourism had differed little from that of the Victorian period, being largely geared to British visitors, with seaside resorts, hydro hotels, fishing, and golf being the principal attractions. The advent of cheap package air tours to resorts abroad where sunshine could be relied upon was a severe challenge that led in 1969 to the creation of the government-funded Scottish Tourist Board (Visit Scotland's predecessor). Scotland still competes internationally thanks to its scenery and rich historical and literary heritage.

A distinctive feature of the Scottish economy was the higher proportion of GDP accounted for by government and public services (28.8 per cent in 2004) compared with the UK average (23.5 per cent). Allocation of public expenditure under the Barnett Formula of

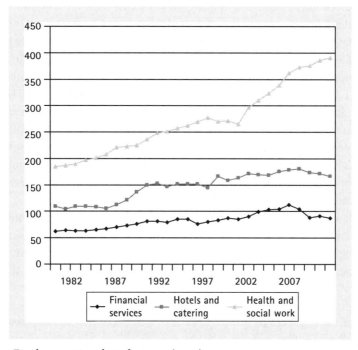

FIGURE 35.4 Employment in selected sectors (000s)

*Sources: Employee jobs by detailed industry, 1982–2009, Office for National Statistics.*

1978 and its later modifications perpetuated a situation that was more generous to Scotland than to England or Wales, and public expenditure per head in Scotland was consistently higher than the UK average. The numbers employed in the public sector increased after devolution in 1999, particularly in health and social work (see Fig. 35.4).[21] However, by 2010 the growth in the UK government's budget deficit and the national debt had reached the limit of financial markets' tolerance, and the expansion of public-sector employment was over.

# REGIONAL DIFFERENCES

As David Newlands points out, neoclassical economic growth theory suggests that differences between regions should decline over time, as prices guide capital to invest where profits are greatest, and labour to move to where wages are highest. On the other hand, theories of cumulative causation suggest that market forces create disparities as regions specialize in different industries, which generate clusters of interlinked firms drawing upon local skills and experience.[22] On the whole, Scottish experience in the late twentieth century suggests that cumulative causation was the dominant source of change, for good or ill. It is instructive to compare the fortunes of Scotland's four largest cities and their surrounding regions. The Glasgow area had been an early example of a successful industrial cluster in the nineteenth century. However, the Clyde Valley Regional Plan of 1946 concluded that shipbuilding had monopolized too many of the west of Scotland's resources, a view endorsed by Sydney Checkland, who noted in his study of Glasgow that heavy engineering discouraged the growth of other industries.[23] The west of Scotland's limited range of industrial skills compared with the English Midlands became all too apparent in the 1960s and 1970s as the Linwood experiment progressed. Edinburgh, on the other hand, had never been dominated by a single industry and, as Scotland's principal administrative, legal, and financial centre, was well placed to benefit from a shift in the economy from industry to services. GDP per head in the Strathclyde region increased by 32.4 per cent in real terms between 1977 and 1995, but Lothian's increased by 57.8 per cent. Strathclyde's share of Scotland's population fell from 49.2 per cent at the time of the 1971 census to 44.4 per cent thirty years later; over the same period Lothian's share rose from 14.3 per cent to 15.4 per cent.

As a result of the North Sea oil boom being concentrated on Aberdeen, the Grampian region's GDP per head increased by 73.8 per cent in real terms between 1977 and 1995; the comparable figure for Tayside, Dundee's hinterland, was 40.7 per cent. Whereas in 1971 the populations of Aberdeen and Dundee had been about the same size, just over

---

[21] The official statistics for employment in health and social work do not distinguish between public and private sector, but most is in the public sector.

[22] David Newlands, 'The Regional Economies of Scotland', in Thomas Devine, Clive Lee, and George Peden, eds., *The Transformation of Scotland: The Economy since 1700* (Edinburgh, 2005), 160–1.

[23] S. G. Checkland, *The Upas Tree: Glasgow 1875–1975* (Glasgow, 1976), 48.

180,000, by 2001 Aberdeen's had risen to 213,000 but Dundee's had fallen to 142,000. Dundee had managed to reduce its dependence on jute through inward investment by American firms in the post-war period, but in the 1970s these largely branch-factory operations began to contract. Multinational oil companies preferred to cluster in and around Aberdeen. By the end of the century the largest employers in Dundee were the National Health Service, the city's two universities, and the local authority. Jim Tomlinson suggests that Dundee is an example of a city that has moved from integration with the international economy, first through jute and then through multinational companies, to increasing disengagement, a process he calls 'deglobalisation'.[24]

Despite falling employment in agriculture, forestry, and fishing, most rural areas did not experience depopulation. Between 1971 and 1997 the Highland Region's share of Scotland's population rose from 3.3 per cent to 4.1 per cent; Dumfries and Galloway's from 2.7 per cent to 2.9 per cent; and the Borders, despite the problems of the textile industry, from 1.9 per cent to 2.1 per cent. In the Highlands the population decline, which had begun in the 1840s, began to be reversed from 1965, when the establishment of the Highlands and Islands Development Board was followed by a marked increase in public expenditure aimed at stimulating economic activity. The granting by the European Union in 1994–9 of Objective 1 status, reserved for regions with less than 75 per cent of average EU income per head, and transitional status in 2000–6, had a similar effect. Improved roads in the Highlands encouraged tourism. In the Lowlands agricultural subsidies benefited market towns indirectly, as well as farmers directly, and the boundary between cities and countryside became increasingly porous as commuters used their cars to turn rural communities into Arcadian suburbs.

Table 35.1 shows how disparities in regional GDP per head increased during the 1980s, with Grampian and Lothian pulling ahead of the rest of the country. Table 35.2 breaks the country down into smaller units, and shows that the city of Glasgow improved its relative position, but Inverclyde and Renfrewshire, and Ayrshire, became relatively poorer. Both tables warn against making sweeping generalizations about the Scottish economy. For example, the Scots have been criticized for lack of enterprise, but the business start-up rate is not uniform across the country. The number of new businesses in 2008 per ten thousand people varied widely between the four principal cities: Aberdeen, 45.2; Edinburgh, 39.5; Glasgow, 32.1; Dundee, 23.2. Out of sixty-four cities in the UK, Aberdeen ranked 10th, Edinburgh 20th, Glasgow 44th, and Dundee 63rd. The stock of VAT-registered businesses also varied markedly, with rural areas typically having rates of three hundred firms per ten thousand people, well above the UK average, but urban areas having rates below two hundred. The data suggest two or three major reasons why business start-up rates differ. One is the expectation of profit, which is linked to GDP and population growth—both highest in and around Edinburgh and Aberdeen. Another is availability of capital, which is linked to home ownership, since property can provide security for loans. Edinburgh and Aberdeen

---

[24] David Newlands, 'The Oil Economy', in W. Hamish Fraser and Clive Lee, eds., *Aberdeen 1800–2000* (East Linton, 2000), 126–52; Jim Tomlinson, 'The Deglobalisation of Dundee, c.1900–2000', *Journal of Scottish Historical Studies*, 29 (2009), 123–40.

have high house prices, and rural areas have much higher rates of home ownership than urban areas with large local-authority housing estates. It has also been suggested that people whose only experience of employment has been in large workplaces like shipyards or steel mills, or with local authorities, may be less entrepreneurial than others, and the urban–rural difference would be consistent with that explanation.

### Table 35.1  Regional GDP per head in Scotland (UK=100)

|                        | 1981  | 1991  |
|------------------------|-------|-------|
| Highland               | 99.2  | 87.3  |
| Grampian               | 120.5 | 134.8 |
| Tayside                | 89.7  | 89.1  |
| Fife                   | 98.7  | 84.7  |
| Lothian                | 102.7 | 110.5 |
| Central                | 100.9 | 87.7  |
| Strathclyde            | 89.8  | 88.3  |
| Borders                | 87.2  | 81.5  |
| Dumfries and Galloway  | 94.3  | 86.6  |
| Scottish average       | 96.3  | 95.8  |

*Source*: Clive Lee, *Scotland and the United Kingdom: The Economy and the Union in the Twentieth Century* (Manchester, 1995), 55.

### Table 35.2  GVA per head in selected areas (UK=100)

|                             | 1995 | 2005 |
|-----------------------------|------|------|
| Shetland                    | 98   | 95   |
| Highlands and Islands       | 75   | 74   |
| Aberdeen and NE Scotland    | 139  | 125  |
| Dundee and Angus            | 96   | 87   |
| Fife and Clackmannan        | 77   | 70   |
| Edinburgh                   | 150  | 159  |
| West Lothian                | 118  | 97   |
| Glasgow                     | 121  | 137  |
| Inverclyde and Renfrewshire | 100  | 79   |
| North Lanarkshire           | 72   | 76   |
| North and East Ayrshire     | 80   | 65   |
| Borders                     | 84   | 66   |
| Dumfries and Galloway       | 84   | 69   |
| Scotland                    | 100  | 95   |

*Source*: *Scottish Economic Statistics* (Edinburgh, 2008), table 1.3.

There were also regional and class disparities in social conditions. While the problems of workless households and of people eking out an existence on social-security benefits have not been restricted to any one region, they are most prevalent in former industrial areas, mainly in the west of Scotland. Neoclassical growth theory may be correct in stating that capital and labour will respond to market forces to achieve an optimum distribution in the long run, but for some communities a generation has not been long enough.

# Unanswered Questions and Future Research

From the vantage point of 2011, when most Scots are visibly more prosperous than when industrial employment peaked in the mid-1960s, the economic changes of the 1980s seem more benign than they did at the time. Even so, it is open to debate whether de-industrialization was unnecessarily abrupt and whether some of its adverse social consequences could have been avoided. Notwithstanding an expansion of higher education, it is not clear that all of the labour force has been provided with the education and skills appropriate to the knowledge-based economy of the future envisaged by Scottish government agencies. There are other questions in a formidable agenda for research on the last fifty years. For example, business historians could investigate why some firms in declining sectors like textiles survived and sometimes prospered. The financial sector is in need of attention, Charles Munn's forthcoming history of the Alliance Trust being a welcome start. Tourism requires a study equivalent to Alastair Durie's ground-breaking book on the pre-1939 period.[25] Comparative urban and regional history could bring out the diversity of Scotland's experience of economic growth and social change.

## Further Reading

Devine, Thomas, *The Scottish Nation 1700–2007* (London, 2006).

Devine, Thomas, Lee, Clive, and Peden, George, eds., *The Transformation of Scotland: The Economy since 1700* (Edinburgh, 2005).

Fraser, W. Hamish, and Lee, Clive, eds., *Aberdeen 1800–2000: A New History* (East Linton, 2000).

Harvie, Christopher, *No Gods and Precious Few Heroes: Twentieth-Century Scotland*, 3rd edn. (Edinburgh, 1998).

Lee, Clive, *Scotland and the United Kingdom: The Economy and the Union in the Twentieth Century* (Manchester, 1995).

Payne, Peter, *Growth and Contraction: Scottish Industry c.1860–1990* (Dundee, 1992).

---

[25] Alastair Durie, *Scotland for the Holidays: Tourism in Scotland c.1780–1939* (East Linton, 2003).

Payne, Peter, 'The Economy', in Thomas Devine and Richard Finlay, eds., *Scotland in the 20th Century* (Edinburgh, 1996), 13–45.

Peat, Jeremy, and Boyle, Stephen, *An Illustrated Guide to the Scottish Economy*, ed. Bill Jamieson (London, 1999).

Phillips, Jim, *The Industrial Politics of Devolution: Scotland in the 1960s and 1970s* (Manchester, 2008).

Saville, Richard, ed., *The Economic Development of Scotland 1950–1980* (Edinburgh, 1985).

Tomlinson, Jim, and Whatley, Christopher, eds., *Jute No More: Transforming Dundee* (Dundee, 2011).

······························································

# CHAPTER 36

# A NEW SCOTLAND? SOCIETY AND CULTURE<sup>*</sup>

······························································

## DAVID McCRONE

SCOTLAND is defined as much by what it has ceased to be as by what it has become. Scotland in the early twentieth century was marked by the dominance of Capital, local and private, by Empire, and by Protestantism. It was a rich and affluent society, but wealth was highly concentrated, and if you were unlucky enough to be at the bottom of the heap, life was short and fairly brutish. By the mid-twentieth century, much of this was being swept away by the legacy of war and the welfare state, one following the other as part of the social bargain. Scotland was 'British' because it was sutured into the fabric of the state. Mid-century was the high point of electoral similarity between Scotland and England, in a classic two-party system as Tories and Labour took over nine of every ten votes in both countries.

So what of Scotland today? In the post-war period, Scotland's economic transformation owed much to the influx of foreign companies, and is subject to the ebb and flow of global capitalism in which it has little choice but to participate. Empire no more; British no more?—not quite, though in truth the vast majority of Scots owe their allegiance to national (Scottish) identity, rather than the state (British) variety. The fact that only four in one hundred people born and living in Scotland give priority to being British over being Scottish is surely a change from the experiences and aspirations of our parents and grandparents. Warfare no longer binds us into being British, and the long process of dismantling the welfare state begun by Mrs Thatcher and the neo-liberals shows no sign of retreating. Above all, the recovery of a parliament at the cusp of the new century is surely the mark of modern Scotland, and lying behind it, the assertion of Home Rule and more self-government.

* I am grateful to Michael Anderson, Lindsay Paterson, and the anonymous referees for their helpful comments.

Our concern is with how Scotland has changed, which begs questions—in what respect, and over what time period. The timescale of this chapter, broadly, is the last twenty-five years, taking us back to the mid-1980s. This chapter will focus on three aspects of our story: Scotland's demography, its social stratification, and social values and attitudes. First of all, population is elemental; Scotland is its people. How demography is patterned and structured is both a reflection of wider social and economic processes, and in turn helps to determine them. Second, there is the issue of how Scotland is stratified in terms of the distribution of power and resources. Once more, there is interesting tension between reality and belief. 'We're a' Jock Tamson's bairns' may be a comforting tale to tell, but it doesn't tell half the story. Finally, and relatedly, there are values and attitudes, how we as Scots see ourselves, and how we translate these into social and political practices.

Lying behind dimensions of change are issues of comparison, whether for example Scotland is changing in different ways and at a different rate than its comparators, most obviously England. The question is whether social change is driven mainly by changes in state policy (e.g. levels of macroeconomic policy), at 'national' (Scottish) levels, or indeed simply reflects structural changes common to all Western developed societies.

# Scotland's People

The population of Scotland has been at or around five million since the middle of the twentieth century, and the most recent official estimates put it at just under 5.2 million. Scotland's aggregate level of population growth is abnormally low. Compared with England, Scotland's population growth has been slower in every decade for more than two hundred years, despite being yoked together in a unitary state for that period.

In 1851 England's population was about six times that of Scotland, and by 1901, seven times. By 2001, the differential was ten to one, and population estimates suggest the gap between England and Scotland will grow. While cautious about population projections, recent data suggest that, in the next twenty-five years Scotland's population will grow by 5 per cent, whereas England's will grow by almost 20 per cent, and Wales and Northern Ireland do not lag far behind with projected population growth of 15 per cent and 11 per cent respectively (General Register Office for Scotland, 2009). It is a surprising fact that, among the twenty-seven countries currently in the European Union, only Hungary, Latvia, and Estonia actually matched Scotland in having smaller populations in 2001 than in 1971.

Scotland's failure to reproduce itself does present something of a puzzle. In part, the answers are historical, reflecting disproportionate levels of emigration and low levels of immigration, coupled with a declining birth rate. In recent years, fewer Scots have emigrated, mainly because the traditional routes to the 'old' Commonwealth countries of Canada, Australia, and New Zealand have fallen off, but it is a complicated picture.

If there has been a falling off in out-migration, and rising in-migration, mainly but not exclusively from places like Poland, changing fertility rates also explain Scotland's low level of population increase. Rates for live births per 1,000 women have been lower in Scotland than other parts of the UK. In crude terms, births in 2001 were only 40 per cent of what they were a century previously. It is, however, not simply a question of absolute decline, but in the general fertility rate, a measure based on the number of women of childbearing age. The baby boom of the 1960s fell away steeply in the 1970s and 1980s, while the rate of decline levelled off thereafter. The dramatic fall in fertility occurred among women in their twenties, whereas rates among older women have increased such that women aged thirty to thirty-four have overtaken women aged twenty-five to twenty-nine. By 2008, women over thirty accounted for half of all Scottish births. These changes in fertility rates reflect the expansion of labour-market participation for younger women, as well as shifts in lifestyle, changes that Scotland shares with comparable countries.

If Scotland's rates of fertility are marginally lower than other British countries, it is Scotland's death rate that marks it as an outlier. From about the early 1950s until the 1990s, the annual number of deaths was stable (between 60,000 and 65,000 each year), while by mid-2000 it stood at the lowest ever recorded figure of 55,000. By 2008, life expectancy[1] for men stood at seventy-five, and for women, eighty, such that men now live six years longer than they did in 1981, and women five years longer. Scotland shares a similar pattern with other comparable countries, but these figures are actually lower than the average for the twenty-seven EU countries (by about four years for men, and five years for women).

Scottish rates of dying are a dubious *cause célèbre*. Deaths from cancer, coronary heart disease, and strokes are significantly higher than for other countries in the UK. This has led epidemiologists to talk about a 'Scottish effect', whereby standardizing mortality ratios by age, sex, and social deprivation still deliver a higher death rate (by around 7+ percentage points) than for the rest of the UK.[2] This is not simply a feature of abnormal levels of social deprivation, for if we compare Glasgow and Liverpool, which are comparable in terms of class structure and levels of poverty, Scotland's largest city has a higher mortality rate. Unusually high death rates are not confined to Glasgow, but occur in west-central Scotland; West Dunbartonshire, Renfrewshire, Inverclyde, and North Lanarkshire have standardized mortality ratios of more than 10 per cent higher than the Scottish average—but none of these match Glasgow City's 27 per cent.[3]

It seems to have something to do with the shifting population geography of Scotland, for there have been significant movements of population in recent years, mainly from west to east, and from urban to rural. The areas that saw the largest population increases

---

[1] That is, how long someone born in 2008 might expect to live, assuming unchanged conditions.

[2] V. Carstairs and R. Morris, 'Deprivation: Explaining Differences Between Scotland and England and Wales', *British Medical Journal*, 299 (1989), 886–9.

[3] General Register Office for Scotland, *Scotland's Population 2009*. Hereafter, Glasgow City will be referred to as 'Glasgow' to distinguish it from the conurbation conventionally referred to as Greater Glasgow.

between 1999 and 2009 were West Lothian (+10 per cent), East Lothian (+9 per cent), and Perth and Kinross (+8 per cent); the greatest population decline occurred in Inverclyde (−6 per cent), Eilean Siar, and West Dunbartonshire (−5 per cent each). Glasgow's position is complicated (its population fell only marginally by −0.5 per cent), but Glasgow's and Edinburgh's populations seem to be converging in size.[4] Indeed, the largest absolute increase in population in any council area between 1999 and 2009 occurred in Edinburgh (+30,000). Whereas in the 1960s, the population of Glasgow was twice that of Edinburgh, by 2008 it was only 20 per cent bigger. True, the estimated population of Greater Glasgow is over 1.1 million, but as a proportion of that figure, Glasgow stands at little over half, compared with almost three-quarters half a century ago. Rural, small-town Scotland including much of the Highlands (but excluding Eilean Siar) show above-average fertility and low mortality, coupled with net in-migration; similarly, the east-coast regions around Edinburgh and Aberdeen, with high levels of inward migration, often from outwith Scotland. Post-industrial Scotland, especially in the west-central region, has lower birth rates, high mortality, levels of morbidity well above the average, and continuing out-migration.[5]

Longevity and a falling birth rate have also helped to change the composition of the population. Scotland now has marginally more people of pensionable age (20 per cent) than under sixteen (18 per cent). The population pyramid shows two bulges reflecting the two baby booms, the late 1940s and the 1960s. In the last decade there has been a significant decrease (almost 10 per cent) in people under sixteen, and between thirty and forty-four, and a rise of over 10 per cent among those over forty-five.

It is not simply a question of an ageing population, but in the way households are formed and re-formed. The number of people getting married in 2008, for example, was the lowest since the late nineteenth century. It is true that more people are cohabiting than ever before, but young people choose to remain unattached rather than enter formal or informal relationships. Marriage has become a minority pursuit among young adults, while a quarter of adults over sixteen have some experience of having been married, but no longer, at least to their original partner.

With these changes have come shifts in the composition of households. Single-adult households are already the most common form, projected to increase by a half in the next twenty years, closely followed by two-adult households, likely to increase by a quarter, changes with obvious implications for housing-stock needs. Concomitant decreases in household forms are likely among larger households (especially containing two or more adults with children), as well as three or more adults, all likely to decrease by one-third. Many Scots brought up to read the best-selling newspaper *The Sunday Post*[6] will

---

[4] In this period Edinburgh grew by 5.7 per cent, largely as a result of net inward migration (GRoS, 2009: table 1.1, p. 20).

[5] L. Paterson, F. Bechhofer, and D. McCrone, *Living in Scotland: Social and Economic Change since 1980* (Edinburgh, 2004).

[6] Founded in 1914, *The Sunday Post* had a circulation of more than a million in the post-Second World War period, before suffering a sharp decline in the past thirty years.

recall the classic cartoon image of the 'Broons'—the parents (maw and paw) and eight children (Daphne, Maggie, Hen, Joe, Horace, The Twins, and The Bairn), as well as Grandpaw Broon. Manifestly, this is a thing of history, if not mythology, for the flat in Glebe Street would surely have been hard-pressed to accommodate eleven people.

The extension of adolescence by education means that most individuals aged sixteen to twenty-four are found in 'large family' households, indicating that most have not yet left home. If we include living with a parent or step-parent, as many as eight out of ten sixteen-year-olds[7] continue to live in the 'family' home. The shift for them into small family units does not come these days until they are aged twenty-five and over. Almost three-quarters of Scottish households do not have children under the age of sixteen living with them, a significant contrast with as recently as the 1980s when two-thirds did. At the beginning of the twentieth century, there were clear class differences in family structures, with working-class families twice the size of middle-class ones,[8] but class differentials of this sort seem to have faded away to parity by the beginning of the twenty-first century. You can no longer tell people's social class by the number of siblings they have.

Surely these demographic changes simply reflect the personal and intimate decisions individuals make about their lives? Scotland is a society that struggles to reproduce itself, unlike England. The combination of falling birth rates, above-average mortality rates, and lower levels of inward migration help to create a different set of political and cultural understandings. 'Welcoming' incomers is not so much a cultural trait as an economic necessity, and Scottish governments have set about policy initiatives to attract migrants (such as 'Smart, Successful Scotland' and The Fresh Talent Initiative).[9] None of Scotland's major political parties have policies to restrict inward migration. Indeed, in-migration to Scotland has been proportionately greater than in England, but unlike its southern neighbour, the flow is mainly from England rather than from abroad. There are 400,000 English-born people living in Scotland, some 8 per cent of its population (comparably, 800,000 Scots-born live in England, reflecting the reality of an integrated labour market).

As Michael Anderson shows in Chapter 2, the distinguishing feature of Scotland has been the propensity of people for geographical mobility, either travelling to England or overseas. If these rates have fallen in the past few decades, this reflects diminishing opportunities for economic migration, notably in the former Dominion countries. There has also been considerable movement away from the cities, notably Glasgow and Dundee, the two most 'industrial' settlements in terms of employment, compared in particular with English cities.

Population changes also matter with regard to Scotland's regional geography. We might see Scotland as dominated by two cultural landscapes:[10] one, that it is a 'people-

---

[7]  Strictly speaking, those in fourth year at secondary school; see Paterson, Bechhofer, and McCrone, *Living in Scotland*, 32.

[8]  Ibid., 35.

[9]  *A Smart, Successful Scotland*, http://www.scotland.gov.uk/Resource/Doc/158455/0042945.pdf (p. 13). The *Fresh Talent: Working in Scotland Scheme* was launched in June 2005.

[10]  For an account of contrasting images of Scotland, see Andrew Blaikie's *The Scots Imagination and Modern Memory* (Edinburgh, 2010).

less place', bereft of population, imagined as rural empty space (most obviously the 'cleared' lands in the Highlands, although population densities were always low); the other, a place of teeming towns, densely populated and dominated by tenements; in George Blake's words, Scotland appears 'overweight with cities'. Both, of course, are cultural fabrications, but meaningful ones. The image is of an 'over-urbanized' Scotland, a country of 'toons'. Take this observation by Willie McIlvanney:[11]

> It seems to me that the thing Scottish writing would have to confront is the Scottish urban experience. Because the truth is for most of us that is where we have been. You take the nexus around Glasgow that's still the eye of the hurricane. I think that's where our understanding of ourselves resides.

In a country with strong regional identities around its four major cities, with distinctive media, football teams, and local cultures,[12] shifts of population to suburbs or beyond reinforce the sense of identity and change. New shifts simply reinforce rather than contradict these senses of distinct places.

## Social Class and Opportunity

Demography, of course, is neither determining nor determined, but it is manifestly connected to patterns of social inequality and social class. Arguably, living in an area of economic decline is harder than living in a more prosperous one—if nothing else, jobs are less easy to come by. On the other hand, being poor in, say, Edinburgh and Aberdeen is not the same as being poor in Glasgow and Dundee. Indeed, it may be worse, if all around you is affluence and prosperity with which you have little connection.

Levels of poverty and deprivation are concentrated in areas subject to de-industrialization. 'Multiple deprivation', measuring domains of income and employment, educational opportunity, health, access to services, and levels of crime, show significant levels of concentration within Scotland.[13] Glasgow continues to have the highest concentrations by a considerable margin, along with Inverclyde, Dundee, West Dunbartonshire, and North Ayrshire. The most deprived area in Scotland in 2009 was the Parkhead/Barrowfield area of east Glasgow. Indeed, there are some stark contrasts within the city itself, with people in east Glasgow having a life expectancy of sixty-eight years, barely improving in more than a decade.[14] The better news is that Glasgow's share

---

[11] Quoted in Jeremy Idle, 'McIlvanney, Masculinity and Scottish Literature', *Scottish Affairs*, 2 (1993) 56.

[12] See the interest in local histories and cultural forms, especially language and patois, and the personification of cities in the works of, for example, Leslie Mitchell ('Lewis Grassic Gibbon'), Hugh MacDiarmid, and Alistair Gray.

[13] Scottish Government, *Scottish Index of Multiple Deprivation 2009 Report*, October 2009 (www. scotland.gov.uk/Topics/Statistics/SIMD/): accessed 10 December 2009.

[14] Health and Well-Being Profiles, *Scottish Population Health Observatory* (Glasgow, 2008).

of deprived areas is diminishing, from 48 per cent in 2006 to 43 per cent in 2009, but this still reflects highly concentrated levels. The city has the highest proportion of its working-age population experiencing employment deprivation (18 per cent), and of these people almost two-thirds live in the most deprived areas, suggesting that individual and aggregate concentrations correlate highly.

Behind this measuring of 'deprivation' is social class, with which Scotland has a curious relationship. On the one hand, class long seems to be the key stratifier of social power, such that Scotland's politics were 'class' politics; on the other hand, the legend of meritocracy and egalitarianism, that 'we're a' Jock Tamson's bairns', is a deep, distinctive cultural marker. In large part, there is a long-standing dialectic between social inequality on the one hand and egalitarianism on the other. Social class helped to define Scotland such that not only did it provide the main structuring dimension of social inequality, but it became almost a proxy for Scotland itself, vis-à-vis England. This was given voice, and reinforcement, by class politics, and the hegemony of the labour movement.

The decline of the Conservatives, the buoyancy of Labour, and the rise of the Nationalists all seemed to give support to this thesis that Scotland was 'different'; that its politics reflected something more structural in its economy and relationship to the means of production. These political developments were premised on Scotland having a larger 'working class' and a smaller bourgeoisie than England (usually typified as inherently Conservative). Thus, it seemed 'obvious' that the growing divergence between Scotland and England was the result of structural class differences, especially as they seemed a convenient way of explaining political changes in the 1970s and 1980s. Scotland was anti-Tory because it was working class. However, the decline of the Conservative Party in Scotland was too stark and too rapid simply to be explained in terms of differential class effects. Instead, and more appropriately, the explanations swung to 'political' factors, namely, Scotland's constitutional relationships with the British state, and the growing 'democratic deficit' whereby Scots got a government at Westminster that they manifestly had not elected. This, perhaps more than anything else, persuaded many to support 'Home Rule' and a devolved Parliament, and if necessary, to use whatever party-political vehicle was most likely to achieve it.[15]

Where has that left our understanding of social class in Scotland? In general terms, its class structure reflects the facts that, as in England and elsewhere, a long-term secular decline away from manual employment has taken place. Further, the loss of indigenous commerce and industry has led to a smaller 'bourgeois' base, but, by and large, the trends are in the same direction as south of the border. Table 36.1 compares social-class distributions in England and Scotland using 2006 data from the British and Scottish Social Attitudes surveys.[16]

Although there are modest differences between England and Scotland, with Scotland having a marginally larger manual working class (+3) and England more managers and

---

[15] A. Brown, D. McCrone, L. Paterson, and P. Surridge, *The Scottish Electorate: The 1997 General Election and Beyond* (Basingstoke, 1999).

[16] A. Park et al., *British Social Attitudes: The 24th Report* (London, 2008), 259–78.

Table 36.1 Social class in England and Scotland

| Per cent by column | England* | Scotland* |
|---|---|---|
| Managers and professionals | 38 | 33 |
| Intermediate | 12 | 10 |
| Employers in small organizations/own account | 9 | 8 |
| Lower supervisory and technical | 13 | 18 |
| Semi-routine and routine workers | 28 | 31 |
| *Base* | *3,695* | *1,594* |

* People resident in the country at the time of the surveys.

professional workers (+5), it is the similarities rather than the differences that are most obvious. The fact that the ratio of managerial and professional workers to those in routine and semi-routine manual employment is virtually 1.5 to 1 (40 per cent to 27 per cent) provides confirmation that Scotland is a very different place than it was a half century before, still less the previous century. The proportion of people in manual work during the twentieth century was much higher; in 1921 it stood at 74 per cent, and even by the 1961 census it was 63 per cent. The fact that it is now less than one-third today reflects how much Scotland, and employment generally, has changed. Men and women have different patterns of employment: proportionally fewer women in higher managerial and professional occupations (−5), lower supervisory and technical (−10), and routine (−7), but more in intermediate clerical and administrative (+10), and semi-routine (+9). In general terms, the declining size of the manual working class, and the growth in professional and managerial employment, reflects changes in the nature of work itself (from manual to automated work, for example), rather than because fewer people these days are in manufacturing or extractive industries.[17] Recent analysis confirms that the largest proportional increases between 2001 and 2008 have occurred in managerial, professional, and associated technical occupations,[18] and that occupations associated with the knowledge economy are more the prerogative of male and full-time work than female and part-time work.

Has Scotland become a 'middle-class' society? Here we have to tread carefully. It is true that fewer people are in manual occupations, and more in non-manual, but we cannot simply translate occupations into social class. Many 'non-manual' occupations these days are 'routine' in being poorly paid and insecure (such as working in a call centre). Nor can we assume that people self-allocate to a social class simply on the grounds of their employment. Scots are far more likely to describe themselves as 'working class' compared with people in England, almost regardless of their own 'objective' class position. The Scottish Elections surveys of 1979 and 1999 asked people to assign themselves to 'working class' or 'middle class'. By 1999, every class showed a majority called

[17]  Paterson, Bechhofer, and McCrone, *Living in Scotland*, 87.
[18]  J. Sutherland, 'Occupational Change in Scotland, 2001–8', *Scottish Affairs*, 69 (2009), 93–121.

themselves 'working class', even the professionals.[19] While, unsurprisingly, those who remained in manual jobs (the 'working class') overwhelmingly (almost 90 per cent) described themselves as 'working class', 80 per cent who had been upwardly mobile into 'middle-class' jobs continued to say they were 'working class'. While in recent years proportionally fewer people in higher professional and managerial employment in Scotland say they are 'working class', it was still a significant minority.[20] The fact that people doing quite similar jobs in Scotland and England are able to describe themselves in different social-class terms tells us that there are important 'cultural' differences about where people place themselves in the social stratification system, and that it is not something simply derived from their 'objective' social conditions.

What about the processes of social mobility, that is, class as 'biography'? Scotland has its egalitarian myth of Jock Tamson's bairns, but there is little to distinguish its processes of social mobility from those of other UK or European countries because they share similar experiences, notably early industrialization and the demise of a peasantry. Because their economic histories are comparable, the British countries (and that includes Northern Ireland, but not the south, which has a quite different economic history) had similar trajectories. By the 1970s, a substantial section of the 'service class', those in senior professional and managerial occupations, was drawn up from the manual working class; as many as one-third in the top 'salariat' had fathers who had been in manual working-class jobs. Modern social mobility, however, does not resemble a game of snakes and ladders such that those who climb up the ladders are balanced by those who slide down the snakes.

Indeed, the transformation of occupational structures in the last fifty years has created a cadre of new non-manual labour, well paid and highly trained, who do not, in the classical Marxist sense, own the means of their own production. We see that in the transformation from a society of manual work to one of administrators and professionals. Expansion at the top allows for movement in from below—mainly through the acquisition of educational capital—while those who are already there by dint of social background take advantage of such opportunities. Economic retrenchment and industrial reorganization under 'Thatcherism' in the 1980s seem to have had very little effect on processes of social mobility and social change, unless, of course, you happened to be a Fife coalminer or a Lanarkshire steelworker.

A few figures make the point. The percentage of men who were in a higher social class than their fathers—that is, who were inter-generationally upwardly mobile—in 1975 was 42 per cent; and in 1997, 47 per cent. For England and Wales, the figures were 43 per cent and 47 per cent respectively. No difference there. Women fared marginally better than men; in 1997, 48 per cent of women in Scotland and 50 per cent in England were in a higher social class than their fathers.[21] Looking at the social origins of people in the

---

[19] Paterson, Bechhofer, and McCrone, *Living in Scotland*, 98–101.

[20] In 2003, 42 per cent so described themselves; see Paterson, Bechhofer, and McCrone, *Living in Scotland*, 99.

[21] To compare women with their fathers and not their mothers reflects the fact that far fewer women were in the paid labour market in the older generation.

'service class', those in social classes I and II,[22] almost half (46 per cent) had fathers who had been manual workers. There was also a lot of self-recruitment, for 32 per cent in the service class had fathers also belonging to that class, with the rest from routine non-manual workers (8 per cent) or self-employed (14 per cent). Only about one-third of the service class was 'self-recruited'. At the other end of the scale, and largely reflecting a shrinking manual working class, as many as 72 per cent of manual workers had fathers who were also manual workers. The manual working class is much more homogeneous in terms of social origins than the 'service class'. Few shift from that class into the manual working class—only 12 per cent of the latter, suggesting that acquiring the necessary educational and social capital to remain in relatively privileged positions keeps the children of the service class in the manner to which they have grown accustomed.

Coming from a relatively privileged class confers benefits such that people's relative mobility rates are reasonably secure. Your chances of remaining in the service class if your origins are there have not changed very much over time. It is the changing structures of social opportunity that account for upward social mobility rather than openness in the system per se. There has been a large amount of absolute mobility, while rates of *relative* mobility—working-class gains at middle-class expense—have not changed very much. Two-thirds of working adults in 2001 have been socially mobile, and most of these—again two-thirds—have been upwardly mobile.[23] The parents of those people born in the 1960s have themselves been upwardly mobile. However, it seems that their children may not be so much downwardly mobile as immobile, because the system has limits. If the top positions fill up, and the structure does not expand to fill the demand, which it might not if occupational change slows, then accommodating incomers and stayers at the upper levels may not be possible. Patterns of absolute and relative mobility differ little between men and women, apart from labour-market effects notably of gender 'segmentation', such that women are mainly in lower non-manual jobs, and men predominate in skilled manual jobs.

The role of educational expansion also plays a role between social origins and destinations, in that acquiring technical and cultural skills 'pays off' in occupational terms. It is, however, not the whole story; the service class has other ways of conferring privilege on their children, by using forms of cultural capital or through social networks, as well as more conventional inherited forms of material capital and wealth. The association between social class of origin and destination is weaker the more educated you are, suggesting that if middle-class children do not achieve the highest educational qualifications, they have other forms of cultural capital available to them to maintain their social position. Growing public and private service sectors have greater amounts of upward mobility compared with 'traditional' sectors, which are more often retrenching, offering fewer opportunities for incomers.

Structural change has its effects on 'non-secular' areas of life. It was once the case that older Roman Catholics were more likely to have been in manual working-class

---

[22] Social classes I and II are mainly professionals, managers, large proprietors, and officials.
[23] C. Iannelli and L. Paterson, 'Social Mobility in Scotland since the Middle of the Twentieth Century', *The Sociological Review*, 54(3) (2006).

jobs than adherents of other religions, giving rise to claims of religious discrimination. These days, younger Catholics have social mobility patterns very similar to
everyone else, suggesting that religion is not a barrier to social mobility, and discounting the notion that active social discrimination is what kept Catholics in their
place. With hindsight, we may have seen the passing of a historical moment, with the
offspring of poor Irish immigrants no longer confined to menial jobs, although
whether this was due to occupational processes rather than active sectarian discrimination is a moot point.[24]

Let us return to our story of social change. While there may be some slowing in rates
of mobility as occupational structures and employment opportunities retract, the lessons of recent history suggest that modern economies have a capacity to generate additional employment opportunities, and that it would take major social and economic
upheaval to have a lasting effect on how people's life chances are affected. What has happened in Scotland is similar to what has happened in other advanced industrial societies, including England. It is not that Scotland is little different from England as regards
how it handles and interprets such processes. As noted earlier, far more people in
Scotland than in England call themselves 'working class', even where they do 'middle-
class' jobs. However, structures are mediated by social and cultural accounts, and in this
respect Scotland is undoubtedly different. In the next section, we will focus particularly
on these values and attitudes.

## SOCIAL VALUES AND ATTITUDES

The most obvious ways in which Scots are different from the English is in relation to
their social identities. While it is true that most Scots, like the English, describe themselves as parents, partners, or in terms of gender, the major difference relates to national
identity.[25] Scots are twice as likely to say they are 'Scottish' than the English are to say
they are 'English'; and far less likely to describe themselves as 'British'. Put another way,
around three-quarters of 'native' Scots[26] give priority to being Scottish (and only 3 per
cent to being British); among the English the figures are 37 per cent and 13 per cent
respectively—the largest number, 46 per cent, are equally English and British.[27] This
state of affairs north of the border has not changed much in a decade, suggesting that
devolution has not made Scots more Scottish; they felt 'Scottish' at the outset, so helping
to fuel the demand for Home Rule in the 1990s.

---

[24] In other words, unskilled manual labour unable to acquire educational and technical skills to be
upwardly mobile rather than an employer operating a 'no Catholics' policy.

[25] See F. Bechhofer and D. McCrone, 'Being Scottish', in Frank Bechhofer and David McCrone, eds.,
*National Identity, Nationalism and Constitutional Change* (London, 2009).

[26] 'Native' here refers to people born and currently living in Scotland.

[27] See Bechhofer and McCrone, 'Being Scottish', 72.

It is important to stress two important aspects of Scottish identity: first, that there is very little variation by gender, age, social class, or religion, indicating that 'being Scottish' is normative and taken for granted. Secondly, there is no straightforward relationship between national identity and 'politics', either in terms of party or constitutional preferences. While it is true that 'exclusive' Scots, those who describe themselves as 'Scottish, not British', are more likely to support the SNP and vote for independence, the relationship is not straightforward, just as the few who emphasize that they are British are not staunch defenders of the Union. It is fair to say that Scottish national identity is, by and large, a matter of culture rather than politics.

What is it that makes people feel Scottish? The main markers of Scottish identity are being born in Scotland, having Scottish parents, and living there—roughly in that order. Being born in a country is an 'accident' of birth—none of us have that kind of control over our lives. What if, through no fault of your own, you don't have the requisite birth marker? Two outlier groups are interesting. Scotland's largest 'minority'—some 400,000, or 8 per cent—are people born in England. Most feel they cannot claim to be Scottish; some say they are British, while others say that they did not realize they were 'English' until they came to live in Scotland. Many of those who have lived long-term north of the border tend to say they 'come from Scotland', as opposed to simply asserting that they *are* Scottish, a much stronger claim. The second outlier group are people who are non-white—around 2 per cent of the Scottish population—mainly of Pakistani origin, who are much more willing to use hybrid forms of identity such as Scottish Muslim[28] than their equivalents south of the border for whom the 'English' (as opposed to the British) descriptor is felt to be unavailable.

Taking the longer historical view, Scottish national identity has had to be more 'civic' than 'ethnic', for its cultural and territorial diversity has meant that there is no singular identity marker such as language or religion indisputable throughout the land. Christopher Smout once expressed this helpfully as having a 'sense of place' rather than a 'sense of tribe', and this has had a long pedigree in Scotland for good reasons:

> If coherent government was to survive in the medieval and early modern past, it had, in a country that comprised Gaelic-speaking Highlanders and Scots-speaking Lowlanders, already linguistically and ethnically diverse, to appeal beyond kin and ethnicity—to loyalty to the person of the monarch, then to the integrity of the territory over which the monarch ruled. The critical fact allowed the Scots ultimately to absorb all kinds of immigrants with relatively little fuss, including, most importantly, the Irish in the 19th century.[29]

This is, of course, not to imply that Scots are morally superior to others; merely that their history of diversity makes for a 'mongrel' people.

Given the push for greater self-government, and above all the election of a (minority) Nationalist government in 2007, might it not be that Scottish national identity is

---

[28]  A. Hussain and W. Miller, *Multicultural Nationalism* (Oxford, 2006).
[29]  T. C. Smout, 'Perspectives on Scottish Identity', *Scottish Affairs*, 6 (1994), 107.

becoming more 'political'? Like much in Scottish life, the answer is not straightforward. In the 2007 election the SNP did much better than previously at persuading supporters of independence to vote for it (previously a sizeable minority voted for other parties, notably Labour), but they also captured a significant number of those who wanted a more powerful parliament (the so-called devolution-max option), as well as a sizeable proportion of people describing themselves as Scottish not British. There is no simple relationship between national identity and political preferences. In similarly 'under-stated nations' to Scotland such as Catalonia and Quebec, we find similar weak associations of this sort, and a capacity of the electorate to play whatever system is to hand to maximum effect. While a minority of Scots claim to want independence (around 25–30 per cent), a clear majority—two-thirds—want a more powerful parliament in the Union.[30] They are much more likely to trust the Scottish Parliament than the British one to work in Scotland's interests, and to credit Holyrood with the successes, and to blame Westminster for the failures, when it comes to policies and outcomes.[31]

Undoubtedly, the major institutional change in Scotland over the last twenty-five years has been the setting up of a devolved Parliament. There is no simple cause-and-effect relationship, however, between political–constitutional change and national identity. In many ways, the Parliament has become another form of institutional distinctiveness and autonomy, without implying that greater self-government will lead inexorably to full and formal independence. At the start of this process in the 1970s and 1980s, many claimed that Scots had different values and attitudes to the English. After all, *they* had elected Mrs Thatcher's right-wing government in 1979, and *we* hadn't. Somehow this reflected different ways of seeing the world; the difference between a commitment to (Scottish) 'collectivist' values on the one hand and (English) 'individualism' on the other.

Stereotypes are rarely to be swallowed whole, even if they might contain a grain of truth. Are Scots more 'left-wing' than the English? And what about the stereotype that they are far less 'liberal' and more 'authoritarian' than their neighbours, as befits a nation inflected with puritanical forms of religion? Caricaturing the English as rampant individualists is inaccurate. England voted for Thatcher's Conservatism *in spite* of its right-wing animus than *because* of it.[32] Support for mildly redistributive policies on taxation and public spending characterized England as well as Scotland. The majority in both societies supports the views that 'there is one law for the rich and one for the poor', 'ordinary people do not get their fair share of the nation's wealth', 'big business benefits at the expense of workers', and 'the gap between those with high incomes and those with low incomes is too large'.[33]

[30]  D. McCrone, 'Conundrums and Contradictions: What Scotland Wants', in Charlie Jeffery and James Mitchell, eds., *The Scottish Parliament 1999–2009: The First Decade* (Edinburgh, 2009).
[31]  A. Park and D. McCrone, 'The Devolution Conundrum?', in Catherine Bromley et al., *Has Devolution Delivered?* (Edinburgh, 2006).
[32]  A. Heath, R. Jowell, and J. Curtice, *The Rise of New Labour: Party Policies and Voter Choices* (Oxford, 2001).
[33]  J. Curtice, D. McCrone, N. McEwen, M. Marsh, and R. Ormston, *Revolution or Evolution? The 2007 Scottish Elections* (Edinburgh, 2009).

The point about such questions is that they show (a) a consistent majority in favour of the 'left-wing' option over the past decade; (b) while Scotland has a marginally higher level of support for the 'leftist' option, the differences from England are modest; (c) if anything, both the English and the Scots have moved away from the leftist position to a degree, possibly because governments of all persuasions have done so themselves, and the electorate simply adjusts to the new political and economic realities of life, however reluctantly. Support for redistribution from the better off to the less well off now stands at 37 per cent in Scotland (down from 50 per cent in 2000) compared with 42 per cent in England (up marginally from 38 per cent in 2000). There is no great difference between England and Scotland with regard to 'liberal/authoritarian' values, and if anything, Scots are marginally more liberal than those south of the border when it comes to 'respect for traditional values', 'stiffer sentences for law breakers', 'schools teaching respect for author- ity', and 'censorship of films and magazines to uphold moral standards'. The majority, however, in both societies support the more 'conservative' positions, with the exception of 'the law should always be obeyed' where only a minority (41 per cent) do so. Those who give priority to being 'Scottish' in terms of identity are more likely to adopt 'left- wing' values than those who say they are 'British', in contrast to people in England for whom 'English' carries no such implication.[34]

We might say that emphasizing your Scottishness is associated with social democratic values. So why should Scotland and England *appear* to be different as regards social and political values? It might seem counter-intuitive to assert greater similarity than differ- ence given political developments in both countries, notably that the Conservative Party does much better south of the border. The key to unlocking the puzzle lies not with regard to values and attitudes per se, assuming that these drive political choices, so much as with the divergence of forms of party competition. Whereas in England Labour and the Conservatives are the main protagonists, the battle in Scotland is between Labour and the SNP, with an electoral system that gives no party a realistic chance of an overall majority. Scottish politics thus focuses around 'social democratic' issues, whereas south of the border the pull is around neo-liberalism and market forces, because the main par- ties have chosen this as their battleground. If Scotland is 'different', it is due to ongoing political and cultural processes creating and shaping these differences, not because there is something ineluctable about them.

## Conclusion

That Scotland has been transformed over the past twenty-five years is not in doubt. For the better?—that is a judgement readers must make, depending on their values and per- spectives. That life for most people has improved cannot be doubted. Compared with

---

[34] M. Rosie and R. Bond, 'Social Democratic Scotland?', in Michael Keating, ed., *Scottish Social Democracy: Progressive Ideas for Public Policy* (Oxford, 2005).

what our parents and grandparents had, Scots are much better off as regards worldly goods. Two-thirds own their own homes, and less than a quarter live in the 'socially rented' sector. Virtually everyone has central heating, a washing machine, fridge, and freezer, mobile phone, and TV sets. There has been a dramatic rise in the numbers with Internet access; from 40 per cent in 2002 to 64 per cent by 2008, including those on the lowest incomes.[35] It is true that by not possessing such consumer goods, a person is likely to feel relatively more deprived given they have become the norm. Perhaps in the days when these items were not at all widespread and when many people were in the same poverty boat, there was comfort in knowing one's neighbours also had to struggle. Older forms of social and community solidarity have eroded, at least among working-class communities such as those tied to particular occupations like mining, steelworking, and fishing. New forms of deprivation have emerged linked to unequal access to goods and services; people's social circumstances dictate the quality of their lives. Being for example a single parent means having fewer savings and worldly goods than anyone else. Concentrated forms of poverty are found still in major cities such as Glasgow and Dundee, and west-central Scotland. Further, economic decline has a compounding effect on those least able to withstand its social impact. Those with more social and economic capital can leave behind those less well endowed as they migrate to places of greater opportunity.

Scotland has become a more unequal society as a result, highlighting the fact that most of the key levers of economic redistribution such as taxation lie with Westminster not Holyrood. There are structural limits to what the Scottish Parliament can do, helping to fuel demands for greater self-government, if currently stopping short of outright independence. Scotland has been transformed symbolically as well as socially by the Parliament. It is the most significant aspect of the last twenty-five years.

Has the end of older solidaristic forms of association left Scots alienated and individualized, reinforced perhaps by new patterns of consumer behaviour? It would be easy to draw that conclusion if we simply looked at what people now possess and consume, as privatized individuals. That would be to ignore both new as well as ongoing forms of social interaction. Around one-third of Scots claim to have carried out voluntary work lasting between one and five hours per week in the previous year,[36] and this is true for most age groups (apart from the very elderly) and all social classes. This involves working with children, schools, young people, local communities, and neighbourhoods. Most people too are involved in cultural activities, going to the pictures, libraries, theatres, museums, and live music events, and as many as two-thirds living in the most deprived communities get involved too. Only a quarter of all Scots said they did none of these things. This, then, is the new Scotland. It is not the society our ancestors knew, but there is enough that would be recognizable to them that they could claim they left us a country in good heart.

---

[35] *Scotland's People*, Annual Report: Results from 2007/2008 Scottish Household Survey (www.scotland.gov.uk/Topics/Statistics/16002) (Edinburgh, 2008): accessed 10 December 2008.

[36] The Scottish Government, *Scottish Household Survey* (Edinburgh, 2008).

## FURTHER READING

Bechhofer, Frank, and McCrone, David, eds., *National Identity, Nationalism and Constitutional Change* (London, 2009).

Brown, Alice, McCrone, David, Paterson, Lindsay, and Surridge, Paula, *The Scottish Electorate: The 1997 General Election and Beyond* (Basingstoke, 1999).

Curtice, John, McCrone, David, McEwen, Nicola, Marsh, Michael, and Ormston, Rachel, *Revolution or Evolution? The 2007 Scottish Elections* (Edinburgh, 2009).

Iannelli, Christina, and Paterson, Lindsay, 'Social Mobility in Scotland since the Middle of the Twentieth Century', in *The Sociological Review*, 54(3) (2006).

Keating, Michael, ed., *Scottish Social Democracy: Progressive Ideas for Public Policy* (Oxford, 2005).

McCrone, David, *Understanding Scotland* (London, 2001).

—— 'Conundrums and Contradictions: What Scotland Wants', in Charlie Jeffery and James Mitchell, eds., *The Scottish Parliament 1999–2009: The First Decade* (Edinburgh, 2009).

Paterson, Lindsay, Bechhofer, Frank, and McCrone, David, *Living in Scotland: Social and Economic Change since 1980* (Edinburgh, 2004).

Smout, Christopher, 'Perspectives on Scottish Identity', *Scottish Affairs*, 6 (1994), 107.

Sutherland, John, 'Occupational Change in Scotland, 2001–8', *Scottish Affairs*, 69 (2009), 93–121.

# Index